THAT'S THE JOINT!

THAT'S THE JOINT!

The Hip-Hop Studies Reader

Murray Forman & Mark Anthony Neal

EDITORS

ROUTLEDGE
OCM 51846137
New York · London

Published in 2004 by
Routledge
270 Madison Avenue
New York, NY 10016
www.routledge-ny.com

Published in Great Britain by
Routledge
2 Park Square
Milton Park, Abingdon
Oxfordshire OX14 RN
www.routledge.co.uk

Routledge is an imprint of the Taylor & Francis Group.

Printed in the United States of America on acid free paper.
Typesetting: Jack Donner, BookType.

10 9 8 7 6 5 4

Library of Congress Cataloging-in-Publication Data

That's the joint! : the hip-hop studies reader / edited by Mark Anthony Neal and Murray Forman.
    p. cm.
 Includes bibliographical references and index.
  ISBN 0-415-96918-2 (hardback : alk. paper) — ISBN 0-415-96919-0 (pbk. : alk. paper)
  1. Rap (Music)—History and criticism. 2. Rap (Music)—Social aspects. 3. Hip-hop.
I. Neal, Mark Anthony. II. Forman, Murray, 1959-
  ML3531.T43 2004
  782.421649'09—dc22

                                                                    2004015140

Dedicated to the memory of
Jason "Jam Master Jay" Mizzel,
R.I.P.

Contents

Foreword

"Sir, please turn around and face me," the airport security employee directed me. As I complied, he continued to methodically search me at the security checkpoint. He reminded me of my son, a tall taffy-faced figure who'd barely left his youth behind. As I caught his eyes when he frisked my outstretched arms, he whispered to me while keeping his professional demeanor.

"Man, I really feel your work on Pac," he gently stated, referring to my book *Holler If You Hear Me: Searching for Tupac Shakur.* "Plus, I've seen *Thug Angel* and *Tupac Vs.*"—two documentaries on the slain rapper in which I'd participated—"and you be puttin' it down."

"May I please place my hands on your chest since my detector went off?" he quizzed me more formally without missing a beat. "Sure, no problem," I replied. "That's where my suspenders are. And I'm glad you like the work." "Fo' sho, fo' sho," he said as he effortlessly slid back into his vernacular voice. "I'm just glad to know that somebody from your generation cares about Pac and hip-hop, and takes the time to listen to what we're saying."

"Alright, sir, I'm finished. You're done. But could you do me a big favor?" "What's that?" I asked.

The young man retreated to a portable booth tucked away at the end of the security line and fetched a dog-eared paperback copy of my book. "If you don't mind, please sign this before you go."

I was moved by his heartfelt compliments. I was even more touched by his eloquent rebuke of the view that his generation is illiterate and wholly fixed on destruction and mindless materialism. We weren't in school, and he wasn't reading my book for a good grade or for extra credit. Like the best students, he read for passion, and for the pleasure and pursuit of critical stimulation. It seemed that he was hungry for a sign among intellectuals and older folk that the huge importance of hip-hop hadn't been smothered by contempt, or just as bad, squandered by undiscriminating enthusiasm. And his delight in me taking Tupac seriously, was an unspoken nod to the fierce crosswinds in which hip-hop is presently caught. There are some who dismiss hip-hop as the dead letter of brazen stereotype-mongering among the severely undereducated and their gaggle of learned and over-interpreting defenders. Other critics claim that the deficits of hip-hop are amplified because they blare beyond the borders of ugly art to inspire youth to even uglier behavior. And others protest that, stripped of politics, history, and racial conscience, hip-hop is little more than sonic pathology that blasts away all the achievement of the civil rights struggle.

The academic study of hip-hop—like hip-hop itself—has been the subject of complaints even from its earliest days. By now, many of the complaints are familiar, even tired. But that hasn't stopped their being repackaged every so often to track the sensational headlines that trumpet the moral transgressions or violent deaths that rattle the rap world. John McWhorter, who's made a career in the public arena by twisting anecdotes of perceived black misbehavior into a questionable analysis of contemporary race, eloquently weighs in with lopsided moralizing in the summer 2003 issue of *City Journal*. "By reinforcing the stereotypes that long hindered blacks," McWhorter argues, "and by teaching young blacks that a thuggish adversarial stance is the properly 'authentic' response to a presumptively racist society, rap retards black success." That's an awfully big burden to carry—the fate of black success—especially for black youth (at least the ones who make a cameo in the anecdote that fronts McWhorter's essay) who appear to McWhorter to embody the "antisocial behavior" encouraged by hardcore rap that preaches "bone-deep dislike of authority."

Many critics, including McWhorter, don't account for the complex ways that some hip-hop artists play with stereotypes to either subvert or reverse them. For instance, amidst all the pimp mythologies and metaphors that weigh heavily on branches of contemporary hip-hop, rappers like Common seize on pimpology's prominence to poke fun at its pervasiveness. But its critics often fail to acknowledge that hip-hop is neither sociological commentary nor political criticism, though it may certainly function in these modes through its artists' lyrics. Hip-hop is still fundamentally an *art form* that traffics in hyperbole, parody, kitsch, dramatic license, double entendres, signification, and other literary and artistic conventions to get its points across. By denying its musical and artistic merit, hip-hop's critics get to have it both ways: they can deny the legitimate artistic standing of rap while seizing on its pervasive influence as an art form to prove what a terrible affect it has on youth. There are few parallels to this heavy-handed wrong-headedness in the criticism of other art forms like films, plays, or visual art, especially when they are authored by non-blacks. These cultural products are often conceded as art—even bad art, useless art, banal art, but *art* nonetheless—while there is a far greater consensus about hip-hop's essential artlessness. That cultural bias—and unapologetic ignorance—informs many assaults on the genre that reinforce the racial gulfs that feed rap's resentment of the status quo.

Of course, not all the barbs aimed at hip-hop are meant exclusively for its artists. Some are directed at the post-civil rights era generation of Black academics who have been prominent in practicing the academic study of hip-hop. Thus, revered intellectuals and writers like Martin Kilson react angrily when they think intellectuals who engage hip-hop don't embrace the values and styles of the civil rights movement. In an online journal of opinion, *The Black Commentator*, Kilson points to several articles from the post-civil rights black intelligentsia to prove that they are "tossing poisoned darts at African Americans' mainline civil rights tradition and its courageous leadership figures." Kilson's criticism of the post-civil rights era black intelligentsia includes a section taking me to task for an op-ed piece I wrote for the *New York Times* about the controversy surrounding the movie *Barbershop* (in which a character jokes about such civil rights era figures as Martin Luther King, Jr. and Rosa Parks). Kilson was part of that chorus of voices decrying the movie for its perceived "irreverence toward African-American civil rights leadership."

Kilson's view that movies like *Barbershop*—as well as hip-hop more generally—"serve as anti-Black ammunition for conservative opponents of African-Americans' civil rights agenda." is not unrepresentative of many older—and truth to be told, younger—black folks' beliefs about hip-hop and those scholars associated with its defense. Many agree with Kilson that "there's nothing whatever that's seriously radical or progressive about hip-hop ideas and values." Many support Kilson's view that hip-hop is politically empty, and is little more "than an updated face on the old-hat, crude, anti-humanistic values of hedonism and materialism."

Critics of hip-hop like Kilson make a point, of course—and it's not a point that's hard to make—that hip-hop is full of problematic expressions. It reeks of materialism; it gorges with stereotypes and offensive language; it spoils with retrogressive views; it is rife with hedonism; and it surely cannot always be said to side with humanistic values. But this argument demands little engagement with hip-hop; these views don't require much beyond attending to surface symptoms of a culture that offers far more depth and color when it's taken seriously and criticized in proper fashion. It is odd that gifted intellectuals should so resolutely stick to superfluous observation, as if afraid of the intellectual credibility or complex truths they might find in a comprehensive study of hip-hop. It would be outlandish to comment on, say, metaphysical poetry without interacting critically with its most inspired poets. At least *read* Donne. And if one were to make hay over the virtues or deficits of nineteenth-century British poetry, or twentieth-century Irish poetry, then one should encounter the full range of Tennyson's or Yeats's work before jumping, or slouching, to conclusions.

Unfortunately, much of the source material for such a study of hip-hop is diffuse and hard to come by. Instead of meaningful critical inquiry we argue about op-eds—and not books. The major points in my *New York Times* op-ed on the brouhaha over *Barbershop*—stirred largely by civil rights leaders—were that films are not scholarly monographs; that folk have the right to express themselves, and if we don't like it, we can criticize them or make our own films; that one film can't possibly represent the entire black experience; that recent scholarship focused on mass movements in the civil rights era veered toward group dynamics being just as important as charismatic leadership; that civil rights organizations *at their worst* shut down free speech; that *at their best* barbershops offered politically incorrect black speech as a bonus of sheared hair; and that art is supposed to get in our faces and not simply soothe or reassure us. What critics of hip-hop miss by neglecting to make concrete engagement with hip-hop culture is the complexity of that culture. I've written a book on rapper Tupac Shakur and one on Dr. King. I don't despise civil rights; I take it so seriously that I engage it at fair length, concluding that, despite his faults, King is the greatest American produced on our native soil!

Critics of hip-hop from an earlier generation, like Kilson, often work from an uniformed view of hip-hop culture and its critics—after all, those of us who study and write about hip-hop aren't just fans. In fact, we sometimes make some of the same criticisms that Kilson and others make, but hopefully from a more informed perspective. What we need are more informed and extended analyses of hip-hop culture, and, for that matter, of civil rights leaders and movements. Unfortunately, there is little serious work from the critics of hip-hop that engages hip-hop with intellectual rigor, rather than knee-jerk negativism.

This opposition to the study of hip-hop is shared by other writers like Hugh Pearson, a Brown University graduate who is appalled by the fact that Ivy League schools would dare offer hip-hop courses. Writing in *Newsday* in the late summer of 2003, Pearson condemns Harvard for housing a hip-hop archive because its scholars deem the art form and culture on which it rests to be an important cultural phenomenon that is worthy of study. Pearson rails at rappers with "a tendency to compose ungrammatical lyrics flowing from the ungrammatical speech patterns that are standard for too many African-Americans." Unlike earlier funk musicians, who "in those days no one considered ... worthy of 'study' at a serious university," Pearson is galled that the Ivy League "will now treat hip-hop as respectable." Pearson has no sense of irony when he pinches a phrase from a man of manifest mediocrity—George W. Bush —who, in accepting the Republican nomination for the presidency at its 2000 convention, spoke of the "soft bigotry of low expectations." It was an unintended autobiography in précis to be sure.

Pearson samples the line to suggest that that's what studying hip-hop in the academy amounts to, instead of a course of study that "extol[s] the positive elements of the African-American community," and that, instead of "[raising] cultural standards ... prefers to make chicken salad out of chicken necks."

In putting down the study of hip-hop—and African-American Studies as well—critics like Pearson believe that it is simply unworthy of serious examination. But we should be willing to take a scholarly look at hip-hop for no other reason than the art form and culture has grabbed global attention and sparked emulation in countless different countries and among widely varied ethnicities. For example, when I was in Brazil recently and went to the "Black Six," a hip-hop club in Rio, I might as well have been in Harlem or Philadelphia. We need to study the way that cultures of articulation and representation have traversed international boundaries and been adopted in fascinating manner in the languages and accents indigenous to their regions—this phenomenon alone is a cause of intellectual curiosity. Because they appear to be ashamed of hip-hop—a feeling shared by many blacks and others who decry the sordid images of hip-hop as the detritus of the culture that should be swept away with the garbage—critics of hip-hop culture are incapable of acknowledging just how interesting and insightful the study of rap has proven in various intellectual settings around the world. Pearson's demand for an exemption from this trend in our nation's most prestigious universities is an odd cry for remedial provincialism—a return to a climate of academic curiosity where only a narrow range of subjects could be legitimately pursued.

This brief genealogy of conflicts should show just why the book you hold in your hand is so critical. By taking the time to present a feverishly productive intellectual accounting of an equally fertile culture of expression, Murray Forman and Mark Anthony Neal have placed at our disposal some of the most intriguing engagements with hip-hop culture. The writers in this volume don't shy away from probing the complex varieties of black identity, even those that skirt close to stereotype as they undress its mauling effects. The contributors to this volume dig deep into hip-hop's rich traditions of expression to generate a criticism equal to the art that inspires it. And these writers have no shame in poring hard and long over hip-hop; assuming its intellectual value without being unduly defensive about its critical status is a shining virtue of the book.

Hip-hop is being studied all over the globe, and the methodologies of its examination are rightfully all over the map. They are multidisciplinary in edifying, exemplary fashion, borrowing from sociology, politics, religion, economics, urban studies, journalism, communications theory, American studies, transatlantic studies, black studies, history, musicology, comparative literature, English, linguistics, and many more disciplines besides. This book makes it plain that hip-hop is no fad, either culturally or intellectually, and that its best artists and intellectuals are as capable of stepping back and critiquing its flows and flaws as the most astute observers and participants in any other genre of musical or critical endeavor. As the academic study of hip-hop enters a new phase—as it matures and expands, as it deepens and opens up even broader avenues of investigation—it needs a summary text, one that captures the many sided features of a dynamic culture that demands rigorous criticism and consideration. That's what you've got in your hands. This is an intellectual mix-tape that heads from all over can feel and learn from each time they take a listen and give a read. It has the same features of the best hip-hop: seductive rhythms, throbbing beats, intelligent lyrics, soulful samples, and a sense of joy that is never exhausted in one sitting. So, like the hottest joints, sit down and savor the vibe of this heady and heartfelt compilation.

Michael Eric Dyson

Acknowledgments

We are grateful to the numerous individuals who expressed their encouragement and offered their assistance in preparing the manuscript for *That's the Joint!* In assembling the essays, we have attempted to be as inclusive as possible; our apologies to several authors who offered their permission to include previously published articles but whose work was ultimately excluded due to prohibitive reprint costs. Thanks are due to the authors who, when contacted, went out of their way to personally assist us, or helped in negotiations with their publishers: Andrew Bartlett, Todd Boyd, Mark Dery, Greg Dimitriadis, Juan Flores, Paul Gilroy, Michael Holman, Cheryl Keyes, Bakari Kitwana, Gwendolyn Pough, Tricia Rose, David Toop, and Rickey Vincent.

Shout outs to: Marcyliena Morgan of the Hip-Hop Archive at Harvard University (especially for hosting the symposium "All Eyez on Me: Tupac Shakur and the Search for a Modern Folk Hero," where several of the authors represented in these pages convened), Knut Aukrust (Oslo, Norway), Michael Eric Dyson (Philadelphia), Emmett Price III (Boston), and Tony Mitchell (holding fort Down Under). "Big Up" to the Northeastern University Hip-Hop Studies Collective: E. P. III, Paul K. Saucier, Geoff Ward, Alan West-Duran, and Nadine Yaver.

The Department of Communication Studies, Northeastern University, provided support in the book's early stages, and we thank the department chair, P. David Marshall, and the administrative staff and work study students for their assistance in the manuscript's preparation. Thanks to Amy Rodriguez for editing assistance, and Matt Byrnie and Mark Henderson of Taylor and Francis for shepherding the project through. Special thanks to Zamawa Arenas for her enduring grace.

Murray Forman
Boston

Introduction

Murray Forman

These words we say, we want y'all to hear
We're gonna make a lot of sense—we're gonna make it clear ...

... We're gonna rock this record and don't you forget
  Ah, that's the joint

"That's the Joint" by The Funky Four + One
(1980, Sugar Hill Records)

In his 1995 paean "Old School" (1995, Interscope), Tupac Shakur pays tribute to hip-hop's formative stages and its pioneers with detailed references to everyday teen practices, clothing styles, and a general attitude or way of being as the cultural underpinnings of hip-hop took shape almost twenty years prior. Calling out to New York City's boroughs, he identifies the locus of hip-hop's origins, proclaiming gratitude to rap music's innovators and citing the essential contribution of local radio stations, DJs, or nightclubs. He also explicitly describes the urban perambulation and mobility of subway rides between Brooklyn and Harlem and the social cohesion of neighborhood block parties "in the projects," noting in his lyrics that early hip-hop was the product of overlapping influences as teens from different neighborhoods moved across the city, mingling in formal and informal urban spaces—literally inhabiting both aboveground and underground environments.

When Shakur intones the phrase "Forget the TV, about to hit the streets and do graffiti / Be careful don't let the transit cops see me," he explains that early hip-hop was characterized by *public actions* that were, in many cases, simultaneously accompanied by *risks* of varying severity. From this vantage, hip-hop can be seen as a series of practices with an evolved history and the ongoing potential to challenge both social norms and legal stricture; in hip-hop, there are always stakes of crucial importance. The song's hook, woven throughout the track in the sampled voice of MC Grand Puba of the rap group Brand Nubian from their recording "Dedication," summarizes the debt and gratitude owed to hip-hop's creative trailblazers and its early supporters: "What more can I say? I wouldn't be here today if the old school didn't pave the way."

In ways similar to those uttered in Shakur's "Old School," contemporary scholars might recognize their own debt to hip-hop's pioneering authors and cultural critics. Since hip-hop's inception in the uptown boroughs of New York, there has emerged a considerable body of written work about the cultural practices and informing attitudes that comprise a hip-hop way of life. For example, in 1978, *Billboard*, the music industry's main trade magazine, printed a short article about the localized phenomenon of DJ street parties and the growing prestige of pioneer DJ Kool Herc, whose music and performance innovations were generating excitement among uptown audiences at the time. Appearing under the title "B-Beats Bombarding Bronx," Robert Ford, Jr.'s, auspicious article reported that, following Herc's lead, "other Bronx DJs have picked up the practice and now B-Beats are the rage all over the borough and the practice is spreading rapidly" (1978: 65). Although it took a few more years for academics to catch on, journalists working the culture beat began following this underground music (even before it was known as "rap") and the attendant cultural practices of break dancing (or B-boying) and graffiti. Attesting to the swift increase of mainstream media coverage, Judy McCoy's library reference guide *Rap Music in the 1980s* (1992) provides a date-specific list graphically displaying the proliferation of rap reviews, artist interviews or profile pieces, and industry analysis.

In their writing, journalists charted the entrepreneurial and artistic personalities involved, the rise of a vital and ever-shifting club scene, and rap and hip-hop's gradual expansion beyond the narrow enclaves of the Bronx and Harlem. The contributions of several of these pioneering authors, including Robert Ford, Jr., Nelson George, Sally Banes, and Michael Holman, are included in *That's the Joint!* Today, this trend continues in the writing of, to name but a few, Jon Caramanica, Davey D, Kevin Powell, Kelefa Sanneh, and Touré who write about hip-hop for the daily press, specialty magazines, and dedicated Web sites. Benchmark films such as Charlie Ahearn's *Wild Style* and Tony Silver and Henry Chalfant's *Style Wars*, both released in 1982, or *The Show* (1995), directed by Brian Robbins, and Peter Spirer's *Rhyme & Reason* (1997), further circulated the images, sounds, and sensibilities of early hip-hop, providing important documentation of the era, as does Doug Pray's more recent production, *Scratch* (2002), a documentary about early DJs and contemporary "turntablists."

The emergence of academically oriented approaches to hip-hop culture is most often traced to the 1984 publication of David Toop's *Rap Attack: African Jive to New York Hip-Hop* and Steven Hager's *Hip Hop: The Illustrated History of Break Dancing, Rap Music, and Graffiti.* They, and others in rapid succession, presented a focused examination of the cultural contexts within which hip-hop evolved and flourished. Though there was often a limiting sense of analytic scope (with many early writers fixating on the culture's marginal status, advancing disputable claims about hip-hop's ostensibly organic roots in a ghetto poverty that were, some argued, disconnected from systems of commerce), these first scholarly forays remain valuable to the contemporary perspective on how hip-hop was viewed at the time and the prevailing sense of its impact and importance in that nascent era. Far from simply seeming outdated, this initial writing on hip-hop still offers historical information that is worth contemplating as today's scholars and young hip-hop "heads" attempt to appraise the current cultural landscape and, tentatively, predict hip-hop's next phase of reinvention.

Paraphrasing Chuck D of Public Enemy, despite relative antagonism and constraint through the 1990s, hip-hop rapidly "bum rushed" the halls of higher education. When, in regard to rap recordings, Paul Gilroy admits, "I don't think anyone actually knows what the totality of its hyperactivity looks like ... I can't keep up with the volume of hip-hop product anymore" (1992: 309), he could just as easily be addressing the contemporary outpouring of articles and books about rap and hip-hop that have circulated into the public sphere through scholarly journals and academic presses. In the eyes of some traditionalists and conservative intellectuals, this new area of study posed a challenge to the hegemony of prevailing academic standards and disrupted disciplinary norms, facilitating comparisons with the far earlier stance of critic Bernard Rosenberg (1957), who cautioned against the worrisome academic incursions of popular culture research in the 1950s, or Allan Bloom, whose 1987 book *The Closing of the American Mind* focused specifically on what he perceived were the erosive influences of popular music among students. Today, having gained a certain respectability and reputation for analytic rigor—having paid its dues and earned its keep—scholarly work on hip-hop is considerably less marginalized within the university.

The "new black intelligentsia," of which Todd Boyd, Michael Eric Dyson, Robin D. G. Kelley, Mark Anthony Neal, and Tricia Rose are among the most conspicuous members, demonstrates a clear understanding of, and affinity with hip-hop. In the writing and lectures of a growing number of progressive black thinkers—not all of whom toil in the university system—there is general concurrence that hip-hop represents an extension of specifically African American cultural traditions but, importantly, it also poses challenges and introduces ruptures to prevailing notions of an unbroken cultural continuum; in this context, Boyd's *The New H.N.I.C.: The Death of Civil Rights and the Reign of Hip Hop* (2002) is a particularly compelling text. Displaying intellectual dexterity while holding hip-hop itself under a harsh critical light, contemporary scholars across the cultural spectrum frequently employ many of hip-hop's inherent strategies that include appropriating and reincorporating academic theories and elucidating the contemporary cultural condition in language that is simultaneously learned *and* hip. A further prominent indicator of the academic embrace of hip-hop may be witnessed in the establishment of various institutes and research centers, including the founding of the Hiphop Archive housed in the W.E.B. Du Bois Institute for African and African American Research at Harvard University. Drawing on the institution's deep resource base to host hip-hop luminaries such as pioneering DJ Afrika Bambaataa and scholars from across the United States, the Harvard-based archive illustrates that hip-hop's social impact and cultural contributions are far too important for teachers and students to ignore and, moreover, avoiding them would be irresponsible since literally millions of people world wide are influenced by hip-hop on a daily basis.

With *That's the Joint!*, we assert that *research and writing, whether in journalistic or academic contexts, is absolutely part of the wider hip-hop culture.* Analyzing, theorizing, and writing about hip-hop are also forms of cultural labor and should accordingly be regarded as consequential facets of hip-hop. Hip-hop's first chroniclers were always more than dispassionate objective observers. They were in many cases fully implicated in the emergent culture of hip-hop, circulating within the same social circles as the prime innovators and entrepreneurs, and they counted themselves among the earliest audience members who cohered at both formal and informal events. Many of today's hip-hop scholars started as journalists, covering hip-hop in their local press, spinning records on campus–community radio stations, writing record reviews, or documenting the proliferating national hip-hop scenes, and many continue to navigate between the media and academia. As a generation of scholars steeped in hip-hop's cultural influences graduated into tenure track positions, teaching students in their teens and twenties who have never known a world without hip-hop, the dynamic interrelations and productive overlay between academic and nonacademic spaces have become more obvious. *That's the Joint!* ideally inhabits this liminal zone where the 'hood and the university converge.

A cursory search of the Internet reveals dozens of undergraduate courses and graduate seminars exclusively focused on hip-hop, and there are scores of single-class modules in a wide range of contexts addressing hip-hop themes and issues. The subtitled reference to "hip-hop studies" in *That's the Joint!* is intentional, advanced with full awareness that, although there is not yet an institutionalized subdiscipline called "hip-hop studies," there is a plethora of hip-hop research across the disciplines and the volume and sophistication of work in various university departments is consistently increasing. Although hip-hop is most frequently analyzed and discussed within the disciplinary contours of African-American studies or popular music studies, it also represents a growing area of research in American studies, cultural studies, communications and media studies, English, ethnic studies, performance studies, sociology, and women's studies. Published writing on rap and hip-hop culture constitutes the new entrant in these fields, jostling against more conventional works. The majority of essays and articles in *That's the Joint!* were selected by surveying references and citations in published hip-hop research in order to gauge the utility of specific essays. This approach was augmented by a review of roughly seventy-five course syllabi and an assessment of readings assigned to students across academic disciplines.

Still, despite its gains in the academy, hip-hop scholarship often remains a peripheral concern among those outside the university—the students enrolled in advanced seminars in "the school of hard knocks"—who tend to experience hip-hop most intensely and who most ardently reproduce the cultural practices and discourses "in the 'hood," which remains the center of hip-hop's production and its symbolic source of meaning and value. There is frequently a defensive attitude expressed among the youth of the extended and variegated hip-hop community that is articulated as skepticism for scholarly engagements with hip-hop. For youth who are most explicitly identified with hip-hop's cultural forms, claims made for and about hip-hop by professors occupying academia's "ivory towers" or "hallowed halls" are frequently met with suspicion, if not outright derision. It is not rare, for instance, to hear critiques among young constituents of "the hip-hop nation" who are convinced that professors with little or no connection to "the 'hood" and, thus, lacking in "street credibility" in their view, are exploiting the culture in order to identify with something cool, exciting, "fresh," or "phat." This viewpoint, inscribed at its worst with a palpable anti-intellectual disdain, suggests that university and college teachers are often most interested in translating hip-hop's cultural forms and practices into abstract theoretical jargon, building their academic careers on the backs of MCs, DJs, B-boys and graffiti artists who forge the objects of scholarly research.

These criticisms are not always without merit; the main criticism voiced among the self-appointed guardians of hip-hop is that scholars, whether consciously or not, often exert their relative authority when conducting research and publishing their findings, and they are eminently capable of appropriating dimensions of hip-hop according to personal or professional agendas. As hip-hop has evolved as a significant—and lucrative—facet of the entertainment industry, emerging as a profoundly influential commercial and cultural force, it has been taken up as a topic of academic inquiry with greater enthusiasm. Yet just as a new generation of artists capitalized on the enhanced value of, for example, rap music or 'hood films in the popular market, so, too, did hip-hop's journalists and scholarly writers proliferate, attaining social status as hip-hop commentators, cultural critics, and professional experts. Mirroring patterns in the recording and film industries and the magazine publishing sector throughout the 1990s, scholarly research on hip-hop also constituted a growth sector among academic publishers and university presses. Hip-hop scholarship, then, is not simply an uninvested or benign study of cultural formations and social practices; it cannot be excluded from the commercial corporate systems through which hip-hop has been constructed, projected, or amplified on the local, regional, national, or global scale. As Tupac Shakur's "Old School" reminds us, hip-hop's cultural practices are thoroughly traced with stakes of varying consequence, and the same holds true for hip-hop scholarship.

The university is surely (and thankfully) not the central site or driving force in contemporary hip-hop culture, yet the work that is taking place in its classrooms is not without stakes. As hip-hop evolves as a regular facet of university curricula it is essential to acknowledge and critique the role of academics in shaping public knowledge about hip-hop. Academics and journalists—in their own ways and in their own far-too-disconnected domains—function as gatekeepers of sorts; gatekeepers of knowledge certainly, but also gatekeepers of discourse. This is to concede that, whether aggressively or through more passive forms, boundaries of language and expression within which the world is made meaningful are being circumscribed.

As hip-hop passes the first quarter century of existence, it is important to address the ways in which knowledge of the culture is constructed, how the character of hip-hop's myriad practices are framed and conveyed both to a general public and to a core of deeply invested participants who, for those working within the academy, are also our students. The articles selected for *That's the Joint!* reflect the disparate discursive patterns through which hip-hop has been addressed, presenting ideas and terminology that may converge in a form of dialogue, but that may also collide and conflict.

Another outcome of hip-hop's academic study is the formation of what might reasonably be termed a "hip-hop canon," encompassing key written works and dominant research themes that are identified with influential scholars. Rap music is so sufficiently established that few hardcore defenders of hip-hop would dispute that, for example, Eric B and Rakim's *Paid in Full* (1987, Island Records) or Public Enemy's *It Takes a Nation of Millions to Hold Us Back* (1988, Def Jam) are hip-hop classics, essential listening, must-have cultural commodities, but it is unlikely that the same would be said of Tricia Rose's go-to text *Black Noise: Rap Music and Black Culture in Contemporary America* (1994). The hip-hop "canon" is not a widely discussed topic, but it is emerging in much the same way that rock or jazz studies evolved, with several key texts becoming enshrined in various forms, not least of which includes course syllabi and academic reading lists. Just as the durability and tenacity of hip-hop and rap annoyed *and* impressed individuals in the culture industries, so, too, has hip-hop endured in relation to the academy. In this context, if hip-hop's cultural producers and earnest constituents "bring the noise" in a maelstrom of beats and rhymes, then academic writers in corresponding fashion "bring the canons." This notion of a hip-hop research canon isolates attention on the academic literature that attempts to explain, define, theorize, and culturally locate hip-hop in relation to myriad factors such as industry structures, policy and regulations, social practices, and collective and subjective identity formation.

Lillian Robinson writes that the canon "is the set of books that make up the Book. This inclusion has a basis in scholarship, the application of certain standards ... to a text" (1997: 142). For Henry Louis Gates, Jr., a canon serves a unifying function as "the commonplace book of our shared culture" (1992: 21), although rigorous and sophisticated analytical perspectives must prevail, for as Gates emphasizes, the canon is also structured on a firm foundation of intellectual "soundness" (1992: 39). Examples of speculative or anecdotal texts on hip-hop abound, and some of these (Light, 1999; Fricke and Ahearn, 2002) are invaluable sources of information, but there is also a solid research corpus displaying rigor, analytical sophistication, and "intellectual soundness." These brief definitions of canonicity are important to hip-hop and the study of its cultural practices because, for whatever else can be said of canon formation, it is a productive enterprise: it produces a sense of history and evolution and it also produces values.

In assembling the articles in *That's the Joint!* we have remained mindful of the complexities of adjudicating the "soundness" of hip-hop writing, self-reflexively assessing our own biases in the evaluation of "standards." This process also reminds us that there are important stakes involved in scholarly writing about hip-hop and in the inclusion of books and articles in course syllabi and curricula, reinforcing the awareness that power is a factor of crucial importance in the "the distribution of cultural capital" and the attendant processes of "exclusion" and "selection" (Guillory, 1993: 6). As university and college educators labor over the definition of their own standards of research rigor or, in preparation of course syllabi, they debate the value and utility of one book or article over another, it is imperative that the power and authority infused in this process is not ignored.

The term "hip-hop nation" has emerged as a cultural commonplace, employed in reference to a relatively coherent social entity founded in shared interests or values and collective practices that bind constituents within a symbolic unity. This "nation" is not precisely placed, lacking agreed-upon boundaries or other demarcating features, but is, in its fuller sense, akin to Benedict Anderson's (1983) concept of "imagined communities." In Anderson's view, national consciousness has been historically related to the rise of "vernacular print markets," "print capitalism," and publishing initiatives supporting a sense of shared identification. As he explains, in more recent times educational systems and the mass media have figured prominently in the manufacture and circulation of nationalist ideologies, diffusing the dominant ideals of "the nation" and establishing its resonant discourses, symbols, and icons.

If there is to be any more talk of the hip-hop nation, then it might be time to speak also of an emergent national literature and press and the possible—even accidental—formation of a canon within which themes and symbols, the circulation of shared knowledge and traditions, are identified, analyzed, and disseminated. As Stephen Gray explains, there is a process by which a literature "comes into its own":

> not just in terms of a prescribable number of acceptably "great" works, but in terms of the whole nexus that supports a literature—its own publishing industry, including newspapers, magazines, and journals, its own self-referencing use of language, its mutual understanding of a set of enfolded norms and values, its own context of myth about the past and the present, its theoretical wing of evaluators like ourselves, its sense of settling in to keep doing a job that has to be continually done, and—most important of all—its own community of readership or audience, which receives the work and feeds back into it reciprocally. (Gray, 1984: 228)

That's the Joint! is conceived within this elaborated cultural framework that shapes the thinking and writing about hip-hop. This book is deliberately heterogeneous, reflecting the diverse and complex character of hip-hop culture, and in presenting historical, theoretical, and journalistic assessments, it adheres to themes and patterns that have defined the study and analysis of hip-hop since its inception. By integrating writing from the popular and academic realms, a clearer picture emerges of what hip-hop is and how it is socially meaningful among its active producers and, in the commercial contexts of the culture industries, among its active audiences.

That's the Joint! includes essays both by authors who are renowned in the area of hip-hop studies and others who, in the early stages of their careers, are lesser known. Some of the work published here is widely acknowledged among hip-hop scholars as groundbreaking research, yet we have also seen fit to reproduce more obscure essays and journalistic reports in order to provide a comprehensive and well-rounded compendium. The articles included in *That's the Joint!* fall under two categories: scholarly writing that is frequently cited in hip-hop research, and popular reporting that is exemplary in its capacity to convey the character or contemporaneous impact of hip-hop practices at particular moments.

The first part of this book simultaneously isolates hip-hop history and its historiography. Encompassing journalistic and historical research, these chapters establish a setting within which to conceive hip-hop's formative stages and to observe the manner in which early writers approached the emergent culture and its diffuse practices. In the second part, the persistent theme of authenticity in hip-hop is under analysis. As hip-hop has evolved into an important commercial enterprise within the entertainment industries, the authenticity debates have intensified; similarly, as a growing number of individuals identify themselves in and through hip-hop's customs, the question of cultural rites of passage, commitments, and belonging urgently arise. The issue of authenticity is most often articulated within the discourse of "the real," a ubiquitous expression that encompasses material and symbolic essences and that is, as these chapters illustrate, primarily traced across the social variables of race, class, and location.

The spatial politics of hip-hop are the object of analysis in the third part. Although hip-hop has always displayed a pronounced spatiality, there has been an ongoing process of transformation, particularly as the identification with localized places and the cultural sphere of "the 'hood" have attained greater importance and urgency. As the chapters in this part suggest, urban space and place are inscribed with competing social values and are sharply defined by the expression of power and authority. The manner in which hip-hop's cultural practitioners portray these cultural spaces and the struggles occurring within them is, thus, a pressing issue in hip-hop scholarship.

Women in hip-hop and the enunciation of gender politics comprise the analytical core of the fourth part. Hip-hop's masculine expressivity is well documented, constituting the dominant voice in the articulation of gender identities. Indeed, the most ferocious attacks on hip-hop often focus on gender issues, with the most vehement opposition targeting rap lyrics and film or video images that feature sexist or misogynist content. The authors in this part adopt an important feminist critique that probes the social characteristics informing black female practices or identities and, through their interrogation of power relations and social structures of male hegemony, they extend the range of perspectives through which hip-hop is rendered meaningful.

The fifth part focuses on the political realities and future political potentials of "the hip-hop generation." Hip-hop has maintained a striking capacity for political insight and social critique, evident in such rap recordings as the 1980 single "How We Gonna Make the Black Nation Rise?" (Clappers) by Brother D and Collective Effort, Grandmaster Flash and the Furious Five's classic track "The Message" (Sugar Hill) from 1982, or the posse cut "Self-Destruction" (Jive) recorded in 1989 by a fellowship of MCs united under the title The Stop the Violence Movement. Through the 1990s, hip-hop's political qualities emerged as a major force, influencing youths across racial, spatial, and class boundaries. The chapters in this part isolate the issues of cultural struggle and resistance as they are expressed by the hip-hop generation, exploring the political conflict and collaboration that have, at various times, determined hip-hop's development.

Hip-hop aesthetics and technology and cultural production are the main themes in parts six and seven, respectively. In the sixth part, the essays explore hip-hop's creative processes and the various aesthetic considerations influencing rap music production, elaborating on both the kinds of technology employed and the logic of technological appropriation that are fundamental to the sonic construction of rap tracks. In the seventh part hip-hop's prodigious creative output is associated with the rationalized apparatuses of the culture industries. Through political economic analyses and interviews with key representatives of the entertainment industry, these chapters present a thorough assessment of hip-hop as a living culture and as a commodified set of cultural practices, detailing the fundamental issues as hip-hop is incorporated into the global flow of commercial sounds and images.

That's the Joint! is not the final word on hip-hop scholarship; rather, it is an accumulation of essays and articles that, from the *first* written words on hip-hop, have addressed its main themes and debates. This book is designed to introduce students to some of the prominent authors in hip-hop studies and to provide a coherent collection of writing that reflects a wide range of issues and the diverse ways of contemplating them. In our efforts to produce a concise, usable text for hip-hop scholars we have attempted to represent the impact of hip-hop on multiple sectors of social life and its significance in multiple academic disciplines.

References

Anderson, Benedict. 1983. *Imagined Communities: Reflections on the Origin and Spread of Nationalism.* New York: Verso.

Bloom, Allan. 1987. *The Closing of the American Mind.* New York: Simon and Schuster.

Boyd. Todd. 2002. *The New H.N.I.C.: The Death of Civil Rights and the Reign of Hip Hop.* New York: New York University Press.

Ford, Robert, Jr. 1978. "B-Beats Bombarding Bronx." *Billboard* (July 1): 65.

Fricke, Jim, and Charlie Ahearn. 2002. *Yes Yes Y'All: The Experience Music Project Oral History of Hip-Hop's First Decade.* Cambridge, Mass.: Da Capo Press.

Gates, Jr., Henry Louis. 1992. *Loose Canons: Notes on the Culture Wars.* New York: Oxford University Press.

Gilroy, Paul. 1992. "It's a Family Affair." In *Black Popular Culture,* edited by Gina Dent, pp. 303–316. Seattle: Bay Press.

Gray, Stephen. 1984. "A Sense of Place in New Literatures, Particularly South African English." *World Literature Written in English,* 24, no. 2 (Autumn): 224–231.

Guillory, John. 1993. *Cultural Capital: The Problem of Literary Canon Formation.* Chicago: University of Chicago Press.

Hager, Steven. 1984. *Hip Hop: The Illustrated History of Break Dancing, Rap Music, and Graffiti.* New York: St. Martin's Press.

Light, Alan, ed. 1999. *The Vibe History of Hip Hop.* New York: Three Rivers Press.

McCoy, Judy. 1992. *Rap Music in the 1980s: A Reference Guide.* Metuchen, N.J.: Scarecrow Press.

Robinson, Lillian. 1997. *In the Canon's Mouth: Dispatches from the Culture Wars.* Bloomington: Indiana University Press.

Rose, Tricia. 1994. *Black Noise: Rap Music and Black Culture in Contemporary America.* Hanover: Wesleyan University Press.

Rosenberg, Bernard. 1957. "Mass Culture in America" In *Mass Culture: The Popular Arts in America,* edited by Bernard Rosenberg and David Manning White, pp. 3–12. New York: Free Press.

Toop, David. 1984. *The Rap Attack: African Jive to New York Hip-Hop.* Boston: South End Press.

Part I

Hip-Hop Ya Don't Stop:
Hip-Hop History and Historiography

Murray Forman

"Back in the day" has emerged as a common expression within hip-hop, most frequently employed to describe the past and to mark moments in the evolution of the hip-hop culture. The phrase is often imbued with a certain nostalgia, acknowledging benchmarks, transitional phases, or influential aesthetic innovations realized within general historical contexts. Yet for all of its rhetorical potency and casual utility it remains an inexact expression, like a form of shorthand that communicates information but lacks precision or accuracy. Over the years the phrase has been applied widely and wildly, and it is not rare to hear narratives about 1970s Bronx block parties, the 1982 release of Grandmaster Flash and the Furious Five's "The Message" (Sugar Hill), the 1988 rise of N.W.A., or the 1993 launch of Bad Boy Entertainment, all framed as occurrences from "back in the day," depending on one's generational vantage.

Although hip-hop's formation is the topic of considerable scholarly analysis (Toop, 1984; Hebdige, 1987; Rose, 1994; Forman, 2002) there is significant value in revisiting hip-hop's histo-riography, including articles published in an industry trade magazine such as *Billboard* or in the popular press, including *The Source* (which bills itself as "the magazine of hip-hop music, culture, and politics"). Essays and social commentary written about the New York City hip-hop scene in the late 1970s and early 1980s offer what Mark Anthony Neal describes as "a real time feel," evoking the crackling energies and broader sensibilities of an emergent cultural sector. Although they may opt for a temporal perspective—positioning the erupting hip-hop phenomena within a historical context—these writings benefit from an immediacy and proximity to events, detailing transitional forces at the instant they occur. They isolate key elements of innovation and sociocultural change, providing insights on the undulating composition of the cultural terrain and identifying the ruptures from which hip-hop's alternative practices emanated.

The evolution of hip-hop corresponds with cultural theorist Raymond Williams's observation that the process of "formal innovation" is gradual, and although "residual" cultural practices from prior eras continue, new "emergent" cultural forms and practices may arise that challenge or disrupt the cultural dominant. Hip-hop constitutes an emergent cultural form, but so, too, does early writing about hip-hop, for as Williams explains in reference to innovation and emer-gent cultural forms,

> there are always important works which belong to these very early stages of particular forms, and it is easy to miss their formal significance by comparison with preceding or succeeding mature examples.... It is then easy to miss one of the key elements in cultural production: innovation as it is happening; innovation in process. (1981: 200)

Though written well before hip-hop's influence and authority were guaranteed—when the shouted declaration "hip-hop, it don't stop" expressed a combination of defensiveness and willful optimism—the articles featured here reflect an awareness that change *was* stirring. They offer a chronicle of an era when hip-hop still constituted an unknown "emergent" force that was being processed and aligned with prevailing cultural experiences and meanings. These articles and essays are, thus, also crucial facets of hip-hop's emergent cultural practices.

The chapters in this section are written by some of hip-hop's earliest commentators who observed *and* participated in its cultural manifestation. They present documentation of hip-hop's formative moments while reacquainting us with the operative discourses and visual descriptions of hip-hop in its primary stages. This is not abstract history written from secondary sources, but a series of accounts framed by writers and critics whose immediate environments were under radical revision as hip-hop's style, vernacular, and sensibilities spread, soon informing the lingua franca of an entire generation.

Sally Banes was an early commentator during hip-hop's formative stages, reporting in the New York press on the rise of breaking and the convergence between B-boying and the related elements of hip-hop including "graffiti" and "verbal dueling" (Banes, 1981: 32). As she observes, breaking began as an articulation of physical presence featuring equal doses of competition and visual display. It was—and remains—an expression of style, which, among its young B-boy leaders, is clearly related to status and social profile. From its beginning, breaking formed a link between the street and the nightclub, and it was a crucial factor in hip-hop's transition from the underground environment, including subway platforms and neighborhood parks, to the mass-mediated realm of mainstream culture. Breaking rapidly ascended in the popular imagination following a barrage of media exposure, first on the pages of urban newspapers and later in several low-budget Hollywood films (such as *Flashdance*, 1983; *Breakin'*, 1984; *Breakin' 2: Electric Boogaloo*, 1984; and *Beat Street*, 1984). Banes also emphasizes the communal character of early B-boy crews and the formation of organized collectives that developed within a coherent system of training, competitions, and show-downs. Arguably faster than any other aspect of hip-hop, breaking acquired a formal infrastructure that was as dynamic as some of the floor moves executed by the young B-boys.

Craig Castleman provides an impressively explicit synopsis of graffiti's rise and evolution in New York City, commencing with the obscure but ubiquitous tags by "TAKI 183" in 1971. As he explains, graffiti rapidly expanded from a casual urban youth practice to a fully evolved cultural pastime, simultaneously acquiring the status as a point of crisis and moral panic among civic authorities. As graffiti was politicized, its young perpetrators were concurrently demonized, pathologized, and criminalized, leading conservative critic Nathan Glazer to claim:

> while I do not find myself consciously making the connection between graffiti-makers and the criminals who occasionally rob, rape, assault, and murder [subway] passengers, the sense that all are part of one world of uncontrollable predators seems inescapable. (1979: 4)

Castleman's chapter offers a convincing explanation of the processes by which young black and Puerto Rican youths were defensively positioned against state power and, as graffiti evolved, its youth practitioners were increasingly placed under police surveillance and constraint. Indeed, this narrative offers a detailed account of the tensions between New York's youth and the city's authority structure that has endured in hip-hop to this day and that has been reproduced throughout the nation and in urban centers around the world wherever hip-hop has taken root. Castleman's perceptive analysis also links the antigraffiti crusade to a narrow, genteel urban aesthetic and internal administrative agendas involving, among other things, budgetary battles pertaining to New York's Metropolitan Transit Authority expenditures. The harsh punitive measures targeting mainly blacks and Latinos through much of the 1970s and early 1980s, along with the implementation of subway "buffing" and cleaning technologies, altered the cultural climate and eventually ended the "golden age" of subway graffiti in New York.

Offering a concise overview of breaking (or B-boying), Michael Holman's historical analysis connects the athletic practice to dance styles and cultural traditions spanning several continents and two centuries. He conjoins the global and the local, indicating the ways in which cultural influences flow across borders and are appropriated in highly particularized conditions. Holman, who reported on the early hip-hop scene and promoted performances at the infamous Negril nightclub, was ideally situated to observe the formation of pioneering B-boy crews who reveled in the simultaneous development of new, innovative moves and the opportunities to show them off in aggressive B-boy competitions with other New York crews. Through his words, the image of a complex system of urban movement and participation emerges. Holman also profiles several of the B-boy innovators whose skill and artistry were influential in opening new opportunities for MCs, DJs, graffiti artists, and B-boys throughout New York.

In two brief articles that were among the first reports on hip-hop in the music industry's primary trade magazine *Billboard*, Robert "Rocky" Ford, Jr., provides first-person accounts of the nascent DJ scene in the Bronx. The location and character of DJ and MC parties, as well as record stores selling the recorded material underlying the DJ's work, are locally situated and Ford's reports reinforce the fact that, in 1978–1979, there already existed a vibrant cultural infrastructure encompassing nightclubs, independent record retail outlets, and audiences. Ford's articles served notice to the music industry that DJ and MC practices were thriving in New York's upper boroughs, and although it took almost another five years for the major entertainment conglomerates to acknowledge hip-hop's cultural legitimacy and importance, black entrepreneurs in the Bronx, Harlem, Queens, and elsewhere nurtured an active scene. Ford's observations reflect the extent to which hip-hop was already part of an entertainment and leisure economy and was, thus, a commercially oriented phenomenon almost from the start. It is also interesting to note how the early MCs did not yet envision rapping as an end in itself but as a bridge to future endeavors in the broadcasting industry.

The Nelson George interview with three of rap music's originators—Afrika Bambaataa, Kool DJ Herc, and Grandmaster Flash—presents a reflective look at the atmosphere within which hip-hop evolved, while detailing the competitive nature of their relations within localized commercial market conditions. George, who for over twenty years has provided astute journalistic and cultural analysis of hip-hop, elicits descriptions of urban social change, technological issues, and aesthetic innovation from hip-hop's "founding fathers" and, through their words, it is evident that the early hip-hop scene was a fragmented amalgamation of practices, interests, and objectives. Rap is a highly appropriative music, borrowing inventively from myriad sources in the creation of new sonic forms. Moreover, rap music relies on the appropriation and rechanneling of music technologies, especially the turntable, mixer, and vinyl record, which, in the hands of DJ trailblazers, were invested with new meanings and applications. Describing the merging of electronic technologies with new lyrical styles and stage craft, George elicits a valuable profile of early hip-hop performance and the formation of what are today acknowledged as established hip-hop conventions. In this interview, one of the more resonant features is the emphasis on family and community as nurturing forces that provide an essential foundation for the work and play among hip-hop's first professional DJs.

REFERENCES

Banes, Sally. 1981. "Breaking Is Hard to Do: To the Beat, Y'All." *The Village Voice* (April 22–28): 31–33.

Forman, Murray. 2002. *The 'Hood Comes First: Race, Space, and Place in Rap and Hip-Hop.* Middletown, CT: Wesleyan University Press.

Hebidge, Dick. 1987. *Cut 'n' Mix: Culture, Identity and Caribbean Music.* London: Methuen.

Glazer, Nathan. 1979. "On Subway Graffiti in New York." *Public Interest*, no. 54 (Winter): 3–11.

Rose, Tricia. 1994. *Black Noise: Rap Music and Black Culture in Contemporary America.* Hanover: Wesleyan University Press.

Toop, David. 1984. *The Rap Attack: African Jive to New York Hip-Hop.* Boston: South End Press.

Williams, Raymond. 1981. *Culture.* London: Fontana Press.

1
Breaking

Sally Banes

Break dancing is a style of competitive, acrobatic, and pantomimic dancing. It began as a kind of game, a friendly contest in which black and Hispanic teenagers outdid one another with outrageous physical contortions, spins, and back flips, wedded to a fluid, syncopated, circling body rock done close to the ground. Breaking once meant only dancing on the floor, but now its definition has widened to include electric boogie, up-rock, aerial gymnastics, and all sorts of other fancy variations.

Although breaking is the newest part of hip-hop culture, it's the part that has made hip hop a media obsession. Five years ago the only people who had ever heard of breaking were the kids in New York's ghettos who did it. They didn't even have a definite name for the form—they sometimes called it "breaking," but they also referred to it as "rocking down," "b-boy," or just "that kind of dancing you do to rap music." By 1980—when the form had already been around for a few years—they weren't even very interested in it anymore. This kind of dancing was a passing fad, they felt, that would soon be replaced by roller disco. But history was to prove them wrong. Not since the twist, in the early sixties, has a dance craze so captured the attention of the media.

By 1984 only a hermit could *not* have known about breaking. It had arrived, not only in the United States but also in Canada, Europe, and Japan. Breaking had been featured in the 1983 Hollywood film *Flashdance*, the independent hip-hop musical film *Wild Style*, and the documentary *Style Wars* (which aired on PBS), served as the inspiration for the 1984 films *Breakin'* and *Beat Street*, and was rumored to be the subject of fifteen forthcoming Hollywood movies. Countless how-to books and videos had hit the market. Breaking had been spotlighted on national news shows, talk shows, and ads for Burger King, Levi's, Pepsi-Cola, Coca-Cola, and Panasonic. One hundred break dancers heated up the closing ceremonies of the 1984 summer Olympics in Los Angeles. And Michael Jackson had given the form national currency.

Breaking made the cover of *Newsweek* in 1984. Newspapers all over the country regularly carried stories on its latest ups and downs. The paradox emerged, as you flipped the pages of the *Washington Post* or the *Los Angeles Times*, that break dancers who'd come up in the ghetto were banned from city streets and shopping malls for causing disturbances and attracting undesirable crowds, while at the same time middle-class housewives and executives could learn to break dance in their spare time at classes proliferating throughout the suburbs. Doctors added to the form's acceptability by giving medical advice on how to survive it unbruised. And the *New York Times* began using breaking as a metaphor even in articles that had nothing to do with hip hop.

By now, break dancing was happening at bar mitzvahs, children's dance recitals, high-school proms, college dances, in prison talent shows, at ballet galas, and on Broadway, as well as in clubs and discos—and, in a second-generation revival, in city parks and on the streets once again. Even President Reagan was delighted by breaking when he saw the New York City Breakers perform in Washington, D.C., at a Kennedy Center gala.

The media hype about break dancing has changed both its form and its meaning. So to talk about break dancing you have to divide it into two stages: before and after media. Before the media turned breaking into a dazzling entertainment, it was a kind of serious game, a form of urban vernacular dance, a fusion of sports, dancing, and fighting whose performance had urgent social significance for the dancers. After media, participation in break dancing was stratified into two levels: professional and amateur. For the pros, break dancing had become a theatrical art form with a technique and a vocabulary that, like ballet's, could be refined and expanded. On this level, competition took on new meaning. It was no longer a battle for control of the streets, for neighborhood fame, or to win your opponent's "colors" (tee-shirt with crew insignia). Now cash prizes, roles in Hollywood movies, and European tours were at stake. For the amateurs, the element of competition had diminished. The appeal was a mixture of getting physically fit, tackling the challenge of breaking's intricate skills, and even becoming more like street kids, who've suddenly become stylish thanks to the meteoric vogue of hip hop.

Breaking first entered media consciousness when Martha Cooper, a photographer who had for years been documenting graffiti, was sent by the *New York Post* to cover "a riot" and found some kids—members of the High Times Crew, friends and relatives from West 175th Street—who claimed they'd been dancing, not fighting, in a subway station. One kid demonstrated some moves to a policeman, who then called in the others one by one. "Do a head spin," he commanded as he consulted a clipboard full of notes. "Do the baby." As each crew member complied, performing on cue as unhesitatingly as a ballet dancer might pirouette across a stage, the police had to admit defeat.

Or so the story goes. But, like ballet and like great battles (it shares elements of both), breaking is wreathed in legends. Since its early history wasn't documented—the *Post* never ran Cooper's photos—it lives on only in memories and has taken on mythological form.

The heroes of these legends are the b-boys, the original break dancers, black and Hispanic teenagers who invented and endlessly elaborate the heady blend of dancing, acrobatics, and warfare that is breaking. Like other forms of ghetto street culture and like the other elements of hip hop, breaking began as a public showcase for the flamboyant triumph of virility, wit, and skill. In short, of style.

The intensity of the dancer's physicality gives breaking a power and energy even beyond the vitality of graffiti and rapping. If graffiti is a way of "publishing," of winning fame by spreading your tag all over the city, breaking is a way of claiming the streets with physical presence, using your body to publicly inscribe your identity on the surfaces of the city, to flaunt a unique personal style within a conventional format. The body symbolism makes breaking an extremely powerful version of two favorite forms of street rhetoric—the taunt and the boast. The razzing takes the form of insulting gestures aimed at your opponent, while the bragging is expressed through acrobatic virtuosity. Breaking is a competitive display of physical and imaginative prowess, a highly codified dance form that in its early stages served as an arena for both battles and artistic invention and that allowed for cracking open the code to flaunt personal inventiveness.

The High Times Crew told the cops they were dancing, not fighting, and as breaking captured mainstream attention it was touted in the media as a transfiguration of gang warfare. Breaking may be a stylized, rhythmic, aesthetically framed form of combat—but it still escalates, at times, into actual violence. Peace is volatile when honor is at stake, and the physical heat of the form itself makes for situations that are highly combustible, as scenes from both *Breakin'* and *Beat Street* show.

Until breaking became frozen and legitimated by media hype, it was, like much of kids' culture in our cities, self-generated and nearly invisible to outsiders, especially adults—who just didn't want to even think about it or know about it, much less watch it. It was both literally and figuratively an underground form, happening in the subways as well as in parks and city playgrounds, but only among those in the know. Its invisibility and elusiveness had to do with the extemporaneous nature of the original form and also with its social context. Breaking jams weren't scheduled; they happened when the situation arose. You didn't get advance notice of a breaking "performance"; you had to be in the right place at the right time. In other words, you had to be part of the crew system that provided social order among the kids of the Bronx, Manhattan, and Brooklyn ghettos.

Since May 1981, when Henry Chalfant presented the Rock Steady Crew at Common Ground in SoHo as part of a graffiti rock show, breaking has taken to theatrical presentation like a duck to water. The first article on the form, by Sally Banes with photos by Martha Cooper, appeared in the *Village Voice* just before the concert, giving breaking instant visibility. By the end of that summer, break dancers had appeared outdoors at Lincoln Center and at other festivals, and endless filming had begun. The Rock Steady Crew signed up for an appearance in *Flashdance*, and kids were already learning to break not from older brothers and cousins on the street, but from watching Rock Steady on TV. Breaking had entered the public eye and left the underground for the mainstream, and this new theatrical context, with a style largely disseminated by the Rock Steady Crew, quickly crystallized the form for spectators.

Through breaking, in its original form, all the pleasures, frustrations, hopes, and fears of adolescence were symbolically played out in public spaces. Breaking was inextricably tied to rapping, both in terms of its style and content and because the rap provides the insistent percussion that drives the dance.

The format of the dance was at first quite fixed. The dancers and onlookers formed an impromptu circle. Each person's turn in the ring was very brief—ten to thirty seconds—but packed with action and meaning. It began with an entry, a hesitating walk that allowed him time to get in step with the music for several beats and take his place "onstage." Next the dancer "got down" to the floor to do the footwork, a rapid, slashing, circular scan of the floor by sneakered feet, in which the hands support the body's weight while the head and torso revolve at a slower speed, a kind of syncopated, sunken pirouette, also known as the helicopter. Acrobatic transitions such as head spins, hand spins, shoulder spins, flips, and the swipe—a flip of the weight from hands to feet that also involves a twist in the body's direction—served as bridges between the footwork and the freeze. The final element was the exit, a spring back to verticality or a special movement that returned the dancer to the outside of the circle.

The entry, the footwork, and the exit were all pretty formulaic, with very little room for showing off personal style, although some dancers created special versions of these elements—Frosty Freeze, for instance, often exited "on point," walking on the tips of his sneakers. The entry, the footwork, and the exit were like the stock expressions and nonsense syllables that sandwich narrative content in a rap. They provided a rhythmic frame for the freeze, an improvised pose or movement, which broke the beat. They also provided a nicely textured, comfortably predictable backdrop against which the freeze stood out in bold relief. And besides their aesthetic function, these segments were a way for the dancer to "tread water" between strokes, to free the mind for strategizing while the body went through familiar, uninventive paces.

The simplest combination of a breaking sequence was entry-footwork-spin-freeze-exit. But turns in the center could be extended by inserting more footwork-spin-freeze segments.

In other words, you might get: entry-footwork-spin-freeze-footwork-spin-freeze-exit. And so on.

The entry, the footwork, and the exit framed the freeze, a flash of pure personal style, which was the most important part of the dance. The main thing about the freeze was that it should be as intricate, witty, insulting, or obscene as possible. "You try to put your head on your arm and your toenails on your ears," explains Ken of the Breakmasters crew. "When you spin on your head," says another b-boy. "When you take your legs and put them in back of your head out of the spin." A dancer might twist himself into a pretzel, or strike a cocky salute. He would quote the sexy poses of a pinup girl, or perhaps present his ass to his opponent in a gesture of contempt. Through pantomime, he might extend the scatological insult even more graphically, pretending to befoul his opponent. Or he might hold his nose, telling the other guy he stinks. He might put his hand to his spine, signaling a move so good it hurts. Sometimes the dancers in the opposing crew joined in, razzing the performer from the sidelines.

Some of the freeze motifs prophetically rehearsed possible futures for the b-boys. Several images quoted sports actions—swimming, rowing a boat—and even more suggested the military. The freeze celebrated the flexibility and budding sexuality of the gangly male adolescent body, and looked forward to sexual adventures or commemorated past ones. The gun imagery of the military pantomimes doubled as phallic imagery. A dancer would often grab his crotch or hump the floor for a memorable finale.

Another important set of motifs in the freeze section was the exploration of body states in a subjunctive mode—things not as they are, but as they might be—comparing and contrasting youthful male vitality with its range of opposites: women, animals (dogs, horses, mules), babies, old age, injury and illness (e.g., a heart attack à la Richard Pryor's routines), and death.

Various dancers had their specialties, especially in the freeze, but also sometimes in the other sections of the dance. Crazy Legs got his name from his rubber-legged way of walking into the ring, a move descended from the Charleston, and he also takes credit for the W, both face-up and face-down. Kip Dee claims he invented the elbow walk. As breaking moved from the streets to the stage, dancers teamed up to make group freezes, a development that has been elaborately extended over the past two or three years.

In the broadest sense, freezes were improvised. Few were devised on the spot; they were imagined and worked out in advance. But they allowed for the greatest range of individual invention, and the choice of which freeze to use at a given time was often an extemporaneous decision. The b-boys used a variety of methods to create new freezes, including techniques, such as accidents and dreams, preferred by shamans and by the Dadaist and Surrealist painters and poets. Not all freezes have names, but to name your speciality—and to write it as graffiti—was a way of laying claim to it, a kind of common-law copyright.

In breaking as street competition, the freeze was the challenge that incited, a virtuosic performance as well as a symbol of identity. As each dancer repeatedly took his turn and, through a series of strategic choices, built excitement with a crescendo of complicated, meaning-packed freezes, he won status and honor for himself and for his group.

The b-boys organized themselves according to neighborhood or family ties into crews, which were networks for socializing, writing graffiti, and rapping, as well as dancing, held together by a strict code of ethics and loyalty. Crews performed in a spirit of friendly competition at jams where the crew leader directed the group's moves. One kid would set up a challenge, and a b-boy from the opposing crew would try to top him, or "burn" him. The crew leader was in charge of sending in new players to spell someone who had run out of moves. Onlookers—more friends, relatives, and neighbors—would judge the contest by consensus. B-boys learned to dance in a system of master-apprentice, referring to each other as father and son—even though the "father" was usually only a few years older than his "son"!—and even chose names that reflected their relationship, like Ty Fly and Kid Ty Fly.

In those days, although there were some girls who joined in, most of the break dancers were boys from the ages of about eight to sixteen. One reason that girls were the exception was that breaking was a specific expression of machismo. Part of its macho quality comes from the physical risk involved—not only the bruises, cuts, scratches, and scrapes, but also the risk of real fighting that might erupt. And part of it is the deliberate attempt to impress the girls.

Breaking was one kind of "rocking," which also included up-rock, a more pantomimic, narrative style of dancing done jumping down and up to standing level, kicking, jabbing, and punching right in a rival's face, without actually touching. In up-rock every move is intended to insult the opponent, and besides actual fighting gestures, a dancer might mime grabbing his rival's private parts, smelling his hand, making a face, and then throwing the offending odor back. Up-rock is funny, but like a rapper's boast it has a mean edge.

The break dancer's "costume" was born of necessity as well as style. Tee-shirts and net over-shirts provide traction on the spins, and sneakers are important to the footwork. Their critical role in the dance is emphasized by making the feet look gigantic and by nearly fetishizing the shoes with embellishments like wide, bright laces loosely tied so that the tongues stick out. The insignia of the crew, as well as colors and outfits that coordinate with those of fellow crew members, play a part in intensifying group solidarity. And the overall look of militarized athleticism creates an image of power and authority. The other accessory for break dancing is a mat, made of cardboard or linoleum, that originally protected the dancers from scraping against concrete.

For the current generation of b-boys, it doesn't really matter that the breakdown is an old name in Afro-American dance for both rapid, complex footwork and a competitive format. Or that a break in jazz means a soloist's improvised bridge between melodies. Or that *break* is a technical term in Haitian voodoo, referring to both drumming and dancing, that marks the point of possession. Katherine Dunham defines the term as "convulsive movements and sharp temporary changes in a ceremonial ... rhythm." Or that in a different Afro-American culture, in French Guiana, there is an old dance called, in Creole, *cassé ko* (translation: breaking the body). All these connections have obvious links with break dancing as we now know it. For the b-boys, memory is short and history is brief; breaking started in the mid-seventies, maybe in the Bronx, maybe in Harlem. It started with Afrika Bambaataa's Zulus. Or with Charlie Rock. Or with Joe, from the Casanovas, from the Bronx, who taught it to Charlie Rock. "Breaking means going crazy on the floor," one b-boy explained back in 1980. "It means making a style for yourself."

As Fab Five Freddy (Fred Braithwaite), the musical director for *Wild Style*, remembers it, breaking began when rapping did, as an intuitive physical response to the music. "Everybody would be at a party in the park in the summer, jamming. Guys would get together and dance with each other, sort of a macho thing where they would show each other who could do the best moves. They started going wild when the music got real funky "—music by groups like SuperSperm and Apache. As the beat of the drummer came to the fore, the music let you know it was time to break down, to freestyle." The cadenced, rhyming, fast-talking epic mode of rapping, with its smooth surface of sexual braggadocio, provided a perfect base for a dance style that was cool, swift, and intricate. The structure of the rap, with its play of quick, varying rhythms going on and off the beat within a steady four-square pulse, is like the off-balance, densely packed, lightning-speed pace of the breaking routine. The sense of inclusiveness, of all being in on a fun time together ("Everybody say ho!" "This is the way we rock the house!" "I am! We are!"), of turn-taking, is there both in the rap and in the dance. At times the lyrics of the rap even dictate the break-dancing moves, as the MC calls out the names of the dancers and the steps.

For the current generation of b-boys the history of breaking may reach back only to recent memory—and even those stories conflict—but of course in a broader sense the history of breaking goes back to the slave trade, when Afro-American dancing was born. Breaking *is* something new and original, born of American ghetto culture in the seventies and (in its latest manifestation) in the eighties, but its basic building blocks are moves from the Afro-American repertory, which includes the lindy and the Charleston and also includes dances from the Caribbean and South America. *Capoeira*, a Brazilian form of martial art that, since slaves were forbidden to practice it, evolved as a dance to disguise itself, bears a striking resemblance to breaking, with its crouching, circling, cartwheeling moves. And, as the Africanist Robert F. Thompson has pointed out, *capoeira* is a pretty direct descendant from Angolan dance. But while breaking is not *capoeira*, but something unique, and while breakers may never have seen *capoeira* until others pointed out to them the similarities of the two forms, the two dance/sport/fight forms have the same roots, just as rapping and the collage of music that comes with it are new and at the same time firmly rooted in a tradition of black and Hispanic music and verbal style.

The main source of the movement in breaking is black dance, but like the rest of hip hop, breaking is an exuberant synthesis of popular culture that draws on everything in its path. Some moves can be traced to the Caribbean, some to the black church, some to the Harlem ballrooms of the twenties and thirties, some to such dances as the lindy and the Charleston, and others to such diverse sources as kung-fu movies—which were immensely popular in the seventies—*Playboy* magazine, French pantomime, cartoons, comics, and TV.

Like any form of dance, breaking is more than the sum of its movements; it is also the way movements are combined, as well as the costumes, music, setting, audience, and the interaction between dancers and spectators. And its context. As an integral part of hip hop, breaking shares many stylistic features with graffiti, rapping, and scratching. Like wild-style graffiti, it emphasizes flamboyance, and the embellishment of the tag finds its parallel in the freeze. The act of writing graffiti is, despite its acceptance on canvas at the Fifty-seventh Street galleries, an act of defacement, and breaking, in its days before media hype, was an act of obscene gestures, a threat. In both graffiti and breaking, each piece or freeze is a challenge, a call to rivals to try to top this, and at the same time a boast that it is unbeatable. Graffiti, rapping, and breaking alike celebrate the masculine heroes of the mass media—Superman and other comic-book heroes, the Saint of detective book and TV fame, athletes, kung-fu masters, and great lovers. The obscure gestural ciphers of breaking find their parallels in the (deliberately) nearly unreadable alphabets of wild-style graffiti, the (deliberately) nearly unintelligible thicket of rap lyrics, and the (deliberately) barely recognizable music that is cut up and recombined in scratching.

Graffiti writers make up new names for themselves, choosing tags partly on the aesthetic grounds that certain letters look good together; break dancers, too, rename themselves, either after their dancing specialty or style—Frosty Freeze, Kid Glide, Spinner, Little Flip—or, like rappers and DJs, with an alliterative name that sounds good—Eddie Ed, Nelly Nell, Kip Dee. And they name their crews in a similar fashion: Breakmasters, Rock Steady, Dynamic Breakers, Magnificent Force, Rockwell, Floormasters, Rockers' Revenge, Supreme Rockers, Furious Rockers. Just as graffiti writers mark off city territory and lay title to it with their tags, breakers claim space by tracing symbols on the streets with their dancing and penetrating public space with their ghetto blasters. To write on subway trains, to strike obscene poses, to wear torn clothing, to scratch records, to talk in secret codes, and to sing one's sexual exploits and other praises are transgressive acts. But it is a mark of our times that even such acts, vivid, proud, and aggressive, transmuting destruction into imaginative creation, can be defused as mainstream culture adopts them. Instead of dreaming of becoming revolutionaries, as they might have in the sixties, in the eighties the b-boys aspire to be stars. And at least for some of them, the dream has already come true.

After media exposure, the form of break dancing immediately began to change as theatrical and other experiences—such as a panel at a conference on the folklore of the Bronx—were brought back to "home base." The folklore conference arranged a jam at a roller disco in the Bronx, and soon after, Henry Chalfant and Tony Silver, the directors of *Style Wars*, shot a battle between the Rock Steady Crew and the Dynamic Rockers (later Dynamic Breakers) at a roller disco in Queens. The stage was set for the scene at the Roxy, a roller disco in Chelsea, in Manhattan, that soon replaced the Negril as the venue for Wheels of Steel hip-hop nights. When *Style Wars* was being filmed, the owner of the Queens disco kept clearing out the circle so the cameramen could get in. The next time Rock Steady was break dancing in the park, the crew's president, Crazy Legs, was walking back and forth saying, "Open up the circle."

By now, the circular format has opened up so far it's become linear, for greater theatrical legibility. Less improvisation takes place as well-worn popular moves become standard. As is often the case in the development of a dance form, acrobatic transitions are elaborated, while the freeze, which once concentrated personal expression, competitive gestural dialogue, and group style into a single significant image, has dwindled away to almost nothing and sometimes even merges with the exit. What once was a dance for adolescents is now the terrain of young adults, professionals whose bodies are less gangly and whose higher level of skill is commensurate with their years of practice. Group choreography and aerial spins, reminiscent of the spectacular balancing acts of circus gymnasts, have added to breaking's theatrical brilliance, as has the influx of electric boogie, popping, locking, ticking, King Tut, the float, and other moves that are not break dancing *per se*, into the genre.

Locking is a comic dance that creates the illusion that a person's joints are stuck in one place while his extremities are swinging in wild, rapid circles. It was originally popularized in the early seventies by dancers on the popular black dance television program *Soul Train*, which spawned a dance group called the Lockers, whose flamboyance made locking and the related popping—where one segment of the body moves while others stay still—nationally known. Fred Berry, star of the seventies television comedy series *What's Happening!!*, Jeffrey Daniels, ex-member of the pop-funk vocal group Shalamar, and choreographer Toni Basil were key members of the dance troupe. Berry's bouncy body and beefy face were symbolic of locking's comic appeal. Daniels, a willowy stick figure with an enormous Afro, not only locked and popped, but did a mean robot (the moves look like they sound)—and, along with Michael Jackson, helped spread the moonwalk, a pantomimed illusion of walking backwards, via Shalamar tours and videos. Basil, a choreographer since the sixties, when she worked on the television series *Shindig!* and the legendary film *The T.A.M.I. Show*, worked throughout the seventies and eighties integrating the Lockers' moves into progressive film and video projects, such as her contribution to the Talking Heads' trailblazing "Once in a Lifetime" video. Another noteworthy ex-Locker is the Latin dancer Shabbadoo, who went on to star in the break dance film *Breakin'*.

The electric boogie is a mimelike movement of the entire body, full of wiggles and robotic head turns, that refined the Lockers' movements into a more fluid, less jerky style. It was inspired by moves seen on a summer replacement television show hosted by mimes Shields and Yarnell. Kids picked up on it from TV, as they had locking, and embellished it, though the mime artists' white gloves are often worn by street dancers. Also via television came the King Tut and its kissing cousin the Egyptian after comedian Steve Martin appeared on *Saturday Night Live* in mock Egyptian garb to perform his hit single "King Tut." With his arms aimed out at sharp right angles, Martin resembled a talking stone carving, and this move was quickly assimilated by youngsters.

All these moves—locking, popping, the electric boogie, the King Tut, and the Egyptian—were similar in that each emphasized arm and upper-body motions, and unlike break dancing, kept the dancers in basically upright positions.

As kids began to learn break-dancing moves by watching the pros on TV or at dance classes, instead of from breakers on the street, the performance style became homogenized. There's now more of a tendency to copy personal style directly instead of making one's own signature. Amateur breaking still happens—in fact, more than ever, as children as well as adults of all classes and ethnic backgrounds get down at school dances, country clubs, shopping malls, in living rooms, and even on street corners, not in the original competitive mode, but as a money-earning public performance.

The flexibility and resilience of breaking is evident in the way it incorporated electric boogie and other new moves, rather than letting itself be replaced by them. B-boys vow that it will never die out but, like ballet, become an honored tradition. Interviewed by the *New York Times*, Kid Smooth, sixteen years old, imagined having a son and that son having a conversation someday with his friends: "One kid says, 'My father is a doctor.' The other kid says, 'My father is a lawyer.' And my kid, he says, 'My father spins on his head.'"

At a time when youth culture is again taking center stage in America, the rest of the country is fascinated by black and Latin kids' street life precisely because of its vivid, flamboyant, energetic *style*. It symbolizes hope for the future—born of a resourceful ability to make something special, unique, original, and utterly compelling out of a life that seems to offer very little. As Fab Five Freddy puts it, "You make a new style. That's what life on the street is all about, just being you, being who you are around your friends. What's at stake is a guy's honor and his position in the street. Which is all you have. That's what makes it so important, that's what makes it feel so good—that pressure on you to be the best. Or to try to be the best. To develop a new style nobody can deal with. If it's true that this stuff reflects life, it's a fast life."

2
The Politics of Graffiti

Craig Castleman

In 1972 subway graffiti became a political issue in New York City. In that year and the two following, a variety of elected and appointed city officials, particularly Mayor John V. Lindsay, devised and debated graffiti-related policies and programs and issued numerous public statements on the subject.

In examining the progress of subway graffiti as a political issue, New York's newspapers and magazines serve as a revealing and important resource, for not only did they report the graffiti policies of public officials but seemingly played a role in motivating and shaping them as well.

By summer 1971 the appearance of the mysterious message "Taki 183" had sufficiently aroused the curiosity of New Yorkers to lead the *New York Times* to send one of its reporters to determine its meaning. The results of his search, published on July 21, 1971, revealed that Taki was an unemployed seventeen year old with nothing better to do than pass the summer days spraying his name wherever he happened to be. He explained, "I just did it everywhere I went. I still do, though not as much. You don't do it for girls; they don't seem to care. You do it for yourself. You don't go after it to be elected president."[1] The reporter interviewed other neighborhood youths, including Julio 204 and Ray A.O. (for "all over"), who were following in the footsteps of Taki, to whom they referred as the king, and he spoke with an official of the MTA who stated that more than $300,000 was being spent annually to erase graffiti. Patrolman Floyd Holoway, a vice-president of the Transit Patrolmen's Benevolent Association questioned by the reporter as to the legal machinery relating to graffiti writing, explained that graffiti was barred only by MTA rules, not by law. Thus writers under the age of sixteen could only be given a lecture, not a summons, even if they were caught in the act of writing on the walls. Adult writers could be charged with malicious mischief and sentenced to up to a year's imprisonment.

Taki confessed that as he grew older, he worried more about facing adult penalties for writing graffiti but admitted, "I could never retire ... besides ... it doesn't harm anybody. I work. I pay taxes too. Why do they go after the little guy? Why not the campaign organizations that put stickers all over the subways at election time?"[2]

The *Times* article presented Taki as an engaging character with a unique and fascinating hobby, and this seemed to have a profound effect on the city's youth. Taki became something of a folk hero, and the ranks of the graffiti writers increased enormously. However, though each day brought numerous new writers to the walls and the subways were marked with names from top to bottom, 1971 brought no further press coverage of graffiti.

In spring 1972 another article on graffiti appeared in the press. It was intended not to help familiarize New Yorkers with the writers but to declare war on them. On May 21 city council president Sanford Garelik told reporters, "Graffiti pollutes the eye and mind and may be one of the worst forms of pollution we have to combat." He called upon the citizens of New York to band together and wage "an all-out war on graffiti" and recommended the establishment of a monthly "antigraffiti day" on which New Yorkers, under the auspices of the Environmental Protection Agency, would scrub walls, fences, public buildings, subway stations, and subway cars.[3]

The *Times*'s management followed up on Garelik's statement by printing an editorial denouncing the "wanton use of spray paint to deface subways." They praised Garelik's "noble concept" of an antigraffiti day but questioned its lasting appeal. Rather than burden the populace with the responsibility for cleaning up graffiti, the *Times* called upon the city administration to ban the sale of spray paint to minors and thus stop graffiti at its source.[4]

Taking his cue from both the *Times*'s and Garelik's suggestions, Mayor Lindsay announced his own antigraffiti program in late June. The mayor's proposal called for the fining and jailing of anyone caught with an open spray can in any municipal building or facility. Lindsay was highly agitated at the time of the announcement, and Robert Laird, his assistant press secretary, admitted to a *Times* reporter that "the unsightly appearance of the subways and other public places created by the so-called graffiti artists has disturbed the Mayor greatly."[5]

Lindsay again addressed the graffiti problem in extemporaneous comments before a large crowd at the rededication ceremonies for Brooklyn's Prospect Park boathouse in late August. Standing before the white ceramic exterior of the newly renovated structure, Lindsay noted that he had asked for tighter legislation against graffiti vandalism but said that police action alone would not cure the problem. Pleading for greater public interest in the problem, the mayor exclaimed, "For heaven's sake. New Yorkers, come to the aid of your great city—defend it, support it and protect it!"[6]

Lindsay's graffiti legislation had been referred to the city council's General Welfare Committee in early August, but the members had shown little inclination to deal with it at that time. (The council meets only twice during the summer months, and committee activity is virtually suspended from July to September.) Impatient with the committee's foot dragging, Lindsay insisted that they hold a special meeting on graffiti on August 31. The mayor asked a number of top administration officials, including the deputy mayor, the parks commissioner, and the MTA chief administrator, to testify in favor of the legislation. But only four members of the fifteen-member committee were present at the session, and no action was immediately forthcoming.[7]

Meanwhile MTA chairman Ronan publicly gave his support to Mayor Lindsay's graffiti campaign. On October 28 he told reporters that he had instructed the transit police to charge "such miscreants with 'malicious mischief,' " and he urged the mayor to stress the seriousness of "this blighting epidemic" to the courts.[8] Later that same day Mayor Lindsay held a ceremony in his office at which he officially commended one of Dr. Ronan's transit policemen, patrolman Steven Schwartz, for his "personal crusade" against graffiti. Schwartz alone had apprehended thirteen writers in the previous six months, a record for graffiti arrests unmatched in the department. The mayor followed up the ceremony with a statement that it was the "Lindsay theory" that graffiti writing "is related to mental health problems." He described the writers as "insecure cowards" seeking recognition.[9]

The General Welfare Committee submitted a graffiti bill to the city council in mid-September stating that the use of markers and spray paint to write graffiti has "reached proportions requiring serious punishment for the perpetrators" and that such defacement and the use of "foul language" in many of the writings is "harmful to the general public and violative of the good and welfare of the people of the city of New York."[10] The bill proposed to eliminate graffiti by making it illegal to carry an aerosol can of paint into a public facility "unless it is completely enclosed in a sealed container." It specified that "no person shall write, paint or draw any inscription, figure or mark of any type" on any public property. Judges were given wide latitude in dealing with such offenses, but the law stated that it was the council's intent that any person guilty of writing graffiti "should be punished so that the punishment shall fit the crime." In this spirit the bill recommended that judges sentence writers "to remove graffiti under the supervision of an employee of the public works office, New York City transit authority or other officer or employee designated by the court."[11] The bill also recommended that merchants selling spray paint or markers be required to register with the Police Department and to keep a record of the names and addresses of all persons who purchase such merchandise.[12]

The day after the General Welfare Committee approved the bill, the *Times* published an editorial stating that graffiti "are day-glo bright and multicolored, sometimes obscene, always offensive." The editorial praised the committee for getting tough with "youthful vandals" and announced that "graffiti are no longer amusing; they have become a public menace."[13]

Perhaps intending to spur the full council on to faster action on the graffiti law, Mayor Lindsay on October 5 announced the formation of a graffiti task force under the direction of his chief of staff, Steven Isenberg. The task force, which included among its members the heads of a number of city agencies, was designed to coordinate "tough new programs" for the enforcement of the expected graffiti legislation.[14] The mayor further stated that

> the ugliness of graffiti and the ugly message—often obscene or racist—has generated widespread support for the City's campaign to end this epidemic of thoughtless behavior. Even those who once possessed mild amusement about graffiti are becoming increasingly indignant at the damage being done.... I know the problem is complex, but we have to roll up our sleeves and solve it. The assault on our senses and on our pocketbooks as we pay the clean-up costs must be stopped.[15]

The graffiti bill was approved unanimously by the full city council on October 11, minus the section on control of the sale of spray paint, which had aroused opposition from merchants and was considered by the council to be "too controversial."[16] Mayor Lindsay, who signed it into law on October 27, was pleased with the bill but warned merchants to "self-regulate" their sales or he would impose further legislation that would make it illegal to sell spray paint to anyone under eighteen years of age.[17]

There was also antigraffiti action on other fronts. Science came to the aid of graffiti fighters with the invention, by E. Dragza of the Samson Chemical Corporation, of an "artproof acrylic polymer hydron" which he named Dirty Word Remover (DWR).[18] On July 31 Mayor Lindsay announced that Dragza's formula, renamed Hydron 300, was to be sprayed on a library in Queens, another in Brooklyn, and a firehouse in the Bronx, to facilitate the removal of graffiti from their walls. The mayor expressed hopes that use of the "Teflon-like coating" would help to make graffiti removal "easier and less costly." The cost of the experiment was set at $5,000.[19] Results of the test were never made public.

Inspired by the growing campaign against graffiti, private citizens also got involved in the "graffiti war" of 1972. In November the Kings County Council of Jewish War Veterans invited "citizens of good will" to join their bucket brigade to clean graffiti off the monument to President John F. Kennedy in Brooklyn's Grand Army Plaza.[20] The Boy Scouts and Girl Scouts staged their own graffiti cleanup day when more than 400 scouts spent a day partially cleaning six IND trains. Each participating scout received a citizenship medallion in honor of his or her achievement from the Avon Products Corporation.[21]

Other New Yorkers devised ingenious solutions to the problem. E.A. Sachs, for example, in a letter to the *New York Times* suggested that the MTA paint subway vehicles with a "multicolored spray" that would "camouflage any attempts at graffiting."[22] M.W. Covington, also in a letter, made the more drastic suggestion that a "massive police assault" be launched against graffitists who deface Central Park monuments.[23] R.H. Robinson of Brooklyn showed great ingenuity in his suggestion that large fines levied on convicted graffitists be divided between the city and persons turning in the graffitists. He noted that he had already assembled a lengthy list of offenders in his own neighborhood.[24] Of more than a dozen letters concerning graffiti that appeared in the *Times* that winter, only one was sympathetic to the writers. The letter writer, P.R. Patterson, hailed youths who paint graffiti for "cheering up the depressing environment in the poorer areas of the city" and accused most people of being "guilty of subduing the desire to mark up subways as a protest against the indignities of the city bureaucracy."[25]

Early in 1973 Steven Isenberg announced that over the year the police had arrested 1,562 youths for defacing subways and other public places with graffiti. Of those arrested, 426 eventually went to court and were sentenced to spend a day in the train yards scrubbing graffiti.[26]

Two weeks after Isenberg's announcement Frank Berry, the executive officer of the transit authority, announced that conventional "quick treatment" graffiti writing had reached the "saturation level" and was being supplanted by "large ... multi-colored inscriptions that may cover one-half or more of a subway car's outer surface." The alarming proliferation of such "grand design" graffiti constituted, according to Berry, distinct danger to riders because "they can block the vision of riders preparing to enter or leave through the door." In light of these new developments Berry called for an increase in the number of graffiti arrests to eliminate the possibility of a "grand design" epidemic.[27]

On February 26 the New York City Bureau of the Budget completed a detailed work plan for Mayor Lindsay's graffiti task force. The report began by stating that antigraffiti efforts in 1972 had cost the city $10 million, yet they had not been sufficient to reduce "the city-wide level of graffiti defacement" below "fifty percent surface coverage," a level that it declared "unacceptable."[28] It thus proposed that the city engage in a graffiti prevention project that would seek to reduce the level of defacement to an acceptable 10 to 20 percent. The cost of such a project was estimated to be $24 million.[29]

Under the control of a project management staff team appointed by the mayor, the proposed project would coordinate efforts by various city agencies and private corporations toward four major project elements:

- Technological improvements: Testing and implementing the use of high-performance paints, coatings, and solvents for graffiti-defaced surfaces.
- Security measures: Testing and implementing increased security measures in those areas of the city where security may deter graffiti vandalism.
- Motivation of graffiti vandals: Testing and implementing psychological measures aimed at either inhibiting vandalism or diverting vandals elsewhere.
- Control of graffiti instruments: Testing and implementing the feasibility of manufacturer and retailer restrictions on packaging and display of graffiti instruments.[30]

Under these categories the report listed nearly one hundred specific tasks, the completion of which would lead to the achievement of the overall objectives. The tasks included "implementing and monitoring psychological field-testing for graffiti vandalism prevention and developing procedures for monitoring of procedures involved in implementation of restrictions." Mayor Lindsay devoted a month to study of the report before releasing it or commenting on it publicly.

Meanwhile on March 26 *New York Magazine* published a long article by Richard Goldstein, "This Thing Has Gotten Completely Out of Hand." His reference was not to the growing graffiti fad but to the city's fight against it. Goldstein, giving the pro-graffiti forces their first published support, stated that "it just may be that the kids who write graffiti are the healthiest and most assertive people in their neighborhoods." He further declared graffiti to be "the first genuine teenage street culture since the fifties. In that sense, it's a lot like rock 'n' roll."[31]

In the same issue the *New York Magazine* management presented a "Graffiti 'Hit' Parade" in which it gave "Taki awards" to a number of graffitists in categories labeled "Grand Design" and "Station Saturation." Award-winning works were reproduced in full color in the magazine. They declared the emergence of grand design pieces a "grand graffiti conquest of the subways" and ridiculed chairman Ronan, Mayor Lindsay, and the *Times* for their attitude toward the new art form. The Taki Awards article also contained a statement in praise of graffiti from pop artist Claes Oldenberg that was reprinted in the catalog for two subsequent UGA exhibitions and was quoted in a number of magazine and newspaper articles about graffiti, as well as Norman Mailer's book, *The Faith of Graffiti*. Said Oldenberg:

> I've always wanted to put a steel band with dancing girls in the subways and send it all over the city. It would slide into a station without your expecting it. It's almost like that now. You're standing there in the station, everything is gray and gloomy and all of a sudden one of those graffiti trains slides in and brightens the place like a big bouquet from Latin America. At first it seems anarchical—makes you wonder if the subways are working properly. Then you get used to it. The city is like a newspaper anyway, so it's natural to see writing all over the place.[32]

The day after the *New York* articles appeared, Mayor Lindsay called a press conference at which he discussed the findings and proposals contained in the graffiti prevention project report. He stated that copies of the work plan would be sent to the heads of the MTA, the Environmental Protection Agency, the board of education, and all other agencies and authorities concerned with graffiti prevention. He ridiculed "those who call graffiti vandalism 'art'" and asked the citizens of New York to join him in denouncing the graffiti vandals. "It's a dirty shame," said the mayor, "that we must spend money for this purpose in a time of austerity. The cost of cleaning up graffiti, even to a partial extent, is sad testimony to the impact of the thoughtless behavior which lies behind ... the demoralizing visual impact of graffiti."[33]

As graffiti continued to appear on subways and other city property, Mayor Lindsay became increasingly angry, not only at supporters of graffiti and the writers themselves but at his own staff for their inability to control the problem. In an interview with a *Sunday News* reporter, Steven Isenberg "smiled when he recalled two times when Mayor Lindsay burst into his office and—with four-letter fervor—ordered him to 'clean up the mess.' One time the Mayor had snipped a ceremonial ribbon at the opening of a Brooklyn swimming pool that was already covered with graffiti and the other time he had spotted a graffiti-laden bus in midtown. 'I certainly got reamed out,' Isenberg recalled."[34]

The mayor's anger over the continued appearance of graffiti on the subways exploded publicly on June 30, 1973. Steven Isenberg explained, "When the Mayor went to mid-town to publicize the parking ticket step-up, he took the subway back to City Hall and what he saw made him madder than hell."[35] Immediately upon his return to his office the mayor called a hurried press conference at which he snapped, "I just came back from 42nd Street in one of [MTA chairman] Dr. Ronan's graffiti-scarred subway cars, one of the worst I've seen yet."[36] The mayor stated that the extent of name marking in the trains and stations was "shocking" and pointed out that the antigraffiti force he had organized the year before had come up with a plan to prevent the writing through increased police surveillance of lay-ups, train yards, and stations. "Since the time the plan was sent to the MTA I haven't heard a word," he said. "I don't think they even bothered to look at it. They don't give a damn and couldn't care less about being responsive to elected officials."[37]

A few months later in an interview with Norman Mailer, Lindsay explained that his aggravation with graffiti was due to the fact that it tended to nullify many of his efforts to provide the city's subway passengers with "a cleaner and more pleasant environment" in which to travel. At that time the mayor was also attempting to justify the city's massive expenditures for new subway cars, which, once covered with graffiti, "did not seem much more pleasant" than the old cars.[38]

The graffiti policies that were established during the Lindsay administration are still being pursued. The MTA continues to scrub trains only to find them immediately redecorated. The police continue to apprehend writers only to see them released, unpunished, by the courts. It would seem that the failure of the city's expensive antigraffiti policies should be a matter of great concern to the press and elected officials; however, the management, expense, and overall wisdom of New York City's antigraffiti policies have not been criticized publicly by either politicians or the press and thus continue unchanged.

Norman Mailer attributed Lindsay's attitude toward graffiti to the fact that the mayor had earlier sought the Democratic presidential nomination in 1972 and that graffiti had been

> an upset to his fortunes, … a vermin of catastrophe that these writings had sprouted like weeds over the misery of Fun City, a new monkey of unmanageables to sit on Lindsay's overloaded political back. He must have sensed the Presidency draining away from him as the months went by, the graffiti grew, and the millions of tourists who passed through the city brought the word out to the rest of the nation: "Filth is sprouting on the walls."[39]

It is doubtful that graffiti played as important a role in Lindsay's declining political fortunes as Mailer speculates. Evidently, however, Lindsay believed that graffiti was a problem significant enough to rate a substantial amount of his attention, and thus it became a political issue during his administration.

The fact that there has been very little reduction in the amount of graffiti that has covered the city's subways since 1971 can be seen as proof that the city's antigraffiti policies have failed. John deRoos, former senior executive director of the MTA, has placed the burden of blame for this failure on the city's judicial system: "Almost all graffiti can be traced to people who have been arrested at least once. But the courts let them off. Six, seven, eight, or nine times."[40] In an interview former transit police chief Sanford Garelik also laid the blame for the failure of the MTA's graffiti arrest policies on the courts: "The transit police are doing their job but what's the use of making arrests if the courts refuse to prosecute? Graffiti is a form of behavior that leads to other forms of criminality. The courts have to realize this … anything else is an injustice to the public."

Chief Judge Reginald Matthews of the Bronx Family Court has replied to such criticism of the courts' handling of graffiti: "Graffiti is an expression of social maladjustment, but the courts cannot cure all of society's ills. We have neither the time nor the facilities to handle graffiti cases; in fact, we cannot always give adequate treatment to far more serious crimes. Graffiti simply cannot be treated by the juvenile justice system as a serious thing, not in New York."

Not everyone in the MTA and the transit police blames the courts. Reginal Lewis, a car maintenance foreman at the MTA, puts the blame on the transit police for "not keeping the kids out of the (train) yards." Detective sergeant Morris Bitchachi, commander of the MTA's ten-member graffiti squad, blamed the city's Department of Social Services for not providing special rehabilitation programs for "known graffiti offenders."

City University professor George Jochnowitz had another idea: "The *New York Times* is ... responsible for the prevalence of graffiti. On July 21, 1971, an interview with Taki 183, a previously unknown graffiti dauber, appeared.... The glorification of this vandal by the nation's most prestigious newspaper was not without effect. Within months a minor problem became a major one."[41]

After 1975 there was little press coverage of graffiti, a reflection of the city government's reluctance to publicize the city's continuing failure to control the graffiti phenomenon. This, combined with the seeming unwillingness of the press to bring criticism upon itself through the publication of other Taki-style reports, led to a near press blackout on the subject of graffiti.

In 1980 the blackout ended when the *New York Times Magazine* published a long article about three graffiti writers: NE, T-Kid, and Seen. Other newspapers followed suit, featuring articles on other writers and on the current state of the graffiti phenomenon.

In September 1981 the mayor's office broke its silence when Mayor Koch declared that "New Yorkers are fed up with graffiti," and announced a 1.5 million dollar program to provide fences and German Shepherd watchdogs for the Corona trainyard. MTA chairman Richard Ravitch had at first rejected the idea, stating that, "fences are not going to work. It is likely that they would be cut and the dogs would get out and perhaps injure someone in the neighboring community."[42] Ravitch quickly gave in to pressure from the mayor, however, and a double set of razor wire-topped fences were quickly installed, between which six dogs patrolled the perimeter of the yard. Mayor Koch and the press were present on the day the dogs were released and the mayor declared, "We call them dogs, but they are really wolves. Our hope is that the vandals will ultimately get the message."[43]

To test the effectiveness of the fences and dogs, all of the trains stored at the yard were painted white and the mayor asked the MTA to inform him immediately if any graffiti was painted on them. For the following three months the trains were watched closely and no graffiti appeared on the outsides of the trains. Declaring the Corona experiment a success, the mayor announced on December 14 that the city would increase its contribution to the MTA by $22.4 million to fund the installation of similar fences at the other eighteen train yards operated by the authority. The mayor stated that the new security installations would not feature attack dogs because, at $3,000 per year apiece, their maintenance had proved too expensive. Instead, coils of razor wire would be placed between the fences. Said Koch, "I prefer to think of these as steel dogs with razor teeth. And you don't have to feed steel dogs."[44] Ravitch said that he was pleased by the mayor's decision to increase transit financing and that the MTA would attempt to complete construction of the new fences within six months.

Privately, MTA officials expressed doubts that the fences would, ultimately, be effective. Graffiti writers did so as well. Said Ali, "We haven't gone over the fences at Corona because it's on a lousy subway line. If they fence a popular yard like Pelham or Coney Island, the writers won't be stopped by razor wire, dogs, or laser towers. We'll get past the fences. Wait and see." Daze said, "All the fences will do is keep most of us out of the yards. We'll still be able to hit the trains in the lay-ups, and we'll bomb the insides and the outsides of in-service trains with tags—big spray-paint tags like nobody's ever seen. The MTA can't stop us from doing that unless they put a cop on every car." Bloodtea continued, "All they're doing is moving graffiti from the outsides of the trains to the insides. It's the inside graffiti—the tags—that the public hates. All the mayor is doing is getting rid of the outside pieces that the public likes, the big colorful pieces."

According to mayoral aide Jack Lusk, the yard-fencing program is the first step in a long-range antigraffiti program. Said Lusk;

"The public hates graffiti and it's up to us to do something about it. Fencing the yards will take care of some of it. Beyond that we're planning a series of antigraffiti television, radio, and print advertisements featuring the slogan. 'Make your mark in society, not on it.' We're also considering sponsoring antigraffiti citizens' groups; legislation banning the sale of spray paint and markers to minors; and possibly the establishment of a special transit court that will handle crimes like graffiti and other forms of vandalism. Even though the mayor does not have direct authority over the MTA, the public holds him responsible for the state of the subways. The public is frightened and disgusted by graffiti and they want us to do something about it. We're going to do whatever is necessary to wipe it out."

Notes

1. "'Taki 183' Spawns Pen Pals," *New York Times*, July 21, 1971, p. 37.
2. Ibid.
3. "Garelik Calls for War on Graffiti," *New York Times*, May 21, 1972, p. 66.
4. "Nuisance in Technicolor," *New York Times*, May 26, 1972, p. 34.
5. "Fines and Jail for Graffiti Will Be Asked by Lindsay," *New York Times*, June 26, 1972, p. 66.
6. "Lindsay Assails Graffiti Vandals," *New York Times*, August 25, 1972, p. 30.
7. Edward Ranzal, "Officials Testify in Favor of Mayor's Graffiti Bill," *New York Times*, September 1, 1972, p. 25.
8. Edward Ranzal, "Ronan Backs Lindsay Antigraffiti Plan," *New York Times*, August 29, 1972, p. 66.
9. Ibid.
10. "Stiff Antigraffiti Measure Passes Council Committee," *New York Times*, September 15, 1972, p. 41.
11. New York Administrative Code, Section 435–13.2 (1972).
12. "Stiff Administrative Measure Passes Council Committee," *New York Times*, September 15, 1972, p. 41.
13. "Scratch the Graffiti," *New York Times*, September 16, 1972, p. 28.
14. "Lindsay Forms 'Graffiti Task Force,'" *New York Times*, October 5, 1972, p. 51.
15. Office of Mayor John V. Lindsay, press release, October 4, 1972.
16. "Antigraffiti Bill One of Four Gaining Council Approval," *New York Times*, October 11, 1972, p. 47.
17. "Lindsay Signs Graffiti Bill," *New York Times*, October 28, 1972, p. 15.
18. "New Chemical May Curb Graffiti," *New York Times*, April 22, 1972, p. 35.
19. Office of Mayor John V. Lindsay, press release, July 31, 1972.
20. "Antigraffiti 'Bucket Brigade' Planned," *New York Times*, November 13, 1972, p. 41.
21. "Boy Scouts Scrub Graffiti Off Walls of Subway Cars," *New York Times*, February 25, 1973, p. 35.
22. E. H. Sachs, Jr., letter, *New York Times*, December 24, 1972, Sec. 8, p. 2.
23. M. W. Covington, letter, *New York Times*, December 26, 1972, p. 32.
24. R. H. Robinson, letter, *New York Times*, June 5, 1972, p. 32.
25. P. R. Patterson, letter, *New York Times*, December 14, 1972, p. 46.
26. *New York Times*, January 14, 1973, p. 14.
27. "Fight against Subway Graffiti Progresses from Frying Pan to Fire," *New York Times*, January 26, 1973, p. 39.
28. Bureau of the Budget of the City of New York, *Work Plan—Graffiti Prevention Project* (February 26, 1973), p. 2.
29. Ibid., p. 3.
30. Ibid., p. 2.
31. Richard Goldstein, "This Thing Has Gotten Completely Out of Hand," *New York Magazine*, March 26, 1973, pp. 35–39.
32. "The Graffiti 'Hit' Parade," *New York Magazine*, March 26, 1973, pp. 40–43.
33. Murray Schumach, "At $10 Million, City Calls It a Losing Graffiti Fight," *New York Times*, March 28, 1973, p. 46.
34. James Ryan, "The Great Graffiti Plague," *New York Daily News Sunday Magazine*, May 6, 1973, p. 33.
35. James Ryan, "The Mayor Charges MTA Is Soft on Graffiti," *New York Daily News*, July 1, 1973, p. 2.

36. Alfred E. Clark, "Persistent Graffiti Anger Lindsay on Subway Tour," *New York Times*, July 1, 1979, p. 47.
37. Ibid.
38. Norman Mailer, *The Faith of Graffiti* (New York: Praeger/Alskog Publishers, 1974).
39. Ibid.
40. Owen Moritz, "The New Subway," *New York Daily News*, December 5, 1978, p. 37.
41. George Jochnowitz, "Thousands of Child-hours Wasted on Ugly Daubings," *New York Post*, October 20, 1978, p. 43.
42. Ari L. Goldman, "Dogs to Patrol Subway Yards," *New York Times*, September 15, 1981, p. 1.
43. Ibid.
44. Ari L. Goldman, "City to Use Pits of Barbed Wire in Graffiti War," *New York Times*, December 15, 1981, p. B-1.

3
Breaking:
The History

Michael Holman

Introduction

In the spring of 1975 the 77th Street fountain in New York City's Central Park was the place to be. On weekends the hip kids from all the boroughs—Brooklyn, Bronx, Manhattan, Queens—came down to the fountain. With their radios, better known as ghetto blasters or boom boxes, they made the fountain a rocking inner city park scene.

The fountain is in a cobblestone area about half a mile square with a big Roman style fountain in the middle, cut out of the trees and grass of Central Park. It was like a hidden valley. Walking through the trees to reach it was like finding a hidden Mayan temple buried deep in a rain forest. Once you got to it, the square was an outside-in block party, rocking and shocking the midday. Most everyone there was Black or Spanish, with Italians, Irish, and some tourists, too. Radios blaring on the same station. Fellows throwing base at the girls. Girls in high heels dancing the Latin hustle on cobblestone. There were old men playing cards, dominoes, grooving to Tito Puente, having a taste. Families were having picnics on the grass hills surrounding the square. Vendors selling ice cream, soda, hot dogs, loose joints and more. To a California kid the way people dressed was hip to the point of being bizarre. How could so many people in one place be so cool?

Platform shoes were history at that point. Only tourists and diehard hippies wore them. Instead it was shoes like marshmallows. Fat toed, colorful shoes with one- to two-inch soles made out of chalk-white rubber. Those hip kids wore jeans, or thirties peg pants, always pressed, with a single one-inch calvary stripe down the leg, with pajama top T-shirts and gangster appleboy hats or baseball hats.

The girls were wearing tight jeans or skirts, high heels or flats, and T-shirts. I can't recall the names of all the stuff they wore or how they got it together, but I do remember that they looked awfully good.

And everywhere there was music and dancing. Some radios rocked James Brown or funk or disco. Tape machines blared Afro-Cuban while three or four live congo players made the sound a little more earthy. If the fellows weren't rapping or dancing with the girls, they were dancing in large groups with each other. They danced in crazy fresh three-, four- or five-man routines. I remember seven or eight guys who had on the street look with marshmallows, striped peg pants and all. They were in a dance formation I recognized as the bus stop, also known as the L.A. hustle. The bus stop was a dance where three or more people joined in military like platoon formations (people in rows side by side). All of the people in the bus stop formation marched forward in unison three steps, then to the side three steps, then to the other side three steps, then stopped and clicked heels, stomped their feet, turned around in place, and started again. There were sometimes thirty or more people in the bus stop formation. Truth can be stranger than fiction.

The way these kids at the fountain were doing the bus stop was completely different from the L.A. hustle as I knew it. At the moment that the usual dancers would stomp their feet and click their heels (like Dorothy in the Wizard of Oz), these New York kids dropped to the ground, spinning on the way, then did a little footwork freeze here, freeze there, then pop back up in time to pick up the rest of the routine. All of a sudden the radio cut to James Brown's live version of Sex Machine and the homeboys got loose. They all dropped the L.A. hustle like a bad joke and started going off on the drop and footwork. At first I thought it was a variation on the L.A. hustle; I realized later that the L.A. hustle was just a little experiment, these drops and footwork were the real deal. Their drop move was crazy fresh! I'd never seen it before. First they hopped, then stepped, then abruptly dropped to a squat with backs straight, on the snare drum note and popped back up into standing leg steps on the bass beats. Each guy had unique leg steps in between the drops, like Ali shuffles, spins, hops with one leg up then dropping down in a squat and coming up fast, all on the beat and with serious finesse. Like this: base-snare-bass-bass-bass, spin-drop-popup-shuffle, shuffle-snare-bass-bass bounce-bounce, drop spinup-snare-bass-bass-snare, step-step drop. They looked like Russian kazotsky dancers with soul.

Their footwork on the ground was bugged out, too. It looked like gymnastic sweeps and other footwork mixed with leg stretch exercises, splits, drops and spins done while squatting low to the ground, using the hands to propel the body. Some of the moves were strange and complicated, at the same time beyond my understanding. But I knew it was something very hip, very special. I liked this dance. It was more than just hip, it looked like fun. What I had witnessed for the first time that fine spring day in Central Park was the beginnings of a dance style that would evolve and later become an international phenomenon called breaking.

Part I

It was the mid-seventies, New York (the disco decade) that gave birth to breakdance style, but its roots date back to ancient Africa, feudal China, and tribal Eurasia.

"Oh no!" you say. "Boring history junk!" Well hold up home boys and home girls, just chill for a few and bust it. To appreciate breaking to the max you've got to understand how it started, and where it came from. After all, the more you know about breaking, the better you will be at (1) doing it, (2) being able to see its influence in other dance and art forms, or (3) impressing strangers with all the stuff you know.

Like most American dances, breaking owes much to eighteenth century American slavery, when African and European dance styles began to mesh. In early America the European and British Americans introduced the minuet, the waltz and the quadrille (the dance you always see in Three Musketeers movies). The African-American slaves introduced a shuffle step dance called the joba that sort of looked like a prehistoric tap dance, the snake hips, and the fishtail.

The hip thing to do if you were a slave was to imitate the master's dances in a mocking way just for fun while incorporating some of your own moves and rhythms. But unlike the highly civilized, properly timed European dances, African dance was about leaps, hops, skips, falls, drops and turns done to unrelenting tribal beats and rhythms. These moves done in combination with the European dance steps looked a little buggy. Like a proper eighteenth century gentleman trying to stay cool with a hot foot, I imagine it looked ridiculous at first, but then so did the L.A. hustle.

From (out of) those new cross cultural dance experimentations and in some of the purely African dances there were styles that resembled and would later, through American dance history, evolve to become the ultimate dance form: breaking.

Similar in style, for example, was the juba, which was done by one or more dancers in a circle of male dancers, each one taking his turn to go off. The steps they used were more like shuffle steps and tap than breaking, but the circle formation deal with one-at-a-time action is close. Within the same period of time, dances that use drops like the bullfrog hop resembled Brooklyn rocking. These slave dance creations soon caught the attention and interest of the masters. They began to see and appreciate their level of difficulty and creativity that went into these dances.

Being the kind-hearted type of chaps they were, the slave masters often let the best of the dancers have it a little easier, and being sporting fellows, the masters would encourage competition. Battles. Here's another important connection to breaking that has existed throughout American dance history. The competition. Every dance form done first by young Black men from the jiggy contest on the plantations of Texas in 1850 to tap dancing of the 20s to the jitterbug of the 30s and 40s to breaking today has always been about who was the best.

Even the electric boogie, which most people think could not have been created without European mime and Marcel Marceau, appeared to have its roots in early America. A dance called the Virginia Essence created by slaves, which combined British clog dancing and African shuffle steps, sounds a lot like the electric boogie. In 1872 ragtime composer Arthur Marshall was quoted as saying, "If a guy could really do it, he sometimes looked as if he was being towed around on ice skates. The performer moves forward without appearing to move his feet at all by manipulating his toes and heels rapidly." If that's not an early moon walk, then what is? Or how about this? A dance that appeared around the turn of the century in Black minstrel shows called Stepping on the Puppy's Tail also had an amazing resemblance to the moon walk. Stepping on the Puppy's Tail was described as moving each foot alternately backwards "like a horse pawing the ground." It just goes to show there's nothing new under the sun, or in this case under the moon.

There, that wasn't so bad. We peeked a look at how colonial American and pre-Civil War American dance had a few ties with breaking.

1. Dancers standing in circles while somebody in the middle does his thing.
2. A little electric boogie action.
3. The beginning of competition in American subculture dance.

In the 1850s Irish citizens emigrated to America. Poor, fleeing from potato famines, many settled in New York City in lower Manhattan, the same neighborhoods as most of New York's Blacks at the time. The Blacks were digging on their national dance called the Irish Jig. Unlike the British Jig (which is like what you see in pirate movies) the Irish Jig was controlled and required more skill. With the back straight and the arms firmly by the side, the legs and feet moved rapidly in complex time and rhythm and made clacking sounds on the floor.

The Blacks, who were doing the juba shuffle dance, combined it with the Irish Jig and developed the tap dance.

What does that have to do with breaking, you ask? Well, since tap has been around so long, it has connections with all the other dances that eventually did evolve into breaking.

At the turn of the century when Black dancers were touring the states with circus and carnivals as minstrels, things were beginning to get interesting. Since live acts in those days were about amazing some hick in the next town just to sell him medicine he didn't need, stage dancing became more spectacular and inventive.

For example, Jim Green, a dancer in a company called A.G. Allen's Mighty Minstrels, was known for a move he did that stopped the show. He'd dance for a while, then fall on the floor and spin around on his butt in time with the music, and he called it the Black Bottom. Hold everything! The first ass spin!?! Word up.

In New York, 1915, during the vaudeville years, a Black tap dancer named Dewey Weinglass, after seeing the Russian dancer Ivan Bankoff at a Broadway theater, started experimenting with Russian steps. He borrowed moves like drops, squats, sweeps, splits, tumbles, and flips and added them to his dance routines. Early in 1911 petite Ida Forsyne, only five feet tall, another American Black vaudeville dancer, used Russian moves in her shows and became a European sensation. She could do what the Russian peasant dancers did since she was so light and tiny. Like Kazotsky (the squatting kick dance that goes with da-da-da-dadadadada-hey!) but even faster. She added her own variations that even the Russian dancers couldn't do, all the way across the stage and return backwards. The first Black American collaborators with Russian dance had definite connections with top rocking, drops, footwork, and a lot of other gymnastic style moves in breaking!

I'd like to stop and make a prediction here. I predict that these Russian-influenced breaking moves will come full circle in the next couple of years as breaking breaks through the Iron Curtain. Russian gymnasts will completely dig it and pick it up as part of their gymnastic floor routines or as a separate gymnastic sport. But don't worry, if there's a battle. The Bronx will brush Moscow for years to come. Why the confidence, you ask? After all, the Eastern Europeans started a lot of this stuff and always do very well at the Olympics, thank you. But the reason they could never take us out is because breaking happens on funky beat of which Russians have no conception. This is also the major distinction between the original European dances and the copies by African-American slaves. The Blacks took stiff rhythms and made them rock. Therefore the Russkies would have to immigrate millions of Black Africans to Russia, and a few million Spanish, show nothing but Bruce Lee and Kung Fu films, wait a couple of hundred years and then battle us!

Flash dancing was a tap dance style that started in the 1920s and like the movie of the same name involved wild acrobatics. This was the time of crazy aerial acts like the Nicholas Brothers, the Four Step Brothers and the Berry Brothers. These dance crews were capable of forward flips with no hands, landing in splits, running up walls into flips (like the movie *Flashdance*), sliding in the splits across 50-foot stages, all of this taking place in between tap dance routines. It's no wonder that the 1983 film *Flashdance* would feature break-dancing, our generation's flash dancing. One dancer known as Pops Whitman was doing moves very similar to the drop moves of 70s New York and the perfected drops of the later 1980s. As described by a colleague, Baby Laurence Jackson, "I'm sure Pops Whitman invented a lot of flash steps. A front and back split that looked effortless but was almost impossible and a Russian twist that was indescribable. He started spinning like a top and went down into a squat and up over and over, each time he came up he was facing his audience with his ankles locked. In my book he was the greatest of all the acrobatic tap dancers."

Sounds like Baby Jackson was talking about New York City Breakers Powerful Pexster! Nothing new under the sun, just rehearsed a few times, that's all. Here's another story from the flash dance days that's pretty cool.

The Nicholas Brothers and the Berry Brothers, considered the top crews in flash dancing, challenged each other to a battle. It happened at New York City's downtown Cotton Club in 1938 while Cab Calloway's orchestra was rocking the house (46 years before the New York City Breakers battled Rock Steady in the film, *Beat Street*.)

The Berry Brothers supposedly took out the Nicholas Brothers, with a fresh move described as unbelievable the two brothers did a flying leap from a platform high above the stage twelve feet into the air and over the heads of Cab Calloway's orchestra. They landed twenty feet away downstage in a split right on the last note of the music. Some say the Nicholas Brothers were better all-around performers and acrobatic dancers, but not as accomplished in the flash acrobatics style for which the Berry Brothers had no rival. Flash acts were seen in more than just nightclubs. In the 30s and 40s hundreds of films were made featuring flash dancing. These films served to "turn on" millions of people in a short period of time to these unique dance styles. Out of those millions, thousands tried the dancing, hundreds perfecting and improving on the styles (which added to dance evolution). The films and television shows that breakers are now appearing in work in very much the same way. In the 50s couples were still doing the swing and jitterbug dances to rock and roll music while rock and roll performers started developing a new style of performance dancing that borrowed from the spectacular dance moves of generations before. Elvis Presley, for example, did something with his legs that dates back to early minstrel dancing called legomania or rubber legs. Jackie Wilson was the rock and roll rhythm and blues star who was famous for splits, spins and other moves from flash dancing of the 20s and 30s.

The dawn of the revolutionary sixties partner dancing gave way to a get it together and let it all hang out freestyle. Sixties youth challenged all established popular dance forms with new steps and moves focusing on expression. While revolting against both orchestrated lifestyles and sounds of the past and the new high technology of the present, Americans got hip to a funky music called rhythm and blues. Safely held in Black American culture for years, rhythm and blues, with its emphasis on tight beats and repetitive rhythm sections, finally had its day of mass popularity. American popular dance became more informal and expressive. In other words, America got loose. Soul and rhythm and blues labels like Decca, Motown, and Philly Sound hit an all-time high in popularity as they supplied America and the world with music tailor-made for the monkey, the jerk, and the mashed potatoes. Just when America was getting used to rhythm and blues, James Brown crashed on the set sing-screaming like a fiend, doing unbelievable sliding and spinning moves into splits, while his band played the funkiest bass rhythms and blues beats anyone had ever heard. He was it. The undisputed king of soul. James Brown combined old minstrel dances like the camel walk and the one-foot slide with 30s flash dances like spins and splits all on the funky rhythm and blues beats of his Fabulous Flames and created a new level of performance dance. Through his music he also created a new wave of popular dance styles.

James Brown created the ultimate dance music because it had unrelenting repetitive beats and rhythms that could make you dance forever. The James Brown sound doesn't speak to your head, it speaks to your body, to your arms and legs, your hips and your rear end, directing, supporting, moving you like a river current. James Brown brought a quality to American Black music which had been missing since tribal Africa. Low down funk. By the late 60s and into the early 70s, at the height of funk influence, popular dance also changed. Dances that imitated characters or animals like the monkey, or the Philly dog gave way to simple dance steps that were more about movement and body control. As music became more structural and steady in rhythm due to the emergence of funk, popular dancing evolved into an even greater form of freestyle. New York, with its history of Black dance and its street-wise culture, was first to develop and perfect freestyle street dancing. A freestyle dancer had confidence in the beat always being there at the same time and place. He could go off into steps, changes, drops, off-beat splits and moves, spins, and then at the last moment fall back to the original steps and on the beat.

Also made popular by James Brown were the bridges or breaks (in tempo and rhythm) in songs. He changed the rhythm and the tempo of the main part of the song to a new high intensity pace for about 15 to 20 seconds, then dropped back to the original beat without losing any timing or rhythm. The breaks lasted such a short time because they were too intense to fill the whole song and were a nice change of pace which made the song more interesting to listen to. For the freestyle dancers in the early 70s who used the more intense breaks to really go off and do the hottest moves, the breaks in the songs weren't long enough. D.J.s like Cool Herc in the Bronx recognized the frustrations of these freestyle dancers and would elongate the breaks in the record by using two of the same records on two turntables and a mixer. He mixed back and forth from record to record, never leaving the break. Now the freestyle dancers had their cake and could eat it too. With more break time, freestyle dancers developed new moves and styles to match the length and intensity of the special mixed breaks. As steps by freestyle dancers became more spectacular and unique, competition to see who was best became more intense. In order to outdo each other, freestyle dancers began dropping to the ground using Russian-style footwork and gymnastics moves like sweeps and splits. Comedy and pantomime in moves or routines helped to zap a judging crowd in freestyle dance battles which usually took place at the first hip-hop jams where break mixing D.J.s supplied the sounds. These freestylists of the early and mid-70s who danced in the breaks of funk and disco records were called B-boys or Break boys, and are the fathers of modern breakdancing. How breaking evolved to become what it is now is in the story ahead. Read on.

PART 2

The first real breakers were the gang members of Black gangs in the Bronx in the late 60s, early 70s. These guys did a dance called the Good Foot, from James Brown's record of the same name. The Good Foot was the first freestyle dance that incorporated moves involving drops and spins and resembled the beginnings of breaking. The best way to describe the Good Foot is to imagine a majorette marching in a parade taking steps raised high at the knee but keeping the leg raised at the knee in the air for a beat before dropping it down and simultaneously raising the other leg, like a stop action drum majorette on beat.

When the gangs disappeared and only party crews remained these Good Foot freestyle dancers hung out with the party crews, and as the party crew D.J.s started developing their techniques the freestyle dancers began to develop their own moves.

As the D.J.s invented new ways to elongate the break beats in the records, dancers had more time to invent and experiment. Soon moves like dropping down to the ground and popping up again on beat became standard and gave these first breakers the nickname of "boie-oie-oings."

Footwork came in when the boie-oie-oings started using their arms and hands to support their bodies in order to free the feet and legs to do gymnastic steps, shuffles and sweeps. In Brooklyn a new step inspired by these drops was being developed called the Brooklyn Rock. Once the first early break moves had been established (drops footwork, sweeps, etc.), a definite style began to develop. The first and longest lasting style was comedy.

Comedy style was developed by the ex-Black Spades Good Foot Dancers who had joined with the D.J. Cool Herc Party Crew called the "Herculoids." D.J. Cool Herc would throw a party and the Herculoids would put on a show of dance style moves called comedy that involved all kinds of pantomime, mime, acting and effects. The three Herculoids most famous for their comedy breakdancing were the "Nigger Twins" (Kevin and Keith Smith) and "Clark Kent." The "Chuch Center," famous for breakdance battles on 1159 Second Avenue in Manhattan, was one of the places where the "Nigger Twins," "Clark Kent" and "Cool Herc" were known to appear for performances. In these shows they would do moves ranging from simple Charlie Chaplin penguin steps and drop routines, in which they'd catch each other in step and on beat, to involved pantomime acts, like dropping to the floor in a freeze while hiding their faces and coming up wearing shaving cream, with a razor in their hand. They would shave the cream all off and on beat! Another way they would try to get a laugh out of an audience would be to go into a freeze and pop up eating a hidden sandwich.

Soon other breakdance crews were challenging the Herculoids with less comedy and more breakdance moves (and battles). Even though the Herculoids' moves were considered crazy they always felt that they'd at least be remembered if they were to lose in breakdance battles. Another early breakdancer, T-LaRock, who is now a rapping M.C., was known for another unusual pantomime routine. He would act as if he were grabbing the head of another breakdancer, taking it off his body, carry it to the middle of the dance floor, set it on the floor, dance around it and stomp on it making fun or humiliating the other dancer.

In 1977 another gang called "The Organization," which later became the world famous "Zulu Nation," put together a breakdance crew called "The Zulu Kings." The Zulu Kings were made up of dancers, Pow Wow (now a rapper with Soulsonic Force), Amid Henderson, Zambu, Aziz Jackson, and Kusa Stokes. The Zulu Kings were the first organized breaking crew to travel around the Bronx challenging other lesser known crews to battles. The Zulu Kings had moves like ass spins, spider walks, footwork, and mime similar to the electric boogie. There were also girl breakdancing crews in the Zulu Nation called the Zulu Queens and the Shaka Queens. Lisa Lee of the rapping group "Us Girls" was one of the Zulu Queens. The girl breakers of that time did not do the floor moves the guys did. They concentrated more on routines and synchronized group moves which pioneered the idea of complex routines for breakers years later. The Jackson 5 and other soul groups were the main inspiration for the routines the girls did. Their routines were choreographed to particular records and at certain moments in the record each girl would do a solo. Double dutch jump roping was also a major influence on the girl breakers of the late 70s.

As breaking became more popular in the Bronx, battles between breakers would take place in school during lunchtime in the cafeteria or in the hallways. A school was a very popular place for the early breakers to practice their moves, especially in the hallways during recess or if a breaker asked his teacher if he could go to the bathroom he always spent a few extra minutes practicing on the hard marble floors of the hallways before coming back to class.

In the old days breaking was done mainly at parties, not outside. And more often in the dark at night and mainly in the winter because that was when people came inside to party. In the old days people would get high before breaking, using this as an excuse for inspiration. This contrasts heavily with the athletic oriented breaker of today who frowns on the use of drugs and alcohol. Breakdancing today is so complex and physical that drugs interfere with one's ability to perform. In the past it was not as involved and as technical as today so this type of behavior was easily accepted. An interview with an early breakdancer, T-LaRock, of the west side of the Bronx, 173rd Street and University Avenue, reveals some interesting history. T-LaRock was part of a crew called the "Undefeated Four" which had M.C.s, D.J.s, and breakers. They battled against other crews like "The Red Devils," featuring the original Mr. Freeze and D.J. Smokie and the Smoketrons, one of the first D.J./M.C. breaker crews to bring sound equipment outside to entertain block parties. Vincent, one of the Smoketrons, was known for the move "the spider," and all the breakdancers of the Smoketrons were considered good. T-LaRock and another breaker named Matthew were known for breaking on toe. Like ballerinas, they would hop to their toes while they did normal breakdance moves. Unlike today the early breakers never allowed anything other than their hands or feet to hit the ground. To allow any other part of your body to hit the ground was considered uncool — it was called "sweeping the floor." The early breakers never did the same move as each other. It was important that each breakdancer come up with his own individual move that was unique. Another breakdancer from the early days known for his super flexibility was Rubber Band. Rubber Band had a sister named Mamma who was also very good at flexible breakdance moves. Though the early breakdance moves were not as complex and as physical as those of the 80s, the early breakers put more emphasis on breaking on beat. Though they did not have the power, speed, and technique of the breakers of the 80s, they had as much style and finesse.

In contrast with the early days of breaking, break dancing today is more premeditated, each move is thought out. In the 70s it was more spontaneous, freestyle.

From the mid to late 70s, breakdancers, who were primarily young Black kids and former gang members, to the early to mid-80s breakdancers of New York, who are predominantly Puerto Rican crew members, there are a couple of years of evolution from the simpler early breakdance steps of the Black kids to the more acrobatic breakdance steps of the Puerto Ricans that need to be traced. How and when did the young Puerto Rican Breakers of New York today pick up the art from the older Black breakdancers of the 70s? Who were the people involved? How did the moves change from simple floor exercise footwork, sweeps, and comedy to the more acrobatic gyroscopic backspins, headspins, and 1990 moves of the future?

In 1977 a dance emerged uptown called "The Freak." The Freak dance was a whole new sensation, again started by the Black kids, in which two or more guys would dance with one girl. The two guys would create a circle around the one girl and on beat do a somewhat physical bump-and-grind dance that became so popular it killed breaking uptown. Then came a dance called "The Spank," and soon breaking was forgotten. If you were into breakdance in late 77–78 you were ridiculed for doing the old thing, the old dance. The Puerto Ricans were impressed by what the Black kids were doing in the mid to late 70s, and they were just getting into breakdancing a little behind the Black kids. But their interest in breaking was much more intense. They were the ones who started taking it to even higher levels of acrobatics and gymnastics. From 1977 when breaking was losing its popularity with the Black kids until 1979–1980 when the Puerto Rican kids and younger Black kids started to make it more acrobatic, more gymnastic, there is a missing link that has to my knowledge never been explained. How and when did the first generation of breakdancers, the Black kids, the gangs and evolved crews like The Zulu Kings, the Herculoids the Smoketrons, pass on and inspire the next generation of breakdancers who were predominantly Puerto Rican?

Some of the breakdancers who were in crews like The Zulu Kings or the Casanovas or the Gestapos, like Joe Joe, Charlie Rock and Rubber Band didn't abandon breakdancing for the "Freak" or the "Spank." They instead began to put together new crews, and these crews during the time period of approximately 1977–1978, were more involved with the Puerto Rican kids who wanted to learn more about breaking. The crew names during this period of time were The Bronx Boys, Sure Sho Crew, 7 Deadly Sins, Rock Steady, East Side Juniors, Rock City Rockers, Def City Boys, Floormaster Dancers (also known as Filthy Mad Dogs, the inspiration for the crew name Floormasters who later became the New York City Breakers), Universal Crew, Cold Crush Crew, and Star Child L-Rock. Joe Joe from the Casanovas with other old school breakers like Spy, Mongo, Jimmy Lee, Rubber Band (mentioned earlier), Lace, and Trac II put together a crew named Rock Steady. One of their young jack members was named Crazy Legs. Crazy Legs, influenced by old school breakers like Rubber Band, Joe Joe, and Mongo, began to develop the new school breakdance moves. Also Lil Lep of the New York City Breakers, one time president of the crew, "Seven Deadly Sins," whose members consisted of Bennie, Reggie, Willski, P-Man, and Gayo. This was another crew that was developing in the middle of the first and second generation of breakdancers. Another member of the Seven Deadly Sins, Cool Sky (whose real name was Victor), taught Lil Lep to break. The Floor-master Dancers taught the Floormasters (current New York City Breakers, Chino Nowell, Tony Lopez, Cory Montalvo, and Matthew Kaban) how to uprock and, as mentioned before, influenced the crew to take the name the Floormasters. A number of other crews existed in this in-between time of 1977–1978, such as Sure Shot crew, The Chosen Few crew, and the Mastermind crew. In those days breaking was more often referred to as rocking. As with the old school many of the moves were simply footwork uprocking, leg steps, the spider, etc. Breakdancers like Crazy Legs, Lil Lep, and other young teenage dancers of the late 70s were being influenced and were developing new moves based on their experiences with the old breakdancers.

Crazy Legs is considered by many to be the main focal point of the transition from old school to new school. Having invented many of the new breakdance moves like backspins and windmills, Crazy Legs is the one to whom many of the new school breakers of today are indebted. But other breakers along the way had their influences on the new school of breaking. Not only breakdancers, but media stars like Bruce Lee and other Kung Fu film stars and martial artists had a major influence on breakdancing culture.

As said before, the popularity of Kung Fu films during the mid- and late 70s around the world, and especially in New York City, has had a great impact on breakdancing style. Many of the breakdancers were avid fans of martial artists like Bruce Lee. A large number of martial arts moves were incorporated into breakdancing through the influence of the films and the interest in martial arts vis-à-vis Bruce Lee. The Chinese, like many other folk around the world, mainly the Russian peasants and African slaves in early America, had a dance or style of movement that was influenced heavily by the animals on which they depended for survival. Instead of manifesting itself in dance like in Africa, or through sports like the gymnastics of the Eurasians and eastern Europeans, the Chinese animal emulation was expressed through martial arts. Styles like the white crane, tiger style, five star praying mantis, eagle, and monkey style were means of expressing body movement and fighting techniques through the imitation of animal movement. By imitating animal movement a human was able to do moves and body movements that served as a martial art. Kung Fu, with its imitation of animal movements, is a stylized form of human expression. Its heavy emphasis on style and rhythm was a natural influence and inspiration to breakdancing. The films featuring Bruce Lee and other great Kung Fu martial artists appealed to the working class aesthetics of the Bronx and the rest of New York street kids. Since most Kung Fu movements hug close to the ground and use the whole body, both the hands and feet, it was a natural influence on breaking moves. Windmills, which are gyroscopic body movements, are very similar to certain Kung Fu moves. Crazy Legs, of the old Rock Steady crew, knew the potential impact of breakdancing and was an exceptional breakdancer himself. His skills and abilities in breakdancing were matched only by his ability to create new moves. As many of the old school breakers began to drop out of breakdancing (since there was no means of reward in those days), Crazy Legs, with his dream of making breakdancing something important, continued looking for good breakers, teaching potential breakers as old members dropped out of Rock Steady. Breakers like Buck Four, whose basement was used for many breakdance meetings and get-togethers and practices on Decatur Avenue in the Bronx, Little Crazy Legs, Take One, and Frosty Freeze were all to be the new members. Also Mr. Freeze, who was influenced and taught by Lil Lep, was the first white kid to be able to break well. Mr. Freeze was from France, and by some mysterious way was relocated to the Bronx. He was heavily into punk rock but gave it up for hip-hop because of his love for breaking.

The only crews to survive from the late 70s early 80s were the Rock Steady crew, The Dynamic Rockers from Queens, and the Floormasters who then reformed to become The New York City Breakers. The Dynamic Rockers later changed their name to the Dynamic Breakers. The New York City Breakers and Rock Steady are obviously the most successful of all the crews to emerge in the early middle 1980s.

4

B-Beats Bombarding Bronx:
Mobile DJ Starts Something with Oldie R&B Disks*

Robert Ford, Jr.

NEW YORK—A funny thing has been happening at Downstairs Records here.

The store, which is the city's leading disco product retailer, has been getting calls for obscure r&b cutouts such as Dennis Coffy's "Son of Scorpio," on Sussex, Jeannie Reynolds' "Fruit Song" on Casablanca, and the Incredible Bongo Band's "Bongo Rock" on Pride.

The requests, for the most part, come from young black disco DJs from the Bronx who are buying the records just to play the 30 seconds or so of rhythm breaks that each disk contains.

The demand for these records, which the kids call B-beats, has gotten so great that Downstairs has had to hire a young Bronxite, Elroy Meighan, to handle it.

According to Meighan the man responsible for this strange phenomenon is a 26-year old mobile DJ who is known in the Bronx as Cool Herc. It seems Herc rose to popularity by playing long sets of assorted rhythm breaks strung together.

Other Bronx DJs have picked up the practice and now B-beats are the rage all over the borough, and the practice is spreading rapidly.

Herc, who has been spinning for five years, says that his unique playing style grew from his fascination with one record, "Bongo Rock." "The tune has a really great rhythm break but it was too short so I had to look for other things to put with it," Herc relates.

Since Herc was not completely satisfied with the new disco product coming out at the time, he started looking in cutout bins for tunes with good rhythm breaks.

Herc's intensive searching for tunes has now even come up with a new remake of "Bongo Rock." The '73 tune has been covered by a group called the Arawak All-Stars on an apparently Jamaican-based label, Arswal Records.

Herc has also found that some of the rhythm breaks get better response when they are played at a faster speed. Herc plays tunes such as the Jeannie Reynolds record at 45 rather than the $33^1/_3$ at which it was recorded.

Herc thinks the popularity of B-beats stems from the kids' dissatisfaction with much of today's disco product. "On most records, people have to wait through a lot of strings and singing to get to the good part of the record," Herc believes. "But I give it to them all up front."

Herc hopes that some day he will be able to produce an entire B-beat album featuring "Bongo Rock" and other obscure numbers. Till then he plans to keep packing them in at the clubs and dances he works in the Bronx.

*From *Billboard*, July 1, 1978, p. 65.

5

Jive Talking N.Y. DJs Rapping Away in Black Discos*

Robert Ford, Jr.

NEW YORK—Rapping DJs reminiscent of early r&b radio jocks such as Jocko and Dr. Jive are making an impressive comeback here—not in radio but in black discos where a jivey rap commands as much attention as the hottest new disk.

Young DJs like Eddie Cheeba, DJ Hollywood, DJ Starski, and Kurtis Blow are attracting followings with their slick raps. All promote themselves with these snappy show business names.

Many black disco promoters now use the rapping DJs to attract young fans to one-shot promotions, and a combination of the more popular names have filled this city's largest hotel ballrooms.

The young man credited with reviving the rapping habit in this area is DJ Hollywood, who started gabbing along with records a few years ago while working his way through school as a disco DJ.

Hollywood is now so popular that he has played the Apollo with billing as a support act. It is not uncommon to hear Hollywood's voice coming from one of the countless portable tape players carried through the city's streets. Tapes of Hollywood's raps are considered valuable commodities by young blacks here.

A close friend and disciple of Hollywood's, Eddie Cheeba, has been working as a mobile jock for five years and talking over the records for the last two. He now travels with an entire show, which includes seven female dancers and another DJ, Easy Gee, who does most of the actual spinning. Cheeba and his Cheeba Crew are now booked two months in advance.

Cheeba says the rapping craze grew out of a need for something more than records.

"These people go to discos every week and they need more than music to motivate them," Cheeba observes. "I not only play records, but I rap to them and they answer me."

Though they often work before crowds in the thousands, Cheeba and most of the popular rapping DJs do not get records from labels or from pools. Most of them buy their own product and do so without complaining.

As DJ Starski puts it, "Most of the records the labels send us won't go up there anyway, so I'd rather buy what I want."

Starski is one of the most popular DJs with high school and college age blacks in the Bronx and Manhattan. He has played almost every major black club and ballroom in the area. He generally works with Cool DJ AJ, who does not rap but is a master of B-beats. B-Beats are series of short rhythm breaks strung together to sound like one song.

*From *Billboard* May 5, 1979, p. 3.

Starski is proud of his ability to excite a crowd with his rapping. "It's a beautiful thing to see a dance floor full of people dancing to your music and answering your rap," Starski says.

Kurtis Blow, the most popular rapping DJ in Queens, hopes disco will be a springboard into broadcasting for him. Blow, a student at CCNY, has been working about a year and got his first break at the now defunct Small's Paradise. Blow built a following at Small's and is now booked solid for weeks.

Cheeba already had a shot at radio during a fill-in run last summer at Fordham's WFUV-FM.

6

Hip-Hop's Founding Fathers
Speak the Truth

Nelson George

Kool DJ Herc. Afrika Bambaataa. Grandmaster Flash. Old School, you say? Hell, these three are the founding fathers of hip-hop music—the progenitors of the world's dominant youth culture. For them, hip-hop is not a record, a concert, a style of dress or a slang phrase. It is the constancy of their lives. It defines their past and affects their view of the future. As DJs in the '70s, these three brothers were the nucleus of hip-hop—finding the records, defining the trends, and rocking massive crowds at outdoor and indoor jams in parts of the Bronx and Harlem.

What hip-hop was and has become is the subject of the first collective interview involving Herc, Bambaataa and Flash—the first time, in fact, that Herc has spoken on record in over ten years. One late summer evening they sat together, first in a Broadway photography studio and later at The Source's offices, telling stories, laughing at old rivalries and setting history straight.

Kool DJ Herc (aka Clive Campbell) used the sound systems of the Caribbean as the model for his mammoth speaker setup. But the sensibility that led him to scout for obscure records and mesh beats from blaxploitation soundtracks with Caribbean dance hits, soul grooves and novelty records was born of the hectic world that was the Bronx during the Carter administration. Hip-hop's sonic montage was conceived by him in city parks and school yards, where crowds flocked to hear him play, grooving to the beats he unearthed. Fact is, there were no B-boys until Herc labeled them so.

If Kool Herc is the base, then Bambaataa and Flash are twin pillars who complemented and extended the original vision. Bam came through New York's early '70s gang banging era unharmed but wiser. Seized by an enormous musical curiosity and a communal vision of African-American empowerment, he founded the Zulu Nation, the single most enduring institution in hip-hop. While labels and clubs have come and gone, the Zulu Nation emerged from the Bronx River Community Center into a collective with adherents around the world. At its center all these years is Bambaataa, who found musical inspiration in rock, Third World music and, most crucially, the electronic instrumentation that would support his breakthrough group, the Soul Sonic Force.

Grandmaster Flash (Joseph Saddler) was a teenager fascinated by records and audio circuitry. Aside from having a wide musical interest, Flash became intrigued with the possibilities the technology surrounding music suggested for innovation. The concept of scratching—now the backbone of hip-hop DJing—came out of his laboratory (with an assist from his friend Grand Wizard Theodore). Flash's introduction of the "beat box" turned DJs from beat mixers to beat makers. And the building blocks of rapping as we know it were laid by the crew that gathered around Flash—initially, Kid Creole, his brother Melle Mel and the late Cowboy.

The conversation that evening was wide ranging, including issues of historical detail and philosophy. Who was the first to scratch a record? Was DJ Hollywood the first hip-hop rapper? What was the relationship between break dancing and rapping? Who first played "Apache"? These and other often-debated questions are addressed by the people who were in the eye of the cultural hurricane.

In a broader sense, Herc, Bambaataa and Flash talk at length about the all-embracing musical curiosity that inspired hip-hop's creation and how debates about "hardcore" and "sell-out" records run contrary to the scene's roots. The wholesale dissing of women, the increasing violence between rival rap posses and the control of rap's manufacture by major corporations troubles them. The camaraderie of these rivals-turned-griots, the good humor in their remembrances and the vivid descriptions of epic park parties are a powerful contrast to the Black-on-Black crime that scars much contemporary hip-hop.

Because of their shared affection and respect, this conversation is not mere nostalgia—it is a testament to why mutual respect is integral to hip-hop's future.

AFRIKA BAMBAATAA: Most people today, they can't even define in words, hip-hop. They don't know the whole culture behind it.

GRANDMASTER FLASH: You know what bugs me, they put hip-hop with graffiti. How do they intertwine? Graffiti is one thing that is art, and music is another.

KOOL DJ HERC: I was into graffiti. That's where Kool Herc came from.

THE SOURCE: Were people doing tags and shit when you were playin'?

BAM: No, they did tags on the wall. See before the whole word hip-hop, graffiti was there before that. But really when the Zulu Nation pulled the whole thing together and we laid down the whole picture. You know, the graffiti and the breakdancers.

HERC: That's where the graffiti artists were congregating at. Going to the Factory West, or going to the Sand Pad, or going down to the Nell Guen on 42nd Street, or going to the Puzzle up there on 167th street, or to the Tunnel. That's where the graffiti guys used to hang out. That's how hip-hop came a long way.

BAM: It was there with the street gang movement. The gangs would've started dying down, but you still had the graffiti crews coming up into the hip-hop culture. Once everything started coming into place, we started doing shows and traveling into different boroughs. Then we started traveling to different states and that's when we threw everything together.

HERC: And the thing about graffiti was, I was the guy with the art. I liked graffiti flyers. My graffiti friend used to do my flyers.

BAM: Sometimes we didn't need flyers, we just say where we gonna be and that's where we at.

HERC: Block party, we gonna be over there, be there! That was it.

FLASH: Or what might happen is, if I'm playin', I'll say "Herc's givin' a party tomorrow in the street," or if Bam's playin', Bam will say, "Flash will be here."

THE SOURCE: Ok, how does breakdancing, or breaking fit into all that?

FLASH: It was basically a way of expressing how the music sounds. Early breakdancing you hardly ever touched the floor. I would say, maybe this is a bad comparison, but it was more like a Fred Astairish type of thing—stylin', the hat, you know, touchin', white laces, finesse, that's where the two intertwined. It was like just one particular couple would draw a crazy crowd in the street. Stylin', nothing sweaty, they wouldn't break a sweat. Just fly. Like Eldorado, like Mike, Sasa, Nigger Twins, Sister Boo.

BAM: You had Mr. Rock, the Zulu Queens, the Zulu Kings.

THE SOURCE: So when did it get involved with guys getting' on the floor?

BAM: Well the first form of breakdancing started with the street gangs with a dance called "Get on the Good Foot" by James Brown. There were a lot of women who was really into the breakdancing too that would tear the guys up in the early stages. But then it all came together.

HERC: They started to bet money.

BAM: The first era lasted for a while then it died down. And then the second generation came.

HERC: The Puerto Ricans carried breakdancing.

FLASH: They took it to the next level for sure.

HERC: They carried all forms of hip-hop music with dancing.

FLASH: It died for a while then it came back and it was this new acrobatic, gymnastic type of style.

BAM: And really with some of them, they had been doing this since '77 and it never really died with them. Especially with the Rock Steady Crew, the New York City Breakers, and a couple of those crews.

THE SOURCE: OK, the phrase B-boy. What does that mean to you?

HERC: The boys that break. When somebody go off in the neighborhood, "Yo, I'm ready to break on somebody," so we just say B-boys, you know, breakers.

THE SOURCE: So it doesn't necessarily mean, he's a dancer? It's an attitude or somebody who does something?

FLASH: You don't have to be a dancer!

HERC: B-boys, these are the boys, these are the boys that break. So we call 'em B-boys.

THE SOURCE: Let me ask you, is there a time where you remember the whole style of the hat sideways attitude coming in? Where you said this is a new style as opposed to what had gone before? Is there a point where you said, "Oh he's a B-boy. This is new."

FLASH: I think when actually dancers started making contact, like doing jump kicks and kicking people on the floor, that's when the hat started going like this [Flash turns his hat sideways]. It was like, "I ain't dancing with you, I'm gonna try to hurt you." That's when the hat went to the side.

BAM: With some of them, they did hurt some. Some people got hurt. When they danced against each other, or especially if they had different crews. All through the time there was a struggle. You had your peaceful moments and you had your straight-up battles.

HERC: After a while guys would start to say, "Well you gonna have to pay to see me dance." Or, "If you want to take me out or discredit me you have to put some money up."

THE SOURCE: Like Basketball. What were the records that made them do that?

ALL: James Brown, "Give It Up, Turn It Loose."

BAM: "Apache" was the national anthem.

HERC: "Just Begun."

FLASH: "Black Heat," remember that one?

BAM: "Family . . . " by Sly and the Family Stone.

THE SOURCE: To find these beats, you would go to Downstairs Records and just find a ton of records?

ALL: No we didn't just go to Downstairs!

FLASH: That was one of Herc's spots.

HERC: That spot to me was where I find shit that wouldn't be nowhere else, or I found something that I could say, "Hey this is good." I'd go to somebody's house and they'd say, "Herc, I know you like records, run through my records. I got a whole lot of stuff there."

FLASH: Or girls' houses for sure. Dope.

HERC: Or going to one of Bam's parties and I hear something and I say, "I could use this with this."

BAM: I took music from around the whole world. I was playin' so much crazy shit, they called me the master of records.

FLASH: He was the man. He was the king of the records.

HERC: When I go to his party, I'm guaranteed to be entertained by some shit I don't hear other people play. Then I step to Mr. Bam, "What's that one?"

THE SOURCE: Tell me five records you might play in a row back in the day?

BAM: Well you would hear something from the Philippines by a group named Please which did a remix for "Sing a Simple Song."

FLASH: You might hear "Fernando" by Bob James, I might play that with a ...

HERC: You might hear "Fat Sap from Africa" or "Seven Minutes of Funk." "Babe Ruth."

FLASH: Or how about on the back side of the Incredible Bongo Band, the other one, "Bongolia."

BAM: You could hear "The Return of Planet Rock" by the Incredible Bongo Band. "Sing, Sing, Sing," "Sex" by Bobby Knight.

THE SOURCE: Who was the first person to take the record in the bathtub and wipe the labels off?

FLASH: That was me. People were getting too close, you know. I will give all due respect to my boys right here, but you know, other people.

HERC: He put us on a wild goose chase [everyone laughs].

BAM: I had a way of telling things from the color of the album. I could know if it was Mercury or Polygram. Then I would try to see who it sounded like.

FLASH: Hey Bam, I followed you on a Saturday with glasses on. I seen one bin you went to, pulled the same shit you pulled, took that shit home—and the break wasn't on the mutha-fucka [everyone is hysterical].

BAM: I used to tell people, "Do not follow me and buy what I buy," and I went into a record store and everyone was waitin' around to see what I pulled. So I pulled some Hare Krishna records [everyone laughs]. It had beats but ...

FLASH: You couldn't play that bullshit. I got a crate full of bullshit.

HERC: If I go somewhere and I hear something, I give the DJ respect. I don't try to say, "I played it." 'Cause the first time I heard "Seven Minutes of Funk," I was with this girl I used to talk to, and we were at this place called The Point, and it was like a movie. The minute we hit the door, people knew who we were, and we didn't know people knew who we were. All we heard was ... [Herc hums the "Seven Minutes of Funk" bassline which was used on EPMD's "It's My Thing"] The further we walk in the party the record was still going. I was like, "That shit is ruff."

THE SOURCE: Who discovered "The Mexican"?

BAM: Herc got "The Mexican."

THE SOURCE: What kind of equipment did you have in the late '70s, early '80s?

FLASH: I had six columns and maybe two bullshit bass bottoms. I didn't have much of a system. I was going to school and I had a messenger job. I also had electronic experience though, so a lot of the stuff I make-shifted. I didn't really hear a real heavy, heavy, heavy system until I heard this man [Herc] out in the park. It was incredible.

THE SOURCE: Where did you get your equipment?

HERC: My old man bought a Sure P.A. system for his band he used to be with. The band fell off and the speakers wound up in my room. My pops was a little strict and told me to not touch 'em. I never did play 'em but another kid in the neighborhood had the same system and played his. So I asked him how to hook up the Sure P.A. to the system. They wouldn't tell me. So I borrowed one of my father's friend's systems 'cause I wouldn't touch the Sure stuff in the house. What they was doing was using one of the channels from the turnta-bles and using the brain itself to power the whole thing. My shit was, I used the pre-amp, used the speakers wires put into a channel, and used the two knobs to mix. I got more sound than they ever got.

THE SOURCE: What kind of turntables were you using?

HERC: At first I started with Gerards [laughs]. Then from there I went downtown and I seen two Technics 1100As and I went and got 'em.

FLASH: They're still the best turntables in the world right now, the 1100A, but you can't find 'em. Because of the tork and the pick-up. You could have the hand the size of a monkey and that thing would still turn. The actual design of that turntable was incredible. I was never able to afford 'em so I had to adjust my touch to cheaper turntables.

THE SOURCE: But the questions is, who started it?

FLASH: There was this family called the Livingstons, OK. There was Gene, Claudio, and this little kid named Theodore. Now, before we actually became Grandmaster Flash and the Furious Five, I kept my equipment at Gene Livingston's house. What he would tell me is because his little brother was so interested was, "Don't let Theodore in the room, don't let Theodore on the turntables!" Now when he went to work, I would tell Theodore to come on in and let me see what you can do. Now, he had an ability to take the needle and drop it and just keep it going. He had such a rhythm that was incredible. I begged Gene for like a year and a half to take this little kid out in the park with us as the team to get larger notoriety. He didn't like the idea of it. After a while this little kid kinda outshined his big brother. So what Theodore did for scratchin' is this—where I had expertise on the back-spin or fakin' the faze, what Theodore would do with a scratch was make it more rhyth-mical. He had a way of rhythmically taking a scratch and making that shit sound musical. He just took it to another level.

THE SOURCE: People don't appreciate how much technical knowledge went into the creation of music. You had to really study turntables and speakers and the entire thing.

FLASH: Break-up plenty of equipment to get what it was.

THE SOURCE: So you had to custom-make everything.

FLASH: I had to custom-make my cue system also. I couldn't afford a mixer with a built-in cue system where you could hear turntable one or two in advance. I had to actually get a single pole–double throw switch, crazy glue it to the top of my mixer, build an external mix on the outside just strong enough to drive a headphone, so when you clicked it over you would hear the other turntable in advance. But this whole idea of hearing the cut ahead of time took three years to come into being.

THE SOURCE: How did you create the beat box?

FLASH: For some reason the world seems to think the beat box is something you do with your mouth. The beat box was an attempt to come up with something other than the tech-niques I created on the turntables to please the crowd. There was this drummer who lived in the Jackson projects who had this manually operated drum box he used to practice his fingering. I begged him to sell it to me. Then I found a way to wire it into my system and called it the beat box. The drummer taught me how to use it. When my partner Disco Bee would shut the music off, I would segue into it, so you couldn't tell where the music stopped and I started.

THE SOURCE: Bam, where do you trace your interest in music to?

BAM: I'll give credit to my mother. When I was growing up in the '60s, I used to hear a lot of the Motown sounds, James Brown sounds, the Stax sounds, Isaac Hayes and all of them. As well as Edith Piaf, Barbra Streisand, the Beatles, the Who, Led Zeppelin. From there I started knowing about a lot of different music and that's when I first heard African music from Miriam Makeeba. I was listening to this sister talk about things about South Africa which I didn't really understand at the time. One movie that grabbed my attention was this movie called Zulu. At the time when you were seeing Black people on TV, you would see us in degrading roles. So to see this movie with Black people fighting for their land was a big inspiration for me. Then here comes this guy that I used to not like at first, I though he was weird and crazy, which was Sly Stone. But once I heard "Sing a Simple Song," "People," and "Stand," I switched totally to this sound of funk. Then I seen the whole Motown start changing. The Temptations started getting psychedelic. I was a gang member by that time. From '69 to about '75 I was in the Black Spades but, like a lot of these young great Black musicians, I was a visionary. I said to myself, "When I get older, I'ma have me a Zulu Nation." I just waited for the right time.

THE SOURCE: You went from gangs to doing parties—how did you make that transition to being a DJ?

BAM: Well before Flash, Herc, all of us, there was Disco DJs happening in the areas. Flowers, Kool DJ Jones, Lovebug Starski, and Kool DJ Dee. Those were who I follow at one time. Then you started hearing the sound that was coming from my brother Kool DJ Herc. Then when I came out with my system, Herc was like an angel looking over me. Then when I changed over to giving my big party, I didn't have to worry about having it packed 'cause I was in control of all the gangs out there anyway. So when I changed over and brought everybody from the street gangs into the Zulu Nation, when I gave the first big function, everyone knew who I was and backed me up.

THE SOURCE: People have always speculated that the rise of hip-hop caused the gangs to disappear in New York or changed them over. What would you say the relationship was to the rise of hip-hop parties to the gangs of New York?

BAM: Well, I would say the women were more important. The women got tired of the gang shit. So brothers eventually started sliding slowly out of that 'cause they had people that got killed. Cops were breakin' down on people. The cops actually had a secret organization called the "purple mothers" that were ex-Vietnam veterans that would roll on gang members. There was a lot of crazy shit going on in the struggle of the gangs and the transition from the gangs dying down and the women putting their foot down. Drugs helped destroy the gangs too. Now one thing people must know, that when we say Black we mean all our Puerto Rican or Dominican brothers. Wherever the hip-hop was and the Blacks was, the Latinos and the Puerto Ricans was, too.

THE SOURCE: What do you think now when people say that there's a certain style of music that's considered hip-hop, and a certain style that's not considered hip-hop? Claims that some records are fake hip-hop records and some are real?

BAM: They're ignorant. They don't know the true forms of hip-hop. Just like I tell 'em, you got all styles of hip-hop, you gotta take hip-hop for what it is. You got your hard beats, you got your gangsta rap, you got your electro-funk sound which came from the party rock sound, you got your Miami bass, you got the go-go from DC. We was playin' go-go years ago. If you really with Teddy Riley, he came to Bronx River parties and heard go-go music and just flipped it up and now you got new jack swing. All of this was all part of hip-hop.

FLASH: It's all about different tastes. It could be hard drums like a Billy Squire record. It could be the bass hitting and drums soft like "Seven Minutes of Funk." It could have the hallway echo effect of "Apache."

HERC: We can't let the media define this for us. Someone says it's got hardcore beats and talkin' about bitches sucking dick, that's hardcore. That same person says that Jazzy Jeff & the Fresh Prince are soft, it's not hip-hop. It is hip-hop. It's just another form. It's about experimenting and being open.

BAM: Different generations have lost the true meaning. We were teaching the public when we did parties in the park.

THE SOURCE: Tell me about doing parties in the park.

HERC: See, the park playin' is like playin' for your people. You give them something free. Sometimes it's hot and a lot of the clubs didn't have no air conditioner. So I gave parties out in the park to cool out while summer's there. To play in the park is to give the fans and the people something.

BAM: We'd play for everybody. You'd play certain records that grabbed the old, you played the straight up hip-hop records . . .

FLASH: You can actually experiment 'cause now you have a wider audience coming. You have like mothers and fathers and a wide spread of people. You can actually test your new-found jams to see how they work on the public right then and there. You'll know right then and there if you got something, as soon as you play it.

BAM: We were selling cassettes of our mixes that were really our first albums. We had luxury cabs like OJ and the Godfathers and Touch of Class that would buy our tapes.

FLASH: How it worked was people would call for a car, and if they had a dope Herc tape, or a dope Bam tape, or a dope Flash tape, that particular customer might stay in the cab all day long. So these cab drivers were making extra money and at the same time they were advertising us. Like Bam said, it was like cuttin' an album, but it was on tape.

THE SOURCE: The first hip-hop I ever heard was on a tape that was sold in Brooklyn. I saw it on Fulton Street, and that's first time I realized it was being passed around the city.

BAM: Circulating. If you look at it, everything's repeating itself now. Look at all the DJ tapes now. You have Ron G, Kid Capri, Doo Wop. All these kids are doing the same things we did twenty something years ago. It's like life is returning back to the surface. Just like your hearing a new rebirth of funk. All of the stuff is coming back, like Pumas . . .

FLASH: Bell bottoms, teardrops, the big high-heel shoes.

THE SOURCE: Talking about style, your two groups were both stylistically influenced by funk groups.

BAM: I could tell you about that. A lot of the rappers used to dress regular and then we got more into presenting people with something. You know, when you're payin' five, ten dollars to come in, you want to see people dressed up.

FLASH: You know what, we was like businessmen. In a very simplistic sort of fashion. It was like three corporations and we carefully did things without realizing it.

BAM: We was businessmen at like thirteen, fourteen. Making our own parties. We had payrolls. Picking the venues or the streets or the centers. Dealing with the politics, or deciding whether you needed police. We dealt with so much business at such a young age.

THE SOURCE: One of the things you hear is that battling the essence of hip-hop. But you're saying that that was something that came afterwards. At the root of it was some kind of fellowship.

FLASH: Yeah. Experimental musically, but it was a fellowship.

THE SOURCE: Would guys roll up who were tryin' to make a rep and challenge you one-on-one?

FLASH: You can't take away three or four years of establishment in one night. You can't do that. You'll just be a statistic. Bam, Herc and myself already had a science on how to control our crowd. At that time you definitely had to earn it. Not in days, weeks, months—it took years to get a little bit of respect. Then you had to pass through one of the three of us.

BAM: You couldn't even come in our areas to play or else you dealt with us with respect. We would make sure you couldn't play one of the clubs or even come into the community.

THE SOURCE: I remember a club called 371. This was DJ Hollywood's club. What did you guys think about that whole scene?

BAM: Hollywood, himself, was more like disco oriented.

THE SOURCE: I've heard Hollywood was the first hip-hop rapper.

FLASH: No, the first people I heard talk on the microphone and do it extremely well and entertain the crowd and wasn't talkin' to the beat of the music, was Herc's people. Coke La Rock. He would just talk while Herc was cuttin'.

HERC: Little phrases and words from the neighborhood that we used on the corner is what we would use on the mic. Like we talkin' to a friend of ours out there in the crowd.

BAM: And when they got rhymin' it came from the Furious when they added Melle Mel.

FLASH: It was Cowboy, then it was Kid Creole, and Melle Mel. There were these dancers Debbi and Terri who used to go through the crowds shouting "Ho!" and people picked up on that. Cowboy came up with a lot of phrases and had a powerful voice that just commanded attention. "Throw your hands in the air!" "Clap to the beat!" "Somebody scream!" all came from Cowboy. Kid Creole and his brother Melle Mel were the first to really flow and have a poetic feel to their rhymes. They were the first rhyme technicians. They were the first to toss a sentence back and forth. Kid would say, "I," Mel would say, "was," Kid would say, "walking," Mel would say, "down." They just tossed sentences like that all day. It was incredible to watch, it was incredible to hear. Along with Coke La Rock with Herc, they were the root. It was Cowboy, Kid Creole and Melle Mel for quite a while before it became the five of us. Like syncopating to the beat of music was incredible. You just didn't get it overnight. You had to play with it, develop it, break things, make mistakes, embarrass yourself. You had to earn it.

THE SOURCE: Is it a real important distinction between Hollywood and what you were doing?

FLASH: He did come in around the same era. He was there and made a mark. It was just he was a softer side of music. Something we might not play, he would jam and kill it. He was a disco rapper. He'd rap over things like "Love is the Message" which I would never play. Things that were on the radio he'd do for the crowds at after-hours clubs.

THE SOURCE: For a lot of people, Disco Fever was the first place where they heard hip-hop.

ALL: No.

THE SOURCE: OK, then what was that place's significance.

FLASH: There was a lot of clubs between Flash, Bam, and Herc. But the clubs started diminishing slowly but surely. Fatalities were happening there, there, and there. Things got a little bad for everybody. This guy Sal at the Fever resisted at first, but then decided to take a chance on it. What happened was the Fever became a later meeting point for a lot of mobile jocks and new stars at the time. At any given time Camacho would walk in there, Herc would walk in there, Kurtis Blow, Sugarhill Gang, a member of the Commodores. I mean it was like this place was quite well known.

HERC: What the Fever did was give hip-hop a place with disco lights, fly, you could come nice. It had a prime location next to the Concourse. It had a downtown atmosphere uptown.

THE SOURCE: When the Sugar Hill Gang made "Rapper's Delight," hip-hop was now on record. You guys were the founders of this style, yet it was a while before you guys got involved with making records. Did you discuss recording in the mid-'70s?

FLASH: I was approached in '77. A gentleman walked up to me and said, "We can put what you're doing on record." I would have to admit that I was blind. I didn't think that somebody else would want to hear a record re-recorded onto another record with talking on it. I didn't think it would reach the masses like that. I didn't see it. I knew of all the crews that had any sort of juice and power, or that was drawing crowds. So here it is two years later, and I hear "To the hip-hop, to the bang to the boogie," and it's not Bam, Herc, Breakout, AJ. Who is this?

HERC: And when I heard [Big Bank] Hank [of the Sugar Hill Gang], I was like, what? I knew Hank. I didn't really appreciate that Hank knew me personally, had been to my house, was from the neighborhood, and never once said, "Herc, I'm doing something." Never, until this day.

BAM: 'Cause he never gave credit to Grandmaster Casanova Fly, who is called Grandmaster Caz these days from the Cold Crush Brothers, for the rhymes.

THE SOURCE: Now did he literally write them and Hank took them?

HERC: Caz used to come to the Sparkle where Hank was a doorman. He used to get on the mic and Hank heard him. That's when Hank saw the scene growing. I went to New Jersey—my girlfriend knew him—and he was working in a pizza shop down there. I just said, "When Sylvia [Robinson, of Sugar Hill Records] hear the real deal, she gonna know." And I was happy to be in the Fever when she seen the truth. And it was hell with them after that. To see Melle Mel and them on stage.

FLASH: 'Cause the cream of the crop like Caz, The Fantastic Five was in there.

THE SOURCE: Again, you guys did eventually make records. You got with Bobby Robinson who had Enjoy Records in Harlem for years.

FLASH: Yeah we got with Bobby. We was playin' at a club on 125th street. All I know was he made me very nervous 'cause I knew what my age bracket was, and here was this old man who came in at about 11:00, and he stayed to the end of the party. So I said to myself, "Either he's the cops, he's somebody's father looking for his daughter, or something's gonna go down here." So then when we were breaking down the equipment at the end of the night, he stepped me and said, "Flash, do you think it's possible that we can get together and possibly put together a record." You know, I went back to the folks, talked about it, and we did it.

THE SOURCE: How much did he pay you?

FLASH: Maybe a thousand a man. Not bad.

THE SOURCE: Almost all the people who came at this point were still Black though, am I right?

BAM: Record companies, yeah they were still Black.

THE SOURCE: It was still a Black thing in the sense that to find out about it you had to be near the grass roots.

FLASH: These were little record companies that were selling records out the trunk of their car. They were only looking for cream of the crop rappers to do this. At that time, all they wanted was what Sylvia was doing.

THE SOURCE: A lot is going on right now. We're talking about '80, '81. We have the first rap records. The music is starting to spread in terms of your appearances outside of the Bronx. Did you get the sense that it was getting out of control?

FLASH: I wanted to push it.

HERC: I was mad when Sugar Hill came first and did their thing.

BAM: I was the one who was always more independent. I would just sit back and watch to see where things were going before I stepped into it. 'Cause I was watching Flash be successful moving his stuff, I was happy. Then this white guy came down and checked us out named Malcolm MacLaren. And Tom Silverman came down and checked me out in Bronx River with Arthur Baker. First Malcolm MacLaren came, 'cause he said, "There's this Black kid playin' all this rock and other type of music to a Black and Spanish audience." When he seen this, he invited me to come play at the Ritz with Bow Wow Wow. So when I came and did that show, I brought everybody together like Rock Steady and all the groups. That's where I first met them and we all came under the Zulu Nation. There was this guy Michael Holman who used to invite me down to DJ at the Mudd Club, then to Negril with my son Afrika Islam, D.St., Whiz Kid.

Then we used to get too big for that so we went to Danceteria and got too big for that until finally the Roxy became our home. Then Flash and them came and played the Ritz on the Sugar Hill tour with Sequence and the West Street Mob. With the Roxy it became like an international world club. Everyone was coming to the Roxy. Then you had the clubs that didn't want hip-hop nowhere down there like the Limelight. They would make a dress code 'cause there were too many Blacks and Puerto Ricans coming into the neighborhood. That's when I started fighting racism down in the club scene. I would say, "If you don't let my Blacks or Puerto Ricans in, I'm gonna leave." That's when we started gettin' power in the clubs.

THE SOURCE: How did you feel about the whole process of going from having parties to doing records?

FLASH: I'd have to say, I wasn't ready. I was content with what I was doing. I think what happened was when Herc stopped playing eight hours a night. Flash stopped playing, Bam stopped playing, the street thing flipped. Like one DJ would play eight different clubs in one night and not really have an audience anymore. You lost your home champion because there was nobody there. I would have personally like to stay away from records a little longer. Not to say that I wouldn't want to make records 'cause records was the next plateau for spreading the musical word.

BAM: Everyone was nervous. It took the excitement away. We didn't have the parties. Everyone would go out and buy the record.

FLASH: It was a thing to me coming into the place at six and taking two-and-a-half hours to set up the sound system and make sure the EQs were right and the crates were right. It was fun.

BAM: Plus a lot of people in the early records were gettin' robbed. That's something a lot of people don't want to talk about it. A lot of people now who know they can make money have to know what the Old School went through.

FLASH: You know what's really sad to know and see, is that these people have never really seen a block party—like a block party that goes ten or twelve hours. Starting at noon and ending at midnight. I mean you have to really be in a party for hours to watch a DJ expand on what he would play. That would separate the men from the boys as far as the DJ is concerned. The way I see it, the less times he repeats something in a ten hour period, the more qualified he is. That's why we would come up with ten-fifteen crates of records. So we wouldn't have to play anything twice.

THE SOURCE: You all seem to feel there's a sense of community about the hip-hop scene during the party era that's never really been recaptured.

BAM: Today it gets sickening with the disrespecting of self. To me a lot of brothers and sisters lost knowledge of self. They're losing respect of the "us syndrome" and getting into the "I syndrome." You can't build a nation with an "I" you got to build a nation with a "us." The disrespecting of the Black women—you got some sisters that go into the category "bitches," although you got a lot of the Black women that don't deserve that.

THE SOURCE: I want to get into the whole area of the media and rap's evolution. How do you feel the history rap has been told? Do you think it has been distorted in any way?

FLASH: There are those out there that made a great attempt to accuracy. Then there are those who are just doing it to make a dollar. I think to this point it hasn't been really told. I'm not going to try to toot my own horn, but I think the only ones that can really tell you the story are Herc, Bam, Breakout and myself. Either you can hear his-story or history, and the only way you gonna hear the real historical views on it is by the people who were actually there—who actually took it from nothing and built into whatever it became to be. Some people don't dig deep enough to find out what happened back then. They just fix it so it's comfortable for the reader, which is really dangerous.

BAM: My thing from studying history and listening to great leaders like Elijah, Malcolm, and Minister Farrakhan, I see that everything is planned by design. Even in the industry, nobody talked to the Black and Latino and said, "Do y'all want to get rid of vinyl?" They never had no survey. But the next thing you know vinyl is out the door and CDs are in. I always told people that there was people in the industry that was tryin' to destroy hip-hop. They couldn't do it. That's why Zulu Nation, TC Islam and all of us are pushing a united hip-hop front. Cause you got a lot of people from the Old School who are really mad. Melle Mel, Kurtis Blow, Kevi Kev, a lot of old timers who didn't get their due respect or even the money that they should have made. You got people who are opening the door that are out of there now who ain't paying no mind where the history come from.

THE SOURCE: When you say Old School guys are mad, who owes them? Where did the point come where they were left behind?

BAM: A lot of the companies, a lot of friction happened between the companies. You had companies that was robbing people by not telling them about publishing. Some artists' albums went gold but they didn't give them no money. You know, here's a leased car instead of royalties.

THE SOURCE: Well let me ask you something—who owns hip-hop now?

BAM: White industry.

HERC: Whites.

BAM: The white industry owns it now because they control all the record companies. And all our people that make money worry about Benz's and big houses and fly girls instead of being Black entrepreneurs. You need to take the business back.

THE SOURCE: Herc, you're one of the people that there's a great mystique or mystery about. Tell us about the decisions you made during the period when rap came out on records.

HERC: I was maintained as far as running the sound system and giving parties. The mic was always open for the MCs. My thing was just playin' music and giving parties. I wasn't interested in making no records.

THE SOURCE: What do you most like about hip-hop culture today?

FLASH: Contrary to the media and to the powers that be, hip-hop has a vibe. Under all the crush and blows, being called a fad, it now has its own category and is stronger than ever. I thank God that I'm here to see it. It's quite a compliment to walk down the street and be told, "Flash do you realize you're a legend?" But a lot of times legends die young and don't get to see what they seeded. I'm glad to see it.

THE SOURCE: What about hip-hop culture at this point do you dislike the most?

FLASH: I think that somebody went around and said that in order to cut a hit record, we have to disrespect our brothers, sisters, mothers and children. What people don't realize here is that hip-hop has a large influence on people. What you say maybe just frivolously, somebody can seriously go out and go do. I'm not sayin' that what we're doing is not right, but it shouldn't be the only way that a record is made. Like if you listen to ten records, seven of them is either disrespecting our sisters, or hurting people.

THE SOURCE: Bam, what do you like most about what's going on now?

BAM: I love that hip-hop has become international. I love when I go to France and hear French hip-hop groups. I love when I go to England and hear British hip-hop groups. I love to see hip-hop groups all through Africa. Hip-hop has taken a lot of brothers and sisters who might be doing negative things and have gotten into the rap world to see other people's way of life. Hip-hop has also had a force to unite people together. You have all people of color trying to understand what's happening with the Black problem. Some are getting educated about negative and positive things.

Nelson: Herc, what aspect of hip-hop culture do you like the most?

HERC: That it's still here. It's giving youth a chance to pay for education if they want to. Giving 'em a chance to go overseas. It's here, it ain't going nowhere. Music was always our way of information—it was the drums. They took it away from us in Africa, now we found it again. The music is our fuckin' drums man. All I could say right now as far as rappers out here today is: be true to the game.

Part II
No Time for Fake Niggas:
Hip-Hop Culture and the Authenticity Debates

Mark Anthony Neal

In an article published in the *New York Times* (August 22, 1999), hip-hop journalist Toure made a principled effort to outline the contours of the hip-hop nation. According to Toure:

> we are a nation with no precise date of origin, no physical land, no single chief. But if you live in the Hip-Hop Nation, if you are not merely a fan of the music but a daily imbiber of the culture, if you sprinkle your conversation with phrases like "off the meter" (for something that's great) or "got me open" (for something that gives an explosive positive emotional release), if you know why Dutch Masters make better blunts than Phillies . . . then you know the Hip-Hop Nation is a place as real as America on a pre-Columbus atlas. (Toure, 1999: 1)

Of course the *New York Times* seems like an odd place to work out the attributes of a seemingly mythical formation that is grounded in the traditions of urbanized black and brown masculinities and black popular expression, but Toure's motivations (and attendant defensive stance) are informed by the very reason that the *New York Times* would sanction the piece in the first place; hop-hop had exploded as one of the most powerful cultural phenomena of the post–civil rights era, and it was an open secret that hip-hop's most visible consumers were young white kids.

Toure acknowledges the changing dynamics of the hip-hop nation, stating that the "Hip-Hop Nation senate is swelling to include whites, women, and Southerners but don't expect that senate to become a true melting pot anytime soon. As long as upper-class white men stay in charge of the United States Senate, urban black men will remain our leading speakers" (p. 1). Here, Toure sounds like the "last black man standing"— making a last ditch effort to mark what authentic hip-hop sounds, and more importantly, looks like. Within hip-hop, mantras like "keepin' it real" (resonant through the 1990s) and the more contemporary "I'm just trying to do me," have expressed the ambivalence of black hip-hop artists and audiences with the commercial success and widespread visibility afforded the genre over the past fifteen years or so. This ambivalence (in some cases expressed as outright disdain for what is perceived as cultural encroachment by whites *and* women) has only increased as a figure like Eminem has become the most celebrated hip-hop artist ever. Despite Toure's claims (and I'm not saying that he is wrong), hip-hop has never been as essentialist as we've been led to believe, owing in part to the fact that, in the picture book of American society, the mythogenic discourses in which black masculinity has been inscribed have often obscured by who else was in the room when black men were being blamed for being "too black, too strong," and too loud.

This section of the book takes its title from Lil Kim's recording "No Time," itself a mid-1990s mantra of authentic hip-hop expressed in the midst of a bicoastal war of words and deeds that ultimately led to the deaths of two of hip-hop's most celebrated wordsmith warriors, Tupac Shakur and Christopher "The Notorious B.I.G." Wallace. The acrimony between the Death Row Records and Bad Boy Entertainment camps with which Shakur and B.I.G., respectively, were associated, contributed to a long simmering feud—what some called a hip-hop "Civil War" of competing sensibilities—pitting East Coast hip-hop artists against those from the West Coast. Because of the significance of New York City in the lore of hip-hop, the East Coast had always been seen as the symbolic center of the hip-hop world. This "coast supremacy" was challenged in the early 1990s as artists such as N.W.A., Ice Cube, Snoop Dog, Warren G, Digital Underground, Tupac, and even Hammer emerged as some of the genre's most bankable performers.

At the core of the East Coast versus West Coast conflict was a fundamental belief that the experiences of those on one coast marked them as more authentic—more gangsta, more ghetto, more hardcore—than those on the other. In other words, one 'hood was deemed more authentically hip-hop, and by extension, more authentically black, than the other.

If the buying public seems indifferent to the various strains of hip-hop, some finding authenticity in a diverse array of hip-hop's forms, many political pundits and public officials have been equally indifferent, though with more sinister designs. Some of these figures, particularly those with conservative political slants, use hip-hop's claim to authenticity against the very communities in struggle that "authentic" rappers ostensibly represent. Citing the example of the infamous Willie Horton commercials funded by the Republican Party during the 1988 presidential election, Michael Eric Dyson observes that the late Republican leader Lee Atwater's "use of Willie Horton viciously played on the very prejudice against black men that has often led blues musicians to express the psychic, personal, and social pain occasioned by racism in American (political) culture." Ironically, Atwater considered himself a patron of the blues tradition. According to Dyson, the desire within hip-hop to "maintain its aesthetic, cultural, and political proximity to its site of original expression: the ghetto poor" means that hip-hop may not be able to withstand the appropriative tendencies exhibited by Atwater.

In his chapter Paul Gilroy openly asks:

> if the 'hood is the essence of where blackness can be found, which 'hood are we talking about? How do we weigh the achievements of one 'hood against the achievements of another? How is black life in one 'hood connected to life in others? Can there be a blackness that connects, articulates, synchronizes experiences and histories across the diaspora space?

Gilroy's comments speak not only to the difficulties of measurement (dating back to the "black is, black ain't" debates of the 1960s), but to the futility of it all, as if there is some value in living in the most insidious crucible of urban disaffection. But valuable it is when it is your claim to fame and potentially translates into CD unit sales and regular rotation on the video channel of your choice.

In his challenging and provocative chapter, Ronald A.T. Judy would have us believe that the very notion of an "authentic" nigger is rife with essentialist views of black life and culture that have not fully taken into account hip-hop's significant impact. According to Judy, "understanding the possibilities of nigga authenticity in the emerging realities of transnational capital is a humbling undertaking . . . the general consensus is 'this nigga is deadly dangerous'," an "assumption that this nigga of the present age is somehow related to the 'bad nigger' of slavery and the postbellum South." Beyond the perhaps simplistic generational distinctions made between the words "nigger" and "nigga," Judy argues that "nigga defines authenticity as adaptation to the force of commodification. . . . Authenticity is hype, a hypercommodified affect whose circulation has made hip-hop global." In Judy's view, hip-hop is an "utterance of a habit of thought toward an increasingly rationalized and fragmented world of global commodification. It is thinking about being in a hypercommodified world" where "nigga designates the scene, par excellence, of commodification, where one is among commodities."

Beyond Judy's theoretical observations of hip-hop's authenticity debates, there have always been concrete queries as to who belongs to the hip-hop nation. For example, in her book *New York Ricans from the Hip Hop Zone* (2003), Raquel Rivera argues that

> identification of hip-hop as African-American must be contextualized in hip-hop's growing commercialization and international popularity, and thus expansion outside of territory where Puerto Ricans are a familiar presence, whether as neighbors, lovers, family, playmates or artists. (Rivera, 2003: 82)

Placing Rivera's observation in the context of hip-hop commodification, Juan Flores asserts that the "commercialization process involves the extraction of popular cultural expression from its original social context and function, it seems that the 'Latinization' of hip-hop has meant its distancing from the specific national and ethnic traditions to which it had most directly pertained." Even the notion of an essentialized Spanish-speaking presence in hip-hop can be challenged if one considers the very different formations of Puerto Rican and Chicano hip-hop. For instance, the Nuyorican experience—the navigation between distinct Puerto Rican sensibilities and those derived from life in New York City—that marked so many of the first generation of Puerto Rican hip-hop artists is very different than those of "La Raza" rappers like Kid Frost and the Aztlan Underground or Cuban-American MC Mellow Man Ace. According to Raegan Kelly in her chapter, "To call yourself Chicano is to claim La Raza, to locate your origin within the struggle of a people for land and for cultural, political and economic self-determination."

In his chapter Robin Kelley easily links bicoastal authenticity debates to the fascination with ghetto life among social scientists and urban ethnographers. According to Kelley, some of these scholars "treat culture as if it were a set of behaviors. They assume that there is one identifiable ghetto culture, and what they observe was it." He adds that "although these social scientists came to mine what they believed was *the* 'authentic Negro culture,' there was real gold in them thar ghettos since white America's fascination with the pathological urban poor translated into massive books sales." Thus, both hip-hop artists (regardless of whether or not they are actually from ghetto) and the scholars who write about them and the environment that produced them have a clear commercial stake in representing the "ghetto real" in their work. Ultimately, Kelley suggests that the real question posed by these ethnographers (and that hardcore rappers readily answer) is "what kind of 'niggers' populate the inner city?"

In his chapter Alan Light suggests that the reality is that hip-hop was often driven by two divergent camps, whether they be the hardcore versus the pop-lite, or the ghetto surreal versus the politically conscious. According to Light, "Hip-hop is first and foremost a pop form, seeking to make people dance and laugh and think. To make them listen and feel, and to sell records, by doing so," but hip-hop also "by definition has a political content . . . rap is about giving voice to a black community otherwise underrepresented, if not silent, in the mass media." Light admits that "these differences are irreconcilable . . . the two strains have been forced to move further apart and to work, in many ways, at cross purposes." Light's comments highlight the diversity inherent in any popular form, but that are largely denied to the African American purveyors of hip-hop music and culture.

Dave Samuels explains that debates over authenticity have little impact on the buying public which, he argues, still views authentic hip-hop as that which is primarily informed by the stock stereotypes of young black men: a virile, hypermasculine figure given to criminality, recklessness, and even "racism." In his chapter Samuels facetiously suggests that when the film *Boyz N the Hood* and the NWA album *Niggaz4life* were released during the summer of 1991, "young black men committing acts of violence were available in a wide variety of formats." Citing the example of Brand Nubian, a hip-hop act that espoused the teachings of the Five-Percent Nation—an off-shoot of The Nation of Islam—Samuels claims, "Anti-white, and, in this case, anti-Semitic rhymes are a shorthand way of defining one's opposition to the mainstream," adding that "racism is reduced to fashion by the rappers who use it and by the white audiences to whom such images appeal." What is crucial to this analysis is Samuels's admission that he doesn't believe that Brand Nubian are wholly invested in their rhetoric, but that they understand that "anti-Semitic slurs and black criminality correspond to 'authenticity,' and 'authenticity' sells."

References

Rivera, Raquel. 2003. *New York Ricans from the Hip Hop Zone*. New York: Palgrave Macmillan.
Toure. 1999. "The Hip-Hop Nation: Whose Is It?" *New York Times*, August 22, Section 2, p. 1.

7

The Culture of Hip-Hop

Michael Eric Dyson

From the very beginning of its recent history, hip-hop music—or rap, as it has come to be known—has faced various obstacles. Initially, rap was deemed a passing fad, a playful and ephemeral black cultural form that steamed off the musical energies of urban black teens. As it became obvious that rap was here to stay, a permanent fixture in black ghetto youths' musical landscape, the reactions changed from dismissal to denigration, and rap music came under attack from both black and white quarters. Is rap really as dangerous as many critics argue? Or are there redeeming characteristics to rap music that warrant our critical attention? I will attempt to answer these and other questions as I explore the culture of hip-hop.

Trying to pinpoint the exact origin of rap is a tricky process that depends on when one acknowledges a particular cultural expression or product as rap. Rap can be traced back to the revolutionary verse of Gil Scott-Heron and the Last Poets, to Pigmeat Markham's "Here Come de Judge," and even to Bessie Smith's rapping to a beat in some of her blues. We can also cite ancient African oral traditions as the antecedents to various contemporary African-American cultural practices. In any case, the modern history of rap probably begins in 1979 with the rap song "Rapper's Delight," by the Sugarhill Gang. Although there were other (mostly underground) examples of rap, this record is regarded as the signal barrier breaker, birthing hip-hop and consolidating the infant art form's popularity. This first stage in rap record production was characterized by rappers placing their rhythmic, repetitive speech over well-known (mostly R&B) black music hits "Rapper's Delight" was rapped over the music to a song made by the popular seventies R&B group Chic, titled "Good Times." Although rap would later enhance its technical virtuosity through instrumentation, drum machines, and "sampling" existing records—thus making it creatively symbiotic—the first stage was benignly parasitic upon existing black music.

As rap grew, it was still limited to mostly inner-city neighborhoods and particularly its place of origin New York City. Rap artists like Funky 4 plus 1, Kool Moe Dee, Busty Bee, Afrika Bambaataa, Cold Rush Brothers, Kurtis Blow, DJ Kool Herc, and Grandmaster Melle Mel were experimenting with this developing musical genre. As it evolved, rap began to describe and analyze the social, economic, and political factors that led to its emergence and development: drug addiction, police brutality, teen pregnancy, and various forms of material deprivation. This new development was both expressed and precipitated by Kurtis Blow's "Those Are the Breaks" and by the most influential and important rap song to emerge in rap's early history, "The Message," by Grandmaster Flash and The Furious Five. The picture this song painted of inner-city life for black Americans—the hues of dark social

61

misery and stains of profound urban catastrophe—screeched against the canvas of most suburban sensibilities:

> You'll grow up in the ghetto living second rate / And your eyes will sing a song of deep hate / The places you play and where you stay, / Looks like one great big alleyway / You'll admire all the number book takers / Thugs, pimps, and pushers and the big money makers / Drivin' big cars, spendin' twenties and tens, and you want to grow up to be just like them / ... It's like a jungle sometimes / It makes me wonder how I keep from goin' under.

"The Message," along with Flash's "New York, New York," pioneered the social awakening of rap into a form combining social protest, musical creation, and cultural expression.

As its fortunes slowly grew, rap was still viewed by the music industry as an epiphenomenal cultural activity that would cease as black youth became bored and moved on to another diversion, as they did with break-dancing and graffiti art. But the successes of the rap group Run-DMC moved rap into a different sphere of artistic expression that signaled its increasing control of its own destiny. Run-DMC is widely recognized as the progenitor of modern rap's creative integration of social commentary, diverse musical elements, and uncompromising cultural identification—an integration that pushed the music into the mainstream and secured its future as an American musical genre with an identifiable tradition. Run-DMC's stunning commercial and critical success almost singlehandedly landed rap in the homes of many black and nonblack youths across America by producing the first rap album to be certified gold (five hundred thousand copies sold), the first rap song to be featured on the twenty-four-hour music video channel MTV, and the first rap album (1987's *Raising Hell*) to go triple platinum (three million copies sold).

On *Raising Hell*, Run-DMC showcased the sophisticated technical virtuosity of its DJ Jam Master Jay—the raw shrieks, scratches, glitches, and language of the street, plus the innovative and ingenious appropriation of hard-rock guitar riffs. In doing this, Run-DMC symbolically and substantively wedded two traditions—the waning subversion of rock music and the rising, incendiary aesthetic of hip-hop music—to produce a provocative musical hybrid of fiery lyricism and potent critique, *Raising Hell* ended with the rap anthem, "Proud to be Black," intoning its unabashed racial pride:

> Ya know I'm proud to be black ya'll, And that's a fact ya'll / Now Harriet Tubman was born a slave, She was a tiny black woman when she was raised / She was livin' to be givin', There's a lot that she gave / There's not a slave in this day and age, I'm proud to be black.

At the same time, rap, propelled by Run-DMC's epochal success, found an arena in which to concentrate its subversive cultural didacticism aimed at addressing racism, classism, social neglect, and urban pain: the rap concert, where rappers are allowed to engage in ritualistic refusals of censored speech. The rap concert also creates space for cultural resistance and personal agency, loosing the strictures of the tyrannizing surveillance and demoralizing condemnation of mainstream society and encouraging relatively autonomous, often enabling, forms of self-expression and cultural creativity.

However, Run-DMC's success, which greatly increased the visibility and commercial appeal of rap music through record sales and rap concerts, brought along another charge that has had a negative impact on rap's perception by the general public: the claim that rap expresses and causes violence. Tipper Gore has repeatedly said that rap music appeals to "angry, disillusioned, unloved kids" and that it tells them it is "okay to beat people up." Violent incidents at rap concerts in Los Angles, Pittsburgh, Cleveland, Atlanta, Cincinnati, and New York City have only reinforced the popular perception that rap is intimately linked to violent social behavior by mostly black and Latino inner-city youth. Countless black parents, too, have had negative reactions to rap, and the black radio and media establishment, although not as vocal as Gore, have voted on her side with their allocation of much less airplay and print coverage to rap than is warranted by its impressive record sales.

Such reactions betray a shallow understanding of rap, which in many cases results from people's unwillingness to listen to rap lyrics, many of which counsel antiviolent and antidrug behavior among the youths who are their avid audience. Many rappers have spoken directly against violence, such as KRS-One in his "Stop the Violence." Another rap record produced by KRS-One in 1989, the top-selling *Self-Destruction*, insists that violence predates rap and speaks against escalating black-on-black crime, which erodes the social and communal fabric of already debased black inner cities across America:

> Well, today's topic is self-destruction, It really ain't the rap audience that's buggin' / It's one or two suckers, ignorant brothers, Tryin' to rob and steal from one another / ... 'Cause the way we live is positive / We don't kill our relatives / ... Back in the sixties our brothers and sisters were hanged. How could you gang-bang? / I never, ever ran from the Ku Klux Klan, and I shouldn't have to run from a black man, 'Cause that's / Self-destruction, ya headed for self-destruction.

Despite such potent messages, many mainstream blacks and whites persist in categorically negative appraisals of rap, refusing to distinguish between enabling, productive rap messages and the social violence that exists in many inner-city communities and that is often reflected in rap songs. Of course, it is difficult for a culture that is serious about the maintenance of social arrangements, economic conditions, and political choices that create and reproduce poverty, racism, sexism, classism, and violence to display a significant appreciation for musical expressions that contest the existence of such problems in black and Latino communities. Also disappointing is the continued complicity of black radio stations in denying rap its rightful place of prominence on their playlists. The conspiracy of silence and invisibility has affected the black print media, as well. Although rapper M.C. Shan believes that most antirap bias arises from outside the black community, he faults black radio for depriving rap of adequate airplay and laments the fact that "if a white rock'n'roll magazine like *Rolling Stone* or *Spin* can put a rapper on the cover and *Ebony* and *Jet* won't, that means there's really something wrong."

In this regard, rap music is emblematic of the glacial shift in aesthetic sensibilities between blacks of different generations, and it draws attention to the severe economic barriers that increasingly divide ghetto poor blacks from middle- and upper-middle-class blacks. Rap reflects the intraracial class division that has plagued African-American communities for the last thirty years. The increasing social isolation, economic hardship, political demoralization, and cultural exploitation endured by most ghetto poor communities in the past few decades have given rise to a form of musical expression that captures the terms of ghetto poor existence. I am not suggesting that rap has been limited to the ghetto poor, but only that its major themes and styles continue to be drawn from the conflicts and contradictions of black urban life. One of the later trends in rap music is the development of "pop" rap by groups like JJ Fad, The Fat Boys, DJ Jazzy Jeff and The Fresh Prince, and Tone Loc. DJ Jazzy Jeff and the Fresh Prince, for example, are two suburbanites from South West Philadelphia and Winfield. (For that matter, members of the most radical rap group, Public Enemy, are suburbanites from Long Island.) DJ Jazzy Jeff and The Fresh Prince's album, *He's the DJ, I'm the Rapper*, sold over three million copies, boosted by the enormously successful single "Parents Just Don't Understand." This record, which rapped humorously about various crises associated with being a teen, struck a chord with teenagers across the racial and class spectra, signaling the exploration of rap's populist terrain. The Fresh Prince's present success as the star of his own Quincy Jones-produced television series is further testimony to his popular appeal.

Tone Loc's success also expresses rap's division between "hardcore" (social consciousness and racial pride backed by driving rhythms) and "pop" (exploration of common territory between races and classes, usually devoid of social message). This division, while expressing the commercial expansion of rap, also means that companies and willing radio executives have increasingly chosen pop rap as more acceptable than its more realistic, politically conscious counterpart. (This bias is also evident in the selection of award recipients in the newly created rap category at the annual Grammy Awards.) Tone Loc is an L.A. rapper whose first single, "Wild Thing," sold over two million copies, topping *Billboard*'s "Hot Singles Chart," the first rap song to achieve this height. Tone Loc's success was sparked by his video's placement in heavy rotation on MTV, which devotes an hour on Saturdays to "Yo! MTV Raps," a show that became so popular that a daily hour segment was added.

The success of such artists as Tone Loc and DJ Jazzy Jeff and The Fresh Prince inevitably raises the specter of mainstream dilution, the threat to every emergent form of cultural production in American society, particularly the fecund musical tradition that comes from black America. For many, this means the sanitizing of rap's expression of urban realities, resulting in sterile hip-hop that, devoid of its original fire, will offend no one. This scenario, of course, is a familiar denouement to the story of most formerly subversive musical genres. Also, MTV's avid acceptance of rap and the staging of rap concerts run by white promoters willing to take a chance on rap artists add further commentary to the sad state of cultural affairs in many black communities: the continued refusal to acknowledge authentic (not to mention desirable) forms of rap artistry ensures rap's existence on the margins of many black communities.

Perhaps the example of another neglected and devalued black musical tradition, the blues, can be helpful for understanding what is occurring among rap, segments of the black community, and mainstream American society. The blues now has a mostly young white audience. Blacks do not largely support the blues through concert patronage or record buying, thus neglecting a musical genre that was once closely identified with devalued and despised people: poor southern agrarian blacks and the northern urban black poor, the first stratum of the developing underclass. The blues functioned for another generation of blacks much as rap functions today: as a source of racial identity, permitting forms of boasting and asserting machismo for devalued black men suffering from social degradation, allowing commentary on social and personal conditions in uncensored language, and fostering the ability to transform hurt and anguish into art and commerce. Even in its heyday, however, the blues existed as a secular musical genre over against the religious traditions that saw the blues as "devil's music" and the conservative black cultural perspectives of the blues as barbaric. These feelings, along with the direction of southern agrarian musical energies into a more accessible and populist soul music, ensured the contraction of the economic and cultural basis for expressing life experience in the blues idiom.

Robert Cray's recent success in mainstreaming the blues perhaps completes the cycle of survival for devalued forms of black music: it originates in a context of anguish and pain and joy and happiness, it expresses those emotions and ideas in a musical language and idiom peculiar to its view of life, it is altered as a result of cultural sensibilities and economic factors, and it undergoes distribution, packaging, and consumption for leisurely or cathartic pleasure through concert attendance or record buying. Also, in the process, artists are sometimes removed from the immediate context and original site of their artistic production. Moreover, besides everyday ways in which the music is used for a variety of entertainment functions, it may occasionally be employed in contexts that undermine its critique of the status quo, and it may be used to legitimize a cultural or social setting that, in negative ways, has partially given rise to its expression. A recent example of this is the late Lee Atwater's positioning himself as a privileged patron of the blues and soul music traditions in the 1989 Bush inauguration festivities, which was preceded by his racist use of the Willie Horton case. Atwater's use of Willie Horton played on the very prejudice against black men that has often led blues musicians to express the psychic, personal, and social pain occasioned by racism in American (political) culture. Rap's visibility may alter this pattern as it continues to grow, but its self-defined and continuing challenge is to maintain its aesthetic, cultural, and political proximity to its site of original expression: the ghetto poor.

Interestingly, a new wave of rap artists may be accomplishing this goal, but with foreboding consequences. For example, N.W.A. (Niggaz With Attitudes) reflects the brutal circumstances that define the boundaries within which most ghetto poor black youth in Los Angeles must live. For the most part they—unlike their socially conscientious counterparts Public Enemy, Boogie Down Productions, and Stetsasonic—have no ethical remove from the violence, gang-bangin', and drugs in L.A.'s inner city. In their song "—Tha Police," N.W.A. gives a sample of their reality:

Fuck the police, comin' straight from the underground. A young nigger got it bad 'cause I'm brown / And not the other color, so police think, / They have the authority to kill a minority / … Searchin' my car looking for the product, / Thinkin' every nigger is sellin' narcotic / … But don't let it be a black and a white one, / 'Cause they'll slam ya down to the street top, / Black police showin' out for the white cop.

Such expressions of violence certainly reflect the actual life circumstances of many black and Latino youth caught in L.A. ghetto living. N.W.A. celebrates a lethal mix of civil terrorism and personal cynicism. Their attitude is both one answer to, and the logical outcome of, the violence, racism, and oppression in American culture. On the other hand, their vision must be criticized, for the stakes are too high for the luxury of moral neutrality. Having at least partially lived the life they rap about, N.W.A. understands the viciousness of police brutality. However, they must also be challenged to develop an ethical perspective on the drug gangs that duplicate police violence in black-on-black crime. While rappers like N.W.A. perform an invaluable service by rapping in poignant and realistic terms about urban underclass existence, they must be challenged to expand their moral vocabulary and be more sophisticated in their understanding that description alone is insufficient to address the crises of black urban life. Groups like N.W.A. should be critically aware that blacks are victims of the violence of both state repression *and* gang violence, that one form of violence is often the response to the other, and that blacks continue to be held captive to disenabling lifestyles (gang-bangin', drug dealing) that cripple the life of black communities.

Also problematic is the sexist sentiment that pervades so much of rap music. It is a rampant sexism that continues to mediate the relations within the younger black generation with lamentable intensity. While it is true that rap's sexism is indeed a barometer of the general tenor and mood that mediates black male-female relations, it is not the role of women alone to challenge it. Reproach must flow from women *and* men who are sensitive to the ongoing sexist attitudes and behavior that dominate black male-female relationships. Because women by and large do not run record companies, or even head independent labels that have their records distributed by larger corporations, it is naïve to assume that protest by women alone will arrest the spread of sexism in rap. Female rappers are certainly a potential resource for challenging existing sexist attitudes, but given the sexist barriers that patrol rap's borders, male rappers must be challenged by antisexist men, especially male rappers who contest the portrayal of women in most rap music. The constant reference to women as "skeezers," "bitches," and "ho's" only reinforces the perverted expression of male dominance and patriarchy and reasserts the stereotyping of women as sexual objects intended exclusively for male pleasure.

Fortunately, many of the problems related to rap—particularly with black radio, media, and community acceptance—have only fostered a sense of camaraderie that transcends in crucial ways the fierce competitive streak in rap (which, at its best moments, urges rappers on to creative musical heights). While the "dis" rap (which humorously musicalizes "the dozens") is alive and well, the overall feeling among rap artists that rap must flourish outside the sanctions of traditional means of garnering high visibility or securing record sales has directed a communal energy into the production of their music. The current state of affairs has also precipitated cooperative entrepreneurial activity among young black persons. The rap industry has spawned a number of independent labels, providing young blacks (mostly men) with experience of heads of their own businesses and with exposure as managers of talent, positions that might otherwise be unavailable to them. Until recently, rap flourished, for the most part, outside of the tight artistic and economic constraints imposed by major music corporations. Although many independent companies have struck distribution deals with major labels—such as Atlantic, MCA, Columbia, and Warner Brothers—it has usually been the case, until the late 1980s, that the inexperience of major labels with rap, coupled with their relatively conservative musical tastes, has enabled the independent labels to control their destinies by teaching the major music corporations invaluable lessons about street sales, the necessity of having a fast rate of delivery from the production of a record to its date of distribution, and remaining close to the sensibilities of the street, while experimenting with their marketing approach in ways that reflect the diversification of styles in rap.

Rap expresses the ongoing preoccupation with literacy and orality that has characterized African-American communities since the inception of legally coerced illiteracy during slavery. Rap artists explore grammatical creativity, verbal wizardry, and linguistic innovation in refining the art of oral communication. The rap artist, as Cornel West has indicated, is a bridge figure who combines the two potent traditions in black cultures: preaching and music. The rap artist appeals to the rhetorical practices eloquently honed in African-American religious experiences and the cultural potency of black singing/musical traditions to produce an engaging hybrid. They are truly urban riots dispensing social and cultural critique, verbal shamans exorcising the demons of cultural amnesia. The culture of hip-hop has generated a lexicon of life that expresses rap's B-boy/B-girl worldview, a perspective that takes delight in undermining "correct" English usage while celebrating the culturally encoded phrases that communicate in rap's idiom.

Rap has also retrieved historic black ideas, movements, and figures in combating the racial amnesia that threatens to relegate the achievements of the black past to the ash heap of dismemory. Such actions have brought a renewed sense of historical pride to young black minds that provides a solid base for racial self-esteem. Rap music has also focused renewed attention on black nationalist and black radical thought. This revival has been best symbolized by the rap group Public Enemy. Public Enemy announced its black nationalism in embryonic form on their first album, *Yo! Bum Rush the Show*, but their vision sprang forward full-blown in their important *It Takes a Nation of Millions to Hold Us Back*. The album's explicit black nationalist language and cultural sensibilities were joined with a powerful mix of music, beats, screams, noise, and rhythms from the streets. Its message is provocative, even jarring, a précis of the contained chaos and channeled rage that informs the most politically astute rappers. On the cut "Bring the Noise," they intone:

> We got to demonstrate, come on now, they're gonna have to wait / Till we get it right / Radio stations I question their blackness / They call themselves black, but we'll see if they'll play this / Turn it up! Bring the noise!

Public Enemy also speaks of the criminality of prison conditions and how dope dealers fail the black community. Their historical revivalism is noteworthy, for instance as they rap on "Party for Your Right to Fight":

Power Equality / And we're out to get it I know some of you ain't wit' it / This party started right in '66 / With a pro-Black racial mix / Then at the hour of twelve / ... J. Edgar Hoover, and he coulda' proved to 'ya / He had King and X set up / Also the party with Newton, Cleaver, and Seale / ... Word from the honorable Elijah Muhummad / Know who you are to be Black / ... the original Black Asiatic man.

Public Enemy troubled even more sociocultural waters with their Nation of Islam views, saying in "Don't Believe the Hype": "The follower of Farrakhan / Don't tell me that you understand / Until you hear the man." Such rap displays the power and pitfalls associated with the revival of earlier forms of black radicalism, nationalism, and cultural expression. The salutary aspect of the historical revival is that it raises consciousness about important figures, movements, and ideas, prompting rappers to express their visions of life in American culture. This renewed historicism permits young blacks to discern links between the past and their own present circumstances, using the past as a fertile source of social reflection, cultural creation, and political resistance.

On the other hand, it has also led to perspectives that do not provide *critical* reflection on the past. Rather, many rappers attempt to duplicate the past without challenging or expanding it. Thus, their historical insight fails to illumine our current cultural problems as powerfully as it might, and the present generation of black youth fails to benefit as fully from the lessons that it so powerfully revives. This is an unfortunate result of the lack of understanding and communication among various segments of the black community, particularly along generational and class lines, problems symbolized in the black community's response to rap. Historical revival cries out for contexts that render the past understandable and usable. This cannot occur if large segments of the black community continue to be segregated from one of the most exciting cultural transformations occurring in contemporary American life: the artistic expression, cultural explorations, political activity, and historical revival of hip-hop artists.

An issue in rap that is closely related to the acknowledgement of history and sources is sampling, or the grafting of music, voices, and beats from another sonic source onto a rap record. The practice of sampling expresses the impulse to collage that characterizes the best of black musical traditions, particularly jazz and gospel. Sampling is also postmodernist activity that merges disparate musical and cultural forms to communicate an artistic message. Sampling is a transgressive activity because rappers employ it to interrupt the narrative flow and musical stability of other musical texts, producing a new and often radically different creation. But rap may potentially take back in its technical appropriation what it has given in its substantive, lyrical achievements: a recognition of history. While sampling permits a rap creator to reconfigure voices and rhythms in creating an alternate code of cultural exchange, the practice may also deprive other artists of recognition or even financial remuneration. The classic case in point is James Brown, who, along with George Clinton, is the most sampled man in rap and the primal progenitor of the beats and rhythms in hip-hop music. Although his voice, rhythms, and beats are often easily identifiable and rap's debt to him is obvious, Brown's benefit has been limited. Recent legal woes connected to the status of rap's practice of creative borrowing may hasten rap's codification of appropriate acknowledgement, particularly in an economic practice similar to the royalty that distinguishes between small bites of music and significant borrowing and quotation.

Rap is a form of profound musical, cultural, and social creativity. It expresses the desire of young black people to reclaim their history, reactivate forms of black radicalism, and contest the powers of despair and economic depression that presently besiege the black community. Besides being the most powerful form of black musical expression today, rap projects a style of self into the world that generates forms of cultural resistance and transforms the ugly terrain of ghetto existence into a searing portrait of life as it must be lived by millions of voiceless people. For that reason alone, rap deserves attention and should be taken seriously; and for its productive and healthy moments, it should be promoted as a worthy form of artistic expression and cultural projection and an enabling source of black juvenile and communal solidarity.

8
Puerto Rocks:
Rap, Roots, and Amnesia

Juan Flores

By the early 1990s, hip-hop had finally broken the language barrier. Though young Puerto Ricans from the South Bronx and El Barrio have been involved in breakdancing, graffiti writing, and rap music since the beginnings of hip-hop back in the 1970s, it was only belatedly that the Spanish language and Latin musical styles came into their own as integral features of the rap vocabulary. By the mid-nineties, acts like Mellow Man Ace, Kid Frost, Gerardo, and El General became household words among pop music fans nationwide and internationally, as young audiences of all nationalities came to delight in the catchy Spanglish inflections and the *guaguancó* and merengue rhythms lacing the familiar rap formats. Mellow Man Ace's "Mentirosa" was the first Latino rap record to go gold in the summer of 1990; Kid Frost's debut album *Hispanic Causing Panic* instantly became the rap anthem of La Raza in the same year; Gerardo as "Rico Suave" has his place as the inevitable Latin lover sex symbol; and El General has established the immense popularity of Spanish-language reggae-rap in the Caribbean and Latin America.

Who are these first Latin rap superstars and where are they from? Mellow Man Ace was born in Cuba and raised in Los Angeles, Kid Frost is a Chicano from East L.A., Gerardo is from Ecuador, and El General is Panamanian. But what about the Puerto Ricans, who with their African American homeboys created hip-hop styles in the first place? They are, as usual, conspicuous for their absence, and the story is no less startling for all its familiarity. Latin Empire, for example, the only Nuyorican act to gain some exposure among wider audiences, is still struggling for its first major record deal. Individual emcees and deejays have been scattered in well-known groups like the Fearless Four and the Fat Boys, their Puerto Rican backgrounds all but invisible. Even rap performers from Puerto Rico like Vico C, Lisa M, and Rubén DJ, who grew up far from the streets where hip-hop originated, enjoy greater commercial success and media recognition than any of the Puerto Rican b-boys from the New York scene.

This omission, of course, is anything but fortuitous and has as much to do with the selective vagaries of the music industry as with the social placement of the Puerto Rican community in the prevailing racial-cultural hierarchy. As the commercialization process involves the extraction of popular cultural expression from its original social context and function, it seems that the "Latinization" of hip-hop has meant its distancing from the specific national and ethnic traditions to which it had most directly pertained. But instead of simply bemoaning this evident injustice, or groping for elaborate explanations, it is perhaps more worthwhile to trace the history of this experience from the perspectives of some of the rappers themselves. For if New York Puerto Ricans have had scant play within the "Hispanic rap market," they have one thing that other Latino rappers do not, which is a history in hip-hop since its foundation as an emergent cultural practice among urban youth.

Such an emphasis is not meant to imply any inherent aesthetic judgment, nor does it necessarily involve a privileging of origins or presumed authenticity. Yet it is easy to understand and sympathize with the annoyance of a veteran Puerto Rican deejay like Charlie Chase when faced with the haughty attitudes he encountered among some of the rap superstars from the Island. "The thing about working with these Puerto Rican rappers," he commented, reflecting on his work producing records for the likes of Lisa M and Vico C, "they are very arrogant! You know, because they are from Puerto Rico, and I'm not, right? I feel kind of offended, but my comeback is like, well, yeah, if you want to be arrogant about that, then what are you doing in rap? You're not a rapper. You learned rap from listening to me and other people from New York!"[1] Actually this apprenticeship was probably less direct than Charlie Chase claims, since they more likely got to know rap through the recordings, videos, and concert appearances of Run DMC, LL Cool J, and Big Daddy Kane than through any familiarity with the New York hip-hop scene of the early years.

Where did those first platinum-selling rappers themselves go to learn the basics of rap performance? Again, Charlie Chase can fill us in, by remembering the shows he deejayed with the Cold Crush Brothers back in the early 1980s.

> When we were doing shows, you know who was in the audience? The Fat Boys. Whodini. Run DMC, L.L. Cool J, Big Daddy Kane. Big Daddy Kane told me a story one time, he said, "You don't know how much I loved you guys." He said, "I wanted to see you guys so bad, and my mother told me not to go to Harlem World to see you guys perform because if she found out I did she'd kick my ass!" And he said, "I didn't care, I went. And I went every week. And I wouldn't miss any of your shows." That's how popular we were with the people who are the rappers today.

To speak of Puerto Ricans in rap means to defy the sense of instant amnesia that engulfs popular cultural expression once it is caught up in the logic of commercial representation. It involves sketching in historical contexts and sequences, tracing traditions and antecedents, and recognizing hip-hop to be more and different than the simulated images, poses, and formulas the public discourse of media entertainment tends to reduce it to. The decade and more of hindsight provided by the Puerto Rican involvement shows that, rather than a new musical genre and its accompanying stylistic trappings, rap constitutes a space for the articulation of social experience. From this perspective, what has emerged as "Latin rap" first took shape as an expression of the cultural turf shared, and contended for, by African Americans and Puerto Ricans over their decades as neighbors, coworkers, and "homies" in the inner-city communities. As vernacular cultural production prior to its commercial and technological mediation, hip-hop formed part of a more extensive and intricate field of social practice, a significant dimension of which comprises the long-standing and ongoing interaction between Puerto Rican and Black youth in the shared New York settings. Not only is the contextual field wider, but the historical reach is deeper and richer as well: the Black and Puerto Rican conjunction in the formation of rap is prefigured in important ways in doo-wop, Latin boogaloo, Nuyorican poetry, and a range of other testimonies to intensely overlapping and intermingling expressive repertoires. Thus when Latin Empire comes out with "I'm Puerto Rican and Proud, Boyee!" they are actually marking off a decisive moment in a tradition of cultural and political identification that goes back several generations.

I have gained access to this largely uncharted terrain by way of conversations and interviews with some of the protagonists of Puerto Rican rap. Early hip-hop movies like *Wild Style* and *Style Wars*, which documented and dramatized the prominent participation of Puerto

Ricans, sparked my initial interest and led to a burst of research (which hardly anyone took seriously at the time) and a short article published in various English and Spanish versions in the mid-1980s. At that time, the only adequate written consideration of Puerto Ricans had to do with their role in the New York graffiti movement, as in the excellent book *Getting Up* by Craig Castleman and an important article by Herbert Kohl. Steven Hager's *Hip-Hop* includes a valuable social history of youth culture in the South Bronx and Harlem at the dawn of hip-hop, with some attention to the part played by Puerto Ricans in graffiti, breakdance, and rap music.[2] Otherwise, and since those earlier accounts, coverage of Puerto Rican rap has been limited to an occasional article in the *Village Voice* or *Spin* magazine, generally as a sideline concern in discussions of wider style rubrics like "Hispanic," "Spanish," or "bilingual" rap. Primary evidence of a historical kind is even harder to come by, since Puerto Rican rhymes were never recorded for public distribution and many have been forgotten even by their authors.

Chasin' the Flash

Charlie Chase calls himself "New York's Number One Puerto Rican DJ," and that's how he's been known since back in the seventies when he was blasting the hottest dance music on the waves of WBLS and in the early eighties when he was deejay for the legendary Cold Crush Brothers. When he says "Number One," he means not only the best but also the first: "When I started doing rap, there were no Hispanics doing it. If there were I didn't know about it. Anyway, I was the first Hispanic to become popular doing what I did. I was a deejay."

Charlie was born in El Barrio in the 1950s, and though his family moved a lot it was always from one Puerto Rican and Black neighborhood to another.

> I grew up in Williamsburg from the age of two to nine. I moved to the Bronx, on Brook Avenue and 141st, ¡que eso por allí es candela! I grew up there from ten to about thirteen, then I moved back to Brooklyn, over in Williamsburg, Montrose Avenue, por allá on Broadway. Then we moved back to the Bronx again, 161st and Yankee Stadium. From there we went to 180th and Arthur, and from there it was Grand Concourse and 183rd, then Valentine and 183rd, then back to 180th. I mean, we moved, man! I've been all over the place, and it's like I've had the worst of both worlds, you know what I mean?

Charlie's parents came from Mayagüez, Puerto Rico. Though family visits to the Island were rare, that Puerto Rican background remained an active influence throughout his upbringing. At home he was raised on Puerto Rican music. "You see I always listened to my mother's records. She was the one who bought all the Latin records. She bought them all. She bought Tito Puente, she was into trios, el Trio Los Condes." Even his career in music seems to have been handed down to him as part of that ancestry.

> I come from a family of musicians. My grandfather was a writer and a musician; he played in bands. So did my father; he played in trios. So I kind of followed in their footsteps. My father left me when I was ten and I never learned music from him; he didn't teach me how to play instruments. For some reason or other, it must have been in the blood, I just picked up the guitar and wanted to learn.

Charlie makes clear that he didn't start off in rap or as a deejay. "I'm a bass player. I played in a Spanish ballad band, merengue band, salsa band, rock band, funk band, Latin rock band. I produced my first album at the age of sixteen and it was a Spanish ballad album. We played with the best, Johnny Ventura, Johnny Pacheco, Los Hijos del Rey, Tito Puente. The name of the group was Los Giramundos." So it turns out that Charlie Chase, famed deejay for the Cold

Crush Brothers, started off gigging in a Latin band when he was fifteen years old and could have had a whole career in salsa. "Yeah," he recalls, "but there was no money in it. There were a lot of people being ripped off.... I said, man, I want to do something else." Fortunately, he did have somewhere to turn, for alongside his inherited Latin tradition there was his dance music and R&B. Talking about his transition to deejaying he remembers:

> I was a music lover. I grew up listening to WABC, Cousin Brucie, Chuck Leonard, all of these guys, and I was always into music. In school I would always have the radio on. It was always a big influence in my life and then I turned into a musician. I started playing with the band, and then a few years later I got into deejaying, and then the deejaying was making more money for me than the band.

It all seems to make sense, I thought, but what about that name? What's a Puerto Rican doing with a name like Charlie Chase? "My name was Carlos," he said. "Charlie is a nickname for Carlos." Fine, I said, but what about Chase? "Chase?" he repeated, hesitantly. "There is a story behind that which I never told anybody, and I don't know if I want to say it. Because when this person reads this, he is going to be so souped." (Little was I to know how much this little story has to say about the situation of young Puerto Ricans in the early days of rap.)

> I made up my name because of Grandmaster Flash. Flash is a friend of mine. I first saw Flash doing this, cutting and all of this, and I saw that and I said, aw, man, I can do this. I was deejaying at the time, but I wasn't doing the scratching and shit and I said, I can do this, man. I'll rock this, you know. And I practiced, I broke turntables, needles, everything. Now "Chase" came because I'm like, damn, you need a good name, man. And Flash was on top and I was down here. So I was chasing that niggah. I wanted to be up where he was. So I said, let's go with Charlie Chase.

There's no telling how "souped" Grandmaster Flash will get when he finds out, but his friend and main rival (along with Grandmaster Theo) back in the days, grew up as Carlos Mandes. "It's Mandes," Charlie emphasized, "m-a-n-d-e-s. Not Méndez." Whatever the origin of his Puerto Rican name, ever since he started chasing the Flash Carlos Mandes has been known, by everyone, as Charlie Chase. He doesn't even like it when "Mandes" appears on the records he wrote. "Nobody knows my name was Carlos Mandes. They'd laugh. They'd snap on me."

Charlie might think that Mandes sounds corny now, but at the time the problem was that it didn't fit. He never tires of telling about how difficult it was to be accepted as a Puerto Rican in rap, especially as a deejay, and because he was so good. "A lot of Blacks would not accept that I was Spanish. You know, a lot of times because of the way I played they thought I was Black, because I rocked it so well." As a deejay he was usually seated in back, behind the emcees and out of sight. In the beginning, in fact, his invisibility was a key to success. "I became popular because of the tapes, and also because nobody could see me. Since they thought I was Black, you know, because I was in the background." Even when they saw him, he says that "they still wouldn't believe it. They are like, 'no, that's not him! That's bullshit! That's not him!' A few years went by and they accepted it, you know. I was faced with a lot of that. You know, being Hispanic you're not accepted in rap. Because to them it's a Black thing and something that's from their roots and shit."

"What the fuck are you doing here, Puerto Rican?" Charlie remembers being faced with that challenge time and again when he went behind the ropes, among the rappers, at the early jams. He had to prove himself constantly, and he recalls vividly the times when it took his homeboy Tony Tone from DJ Breakout and Baron to step in and save his skin. "I turn around and see him breaking on them and I hear what he's saying and I'm like, oh shit!" As tough as it got, though, Charlie knew very well that he wasn't out of place. "I was the type of kid that, you know, I always grew up with Black people.... My daughter's godfather is Black. He's like my brother, that guy."

But the best proof was that Charlie was with the Cold Crush Brothers, who were all Black. "We all grew up in the streets, man. It's like a street thing. Once you see that the guy is cool, then you're accepted, everything flows correctly." And it's not that Charlie just did everything like the other brothers, to fit in. Aside from his "mancha de plátano," those indelible earmarks of the Puerto Rican, he had his own personal style about him that he wasn't about to give up just to be one of the boys. He remembers about Cold Crush that "the only thing was, it was a trip when it came to the dressing bit. You see, I don't dress like the average hip-hopper and never did. They wanted to wear Kangols, Martin X, and these British walkers and all that stuff at the time, and I was like, that's not me, fellas. That's not me, man. At that time, I combed my hair back in a DA." Not only did he refuse to fit the mold, but Charlie's insistence helped the group arrive at the look that helped to establish their immense popularity in those years. "We came up with a look that everybody copied afterwards, which we all felt comfortable with. It was the leather and stud look, which we popularized in rap and through that look we became hard."

Besides, as alone as he was sometimes made to feel, Charlie knew that he wasn't the only Puerto Rican who was into rap. "Hispanics always liked rap, young Puerto Ricans were into it since the beginning. I wasn't the only one who felt the same way about music like that. There were plenty of them, but they didn't have the talent, they just enjoyed it. Me, I wanted to do it, you know. Forget it, there were plenty of people. I mean, when you grow up in the streets, it's a street thing, man." In its street beginnings, Puerto Ricans were an integral part of the rap scene, and not only as appreciative fans. Though their participation in production and performance was submerged (far more so than in breaking and graffiti), they were an essential and preponderant presence in the security crews that, in the gang environment, made the whole show possible. "It was rough, man," Charlie recalls.

All of my crew, the whole crew, were Spanish, maybe two or three Black guys. They were all Spanish, and when we jammed we had bats. If you crossed the line or got stupid, you were going to get batted down, alright? And that was that. That was my crew, they would help me with records, they were security. The guys in my group were Black, but the rest of the guys, security, were Hispanic.... People'd be like, yo, those are some wild Spanish motherfuckers. Don't mess with them, man.

But with a little coaxing Charlie will even call to mind some other Puerto Rican rappers from those days. There was Prince Whipper Whip and Ruby D (Rubén García) from the Fantastic Five, OC from the Fearless Four with Tito Cepeda, Johnny who was down with Master Don and the Def Committee. "Then there was this one group," Charlie recalls, "that wanted to do Latin rap songs, way back. And they had good ideas and they had great songs, but they just didn't have enough drive, you know? They had a great idea, they had a routine. They had these crazy nice songs, but they just weren't ambitious enough.... Robski and June Bug, those were the guys." Years before anybody started talking about "Latin rap," Robski and June Bug were busy working out Spanglish routines and even rendering some of the best rhymes of the time into Spanish. "They took our songs and translated them into Spanish. They blew our heads, man! It was weird, because they actually took everything we said and turned it into Spanish and made it rhyme. And they did a good job of it."

But in those days using Spanish in rap was still a rarity, especially in rhymes that were distributed on tapes and records. It wasn't only lack of ambition that prevented Robski and

June Bug from making it, "'cause at that time," Charlie says, "a lot of people were doing it underground, but they couldn't come off doing it, they couldn't make money doing it. The people that did it, did it in parties, home stuff, the block, they were the stars in their ghetto." But Charlie himself, "chasing the Flash," was with the first rap group to be signed by CBS Records, the first rap group to tour Japan, the group that played in the first hip-hop movie, *Wild Style*. At that level, rapping in Spanish was still out of the question. Charlie explains what it was like for him to face this constraint, and gives a clear sense of the delicate generational process involved in the entry of bilingualism into commercially circumscribed rap discourse.

> I always stressed the point that I was Hispanic doing rap music, but I couldn't do it in Spanish, you understand? But that was my way of opening the doors for everybody else to do what they're doing now. You see, there are certain degrees, certain levels and steps that you have to follow. And being that I was there at the very beginning, that was the I way I had to do it, That was my contribution. I feel sorry that I couldn't do it then, but I want to do it now and I'm making up for it, because now I can.... I wanted everybody to know that I was Spanish, rocking, ripping shit up. In a Black market.

At that early stage in negotiating Puerto Rican identity in rap, the key issue was not language but what Charlie calls "the Latin point of view"; pushing rhymes in Spanish was not yet part of the precarious juggling act.

> For me it's the Latin point of view. You see, what I emphasize is that I'm Hispanic in a Black world. Not just surviving but making a name for myself and leaving a big impression. Everything that happened to me was always within the Black music business, and I always was juggling stuff all of the time, because I had to be hip, I had to be a homeboy. But I also had to know how far to go without seeming like I was trying to kiss up or something, or "he's just trying to be Black." When you deal with the people I deal with, especially at a time when rap was just hard core and raw, you're talking about guys who were *títeres*, you know, tough guys. I had to juggle that. I had to play my cards correct.

If Spanish wasn't yet part of the "Latin point of view," the music was, especially the rhythmic texture of the songs, which is where as the deejay Charlie was in control. He remembers sneaking in the beat from the number "Tú Coqueta," right "in the middle of a jam. I'm jamming. I throw that sucker in, just the beat alone, and they'd go off. They never knew it was a Spanish record. And if I told them that they'd get off the floor." Even the other rappers couldn't tell because the salsa cuts seemed to fit in so perfectly. "It was great! I would sneak in Spanish records. Beats only, and if the bass line was funky enough, I would do that too. Bobby Valentín stuff. He played bass with the Fania All-Stars, and he would do some funky stuff." As a bassist in Latin bands, Charlie knew the repertoire to choose from.

But he also knew that he had to walk a fine line and that he was ahead of his time, not only for the R&B-savvy rappers but for Latin musical tastes as well. In fact it was because of the resistance he faced from the Latin musicians, and not only the better pay, that Charlie decided to leave Los Giramundos and go into rap full time.

> Sometimes I'd go to gigs and in between songs I'd start playing stuff from rap music and the drummer would like it too, and he'd start doing some stuff. And sometimes people would get up to dance to it and the rest of the guys in the band would get furious at us, and they would say, "What are you doing? If you're not going to play a song, don't do it." They would break on me. They didn't want that stuff.

Not that Charlie didn't try to interest Latin musicians in mixing some elements of rap into their sound. He especially remembers working on a record concept with Willie Colón.

> He could have had the first Latin hip-hop record out and it would have been a hit. It was a singing rap. He was singing, right, there was a little bit of rap, and I was scratching. I did the arrangements. What happened was, the project was being held and held and held. What happened? He put out the record, an instrumental! He took out all the raps, then he overdubbed. Killed the whole project. He slept on it.

But as Charlie learned early on, when it comes to the emergence of new styles in popular music it's all a matter of timing. He himself had trouble relating to the use of Spanish in rap when he first heard it on record. Back in 1981 the group Mean Machine came out with the first recorded Spanish rhymes in their "Disco Dream," a side that deeply impressed some of the present-day Latino rappers like Mellow Man Ace and Latin Empire when they first heard it, though that was some years after it was released. But Charlie knew Mean Machine when they started and recalls his reaction when "Disco Dream" first came out. "It was strange, and it was new. At first I didn't jive with it because I was so used to it and I myself got so caught up in that whole R&B thing that when I heard that, it didn't click with me. And I was like, 'Naw, this is bullshit!'" But with time tastes changed, as did Charlie's understanding of himself and his own role. "And then," he goes on, "something made me realize one day that, wait a minute, man, look at you, what are you? You don't rap like they do, but you're Hispanic just like them, trying to get a break in the business. And I said, if anything, this is something cool and new."

Seen in retrospect, Mean Machine was only a faint hint of what was to become Latino rap in the years ahead. The Spanish they introduced amounted to a few party exhortations rather than an extended Spanish or bilingual text. Charlie draws this distinction, and again points up the changing generations of Latino presence in rap.

"The way that they did it was not like today. Today it's kind of political, opinionated, and commercial, and storytelling. What they did was that they took a lot of Spanish phrases, like 'uepa' and 'dale fuego a la lata, fuego a la lata,' stuff like that, and turned them into a record." However perfunctory their bilingualism and fleeting their acclaim, Mean Machine's early dabbling with Spanglish rhymes did plant a seed. Puerto Rock of Latin Empire attests to the impact "Disco Dream" had on them:

> They didn't continue. After one record, that was it. I know them all, we keep in contact. Mr. Schick came out with, "Tire su mano al aire / Yes, means throw your hands in the air / y siguen con el baile means / dance your body till you just don't care." And then it ended up with, "Fuego a la lata, fuego a la lata / agua que va caer." So we were like bugging! We were more or less doing it but in English and got crazy inspired when we heard that record. We was like, Oh, snap! He wrote the first Spanish rhyme! We was skeptical if it was going to work, and when we heard the record we were like, it's going to work.[3]

The disbelief and strategic invisibility that surrounded Latino participation in rap performance in the early years gave way to a fascination with something new and different. Charlie sees this process reflected in the changing fate of his own popularity among hip-hop audiences. "It was kind of complicated," he recalls. If at first he became popular because "nobody could see me," he later became even more popular because "everyone found out I was Hispanic. And it was like, 'yo, this kid is Spanish!' and 'What? Yo, we've got to see this!'" Once he began to feel this sense of curiosity and openness, a new stage appeared in rap history, and Charlie was quick to recognize its potential, commercially and politically. He tells of how his enthusiasm caught the attention among some of the Latin musicians, especially his friend Tito Puente, who seemed to be fondly reminded of their own breakthrough a generation before.

> These guys, they love it. Because for one, it's for them getting back out into the limelight again, you know, in a different market.... The musicians are very impressed to see that somebody like me wants to work with them in my style of music. And when I tell them about my history they are very impressed because in their day, when they came out, they were the same way. When Tito Puente came out, he was doing the mambo and it was all something new. It was all new to him, too. So he can relate to what I'm doing. And for him it's almost like a second coming.

After the decade it has taken for Puerto Rican rap to come into its own, Charlie now feels that the time is right for the two sides of his musical life to come together, and for full-fledged "salsa-rap" to make its appearance.

> For this next record I want to do a project, where I want to get all the East Coast rappers together, I want to get POW, I want to get Latin Empire, I want to get a few other guys that are unknown but that are good. I want to join them, I want to bring in Luis "Perico" Ortíz, I want to bring Tito, I want to bring Ray Barretto, you know. Bring them to handle all the percussion stuff and then my touch would be to bring in the rap loops, the beats, the bass lines, the programming. I'll program and also arrange it. And they will come in, Luis "Perico" would do the whole horn section, Tito would come in and handle all the percussion section, and Ray Barretto would handle the congas. And I would get my friend Sergio who is a tremendous piano player, a young kid, he's about twenty-four, twenty-five now, he works for David Maldonado. I just want to kick this door wide open, once and for all, and that's the way I'm going to do it.

As ambitious as such a project may sound, bringing together Puerto Rican musicians across musical traditions is only half of Charlie's strategy for promoting Latino unity. For "if any Hispanics want to make it in this business," he claims, "they've got to learn to pull together, no matter where you're coming from, or it's not going to work. It's not going to work, man. Kid Frost on the West Coast right now, he's got a little thing going. He and I are working around a few things. He's got his Latin Alliance on the West Coast. I've got a lot of Latin people who work with me on this. I'm trying to form something here where we can merge, cover the whole United States. That's the best way we can do it, if we unify."

Yet with his repeated emphasis on Latino unity, Charlie has more than commercial success in mind. His own experience, he now feels, leads him to set his sights on the political and educational potential of his musical efforts.

> Because what I did, I had to unite with Black people to get my success and become Charlie Chase, "New York's Number One Puerto Rican DJ." Ironically, I did it with Black people. Which proves, man, that anybody can get together and do it. If I did it with Black people, then Hispanics can do it with Hispanics and do a much better job. That's my whole purpose right now. I mean, I have made my accomplishments, I have become famous doing my thing in rap, I have respect. Everybody knows me in the business. I have all of that already, man. I've tasted the good life, I've toured the world, I've done all of that. Now I want to do something meaningful and helpful. Hopefully, because a lot of kids are being steered the wrong way.

Puerto Rocks

Moving into the 1990s, then, the prospects and context have changed for Latino rap. Hugely popular albums like *Latin Alliance, Dancehall Reggaespañol* and *Cypress Hill* have been called a "polyphonic outburst" marking the emergence of "the 'real' Latin hip-hop." Kid Frost's assembly of Latin Alliance is referred to as "a defining moment in the creation of a nation-wide Latino/Americano hip-hop aesthetic." Unity of Chicanos and Puerto Ricans, which has long eluded politicos and admen, is becoming a reality in rap, and its potential impact on the culture wars seems boundless: "Where once the folks on opposite coasts were strangers, they've become one nation 'kicking Latin lingo on top of a scratch', samplin' substrate.... There is no question that we are entering an era when the multicultural essence of Latino culture will allow for a kind of shaking-out process that will help define the Next Big Thing."[4] Not only is the use of Spanish and bilingual rhyming accepted, but it has even become a theme in some of the best-known rap lyrics, like Kid Frost's "Ya Estuvo," Cypress Hill's "Funky Bi-lingo," and Latin Empire's "Palabras." Latino rappers are cropping up everywhere, from the tongue-twisting, "trabalengua" Spanglish of one Chicago-Rican group to the lively current of Tex-Mex rap in New Mexico and Arizona.[5] And it's not only the rappers themselves who have been building these bicultural bridges: Latin musical groups as varied as El Gran Combo, Wilfredo Vargas, Manny Oquendo's Libre, and Los Pleneros de la 21 have all incorporated rap segments and numbers into their repertoires.

But while he shares these high hopes, a seasoned veteran of "the business" like Charlie Chase remains acutely aware of the pitfalls and distortions involved. After all, he had witnessed firsthand what was probably the first and biggest scam in rap history, when Big Bad Hank and Sylvia Robinson of Sugar Hill Records used a rhyme by his close friend and fellow Cold Crush brother Grandmaster Cas on "Rapper's Delight" and never gave him credit. The story has been told elsewhere, as by Steven Hager in his book, but Charlie's is a lively version.

This is how it happened. Hank was working in a pizzeria in New Jersey, flipping pizza. And he's playing Cas' tape, right? Sylvia Robinson walks in, the president of Sugar Hill. She's listening to this, it's all new to her. Mind you, there were never any rap records. She says, "Hey, man, who's this?" He says, "I manage this guy. He's a rapper." She says, "Can you do this? Would you do this on a record for me?" And he said, "Yeah, sure. No problem." And she says, "Okay, fine." So he calls Cas up and says, "Cas, can I use your rhymes on a record? Some lady wants to make a record." You see what happened? Cas didn't have foresight. He couldn't see down the road. He never imagined in a million years what was going to come out of that. He didn't know, so he said, "Sure, fine, go ahead." With no papers, no nothing. And it went double platinum! Double platinum! "Rapper's Delight." A single. A double platinum single, which is a hard thing to do.

Charlie doesn't even have to go that far back to reflect on how commercial interests tend to glamorize and, in his word, "civilize" rap sources. He tells of his own efforts to land a job as an A&R (artist and repertoire) person with a record label. "All of this knowledge, all of this experience. I have the ear, I'm producing for all of these people. I mean, I know. You cannot get a more genuine person than me. I can't get a job." The gatekeepers of the industry could hardly be farther removed from the vitality of hip-hop. "I go to record labels to play demos for A&R guys that don't know a thing about rap. They talk to me and they don't even know who I am. White guys that live in L.A. Forty years old, thirty-five years old, making seventy, a hundred thousand a year, and they don't know a thing! And they're picking records to sell, and half of what they're picking is bullshit. And I'm trying to get somewhere and I can't do it."

As for promoting bilingual rap, the obstacles are of course compounded, all the talk of "pan-Latin unity" notwithstanding. "Not that long ago," Charlie mentions, "Latin Empire was having trouble with a Hispanic promoter at Atlantic Records who wouldn't promote their records. You know what he told them? (And he's a Latino.) He told them, 'Stick to one language.' And that's negative, man. You're up there, man, pull the brother up." And of course it's not only the limits on possible expressive idioms that signal a distortion but the media's ignorance of rap's origins. *Elle* magazine, for example, announced that Mellow Man Ace "has been crowned the initiator of Latin rap," their only evident source being Mellow Man himself: "I never thought it could be done. Then in 1985 I heard Mean Machine do a 20-second Spanish bit on their 'Disco Dream.' I bugged out." And the Spanish-language *Más* magazine then perpetuated the myth by proclaiming that it was Mellow Man Ace "quien concibió la idea de hacer rap en español" ("whose idea it was to do rap in Spanish").[6]

The problem is that in moving "from the barrio to *Billboard*," as Kid Frost puts it, Latino rappers have faced an abrupt redefinition of function and practice. The ten-year delay in the acceptance of Spanish rhymes was due in no small part to the marketing of rap, through the eighties, as a strictly African American musical style with a characteristically Afrocentric message. Charlie Chase confronted this even among some of his fellow rappers at the New Music Seminar in 1990 and appealed to his own historical authority to help set the record straight.

> I broke on a big panel. Red Alert, Serch from Third Base, Chuck D, the guys from the West Coast, these are all my boys, mind you, these are all of my friends. So I went off on these guys because they were like "Black this, and Black music," and I said "Hold it!" I jumped up and I said, "Hold up, man. What are you talking about, a Black thing, man? I was part of the Cold Crush Brothers, man. We opened doors for all you guys." And the crowd went berserk, man. And I grabbed the mike and I just started going off. I'm like, "Not for nothing, man, but don't knock it. It's a street thing. I liked it because it came from the street and I'm from the street. I'm a product of the environment." I said that to Serch, I pointed to Serch, 'cause that's his record from his album. And I said, "Yo, man, rap is us. You're from the street, that's you man, that's rap. It ain't no Black, White or nothing thing, man. To me, rap is colorblind, that's that!" The niggahs were applauding me and stuff. I got a lot of respect for that.

Latin Empire has had to put forth the same argument in explaining their own project. As Rick Rodríguez aka "Puerto Rock" puts it, "When it comes to hip-hop I never pictured it with a color." They too are a "product of the environment" and see no need to relinquish any of their Puerto Rican background. "Our influence," Puerto Rock says, "is the stuff you see around you. Things you always keep seeing in the ghetto. But they don't put it in art. It's streetwise. The styles, the fashions, the music is not just for one group. Everybody can do it. But too many Puerto Ricans don't understand. There's a big group of Latinos that's into hip-hop, but most of them imitate Black style or fall into a trance. They stop hanging out with Latin people and talking Spanish. I'm proving you can rap in Spanish and still be dope." Puerto Rock's cousin and partner in Latin Empire, Anthony Boston aka MC KT, has had to deal even more directly with this stereotype of rap, as he is often mistaken for a young African American and was raised speaking more English than Spanish. KT's rhymes in "We're Puerto Rican and Proud!" serve to clarify the issue:

> I rarely talk Spanish and a little trigueño
> People be swearin' I'm a moreno
> Pero guess what? I'm Puertorriqueño.
> Word'em up.

All jokes aside, I ain't tryin' to dis any race
And

Puerto Rock
He'll announce everyplace ...

M.C. KT
That I'll perform at, so chill, don't panic
It is just me, Antonio, another deso Hispanic.

To drive the point home, the initials KT stand for "Krazy Taino": "It's fly," Puerto rock comments. "With a 'K,' and the 'r' backwards like in Toys-"R"-Us. In our next video he's going to wear all the chief feathers and that. Nice image. With all the medallions and all that we've got. Like in Kid Frost in his video, he wears the Mexican things. That's dope, I like that. Tainos have a lot to do with Puerto Ricans and all that, so we're going to boost it up too. Throw it in the lyrics."

But KT didn't always signal the Puerto Rican cultural heritage, and in fact the derivation of their names shows that their struggle for identity has been a response against the stereotyped symbolism of rap culture. "MC KT is his name because before Latin Empire we were called the Solid Gold MCs. KT stood for karat, like in gold." The group gave up the faddish cliché Solid Gold because they had no jewelry and didn't like what it stood for anyway. When they started, in the early eighties, "We worked with a few different trend names. We started off with our name, our real names, our nicknames. Like Tony Tone, Ricky D, Ricky Rock, all of that. Everything that came out, Rick-ski, every fashion. Double T, Silver T, all of these wild Ts." After trying on all the conformist labels, Rick finally assumed the identity that was given him, as a Puerto Rican, in the African American hip-hop nomenclature itself; he came to affirm what marked him off. "And then I wound up coming up with Puerto Rock," he explains, "and I like that one. That's the one that clicked the most. The Puerto Ricans that are into the trend of hip-hop and all that, they call them Puerto Rocks. They used to see the Hispanics dressing up with the hat to the side and all hip-hop down and some assumed that we're supposed to just stick to our own style of music and friends. They thought rap music was only a Black thing, and it wasn't. Puerto Ricans used to be all crazy with their hats to the side and everything. So that's why they used to call the Puerto Ricans when they would see them with the hats to the side, 'Yo, look at that Puerto Rock, like he's trying to be down.' They used to call us Puerto Rocks, so that was a nickname, and I said, 'I'm going to stick with that. Shut everybody up.'"

The name the group's members chose to replace Solid Gold was arrived at somewhat more fortuitously, but equally reflects their effort to situate themselves in an increasingly multicultural hip-hop landscape.

Riding around in the car with our manager, DJ Corchado, we were trying to think of a Latin name. We was like, the Three Amigos, the Latin Employees, for real, we came up with some crazy names. We kept on, 'cause we didn't want to limit ourselves, with Puerto Rican something, yeah, the Puerto Rican MCs. We wanted Latin something, to represent all Latinos. So we was the Two Amigos, the Three Amigos, then we came up with many other names, Latin Imperials, Latin Alliance. And then when we were driving along the Grand Concourse my manager's car happened to hit a bump when I came out with the Latin Employees. Joking around, we were just making fun and when the car hit the bump my manager thought I said "Empire." I was like, what? Latin Empire! I was like, yo, that's it! As soon as they said it, it clicked. It's like a strong title, like the Zulu Nation.

Groping for names that click, of course, is part of the larger process of positioning themselves in the changing cultural setting of the later eighties. The decision to start rhyming in Spanish was crucial and came more as an accommodation to their families and neighbors than from hearing Mean Machine or any other trends emerging in hip-hop. "In the beginning it was all in English and our families, all they do is play salsa and merengue, they thought you were American. They considered it noise. "'Ay, deja ese alboroto,' 'cut out that racket,' you know. We said, 'Let's try to do it in Spanish, so that they can understand it, instead of complaining to us so much.' They liked it. They was like, 'Oh, mi hijo.'" And when they tried out their Spanish with the mostly Black hip-hop audiences, they were encouraged further. "We used to walk around with the tapes and the big radios and the Black people behind us, 'Yo, man, that sounds dope, that's fly!' They be like, 'yo, I don't understand it, man, but I know it's rhyming and I hear the last word, man, that's bad' they be telling us. We was like, oh, snap! Then I used to try to do it in the street jams and the crowd went crazy."

Acceptance and encouragement from the record industry was a different story, especially in those times before Mellow Man Ace broke the commercial ice. Atlantic did wind up issuing "We're Puerto Rican and Proud," but not until after "Mentirosa" went gold, and then they dragged their feet in promoting it. Since then, aside from their tours and the video "Así Es la Vida" which made the charts on MTV Internacional, Latin Empire has been back in the parks and community events. They believe strongly in the strong positive messages of some rap and have participated actively in both the Stop the Violence and Back to School campaigns. They pride themselves on practicing what they preach in their antidrug and antialcohol rhymes. They continue to be greeted with enthusiastic approval by audiences of all nationalities throughout New York City, and on their tours to Puerto Rico, the Dominican Republic, and, most recently, Cuba.

Their main shortcoming, in the parlance of the business, is that they don't have an "act," a packaged product. As the author of "The Packaging of a Recording Artist" in the July 1992 issue of *Hispanic Business* suggests, "To 'make it' as a professional recording act, you must have all the right things in place. Every element of what a recording act is must be considered and exploited to that act's benefit. The sound, the image, the look—all these factors must be integrated into a single package and then properly marketed to the public." In the packaging and marketing process, the artists and the quality of their work are of course secondary; it's the managers, and the other gatekeepers, who make the act. The article ends, "So while quality singing and a good song are the product in this business, they don't count for much without strong management."[7]

The pages of *Hispanic Business* make no mention of Latin Empire, concentrating as they do on the major Hispanic "products" like Gerardo, Exposé, and Angelica. What they say about Kid Frost is most interesting because here they are dealing with a Latino rapper who is "on his way to stardom in the West Coast Hispanic community" and cannot be expected to "lighten up on who he is just to get that cross-over audience." Clearly the main danger of the artist crossing over is not, from this perspective, that he might thereby sacrifice his focus and cultural context, but that he could lose out on his segment of the market. "It's so tempting for an artist to do that once they've gained acceptance. But you risk losing your base when you do that and you never want to be without your core audience. That's why we work as a team and always include our artists and their managers in the packaging and marketing process."[8]

Latin Empire's members can't seem to get their "act" together because they remain too tied to their base to endure "strong management." Their mission, especially since rap "went Latin," is to reinstate the history and geography of the New York Puerto Rican contribution to hip-hop and counteract the sensationalist version perpetrated by the media. In some of their best-known numbers like "El Barrio," "Mi Viejo South Bronx" and "The Big Manzana," they take us deep into the Puerto Rican neighborhoods and back, "way back, to the days of *West Side Story*," when the New York style originated. Tracing the transition from the gang era to the emergence of the "style wars" of hip-hop, they tell their own stories and dramatize their constant juggling act between Black and Latino and between Island and New York cultures. In another rhyme, "Not Listed," they "take hip-hop to another *tamaño* [level]" by emphasizing the particular Puerto Rican role in rap history and countering the false currency given new arrivals. They end by affirming these ignored roots and rescuing the many early Puerto Rican rappers from oblivion:

> Y'all need to see a médico
> but we don't accept Medicaid
> we don't give no crédito
> we only give credit where credit is due
> we got to give it to the Mean Machine
> and the other brothers who were out there
> lookin' out for Latinos
> some kept it up, some chose other caminos
> but we can't pretend that they never existed
> cause yo, they were out there, just not listed.

In another of their rhymes Latin Empire's members address the music business itself, lashing out at the counterfeits and subterfuges facing them in their "hungry" battle for a fair record deal. Some of "Kinda Hungry" sounds like this:

> Yeah that's right I'm hungry,
> in other words, yo tengo hambre.
> Those who overslept caught a calambre.
> Fake mc's hogging up the posiciones,
> but all we keep hearing is bullshit canciones.
> Don't be feeding mis sueños.
> You might be the head of A&R but I want to meet the dueños.
> So I can let 'em know como yo me siento
> and update 'em on the Latino movimiento
> 'cause I'm getting tired of imitadores
> that shit is muerto, that's why I'm sending you flores,
> En diferentes colores.
> I'm like an undertaker ...
> I still don't understand how they allowed you to make a
> rap record que no sirve para nada.
> I'll eat 'em up like an ensalada.
> Speakin' about food you want comida?
> Na, that's not what I meant,
> what I want is a record deal en seguida
> so we can get this on a 24 track
> put it out on the market and bug out on the feedback.
> Huh, tú no te debas cuenta,
> a nigga like me is in effect en los noventas.
> Straight outta Vega Baja
> the other candidates?
> I knock 'em out the caja, knock 'em out the box
> because I'm not relajando I truly feel it's time

> I started eliminando mc's givin' us a bad nombre.
> I can't see TNT nor my righthand hombre
> the Krazy Taino sellin' out,
> there's no way, there's no how,
> that's not what we're about.
> We're all about looking out for my gente,
> here's some food for thought, comida para la mente.

With all their "hunger" for recognition, members of Latin Empire also feel the burden of responsibility for being the only Nuyorican rap group given any public play at all. They realize that, being synonymous with Puerto Rican rap, they are forced to stand in for a whole historical experience and for the rich variety of street rappers condemned to omission by the very filtering process that they are confronting. A prime example for them of the "not listed" is the "righthand hombre" mentioned here, MC TNT. Virtually unknown outside the immediate hip-hop community in the South Bronx, TNT is living proof that hardcore, streetwise rhyming continues and develops in spite of the diluting effects and choices of the managers and A&R departments. Frequently, Puerto Rock and KT have incorporated TNT into many of their routines, and his rhymes and delivery have added a strong sense of history and poetic language to their presentations.

Like Puerto Rock, TNT (Tomás Robles) was born in Puerto Rico and came to New York at an early age. But in his case, childhood in the rough neighborhoods on the Island figures prominently in his raps, as in this autobiographical section interlaced with samples from Rubén Blades's salsa hit "La Vida Te Da Sorpresas":

> Este ritmo es un invento
> Cuando empiezo a rimar le doy el roo por ciento
> No me llamo Chico, o Federico
> Dónde naciste? Santurce, Puerto Rico
> Cuando era niño no salía'fuera
> porque mataban diario en la cantera
> Esto es verdad, realidad, no un engaño
> mi pae murió cuando yo tenía seis años
> La muerte me afectó con mucho dolor
> pues mi mae empaquetó y nos mudamos pa' Nueva York
> cuando llegué era un ambiente diferente
> pero no me arrepentí, seguí para frente
> y por las noches recé a Dios y a la santa
> porque en mi corazón el coquí siempre canta.

[This rhyme is an invention / When I start to rhyme I give it 100 percent / My name isn't Chico or Federico / Where were you born? / Santurce, Puerto Rico / When I was a boy I didn't go out / 'cause there were killings / in the quarry every day / This is true, reality, not a hoax / my father died when I was six / his death caused me a lot of pain / well my mother packed up and we moved to New York / when I arrived it was a very different atmosphere / but I didn't regret it, I moved ahead / and at night I prayed to God and the holy mother / because in my heart the *coquí* frog always sings.]

By the late 1970s, as an adolescent, TNT was already involved in the gang scene in the South Bronx and took part in the formation of Tough Bronx Action and the Puerto Rican chapters of Zulu Nation. By that time he was already playing congas in the streets and schoolyards and improvising rhymes. When he first heard Mean Machine in 1981, he recalls, he already had notebooks of raps in Spanish, though mostly he preserved them in his memory.

TNT also goes by the epithet "un rap siquiatra" ("a rap psychiatrist"): in his lively, storytelling rhymes he prides himself on his biting analysis of events and attitudes in the community. He responds to the charges of gangsterism by pointing to the ghetto conditions that force survival remedies on his people. "Livin' in a ghetto can turn you 'to a gangster" is one of his powerful social raps, and in "Get Some Money" he addresses the rich and powerful directly: "he threw us in the ghetto to see how long we lasted / then he calls us a little ghetto bastard." His "Ven acá tiguerito tiguerito," which compares with anything by Kid Frost and Latin Alliance in sheer verbal ingenuity, captures the intensity of a combative street scene in El Barrio and is laced with phrases from Dominican slang. His programmatic braggadocio is playful and ragamuffin in its effect, yet with a defiance that extends in the last line to the very accentuation of the language:

> Soy un rap siquiatra un rap mecánico
> óyeme la radio y causo un pánico
> te rompo el sistema y te dejo inválido
> con un shock nervioso te ves bien pálido
> no puedes con mi rap
> aléjate aléjate
> tómate una Contact y acuéstate
> o llame a los bomberos que te rescaten.

[I'm a rap psychiatrist, a rap mechanic hear me on the radio and I cause a panic / I break your system and I leave you an invalid / with a nervous shock you look pretty pale / you can't deal with my rap / go away, go away / take a Contac and go to bed / or call the firefighters to come rescue you.]

By the mid-1990s, at twenty-five, MC TNT was already a veteran of Spanish rap battles, still "unlisted" and awaiting his break, yet constantly working on his rhymes and beats every moment he can shake off some of the pressure. He is the closest I have run across to a rapper in the tradition of Puerto Rican plena music, since like that of the master *pleneros* his work is taking shape as a newspaper of the barrios, a running, ironic commentary on the untold events of everyday Puerto Rican life. When all the talk was of referendums and plebiscites to determine the political status of Puerto Rico, TNT had some advice for his people to contemplate:

> Puerto Rico, una isla hermosa,
> donde nacen bonitas rosas,
> plátanos, guineos y yautía,
> Sasón Goya le da sabor a la comida.
> Y ¿quién cocina más que la tía mía?
> Pero el gobierno es bien armado,
> tratando de convertirla en un estado.
> Es mejor la dejen libre (asociado?).
> Cristóbal Colón no fue nadie,
> cruzó el mar con un bonche de salvajes.
> Entraron a Puerto Rico rompiendo palmas,
> asustando a los caciques con armas.
> Chequéate los libros, esto es cierto.

pregúntale a un cacique pero ya está muerto.
¿Cómo él descubrió algo que ya está descubierto?
Boricua, ¡no te vendas!

[Puerto Rico, a beautiful island / where there are pretty roses, / plantains, bananas, and root vegetables, / Goya seasoning gives the food flavor / And who cooks better than my own aunt? / But the government is well armed, / trying to convert it into a state / It's better to leave it free (associated?) / Christopher Columbus was nobody, / he crossed the sea with a bunch of savages, / they entered Puerto Rico destroying the palm trees, / terrifying the Indian chiefs with their weapons. / Check out the books, this is true, / ask one of the Indian chiefs but they're already dead. / How could he discover something already discovered? / Puerto Rico, don't sell yourself!]

Like other Latino groups, Puerto Ricans are using rap as a vehicle for affirming their history, language, and culture under conditions of rampant discrimination and exclusion. The explosion of Spanish-language and bilingual rap onto the pop music scene in recent years bears special significance in the face of the stubbornly monolingual tenor in today's public discourse, most evident in the crippling of bilingual programs and services and in the ominous gains of the "English Only" crusade. And of course along with the Spanish and Spanglish rhymes, Latino rap carries an ensemble of alternative perspectives and an often divergent cultural ethos into the mainstream of U.S. social life. The mass diffusion, even if only for commercial purposes, of cultural expression in the "other" language, and above all its broad and warm reception by fans of all nationalities, may help to muffle the shrieks of alarm emanating from the official culture whenever mention is made of "America's fastest-growing minority." Latin rap lends volatile fuel to the cause of "multiculturalism" in our society, at least in the challenging, inclusionary sense of that embattled term.

For Puerto Ricans, though, rap is more than a newly opened window on their history; rap *is* their history, and Puerto Ricans are an integral part in the history of hip-hop. As the "Puerto rocks" themselves testify in conversation and rhyme, rapping is one of many domains within a larger field of social and creative practices expressive of their collective historical position in the prevailing relations of power and privilege. Puerto Rican participation in the emergence of hip-hop music needs to be understood in direct, interactive relation to their experience in gangs and other forms of association among inner-city youth through the devastating blight of the seventies. "Puerto rocks" are the children of impoverished colonial immigrants facing even tougher times than in earlier decades. They helped make rap what it was to become, as they played a constitutive role in the stylistic definition of graffiti writing and breakdancing.

In addition to these more obvious associations, the formative years of rap follow closely the development of both salsa and Nuyorican poetry, expressive modes which, especially for the young Puerto Ricans themselves, occupy the same creative constellation as the musical and lyrical project of bilingual and bicultural rap. Musically, rap practice among Puerto Ricans is also informed by the strong antecedent tradition of street drumming and, at only a slight remove, their parallel earlier role in styles like doo-wop, boogaloo, and Latin jazz. In terms of poetic language, Spanglish rap is embedded in the everyday speech practices of the larger community over the course of several generations, and even echoes in more than faint ways the tones and cadences of lyrics typical of plena, bomba, and other forms of popular Puerto Rican song.

Like these other contemporaneous and prefiguring cultural practices, the active presence of Puerto Ricans in the creation of rap bears further emphatic testimony to their long history of cultural interaction with African Americans. Hip-hop emerged as a cultural space shared by Puerto Ricans and Blacks, a sharing that once again articulates their congruent and inter-mingling placement in the impinging political and economic geography. It is also a sharing in which, as the story of rap reveals, the dissonances are as telling as the harmonies, and the distances as heartfelt as the intimacy. The Puerto Ricans' nagging intimation that they are treading on Black turf and working in a tradition of performative expression most directly traceable to James Brown and Jimmy Castor, the dozens and the blues, makes rap into a terrain that is as much contested as it is coinhabited on equal terms. Jamaican dubbing, with its strong Caribbean resonance, serves as a bridge in this respect, just as reggae in more recent years is helping to link rap to otherwise disparate musical trends, especially in its reggaespañol dance-hall versions. In the historical perspective of Black and Puerto Rican interaction, rap is thus a lesson in cultural negotiation and transaction as much as in fusions and crossovers, especially as those terms are bandied about in mainstream parlance. If multiculturalism is to amount to anything more than a wishful fancy of a pluralist mosaic, the stories of the "Puerto rocks" show that adequate account must be taken of the intricate jostling and juggling involved along the seams of contemporary cultural life.

What is to become of Latino rap, and how we appreciate and understand its particular messages, will depend significantly on the continuities it forges to its roots among the "Puerto rocks." Recuperating this history, explicitly or by example, and "inventing" a tradition diver-gent from the workings of the commercial culture, makes for the only hope of reversing the instant amnesia that engulfs rap and all forms of emergent cultural discourse as they migrate into the world of pop hegemony. Charlie Chase, TNT, and the other "Puerto rocks" were not only pioneers in some nostalgic sense but helped set the social meaning of rap practice prior to and relatively independent of its mediated commercial meaning. That formative partici-pation of Latinos in rap in its infancy is a healthy reminder that the "rap attack," as Peter Toop argued some years ago now, is but the latest outburst of "African jive," and that the age-old journey of jive has always been a motley and inclusive procession. And as in Cuban-based salsa, the Puerto Rican conspiracy in the present volley shows how creatively a people can adopt and adapt what would seem a "foreign" tradition and make it, at least in part, its own. To return to the first "Puerto rock" I talked with in the early 1980s, I close with a little rhyme by MC Rubie Dee (Rubén García) from the South Bronx:

> Now all you Puerto Ricans you're in for a treat,
> 'cause this Puerto Rican can rock a funky beat.
> If you fall on your butt and you start to bleed,
> Rubie Dee is what all the Puerto Ricans need.
> I'm a homeboy to them 'cause I know what to do,
> 'cause Rubie Dee is down with the black people too.[9]

Notes

1. Quotes of Charlie Chase are from my interview with him, "It's a Street Thing!" published in *Calalloo* 15.4 (Fall 1992): 999–1021.
2. See my article, written in 1984, "Rappin', Writin' and Breakin': Black and Puerto Rican Street Culture in New York City," *Dissent* (Fall 1987): 580–84 (also published in *Centro Journal* 2.3 [Spring 1988]: 34–41). A shortened version of the present chapter appeared as "'Puerto Rican and Proud, Boy-ee!': Rap, Roots, and Amnesia," in Tricia Rose and Andrew Ross, eds., *Microphone Fiends: Youth Music and Youth Culture*, pp. 89–98 (New York: Routledge, 1994). Other references are Craig Castleman, *Getting Up: Subway Graf-fiti in New York* (Cambridge: MIT Press, 1982); Herbert Kohl, *Golden Boy as Anthony Cool: A Photo Essay on Naming and Graffiti* (New York: Dial, 1972); Steven Hager, *Hip-Hop: The Illustrated History of Break Dancing, Tap Music, and Graffiti* (New York: St. Martin's, 1984). See also David Toop, *The Rap Attack: African Jive to New York Hip-Hop* (Boston: South End, 1984).
3. Quotes from Latin Empire are from my interview with them, "Puerto Raps," published in *Centro Journal* 3.2 (Spring 1991): 77–85.

4. Ed Morales, "How Ya Like Nosotros Now?" *Village Voice*, November 26, 1991, 91.

5. For an overview of Latino rap, see Mandolit del Barco, "Rap's Latino Sabor," in William Eric Perkins, ed., *Droppin' Science: Critical Essays on Rap Music and Hip-Hop Culture* (Philadelphia: Temple University Press, 1996), 63–84.

6. Elizabeth Hanley, "Latin Raps: Nuevo ritmo, A New Nation of Rap Emerges," *Elle*, March 1991, 196–98; C.A., "El rap latino tiene tumbao," *Más* 2.2 (Winter 1990): 81.

7. Joseph Roland Reynolds, "The Packaging of a Recording Artist," *Hispanic Business* 14.7 (July 1992): 28–30.

8. Ibid.

9. Cited in Flores, "Rappin', Writin', and Breakin.'"

9

It's a Family Affair

Paul Gilroy

The complicated phenomena we struggle to name as black nationalism, cultural nationalism, and neonationalism have now been so reconfigured that our essentially nineteenth-century, or maybe even eighteenth-century, understanding of them has to be abandoned. Everywhere, as a result of both internal and external pressures, the integrity of the nation-state as the primary focus of economic, political, and cultural action, has been compromised. The impact of this on nationalist ideologies (black and otherwise) is particularly important and needs to be taken into account. I am not satisfied with just pinning the prefix "neo" onto nationalism and feeling that we've done the job of analyzing it. If we are to distinguish the contemporary discourses of black nationalism from the black nationalisms of the past, we have to examine the novel modes of information and cultural production in which they circulate.

Perhaps the easiest place to begin is to think about the changes in information and communication technologies that have taken all nationalisms away from their historic association with the technology of print culture. This is one way of conceptualizing the changed notions of space and time we associate with the impact of the postmodern and the postindustrial on black cultures. If we are to think of ourselves as diaspora people, how do we then understand the notion of space? How do we adjust our understanding of the relationship between spatialization and identity formation in order to deal with these techno-cultural changes? One thing we might do is take a cue from Manuel Castells,[1] who describes the shift from an understanding of space based on notions of place and fixity to an understanding of place based on flows. Or, what another exiled Englishman, Iain Chambers, introduces in his very suggestive distinction between roots and routes.[2] (I don't think this pun has quite the same force in American versions of English.) If we're going to pick up the vernacular ball and run with it, then maybe the notion of the crossroads—as a special location where unforeseen, magical things happen—might be an appropriate conceptual vehicle for rethinking this dialectical tension between cultural roots and cultural routes, between the space marked out by places and the space constituted by flows. The crossroads has a nicely Africalogical sound to it too: a point at which the flows of black popular cultures productively intersect.

These issues point to the way we will have to refine the theorizing of the African diaspora if it is to fit our changed transnational and intercultural circumstances. Though the current popularity of Afrocentrism points to other possibilities, we might consider experimenting, at least, with giving up the idea that our culture needs to be centered anywhere except where we are when we launch our inquiries into it. Certainly, we will have to find a better way to deal with the obvious differences between and within black cultures—differences that live on under the signs of their disappearances, constituting boundaries that stubbornly refuse to be erased.

I wish I had five bucks for every time I've heard the trope of the family wheeled out to do the job of recentering things when the debates of the last few days promised to question the spurious integrity of ideal racial culture. The trope of the family is especially significant right now when the idea of belonging to a nation is only infrequently invoked to legitimate the essence of today's black political discourses. Certainly in England, and probably in the United States, as well, there are a number of other legitimization strategies, but the invocation of "race" as family is everywhere. Its dominance troubles me because, at the moment, in the black English constituency out of which I speak, the trope of the family is not at the center of our discussion of what a black politics could or should be. And I'll return to that point later.

Afrocentricity names itself "systematic nationalism" (that's what Molefi Kete Asante calls it),[3] but it is stubbornly focused around the reconstitution of individual consciousness rather than around the reconstruction of the black nation in exile or elsewhere. The civic, nation-building activity that defined the Spartan-style aspirations of black nationalism in the nineteenth century has been displaced in favor of the almost aesthetic cultivation of a stable, pure, racial self. The "ism" in that nationalism is often lacking, too; it is no longer constructed as a coherent political ideology. It appears more usually as a set of therapies—tactics in the never-ending struggle for psychological and cultural survival. In some nonspecific way, then, a new idea of Africanness, conveniently disassociated from the politics of contemporary Africa, operates transnationally and interculturally through the symbolic projection of "race" as kinship. It is now more often a matter of style, perspective, or survivalist technique than a question of citizenship, rights, or fixed contractual obligations (the things that defined nationality in earlier periods).

Indeed, though contemporary nationalism draws creatively on the traces of romantic theories of national belonging and national identity, derived from the ethnic metaphysics of eighteenth-century Europe, Afrocentric thinking attempts to construct a sense of black particularity *outside* of a notion of a national identity. Its founding problem lies in the effort to figure sameness across national boundaries and between nation-states. The first sentence of Asante's "Nia—The Way" can be used to illustrate this: "This is the way that came to Molefe in America."[4] But the text's elisions of African-American particulars into African universals belie this modesty. Look also at the moment in the same text where the author struggles with the fact that only thirty-seven percent of the blacks who live in the Western hemisphere live in the United States. Forty percent, he muses to himself, live in Brazil. What do we do about that? Where are their inputs into Africalogical theory?

The understanding of blackness that emerges routinely these days gets projected, then, onto a very different symbolic landscape than it did in either nineteenth-century black nationalism, in Garveyism, or in the nationalism of the Black Power period. The new popular pantheon of black heroes is apparently a diasporic one—Marcus, Malcolm, Martin, Marley, Mandela, and *Me*! The narcissistic momentum of that masculine list is another symptom of a cultural implosion that must work against the logic of national identity. The flow is always inward, never outward; the truth of racialized being is sought, not in the world, but in the psyche. I know that the moment of epistemological narcissism is necessary in building movements that actually move, but doesn't it abandon the world of public politics, leaving us with a form of therapy that has little to offer beleaguered communities?

Some of the rhetoric of nationalism, however, does remain. It's there in the service of groups like the Five Percent Nation and the Nation of Islam. But for them it legitimates an ideology of separation that applies as viciously within the race as it does between blacks and whites. If there is still a coherent nationalism in play though—and I say this from my own perch in London—I want to suggest that it is the nationalism of black Americans. This nationalism is a powerful subtext in the discourse of Afrocentricity, but it has evolved from an earlier period in black U.S. history. It is a very particular way of looking at the world that, far more than it expresses any exilic consciousness of Africa, betrays a distinctively American understanding of ethnicity and cultural difference. The family is the approved, natural site where ethnicity and racial culture are reproduced. In this authoritarian pastoral patriarchy, women are identified as the agents and means of this reproductive process.

This is where the question of the family begins to bite: representations of the family in contemporary black nationalism, transcoded—maybe wrongly—from London, appear to mark the site of what can, at the least, be called an ambivalent relationship to America. So, recognizing this, I don't want to call it Afrocentrism any more. I want to call it Americocentrism. And I want to suggest that it has evolved in a very uneasy mode of coexistence with the pan-African political discourses that gave birth to it. Of course, the identification with Africa, on which that Americocentrism is premised, is necessarily partial and highly selective. Contemporary Africa, as I have said, appears nowhere. The newly invented criteria for judging racial authenticity are supplied instead by restored access to original African forms and codes. It is significant, however—and this is where the trope of the family begins to look like a disaster for black feminism—that those definitions of authenticity are disproportionately defined by ideas about nurturance, about family, about fixed gender roles, and generational responsibilities. What is authentic is also frequently defined by ideas about sexuality and patterns of interaction between men and women that are taken to be expressive of essential, that is, racial, difference. This authenticity is inseparable from talk about the conduct and management of bitter gender-based conflicts, which is now recognized as essential to familial, racial, and communal health. Each of these—the familial, the racial, the communal—leads seamlessly into the next. Where was that heavy chain of signifiers forged? Whose shackles will it make? How does that conjunction reveal the impact, not just of an unchanged Africa, but of a contemporary America?

Now, the changed status of nationality in black political discourse can also be felt in the way the opposition between the local and the global has been reinscribed in our culture and in our consciousness. Today, we are told that the boys, and the girls, are from the 'hood—not from the race, and certainly not from the nation. It's important that the 'hood stands in opposition to foreign things—if you remember John Singleton's film—in opposition to the destructive encroachments of Seoul-to-Seoul Realty or the idea of turning the ghetto into black Korea. (Does Singleton's choice of that proper name for the Korean menace signal a rebuke to Soul II Soul?)

From London, the untranslatability of the term "hood" troubled me. I thought it marked a significant shift away from the notion of the ghetto, which is eminently exportable, and which carries its own very interesting intercultural history that we should be able to play with. But, if the 'hood is the essence of where blackness can now be found, which 'hood are we talking about? How do we weigh the achievements of one 'hood against the achievements of another? How is black life in one 'hood connected to life in others? Can there be a blackness that connects, articulates, synchronizes experiences and histories across the diaspora space? Or is it only the sign of Larry Fishburne's patriarchal power that holds these different local forms of blackness together?

This matters not just because images of black sociality not derived from the family seem to have disappeared from our political cultures, but also because, if Tim Dog is to be believed, Compton is as foreign to some blacks in New York as Kingston, London, Havana, Lagos, Aswan, or Capetown—possibly even more so. His popular outrage against West Coast Jheri curls and whack lyrics registers (as does his claim that all that gang shit is for dumb mother-fuckers) disappointment and frustration that the idea of a homogeneous national community has become impossible and unthinkable. Maybe this is what happens when one 'hood speaks to another.

> Ah, shit. Motherfucker step to the ring and cheer.
> The Tim Dog is here.
> Let's get right down to the nitty gritty.
> And talk about a bullshit city.
> Talking about niggers from Compton.
> They're no comp and they truly ain't stompin'.
> Tim Dog, a black man's task,
> I'm so bad, I wear Superman's mask.
> All you suckers that rip from the West Coast,
> I'll dis' and spray your ass like a roach.
> You think you're cool with your curls and your shades,
> … and you'll be yelling outrage.
> A hard brother that lives in New York.
> We suckas are hard, and we don't have to score.
> Shut your mouth, or we come out stompin'.
> And yo Easy, fuck Compton.[5]

Now, I don't pretend to understand everything Tim Dog's performance means here in the United States, but in London it has a very particular meaning. This has to do with a bewilderment about some of the self-destructive and sibling-cidal patterns of sociality that have been a feature of black U.S. inner-urban life. The same tension between the local and the global—implosion at one end, dissemination at the other—is, again, part of the story. Of course, when these things come down the transnational wire to us in Europe and to black folks in other parts of the world, they become metaphysical statements about what blackness is. And we have to deal with them on that basis.

Obviously, there are other voices, and there are other subject positions. In fact, one of the things I find troubling in debates about rap is that I don't think anyone actually knows what the totality of its hypercreativity looks like. I am a compulsive consumer (user, actually) of that culture, but I can't keep up with the volume of hip-hop product anymore. I don't know if anyone can. There is simply too much of it to be assimilated, and the kinds of judgments we make have to take that volume into account. It's a flood—it's not a flow, it's a flood, actually—and just bobbing up and down in the water is not enough.

But when we come back to the family, the idea of hip-hop as a dissident, critical space looks more questionable. Ironically, it is precisely where the motivation is constructive that the pastoral patriarchy of race as family gets reproduced. Another voice I want to present answers, in a sense, the calculated nihilism of Tim Dog. It's an attempt, by KRS 1 (Chris Parker), to locate the politics of race in what he describes as the opposition between civilization and technology—an interesting opposition because of its desire to hold onto the narrative of civilization and make it part of a grand narrative of black development. But this attempt is notable not just for its humanism—humanity versus technology—but for the extraordinary emphasis that falls on the family. I wonder how much the trope of the family allows him to hold the very diverse forces of this new racialized humanism together.

> Be a Man, not a sucker.
> And don't disrespect your baby's mother.
> When the pressure's on, don't run for cover.
> We gotta move on and be strong for one another.

You can't just be a lover, build the nation.
We gotta start with better relations.
'Cause the family is the foundation.
We're here to heal, and we're here for the duration.
Multi-educating.

Definitely develop your African mind because we are all family. And once we see that we are all brothers and sisters no matter what, we go far beyond the nuclear family—from an Afrocentric point of view.[6]

I don't want to be forced into the position of having to point out that it may not help to collapse our intraracial differences into the image of ourselves as brothers and sisters any more than I want to be forced into the position of saying that we don't all recognize our own images in the faces of Clarence Thomas and Anita Hill (which adorn the posters for this event) but that is some of what this Americocentric obsession with family brings to mind. I recognize that the discourse of racial siblinghood is a democratic one. I know it emerged from the communitarian radicalism of the church and that, as W.E.B. Du Bois pointed out long ago in *The Souls of Black Folk*, this happened in a period before the slaves enjoyed the benefits of nuclear family life. The political language of brotherhood and sisterhood can be used in ways that accentuate an image of community composed of those with whom we disagree. From this perspective, the differences we still experience, in spite of white supremacy's centripetal effects, might be seen as a precious and potentially productive resource. However, at the moment, the wind is blowing in another direction.

Obviously, not all of this popular culture wants to bury its differences in images of an organic, natural, racial family. And I have been especially engaged by the voices within hip-hop culture that have sought other strategies for living with difference and building on the hybrid qualities of the form itself to affirm the value of mixing and what might be called creolization. There are some absorbing poetic attempts to explore the consequences of a new political ontology and a new historicity. I am excited, for example, by Rakim's repeated suggestion that "it ain't where you're from, it's where you're at." It grants a priority to the present, emphasizing a view of identity as an ongoing process of self-making at a time when myths of origins hold so much appeal. Sometimes that kind of idea is strongest where the Caribbean styles and forms, very often dominated by pan-African motifs, are most developed. Caribbean popular cultures have their own rather more mediated and syncretized relationships to Africa. But it's also important to remember that reggae has constructed its own romance of racial nihilism in gun culture, misogyny, and machismo.

Rebel MC's "Wickedest Sound" comes from London and points to a different notion of authenticity.[7] Its racial witness is produced out of semiotic play rather than ethnic fixity, and a different understanding of tradition emerges out of the capacity to combine the different voices, styles, and motifs drawn from all kinds of sources in a montage of blackness(es). This version of the idea of authenticity, premised on a notion of flows, is also alive in diaspora culture. It's dear to me because it appeared within the version of hip-hop culture that we have produced in London. There are, of course, African-American traces here struggling to be heard among the Caribbean samples, but, happily, the trope of race as family is nowhere in sight.

Against this playful, vibrant, postracial utopia—which argues that there is no betrayal in the acknowledgment of a white listening public—an Americocentric, postnationalist essence of blackness has been constructed through the dubious appeal to family.

There have been other periods in black political history where the image of race as family has been prominent. The nineteenth-century ideas of a nationality exclusively concerned with male soldier-citizens were produced in a period when an anti-imperialist or an anti-racist political project among diaspora blacks was unthinkable. We would do well to reconsider them now because they haunt us. In *Africa or America*, Alexander Crummell drew his theory of nationality and racial personality from the work of Lord Beaconsfield (Benjamin Disraeli):

> Races, like families, are organisms and the ordinance of God. And race feeling, like family feeling, is of divine origin. The extinction of race feeling is just as possible as the extinction of family feeling. Indeed, race is family. The principle of continuity is as masterful in races as it is in families, as it is in nations.[8]

This discourse of race as community, as family, has been born again in contemporary attempts to interpret the crisis of black politics and social life as a crisis solely of black masculinity. The family is not just the site of cultural reproduction; it is also identified as the mechanism for reproducing the cultural dysfunction that disables the race as a whole. And since the race is nothing more than an accumulation of families, the crisis of black masculinity can be fixed. It is to be repaired by instituting appropriate forms of masculinity and male authority, intervening in the family to rebuild the race.

Even hip-hop culture—the dissonant soundtrack of racial dissidence—has become complicit with this analysis. It's interesting, in thinking about the changing resonance of the word "nation" in black culture, that reports say Michael Jackson wants to call his new record company Nation Records. (One of the extraordinary things about the Jacksons is that they have turned their dysfunctionality as a black family into such an interesting marketing strategy.) Images of the black family complement the family tropes of the cultural forms themselves. These images are all around us in the selling of black popular culture. They are so visible in the marketing of Spike Lee and his projects that they point to the value of reading his oeuvre as a succession of Oedipal crises.

On the strange kind of cultural loop I live, I saw Marlon Riggs's powerful film *Tongues United* for the second time on the same night I first saw *Boys N the Hood*. (We get these things in a different sequence than in the States.) Listening to that authoritative voice saying that black men loving black men was *the* revolutionary act—not *a* revolutionary act but *the* revolutionary act—the force of that definite article set me to thinking about *Boyz N the Hood*. I know there are differences between these two projects. I have an idea of where some of them dwell. But aren't there also similarities and convergences in the way that love between men is the common focus of these "texts"?[9]

Let me say why I think the prominence of the family is a problem. Spreading the Oedipal narrative around a bit can probably produce some interesting effects, but this bears repeating: the trope of the family is central to the means whereby the crisis we are living—of black social and political life—gets represented as the crisis of black masculinity. That trope of the family is there, also, in the way conflict, within and between our communities, gets resolved through the mystic reconstruction of the ideal heterosexual family. This is the oldest conservative device in the book of modern culture. Once again, *Boyz N the Hood* is the most obvious illustration of an authentically black and supposedly radical product that is complacently comfortable working within those deeply conservative codes. In Isaac Julien's recent film *Young Soul Rebels*, the fragile image of nonfamilial community that appears has been much criticized. It's the point at which the film ends and a kind of surrogate, joyfully disorganic, and synthetic kin group constitutes itself slowly and tentatively—in and around desire, through music, affirmation, celebration, and play.

Lest this look like a binary split between conservative, familial Americana and the truly transgressive counterculture of black Britons, I want to amplify what I take to be a similar note of disorganicity in the way that kinship can be represented. It is drawn from an American hip-hop record popular on both sides of the Atlantic right now—a tune called "Be a Father to Your Child" by Ed O.G. and Da Bulldogs.[10] It's been very popular in London, partly because of the sample it uses—a seventies black nationalist love song called "Searching" from Roy Ayers—which gets transposed into a different conceptual key by this contemporary appropriation. Two things interest me about this cut. First of all, the object of desire in the original version of the tune was gendered female; it is about searching for the love of a black woman. In the Ed O.G. version, the object of desire is ungendered. I found the opening up of that signifier suggestive. It means that when Ed O.G. talks about familial obligation, he's not saying be a father to your son—he's saying be a father to your child.

Second, and more important, Ed O.G. makes the pragmatic *functionality* of family the decisive issue, not the biological payback involved in family life. If you are responsible for producing a child with someone, he says, and that child is being supported by somebody else who is prepared to father it effectively when you fail, then back off and let him get on with it—even if that person is not the biological parent. That small gesture is something I want to celebrate. I think it shows—though I don't want to sound prescriptive about this—that the struggle over the meaning of family is alive within the culture, that a critical perspective on these complex questions isn't something that needs to be imported into that vernacular from outside by people like us. We don't play that role.

> Hey yo, be a father.
> It's not, Why bother?, son.
> A boy can make 'em, but a man can raise 'em.
> And if you did it, admit it. Then stick with it.
> Don't say it ain't yours, 'cause all women are not whores.
> Ninety percent represent a woman that is faithful.
> Ladies can I hear it?
> *Thank you.*
> When a girl gets pregnant, her man is gonna run around,
> dissin' her for now, but when it's born he wants to come around
> talkin' that I'm sorry for what I did.
> And all of a sudden, he now wants to see his kid.
> She had to bear it by herself and take care of it by herself.
> And givin' her some money for milk don't really help.
> Half of the fathers and sons and daughters don't even want to take 'em.
> But it's so easy for them to make 'em.
> It's true, if it weren't for you, the child wouldn't exist.
> Afterwards, he's your responsibility, so don't resist.
> Be a father to your child …
> See, I hate when a brother makes a child and then denies it.
> Thinkin' that money is the answer, so he buys it
> a whole bunch of gifts and a lot of presents.
> It's not the presents, it's your presence and the essence
> of bein' there and showin' the baby that you care.
> Stop sittin' like a chair and havin' your baby wondering
> where you are or who you are.
> Who you are is daddy.
> Don't act like you ain't 'cause that really makes me mad, G,
>   to see a mother and a baby suffer.
> I had enough o' brothers who don't love the
> fact that a baby brings joy into your life.
> You can still be called daddy if the mother's not your wife.

Don't be scared, be prepared.
'Cause love is gonna getcha.
It'll always be your child, even if she ain't witcha.
So, don't front on your child when it's your own,
'cause if you front now then you'll regret it when it's grown.
Be a father to your child …
Put yourself in his position and see what you've done.
But just keep in mind that you're somebody's son.
How would you like it if your father was a stranger,
and then tried to come into your life and tried to change the
way that your mother raised ya.
Now wouldn't that amaze ya?
To be or not to be.
That is the question.
When you're wrong, you're wrong.
It's time to make a correction.
Harrassin' the mother for bein' with another man.
But if the brother man can do it better than you can, *let 'im.*
Don't sweat 'im, dude.
Let him do the job that you couldn't do … [11]

I'll end by saying that even the best of this familialization of politics is still a problem. I don't want to lose sight of that. I want to have it both ways: I want to be able to valorize what we can recover; and I want to be able to cite the disastrous consequences that follow when the family supplies not just the only symbols of political agency we can find in the culture, but the only object upon which that agency can be seen to operate as well. Let's remind ourselves that there are other possibilities. Historically, black political culture's most powerful notions of agency have been figured through the sacred. They can also get figured through the profane, and there, a different idea of worldly redemption can be observed. Both of these possibilities come together for me in the traditions of musical performance that culminate in hip-hop. In them, we find what I call the ethics of antiphony—a kind of ideal communicative moment in the relationship between the performer and the crowd that surpasses anything the structures of the family can provide.

Notes

1. Manuel Castells, *The Informational City* (Oxford: Basil Blackwell, 1991).
2. This distinction has also been employed in similar ways by Dick Hebdige and James Clifford. See Iain Chambers, *Border Dialogues* (New York: Routledge, 1990).
3. Molefi Kete Asante, *Afrocentricity* (Trenton, N.J.: Africa World Press, 1988).
4. Ibid.
5. Tim Dog, *Fuck Compton* [EP], Columbia Records, 1991. CD/Cassette.
6. H.E.A.L. [Human Education Against Lies], KRS 1, "Family Got to Get Busy," *Civilization Against Technology*, Elektra/Asylum Records, 1991. CD/Cassette.
7. Rebel MC, "Wickedest Sound," *Black Meaning Good*, Desire Records LUVCD12.
8. Alexander Crummell, *Africa or America* (Springfield, Mass.: Willey and Co., 1891), 46.
9. I use the word "texts" in quotation marks because I don't think any analysis that appropriates these cultural forms exclusively as texts will ever be adequate.
10. Ed O.G. & Da Bulldogs, *Life of a Kid in the Ghetto*, Mercury Records, 1991. CD/Cassette.
11. Ibid.

10

Hip-Hop Chicano:

A Separate but Parallel Story

Raegan Kelly

What's up Homie? Don't you know me?
Si mon.
Ain't you the brother of the mas chingon?
Straight up, and I'm down with the Raza
Kid Frost got my back
Boo Yaa's en la casa
Cause every day things get a little crazier
As I step to the microphone area
First I call my city
Puro Los Angeles
[lights up & cops a hit] Yeah homes
That's what the ganga says ...

Cypress Hill, "Latin Lingo"

Laying claim to the gangsta persona is a favorite theme in hiphop. Reading the wax, Toddy Tee, Schooly D, and NWA get major props ... but for the concepts of *carnelismo, calo* terminology (homeboy, OG, etc.), the pachuco/cholo/gangsta style of dress, and the lowered ride, proper respect is due the *varrio*.

Chicano gangs, or "street syndicates," have been a fact of life in LA since the early 1930s (some claim earlier); accordingly their history, memory, and culture are long and strong. Defined by Martin Sanchez Jankowski as (roughly) adaptational organizations whose primary goal is survival through self-reliance,[1] "gang youth," while always a target of the media and law enforcement, have become, in LA at least, social pariahs without peer. To take pride visibly in this position is one way of inverting it, but the presence of colors, oversized Dickies, pendeltons, street lingo and fire power within the language and style of hiphop is only in small part fantasy-fulfillment—many of those who talk the talk have walked the walk.

Paralleling the development of gang culture were the rise of the lowrider and the zoot suiter in LA. In the *varrio*, self-reliance and brown pride go hand in hand, and a large percentage of brown hiphop integrates commentary on race and cultural difference into straightforward narratives of life on the streets. Sen Dogg of Cypress Hill exemplifies the West Coast B-boy in "Latin Lingo"—he declares his homies, his Raza, his hood, LA hiphop (and, of course, a phat blunt) in a particularly West Coast combination of English, *pachuquismo*, and hiphop slang.

Both linguistically and stylistically, aspects of the West Coast gangsta, whether it be Kid Frost, Ganxsta Ridd (of the Boo Yaa Tribe) or Ice Cube in a pendelton, Dickies and a lowered '63 S.S., originated with *pachucos* and Zoot Suiters of 1940s *varrios* of east Los Angeles.

Like the "Teddy Boy" of Harlem, the *pachuco* was the ultimate expression of cultural resistance, anarchy, and (in)difference in the North American south west of the 1940s. Generally identified as Chicano gang members (although most were not)[2] *pachucos* sported pompadours, wide-shouldered extra-long fingertip coats, high-waisted "drape" pants with pegged ankles and reat pleats, wide-brimmed hats, long watch chains, and *fileros*. Much has been written in detail about the "Zoot Suit Riots" that took place in Los Angeles in 1943, but what matters is precisely what caused civilians and sailors to roam the streets in mobs looking for young Chicanos to beat down. In *The Zoot-Suit Riots*, Mauricio Mazon describes their hatred as being comprised of a mixture of patriotic fervour and fear (mixed with envy) of difference, and of themselves.

To the good citizens of LA, "[Zoot Suiters] seemed to be simply marking time while the rest of the country intensified the war effort."[3] *Pachucos* openly smoked marijuana, spoke their own tongue, had their own style of music, dance and dress. Most infuriating, however, was that *pachucos* and zoot suiters spent so much time developing their own insular culture while good "patriotic" Americans built bombers 9-to-5 and went off to war. *Pachucos* didn't have a good "work ethic." They didn't seem to care, had their own set of priorities, and this pissed people off. (The attacks weren't completely symbolic, of course—it was around this time that the California Youth Authority camps were established, and an increasingly militant approach to law enforcement in Los Angeles was adopted.[4]

The Lowered Ride

Although the east side of Los Angeles was generally regarded as being overrun by gangs, violence, and an undocumented workforce,[5] what was to become one of the largest *varrios* in the south west had its own fast developing political, musical and street culture. In the early fifties a "basic car plan" was initiated by the First Street Merchants and the sheriff's department, and the tradition of car clubs began among east Los Angeles youth.[6] Originally designed to provide an alternative to gangs, car clubs became a focal point for social life in the *varrio*, providing a place to work, hang out, listen to music, gain knowledge of self-expression and cultural identity through the art of car customizing.

Chicanos have been customizing cars since the forties. The concept of a fully customized car, top to bottom, front to back, inside and out, took years to develop, but from the very beginning it was treated as an art form. Generally starting with a used American standard, a clay model, and much ingenuity and love, customizers take bits and pieces off different automobiles out of scrap yards, alter them and put them together to create a totally new and unique car. Bill Hines is one of *Lowrider* magazine's "Legends of Lowriding"; his first custom was a '41 Buick convertible with "chopped top" and a Cadillac front end. Known to some as the "King of Lead" for his ability totally to rework a body with a lead paddle and a spray gun, he was also one of the first to design a hydraulic lift system for raising and lowering custom cars (using modified aircraft landing gear parts), California-style, in 1964. (The first lifted custom was purportedly done by the Aguirres of San Bernardino, California, on a 1956 Corvette).[7] Hydraulics served a dual function—to raise a lowered vehicle for driving long distances (protect the underside), and to keep the cops away (riding too slow was a ticketable offense). "I remember a guy with this candy turquoise '63 Ford ... that wanted to fool the cops. So, he had me juice it in front and back. He'd cruise with it laid until the cops spotted him. They couldn't figure it out. They didn't know what a lift was."[8]

To drive a beautifully customized ride low and slow down one of LA's main thoroughfares is an expression of pride, pride in being different, taking one's time, being Chicano. Jesse

Valdez, another of the original lowriders and former leader of one of LA's best-known car clubs, The Imperials, remembers the heyday of lowriding: "In '66, '67, '68—we'd cruise Downey, Paramount, Whittier. That's when everybody was lowriding; Chicanos, black guys, white guys."[9] Whittier Boulevard, a unifying site for east LA through to the mid-seventies, was the site of the Eastside Blowouts, the Chicano political protests of '71–72; it provided a focal point for the *muralista* movement of the same time and Luis Valdez's 1979 movie *Boulevard Nights*. (Valdez's film, a classic Hollywood document of *varrio* street life in LA, opened ironically just after the boulevard was permanently closed to cruisers.) Favorites of the car culture tended to be instrumentals with sparse lyrics and heavy basslines—"Whittier Boulevard" by Thee Midniters, "Lowrider" by WAR (previously Señor Soul), "More Bounce" by Zapp.

Latin Lingo

> Calo is the privileged language of the Mexican-American barrio … (It) was neither a *pachuco* nor a new world contribution. Calo has its ancient roots buried deeply in the fertile gypsy tongue (Calé, Romano, Zincalo and Calogitano …) … fractured in spelling, crippled in meaning; mutilated French, English, Italian, and the dead languages of Latin, Greek, and Hebrew, plus medieval Moorish, Calo, originally *Zincalo*, was the idiom of the Spanish Gypsies—one of the many minorities in Spain. The *conquistadores* brought Calo to the New World. Already identified by the upper classes as the argot of the criminal, the poor, and the uneducated, Calo and its variants became well known to the conquered Indian …
>
> Mauricio Mazon, *The Zoot-Suit Riots*, p. 3

To followers of scat and the spoken-word traditions of jazz and bebop, Calo probably sounds little different than the jive scat of Cab Calloway or the inverted *Vout* language of Slim Gaillard. In some ways today it operates much like early hepster phraseology—hip Calo terms like homeboy and loc have completely penetrated hiphop and gang culture. But for the *pachucos* of the forties and in the *varrios*, of today, Calo is also an important way to mark cultural difference/peripherality through language. Frequently referred to as "Spanglish" (half English, half Spanish) Calo is in fact a tongue all its own, a "living language" whose words and meanings change from location to location and person to person.

> Muy Loco, Crazy
> Ever since I come from Mexico
> I don't want to do the Mambono
> All I want to do is go go go
> When the crazy band she starts to blow
> All the *señoritas* say to me
> Come on Pancho dance with me
> Pancho Pancho don't go to the Rancho
> Til you do the Pancho Rock with me
> Lalo Guerrero and His Orchestra, "Pancho Rock"

The great Latin bandleader Lalo Guerrero was one of the first to incorporate Calo into the Los Angeles club scene in the forties. *Pachuco* and zoot cultures gravitated towards the big band sound, which Guerrero fused with the structures of swing and rumba in songs like "Chuco Suave," "Marijuana Boogie," and "Vamos a bailar."[10] Another Calo favorite was the Don Tosti band's "Pachuco Boogie," characterized by Johnny Otis as Chicano Jump Blues, "which consisted of a jump type shuffle with either Raul [Diaz] or Don [Tosti] rapping in Calo about getting ready to go out on a date. Very funny stuff and another candidate for the title of the first rap record."[11]

Through the fifties and sixties East Los Angeles developed an active recording and club scene, which, as Steven Loza explains in *Barrio Rhythm*, "was integrally related to the black music experience, for musical as well as economic reasons."[12] The influence went both ways, and in 1952 African American saxophonist Chuck Higgins released the hit single "Pachuco Hop." Loza quotes Ruben Guevara's description of the east LA music scene in the late fifties and early sixties at El Monte Legion Stadium, which reads like an early description of Go-Go:

> A lot of Anglo kids copied not only the styles (hair, dress) but the dances, the most popular of which were the Pachuco Hop, Hully Gully, and the Corrido Rock ... the Corrido was the wildest, sort of an early form of slam dancing. Two or three lines would form, people arm in arm, each line consisting of 150 to 250 people. With the band blasting away at breakneck rocking tempo, the lines took four steps forward and four steps back, eventually slamming into each other (but making sure that no one got hurt).... After the dance, it was out to the parking lot for the grand finale. Where's the party? *Quien tiene pisto? Mota?* Who's got the booze? Weed? Rumors would fly as to which gangs were going to throw *chingasos*—come to blows. The Jesters Car Club from Boyle Heights, which dominated the Eastside, would parade around the parking lot in their lavender, maroon or gray primered cars, wearing T-Timer shades (blue or green colored glasses in square wire frames).[13]

Latin and Afro-Cuban rhythms seem to have penetrated the early hiphop scene at least a decade before we hear any bilingual or Calo phraseology. In the early seventies, at the same time as lowriders in Califas were bumpin' the sounds of Tierra, Señor Soul, and Rulie Garcia and the East LA Congregation, Jimmy Castor was creating hiphop beats in New York using a fusion of "one-chord riffing, a Sly Stone pop bridge, fuzz guitar, timbales breaks, and an idealistic lyric applicable to any emergent movement."[14] David Toop credits Jimmy Castor with being a hiphop innovator, at the center of the Latin soul movement in the sixties and highly influenced by Latin masters like Cal Tjader, Chano Pozo, and Tito Puente.[15] Seven years later Afrika Bambaataa would redefine "influence," straight cutting Slim Gaillard's unique *Vout* lyrics into the mix.

In *Hip-Hop: The Illustrated History*, Steven Hager describes the early tagging and writing scene in 1970s New York as being racially integrated: the first tagger on record, Taki 183, was Greek; the second, Julio 204, was Chicano; and Tracy 168, a young white kid living in Black Spades territory, founded one of the scene's largest crews, "Wanted," in 1972.[16] The internationally known Lee Quinones and Lady Pink (stars of *Wild Style*)[17] were both Puerto Rican, as were the members of the all-time great breaking group, the Rock Steady Crew.

In the Bronx, funk and early hiphop entered the already hot Puerto Rican street and dance scene around 1977–78, with members of the Zulu Nation schooling Puerto Ricans in the ways of breakdancing and Puerto Rican DJs like Charlie Chase spinning funk and sporting early B-boy styles at their then disco-dominated block parties.[18] Rammelzee ('Ramm-elevation-Z—Z being a symbol of energy which flows in two directions)[19] and RubyD, recently dubbed the Puerto Rican Old School by West Coast Puerto Rican funkster Son Doobie of Funkdoobiest, rocked the mike all over NYC. The 1983 hit "Beat Bop" (Rammelzee vs. K-Rob) showcases what Rammelzee is known best for—what he dubbed "slanguage,"[20] an ingenious combination of freestyle metaphor and over-the-top hiphop drops delivered in the Shake Up King's particular nasal drawl:

Just groovin' like a sage y'all
Break it up, yeah, yeah, stage y'all
Like a roller coaster ride that can make ya bump
Groovin with the rhythm as you shake yer rump—rock rock ya don't stop
You got it now baby—ya don't stop
Just hiphop the day, yeah doobie doo
Yeah scoobie doo, whatcha wanna do crew?
Just freak it, ya baby, just freak up, ya ya baby
Drink it up here, I know my dear
I can rock you out this atmosphere
Like a gangster prankster, number one bankster
Got much cash to make you thank ya
Rock on to the break a dawn—Keep it on now keep it on
I know Zee Zee that can rock quick
Like a high kind a class
Hand yer rhythm to the stick ...

"Beat Bop," Rammelzee vs. K-Rob

In 1980 a young Samoan dancer named Sugar Pop would move west from the streets of New York to bring breaking to the poplockers of south central, Venice and Hollywood in Los Angeles. One of the groups Sugar Pop encountered was the Blue City Crew, a group of Samoan poplockers coming out of Carson in south LA. In Topper Carew's movie *Breakin and Entering* about the early eighties breaking scene in LA, the crew talks about how the advent of street dancing correlated with a drop in gangbanging in the hoods and *varrios* of LA—homies were taking their battles to the dance floor. "In LA it ain't like that.... If you got the moves, you can hold down. That's all it is."

It was also around this time that hiphop started to penetrate the LA Chicano dance scene. In the mid- to late seventies Chicanos were throwing giant dance parties at Will Rogers State Beach, Devonshire Downs and in parks and roller rinks in the San Fernando Valley, complete with battling mobile DJs, hundreds of Curwen Vegas, MCs to keep the crowd hyped and, of course, circling helicopters. Precursors of today's massive rave scene (which are approximately 75 percent Chicano in Los Angeles), the music of choice at these parties was alternative/new wave, disco, and early techno-based hiphop (Egyptian Lover, Magic Mike, Melle Mel, Grandmaster Flash). Due to popular demand, in 1983–1984 Uncle Jam's Army set up special Valley-side gigs at the Sherman Square roller rink in Sherman Oaks. Young Chicano, Latino, and Samoan MCs, many of them former dancers, were working their way through the LA house party scene at this time, but one of the earliest to make it to wax was Arthur Molina, Jr. (aka Kid Frost) in 1984 with the single "Rough Cut." The music, written by David Storrs of Electrobeat Records (the same Storrs who wrote the music for Ice T's "Body Rock"),[21] has a decidedly early West Coast flavor, but lyrically the song bears a strong resemblance to Run DMC's "It's Like That," also released in 1984.

Sometimes you wait around
Rockin' cold hard streets
People strugglin' hard
Just tryin' to make ends meet
I just stand tough
hold down my feet
Never understand the meaning
of the word Defeat
So you see it's like that

And that's the way it is
But when I'm on the microphone, it goes something like this:
Body breakin' Booty shakin'
Good money for the makin'
You just put it in my pocket
Cause you know I got talent
It's Rough, it's Tough
Let me see if you can handle my stuff
It's Rough Rough Rough Rough Rough …

Kid Frost, "Rough Cut"

The earliest bilingual hiphop song that I've heard on record is out of New York—Carlos T (aka Spanish Fly) and the Terrible Two's hit "Spanglish."[22] Rapping over a classic Grandmaster Flash beat the Terrible Two dominate the song in English, with Carlos T coming in short and fast. "This is the way we harmonize, everybody, everybody, I said Danse funky danse, y que danse, todo mundo, todo mundo."

In 1989 the Cuban-born Mellow Man Ace kicked bilingual lyrics throughout his album *Escape from Havana*, generally alternating line for line between English and Spanish, as in "Mentirosa," or verse for verse, as he does in "Rap Guanco," over the Kool and the Gang bassline from Lightnin' Rod's[23] cut "Sport" on the *Hustlers' Convention* album of 1973:

… I'm the lyrical, miracle founder of the talk style
Put together intelligently wild
And what I came up with is called Rap Guanco
Different than house, nothing like GoGo
And if you're wonderin' damn how'd he start this
Well, last year I opened my own market
Cause it was time for somethin' new to come along and I thought
A bilingual single, that can't go wrong …
    …
Ahora si que vengo [And now yes I'm coming]
Sabroso si caliente … [Flavor very hot] …

Mellow Man Ace, "Rap Guanco"

A year later, Kid Frost hit the streets with his classic adaptation of the Gerald Wilson/El Chicano tune "Viva La Tirado," "La Raza," matching in syntax and lingo the Pachuco street slang (Calo) of East LA.

Quevo
Aqui'stoy MC Kid Frost
Yo estoy jefe [I am in charge]
My *cabron* is the big boss
My *cuete* is loaded [pistol/rod]
It's full of *balas* [bullets]
I'll put it in your face
And you won't say *nada.* [nothing]
Vatos, cholos, call us what you will [Chicano homeboys, lowriders]
You say we are assassins,
Train ourselves to kill
It's in our blood to be an Aztec warrior

Go to any extreme
And hold to no barriers
Chicano and I'm brown and proud
Want this *chingaso*? [smack, wack, as in "beat down"]
Si mon I said let's get down

...

The foreign tongue I'm speaking is known as Calo
Y sabes que, loco? [And you know what, loc?]
Yo estoy malo [I am mean/bad]
Tu no sabes que I think your brain is hollow? [Don't you know that ...]

...

And so I look and I laugh and say *Que pasa?* [What's happening?]
Yeah, this is for La Raza.

Kid Frost, "La Raza," Hispanic Causing Panic

"La Raza" is important for several reasons. It marks a radical change in Kid Frost's work—the distance between the non-committal "So rough, so tough" of "Rough Cut" and "It's in our blood to be an Aztec warrior / Go to any extreme" marks a change in consciousness, at least of his perception of hiphop as a language of consciousness. Frost's use of Calo is an appeal to the authenticity of the streets and the *pachuco* lifestyle, but within the context of the song it is also a nod to Chicano pride, as is the claim "Chicano and I'm brown and proud." The term Chicano, derived from *mechicano* and once considered derogatory and indicative of lower-class standing, applies to all people of Mexican descent/all people of indigenous descent. To call yourself Chicano is to claim La Raza, to locate your origin within the struggle of a people for land and for cultural, political and economic self-determination. Also, Frost's use of an El Chicano hit, as opposed to the less culturally specific beat of "Rough Cut," is a nod to the *veteranos* (who to this day remain partial to Oldies over hiphop).

The early nineties have been watershed years for Chicano hiphoppers—a peak moment being the 1991 release of Cypress Hill's first album. Showcasing the combined talents of Mellow Man Ace's brother Sen Dogg, B-Real, DJ Muggs, *Cypress Hill* integrates the best of Rammelzee's hiphop tricknology, the Calo rap of Don Tosti and Raul Diaz, bad-ass West Coast gangsta mythology, humor, and trademark beats.

Gangsta Rid, What's up Y'all?
"It's a tribe thing ... "

...

"Hey where you from homies?"
It's on
He sees 'em reach for his gun
Buckshot to the dome
He jumps in the bomb
Homies in tha back but she just wants to go home
But he trips to the store
Homeboy needs a 40
White boy's at the counter
Thinkin' "O Lordy Lordy"
Pushin' on the button
Panickin' for nuttin'
Pigs on the way
Hey yo he smells bacon ...

...

Scooby doo y'all, scooby doo y'all
A scooby doo y'all
A doobie doobie doo y'all ...

Cypress Hill, *Hole in the Head*, 1991

It's a Tribe Thing

I am a revolutionary ... because creating life amid death is a revolutionary act. Just as building nationalism in an era of imperialism is a life-giving act.... We are an awakening people, an emerging nation, a new breed.

Carlos Muñoz, Jr., *Youth Identity, Power*, p. 76

Corky Gonzales's Crusade for Justice in 1969 brought people from every corner of the *varrio* together in the name of self-determination and La Raza. One of the concepts put forth during the course of the conference was that Chicano students, needing "revolutionary role models," would do well to emulate their brothers and sisters in the streets, the *vatos locos* of the *varrio*, *Carnelismo*, or the code of absolute love in Chicano gangs, was to be adopted by radical student nationalists as the locus of their developing ideology.[24]

The Chicano hiphop that has made it to wax in the last two years frequently assimilates some combination of street mentality and nationalist politics, whether it be as simple as giving the nod to brown pride, or as complex as the cultural nationalism of Aztlan Underground. The gangsta presently dominates brown hiphop, good examples being Proper Dos (west LA), RPM (Valley), Street Mentality (Pico/Union), The Mexicanz (Long Beach) and Brown Town (east LA), to name a few. The music: generally simple beats, frequently scary, down with ganga, *rucas* and *cuetes*, sometimes intentionally educational, and occasionally hilarious. Groups like Of Mexican Descent represent a new generation of lyrical wizards, working in two tongues, with breath control, and kicking knowledge of self.

Cypress Hill are at the center of one of LA's finer hiphop posses, the Soul Assassins. The more recent group Funkdoobiest (consisting of Puerto Rican and Sioux MCs and a Mexican DJ) are down, as well as the Irish American group House of Pain, and allied are the Samoan brothers of the Boo Yaa Tribe, Mellow Man Ace, and Kid Frost. For me, the Soul Assassins represent some of the most radical (and difficult) aspects of living in Los Angeles. On one hand they describe the celebration of difference through hiphop (and the fierce potential in collaboration and in the music), on the other, their lyrics frequently demarcate territorial and personal boundaries (BOOM-in-your-face). But at its most elemental, the beats of hiphop are about walking all over those boundaries with no apologies.

Out of the east we've heard from groups like the Puerto Rican Powerrule (New York), and Fat Joe the Gangsta (Bronx), there's a Brewley MC in Puerto Rico, and reggae español posses in Panama and Mexico, but brown hiphop seems to be coming to fruition on the West Coast. Although the Latin Alliance project didn't hold, hopefully the concept was not outmoded but a little ahead of its time. In a city where 10 per cent of the world's population of El Salvadorans lives around MacArthur Park (downtown), the possibilities for cross-cultural collaboration and unity seem, well, massive. And with cats like Kid Frost, Cypress, AUG, Proper Dos, and OMD sharpening their skills in every corner of LA, hiphop is where to make it happen. After all, it still remains true that (referring back to the Samoan brother from Carson City) in LA hiphop if you are down, you can hold down.

Special Thanks to Bulldog and Tate.

Notes

1. Martin Sanchez Jankowski, *Islands in the Street*, Berkeley, Los Angeles and Oxford, 1991, pp. 25–7.
2. Mauricio Mazon, *The Zoot-Suit Riots; The Psychology of Symbolic Annihilation*, Austin, 1984, p. 5.
3. Ibid, p. 9.
4. Ibid, p. 108.
5. Steven Loza, *Barrio Rhythm; Mexican American Music in Los Angeles*, Urbana and Chicago, 1993, p. 42.
6. Ibid.
7. Dick DeLoach, "Bill Hines: The King of Lead," *Lowrider Magazine*, April 1992, p. 52.
8. Ibid, p. 53.
9. Dick DeLoach, "Jesse Valdez and Gypsy Rose," *Lowrider Magazine*, October 1992, p. 56.
10. *Barrio Rhythm*, p. 71
11. Ibid, p. 81.
12. Ibid.
13. Ibid, p. 83.
14. David Toop, *Rap Attack 2: African Rap to Global Hip Hop*, London and New York, 1991, p. 22.
15. Ibid, p. 24
16. Steven Hager, *Hip-Hop: The Illustrated History*, p. 21.
17. *Wild Style*, Charlie Ahearn, 1981. A 35mm rap-umentary about the early integration of the different elements of hiphop culture in New York. Also starring Fred Braithwaite and Patty Astor.
18. *An Illustrated History of Hip Hop*, p. 81.
19. *Rap Attack 2*, p. 122.
20. Ibid.
21. Billy Jam, liner notes on *West Coast Rap, The First Dynasty*, Vol. 2, 1992, Rhino Records.
22. On *Greatest Hits of the Zulu Nation*, circa 1982.
23. AKA Jalal of the Last Poets.
24. Carlos Muñoz, Jr., *Youth, Identity, Power: The Chicano*, Verso, 1989, p. 76.

Further Reading

Rodolfo F. Acuna, *A Community Under Siege: A Chronicle of Chicanos East of the Los Angeles River; 1945–1975.* Monograph no. 11/Chicano Studies Research Center Publications, Los Angeles: University of California 1984.

Rodolfo F. Acuna, *Occupied America; A History of Chicanos,* New York: HarperCollins 1988.

Dick DeLoach, "Bill Hines: The King of Lead," *Lowrider Magazine* 14, 1992, pp. 52–3.

Dick DeLoach, "Jesse Valdez and Gypsy Rose," *Lowrider Magazine* 14, 1992, pp. 56–8.

Willard Gingerich, "Aspects of Prose Style in Three Chicano Novels: *Pocho, Bless Me, Ultima* and *The Road to Tamazunchale* in ed. Jacob Ornstein-Galicia, *Form and Function in Chicano English*, Rowley, Massachusetts: Newbury House 1994.

Steven Hager, *Hip-Hop: The Illustrated History, Rap Music and Graffiti,* New York: St. Martin's Press, 1984.

Martin Sanchez Jankowski, *Islands in the Street*, Berkeley, Los Angeles and Oxford: University of California Press 1991.

George Lipsitz, *Time Passages; Collective Memory and American Popular Culture,* Minneapolis: University of Minnesota Press 1990.

Steven Loza, *Barrio Rhythm: Mexican American Music in Los Angeles,* Urbana and Chicago: University of Illinois Press 1993.

Mauricio Mazon, *The Zoot-Suit Riots; The Psychology of Symbolic Annihilation,* Austin: University of Texas Press 1984.

Carlos Muñoz Jr, *Youth, Identity, Power; The Chicano Movement,* London and New York: Verso 1989.

Harry Polkinhorn, Alfredo Velasco and Mal Lambert, *El Libro De Calo; Pachuco Slang Dictionary*, San Diego: Atticus Press 1983.

Stan Steiner, *La Raza: The Mexican Americans*, New York, Evanston, and London: Harper & Row 1970.

David Toop, *Rap Attack 2: African Rap to Global Hip Hop*, London and New York: Serpent's Tail 1991.

11

On the Question
of Nigga Authenticity

R.A.T. Judy

Almost every law and method ingenuity could devise was employed by the legislatures to reduce the Negroes to serfdom,—to make them slaves of the state, if not of individuals.... [T]he Negro is coming more and more to look upon law and justice, not as protecting safeguards, but as sources of humiliation and oppression.

W.E.B. Du Bois, *The Souls of Black Folk*

Real Niggaz don't die.

Dr. Dre

The straight up nigga.—There is the story of the hard-core OG, down with the One Percent Nation, who kicked the pure fact in 1991 and declared this the era of the nigga.

"It is the end of black folk, and the beginning of global niggadom," he proclaimed.

The brother got props from a serious transnational corporation that gave his record global distribution in two media formats: audio and video. It was picked up and echoed in all formats of the news media, becoming a great event. Folks started buggin', and a panic set in. In other words, there was considerable acrimony. How has this brother gotten so lost? some asked. Why would a serious transnational corporation be associated with a nigger? asked others who had considerable capital investment but little understanding of the communicability of affect. Those concerned with the OG's soul wondered out loud where we have come to as a people. They wanted to know if this was the beginning of the end of black folk. Have our children come to achieve what four hundred years of slavery and oppression could not, the death of black folk?

The OG stepped to these believers and busted 'em out.

"This is not the beginning of the end of black folk," he said.

"They are always already dead wherever you find them. The nurturing haven of black culture which assured memory and provided a home beyond the ravishing growth of capitalism is no longer. There cannot be any cultural authenticity in resistance to capitalism. The illusion of immaterial purity is no longer possible. It is no longer possible to be black against the system. Black folk are dead, killed by their own faith in willfully being beyond, and in spite of, power. Will beyond power has no passion, only affect. Black folk have killed themselves by striving to conserve themselves in a willful affect—the productive labor of modern subjects, a.k.a. work. Black folk, who have always been defined in relation to work, went the way of work.

"There is a motto circulating these days: Real Black Folks Work. And where else can you find real black folk except in the killing fields, which is, by definition, the place for nonproductive consumption—the end of work? The killing fields, then, are the place of non-work for complete consumption of needless workers. Real black folk are already dead, walking around consuming themselves in search of that which is no longer possible, that which defines them. Understand that the killing fields are everywhere; and whoever is born after us in the killing fields will belong to a higher history, the history of the nigga. You all are upset by this because you don't know what it is to be a nigga. A nigga is that which emerges from the demise of human capital, what gets articulated when the field nigger loses value as labor. The nigga is unemployed, null and void, walking around like … a nigga who understands that all possibility converts from capital, and capital does not derive from work."

After this, the OG's record sales grew rapidly; so did the acrimony, and increasing pressure was put on the transnational corporation to be responsive to community standards of decency. No Niggaz Allowed was the sentiment, and the OG was censured. Ending his contractual relation with the transnational, he dropped more science.

"You all ain't ready yet. You cannot even hear what is being spoken by your own children, let alone understand, because you got your heads up your asses and are on capitalism's dick. You may think I'm too early, but I'm just in time. Some straight up niggaz with attitude done already busted some serious nigga moves."

At the same time he ended his contractual relation with the transnational, he incorporated his own independent label and hooked up with another transnational network of distribution. When called to account for his own blatant embrace of capitalism, his only reply was: "It's a home invasion."

Understanding the possibilities of nigga authenticity in the emerging realities of transnational capital is a humbling undertaking. From the pulpit to the lectern, from the television news desk to the op-ed pages of the leading papers, the general consensus is "this nigga is deadly dangerous." It is this nigga who gang-bangs, this nigga who is destroying the fabric of society, who has spread across the country like an infestation, bringing an epidemic of death and despair to black America. All this, on the assumption that this nigga of the present age is somehow related to the "bad nigger" of slavery and the postbellum South, an assumption that remains to be tested.

Citing Leon R. Harris's 1925 essay, "The Steel-Drivin' Man," as its principal literary quotation, the *Oxford English Dictionary* defines *nigga* as a southern pronunciation of *nigger*, whose variant forms are *niggah, nigguh,* and *niggur*: "Howdy niggahs, … how's you all dis mawnin'."[1] The next quotation is from Chester Himes's *Black on Black*: "Niggah, ef'n yo is talkin' tuh me, Ah ain' liss'nin'."[2] The *h* gets dropped in Paulette Cross's recording of a joke told to her by Ronald Taylor, of Milwaukee, Wisconsin, in 1968: "There's this uh—black cat from the north, ya know, he's a bad nigga.… There's this nigga who went to the 'Sip, you know, uh—Mississippi.… They end up losing all of their money to that big nigga who is supposed to be the epitome of 'nigga-ness'."[3] The irregular spelling of the term persisted, however, well into the mid-seventies, which is when the OED's citations end. *Nigga* became the dominant form with the emergence of hard-core gangster rap, as a particular expression of hip-hop around 1987. Since then, real niggaz have been associated with hip-hop and hard-core rap, and the latter identified as an index of social malaise. As Joe Wood discovered in his search for "the real thing" in Mississippi, the domain of "real niggaz" is global:

Down here, traditional blues has lost stagger lee's [*sic*] spirit to hip-hop's real niggaz.... Folks do listen to other music, but the essential music—the "real" thing—is the nihilistic capitalistic hard-core hip-hop rap shit.... [W]e want the real niggaz even when they're fronting all that bitch shit because of this: in America, violence and making dollars make for respect and those motherfuckers are getting it.[4]

Employing *nigga* in this way leads to consideration of the seemingly unavoidable question of authenticity in relation to commodification: Can a commodified identity be authentic? Understanding the movement from nigger to nigga means recalling the historical systematic employment of nigger as an exchange value, as well as giving some consideration to a set of problems specific to the issue of human capital at the end of political economy. The objective is to determine whether or not hard-core gangster rap's employment of the category nigga is an attempt to think an African American identity at the end of political economy, when work no longer defines human being.

Nigga to Nigger

What is hard-core rap? We know it is an expression of something called hip-hop. What is hip-hop? It is a kind of utterance: "Hip-hop hooray ho hey ho," an utterance of a habit of thought toward an increasingly rationalized and fragmented world of global commodification. It is thinking about being in a hypercommodified world. Rap is a way of this thinking that cannot itself be rigorously thought about without thinking hip-hop. To think about rap is to think about hip-hop, although not necessarily in the way of hip-hop. Thinking about rap in the way of hip-hop is to think it hard core, to think it like a nigga.

Thinking about the nigga, to put it schematically, lies at the crux of two genealogical procedures.[5] One, which traces the origins of rap to recognized African American rhetorical forms (toasts, shouts, and various forms of signifying or verbal games) and tropes, leads to a kind of utopian historicism that is grounded in the concept of the morally legitimate tradition of African American resistance to dehumanizing commodification. This account allows for a morally legitimate form of rap that is stylistically hard core, while still belonging to the tradition of the African American liberation struggle dating back to spirituals, a struggle characterized by the deification of "knowledge as possessing an inherent power that emancipates."[6] The other genealogy traces the development of gangster rap as a rupture in this morally legitimate tradition of resistance, whose origin is not in the form of rap itself but in a moral malaise engendered by the conditions of capitalism's hegemony over all aspects of life.

We are not yet accustomed, however, to thinking at the crux, to thinking hard core. Instead, the predominant thinking about rap is obsessed with the question of its historical and ideological significance for African American society. In turning to the question of significance we are concerned with rap's significance *for*. Rap is *for* African American society. It is an expression of this society's utterance. It serves this society's purpose: the constitution of subjects of knowledge. This is also a conservative purpose; it aims at keeping the African American experience through its conversion into knowledge. Knowledge gives significance to experience; in so doing it liberates significance from experience. What is this significance, and how is it liberated in knowledge? Of significance is the difference between having experience and knowing it, between being a slave and knowing oneself in slavery. This is the difference of the knowing that adheres to an ancient oracular utterance: "Know your self." The slave who knows him- or herself to be other than the experience of slavery, knows him- or herself to be in that knowing. Whatever the nature of the experience, however cruel the task at hand, however abject the economy of phenomenal bodies as commodities, the slave knows him- or herself as being heterogeneous from the it that is used up in slave labor. Knowledge liberates in announcing the heterogeneity of the instance of self-knowing, of apperception, from experience. Such self-knowing is what is called human nature. The human is that creature which knows itself knowing. The human can be enslaved but never *is* a slave. The human can be designated a phenomenal thing of the slave experience, *nigger*, but never *is* a nigger. This is a liberal knowledge that presumes the universality of apperception without knowing it and makes the human the significance of experience. The purpose of African American society, then, is the liberation of humans as subjects of knowledge from the subject of experience, from the commodified nigger of slavery.

Thinking about hard-core rap in terms of its significance for African American society is a way of disposing of it, unless we are willing to think it *with* the commodified nigga. Thinking with the nigga is to become concerned with it as an expression of an emergent utterance—hip-hop—which does not work according to the purpose of liberal knowledge. Yet, because we have failed to think about rap at the crux, *nigga* is misread as *nigger*. Once this association is made, the departure of hard core from the purpose of African American society can only be thought of as regressive. In this regressive thought, the hard-core nigga is an expression of angry, self-destructive violence, the armed and insatiable beast of capitalism that knows only exchange-value and the endless pursuit of greater pleasure: "You know that the jungle creed says that the strongest must feed on any prey at hand." The nigga of hard core blurs with the gang-banger, mackdaddy, new-jack, and drug-dealer, becoming an index of the moral despair engendered by a thoroughly dehumanizing oppression, and hence inevitably bearing a trace of that dehumanization: "And I was branded a beast at every feast before I ever became a man." In regressive thought, the hard-core nigga is the *bad nigger* become *gangster*.[7] In this way, we are prevented from truly thinking about the significance of hard-core rap.

Truly thinking about the significance of hard-core gangster rap requires that we disengage the question of its significance from that of its significance for African American society. The place to begin this disengagement is the identification of nigga with bad nigger. In order to establish hard-core rap's connection to the African American tradition, it has become convenient to differentiate between morally legitimate hard-core rappers and those who are amoral or nihilistic.[8] The former, the heroic *badmen* hard-core rappers, are considered to be a continuation of the *badman* figure of African American folklore—a Railroad Bill, who may be either radically secular or religious. This differentiation is of some use here, because it goes directly to the problematic relationship between nigger and nigga that frames this discussion. It is particularly so in its identification of the hard-core nigga with the *bad nigger*, who, like the *badman*, is a figure of folklore.

Someone who has elaborated this differentiation and identification to a considerable extent is Jon Michael Spencer. But what does Spencer mean by bad nigger and badman; what definition does he give of these terms? He doesn't give a definition of the bad nigger as such, but provides negative example and explanation: "The attitude of the 'bad nigger' is not negritude, it is narcissism and hedonism, and it is genocidal. The 'bad nigger' is not viewed as a hero by the masses of the black community, whose safety and moral stability he threatens." He has considerably more to offer, by way of definition, on the badman.

> The hard-core rappers, who engage in the insurrection of subjugated knowledges are "badmen" practicing self-determinative politico-moral leadership. They are ... political rappers ... who speak "attitudinally" but with knowledge about the conditions that the establishment has effected in their communities: social jingoism (such as black stereotyping) and civil terrorism (such as police-on-black crime). In response, the political rappers, alongside a new group of Christian rappers, advocate the formation of community; unity over disunity, economic self-determination over black-on-black crime and "gang banging."

For them it is knowledge, and only knowledge, that can lead to the overcoming of the fear, deception, and hatred that cause division and disrupt community.[9]

The difference is attitudinal, then; it is a difference in order and type of knowledge. The badman possesses a knowledge of self, which the bad nigger lacks. This knowledge is of political significance, in that it is the basis for a type of morality, or self-government, which then forms the basis for community self-determination, which belongs to economy.

Leaving aside the question of the bad nigger for the moment in order to focus on the badman as the source of hard core's legitimate genealogy, attention is drawn to the fact that Spencer defines politics in terms of how self-government relates to the art of properly governing the community and identifies the latter with economy. This is no small point. In Spencer's definition of the badman, we hear an echo of the liberal concept of political economy, the notion that the upward continuity of government defines community: effective good government of the community derives upward from good government of family, which derives from individual morality, or self-government. Spencer has drawn a very tight circle, whose epicenter is reason, or the epistemological project of modernity. The badman who has self-knowledge is, by definition, the subject of knowledge. In this sense, the function of the badman is pedagogical, providing a model of the formation of the leader; hence Spencer's definition of him as "practicing self-determinative politico-moral leadership." There is a downward continuity involved in this model of leadership in the implication that when the community is well run, then the head of the family will know how to properly govern his family (this is the idea of role-modeling that has become the sine qua non of grass-roots community work among urban African Americans today), which means that individuals will behave as they should. They will *police* themselves.

It is extremely significant that the positive force of Spencer's badman is his strong sense of social propriety, his understanding that strict obedience to social codes is essential for collective survival. The badman is the self-consciously representative black, he is an instantiation of morality above the law. Keep in mind that for Spencer, the question of morality in rap is a question of authenticity; the heroic badman is a figure of legitimate moral resistance to white oppression. It is a figure that recurs in various expressions of black folklore and popular culture, from the stories of High John the Conqueror to the blues. As the present-day avatar of this figure, the *badman* hard-core political rapper lets rap belong to a continuous tradition of community conservation as the moral response to a singular form of oppression. According to Spencer, that tradition is rooted in the African American spiritual-blues impulse, which is a kind of oppositional knowledge, a joyous science that is dropped by hard-core gospel rappers, such as PID (Preachers in Disguise), ETW (End Time Warriors), D-Boy Rodriguez, and MC Hammer—badman as *homo Africanus Americanus moralis*.

The problem is that the most vital and resilient form of rap is the hard-core nigga gangster rap (so much so that even pop rap icon LL Cool J moved into the ranks of rhetorical bangers with his single "Here's How I'm Comin' "). This popularity of the nigga is what prompted Spencer to differentiate between the badman and the bad nigger in the first place. To understand this, we must take up again the question of the bad nigger that was set aside earlier. The objective of the argument for the heterogeneity of the badman and bad nigger is to establish rap's authenticity as an African American form by rescuing it from the "genocidal" tendencies of the bad nigger.

Its centrality to Spencer's argument notwithstanding, the sharp distinction between these two figures is a radical departure from how their relationship has been understood by those who know about such things. Since Brearely's 1939 essay, "Ba-ad Nigger," folklorists and historians of African American slave culture have understood the postbellum folklore figure of the badman to derive from the antebellum bad nigger.[10] The folklorist John W. Roberts has recently disputed this association.[11] The basis of that critique is Roberts's analysis of the sociopolitical circumstance under which late-nineteenth-century African American folklore developed. Given that both the badman and the bad nigger are characterized in terms of their resistance to the law, the most significant aspect of postbellum sociopolitical circumstances relative to these figures is the law. As W.E.B. Du Bois remarked in *The Souls of Black Folk* (1902), and subsequently analyzed in *Black Reconstruction* (1935), the systematic use of the law by white authorities to disenfranchise blacks after the resumption of home rule in the South caused blacks to make avoidance of the law a virtue.[12] Roberts elaborates this into the argument that maintaining internal harmony and solidarity within one's own community was a form of protection against the law of the state. In this understanding, the black community becomes the police in order to not give the police any reason or cause to violate it.

In other words, Roberts anticipates Spencer and claims that the postbellum black community was, in fact, self-policing in order to preempt any intrusion from the external law of the state. Concurring with the generally accepted interpretation of the bad nigger as anticommunitarian, flaunting the morality of the community as well as the law, Roberts argues the illogic of a newly emancipated people, striving to establish and defend their right to participate in the general community of America, celebrating a figure that challenged the very virtue of morality on which community survival depended. The bad nigger was not only uncelebrated in the black community but despised as a threat to civil society. By contrast, according to Roberts, the badman of black folklore challenges the unjustness of the law of the state, while preserving the moral law of the community.

The disassociation of the badman and bad nigger as two distinct tropes addresses Spencer's essential concern with hard-core political rap, which is how it can be employed to reconstitute a community in crisis. The badman political hard-core rapper will regain the morality that Roberts claims preserved the postbellum community from both the law and bad niggers. But what category of individual did this community consist of? Apparently, they were neither badmen nor bad niggers, but something else. What both Spencer and Roberts forget is that there were niggers other than bad ones. This is a vexing issue, precisely because *nigger* was for quite some time the term used to designate African American slaves as commodity. Understandably, Spencer may have elided this issue for fear that it would distract too much from the paramount question of hard-core rap's amorality. In fact, it goes right to the heart of the matter. For understanding nigga as the analog of bad nigger, and the latter as the index of devastating amorality, first requires an examination of the presupposed community of niggers. Can there even be a "community" of niggers, as opposed to a "bunch" or a "collection"? This involves determining the basis for differentiating between the bad nigger and that which is simply a nigger. Doing that means a philological digression.

Niggerdom

According to the *Oxford English Dictionary*, *nigger* belongs to the French *negre*, which, like its Spanish cognate, *negro*, was used in early modern time to designate black people. It appears to have come into English through the Dutch, sometime in the sixteenth century, and by the seventeenth century, it appeared in variant forms: *neeger, neager, negar, negre*. In its earliest known literary reference of 1587, it is already associated with slavery: "There were also in her 400 neegers, whome they had taken to make slaves."[13] By the time it reaches the Virginia colony, it simply designates black people as slave-labor, as in Captain John Smith's 1624 observation: "A Dutch man of warre that sold us twenty Negars."[14] The Latinate, *niger*, was used by Hellowes in 1574: "The Massgets bordering upon the Indians, and the Nigers of Aethiop, bearing witnes"; and by Reginald Scot in 1584 in the precise sense of black-of-color: "A skin like a Niger."[15] By the time Samuel Sewall began writing his *Diary*, the appellation also referred to slave-labor as property: "Jethro, his Niger, was then taken" (1 July 1676); "Met a Niger Funeral" (20 October 1712).[16] In 1760, G. Wallace argued "Set the Nigers free, and, in a few generations, this vast and fertile continent would be crouded with inhabitants."[17] Robert Burns added the second g to the Latinate in 1786: "How graceless Ham leugh at his Dad, Which made Canaan a nigger."[18] Hence, *niggerdom* as the designation of black people in general, whose despised status Henry Fearon (1818) thought was deserved—"The bad conduct and inferior nature of niggars (negroes),"[19]—and William Faux (1823) lamented—"Contempt of the poor black or nigger, as they are called, seems the national sin of America."[20]

Of particular importance in this regard is the belonging-togetherness of the categories *nigger* and *work*, an association articulated in the American English expression "to work like a nigger," as in George Eliot's incidental remarking in 1861: "Charles ... will ... work like a nigger at his music";[21] or Twain's more renowned "He laid into his work like a nigger."[22] *Nigger* could mean exceptionally hard work, because niggers, by definition, are labor commodities (i.e., nigger is an index of productive labor that is somebody else's property). A nigger is both productive labor and value, a quantitative abstraction of exchange: the equivalent of three-fifths of a single unit of representational value. The value of the nigger is not in the physical body itself but in the energy, the potential force, that the body contains. That force is there in the nigger body, standing-in-reserve, as it were, for its owner to consume as he/she likes. That force is the thing that the planter owns. It is the property of the planter that is the nigger. The nigger is that thing.

Understanding the thingness of the nigger in the context of knowing a bad nigger from that which is simply a nigger leads to consideration of the relationship between things and humans, which is a question of commodification. Fearon's identification of *nigger* and *negro* leads to such a consideration. In spite of the casualness of his identification, such has not always been obvious. Whereas *neger* comes into English through Dutch already associated with the commodification of black peoples' labor, and hence is far more a substantive, *negro*, and its variant, *negroe*, first occur in the literary record as anglicizations of the Spanish and Portuguese descriptive adjective, *negro*. In 1555, Richard Eden, translating Pedro Martir de Angleria's *Decadas del Nuevo Mundo*, writes, "They are not accustomed to eate such meates as doo the Ethiopians or Negros."[23] And, in 1580, Frampton states that in "all Ginea the blacke people called Negros doe use for money ... certayne little snayles." The confusion of *negro* with *niger* is already noticeable, however, in Sewall's *Diary*, when after regularly referring to "Nigers," he claims to have "essay'd ... to prevent Indians and Negros being Rated with Horses and Hogs" (22 June 1716). Given Sewall's effort to disabuse the colonists of the notion that black-labor was their property, his employment of "Negro" as a substantive synonymous with "Niger" can be understood as his attempt to define "Negros" as humans, hence his capitalization of the terms. Be that as it may, *negro* was generally employed in the lower-case as a descriptive adjective of color until the twentieth century, when Booker T. Washington, among others, began to agitate for its capitalization as a positive racial designation, preferred over *colored*. Accordingly, *negro* or *Negro* was utilized to designate a human identity, in opposition to *nigger*, which designated a commodity-thing. The widespread use of the appellation *nigger* among antebellum slaves as an approbatory term of affiliation can be taken as an ironic "misnaming." It is a paralipsis that reveals the historical order of appellation, turning the nigger-thing back into the black (negro) human who forms community bonds.

Now, if a negro is a black human, and a nigger is a thing or a human-become-thing, what is a bad nigger? John Little, a fugitive slave living in Canada, wrote in 1856 that "a 'bad nigger' is the negro who is put in the stocks or put in irons.... 'Boy, what have you got that on you for? That shows a damned bad nigger ... if you weren't a bad nigger you wouldn't have them on.' "[24] Little draws attention to the double entendre of *bad nigger* in the antebellum South. In the view of the white planters, *bad nigger* designated an obstreperous, dangerous nigger, who threatened the order of the plantation by refusing to submit to its laws. For the slaves, *bad nigger* indicated an individual who, in challenging the laws of slavery, refused to be a nigger-thing.

A bad nigger, then, is an oxymoron: rebellious property. In rebellion, the bad nigger exhibits an autonomous will, which a nigger as commodity-thing is not allowed to exhibit. There is little more dangerous than a willful thing; through the exhibition of autonomous will, the bad nigger marks the limits of the law of allowance by transgressing it. The bad nigger frightens both white planter and other slaves because he/she reveals the impossibility of completely subjugating will; it can only be eliminated in death, and the bad nigger, by defin-ition, does not fear death. The bad nigger embraces death, and in that embrace steps beyond standing-in-reserve, beyond thingness. This frightens the planter, not only because the force that he understood to be his property is being withheld but because it is withheld through an unknowable agency, through the will of another, an unbridled, lawless force. The bad nigger indicates individual sovereignty, which is to say he is self-possessed.

What is at stake here is not the obvious problem of the bad nigger embodying the Enlight-enment subject (i.e., exhibiting the characteristics of the autonomous subject who is the cornerstone of both civil society and the state). The real threat of the bad nigger is in exhibiting the groundlessness of the sovereign individual. Being a nigger appearing as a human, the bad nigger indicates the identification of human with thing, that the human can only be among things, cannot be beyond or abstracted from things. The bad nigger is the human-cum-thing. Little noted this when he remarked that "the man who was a 'bad nigger' in the South is here [in Canada] a respected, independent farmer."[25] Another instance of paralipsis, Little's conversion of bad nigger into respected independent farmer reveals the contrariness of liberal civil society. The bad nigger indexes a radical incommensurability, on the one hand exhibiting the individual sovereignty that forms the basis of moral order in liberal theories of political economy; on the other, embodying the lawlessness that morality is supposed to contain. We should not fail to note that Little's bad nigger starts out "the negro who is put in the stocks or put in irons," marking once again the ironic movement from nigger to negro. That which is called simply nigger is essentially the black human. The difference between the bad nigger and the simple nigger, then, is that the former indexes the open-ended possibilities of being among things—lawlessness; and the latter, converted into the negro, is the basis for community identity and collective resistance against continued dehumanization under capitalism—a community of moral beings. The bad nigger, by definition, is that human-cum-thing that is not subject to work. This thingness of the human puts into jeopardy community, when the latter is understood as being based on the communicability of senti-ments or feelings.

Das Nigga Affekt

Although we have a keener sense of what a bad nigger is in relation to a simple nigger, that under-standing has only enabled a beginning or preliminary exploration of the possibilities of nigga authenticity. Very schematically, we can say that in regressive thought, the nigga is conflated with the bad nigger as *homo criminalis*, constituting a threat to the survival of the commu-nity by giving the police cause to attack. But what is the relationship between the police and this community? To summarize what we have discovered thus far about the latter, it is a community of moral beings, grounded in values that transcend the domain of things. In community, through moral-based knowledge, the nigger-thing becomes the negro-subject. The police, as agents of the state, work to maintain the order of things, to enforce the laws of property. In other words, the function of the police, as officers of the courts, is to turn the negro back into a nigger. In the legal system, one is a nigger-thing; only in the community is one a human-subject. Because the moral order enables this negro-subject—*homo Africanus Americanus moralis*—it must be preserved at all times and cost. The state-authorized armed regulatory force of the police must be kept out. This is achieved through the community's governing itself. In this perspective, it is society, not just police in the narrow sense of the authorized armed regulatory force, but police in the broader sense of governmentality, that the nigga threatens to undermine.

In terms of governmentality, hard-core nigga gangster rap is an index of a general crisis of morality in the black community. Spencer recognizes this moral crisis as issuing from a collapse in the overall social fabric, resulting in the dissolution of the family. The broader social crisis results, in turn, from an inability to distinguish any longer the domain of economy from those of culture and politics. The result is the end of morality as the basis for identity beyond commodification. Another way of putting things is that the identification of society as economy has led to the displacement of the negro-subject with the nigger-thing from *within* the community. Although the crisis Spencer refers to as the emergency of black initially resulted from the emergence of an unbridled transnational capitalism, he understands its principal agent to be hard-core rap itself. More precisely, Spencer understands the hyper-commodification of the hard-core nigga to be a chief component in the demise of black people.

In response, the badman hard-core political rapper is called for in social defense, which we should not forget was the slogan of the penal theory put forward by Franz von Liszt ("Die Aufgaben und die Method der Strafrechtswissenschaft") and the social school of law. In that theory, social defense involves intimidation, in the instance of occasional delinquents, and neutralization, in the case of hardened criminals. Between these two extremes are the various modes of preventive intervention collectively called "social hygiene" in the International Union of Penal Law. The aim of social hygiene is to eradicate the social conditions that breed the criminal, or, as it were, the nigga. The police, then, is the order of governmentality called community—that is, the disciplinary practices that construct society as an economy of well-managed individuals. What does it mean, though, when community is identified with moral police? Here, it means that any nigger who doesn't obey the law and take moral responsibility for his actions is a bad nigger.

It is a grave error, however, to identify the bad nigger with the hard-core gangster rapper, because regressive thought cannot comprehend the hard-core nigga. When the Original Gangster, Ice-T, exclaims, "I'm a straight up nigga," he is reiterating the difference between a nigga being and being a nigga.[26] Knowing that difference requires an understanding of what is the nature of experience in a global economy. When the OG further points out how the process of consuming rap is tantamount to the "niggafication" of white suburban youth, he is doing more than remarking on the inevitability of popular culture's dissemination; he is also remarking on the equally inevitable loss of experience to commodified affect.[27] This is the age of hypercommodification, in which experience has not become commodified, it is commodification, and *nigga* designates the scene, par excellence, of commodification, where one is among commodities. Nigga is a commodity affect. The OG offers exhibition of this, on the one hand, reminding us that his rhymes come from "experience," and, on the other hand, claiming that virtually everyone involved in the commodified affect of his experience is a nigga:

> I'm a nigga, not a colored man,
> or a black, or a Negro.
> or an Afro American, I'm all that.
> Yes! I was born in America true,
> does South Central
> look like America to you?

> I'm a nigga, a straight up nigga
> from a hard school. ...
> I'm a nigga in America,
> and that much I flaunt,
> cause when I see what I like,
> yo I take what I want.
> I'm not the only one,
> That's why I'm not bitter,
> cause everybody is a nigga to a nigga.[28]

The nigga is constituted in the exchange of experience for affect. This is not identical with the bad nigger who jeopardized community by insisting on having unmediated free experience. Such an insistence requires an essential innocence of identity, a way of understanding experience that is simply impossible right now. A nigga forgets feelings, recognizing, instead, that affects are communicable, particularly the hard-core ones of anger, rage, intense pleasure. One can belong with millions of others in an asynchronic moment of consumption of the same affect, the same passion. This is not empathy. The possibility of the nigga rests on the twofold of experience and affect, and the fact that experience is essentially unfungible; it cannot be sold as is but must be abstracted and processed by the formulaic functions of transnational capitalism. Knowing this, the hard-core gangster rapper traffics in affect and not values. In this sense, hard-core rap is the residual of the nonproductive work of translating experience into affect—it is pulp fiction, drawing into its web all the real nigga experiences it can represent in the affective constitution of niggaz.

The status as being at once both rooted in experience and available for appropriation marks nigga as the function by which diverse quotidian experiences and expressions are "authenticated" as viable resistance to the dominant forms of power. Nigga realizes that the end of political economy involves a shift in the technologies of government, and not a general problem of government. A crucial aspect of hard-core rap is how it strives to expose and problematize the technologies of government by constantly becoming an expression of overflowing energy that is pregnant with future. This is why, at those moments in which rap's appropriation by the transnational economy appears to signal its comprehension and diluting, hard core is reclaimed as the source (i.e., KRS-1, Run-DMC, Naughty by Nature). When Public Enemy released "Don't Believe the Hype" in 1989, they were marking how popular culture is itself a technology of government. That is to say, designating the contradiction (other/appropriate) that is constitutive of popular culture, *nigga* defines *authenticity* as adaptation to the force of commodification. Rap becomes an authentic African American cultural form against its appropriation as transnational popular culture.

Authenticity, then, is produced as the value everybody wants precisely because of the displacement of political economy with economy; it is not engendered by virtue of its relation to that which has to be protected from commodification so that African Americans might know themselves as a collective identity against a particular social, political, and historical threatening reality. Authenticity is hype, a hypercommodified affect, whose circulation has made hip-hop global—which is why the immanent critique of rap fails. This is not to suggest that rap is no longer African American but rather that one condition of being African American is participating in the consumption of rap. Put differently, hard-core rap, in its formal and rhetorical strategies, is akin to the blues as understood by Ralph Ellison: an oppositional cultural movement that is thoroughly symbolic in the face of political domination. But, whereas the blues is a collective response to political domination, the hegemony rap contends with is of another order, the global hypercommodification of cultural production, in which the relation of cultural object to group being no longer matters politically. Nigga is not an essential identity, strategic or otherwise, but rather indicates the historicity of indeterminate identity.

With regard to understanding nigga authenticity, then, the question is not what is nigga authenticity but whether or not nigga can be either authentically or inauthentically. Understanding whether nigga can be either authentically or inauthentically is an existential task. In other words, nigga poses an existential problem that concerns what it means (or how it is possible) to-be-human. In contrast, the badman and bad nigger pose a moral problem that concerns the structures and relations of humans—their governability. There is a familiar cast to this formulation of authenticity. Hard-core's nigga returns us to the existentialist preoccupation with the difference between the subject of knowledge and the subject of experience. In these terms, the question of nigga authenticity is an ontological question about the a priori features of human being, and the structures it is concerned with have to do with the habits of thought by which certain *types* of consciousness are possible. The moral-political question is concerned with particular acts, decisions, or modes of behavior—it is an ontical question.

In the reading of nigga as an index of black emergency, it is presupposed that authentic being derives from morality. That is, the nigger becomes the negro through moral behavior, or good works, founded on morality as a governmental habit of thought (police as internalized control). At the root of the despair about the demise of black morality is the recognition that ontical matters are made possible by the habits of thought of human being. With this recognition, we understand that it is an error to think that being negro existentially (i.e., being a black human) results from a particular set of morally determined social decisions and acts. To think in this way is to turn away from the question of what it means to-be-human, precisely because it refuses to take care of the question of how a person really is. Moral behavior, by definition, is an ontologically inauthentic way to be. Still, in understanding the hard-core nigga to be amoral, even this way of thinking recognizes in the nigga an emergent habit of thought at the end of black morality. As such, the question of nigga authenticity is not a moral question but is about the very possibility of being human: it is a strictly existential matter. In wanting to understand what it is to be a real nigga, it is crucial to remember that humans are the entities to be analyzed. To be nigga is ontologically authentic, because it takes care of the question of how a human really is among things. Niggadom, then, is a new dogmatics—that is, an attempt to formulate an ontology of the higher thinking called "hip-hop science."[29]

Notes

1. Leon R. Harris, "The Steel-Drivin' Man," *The Messenger* 7 (1925): 386–87, 402.
2. Chester Himes, "Black on Black," in *Black on Black, Baby Sister, and Selected Writings of Chester Himes* (Garden City, N.Y.: Doubleday, 1973), 139.
3. Paulette Cross, *The Folklore Forum* 2, no. 6 (Nov. 1969): 140–61.
4. Joe Wood, "Niggers, Negroes, Blacks, Niggaz, and Africans," *Village Voice* (17 Sept. 1991), 28–29.
5. With three notable exceptions, by and large, the thirteen significant books on rap published in the past ten years have focused on its genealogy. There is a preoccupation with pointing out rap's "authentic origins" in antecedent African American forms of expression. David Topp's *Rap Attack: African Jive to New York Hip Hop* (Boston: South End, 1984) leads the way as an example of popular ethnography. In this same category is Havelock Nelson and Michael A. Gonzales's *Bring the Noise: A Guide to Rap Music and Hip-Hop Culture* (New York: Harmony, 1991). Six of the books are journalistic, and more than a little impressionistic, exposés: see Nelson George et al., *Fresh Hip-Hop Don't Stop* (New York: Random House, 1985), Nelson George, *Buppies, B-Boys, Baps and Bohos* (New York: HarperCollins, 1992), Steven Hager, *Hip Hop: The Illustrated History of Break Dancing, Rap Music, and Graffiti* (New York: St. Martin's Press, 1984), Keith Elliot, *Rap* (Minneapolis: Lerner Publications, 1987), Mark Costello and David Wallace, *Signifying Rappers: Rap and Race in the Urban Present* (New York: Ecco Press, 1990), and William Hauck Watkins, *All You Need to Know about Rappin'* (Chicago: Contemporary Books, 1984). Houston Baker's *Black Studies, Rap, and Academy* (Chicago: University of Chicago Press, 1993) is a meditation on rap's significance for academics, and Bill Adler's *Tougher than Leather: The Authorized Biography of Run-DMC* (New York: New Amsterdam Library, 1987) is a group biography. Of the exceptions mentioned earlier,

two of them—Tricia Rose's *Black Noise: Rap Music and Black Cultural Resistance in Contemporary American Popular Culture* (Middletown, Conn.: Wesleyan University Press, 1994), and Joseph D. Eure and James G. Spady's *Nation Conscious Rap* (New York: PC International, 1991)—are attempts to elaborate on rap in the context of what might be termed the political economy of hip-hop. The third exception— Greg Tate's *Flyboy in the Buttermilk* (New York: Simon and Schuster, 1992)—is an exhibition of hip-hop aesthetic critique. As for journal and newspaper articles, the contributions of Greg Tate to *Village Voice*, and of Jon Pareles to the *New York Times* have been prodigious. Finally, Jon Michael Spencer's academic journal, *Black Sacred Music: A Journal of Theomusicology*, became a forum for scholarship on rap, in vol. 5, no. 1 (Spring 1991), a special issue, entitled *The Emergency of Black and the Emergence of Rap*.

The dominant tendency is to categorize rap into periods of development, with each successive period characterized by rap's greater, more diversified circulation. The model for this periodization has been David Topp's *Rap Attack: African Jive to New York Hip Hop*, whose paramount concern was with establishing rap's "rootedness" in African American forms of cultural expression. Following Topp's model, Ronald Jemal Stephens delineates three definitive periods of rap. The first period, dating from roughly 1973 to 1985, Stephens calls the "boogie woogie hip-hop wave," the hallmark of which are the Sugarhill Gang's 1979 "Rapper's Delight," and the 1982 release of Grandmaster Flash and the Furious Five's "The Message" ("Nation of Islam Ideology in the Rap of Public Enemy," in *Black Sacred Music*). Michael Eric Dyson calls this same period "message rap" ("The Three Waves of Contemporary Rap Music," in *Black Sacred Music*). The second period, the rock 'n' roll hip-hop wave (which Dyson calls "pop rap") is marked by the success of Run-DMC's "King of Rock," Tone Loc's "Wild Thing," as well as that of LL Cool J. The third period Stephens calls the "hard-core hip-hop wave." In spite of some differences of the defining moments of rap's development—for example, Dyson identifies periods solely on the basis of lyrical themes, while Stephens follows changing economies of circulation as well as lyrical content—the tertiary periodization of rap appears to be the dominant analytical model.

6. Spencer, *The Emergency of Black*, 2.
7. Writing for the *New York Times* in 1990, Jon Pareles identifies hard-core "gangster rap" as a style initiated by KRS-1 but commonly associated with the Los Angeles rappers Ice-T, Ice Cube, and NWA, and the Houston-based Geto Boys. He delineates its definitive features as rapid-fire style of delivery and "terrifying" lyrical thematics. Among the latter are: "scenes of inner-city violence, sometimes as cautionary tales, sometimes as fantasies and sometimes as chronicles without comment; detailed put-downs (with threats of violence) of anyone the rappers dislike; at least a song or two per album about sexual exploits; belligerent foul-mouthed personas … the bad guys from innumerable police shows [who,] armed and desperate, [tell] the story the way they see it; the denouncing of ghetto violence as genocidal and aimed at black youth [Pareles calls this the political theme]; the connection of crime and drugs to poverty or [poverty-induced] insanity; machismo, or the translation from boyhood to manhood through combat or sexual exploits; and a reflexive, unquestioning homophobia and a sexism that easily slides into misogyny, as general sensation turns back onto the closest targets" (Jon Pareles, "Gangster Rap: Life and Music in the Combat Zone," *New York Times*, 7 Oct. 1990). Pareles further characterizes gangster rap as being formally hybrid, a jumble of "brilliance and stupidity, of vivid story telling and unexamined consciousness … mock-documentaries, political lessons, irony, and self promotion." The focus of Pareles's article is on the Geto Boys, whose first major release of 1989 was released by the Rap-a-Lot label but rejected by the record pressing plant and withdrawn from circulation by its distributor, Geffen Records. Pareles reviews the remix re-release of the tracts of this album. These remixes appeared on a second release by the Geto Boys, entitled *The Geto Boys*, without a distributor's name and with a disclaimer by Def American Recordings, stating that its manufacturer and distributor "do not condone or endorse the content of this recording, which they find violent, sexist, racist, and indecent." *The Geto Boys* is most definitely all of this, graphically describing murder, rape, and mutilation. However, the leap in Pareles's logic is that of example: in other words, holding that a definite and specific instantiation of a discourse is generalized by analogy. The Geto Boys becomes the synecdoche of a loosely knit collection of rappers: Ice Cube, NWA, CPO, Kool G Rap, DJ Polo, and Audio Two, all of whom become categorized as gangster rappers.
8. Spencer, *The Emergency of Black*, 1–13.
9. Spencer, *The Emergency of Black*, 8.
10. Eugene Genovese draws heavily from Brearely's elaborations, emphasizing the nihilistic aspect of the "baad nigger" and associates him with the badman of folklore. See *Roll Jordan Roll: The World the Slaves Made* (New York: Vintage, 1972), 436–37, 625–29.
11. John W. Roberts, *From Trickster to Badman: The Black Folk Hero in Slavery and Freedom* (Philadelphia: University of Pennsylvania Press, 1989), 171–219.
12. W.E.B. Du Bois, *The Souls of Black Folk* (1902; reprint, New York: Fawcett, 1961), 31, 131; *Black Reconstruction in America, 1860–1880* (1935; reprint, New York: Atheneum, 1962).
13. *Oxford English Dictionary*, compact ed., 1982.

14. Captain John Smith, *A True Relation of Virginia* (1608; reprint, Boston: Wiggin and Lunt, 1866).

15. Reginald Scot, *Discoverie of Witchcraft* (1584; reprint, Totowa, N.J.: Rowman and Littlefield, 1973), 122.

16. Samuel Sewall, *Diary of Samuel Sewall, 1674–1729*, ed. M. Halsey Thomas (New York: Farrar, Straus and Giroux, 1973).

17. *Oxford English Dictionary*, compact ed., 1982.

18. Robert Burns, "Ordination," in *The Complete Works of Robert Burns* (New York: Houghton, Mifflin and Company, 1987).

19. Henry Bradshaw Fearon, *Sketches of America; a Narrative of a Journey of Five Thousand Miles Through the Eastern and Western States of America; Contained in Eight Reports Addressed to the Thirty-nine English Families by Whom the Author Was Deputed, in June 1817, to Ascertain Whether Any and What Parts of the United States Would be Suitable for Their Residence. With Remarks on Mr. Birkbeck's "Notes" and "Letters"* (London: Longman, Hurst, Rees, Orme, and Brown, 1818), 46.

20. William Faux, *Memorable Days in America: Being a Journal of a Tour to the United States, Principally Undertaken to Ascèrtain, by Positive Evidence, the Condition and Prospects of British Emigrants; Including Account of Mr. Birkbridge's Settlement in Illinois* (London: W. Simpkin and R. Marshall, 1823), 9.

21. George Eliot, Letter dated 13 Apr. 1861, in *The Yale Edition of the George Eliot Letters*, 9 vols. (New Haven: Yale University Press, 1975), 3:404.

22. Mark Twain, *A Tramp Aboard* (Hartford, Conn.: American Publishing Company, 1879), 40.

23. Pedro Martir de Angleria, *Decades of the Newe Worlde or West India*, trans. Richard Eden (Londini: In aedibus Guilhelmi Powell, 1555), 239.

24. Benjamin Drew, *A North-Side View of Slavery. The Refugee: or the Narratives of Fugitive Slaves in Canada. Related by Themselves, with An Account of the History and Condition of the Colored Population of Upper Canada* (1856; reprint, New York: Negro Universities Press, 1968), 203, 219–20.

25. Drew, *A North-Side View of Slavery*, 219–20.

26. Ice-T, "Straight up Nigga," *Original Gangster* (New York: Sire Records), 1991.

27. Ice-T, *The Ice-Opinion: Who Gives a Fuck*, ed. Hedi Siegmund (New York: St. Martin's Press, 1994), 144–45.

28. Ice-T, "Straight up Nigga," *Original Gangster*.

29. Of course, in pursuing such a science, we are well advised to recall Dilthey's qualification: "All dogmas need to be translated so as to bring out their universal validity for all human life. They are cramped by their connection with the situation of the past in which they arose" (Graf Paul Yorck to W. Dilthey, in Rudolph Bultmann, "New Testament Mythology" in *Kerygma and Myth*, ed. Hans-Werner Bartsch, trans. Reginald H. Fuller [London: SPCK, 1960], 23).

12

Looking for the "Real" Nigga:
Social Scientists Construct the Ghetto

Robin D.G. Kelley

Perhaps the supreme irony of black American existence is how broadly black people debate the question of cultural identity among themselves while getting branded as a cultural monolith by those who would deny us the complexity and complexion of a community, let alone a nation. If Afro-Americans have never settled for the racist reductions imposed upon them—from chattel slaves to cinematic stereotype to sociological myth—it's because the black collective conscious not only knew better but also knew more than enough ethnic diversity to subsume these fictions.

Greg Tate, *Flyboy in the Buttermilk*

The biggest difference between us and white folks is that we know when we are playing.

Alberta Roberts, quoted in John Langston Gwaltney, *Drylongso*

"I think this anthropology is just another way to call me a nigger." So observed Othman Sullivan, one of many informants in John Langston Gwaltney's classic study of black culture, *Drylongso*.[1] Perhaps a kinder, gentler way to put it is that anthropology, not unlike most urban social science, has played a key role in marking "blackness" and defining black culture to the "outside" world. Beginning with Robert Park and his protégés to the War on Poverty inspired ethnographers, a battery of social scientists have significantly shaped the current dialogue on black urban culture. Today sociologists, anthropologists, political scientists, and economists compete for huge grants from Ford, Rockefeller, Sage, and other foundations to measure everything measurable in order to get a handle on the newest internal threat to civilization. With the discovery of the so-called underclass, terms like *nihilistic, dysfunctional,* and *pathological* have become the most common adjectives to describe contemporary black urban culture. The question they often pose, to use Mr. Othman Sullivan's words, is what kind of "niggers" populate the inner cities?

Unfortunately, too much of this rapidly expanding literature on the underclass provides less an understanding of the complexity of people's lives and cultures than a bad blaxploitation film or an Ernie Barnes painting. Many social scientists are not only quick to generalize about the black urban poor on the basis of a few "representative" examples, but more often than not, they do not let the natives speak. A major part of the problem is the way in which many mainstream social scientists studying the underclass define *culture*. Relying on a narrowly conceived definition of culture, most of the underclass literature uses *behavior* and *culture* interchangeably.

My purpose, then, is to offer some reflections on how the culture concept employed by social scientists has severely impoverished contemporary debates over the plight of urban African Americans and contributed to the construction of the ghetto as a reservoir of pathologies and bad cultural values. Much of this literature not only conflates behavior with culture, but when social scientists explore "expressive" cultural forms or what has been called "popular culture" (such as language, music, and style), most reduce it to expressions of pathology, compensatory behavior, or creative "coping mechanisms" to deal with racism and poverty. While some aspects of black expressive cultures certainly help inner city residents deal with and even resist ghetto conditions, most of the literature ignores what these cultural forms mean for the practitioners. Few scholars acknowledge that what might also be at stake here are aesthetics, style, and pleasure. Nor do they recognize black urban culture's hybridity and internal differences. Given the common belief that inner city communities are more isolated than ever before and have completely alien values, the notion that there is one discrete, identifiable black urban culture carries a great deal of weight. By conceiving black urban culture in the singular, interpreters unwittingly reduce their subjects to cardboard typologies who fit neatly into their own definition of the "underclass" and render invisible a wide array of complex cultural forms and practices.

"It's Just a Ghetto Thang": The Problem of Authenticity and the Ethnographic Imagination

A few years ago Mercer Sullivan decried the disappearance of "culture" from the study of urban poverty, attributing its demise to the fact that "overly vague notions of the culture of poverty brought disrepute to the culture concept as a tool for understanding the effects of the concentration of poverty among cultural minorities."[2] In some respects, Sullivan is right: the conservatives who maintain that persistent poverty in the inner city is the result of the behavior of the poor, the product of some cultural deficiency, have garnered so much opposition from many liberals and radicals that few scholars are willing even to discuss culture. Instead, opponents of the "culture of poverty" idea tend to focus on structural transformations in the U.S. economy, labor force composition, and resultant changes in marriage patterns to explain the underclass.[3]

However, when viewed from another perspective, culture never really disappeared from the underclass debate.[4] On the contrary, it has been as central to the work of liberal structuralists and radical Marxists as it has been to that of the conservative culturalists. While culturalists insist that the behavior of the urban poor explains their poverty, the structuralists argue that the economy explains their behavior as well as their poverty.[5] For all their differences, there is general agreement that a common, debased culture is what defines the "underclass," what makes it a threat to the future of America. Most interpreters of the "underclass" treat behavior as not only a synonym for culture but also as the determinant for class. In simple terms, what makes the "underclass" a class is members' common behavior—not their income, their poverty level, or the kind of work they do. It is a definition of class driven more by moral panic than by systematic analysis. A cursory look at the literature reveals that there is no consensus as to precisely what behaviors define the underclass. Some scholars, like William Julius Wilson, have offered a more spatial definition of the underclass by focusing on areas of "concentrated poverty," but obvious problems result when observers discover the wide range of behavior and attitudes in, say, a single city block. What happens to the concept when we find people with jobs engaging in illicit activities and some jobless people depending on church charity? Or married employed fathers who spend virtually no time with their kids and jobless unwed fathers participating and sharing in child care responsibilities? How does the concept of underclass behavior hold up to Kathryn Edin's findings that many so-called welfare-dependent women must also work for wages in order to make ends meet?[6] More importantly, how do we fit criminals (many first-time offenders), welfare recipients, single mothers, absent fathers, alcohol and drug abusers, and gun toting youth all into one "class"?

When we try to apply the same principles to people with higher incomes, who are presumed to be "functional" and "normative," we ultimately expose the absurdity of it all. Political scientist Charles Henry offers the following description of pathological behavior for the very folks the underclass is supposed to emulate. This tangle of deviant behavior, which he calls the "culture of wealth," is characterized by a "rejection or denial of physical attributes" leading to "hazardous sessions in tanning parlors" and frequent trips to weight-loss salons; rootlessness; antisocial behavior; and "an inability to make practical decisions" evidenced by their tendency to own several homes, frequent private social and dining clubs, and by their vast amount of unnecessary and socially useless possessions. "Finally," Henry adds, "the culture of the rich is engulfed in a web of crime, sexism, and poor health. Drug use and white collar crime are rampant, according to every available index.... In sum, this group is engaged in a permanent cycle of divorce, forced child separations through boarding schools, and rampant materialism that leads to the dreaded Monte Carlo syndrome. Before they can be helped they must close tax loopholes, end subsidies, and stop buying influence."[7]

As absurd as Henry's satirical reformulation of the culture of poverty might appear, this very instrumentalist way of understanding culture is deeply rooted even in the more liberal social science approaches to urban poverty. In the mid- to late 1960s, a group of progressive social scientists, mostly ethnographers, challenged the more conservative culture-of-poverty arguments and insisted that black culture was itself a necessary adaptation to racism and poverty, a set of coping mechanisms that grew out of the struggle for material and psychic survival.[8] Ironically, while this work consciously sought to recast ghetto dwellers as active agents rather than passive victims, it has nonetheless reinforced monolithic interpretations of black urban culture and significantly shaped current articulations of the culture concept in social science approaches to poverty.

With the zeal of colonial missionaries, these liberal and often radical ethnographers (mostly white men) set out to explore the newly discovered concrete jungles. Inspired by the politics of the 1960s and mandated by Lyndon Johnson's War on Poverty, a veritable army of anthropologists, sociologists, linguists, and social psychologists set up camp in America's ghettos. In the Harlem and Washington Heights communities where I grew up in the mid- to late 1960s, even our liberal white teachers who were committed to making us into functional members of society turned out to be foot soldiers in the new ethnographic army. With the overnight success of published collections of inner city children's writings like *The Me Nobody Knows* and Caroline Mirthes's *Can't You Hear Me Talking to You?*, writing about the intimate details of our home life seemed like our most important assignment.[9] (And we made the most of it by enriching our mundane narratives with stories from *Mod Squad*, *Hawaii Five-O*, and *Speed Racer*.)

Of course, I do not believe for a minute that most of our teachers gave us these kinds of exercises hoping to one day appear on the *Merv Griffin Show*. But, in retrospect at least, the explosion of interest in the inner city cannot be easily divorced from the marketplace. Although these social scientists came to mine what they believed was the "authentic Negro culture," there was real gold in them thar ghettos since white America's fascination with the pathological urban poor translated into massive book sales.

Unfortunately, most social scientists believed they knew what "authentic Negro culture" was before they entered the field. The "real Negroes" were the young jobless men hanging out on the corner passing the bottle, the brothers with the nastiest verbal repertoire, the pimps and hustlers, and the single mothers who raised streetwise kids who began cursing before they could walk. Of course, there were other characters, like the men and women who went to work every day in foundries, hospitals, nursing homes, private homes, police stations, sanitation departments, banks, garment factories, assembly plants, pawn shops, construction sites, loading docks, storefront churches, telephone companies, grocery and department stores, public transit, restaurants, welfare offices, recreation centers; or the street vendors, the cab drivers, the bus drivers, the ice cream truck drivers, the seamstresses, the numerologists and fortune tellers, the folks who protected or cleaned downtown buildings all night long. These are the kinds of people who lived in my neighborhood in West Harlem during the early 1970s, but they rarely found their way into the ethnographic text. And when they did show up, social scientists tended to reduce them to typologies—"lames," "strivers," "mainstreamers," "achievers," or "revolutionaries."[10]

Perhaps these urban dwellers were not as interesting, as the hard-core ghetto poor, or more likely, they stood at the margins of a perceived or invented "authentic" Negro society. A noteworthy exception is John Langston Gwaltney's remarkable book, *Drylongso: A Self-Portrait of Black America* (1981). Based on interviews conducted during the 1970s with black working-class residents in several Northeastern cities, *Drylongso* is one of the few works on urban African Americans by an African American anthropologist that appeared during the height of ghetto ethnography. Because Gwaltney is blind, he could not rely on the traditional methods of observation and interepretation. Instead—and this is the book's strength—he allowed his informants to speak for themselves about what *they* see and do. They interpret their own communities, African American culture, white society, racism, politics and the state, and the very discipline in which Gwaltney was trained—anthropology. What the book reveals is that the natives are aware that anthropologists are constructing them, and they saw in Gwaltney—who relied primarily on family and friends as informants—an opportunity to speak back. One, a woman he calls Elva Noble, said to him: "I'm not trying to tell you your job, but if you ever do write a book about us, then I hope you really do write about things the way they really are. I guess that depends on you to some extent but you know that there are more of us who are going to work every day than there are like the people who are git'n over."[11] While his definition of a "core black culture" may strike some as essentialist, it emphasizes diversity and tolerance for diversity. Gwaltney acknowledges the stylistic uniqueness of African American culture, yet he shows that the central facet of this core culture is the deep-rooted sense of community, common history, and collective recognition that there is indeed an African American culture and a "black" way of doing things. Regardless of the origins of a particular recipe, or the roots of a particular religion or Christian denomination, the cook and the congregation have no problem identifying these distinct practices and institutions as "black."

Few ghetto ethnographers have understood or developed Gwaltney's insights into African American urban culture. Whereas Gwaltney's notion of a core culture incorporates a diverse and contradictory range of practices, attitudes, and relationships that are dynamic, historically situated, and ethnically hybrid, social scientists of his generation and after—especially those at the forefront of poverty studies—treat culture as if it were a set of behaviors. They assume that there is one identifiable ghetto culture, and what they observed was it. These assumptions, which continue to shape much current social science and most mass media representations of the "inner city," can be partly attributed to the way ethnographers are trained in the West. As James Clifford observed, anthropologists studying non-Western societies are not only compelled to describe the communities under interrogation as completely foreign to their own society, but if a community is to be worthy of study as a group it must possess an identifiable, homogeneous culture. I think, in principle at least, the same holds true for interpretations of black urban America. Ethnographers can argue that inner city residents, as a "foreign" culture, do not share "mainstream" values. Social scientists do not treat behavior as situational, an individual response to a specific set of circumstances; rather, inner city residents act according to their own unique cultural "norms."[12]

For many of these ethnographers, the defining characteristic of African American urban culture was relations between men and women. Even Charles Keil, whose *Urban Blues* is one of the few ethnographic texts from that period to not only examine aesthetics and form in black culture but take "strong exception to the view that lower-class Negro life style and its characteristic rituals and expressive roles are the products of overcompensation for masculine self-doubt," nonetheless concludes that "the battle of the sexes" is precisely what characterizes African American urban culture.[13] Expressive cultures, then, were not only constructed as adaptive, functioning primarily to cope with the horrible conditions of ghetto life, but were conceived largely as expressions of masculinity. In fact, the linking of men with expressive cultures was so pervasive that the pioneering ethnographies focusing on African American women and girls—notably the work of Joyce Ladner and Carol Stack—do not explore this realm, whether in mixed-gender groupings or all-female groups. They concentrated more on sex roles, relationships, and family survival rather than expressive cultures.[14]

Two illuminating examples are the debate over the concept of "soul" and the verbal art form known to most academics as "the dozens." In the ethnographic imagination, "soul" and "the dozens" were both examples par excellence of authentic black urban culture as well as vehicles for expressing black masculinity. The bias toward expressive male culture must be understood within a particular historical and political context. In the midst of urban rebellions, the masculinist rhetoric of black nationalism, the controversy over the Moynihan report, and the uncritical linking of "agency" and resistance with men, black men took center stage in poverty research.[15]

Soul was so critical to the social science discourse on the adaptive culture of the black urban poor that Lee Rainwater edited an entire book about it, and Ulf Hannerz structured his study of Washington, D.C., on it.[16] According to these authors, *soul* is the expressive lifestyle of black men adapting to economic and political marginality. This one word supposedly embraces the entire range of "Negro lower class culture"; it constitutes "essential Negroness." Only authentic Negroes had soul. In defining *soul*, Hannerz reduces aesthetics, style, and the dynamic struggle over identity to a set of coping mechanisms. Among his many attempts to define *soul*, he insists that it is tied to the instability of black male-female relationships. He deduced evidence for this from his findings that "success with the opposite sex is a focal concern in lower-class Negro life," and the fact that a good deal of popular black music—soul music—was preoccupied with courting or losing a lover.[17]

Being "cool" is an indispensable component of soul; it is also regarded by these ethnographers as a peculiarly black expression of masculinity. Indeed, the entire discussion of cool centers entirely on black men. Cool as an aesthetic, as a style, as an art form expressed through language and the body, is simply not dealt with. Cool, not surprisingly, is merely another mechanism to cope with racism and poverty. According to Lee Rainwater and David Schulz, it is nothing more than a survival technique intended to "make yourself interesting and attractive to others so that you are better able to manipulate their behavior along lines that will provide some immediate gratification." To achieve cool simply entails learning to lie and putting up a front of competence and success. But like a lot of adaptive strategies, cool is self-limiting. While it helps young black males maintain an image of being "in control," according to David Schulz, it can also make "intimate relationships" more difficult to achieve.[18]

Hannerz reluctantly admits that no matter how hard he tried, none of the "authentic ghetto inhabitants" he had come across could define *soul*. He was certain that soul was "essentially

Negro," but concluded that it really could not be defined, for to do that would be to undermine its meaning: it is something one possesses, a ticket into the "in crowd." If you need a definition you do not know what it means. It's a black (male) thang; you'll never understand. But Hannerz obviously felt confident enough to venture his own definition, based on his understanding of African American culture, that *soul* was little more than a survival strategy to cope with the harsh realities of the ghetto. Moreover, he felt empowered to determine which black people had the right to claim the mantle of authenticity: when LeRoi Jones and Lerone Bennett offered their interpretation of soul, Hannerz rejected their definitions, in part because they were not, in his words, "authentic Negroes."[19]

By constructing the black urban world as a single culture whose function is merely to survive the ghetto, Rainwater, Hannerz, and most of their colleagues at the time ultimately collapsed a wide range of historically specific cultural practices and forms and searched for a (*the*) concept that could bring them all together. Such an interpretation of culture makes it impossible for Hannerz and others to see soul not as a thing but as a discourse through which African Americans, at a particular historical moment, claimed ownership of the symbols and practices of their own imagined community. This is why, even at the height of the Black Power movement, African American urban culture could be so fluid, hybrid, and multinational. In Harlem in the 1970s, Nehru suits were as popular and as "black" as dashikis, and martial arts films placed Bruce Lee among a pantheon of black heroes that included Walt Frazier and John Shaft. As debates over the black aesthetic raged, the concept of soul was an assertion that there are "black ways" of doing things, even if those ways are contested and the boundaries around what is "black" are fluid. How it manifests itself and how it shifts is less important than the fact that the boundaries exist in the first place. At the very least, *soul* was a euphemism or a creative way of identifying what many believed was a black aesthetic or black style, and it was a synonym for black itself or a way to talk about being black without reference to color, which is why people of other ethnic groups could have soul.

Soul in the 1960s and early 1970s was also about transformation. It was almost never conceived by African Americans as an innate, genetically derived feature of black life, for it represented a shedding of the old "Negro" ways and an embrace of "Black" power and pride. The most visible signifier of soul was undoubtedly the Afro. More than any other element of style, the Afro put the issue of hair squarely on the black political agenda, where it has been ever since. The current debates over hair and its relationship to political consciousness really have their roots in the Afro. Not surprisingly, social scientists at the time viewed the Afro through the limited lens of Black Power politics, urban uprising, and an overarching discourse of authenticity. And given their almost exclusive interest in young men, their perspective on the Afro was strongly influenced by the rhetoric and iconography of a movement that flouted black masculinity. Yet, once we look beyond the presumably male-occupied ghetto streets that dominated the ethnographic imagination at the time, the story of the Afro's origins and meaning complicated the link to soul culture.

First, the Afro powerfully demonstrates the degree to which soul was deeply implicated in the marketplace. What passed as "authentic" ghetto culture was as much a product of market forces and the commercial appropriation of urban styles as experience and individual creativity. And very few black urban residents/consumers viewed their own participation in the marketplace as undermining their own authenticity as bearers of black culture. Even before the Afro reached its height of popularity, the hair care industry stepped in and began producing a vast array of chemicals to make one's "natural" more natural. One could pick up Raveen Hair Sheen, Afro Sheen, Ultra Sheen, Head Start vitamin and mineral capsules, to name a few. The Clairol Corporation (whose CEO supported the Philadelphia Black Power Conference in 1967) did not hesitate to enter the "natural" business.[20] Listen to this Clairol ad published in *Essence Magazine* (November 1970):

No matter what they say ... Nature Can't Do It Alone! Nothing pretties up a face like a beautiful head of hair, but even hair that's born this beautiful needs a little help along the way.... A little brightening, a little heightening of color, a little extra sheen to liven up the look. And because that wonderful natural look is still the most wanted look ... the most fashionable, the most satisfying look you can have at any age ... anything you do must look natural, natural, natural. And this indeed is the art of Miss Clairol.

Depending on the particular style, the Afro could require almost as much maintenance as chemically straightened hair. And for those women (and some men) whose hair simply would not cooperate or who wanted the flexibility to shift from straight to nappy, there was always the Afro wig. For nine or ten dollars, one could purchase a variety of different wig styles, ranging from the "Soul-Light Freedom" wigs to the "Honey Bee Afro Shag," made from cleverly labeled synthetic materials such as "Afrylic" or "Afrilon."[21] Second, the Afro's roots really go back to the bourgeois high fashion circles in the late 1950s. The Afro was seen by the black and white elite as a kind of new female exotica. Even though its intention, among some circles at least, was to achieve healthier hair and express solidarity with newly independent African nations, the Afro entered public consciousness as a mod fashion statement that was not only palatable to bourgeois whites but, in some circles, celebrated. There were people like Lois Liberty Jones, a consultant, beauty culturist, and lecturer, who claimed to have pioneered the natural as early as 1952! She originated "Coiffures Aframericana" concepts of hair styling which she practiced in Harlem for several years from the early 1960s.[22] More importantly, it was the early, not the late, 1960s, when performers like Odetta, Miriam Makeba, Abby Lincoln, Nina Simone, and the artist Margaret Burroughs began wearing the "au naturelle" style—medium to short Afros. Writer Andrea Benton Rushing has vivid memories of seeing Odetta at the Village Gate long before Black Power entered the national lexicon. "I was mesmerized by her stunning frame," she recalled, "in its short kinky halo. She had a regal poise and power that I had never seen in a 'Negro' (as we called ourselves back then) woman before—no matter how naturally 'good' or diligently straightened her hair was." Many other black women in New York, particularly those who ran in the interracial world of Manhattan sophisticates, were first introduced to the natural through high fashion models in au naturelle shows, which were the rage at the time.[23]

Helen Hayes King, associate editor of *Jet*, came in contact with the au naturelle style at an art show in New York, in the late 1950s. A couple of years later, she heard Abby Lincoln speak about her own decision to go natural at one of these shows and, with prompting from her husband, decided to go forth to adopt the 'fro. Ironically, one of the few salons in Chicago specializing in the au naturelle look was run by a white male hairdresser in the exclusive Northside community. He actually lectured King on the virtues of natural hair: "I don't know why Negro women with delicate hair like yours burn and process all the life out of it.... If you'd just wash it, oil it and take care of it, it would be so much healthier.... I don't know how all this straightening foolishness started anyhow." When she returned home to the Southside, however, instead of compliments she received strange looks from her neighbors. Despite criticism and ridicule by her co-workers and friends, she stuck with her au naturelle, not because she was trying to make a political statement or demonstrate her solidarity with African independence movements. "I'm not so involved in the neo-African aspects of the 'au naturelle' look," she wrote, "nor in the get-back-to-your-heritage bit." Her explanation was simple: the style was chic and elegant and in the end she was pleased with the feel of her hair. It is fitting to note that most of the compliments came from whites.[24]

What is also interesting about King's narrative is that it appeared in the context of a debate with Nigerian writer Theresa Ogunbiyi over whether black women should straighten their hair or not, which appeared in a 1963 issue of *Negro Digest*. In particular, Ogunbiyi defended the right of a Lagos firm to forbid employees to plait their hair; women were required to wear straight hair. She rejected the idea that straightening hair destroys national custom and heritage: "I think we carry this national pride a bit too far at times, even to the detriment of our country's progress." Her point was that breaking with tradition is progress, especially since Western dress and hairstyles are more comfortable and easier to work in. "When I wear the Yoruba costume, I find that I spend more time than I can afford, re-tying the headtie and the bulky wrapper round my waist. And have you tried typing in an 'Agbada'? I am all for nation-alisation but give it to me with some comfort and improvement."[25]

Andrea Benton Rushing's story is a slight variation on King's experience. She, too, was a premature natural hair advocate. When she stepped out of the house sporting her first Afro, perhaps inspired by Odetta or prompted by plain curiosity, her "relatives though I'd lost my mind and, of course, my teachers at Juilliard stole sideways looks at me and talked about the importance of appearance in auditions and concerts." Yet, while the white Juilliard faculty and her closest family members found the new style strange and inappropriate, brothers on the block in her New York City neighborhood greeted her with praise: " 'Looking good, sister,' 'Watch out, African queen!' " She, too, found it ironic that middle-class African woman on the continent chose to straighten their hair. During a trip to Ghana years later, she recalled the irony of having her Afro braided in an Accra beauty parlor while "three Ghanaians (two Akan-speaking government workers and one Ewe microbiologist) ... were having their chemically-straightened hair washed, set, combed out, and sprayed in place."[26]

No matter what spurred on the style or who adopted it, however, the political implications of the au naturelle could not be avoided. After all, the biggest early proponents of the style tended to be women artists whose work identified with the black freedom movement and African liberation. In some respects, women such as Abby Lincoln, Odetta, and Nina Simone were part of what might be called black bohemia. They participated in a larger community—based mostly in New York—of poets, writers, musicians of the 1950s, for whom the emancipation of their own artistic form coincided with the African freedom movement. *Ebony, Jet,* and *Sepia* magazines were covering Africa, and African publications such as *Drum* were being read by those ex-Negroes in the States who could get their hands on it. The Civil Rights movement, the struggle against apartheid in South Africa, and the emergence of newly independent African nations found a voice in recordings by various jazz artists, including Randy Weston's *Uhuru Afrika*, Max Roach's *We Insist: Freedom Now Suite* (featuring Abby Lincoln, Roach's wife), Art Blakey's "Message from Kenya" and "Ritual," and John Coltrane's "Liberia," "Dahomey Dance," and "Africa." Revolutionary political movements, combined with revolutionary experiments in artistic creation—the simultaneous embrace and rejection of tradition—forged the strongest physical and imaginary links between Africa and the diaspora.[27] Thus, it is not surprising that Harold Cruse, in one of his seminal essays on the coming of the new black nationalism, anticipated the importance of the style revolution and the place of the au naturelle in it. As early as 1962, Cruse predicted that in the coming years "Afro-Americans ... will undoubtedly make a lot of noise in militant demonstrations, cultivate beards and sport their hair in various degrees of la mode au natural, and tend to be cultish with African- and Arab-style dress."[28]

Of course, he was right. By the mid-1960s, however, the Afro was no longer associated with downtown chic but with uptown rebellion. It was sported by rock-throwing black males and black-leathered militants armed to the teeth. Thus, once associated with feminine chic, the Afro suddenly became the symbol of black manhood, the death of the "Negro" and birth of the militant, virulent Black man.[29] The new politics, combined with media representations of Afro-coifed black militants, profoundly shaped the ethnographic imagination. As new narratives were created to explain the symbolic significance of the natural style, women were rendered invisible. The erasure of women, I would argue, was not limited to histories of style politics but to ghetto ethnography in general.

The masculinism of soul in contemporary ghetto ethnography has survived to this day, despite the last quarter-century of incisive black feminist scholarship. The ethnographic and sociological search for soul has made a comeback recently under a new name: the "cool pose." In a recent book, Richard Majors and Janet Mancini Bilson have recycled the arguments of Lee Rainwater, Ulf Hannerz, Elliot Liebow, and David Schulz, and have suggested that the "cool pose" captures the essence of young black male expressive culture. Like earlier constructors of soul, they too believe that the "cool pose" is an adaptive strategy to cope with the particular forms of racism and oppression black males face in America. "Cool pose is a ritualized form of masculinity that entails behaviors, scripts, physical posturing, impression management, and carefully crafted performances that deliver a single, critical message: pride, strength, and control." Echoing earlier works, the cool pose is also a double-edged sword since it allegedly undermines potential intimacy with females.[30] By playing down the aesthetics of cool and reducing the cool pose to a response by heterosexual black males to racism, intraracial violence, and poverty, the authors not only reinforce the idea that there is an essential black urban culture created by the oppressive conditions of the ghetto but ignore manifestations of the cool pose in the public "performances" of black women, gay black men, and the African American middle class.

A more tangible example of black urban expressive culture that seemed to captivate social scientists in the 1960s is "the dozens." Yet, in spite of the amount of ink devoted to the subject, it has also been perhaps the most misinterpreted cultural form coming out of African American communities. Called at various times in various places "capping," "sounding," "ranking," "bagging," or "dissing," virtually all leading anthropologists, sociologists, and linguists agree that it is a black male form of "ritual insult," a verbal contest involving any number of young black men who compete by talking about each other's mama. There is less agreement, however, about how to interpret the sociological and psychological significance of the dozens. In keeping with the dominant social science interpretations of the culture concept, so-called ritual insults among urban black youth were either another adaptive strategy or an example of social pathology.

The amazing thing about the sociological and ethnographic scholarship on the dozens, from John Dollard's ruminations in 1939 to the more recent misreadings by Roger Lane and Carl Nightingale, is the consistency with which it repeats the same errors. For one, the almost universal assertion that the dozens is a "ritual" empowers the ethnographer to select what appears to be more formalized verbal exchanges (e.g., rhyming couplets) and ascribe to them greater "authenticity" than other forms of playful conversation. In fact, by framing the dozens as ritual, most scholars have come to believe that it is first and foremost a "contest" with rules, players, and mental scorecard rather than the daily banter of many (not all) young African Americans. Anyone who has lived and survived the dozens (or whatever name you want to call it) cannot imagine turning to one's friends and announcing, "Hey, let's go outside and play the dozens." Furthermore, the very use of the term *ritual* to describe everyday speech reinforces the exoticization of black urban populations constructing them as Others whose investment in this cultural tradition is much deeper than trying to get a laugh.[31]

These problems, however, are tied to larger ones. For example, white ethnographers seemed oblivious to the fact that their very presence shaped what they observed. Asking their subjects to "play the dozens" while an interloper records the "session" with a tape recorder and notepad has the effect of creating a ritual performance for the sake of an audience, of turning spontaneous, improvised verbal exchanges into a formal practice. More significantly, ethnographers have tailor-made their own interpretation of the dozens by selecting what they believe were the most authentic sites for such verbal duels—street corners, pool halls, bars, and parks. In other words, they sought out male spaces rather than predominantly female and mixed-gender spaces to record the dozens. It is no wonder that practically all commentators on the dozens have concluded that it is a boy thing. The fact is, evidence suggests that young women engaged in these kinds of verbal exchanges as much as their male counterparts, both with men and between women. And they were no less profane. By not searching out other mixed-gender and female spaces such as school buses, cafeterias, kitchen tables, beauty salons, and house parties, ethnographers have overstated the extent to which the dozens were the sole property of men.[32]

Folklorist Roger Abrahams, who pioneered the study of the dozens in his book on black vernacular folklore "from the streets of Philadelphia," is one of the few scholars to appreciate the pleasure and aesthetics of such verbal play. Nevertheless, he argues that one of the primary functions of the dozens is to compensate for a lack of masculinity caused by too many absent fathers and domineering mothers, which is why the main target of insults is an "opponent's" mother. "By exhibiting his wit, by creating new and vital folkloric expression, [the dozens player] is able to effect a temporary release from anxiety for both himself and his audience. By creating playgrounds for playing out aggressions, he achieves a kind of masculine identity for himself and his group in a basically hostile environment."[33] David Schulz offers an even more specific interpretation of the dozens as a form of masculine expression in an environment dominated by dysfunctional families. He writes: "Playing the dozens occurs at the point when the boy is about to enter puberty and suffer his greatest rejection from his mother as a result of his becoming a man. The dozens enables him to develop a defense against this rejection and provides a vehicle for his transition into the manipulative world of the street dominated by masculine values expressed in gang life." It then serves as a "ritualized exorcism" that allows men to break from maternal dominance and "establish their own image of male superiority celebrated in street life."[34]

Allow me to propose an alternative reading of the dozens. The goal of the dozens and related verbal games is deceptively simple: to get a laugh. The pleasure of the dozens is not the viciousness of the insult but the humor, the creative pun, the outrageous metaphor. Contrary to popular belief, mothers are not the sole target; the subjects include fathers, grandparents, brothers, sisters, cousins, friends, food, skin color, smell, and hairstyles. I am not suggesting that "your mama" is unimportant in the whole structure of these verbal exchanges. Nor am I suggesting that the emphasis on "your mama" has absolutely nothing to do with the ways in which patriarchy is discursively reproduced. However, we need to understand that "your mama" in this context is almost never living, literal, or even metaphoric. "Your mama" is a generic reference, a code signaling that the dozens have begun—it signifies a shift in speech. "Your mama" is also a mutable, nameless body of a shared imagination that can be constructed and reconstructed in a thousand different shapes, sizes, colors, and circumstances. The emphasis on "your mama" in most interpretations of the dozens has more to do with the peculiar preoccupation of social science with Negro family structure than anything else. Besides, in many cases the target is immaterial; your mama, your daddy, your greasy-headed granny are merely vehicles through which the speaker tries to elicit a laugh and display her skills. In retrospect, this seems obvious, but amid the complicated readings of masculine overcompensation and ritual performance, only a handful of writers of the period—most of whom were African Americans with no affiliation with the academy—recognized the centrality of humor. One was Howard Seals, who self-published a pamphlet on the dozens in 1969 titled *You Ain't Thuh Man Yuh Mamma Wuz*. In an effort to put to rest all the sociological overinterpretation, Seals explains: "The emotional tone to be maintained is that of hilariously, outrageously funny bantering."[35] Compare Seals's comment with linguist William Labov, who, while recognizing the humor, ultimately turns laughter into part of the ritual and thus reinforces the process of Othering:

The primary mark of positive evaluation is laughter. We can rate the effectiveness of a sound in a group session by the number of members of the audience who laugh.

A really successful sound will be evaluated by overt comments ... the most common forms are: "Oh!," "Oh shit!" "God damn!," or "Oh lord!" By far the most common is "Oh shit!" The intonation is important; when approval is to be signalled the vowel of each word is quite long, with a high sustained initial pitch, and a slow-falling pitch contour.[36]

Without a concept of, or even an interest in, aesthetics, style, and the visceral pleasures of cultural forms, it should not be surprising that most social scientists explained black urban culture in terms of coping mechanisms, rituals, or oppositional responses to racism. And trapped by an essentialist interpretation of culture, they continue to look for that elusive "authentic" ghetto sensibility, the true, honest, unbridled, pure cultural practices that capture the raw, ruffneck "reality" of urban life. Today, that reality is rap. While studies of rap and Hip Hop culture have been useful in terms of nudging contemporary poverty studies to pay attention to expressive cultures, they have not done much to advance the culture concept in social science. Like its progenitor, the dozens, rap or Hip Hop has been subject to incredible misconception and overinterpretation. Despite the brilliant writing of cultural critics like Tricia Rose, Greg Tate, George Lipsitz, Brian Cross, James Spady, dream hampton, Seth Fernando, Jonathan Scott, Juan Flores, Toure, and others, a number of scholars have returned to or revised the interpretive frameworks developed by the previous generation of ethnographers.[37]

For example, in a very recent book on poor black youth in postwar Philadelphia, Carl Nightingale suggests that the presumed loss of oral traditions like toasting (long, often profane vernacular narrative poetry performed orally) and the dozens, and the rise of rap music and similar commercialized expressive cultures partly explains the increase in violence among young black males. The former, he argues, has played a positive role in curbing violence while the latter is responsible for heightening aggression. He thus calls on young black men to return to these earlier, presumably precommercial cultural forms to vent emotions. Nightingale advocates resurrecting the ring shout, drumming, singing the blues, even toasting, to express black male pain and vulnerability.

The suggestion that rap music has undermined black cultural integrity is made even more forcefully in a recent article by Andre Craddock-Willis. He criticizes nearly all rap artists—especially hard-core gangsta rappers—for not knowing the "majesty" of the blues. The Left, he insists, "must work to gently push these artists to understand the tradition whose shoulders they stand on, and encourage them to comprehend struggle, sacrifice, vision and dedication—the cornerstones for the Black musical tradition."[38] (A tradition, by the way, that includes the great Jelly Roll Morton, whose 1938 recording of "Make Me a Pallet on the Floor" included lines like: "Come here you sweet bitch, give me that pussy, let me get in your drawers / I'm gonna make you think you fuckin' with Santa Claus.")[39]

On the flip side are authors who insist that rap music is fundamentally the authentic, unmediated voice of ghetto youth. Tommy Lott's recent essay, "Marooned in America: Black Urban Youth Culture and Social Pathology," offers a powerful critique of neoconservative culture-of-poverty theories and challenges assumptions that the culture of the so-called underclass is pathological, but he nevertheless reduces expressive culture to a coping strategy to deal with the terror of street life. For Lott, the Hip Hop nation is the true voice of the black lumpen-proletariat whose descriptions of street life are the real thing. "As inhabitants of extreme-poverty neighborhoods," he writes, "many rap artists and their audiences are entrenched in a street life filled with crime, drugs, and violence. Being criminal-minded and having street values are much more suitable for living in their environment." Of course, most rap music is not about a nihilistic street life but about rocking the mike, and the vast majority of rap artists (like most inner city youth) were not entrenched in the tangled web of crime and violence. Yet, he is convinced that Hip Hop narratives of ghetto life "can only come from one's experiences on the streets. Although, at its worst, this knowledge is manifested through egotistical sexual boasting, the core meaning of the rapper's use of the term 'knowledge' is to be *politically* astute, that is, to have a full understanding of the conditions under which black urban youth must survive."[40]

By not acknowledging the deep visceral pleasures black youth derive from making and consuming culture, the stylistic and aesthetic conventions that render the form and performance more attractive than the message, these authors reduce expressive culture to a political text to be read like a less sophisticated version of *The Nation* or *Radical America*. But what counts more than the story is the "storytelling"—an emcee's verbal facility on the mic, the creative and often hilarious use of puns, metaphors, similes, not to mention the ability to kick some serious slang (or what we might call linguistic inventiveness). As microphone fiend Rakim might put it, the function of Hip Hop is to "move the crowd." For all the implicit and explicit politics of rap lyrics, Hip Hop must be understood as a sonic force more than anything else.

Despite their good intentions, ignoring aesthetics enables these authors not only to dismiss "egotistical sexual boasting" as simply a weakness in political ideology but also to mistakenly interpret narratives of everyday life as descriptions of personal experience rather than a revision of older traditions of black vernacular poetry and/or appropriations from mainstream popular culture. To begin with rap music as a mirror image of daily life ignores the influences of urban toasts and published "pimp narratives," which became popular during the late 1960s and early 1970s. In many instances the characters are almost identical, and on occasion rap artists pay tribute to toasting by lyrically "sampling" these early pimp narratives.[41]

Moreover, the assumption that rappers are merely street journalists does not allow for the playfulness and storytelling that is so central to Hip Hop specifically, and black vernacular culture generally. For example, violent lyrics in rap music are rarely meant to be literal. Rather, they are more often than not metaphors to challenge competitors on the microphone. The mic becomes a Tech-9 or AK-47, imagined drive-bys occur from the stage, flowing lyrics become hollow-point shells. Classic examples are Ice Cube's "Jackin' for Beats," a humorous song that describes sampling other artists and producers as outright armed robbery, and Ice T's "Pulse of the Rhyme" or "Grand Larceny" (which brags about stealing a show).[42] Moreover, exaggerated and invented boasts of criminal acts should sometimes be regarded as part of a larger set of signifying practices. Growing out of a much older set of cultural practices, these masculinist narratives are essentially verbal duels over who is the "baddest." They are not meant as literal descriptions of violence and aggression, but connote the playful use of language itself.[43]

Of course, the line between rap music's gritty realism, storytelling, and straight-up signifyin(g) is not always clear to listeners nor is it supposed to be. Hip Hop, particularly gangsta rap, also attracts listeners for whom the "ghetto" is a place of adventure, unbridled violence, erotic fantasy, and/or an imaginary alternative to suburban boredom. White music critic John Leland, who claimed that Ice Cube's turn toward social criticism "killed rap music," praised the group NWA because they "dealt in evil as fantasy: killing cops, smoking hos, filling quiet nights with a flurry of senseless buckshot." This kind of voyeurism partly explains NWA's huge white following and why their album *Efil4zaggin* shot to the top of the charts as soon as it was released. As one critic put it, "In reality, NWA have more in common with a Charles Bronson movie than a PBS documentary on the plight of the inner-cities." NWA members have even admitted that some of their recent songs were not representations of reality "in the hood" but inspired by popular films like *Innocent Man* starring Tom Selleck, and *Tango and Cash*.[44]

Claims to have located the authentic voice of black ghetto youth are certainly not unique. Several scholars insist that Hip Hop is the pure, unadulterated voice of a ghetto that has grown increasingly isolated from "mainstream" society. Missing from this formulation is rap music's incredible hybridity. From the outset, rap music embraced a variety of styles and cultural forms, from reggae and salsa to heavy metal and jazz. Hip Hop's hybridity reflected, in part, the increasingly international character of America's inner cities resulting from immigration, demographic change, and new forms of information, as well as the inventive employment of technology in creating rap music. By using two turntables, and later digital samplers, deejays played different records, isolated the "break beats" or what they identified as the funkiest part of a song, and boldly mixed a wide range of different music and musical genres to create new music. And despite the fact that many of the pioneering deejays, rappers, and break dancers were African American, West Indian, and Puerto Rican and strongly identified with the African diaspora, rap artists wrecked all the boundaries between "black" and "white" music. Deejay Afrika Islam remembers vividly the time when Hip Hop and punk united for a moment and got busy at the New Wave clubs in New York during the early 1980s. Even before the punk rockers sought a relationship with uptown Hip Hop deejays, Afrika Islam recalls, in the Bronx they were already playing "everything from Aerosmith's 'Walk This Way' to Dunk and the Blazers." Grand Master Caz, whose lyrics were stolen by the Sugarhill Gang and ended up in *Rapper's Delight* (the first successful rap record in history), grew up in the Bronx listening to soft rock and mainstream pop music. As he explained in an interview, "Yo, I'd bug you out if I told you who I used to listen to. I used to listen to Barry Manilow, Neil Diamond, and Simon and Garfunkel. I grew up listening to that WABC. That's why a lot of the stuff that my group did, a lot of routines that we're famous for all come from all white boy songs."[45]

If you saw a picture of Caz, this statement would seem incongruous. He looks the part of an authentic black male, a real ruffneck, hoodie, "G," nigga, criminal, menace. And yet, he is a product of a hybrid existence, willing to openly talk about Simon and Garfunkel in a book that I could only purchase from a Nation of Islam booth on 125th Street in Harlem. He is also the first to call what he does "black music," structured noise for which the beat, no matter where it is taken from, is everything. Moreover, like the breakers who danced to his rhymes, the kids who built his speakers, the deejay who spun the records, Caz takes credit for his creativity, his artistry, his "work." This is the "black urban culture" which has remained so elusive to social science; it is the thing, or rather the process, that defies concepts like "coping strategy," "adaptive," "authentic," "nihilistic," and "pathological."

Revising the Culture Concept: Hybridity, Style, and Aesthetics in Black Urban Culture

Aside from the tendency to ignore expressive/popular cultural forms, and limit the category of culture to (so-called dysfunctional) behavior, the biggest problem with the way social scientists employ the culture concept in their studies of the black urban poor is their inability to see what it all means *to the participants and practitioners*. In other words, they do not consider what Clinton (George, that is) calls the "pleasure principle." If I may use a metaphor here, rather than hear the singer they analyze the lyrics; rather than hear the drum they study the song title. Black music, creativity and experimentation in language, that walk, that talk, that style, must also be understood as sources of visceral and psychic pleasure. Though they may also reflect and speak to the political and social world of inner city communities, expressive cultures are not simply mirrors of social life or expressions of conflicts, pathos, and anxieties.

Paul Willis's concept of "symbolic creativity" provides one way out of the impasse created by such a limited concept of culture. As Willis argues, constructing an identity, communicating with others, and achieving pleasure are all part of symbolic creativity—it is literally the labor of creating art in everyday life. Despite his distrust of and vehement opposition to "aesthetics," he realizes that, in most cases, the explicit meaning or intention of a particular cultural form is not the thing that makes it attractive. The appeal of popular music, for example, is more than lyrical: "Songs bear meaning and allow symbolic work not just as speech acts, but also as structures of sound with unique rhythms, textures and forms. Thus, it is not always what is sung, but the *way* it is sung, within particular conventions or musical genres which gives a piece of music its communicative power and meaning."[46] Indeed, words like *soul* and *funk* were efforts to come up with a language to talk about that visceral element in music, even if they did ultimately evolve into market categories. Over two decades ago, black novelist Cecil Brown brilliantly captured this "thing," this symbolic creativity, the pleasure principle, soul, or whatever you want to call it. Writing about the godfather of soul, James Brown, he argued that his lyrics are less important than how they are uttered, where they are placed rhythmically, and "how he makes it sound." "What, for instance, does 'Mother Popcorn' mean? But what difference does it make when you're dancing to it, when you are feeling it, when you are it and it you (possession). It's nothing and everything at once; it is what black (hoodoo) people who never studied art in school mean by art."[47]

Yet to say it is a "black" thing doesn't mean it is made up entirely of black things. As Greg Tate makes clear in his recent collection of essays, *Flyboy in the Buttermilk*, and in the epigraph to this chapter, interpreters of the African American experience—in our case social scientists—must bear a large share of the responsibility for turning ghetto residents into an undifferentiated mass. We can no longer ignore the fact that information technology, new forms of mass communication, and immigration have made the rest of the world more accessible to inner city residents than ever before.[48] Contemporary black urban culture is a hybrid that draws on Afrodiasporic traditions, popular culture, the vernacular of previous generations of Southern and Northern black folk, new and old technologies, and a whole lot of imagination. Once again, James Clifford's ruminations on the "predicament of culture" are useful for exposing the predicament of social science. He writes: "To tell … local histories of cultural survival and emergence, we need to resist deep-seated habits of mind and systems of authenticity. We need to be suspicious of an almost-automatic tendency to relegate non-Western (read: black) peoples and objects to the pasts of an increasingly homogeneous humanity."[49]

Notes

1. John Langston Gwaltney, *Drylongso: A Self-Portrait of Black America* (New York: Random House, 1980), xix.
2. Mercer L. Sullivan, "Absent Fathers in the Inner City," *The Annals* 501 (January 1989): 49–50.
3. Recent proponents of a new "culture of poverty" thesis include Ken Auletta, *The Underclass* (New York: Random House, 1982); Nicholas Lemann, "The Origins of the Underclass: Part I," *Atlantic Monthly* 257 (June 1986): 31–61, and "The Origins of the Underclass: Part II," *Atlantic Monthly* 258 (July 1986): 54–68; Nicholas Lemann, *The Promised Land: The Great Black Migration and How It Changed America* (New York: Knopf, 1991); Charles Murray, *Losing Ground: American Social Policy, 1950–1980* (New York: Basic Books, 1984); and Lawrence Mead, *The New Dependency Politics: Non-Working Poverty in the U.S.* (New York: Basic Books, 1992). These works are quite distinct in scope, methods, and ideology from the pioneering studies of Oscar Lewis, who introduced the "culture of poverty" idea to American social science. Unlike the more recent works, he did not argue that poor people's behavior is the *cause* of their poverty. Rather, he insisted that capitalism impoverished segments of the working class, who were denied access to mainstream institutions. The culture they created to cope with poverty and disfranchisement was passed down through generations and thus led to passivity and undermined social organization. Lewis had no intention of using the culture-of-poverty thesis to distinguish the "deserving" from the "undeserving poor." See Oscar Lewis, *The Children of Sanchez* (New York: Random House, 1961) and *La Vida: A Puerto Rican Family in the Culture of Poverty, San Juan and New York* (New York: Random House, 1966).

   Critics of the culture-of-poverty thesis are many, and they do not all agree with each other as to the relative importance of culture or the causes of poverty. See especially Charles Valentine, *Culture and Poverty: Critique and Counter-Proposals* (Chicago: University of Chicago Press, 1968); Herbert J. Gans, "Culture and Class in the Study of Poverty: An Approach to Antipoverty Research," in *On Understanding Poverty: Perspectives from the Social Sciences*, ed. Daniel Patrick Moynihan (New York: Basic Books, 1968); Sheldon Danziger and Peter Gottschalk, "The Poverty of *Losing Ground*," *Challenge* 28 (May–June 1985): 32–38; William Darity and Samuel L. Meyers, "Does Welfare Dependency Cause Female Headship? The

Case of the Black Family," *Journal of Marriage and the Family* 46, no. 4 (1984): 765–79; and Mary Corcoran, Greg J. Duncan, Gerald Gurin, and Patricia Gurin, "Myth and Reality: The Causes and Persistence of Poverty," *Journal of Policy Analysis and Management* 4, no. 4 (1985): 516–36.

4. Michael Katz, "The Urban 'Underclass' as a Metaphor of Social Transformation," in *The Underclass Debate: Views from History*, ed. Michael Katz (Princeton, N.J.: Princeton University Press, 1993), 3–23.

5. The most prominent of the structuralists adopt some cultural explanation for urban poverty, suggesting that bad behavior is the outcome of a bad environment. William Julius Wilson's most recent work argues that the lack of employment has eroded the work ethic and discipline of the underclass, leading to behaviors that allow employers to justify not hiring them. See especially William Julius Wilson, *When Work Disappears: The World of the New Urban Poor* (New York: Knopf, 1996); William J. Wilson, *The Truly Disadvantaged: The Inner City, the Underclass, and Public Policy* (Chicago: University of Chicago Press, 1987); David T. Ellwood, *Poor Support: Poverty in the American Family* (New York: Basic Books, 1988); Elijah Anderson, *Streetwise: Race, Class, and Change in an Urban Community* (Chicago: University of Chicago Press, 1990); Elijah Anderson, "Sex Codes and Family Life among Poor Inner City Youth," *The Annals* 501 (January 1989): 59–78; Troy Duster, "Social Implications of the 'New' Black Underclass," *Black Scholar* 19 (May–June 1988): 2–9; Christopher Jencks, *Rethinking Social Policy: Race, Poverty, and the Underclass* (Cambridge: Harvard University Press, 1992); Mark S. Littman, "Poverty Areas and the Underclass: Untangling the Web," *Monthly Labor Review* 114 (March 1991): 19–32; Jacqueline Jones, *The Dispossessed: America's Underclasses from the Civil War to the Present* (New York: Basic Books, 1992); Douglas G. Glasgow, *The Black Underclass: Unemployment and Entrapment of Ghetto Youth* (New York: Random House, 1981); William Julius Wilson and Loic J. D. Wacquant, "The Cost of Racial and Class Exclusion in the Inner City," *The Annals* 501 (January 1989): 8–25; John D. Kasarda, "Caught in a Web of Change," *Society* 21 (November/December 1983): 41–47; John D. Kasarda, "Urban Industrial Transition and the Underclass," *The Annals* 501 (January 1989): 26–47; Maxine Baca Zinn, "Family, Race, and Poverty in the Eighties," *Signs* 14, no. 4 (1989): 856–74; Mary Corcoran, Greg J. Duncan, and Martha S. Hill, "The Economic Fortunes of Women and Children: Lessons from the Panel Study of Income Dynamics," *Signs* 10, no. 2 (1984): 232–48; Mary Jo Bane, "Household Composition and Poverty," in *Fighting Poverty: What Works and What Doesn't*, eds. Sheldon Danzinger and Daniel Weinberg (Cambridge: Harvard University Press, 1986); David Ellwood, *Poor Support* (New York: Basic Books, 1988); Barry Bluestone and Bennett Harrison, *The Deindustrialization of America* (New York: Basic Books, 1982); Richard Child Hill and Cynthia Negrey, "Deindustrialization and Racial Minorities in the Great Lakes Region, USA," in *The Reshaping of America: Social Consequences of the Changing Economy*, eds. D. Stanley Eitzen and Maxine Baca Zinn (Englewood Cliffs, N.J.: Prentice-Hall, 1989); Elliot Currie and Jerome H. Skolnick, *America's Problems: Social Issues and Public Policy* (Boston: Little, Brown and Co., 1984); Carl Nightingale, *On the Edge: A History of Poor Black Children and Their American Dreams* (New York: Basic Books, 1993); and Staff of *Chicago Tribune*, *The American Millstone: An Examination of the Nation's Permanent Underclass* (Chicago: Contemporary Books, 1986). While most of these authors focus on deindustrialization and the effects of concentrated poverty, Douglas S. Massey and Nancy A. Denton have argued that racial segregation is the key to explaining the persistence of black urban poverty. See their *American Apartheid: Segregation and the Making of the Underclass* (Cambridge: Harvard University Press, 1993).

6. Kathryn Edin, "Surviving the Welfare System: How AFDC Recipients Make Ends Meet in Chicago," *Social Problems* 38 (November 1991): 462–74.

7. Charles P. Henry, *Culture and African-American Politics* (Bloomington, Ind.: Indiana University Press, 1990), 12–13. Likewise, social philosopher Leonard Harris asks us to imagine what would happen if we used the same indices to study the "urban rich": "Suppose that their behavior was unduly helpful to themselves; say they rarely married, had more one-child families, were more likely than previous rich to be sexual libertines practicing safe sex, were health conscious, and were shrewd investors in corporate and ghetto property without moral reflection." Leonard Harris," Agency and the Concept of the Underclass," in *The Underclass Question*, ed. Bill E. Lawson (Philadelphia: Temple University Press, 1992), 37.

8. Lee Rainwater, *Behind Ghetto Walls: Black Families in a Federal Slum* (Chicago: Aldine Publishing Co., 1970); Elliot Liebow, *Tally's Corner: A Study of Negro Streetcorner Men* (Boston: Little, Brown and Co., 1967); Ulf Hannerz, *Soulside: Inquiries into Ghetto Culture and Community* (New York: Columbia University Press, 1969); Carol B. Stack, *All Our Kin: Strategies for Survival in a Black Community* (New York: Harper and Row, 1974); Betty Lou Valentine, *Hustling and Other Hard Work: Life Styles in the Ghetto* (New York: Free Press, 1978); Joyce Ladner, *Tommorrow's Tommorrow: The Black Woman* (Garden City, N.Y.: Anchor, 1971); David Schulz, *Coming Up Black: Patterns of Ghetto Socialization* (Englewood Cliffs, N.J.: Prentice-Hall, 1969).

9. Stephen M. Joseph, ed., *The Me Nobody Knows: Children's Voices from the Ghetto* (New York: Avon Books, 1969); Caroline Mirthes and the Children of P.S. 15, *Can't You Hear Me Talking to You?* (New York: Bantam Books, 1971).

10. These typologies are drawn from Hannerz, *Soulside*; William McCord, John Howard, Bernard Friedberg, Edwin Harwood, *Life Styles in the Black Ghetto* (New York: W. W. Norton, 1969).

11. Gwaltney, *Drylongso*, xxiv, xxxii.

12. James Clifford, "On Collecting Art and Culture," in *The Predicament of Culture: Twentieth-Century Ethnography, Literature, and Art* (Cambridge: Harvard University Press, 1988), 246. Don't get me wrong. The vast and rich ethnographic documentation collected by these scholars is extremely valuable because it captures the responses and survival strategies hidden from economic indices and illuminates the human aspects of poverty. Of course, these materials must be used with caution since most ethnographies do not pay much attention to historical and structural transformations. Instead, they describe and interpret a particular community during a brief moment in time. The practice of giving many of these communities fictitious names only compounds the problem and presumes that region, political economy, and history have no bearing on opportunity structures, oppositional strategies, or culture. For an extended critique, see Andrew H. Maxwell, "The Anthropology of Poverty in Black Communities: A Critique and Systems Alternative," *Urban Anthropology* 17, nos. 2 and 3 (1988): 171–92.

13. Charles Keil, *Urban Blues* (Chicago: University of Chicago Press, 1966), 1–12, 23.

14. Stack, *All Our Kin*; Ladner, *Tommorrow's Tommorrow*. This dichotomy also prevails in Anderson's more recent *Streetwise*.

15. Lee Rainwater, ed., *Soul* (Trans-Action Books, 1970), 9.

16. Rainwater, *Soul* (especially essays by John Horton, Thomas Kochman, and David Wellman); Ulf Hannerz, "The Significance of Soul" in *ibid.*, 15–30; Hannerz, *Soulside*, 144–58. For other interpretations of soul, see Keil, *Urban Blues*, 164–90; William L. Van Deburg, *New Day in Babylon: The Black Power Movement and American Culture, 1965–1975* (Chicago: University of Chicago Press, 1992), 194–97; Claude Brown, "The Language of Soul," in *Mother Wit from the Laughing Barrel: Readings in the Interpretation of Afro-American Folklore*, ed. Alan Dundes (New York: Garland Publishing Co., 1981), 232–43; and Roger D. Abrahams, *Positively Black* (Englewood Cliffs, N.J.: Prentice-Hall, 1970), 136–50.

17. Hannerz, "The Significance of Soul," 21.

18. Schulz, *Coming Up Black*, 78, 103; Rainwater, *Behind Ghetto Walls*, 372. See also John Horton, "Time and Cool People," in Rainwater, *Soul*, 31–50.

19. Hannerz, "The Significance of Soul," 22–23.

20. Robert L. Allen, *Black Awakening in Capitalist America: An Analytic History* (Garden City, N.Y.: Doubleday, 1969), 163; Van Deburg, *New Day in Babylon*, 201–2.

21. Van Deburg, *New Day in Babylon*, 201–2.

22. Lois Liberty Jones and John Henry Jones, *All about the Natural* (New York: Clairol, 1971).

23. Andrea Benton Rushing, "Hair-Raising," *Feminist Studies* 14, no. 2 (1988): 334; Jones and Jones, *All about the Natural*; Helen Hayes King and Theresa Ogunbiyi, "Should Negro Women Straighten Their Hair?" *Negro Digest* (August 1963): 68.

24. King and Ogunbiyi, "Should Negro Women Straighten Their Hair?" 69–70, 71.

25. King and Ogunbiyi, "Should Negro Women Straighten Their Hair?" 67–68.

26. Rushing, "Hair-Raising," 334, 326.

27. Harold Cruse, *Rebellion or Revolution?* (New York: Morrow, 1968); Norman C. Weinstein, *A Night in Tunisia: Imaginings of Africa in Jazz* (New York: Limelight Editions, 1993); Penny von Eschen, *Democracy or Empire: African Americans, Anti-Colonialism, and the Cold War* (Ithaca, N.Y.: Cornell University Press, 1997); Immanuel Geiss, *The Pan-African Movement* (London: Methuen and Co., 1974); Robert Weisbord, *Ebony Kinship: Africa, Africans, and the Afro-American* (Westport, Conn.: Greenwood Press, 1973); P. Olisanwuch Esedebe, *Pan-Africanism: The Idea and Movement, 1776–1963* (Washington, D.C.: Howard University Press, 1982).

28. Cruse, *Rebellion or Revolution?*, 73.

29. As Linda Roemere Wright's research reveals, ads and other images of Afrocoifed women in *Ebony* magazine declined around 1970, just as the number of images of black men with Afros was steadily rising. See Linda Roemere Wright, "Changes in Black American Hairstyles from 1964 through 1977, As Related to Themes in Feature Articles and Advertisements" (M.A. thesis, Michigan State University, 1982), 24–25.

30. Richard Majors and Janet Mancini Billson, *Cool Pose: The Dilemmas of Manhood in America* (New York: Lexington Books, 1992), 4.

31. Historian Roger Lane treats the dozens as a manifestation of a larger pathological culture: "Afro-American culture was marked by an aggressively competitive strain compounded of bold display, semi-ritualistic insult, and an admiration of violence in verbal form at least. 'Playing the dozens,' a contest involving the exchange of often sexual insults directed not only at the participants but at their families, especially their mothers, was one example of this strain." Lane, *Roots of Violence in Black Philadelphia, 1860–1900* (Cambridge: Harvard University Press, 1986), 146–47. See also Roger D. Abrahams, *Deep Down in the Jungle: Negro Narrative Folklore from the Streets of Philadelphia*, new ed. (Chicago: Aldine,

1970), 52–56; Herbert Foster, *Ribin', Jivin', and Playin' the Dozens* (Cambridge, Mass.: Ballinger, 1986); Thomas Kochman, *Black and White Styles in Conflict* (Chicago: University of Chicago Press, 1981), 51–58; Majors and Billson, *Cool Pose*, 91–101; and Nightingale, *On the Edge*, 26–28. There are some remarkable exceptions, such as the work of linguists, historians, literary scholars, and first-person practitioners, who treat the dozens as a larger set of signifying practices found in black vernacular culture or focus on the art and pleasures of verbal play. For these authors, the dozens is not merely a mirror of social relations. See Claudia Mitchell-Kernan, "Signifying, Loud-talking, and Marking," in *Rappin and Stylin' Out: Communication in Urban Black America*, ed. Thomas Kochman (Urbana, Ill.: University of Illinois Press, 1972); H. Rap Brown, *Die, Nigger, Die* (New York: Dial, 1969); *Geneva Smitherman, Talkin' and Testifyin': The Language of Black America* (Boston: Houghton Mifflin Co., 1977), 128–33; Henry Louis Gates, Jr., *The Signifying Monkey: A Theory of African-American Literary Criticism* (New York: Oxford University Press, 1988), especially 64–88; and Houston Baker, *Long Black Song: Essays in Black American Literature and Culture* (Charlottesville, Va.: University Press of Virginia, 1972), 115. Despite disagreements between Baker and Gates, both try to make sense of black vernacular culture—including the dozens—as art rather than sociology. Although Lawrence Levine took issue with the functionalist approach to the dozens over fifteen years ago, he did not reject it altogether. He suggests that the dozens helped young black children develop verbal facility and learn self-discipline. See Lawrence Levine, *Black Culture and Black Consciousness: Afro-American Folk Thought from Slavery to Freedom* (New York: Oxford University Press, 1977), 345–58.

32. Levine, *Black Culture and Black Consciousness*, 357. A beginning is Marjorie Harness Goodwin, *He-Said-She-Said: Talk as Social Organization among Black Children* (Bloomington, Ind.: Indiana University Press, 1990), especially 222–23. However, Goodwin emphasizes "ritual insult" as a means of dealing with disputes rather than as an art form and thus is still squarely situated within social scientists' emphasis on function over style and pleasure.

33. Roger D. Abrahams, *Deep Down in the Jungle*, 60, 88–96; see also Roger D. Abrahams, *Talking Black* (Rowley, Mass.: Newbury House Publishers, 1976).

34. Schulz, *Coming Up Black*, 68. In McCord, et al. *Life Styles in the Ghetto*, Edwin Harwood argues further that the lack of a father leads to violent uprisings and low self-esteem among black male youth: "Negro males who are brought up primarily by mothers and other female relatives pick up from them their hostility toward the males who are not there, or if they are, are not doing worth-while work in society. In such an environment it must be difficult to develop a constructive masculine self-image and the ambivalent self-image that does emerge can only be resolved in ways destructive both to the self and the society, through bold and violent activities that are only superficially masculine. If this analysis is correct, then the Negro youth who hurls a brick or an insult at the white cop is not just reacting in anger to white society, but on another level is discharging aggression toward the father who 'let him down' and females whose hostility toward inadequate men raised doubts about his own sense of masculinity" (32–33).

35. Eugene Perkins, *Home Is a Dirty Street: The Social Oppression of Black Children* (Chicago: Third World Press, 1975), 32.

36. William Labov, *Language in the Inner City: Studies in the Black English Vernacular* (Philadelphia: University of Pennsylvania Press, 1972), 325. David Schulz, however, does not even trust the laughter of his subjects. He writes, "With careful listening one becomes suspicious of the laughter of the ghetto. So much apparent gaiety has a purpose all too often in the zero-sum contest system of interpersonal manipulation for personal satisfaction and gain" (Schulz, *Coming Up Black*, 5).

37. See, for example, Venise T. Berry, "Rap Music, Self-Concept and Low Income Black Adolescents," *Popular Music and Society* 14, no. 3 (Fall 1990); Nightingale, *On the Edge*, 132–33, 162–63, 182–84; Wheeler Winston Dixon, "Urban Black American Music in the Late 1980s: The 'Word' as Cultural Signifier," *Midwest Quarterly* 30 (Winter 1989): 229–41; Mark Costello and David Foster Wallace, *Signifying Rappers: Rap and Race in the Urban Present* (New York: Ecco, 1990); and Andre Craddock-Willis, "Rap Music and the Black Musical Tradition: A Critical Assessment," *Radical America* 23, no. 4 (June 1991): 29–38. The case of Hip Hop might be unusual since social scientists working on the black urban poor have been conspicuously silent, leaving most of the discussion to music critics and cultural studies scholars. The result has been a fairly sophisticated body of work that takes into account both aesthetics and social and political contexts. See, for example, Tricia Rose, *Black Noise: Rap Music and Black Culture in Contemporary America* (Hanover, N.H.: Wesleyan University Press, 1994); Tricia Rose, "Black Texts/Black Contexts," in *Black Popular Culture*, ed. Gina Dent (Seattle: Bay Press, 1992), 223–27; Tate, *Flyboy in the Buttermilk*; Juan Flores, "Puerto Rican and Proud, Boy-ee!: Rap, Roots, and Amnesia," in *Microphone Fiends: Youth Music and Youth Culture*, ed. Tricia Rose and Andrew Ross (New York: Routledge, 1994), 89–98; William Eric Perkins, ed., *Droppin' Science: Critical Essays on Rap Music and Hip Hop Culture* (Philadelphia: Temple University Press, 1996); Joseph G. Eure and James G. Spady, *Nation Conscious Rap* (Brooklyn: P. C. International Press, 1991); James G. Spady, Stefan Dupree, and Charles G. Lee, *Twisted Tales in the Hip Hop*

Streets of Philadelphia (Philadelphia: UMUM LOH Publishers, 1995); Brian Cross, *It's Not About a Salary ... Rap, Race and Resistance in Los Angeles* (London: Verso, 1993); Michael Eric Dyson, *Reflecting Black: African-American Cultural Criticism* (Minneapolis: University of Minnesota Press, 1993); George Lipsitz, *Dangerous Crossroads: Popular Music, Postmodernism, and the Poetics of Place* (London: Verso, 1994); Jeffrey Louis Decker, "The State of Rap: Time and Place in Hip Hop Nationalism," *Social Text* 34 (1989): 53–84; Jonathan Scott, "'Act Like You Know': A Theory of Hip Hop Aesthetics" (unpublished paper in author's possession, 1994); and S. H. Fernando, *The New Beats: Exploring the Music, Culture and Attitudes of Hip Hop* (New York: Anchor Books, 1994). Two good general histories are Steve Hager, *Hip Hop: The Illustrated History of Breakdancing, Rap Music, and Graffiti* (New York: St. Martin's Press, 1984); and David Toop, *Rap Attack 2* (London: Pluto Press, 1991).

38. Craddock-Willis, "Rap Music and the Black Musical Tradition," 37.

39. "Rockbeat," *Village Voice* 39, no. 4 (January 25, 1994): 76.

40. Tommy Lott, "Marooned in America: Black Urban Youth Culture and Social Pathology," in *The Underclass Question*, ed. Bill E. Lawson (Philadelphia: Temple University Press, 1992), 71, 72, 80–81.

41. Digital Underground's song "Good Thing We're Rappin'," *Sons of the P* (Tommy Boy Records, 1991) is nothing if not a tribute to the pimp narratives. One hears elements of classic toasts, including "The Pimp," "Dogass Pimp," "Pimping Sam," "Wicked Nell," "The Lame and the Whore," and perhaps others. Even the meter is very much in the toasting tradition. (For transcriptions of these toasts, see Bruce Jackson, *"Get Your Ass in the Water and Swim Like Me": Narrative Poetry from Black Oral Tradition* [Cambridge: Harvard University Press, 1974], 106–30.) Similar examples which resemble the more comical pimp narratives include Ice Cube, "I'm Only Out for One Thing," *AmeriKKKa's Most Wanted* (Priority Records, 1990) and Son of Bazerk, "Sex, Sex, and More Sex," *Son of Bazerk* (MCA Records, 1991).

42. Other examples include Capital Punishment Organization's aptly titled warning to other perpetrating rappers, "Homicide," *To Hell and Black* (Capitol Records, 1990); NWA's "Real Niggaz," *Efil4zaggin* (Priority Records, 1991); Dr. Dre's "Lyrical Gangbang," *The Chronic* (Deathrow/Interscope Records, 1992); Ice Cube's, "Now I Gotta Wet'cha," *The Predator* (Priority Records, 1992); Compton's Most Wanted's, "Wanted" and "Straight Check N' Em," *Straight Check N' Em* (Orpheus Records, 1991); as well as many of the songs on Ice Cube, *Kill at Will* (Priority Records, 1992); Ice T, *OG: Original Gangster* (Sire Records, 1991); Ice T, *Power* (Warner Bros., 1988); NWA, *100 Miles and Runnin'* (Ruthless Records, 1990). See also chapter 8 of my book *Race Rebels: Culture, Politics, and the Black Working Class* (New York: The Free Press, 1994).

43. Ice T [and the Rhyme Syndicate], "My Word Is Bond," *The Iceberg/Freedom of Speech ... Just Watch What You Say* (Sire Records, 1989); Ice Cube, "J. D.'s Gafflin'," *AmeriKKKa's Most Wanted* (Priority Records, 1990). West Coast rappers also create humorous countercritiques of gangsterism, the most penetrating is perhaps Del tha Funkee Homosapien's hilarious, "Hoodz Come in Dozens," *I Wish My Brother George Was Here* (Priority Records, 1991).

44. See John Leland, "Rap: Can It Survive Self-Importance?" *Details* (July 1991): 108; Frank Owen, "Hanging Tough," *Spin* 6, no. 1 (April 1990): 34; and James Bernard, "NWA [Interview]," *The Source* (December 1990): 34.

45. Quoted in Spady and Eure, *Nation Conscious Rap*, xiii, xxviii. On the early history of Hip Hop in New York, see Rose, *Black Noise*; Hager, *Hip Hop*; and Toop, *Rap Attack 2*.

46. Paul Willis, *Common Culture: Symbolic Work at Play in the Everyday Cultures of the Young* (Boulder, Colo.: Westview Press, 1990), 1–5, 65.

47. Cecil Brown, "James Brown, Hoodoo and Black Culture," *Black Review* 1 (1971): 184.

48. For insightful discussions of the way information technology in the late twentieth century opened up new spaces for building cultural links between black urban America and the African diaspora, see Lipsitz, *Dangerous Crossroads*; and Paul Gilroy, *The Black Atlantic: Modernity and Double-Consciousness* (Cambridge: Harvard University Press, 1993).

49. James Clifford, *The Predicament of Culture: Twentieth-Century Ethnography, Literature, and Art* (Cambridge: Harvard University Press, 1988), 246.

13

About a Salary or Reality?

Rap's Recurrent Conflict

Alan Light

In 1990, rap dominated headlines and the pop charts as never before. Large segments of the American public were introduced to rap—or at least forced to confront its existence for the first time—through a pack of unlikely and sometimes unseemly performers. The year started with the January release of Public Enemy's single "Welcome to the Terrordome," which prompted widespread accusations (in the wake of remarks made by Professor Griff, the group's "Minister of Information," that Jews are responsible for "the majority of wickedness that goes on across the globe") that rap's most politically outspoken and widely respected group was anti-Semitic. The obscenity arrest of 2 Live Crew in June filled news, talk shows, and editorial pages for weeks. The concurrent rise of graphic, violent "Gangster Rap" from such artists as Ice Cube and the Geto Boys stoked these fires, even if their brutal streetscapes often made for complex, visceral, and challenging records.

It's easy to vilify any or all of these artists. *Newsweek* lumped several of them together and ran a cover story (19 March 1990) entitled "Rap Rage," which proved to be a savage attack on the form (including, by some curious extension, the heavy-metal band Guns n' Roses) as "ugly macho boasting and joking about anyone who hangs out on a different block," and as having taken "sex out of teenage culture, substituting brutal fantasies of penetration and destruction." Certainly, Luther Campbell and 2 Live Crew aren't exactly the First Amendment martyrs of the ACLU's dreams; their music consists of junior high-school locker-room fantasies set to monotonous, mighty uninspired beats. The "horror rap" of the Geto Boys is deliberately shocking, and songs such as "Mind of a Lunatic," in which the narrator slashes a woman's throat and has sex with her corpse, raise issues that are a long way from the Crew's doo-doo jokes. Public Enemy, for all of its musical innovation and political insight, has an uncanny knack for talking its way deeper into trouble, and leader Chuck D.'s incomprehensible waffling during the Griff incident, first dismissing Griff, then breaking up the group, then reforming and announcing a "boycott of the music industry," was maddening and painful to watch.

But there was also a different side to the rap story that was at least as prominent in 1990. MC Hammer's harmless dance-pop *Please Hammer Don't Hurt 'Em* became the year's best-selling album and rap's biggest hit ever. It was finally displaced from the top of the charts by white superhunk Vanilla Ice's *To the Extreme*, which sold five million copies in twelve weeks, making it the fastest-moving record in any style in five years.

Hammer has been defended by the likes of Chuck D. for being rap's first real performer, a dancer/showman/business tycoon of the first order, but his simplistic regurgitation of hooks from familiar hits quickly wears thin. Vanilla Ice not only lacks Hammer's passable delivery, he also manufactured a none-too-convincing false autobiography to validate his appropriation of black culture and subsequent unprecedented commercial success. Both are given to a self-aggrandizement so far beyond their talents that the biggest problem is simply how annoying they are.

There's nothing criminal about bad music or even simple-mindedness. And it's nothing new for the most one-dimensional, reductive purveyors of a style to be the ones who cash in commercially. But the most unfortunate result of the year of Hammer, Ice, and the Crew is that it may have determined a perception of rap for the majority of America. Any definitions of rap formed by the millions of Americans introduced to it in the last year would probably (and, sad to say, reasonably) center on a simplified analysis of the genre's basest cultural and sociological components and the most uninspired uses of its musical innovation.

If, in 1990, people new to rap gave it any thought at all, they would have concentrated on the crudeness of 2 Live Crew—who may have a constitutional right to be nasty, but there is no way around the ugliness of their lyrics. Newcomers might (understandably, given much of the mainstream press coverage) have dismissed Public Enemy, self-styled "prophets of rage," as mere traffickers in hate. Whatever one thinks of the controversial sampling process, in which pieces of existing records are isolated and digitally stored and then reconstructed as a kind of montage to form a new musical track, the derivative, obvious samples of Hammer and Ice represented the triumph of the technology at its worst. And rap diehards and novices all had to contend with the cheers of "go, white boy, go" as Vanilla Ice became the biggest star yet to emerge from this black-created style.

This has made for a lot of sociocultural analysis and interpretation, which is perfectly appropriate; rap is unarguably the most culturally significant style in pop, the genre that speaks most directly to and for its audience, full of complications, contradictions, and confusion. But what gets lost in this discussion, tragically, is that rap is also the single most creative, revolutionary approach to music and to music making that this generation has constructed.

The distance between MC Hammer and the Geto Boys seems to be the final flowering of a contradiction built into rap from its very beginning. Though the polarity may seem inexplicable—is it progress now that we hear not just "how can both be called music?" but "how can both be called rap?"—it is actually a fairly inevitable progression that has been building for years. We can be sure that rap artists are more aware than anyone of the current condition; a press release touting the new group Downtown Science quotes rapper Bosco Money's definitive statement of purpose for 1990: "Our crusade is to fuse street credibility with a song that's accessible to the mainstream."

Rap, however, has seen problematic moments before, times when people were sure it was dead or played out or irrelevant. It has, with relatively alarming frequency for such a young art form, repeatedly found itself at seemingly impassable stylistic crossroads. Off and on for years, it has been torn between the apparently irreconcilable agendas inherent in such a radical pop creation. Throughout the decade of its recorded existence, though, rap has always emerged stronger due to its openness to musical and technological innovation and diversification.

We should not forget that 1990 was also the year that the bicoastal post-Parliament-Funkadelic loonies in Digital Underground had a Top 10 hit with "The Humpty Dance," and Oakland's gratuitously nasty Too Short released his second gold-selling album. L.L. Cool J was booed at a Harlem rally for not being political enough, but then recorded an "old-school" style album that reestablished him as a vital street force. It was a year when Public Enemy, so recently a strictly underground phenomenon, shipped over a million copies of the *Fear of a Black Planet* album; a year when the Gangster scene redefined "graphic" and Hammer and Ice redefined "crossover." It was a year when there could be no more arguing that rap sounded like any one thing, or even any two things. Despite the increasing perception among insiders that rap is a sellout or, to outsiders, that it's just a cheap, vulgar style, it is this expansion and flexibility that is the real story of rap's decade on record.

Five years before Vanilla Ice, rap had made its initial breakthrough into mainstream culture, but it looked like it had gone as far as it was going to go. Rap records had managed to cross over to the pop charts as novelty hits on occasion, beginning in 1980 with the startling Top 40 success of the Sugarhill Gang's "Rapper's Delight." By 1985, hip-hop culture, rap, graffiti, and especially breakdancing were receiving widespread popular attention; after a brief break-dancing sequence drew notice in the movie *Flashdance*, other movies like *Breakin'* and *Beat Street* quickly followed, and breakdancing became a staple in young American culture, turning up everywhere from TV commercials to bar mitzvah parties. The soundtrack to all this head spin-ning and 7-Up drinking was an electrosynthesized hip-hop, with lots of outer space imagery, sounds and styles borrowed from the year's other rage, video games, and featuring a burbling, steady electronic pulse (Jonzun Crew's "Pack Jam" is the most obvious example, but the style's real masterworks were Afrika Bambaataa and Soulsonic Force's "Planet Rock" or "Looking for the Perfect Beat"). Maybe it was the rapidity of its appropriation by Hollywood and Madison Avenue, maybe it was just too obviously contrived to last, but the breakdancing sound and look quickly fell into self-parody—much of it was dated by the time it even got released.

There was, at the same time, another strain of rap that wasn't quite as widely disseminated as the break-beat sound but would prove to have a more lasting impact. Grandmaster Flash and the Furious Five's 1982 hit "The Message" offered a depiction of ghetto life so compelling and a hook so undeniable ("Don't push me / 'Cause I'm close to the edge") that it became a pop hit in spite of the fact that it was the hardest-hitting rap that had ever been recorded. (Harry Allen, Public Enemy's "media assassin," recently offered an alternate view when he wrote that the song was the "type of record white people would appreciate because of its picturesque rendition of the ghetto.") In its wake, "socially conscious" rap became the rage. Plenty of junk, including Flash's top rapper Melle Mel's follow-ups "New York, New York" (which was listenable if awfully familiar) and "Survival" (which was just overblown overkill), was released in attempts to cash in on this relevance chic, but the most important and influential rappers to date were also a product of "The Message." Run-DMC's first album came out in 1984.

With its stripped-to-the-bone sound, crunching beats, and such accessible but street-smart narratives as "Hard Times" and "It's Like That," in addition to more conventional rap boasting, the album *Run-DMC* was the real breakthrough of the underground. One irony was that the three members of the group came from black middle-class homes in Hollis, Queens, and their "B-Boy" gangster wear was just as much a costume as the cowboy hats and space suits of Grandmaster Flash or Afrika Bambaataa. "With Run-DMC and the suburban rap school," says producer and co-founder of Def Jam Records Rick Rubin, "we looked at that [ghetto] life like a cowboy movie. To us, it was like Clint Eastwood. We could talk about those things because they weren't that close to home." This "inside" look at the street, though, was enough to impress an unprecedented, widespread white audience when combined with Run and DMC's rapid-fire, dynamic delivery. To the street kids, the group's sound was loud and abrasive—and therefore exciting and identifiable. "It wasn't a hard record to sell to the kids on the street," says Def Jam's president (and Run's brother) Russell Simmons. "But it was a hard record to sell to a producer or the rest of the industry. There was no standard to compare it to."

Run-DMC was the first great rap album. Even as David Toop was writing in *The Rap Attack* (now out of print, Toop's book is one of very few decent extended writings on hip-hop) that "rap is music for 12-inch singles," *Run-DMC*'s release demonstrated that the form could be sustained for longer than six or seven minutes. The next year, though, as breakdance fever continued to sweep the nation, the group released *King of Rock*. It sold over a million copies, but the group sounded tired. The title song and its video were funny, crunching classics, but the in-your-face rhymes and jagged scratching style seemed stale. The tracks which experi-mented with a rap-reggae mix were flat and unconvincing. And though seventeen-year-old hotshot LL Cool J was the first and best rapper to pick up on the Run-DMC style in his spectacular debut *Radio*, he was obviously second-generation, not an innovator. It was 1985, rap had been split down the middle into two camps, and it was becoming harder to care about either one.

What has sustained rap for its (ten-year? fifteen? decades-old? the argument continues ...) history is its ability to rise to the challenge of its limitations. Just at the points at which the form has seemed doomed or at a dead end, something or someone has appeared to give it a new direction. If 1985 was hip-hop's most desperate hour (the rap magazine *The Source* recently referred to this era as "The Hip-Hop Drought"), in 1986 it rose triumphant from the ashes. Run-DMC was at the forefront of this renaissance, but it was the group's producer, Rick Rubin, who inspired it. He thought that a cover, a remake of a familiar song, would be a way to make the group's new album a "more progressive" record. "I went through my record collection," Rubin recalls, "and came up with [Aerosmith's] 'Walk This Way,' which really excited me because the way the vocals worked it was already pretty much a rap song. It would be cool to have a high-profile rap group doing a traditional rock & roll song and really not having to change that much."

Rubin brought Aerosmith's lead singer Steven Tyler and guitarist Joe Perry into the studio with Run-DMC and the resultant "Walk This Way" collaboration made rap palatable to white, suburban youth across the country. It reached Number 4 on the pop singles charts and catapulted the *Raising Hell* album to multimillion selling heights. The recent massive successes of Michael Jackson and Prince had been exceptional crossover developments, opening up MTV to black artists and reintroducing these artists to pop radio. "Walk This Way" drove those opportunities home, and it did so without compromising what made rap so special, so vibrant; the beats and aggressive, declamatory vocals made it an undeniable rap record, heavy-metal guitars or no.

Rap was established as a viable pop form, at least as long as its connections to the traditional rock and roll spirit were made explicit. Nowhere was that connection more obvious than with the next major development in hip-hop. Hot on the heels of *Raising Hell* came the Beastie Boys' *Licensed to Ill*, at the time the biggest-selling debut album in history. The Beasties were three white Jewish New Yorkers who had played together in a punk-hardcore band before discovering rap and hooking up with Rick Rubin. For them, rap wasn't a way to establish racial pride or document hard times: it was a last vestige of rock and roll rebellion, a vaguely threatening, deliberately antagonistic use for their bratty, whiny voices.

Licensed to Ill sometimes rang hollow when the Beastie Boys rhymed about a criminal, decadent life beyond the fantasies of their listeners, but when it worked—as in their breakthrough hit "Fight for Your Right [to Party]"—you could hear young America laughing and screaming along. Their rhymes were simple and unsophisticated compared to those of Run or LL Cool J, but that made it easier for their audience of rap novices to follow. Besides, technical prowess wasn't what their yelling and carousing was about.

The strongest legacy of the album, however, was purely technical. *Licensed to Ill* introduced a newly expanded rap public to the concept of sampling. Until this time, rappers were backed up by DJs who would spin records, cross-cutting between favorite beats on multiple turntables, scratching and cutting up breaks from other songs as a musical track by manually manipulating the records under the needle (the definitive scratch record was Grandmaster Flash's cataclysmic "Grandmaster Flash on the Wheels of Steel"). The advent of the digital sampler meant that a machine could isolate more precise snippets of a recording and loop or stitch them into a denser, more active backdrop. One drumbeat or a particularly funky James Brown exclamation could form the backbone of an entire track, or could just drift in for a split second and flesh out a track.

The Beasties were the perfect group to exploit this technology, because the musical accompaniment they sought was the sound they and Rubin had grown up with, heavy on Led

Zeppelin riffs and TV show themes, and packed with in-jokes and fleeting goofy references. Along with a handful of dance singles, most notably "Pump Up the Volume" by a British production duo called M/A/R/R/S, the Beasties made this bottomless, careening flow of juxtaposed sound familiar to the world. After "Walk This Way" made suburban America a little more open to the idea of rap, the Beasties, with the novelty of their personalities, attitude, and sound (and, of course, their color), won huge battalions of teenagers over to the form. But just as significantly, they rewrote the rules regarding who could make this music and what, if anything, it was supposed to sound like.

Surprisingly, in the wake of the Beastie Boys, there was not a massive, immediate explosion of white rappers. In fact, within the rap community the Beasties were cause for backlash more than celebration, and the next critical development was a move toward music "blacker" than anything ever recorded. Public Enemy emerged out of the hip-hop scene at Long Island's Adelphi University, encouraged by, once again, Rick Rubin. Their first album, 1987's *Yo, Bum Rush the Show*, didn't have the militant polemics that would characterize their later, more celebrated work, but it did have a sound and attitude as new to the listening public as the Beasties or Run or Flash had been. "When we came into the game, musicians said we're not making music, we're making noise," said producer Hank Shocklee, "so I said, 'Noise? You wanna hear noise?' I wanted to go out to be music's worst nightmare." With such open defiance, Public Enemy sculpted jarring, screeching musical tracks and wrote of the hostility they felt from and toward the white community. Public Enemy was offering an extension of rap's familiar outlaw pose, but they grounded it in the realities of contemporary urban life, with a sharp eye for detail and a brilliant sonic counterpoint that raised rap to a new level of sophistication.

If rap had crossed over, however tentatively, Public Enemy was not going to allow anyone to forget that this music came from the streets and that no rappers should feel any responsibility to take it away from there. Having found a pop audience and the kind of mass acceptance any pop form strives for from its inception, rap was now faced with the challenge of retaining its rebel stance and street-reality power. Public Enemy went on the road, opened for labelmates the Beastie Boys, and featured an onstage security force dressed in camouflage and bearing replicas of Uzis. They intimidated the young Beasties crowd and didn't really catch on with rap devotees until "Rebel without a Pause" exploded in urban black communities months later.

Rappers could now sell a million records without ever being picked up by pop radio or crossing over, and the artists were becoming aware of the kind of power that such independence meant. "Rap is black America's CNN," said Chuck D., and he would go on to claim that Public Enemy's goal was to inspire five thousand potential young leaders in the black community. This mindset ran through the work of Boogie Down Productions, who came out as hard-core gangster types (championing the honor of the Bronx in hip-hop's ongoing borough supremacy battles), but soon brought rapper KRS-One's intelligence and social concern up front in raps like "Stop the Violence." The Public Enemy mindset was there in the menacing, slow-flowing style of Eric B. & Rakim, who made the sampling of James Brown rhythm tracks and breaks the single most dominant sound in hip-hop. It was there even in the less revolutionary work of EPMD (the name stands for Erick and Parrish Making Dollars), hardly oppositional in their priorities, but uncompromisingly funky above all else.

It was an attitude that reached its fruition in 1988 when Public Enemy released *It Takes a Nation of Millions to Hold Us Back*, rap's most radical extended statement and still the finest album in the genre's history. Chuck D. castigated radio stations both black and white, fantasized about leading prison breaks, eulogized the Black Panthers, and thunderously expanded rap's range to anything and everything that crossed his mind. Shocklee and Company's tracks were merciless, annoying, and sinuous, using samples not for melodic hooks or one-dimensional rhythm tracks but as constantly shifting components in an impenetrably thick, dense collage. *It Takes a Nation* exploded onto city streets, college campuses, and booming car systems; it was simply inescapable for the entire summer. Jim Macnie wrote in the *Village Voice* that "it seemed that no one ever put in the cassette, no one ever turned it over, it was just on."

After that album, politics and outspokenness were de rigueur, simple boasting way out of style. Public Enemy's sound couldn't be copied—It still hasn't been rivaled—but that screech, once so foreign and aggressive, was soon filling dance floors in hits like Rob Base and D.J. E-Z Rock's propulsive smash "It Takes Two." Public Enemy had thrown down the gauntlet, as much musical and technological as lyrical and political, and they could just wait and see when and how the hip-hop community would respond.

Public Enemy's artistic and commercial triumph crystallized two lessons that had been developing in hip-hop for some time. Number one: anything was now fair game for rap's subject matter. Number two: a rap album could sell a lot of copies without rock guitars. Rap had, after struggling with its built-in contradictions for several years, established its long-term presence as a pop style without being required to compromise anything. Terms like "underground" and "street" and "crossover" were becoming less clear as records that would never be allowed on pop radio were turning up regularly on the pop sales charts. It didn't take long for these successes sans radio and the expansion of rap's subject matter to sink in and to set in motion the forces that put rap in the unsettled, divided condition it faces today.

The most visible immediate result was geographic. Virtually all of the rappers mentioned thus far have been residents of New York City or its environs. In 1988, galvanized by Public Enemy's triumphs, the rest of the country began to compete. Most significantly, five young men from the Los Angeles district of Compton joined together and recorded their first single, "Dope Man," which may or may not have been financed by their founder Eazy-E's drug sales profits. This group called themselves Niggas With Attitude (N.W.A.), and demonstrated that the West Coast was in the rap game for real. Their only real precursor in Los Angeles was Ice-T, the self-proclaimed inventor of "crime rhyme" whose sharp, literate depictions of gang life were inspired by ghetto novelist Iceberg Slim. N.W.A. took Ice-T's direct, balanced, and morally ambiguous war reporting to the next level with brutal, cinematically clear tales of fury and violence. The titles said it all: "Gangsta Gangsta" or even, in a gesture truly unprecedented for a record on the pop charts "[Fuck] tha Police."

Rap's single biggest pop hit in 1988 didn't come from New York or Los Angeles, however, but out of Philadelphia. DJ Jazzy Jeff and the Fresh Prince released a pleasant trifle chronicling teen suburban crises called "Parents Just Don't Understand," which hovered near the top of the pop charts all summer (Fresh Prince went on to become the first rapper to star in a prime-time sitcom). *Yo! MTV Raps* debuted on the music-video network and not only gave hip-hop a national outlet, but quickly became the channel's highest-rated show. Miami's 2 Live Crew released *Move Somethin'*, which went platinum long before they became hip-hop's most famous free-speech crusaders, and cities such as Houston and Seattle were establishing active rap scenes.

A dichotomy was firmly in place—rappers knew that they could cross over to the pop charts with minimal effort, which made many feel an obligation to be more graphic, and attempt to prove their commitment to rap's street heritage. As with the division first evident in 1985, rap had split into two camps with little common ground, and the polarization again led to a period of stagnation. N.W.A.'s *Straight Outta Compton* simply defined a new subgenre—hard-core, gangster rap—so precisely that those who followed in their path sounded like warmed-over imitators. On the other side, like the breakdance electro-rap before it, poppy MTV-friendly hip-hop quickly grew stale. L.A.'s Tone-Löc, possessor of the smoothest, most laid-back drawl in rap history, released "Wild Thing," the second best-selling single in history (right behind "We Are the World"), but it didn't feel like a revolution anymore.

Into the abyss in early 1989 jumped De La Soul, heralding the "DAISY Age" (stands for "da inner sound, y'all," and hippie comparisons only made them mad) and sampling Steely Dan, Johnny Cash, and French language instruction records on their debut album *3 Feet High and Rising*. After two full years of James Brown samples, with the occasional Parliament-Funkadelic break thrown in, it took De La Soul to remind everyone that sampling didn't have to mean just a simpler way to mix and cut records. It was a more radical structural development than that—sampling meant that rap could sound like anything. Michael Azerrad wrote in *Rolling Stone* that many saw the group as "the savior of a rap scene in danger of descending into self-parody." It's an unnecessarily sweeping statement—there were still first-rate hip-hop albums being released—but De La Soul did quickly and assuredly reenergize the form. It was the group's peculiar vision, their quirky intelligence and, just as significantly, their awareness of the true possibilities of sampling technology that made possible such a leap forward.

In De La Soul's wake came a new look (colorful prints, baggy jeans, Africa medallions) and music from De La Soul's cohorts in the Native Tongues movement, including the Jungle Brothers and A Tribe Called Quest. The sound was varied, funny, and gentle, and the "Afro-centric" emphasis of the rhymes was warm, ecologically and socially concerned, and not too preachy. Soon there was also a whole new audience; De La Soul acquired a large collegiate following, drawn to their looser grooves, accessible hooks, and appealing goofiness. This was rap that was nonthreatening, politically correct, and didn't have the tainted feel of a crossover ploy.

In addition, De La Soul helped introduce Queen Latifah and Monie Love to the public, and thus proved instrumental in the emergence of a new generation of women rappers in 1989. Women had been part of rap from the beginning; the three women in Sequence comprised one of the first rap groups to sign a recording contract, and Salt-n-Pepa had several major hits, including "Push It," one of 1988's biggest dance hits. Latifah, however, was something new. In the face of ever-increasing graphic misogyny, she (and MC Lyte, Monie, and then in 1990 Yo-Yo and numerous others) offered a strong female alternative. For all of the attention given to 2 Live Crew or N.W.A.'s "A Bitch Iz a Bitch," rap was allowing a voice for women that was far more outspoken, far more progressive than anything found in other styles of pop music.

Ultimately, this new strain of headier hip-hop offered some kind of uncompromised middle ground between rap's pop and gangster sides, but it didn't slow down their ever-widening divergence. This "new school" became its own movement, while the two camps were far too entrenched to adapt the lessons of the DAISY age to their music. Los Angeles continued to dominate the East Coast in producing new sounds and styles. Young MC, a University of Southern California economics major who had helped write Tone-Lōc's hits, recorded his own raps that featured even more danceable grooves and middle-class lyric concerns, and became a star on his own. The members of N.W.A., meanwhile, took to the road with the threat of arrest hanging over their heads if they chose to perform "[Fuck] tha Police," and by the end of 1989 had received an ominous "warning letter" from the FBI. After a decade on record, the biggest challenge hip-hop faced was not survival, but avoiding overexposure and irreparable co-optation.

Hip-hop is first and foremost a pop form, seeking to make people dance and laugh and think, to make them listen and feel, and to sell records by doing so. From its early days, even before it became a recorded commodity, it was successful at these things—Russell Simmons recalls promoting rap parties with DJ Hollywood and drawing thousands of devoted New Yorkers years before rap made it to vinyl. "It's not about a salary / It's all about reality," rap N.W.A.; even if they didn't claim that life "ain't nothing but bitches and money" on the same album, the fallacy would be clear. On a recent PBS rap special, San Francisco rapper Paris said that "[e]verybody gets into rap just to get the dollars or to get the fame."

At the same time, rap by definition has a political content; even when not explicitly issues-oriented, rap is about giving voice to a black community otherwise underrepresented, if not silent, in the mass media. It has always been and remains (despite the curse of pop potential) directly connected to the streets from which it came. It is still a basic assumption among the hip-hop community that rap speaks to real people in a real language about real things. As *Newsweek* and the 2 Live Crew arrest prove, rap still has the ability to provoke and infuriate. If there is an up side to this hostile response, it is that it verifies rap's credibility for the insider audience. If it's ultimately about a salary, it's still about reality as well. Asked why hip-hop continues to thrive, Run-DMC's DJ Jam Master Jay replied, "because for all those other musics you had to change or put on something to get into them. You don't have to do that for hip-hop."

At a certain level, these differences are irreconcilable. Since Run-DMC and the Beastie Boys established rap's crossover potential, and Public Enemy demonstrated that pop sales didn't have to result from concessions to more conventional pop structures, the two strains have been forced to move further apart and to work, in many ways, at cross-purposes. It is a scenario familiar in the progression of rock and roll from renegade teen threat to TV commercial music. Perhaps more relevant, the situation is reminiscent of punk's inability to survive the trip from England, where it was a basic component of a radical life, to America, where it was the sound track to a fashionable lifestyle.

If this conflict is fundamental to all pop that is the product of youth culture, it is heightened immeasurably by rap's legitimately radical origins and intentions. But success with a wide, white audience need not be fatal to the genre. The rage directed by much of the rap community at Hammer and Vanilla Ice is ultimately unwarranted—if they make bad records, they're hardly the first, and if that's what hits, it's not going to take the more sophisticated listeners away.

Rap has thus far proven that it can retain a strong sense of where it comes from and how central those origins are to its purpose. If this has sometimes meant shock value for its own sake—which often seems the norm for recent Gangster records, such as N.W.A.'s *100 Miles and Runnin'*—and if that is as much a dead end as Hammer's boring pop, the legacy of De La Soul is that there are other ways to work out rap's possibilities. Some of the best new groups, such as Main Source and Gang Starr, may have disappeared by the time this article appears, but they have been integrating melody, live instruments, and samples from less familiar sources into their tracks, learning from De La Soul and Digital Underground and company that hip-hop has other roads still left untrodden.

The paradigmatic hip-hop figure of 1990 would have to be Ice Cube, formerly N.W.A.'s main lyricist. He recorded *AmeriKKKa's Most Wanted* with Public Enemy's production team, the first real collaboration between the two coasts, and it ruled the streets for most of the year. The album's layered, crunching, impossibly dense sound set a new standard for rap production, the progression we've been waiting for since *It Takes a Nation of Millions to Hold Us Back.* Ice Cube's technical verbal prowess is astonishing; his razor-sharp imagery is cut up into complicated internal rhymes, then bounced over and across the beat, fluid but never predictable, like a topflight bebop soloist.

The content, though, is somewhat more troublesome. When rhyming about the harsh realities of ghetto life, Ice Cube is profane, powerful, and insightful. When writing about women—make that bitches, since he uses that word a full sixty times on the album—things get more disturbing. He has defended "You Can't Fade Me," a first-person account of contemplating murderous revenge on a woman who falsely accuses him of fathering her expected child, by saying that he's just telling a story and illustrating that people really do think that way. It's a fair enough defense, but it's hard to believe that many listeners won't hear it as Ice Cube's own attitude. If part of rap's appeal is the "reality" of the rappers, their lack of constructed stage personae and distance from the audience, Ice Cube simply doesn't establish the constructedness sufficiently to make the song's "objective" narrative effective.

But here's the surprise. At a press conference late in 1990, Ice Cube said that "a lot of people took mixed messages from my album, so I'm just going to have to try to make my writing clearer in the future." It's something rappers have always had a hard time doing—when a performance style is so rooted in boasting and competition, admitting that you might be wrong or even just imperfect is a risky matter. If Public Enemy had been willing to take such an attitude, of course, they could have handled the Griff affair much more gracefully. But if Ice Cube is sincere about improving his expression without compromising it (and his moving, somber antiviolence track "Dead Homiez" bodes well), he may have shown us the future. Like De La Soul's radical rewriting of sampling and hip-hop personae, gangster rap that moves beyond gore and shock is evidence that rap is not trapped in a dead-end dichotomy.

Writing about rap always has a certain dispatches-from-the-front-lines quality; sounds and styles change so fast that by the time any generalizations or predictions appear, they have often already been proven false. At any moment, a new rapper or a new attitude or a new technology may appear and the troubled times hip-hop faced in 1990 will be nothing but ancient history. This may be its first real struggle with middle age, but rap has never failed to reinvent itself whenever the need's been there.

14

The Rap on Rap:

The "Black Music" that Isn't Either

David Samuels

This summer Soundscan, a computerized scanning system, changed *Billboard* magazine's method of counting record sales in the United States. Replacing a haphazard system that relied on big-city record stores, Soundscan measured the number of records sold nationally by scanning the bar codes at chain store cash registers. Within weeks the number of computed record sales leapt, as demographics shifted from minority-focused urban centers to white, suburban, middle-class malls. So it was that America awoke on June 22, 1991, to find that its favorite record was not *Out of Time*, by aging college-boy rockers R.E.M., but *Niggaz4life*, a musical celebration of gang rape and other violence by N.W.A., or Niggers With Attitude, a rap group from the Los Angeles ghetto of Compton whose records had never before risen above No. 27 on the Billboard charts.

From *Niggaz4life* to *Boyz N the Hood*, young black men committing acts of violence were available this summer in a wide variety of entertainment formats. Of these none is more popular than rap. And none has received quite the level of critical attention and concern. Writers on the left have long viewed rap as the heartbeat of urban America, its authors, in Arthur Kempton's words, "the pre-eminent young dramaturgists in the clamorous theater of the street." On the right, this assumption has been shared, but greeted with predictable disdain.

Neither side of the debate has been prepared, however, to confront what the entertainment industry's receipts from this summer prove beyond doubt: although rap is still proportionally more popular among blacks, its primary audience is white and lives in the suburbs. And the history of rap's degeneration from insurgent black street music to mainstream pop points to another dispiriting conclusion: the more rappers were packaged as violent black criminals, the bigger their white audiences became.

If the racial makeup of rap's audience has been largely misunderstood, so have the origins of its authors. Since the early 1980s a tightly knit group of mostly young, middle-class, black New Yorkers, in close concert with white record producers, executives, and publicists, has been making rap music for an audience that industry executives concede is primarily composed of white suburban males. Building upon a form pioneered by lower-class black artists in New York between 1975 and 1983, despite an effective boycott of the music by both black and white radio that continues to this day, they created the most influential pop music of the 1980s. Rap's appeal to whites rested in its evocation of an age-old image of blackness: a foreign, sexually charged, and criminal underworld against which the norms of white society are defined, and, by extension, through which they may be defied. It was the truth of this latter proposition that rap would test in its journey into the mainstream.

"Hip-hop," the music behind the lyrics, which are "rapped," is a form of sonic bricolage with roots in "toasting," a style of making music by speaking over records. (For simplicity, I'll use the term "rap" interchangeably with "hip-hop" throughout this article.) Toasting first took hold in Jamaica in the mid-1960s, a response, legend has it, to the limited availability of expensive Western instruments and the concurrent proliferation of cheap R&B instrumental singles on Memphis-based labels such as Stax-Volt. Cool DJ Here, a Jamaican who settled in the South Bronx, is widely credited with having brought toasting to New York City. Rap spread quickly through New York's poor black neighborhoods in the mid- and late 1970s. Jams were held in local playgrounds, parks, and community centers, in the South and North Bronx, Brooklyn, and Harlem.

Although much is made of rap as a kind of urban streetgeist, early rap had a more basic function: dance music. Bill Stephney, considered by many to be the smartest man in the rap business, recalls the first time he heard hip-hop:

> The point wasn't rapping, it was rhythm, DJs cutting records left and right, taking the big drum break from Led Zeppelin's "When the Levee Breaks," mixing it together with "Ring My Bell," then with a Bob James Mardi Gras jazz record and some James Brown. You'd have 2,000 kids in any community center in New York, moving back and forth, back and forth, like some kind of tribal war dance, you might say. It was the rapper's role to match this intensity rhythmically. No one knew what he was saying. He was just rocking the mike.

Rap quickly spread from New York to Philadelphia, Chicago, Boston, and other cities with substantial black populations. Its popularity was sustained by the ease with which it could be made. The music on early rap records sounded like the black music of the day: funk or, more often, disco. Performers were unsophisticated about image and presentation, tending toward gold lamé jumpsuits and Jericurls, a second-rate appropriation of the stylings of funk musicians like George Clinton and Bootsy Collins.

The first rap record to make it big was "Rapper's Delight," released in 1979 by the Sugar Hill Gang, an ad hoc all-star team drawn from three New York groups on Sylvia and Joey Robinson's Sugar Hill label. Thanks to Sylvia Robinson's soul music and background, the first thirty seconds of "Rapper's Delight" were indistinguishable from the disco records of the day: light guitars, high-hat drumming, and handclaps over a deep funk bass line. What followed will be immediately familiar to anyone who was young in New York City that summer:

> I said, hip-hop, de-hibby, de-hibby-dibby,
> Hip-hip-hop you don't stop.
> Rock it out, Baby Bubba to the boogie de-bang-bang,
> Boogie to the boogie to be.
> Now what you hear is not a test,
> I'm rapping to the beat ...
> I said, "By the way, baby, what's your name?"
> She said, "I go by the name Lois Lane
> And you can be my boyfriend, you surely can
> Just let me quit my boyfriend, he's called Superman."
> I said, "he's a fairy, I do suppose
> Flying through the air in pantyhose ...
> You need a man who's got finesse
> And his whole name across his chest" ...

Like disco music and jumpsuits, the social commentaries of early rappers like Grandmaster Flash and Melle Mel were for the most part transparent attempts to sell records to whites by any means necessary. Songs like "White Lines" (with its anti-drug theme) and "The Message" (about ghetto life) had the desired effect, drawing fulsome praise from white rock critics, raised on the protest ballads of Bob Dylan and Phil Ochs. The reaction on the street was somewhat less favorable. "The Message" is a case in point. "People hated that record," recalls Russell Simmons, president of Def Jam Records. "I remember the Junebug, a famous DJ of the time, was playing it up at the Fever, and Ronnie DJ put a pistol to his head and said, 'Take that record off and break it or I'll blow your fucking head off.' The whole club stopped until he broke that record and put it in the garbage."

It was not until 1984 that rap broke through to a mass white audience. The first group to do so was Run-DMC, with the release of its debut album, *Run-DMC*, and with *King of Rock* one year later. These albums blazed the trail that rap would travel into the musical mainstream. Bill Adler, a former rock critic and rap's best-known publicist, explains:

> They were the first group that came on stage as if they had just come off the street corner. But unlike the first generation of rappers, they were solidly middle class. Both of Run's parents were college-educated. DMC was a good Catholic schoolkid, a mama's boy. Neither of them was deprived and neither of them ever ran with a gang, but on stage they became the biggest, baddest, streetest guys in the world.

When Run-DMC covered the Aerosmith classic "Walk This Way," the resulting video made it onto MTV, and the record went gold.

Rap's new mass audience was in large part the brainchild of Rick Rubin, a Jewish punk rocker from suburban Long Island who produced the music behind many of rap's biggest acts. Like many New Yorkers his age, Rick grew up listening to Mr. Magic's Rap Attack, a rap radio show on WHBI. In 1983, at the age of 19, Rubin founded Def Jam Records in his NYU dorm room. (Simmons bought part of Def Jam in 1984 and took full control of the company in 1989.) Rubin's next group, the Beastie Boys, was a white punk rock band whose transformation into a rap group pointed rap's way into the future. The Beasties' first album, *Licensed to Ill*, backed by airplay of its anthemic frat-party single "You've Got to Fight for Your Right to Party," became the first rap record to sell a million copies.

The appearance of white groups in a black musical form has historically prefigured the mainstreaming of the form, the growth of the white audience, and the resulting dominance of white performers. With rap, however, this process took an unexpected turn: white demand indeed began to determine the direction of the genre, but what it wanted was music more defiantly black. The result was Public Enemy, produced and marketed by Rubin, the next group significantly to broaden rap's appeal to young whites.

Public Enemy's now familiar mélange of polemic and dance music was formed not on inner-city streets but in the suburban Long Island towns in which the group's members grew up. The children of successful black middle-class professionals, they gave voice to the feeling that, despite progress toward equality, blacks still did not quite belong in white America. They complained of unequal treatment by the police, of never quite overcoming the color of their skin: "We were suburban college kids doing what we were supposed to do, but we were always made to feel like something else," explains Stephney, the group's executive producer.

Public Enemy's abrasive and highly politicized style made it a fast favorite of the white avant-garde, much like the English punk rock band The Clash ten years before. Public Enemy's music, produced by the Shocklee brothers Hank and Keith, was faster, harder, and more abrasive than the rap of the day, music that moved behind the vocals like a full-scale band. But the root of Public Enemy's success was a highly charged theater of race in which white listeners became guilty eavesdroppers on the putative private conversation of the inner city. Chuck D denounced his enemies (the media, some radio stations), proclaimed himself "Public Enemy #1," and praised Louis Farrakhan in stentorian tones, flanked onstage by black-clad security guards from the Nation of Islam, the SIWs, led by Chuck's political mentor, Professor Griff. Flavor Flav, Chuck's homeboy sidekick, parodied street style: oversize sunglasses, baseball cap cocked to one side, a clock the size of a silver plate draped around his neck, going off on wild verbal riffs that often meant nothing at all.

The closer rap moved to the white mainstream, the more it became like rock 'n' roll, a celebration of posturing over rhythm. The back catalogs of artists like James Brown and George Clinton were relentlessly plundered for catchy hooks, then overlaid with dance beats and social commentary. Public Enemy's single "Fight the Power" was the biggest college hit of 1989:

> Elvis was a hero to most
> But he never meant shit to me, you see
> Straight-up racist that sucker was simple and plain
> Motherfuck him and John Wayne
> 'Cause I'm black and I'm proud
> I'm ready and hyped, plus I'm amped
> Most of my heroes don't appear on no stamps
> Sample a look back, you look and find
> Nothing but rednecks for 400 years if you check.

After the release of "Fight the Power," Professor Griff made a series of anti-Semitic remarks in an interview with the *Washington Times*. Griff was subsequently asked to leave the group, for what Chuck D termed errors in judgment. Although these errors were lambasted in editorials across the country, they do not seem to have affected Public Enemy's credibility with its young white fans.

Public Enemy's theatrical black nationalism and sophisticated noise ushered in what is fast coming to be seen as rap's golden age, a heady mix of art, music, and politics. Between 1988 and 1989 a host of innovative acts broke into the mainstream. KRS-One, now a regular on the Ivy League lecture circuit, grew up poor, living on the streets of the South Bronx until he met a New York City social worker, Scott La Rock, later murdered in a drive-by shooting. Together they formed BDP, Boogie Down Productions, recording for the Jive label on RCA. Although songs like "My Philosophy" and "Love's Gonna Get 'Cha (Material Love)" were clever and self-critical, BDP's roots remained firmly planted in the guns-and-posturing of the mainstream rap ghetto.

The ease with which rap can create such aural cartoons, says Hank Shocklee, lies at the very heart of its appeal as entertainment: "Whites have always liked black music," he explains. "That part is hardly new. The difference with rap was that the imagery of black artists, for the first time, reached the level of black music. The sheer number of words in a rap song allows for the creation of full characters impossible in R&B. Rappers become like superheroes. Captain America or the Fantastic Four."

By 1988 the conscious manipulation of racial stereotypes had become rap's leading edge, a trend best exemplified by the rise to stardom of Schoolly D, a Philadelphia rapper on the Jive label who sold more than half a million records with little mainstream notice. It was not that the media had never heard of Schoolly D: white critics and fans, for the first time, were simply at a loss for words. His voice, fierce and deeply textured, could alone frighten listeners. He used it as a rhythmic device that made no concessions to pop-song form, talking evenly about smoking crack and using women for sex, proclaiming his blackness, accusing other rappers of not being black enough. What Schoolly D meant by blackness was abundantly clear.

Schoolly D was a misogynist and a thug. If listening to Public Enemy was like eavesdropping on a conversation, Schoolly D was like getting mugged. This, aficionados agreed, was what they had been waiting for: a rapper from whom you would flee in abject terror if you saw him walking toward you late at night.

It remained for N.W.A., a more conventional group of rappers from Los Angeles, to adapt Schoolly D's stylistic advance for the mass white market with its first album-length release, *Straight Out of Compton*, in 1989. The much-quoted rap from that album, "Fuck the Police," was the target of an FBI warning to police departments across the country, and a constant presence at certain college parties, white and black:

> "Fuck the Police" coming straight out the underground
> A young nigger got it bad 'cause I'm brown
> And not the other color. Some police think
> They have the authority to kill the minority …
> A young nigger on the warpath
> And when I'm finished, it's gonna be a bloodbath
> Of cops, dying in L.A.
> Yo, Dre I've got something to say: Fuck the Police.

Other songs spoke of trading oral sex for crack and shooting strangers for fun. After the release of *Straight Out of Compton*, N.W.A.'s lead rapper and chief lyricist, Ice Cube, left the group. Billing himself as "the nigger you love to hate," Ice Cube released a solo album, *Amerikkka's Most Wanted*, which gleefully pushed the limits of rap's ability to give offense. One verse ran:

> I'm thinking to myself, "why did I bang her?"
> Now I'm in the closet, looking for the hanger.

But what made *Amerikkka's Most Wanted* so shocking to so many record buyers was the title track's violation of rap's most iron-clad taboo—black on white violence:

> Word, yo, but who the fuck is heard:
> It's time you take a trip to the suburbs.
> Let 'em see a nigger invasion
> Point blank, on a Caucasian.
> Cock the hammer and crack a smile:
> "Take me to your house, pal … "

Ice Cube took his act to the big screen this summer in *Boyz N the Hood*, drawing rave reviews for his portrayal of a young black drug dealer whose life of crime leads him to an untimely end. The crime-doesn't-pay message, an inheritance from the grade-B gangster film, is the stock-in-trade of another L.A. rapper-turned-actor, Ice-T of *New Jack City* fame, a favorite of socially conscious rock critics. Tacking unhappy endings onto glorifications of drug dealing and gang warfare, Ice-T offers all the thrills of the form while alleviating any guilt listeners may have felt about consuming drive-by shootings along with their popcorn.

It was in this spirit that "Yo! MTV Raps" debuted in 1989 as the first national broadcast forum for rap music. The videos were often poorly produced, but the music and visual presence of stars like KRS-One, LL Cool J, and Chuck D proved enormously compelling, rocketing "Yo!" to the top of the MTV ratings. On weekends bands were interviewed and videos introduced by Fab Five Freddie; hip young white professionals watched his shows to keep up with urban black slang and fashion. Younger viewers rushed home from school on weekdays to catch ex-Beastie Boys DJ Dr. Dre, a sweatsuit-clad mountain of a man, well over 300 pounds, and Ed Lover, who evolved a unique brand of homeboy Laurel and Hardy mixed with occasional social comment.

With "Yo! MTV Raps," rap became for the first time the music of choice in the white suburbs of middle America. From the beginning, says Doug Herzog, MTV's vice president for programming, the show's audience was primarily white, male, suburban, and between the ages of 16 and 24, a demographic profile that "Yo!"'s success helped set in stone. For its daytime audience, MTV spawned an ethnic rainbow of well-scrubbed pop rappers from MC Hammer to Vanilla Ice to Gerardo, a Hispanic actor turned rap star. For "Yo" itself rap became more overtly politicized as it expanded its audience. Sound bites from the speeches of Malcolm X and Martin Luther King became de rigueur introductions to formulaic assaults on white America mixed with hymns to gang violence and crude sexual caricature.

Holding such polyglot records together is what *Village Voice* critic Nelson George has labeled "ghettocentrism," a style-driven cult of blackness defined by crude stereotypes. P.R. releases, like a recent one for Los Angeles rapper DJ Quik, take special care to mention artists' police records, often enhanced to provide extra street credibility. When Def Jam star Slick Rick was arrested for attempted homicide, Def Jam incorporated the arrest into its publicity campaign for Rick's new album, bartering exclusive rights to the story to *Vanity Fair* in exchange for the promise of a lengthy profile. Muslim groups such as Brand Nubian proclaim their hatred for white devils, especially those who plot to poison black babies. That Brand Nubian believes the things said on its records is unlikely: the group seems to get along quite well with its white Jewish publicist, Beth Jacobson of Electra Records. Anti-white, and, in this case, anti-Semitic, rhymes are a shorthand way of defining one's opposition to the mainstream. Racism is reduced to fashion, by the rappers who use it and by the white audiences to whom such images appeal. What's significant here are not so much the intentions of artist and audience as a dynamic in which anti-Semitic slurs and black criminality correspond to "authenticity," and "authenticity" sells records.

The selling of this kind of authenticity to a young white audience is the stock-in-trade of *The Source*, a full-color monthly magazine devoted exclusively to rap music, founded by Jon Shecter while still an undergraduate at Harvard. Shecter is what is known in the rap business as a Young Black Teenager. He wears a Brooklyn Dodgers baseball cap, like Spike Lee, and a Source T-shirt. As editor of *The Source*, Shecter has become a necessary quote for stories about rap in *Time* and other national magazines.

An upper-middle-class white, Shecter has come in for his share of criticism, the most recent of which appeared as a diatribe by the sometime critic and tinpot racist Harry Allen in a black community newspaper, *The City Sun*, which pointed out that Shecter is Jewish. "There's no place for me to say anything," Shecter responds. "Given what I'm doing my viewpoint has to be that whatever comes of the black community, the hip-hop community which is the black community, is the right thing. I know my place. The only way in which criticism can be raised is on a personal level, because the way that things are set up, with the white-controlled media, prevents sincere back-and-forth discussion from taking place." The latest venture in hip-hop marketing, a magazine planned by Time Warner, will also be edited by a young white, Jonathan van Meter, a former Condé Nast editor.

In part because of young whites like Shecter and van Meter, rap's influence on the street continues to decline. "You put out a record by Big Daddy Kane," Rubin says, "and then put out the same record by a pop performer like Janet Jackson. Not only will the Janet Jackson record sell ten times more copies, it will also be the cool record to play in clubs." Stephney agrees: "Kids in my neighborhood pump dance hall reggae on their systems all night long, because that's where the rhythm is.... People complain about how white kids stole black culture. The truth of the matter is that no one can steal a culture." Whatever its continuing significance in the realm of racial politics, rap's hour as innovative popular music has come and gone. Rap forfeited whatever claim it may have had to particularity by acquiring a mainstream white audience whose tastes increasingly determined the nature of the form. What whites wanted was not music, but black music, which as a result stopped really being either.

White fascination with rap sprang from a particular kind of cultural tourism pioneered by the Jazz Age novelist Carl Van Vechten. Van Vechten's 1926 best seller *Nigger Heaven* imagined a masculine, criminal, yet friendly black ghetto world that functioned, for Van Vechten and for his readers, as a refuge from white middle-class boredom. In *Really the Blues*, the white jazzman Mezz Mezzrow went one step further, claiming that his own life among black people in Harlem had physically transformed him into a member of the Negro race, whose unique sensibility he had now come to share. By inverting the moral values attached to contemporary racial stereotypes, Van Vechten and Mezzrow at once appealed to and sought to undermine the prevailing racial order. Both men, it should be stressed, conducted their tours in person.

The moral inversion of racist stereotypes as entertainment has lost whatever transformative power it may arguably have had fifty years ago. MC Serch of 3rd Bass, a white rap traditionalist, with short-cropped hair and thick-rimmed Buddy Holly glasses, formed his style in the uptown hip-hop clubs like the L.Q. in the early 1980s. "Ten or eleven years ago," he remarks, "when I was wearing my permanent-press Lee's with a beige campus shirt and matching Adidas sneakers, kids I went to school with were calling me a 'wigger,' 'black wannabe,' all kinds of racist names. Now those same kids are driving Jeeps with MCM leather interiors and pumping Public Enemy."

The ways in which rap has been consumed and popularized speak not of cross-cultural understanding, musical or otherwise, but of a voyeurism and tolerance of racism in which black and white are both complicit. "Both the rappers and their white fans affect and commodify their own visions of street culture," argues Henry Louis Gates Jr. of Harvard University, "like buying Navajo blankets at a reservation road-stop. A lot of what you see in rap is the guilt of the black middle class about its economic success, its inability to put forth a culture of its own. Instead they do the worst possible thing, falling back on fantasies of street life. In turn, white college students with impeccable gender credentials buy nasty sex lyrics under the cover of getting at some kind of authentic black experience."

Gates goes on to make the more worrying point: "What is potentially very dangerous about this is the feeling that by buying records they have made some kind of valid social commitment." Where the assimilation of black street culture by whites once required a degree of human contact between the races, the street is now available at the flick of a cable channel—to black and white middle class alike. "People want to consume and they want to consume easy," Hank Shocklee says. "If you're a suburban white kid and you want to find out what life is like for a black city teenager, you buy a record by N.W.A. It's like going to an amusement park and getting on a roller coaster ride—records are safe, they're controlled fear, and you always have the choice of turning it off. That's why nobody ever takes a train up to 125th Street and gets out and starts walking around. Because then you're not in control anymore: it's a whole other ball game." This kind of consumption—of racist stereotypes, of brutality toward women, or even of uplifting tributes to Dr. Martin Luther King—is of a particularly corrupting kind. The values it instills find their ultimate expression in the ease with which we watch young black men killing each other: in movies, on records, and on the streets of cities and towns across the country.

Part III

Ain't No Love in the Heart of the City:

Hip-Hop, Space, and Place

Murray Forman

Themes of space and place are profoundly important in hip-hop. Virtually all of the early descriptions of hip-hop practices identify territory and the public sphere as significant factors, whether in the visible artistic expression and appropriation of public space via graffiti or B-boying, the sonic impact of a pounding bass line, or the discursive articulation of urban geography in rap lyrics. The dominant narrative of hip-hop's growth and development has traditionally described its formative stages in the streets, parks, community centers, and nightclubs of the Bronx and Harlem, documenting its gradual spread across New York's boroughs and throughout the northeast until it had penetrated virtually all regions and urban centers in the United States (Fernando 1994; Ogg and Upshal 1999). Moreover, most accounts tend to detail the localized struggles against adversity within urban ghetto environments as young black and Latino youths confronted authority and repression in their various forms. Through these tellings, a particular image of hip-hop has been circulated, one that binds locale, resistance, innovation, affirmation, and cultural identity within a complex web of spatialized meanings and practices.

Space and place are important factors that influence identity formation as they relate to localized practices of the self. For instance, graffiti has traditionally been integrated as a spatial practice and among the impressive features of the handwritten tag "TAKI 183" that proliferated in New York in the early 1970s is its emphasis on locality (celebrating 183 Street as the young writer's home turf) and its ubiquity throughout the city. As the ink marker tags evolved into larger and more fully realized spray art pieces, the metal canvases of New York's Metropolitan Transit Authority subways presented a mobile medium that privileged space and facilitated young artists' expansive reach while providing billboard-size surfaces that promoted individuals or entire graffiti crews.

Similarly, in rap the definition of one's environment and the urban spaces of home terrain is a conventional aspect of the form. MC Rakim's flowing statement "Now if you're from Uptown, Brooklyn bound, the Bronx, Queens, or Long Island Sound, even the other states come right and exact, it ain't where you're from but where you're at" ("I Know You Got Soul," 1987, 4th and Broadway) still reverberates within hip-hop even as the discourses and lyrical articulation of race, space, and place have advanced to a point where they begin to undermine Rakim's original concept. Although his line is widely referenced, it does, in fact, seem to matter a great deal "where you're from" *and* "where you're at." These are interconnected themes that are not easily segmented or compartmentalized. The tales of originary sites of significance that describe local places and place-based activities emerge as crucial indicators for the shaping of attitudes and identities among hip-hop's entrepreneurs including Def Jam founder Russell Simmons,

James Smith of Rap-A-Lot Records, or Bad Boy Entertainment creator P. Diddy as well as among artists such as Tupac Shakur or Eminem. Can Jay-Z be realistically disconnected from Brooklyn or Nas from Queens? Can Snoop Dogg be comprehended without acknowledging his Long Beach, California, roots and can Outkast be isolated from Atlanta? Where these individuals are from is an essential element of who they are and what they project, whether in a broader regional sense of space or in more finely nuanced and closely delineated scale of place.

Since rap music's inception, its lyrics have articulated the details of place with ever greater specificity. In the process, MCs have transformed the abstract notion of space into a more closely defined locus of experience as the close-knit relations that cohere within neighborhoods and city blocks are granted discursive primacy. If space is a broadly configured dimension, place, as framed within discourses of the 'hood, constitutes a microscale of experience that has, since roughly 1988, achieved greater significance within hip-hop; today, "the 'hood" prevails as hip-hop's dominant spatial trope. The emphasis on the geocultural character of "the 'hood" can be heard in Scarface's 2002 recording "On My Block" (Def Jam South) when he proclaims "on my block it ain't no different than the next block," suggesting the continuity of a localized environment, individuated places that are linked across urban space. With over a decade of experience in the rap music industry, Scarface's identification with his block and his 'hood is also infused in the expressive voice of a rap elder, someone who has been impacted and molded by his connection to the 'hood and who, approaching middle age, finds himself in a unique physical and mental state from which to analyze the allure and character of his immediate surroundings. For him, the local remains a touchstone, linked to roots and the foundations of personal character.

Addressing rap music's inception within the geographic and cultural environments of uptown New York, David Toop names people and places that were integral to the establishment of a vital hip-hop scene. Toop's chapter introduces a rationale for developments in rap, citing the nexus of cultural influences, especially those of the Caribbean and African American communities, and he details the rise of prominent innovators who merged artistry with commerce as they honed their hip-hop talents. Throughout his chapter, he explicitly refers to local schools, housing projects, community centers, public parks, and nightclubs, reinforcing the vitality of the city's uptown boroughs and the spatial concentration of early hip-hop.

Davarian Baldwin offers a sophisticated reading of spatial practices and social power that are aligned across multiple dimensions and that are often intensely inflected by aspects of race, class, and gender. As Baldwin explains, space may refer to material, lived environments, but it is also politicized in myriad ways and the spatial character of any environment is often forged through the political alliances or antagonisms that unfold within social relations. Baldwin interrogates the often-stated authority of the ghetto as the root of "real" hip-hop, challenging prevalent attitudes that assert the "truth" of compressed urban enclaves and nominate the 'hood as today's dominant locus of hip-hop identity. In his analysis, however, Baldwin acknowledges that the ghetto and the 'hood function within a symbolic economy where the spatial value of any given location is assessed in relation to other places and spaces. Properly foregrounding the representational images and narratives of ghetto spaces that proliferate in the media, Baldwin offers an insightful critique of the manifold articulations of "the real" and the ways they are interpreted and made meaningful among audiences and consumers, both white and black. The specific references to the infamous east-west animosities that prevailed throughout much of the 1990s are convincingly framed within a discursive conflict pertaining not simply to geographies of difference but to underlying ideological formations relating to distinctions across the geopolitical landscape of U.S. blackness in which "ghettocentricity" emerges as "a counter move to the Afrocentricity and white supremacy of the day."

In my own contribution, I explain hip-hop's emergence and expansion in the context of localized labor and industrial capital. Hip-hop is not newly commercialized, having been integrated into highly localized marketing and promotional infrastructures since its inception, yet what is often overlooked in critical studies is how various enabling or restrictive factors operating at differing scales of influence have affected the growth and evolution of hip-hop at each stage of its development. A fundamental issue in the study of space and place includes the role of the posse, crew, or clique. As Greg Tate observes, "every successful rap group is a black fraternal organization, a posse" (1992: 134) and this chapter explores the ways in which the posse formation is integrated into the particular creative processes of rap music. Finally, the chapter examines specific lyrical examples in order to chart some of the more prominent discursive shifts that have, over time, altered the spatial emphasis of rap music and hip-hop culture as the initial emphasis of the ghetto was subsumed by a pronounced articulation of themes and imagery from "the 'hood."

Although members of the hip-hop generation display their affective alignment with the 'hood, the constituent elements of hip-hop have also expanded on a global scale, disseminated through the transnational mass media. A growing body of scholarly research (Mitchell 2001) indicates that today hip-hop is also part of the everyday practices and experience of youths around the world as they combine its expressive forms with their own national and local inflections. DJs, MCs, B-boys, and graffiti artists in dispersed global contexts are actively integrating hip-hop with their own cultural experiences, creating new locally relevant meanings and redefining their social environments as they do so. Andy Bennett's contribution is, thus, representative of this more recent thread in the study of global hip-hop.

As a dynamic cultural form and highly promoted set of cultural commodities, hip-hop has entered the consciousness of audiences and observers on a global scale. How it is packaged and promoted and, correspondingly, how audiences have adopted *and* adapted it within their own daily conditions is a crucial issue for, as Bennett notes, hip-hop's international mobility is fraught with questions concerning authenticity in the face of the appropriation of African American cultural practices. Bennett offers an impressive ethnographic analysis of localized hip-hop scenes, remaining cognizant of the fact that the local and the global are inextricably imbricated through contemporary cultural circuits and media flows (what Robertson [1995] has termed "the glocal" or that Robins [1991] refers to as "the global-local nexus"). The two urban research sites in Bennett's study reveal distinct ways that hip-hop is made meaningful according to local and national traditions, as well as identifying the different cultural stakes involved for the young hip-hop fans and artists in Newcastle, UK, and Frankfurt am Main, Germany.

REFERENCES

Fernando, S. H. 1994. *The New Beats: Exploring the Music, Culture, and Attitudes of Hip-Hop*. New York: Anchor Books.

Hebdige, Dick. 1987. *Cut 'n' Mix: Culture, Identity and Caribbean Music*. London: Comedia.

Mitchell, Tony, ed. 2001. *Global Noise: Rap and Hip-Hop Outside the USA*. Middletown, CT: Wesleyan University Press.

Ogg, Alex, and David Upshal. 1999. *The Hip Hop Years: A History of Rap*. New York: Fromm International.

Robertson, Roland. 1995. "Glocalization: Time-Space and Homogeneity-Heterogeneity." In *Global Modernities*, edited by Mike Featherstone, Scott Lash, and Roland Robertson. Thousand Oaks, CA: Sage.

Robins, Kevin. 1991. "Tradition and Translation: National Culture in its Global Context." In *Enterprise and Heritage: Crosscurrents of National Culture*, edited by John Corner and Sylvia Harvey. New York: Routledge.

Rose, Tricia. 1994. *Black Noise: Rap Music and Black Culture in Contemporary America*. Hanover, NH: Wesleyan University Press.

Tate, Greg. 1992. *Flyboy in the Buttermilk: Essays on Contemporary America*. New York: Fireside.

15

Black Empires, White Desires:
The Spatial Politics of Identity in the Age of Hip-Hop

Davarian L. Baldwin

We have reached the point where our popular culture threatens to undermine our character as a nation.

Bob Dole

People are outraged, man, you get to the point where you're constantly hearing over and over talk about mugging people, killing women, beating women, sexual behavior. When young people see this—14, 15, 16 years of age—they think this is acceptable behavior.

Rev. Calvin O. Butts

I have seen a rise lately in the disrespect of black women.... Are we the ones influencing the world? If that was the case, what music was Bill Clinton listening to when he whirlpooled Lani Guinier?

Joseph Simmons (of Run DMC)

1997 was a pivotal year for black popular culture in general and hip hop in particular. Caught in the crossfire of the William Bennett/C. Delores Tucker censorship movement, the deaths of Tupac Shakur and the Notorious BIG (in a so-called East/West Coast battle), and an increase in its consumption (especially of "gangsta rap") among suburban white youth, hip hop has been placed under the "microscope and found ... to be the source of all that is wrong with American society" (Diawara, 1993, 2). From the right, hip hop is attacked as a practice that started in urban America but is infecting the morals and family values of suburban teens. At the same time, sectors of the left and the black middle-class distance themselves from hip hop because of its misogyny and homophobia. The critique of hip hop as a black popular culture form that exists as an outside threat or infection, ravaging "American" (and black middle-class) culture and values, must be understood within a history of identification located squarely in the ideological and material spaces of colonialism, racism, and national identity. The ability to fix hip hop as pure difference from the norm or as the source of wrongdoing must be interrogated. It suggests that there is an already-agreed-upon national character

159

threatened by a deviant popular culture (Dole) and leaves unquestioned the border where national character ends and popular culture begins.[1]

Hip hop itself is not purely a U.S., let alone black, cultural form. However, it is not an understatement to say that the deviancy or threat in popular culture is racialized, particularly through old narratives of the dysfunction of the black family (Kelley, 1997). These stories are now being deployed to identify the source of the problem within hip hop culture. After the death of the Notorious BIG, *Village Voice* writer Toure suggests this vision: "I can see now that the murder and killings are coming from the same hands that make the beats and rhymes; how is living in hip hop any different than living in the dysfunctional black family writ large?" (1997, 30).

For many, it appears that the hip hop nation and the nation at large are no longer safe from the deviancy that the black family produces. Discourse on the black family with its female-headed home becomes shorthand to make sense of the supposedly unique violence and sexuality in certain genres of hip hop. The lazy connections made between mythologies of dysfunctional black families and hip hop ignore the performative aspects of black popular culture. These narratives understand the deviancy in hip hop to be an uncomplicated (re)presentation of black culture (Fanon, 1967). The performance of hip hop as a black cultural form, for better or worse, becomes a reference for "authentic" blackness. As an action and reaction against conservative and liberal backlash,[2] at times hip hop attempts to counter negative notions of blackness with its own "racial authenticity," where the position of absolute difference is self-induced. Racial authenticity is best articulated in these instances through the stance that the artistic production is pure and untouched by any means of dilution.[3]

Within black communities, this process of black authenticity has historically oscillated between the binaries of excess and austerity. As Greg Tate contends, "the controversies surrounding hip hop in the black community have revived an ongoing debate over who best tells black stories: our blues people or our bourgeoisie" (1997, 70). In order to combat the "negative" idealizations of blackness, middle-class moral purists (even draped in kente cloth) attack the sexual frankness of hip hop as "excessive" and tend to support what is understood as "positive rap" because of its Afrocentric rhetoric and/or political awareness,[4] where as some "Ghettocentric" advocates defend the explicit lyrics as reality-based and resent the possibilities of censorship as dilutions of the authentic "realness" of black experiences. This position in hip hop is exemplified by the characterization of the "keepin-it-real nigga."

It must be noted that these positions are not set in stone and often overlap and intersect. For example, a third position might be the one articulated by KRS-One, which contains a nationalist hip hop edge but is rooted in nostalgia, not for Africa's golden era, but for a hip hop golden age. In the midst of hip hop's international growth and change, this "reaching back" for better times attempts to figure out "what went wrong, and why did hip hop become the revolution that failed?" Instead of attempting to "keep it real," this position is set on correcting rap music's ills, so that, as a culture, the hip hop nation can "keep it right." In what way are the articulations of the "keepin'-it-real nigga" or the "African" complicit with a white patriarchal order by designating what behaviors, sexualities, and representations will be accepted into the space of black popular culture? In what way is the masking of these performances as "natural," "accurate," or "real" complicit with the traditional order, and in what way are they disruptive?

Ironically, both extreme critiques and defenses of hip hop as an authentic representation of black life converge upon a certain refashioning of the infamous Moynihan (1965) report. When black families and women are the point of focus, representations of black women stand in for authentic blackness. In turn, the visibility of black female purity or contamination signifies the success or failure of black culture; women's bodies become the terrain on which battles over black authenticity are waged. In this context, C. Delores Tucker is able to attend a Time Warner board meeting and exclaim that Lil' Kim's songs must be banned. As an example of what she calls "pornographic," Tucker quotes "No Time": "No money, money / No licky, licky / Fuck the dicky, dicky and the quickie" (1996). Kim's lyrics could be (and have been) read as part of a long musical history of black women taking a stance for sexual and economic self-satisfaction (Rose, 1994; Davis, 1998). However, alternative voices are now silenced as deviant, as false articulations of blackness, and therefore irrelevant. The primacy of familial and traditional values nearly overrides any focus on social/sexual inequalities. But the insistence on making an artist like Kim irrelevant also shows the centrality of her work. Despite the attempts to repress and regulate personal and interpersonal black conduct, artists like Kim have emerged as part of a hip hop-inspired black bourgeois aesthetic.

This aesthetic rejects both black petit-bourgeois respectability and ghetto authenticity. Its practitioners accept the black bourgeois notion of upward mobility without rejecting the desires and consumption habits of the black working class. This new black aesthetic offers a new identity outside the workplace by endorsing the consumption of luxury goods. As a form of "dressing up," it also offers a status for subordinate groups that blurs distinctions between themselves and their oppressors (Kelley, 1994, 167–69). They are changing what it means to be black and middle class in ways that make our proponents of traditional values cringe because they refuse to be disciplined into puritan characterizations of normative middle-class behavior. They have all the trappings of the middle and elite classes but wear Versace and Armani in a different way, drive their Bentleys to different places, and play out private inequalities in public arenas.

This black aesthetic potentially de-naturalizes the divides of black/white, male/female, authentic/commodified, and challenges normative notions of hip hop as a space that can purify the impure. It debunks the contention that if hip hop were practiced in its truest form, it could bring in the straying brothers and sisters who lack "knowledge of self" or who "ain't keepin it real," as if such pronouncements of identity were ever stable. The artists remind us that "in concept, hip hop was never anti-capitalist, pro-black or intentionally avant-garde. Up until Public Enemy, hip hop's intent was never to shock the world but to sell the market on its novelty and profitability" (Tate, 1997, 70). Hip hop as a musical form could never follow the traditional association of commodification with cooptation, because the revolution of hip hop was fought out within the circuits of the market. These artists have begun to discover that a black politics can also be organized within the processes of consumption.

In the same way as we consume these artists, they consume other American cultural icons. Through their performance of gangsters, rich women, and corporate culture icons, the new gangsta rappers like Biggie, Lil' Kim and Jay-Z are living the American dream of commodity obsession and appropriation. However, the appropriation of cultural icons is not a new formulation. Throughout the 20th century, Americans of all hues who have been marginalized as ethnic or "other" have utilized the "gangsta" as a site of socio-economic mobility. In this particular moment, the grammar of the gangsta's "hustle" or "game" has become the language of the culture industry. Hip hop artists and other culture workers have become "playas," and those who attempt to stop black progress in the game have become dubbed "playa haters." These workers have aesthetically, and begun to materially, appropriate the culture industry as a site for black institution-building and contestation.

Their music describes the American entrepreneur, for whom competitiveness is a way of life. While they don't like government restrictions any more than the Republicans and endorse rampant individualism within the markets, they also expose how the fervor for deregulation extends to everything except certain genres of the American music industry, genres which dominate the world market. In addition to money makers, these lyricists speak to the inequalities, restrictions, and uneven developments that have been aimed at African-Americans and women in their quest for the "American dream."

In the current backlash against gangsta rap, however, may be heard a decline-and-fall narrative that understands hip hop to be over-commodified and calls for a return to the roots of street parties and the "yes yes y'all" freestyle rhyme, which exemplifies a pre-commodified, undiluted era. This can be heard in KRS-One's 1997 hit, "Rapture," where the hook to the song says, "step into a world where hip hop is real." In the video, we see the re-invocation of a bygone era in the historic Boogie Down South Bronx, where breakdancers and graffiti artists don the early 80s fashions of warm-up suits and Puma sneakers while performing a corrective memory of the old-school concert as a utopic space.

But this utopic space has been (re)constructed in 1997, where people no longer perform or consume hip hop in the same ways. This video intentionally decontextualizes hip hop's transformations in the pursuit of a fictive realness. Such an excavation of a hip hop past doesn't question whether hip hop was ever purely outside the circuits of commodification or consistently and totally oppositional. Rather, it assumes the location of the South Bronx and the rhyming of KRS-One as correctives to contemporary hip hop. Through performances like the one above, hip hop becomes visually fixed through the designation of which images and behaviors will exemplify an "authentic" black cultural practice. However, the new gangsta/playa aesthetic is not a full embrace of marketplace ideology and commodified cultural production. The identities produced therein are important sites for a black politics at the end of the 20th century.

The general critiques circulating around gangsta rap highlight the patriarchal masculinity, drugs, sex, gunplay, and consumption habits without either remembering the Dapper Dan and Gucci days of hip hop's "golden age" or noting the earlier progressive move that gangsta rap was making against the evolution of nation-conscious hip hop in the early 90's. What many now term "positive" or conscious rap had begun to evoke a sense of gatekeeping that designated who was and was not authentically black.

"Moving on Up": Black Respectability in the Era of Nation-Conscious Hip Hop

The massive economic and cultural reorganization of life in the 1980s pulled black people in all directions. At the same time that a black middle-class was growing (in part due to affirmative action), a larger critical mass of African-Americans were left behind in the urban enclaves of all the major U.S. cities and rural locations. The Brooklyn Heights location of the *Cosby Show* and hip hop's "Boogie Down" South Bronx were talking to each other in previously unthinkable ways. The desire for upward class mobility through the market was confronting the black cultural form of hip hop, which in some ways was marketable because of its origins in urban poverty. The urban origins of hip hop and its artists' desire to become, as Eric B. and Rakim stated, "Paid in Full" (1987), were met by black audiences, who were grappling with what it meant to be paid and black. Up to this point, authentic blackness in hip hop was associated with the inner city. When African-Americans became more upwardly mobile in the 1980s, with (for example) many black youths entering the nation's elite universities, anxieties grew within the black middle class over its relationship to blackness. Black people's "moving on up" was accompanied by a sense of alienation from authentic spaces.

The icons of Afrocentricity and Africa itself served as bridges between upward mobility and historically black experiences. The notion that success and academic achievement were necessarily white experiences was met with a wave of Afrocentricity, where the study and consumption of Afrocentric goods and literature could justify a class distinction without raising issues of black authenticity. Designer wear and bourgeois habits were legitimized with, respectively, kente cloth and reconstructed Yoruba origins.

Concurrently, as hip hop became more mainstream, the nation-conscious Afrocentric genre grew. It does not seem a coincidence that in 1988, the formerly "criminally-minded" (1986) KRS-One took on the role of Malcolm X in "By All Means Necessary" (1988) and Long Island-based Public Enemy, who in 1986 were "rollin in their 98 Olds-mobile" began to state that "It

Takes a Nation of Millions to Hold [Them] Back" (1988). In part, nation-conscious rap became a cipher to understand blackness in arenas of upward mobility and hip hop's national growth. As well, this music shared its terrain with an African-American and white college-age audience who used African and Black Power fashions, hairstyles, and rhetoric to demonstrate political acts of rebellion and resistance. The academic Afrocentricity of Molefi Asante countered dominant academic politics by positioning "Africa" at the center of study and analysis (1987, 187).

Afrocentricity served as a powerful tool for African-American students as their professors and administrators questioned the validity of integrating multicultural education into the canon and strengthening African-American Studies programs. The aesthetic of the "African" became a stance where students could mount a counterattack against the academic claims that African-Americans had no culture worthy of the canon. Afrocentricity served as a safe space in threatening academic waters, a complement to nationhood rhetoric within the Reagan/Bush regime, and a language to maintain borders around the definition of hip hop during its national expansion.

The move toward empowering black populations outside urban spaces through a kind of Afrocentric/nation-conscious hip hop form was not entirely new. Its roots are visible in the collective known as the "Native Tongues," which was roughly comprised of the Jungle Brothers, A Tribe Called Quest, Queen Latifah, Monie Love, and De La Soul (Boyd, 1995, 299). Their origins point even further back toward the Universal Zulu Nation of the Bronx-based Afrika Bambaataa, who in the late 70s was hell-bent on not just transmitting his Kraftwerk-inspired "techno funk" to the nation, but on making the "Planet Rock."

Native Tongues followed in Bambaataa's footsteps by not letting their musical influences or artistic vision be impeded by fictive standards of how hip hop should sound. For example, De La Soul's first single "Me, Myself and I" ironized earlier rap posturings by counterpoising the popular b-boy stance to "being one's self." De La Soul is known for initiating hip hop's breakaway from the recycling of the same James Brown beats by introducing the samples of everything from Steely Dan to Disney. Introducing a class consciousness, De La Soul was also clear about being from a relatively affluent Long Island background, stating that this heavily influenced their sound and aesthetics, which ran contrary to the stereotypical urban style. Within this distinction, they rejected what had become the authentic style of sweatsuits, gold chains, and Kangol hats by presenting their bohemian style of flowered shirts, dreaded hair, and African medallions.

Released in 1988, "Me, Myself and I" attempted to open a space where blackness could be understood through parody and the interrogation of multiple identities within hip hop, while simultaneously making subtle political statements to the nation at large:

> Glory, glory hallelu
> glory for plug one and two
> But that glory's been denied by
> kudzids and gookie eyes
> people think they dis my person by
> stating I'm darkly packed
> I know this so I point at Q-Tip and he
> states "Black is Black"
> mirror, mirror on the wall
> shovel chestnuts in my path
> please keep all nuts with the nuts
> so I don't get an aftermath
> but if I do I'll calmly punch them in

> the 4th day of July
> cause they tried to mess with 3rd
> degree
> that's Me, Myself and I

In this song, De La Soul is exploring issues of cultural individualism within blackness through an ironic reference to American patriotism. They are asking that the rhetoric of cultural freedom be applied both inside and outside of "the race." But the political impetus of this Afrocentric style became statically and dangerously interpreted as the only option within blackness, a turn that may have prompted De La Soul to title their second album *De La Soul Is Dead*. The "Soul" in Afrocentric rap began to articulate an essentialist position that equated musical "soul" with a particular black nationalist, Afrocentric identity, instead of allowing for a multiplicity of black experiences to be heard. Afrocentric versions of nation-conscious rap deployed the sunny disposition of Egypt and a re-imagined Egyptian/African culture as sources of racial legitimacy in the face of racial oppression. But in its attempts to create a powerful picture of black life, Afrocentrism expected blacks to live up to an imagined identity based on a particular version of African-American history and painted over issues of gender with broad strokes. Black life was articulated primarily in the voice of black men, and if not from men, then from the position of patriarchy.[5]

The "fertile" soil of Egypt and "Mother Africa" were fetishized as female objects, primarily valuable for their production of melanin babies, otherwise known as the "original black man." Taking material from Asante, psychologist Frances Cress Welsing, and even 18th century white scholars (like the biologist Gregor Mendel), the melanin in black skin or the culture of African people is understood as making the black man naturally good, artistic, and superior.

As Jeffrey Decker has stated, work by the artist Isis was emblematic of this phenomena. In her music video "The Power of Myself Is Moving," she plays the part of a fertility goddess along the Nile: "I'm a self coming forth a creature bearing life / a renaissance, a rebirth" (1990). Even through a female voice, the message evokes the patriarchal order where women are revered solely for their inherent nurturing and reproductive skills. Because the black woman bears the seed of the black nation, she is viewed as an "object" that must be protected from both interracial and intraracial contamination.

As stated earlier, the absence of any discussion of intraracial class conflict is a crucial over-sight in Afrocentric work. However, anxieties over class-based behaviors emerge through a rigid representation of regional differences and gendered behavior. One of the key groups to articulate this phenomenon was Arrested Development, which Todd Boyd rightly lauds for relocating hip hop outside urban spaces into the landscapes of the rural South, while also crit-icizing the group for its romanticization of this locale: "Arrested Development argues for a kind of cultural innocence or purity. This notion of purity is exemplified through a juxtapo-sition of the harsh urban realities of the street prominent in contemporary rap and their embrace of the premodern "country," the simplicity of a rural landscape" (1995, 300). Arrested Development promotes the romantic rural by defining and denigrating its other: the urban subject.

This rural-urban dichotomy creates a class hierarchy between the positive images of pastoral Afrocentric rap and the depressing dangers of urban experiences. A binary, expressed this time in terms of the "true black self," is established between the haves and have-nots: "Now I see the importance of history / why my people be in the mess that they be / many journeys to freedom made in vain / by brothers on the corner playing ghetto games" (1992). This trope of "knowledge to be acquired" through mastering designated Afrocentric texts and behaviors is understood as the entryway to authentic blackness. The revisionist Southern history of Arrested Development (AD) can easily be mapped onto the "return to family values" narrative, best depicted in idealization of rural New England communities by white conservatives like Newt Gingrich. In both narratives, place and family space became the loci for the creation of "proper values." As well, both rhetorics claim to speak from the position of the popular or "everyday people," while masking their privileged class positions.

Scholars like Boyd have prized AD for their positive and progressive gender politics. However, I am skeptical of such a position, because the voices of their women rappers are constrained by their role as a prize. In AD's work, the "black queen" serves as an object that must not be contaminated by "niggas." In the video "People Everyday," black men are performing the stance of the "urban nigga"—drinking 40's and grabbing their crotches— when an "African queen" approaches and one of the men grabs her butt. Simultaneously, Speech[6] can be heard in a voiceover criticizing their behavior: "My day was going great and my soul was at ease / until a group of brothers / started buggin out / drinking the 40 ounce / going the nigga route / disrespecting my black queen / holding their crotches and being obscene" (1992). The woman is given no agency and the nigga performs the stereotypical deviant role that gives the African the opportunity to do his duty and step in to protect his queen. An analogy is made between the ability of the African man to protect his woman and the intrinsic strength of the African identity: "That's the story y'all / of a black man / acting like a nigga / and get stomped by an African" (1992). Even in the midst of gender inclusion, masculine aggression rears its ugly head. The radical right's vision of the patriarchal family is upheld, but now in blackface and kente cloth. But what happens when the nigga speaks back?

"The Nigga You Love to Hate": Class Conflicts in the "G-Funk" Era

Rather than evading the nigga, gangsta rap actually engaged and mimicked the position of nigga as other, as performance. In the next section I, along with Robin Kelley and other scholars, postulate that the earliest manifestations of gangsta rap attempted to speak back to the middle-class-oriented position of nation-conscious rap. Kelley argues that, "L.A. gangsta rappers are frequent critics of black nationalists [as well]. They contend that the nationalist focus on Africa—both past and present—obscures the daily battles poor black folk have to wage in contemporary America" (1994, 212). In some regards, nation-conscious rap assumed that everyone agreed on the definition of "knowledge of self" and, in turn, blackness. Gangsta rap, however, provides another perspective on black life.

As well, gangsta rappers saw no inherent negativity in the term "nigga," defining themselves as niggas in defiance of the dominant society, both black and white. As hip hop was continuing to expand, more tensions arose around the definition of hip hop as a representation of blackness. Although hip hop originated and was most successful in urban New York and on the East Coast, the emergence of gangsta rap shifted the focus in hip hop to the lived experience of the post-industrial city on the West Coast, particularly Los Angeles.

The highly popular N.W.A. (Niggas With Attitude) album, *Straight Outta Compton* was released in 1988 at the same time that nation-conscious rap was becoming popular. However, it wasn't until the early 90s—when N.W.A.'s *efil4zaggiN* (Niggaz 4 life) reached number one on the *Billboard* charts before it was even released, Snoop Doggy Dogg was introduced on the *Deep Cover* soundtrack, and Dr. Dre's multi-platinum album *The Chronic* was heard on every street corner and video station—that everyone was forced to realize that gangsta rap was a force to be reckoned with. The West Coast began to dismantle New York's monopoly of hip hop and critiqued nation-conscious rap's politically correct disciplining of black bodies. Unlike the critiques of black nihilism that wax nostalgic for a bygone black community (West, 1993), gangsta rappers aren't anti-nationalist or apolitical, but they do oppose a political correctness which obscures the historical realities of class, gender, and locational difference within the representation of black communities.

On "Dre Day," Dr. Dre retorts: "no medallions / dreadlocks / or Black fist it's just that gangsta glare / with gangsta rap that gangsta shit, / brings a gang of snaps" (1992). Instead of seeing this position as exemplifying a movement of anti-politics, I see it as a shift in the way in which politics is articulated. In hindsight, it is an attempt to break the stranglehold of nation-conscious rap on hip hop expression. The political language of nation-conscious rap, in its most general sense, was traded in for the grammar of the hood and the particular day-to-day struggles of black people.

In gangsta rap, the nigga acquired a locational and economic specificity. Kelley argues that the experiences of young black men in the inner city were not universal to all black people, and furthermore, that "nigga does not mean black as much as it means being a product of the post-industrial ghetto" (1994, 210). This process exposes the limitations of politics based on skin color. Gangsta rap can be understood as resistance, where the nigga is seen as a performative identity that is not solely accessed by a black constituency.

Thus, we are encouraged to analyze the nigga within the American mainstream, especially since so much of the work in gangsta rap is inspired by popular action-adventure and gangster films and its biggest registered consumers are suburban white teens. Because of this phenomenon, we must think critically about white youth's influence over creating and maintaining the gangsta subject by purchasing the music. The gangsta subject would not continue to exist in commodified form if there were not buyers waiting for the product. Gangsta rap deals in fantasy and evil, constructing marketable stories that tell as much about its white teen listeners' desires as about its practitioners. In what ways do the consumption of and desire for a genre help to continue its existence?

The problematics that supposedly originate in the nigga subject are turned back onto America and its political/economic/racial regime. In Kelley's essay, a Chicano gang member makes visible his relation to the economic order in regard to his "deviant" behavior: "I act like they do in the big time, no different. There ain't no corporation that acts with morals and that ethics shit and I ain't about to either. As they say, if it's good for General Motors, it's good enough for me" (1994, 196). The desires of the "gangsta" are exposed equally as the desires of its consumers and creators, problematizing the belief in a pure pathological difference based on race. In other words, the behaviors of the nigga are found in all segments of American life.

Through the performance of the nigga, the gangsta rapper fights against fixity and attempts to make visible the multiple registers through which the hood, racial pathologies, and the nigga are actualized. In gangsta rap, individualism and criminality are continually tied to America culture. As Ice-T states: "America stole from the Indians sure and prove / what's that? / a straight up nigga move!" (1991). But in this position of rebelliousness, gangsta rap and the nigga became idealized as Ghettocentric, a counter move to the Afrocentricity and white supremacy of the day.

The nigga became the embodiment of black defiance against all comers through a highly masculinist imaginary, where the nigga was strong when he wasn't a "punk," "bitch," or "pussy." The project of uncovering the racially hybrid subjectivity of the nigga is halted when the nigga is flaunted as the only "real" black identity. The tropes of masculinity, promiscuity, and violence become naturalized as inherently black. However, this form of identification is no different from most young men in patriarchal societies who come to associate masculinity with aggression and violence. Blackness as hypermasculine becomes a romanticized position of strength and opposition that hopes to create "safe spaces" of uncontested male power. Furthermore, the belief that black family structures are deviant because of the instability of its women is a narrative that may also be found in gangsta rap.

The male rapper begins to call for the restoration of the patriarchal order, because for him, the female is fixed as a threat to the progress of his success or hustle. In the same way that gangsta rap performs the violence of an idealized America, it also calls upon traditional tales of black women as scapegoats for problems within the nation(hood). "African-American women are often portrayed as welfare queens making babies merely to stay on public assistance or 'gold-diggers' who use their sexuality to take black men's meager earnings" (Kelley, 1994, 217). This narrative can be found in Dr. Dre's song "Bitches Ain't Shit But Hoes and Tricks," or E-40's "Captain Save a Ho," in which men are chastised for taking care of a woman and her children, especially if they aren't his own. During this song's popularity, a man who listened to his girlfriend or spent too much time with a woman was accused of "having an S on his chest" because he was "savin' em" (his woman was in control). The woman is seen as putting the man's freedom in jeopardy by hustling him for his money and time.

At its most progressive, gangsta rap analyzes the contingent relationship between poverty and a racialized political economy but at the same time can explain women in poverty in terms of a behavioral problem, claiming that all a woman wants is to take you for your goods. Tricia Rose explains how black males fear the assertion of a strong woman's sexuality: within gangsta spaces, there is no guarantee that heterosexual male desires will be met because of women's capacity to reject or manipulate men's advances (1991). This is not a new narrative and indeed is based on longstanding fears of women's ability to trap men (e.g., through pregnancy), when sexual exchange is able to produce money and goods (Kelley, 1994, 219).

Just as the purified space of the black nationalist is insecure, so also is the stability of the gangsta. The terrain where black men attempt to assert their masculinity or evade the issues of class is always highly contested. Male gangsta rappers expose the vulnerability of heterosexual male desire in their exaggerated stories of dominance over female representations of black life.

The degree of anxiety expressed in these heavy-handed fantasies explains both an intense desire and distrust of women and the way in which their (in)subordination disrupts racial authenticity. However, gangsta rap is *not* vying for a sanitized vision of Africa, complete with corrective gender and class relationships. It forces us to deal with the everyday in a way that can't justify the harsh denigration of female and working-class desires, particularly in the marketplace. Gangsta rap seems suited for engaging the social contradictions and ambiguities of urban life.

In the context of racial distinctions, while gangsta rap's white consumers and critics are identifying the gangsta as something "other" than themselves or the white middle-class values they purport to inherit, these artists are parodying "normative" behavior. Peter Stallybrass and Allon White argue that:

The "top" attempts to reject and eliminate the "bottom" for reasons of prestige and status, only to discover, not only that it is in some way frequently dependent upon the low-Other, but also that the top *includes* the low symbolically, as a primary eroticized constituent of its own fantasy life. The result is ... a psychological dependence upon precisely those others which are being rigorously opposed and excluded at the social level. It is for this reason that what is socially peripheral is so frequently *symbolically* central. (5, 1986)

Although gangsta rap has been constructed as deviant from middle-class normativity, examining the social texts of desire and consumption shows its relationship to those very norms. For example, the "vulgar" black female deviance performed or commented on in gangsta rap is not nor can be discretely separated from the sense of entitlement clothed in middle-class normative respectability. The gangsta performance forces those who embrace white middle-class patriarchy to stare the black gangsta in the face and see him- or herself. This shift to gangsta music has allowed black men and women trapped by oppressive systems to reinvent themselves through new performative acts, a reinvention defined by Manthia Diawara as the "defiant tradition in black culture that challenges every attempt to police the black body or mind" (1993, 4).

The Wretched of the Earth: Pleasure, Power, and the Hip Hop Bourgeoisie

Earlier conservative idealizations of black life evaded an engagement with the black body through policing it, whereas Diawara's notion of the "black good life society" "emphasizes the necessity for a productive space which is accompanied by consumption, leisure, and pleasure in black people's relation to modernity" (1993, 7). This engagement with pleasure and commodity consumption addresses realities that black middle-class and black church aesthetic forms often shun.

These traditional forms have historically functioned within ideologies that separate intellect and pleasure, mind and body, and have been articulated within the binary of a harsh middle class/working class divide. Historically, it has been black people's responsibility to link pleasure or freedom with the non-material. L.A.-based gangsta rap reopened a space where it is not sinful to link black pleasure with materialism. Rather than finding a politics through positive imaging, the "black good life" seeks a politics through performance and refashions identity through irony and play. If moral and cultural correctness is seen as denial, then open representations of sexuality and grotesque and carnivalesque characterizations/eroticizations of violence can be understood as potentially liberating.

The performance of so-called deviant acts and direct confrontations with black stereotypes create black industries, as well as make visible the social construction of what appear as natural black characteristics. These performances expose the interracial and intraracial formation of the nigga identity and "take ethical decisions away from the church, out of the moral and religious arena, and place them squarely at the feet of material well being and pleasure" (Diawara, 1993, 7). I argue that the backlash against the new cadre of male and female gangsta rappers, whether it be voiced by C. Delores Tucker, William Bennett, Rev. Calvin Butts, or hip hop purists, is mobilizing around an ethic that purports to speak "for the people" but in actuality does not. The gatekeepers of "authentic blackness" are anxiety-ridden over public displays of the black good life society, exemplified in the emergence of a new hip hop identity; a black middle-class aesthetic that will not be policed by traditional notions of morality and class status.

Confident in the freedom offered by the pleasures and profits of performing gangsta, New York-based Lil' Kim, Foxy Brown, Jay-Z, and The Notorious BIG are exemplars of this hip hop shift. Consequently, these artists are specifically attacked for their lines of commodity endorsements from Versace to Lexus and for their obsession with Italian-American mobsters. Yet, in the same way that white supremacy has created the nigga as a repository for its own not-so-laudable activities, "gangsta/playa" rappers have taken white American commodities as signs of achieving "the dream." By performing the roles of Italian-American mobsters and movie characters, they continue to question the idea that gangsta behaviors in hip hop are inherently an extension of deviant, let alone black, culture. At the same time, their gangsta performance critiques the notions of blackness expressed through ghetto authenticity or black bourgeois respectability. This version of gangsta rap questions the fictive boundaries placed around class status as a means of social exclusion.

One way in which upward mobility has historically been policed is by the coupling of class status with behavioral dictates. As working-class blacks advance financially through the entertainment arena, they are expected to change their behaviors in a way that "properly" suits their new economic status. However, the privacy traditionally afforded middle-class citizens is not given to these black cultural workers, who are placed under strict scrutiny as if their social advancement warranted a special kind of public attention. So many perceptions are shaped by the "you can take a nigga out of the hood, but you can't take the hood out of the nigga" narrative, that entertainment and sports pages begin to look like the Metro section. But I wonder if these entertainers are becoming more of an embarrassing spectacle, or whether there are larger anxieties about the changing composition of the American middle and upper class? This belief that particular behaviors can be linked to a specific class standing hardly ever makes visible that entrée into the normative middle-class space has historically been acquired and maintained through not-so-middle-class behaviors.

Instead of reacting to "culture of poverty" rhetorics by disassociating blackness from American culture, these gangsta collectives have crowned themselves Junior M.A.F.I.A., The Firm, and Roc-A-Fella (Rockefeller) Records. They problematize the lines drawn between legality and illegality, morality and immorality, by articulating not the culture of poverty but mainstream American culture. This American tale potentially tears the racial and economic structure of U.S. life away from the current trends in neo-Social Darwinist ideology (i.e., that there is something particular to black culture that is intrinsically deviant). Critics of gangsta rap hold to the claim that inherent to the middle-class identity are distinguishably different values. The lyrics of the new gangstas make it clear that the rhetoric of individualism pays homage to traditional mainstream values that are being used "to redistribute more income, wealth and power to classes that are already most affluent in those aspects" (Gans, 1995, 7).

Born amidst the same media that chain black identity to cultural pathology, this new black-entertainment middle class has viewed the slippery slope of ethical behavior in American life. They were children of the 1980s Yuppie and Buppie culture, when conspicuous consumption was a normative, elite class behavior. These artists have witnessed on television and movie screens the prominence of John Gotti, Manuel Noriega, and Saddam Hussein, all as a result of U.S. state intervention. For them, corporate culture *is* gangsta culture. Could witnessing and experiencing life within the American context have possibly encouraged and nurtured the violation of so-called family values within marginal communities? Jay-Z, owner of Roc-A-Fella Records, seems to think so:

> Your worst fear confirmed
> me and my fam'(ily) roll tight like the firm
> gettin' down for life, that's right, you betta learn
> why play with fire, burn
> we get together like a choir, to acquire what we desire
> we do dirt like worms, produce g's [thousands of dollars] like sperm
> Til legs spread like germs ...
> I sip fine wines and spit vintage flows—what y'all don't know?
> 'Cuz you can' knock the hustle
> Y'all niggas lunchin' punchin' a clock
> function is to make and lay back munchin'
> sippin' Remy on the rocks
> my crew, something to watch
> notin' to stop
> un-stoppable ...
> you ain't havin' it? Good me either
> Let's get together and make this whole world believe us, son
> at my arraignment screamin'
> All us blacks got is sports and entertainment—until we're even
> thievin' as long as I'm breathin'
> can't knock the way a nigga eatin' fuck you even
> (1996)

These lyrics might easily seem to promote illegality, self-indulgence, misogyny, and crudely hedonistic tendencies; however, they also provide a critique of the socio-economic structure that prevents many African-Americans access to decent wage labor. Jay-Z makes clear that large populations of African-Americans are still excluded from middle-class consumption except through sports and entertainment. On Jay-Z's latest album, he is inspired by the hook in the theme song from the musical *Annie*. While the song refers to a little white orphan, Jay-Z argues that "instead of treated we get tricked / instead of kisses we get kicked / it's a hard knock life" is an archetypal "ghetto anthem" (1998). Both sets of lyrics endorse a hustler's mentality, a strategic manipulation of the opportunities made available in light of socio-economic inequalities. This perspective suggests that consumption and pleasure could serve as working-class critiques of middle-class ideals and also utilizes the trope of the gangsta/playa to appropriate the terrain of the "free" market for black institution-building.

Another example of this manipulation of black identity is the platinum-selling artist, The Notorious BIG (aka Biggie Smalls). Before his untimely death, Biggie was one of the artists who freed hip hop from the tight grip of the "keepin it real" persona. After the Ghettocentric turn, rappers were forced to write their rhymes as if they reflected authentic lived experience. So as "keepin it real" in gangsta rap became prevalent, artists competed with one another to see who could depict the most devastatingly grim "personal" narratives. Biggie, however, was unabashed about his goal of upward mobility within the narratives of his ghetto background. He did not feel that he had to stay in the ghetto or necessarily back up his lyrics with authentic acts. In his first single, "Juicy," Biggie remarks, "fifty-inch screen / money green leather sofa / got two cars / a limousine / with a chauffeur / phone bill about two g's fat / no need to worry / my accountant handles that / and my whole crew is lounging / celebratin' everyday / no more public housing" (1994).

In his short career, Biggie took advantage of what was marketable and was never bound by the New York-centric formalism about how real hip hop should sound. In fact, he worked with Luke Skyywalker, Bone Thugs-n-Harmony, and even Michael Jackson, collaborations that would suffice to bar most from the "authentic" hip hop nation. He didn't totally leave the hood behind, but he was more self-conscious in his "performance" of the gangsta lifestyle.

On a number of occasions, Biggie stated that The Notorious BIG was nothing but a character or role that he performed; *he* was Christopher Wallace. In fact, the name "Biggie Smalls" comes from the 70s film *Let's Do It Again,* starring Sidney Poitier and Bill Cosby. Biggie even goes as far as to assume the role of a white movie figure, Frank White, from the film *King of New York*, and concluded his rhymes by exclaiming "MAFIOSO!"

This performance of Mafia culture begs the questions: whose culture is deviant? Isn't the acceptance of certain gangsta ethics in mainstream entertainment deviant? The rise of Roc-A-Fella, Death Row, and Bad Boy, with their commodification of illegality, cannot be divorced from the actual rise during Prohibition of the Irish-American Kennedy family or the Italian-American Gambino family. Likewise, these artists' conspicuous consumption habits cannot be seen as distinct from the mansion-and-yacht stories of Larry Ellison at Oracle, Jim Clark at Netscape, and Bill Gates at Microsoft, complete with feuds over who has the biggest "Cyber Boy Toy" (Kaplan, 1998), whose Horatio Alger narratives have served as models for this country's "formal" economy.

The posthumous indictment of Biggie at his 1997 memorial by Khallid Muhammad couldn't be more correct: "wearing the white man's clothes, showing up on TV dressed like you're Al Capone Baby Face Nelson, ugly as you are" (Marriott, 1997). Indeed, Biggie's is an ugly and messy performance that illuminates the muddled realities of racial and national identity and concurrently unfolds along the axis of gender. Even in his misogynist lyrics, Biggie wasn't shy about passing the mic. He gives props to "the honeys getting money, playing niggas like dummies" (1994). From this gangsta genre emerged a cadre of women artists headed by Lil' Kim of Junior M.A.F.I.A. and Foxy Brown of "The Firm."

These women questioned normative notions of male-female relations; in their stories, they acquire capital, express dissatisfaction with sexual partners, and reverse stereotypical gender roles. Foxy Brown declares:

> No more sex me all night
> thinking it's alright
> while I'm looking over your shoulder
> watching your whole life
> you hate when it's a ball right ladies this ain't hand ball
> nigga hit these walls right
> before I call Mike
> in the morning when it's all bright
> eggs over easy
> hope you have my shit tight
> when I open my eyes
> while I'm eating getting dressed up
> this ain't your pad
> I left money on the dresser
> find you a cab
> (1996)

In most scenarios, black males monopolize blackness through a relegation of the black female to the role of fetish, but here men have become the objects of desire. When patriarchal desires suddenly become articulated in a female voice, these desires are deemed "unnatural." Questions emerge as to what is ladylike and why a woman can't get hers like any man?[7]

Female identity in these musical texts becomes performance by coupling highly materialistic and aesthetically violent and excessive personas with infectious beats and rhymes.

The rhymes make it obvious that the relentless pursuit of status, power, and sexual satisfaction is not gender-specific, and thus reverse the objectification of women as sexual objects by viewing men as accesses to pleasure and capital accumulation, if necessary, through sexual exchange. Lil' Kim debunks the old myth that women only give sex for love and men only give love for sex; she makes it clear that the terms on which masculinity will be recognized will be her economic and sexual self-satisfaction:

> I knew a dude named Jimmy
> he used to run up in me
> night time pissy drunk
> off the Henne and Remy
> I didn't mind it
> when he fucked me from behind
> It felt fine
> especially when he used to grind it
> he was a trip
> when I sucked his dick
> he used to pass me bricks
> credit cards and shit
> I'd suck 'im to sleep
> I took the keys to the jeep
> tell him I'd be back
> go fool with some other cat …
> it was something about this dude I couldn't stand

something that coulda made his ass a real man
something I wanted
But I never was pushy
the motherfucker never ate my pussy
(1996)

In a *Vibe* interview, Lil' Kim describes this sexual commerce as the American way: "Sex … Money is power to me. It's not power alone, but you wanna have money to get the girls. To me, men like what women like, or they learn to like it" (Good, 1997, 176). She and her fellow female artists have understood that "sex sells" and have indirectly initiated a transformation of the color-coded and gender-laden rules by which social relations are scrutinized. This is in no way a proto-feminist position; neither Kim nor Foxy increases the value of women's sexuality. Nonetheless, their performances in the cultural marketplace open up a dialogue about "natural" gender roles and explore issues of female pleasure.

However, the power in articulating bodily pleasure is not purely narcissistic; indeed, it is not just about individual freedom but also concerns the transformation of institutions. Transgressions of black/white, male/female binaries have led artists to challenge the "old-school" belief that "real" hip hop must reside only outside the market. We then begin to remember that hip hop nationalism or nation-conscious rap was created through commodification and market growth. Even the idea of a hip hop national consciousness was raised through the market and utilized market tools, including records, tapes, and stage shows. For example, the "Fresh Fests" of the mid-80s did more than make money; they became a medium to circulate and exchange dance steps, clothing styles, lyrics, and ideas. The commodification of hip hop fashions and aesthetics became a common point of reference for its fans nationwide. The concept of a national consciousness or hip hop nation was not diluted but was in many ways strengthened through the circuits of mass media.

Technological advances within the market such as the music video have revealed the regional and aesthetic diversity of hip hop. Music videos allowed regional artists the space to craft personal and social narratives and "represent" their home not only with visuals but by contextualizing the style and delivery of their rhymes to a national audience without fear of retribution. An example of the power of musical/visual context is the artist Tongue Twista from the group Do or Die. Before Do or Die's breakthrough single "Po Pimps" (Emotions), Tongue Twista had been considered a one-hit wonder in the late 80s, when he was performing Afrocentric styles, wearing African beads and Cross-Colors gear. His claim to fame was recognition by the *Guinness Book of World Records* as "the world's fastest rapper." But thanks to the space opened up by music videos and other alternative outlets, we may now learn that his rapid rhyme style can be located within a Midwest/Southern-influenced hip hop aesthetic identifiable by its staccato delivery blended with doo-wop harmonies and laid over rich Stax-style horns and bass lines. In addition, music video production has enabled the formation of black directors, camera operators, and production crews. Due to video training, these positions have bypassed the white male unions that control apprenticeship systems and employment networks. A perfect example of this breakthrough is F. Gary Gray, who started out directing hip hop/R&B videos and who in 1995 parlayed these skills into a highly successful feature film, *Friday*.

For the regional developments in gangsta/playa hip hop, technological innovations have made it easier and cheaper to own recording studios and gain access to other professional recording resources. Ironically, when conservatives like C. Delores Tucker led the backlash against "gangsta rap," its listeners were drawn closer together. The major labels that produced gangsta rap decided to stop manufacturing it at the same pace. However, while the production side submitted to "public opinion," consumers utilized music technologies to rework the genre based on regional tastes. The consumers of gangsta rap realized that they had more in common musically with the South, West, and Midwest than with the Northeast. For so long, New York had dictated what "real hip hop" is and how it should sound and look.[8] In the face of resistance from both conservative movements and "old school" purists, independent compilations were circulated locally that included artists from emerging Southern and Midwestern versions of California-based gangsta rap. Due to the regional desire for the music, car-trunk distribution turned into independent label empires.

This process has encouraged the formation of semi-independent hip hop labels nationwide, including Death Row and Ruthless Records in Los Angeles; Sick Wit It Records in Vallejo, California; Rap-A-Lot and Suave House Records in Houston; Fully Loaded Records in Decatur, Georgia; So So Def Records in Atlanta; Blackground Records in Virginia; and the Cash Money Clique in New Orleans. While these developments are laudable, it has not been easy for female artists to take advantage of this phenomenon. With the notable exceptions of Queen Latifah, Missy Elliott, and Lil' Kim, women artists/entrepreneurs have not been able to utilize this gangsta grammar to build independent labels. However, artists have been encouraged to look at the relationship between work and culture and to understand the business side of music. The No Limit Empire, headed by Master P, is something to take special note of. P inaugurated the two-pronged strategy of high production (between April 1996 and March 1997, his label released seven albums) and business autonomy that is more reminiscent of West Indian dancehall culture: "You have a product, a rap product. It belongs to you. And you're just going to give somebody 85% of what you make on the product? To do what? Organize your life, basically call you in the morning and tell you to be across town at such and such a time … shit, I can wake my own damn self up" (Green, 1997, 100). The only aspect of P's business that is not self-contained is a distribution deal with Priority Records.[9]

Probably the most important aspect of P's business is his engagement with multiple media. Unlike conventional black media entrepreneurs, he feels that nothing is beyond his grasp. Instead of trying to pitch a film deal to a movie conglomerate, P conceived, marketed, and created his own visual autobiography, *I'm 'Bout It*. He released it himself, taking it straight to video and distributing it through record stores and the Blockbuster Video chain. In 1997, the film had sold over 250,000 units and has surpassed video giants like *Jurassic Park* in weekly sales.

The strategic marketing of P's film projects used the subversive strategies of the new independent labels. Each No Limit CD is packaged with ads about upcoming work. His projects are a success because he eliminates intermediaries and up-front advances from other sources. P states: "Of course they gonna pop some money at you … but how much money can they pop at me that I ain't already seen? That's how white boys do ya. That's how they get our ideas, our inventions" (Jackson, 1998, 74). Master P's aim is to maintain ownership over the means of production by being clear about the consumption habits and tastes of his consumer base.

Whether an artistic flop or a stroke of marketing genius, *I'm Bout It* has been hailed as paving the way for a new wave of independent hip hop films from cities outside New York or L.A. While Master P was working on his second film, a comedy called *I Got the Hookup*, other black entrepreneurs and aspiring film-makers had been given an example of how to be "playas in the game." From Bruce Brown's D.C.-based *24–7* (1997), which is driven by a hip hop and go-go soundtrack, to Robert Hayes's urban crime drama *Winner Takes All* (1998), which depicts the post-industrial landscape of Louisville, Kentucky, a wide range of black filmic expressions abound. The strength of this new wave of filmmaking lies in its manipulation of technologies as a means of autonomy. The first wave of hood films in the early 90s (*Boyz in the Hood, Menace II Society*) were largely dependent on multimedia conglomerates for distribution and heavily targeted by the gatekeepers of "official" depictions of black life. But the new movie-makers no longer have to bow down to revenue sources or critics. They can go straight to TV or DVD or sell films in record stores. These filmmakers are breaking the rules of conventional budgets, subject matter, marketing, and distribution (Shaw, 1998, 102).

Conclusion

I don't want to suggest that these transgressions of the black/white, male/female authentic/commodified binaries contain any overtly political agenda, because, as we've seen, two artists have died over these attempts to build black empires. Biggie, who labeled himself the "Teflon Don" (aka Mafia boss John Gotti), was not invincible. Concurrently, young children are performing these identities to death, which only fuels the debate for hip hop's critics. Nonetheless, hip hop cannot be singled out without scrutinizing George Bush's endorsement of the violent and misogynist Arnold Schwarzenegger film *True Lies* as "friendly to families" (Pareles, 1995).

Moreover, hip hop can't be seen as all that is wrong with American life. The cultural oscillations of hip hop and the current gangsta trends bear witness to our national history. This music cannot be divorced from the numerous American-dream stories of this nation. Like early gangsta and Afrocentric rappers, the new rappers are not trying to hold black identity to some place of total opposition to consumption, commodification, or social mobility. They are claiming their U.S. citizenship by partaking of conspicuous consumption and performing the identities of a U.S. gangsta government and elite-class capitalists.

The gangsta/playa and the subject matter associated with this icon can now be understood as a strategy, a work in progress. This is a position of maneuverability, which in its present form doesn't endorse the cult of authenticity that must explicitly be a "pure" counter to the mainstream. Womanhood is not purely fetishized as the African Queen or the Streetcorner Ho. While one can still see black women being singled out as locations of deviance, so-called deviant tropes are seen as central to constructing not only successful black women but also, as Lil' Kim charges, "Miss Ivana ... Zsa Zsa Gabor, Demi Moore, Princess Diana and all them rich bitches" (1996). For so long, space had been the chief signifier of racial difference, and freedom and movement had become white prerogatives. Yet these artists are now turning static space into sites of creative play and parody. They are appropriating and rearticulating each and every identity like music samples, cutting and scratching the rigid binaries until they are no longer comprehensible. Democracy, nationhood, and struggles over identity are being theorized through the circuits of desire and spectacle and are best summed up by Jay-Z, who doesn't ask to "Rock the Vote" or "Just Say No," but "Can I live?"

Notes

1. Jon Pareles, "Rapping and Politicking: Showtime on the Stump," *New York Times*, June 11, 1995.
2. Michel Marriott, "Hard Core Rap Lyrics Stir Backlash," *New York Times*, August 15, 1995.
3. Marriott, "Hard Core Rap Lyrics Stir Backlash."
4. This class-based form of policing black bodies can be found in all aspects of black life. One important example was covered by *Village Voice* writer Lisa Jones in a review of a book entitled *Basic Black: Home Training for Modern Times* (ed., Elyse Hudson and Karen Grisby Bates; 1997). These women attempt to map "down-home training" onto the typical etiquette book: teaching black people how to receive first-class service in a first-class restaurant, telling black folk to avoid talking to characters on movie screens, etc. In music, this backlash can be found in the black media's embrace of the hip hop/soul artists Erykah Badu in 1997 and Lauryn Hill in 1998. Without minimizing these artists' talent, they were both praised for their mixture of Afrocentric/Rastafarian/Five-Percenter ideology and "old-school" credibility. Badu and Hill became exemplars of the "purist" revival against "negative" female artists like Lil' Kim, and have been particularly lauded for dressing and acting with self-respect and dignity.
5. Within the nation-conscious genre, not all groups or artists ignored issues of class or gender, e.g., Queen Latifah or the L.A.-based group The Coup. However, this essay is attempting to take note of a general "common sense" that located black authenticity within the simultaneous reverence for and restriction of

the black woman. For example, see Decker's analysis of Public Enemy's song "She Watched Channel Zero." True, as Queen Latifah has commented, the women of the nation-conscious genre were not called bitches or hoes, but "queen" status also restricts the ways in which black femininity can be displayed. The weight of the queen's crown was sometimes too heavy a burden to bear.

6. Speech, the lead rapper of Arrested Development, belongs to a prominent black family in Milwaukee, Wisconsin, that runs a black-owned newspaper, *The Community Journal*, where his op-ed "racial uplift" pieces ran in his series, "20th-Century African." This series was known for its catchy and suggestive byline, "Here's the run-down, so you don't get gunned down." This phrase and column foreshadow the urban/African divide that becomes so prominent in his musical ideology.

7. While Foxy's disruption of gender roles within black communities is encouraging, it appears that her exploration of sexuality also reinforces the same patriarchal order. On her new album, *China Doll*, Foxy locates her sexual freedom within the stereotypical image of the exotic Asian woman.

8. In the 1980s, Miami Bass had been marginalized from hip hop as not "real" because it focused more on beats than lyrics. But as other regional versions of hip hop have gained economic and technological resources, this idea of "realness" was exposed as particular to the Northeast. Although conversation in this area is just beginning to emerge, New Yorkers have tended to see hip hop in other regions as "country," "bama," and unsophisticated. However, newer groups like Outkast and Goodie Mob from Atlanta and Timbaland and Missy Elliott from Portsmouth, Virginia, have gone on to parody and play with stereotypes aimed at the "Dirty South."

9. While it is encouraging that black artists/entrepreneurs are breaking into the production side of the music industry, they have yet to shatter the final frontier of the business: distribution. For example, two of gangsta/playa rap's powerhouse semi-independent labels, No Limit and Death Row, are both distributed by Priority Records. Until these labels develop distribution autonomy, they will be forever bound to the structural dictates of the music industry's multinationals.

Bibliography

Books

Asante, Molefi Kete. *The Afrocentric Idea*. Philadelphia: Temple UP, 1987.

Barnekov, Timothy, Robin Boyle, and Daniel Rich. *Privatism and Urban Policy in Britain and the U.S.* New York: Oxford UP, 1996.

Brown, Elaine. *A Taste of Power*. New York: Pantheon, 1992.

Davis, Angela. *Blues Legacies and Black Feminism: Gertrude "Ma" Rainey, Bessie Smith, and Billie Holiday*. New York: Pantheon Books, 1998.

Fanon, Frantz. *Black Skin. White Masks*. Trans. Charles Lam Markmann. New York: Grove, 1967.

Gans, Herbert J. *The War Against the Poor: The Underclass and Anti-Poverty Policy*. New York: Basic Books, 1995.

Kelley, Robin D. G. *Race Rebels*. New York: Free Press, 1994.

Moynihan, Daniel Patrick. *The Negro Family: The Case for National Action*. Washington, D.C.: Office of Policy Planning and Research, U.S. Department of Labor, 1965.

Rose, Tricia. *Black Noise: Rap Music and Black Culture in Contemporary America*. Hanover, NH: Wesleyan UP/UP of New England, 1994.

Stallybrass, Peter, and Allon White. *The Politics and Poetics of Trangression*. Ithaca: Cornell UP, 1986.

West, Cornel. *Race Matters*. Boston: Beacon, 1993.

Articles

Boyd, Todd. "Check Yo'Self. Before You Wreck Yo'Self: Variations on a Political Theme in Rap Music and Popular Culture." Black Public Sphere Collective (ed.). *The Black Public Sphere*. Chicago: U. of Chicago P., 1995.

Decker, Jeffrey Louis. "The State of Rap: Time and Place in Hip Hop Nationalism." Andrew Ross and Tricia Rose (eds.), *Microphone Fiends: Youth Music and Youth Culture*. New York: Routledge, 1994.

Diawara, Manthia. "A Symposium on Popular Culture and Political Correctness." *Social Text*, 1993.

Gilroy, Paul. "Revolutionary Conservatism and the Tyrannies of Unanimism." *New Formations* 28. Spring 1996.

———. "After the Love Has Gone: Bio-Politics and Etho-Poetics in the Black Public Sphere." Black Public Sphere Collective (ed.), *The Black Public Sphere*. Chicago: U. of Chicago P., 1995.

Good, Karen R. "More Than a Lil' Bit." *Vibe*. September 1997.

Green, Tony. "Stairway to Heaven." *Vibe*. June–July 1997.

Hall, Stuart. "The After-life of Frantz Fanon: Why Fanon? Why Now? Why "Black Skin, Where Masks?" Alan Read (ed.), *The Fact of Blackness*. Seattle: Bay Press, 1996.

———. "What Is This 'Black' in Black Popular Culture?" Gina Dent (ed.), *Black Popular Culture*. Seattle: Bay Press, 1992.

Jackson, Scoop. "Soldiers on the Set." *Vibe*. May 1998.

Jones, Lisa. "Home(girl) Training." *Village Voice*. March 19, 1997.

Kaplan, Tony. "Cyber Boy Toys." *Time*. July 1998.

Marriott, Michel. "At a Ceremony for Shakur. Appeals for Peace." *New York Times*. September 23, 1996.

———. "Hard Core Rap Lyrics Stir Backlash." *New York Times*. August 15, 1993.

Pareles, Jon. "Rapping and Politicking: Showtime on the Stump." *New York Times*. June 11, 1995.

Rose, Tricia. "A Symposium on Popular Culture and Political Correctness. *Social Text*. 1993.

———. "Never Trust a Big Butt and a Smile." *Camera Obscura*. #23, 1991.

Shaw, William. "Bustin' a Movie." *Details*. March 1998.

Smith, R. J. "Bigger Than Life." *Village Voice*. March 19, 1997.

Tate, Greg, "Funking Intellect." *Vibe*. June/July 1997.

Toure. "Bigger Than Life." *Village Voice*. March 19, 1997.

Weinraub, Bernard. "National Desk." *New York Times*. June 1, 1995.

Discography

Arrested Development. "People Everyday." *3 Years, 5 Months and 2 Days in the Life Of.* Chrysalis, 1992.

De La Soul. "Me, Myself and I." *3 Feet High and Rising*. Tommy Boy, 1988.

Dr. Dre. "Dre Day." *The Chronic*. Death Row Interscope, 1992.

Eric B. and Rakim. *Paid in Fall*. Island, 1987.

Foxy Brown. "Ill Nana." *ILL NANA*. Rush Recordings, 1996.

Ice Cube. "Species (Tales from the Darkside)." *AmeriKKKa Most Wanted*. Priority, 1990.

Ice T. "New Jack Hustler." *OG: Original Gangster*. Sire, 1991.

Isis. "The Power of Myself Is Moving." *Rebel Soul*. 4th and Broadway, 1990.

Jay-Z. "Can't Knock the Hustle." *Reasonable Doubt*. Roc-A-Fella/Priority, 1996.

———. "Hard Knock Life." *Hard Knock Life* Vol. II. Roc-A-Fella/Def Jam, 1998.

KRS-One. *Criminal Minded*. Sugar Hill, 1986, Reprint, 1991.

———. *By All Means Necessary*. Jive, 1988.

Lil' Kim. *Hard Core*. Big Beat, 1996.

The Notorious BIG *Ready to Die*. Arista, 1994.

N.W.A. *Straight Outta Compton*. Ruthless, 1988.

Public Enemy. "My 98 Oldsmobile." *Yo! Bum the Rush Show*. Def Jam, 1987.

———. "She Watched Channel Zero." *It Takes a Nation of Millions to Hold Us Back*. Def Jam, 1988.

———. "Welcome to the Terrordome." *Fear of a Black Planet*. Def Jam, 1990.

16

Hip-Hop am Main, Rappin' on the Tyne:

Hip-Hop Culture as a Local Construct in Two European Cities

Andy Bennett

Aa dee it coz aa can green eggs and ham,
People always tell iz that am just like me mam,
Aa wuz born aa was bred in smelling distance
o the tyne,
An a couldn't give a toss that the fogs not mine,
Aa like me blaa an a like a pint,
But ave never needed speed for an alreet neet,
Aa divvent drive a car'coz they just get twoced,
Me ken's kanny safe it's on top of a shop ...

Ferank, Newcastle poet and rapper, 1994

Among contemporary youth cultural forms, hip hop has attracted a great deal of interest from academic theorists and researchers. It is also fair to say that hip hop is one of the most contested cultural forms from the point of view of its representation in academic texts. Much of the debate surrounding hip hop relates to the issue of authenticity. Thus, while some theorists maintain that the authenticity of hip hop remains firmly rooted in its origins and continuing significance as an African-American street culture, others suggest that the themes and issues expressed in hip hop contribute to the musicalized dialogue that is held to exist between those displaced peoples of African origin who collectively make up the African-diaspora. More recently, a new school of hip hop theorists, in considering the existence of hip hop culture outside the African-American and wider African-diasporic world, have contested earlier interpretations of hip hop, suggesting instead that hip hop is culturally mobile; that the definition of hip hop culture and its attendant notions of authenticity are constantly being "remade" as hip hop is appropriated by different groups of young people in cities and regions around the world.

In this chapter I want to consider some of the different sociological arguments that have been used to explain the cultural significance of hip hop. I will then offer my own interpretation of the cultural work performed by hip hop in the form of an ethnographic study that examines the local hip hop scenes in two European cities, Frankfurt am Main, Germany, and Newcastle upon Tyne, England. Through a consideration of hip hop's significance in these two cities, I will suggest that arguments and discussions among young people concerning the merits of hip hop as an authentic form of cultural expression correspond closely with the differing local contexts in which hip hop culture is played out. In exploring the relationship between hip hop and the local, I will also refer to comparable studies of "local" hip hop cultures in Italy, France, Southern Ireland, Sweden, Australia, New Zealand, and Japan.

The Origins and Sociological Representation of Hip Hop

There is a general consensus among both academic and non-academic accounts of hip hop that the style originated in the South Bronx area of New York during the early 1970s. A key figure in the creation of hip hop was an ex-street gang member known as Afrika Bambaataa. Aware of the inner-city tensions that were being created as a consequence of urban renewal programs and economic recession, Bambaataa formed "The Zulu Nation" in an attempt to "channel the anger of young people in the South Bronx away from gang fighting and into music, dance, and graffiti"[1] (Lipsitz, 1994, p. 26). Hip hop has since become more widely known because of rap, the aspect of its style that has been most successfully commercialized. Rap is a narrative form of vocal delivery in which rhyming lyrics are spoken or "rapped" in a rhythmic patois over a continuous backbeat. According to Keyes, the distinctive vocal technique employed in rapping "can be traced from African bardic traditions to rural southern-based expressions of African Americans—toast, tales, sermons, blues, game songs, and allied forms—all of which are recited in a chanted rhyme or poetic fashion" (1991, p. 40). The backbeat or "breakbeat" in rap is provided by a DJ who uses a twin-turntable record deck to "mix" sections of vinyl recordings together in a way that seamlessly recombines aspects of existing songs and instrumental passages into a new musical piece (Back, 1996a, p. 192). A further technique employed by rap DJs is "scratching," where the records themselves are used to a rhythmic, percussive effect by rapidly running their grooves to and forth against the record player's stylus to produce a scratching sound (Rose, 1994b).

If there is agreement among theorists as to hip hop's point of origin and the socio-economic conditions from which it emerged, there is much less agreement concerning the ethnic dimensions of hip hop and its significance as a form of cultural expression. Thus, according to one school of thought, the significance of hip hop as a cultural form orientates exclusively around its dialogue with the experience of African-American youth. Beadle, for example, has suggested that rap is "to the black American urban youth more or less what punk was to its British white counterpart" (1993, p. 77). Thus, argues Beadle, relying only upon the ability to "talk in rhythm," rapping has become the perfect "vehicle for pride and for anger, for asserting the self worth of the community" (ibid., p. 85). Similarly, Light defends the essential "blackness" of hip hop in the face of its commercialization and "white" imitations by groups such as the Beastie Boys. According to Light, hip hop "is about giving a voice to a black community otherwise underrepresented. . . . It has always been and remains (despite the curse of pop potential) directly connected with the streets from which it came" (1992, p. 232). The notion of hip hop as a purely African-American cultural form has been further fuelled by its reception among sections of white U.S. society. Rap music, and in particular "*gangsta rap*" with the often violent and misogynistic overtones of its lyrics, has instilled a form of moral panic among the U.S. white middle classes. According to Sexton, attempts by white institutions, notably the Parents Music Resource Center (see Epstein et al., 1990), to censor rap lyrics has led in turn to a form of "clinical paranoia" among black hip hop circles in the U.S. (1995, p. 2). Similarly, African-American writer Dyson argues that: "While gangsta rap takes the heat for a range of social maladies from urban violence to sexual misconduct, the roots of our racial misery remain buried beneath moralizing discourse that is confused and sometimes dishonest" (1996, p. 178). While debates concerning the legitimacy of such claims continue, the point remains that rap and hip hop are being discussed exclusively in African-American terms, a trope that also conveniently excludes the involvement of Puerto-Rican and white youth in the development of hip hop (Flores, 1994; Mitchell, 1998). Indeed, one could go as far as to say that such readings of hip hop historicize and sociologize the latter in a way that closes off any consideration of its significance in non-African-American contexts. This aspect of African-American-centered writing on hip hop is exemplified by Potter, who, in response to the growth of interest in hip hop outside the U.S., suggests that "there is always a *danger* that it will be appropriated in such a way that its histories are obscured and its message replaced by others" (1995, p. 146; my emphasis).

The implied notion in the work of Potter that hip hop's only authentic cultural resonance is with the experience of inner-city African-Americans is challenged by a number of theorists who argue that hip hop, while it may indeed have emerged from the ghettos of U.S.-America, is, like other aspects of African-American culture, historically rooted in the removal by force of native Africans from their homelands during the western slave trade of the sixteenth to nineteenth centuries (Lipsitz, 1994). Despite the gradual abolition of slavery in Europe and America during the nineteenth century, the African-diaspora created by the slave trade has continued to grow as people have left Africa and former slave colonies such as the West Indies in order to escape political and religious persecution or in an attempt to secure a better standard of living and better opportunities for themselves and their children (see, for example, Foner, 1978; Hebdige, 1987). Against this African-diasporic backdrop, it is suggested, cultural forms such as music function as "privileged site[s] for transnational communication, organization and mobilization" (Lipsitz: 1994, p. 34). This argument is central to a study by Cobley and Osgerby of Afro-Caribbean hip hoppers, in the Peckham district of London, whose attachment to hip hop, it is argued, is "engendered by diasporic identification" with African-Americans (1995, p. 11). The centrality of the African-diaspora to the cultural dialogue of hip hop is similarly emphasized in the work of Decker, who points to what he identifies as the Afro-centric sensibilities expressed in the work of U.S.-based rap groups such as Arrested Development. According to Decker, such Afro-centricism attempts "to reverse a history of Western economic dependency and cultural imperialism by placing a distinctly African value system … at the center of the worldview" (1994, p. 111).

Such work is arguably more useful in assessing hip hop's increasingly global significance than are studies that center exclusively around the latter's African-American properties. At the same time, however, there remains a danger of essentializing hip hop as a "black" cultural form. Indeed, it is increasingly evident that the appeal of hip hop is not merely limited to young people connected with the African-diaspora. On the contrary, hip hop and its various cultural activities appear to attract young people from very diverse socio-cultural backgrounds. Significant in this respect is the work of Gilroy, who challenges the contested blackness of hip hop through his positioning of the African-diaspora as a dynamic cultural force whose rootedness in the development of western capitalism has transformed it into a primary influence on global popular culture. Thus states Gilroy, "the transnational structures which brought the black Atlantic world into being have themselves developed and now articulate its myriad forms into a system of global communications constituted by flows" (1993, p. 80). In this way, argues Gilroy, "black" culture becomes a global culture, its styles, musics, and images crossing with a range of different national and regional sensibilities throughout the world and initiating a plurality of responses.

Gilroy's views and their implications for the interpretation of hip hop's cultural significance are developed in a new body of work that collectively examines the role of hip hop in a range of globally and culturally diffuse settings. Mitchell's research on hip hop in Europe and Oceania illustrates wide-ranging uses of rap and other aspects of the hip hop style in these areas of the world. Thus, in France and Italy hip hop has become a vehicle for the discussion of subjects such as "racism [and] police harassment," while in New Zealand Maori rap groups campaign for the rights of indigenous peoples around the world (1996, pp. 40, 244–50). Fillipa (1986) provides further insight into the localization of rap and hip hop in the context of Europe with an account of rap's incorporation into the suburban and rural cultures of southern Italy. Bjurström considers the significance of hip hop among the youth of ethnic minority groups in Sweden as a form of collective resistance to the white skinhead style, suggesting that hip hop and skinhead represent "the most conspicuous opposite poles in the ethnic-stylistic warfare of Swedish youth culture" (1997, p. 49). The diversity of hip hop culture at a global level is further illustrated by Harpin in a review of Southern Irish rap group Scary Eire, who, according to Harpin, "turn local problems, like high unemployment and the cost of everyday living, into sharp rhymes" (1993, p. 58). Finally, Condry's (1999) research into the significance of hip hop among Japanese youth illustrates how local hip hoppers use their musical and stylistic preferences as a means of marking themselves out from what they consider to be the "mainstream" youth of Japan. As such work begins to reveal, the commercial packaging of hip hop as a global commodity has facilitated its easy access by young people in many different parts of the world. Moreover, such appropriations have in each case involved a reworking of hip hop in ways that engage with local circumstances. In every respect then, hip hop is both a global and a local form.

Global, Local, and "Glocal" Cultures

There has been considerable debate among cultural theorists as to the effects of globalization on local cultures. One school of thought has maintained that globalization can have only a pathological effect on local differences, which are gradually eroded away by a one-directional flow of cultural commodities from the west, thus producing, according to Ritzer (1993), a gradual "McDonaldization" of the world. Such views have been challenged by theorists such as Lull (1995), whose concept of *cultural reterritorialisation* provides a framework for an understanding of cultural products as malleable resources that can be *reworked*, that is, inscribed with new meanings that relate to the particular local context within which such products are appropriated. Lull's approach is developed by Robertson who illustrates more graphically the interplay between the global and the local. Thus, argues Robertson:

> It is not a question of *either* homogenization or heterogenization, but rather the ways in which both of these tendencies have become features of life across much of the late-twentieth-century world. In this perspective the problem becomes that of spelling out the ways in which homogenizing and heterogenizing tendencies are mutually implicative. (1995, p. 27)

Robertson suggests that the crossing of such tendencies is best considered in terms of a process of *glocalization*. While it could be argued that each of the musical forms and stylistic sensibilities considered in this study is in one way or another illustrative of such a process of glocalization, it seems to me that hip hop, particularly in view of the often fractious "in-scene" debates that accompany its appropriation in local contexts, provides an especially animated example of a "glocal" culture. Beginning with a study of the local hip hop scene in Frankfurt am Main, Germany, I will now consider how the localization of hip hop, rather than being a smooth and consensual transition, is fraught with tensions and contradictions as young people attempt to reconcile issues of musical and stylistic authenticity with those of locality, identity and everyday life.

Hip Hop am Main

Frankfurt am Main is an international center. The city's population currently stands at around six hundred thousand people of whom approximately 25 per cent are foreign in origin. Many of Frankfurt's foreign residents, particularly the large Turkish and Moroccan populations, live in the city as "Gastarbeiter" (guest workers)[2] while many more have fled religious or political persecution in their home countries. Additionally, Frankfurt is the banking center of Germany and a central European base for a range of multinational companies. Consequently, the city's shopping areas, business quarters and suburbs are filled with the sights and sounds of a variety of different national cultures. Indeed, the Frankfurter Flohmarkt (flea market), held each Saturday on the south bank of the River Main, illustrates perfectly the mix of cultures that exist side by side in the city. To walk through the Flohmarkt is to experience at first hand the multicultural atmosphere of Frankfurt. Hip hop in Frankfurt also owes much to the international flavor of the city, albeit an internationalism borne out of somewhat different historical circumstances. As with other German cities, early experimentations with hip hop in Frankfurt were largely influenced by the African-American rap groups featured on American Forces Network (AFN), the radio station and TV channel established to serve personnel of the U.S. Army, which maintained a presence in central Germany between 1945 and 1996. Similarly, the presence of several large U.S. Army bases in and around Frankfurt meant that the local citizens were kept constantly in touch with many aspects of U.S. culture—particularly U.S. films, shown both in German and in their original English versions, U.S.-style diners and, most importantly, U.S. music and fashion. Thus, as one interviewee explained: "Frankfurt was introduced very early to soul, funk and so on. There were so many GIs here and they had such a great influence. So many new clubs opened while they were over here."

Similarly, a second interviewee gave the following account:

When I was about seven years old my family moved to Ginnheim [a town just outside of Frankfurt]. On both sides of the apartment block where I lived were American Army quarters. The guys on one side used to listen to heavy metal music and the guys on the other played soul, funk and rap and stuff all the time.

It was due to this abundant supply of U.S. American cultural resources and information that the first Frankfurt hip hop "posses" and rap "crews" were formed. Sachsenhausen, a district in the south of Frankfurt and a principal location for live music venues in the city, is generally acknowledged as the place where the live hip hop scene in Frankfurt began. A local rapper of Spanish-German origin who worked in one of the district's bars remembers it thus:

During the mid-1980s Sachsenhausen was a traditional meeting point for American GIs, many of whom were into hip hop. As a consequence, it was also the crystallization point for the local hip hop scene. And that set a precedent y'know. In the beginning the Frankfurt hip hop scene modeled itself very much on the example set by the GIs.

As a general trend, however, this stage in the development of Frankfurt hip hop was rather short lived. A large percentage of Frankfurt's hip hop following comprises young people from the city's numerous North African, South East Asian and southern European ethnic minority groups. In due course, a number of these young people, particularly those who came from Gastarbeiter families and whose social status in Germany remained decidedly unclear, began to make the realization that, as with African-Americans, theirs was a "distinct mode of lived [ethnicity]" which demanded its own localized and particularized mode of expression (Gilroy,

1993, p. 82). As a result of this, such groups began to seek ways in which to rework hip hop into a form that could be used as a vehicle for the expression of more locally relevant themes and issues.

The Localization of Hip Hop in Frankfurt

> We've found our way of communicating … and now the German rappers have got to do that too [African-American rapper commenting upon rap in Germany].[3]

In Frankfurt, as with other German cities, an early attempt to rework hip hop into a medium for the expression of local themes and issues came as a number of local rap groups began incorporating German lyrics into their music. If much has been written about the cultural significance of popular music lyrics (see, for example, Denzin, 1969; Laing, 1971), rather less attention has been focused upon the cultural significance of the language in which they are sung. Arguably, however, language in popular music cannot be assessed merely in terms of the themes and issues that it conveys or in relation to the sound or "grain" of the voice (Barthes, 1977). Rather, the simple fact of language itself can also play a crucial role in informing the cultural sensibilities that become inscribed within conventions of musical taste. One might think, for example, of the nationalist sentiment encapsulated in the Welsh "Celtic rock" movement of the 1970s when the fact of performing and listening to lyrics written in Welsh became a form of political statement in itself (Wallis and Malm, 1984, pp. 139–143). Similarly, in many former Eastern bloc countries, English-language popular music became highly fashionable among young people, not primarily because the lyrical content of the songs was understood but because of the counter-cultural stance that could be implied through listening to such music (Easton, 1989; Pilkington, 1994).

Parallel notions of language as a signifier of particular cultural sensibilities can be identified with the turn towards German-language rap within the Frankfurt hip hop scene. In switching over from English to German-language rapping, it could be argued, a new measure of accuracy was made possible between localized social experience and linguistic representation. For many young Frankfurt hip hoppers, German, if not their mother tongue, had become their adopted tongue following many years of living in the country. Thus, at a fundamental level it was much easier for these young people to rap in German than in English, their knowledge of English being for the most part very limited. At the same time, however, a more ideological motive can also be seen to underpin the move towards German-language rap. Thus, among many Frankfurt rappers and rap fans whom I interviewed, it was argued that only when local rappers started to write and perform texts in the German language did their songs begin to work as an authentic form of communication with the audience. Frankfurt rap group United Energy gave me the following account of their own move towards rapping in German:

> In the beginning people didn't think that rapping would sound like it should if we tried to do it in German. But then people began to realise that it was too limiting rapping in English, because their knowledge of the language wasn't good enough. So now a lot of rappers have begun to rap in German and it's just better, more effective. Anyway, we're living in Germany, so we should rap in German.

Mitchell (1996) identifies similar motives underpinning the popularity of Italian-language rap. In particular, argues Mitchell, the use of regional dialect in Italian rap has become a dominant market of hip hop's significance in the articulation of local identity. Mitchell also illustrates how the turn towards rapping in Italian has facilitated rap's use as a means of engaging with more nationally felt issues such as neo-Fascism and racism. Comparable examples of such nationally felt issues, and their manifestation at local level, inform the move towards German language rap in Frankfurt and other German cities.

"Ich habe einen grünen Pass"

Two thematic issues that appear regularly in German-language rap songs concentrate respectively upon the fear and anger instilled in ethnic minority groups by racism and the insecurity experienced by many young members of such groups over issues of nationality. The first theme has in recent years become one of national concern in Germany. Since the German reunification in October 1990, there has been a steady rise in neo-Fascist attacks against Gastarbeiter and refugees in Germany[4] (Fekete, 1993, p. 162). This in turn has led to growing support in Germany for anti-Fascist movements such as "Rock gegen Rechts" (Rock Against Racism).[5] A point often made by German rappers, however, is that despite the well-meant intentions of antiracism concerns, neo-Fascists and other racist groups will not single out people on ideological grounds but will go for the easy targets, those who can be identified by the color of their skin. This was the theme of amateur Frankfurt rap band Extra Nervig's song "Gib die Glatzen keine Chance!"[6] (Stop the skinheads!).

> You tell me you're on my side,
> Well your fancy words are fine,
> But you're not kicked to the ground,
> Just because of the way you look …

While there are fewer incidents of racial violence in Frankfurt than in other German cities, although this is on the increase, racism is often experienced in other ways. As I have already pointed out, much of Frankfurt's non-German population is made up of Gastarbeiter (guest workers) who, as with the Asians and Afro-Caribbeans who emigrated to Britain from the 1950s onwards, were called upon to meet the increasing demand for manual laborers in post-war western Europe. Because many Gastarbeiter have a relatively poor command of the German language and occupy minor positions in the labor market, they are often regarded as second-rate citizens, a label that is also ascribed to their children despite the fact that they have been born and educated in Germany, speak the language fluently and often have a skilled trade and, increasingly, a college or university qualification. This problem is, in turn, compounded by the issue of citizenship, which, in contrast to many other countries, is not given automatically to any child who is born in Germany. As a consequence, those people who have acquired German citizenship often find that they are subject to the same sort of stigmatization as those who have not. The term "Asylant" or "Asylbewerber" (a person seeking political asylum) is often carelessly used in youth clubs, cafes and other public places and can be very offensive, especially to those in possession of German citizenship.

Rap group Advanced Chemistry's song "Fremd im eigenen Land" (A Foreigner in My Own Country), along with its simple yet effective promotional video, was one of the first German rap songs to underline the severity of this type of misunderstanding and the hurt that it can cause. Performed by three rappers, each holding German citizenship, but with respective origins in Haiti, Ghana and Italy, the song chronicles the struggle of each to be accepted as German and orientates around the phrase "Ich habe einen grünen Pass, mit einem Goldenen Adler drauf"—"I have a green passport, with a golden eagle on it" (this being the design of the old German passport). In the video, each member of the group is questioned about his nationality. On one occasion group member Frederick Hahn is approached by a white German youth who asks, "Where do you come from, are you African or American?" When Hahn replies that he is German the youth begins to ridicule him and accuses him of lying, only retreating when Hahn produces his passport and sarcastically retorts, "Is this the proof you're looking for?" In a further scene, another member of Advanced Chemistry is asked by a white girl if he is "going home later?," as in back to his "home" country, to which Hahn replies "always the same stupid questions ... I've been living in this country for twenty years." In an interview with journalist Lee Harpin, Advanced Chemistry spoke of their concern to expose the racial exclusion suffered by Germany's ethnic minority groups. Thus, as one of the group explained:

> We rap in German in order to reach our own public, in order that they understand our problem ... it's a fact of life that if you're not recognized as a full German citizen you face constant harassment and identity checks. (1993, pp. 59–60)

Since the release of "Fremd im eigenen Land," a number of German-language rappers in Frankfurt have endeavored to develop its theme and have also used the rap medium to explore a range of similar issues. The resulting work by groups such as United Energy and Extra Nervig has consolidated in the minds of many of those who attend their performances the link between rap as a politicized discourse and the various insecurities experienced by members of ethnic minority groups in Frankfurt. Indeed, the centrality of rap and hip hop within local strategies of resistance to issues such as racism and racial exclusion is not limited to Germany but can also be seen in a range of other European contexts. Mitchell, for example, has noted how French rap artists such as MC Solaar focus on issues of racism in their country while in Italy hip hop provides a powerful critique against the growing support for Fascist ideology and far right political groups (1996, pp. 40, 149–50). Similarly, Bjurström's work on ethnicity and identity in Sweden illustrates how local hip hop fans have embraced Swedish rapper Papa Dee's tongue-in-cheek claim to be an "Original Black Viking" as a means of negotiating the hostility exhibited by white racist agitators who "celebrate the mythical Viking as an ancestor to German Nazists [sic] and their modern counterparts" (1997, p. 54).

By the same token, however, to claim that hip hop's role in opposition to locally manifested instances of racism and Fascism must in each case involve such forms of dialogic engagement with issues of nation and national identity is oversimplistic. Thus, to return to the context of Germany, while the lyrical themes of groups such as Advanced Chemistry may find appeal among some sections of Germany's ethnic minority youth, for others the mutuality of German-language rap with the desire to be seen as "German" is viewed negatively and has resulted in alternative forms of local hip hop culture which actively seek to rediscover and, in many cases, reconstruct notions of identity tied to traditional ethnic roots.[7] This, is particularly so in the case of Frankfurt where the percentage of ethnic minority inhabitants is higher than in most other German cities. During a conversation with a group of hip hoppers from Nordweststadt, a particularly multiethnic area of Frankfurt with a large number of Gastarbeiter families, I noted how German-language rap groups such as Advanced Chemistry were continually criticized for their failure to acknowledge any form of ethnic identification other than that symbolized by their German passports, a failure that was perceived to amount to a symbolic betrayal of the right of ethnic minorities to "roots" or to any expression of cultural heritage. Thus, as a young Turkish woman put it: "I think that they [Advanced Chemistry] should be proud of their roots. When people say to me 'are you German?', I say 'no I'm not' and I'm not ashamed to say that."

Such sentiments are encapsulated in the Turkish rap styles that are also an integral part of the Frankfurt hip hop scene. In the same way that Asian musicians in Britain have experimented with western popular music and traditional bhangra styles learned from cassette tapes acquired in Asian shops (see Banerji and Baumann, 1990, p. 144), so young Turkish people living in German cities are able to obtain cassette recordings of traditional songs and music very cheaply from local shops established to cater for their cultural needs. Using rhythms and melodies learned or sampled from such cassettes, traditional Turkish musical styles have been fused with African-American rap styles to produce a distinctive variation of the rap sound. If German-language rap has come to signify the voice of the second-generation immigrant attempting to integrate into German society, then Turkish rap works to a broadly opposite effect, the whole Turkish rap movement translating into a singly defiant message aimed at the Turk's white German hosts.

While employed as a youth worker in Frankfurt, I was invited to sit on the judging panel of a talent competition for local bands in the neighboring town of Schwalbach. As well as those bands taking part in the competition, a number of other local groups had been booked to provide entertainment between the various heats, including a Turkish rap group. Prior to the group's performance, an incident occurred in which some of the young Turkish people who had come specially to see the group began hurling eggs at a white group performing "Deutsch-rock" (rock music with German lyrics). The Deutsch-rock group's performance had to be temporarily interrupted while those responsible for the disruption were removed from the building. When the group returned to the stage their singer attempted to quell the situation by assuring the audience that, although the songs performed were in German, their lyrics were not racist and should not be regarded as such. Nevertheless, the young Turkish people remaining in the hall continued to act in a hostile fashion and accused the group of being Nazis. Later, as the Turkish rap group took to the stage, a large cheer went up and those who had come to see them moved onto the dance floor in a symbolic show of defiance regarding the incident that had occurred previously. Although many white Germans in the hall appeared to appreciate the music, few of them ventured onto the dance floor, wary of the nationalistic fervor that was manifesting itself there.

Scenes within Scenes

The two versions of hip hop examined above importantly illustrate how, even within the same city or region, hip hop scenes can be crossed by competing knowledges and sensibilities which, although working out of the same nexus of local experience, generate a multiplicity of musicalized and stylized solutions to the often problematic issue of place and identity. Interestingly, while researching in Frankfurt, I identified a third hip hop sensibility which, while also acting as a resource via which the youth of ethnic minorities are able to mark themselves out from the city's white population, relies upon an altogether different strategy to that of actively reworking hip hop. Rather, this realization of the hip hop identity relates to the possibility that it presents for the formulation of a romanticized association with the African-American experience. It is significant that in much of the work that focuses on non-U.S. examples of hip hop, there is an implication that "localization" necessarily involves some element of stylistic and musical transformation in hip hop. Thus, for example, Mitchell argues that the development of an Australian hip hop scene has been given some degree of "official recognition" by the release in 1995 of a compilation of rap tracks by Australian artists whose musical and stylistic direction indicates that the local hip hop scene "no longer needs 'supporting'" (1998, pp. 9–10). It seems to me, however, that there is a danger here of essentializing the process of localization so that it becomes synonymous with obvious innovation. In this way such an interpretation of "localization" overlooks some of the more subtly nuanced properties of appropriation and transformation for which Robertson (1995), as previously noted, coins the term *glocality*. Arguably then, the process of localization, as this relates to rap and hip hop, or indeed other forms of music and style, need not involve any obvious physical transformations of musical and stylistic resources but may, alternatively, rely on localized affinities, which are experienced more at the level of the experiential and which, in turn, demand a more abstract form of analytical engagement with the situating properties of local environments.

Thus, returning to the context of Frankfurt, I would argue that the African-American-based hip hop sensibility described above could also be seen as the expression of a "local" hip hop culture in that its origins are similarly rooted in the recent socio-historical context of Frankfurt. I have previously noted above how the Frankfurt hip hop scene developed in part because of the influence of African-American GIs whose impromptu rap performances in the city's clubs, bars and other public spaces encouraged imitation among local hip hop enthusiasts. Thus, in this sense, African-American representations of hip hop could be said to have been a "part" of the local scene from the outset. Furthermore, now that the U.S. army's occupation of central Germany has officially ended, there are clear indications that African-American hip hop will not only continue to be highly influential in Frankfurt but is also set to remain an integral part of the local hip hop scene. Thus, as a journalist working for a local hip hop magazine explained to me:

> Infrared [a small independent hip hop label in Frankfurt] have recently signed a U.S. rap group called Poverty. They were all stationed over here in the army and now they want to stay here and try and develop their career as a rap group. You get that quite a lot. Or American soldiers stationed over here invite relatives over who are into rap and hip hop and they like it here so they decide to stay. In the U.S. there's a lot of competition, very hard competition, between rappers … on every street corner there are ten rappers trying to get a recording deal. It's a lot easier for them over here, particularly if they come from the ghetto, the way of life is much less aggressive here … and the labels are often attracted to them, not least of all because they know that with any luck they can sell their records in the U.S. which means a lot of money for them.

The continuation of African-American hip hop's acutely physical presence within the local Frankfurt scene in turn ensures that it also continues to play a role in the formulation of local hip hop sensibilities. Thus, even today, for many enthusiasts hip hop continues to make "authentic" sense only in its African-American context. As one young hip hopper argued:

> How can you talk about German hip hop, what meaning does it have? What are you gonna do, sing about the ghetto? I'm into hip hop because of where it's at now y'know. It's a good style, you shouldn't mess with it. Some of those black guys are so cool. I look up to them and respect them…. When I go out on the street, they're the ones I'm thinking about, that's who I wanna be like y'know.

At the same time, however, it seems to me that this form of aesthetic attachment to the genre also derives from other distinctive forms of physical and visual experience acquired in Frankfurt's local environment. To put this another way, it could be argued that there is a direct correspondence between the significance of African-American-style hip hop as an authentic cultural practice in Frankfurt and the various terrains, both physical and symbolic, of the city itself. In many of the conversations I had with devotees of German-language rap, strong opinions were voiced against those who continue to listen to African-American rap artists. On one occasion, in speaking about the popularity of U.S.-style "gangsta rap" in Frankfurt, a German-language rapper explained to me:

> There are people who don't understand a word of English, but they like the music so they pretend that they understand what they're listening to and I personally have a problem with

that. For a lot of people, the commercial side of it, the image and the clothes are more important than the music and I find that ridiculous. They pretend to be "gangsta" rappers from the USA and yet we've got enough social problems here which need to be addressed.

It is interesting to note the way in which the word "pretend" is used in the above account to denote a form of "playing" or "acting" out a role, which, according to the interviewee, is how those who favor the African-American style of hip hop must inevitably come to understand their aesthetic attachment to the hip hop genre. An interesting analogy between public life and the conventions of theatrical performance is offered by Chaney. It seems to me that Chaney's conceptualization of the modern city center as "a stage for public drama," together with its underlying implication that the modern urban experience, rather than complying with a commonly acknowledged and "objective" social narrative, comprises a series of competing fictive interpretations, provides a fitting theoretical starting point for a further exploration of the deeply ingrained visions of America that continue to inform much of the hip hop culture acted out in the streets of Frankfurt (1993, p. 68). If, on the one hand, Frankfurt's multiple fictions of collective life are sustained by the multicultural composition of the city, since 1945 the changing face of the city itself has increasingly enhanced the flow of public drama. In particular, U.S.-directed post-war redevelopment has brought with it a variety of structures, surfaces and images which have met head on with the increasing flow of popular culture resources from the U.S. to produce an enduring visage of America in Frankfurt.

The View from "Mainhatten"

During the Second World War, Frankfurt was heavily bombed by enemy aircraft and much of the city center completely destroyed. After the war, reconstruction work was facilitated in Frankfurt and other German cities with considerable financial assistance from the U.S. government in the form of an ambitious loan package known as the Marshall Plan (Mayer, 1969). While care was taken in certain parts of the city to restore buildings as they had appeared in the pre-war years, in other areas modern high rise constructions (Hochhäuse) replaced bomb damaged eighteenth- and nineteenth-century German architecture. In the city center, such redevelopment programs completely revised the appearance of the old business quarters and shopping districts. Indeed with its futuristic skyline, notably the Bundesbank, a high rise, glass fronted building with a twin tower design, and the more recently erected Messeturm (trade center), Frankfurt city center has taken on the look and feel of a modern North American city. It is perhaps of little surprise then that this part of Frankfurt has become known locally as "Mainhatten." Indeed, when such elements of local urban folklore are read in conjunction with a prolonged absorption in Frankfurt's impressive infrastructure of consumer, leisure and public transport facilities, the city center increasingly comes to resemble the physical realization of Baudrillard's (1988) "cinematographized" U.S., which, Baudrillard argues, has become the primary way in which non-Americans experience the U.S. and thus construct images and ideas concerning the nation, its people and culture (see also Smart, 1993 and Gane, 1993).

Such a visage is perhaps most evident in the pedestrianized shopping precinct known as the "Zeil" and two adjacent open areas, the "Konstablerwache" and the "Hauptwache," which are each built over main intersections of the Frankfurt underground system. Over the years, these locations have become central meeting places for young people, accommodating skateboarders, breakdancers, buskers, street artists and the like. On either side of the "Zeil" familiar U.S. icons, such as the Disney Store and McDonald's, as well as a number of imitation U.S.-style fast food outlets, amplify the illusion that this is indeed a scene from a U.S. city.

Similarly, the main entrance to Hertie, a large department store, is bedecked on either side and above with multiple TV screens which provide visitors to the Zeil with a twenty-four hour transmission of American MTV.

In the context of this scenario it is easy to see how a version of hip hop culture grounded in notions of African-American style and a form of romanticized association with African-American street culture has become as much a part of Frankfurt's convoluted urban narrative as the politicized German-language variation of hip hop considered above. Offering as they do, a sonic and visual backdrop of Americana, public spaces such as the Zeil provide a perfect stage for the acting out of a hip hop sensibility that imagines itself to be a part of the African-American experience. In this sense, the Zeil becomes simultaneously "both a real and an imaginary place" (Chambers, 1992, p. 188). Speaking about the popularity of U.S. rap in Frankfurt and attempting to account for this, the manager of a local independent record label specializing in rap made a number of points that add weight to the above observation. Thus, he argued:

> The thing about hip hop that people keep forgetting, is that it's not just one definite thing. It's a lot of things, different sounds, different styles, different feelings. You can basically do with it what you want.... A lot of kids here go for the groove and the image. They see the videos, they see the clothes and the "cool image" and the kids enjoy that, they want to be like that. They're just play acting the whole thing. And you know, Frankfurt is this big international city ... there's lots going on here, movies, gigs. It's got really Americanized y'know. There's lots of places to go where you can hang out with your friends on the street, listen to your music real loud ... just like in the States. English is used a lot here too and even if a lot of the kids don't know it so well they're used to the sound of it and they can pick out key phrases. And that influences tastes in rap music. English [that is, African-American] rap is simply cool, it's in, and you can relate it to what's going on in the street here.

In the social context of Frankfurt am Main then, collective notions of hip hop and its significance as a mode of cultural expression are governed by a range of differing local factors which have, in their turn, given rise to a number of distinctive localized variations in the formulation of hip hop authenticity. It follows, therefore, that if notions of hip hop authenticity are intimately bound up with forms of local knowledge and experience then, in the context of other urban and regional locations with differing social circumstances and conditions, versions of hip hop culture and debates concerning its authentic usage will be based around a rather different range of social and aesthetic criteria. In order to illustrate this point more conclusively, I want now to conduct a further examination of hip hop culture and its attendant notions of authenticity as these are realized in the context of a different local urban setting, Newcastle upon Tyne in northeast England.

Rappin' on the Tyne

In terms of both its socio-economic history and ethnic composition, the cultural context of Newcastle upon Tyne is markedly different to that of Frankfurt am Main. Newcastle is a predominantly white, working-class post-industrial city. Thus, although small Asian and Afro-Caribbean minorities do exist in Newcastle, their influence upon its cultural environment, including the local music and club scene, has been nominal as compared with other British cities with larger Asian and Afro-Caribbean populations. This is also true of the small hip hop scene that has grown up around Newcastle, the neighboring city of Gateshead and a number of outlying towns and villages, such as Blythe and Cramlington, this scene being dominated by white male enthusiasts. Indeed, the male-centered nature of the Newcastle hip hop scene is another factor that sets it apart from the Frankfurt scene which, although also largely male, is characterized by a growing number of female hip hop enthusiasts and rap groups. This is indicative of both the wider acceptance in Germany of women and girls taking part in music-making activities and the emphasis upon music as a learning resource, which has in turn led to the establishment of numerous community-based music-making projects, many of which offer courses and workshops exclusively for women and girls (see Meinig, 1993; Pohl, 1993; Bennett, 1998). In Britain, by contrast, it could be argued that women and girls wishing to become involved in music-making activities continue to be confronted by indifference and hostility from their male peers. Cohen, for example, notes that girls were discouraged from taking part in community music projects in Liverpool for fear of being "criticized for wanting to do something that was mainly a boy's activity" (1991, p. 204; see also Bayton, 1988). Similar sensibilities appear to prevent the participation of women in the Newcastle hip hop scene. Thus, although none of my male interviewees claimed to object to female hip hoppers, their code of speech contained a number of male-centered terms such as "new jack" and "homeboy," which suggested that they considered hip hop culture to be an essentially male-orientated pursuit.

Hip Hop and "Whiteness"

The issue of white British working-class youth appropriating African-American and other black musical forms is one that has long been addressed by theorists of youth culture and popular music. Significantly, however, there has been little attempt to study white appropriations of hip hop in the context of the UK. The essential "whiteness" of hip hop culture in Newcastle, in addition to providing an ideal setting for beginning such an enquiry, also casts further light on the micro-social issues that inform the "localization" of hip hop. In many parts of the UK, the localization of hip hop has involved its appropriation by Afro-Caribbean and Asian youth, whose collective use of the style has turned partly on its deemed failure to translate into white terms. Such a belief is manifest among Afro-Caribbean hip hoppers in Cobley and Osgerby's (1995) research on the hip hop scene in London's Peckham district. According to Cobley and Osgerby, while Afro-Caribbean hip hopper's acknowledged white appropriations of the hip hop style they refused to take such appropriations seriously, much less view them as authentic expressions of hip hop culture. Similarly, Ashwani Sharma's account of London and Midlands-based Asian rap groups, such as Asian Dub Foundation, Fun Da Mental, Hustlers HC and ADF, argues that these groups' bhangra—rap fusions — perform an instrumental function in the marking out of a "*strategic* Asian identity" through their articulation of "significant dimensions of Asian cultural and political life in Britain" (1996, pp. 44–45). Finally, Back, in considering hip hop's translation in the context of south London, suggests that it has moved beyond its initial focus "on particular British circumstances" and now appropriates "the language of black New York ... to document and mythologize happenings in South London" (1996, pp. 207–9). As will shortly become evident, such discourses and sensibilities of African-American hip hop also feature in the Newcastle hip hop scene but are translated into white terms. That such a translation is possible in Newcastle, while remaining problematic in other British cities, has much to do with the ethnic composition of the local urban population which, as previously noted, is predominantly white. Indeed it could be argued that the essential "whiteness" of Newcastle and, by definition, the local hip hop scene, facilitates a highly particularized series of responses to the "black" characteristics of the hip hop style which, among certain sections of the local hip hop community, amounts to a celebration of blackness in the absence of blackness.

A general supposition of those who have attempted to account for the appropriation of

African-American musics by white British working-class youth is that the structural position of white working-class Britons and African-Americans is sufficiently similar to allow for African-American musics to perform a binary role in which the oppressions experienced by each group are simultaneously addressed. Thus, for example, Chambers has suggested that the "oppositional values" contained in African-American music also "symbolize and symptomatize the contradictions and tensions played out in [white] British working class youth" (1976, p. 166).[8] Certainly one could argue that sections of white working-class youth may appropriate black music and aspects of black style in symbolic recognition of their felt affinity with African-American and other black ethnic minority groups. At the same time, however, it is also important to acknowledge the actively constructed nature of such a cultural association rather than viewing it simply as a product of structural circumstances. In this sense then, the use of black music and style on the part of the white working-class youth becomes a particular form of lived sensibility; a reflexive lifestyle "strategy" (Chaney, 1996, pp. 112–125). Moreover, if this line of argument is followed to its logical conclusion, it follows that a number of other actively constructed ideological positions may also be articulated by white working-class youth via their appropriation of black musical forms in which symbolic associations with the fact of "blackness" itself are considered to be less important. To this must be added the significance of place. It is often taken for granted that white British appropriations of black music and style routinely take place in settings where a prominent black population serves as a continual point of reference for such appropriations. This is the case with Jones's (1988) research on white appropriations of reggae, which was carried out in a mixed-race area of Birmingham, and is also evident in Hebdige's work on the origins of mod and skinhead culture (1976a, 1976b, 1979). In reality, however, white working-class youth's experimentation with black music and style occurs in a range of differing local contexts and thus against a variety of referential socio-cultural backdrops which may or may not include an established black population.

Black Music in the Northeast

The northeast region of England has a long established tradition of appropriation from African-American music. During the 1960s, Newcastle group the Animals achieved international success with a style of music based closely on the urban blues of African-American artists such as Robert Johnson (Gillett, 1983, pp. 269–272). Rhythm and blues continues to be immensely popular in the area with a significant number of local "R&B" groups performing in local pubs and clubs, while each August the County Durham town of Stanley plays host to an internationally renowned blues festival. Similarly, during the 1970s, a number of dance venues in small towns in the neighboring region of East Yorkshire featured "Northern Soul," an all-white "underground" soul scene that centers around rare black soul imports primarily from the U.S. (see Milestone, 1997). Significantly, in the case of northeast England, such white appropriations of black music and style have largely taken place without physical reference to a local black population. As such, the point raised above positing the issue of black "association" as something that is actively constructed by white youth in their appropriation of black music and style, rather than as a structurally determined "given" of such appropriation, is perhaps more clearly illustrated. Indeed, the consciously articulated nature of black association in the northeast region is particularly evident when one considers the competing sensibilities that characterize the local hip hop scene in Newcastle. At the center of this scene, a hardcore of hip hop enthusiasts share the belief that their intimate understanding of hip hop's essential "blackness" as the key to its relevance for the white working-class experience guarantees them a form of aesthetic supremacy over other local white hip hop fans who, according to this group, have no such understanding of the genre and thus no authentic claim to the title "hip hopper." Conversely, a number of other local hip hop enthusiasts firmly reject the notion that hip hop can be understood only in terms of its African-American context and attempt to rework it as a platform for the expression of issues that relate more directly to their own day to day experiences. I want now to consider each of these responses to hip hop in turn. In doing so, I hope to illustrate how, as with the various hip hop sensibilities examined in the case of Frankfurt, these responses, despite their obvious stylistic differences, are each intimately bound up with the particularities of local experience.

"You Into that 'Nigger Music' Then?"

In his study of the music scene in Austin, Texas, Shank (1994) draws attention to the important role played by local independent record shops in authenticating particular scenes by providing a space for like-minded individuals to meet, discuss their tastes in music and argue over the merits of particular tracks and artists, thus positioning themselves in relation to other music scenes located in the same city or town. In the context of the Newcastle hip hop scene, a comparable role is performed by Groove. Groove is a tiny independent record shop in the center of Newcastle dealing exclusively in U.S. rap which is specially imported and, consequently, not readily available in the high street chain stores. The proprietor of Groove, a white Newcastle man named Jim, is a devotee of African-American rap music and hip hop culture. Having listened to soul music during his teens, he then turned to rap as it became more widely available in Britain during the 1980s. Groove has become something of a meeting point for those who believe, like Jim, that rap and hip hop can only be understood in terms of their African-American cultural context. On the surface, the group of local hip hop enthusiasts who frequent Groove appear to correspond unproblematically with the commonly expounded sociological thesis that African-American dance music is somehow able to connect with the experiential world of white working-class youth in Britain. Below is an extract from a discussion I conducted with Jim and several of the regular visitors to Groove during which I asked them to comment on the issue of *white* hip hop:

> A.B.: There are a lot of white rap fans in Newcastle who are using hip hop to talk about their own experiences.
>
> Jim: There's no such thing as white hip hop.
>
> A.B.: Why is that?
>
> Jim: Because hip hop is a black music. As white people we should still respect it as black music.
>
> Jeff: All the time before, white people were into black music, hip hop's just the same. There's a message in black music which translates for white working-class people.
>
> A.B.: What is that?
>
> Dave: It's about being proud of where you come from ...
>
> Jeff: Yeah and because it [black music] offers a strength and intelligence which no British culture does.
>
> Jim: The trend at the moment is to be real ... to rap in your own accent and talk about things close to you ... don't try to be American like. But that's why British hip hop will always be shite.... I went to New York, well actually to Cleveland near New York, and stayed with a black family. It was brilliant, it changed my life. You can't talk about white hip hop, it doesn't exist.

Clearly then, among the Groove regulars there is a shared sense of belief that the essential blackness of hip hop is also the key to its use by white working-class youth as an authentic mode of cultural expression. Interestingly, however, when the wider cultural context of

Groove and those who frequent it is studied in more detail, it becomes evident that such a belief in the nature of hip hop carries a level of symbolic importance that goes beyond a shared sense of affinity with the African-American experience. Within the local Newcastle music scene, Groove has a reputation for being one of the few "specialist" record shops in the city. As such the shop enjoys something of an "outsider" status. Indeed, as a local hairdresser and popular music enthusiast who is familiar with Groove suggested to me one day as I sat in his chair: "I can't see how he [Jim] makes any money from that business. It's more a labor of love for him really."

In many ways, the above observation constitutes a highly sensitive reading of Groove and the type of cultural work that it performs. In the context of Newcastle, Groove, although ostensibly a business venture, at the same time plays host to a type of self-styled local hip hop elite in which an intimate understanding of hip hop's black roots is combined with a comprehensive knowledge of rap music and what, on the basis of the group's understanding of the music's cultural significance, counts as good or bad rap. This form of local "cultural capital," into which the local reputation of Groove is included, is then used as a way of articulating the group's difference from the "new jacks," a term given to those who are considered to be hip hop "tourists," that is, those who listen indiscriminately to rap music before moving on to a new trend. Thus, as Jim pointed out:

> These new jacks, you can spot them a mile off. They're just into hip hop 'cause it's trendy like. They come in here and they don't know what the fuck they're talking about. They'll buy about one record a month for a year or something and then get into something else, house or something.

Marks has suggested that white appropriations of black musical forms are often symbolically transformed into "badge[s] of exclusivity," particularly if such conspicuous displays of black taste on the part of young whites enable them to "manifest their difference from the cultural mainstream" (1990, p. 105). Clearly, this observation goes some way towards explaining the shared sensibility of those local hip hop enthusiasts who frequent Groove and their collective response towards the perceived fickleness of the new jacks' attachment to the genre.

Arguably, however, there is a further reason why these and other like-minded local hip hop enthusiasts are so passionate in their symbolic association with African-American culture. In a Birmingham-based study Jones has noted how young whites' "displays of affiliation to black culture" result on occasion in them becoming "the objects of a 'deflected' form of racism" (1988, p. 199). In the social context of Newcastle, perhaps because of the city's predominately white populace, such physical challenges to forms of black association occur more frequently. On one particular evening, I accompanied a group of local hip hop enthusiasts, several of whom were regular customers at Groove, to a bar in the center of Newcastle where a weekly "hip hop" night was being held. On the way to the bar the group, who were dressed in typical African-American hip hop style clothes such as loose fitting shorts, basketball caps, designer training shoes and sunglasses, attracted comments such as "are you going to a fancy dress party?" and were also subject to several shouts of "wigger" (white nigger) from other young club and pub-goers. The use of "wigger" in this context is particularly significant in that it involves a localized reworking of the term. Cobley and Osgerby note how in London, Afro-Caribbean hip hop enthusiasts use "wigger" as a way of marking out the deemed inauthenticity of "white youth [who] appropriate 'black' styles" (1995, p. 6). In the context of Newcastle, however, "wigger's" white on white application suggests that it is being used as a way of stigmatizing those who are seen as "wanting to be black" and thus deviating from the locally established norm. Clearly, such "deflected" racism cannot be equated with the systematic abuse and physical violence that continues to be directed at ethnic minorities in Britain by white racist groups. It does, however, suggest the need for a broader consideration of the factors contributing to racist behavior and the ways in which the symbolic alliance of whites with African-American and other ethnic minority groups, through mediums such as music and style, might be viewed as a form of cultural betrayal by other sections of white youth.

Such a view is substantiated via other accounts I received of the deflected racism encountered by hip hop enthusiasts in Newcastle. Thus, for example, as another Groove regular explained: "I used to work in a record shop and I'd always be getting loads of shit from the customers ... they'd say 'what do you like this nigger music for?' Or, 'you only like this music 'cause it's black.'" The particular hostility of deflected racism in "white" settings is graphically portrayed in the following account by a white hip hop enthusiast from Glasgow, another British city with a predominantly white population, whose expertise in breakdancing had led him to move down to Newcastle where he worked part-time in a local dance school. This hip hopper's account of his experiences in Glasgow is comparable with those of the Newcastle hip hoppers noted above. Thus, he explained:

> We were always different like ... 'cause we always used to go in the park and that and you'd get these idiots comin' up and saying "what yoos doin' there, that breakdancin'?" ... and they'd do us in.... And we used to go to nightclubs and that and the DJ was one of our mates. He'd clear the floor and say "right we're havin' some breakdancers up now, some really hardcore hip hoppers," and they'd all start spittin' on us.

If the essential whiteness of given local settings can lead to such expressions of prejudice and hostility regarding white associations with "blackness," at the same time those who are stigmatized for their "deviant" identity politics often use the fact of such negative responses as a key resource when marking out a cultural territory for themselves. Thus, in the case of the Newcastle hip hoppers, the displays of hostility that they encountered resulted in them becoming even more forthright in terms of their "black association," this symbol of "exclusivity" being turned around and worn with an air of defiance in the face of a crowd whose racism, it was argued, went hand in hand with its small-mindedness and conservative tastes in music and fashion. Thus, as one of the group exclaimed: "I fucking hate the town scene, all that crap commercial music and fashion stuff. As far as I'm concerned it has nothing to do with my life whatsoever!" Within the group then, there was a carefully fashioned sensibility which dictated that in being frank about their dedication not only to African-American hip hop but also to the stylistic and ideological forms of address they deemed to be a part of it, they were in turn revealing an honesty and integrity within themselves, thus setting the group apart from the small town mentality that was deemed to prevail in Newcastle. Indeed, one could go as far as to argue that for this particular group of hip hoppers, their staunchly adhered-to hip hop identity had become a form of external faith, the latter being reconfirmed each time the group was subject to abuse by "non-believers." As such, incidents of abuse had become not so much insulting experiences or tests of patience, but rather provided the group with a platform for displays of collective martyrdom to their cause. This "localized" response on the part of white youth to African-American hip hop style further emphasizes the point made in relation to the continuing significance of African-American hip hop in Frankfurt. Thus, in relation to Groove and those hip hop enthusiasts whose shared discourse of authenticity and integrity revolves around being a part of the Groove "scene," the local significance of rap and hip hop derives not from any obvious physical reworking of the latter but more from a locally forged sense of affinity with hip hop based upon a sense of its *strength and intelligence* in comparison to what is seen as a fickle and undiscerning local mainstream youth culture.

A "Street Thing!"

A somewhat different if equally constructed hip hop sensibility can be seen in relation to those individuals who make up what could be termed Newcastle's *white* hip hop culture. For these local enthusiasts, hip hop's use as an authentic mode of expression does not center around the form of felt association with the African-American experience shared by those individuals who frequent Groove. Rather, there is a commonly held view among *white* hip hoppers that the essence of hip hop culture relates to its ready translation into a medium that directly bespeaks the white British working-class experience. Thus as one self-styled "Geordie" rapper explained to me:

> Hip hop isn't a black thing, it's a street thing y'know, where people get so pissed off with their environment that they have to do something about it. And the way to do it and get the word to the people is to do it creatively, be it writing on a wall or expressing it in a rap … or wearing baggy clothes y'know. It's all part of this one thing of going "oh look man, we've had enough of this and we're gonna change it in our way."

An interesting comparison here is a study by Maxwell of the hip hop scene in Sydney, Australia. According to Maxwell, although the Sydney hip hoppers' realization of their scene involved taking "the simulacrum of a culture which they had accessed through the electronic media" the physical realization of this simulacrum brought it into contact with a new reality, one located in the streets and neighborhoods of Sydney (1994, p. 15). In a similar fashion *white* hip hop enthusiasts in Newcastle are attempting to rework the hip hop style so that it becomes a form of address that resonates intimately with the nature of their own particular local circumstances. I want now to consider two specific examples of the way in which hip hop has been taken up by white working-class youth in Newcastle as a way of addressing issues encountered on a day to day basis in the city.

"Am that Dreadlock Hippy Bastard that Comes from the Toon"

This chapter begins with an extract from "Aa dee it coz aa can" (I do it because I can) by Ferank, a Newcastle poet and rapper. Originally written as a poem, "Aa dee it coz aa can" was later recorded as rap. As with much of Ferank's work, this rap deals directly with his own experiences of living in Newcastle and is performed in a local Geordie accent, a feature that Ferank feels adds an important element of authenticity to his style. Thus, he argues: "I'm not American, so it's pointless for me to do a rap in an American accent.... Anyway, the Geordie accent that myself and other rappers up here are using is a dialect, just like patois, and so it should be used." "Aa dee it coz aa can," which is essentially a commentary on aspects of Newcastle life and the local Geordie culture, works at a number of different levels. Thus, in one sense the rap is intended to deliver a firm message to those living in other places, both in Britain and abroad, whose impressions of Newcastle are dominated by the notion of the typical Geordie stereotype. Using his own starkly profiled local identity as a springboard, Ferank attempts to demonstrate, through the medium of his informed reading and poetical summary of the local situation, that the stereotypical image of the Geordie character is erroneous. As Ferank explained to me:

> I was tryin' to change people's perceptions of what they think o' Geordies. Flat caps and this Geordie pride thing which I don't feel. Eh, I'm proud o' where I come from and of the people that I care for and who care for me. But eh, there's a lot of malice in this town and a lotta people who need an education. And I'd like to think that I've had one of sorts, and I've

always been from here. So it was kinda sayin' "oh look man for fuck's sake, I might be from here but I'm not your typical Geordie!." While I am … while I should be accepted as the most typical Geordie.

At the same time, however, "Aa dee it coz aa can" also criticizes the cultural conservatism that Ferank identifies with sections of Newcastle's population, especially when confronted with someone who fails to conform with accepted conventions of appearance such as dress and hairstyle. It is Ferank's opinion that such conservatism is destined to remain a part of the city's character for a long time to come as, from a very early age, children are indoctrinated by their parents into believing that those who are in some way "individual" or "eccentric" in their appearance or manner are misfits and should therefore be subject to a form of systematic stigmatization. Again, as Ferank himself explained to me:

When I'm out in the street I'll get someone pass a comment on how I look, within earshot of myself and they don't mind if I hear. Y'know … and that's their attitude to everything here…. Like I'll walk past kids in the street and they'll be with their parents and that and even the parents'll join in wi' like "look at the state o' him, they look like bloody rats' tails in 'is hair." Y'know, they're really blatant about it…. These people need an education. You can't get away with that, you gotta expect a reaction. And they normally get one from me…. They get it in a rhyme, they're there y'know. And maybe they'll see themselves and go "oh hang on a sec … I need to think a little differently about what I'm sayin."

Ferank's visual image combines a dreadlock hairstyle with a broadly eclectic if eccentric dress sense in which brightly colored garments are often combined to dazzling effect. Thus, as he explains: "I love to dress up myself, I always have. So amongst my mates it's like, 'whoa fuckin' hell, look what Ferank's got on!'" In his rap, Ferank contrasts the playfulness implied in his own chosen image with the harsh reactions which this image often elicits and makes it pointedly clear that, whatever others may think of him, he is determined to stand by his right to be an individual.

It shouldn't really matter that me skeets are aal tatty, An a wear funny clothes wi' me dreads aal natty, 'Coz underneath am just like yeez, Or have aa just managed to outrun the disease … An me eyes just sing the sad, sad song, Of the hatred the parents install in tha young … aal never shaddap an aal never siddoon, 'Am that dreadlock hippy bastard that comes from the toon.

While Ferank describes his work as a form of protest against the conservatism he encounters on the streets of Newcastle, there is a clear sense in which, at a deeper level, he is also exposing the contradictions inherent in the sensibilities of a local white youth culture that collectively appropriates black cultural resources while simultaneously stigmatizing certain individual experimentations with black style as in some way going "too far." In many respects, Ferank's personal battle for self-expression serves to reconfirm the fact that many young whites, especially those who live in predominantly white areas, maintain a double standard in which an acceptance of black music and style goes hand in hand with an intolerance of black minority groups. While Ferank, who is regarded as a white "imitator," remains untouched by the more brutal and disturbing aspects of such intolerance, the reactions of local white youth to his experiments with aspects of black style serve as telling reminders of considerable local variations which characterize racial tolerance and multiculturalism in Britain.

At the same time, Ferank's work illustrates another of the ways in which hip hop is being modified or reworked by white working-class youth in Newcastle so that it becomes a more localized and, in Ferank's case, highly personalized mode of expression. Indeed, it is clear from Ferank's own account of the meanings underlying his work that his personal attachment to hip hop results directly from the artistic license it grants him. Through the medium of hip hop Ferank is able to publicly voice feelings and opinions that would otherwise find little scope for expression. In this sense, a further similarity can be seen between the *white* hip hop culture of Newcastle and the German-language rappers of Frankfurt in that both of them consider hip hop's value as an authentic mode of expression to be primarily rooted in the power it gives them as individuals to comment upon the nature of their own day to day experiences. This form of attachment to hip hop is further illustrated below where a second "Geordie" adaptation of the hip hop sensibility is considered.

The "Broon Ale" Ward

Ferank is often to be heard performing his raps at Mac's Bar, one of the few venues in Newcastle that provides an opportunity for local rappers to air their skill in a live situation. While much of Ferank's work is composed beforehand, many of the rappers who frequent Mac's Bar engage in a form of rapping known as "freestyle." Basically, this involves taking a particular theme and verbally improvising a series of ideas and points of view around the chosen theme. This form of rapping has also become a primary way in which local *white* rappers address issues that are particular to Newcastle and its people. Indeed, in many ways, "freestyling" provides a more effective form of local address than written rap as it enables the rapper to engage in a relatively spontaneous form of discourse. Thus, snippets of local "street" gossip and more widely acknowledged local themes and issues can be verbally woven together with pieces of local urban folklore to produce particularly pointed, hard-hitting and, on occasion, humorous cameos of local social life. The following account is drawn from a conversation with a member of one particular group of freestyle rappers who regularly perform at Mac's Bar:

> We used to use a lot of "Americanisms" in our raps, but then when we started comin' down here we heard pure Geordie rap. Like with Ferank … it was just like "oh yeah check out Ferank's flow." And then people'd be sayin' to us "why don't you do a rap theme about like eh, like an American rap crew would do a song about Crack and about how it's affecting their city an' that?" An' we started thinkin' "well aye why not, let's 'ave a go at doin' something about Newcastle Brown Ale" because there's lots of "isms" for Newcastle Brown Ale. "The Dog," "Geordie into space," all these different names and it's … y'know all these different reputations it's got. They used to have a ward up at the General [hospital] which was the "Broon Ale" ward [owing to the number of people admitted with injuries caused through fighting when drunk]. So we thought, "yeah, that's the stuff we should be rappin' about," it's like our version of "Crack on the streets" with a bit a' humour in there an' all y'know.

While the notion of a white Newcastle rap group rapping about the local drinking culture may initially seem rather comical, it is important to understand the local circumstances to which the group is responding. As with many of those young people involved in the Newcastle dance music scene, there is growing cynicism among local hip hoppers concerning the city center pub and club scene and the aggressive, masochistic atmosphere that often manifests itself there. Thus, in a very real sense, by rapping about the problems of excessive drinking and alcohol-related violence, the white rap group quoted above are addressing an aspect of their local environment which, they feel, needs to be acknowledged and changed. Additionally, it is also widely held among members of Newcastle's hip hop scene that the possibility of staging hip hop nights in the city is being continually reduced because of the more commercially successful mainstream club nights that increasingly dominate Newcastle's night-time economy. Consequently, the freestyle raps heard in Mac's Bar assume a dual resonance in that they not only attack the senseless violence that characterizes the local mainstream club scene but also deal with the latter's steady encroachment on the hard-won club space of Newcastle's more underground and alternative youth cultures.

The obvious connection of such "home grown" rap with the shared sensibilities of local hip hoppers is clearly evidenced by the particular type of listening sensibility that it appears to invoke in Mac's Bar. When the "freestylers" take to the floor, usually towards the end of the evening, the audience, who have up to that point been lazily dancing to a mix of mainly U.S. rap sounds, stop dancing and gather around the performers to listen to their raps. In doing so they are acknowledging the fact that the improvised stories these local rappers are relating work out of a shared stock of local knowledges and experiences that are in many ways uniquely relevant to Newcastle and the surrounding area. In listening to the "freestylers," regulars at Mac's Bar are receiving accounts of their own lives depicted via a form of quickfire verbal reference to locations and events, names and faces with which they are all intimately familiar. Again, this instance of local hip hop activity is indicative of the close links that prefigure collective notions of authenticity, identity and local experience in hip hop. When the Geordie rappers take to the floor, there is an obvious shift in the audience's response. From the point of view of the audience, the music ceases to provide purely a rhythm for dancing or a background noise over which to talk and becomes something to be listened to, something that actively involves them. In drawing around the stage to listen to the Geordie rappers, the audience collectively endorse the more locally relevant focus of the rappers' messages, thus celebrating its particularized "authenticity."

The purpose of this chapter has been to demonstrate how hip hop cultures and attendant notions of authenticity are in each case a product of locality, that is to say, the particular local circumstances under which hip hop is appropriated and subsequently used as a collective form of expression. Using examples of different local hip hop scenes, I have attempted to illustrate how, in each instance, the particular version, or versions, of hip hop culture created, together with attendant debates as to which individuals are *authentically* portraying the hip hop sensibility, is underpinned by a stock of distinctive local knowledges. In each of the local hip hop cultures examined here, the particular characteristics of the wider social context have been shown to greatly influence the manner in which enthusiasts frame their association with the hip hop genre. In addition to looking at localized receptions of recorded rap music, during the course of this chapter I have also made some consideration of how live performances by local rappers can similarly serve to articulate notions of local identity. If "recorded" musical texts can be reworked by audiences to act as powerful statements of regional place and identity, then local "live" music scenes and the musicians who participate in them can also play a crucial role in the communicating such themes and issues to local audiences.

Notes

1. Aside from rap music, "graffiti" is perhaps the most characteristic aspect of hip hop culture. However, because of the nature of this chapter's enquiry, which focuses primarily upon the local significance of rap, it will not be possible to engage in any in-depth discussion of hip hop graffiti. For a more informed analysis of the latter, see Lachmann (1988), Brewer and Miller (1990) and Deppe (1997).
2. "Gastarbeiter" is the term applied to those individuals, typically from Turkey and Morocco, who have been granted special permission to enter Germany in order to meet the country's demand for unskilled manual labor.
3. Excerpt from the documentary *Lost in Music* broadcast on ZDF, March 1993.
4. This is particularly so in the former East Germany where the influx of capitalism from the west has not,

as was expected, led to a better quality of life but has rather resulted in high levels of unemployment and related social problems such as homelessness.

5. For an account of the Rock gegen Rechts movement see de Cologne (1980).
6. The term "*Glatzen*" (plural of *Glatze*) derives from the German adjective *glatt* which means "smooth." "*Glatze*" is a slang term often applied to a bald person. In the wake of the neo-Fascist movement in Germany the term has been appropriated by opposers of the movement and used in relation to all German skinheads as a way of linking them with neo-Nazi ideology. This automatic association of "skinhead" culture with the neo-Fascist movement is, however, largely inaccurate. In Germany, as in Britain, many skinheads are themselves anti-Facists. For a fuller account of this general misunderstanding and the special problems it has caused for skinheads in Germany, see Farin and Seidel-Pielen (1994).
7. It should be pointed out that German-language rap is almost exclusively performed by groups who originate in whole or in part from Germany's ethnic minorities. "All white" German-language rap groups, the most famous example of which is Die Fantastichen Vier, remain conspicuously apolitical in their music. This has lead to criticism from more politicized German-language rap groups such as Advanced Chemistry, who have suggested in a TV interview that Die Fantastichen Vier are a "hit pop" group whose style is little more than a fashionable pastiche of hip hop culture.
8. For historical accounts of white appropriations of black music in Britain, see Oliver (1990) and Fryer (1998).

References

Back, L. (1996) *New Ethnicities and Urban Culture: Racisms and Multiculture in Young Lives*, UCL Press, London.

Banerji, S. and Baumann, G. (1990) Bhangra 1984–88: Fusion and Professionalisation in a Genre of South Asian Dance Music in P. Oliver (ed.) *Black Music in Britain: Essays on the Afro-Asian Contribution to Popular Music*, Open University Press, Milton Keynes.

Barthes, R. (1977) The Grain of the Voice in S. Frith and A. Goodwin (eds) (1990) *On Record: Rock, Pop and the Written Word*, Routledge, London.

Bayton, M. (1988) How Woman Become Rock Musicians in S. Frith and A. Goodwin (eds) (1990) *On Record: Rock, Pop and the Written Word*, Routledge, London.

Beadle, J.J. (1993) *Will Pop Eat Itself?: Pop Music in the Sound Bite Era*, Faber & Faber, London.

Bennett, A. (1988) The Frankfurt Rockmobil: A New Insight into the Significance of Music-Making for Young People, *Youth and Policy*, 60: 16–29.

Bjurström, E. (1997) The Struggle for Ethnicity: Swedish Youth Styles and the Construction of Ethnic Identities, *Young: Nordic Journal of Youth Research*, 5(3): 44–58.

Brewer, D.D. and Miller, M.L. (1990) Bombing and Burning: The Social Organization and Values of Hip Hop Graffiti Writers and Implications for Policy, *Deviant Behavior*, 11: 345–69.

Chambers, I. (1976) A Strategy for Living: Black Music and White Subcultures in S. Hall and T. Jefferson (eds) *Resistance Through Rituals: Youth Subcultures in Post-War Britain*, Hutchinson, London.

Chambers, I. (1992) Cities Without Maps in J. Bird, B. Curtis, T. Putnam, G. Robertson, and L. Tickner (eds) *Mapping the Futures: Local Cultures, Global Change*, Routledge, London.

Chaney, D. (1993) *Fictions of Collective Life: Public Drama in Late Modern Culture*, Routledge, London.

Chaney, D. (1996) *Lifestyles*, Routledge, London.

Cobley, P. and Osgerby. W. (1995) Peckham Clan Ain't Nothin' to Fuck With: Urban Rap Style in Britain' unpublished paper presented at the Youth 2000 conference, University of Teesside, Middlesborough.

Cohen, Sara (1991) *Rock Culture in Liverpool: Popular Music in the Making*, Clarendon Press, Oxford.

de Cologne, F. (1980) *Rock gegen Rechts: Beiträge zu einer Bewegung*, Weltkreis, Dortmund.

Condry, I. (1999) The Social Production of Difference: Imitation and Authenticity in Japanese Rap Music in H. Fehrenbach and U. Poiger (eds) *Transactions, Transgressions, Transformations American Culture in Western Europe and Japan*, Providence, RI, Berghan Books.

Decker, J.L. (1994) The State of Rap: Time and *Place in Hip Hop Nationalism in A. Ross and T. Rose (eds) Microphone* Fiends: Youth Music and Youth Culture, Routledge, London.

Denzin, N.K. (1969) Problems in Analyzing Elements of Mass Culture: Notes on the Popular Song and Other Artistic Productions, *American Journal of Sociology*, 75: 1035–38.

Deppe, J. (1997) *Oden: On the Run — Eine Jugend in der Graffiti-Szene*, Schwarzkopf & Schwarzkopf, Berlin.

Dyson, M.E. (1996) *Between God and Gangsta Rap: Bearing Witness to Black Culture*, Oxford University Press, New York.

Easton, P. (1989) The Rock Music Communit' in J. Riordan (ed.) *Soviet Youth Culture*, Indiana University Press, Bloomington and Indianapolis.

Epstein, J.S., Pratto, D.J. and Skipper Jr., J.K. (1990) Teenagers, Behavioral Problems, and Preferences for Heavy Metal and Rap Music: A Case Study of a Southern Middle School, *Deviant Behavior*, 11: 381–94.

Farin, K. and Seidel-Pielen, E. (1994) *Skinheads*, Verlag C.H. Beck, München.

Fekete, L. (1993) Inside Racist Europe in T. Bunyan (ed.) *Statewatching the New Europe: A Handbook on the European State*, Statewatch, London.

Filippa, M. (1986) Popular Song and Musical Cultures in D. Forgacs and R. Lumley (eds) *Italian Cultural Studies: An Introduction*, Oxford University Press, Oxford.

Flores, J. (1994) Puerto Rican and Proud, Boyee!: Rap Roots and Amnesia in A. Ross and T. Rose (eds) *Microphone Fiends: Youth Music and Youth Culture*, Routledge, London.

Foner, N. (1978) *Jamaica Farewell: Jamaican Migrants in London*, Routledge & Kegan Paul, London.

Gane, M. (ed.) (1993) *Baudrillard Live: Selected Interviews*, Routledge, London.

Gillett, C. (1983) *The Sound of the City: The Rise of Rock and Roll*, 2nd edn, Souvenir Press, London.

Gilroy, P. (1993) *The Black Atlantic: Modernity and Double Consciousness*, Verson, London.

Harpin, L. (1993) One Continent Under a Groove, *ID: The Europe Issue*, 16 May: 58–60.

Hebdige, D. (1976a) The Meaning of Mod in S. Hall and T. Jefferson (eds) *Resistance Through Rituals: Youth Subcultures in Post-War Britain*, Hutchinson, London.

Hebdige, D. (1976b) Reggae, Rastas and Rudies in S. Hall and T. Jefferson (eds) *Resistance Through Rituals: Youth Subcultures in Post-War Britain*, Hutchinson, London.

Hebdige, D. (1979) *Subculture: The Meaning of Style*, Routledge, London.

Hebdige, D. (1987) *Cut 'n' Mix: Culture, Identity and Caribbean Music*, Routledge, London.

Jones, S. (1988) *Black Culture, White Youth: The Reggae Tradition from JA to UK*, Macmillan, London.

Keyes, C.L. (1991) Rappin' to the Beat: Rap Music as Street Culture Among African Americans, Doctoral thesis published by University Microfilms International, Ann Arbor, Michigan.

Lachmann, R. (1988) Graffiti as Career and Ideology, *American Journal of Sociology*, 94(2): 229–50.

Laing, D. (1971) Listen to Me in S. Frith and A. Goodwin (eds) (1990) *On Record: Rock, Pop and the Written Word*, Routledge, London.

Light, A. (1992) About a Salary or Reality?: Rap's Recurrent Conflict in A. DeCurtis (ed.) *Present Tense: Rock and Roll and Culture*, Duke University Press, London.

Lipsitz, G. (1994) *Dangerous Crossroads: Popular Music, Postmodernism and the Poetics of Place*, Verso, London.

Lull, J. (1995) *Media, Communication, Culture: A Global Approach*, Polity Press, Cambridge.

Marks, A. (1990) Young, Gifted and Black: Afro-American and Afro-Caribbean Music in Britain 1963–88 in P. Oliver (ed.) *Black Music in Britain: Essays on the Afro-Asian Contribution to Popular Music*, Open University Press, Milton Keynes.

Maxwell, I. (with Bambrick, N.) (1994) Discourses of Culture and Nationalism in Contemporary Sydney Hip Hop, *Perfect Beat*, 2(1): 1–19.

Mayer, H.C. (1969) *German Recovery and the Marshall Plan, 1948–1952*, Edition Atlantic Forum, New York.

Meinig, U. (1993) Von "e-Moll" und "langen Fingernägeln" — eine Mädchen-Rockband in Hamburg-Eidelstadt in W. Hering, B. Hill, and G. Pleiner (eds) *Prasixhandbuch Rockmusik in der Jugendarbeit*, Leske & Budrich, Opladen.

Milestone, K. (1997) Love Factory: The Sites, Practices and Media Relationships of Northern Soul in S. Redhead, D. Wynne and J. O'Connor (eds), *The Clubcultures Reader: Readings in Popular Cultural Studies*, Blackwell, Oxford.

Mitchell, T. (1996) *Popular Music and Local Identity: Rock, Pop and Rap in Europe and Oceania*, Leicester University Press, London.

Pilkington, H. (1994) *Russia's Youth and its Culture: A Nation's Constructors and Constructed*, Routledge, London.

Pohl, M. (1993) Mädchen — und Frauenrockbands in der Jugendarbeit in W. Hering, B. Hill, and G. Pleiner (eds) *Praxishandbuch Rockmusik in der Jugendarbeit*, Leske & Budrich, Opladen.

Potter, R. (1995) *Spectacular Vernaculars: Hip hop and the Politics of Postmodernism*, State University of New York Press, New York.

Ritzer, G. (1993) *The McDonaldization of Society: An Investigation into the Changing Character of Contemporary Social Life*, Pine Forge Press, London.

Robertson, R. (1995) Glocalization: Time-Space and Momogeneity-Heterogeneity in M. Featherstone, S. Lash and R. Robertson (eds) *Global Modernities*, Sage, London.

Rose, T. (1994) *Black Noise: Rap Music and Black Culture in Contemporary America*, Wesleyan University Press, London.

Sexton, A. (1995) Don't Believe the Hype: Why Isn't Hip-Hop Criticism Better? in A. Sexton (ed.) *Rap on Rap: Straight-Up Talk on Hip-Hop Culture*, Delta, New York.

Shank, B. (1994) *Dissonant Idententies: The Rock 'n' Roll Scene in Austin, Texas*, Wesleyan University Press, London.

Sharma, A. (1996) Sounds Oriental: The (Im)possibility of Theorizing Asian Music Cultures in S. Sharma, J. Hutnyk and A. Sharma (eds) *Dis-Orienting Rhythms: The Politics of the New Asian Dance Music*, Zed Books, London.

Smart, B. (1993) Europe/America: Baudrillard's Fatal Comparison in C. Rojek and B.S. Turner (eds) *Forget Baudrillard?*, Routledge, London.

Wallis, R. and Malm, K. (1984) *Big Sounds from Small Peoples: The Music Industry in Small Countries*, Constable, London.

17

"Represent":
Race, Space, and Place in Rap Music

Murray Forman

Say somethin' positive, well positive ain't where I live
I live around the corner from West Hell
Two blocks from South Shit and once in a jail cell
The sun never shined on my side of the street, see?

> Naughty By Nature, "Ghetto Bastard
> (Everything's Gonna Be Alright)," 1991, Isba/Tommy Boy Records

If you're from Compton you know it's the 'hood where it's good

> Compton's Most Wanted, "Raised in Compton," 1991, Epic/Sony

Introduction

Hip hop's[1] capacity to circumvent the constraints and limiting social conditions of young Afro-American and Latino youths has been examined and celebrated by cultural critics and scholars in various contexts since its inception in the mid-1970s. For instance, the 8 February 1999 issue of the U.S. magazine *Time* featured a cover photo of ex-Fugees and five-time Grammy award winner Lauryn Hill with the accompanying headline "Hip-Hop Nation: After 20 Years—how it's changed America." Over the years, however, there has been little attention granted to the implications of hip hop's spatial logics. *Time*'s coverage is relatively standard in perceiving the hip hop nation as a historical construct rather than a geo-cultural amalgamation of personages and practices that are spatially dispersed.

Tricia Rose (1994) arguably goes the furthest in introducing a spatial analysis when she details the ways that hip hop continually displays a clever transformative creativity that is endlessly capable of altering the uses of technologies and space. Her specific references to hip hop culture and space stress the importance of the "postindustrial city" as the central urban influence, "which provided the context for creative development among hip hop's earliest innovators, shaped their cultural terrain, access to space, materials, and education" (1994, p. 34). As this suggests, the particularities of urban space themselves are subjected to the deconstructive and reconstructive practices of rap artists. Thus, when, in another context, Iain Chambers refers to rap as "New York's 'sound system' ... sonorial graffiti" with "the black youth culture of Harlem and the Bronx twisting technology into new cultural shape" (1985, p. 190), he opens the conceptual door onto corresponding strategies that give rise to the radical transformation of the sites where these cultures cohere and converge or the spaces that are reimagined and, importantly, remapped. Rap artists therefore emerge not only as aberrant users of electronic and digital technologies but also as alternative cartographers for what the Samoan-American group Boo Yaa Tribe has referred to in an album title as "a new funky nation."

Indeed, there is very little about today's society that is not, at some point, imbued with a spatial character and this is no less true for the emergence and production of spatial categories and identities in rap music and the hip hop cultures of which it is a central component. Rap music presents a case worthy of examination and provides a unique set of contexts for the analyses of public discourses pertaining to youth, race, and space. Rap music is one of the main sources within popular culture of a sustained and in-depth examination and analysis of the spatial partitioning of race and the diverse experiences of being young and black in America. It can be observed that space and race figure prominently as organizing concepts implicated in the delineation of a vast range of fictional or actually existing social practices that are represented in narrative and lyrical form. In this chapter, I seek to illuminate the central importance of spatiality in the organizing principles of value, meaning, and practice within hip hop culture. My further intent is to explore the question of how the dynamics of space, place, and race get taken up by rap artists as themes and topics and how they are located within a wider range of circulating social discourses. The prioritization of spatial practices and spatial discourses that form a basis of hip hop culture offers a means through which to view both the *ways* that spaces and places are constructed and the *kinds* of spaces or places that are constructed.

The chapter traces the way in which hip hop's popularity spread from New York to other U.S. cities, most notably Philadelphia and Los Angeles but eventually more geographically marginal cities such as Seattle, and it discusses changes that have taken place in rap production, particularly the rise of artist-owned labels. Such developments encouraged the emergence of distinctive regional rap sounds and styles, as well as strong local allegiances and territorial rivalries, as the identities and careers of rap acts became more closely tied to the city and to its specific neighborhoods ('hoods) and communities. The chapter examines the effects of all this on the spatial discourse of rap. It points to a gradual shift within rap from a concern with broad, generalized spaces, to the representation of specific named cities and 'hoods (as illustrated by Gansta Rap from the Californian city of Compton which celebrates and glorifies Compton as well as the street warrior and gang rivalry) and the representation of smaller-scale, more narrowly defined and highly detailed places (as illustrated by rap from the North West city of Seattle which has a distinctively local flavor).

Locating Hip Hop

Describing the early stages of rap music's emergence within the hip hop culture for an MTV "Rap-umentary," Grandmaster Flash, one of the core DJs of the early scene, recalls the spatial distribution of sound systems and crews in metropolitan New York:

> We had territories. It was like, Kool Herc had the west side. Bam had Bronx River. DJ Breakout had way uptown past Gun Hill. Myself, my area was like 138th Street, Cypress Avenue, up to Gun Hill, so that we all had our territories and we all had to respect each other.

The documentary's images embellish Flash's commentary, displaying a computer generated map of the Bronx with colored sections demarcating each DJ's territory as it is mentioned, graphically separating the enclaves that comprise the main area of operations for the competing sound systems.

This emphasis on territoriality involves more than just a geographical arrangement of cultural workers and the regionalism of cultural practices. It illuminates a particular relationship to space or, more accurately, a relationship to particular places. As Flash conveys it, the sound systems that formed the backbone of the burgeoning hip hop scene were identified by their audiences and followers according to the overlapping influences of personae and turf. The territories were tentatively claimed through the ongoing cultural practices that occurred within their bounds and were reinforced by the circulation of those who recognized and accepted their perimeters. It is not at all insignificant that most of the dominant historical narratives pertaining to the emergence of hip hop (i.e., Hager 1984; Toop 1984) identify a transition from gang-oriented affiliations (formed around protection of turf) to music and break dance affiliations that maintained and, in some cases, intensified the important structuring systems of territoriality.

Flash's reference to the importance of "respect" is not primarily addressing a respect for the skills or character of his competitors (although, elsewhere [George 1993] he acknowledges this as well). Rather, his notion of respect is related to the geographies that he maps; it is based on the existence of circumscribed domains of authority and dominance that have been established among the various DJs. These geographies are inhabited and bestowed with value, they are understood as lived places and localized sites of significance, as well as being understood within the market logic that includes a product (the music in its various live or recorded forms) and a consumer base (various audience formations). The proprietary discourse also implies, therefore, that even in its infancy hip hop cartography was to some extent shaped by a refined capitalist logic and the existence of distinct market regions. Without sacrificing the basic geographic components of territory, possession and group identity that play such an important role among gang-oriented activities, the representation of New York's urban spaces was substantially revised as hip hop developed.

Clearly, however, the geographical boundaries that Flash describes and which are visually mapped in the documentary were never firm or immovable. They were cultural boundaries that were continually open to negotiation and renegotiation by those who inhabited their terrains and who circulated throughout the city's boroughs. As the main form of musical expression within the hip hop culture, the early DJ sound systems featured a series of practices that linked the music to other mobile practices, such as graffiti art and "tagging." Together, these overlapping practices and methods of constructing place-based identities, and of inscribing and enunciating individual and collective presence, created the bonds upon which affiliations were forged within specific social geographies. Hip hop's distinct practices introduced new forms of expression that were contextually linked to conditions in a city comprised of an amalgamation of neighborhoods and boroughs with their own highly particularized social norms and cultural nuances.

Hip Hop, Space, and Place

Rap music takes the city and its multiple spaces as the foundation of its cultural production. In the music and lyrics, the city is an audible presence, explicitly cited and digitally sampled in the reproduction of the aural textures of the urban environment. Since its inception in the mid- to late 1970s, hip hop culture has always maintained fiercely defended local ties and an in-built element of competition waged through hip hop's cultural forms of rap, breakdancing and graffiti. This competition has traditionally been staged within geographical boundaries that demarcate turf and territory among various crews, cliques, and posses, extending and altering the spatial alliances that had previously cohered under other organizational structures, including but not exclusive to gangs. Today, a more pronounced level of spatial awareness is one of the key factors distinguishing rap and hip hop culture from the many other cultural and subcultural youth formations currently vying for attention.

Throughout its historical evolution, it is evident that there has been a gradually escalating urgency with which minority youth use rap in the deployment of discourses of urban locality or "place," with the trend accelerating noticeably since 1987–1988. With the discursive shift from the spatial abstractions framed by the notion of "the ghetto" to the more localized and specific discursive construct of "the 'hood" occurring in 1987–1988 (roughly corresponding with the rise and impact of rappers on the U.S. West Coast), there has been an enhanced emphasis on the powerful ties to place that both anchor rap acts to their immediate environments and set them apart from other environments and other 'hoods as well as from other rap acts and their crews which inhabit similarly demarcated spaces.

Commenting in 1988 on rap's "nationwide" expansions beyond New York's boroughs, Nelson George writes, "Rap and its Hip Hop musical underpinning is now the national youth music of black America ... rap's gone national and is in the process of going regional" (George 1992, p. 80). George was right, as rap was rising out of the regions and acts were emerging from the South (Miami-based 2 Live Crew or Houston's The Geto Boys), the Northwest (Seattle's Sir Mix-A-Lot and Kid Sensation), the San Francisco Bay area (Digital Underground, Tupac, Too Short), Los Angeles (Ice T, N.W.A.) and elsewhere. Indeed, the significance of the east-west split within U.S. rap cannot be overstated since it has led to several intense confrontations between artists representing each region and is arguably the single most divisive factor within U.S. hip hop to date. Until the mid-1990s, artists associated with cities in the Midwest or southern states often felt obligated to align themselves with either East or West, or else they attempted to sidestep the issue deftly without alienating audiences and deriding either coast. In the past several years, however, Houston, Atlanta, and New Orleans have risen as important rap production centers and have consequently emerged as powerful forces in their own right.

Today, the emphasis is on place, and groups explicitly advertise their home environments with names such as Compton's Most Wanted, Detroit's Most Wanted, the Fifth Ward Boyz, and South Central Cartel, or else they structure their home territory into titles and lyrics, constructing a new internally meaningful hip hop cartography. The explosion of localized production centers and regionally influential producers and artists has drastically altered the hip hop map and production crews have sprung up throughout North America. These producers have also demonstrated a growing tendency to incorporate themselves as localized businesses (often buying or starting companies unrelated to the music industry in their local neighborhoods, such as auto customizing and repair shops) and to employ friends, family members and members of their wider neighborhoods. Extending Nelson George's observation, it now seems possible to say that rap, having gone regional, is in the process of going local.

The Regional Proliferation of Artist-Owned Record Labels

Reflecting on the intensification of regional rap activity within the U.S. during what might be defined as the genre's "middle-school" historical period,[2] Nelson George writes that 1987 was "a harbinger of the increasing quality of non-New York hip hop," citing as evidence the fact that three of the four finalists in the New Music Seminar's DJ Competition were from "outside the Apple—Philadelphia's Cash Money, Los Angeles's Joe Cooley, and Mr. Mix of Miami's 2 Live Crew" (George 1992, p. 30). In the pages of *Billboard*, he observed that despite New York's indisputable designation as the "home" of rap, Philadelphia rappers in particular (most notably, DJ Jazzy Jeff and the Fresh Prince) were making inroads on the scene and on the charts, making it "rap's second city" (George, ibid.). This expansion was facilitated by the emergent trend in the development of artist-owned independent labels and management companies which entered into direct competition with non-artist-owned companies.

After years of bogus contracts, management conflicts, and poor representation, a growing number of artists began dividing their duties between recording or performing, locating and producing new talent, and managing their respective record companies. By forming self-owned labels and publishing companies and establishing themselves as autonomous corporate entities, forward-thinking rap artists were also able to maintain greater creative control over their production while ensuring increased returns on their sales. In a rather excessive discourse, artists spoke of throwing off the corporate shackles of the recording industry as well as invoking the quite separate issues of building something of which one can be proud or being remunerated in a more lucrative manner.

Once several key labels such as Luther Campbell's Skyywalker Records and Eazy-E's Ruthless Records had been established and had proven the viability of the venture, their initiatives were rapidly reproduced as numerous artists followed suit. For many recording artists, to gain wealth and material renumeration for their work suddenly meant learning the production and management side of the industry and exercising entrepreneurial skills as well. As the trend expanded, small artist-owned and operated labels burgeoned and another tier was added to the industry. With the rise of artist-owned labels there was also an increased emphasis on regional and local affiliations and an articulation of pride and loyalty in each label, its artist roster, and the central locale of operation.

Rap is characteristically produced within a system of extremely close-knit local affiliations, forged within particular cultural settings and urban minority youth practices. Yet the developments in the rap industry, whereby production houses or record labels might be identified on the basis of their regional and local zones of operation, are not unique to this current period. For instance, independent "race record" labels, which targeted blacks in the South and in larger northern urban centers throughout the 1920s and 1930s, flourished in part due to the enhanced mobility of black populations which maintained their affinities for the various regional blues styles. Nelson George's consistent attention to black musical tradition, the music industry's gradual permutations, and rap's growing national influence led him to note in *Billboard* that "regional music used to be the backbone of black music and—maybe—it will be again" (31 May 1986, p. 23). He recalls black American musical production in the immediate post–World War II period when independent labels were dispersed across the nation, recording locally and regionally based artists while servicing the needs of black music consumers within these regional markets.

Examining the history of black popular music in the 1960s and 1970s, the names Motown, Stax, or Philadelphia International Records (PIR) evoke images of composers, producers and musical talent working within very specific studio contexts in Detroit, Memphis, and Philadelphia. The dispersed independent labels and production sites that operated from the 1950s through the 1970s are therefore culturally meaningful and relevant to descriptions of black music of the period as they convey an idea of consistency and identifiable signature sounds or styles.[3] This trend has continued with rap, with more pronounced and explicit connection to specific locales and the articulations of geography, place and identity that sets the genre apart from many of its musical predecessors.

Of the smaller labels that had thrived in the 1950s, 1960s, and 1970s, most disappeared as musical tastes shifted, as economic transitions evolved, or as the industry majors swallowed them or bumped them out of the market by introducing their own specialty labels. Towards the end of the 1980s, the U.S. music industry was no longer even primarily American, with the major parent companies being massive transnational entities with corporate offices based in several countries. Yet, in both rock and rap there was a resurgence of regional production in the mid- to late 1980s and, with it, the resurgence of regionally distinct styles. In the black music sector these were exemplified by the Minneapolis funk that was a trademark of artists like Prince, The Time, Jimmy Jam and Terry Lewis, or Jesse Johnson; the Washington, D.C. go-go sound of Chuck Brown, Redd and the Boys, and especially Trouble Funk; and from Chicago, house music exemplified by DJ Frankie Knuckles. Rap production in New York, Los Angeles, and Miami also began to display regionally distinct "flavors" to a greater extent as individual producers emerged with their own trademark styles and influences. Individual studios such as Chung King in New York also became associated with specific production styles and sounds in rap.

As evidence of the arrival of artist-owned labels in the rap business, in December, 1989, *Billboard* featured advertisements in a special section on rap that illustrated the trend. Among these were ads for Eazy-E's Ruthless Records (Compton, CA), Luther Campbell's Skyywalker Records (Miami, FL), and Ice T's Rhyme Syndicate (South Central LA). Appearing alongside these were advertisements for the established independent rap labels Def Jam, Tommy Boy and Jive as well as ads for the newer "street" divisions of major labels including Atlantic ("The Strength of the Street"), MCA ("Wanna Rap? MCA Raps. Word!") and Epic ("Epic in Total Control. No Loungin', Just Lampin"). The phenomenon has since evolved to the extent that artist-owned operations have become relatively standard in the industry, existing as influential players alongside the major labels.

As a later entrant, Death Row Records (initiated in 1992 by principal investors Suge Knight and former member of the rap group Niggaz with Attitude [N.W.A.] Dr. Dre) flourished through a lucrative co-ownership and distribution alliance with upstart Interscope Records, which was itself half-owned by Time Warner's Atlantic Group. Although a series of misfortunes in 1996–97 decimated the label,[4] it rose to virtual dominance in the rap field between 1992 and 1997 with top-charting releases by Dr. Dre, Snoop Doggy Dogg, and Tupac Shakur as well as the soundtrack albums *Deep Cover* (1992) and *Murder Was the Case* (1994). One of the factors that characterized Death Row Records from its inception and which is common to the dozens of artist-owned and operated rap labels to emerge in the late 1980s and early 1990s, however, is an organized structure rooted in localized "posse" affiliations.

Homeboys and Production Posses

Greg Tate suggests that, "every successful rap group is a black fraternal organization, a posse" (1992, p. 134). On the same theme, Tricia Rose writes that "rappers' emphasis on posses and neighborhoods has brought the ghetto back into the public consciousness" (1994, p. 11). For Public Enemy's Chuck D, posse formations are a necessary response to the fragmentive effects of capitalism: "the only way that you exist within that mould is that you have to put together a 'posse', or a team to be able to penetrate that structure, that block, that strong as steel structure that no individual can break" (Eure and Spady 1991, p. 330). As each of these commentators suggests, the posse is the fundamental social unit binding a rap act and its production crew together, creating a collective identity that is rooted in place and within which the creative process unfolds. It is not rare for an entire label to be defined along posse lines with the musical talent, the producers and various peripheral associates bonding under the label's banner.

With collective identities being evident as a nascent reference throughout rap's history in group names like The Sugarhill Gang, Doug E. Fresh and the Get Fresh Crew, X-Clan, or the 2 Live Crew, the term "posse" was later unambiguously adopted by rap artists such as California's South Central Posse or Orlando's DJ Magic Mike, whose crew records under the name "the Royal Posse." In virtually all cases, recording acts align themselves within a relatively coherent posse structure, sharing labels and producers, appearing on each other's recordings and touring together.

The term posse is defined as a "strong force or company" (*Concise Oxford Dictionary*, 1985) and for many North Americans it summons notions of lawlessness and frontier justice that were standard thematic elements of Hollywood westerns in the 1940s and 1950s. This is, in fact, the basis of the term as it is applied within rap circles, although its current significance is related more precisely to the ways in which the Jamaican posse culture has over the years adapted the expressive terminology and gangster imagery of the cinema to its own cultural systems. In her illuminating research on the sinister complexities of the Jamaican posse under-world, Laurie Gunst (1995) explains how the posse system grew under the specific economic, political, and cultural conditions of mid-1970s Jamaica, evolving into a stratified and violent gang culture that gained strength through the marijuana, cocaine, and crack trade. As she explains, the Jamaican posse system has, since 1980, been transplanted to virtually every major North American city.

The Jamaican posse expansion is important in this context as it coincides almost precisely with the emergence of rap and hip hop in New York's devastated uptown ghetto environments. This connection is strengthened when rap's hybrid origins that were forged in the convergence of Jamaican sound systems and South Bronx funk are considered. The concept of the posse has, through various social mechanisms and discursive overlays, been traced upon many of rap's themes, images, and postures that take the forms of the pimp, hustler, gambler and gangster in the music's various sub-genres that evolved after 1987. Rap has also been influenced by the gangland models provided by the New York mafia and Asian Triad gangs.

Since roughly 1987 hip hop culture has also been influenced by alliances associated with West Coast gang systems. Numerous rap album covers and videos feature artists and their posses representing their gang, their regional affiliations or their local 'hood with elaborate hand gestures. The practice escalated to such an extent that, in an effort to dilute the surging terri-torial aggression, Black Entertainment Television (BET) passed a rule forbidding explicitly gang-related hand signs on its popular video programs.

"The 'Hood Took Me Under": Home, Turf and Identity

It is necessary to recognize that the home territory of a rapper or rap group is a testing ground, a place to hone skills and to gain a local reputation. This is accurately portrayed in the 1992 Ernest Dickerson film *Juice* where the expression "local" is attributed to the young DJ Q, in one instance suggesting community ties and home alliances whereas, in another context, it is summoned as a pejorative term that reflects a lack of success and an inability to mobilize his career beyond the homefront. In interviews and on recordings most rappers refer to their early days, citing the time spent with their "home boys," writing raps, perfecting their turntable skills, and taking the stage at parties and local clubs or dances (Cross 1993). Their perspective emerges from within the highly localized conditions that they know and the places they inhabit.

As a site of affiliation and circulation, the 'hood provides a setting for particular group interactions which are influential in rap music's evolution. In rap, there is a widespread sense that an act cannot succeed without first gaining approval and support from the crew and the 'hood. Successful acts are expected to maintain connections to the 'hood and to "keep it real" thematically, rapping about situations, scenes and sites that comprise the lived experience of the 'hood. At issue is the complex question of authenticity as rap posses continually strive to reaffirm their connections to the 'hood in an attempt to mitigate the negative accusations that they have sold out in the event of commercial or crossover success. Charisse Jones has noted a dilemma confronting successful rap artists who suddenly have the economic means to "get over" and leave the 'hood. As she writes in the *New York Times* (24 September 1995, p. 43), contemporary artists such as Snoop Dogg or Ice T are often criticized for rapping about ghetto poverty and gang aggression while living in posh suburban mansions.

Those who stay in the 'hood generally do so to be closer to friends and family, closer to the posse. While a common rationale for staying in the 'hood is familiarity and family bonds, in numerous cases artists also justify their decisions to stay along a creative rationale, suggesting that the 'hood provides the social contexts and raw resources for their lyrics. Others leave with some regret, suggesting that the 'hood may constitute "home" but its various tensions and stresses make it an entirely undesirable place to live (this is even more frequent among rappers with children to support and nurture); there is no romanticizing real poverty or real danger.

The 'hood is, however, regularly constructed within the discursive frame of the "home," and the dual process of "turning the 'hood out" or "representing" (which involves creating a broader profile for the home territory and its inhabitants while showing respect for the nurture it provides) is now a required practice among hardcore rap acts. The posse is always explicitly acknowledged and individual members are greeted on disk and in live concerts with standard "shout outs" that frequently cite the streets and localities from which they hail. This continual reference to the important value of social relations based in the 'hood refutes the damning images of an oppressed and joyless underclass that are so prevalent in the media and contemporary social analyses. Rap may frequently portray the nation's gritty urban under-side, but its creators also communicate the importance of places and the people that build community within them. In this interpretation, there is an insistent emphasis on support, nurture and community that coexists with the grim representations that generally cohere in the images and discourses of ghetto life.

As in all other popular music forms, "paying dues" is also part of the process of embarking on a rap music career, and the local networks of support and encouragement, from in-group affiliations to local club and music scenes, are exceedingly important factors in an act's profes-sional development. One way that this is facilitated is through the posse alliances and local connections that form around studios and producers. For example, in describing the produc-tion house once headed by DJ Mark, The 45 King, the rap artist Fab 5 Freddy recalls that "he had this posse called the Flavor Unit out there in New Jersey.... He has like a Hip Hop training room out there, an incredible environment where even if you weren't good when you came in, you'd get good just being around there" (Nelson and Gonzales 1991, p. xiii).[5] This pattern is replicated in numerous instances and is also exemplified by the production/posse structure of Rap-A-Lot Records in Houston (home to acts such as the Geto Boys, Scarface, Big Mike, Caine, and The Fifth Ward Boyz) where the company was forced to relocate its offices because "artists were always kicking it there with their posses like it was a club" (*Rap Sheet*, October 1992, p. 18). By coming up through the crew, young promising artists learn the ropes, acquire lessons in craft and showmanship, attain stage or studio experience and exposure and, quite frequently, win record deals based on their apprenticeships and posse connections.

Few rap scholars (Tricia Rose and Brian Cross being notable exceptions) have paid atten-tion to these formative stages and the slow processes of developing MC and DJ skills. There is, in fact, a trajectory to an artist's development that is seldom accounted for. In practice, artists' lyrics and rhythms must achieve success on the home front first, where the flow, subject matter, style and image must resonate meaningfully among those who share common bonds to place, to the posse and to the 'hood. In this sense, when rappers refer to the "local flavor," they are identifying the detailed inflections that respond to and reinforce the significance of the music's particular sites of origin and which might be recognized by others elsewhere as being unique, interesting and, ultimately, marketable.

The Spatialization of Production Styles

The posse structures that privilege place and the 'hood can be seen as influential elements in the evolution of new rap artists as well as relevant forces in the emergence of new, region-ally definable sounds and discourses about space and place. For example, critics and rappers alike acknowledge the unique qualities of the West Coast G-funk sound which defined a production style that emerged with Dr. Dre's work on the *Deep Cover* soundtrack and the release of his 1992 classic *The Chronic* (Death Row/Interscope), and arguably reached its apex with the 1994 release of Warren G's *Regulate … G Funk Era* (Violator/Rush Associated Labels). Other local artists in this period, such as the Boo Yaa Tribe, Above the Law, Compton's Most Wanted, and DJ Quik, also prominently featured variations on the G-funk sound and reinforced its influence in the industry as an identifiable West Coast subgenre. G-funk makes ample use of standard funk grooves by artists including George Clinton, Bootsy Collins, Gap Band, or the late Roger Troutman, and is characterized as being "laid-back" and sparse, featuring slow beats and longer sample loops. While it was regarded as a regionally distinct sound, it was also often related specifically to Dr. Dre's production style and was comparatively categorized by its difference from the more cacophonous East Coast jams (recognizable in the early work of the Bomb Squad, the production crew of the rap act Public Enemy). As Brian Cross (1993) notes, however, the impact of the G-funk style among California rap acts is also related to the extended influence of late 1970s funk music in the Southwest that was a consequence of limited access to independently produced and distributed rap product in the early 1980s, delaying rap's geographic expansion from New York to the Los Angeles area.

Explaining the Bomb Squad's production processes following the release of Public Enemy's *Fear of a Black Planet* (1990, Def Jam), Chuck D describes his production posse's familiarity with various regional styles and tastes and their attempts to integrate the differences into the album's tracks. As he states:

> Rap has different feels and different vibes in different parts of the country. For example, people in New York City don't drive very often, so New York used to be about walking around with your radio. But that doesn't really exist anymore. It became unfashionable because some people were losing their *lives* over them, and also people don't want to carry them, so now it's more like "Hey, I've got my Walkman." For that reason, there's a treble type of thing going on; they're not getting much of the bass. So rap music in New York City is a headphone type of thing, whereas in Long Island or Philadelphia … it's more of a bass type thing. (Dery 1990, p. 90)

These regional distinctions between the "beats" are borne out in the example of the Miami production houses of Luther Campbell or Orlando's Magic Mike. In Florida (and to some extent, Georgia) the focus is on the bass—Florida "booty bass" or "booty boom" as it has been termed—which offers a deeper, "phatter," and almost subsonic vibration that stands out as a regionally distinct and authored style.[6] Within U.S. rap culture, artists and fans alike reflect an acute awareness that people in different parts of the country produce and enjoy regional variations on the genre; they experience rap differently, structuring it into their social patterns according to the norms that prevail in a given urban environment. Thus, the regional taste patterns in South Florida are partially influenced by the central phenomenon of car mobility and the practice of stacking multiple 10- or 15-inch bass speakers and powerful sub-woofers into car trunks and truck beds.

Add to these stylistic distinctions the discursive differences within rap from the various regions (i.e., the aforementioned Gangsta Rap from the West Coast crews, the chilling, cold-blooded imagery from Houston's "Bloody Nickle" crews on Rap-A-Lot Records, or the "pimp, playa and hustla" themes that are standard among Oakland and San Francisco cliques), the localized posse variations in vocal style and slang, or the site-specific references in rap lyrics to cities, 'hoods, and crews, and a general catalogue of differences in form and content becomes clearly audible. What these elements indicate is that, while the rap posse provides a structured identity for its members, it can also provide a referential value to the production qualities and the sound of the musical product with which it is associated.

Rap's Spatial Discourse

In his enquiry into the cultural resonance and meanings of the term "the 'hood," Paul Gilroy poses the question, "how is black life in one 'hood connected to life in others? Can there be a blackness that connects, articulates, synchronizes experiences and histories across the diaspora space?" (1992, p. 308). He criticizes the idea of "nation" that has emerged as an important structuring concept in American hip hop culture (mainly after 1987) and remains skeptical of the value invested in the discourses of "family" unity (communicated in the rhetoric of black brotherhood and sisterhood) when there is so much territorial antagonism evident in the strands of rap that privilege the spatialities of gang culture and turf affiliation. Gilroy expresses his perplexity with the closed contours that the 'hood represents, suggesting that its inward-turning spatial perspectives inhibit dialogue across divided social territories and cultural zones. He further argues that redemptive attempts to appeal to either the black "nation," or to the "family" of internationally dispersed blacks in the rap subgenre known as "message rap" are ill-conceived and based in a particularly North Americanist viewpoint that harbors its own exclusive and hierarchically stratified biases.

Perhaps more in line with Gilroy's expansive, trans-Atlantic visions of rap's diasporic potential is the track "Ludi" (1991, Island Records) by the Canadian act the Dream Warriors. Based in Toronto, the group is part of one of the world's largest expatriate Caribbean communities. Like Gilroy's London, Toronto could be seen as an

> important junction point or crossroads on the webbed pathways of black Atlantic political culture. It is revealed to be a place where, by virtue of factors like the informality of racial segregation, the configuration of class relations, the contingency of linguistic convergences, global phenomena such as anti-colonial and emancipationist political formations are still being sustained, reproduced, and amplified. (Gilroy 1992, p. 95)

In mapping a cultural "crossroads," the song "Ludi" utilizes an early reggae rhythm and a lightly swinging melody (based on a sample of the Jamaican classic "My Conversation," released in 1968 by The Uniques) that taps into a particularly rich moment in the evolution of the reggae style and revives a well-known Jamaican track while relocating it within the performative contexts of hip hop.

"Ludi" (which refers to a board game) begins with rapper King Lou stating that the song is for his mother—who wants something to dance to—and his extended family to whom he offers the musical sounds of their original home environment. The family to which he refers is not, in the immediate sense, the family of black-identified brothers and sisters that cohere within nationalistic and essentialist discourse but literally his siblings. He then expands his dedication to the wider "family" of blacks with a comprehensive roll-call of the English and Spanish-speaking Caribbean islands and Africa which inform (but by no means determine) his cultural identity. There is no attempt to privilege an originary African heritage nor is there a nostalgic appeal to the Caribbean heritage. This extensive list recognizes Toronto's hybrid Afro-Caribbean community and refers directly to a locally manifested culture of international black traditions (rather than a single tradition of essentialist blackness) within which the Dream Warriors developed as young artists. The song's bridge also reinforces the Caribbean connection by making several references to the turntable practices of Jamaican sound systems that are mainstays throughout internationally dispersed Caribbean communities.

Later in the track, King Lou's cohort, Capital Q, reminds him that "there are other places than the islands that play Ludi. Why don't you run it down for the people?" Herc, employing a distinctly Jamaican DJ "toaster" dialect, King Lou provides a wider expression of black diasporic identification as he expands his list to include Canada, the UK, and the United States, countries where the Afro-Caribbean presence is the largest and most influential. He concludes by mentioning his international record labels 4th and Broadway and Island Records and, finally, names the influential Toronto-based independent production house, Beat Factory, that first recorded the group. In this last reference to Beat Factory he effectively returns the scale to the local, closing the circle that positions the Dream Warriors within a global/local system of circulation.

There is no simple means of assessing the impact of this expansive global/local perspective but, within Gilroy's innovative theoretical *oeuvre*, the track can be celebrated for the ways in which its musical and lyrical forms reinforce the dispersed geographies of contemporary black cultures without falling victim to the conservative reductions of black essentialism. Without cleaving towards either the rhetorical rigidity of black nationalist Rap or the nihilistic vitriol of gangster rappers ("niggaz with (bad) attitude"), the Dream Warriors present an alternative path. As "Ludi" illustrates, the group unselfconsciously articulates an evolving hybrid identity informed by transnational migrations that are actively manifested on local grounds.

On the other end of the rap spectrum is the example of artists who mainly operate within a discursive field featuring spatialized themes of intense locality. Whereas the proponents of Message Rap evoke an expanded vision of black America, it is in contrast to the ghettocentric visions of urban black experience that also emerge in the genre, mainly within the lyrics of Gangsta Rap. Despite many shared perspectives on black oppression and systemic injustices, there exists a tension in the interstices between the expansive nationalisms of Message Rap and the more narrowly defined localisms of Gangsta Rap with its core emphasis on "the 'hood." This distance is widened in view of the unapologetic claim among numerous studio gangstas who, like the rap artist Ice Cube on the N.W.A. track "Gangsta, Gangsta" (1988, Ruthless/Priority), claim that "life ain't nothin' but bitches and money." The two subgenres are addressing generally common phenomena in their focus on black struggles for empowerment, yet they are deploying spatial discourses and programs of action that do not fit easily together.

The emergence of an intensified spatial terminology was not a sudden occurrence, but by 1987 when New York's Boogie Down Productions (also known as BDP), featuring rap acts such as KRS-1, Eazy-E, and Ice T broke onto the scene, the privileging of localized experience rapidly acquired an audible resonance. From New York, BDP released "South Bronx" (1987, B-Boy), a track that aggressively disputes the allegations of various rappers from Queens who, in the aftermath of Run-DMC's commercial successes, claimed that they were rap's true innovators. KRS-1's lyrics reaffirm his home turf in the South Bronx borough as the birthplace of hip hop, reinforcing the message in the now-classic chorus with its chant "South Bronx, the South, South Bronx."

Giving name to South Bronx locales and to the artists who inhabited them, anchors his testimony. He attempts to prove its dominance by recounting the genre's formative stages with close attention to locally specific and highly particularized details:

> Remember Bronx River, rolling thick
> With Cool DJ Red Alert and Chuck Chillout on the mix
> While Afrika Islam was rocking the jams
> And on the other side of town was a kid named Flash
> Patterson and Millbrook projects
> Casanova all over, ya couldn't stop it
> The Nine Lives crew, the Cypress Boys
> The Real Rock Steady taking out these toys

> As hard as it looked, as wild as it seemed
> I didn't hear a peep from Queen's ...
> South Bronx, the South South Bronx ...

The references to people and places provide a specificity that is comparatively absent in Eazy-E's important (but often overlooked) single release "Boyz-n-The Hood" (1988, Ruthless/Priority) from the same general period. Musically, "Boyz-n-The-Hood" is considered to have done little to advance the genre aesthetically. Yet, in its uncompromising linguistic turns and startling descriptions of homeboy leisure (involving beer, "bitches," and violence), it was riveting and offered a new hardcore funky model for masculine identification in hip hop:

> 'Cause the boyz in the hood are always hard
> Come talkin' that trash and we'll pull your card
> Knowin' nothin' in life but to be legit
> Don't quote me boy, 'cause I ain't sayin' shit

Describing the LP *Eazy-Duz-It* on which the single first appeared, Havelock Nelson and Michael Gonzales explain that it "overflows with debris from homophobia to misogyny to excessive violence. And yet, anyone who grew up in the project or any Black ghetto knows these extreme attitudes are right on target" (1991, p. 81). Despite such claims to authenticity, however, it is important to acknowledge that the rugged discourses and sensational imagery of violence and poverty are highly selective and are drawn from a range of mundane, less controversial and less marketable urban experiences.

Eazy-E's "Boyz-n-The Hood" reflects many of rap's earlier modes of spatial representation that conceive of the ghetto landscape as a generalized abstract construct, as *space*. The introduction of the terminology of the 'hood, however, also adds a localized nuance to the notion of space that conveys a certain proximity, effectively capturing a narrowed sense of *place* through which young thugs and their potential victims move in tandem. Claims to the representation of authentic street life or 'hood reality emerged with sudden frequency following the rise of Eazy-E and N.W.A., who were among the first to communicate detailed images of closely demarcated space in this manner. This suggests that "reality," authenticity and reduced spatial scales are conceptually linked among those who developed "Boyz-n-The Hood" is ultimately its influence on the popularization of a new spatial vocabulary that spread throughout hip hop from all regions as artists from the West Coast gained prominence in the field.

By most accounts, the spatial discourse that coheres around the concept of the 'hood emerges in rap by California-based artists with the greatest frequency and force. But in the popular media as well as in academic treatises, the focus on West Coast rap in this period tends to be on the expressions of "gangsta" violence and masculine aggression to the exclusion or minimization of prevalent spatial elements. For example, as David Toop writes, "the first release on Ruthless Records, launched by rapper Eazy-E and producer Dr. Dre in 1986, was like a tabloid report from the crime beat fed through a paper shredder" (1991, p. 180). The very term "gangsta rap" is more concretely concerned with the articulation of criminality than any other attributes that may emerge from its lyrical and visual texts. Having become sedimented in the popular lexicon as the key or trademark term for the subgenre, it is difficult to challenge critically the primacy of criminality and to replace it with a spatiality that precedes the "gangsta-ism" that saturates the lyrical texts. The criminal activities that are described in gangsta rap's intense lyrical forms are almost always subordinate to the definitions of space and place within which they are set. It is, therefore, the spatialities of the 'hood that constitute the ascendant concept and are ultimately deserving of discursive pre-eminence.

Since rap's invention, it has become somewhat of a convention for the rapper to be placed at the center of the world, as the subject around which events unfold and who translates topophilia (love of place) or topophobia (fear of place) into lyrics for wider dissemination. This is illustrated in Ice T's "Intro" track on his debut album *Rhyme Pays* (1987, Rhyme Syndicate/Sire). As an introduction, the track allows Ice T to present his hip hop curriculum vitae which is explicitly defined in spatial terms:

> A child was born in the East one day
> Moved to the West Coast after his parents passed away
> Never understood his fascination with rhymes or beats
> In poetry he was considered elite
> Became a young gangster in the streets of LA
> Lost connections with his true roots far away ...

The description of a personal exodus embarked upon by the young rapper under conditions of extreme adversity is crucial to the construction of mystique and legend. Describing his entry into LA gang culture and the rap scene in the magazine *Rap Pages*, Ice T identifies cities, neighborhoods, high schools and housing projects that have meaning to him and to those familiar with these areas:

> I went to a white school in Culver City, and that was chill, but I was livin' in Windsor Hills near Monterey Triangle Park.... When I got to high school all the kids from my area were gettin' bussed to white schools and I didn't want to go to them schools. So me and a few kids from the hills went to Crenshaw. That's where the gangs were. (*Rap Pages*, October 1991, p. 55)

Here, place is a lens of sorts that mediates one's perspective on social relations. It offers familiarity and it provides the perspectival point from which one gazes upon and evaluates other places, places that are "other" or foreign to one's own distinctly personal sites of security and stability (no matter how limited these may be). Ice T may be from the East, but he is shaped by Los Angeles and it is the spaces and places of LA that provide the coordinates for his movement and activities.

Ice T (ibid.) goes on to make the distinction between East Coast rap and the emerging LA "gangsta" style, noting that the latter developed out of a desire to relate incidents and experiences with a more specific sense of place and, subsequently, greater significance to local youths who could recognize the sites and activities described in the lyrics. In this regard, rap offers a means of describing the view from a preferred "here," of explaining how things appear in the immediate foreground (the 'hood) and how things seem on the receding horizon (other places).

Adopting a boastful tone and attitude, Ice T also locates his origins in the New Jersey–New York nexus, essentially fixing his own "roots" in hip hop's cultural motherland. Ice T is in this mode clearly centering himself, building his own profile. In the process, he relates a history that invests supreme value in New York as the first home of hip hop, naturalizing his connections to the art form and validating his identity as a tough, adaptive and street-smart LA hustler, the self-proclaimed "West Coast M.C. king." Ice T's references to New York illuminate the spatial hierarchy that existed at the time; the Northeast was still virtually unchallenged as the dominant zone of hip hop cultural activity. Battles among rap's pioneers and upstarts were still being waged on the local, interborough scale in New York although, gradually, New York's monopoly on rap production and innovation was lost as various other sites of production emerged. The rise of the LA rap sound and the massive impact of the gangster themes after 1987 resulted in the first real incursion on New York's dominance. This development had the additional effect of polarizing the two regions as the aesthetic distinctions based on lyrical content and rhythmic styles became more defined and audiences began spending their consumer dollars on rap from the nation's "West side."

"The West Side Is the Best Side": Representing Compton

The West's arrival was heralded by a deluge of recordings that celebrated and glorified the street warrior scenarios of the California cities of South Central Los Angeles (with help from the 1988 Dennis Hopper film *Colors* and Ice T's galvanizing title song on the soundtrack), Oakland and, especially, Compton. Starting with NWA's "Straight Outta Compton" (1988, Ruthless/Priority), numerous recordings circulated the narrative imagery of vicious gang-oriented activities in Compton, including the tracks "Raised in Compton" (1991, Epic) and "Compton 4 Life" (1992, Epic) by the group Compton's Most Wanted, and DJ Quik's "Born and Raised in Compton" (1991, Profile) or "Just Lyke Compton" (1992, Profile). Appearing on the cover of his album *Way 2 Fonky* (1992, Profile), DJ Quik poses alongside a chain-link fence topped with razor wire, sporting a jacket emblazoned with the Compton logo, proudly advertising his home territory. Through these multiple means of signification the city of Compton rapidly gained a notoriety informed by the image of tough and well-armed homeboys and the ongoing deadly conflict between rival gangs operating with a near-total lack of ethics or moral conscience. This last point can be most clearly discerned in the ubiquitous refrain that "Compton niggaz just don't give a fuck."

Tricia Rose and Brian Cross situate the rise of Compton-based rap in two quite different frames of understanding. Rose writes that

> during the late 1980s Los Angeles rappers from Compton and Watts, two areas severely paralyzed by the postindustrial economic redistribution, developed a West coast style of rap that narrates experiences and fantasies specific to life as a poor young, black, male subject in Los Angeles. (1994, p. 59)

Her assessment situates the phenomenon of West Coast styles and lyrical forms in an internally based set of socio-economic conditions that are responsive to transitions within a complex convergence of global and local forces, or what Kevin Robins (1991) refers to as "the global/local nexus."

Brian Cross locates the rise of Compton's rap scene within a wider and more appropriate cartographic relation to New York and other California locales:

> Hiphop Compton, according to Eazy, was created as a reply to the construction of the South Bronx/Queensbridge nexus in New York. If locally it served notice in the community in which Eazy and Dre sold their Macola-pressed records (not to mention the potential play action on KDAY), nationally, or at least on the East Coast, it was an attempt to figure Los Angeles on the map of hiphop. After the album had gone double platinum Compton would be as well known a city in hiphop as either Queens or the Bronx. (Cross 1993, p. 37)

Refuting Rose's interpretation, the general narrative content of "Straight Outta Compton" sheds little light on the city or its social byways and does not demonstrate any particular concern with the locality's economics. Its basic function as a geographical backdrop actually follows the same standard constructions of abstract space heard in Grandmaster Flash and the Furious Five's "New York, New York," recorded five years earlier, or in Eazy-E's solo effort, "Boyz-n-The-Hood."

Without detailed spatial descriptions of landmarks and environment, Compton does not emerge as a clearly realized urban space on the N.W.A. track even though it is the group's home town. The California city is instead treated as a bounded civic space that provides both specificity and scale for the communication of a West Coast Rap presence. The group is "representing" their home territory and the song's release was their bold announcement that the "boyz" from the 'hoods of Compton were "stompin'" onto the scene and could not be avoided by anyone who paid attention to developments in the business. The Compton and South Central LA crews were not only serving notice to their neighboring communities that they were in charge, but they were also serving notice to New York and the entire hip hop nation that the new sound had arrived and the balance of power (forged in a mix of arrogance and inventiveness) had tipped towards the West. This was the beginning of a decade-long antagonism between East and West Coast rap that has too frequently proven that the gangster themes comprising the lyrical content are based in more than mere lip service or masculine posturing.

On the track "Raised in Compton" (1991, Epic/Sony), MC Eiht of the rap group Compton's Most Wanted explicitly racializes the urban spaces of the city, more fully addressing the specificities of its cultural character and providing a further sense of the place that he recognizes as his formative home. He reproduces several of the general elements that N.W.A. had already imposed on Compton's representational repertoire, but for him the city also has a personally meaningful history that is manifested in his identity as a gangster turned rapper:

> Compton is the place that I touched down
> I opened my eyes to realize that I was dark brown
> And right there in the ghetto that color costs
> Brothers smothered by the streets meaning we're lost
> I grew up in a place where it was go for your own
> Don't get caught after dark roaming the danger zone
> But it was hell at the age of twelve
> As my Compton black brothers were in and out of jail

The attempt to historicize his relations to the city and the 'hood makes this track slightly more complex than "Straight Outta Compton," as MC Eiht's bonds to the localized Compton environment are defined as the product of an evolving growth process, as a child becomes a man. Subjective history, conveyed here in an almost testimonial form, and the experiences of space, together offer relevant insights on the social construction of a gangster attitude or a gang member's *raison d'être*.

George Lipsitz isolates similar tendencies with his focus on the socio-political importance of merging musical and non-musical sources of inspiration and experience among California chicano rock musicians since the 1960s.

> As organic intellectuals chronicling the cultural life of their community, they draw upon street slang, car customizing, clothing styles, and wall murals for inspiration and ideas.... Their work is intertextual, constantly in dialogue with other forms of cultural expression, and most fully appreciated when located in context. (Lipsitz 1990, p. 153)

Like the California chicano music Lipsitz describes, "Raised in Compton" explicitly highlights a customized car culture, urban mobility and the sartorial codes of the Compton streets ("T-shirt and khakis"). In its inclusiveness of the minor details that are, in practice, part of the daily norm for many urban black youth in the cities surrounding Los Angeles, the song accesses the spatial and racial characteristics of the city of Compton that have influenced and shaped the man that MC Eiht has become. The closely detailed articulation of spatial specifics (place names and site references, etc.) is still lacking but there is also a rich description of some of the social formations that are spatially distributed and which reproduce the forces underlying the black teen gangster ethos with which MC Eiht, and many others, so clearly identify.

Maintaining the gang member's pledge to defend the gang (or the "set") and the 'hood forever is the theme of MC Eiht's "Compton 4 Life" (1992, Epic/Sony). This track also offers a personal profile that ties MC Eiht into the neighborhood environment and inextricably links him with the deeper gang structures that prevail. Mid-point in the track he challenges outsiders to "throw up your 'hood 'cause it's Compton we're yellin," in a calculated "turf" statement that is entirely consistent with the structures of spatial otherness that are fundamental to LA gang culture. Eiht and other gangsta rappers enter into the discourses of alienation and social disenfranchisement as a negative factor compelling them towards a criminal lifestyle. Yet they also expound their own versions of alienating power, drawing on the imagery and codes of the street and entering into a discourse of domination that subjugates women, opposing gang members or those who are perceived as being weaker and thus less than them. Framed in terms of gun violence and human decimation, these expressions are intended to diminish the presence of others who represent other cities and other 'hoods. This is the articulation of control through domination, ghetto style.

Spatial domination and geo-social containment are conceived in the threatening form of "one time" or "five-o" (the police) and other gang members, each of whom constitute unavoidable negatives of life in the 'hood. Defeating the enemy forces is the ultimate goal, but in establishing the competitive dynamic, MC Eiht acknowledges that, even in victory, the local streets and the 'hood impose their own kind of incarcerating authority:

> Compton 4 Life
> Compton 4 Life
> It's the city where everybody's in prison
> Niggers keep taking shit 'cause ain't nobody givin'
> So another punk fool I must be
> Learn the tricks of the trade from the street
> Exist to put the jack down, ready and willin'
> One more Compton driveby killin'

There is a brief pause in the rhythm that could be heard as hanging like doom, stilling the song's pace and flow and creating a discomforting gap in the track. When the chorus "Compton 4 Life" suddenly breaks in with the final echoing syllable, it becomes clear that the title is formed around a double entendre: it is an expression of spatial solidarity and loyalty to the 'hood, yet it also refers to the pronouncement of a life sentence and the apparent hopelessness of eternal imprisonment in the city's streets and alleys.

As "Straight Outta Compton," "Raised in Compton" and "Compton 4 Life" suggest, "our sensibilities are spatialized" (Keith and Pile, 1993 p. 26). This point is made resonant when considering Compton artist DJ Quik's mobile narrative on the track "Jus Lyke Compton" (1992, Priority), in which he witnesses and describes the nation-wide impact of the Compton mythology, and Bronx-based rapper Tim Dog's defensive articulation of Bronx pride in the lyrical assassinations of N.W.A. and all Compton artists on the track "Fuck Compton" (1991, Ruffhouse/Columbia). Compton's central significance is maintained through the lyrical representation of activities that are space-bound and which are then discursively traced onto the identities of the rappers who "claim" Compton as their own. The issue of whether or not the tracks refer back to a consistently verifiable reality is rendered moot by the possibilities they present as textual spaces of representation. Artists discursively locate themselves in an array of images and practices within the texts, constructing a relatively coherent identity out of the urban debris that is evidently a crucial aspect of the Compton they experience.

Despite claims by critics of gangsta rap, such as David Samuels (*New Republic*, 11 November, 1991), or folk musician Michelle Shocked, who suggests that "Los Angeles as a whole and South Central specifically bear little resemblance to the cartoon landscape—the Zip Coon Toon Town—of gangsta rap" (*Billboard*, 20 June, 1992, p. 6), the subgenre's narrative depictions of spaces and places are absolutely essential to an understanding of the ways that a great number of urban black youths imagine their environments and the ways that they relate those images to their own individual sense of self. The spaces of Compton and other similar black communities that emerge through their work are simultaneously real, imaginary, symbolic and mythical. With this in mind, the question that should be asked is not "is this real and true," but "why do so many young black men choose these dystopic images of spatial representation to orient their own places in the world?" By framing the question thus, the undeniable fascination with the grisly mayhem of the lyrical narratives is displaced and one can then embark on a more illuminating interrogation of the socio-spatial sensibilities at work.

Representing the Extreme Local: The Case of Seattle

By the end of the 1980s, Rap artists had provided an assortment of spatial representations of New York and Los Angeles that were both consistent with and divergent from the prevailing image-ideas of those urban centers. Rap artists worked within the dominant representational discourses of "the city" while agitating against a history of urban representations as they attempted to extend the expressive repertoire and to reconstruct the image-idea of the city as they understood it. This proved to be a formidable challenge since New York and LA exist as urban icons, resonant signs of the modern (New York) and postmodern (LA) city. They are already well defined, the products of a deluge of representational images, narrative constructions and social interactions.

Rap's emergence from city spaces that are comparatively unencumbered by a deep history of representational images, which carry less representational baggage, presents a unique opportunity for lyrical innovators to re-imagine and re-present their cities. As a traditional frontier city and a prominent contemporary regional center, Seattle might, in this light, be conceived as an *under*represented city that lacks the wealth of representational history common to the larger centers to the South and the East.

In the mid-1980s the Pacific Northwest was, for much of the U.S., a veritable hinterland known best for its mountains, rivers and forests and as the home of Boeing's corporate and manufacturing headquarters. In the music industry, Jimi Hendrix was perhaps Seattle's most renowned native son, but the city was otherwise not regarded as an important or influential center for musical production or innovation. The city's profile changed considerably with the rise of Bill Gates's Microsoft corporation in the outlying area and the emergence of the Starbuck's coffee empire and, by 1990, it was also garnering considerable attention as the source of the massively influential (and commercially successful) "Grunge/Alternative" music scene that spawned bands such as Hole, Nirvana, Pearl Jam, Soundgarden, and the SubPop label. Music has subsequently emerged as an essential element in the construction of Seattle's contemporary image although the industry's rock predilections have not been as favorable to the city's rap and R&B artists.[7]

In the spring of 1986, Seattle rapper Sir Mix-A-Lot's obscure track "Square Dance Rap" (NastyMix Records) made an entry onto *Billboard* magazine's Hot Black Singles chart. The release failed to advance any radical new aesthetic nor did it make a lasting contribution to the rap form. Its relevance, however, is in its capacity to reflect the diverse regional activity in rap production at that time as artists and labels attempted to establish themselves within the rapidly changing conditions fostering regional and local expansion. Mix-A-Lot's emergence illustrates the fact that rap was being produced in isolated regions and, as the track's chart status suggests, that it was selling in significant volume within regional "home" markets.

Despite this, an advertisement for Profile Records appearing six years later in *Billboard*'s "Rap '92 Spotlight on Rap" (28 November 1992), portrays the proliferation of industry activity with a cartographic cartoon entitled "Rap All Over the Map: The Profile States of America." New York, Chicago, Dallas, St Louis, Vallejo and Los Angeles are all represented with the names of acts and their respective regions and cities of origin. The Pacific Northwest is conspicuously labelled "uncharted territory," which refers to Profile's inactivity there but which also reproduces the dominant image of the region as a distant and unknown frontier in the view of those from the nation's larger or more centralized rap production sites.

Regardless of the advertisement's centrist biases, the fact that Seattle was at this stage on the charts (and, in hip hop parlance, "in the house") indicates that rap's consumer base had extended geographically and, moreover, that new and unforeseen sites of production such as Seattle were also being established. In an interesting spatial inversion, Bruce Pavitt, co-founder of the Alternative-oriented SubPop label, actually regarded Seattle's spatial marginality as a positive factor for local musicians, stating that, "one advantage Seattle has is our geographical isolation. It gave a group of artists a chance to create their own sound, instead of feeling pressured to copy others" (*Billboard*, 18 August 1990, p. 30). Sir Mix-A-Lot slowly solidified his Northwest regional base. His single "Baby Got Back" reached the number one position on the *Billboard* pop charts, eventually selling double platinum.

Displaying pride in his Northwestern roots, Sir-Mix-A-Lot provides an excellent example of the organization of spatial images and the deployment of a spatial discourse. In general terms, details that might be overlooked speak volumes about space and place, presenting additional information about the ways that an individual's daily life is influenced by their local environments and conditions. For instance, the standard group photo in the inner sleeve of *Mack Daddy* depicts Mix-A-Lot's Rhyme Cartel posse wearing wet-weather gear consisting of name-brand Gore Tex hats and jackets. This is a totally pragmatic sartorial statement from the moist climate of the Pacific Northwest that remains true to hip hop's style-conscious trends. It displays a geographically particular system of codes conveying regionally significant information that, once again, demonstrates hip hop's capacity to appropriate raw materials or images and to invest them with new values and meanings.

Of all the CD's tracks, "Seattle Ain't Bullshittin'" is exceptional for the manner in which it communicates a sense of space and place with clarity, sophistication and cartographic detail. Establishing himself on the track as a genuine Seattle "player," as the original Northwestern "Mack Daddy" (a term for a top level pimp), Mix-A-Lot bases his claim to local prestige in his persona as a former Seattle hustler who successfully shifted to legitimate enterprises as a musician and businessman. He adopts a purely capitalist discourse of monetary and material accumulation, reproducing the prevailing terms of success and prosperity that conform to both the dominant social values and the value system inherent within the rap industry.

As the title suggests, Seattle is the centerpiece to the track. This is clear from the beginning as Mix-A-Lot and posse member the Attitude Adjuster ad lib over a sparse guitar riff:

> Boy, this is S.E.A.T.O.W.N., clown (forever)
> Sea Town, Yeah, and that's from the motherfuckin' heart
> So if you ain't down with your hometown
> Step off, punk
> Mix, tell these fakes what the deal is ...

As the bass and drums are dropped into the track, Mix-A-Lot lyrically locates himself as a product of Seattle's inner-city core known as the CD (or Central District):

> I was raised in the S.E.A. double T.L.E.
> Seattle, home of the CD, nigga
> 19th and, yes, Laborda,
> pimpin' was hard ...
> It wasn't easy trying to compete with my homies in the CD

Seattle's Central District is home to a sizeable concentration of black constituents who comprise roughly 10 per cent of Seattle's total population. Mix-A-Lot's portrayal of the CD neighborhood is not explicitly racialized yet the references to pimping and competition among "homies in the CD" easily fall into a common, even stereotypical definition of "the 'hood" that is pervasive throughout rap of the period.

The Attitude Adjuster states at one point that "it ain't nothing but the real up" that are evident in Seattle as well as the rest of the nation. Unlike most major American cities, Seattle's black presence does not have a huge defining influence on its urban character: black youths are a socially marginalized constituency within a geographically marginal city. The Attitude Adjuster's pronouncement may suggest a hint of defensiveness but it also gives voice to the region's black hip hop constituency that is, as the subtext implies, just as "hardcore" as that of other urban centers.

Having established his ghetto credentials, Mix-A-Lot expounds on several spatially oriented scenarios, shifting scale and perspective throughout the track with his descriptions of local, regional and national phenomena:

> So even though a lot of niggas talk shit
> I'm still down for the Northwest when I hit the stage
> Anywhere U.S.A.
> I give Seattle and Tacoma much play
> So here's to the Criminal Nation
> And the young brother Kid Sensation
> I can't forget Maharaji and the Attitude Adjuster
> And the hardcore brothers to the west of Seattle
> Yeah, West Side, High Point dippin' four door rides ...

Mix-A-Lot adopts the role of Seattle's hip hop ambassador, acknowledging his own national celebrity profile while accepting the responsibilities of "representing" the Northwest, his record label and posse, and fellow rap artists from "Sea Town." Exploiting his access to the wider stage, he elevates the local scene, bringing it into focus and broadcasting the fact that hip hop is an important element of the Seattle lifestyle for young blacks living there as well.

The perspective shifts again as Mix-A-Lot adopts an intensely localized mode of description, recalling the days when he "used to cruise around Seward Park," moving out of the bounded territory of the city's Central District that is the posse's home base. Seattle is cartographically delineated here through the explicit naming of streets and civic landmarks that effectively identify the patterned mobility of the crew:

> Let's take a trip to the South End,
> We go west, hit Rainier Ave. and bust left,
> ... S.E.A. T.O.W.N., yo nigger is back again
> ... Gettin' back to the hood,

Me and my boys is up to no good,
A big line of cars rollin' deep through the South End,
Made a left on Henderson,
Clowns talkin' shit in the Southshore parking lot
Critical Mass is begging to box
But we keep on going because down the street
A bunch of freaks in front of Rainier Beach
Was lookin' at us, they missed that bus
And they figure they could trust us ...

With its references to the city's crosstown byways and meeting places, the track success-fully communicates an image of the common, "everyday" leisure practices of the Rhyme Cartel posse while also retaining a privileged local or place-based perspective that resonates with greater meaning for all Seattle or Tacoma audience members. This audience will undoubtedly recognize its own environment and the track will consequently have a different and arguably more intense affective impact among Seattle's listeners and fans. Unlike Compton, which was popularized through a relentless process of reiteration by numerous artists, Seattle is repre-sented much less frequently: "Seattle Ain't Bullshittin' " is a unique expression of Northwest identity. For example, there is no similar track on the Seattle-based Criminal Nation's *Trouble in the Hood* which was also released in 1992 (NastyMix/Ichiban), although references to the region are sprinkled throughout several tracks and on the liner sleeve one group member sports a Tacoma T-shirt identifying his home town.

In 1992, the trend towards such closely demarcated spatial parameters was not yet a common characteristic in rap, although it was increasingly becoming a factor in both lyrical and visual representations. Rather than an expression of a narrow social perspective cele-brating the local to the exclusion of other wider scales, "Seattle Ain't Bullshittin' " demon-strates a rather successful method of representing the hometown local "flavor" on an internationally distributed recording.

Conclusion

Rap music's shift towards a self-produced discourse introducing the 'hood as a new spatial concept delimiting an "arena of experience" can be weighed against larger trends currently restructuring global and national economies, transforming national and regional workforces, and, often, devastating urban localities. As numerous supporters have suggested, rap emerges as a voice for black and Latino youth which, as a large subset of North America's socially disen-franchised population, is at risk of being lost in the combined transformations of domestic and global economies that are altering North America's urban cultures today. The discourse of space encompassed by the term "'hood" may in this context also be interpreted as a response to conditions of change occurring at a meta-level, far beyond the scale of the local (and the influence of those who inhabit it).

The requirement of maintaining strong local allegiances is a standard practice in hip hop that continues to mystify many critics of the rap genre. It is, therefore, imperative to recognize and understand the processes that are at work and to acknowledge that there are different messages being communicated to listeners who occupy different spaces and places and who iden-tify with space or place according to different values of scale. It is precisely through these detailed image constructions that the abstract spaces of the ghetto are transformed into the more proximate sites of significance or places of the 'hood. Looking beyond the obvious, spatial discourse provides a communicative means through which numerous social systems are framed for consideration. Rap tracks, with their almost obsessive preoccupation with place and locality, are never *solely* about space and place on the local scale. Rather, they also identify and explore the ways in which these spaces and places are inhabited and made meaningful. Struggles and conflicts as well as the positive attachments to place are all represented in the spatial discourses of rap. This is not a display of parochial narrowness but a much more complex and interesting exploration of local practices and their discursive construction in the popular media.

Notes

1. As an indication of the distinctions between rap and the more encompassing hip hop culture, rap artist KRS-One has said "rap is something you do, hip-hop is something you live" (quoted in *The Source*, June 1995, p. 40). Rap is the music of hip hop and its central form of articulation and expression.
2. Hip hop's timeline can be roughly divided into three general eras: old school refers to the period from 1978–86; middle school covers the period between 1987–1992; and new school extends from 1993–1999. In some cases, the present is referred to as "now school."
3. See Reebee Garofalo (1997, pp. 257–264); see also, Brian Ward (1998).
4. The factors leading to the demise of Death Row include the murder of its marquee star Tupac Shakur, Suge Knight's nine-year sentence for probation violations, an FBI investigation of possible gang-related enterprises including money laundering, and the desertion of its key producer Dr. Dre. In 1998, the artist Snoop Doggy Dogg defected to Master P's New Orleans-based No Limit Records.
5. The Flavor Unit posse at the time included such Rap notables as Queen Latifah, Monie Love, Apache, Lakim Shabazz, and Naughty By Nature who, perhaps more than the rest, explicitly refer to their origins as New Jersey rappers hailing from 118th Street, "Illtown," in East Orange. After internal restructuring, the posse's most bankable star, Queen Latifah, emerged as the executive head of Flavor Unit Management.
6. For a detailed examination of the Florida "bass" phenomenon, see the special feature of *The Source*, March 1994.
7. Addressing the relatively minor industry consideration for Seattle's black artists, Sir Mix-A-Lot's Rhyme Cartel Records released the conspicuously titled *Seattle ... The Dark Side* in 1993. The cover prominently proclaims that the release "flips the script. No Grunge ... just Rap and R&B ... Sea Town Style."

References

Chambers, Iain. 1985. *Urban Rhythms: Pop Music and Popular Culture* (London)

Cross, Brian. 1993. *It's Not About A Salary: Rap, Race, and Resistance in Los Angeles* (London)

Dery, Mark. 1990. "Public enemy: confrontation," *Keyboard*, September

Eure, Joseph and Spady, James (eds.). 1991. *Nation Conscious Rap* (New York)

Garofalo, Reebee. 1997. *Rockin' Out: Popular Music in the USA* (Boston)

George, Nelson. 1986. "The Rhythm and the Blues," in *Billboard*, May 31, p. 23

———. 1992. *Buppies, B-Boys, Baps and Bohos: Notes on Post-Soul Black Culture* (New York)

———. 1993. "Hip-hop's founding fathers speak the truth," *The Source*, November

Gilroy, Paul. 1992. "It's a Family Affair," in *Black Popular Culture*, (ed.) Gina Dent (Seattle)

Gunst, Laurie. 1995. *Born Fi Dead: A Journey Through the Jamaican Posse Underworld* (New York)

Hager, Steve. 1984. *Hip Hop: The Illustrated History of Break Dancing, Rap Music, and Graffiti* (New York)

Jones, Charisse. 1995. "Still hangin' in the 'hood: rappers who stay say their strength is from the streets," *The New York Times*, 24 September, pp. 43–46

Keith, Michael and Pile, Steve (eds.). 1993. *Place and the Politics of Identity* (New York)

Lipsitz, George. 1990. *Time Passages: Collective Memory and American Popular Culture* (Minneapolis)

Nelson, Havelock and Gonzales, Michael. 1991. *Bring the Noise: A Guide to Rap Music and Hip Hop Culture* (New York)

Pike, Jeff. 1990. "At long last, Seattle is suddenly hot," *Billboard*, 18 August, pp. 30–34

Rap Pages, 1991. "The world according to Ice-T," October, pp. 54–67

Rap Sheet, 1992. "The bloody 5: a day in the hood," October, pp. 18–26

Robins, Kevin. 1991. "Tradition and translation: national culture in its global context," in *Enterprise and Heritage Crosscurrents of National Culture*, (eds.) John Corner and Sylvia Harvey (New York)

Rose, Tricia. 1994. *Black Noise: Rap Music and Black Culture in Contemporary America* (Hanover)

Samuels, David. 1991. "The rap on rap," *The New Republic*, 11 November

Shocked, Michelle, and Bull, Bart. 1992. "LA riots: cartoons vs. reality," *Billboard*, 20 June, p. 6

The Source, 1994. Special Issue: Miami Bass, March

Tate, Greg. 1992. "Posses in effect: Ice-T," in *Flyboy in the Buttermilk: Essays on Contemporary America* (New York)

Toop, David. 1984. *The Rap Attack: African Jive to New York Hip Hop* (Boston)

———. 1991. *Rap Attack: African Rap to Global Hip-Hop* (New York)

Ward, Brian. 1998. *Just My Soul Responding: Rhythm and Blues, Black Consciousness, and Race Relations* (Berkeley)

18
Rap and Hip-Hop:
The New York Connection

Dick Hebdige

I went into Body Music [a black owned record shop in Tottenham specialising in soul and reggae] the other day and asked for The Lord's Prayer. The guy serving sez: "Certainly sir. Do you want it wrapped?"

I sez: "Yes please."

He sez [to a hip hop beat]:

"Our father which art up there, hallowed by Thy name.

Thy kingdom come, Thy will be done for ever more amen." [pronounced ah-main!].

> Joke told me by a white Tottenham reggae fan

Anybody who picks up the wax is a friend in my heart.

> DJ Kool Herc

Rap is DJ and MC music. Like talk over and toasted reggae it relies on pre-recorded sounds. In the case of rap the basic beat comes from hard funk rather than Jamaican rhythms, and it is true that there are important differences between rap and reggae. But the process leading to the production of DJ reggae and rap is basically the same. The MCs "rap"—speak and in some cases half sing—their lines in time to rhythms taken from records. And the content of these raps is similar, too. There are boast raps, insult raps, news raps, "message" raps, nonsense raps, party raps and motherly or fatherly, sisterly or brotherly advice raps, just as there are in DJ reggae. There are also other similarities. Just as reggae is bound up with the idea of roots and culture, so rap is rooted in the experience of lower class blacks in America's big northern cities.

The culture that grew up round rap is sometimes called "hip hop." Hip hop culture involves dance, dress, language and wild style graffiti. At its core it also involves an attitude. In the words of Afrika Bambaataa, a leading hip hop DJ: "It's about survival, economics and keeping our people moving on."[1] Rap did for poor blacks in America in the 1980s what reggae had done for the "sufferers" in Jamaica a decade earlier. It got them noticed again and it helped to forge a sense of identity and pride within the local community. Like reggae, the music later found an international audience. And then the sense of identity and pride that went along with rap became available to other people who listened to the music. The hip hop attitude and culture grew up with the music wherever rap was performed or played. By the 1980s hip hop began to receive a further boost with the release of films like *Wild Style* and *Beat Street*.

Both reggae and rap also grew out of city slum environments. Rap started in the South Bronx of New York, which had been a mainly black and Hispanic ghetto for decades. By 1930 nearly a quarter of the people who lived there were West Indian immigrants. And most of the Spanish speakers living in the Bronx nowadays either came originally from Caribbean islands like Puerto Rico and Cuba or are the children of Caribbean immigrants. The Cubans began arriving in the Bronx in the 1930s and 1940s and the Puerto Rican community goes back even further. There are now three million Puerto Ricans living in New York—as many as live in Puerto Rico itself. The Bronx had never been prosperous. But in the 1960s it went into a sudden decline and by the end of the decade it had become the poorest, toughest neighborhood in the whole of New York City.

The Beginning of Hip Hop

In 1967 a DJ called Kool Herc emigrated to the States from Jamaica and came to live in the West Bronx. Herc knew the Jamaican sound system scene, and had heard the early talk-overs of the new DJs like U Roy. By 1973 Herc owned his own system. This was much louder and more powerful than other neighborhood disco set-ups, and it had a much fuller and crisper sound. But when he began dee-jaying at house parties he found that the New York black crowd would not dance to reggae. So he began talking over the Latin-tinged funk that he knew *would* appeal. To start with he merely dropped in snatches of street slang, like the very first toaster DJs who worked for Coxsone Dodd's system in the 1950s. He would shout phrases like "Rock on my mellow! This is the joint!" The talk was meant to keep the people dancing and to add the excitement that comes from "live" performance. Gradually he developed a style that was so popular that he began buying records for the instrumental breaks rather than for the whole track. The lead guitar or bass riff or sequence of drumming that he wanted might only last fifteen seconds. Rather than play the whole record straight through he would play this same part several times over, cutting from one record deck to the other as he talked through the microphone. This meant buying several copies of the same record. And it also meant that Herc had to have a very precise sense of timing. He used the headphones that DJs use to cue up their records so that he could cut from one copy of a record to another at exactly the right point.

Kool Herc found that the drumming on a record called *Apache* by The Incredible Bongo Band was particularly suited to his needs. The Incredible Bongo Band was a Jamaican disco group and their version of *Apache* was released in 1974. But it had been written for the Shadows, Cliff Richard's backing group, in 1960. It had then been "covered" by an American group called The Ventures, who had a minor hit with it in the States. The Incredible Bongo Band used conga drums instead of the standard pop music drum kit. And they laid more stress on the percussion. Thanks to Kool Herc, *Apache* could be heard all over the Bronx in 1975.

The style Herc had invented became known as the "beats" or the "break-beats." And he can be credited with another first. As the switching between record decks got faster and more complicated it required a lot of concentration. Herc couldn't "rap" and operate the records at the same time. So he employed two MCs, Coke-la-Rock and Clark Kent, to do the rapping for him. The MCs would put on a show for the crowd, dancing in front of the decks and bouncing lines off each other. The first MC dance team had arrived.

Soon other DJs began copying Herc's style and adding their own refinements. A DJ called Theodor invented a technique called "scratching." This involves spinning a record backwards and forwards very fast while the needle is in the groove. When handled in this way, a record can be turned into a percussive instrument. Scratching was used to foreground the beat even further.

Grandmaster Flash (Joseph Saddler) was another Bronx DJ who helped to create the hip hop style. His parents came from Barbados and his father had a big collection of Caribbean and black American records. Flash was fascinated not just by the music but by the records themselves. For him they were things to be looked at, touched and handled, not just played:

> My father was a very heavy record collector. He still thinks that he has the stronger collection. I used to open his closets and just watch all the records he had. I used to get into trouble for touching his records, but I'd go right back and bother them.[2]

After graduating in electronics, Flash began combining his two main interests: sound technology and hard funk. He made his own system and would play at night in local parks. To get the power he needed to operate the system he would run a cable from the decks and amplifier to the nearest street light. Flash became an expert at *punch phasing*. This is when the DJ hits a particular break on one deck while the record on the other turntable is still playing. The punch works in hip hop like a punctuation mark in a sentence. It helps to give shape to the flow of sounds on the record in the same way that a comma or a full stop helps to shape the flow of written language. And just as punctuation brings time to the pages of this book by telling the reader when to pause, so the punch in hip hop can be used to accentuate the beat and the rhythm for the dancing crowd. Flash was also one of the first hip hop DJs to work with a beat box: a machine that produces an electronic drum beat. Together with his MC crew—headed in those days by Melle Mel—Grandmaster Flash and the Furious Five produced a hard rapping style that became their trademark. As Flash leapt from deck to deck using multiple turntables Mel would rap in an aggressive, staccato style to the raw, stripped down electronic beat:

> Rappin' on the mike, makin' cold, cold cash
> With a joker spinnin' for me called DJ Flash.[3]

Afrika Bambaataa was another major figure right from the early days. He ran a sound system at the Bronx River Community Center. Today he is a figurehead for hip hop. He acts as an ambassador and spokesman for the music and its culture, just as Bob Marley did for reggae. Afrika Bambaataa is the name of a famous nineteenth-century Zulu Chief; it means "Affectionate Leader." And Bambaataa takes this role seriously. In 1975 he started an organization for funk loving street kids, later known as the Zulu Nation. Bambaataa based his Nation on the idea of the Zulu military system, and tried to adapt the structure of the black New York street gangs accordingly. Bambaataa had himself been a member of the Black Spades—New York's biggest black gang in the 1960s and early 1970s. But he had seen how violence and heroin had destroyed the gangs. In the Zulu Nation he set out to replace "rumbles" (fights) and drugs with rap, dance and hip hop style. He wanted to turn the gang structure into a positive force in the ghetto. Bambaataa's dream is that a sense of community can be created *within* the community rather than being imposed by people coming from outside. He believes that through organizations like the Zulu Nation the people at the bottom of society will learn how to help themselves and each other.

This vision is not unlike Marley's (or Manley's, for that matter). Bambaataa became interested in the politics of race and culture through the Black Muslims, a militant black sect. During the 1960s the Black Muslims won many converts, including Cassius Clay—Mohammed Ali, the great boxing champion. They helped to create a new mood of confidence in the black ghettoes of the Western world. The Black Muslims talked about the need for self-help and communal solidarity. And Bambaataa wanted to link music up to the issues the Muslims were raising. We have seen how Bob Marley had helped to steer reggae music through the rude boy era towards the Rastafarian themes of roots and culture. And at about the same time, Bambaataa was trying to guide black street kids through the gang phase towards a sense of collective solidarity and a more constructive attitude. By the early 1980s, the Zulu Nation had thousands of members worldwide.

By this time a style had grown up round hip hop. Crews of break-dancers (called B-boys and B-girls) had developed acrobatic dance routines that stretch the human body to its limits. First there was the Floor Lock. In this move, the dancers support themselves on one hand while spinning their bodies round and kicking out their legs. Then other moves were added. There was the Handglide or Flow (spinning while balanced on one elbow).[4] There was the Backspin, the Headspin, the Windmill (using the shoulders as the pivot). There was Lofting (diving in the air and landing on the hands). And once you had committed a Suicide (fallen forward with the hands at the sides and landed flat on your back) you could (if you were still alive!) freeze into a posture that told the crowd that the routine was over. Then there was another set of dance moves sometimes called "electric boogie." These include the Tick, the Mannequin or Robot, the King Tut, the Wave and the Pop, the Float and the Moonwalk glide. All these moves require the dancer to snap and twitch muscles in time to the music in a highly disciplined way. The Lock It is a dance mime version of laughing (slapping hands on the knees, etc.). Then there is "uprock," which is a fighting dance based loosely on kung fu moves. And around 1982 "freestyle" came in. As the name suggests freestyle leaves the B-girl or B-boy to improvise like the jazz dancers of the 1940s bebop era. Rival dance crews fight dancing duels drawing on these different dance styles. The aim is to burn off the opposition by suddenly performing an Unnamed Move (a move that hasn't been seen before and so can't be matched straightaway).

Obviously the emphasis on dancing influenced the dress. The clothes worn by B-dancers had to be comfortable, and washable. There could be nothing stiff or formal about them. So they started combining casual clothes and sportswear. After all, break-dancing, body popping and uprock are just as much athletic and competitive sports as baseball or football. The early B-style consisted of anoraks and sweatshirts with hoods, bellbottom jeans, tennis shoes and white sailors' caps with the brim sticking straight out in front. Later the style was modified: in came straight leg jeans, leather jerkins and bomber jackets, sweat shirts and trainers. Caps were worn back to front and on the back of the head.

The wild style graffiti had grown out of the fad among street gangs for "scribbling" their gang names on walls. In the hip hop era this became an art form in its own right. Individual artists used magic markers and spray paint to scribble their "tags" (nicknames) on every surface they could find. Subway trains were a favorite target. Soon the grey carriages of the New York underground system were lost beneath a wild riot of dayglo colours and ornate script. Some graffiti art is now so highly prized that it's sold for thousands of dollars in the New York galleries.

Beat and Voice: The Vital Mix

At the center of the hip hop culture was audio tape and raw vinyl. The radio was only important as a source of sounds to be taped. The break-dancers associated the black radio stations with disco: this was seen as the "official" black music of the mid- to late 1970s. The hip hoppers "stole" music off air and cut it up. Then they broke it down into its component parts and remixed it on tape. By doing this they were breaking the law of copyright. But the cut 'n' mix attitude was that no one owns a rhythm or a sound. You just borrow it, use it and give it back to the people in a slightly different form. To use the language of Jamaican reggae and dub, you just *version* it. And anyone can do a "version." All you need is a cassette tape recorder, a cassette, a pair of hands and ears and some imagination. The heart of hip hop is in the cassette recorder, the drum machine, the Walkman and the big portable—(well, just about!)—ghetto blasters. These are the machines that can be used to take the sounds out on to the streets and the vacant lots, and into the parks.

It wasn't that the break-dancers didn't like artists like James Brown, Chic or Hamilton Bohannon, who got played on the black radio stations. Because they *loved* the funk these people played. And funk rhythm is the backbone of hip hop culture. It was just that the black street kids wanted to bypass the retail outlets. They wanted to undermine the system that had taken artists like James Brown from the ghetto and put them up there out of reach with all the other show business stars. By taping bits of funk off air and recycling it, the break-dancers were setting up a direct line to their culture heroes. They were cutting out the middlemen. And anyway, who *invented* music in the first place? Who ever *owned* sound and speech?

James Brown, the godfather of funk, gave his seal of approval to hip hop culture in 1984. He joined forces with Bambaataa in that year to make a six-part rap record called *Unity*—a plea for peace ("We must push the button for life [the record button on a cassette machine] and nothing else"). And Brown had even hinted at the hip hop option in an old-style rap record called *Get Up, Get Into It, Get Involved* which he'd released way back in 1970:

> You can be like a tape deck, you know
> They can plug you in.
> Say what you wanna say
> Don't let them do it.[5]

But it wasn't long before the hip hop sound could be heard on the radio, and eventually it was itself recorded on vinyl. In 1979 two rap records appeared from nowhere. First there was *King Tim 111 (Personality Jock)* by Fatback, a Brooklyn-based funk band. This was followed by *Rapper's Delight* by the Sugar Hill Gang. The second record was closer to the Bronx style and it crept into the bottom of the U.S. Top 40. It later became an international hit. A flood of rap records followed, although it was some time before the *originators* of the hip hop style got into the studio.

In the early 1980s, Grandmaster Flash and the Furious Five released two classic hard hip hop hits: *Adventures of Grandmaster Flash and the Furious Five on the Wheels of Steel* and *The Message*. The first record is an extraordinary adventure in itself. It is so raw and the cuts are so violent that it sounds more live than a live performance by a punk band. And yet it is built entirely out of second-hand materials. The record is a startling mix of different sounds: the bass line from the rock group Queen's 1980 hit *Another One Bites the Dust* is mixed with a riff from *Good Times*, Chic's disco hit from 1979. These are then mixed with snatches from four or five other rap records. Finally, towards the end of the record, a man and a young child read out extracts from an incomprehensible fairy story. All this is jumbled up and scratched together. The record is full of breaks and silences. But it is held together by the stuttering rhythm. Flash keeps holding the needle back, tearing great empty holes in the web of sound. But however long he waits, he always comes back to hit the mix with the right sound at the right time. He never misses the beat. And some of the sounds he "quotes" are really risky. At one point he mixes in a snatch of Latin salsa. The screaming horns and the eight-bar beat jar against the steady 4/4 time of the Queen bass. And yet somehow it works beautifully. *Adventures on the Wheels of Steel* is an electro boast. Flash is challenging any other hip hop DJ to a cut 'n' mix contest. He knows in his bones he can "flash fastest." The record is about taking sound to the very edge of chaos and pulling it back from the brink at the very last millisecond. On this record Flash is playing chicken with a stylus.

Grandmaster Flash's second classic rap single, *The Message*, plays the same game. Only this time the edginess is in the rap itself. The rhythm is much slower, moodier and steadier than on the earlier release. As the beat pulses along, a synthesizer trips gently up and down the scales in time to the beat. Four beats up, four straight beats. Four beats down, four straight beats. At the beginning of the record this is fine. It's a relief from the pared-down percussion. And it sounds quite lighthearted and playful. But it goes on and on. The beat becomes a kind of metaphor for being locked up. It's as if you're having to live for as long as the record lasts in a space as cramped as a South Bronx tenement. It's like hearing somebody drumming their fingers on a table as you're trying to read. By the end of the record the synthesizer tripping up and down the scales is beginning to sound like somebody running a stick along a railing or a metal mug along the bars of a prison window. Suddenly the hypnotic beat is joined by a man's voice. The voice mutters right up against your ear: "It's like a jungle sometimes / Sometimes I wonder how I keep from going under." This is repeated once and then the voice launches into a syncopated rap on the theme of living in a tenement slum. The voice conjures up vivid, sour images: broken glass is everywhere (there is the sound of a bottle breaking in the background). The voice tells us a story about a crazy bag lady living in the street. Then we get another story about a girl falling in front of a train, losing an arm and having it sewn on again. None of these bits and pieces add up to anything much. Sometimes the voice starts rapping about the pressure of living as a poor black in America:

> You gotta have money, ain't a damn thing funny
> You gotta have a con in this land of milk and honey.

There's nothing stable or coherent in the world this record creates for us. The only constant is the menacing pulse of the beat with the stick being run up and down, up and down along the bars. At regular intervals the voice moves down into a brooding register and barks out the following lines, dropping each syllable like a bomb on the beat:

> Don't push me 'cos I'm close to the edge
> I'm tryin' hard not to lose my head
> It's like a jungle some times
> Sometimes I wonder how I keep from going under.

This sequence is repeated a few times. Each sequence contains a different story. At the end of each story, the voice returns us to the edge.

Then suddenly the record launches into the main narrative. At last we get the message of the song. This time the story is all too coherent. The sequence of events it describes has a horribly inevitable feel about it. The message tells how a young boy living in a ghetto drifts out of school and into crime, gets an eight-year prison sentence for armed robbery, is sexually assaulted by older prisoners and ends up hanging himself in his cell. The message is directed at the listener, who is addressed as the young boy in the story. It's as though we are listening to the voice of someone talking to the corpse or the ghost of his younger brother. The message is: "don't hero worship gangsters or get involved in crime." The rap ends with the lines that started the song as the unremitting beat fades out into silence. *The Message* is a study in mood creation. The flat voice and thudding beat together take the listener across the border into a cold, bleak landscape. This time we are not being led to the Promised Land by Dennis Brown and Aswad. This time we are being led by the ears into hell. But what is so disconcerting and extraordinary about this record is that it mixes its moral with a slinky beat which is as irresistible to dance to as Sly Stone's *I Wanna Thank You (for letting me be myself)*.

Afrika Bambaataa likes mixing things up, too. He has been known to cut from salsa to Beethoven's Fifth Symphony to Yellow Magic Orchestra to calypso through Kraftwerk via video game sound effects and the *Munsters* television series' theme tune back to his base in James Brown. And in 1982 he made a record with the Soul Sonic Force called *Planet Rock* that was a big hit. In its own way, *Planet Rock* is as bizarre as *Adventures on the Wheels of Steel*. But the Soul Sonic Force didn't use the edgy staccato rapping style of the Furious Five. Instead their voices weave in and out of the pulsing party beat with lines like "More bounce to the ounce" and "Planet Rock. It just don't stop it's gonna drive you nuts!" Meanwhile Bambaataa mixes in snatches of song and sound effects round the steady electronic beat. The rhythm of a rap record by Captain Sky called *Super Sporm* is crossed with the computer-generated rhythms and melodies of records like *Trans-Europe Express* and *Numbers* by the German electro group, Kraftwerk. This is then mixed up with the theme from the Clint Eastwood Spaghetti Western *For a Few Dollars More*. (The Eastwood themes composed by Ennio Morricone had also made a powerful impact on dub producers like Lee "Scratch" Perry in Jamaica in the 1970s.)

The daring of Bambaataa's mixes and the black political input that he has made into hip hop have inspired other artists. Air Force One built a hip hop record round Ronald Reagan's famous gaffe when he made a "joke" at a TV station. Reagan had claimed in jest that he had the solution to the Russian "problem." "Ladies and gentlemen, fellow Americans," he says, barely able to restrain the laughter, "We begin bombing in five minutes." President Reagan was unaware that he was being recorded at the time. *See the Light, Feel the Heat* begins with Reagan's "announcement." The phrase "We begin bombing" is picked out and repeated several times as the funk rhythm breaks and crashes in a series of explosions round Reagan's voice. And each time the phrase comes back into the mix, the voice has become more distorted. Reagan's little "joke" gets less and less funny each time it's relayed. By using tape loops, echoes and breaks, by speeding up and slowing down the tape, Air Force One make a political statement without having to say anything directly. This technique has been used on many other records to undermine the official voices of authority. It has even been used in Britain by "scratch" video artists. People like the Duvet Brothers and George Barker tape television programs—including news reports—off air, using domestic video cassette recorders. By re-editing the extracts, they change the meaning of what people in power think they're saying.

In a more respectful vein, the words of 1960s black leaders have been recycled in rap and soul. The voices of Martin Luther King, the Civil Rights leader, and Malcom X, spokesman for the Black Muslims, have both been brought back from the grave in this way. In *No Sell Out*, for instance, on Tommy Boy records, Malcom X's voice is heard "testifying" for the black experience in urban America in lines like: "The only thing that power respects *is* power.... There will be no flim-flam, no sell out." Malcom X's hard, no-nonsense style of delivery fits the funk beat perfectly. This is no coincidence. When Malcom X was alive and making speeches, he drew on the rapping traditions in black street culture, jive and jazz. Malcom X's widow, Mrs. Betty Shabazz, is aware of her late husband's connection to the rhythms of the street. And she gave her permission for Keith LeBlanc to use her late husband's voice on *No Sell Out*. It was Bambaataa who paved the way for that connection between the street, black politics and the studio to be opened up again in the 1980s.

Malcolm McLaren, who managed the British punk group The Sex Pistols in the 1970s, has called *Planet Rock* "the rootsiest folk music around."[6] And though they may seem poles apart, Bambaataa and McLaren share a lot of common ground musically. They both wage war on people's prejudices about popular music. In 1982, McLaren made an album called *Duck Rock* that used rap, African Zulu, Latin, and Burundi rhythms, bits of patter recorded off radio and Appalachian hillbilly music. In his turn, Bambaataa took inspiration and musical ideas from white punk and new wave music. He would mix up the theme from *The Pink Panther* with fragments from The Beatles, The Monkees and the Rolling Stones to create a dance beat that sounded like solid black funk. His aim was to get people to dance their way beyond their own prejudices. Jerry Dammers expressed a similar attitude in 1980 when he produced the album *More Specials*, which included muzak:

> I listen to anything basically … it doesn't matter how good or bad it is, if you listen to it enough, you learn to like it. There's no such thing as good or bad music. I'd really like to destroy people's ideas of good and bad music so that eventually people will hear a record and they won't even know if they like it or not. That's my ambition … [7]

And Horace Gentleman backed up Dammers' decision to move away from ska to draw on other musics: "What we came up with [on *More Specials*] is the songs side and the muzak side—the aim was to make it more international."[8]

When taken to its logical conclusion in rap, cut 'n' mix suggests that we shouldn't be so concerned about where a sound comes from. It's there for everyone to use. And every time a new connection is made between different kinds of music, a new channel of communication opens up.

The connections between rap and Caribbean music didn't have to be forced. A high proportion of the black population in the Bronx came originally from the West Indies. The area has its Puerto Rican and Cuban communities, too. And when these people came from the Caribbean, they brought their own music with them.[9] The streets of the South Bronx had been throbbing to the African-based Latin rhythms of the Cuban rumba, the mamba and the cha-cha-cha for decades. The Puerto Rican "danzon," which is based on European violin music, faded away when it was transplanted to New York. But the *plena*, with its African shuffle rhythm, survived and flourished. These Latin rhythms were sometimes blended with black American music. For instance, in the 1960s there was a craze in New York for Latin soul. And the heavy funk beat of hip hop is regularly lifted by a dash of up-tempo salsa. Salsa means "sauce" in Spanish, and it was South American listeners who first used the term to refer to New York Latin music in the 1940s and 1950s. Tito Puente, the great salsa percussionist and band leader, produces his own brand of the music, which draws on santeria rhythms. Puente is himself a priest of the Santeria faith. And now the Bronx throbs to the sound of the Santeria drums as well as the salsa protest songs of Ruben Blades from Panama and Celia Cruz, the Cuban "queen of salsa."

As we have seen, there is a reggae-rap connection through DJ Kool Herc. And rap got exported back to Jamaica, too. Joe Gibbs cut a version of *Rapper's Delight* in 1979. On one side of the record, a duo called Xanadu and Sweet Lady rap the song New York fashion. On the other side, *Rocker's Choice*, they toast it Trenchtown style. And rap and reggae have a common root in a record called *Love Is Strange* by Mickey and Sylvia. This record was released in 1956 at the time when ska and soul and rock 'n' roll were just beginning. On this record, guitarist Mickey Baker and vocalist Sylvia Vanderpool sing a bantering duet over a lilting Caribbean-flavored shuffle rhythm. In the middle there is a sort of mini-rap between the two. Mickey asks Sylvia how she calls her lover boy. As Mickey keeps asking the question: "And if he *still* doesn't answer?," Sylvia calls back to him in a voice that gets sexier and sexier. The record made the top twenty in the States. It was a hit in Jamaica too. It is sometimes classified as a "rhythm and blues calypso hit."[10] And almost a quarter of a century later, it was Sylvia Vanderpool who set up Sugarhill Records with her husband. This was the company that released the first Bronx-style rap by the Sugarhill Gang before going on to record Grandmaster Flash and the Furious Five.

Some of the other strands that were woven into rap went into the making of reggae as well. David Toop has done some extraordinary detective work on where New York rap came from:

> Rap's forebears stretch back through disco, street funk, radio djs, Bo Diddley, the be-bop singers, Cab Calloway, Pigmeat Markham, the tap dancers and comics, the Last Poets, Gil Scott-Heron, Muhammad Ali, a cappella and doo-wop groups, ring games, skip rope rhymes, prison and army songs, toasts, signifying and the dozens, all the way back to the griots of Nigeria and Gambia.[11]

The mix is very rich. The radio DJs Toop refers to were the jive-talkers of the be-bop era like Daddy O Daylie, Dr. Hep Cat and Douglas Jocko Henderson (the "Ace from Space"). These DJs used the human voice as an instrument so that the rhythm and sound of the words became more important than their meanings. As far as the early sound system operators in Jamaica were concerned, the patter of the DJs was as important as the records they played. The first recorded toasts, like Sir Lord Comic's *Ska-ing West*, used the jive slang of the American radio DJs, and U Roy released a record called *Your Ace from Space* no doubt in tribute to Jocko Henderson. Bo Diddley was famous for one record—an R&B boast song called *Bo Diddley* that he recorded in 1955. The song has a strong African beat which is made even more pronounced by the maracas in the background. It is based on a rhythm sometimes called the "postman's knock" which was later used by Johnny Otis on *Willie and the Hand Jive* and by the Rolling Stones on *Not Fade Away*. Diddley calls out the boasts over this rhythm while the backing singers sing out the line "Hey, Bo Diddley." And it was this kind of raw, shuffle-rhythmed R&B that the sound system operators were playing in the Jamaican yards in the 1950s. In the 1930s and 1940s jazz bandleaders like Cab Calloway and singers like Slim Gaillard had invented nonsense languages. They got the audiences to join in by singing out lines that the crowd chanted back. You can hear the same silly call and response routines whenever Eek a Mouse takes the stage today.

A cappella means "without instruments." In America in the 1950s there were literally hundreds of black street corner groups who tried to follow the success of doo-wop stars like The Platters. And soon there was a spate of vocal harmony groups in Jamaica too. (The voice is an instrument *everyone* can afford!) First there were the duos like Higgs and Wilson, and Jackie and Roy. In the late 1950s a Jamaican group called the Jivin' Juniors had an R&B hit with a record called *Sweet as an Angel*. And the vocal harmonies of groups like the Wailers had their roots in the same tradition.

Finally there were the old word games called "signifying" and the "dozens" in the States. These can be traced back to the West African roots and the griots. And versions of these boasting, insult and trickster games are played throughout the Caribbean. Always the vital mix is voice and rhythm. This is the mix that binds communities together across continents. And it's true even when the rhythms come out of a Roland TR 808 computerized drum machine. In the end it doesn't matter whether the voices are singing or shouting, rapping or toasting. They can be interrupted by video game bleeps and out-takes from Ronald Reagan speeches, and it still doesn't matter. Even when the vocalist is talking fast-style on a microphone in London about something called the *Cockney Translation*, the vital mix survives.

Notes

1. Afrika Bambaataa quoted in Steven Hager, "Afrika Bambaataa's Hip Hop," in *Voice*, 21 September, 1982.
2. Grandmaster Flash quoted in Steven Harvey, "Spin Art," in *New York Rocker*, January, 1982.
3. Grandmaster Flash and The Furious Five quoted in Hager, op. cit., September, 1982.
4. See Mr. Fresh and The Supreme Rockers, *Breakdancing*, Corgi, 1982.

5. James Brown quoted in David Toop, *The Rap Attack: African Jive to New York Hip Hop*, Pluto Press, 1984.

6. Malcom McLaren quoted in Hager, September, 1982.

7. Jerry Dammers quoted in Miles, *The Two-Tone Book for Rude Boys*, Omnibus, 1981.

8. Horace Gentleman, quoted ibid.

9. See Jeremy Marre and Hannah Charlton, *Beats of the Heart-Popular Music of the World*, Pluto Press, 1985.

10. Charlie Gillett, *Sound of the City: The Rise of Rock and Roll*, Outerbridge and Dienstfrey, 1970.

11. David Toop, op. cit., 1984.

19
Uptown Throwdown

David Toop

Saturday night at The Roxy on West 18th. Trouble Funk, the heaviest of heavy funk 'n rap groups from the Washington go-go scene, are just finishing a marathon set which runs the gamut of modern black music. Each number lasts around 30 minutes—segues of their own releases, "Pump Me Up," "Drop the Bomb," "Trouble Funk Express," intercut with quotes from "Alexander's Ragtime Band," "Atomic Dog," "Work That Sucker to Death," *The Munsters* theme, Taana Gardner's "Heartbeat," Kraftwerk's "Trans-Europe Express," all powered by the rock-hard drumming of Mack Carey. The dancers are going crazy as the group chant "drop the bomb on the white boy too," forming a circle and challenging one another's moves. The last note dies and they file off the stage. Afrika Bambaataa, the imposing presence on the DJ plat-form, drops the needle onto Michael Jackson's "P.Y.T.," the sweetest dance tune from *Thriller*.

Bambaataa may look mean when he's at the turntables but he also looks comfortable. A large man, dressed casually in sweatshirt and trainers, his image could be described as homely—certainly a million miles from the sci-fi warrior of his publicity pictures. He has a reputation for being iconoclastic in his record choices and there is no doubt that "P.Y.T." is a shock to the system after 90 minutes of Trouble Funk's intense bombardment of comic-strip and electronic images. The atmosphere lightens up and Bam gets to work with Soul Sonic's scratch DJ, Jazzy Jay.

Two days later, in Arthur Baker's new studio, Shakedown Sound, Bambaataa is being uncharacteristically vehement about Tommy Boy Records boss Tom Silverman's reluctance to have Soul Sonic Force and Shango sharing the same stage in the inproduction movie *Beat Street*. His more usual soft-spoken manner and apparent awkwardness belie his importance as a figurehead for many black youths in the Bronx and a pioneer in the roots development and eventual international success of hip hop. His name is taken from a nineteenth-century Zulu chief (it means Chief Affection) and, ironically enough, it was the British film *Zulu* which gave him the idea in the early 1960s to form the Zulu Nation, a loose organization dedicated to peace and survival which has since spread outwards from the Bronx to other parts of America. Bambaataa outlines the development:

> The Zulu Nation. I got the idea when I seen this movie called *Zulu* which featured Michael Caine. It was showing how when the British came to take over the land of the Zulus how the Zulus fought to uphold their land. They were proud warriors and they was fighting very well against bullets, cannons and stuff. They fought like warriors for a land which was theirs. When the British thought they'd won the next thing you see is the whole mountain full with

233

thousands of Zulus and the British knew they was gonna die then. But the Zulus chanted—praised them as warriors and let them live. So from there that's when I decided one of these days I hope to have a Zulu Nation too.

And then, as the years went by, through all the civil rights movement, human rights, Vietnam war and all the folk and rock that was happening—all the change of the '60s that was happening to the whole world—it just stayed with me to have some type of group like that.

Bambaataa was once a member of The Black Spades, the largest black gang in New York. Although he concedes that the gang era was tough he determinedly looks on the positive side:

To me, the gangs was educational—it got me to learn about the streets, and The Black Spades they had a unity that I couldn't find elsewhere. I've been in a lot of different gang groups but The Black Spades had a unity among each other. The gang was like your family. You learned about how to travel around the New York streets. A lot of times when there were no jobs for youths, no trips happening in the Community Centers so the gangs got them there. If the gangs, 'scuse the expression, tore shit up, the government would start sending people to speak to you, throwing in money to calm the gangs down. America is raised on violence. Only time America really listens is when somebody starts getting violent back.

His downplaying of gang warfare is a response to what he sees as the media's thirst for negative stories and sensationalism. That notwithstanding, the gangs escalated their rivalry to a frightening level of violence between 1968 and 1973. This internal destructiveness can only have contributed to their demise in 1974. Bambaataa puts it down to pressures from the City, drugs and the reaction of women against the fighting among the men.

In his classic study of a black Chicago gang of the '60s, the *Vice Lord Nation*, R. Lincoln Keiser documents the changes that caused the gang to evolve from a social group into an organized fighting gang and latterly, under the influence of Black Nationalism, into a community group:

The club was now legally incorporated, and had received a substantial grant from government sources to undertake self-help projects. The group had started a restaurant called "Teen Town," begun an employment service, and opened a recreation center called "House of Lords." They had entered into agreements with both the Cobras and the Roman Saints, and all three of the clubs had co-operated in community help projects. The Vice Lords were strongly involved in Black pride and Black consciousness programs. A staff of both Whites and Blacks was working in the Vice Lord office on legal problems faced by members of the Lawndale community.

To outsiders the gangs may have seemed like uncontrolled mayhem but each gang had its own structure, method of operation and recognized leaders. Bambaataa joined a division of The Black Spades formed at Bronx River Project in 1969. Through the influence of his mother his main interest was music, but he was also aware of politics within the black community:

In the '60s, that's when I was young and I was seeing a lot of things that was happening around the world. What got me excited first was when James Brown came out with "Say It Loud, I'm Black and I'm Proud." That's when we transcend from negro to black. Negro to us was somebody who needed to grow into a knowledge of themself. There was no land called negroland. Everbody in America—when they came here they knew what country they was from. If you were Italian you called yourself Italian-American, but the blacks didn't know which way they was going. They was brainwashed—all this stuff was put into our mentality. Black was evil, turn the other cheek, believe all the stuff that the Bible is telling you. The Bible contradicts itself. So Martin Luther King was the thing that was happening because he was fighting for civil rights, but Malcolm X was more on the aggressive side. Myself, I was more on the Malcolm X way of thinking. I respect Martin Luther King for what he was doing.

The '60s was a beautiful time because that's when you saw change—not just in America but happening all around the world. I was watching all of that and then later when gangs was fading out I decided to get into the Nation of Islam. It put a big change on me. It got me to respect people even though they might not like us because we was Muslims. The Nation of Islam was doing things that America had been trying to for a while—taking people from the streets like junkies and prostitutes and cleaning them up. Rehabilitating them like the jail system wasn't doing.

Bambaataa's dream of having his own Zulu Nation had to wait until the gang scene had faded. While still in high school he started a group called The Organization that lasted for two years, and with the emergence of the hip-hop scene he changed the name to the Zulu Nation:

There were five members and we used to call them Zulu Kings. They were break-dancers. They were taking out a lot of talent that was happening in high schools and clubs and winning trophies and then more people wanted to join. As we kept playing from place to place more people came and joined and it got large like that. It started stretching from the Bronx to Manhattan, Yonkers, upstate New York to Connecticut to a lot of other places. When people used to leave and go to other states they'd build Zulu Nations according to their own way of thinking.

Mr. Biggs, one of the rappers in Soul Sonic Force, the group who hit big with "Planet Rock," backtracks to their beginnings in hip hop:

I was rapping before the Zulu Nation even started. I started rapping back in about 1974— just me and Bambaataa and a guy by the name of Cowboy (not the one that's with Grandmaster Flash), and this girl called Queen Kenya. Bam had just been given a new DJ set for a graduation present when he got out of high school and he started spinning records. I just picked up a mike one time, just playing around rapping, and I just kept rapping from there.

In those early days each DJ was strong in his own district and was supported by local followers. Few had access to the big clubs so the venues were block parties and schools or, in the summer, the parks. A party in the park would entail wiring the sound system to a lamp post or going to the house nearest the park, paying the owner and running a cable to their electricity. Then the party could go on until the police broke it up. DJs like Kool Dee, Flowers, Pete DJ Jones, Maboya and Smokey were all popular at the time, but for many partygoers the attention shifted to a Jamaican jock called Kool DJ Herc.

Initially, Herc was trying out his reggae records but since they failed to cut ice he switched to Latin-tinged funk, just playing the fragments that were popular with the dancers and ignoring the rest of the track. The most popular part was usually the percussion break. In Bambaataa's words:

Now he took the music of like Mandrill, like "Fencewalk," certain disco records that had funky percussion breaks like The Incredible Bongo Band when they came out with "Apache" and he just kept that beat *going*. It might be that certain part of the record that everybody waits for—they just let their inner self go and get wild. The next thing you know the singer comes back in and you'd be mad.

A conga or bongo solo, a timbales break or simply the drummer hammering out the beat—these could be isolated by using two copies of the record on twin turntables and playing the one section over and over, flipping the needle back to the start on one while the other played through. The music made in this way came to be known as beats or break beats.

Break-beat music and the hip-hop culture were happening at the same time as the emergence of disco (in 1974 known as *party music*). Disco was also created by DJs in its initial phase, though these tended to be club jocks rather than mobile party jocks—records by Barry White, Eddie Kendricks and others became dance floor hits in New York clubs like Tamberlane and Sanctuary and were crossed over onto radio by Frankie Crocker at station WBLS. There were many parallels in the techniques used by Kool DJ Herc and a pioneering disco DJ like Francis Grasso, who worked at Sanctuary, as they used similar mixtures and superimpositions of drumbeats, rock music, funk and African records. For less creative disco DJs, however, the ideal was to slip-cue smoothly from the end of one record into the beginning of the next. They also created a context for the breaks rather than foregrounding them, and the disco records that emerged out of the influence of this type of mixing tended to feature long introductions, anthemic choruses and extended vamp sections, all creating a tension that was released by the break. Break-beat music simply ate the cherry off the top of the cake and threw the rest away.

In the words of DJ Grandmaster Flash:

Disco was brand new then and there were a few jocks that had monstrous sound systems but they wouldn't dare play this kind of music. They would never play a record where only two minutes of the song was all it was worth. They wouldn't buy those type of records. The type of mixing that was out then was blending from one record to the next or waiting for the record to go off and wait for the jock to put the needle back on.

Flash has become world famous through Sugarhill releases like "The Message," yet Herc faded from view despite his innovations in both mixing and rapping. Part of the reason for his demise was a fight at the Executive Playhouse in which he intervened and was stabbed, yet Flash also claims he had limitations as a mixer:

Herc really slipped up. With the monstrous power he had he couldn't mix too well. He was playing little breaks but it would sound so sloppy. I noticed that the mixer he was using was a GLI 3800. It was a very popular mixer at that time. It's a scarcity today but it's still one of the best mixers GLI ever made. At the time he wasn't using no cueing. In other words, the hole was there for a headphone to go in but I remember he never had headphones over his ears. All of a sudden, Herc had headphones but I guess he was so used to dropping the needle down by eyesight and trying to mix it that from the audio part of it he couldn't get into it too well.

Herc's sound system was so powerful that when he held a block party nobody tried to compete. He would even occasionally shame Flash in public, demonstrating the superiority of his set-up over Flash's home-made rig. Grandmaster Flash's entry into mixing stemmed both from his fascination for his father's record collection and his mother's desire for him to study electronics:

My father—he was a record collector. I think what really made me interested into wanting to get into records was because I used to get scolded for touching his records. When I was living in this town up in the Bronx called Throgs Neck he used to have this closet and in this closet were some of the classics. I mean like Benny Goodman, Artie Shaw, all the popular stuff of the time. He would close it but sometimes he would forget to lock it. He would always tell my mother, "Don't let Joseph go in there and touch the records." So what I would do—when my mother's back was turned or she was in the kitchen I would tiptoe up to the closet, turn the knob, go inside the closet and take a record. I would attempt to turn the stereo on. The stereo had a little red light at the bottom of the speaker and that red light really intrigued me. Every time I'd get caught I'd get scolded or I'd get beat. Think I learned my lesson? Hell no!

I was in this place called Grier School, Hope Farm, New York upstate, where I had to stay when my mother had gotten sick. Up there they wanted parental advice on what you wanted your son or daughter to be into, so my mother chose electronics because I always had a knack of tinkering with things and taking things apart.

From there, I came out of Grier School and my mother put me into Samuel Gompers vocational high school in the Bronx there, 147th Street and Southern Boulevard. From there I caught the knack of dealing with televisions, hi-fi stereo and stuff, and that's where I really started to get a love for *sound*. We grew up underprivileged so we didn't really have the money for me to get a really nice sound system for my room. I'd get stuff that was half-disabled and put it back the best way I possibly can.

Flash was one of the first to pick upon Herc's break-beat music that, after less than a year, was becoming the dominant style in the Bronx. He began by playing records for small parties on Fox Street or Hoe Avenue, Faile Street, where there were a few empty apartments. The music was Jimmy Castor, Barry White, James Brown, Sly and the Family Stone and The Jackson Five. As his popularity grew he became aware of his own inability to synchronize beats:

I was in the experimentation phase of trying to lock the beat together. I had to be able to hear the other turntable before I mixed it over. This is when I met Pete DJ Jones. He was a big tall guy, six and some change—he was a sit-down DJ but his knees was like HUGE. I'm saying to myself, wow, how can he take these records and blend them on time, keep this music going without missing a beat? So, I finally got the heart to ask him if I could play on his system. I think he told me no twice. Then after a while he'd heard about me playing for the kids and he gave me permission to play on his system. He told me what to do and to my amazement, wow, you can actually hear the other turntable before you play it out to the people.

I knew what it was because I was going to the technical school for electronics. I knew that inside the unit it was a single pole, double throw switch, meaning that when it's in the center it's off. When it's to the left you're listening to the left turntable and when it's to the right you're listening to the right turntable. I had to go to the raw parts shop downtown to find me a single pole double throw switch, some crazy glue to glue this part to my mixer, an external amplifier and a headphone. What I did when I had all this soldered together, I jumped for joy—I've got it, I've got it, I've got it!

I knew how to blend. Right away, when I got on Pete's set, I know how to blend. That just came naturally. My main objective was to take small parts of records and, at first, keep it on time, no tricks, keep it on time. I'm talking about very short beats, maybe 40 seconds, keeping it going for about five minutes, depending on how popular that particular record was.

After that, I mastered punch phasing—taking certain parts of a record where there's a vocal or drum slap or a horn. I would throw it out and bring it back, keeping the other turntable playing. If this record had a horn in it before the break came down I would go—BAM, BAM, BAM-BAM—just to try this on the crowd.

The crowd, they didn't understand it at first but after a while it became a thing. After I became popular with it I wanted to get more popular, but a lot of places where they heard *of* me I would ask them if I could get on their turntables. A few clubs I used to go to, even Disco Fever, they'd say, "No man, I heard you be scratching up people's records, man. I heard you get a wild crowd too, man. You ain't playing on my set."

A scratch is *nothing* but the backcueing that you hear in your ear before you push it out to the crowd. All you have to know is mathematically how many times to scratch it and when to let it go—when certain things will enhance the record you're listening to. For instance, if you're playing a record with drums—horns would sound nice to enhance it so you get a record with horns and slip it in at certain times.

A large part of the disc jockeys' mystique and power is their resourcefulness in finding unknown or obscure records that can move a crowd. These can be rarities, white-label pre-releases, acetates, unreleased tapes or simply good songs that slipped through the net at the time they were released. Given the obvious difficulty of identifying tunes in the non-stop collages of the b-boy style, the most creative DJs in the Bronx were able to build up strong local reputations as "masters of records"—the librarians of arcane and unpredictable sounds that few could match. In time-honoured fashion their secrecy extended to soaking records in the bath to peel off the center labels or giving records new names. Previously jealously guarded lists, emerging gradually at the beginning of 1984, make bizarre reading. Bambaataa was one of the most outrageous:

The Bronx wasn't really into radio music no more. It was an anti-disco movement. Like you had a lot of new wavers and other people coming out and saying, "Disco sucks." Well, the same thing with hip hop, 'cos they was against the disco that was being played on the radio. Everybody wanted the funky style that Kool Herc was playing. Myself, I was always a record collector and when I heard this DJ, I said, "Oh, I got records like that." I started digging in my collection.

When I came on the scene after him I built in other types of records and I started getting a name for master of records. I started playing all forms of music. Myself, I used to play the weirdest stuff at a party. Everybody just thought I was crazy. When everybody was going crazy I would throw a commercial on to cool them out—I'd throw on *The Pink Panther* theme for everybody who thought they was cool like the Pink Panther, and then I would play "Honky Tonk Woman" by The Rolling Stones and just keep that beat going. I'd play something from metal rock records like Grand Funk Railroad. "Inside Looking Out" is just the bass and drumming ... rrrrrmmmmmmmm ... and everybody starts freaking out.

I used to like to catch the people who'd say, "I don't like rock. I don't like Latin." I'd throw on Mick Jagger—you'd see the blacks and the Spanish just *throwing* down, dancing crazy. I'd say, "I thought you said you didn't like rock." They'd say, "Get out of here." I'd say, "Well, you just danced to The Rolling Stones." "You're kidding!"

I'd throw on "Sergeant Pepper's Lonely Hearts Club Band"—just that drum part. One, two, three, BAM—and they'd be screaming and partying. I'd throw on The Monkees, "Mary Mary"—just the beat part where they'd go "Mary, Mary, where are you going?"—and they'd start going crazy. I'd say, "You just danced to The Monkees." They'd say, "You liar. I didn't dance to no Monkees." I'd like to catch people who categorize records.

Through listening to the type of records that were popular in the beginnings of hip hop (and have remained popular) it becomes easier to understand how the better-known aspects of the culture—rapping, scratching, beat-box music—came to evolve. A b-boy classic like James Brown's "Get Up, Get Into It, Get Involved," released in late 1970, is an up-tempo call and answer routine between Brown and singer Bobby Byrd. For most whites at the time, this was the most meaningless type of James Brown release, but for those young blacks still living in areas like the Bronx and Harlem every phrase had a message.

The record is a single, harsh, seesawing guitar riff with the bass rumbling upfront in the mix and the drummer playing loose funk with the hi-hat cymbal opened then choked shut on the fourth beat of the bar. There is no bridge: the only change in the structure comes half-way through, with a drum break where James shouts, "Fellers, I want you to hit me." the band shout back "Yeah" and the horns hit, "Hit me" … BAM … "Alright, hit me" … BAM … "Hey" … BAM.

The effect is identical to the kind of punch phasing using horns over drum tracks that can be heard on bootlegs of b-boy parties. The break is followed by a tortured rock guitar solo and at the end Brown shouts the prophetic, "You can be like a tape deck, you know … they can plug you in … say what they want you to say … don't let 'em do it." The last phrase is repeated four times, with Bobby Byrd shouting back a resist and survive NO each time.

Most of the words—phrases like "get an education" and "do it one time … get it right"—are shouted or rapped over the music, with Brown's voice rising to a scream towards the close. The general message—a positive exhortation not to waste your life or be manipulated by others—was part of a series of records that encouraged black youth to stay in school, avoid succumbing to hard drugs and be proud of the color of their skin.

The other important break-beat records had some or all of the same ingredients—a funky beat, a positive message, a drum break and some rock guitar: Jimmy Castor's "It's Just Begun," Rufus Thomas's "Do the Funky Penguin" and "The Breakdown," Baby Huey and the Babysitters' "Listen to Me," The Isley Brothers' "Get Into Something" and Dyke and the Blazers' "Let a Woman Be a Woman—Let a Man Be a Man." Other records with drum breaks that could be used to construct new tunes were "Johnny the Fox Meets Jimmy the Weed" by Thin Lizzy (released as a bootleg mix on Dirt Bag Records and called "Johnny the Fox" by Skinny Lizzy); "The Big Beat" by heavy-metal guitarist Billy Squire (also released as a bootleg record featuring just the opening bars of the song) and "Scorpio" by Dennis Coffey, a white session guitarist. "Scorpio" (an inspiration in name if nothing else to the 1982 electro track by Grandmaster Flash and the Furious Five) was included on one of Paul Winley's *Super Disco Brakes* anthologies. The first volume of *Super Disco Brakes* includes New Birth's peculiar Sly Stone-meets-psychedelia fusion, "Gotta Get a Knutt," which can be heard on another bootleg, *Live Convention '82* (volume two), recorded at T Connection.

Live Connection '82 (Disco Wax Records) begins with an extract from "Academy Awards," a track from Masterfleet's 1973 album *High on the Seas* featuring Star Trek actress Nichelle Nichols. After fragments of the "Good Times" bass riff, some Sly Stone, "Gangster Boogie" and a litany of guest DJs and MCs who are "in the house," there is a five-minute 27-second rap which uses the first six bars (13 seconds in total) of "Do the Funky Penguin" cut together by the Grand Wizard Theodore:

> It's like a one for the treble and two for the bass
> Theodore—let's dog the place
> You don't stop, you don't stop, that body rock
> Just clap your hands, it's the sure shot sound
> Brace yourself—for the one that goes down
> Got a little news that you all can tell

Theodore—he got the clientele
All night, y'all, if it's alright
All night, y'all, if it's alright
Porto Rico, Porto Rico
Make money, make money, make money into the Patty Duke
Throw your hands in the air
Wave 'em like you just don't care
Getting down with these sure-shot sounds your body say oh yeah
Yeah, a little louder, little louder
You don't stop, you don't, you won't don't don't
You won't don't don't, you don't don't stop the body rock
Because the people in the back—you ain't the wack
But—don't stop the body rock
The people in the middle, let me see you wiggle
(but don't stop that body rock)
The people on the side—let's ride
(but don't you stop that body rock)
The girls in the rear, you come up here
(but don't you stop that body rock)
Young lady in the blue, I'm talking to you
(but don't you stop that body rock)
Young lady in the brown, you know you're down
(don't stop that body rock)
Young lady in the green, you're looking real clean
(don't you stop that body rock)
Young lady in the black, you ain't the wack
(you ain't thinking 'bout stopping that body rock)
Young lady in the white, she'll bite all night
(but don't you stop that body rock)
Young lady in the yellow got a faggot for a fellow
(but don't you stop that body rock)
'Cos the body rock is sho nuff the shot
(but you won't stop, you don't stop)
Ain't thinking 'bout stopping that body rock
Punk rock, rock the house
Patty Duke, y' all, get cute y' all
Patty Duke, y' all, get cute y' all
Gonna tell you little something, I'm one of a kind
But now I'm gonna rock—the zodiac signs
Pisces—rock the house
Aquarius—rock the house
And Gemini—said get on high
Scorpio—you're the go
Pisces—the higher degree
Just the beat beat beat, the beat beat the beat
Patty Dukeing to the rhythm, get up out your seat
Young ladies—are you with me?
Young ladies—are you with me?
Young ladies in the house say OWW
Say OWW—to the beat, y' all

You don't quit, you don't quit
You don't quit, you don't quit quit
The sure-shot shit
It's like superstition with a bag of tricks
I say this is the way we harmonise
This is the way we turn it up
This is the way we turn it up

And the beat goes on. Raps like these, with their eulogies to the young ladies in blue, red, etc., are reminiscent of black dance music from all eras—country blues and jug bands, piano blues like "Pinetop's Boogie-Woogie," the shouters like Big Joe Turner, the electric blues of John Lee Hooker and Junior Wells, the rock 'n roll of Larry Williams and Little Richard—not great poetry but dancehall rhymes.

As has already been shown, rapping has roots in a variety of sources, but for the hip-hop purists it is again Kool DJ Herc who was the first to come up with a Bronx MC style. Bambaataa remembers:

There's a lot of people trying to take credit like Cheeba and DJ Hollywood—the disco type of DJs that was out there—but I challenge any of these people to sit down and base their facts on when they started to do what we was doing in the street. A lot of these people who claim to be the start of it was doing rapping something like Frankie Crocker or talk like disco-style radio-type rapping. Herc took phrases, like what was happening in the streets, what was the new saying going round the high school like "rock on my mellow," "to the beat y'all," "you don't stop," and just elaborated on that.

Bambaataa sees a connection between Herc's Jamaican origins and his rapping: "He knew that a lot of American blacks were not getting into the reggae of his country. He took the same thing that they was doing—toasting—and did it with American records, Latin or records with beats."

Rappers like Mr. Biggs are more inclined to give some credit to Eddie Cheeba and DJ Hollywood for their part in the general development of rap, even though their sources were the radio rather than the schoolyard. DJ Hollywood was in fact rapping over disco records between acts at Harlem's Apollo Theatre. Kurtis Blow, whose smooth style is closer to this kind of combined DJ/MC, remembers Hollywood as the rap innovator, although the Hollywood rhyme he recites from memory is word-for-word Isaac Hayes's badman rap "Good Love 6–9969" from his 1975 album *Use Me*. Ike's career may have been on the wane by that time, but his influence was obviously still alive in the streets.

Flash also gives Hollywood credit: "He was one of the greatest solo rappers that ever there was. That boy could blaze a crowd—the rhymes he says. I expected him to shoot right to the top—he had a chance before we did." Hollywood also played at Club 371 and his style was capable of appealing to the older fans as well as the b-boys.

Lil Rodney Cee, now with Double Trouble, recalls the formative years of MCs in the middle 1970s:

The way rap is *now*—it isn't the way it was *then*. Whereas then it was just phrases; the MC would say little phrases like, "To the Eastside, make money. To the Westside, make money," or "To the rock, rock, rock, to the rock, rock, rock." In '77–'78 I was with The Magnificent Seven. We was playing in the streets. Rap, then, was only a street thing. At that time, everything was happening at once. B boying was happening at the same time as DJing and rapping came out. Everything was strictly competitive.

The groups that came out was in strict competition, so when we did play in the wintertime we rented small clubs, disco-theques, recs, boys' clubs, PALs. We charged little bits of money and people came and that's what we did in the wintertime. With the money that we made we invested in our sound system for the summertime. That was the basic foundation of what every group did to start off and get into the rap industry.

At the time it wasn't groups rapping—it was solo MCs and they would have a DJ. It would be one DJ and one MC. They would just come out and the people liked it. The more they did the more it got into a unified stage. We said, "Hey, we should get more MCs."

Along with his partner in Double Trouble, KK Rockwell, Rodney was in one of the very first rap groups, Funky Four Plus One More. He recalls the emergence of rap styles and the competitiveness:

The first MC that I know of is Cowboy, from Grandmaster Flash and the Furious Five. He was the first MC to talk about the DJ. He would talk for Grandmaster Flash and say how great Flash is—you know, "the pulsating, inflating, disco shaking, heartbreaking, the man on the turntable" and that's all it was. And then, to have fun, it got into—okay, everybody came from all different places to hear the music so when they came they all were into whatever they were into whether it was graffiti, dancing, b boying—the b boys were strictly in competition, too.

An uptown group would battle a downtown group. What I mean by battle is that they could come and they would say, "Okay. Us four are better than your four," and we would go at it. We would pick one and we would dance against each other. We'd do one move and they'd do a move and the crowd liked it. That's where the competition came in. This is before any records, before any money was made. This was from our hearts.

Grandmaster Flash and the Furious Five embody the gradual move from underground to overground. Dressed in red leathers (old-style DC Comics Flash) and working his way through a pack of Lucky Spike bubblegum, Flash waxes nostalgic over the good old days. The contradictions of roots culture in the marketplace have hit very hard; five years after the first rap records and 10 years since hip hop began to stir, most groups and soloists are gathering themselves to launch out on the second phase in the music business, often with a sobering hindsight wisdom that show business can be no business at all. As a 17-year-old the chances of having good financial and legal advice are very slim. Flash is very conscious that pioneer rappers like DJ Hollywood and Busy Bee Starski have not had the breaks of other, lesser talents, and he is also depressed by the changes that have inevitably wrung the verve out of the scene as a whole. His career shows the process in microcosm:

I had to prove to myself that I could rock a crowd, so as opposed to making them pay I tried it for free. Meaning that I would go in the park and play—St Mary's, 23 Park, 63 Park— these are various parks I used to play at and just do this new thing called scratching and called phasing and see if they would like it. And it just so happened that they did like it. Not knowing, all the time I was doing this, that there were people following me—older men following me. They made a proposal to me: "Flash, let's take it on the inside for a dollar or two and see how this works."

At that time, with my mixing ability, once I warmed up and really got into it, the crowd would stop dancing and just gather round as if it was a seminar. This was what I didn't want. This wasn't school—it was time to shake your ass. From there I knew it was important to have vocal entertainment. There were quite a few MCs, as we called it before the industry called it rap, that tried out for the job to rap with me and the first member of the crew to really pass the test was Keith Wiggins, known as Cowboy.

He had a Simon Says-ish type of style. The particular MC I was looking for was somebody who could complement scratching. This person had to be able to talk with all the obscure scratching I was doing. I'm doing all this but I'm doing it all on time so you have to have the ear to really know. Even now, I might walk into a club and if I'm cutting and keeping it going they rap, but if I stop on time to the beat they get lost. There's some that can't really catch on to it when the music's being phased in and out to the beat. Cowboy, he was superb at it. As far as that "Ho," "Clap your hands to the beat" and "Say oh yeah," I'd have to give him credit for being one of the creators of that.

From there I had gotten Melvin Glover who had almost like a scholastic type of style. From there I had got Danny—he could say rhymes from now to doomsday. He was a person who run his mouth but he could also talk with the sort of obscure scratching I was doing. So it was like Grandmaster Flash and the Three MCs. It worked pretty good. From there I was ready to take it to the inside.

We tried in this club called the Back Door at 169th Street and Boston Road for a dollar. We would party from like 10 at night till 7 in the morning. When we were playing at the Back Door we had diehard fans—it was to a point where kids were sneaking out the house. I try to keep a rapport with some of my close fans and with their parents. I'd even give them the cab fare to get home after the party. I would sit down with some of the mothers and like, "Flash, they won't go to school. They won't go to church but let them hear about you playing at the Back Door—boy, they'll get up, get dressed and they'll definitely be there."

It was like an omen. If you don't come to a Flash party it's something you missed. If you weren't there you felt like an onion—you had to be there, even against your mother's and father's wishes. Then after a while there were crews being created—this was when crews were *really* being created seven or eight years ago. The Malachi Crew, oh, there were so many crews.

Flash's number-one fan, his minder Kevin, has a good memory for crews: "The Casanovas, The Potheads, The Cheeba Crew, there was a crew for every block." He also remembers some of the wilder turntable trickery of the time:

He did this shit one day that fascinated me. See, I was a devoted fan. I wasn't down with the crew—now I am. It was at Roosevelt High School or Bronx River, one of those two. Him and Mike and Disco B were doing their Terrible Trio thing. Flash would cut the record and move out of the way, then Disco B would do it then Flash would do it then Mike would do it. Then they had this other thing they did where they would pop up out of nowhere—from this angle you couldn't see them. It was a different DJ every second—"Good times … good times … good times." The most phenomenal was at Roosevelt. This nigger did this shit. He drop back. He fell back—I thought he'd bust his *ass*. What it was, he had kicked off his shoe and *kicked* the fader. It was perfectly on time. The crowd went *wild*—I mean, niggers was pushing and falling and shit!

Taking this kind of DJ style from community venues into the commercial world of the clubs (no matter how small) involved an inevitable growth in following. Flash recalls the nights at the Back Door:

It was a big success but it was a small place. We would open the doors at 11 o'clock, and 12 o'clock the doors would be *closed*. It was a thing where I would have to pace it. Eleven to 12.30 I would play cool-out hustle music for the calm people, the sophisticated b boy people in the place that wanted to do the hustle or dance proper. But from 1 to 2.30, that's like grab your partner 'cos I'm playing the hottest shit in the crates. My assistant pulls out the *powerful* shit—I'd set up the order according to beats-per-minute, tempo and I'd say, "Hand it to me, man, just like that," and once I'd start playing that shit the crowd would just go. The Incredible Bongo Band, "Bongo Rock," "Johnny the Fox," "The Bells"—Bob James—"Mardi Gras." Me watching them enjoy themselves so much I would really like "pop pop pop pop poppoppop u u u u." I would like break the shit down to eighth, sixteenth notes. It amazed me sometimes.

Bob James was like 102 beats-per-minute and I would go from 102 beats-per-minute to 118 so from there it was like Bob James, James Brown, Donald Byrd, Roy Ayers to John Davis and the Monster Orchestra, "I Can't Stop," and that's like the ultimate, you know. From there I would keep it going but I would give myself a break because for about 50 minutes I'm bending down uncomfortably. I'd put on "Dance to the Drummer's Beat," which is a fairly long break, about four minutes, let it play for a while and then play the slow jams, the real oldies. After you sweat and you're tired you appreciate it: "Oh, he finally slowed it down." The Delfonics, The Moments, The Five Stairsteps—the real slow, out-of-date stuff that was really love songs. I had all that stuff in my crates. I had something like 45 crates behind me.

Flash and Kevin reminisce by singing the chorus of The Delfonics' "For the Love I Gave To You" and recalling how Flash would cut mix the same line over and over, keeping the romantic dancers going for over a minute on the same spot. Eventually, the crowd at the Back Door swelled beyond capacity to the point of discomfort:

So it was to a point where we had to move the corporation down the block to Freeman Street. It was this place called the Dixie Club. That became our new home. The crowd got monstrous and the high school students, who had heard of me and really used to down me, they came to the parties a few times—got a taste of it—they really enjoyed that. We gave them a good time. So they would go to their school organizations and say, "You want Flash." After a while we started knocking all the schools off—Roosevelt, Taft, Monroe, Bronx River. It wasn't so much a party—it was a commercial thing where we were getting hired on a professional basis. By that time we had built up a pretty decent sound system.

A year and a half, two years later, the pinnacle of a DJ's group's career, before it was recording, was who can make it to The Audubon. Once you've played there you are famous throughout the five boroughs. The place held 3,000 people so you're bound to get people from all over the place. It was real strange. The people who were working with me, they said, "Flash, we've played all the schools. We're growing out of the Dixie Club. We've grown out of most gymnasiums we've played in. I want to take you to this place, Flash. I've already rated it and I'm setting it up for the next month."

Adventures on the Wheels of Steel: Grandmaster Flash at Broadway International

He takes me to this building—this place is like a block and a half *long*. I said, "No, please. Let's not try *this* step." He says, "Flash, there's no other place that you can try. Anything smaller than this would be a step down. Give me a month to publicize it." After that day he showed me, I would go down there by myself for about four or five days and think, "I'm not ready for this place. This is too big." The Fire Department sign says "3,000 people. No More." I said to myself, "I'll be lucky to get 400 in this motherfucker, talk about *3,000!*"

So the night came. After a month publicizing me everyone who was interested knew about this big affair. So I bring my sound system in there. It's not really powerful enough to rock this whole place but I put it up high. Strategically, if you put it up high the sound might not be strong but you can at least hear it. The night before I had come up with a way to cut without cueing and I showed it to this guy named Georgie George and Melvin. And Melvin—Melle Mel—as soon as he had seen it he made up a routine. I said, "I'm not ready to do this shit," but it was too late. I didn't want to back out.

So the Audubon comes. Open the doors 11 o'clock. It was like 200 or 300 people. I left out 'cos I was kind of embarrassed, you know, and came back about 12.30, 1 o'clock. This place was JAM PACKED FULL! I said, "Oh shit!" Kool DJ AJ was playing with us. He was pumping the crowd. Everybody was there—the gangsters, the scramblers, the little kids. I went downstairs—the line was around the corner. The shit is jumping off.

We played. Melvin says, "Stop the music" and introduces me—"The world's greatest DJ—Grandmaster Flash." Everybody thought I was going to do regular stuff. I went into my spinning back, turning backwards. The crowd was screaming. I said, "I'm not gonna get nervous. If I let my emotions get to me I'm going to fuck up and it's gonna jump out of the grooves." I'm trying to stay steady. After a while, I had to do the other thing, which is taking the needle and dropping it with no cueing at all—keeping the beat on time. It was taking one beat—dropping it and counting. This is blind—BAM—BAM—I kept it on time. I did it about 10 times. Backed off and the crowd went berserk. The fucking floor was like about to cave in. After that night I felt so good. That was September 2nd 1976.

I was ready to try that shit again. Two months later we tried it and after a while what had happened was other corporations, other b boy groups, were going in there and tearing the place up, breaking out the windows and then the news media and the cops started talking bad about it. . . . "These groups, they call themselves b boys, they're coming down to rent the place and bringing all these wild people. People are getting shot and windows are getting broken out." So the Audubon was out. There was no superlarge place that you could play in.

We was doing it with just us and one other DJ. Other groups that didn't have the heart to go in by themselves were going in there with six or seven DJ groups. Seven or eight different sound systems—it was too confusing. This person was taking too long to turn on or this person's system was fucking up and once you've got that big mass of people you have to keep them entertained. So after a while motherfuckers was getting shot and this and that, so by the time we went back after the third time our clientele was getting kind of scared so we gave it up. Then we started knocking off schools—older places, the Savoy Manor Ballroom, the Renaissance Ballroom—all the posh clubs. For three years things were going great, then all of a sudden you hear on the radio, "To the hip hop, hippedy hop, you don't stop." I'm saying to myself, "I know of anybody else from here to Queens or Long Island that's doing this. Why don't I know of this group called The Sugarhill who? The Sugarhill Gang. They don't know of me and I don't know them. Who are these people?"

They got a record on the radio and that shit was haunting me because I felt we should have been the first to do it. We were the first *group* to really do this—someone took our shot. Every night I would hear this fucking record on the radio, 92KTU, 98, BLS, rock stations. I was hearing this shit in my dreams.

Part IV
I'll Be Nina Simone Defecating on Your Microphone:
Hip-Hop and Gender

Mark Anthony Neal

I could do what you do, EASY! Believe me / frontin' niggaz gives me heebee-geebees
so while you imitatin' Al Capone / I be Nina Simone and defecating on your microphone
                                    Lauryn Hill, "Ready Or Not" (*The Score*, 1996)

Rap music and hip-hop culture have often been singularly cited for the transmission and reproduction of sexism and misogyny in American society. With tracks like Akinelye's "Six-Foot Blow Job Machine" and 2 Live Crew's "Me So Horny," hip-hop is perhaps too easy a target. As sexism and misogyny are largely extensions of normative patriarchal privilege, their reproduction in the music of male hip-hop artists speaks more powerfully to the extent that these young men (particularly young black men) are invested in that privilege than it does to any evidence that they are solely responsible for its reproduction. As journalist Kevin Powell eloquently cautions in the introduction to Ernie Paniccioli's collection of classic hip-hop photographs, *Who Shot Ya?* (2002), "it is wrong to categorically dismiss hip-hop without taking into serious consideration the socioeconomic conditions (and the many record labels that eagerly exploit and benefit from the ignorance of many of these young artists) that have led to the current state of affairs. Or, to paraphrase the late Tupac Shakur, we were given this world, we did not make it." But there is also no denying the fact that hip-hop's grip on American youth allows for the circulation of sexist and misogynistic narratives in a decidedly uncritical fashion.

The embrace of patriarchal privilege by some male hip-hop artists partly explains the marginalization of women among hip-hop artists, particularly when those women don't conform to the normative roles assigned to women within hip-hop (the chicken-head groupie, oversexualized rhyme-spitter, baggy clothed desexualized mic-fiend are prime examples). Thus, many female raps artists are less concerned with challenging the circulation of sexism and misogyny (Sarah Jones's "Your Revolution" notwithstanding) than they are with simply being recognized as peers alongside male rappers. This is in part what Lauryn Hill asks us to consider in her verse from The Fugees's "Ready or Not." Extolling the legacy of the legendary jazz vocalist and activist Nina Simone, Hill champions a notion of hard-core hip-hop that is not rooted in the Mafioso fantasy of the day, but that goes back to the risky aesthetic and political choices made by a woman who, at the height of the civil rights movement in the 1960s, spoke "truth to power" in songs like "Mississippi Goddam" and "Four Women." Hill's lyrical phrase represents a legitimate critique of the hypermasculinity and phallocentrism that pervades hip-hop—a critique that is clearly gendered in its intent.

What Hill and many other female rap artists, including Salt-N-Pepa, Eve, MC Lyte, Queen Latifah, Bahamadia, and Missy Elliot, are really asking for is a respect for woman-centered narratives that exist alongside, and not necessarily in competition with, those of their male peers. As Hill attests, however, these women are ready and more than willing to battle. Accordingly, each of the five women whose essays are collected in this section speak to a complex and multifaceted notion of gender and femininity in hip-hop. While the chapters are clearly in dialogue with one another—Tricia Rose's "Never Trust a Big Butt and a Smile" being the now-legendary opening salvo in scholarly criticism of hip-hop—these chapters are not simply echoing the party line from some mythical center of feminist thought. These are works that complicate our sense of the obvious gender problems within hip-hop.

UCLA ethnomusicologist Cheryl Keyes charts the formation of "four distinct categories of women rappers" within the hip-hop performance tradition. Drawing on Jacqueline Bobo's concept of "interpretive community," Keyes examines the observations of female performers and audiences, identifying the "Queen Mother," "Fly Girl," "Sista with Attitude," and "Lesbian" as the dominant figures within female hip-hop performance, adding that "each category mirrors certain images, voices, and lifestyles." The most provocative of these figures is the "Fly Girl." According to Keyes, "Rap's fly girl image … highlights aspects of black women's bodies considered undesirable by American mainstream standards of beauty." Citing the example of Salt-N-Pepa, hip-hop's quintessential "Fly Girls," Keyes asserts, "they portray via performance the fly girl as a party-goer, and independent woman, but additionally, an erotic subject rather than an objectified one."

Journalist Joan Morgan also finds value in the identity of hip-hop's "Fly Girl" and the associated erotic power she possesses. In the opening pages of her book, *When Chickenheads Come Home to Roost: My Life as a Hip-Hop Feminist*, Morgan relishes the opportunity to replicate the "proper Bronx Girl Switch" that she watched "project girls" employ when she was a young girl growing up in the Bronx. As she notes, these were woman-girls who could "transform into Black Moseses capable of parting seas of otherwise idle Negroes." Given the reverence for the South Bronx in hip-hop lore, it is not a stretch to suggest that the prototype for the hip-hop "Fly Girl" may have been born on the streets of New York's uptown borough.

It is in the context of black female sexuality that Morgan posits a hip-hop feminism that champions both a critical discourse around gender in hip-hop and the pleasures associated with flaunting the very female sexuality that is regularly objectified by some hip-hop artists. As Morgan queries in one passage:

> Is it foul to say that imagining a world where you could paint your big brown lips in the most decadent of shades, pile your phat ass into your fave micromini, slip your freshly manicured toes into four-inch fuck-me sandals and have not one single solitary man objectify—I mean roam his eyes longingly over all intended places—is, like, a total drag to you?

Morgan, in fact, uses the power of female eroticism to flip hip-hop sexual politics on it's head as she brazenly asks, "how come no one ever admits that part of the reason women love hip-hop—as sexist as it is—is 'cuz all that in-yo-face testosterone makes our nipples hard."

Morgan opens *When Chickenheads Come Home to Roost* reminiscing about being a young girl, disappointed that she couldn't accompany her mother to a performance of Ntozake Shange's drama *for colored girls who have considered suicide / when the rainbow is enuf*. Here, Morgan is the ten-year-old girl dreaming of black feminist possibilities.

Treading similar ground within the context of hip-hop, Kyra Gaunt finds these possibilities in the very "girl" games that Morgan herself likely played as a child. Exploring the concept of "play" in black expressive culture, Gaunt writes, "Black girls' musical games promote the skillful development of musical authority that reflects blackness, gender, individual expressive ability, and the very musical styles and approaches that later contribute to adult African-American musical activity."

Challenging the pervasive notion that women exist in hip-hop solely as "chickenhead" groupies, Gaunt posits female hip-hop fans as "nurturing a 'real' appreciation or understanding of the creativity and production (the work) involved in rap music." Specifically linking the games of black girls to hip-hop music and culture, Gaunt argues:

> Play is considered an experience or an act that is performed for its own sake, for pleasure or reward known as *flow*. The rewards for flow experience are said to be intrinsic, often marked by imaginative creativity, improvisation, and adventurousness.... Coincidentally, flow is the same word rappers in hip-hop use to characterize the creative energy they experience when writing, performing, or extemporaneously "freestyling" rhymes or spinning records.

In a particularly fascinating segment of Gaunt's chapter, she discusses black girls' game-songs that reference black female sexuality, such as "Mailman, Mailman," where the postal worker warned about the "lady with the African booty," and "I'm a Nut." "Mailman, Mailman," Gaunt notes, "exploits the powerful meanings of movement and display in the black female body."

Such sentiment could have been echoed in any number of hip-hop recordings, including LL Cool J's "Big Ole Butt" and Sir Mix-O-Lot's "Baby Got Back," but it was a recording by the hip-hop/R&B hybrid group Bell Biv Devoe (BBD) that put the power of black female sexuality into a hip-hop context.

BBD's "Poison" featured the refrain, "never trust a big butt and a smile," a phrase that was adapted into a ground-breaking critique of gender and hip-hop by noted hip-hop scholar Tricia Rose. In her comments about the song, which she extends to men in general, Rose suggests, "'Poison' explains both their intense desire for and profound distrust of women." Rose then states, "the capacity of a woman to use her sexuality to manipulate *his* desire for *her* purposes is an important facet of the sexual politics of male raps about women."

In accord with the chapters in this section, Rose refuses to discuss gender in a strict, male versus female context. For Rose, such a rigid framework fails to acknowledge that

> One of the remarkable talents black women rappers have is their capacity to attract a large male following and consistently perform their explicitly pro-woman material. They are able to sustain dialogue with and consequently encourage dialogue between young men and women that supports black women and challenges some sexist male behavior.

Thus, throughout her chapter Rose focuses on themes in female hip-hop, such as failed relationships, the lyrical dexterity of women rappers, black female sexual expression, and the relationship of black women rappers to white feminism. Of the latter dynamic, Rose notes, "in the case of black women, the realities of racism link black women to black men in a way that challenges cross-racial sisterhood," a sentiment subsequently echoed several years later in Morgan's *When Chickenheads Come Home to Roost*. Most important to Rose is the fact that black women rappers "have expanded rap's territory and have effectively changed the interpretive framework regarding the work of male rappers," transforming the dominant gendered discourses in public circulation.

It is in the spirit of Rose's comments that Gwendolyn Pough's chapter completes the section. Although Pough does not offer an explicit critique of hip-hop and gender, her work acknowledges the impact of gender on the wider field of hip-hop studies. While women critics and scholars have always been a part of the critical community that enunciated the significance of hip-hop music and culture, very often they've been relegated to a limited role, providing the "gender critique." The underlying theme of Pough's chapter is that hip-hop possesses untapped potential. Noting that young white men represents hip-hop's core audience, Pough queries, "Imagine if that same consuming audience became immersed in not just rap music but also a hip-hop toward change? ... I mean really imagine the future presidents and CEOs of this country's White patriarchal power structure really getting down with a hip-hop movement towards change?" Pough's observations about the undisputed whiteness of hip-hop's primary consumers could easily be extended to encompass hip-hop's relationship to feminist thought and thinkers. As Nas says, "Imagine that!"

20

Translating Double-Dutch to Hip-Hop:
The Musical Vernacular of Black Girls' Play

Kyra D. Gaunt

> The black cultural aesthetic is essentially both oral-aural and motor, focusing on action, performance and expression. The young black girl learns the significance of perfecting performer roles ... by trying seriously to learn the current dances, by imitating adults' *[ways of being]* "hip" and "cool."[1]
> She performs within the circle of friends whose actions and song continually cue her: "This is play; do your thing."[2]

These comments capture the ideals of black cultural performance as observed in ring games, hand-clapping games, and double-dutch jump rope. These observations reveal the often overlooked significance of the musical behavior (songs, rhymes, chants, rhythmic hand claps, and dance) associated with the daily rituals of many young black girls. Black girls' musical games promote the skillful development of musical authority that reflects blackness, gender, individual expressive ability, and the very musical styles and approaches that later contribute to adult African-American musical activities. I intend to show how these games act as oral, rather than written, *études*[3] for learning simple and complex black musical aesthetics. These *études* are the first autonomous avenue for black girls to learn the "rules" for making music *sound* "black."

The musical phenomena within African-American girls' games offers an avenue for theorizing about women's participation in contemporary black music culture.[4] My primary interest in this essay is how the games black girls play provide insight into black women's "ambivalent" participation in hip-hop music. I am particularly interested in how this operates given the contemporary appeal and contested opinions concerning the music of hip-hop culture, one of the most influential roles of popular music making in the United States today. Women's "real" musical behavior (what they actually do musically and what it means to them) is transformed and eclipsed by not only hegemonic discourses surrounding African-American women's so-called ideal and so-called dysfunctional social roles, but also by inflated discourse about black music as a "male" culture.

Indeed, we might conclude that black women make music not only *sound* blackness, but sound *black* woman-ness, as well. I will present a redefinition, a reinterpretation of women's "real" musical experiences that will allow an appreciation of their experiences as central, rather than peripheral, to black popular music culture.

"Its a Man's Man's Man's World (But It Wouldn't Be Nothing without a Woman or a Girl)"[5]

The serious study of contemporary popular music (what I like to think of as contemporary folk music) from an ethnomusicological perspective is a recent occurrence. Formerly, the study of folk music investigated so-called preliterate or nonliterate music cultures—*pre*modern or *pre*urban. The study of gender in ethnomusicology emerged as a scholarly pursuit only in the early 1980s. Next to nothing has been written about African-American women's musical experience, even when compared to that of other African diasporan women (who are also underrepresented). Thus, women are rarely represented as generators (composers, producers, "leaders," or performers) of black music culture and style in spite of their actual participation. They are more often perceived as subsidiary to the "real" players of musical invention as imitators, followers, dancers, or idolizing fans. Women's musical involvement is often perceived as a reflection of, or a response to, men's participation. However, if one considers double-dutch and hand-clapping games as musical activity, African-American girls' and women's musical authority is evident.

Black popular music has recalled and signified the emotional and cultural experience of blacks in the United States more than any other cultural medium since 1920 (the year of the first "race" record). The terms associated with black music making (such as syncopation, improvisation, "ragging" and ragtime, bop, swing, being "on time," groove, bridge, etc.) often signify a way of encoding both musical and nonmusical experiences associated with black identity. Words such as *hard, cool, improvisation*, and *gangsta* can have different, often derogatory and disenfranchised meanings for black women.

A central obstacle to understanding black women's musical experience in contemporary culture is that "blackness" has been overwhelmingly imagined, talked about, and personified through the experience of heterosexual black men. These specifically male configurations have been primarily projected by the exponents of black bourgeois values and the authenticating values of street or ghetto "underclass" life since the late 1960s. Surveying the precursors of contemporary black music, we can perceive the canonizing of a heterosexual and masculine authority simply by remembering the "greats": the striding ragtime contributions of Scott Joplin (1868–1917) and Jelly Roll Morton (1885–1941); "hard" bop to "cool" jazz by "cats" Dizzy Gillespie (1917–1993) and Miles Davis (1926–1991), the interpretive gestures of hip-hop's "b-boys" breaking, writing, rhyming, and cutting (breakdancers, graffiti writers and artists, rapping MCs, and turntable-spinning disk jockeys); and in the quintessential gangsta persona and posse of West Coast rap in the 1990s.

When one evaluates musical expressions in culture, rather than through dominant modes of historicized memory and theories of mass production and consumption, women's performance is uncovered. We are most likely to see it in leisure and play, which often produce and ritualize the musical sounds and somatic expression found in black visual representations of popular music. The application and understanding of a theory about play is useful here.

Play is considered an experience or an act that is performed for its own sake, for pleasure or reward known as *flow*. The rewards for flow experience are said to be intrinsic, often marked by imaginative creativity, improvisation, and adventurousness—unbounded and fearless exploration.[6] Coincidentally, *flow* is the same word rappers in hip-hop culture use to characterize the creative energy they experience when writing, performing, or extemporaneously "freestyling" rhymes or spinning records. Flow is also used as a communal sensibility—"Me an' the crew was *flowin'* hard." Hip-hoppers also use flow to communicate the feeling of a never ending performance. Flow, in any case, is not simply about random improvisation, formless and idle. In considering play as cultural expression, we must avoid erroneous assumptions about a lack of formal ways of behaving and performing that lead to perceptions of randomness. Play does involve codes of formality. For example, the codes for play performance tend to readily allow for more individualized and improvisatory expression than is common to, for instance, recorded music (for play is not expected to be recreated relatively the same way in each performance). In play, variation or improvisation on several levels is a more prominent ideal of expression, just as in jazz or hip-hop improvisation.

"That's the Way We Flow": Girls' Musical Play[7]

Black girls' fancy footwork and skillful execution abound when turning the ropes of double-dutch. The skipping of the ropes, the sounds on the pavement, act as a timeline for musicalized gestures and rhymes. Musical creativity is learned and practiced through the body and voiced through tuneful rhymes sung in unison. Often these game songs feature verses that describe the "body musicking," (the act of making the body "dance") that accompanies the rhymes. The long practiced ring game known as "Little Sally Walker" is one example:

> Rise, Sally, rise!
> Wipe your weepin' eyes.
> Put your hands on your hip
> and let your backbone slip.
> Ahhh! Shake it to the east,
> Shake it to the west,
> Shake it to the very one that you love the best.

With each presentation and repetition of this verse, a new girl enters the center of the ring, into the gaze of her sisters in play. This game is also played by boys, but usually the game is performed by girls who share and imagine themselves through playful musical behavior. The girl in the center responds to the words of the verse as she acts out the role of Sally by shaking her "bass-heavy" hips to the east and west in her own stylish manner. Individual girls soon learn to experiment with snatches of steps observed among more experienced movers and shakers.

"Here [in a ring game] she need not fear the taboos of the 'serious' world, as she performs within the circle of friends whose actions and song continually cue her: 'This is play; do your thing.'"[8] This kind of expressive activity is rarely found among young black girls outside the ring in formal or public settings. To do so might seem out of place, as if showing off, which is not well regarded in certain public circumstances. Because social dance tends to thrive in adult settings, expressive social dance might be closely associated with adult sexual behavior or inspire the notion that such behavior carries sexualized meaning about its performer. Thus, the dance could be considered somewhat taboo.[9]

Shaking one's hips is central to many black dance styles, whether it be individualized dance or "hand-dancing"[10] characterized by constant hand-holding and turning between partners that is patterned after African-American dances—the Lindy Hop and jitterbug. The African-American social dances that allow for expression of individual style include the older forms of the 1950s and 1960s—the bop, the Twist, the Tightrope, the Dog, the Australian Slop—and more recent styles from the 1970s to the present—the Bump, the Smurf, the Womp, the Bogle, and the Pepperseed (these last two are Jamaican-derived via enclaves in New York City).

Girls graduate from ring games to hand-clapping. Hand-clapping games, in some urban areas, are actually known as "cheers" or "scolds," and among some groups of girls these games have no specific name at all. Hand-clapping games are played primarily by younger girls of generally the same age until the fifth or sixth grade. These games are played by two or four partners (the latter is called a "bridge"). Hand-clapping games are more complex than ring games because they require more specialized cooperative skill and an equitably shared knowledge among players. Hand-clapping play is structured by a repeated pattern that may include a series of clapping gestures (which incorporate individual clapping and motions cooperatively executed with a partner). Other gestures involve snapping one's fingers and a host of metrical motions involving slapping parts of the body to produce different timbres—knees, thighs, chest, head, mouth). Silences, especially accompanied by gestures, are also common to this play. Patterns of aural gestures usually articulate a four-beat time frame of strong and weak beats similar to most black popular music. For example, in hip-hop it is common to hear a four-beat pattern where a bass sound marks beats 1 and 3, while a treble-voiced sound marks beats 2 and 4.

Along with these motor skills must be learned a repertoire of synchronized musical tunes or songs. A tuneful melodic verse may or may not be accompanied by a refrain—a repeated text or phrase that recurs in a song or poem. The alternation of verse and chorus reflects a textual form of call and response common in most forms of popular music. Hand-clapping game songs, as well as double-dutch, may feature in part or throughout a tuneful declamatory style (using two to five pitches within a narrow range). This style closely resembles the melodic orientation of rapping found in hip-hop music: a narrow range of pitches used to carry the ideas of the narrative or theme synchronized with other musical activity such as segments of previously recorded music woven together by a disk jockey. In the case of hand-clapping games, cheers, and double-dutch, segments may be interchanged with material from other game-songs or may borrow musical ideas from popular and secular folk music.

In the melodic display of girls' game songs, the use of variable intonation of pitch, inflection and tone color, linguistic nuance, and rhythmic articulations of phonics reflects equally complex but different melodic sensibilities from those of music that employs expansive melodies of six to twelve pitches. It is rhythm that is heard most, and it is rhythm that has become synonymous with black music. However, rhythm is not the sole aspect of black musical sound that makes its sound "black."

An Identifiable Black Musical Style

Defining musical behavior as a reflection of racial identity has become a sensitive issue in musical circles. However, musicologists Samuel A. Floyd Jr., director of the Center for Black Music Research in Chicago, and Olly Wilson, a noted University of California composer and scholar, distinguish some of the traits of an identifiable black style. Floyd develops his framework from the evolution of a slave practice known as the ring shout.

> The shout was an early Negro "holy dance" in which "the circling about ... is the prime essential." ... [Participants performed] "jerking," "hitching" motions, particularly in the shoulders. These movements were usually accompanied by a spiritual, sung by lead singers, "based" by others in the group (probably with some kind of responsorial device and by hand-clapping and knee-slapping). The "thud" of the basic rhythm was continuous, without pause ... and the singing that took place in the shout made use of interjections of various kinds, elisions, blue-notes, and call-and-response devices, with the sound of the feet against the floor serving as an accompanying device.[11]

Wilson more specifically defines a set of conceptual approaches or tendencies in African-American musical style. Wilson's conceptional approaches include complex metrical textures, the performance of melodies sung like speech (or played in a percussive manner), frequently overlapping and sometimes complex call-and-response patterns, a high density of discrete musical events (especially the weaving of short motivic ideas with contrasting sound colors and textures), and the inseparability of music and dance and/or stylized movement as a part of the music-making process.[12]

We find many of these traits in girls' musical games. For example, the shapes and sizes of the parts of the body, the light or heavy stress placed on gestures and movement, can create a sound that represents the different musical timbres we are accustomed to hearing in the rhythm section of popular music. The hand claps can reflect the use of the snare drum on the backbeat (beats 2 and 4 of a four-beat pattern) or can be used for off-beat syncopation. As the feet stomp on pavement or a floor, the sound can resemble the thud or slap of a string or electric bass guitar. Of course, these traits could not be simply combined like a recipe for creating black music. Certain ingredients are learned culturally and contribute to a social interplay that cannot be dissected.

Other traits of music making or sounding "blackness" common to African-American and African diasporan music involve the incorporation of speechlike or raplike oral delivery as a form of melody; the incorporation of any musical sound or noise as music; and the nuances of vowel sounds and other phonations, including consonants, as pitched musical sound. The last point can be more readily understood as the exploitation of the brightness and darkness of vowels and consonants, the range of vocal or sound color that can include nasal qualities, huskiness, grittiness, smoothness, and so forth, that are shaped by certain phonetic combinations. The significance of language as musical sound is largely implicated in these last few traits. Some believe that this is a sign of the retention of the tonal variation of African languages, contributing to a "kaleidoscopic" variation in black musical expression or a "heterogeneous sound ideal."[13] This is more complicated than thinking black music is merely about rhythm. Black musical style is a marriage of rhythms of melodies, the body, and language.

Double-Dutch Jump Rope: Black Girls' Delight

Double-dutch is unique among traditional practices for African-American girls. It is performed by three to four girls at a time, but more can play by taking turns in rotation. It is often played on the side-walk, on an asphalt blacktop at a playground, or in the middle of the street. One extra-long rope—a clothesline—is all that is needed, but two ropes about ten feet long are ideal.

Two girls, designated turners, twirl the ropes so that they cut the air with a taut momentum. They alternately loop the ropes toward each other, creating an ellipsoidal space tall and wide enough for players to jump and perform stylized moves within it. One task of the turners, in addition to making sure the ropes do not stop turning, is to make constant adjustments so the space within the ropes fits the articulations of the moving bodies. Girls of varied body types excel at this play as both turners and jumpers. Double-dutch, like ring games and hand-clapping games, has a repertoire of songs that accompany it that draw from jingles, children's rhymes, and popular song.

> I went downtown
> To see James Brown.
> He gave me a nickel
> To buy a pickle.
> The pickle was sour.
> He gave me a flower.
> The flower was dead,
> So this is what he said:
> Hopping on one foot, one foot, one foot.
> Hopping on two foot, two foot, two foot.
> Hopping on three foot …
> Hopping on four foot … [14]

Although this game-song does not literally quote James Brown's music, the lyrics are clearly playing ideas about the "Godfather of Soul" with his emphatic dance and stage persona—"Dance on the good foot!"[15] Brown is the epitome of coordinating movement with a range of vocal expression, rhymes, and speech about movement.

Seizing the optimal moment to enter the circling ropes of double-dutch, one or two girls leap inside immediately, alternating their feet to avoid the skip of the ropes as they pass under them. The jumpers execute styles of movement, from simple to complex choreographed activity (which may or may not be dance) while continuing to shift their weight from the left foot to the right. If an arm or leg movement isn't timed well or is out of place, the rope will stop and the turn is over. The goal is to perpetuate jumping inside the ropes for as long as possible. At times, girls improvise a popular dance move (such as doing the Bump with a partner as they stay within the turning ropes). All movements, improvised or choreographed, must be "in time" with the metrical skips of the ropes—the musical time line. The skips against the pavement serve as a basic rhythmic pulsation, an inconspicuous and conscious rhythmic time line for both rhymes and somatic rhythms.

Double-dutch requires much more coordination, agility, strength, and sensitivity to kinesthetic timing in the body than other girls' games. The body is constantly in motion, resisting and reacting to the gravity pull of the incessant jumping over the turning ropes. It is truly a concerted and musical effort on the part of the jumper(s) and the turners. Although jumpers and turners can be interchangeable, many girls tend to specialize in jumping or turning. But all girls memorize the tuneful rhymes that accompany the practice.

As girls grow older, the musical lessons that were learned, memorized, and danced through the various musical *études* of girls' play are transformed again and again into newer and more mature or adult social activities. They may be employed in the cheerleading associated with male varsity sports in junior and senior high school, and later at some colleges. Here, girls still may be able to compose new cheers in the black style of their former activities, and many of these cheers are then circulated among other cheerleading squads over time and around the country. An apparent difference occurs at these levels due to the interracial and intercultural interactions of institutional education. One is more likely to find black styles of cheerleading in urban areas or at predominantly and historically black institutions. Also, in college and university settings, African-American women may employ their skills in the service of a black Greek-letter organization (sororities such as Alpha Kappa Alpha, Delta Sigma Theta, and Sigma Gamma Rho) where "step shows" are common to group expression in black social settings. Throughout African-American women's lives, dancing may incorporate the lessons of girls' games through the constantly evolving styles of black "street" expression. "Doing your thing" has no age limit and can become quite serious even in its playfulness.

The many black women I have interviewed about the musical experiences during their lives support the cultural opinion that black girls see themselves as active and primary agents of the tradition of hand-clapping games, cheers, and particularly double-dutch. There is a way in which black girls make meaning of these activities that differs from other groups, though there may be commonalities. These activities clearly are connected to musical expression—singing, rhyming, dancing, and rapping. Girls' games encode group identity through the use of idiomatic black linguistics and cultural images.

"Here Come the Lady with the African Booty": Gestures toward Sexuality in Girls' Games

In her assessments of women, gender, and music, ethnomusicologist Ellen Koskoff is not surprised that the "majority of existing descriptions of women's musical activities and rationales for their behavior focus on [women's] primary social roles, for these roles are central to women's gender identity."[16] African-American women's gendered social roles have been plagued by myths about their sexuality (the mythical image of a sexually insatiable Jezebel comes to mind), myths about teenage pregnancy and single motherhood, myths about black women as matriarchs (evoking the image of the ugly Sapphire who usurps men's dominance), myths about black women's incompetence as mothers unable to raise their sons "right," and exaggerated myths about black women's marketability in the workplace relative to black men in a racist society. All of these stereotypes of black female identity contribute to the difficulty (the downright *unattractiveness*) of viewing or hearing the musical activities of black girls and women as reflecting authority and expertise in black music making.

It is through the autonomous experiences of women who once played and performed cheers among themselves—as opposed to standing saddle-shoed on the sidelines of boys' or men's activities—who once played hand-clapping games, who once enjoyed ring games, and who thrilled at trying and sometimes even failing at double-dutch, that we can recoup women's musical participation as a sign of "flow." We are beginning to see how the musical aspects of these games are transmitted, but how are these musical activities interpreted through the socialized assumptions about race and gender? Given the myths about black women's sexuality and their "dysfunctional" roles, are these games (with their musicalized gestures, dance, and behavior) interpreted as "sexual"? Are girls playing with proverbial fire? Koskoff writes:

> Sexuality, both self- and other-defined, affects music performance in three important ways: (1) performance environments may provide a context for sexually explicit behavior, such that music performance becomes a metaphor for sexual relations; (2) the actual or perceived loss of sexuality may change women's musical roles and/or statuses; and (3) cultural beliefs in women's inherent sexuality may motivate the separation of or restriction imposed upon women's musical activities; … young girls, older women, homosexual and "marginal" women (i.e., those who may be of childbearing years but are perceived as if "sexless" for other reasons)—may assume certain musical roles that deny or negate their sexuality.[17]

Let us look at two examples of sexual references in the lyrics of hand-clapping games played by African-American girls. In these games black girls play freely with idioms of sexuality. "Mailman, Mailman" was recorded by Carol Merrill-Mirsky from an eight-year-old African-American girl, Devonne, at King Elementary School in Los Angeles. I recorded "I'm a Nut" from twin sisters Jasmine and Stephanie in a predominantly African-American suburb of Detroit.[18]

> Mailman, mailman, do your duty,
> Here come the lady with da African booty.
> She can do da wah-wah, she can do da splits,
> She can do anything to make you split, so split!

On the surface Devonne's song frames the power of a black woman's "African" butt (or "booty" in the black vernacular). The mailman, doing his job by delivering the mail (male), is being warned about this Africanized (read: primal?) black woman who can do all kinds of tricks to make him succumb to her whim. It is not surprising that girls' games reflect stereotypical racial and gender ideology. However, girls are obviously employing these lyrics as a positive and playful identification. Maybe this game-song is symbolically calling attention to the advanced skill and performative traditions of girls playing hand-clapping games or dancing—countering the power of one kind of work with the power of displaying styles—dance. There is an obvious possibility that black female movement can overpower male duty. This game-song exploits the powerful meanings of movement and display in the black female body.

This is articulated through third-person narration and rhyme. The power of the body is matched by the powerful idioms of sexuality—words that convey an ineffable activity (the "wah-wah"). The "wah-wah" clearly alludes to powerful movement involving "da African booty." The "wah-wah" might have a vague but racial-musical connection to the dance called the Watusi that supposedly imitated the Tutsi ethnic dances of Rwanda and Burundi.[19]

Hazel Carby recalls that at one time illicit sexual behavior was a "natural" consequence of certain modern forms of dancing in black social contexts.[20] Such perceptions in the late 1920s led to moral panic among whites and middle-class blacks concerning black women's lack of control over their sexual behavior or displays of sexuality. Such displays offended upper-class sensibilities and were considered "pathological" and in need of institutional control. If black urban life was synonymous with "commercialized vice," then urban women were precariously at risk. In girls' game playing, beyond any institutional control, sexual behavior and references to sex are neutralized and do not reflect actual behavior. "Doing your thing" here does not mean doing *the* thing, having sex.

In the second example, the implication of sexuality again surfaces. A wildness of behavior is captured and expressed through the words and movements. The girls perform a series of hand claps that involve slapping the chest, which is an unusual gesture in most hand-clapping games. But the chest slaps effectively sound a bass-heavy thud characteristic of black popular music's emphasis on beats 1 and 3.

> I'm a nut [answered by clapping patterns highlighted by chest slaps]
> In a hut [clapped response]
> I met my boyfriend [indecipherable]
> This was interrupted by "Jasmine! Stop!" They regrouped and started again.
> I'm a nut
> In a hut
> I stole my mommy's pockie-book.
> I'm cra—zy!
> I'm foo—lish!
> I'm burning, burning, hot ta hot.
> I'm burning, burning, hot ta hot.
> I'm burning, burning, hot ta hot, SO WHAT!

Jasmine and Stephanie performed these games under their mother's watchful eye. They executed a series of different hand-clapping games for me without pause, with the exception of "I'm a nut." Here they seemed to stop and correct themselves in certain places (apparently in a conscious effort to censor their play under their mother's "religious" eye). Stephanie initiated the censoring. If the phrases had not been censored, there would appear to have been a kind of erotic-erasure inherent in the game itself (without Stephanie's help). The "so what!" erases the possibility of taking what came before seriously. These nine-year-old girls had previously shared their awareness of male genitalia when relating a bit of gossip from school: another girl accused Jasmine of touching a classmate's "thing." During their performance of "I'm a nut," therefore, I was aware that they knew something about sexuality.

In a study on dance among women in Trinidad, Daniel Miller notes that when women express signs of heterosexual behavior among themselves away from men (or in this case a mother), it is not about sex or directed toward men, it is autosexuality.[21] African-American girl's games, like the dance among Trinidadian women at Carnival, make *use* of the idiom of sexuality rather than being *about* sexuality.[22] Miller asserts, "Symptomatic of a more general avoidance of institutionalized relationships … there develops a more flexible moral code which allows affectivity to emerge through the construction rather than the fulfillment of a relationship."[23]

As an oral-kinetic *étude*, "I'm a Nut" highlights the musical interaction of the vocal line and the body musicking. Although the metrical structure appears to be in four-four time, the metrical orientation does not lend itself to a quantitative conception of time—counting "one-two-three-four." The reiterated kinetic experience associated with the body-musicking is marked by the sensation and visual appearance of the emphatic chest slaps. Snarelike hand claps fall on beats 2 and 4, in alternation with the heavy-toned chest slaps on 1 and 3. The body musicking works in tandem with the vocal part on two levels. On one level, there is a call and response, a dialogue, between the vocal part and the body musicking. On another level, the risqué text—"I'm burnin', burnin' hot-ta-hot"—works in tandem with the musical tension experienced aurally and kinetically. Sexuality, as it is obliquely apparent in hip-hop texts, plays a critical role in shaping musical aesthetics within a performance event that is not explicitly about sexual relations. But "I'm a Nut" (as well as Jasmine's and Stephanie's specific performance of it) does allow girls to safely and freely voice and play out real and imagined ways of being black, female, and sexual through cultural musical expression.

The Transformation and Re-Interpretation of Women's Participation in the Culture: The Case of Double-Dutch

> Jibber this, and jibber that,
> Jibber kill the alley cat.[24]

In the early 1970s, there were concerns about the idle minds *and bodies* of girls in the streets and neighborhoods of New York City. In the streets, girls are "in trouble," a code reference to girls' sexual activity and, oftentimes, consequent pregnancy. In response to these concerns, in 1973 two officers of the New York City Police Department, David Walker and Ulysses Williams, who served in the Harlem community affairs division, initiated formalized double-dutch competitions and tournaments. By 1975, Walker and others had formed the American Double-Dutch League (ADDL), which now conducts local, national, and international competitions every year. Groups such as the 4-H Club, the Girl Scouts, the Salvation Army, and various justice and police recreational departments have sponsored teams during the league's twenty-year history.

When Walker was considering an avenue for channeling girls' behavior, he noticed how black girls in the city liked to show off while playing double-dutch and observed that they liked to teach each other rhymes. He was sincerely concerned that girls did not have a citywide athletic event. Boys had basketball, football, and baseball. Then he remembered his sister, who had spent hours playing double-dutch as a child.[25]

Walker commented in an interview that young inner-city girls "are loners, going from toys to boys at an early age."[26] The implication of Walker's rhyme is that *toys* (employed in the play activities of younger girls) are transformed into another sort of game playing with *boys* as girls get older. The detective's words also echo stereotypical perceptions that apply to female fandom in rap music—girls and women chasing after male rap stars rather than nurturing a "real" appreciation or understanding of the creativity and production (the work) involved in rap music. Women's participation is reduced to being about the play of "catching a man"—sexual relationships and sexual politics ("Here come the lady with da African booty"). These are the games African-American women play according to the hegemonic discourse of rap.

Walker and Williams applied a set of rules and guidelines (written by Williams) that formalized the double-dutch tournaments. By 1995, the cost of the rule book was $30. In order to compete, official ADDL ropes must be purchased, only athletic wear is allowed in competition, and each singles or doubles team is required to have a parental sponsor. As of 1980, the rules allow for the inclusion of boys (one boy allowed per singles team, two boys per doubles team).[27] The competition requires participation in compulsory rounds and freestyle rounds not unlike athletic competition in ice skating or gymnastics. Each double-dutch team must qualify to move on to compete in the final rounds. Within the compulsory competition, the officers devised a speed element (likely as a result of their interest in transforming the game into a sport). In street double-dutch, the idea of absolute speed (speed for speed's sake) was never highly regarded. Rather, the appeal was the adventure and skill of cooperative play among black girls. Brought together by school, neighborhood, or other kinship systems, girls develop a repertoire of old and new game songs in which improvised choreography and rhymes structure the adventure. Officers Walker and Williams named the acts executed in the freestyle competition *tricks*, akin to acrobatic feats. The rule book encourages teams to use various props (batons, balls, extra ropes, etc.).[28] Translating double-dutch from the street to the stage of competitive sport ultimately precipitated the loss of the rhymed songs that were integral to girls' games. In my interviews with David Walker and organizers of the ADDL competition, I heard no explanation for the loss of the verbal dimension of double-dutch.[29] I concluded that organizers consciously or unconsciously disapproved of the sexualized expression of many of the game songs. Organizers might have been making a conscious effort to make double-dutch accessible to girls (and later boys) of all ethnic and racial groups.

Institutionalizing the sport, with all the equipment, cross-country travel, and a $30 rule book, situates adults at the center of the perpetuation and arbitration of double-dutch. These adults are often parents and justice and police officers who wish to create a "respectable" sport for competition. The theme for the 1995 World Invitational competition was "Rope, not Dope." Making double-dutch a "sport" has transformed girls' games possibly in response to fears about what African-American girls do with leisure time. Leisure time (once play time) becomes a dangerous period for girls entering puberty. Sexuality and its meanings for African-American women also get transformed and reinterpreted in the context of hip-hop music despite female participation in hip-hop through double-dutch.

The first presentation of rap overseas was a European tour in 1982 featuring representative subcultural expressions from New York City. "Also aboard [the New York City Rap Tour] were the breakdancing Rock Steady Crew, *the Double Dutch Girls*, and the graffiti artists."[30] With the emergence of rap as recorded music in 1979, public interest peeked into hip-hop culture and its performative street culture and dance party scene performed by the "troubled" youth of the South Bronx (and soon thereafter other New York boroughs).[31] Since the early 1980s, the expressive acts of hip-hop have been generally cast as male. By the mid-1990s, girls' double-dutch rope jumping would no longer appear to be emblematic of hip-hop culture and would rarely, if ever again, appear as part of a bill for a touring rap concert. Ironically, even female rappers seem to disregard girls' musical activities as generally reflective of black musical aesthetics or hip-hop aesthetics. One of the few examples of recognition in a hip-hop magazine of the 1990s was expressed by Leslie Segar, a top hip-hop choreographer. Segar noted in a 1993 interview that double-dutch represented an "old school" influence that contributes to hip-hop choreography.[32] One way to understand the "erasure" of double-dutch from the collective memory of hip-hop culture is as the result of the politics of gender, the masculinization of rap. The imposition of masculinity and maleness on conceptions of music performance has been challenged only as a matter of nonmusical history.[33] Assumptions about gender in black music contribute to the belief that males and females have different musical spheres and experiences. In the black popular culture of the 1990s, nowhere is this more evident than in rap music and hip-hop culture. Most rap artists signed to major recording labels are men, most disk jockeys are men, and most fans have been characterized as men. The culture has been documented almost exclusively by men, through male experience, which has led to obvious assumptions that hip-hop culture is exclusive to African-American urban men (erasing not only women's contribution to its origins but also that of Latinos, West Indians, and whites).

Consequently, hip-hop culture has become associated with earlier expressive forms and traditions thought to also be exclusive to black men. Anthropologists collected linguistic practices primarily among African-American men on urban streets involving rhymes, indirection, and metaphor, such as "the dozens" or "cappin'." Rapping as it is expressed in hip-hop music was influenced by these and other antecedents involving tuned and inflected vocal expressivity—the "spiritual" sermon tradition, the rhymes and jive-talk of black radio disk jockeys, and even the poetic banter of Muhammed Ali (former world heavyweight boxing champion). These so-called progenitors of rapping all are connected to constructions of black male authority and privilege—the leader of the black church, the voice and musical personality of black radio, and the male bravado and physical power of black male athletes. Re-remembering these histories as "male" ritualizes and reproduces patriarchal ideologies within and outside black communities.

If one sees the interconnectedness of the black musical activities in both cultural and commercial settings, then an analysis of black girls' games suggests a reinterpretation of women's participation in contemporary hip-hop culture. This perspective is important, given the rampant criticism of misogyny and misrepresentations of women in both commercial and "underground" rap music. If one accepts that the music of hip-hop culture embodies and articulates musical activities that are common to African-American girls' experience, then women's reception of rap might serve as a vehicle for remembering (consciously or subconsciously) their own distinctly female-oriented musical experiences. This explains women's participation as the recovery of a distinctly female mode of expression within a "male" domain of commercial production. It is the ideological power of maleness in a mass-mediated hip-hop culture that makes it so difficult to fully appreciate African-American women's creative and expressive participation as anything other than subsidiary to men's. From such a distorted viewpoint, women are simply perceived as acting out myths and stereotypes. Girls and women play and live out their lives through a complex form of identity politics that questions prevailing constructions of maleness and femaleness.

This masculinized view of rap places female participants in rap and hip-hop culture in the precarious position of being attracted to a musical expression that is apparently "bad" for them, that "talks bad" about them, and therefore diminishes their social capacity and respectability as African-American women. Therein, silence is golden. Women appear as mute and unconscious daughters of the hip-hop revolution. Equipped in this distorted reality with an entire body of methods and meanings ("niggaz," "bytches," booty-shaking, hip-gyrating, singing, and speakingly vulgarly), black girls and women are actually excavating hidden treasures—girls' games.

Conclusion: Can There Be a Way of "Sounding" Black Woman-ness in Musical Behavior?

Olly Wilson described African-Americans' approach to style as a way of making music *sound* "blackness."[34] If "blackness" has been constructed in letters and literature and in very public music performance as primarily male, we can reinterpret "blackness" in music by considering the not-so-public music making of women and girls. In cultural settings where meanings are not solely defined by written and recorded discourse, "blackness" can include and be represented by women and their gendered experience. This view offers a rare opportunity to reinscribe women's musical experience into making music *sound* "blackness" and "femaleness." The apparent emphasis on male authority, male performance, and exclusively male social experiences in the institutionalization of rap music has nearly eclipsed the presence and performance of girls and women.

The games that African-American girls play suggest that both women and girls should recognize signs of their own private play in hip-hop music in addition to hearing it as an expression of black male life. Stuart Hall defines popular culture as the site "where we discover and play with the identifications of ourselves, where we are imagined, where we are represented, not only to the audiences out there who do not get the message, but to ourselves for the first time."[35] Women often must look beyond the publicness of popular culture to fully and playfully imagine their identities. When this is accomplished, African-American women will recognize the male *and* the female in their appreciation of rap music.

Notes

1. Rainwater 1970, 220.
2. Brady 1975, 9.
3. *Etudes* usually refers to musical exercises in written form underlining a melodic, rhythmic, or technical skill intended for application to "real" performances.
4. This essay is based on research conducted for my doctoral dissertation. In addition to field work investigating girls' play, I include oral interviews concerning the musical experiences of African-American women (ages 18–56) born in U.S. cities such as New York, Chicago, Memphis, Pittsburgh, Washington, D.C., and Detroit. See Gaunt 1995, 1997.
5. Brown and Newsome 1991. Composed in 1965, this song is attributed to both Betty Newsome and James Brown; however, Newsome claims she composed it herself and Brown simply "rearranged it" (White and Bronson 1993, 17).
6. Csikszentmihalyi and Csikszentmihalyi 1988, 29.
7. "That's the Way We Flow" refers to Queen Latifah 1991.
8. Brady 1975, 9.
9. Black social dance styles may occur simultaneously in sacred and secular settings.
10. Friedland (1993, 69) documents local opinion holding that "hand-dancing," a black social dance, was developed in Washington, D.C., during the Motown era beginning in the 1950s. The rapid transmission of black dance styles across the country since then has been advanced by (1) black migration between the North and the South and along the East Coast, (2) televised local and national dance shows, as well as (3) popular touring acts on the "Chitlin' Circuit" and other touring networks. Similar claims concerning "hand-dancing" might be made by blacks in other cities.
11. Floyd 1991, 266.
12. Wilson 1992, 328–29.
13. Wilson 1992.
14. Riddell 1990, 138–40.
15. Ibid.
16. Koskoff 1987, 4.
17. Ibid., 6.
18. Merrill-Mirsky 1988, 179, 213.
19. My mother, who grew up in Washington, D.C., recalls this vernacular dance among her teenage peers in the 1950s. She also recalls that a popular song accompanied the dance with the refrain "Wah-wah-tusi."
20. Carby 1992.
21. Miller 1991, 333.
22. Ibid., 335.
23. Ibid., 331.
24. Jones and Hawes 1972, 45.
25. Walker and Haskins 1986, 15.
26. Goodwin 1980, 87.
27. Walker and Haskins 1986, 26.
28. Ibid., 54.
29. David Walker is no longer directly affiliated with the ADDL and has initiated another double-dutch organization, the International Double-Dutch League.
30. Adler and Beckman 1991, 17, emphasis added.

31. I date the formulation of an identifiable hip-hop culture as sometime between 1971 and 1973, according to information from several primary sources, although many aspects of the culture—rapping, certain dance patterns, graffiti—previously existed (George 1985; Toop 1991; Eure and Spady 1991).
32. Allah 1993, 48.
33. See Brown 1994.
34. Wilson 1992.
35. Hall 1992, 32.

References

Adler, Bill, and Janette Beckman (1991) *Rap: Portraits and Lyrics of a Generation of Black Rockers*, St. Martin's Press, New York.

Allah, Bilal (1993) Hip-hop's Fly Choreographers, *Rap Pages*, August, 48–51.

Brady, Margaret K. (1975) 'This Little Lady's Gonna Boogaloo': Elements of Socialization in the Play of Black Girls in *Black Girls at Play: Folkloristic Perspectives on Child Development*, 11–56. Austin, Tex.: Early Elementary Program, Southwest Educational Development Laboratory.

Brown, Elsa Barkley (1994) Negotiating and Transforming the Public Sphere: African American Political Life in the Transition from Slavery to Freedom,. *Public Culture 7* (fall): 107–146.

Brown, James, and Betty Newsome (1991) It's a Man's Man's Man's World, *20 All-Time Greatest Hits.* Performed by James Brown. Compact Disc. Polydor 314 511 326-2 (1965, King Records, 6035).

Carby, Hazel V. (1992) Policing the Black Woman's Body in an Urban Context, *Critical Inquiry 18* (summer): 738–755.

Csikszentmihaly, Mihaly, and I.S. Csikszentmihaly (1988) *Optimal Experience: Psychological Studies of Flow in Consciousness.* Cambridge: Cambridge University Press.

Eure, Joseph D., and J.G. Spady (1991) *Nation Conscious Rap*, PC International Press, Philadelphia.

Floyd, Samuel A., Jr. (1991) Ring Shout! Literary Studies, Historical Studies, and Black Music Inquiry, *Black Music Research Journal* (fall): 265–287.

Friedland, Lee Ellen (1993) Generations of African American Social Dance in Washington, D.C.: Hand Dancing, Hip-Hop, and Go-Go in *1993 Festival of American Folklife, July 1–July 5 1993*, 69–72. Smithsonian Institution, Washington.

Gaunt, Kyra D. (1995) African-American Women from Hopscotch to Hip-Hop in Angharad Valdi (ed) *Feminism, Multiculturalism, and the Media: Global Diversities*, Sage Publications, Thousand Oaks

———. (1997) The Games Black Girls Play: Music, Body, and 'Soul.' Ph.D. diss., University of Michigan.

George, Nelson (1985) *Fresh: Hip-Hop Don't Stop.* Random House, New York.

Hall, Stuart (1990) Cultural Identity and Diaspora in Jonathan Rutherford (ed) *Identity: Community, Culture, Difference*, Lawrence and Wishart, London.

Jones, Bessie, and Bess Lomax Hawes (1972) *Step It Down: Games, Plays, Songs and Stories from Afro-American Heritage*, Harper and Row, New York.

Koskoff, Ellen (1987) An Introduction to Women, Music, and Culture in *Women and Music in Cross-Cultural Perspective*, 1–23, University of Illinois Press, Urbana.

Merrill-Mirsky, Carol (1988) Eeny Meeny Pepsadeeny: Ethnicity and Gender in Children's Musical Play, Ph.D. diss., University of California, Los Angeles.

Miller, Daniel (1991) Absolute Freedom in Trinidad, *Man* n.s. 26 (June): 323–341.

Rainwater, Lee (1970) *Behind Ghetto Walls*, University of Chicago Press, Chicago.

Riddell, Cecelia (1990) Traditional Singing Games of Elementary School Children in Los Angeles, Ph.D. diss., University of California, Los Angeles.

Toop, David (1991) *Rap Attack 2: African Rap to Global Hip Hop*, 2nd ed., Serpent's Tail, New York.

Walker, David, and James Haskins (1986) *Double Dutch*. Enslow Publications, Hillside, N.J.

White, Adam, and Fred Bronson (1993) *The Billboard Book of Number One Rhythm and Blues Hits*, Billboard Books, New York.

Wilson, Olly (1992) The Heterogeneous Sound Ideal in African-American Music in Josephine Wright (ed) with Samuel Floyd, 327–338 *New Perspectives on Music: Essays in Honor or Eileen Southern*, Harmonie Park Press, Warren, Mich.

21

Empowering Self,
Making Choices, Creating Spaces:

Black Female Identity via Rap Music Performance

Cheryl L. Keyes

Critics and scholars have often associated rap music with urban male culture. However, females have been involved in the history of this music since its early years. This article explores Black women's contribution to and role in shaping rap music. In examining female rappers, this study engages an interdisciplinary model that employs cultural studies, feminist theory, and mass mediation theory of popular culture, and it employs an ethnographic concept, the "interpretive community," in its analysis.

Observers of rap music began to notice the proliferation of successful female rap acts during the 1990s. Though rap has often been presented as a male-dominated form by the media, women have been a part of the rap scene since its early commercial years. In general, "females were always into rap, had their little crews and were known for rocking parties, schoolyards, whatever it was; and females rocked just as hard as males [but] the male was just first to be put on wax [record]" (Pearlman 1988:26). Rap music journalist Havelock Nelson notes, "While women have always been involved artistically with rap throughout the '80s, artists like [MC] Lyte, [Queen] Latifah, Roxanne Shanté, and [Monie] Love have had to struggle to reach a level of success close to that of male rappers" (1993:77). Challenging male rappers' predominance, female rap artists have not only proven that they have lyrical skills; in their struggle to survive and thrive within this tradition, they have created spaces from which to deliver powerful messages from Black female and Black feminist perspectives.

Data utilized in this study derive from interviews (1993–1996) with "cultural readers" (Bobo 1995)—African American female performers, audience members, and music critics—referred to in this essay as an "interpretive community." In *Black Women as Cultural Readers*, film critic–scholar Jacqueline Bobo explores the concept of "interpretive community" as a movement comprising Black female cultural producers, critics and scholars, and cultural consumers (1995:22). She writes,

> As a group, the women make up what I have termed an interpretive community, which is strategically placed in relation to cultural works that either are created by black women or feature them in significant ways. Working together the women utilize representations of black women that they deem valuable in productive and politically useful ways. (1995:22)

Because much of the criticism of Black female independent film makers' works stems from male or white perspectives, Bobo finds it necessary to distinguish the interpretive community—Black women involved in making or consuming these films—in order to accurately determine the actual intent and effect of these films. Bobo's thesis of the interpretive commu-nity is appropriate to this examination of women in rap because rap music is a form transmitted by recorded and video performances. More importantly, the classifications of women rappers are based on the constructions of an interpretive community, as observed via recorded perfor-mance and personal interviews. When rapper MC Lyte was asked, for example, if she felt that there is a distinct female rap category, she separated women rappers into three groups, referred to as "crews," reigning in three periods—the early 1980s, the mid-1980s through the early 1990s, and the late 1990s: "Sha-Rock, Sequence, to me, that's the first crew. Then you got a second crew, which is Salt-N-Pepa, Roxanne Shanté, The Real Roxanne, me, Latifah, Monie [Love], and Yo-Yo.... Then after that you got Da Brat, Foxy Brown, Lil' Kim, Heather B" (1996).[1]

Queried about specific categories, both rap music performers and female audience members frequently used the buzzwords *fly* and *attitude* (as in "girlfriend got attitude"), leading me to more clearly discern the parameters of categories. My initial category of "Black Diva" in early interviews for the grand posture of these women was later revised to "Queen Mother" after one female observer convincingly said *diva* denotes a posture of arrogance and pretentiousness as opposed to that of a regal and self-assured woman, qualities that she iden-tified with the Queen Latifah types (see Penrice 1995).

In the female rap tradition, four distinct categories of women rappers emerge in rap music performance: "Queen Mother," "Fly Girl," "Sista with Attitude," and "Lesbian." Black female rappers can, however, shift between these categories or belong to more than one simultaneously. More importantly, each category mirrors certain images, voices, and lifestyles of African American women in contemporary urban society. Let us now examine the four categories or images of Black women introduced to rap by specific female rappers or emcees (MCs) and considered by the interpretive community in general as representative of and specific to African American female identity in contemporary urban culture.

Queen Mother

The "Queen Mother" category comprises female rappers who view themselves as African-centered icons, an image often suggested by their dress. In their lyrics, they refer to themselves as "Asiatic Black women," "Nubian queens," "intelligent Black women," or "sistas droppin' science to the people," suggestive of their self-constructed identity and intellectual prowess. The "queen mother" is, however, associated with African traditional court culture. For instance, in the 16th-century Benin Kingdom of southeastern Nigeria, she was the mother of a reigning king. Because of her maternal connection to the king, she garnered certain rights and privileges, including control over districts and a voice in the national affairs of the state. During his reign, a commemorative head made of brass was sculpted in her honor adorned with a beaded choker, headdress, and crown, along with a facial expression capturing her reposed manner.[2]

It is certainly possible that female rap artists may know of the historical significance of African queens; women in this category adorn their bodies with royal or Kente cloth strips, African headdresses, goddess braid styles, and ankh-stylized jewelry. Their rhymes embrace Black female empowerment and spirituality, making clear their self-identification as African, woman, warrior, priestess, and queen. Queen mothers demand respect not only for their people but for Black women, who are "to be accorded respect by ... men," observes Angela Y. Davis (1998:122). Among those women distinguished by the interpretive community as Queen Mother types are Queen Kenya, Queen Latifah, Sister Souljah, Nefertiti, Queen Mother Rage, Isis, and Yo-Yo.

Queen Kenya, a member of hip-hop's Zulu Nation, was the first female MC to use *Queen* as a stage name.[3] But the woman of rap who became the first solo female MC to commercially record under the name "Queen" is Dana "Queen Latifah" Owens. Queen Latifah's initial singles "Princess of the Posse" and "Wrath of My Madness" (1988), followed by her debut album *All Hail the Queen* (1989), established her regal identity. They include such lyrics as, "You try to be down, you can't take my crown from me," and, "I'm on the scene, I'm the Queen of Royal Badness." Latifah, whose Arabic name means "feminine, delicate, and kind," explains the origin of her stage name:

> My cousin, who's Muslim, gave me that name [Latifah] when I was eight. Well [in rap], I didn't want to be MC Latifah. It didn't sound right. I didn't want to come out like old models. So *queen* just popped into my head one day, and I was like, "Me, Queen Latifah." It felt good saying it, and I felt like a queen. And you know, I am a queen. And every Black woman is a queen. (1993)

Latifah's maternal demeanor, posture, and full figure contribute to the perception of her as a queen mother. Although Queen Latifah acknowledges that others perceived her as motherly even at age 21, she tries to distance herself from the label: "I wish I wasn't seen as a mother, though. I don't really care for that. Just because I take a mature stance on certain things, it gives me a motherly feel … maybe because I am full-figured. I am mature, but I'm twenty-one" (quoted in Green 1991:33). The ambiguity of Latifah's motherly image follows what feminist scholars Joan Radner and Susan Lanser identify as a form of coding in women's folk culture called *distraction*: a device used to "drown out or draw attention away from the subversive power of a feminist message" (1993:15). Queen Latifah finds that her stature and grounded perspective cause fans to view her as a maternal figure or as a person to revere or, at times, fear. However, Latifah attempts to mute her motherly image offstage, as evidenced in the above interview, indicating to fans that she remains, nonetheless, a modest, down-to-earth, and ordinary person in spite of her onstage "Queen of Royal Badness" persona.

Despite the ambiguity, Queen Latifah represents a particular type of mother figure to her audience. In *Black Feminist Thought*, sociologist Patricia Hill Collins recognizes that, in the African American community, some women are viewed as "othermothers." Collins explains.

> Black women's involvement in fostering African-American community development forms the basis for community-based power. This is the type of "strong Black woman" they see around them in traditional African-American communities. Community othermothers work on behalf of the Black community by expressing ethics of caring and personal accountability which embrace conceptions of transformative and mutuality … community othermothers become identified as power figures through furthering the community's well-being. (1990:132)

Queen Latifah's othermother posture is no doubt reflected most vividly through her lyrics, which, at times, address political-economic issues facing Black women and the Black community as a whole. In Latifah's song "The Evil that Men Do" (1989) from *All Hail the Queen*, "she isolates several of the difficulties commonly experienced by young black women [on welfare]" (Forman 1994:44) and shows how the powers that be are apathetic to Black women who are trying to beat the odds:

> Here is a message from my sisters and brothers, here are some things I wanna cover.
> A woman strives for a better life
> but who the hell cares because she's living on welfare.
> The government can't come up with a decent housing plan
> so she's in no man's land

it's a sucker who tells you you're equal …
Someone's livin' the good life tax-free
'cause some poor girl can't be livin' crack free
and that's just part of the message
I thought I should send you about the evil that men do. (quoted in Forman 1994:44)

Another example of Queen Latifah's role as queen mother of rap resonates in her platinum single "Ladies First" (1989), ranked in the annals of rap music history as the first political commentary rap song by a female artist. The lyrics of "Ladies First" respond primarily to males who believe that females cannot create rhymes:

Some think that we [women] can't flow
Stereotypes they got to go.
I gonna mess around and flip the scene into reverse
With a little touch of ladies first.

The video version is far more political, containing live footage of South Africa's apartheid riots overlaid with photographic stills of Black heroines—Winnie Mandela, Rosa Parks, Angela Davis, Harriet Tubman, and Madame C.J. Walker.[4] Pan-Africanism is tacitly evoked with these images—South Africa's political struggle against segregation and a salute to Winnie Mandela, the mother of this struggle, who is presented among U.S. Black women—reminders of Black liberation. Additionally, the bond between Black women in the United States and the United Kingdom is alluded to through the appearance of Monie Love of England, whom Queen Latifah refers to as "my European partner." These images locate Latifah as a queen mother and equal partner among those Black queens who struggled for the freedom of Black people.

Perceived by the interpretive community as a queen mother of rap, Queen Latifah opened the doors for other Afrocentric female MCs, such as Sister Souljah. Souljah, a former associate of the Black nationalist rap group Public Enemy, launched her first LP in 1992. The LP, *360 Degrees of Power*, features the rap single "The Final Solution: Slavery's Back in Effect," in which "Souljah imagines a police state where blacks fight the reinstitution of slavery" (Leland 1992:48). With her candid and somewhat quasipreachy style of delivery, she earned the title "raptivist" from her followers. Souljah's fame grew after her speech at the Reverend Jesse Jackson's Rainbow Coalition Leadership Summit in 1992, where she chided African Americans who murder one another for no apparent reason by figuratively suggesting, "Why not take a week and kill white people[?]" (Leland 1992:48). As a consequence, Souljah was ridiculed as a propagator of hate by presidential candidate Bill Clinton. In the wake of the controversy, her record sales plummeted dramatically while her "raptivist" messages skyrocketed with television appearances on talk shows like *The Phil Donahue Show* and speeches on the university lecture circuit. While Sister Souljah advocates racial, social, and economic parity in her rap messages, she also looks within the community to relationship issues between Black men and women in her lyrics and her semiautobiographical book *No Disrespect* (1994:xiv).

Although Nefertiti, Isis, and Queen Mother Rage are categorized as queen mothers via their names, lyrics, or attire, female rapper Yo-Yo is also regarded by the interpretive community as a queen mother.[5] Her lyrics illustrate her political ideology of Black feminism and female respectability, as advanced by her organization, the Intelligent Black Women Coalition (I.B.W.C.), which she discusses on her debut LP *Make Way for the Motherlode* (1991). But Yo-Yo's image—long auburn braids and very short tight-fitting *pum-pum* shorts (worn by Jamaican dance hall women performers)—and her gyrating hip dancing also position her in the next category, "Fly Girl."

Fly Girl

Fly describes someone in chic clothing and fashionable hairstyles, jewelry, and cosmetics, a style that grew out of the blaxploitation films of the late 1960s through the mid-1970s. These films include *Shaft* (1971), *Superfly* (1972), *The Mack* (1973), and *Foxy Brown* (1974), a film that inspired one MC to adopt the movie's title as her moniker. The fly persona in these films influenced a wave of Black contemporary youth who, in turn, resurrected flyness and its continuum in hip-hop culture. During the early 1980s, women rappers, including Sha Rock of Funky Four Plus One, the trio Sequence, and soloist Lady B, dressed in what was then considered by their audiences as fly.

They wore short skirts, sequined fabric, high-heeled shoes, and prominent makeup. By 1985, the hip-hop community further embraced the fly image via the commercial recording of "A Fly Girl," by the male rap group Boogie Boys, and an answer rap during the same year, "A Fly Guy," by female rapper Pebblee-Poo. The Boogie Boys describe a fly girl as a woman "who wants you to see her name, her game and her ability"; to do so, "she sports a lot of gold, wears tight jeans, leather mini skirts, a made-up face, has voluptuous curves, but speaks her mind" (1987).

By the mid-1980s, many female MCs began contesting the "fly girl" image because they wanted their audiences to focus more on their rapping skills than on their dress styles. Despite this changing trend, the female rap trio Salt-N-Pepa—Salt, Pepa, and Spinderella—nevertheless canonized the ultimate fly girl posture of rap by donning short, tight-fitting outfits, leather clothing, ripped jeans or punk clothing, glittering gold jewelry (i.e., earrings and necklaces), long sculpted nails, prominent makeup, and hairstyles ranging from braids and wraps to waves, in ever-changing hair coloring.

Rap's fly girl image is, however, far more than a whim, for it highlights aspects of Black women's bodies considered undesirable by American mainstream standards of beauty (Roberts 1998). Through performance, Salt-N-Pepa are "flippin da script" (deconstructing dominant ideology) by wearing clothes that accent their full breasts and rounded buttocks and thighs, considered beauty markers of Black women by Black culture (Roberts 1998). Moreover, they portray via performance the fly girl as a party-goer, an independent woman, but, additionally, an erotic subject rather than an objectified one.

Female rappers' reclamation of the *fly* resonates with the late Audre Lorde's theory of the erotic as power (Davis 1998:172). In Lorde's influential essay, "Uses of the Erotic," she reveals the transformative power of the erotic in Black women's culture: "Our erotic knowledge empowers us, becomes a lens through which we scrutinize all aspects of our existence, forcing us to evaluate those aspects honestly in terms of their meaning within our lives" (1984:57). Cultural critic and scholar bell hooks further articulates that Black women's erotic consciousness is textualized around issues of body esteem: "Erotic pleasure requires of us engagement with the realm of the senses … the capacity to be in touch with sensual reality; to accept and love our bodies; [to work] toward self-recovery issues around body esteem; [and] to be empowered by a healing eroticism" (1993:116, 121–122, 124).

Black fly girls express a growing awareness of their erotic selves by sculpting their own personas and, as folklorist Elaine Lawless (1998) puts it, "writing their own bodies." For example, Salt-N-Pepa describe themselves as "women [who have] worked hard to keep our bodies in shape; we're proud to show them off": moreover, "we're not ashamed of our sexuality; for we're Salt-N-Pepa—sexier and more in control" (quoted in Rogers 1994:31).

Another aspect of the fly girl persona is independence. Salt notes that "the image we project reflects the real independent woman of the '90s" (quoted in Chyll 1994:20). But for many women of rap, achieving a sense of independence from an entrepreneurial perspective has not been easy. For instance, it is common knowledge in the rap community that during Salt-N-Pepa's early years, their lyrics and hit songs ("I'll Take Your Man," "Push It," "Tramp," and "Shake Your Thang") were mainly written by their manager/producer Hurby "Luvbug" Azor, until the *Black's Magic* (1990) LP, on which Salt (Cheryl James) ventured into writing and producing the single "Expression," which went platinum. *Black's Magic* also contains Salt-N-Pepa's "Let's Talk about Sex" (written by Azor), which Salt later rewrote for a public service announcement song and video "Let's Talk about AIDS" in 1992.

On Salt-N-Pepa's fourth LP, *Very Necessary* (1993), the group wrote and produced most of the selections. The songs "Shoop" and "Whatta Man" from that album stand out as celebratory songs that deserve note.[6] In the video versions of both songs, the three women scrutinize desirable men, ranging from business types to "ruffnecks" (a fly guy associated with urban street culture). The "Shoop" video turns the tables on the male rappers; in it "ladies see a bunch of bare-chested, tight-bunned brothers acting like sex *objects*, servicing it up to us in our videos," said Salt (quoted in Rogers 1994:31, emphasis added). In "Whatta Man," on the other hand, Salt-N-Pepa praise their significant others in the areas of friendship, romance, and parenting as the female rhythm and blues group En Vogue joins them in singing the chorus, "Whatta man, whatta man, whatta man, whatta mighty good man."

Other women whom the interpretive community categorizes as *fly* are Left-Eye and Yo-Yo. Left Eye is the rapper of the hip-hop/rhythm and blues hybrid group TLC (*T-Boz, Left* Eye, and Chili). When TLC first appeared on the music scene with the debut LP *Ooooooooohhh ... On the TLC Tip* (1992), their baggy style of dress ran counter to the revealing apparel of hip-hop's typical fly girl and invited their full-figured audience to do the same. TLC's T-Boz said, "We like to wear a lot of baggy stuff because for one, it's comfortable, and two, many of our fans don't have the so-called perfect figure; we don't want them to feel like they can't wear what we're wearing" (quoted in Horner 1993:16). Throughout the 1990s, TLC remained steadfast with the message to women of all sizes regarding mental and physical wellness and body esteem, as underscored in both music and video performances of the single "Unpretty" (1999).

Like Salt-N-Pepa, TLC has made delivering "safe sex" messages *a priority*. While both groups do so through lyrics, TLC underscores the messages visually through wearing certain accoutrements. Left Eye of the trio wears a condom in place of an eyeglass lens, while other members of the group attach colored condom packages to their clothes. TLC's warning about unprotected sex, emphasized by the condoms they wear, is conveyed powerfully in their award-winning "Waterfalls" from their second LP, *CrazySexyCool* (1994). The message is amplified in the video: A man decides to follow his partner's wish not to use a condom. Following this encounter, he notices a lesion on his face, which suggests that he has contracted the virus that causes AIDS. TLC's espousal of being fly and sexually independent undoubtedly comes hand in hand with sexual responsibility via their lyrics and image.

Like TLC, Yo-Yo also delivers a serious message, which earns her a place among the queen mothers. But her gyrating hips, stylish auburn braids, short, tight-fitting outfits, and pronounced facial makeup also categorize her as fly. Yo-Yo writes about independent, empowered Black women, championing African American sisterhood in "The I.B.W.C. National Anthem" and "Sisterland" from *Make Way for the Motherlode* (1991). She takes on sexuality in "You Can't Play with My Yo-Yo" and "Put a Lid on It," which, as their titles suggest, explore being sexually in control and being sexually irresponsible.

In 1996, Yo-Yo moved beyond the shadow of her mentor Ice Cube with her fourth LP, *Total Control*, for which she served as executive producer. Following this success, Yo-Yo began a column entitled "Yo, Yo-Yo" in the hip-hop magazine *Vibe*, in which she addresses questions about male-female relationships and interpersonal growth in the name of I.B.W.C.

Since the late 1990s, female MC, songwriter, and producer Missy "Misdemeanor" Elliott has joined the fly girl ranks. Mesmerized by her debut LP *Supa Dupa Fly* (1997) and her single "The Rain," female fans also admire her finger-wave hairstyle, known to some as "Missy [finger] waves," and her ability to carry off the latest hip-hop fashions on her full-figured frame. Elliott has occasionally appeared in television advertisements for the youth fashion store Gap. She no doubt succeeds as a full-figured *fly* woman, breaking new ground in an area too often seen as off-limits to all but the most slender and "correctly" proportioned. In staking her claim to rap music's fly girl category, Elliott further reclaims sexuality and eros as healing power for all Black women, regardless of size. However, with her single "She's a Bitch" from her sophomore LP *Da Real World* (1999), Missy "Misdemeanor" Elliott appends another image to her fly girl posture. Her usage of *bitch* makes a self-statement about being a mover and shaker, on- and offstage, in rap's male-dominated arena, and thus she shares much in common with the next category, "Sista with Attitude."

Sista with Attitude

According to Black English scholar Geneva Smitherman, "'tude, a diminutive form of attitude, can be defined as an aggressive, arrogant, defiant, I-know-I'm-BAD pose or air about oneself; or an oppositional or negative outlook or disposition" (1994:228). Prototypes of this category are grouped according to "'tude": Roxanne Shanté, Bytches with Problems (BWP), and Da Brat are known for their frankness; MC Lyte exudes a hardcore/no-nonsense approach; Boss is recognized for her gangsta bitch posture; and Mia X advances a militaristic stance, all in the name of her predominantly male posse No Limit Soldiers.[7]

In general, "Sista with Attitude" comprises female MCs who value attitude as a means of empowerment and present themselves accordingly. Many of these "sistas" (sisters) have reclaimed the word *bitch*, viewing it as positive rather than negative and using the term to entertain or provide cathartic release. Other sistas in the interpretive community are troubled by that view. These women, such as Lauryn Hill, have "refused to be labeled a 'bitch' because such appellations merely mar the images of young African American females" (1994; see also Harmony, quoted in Donahue 1991). The reclaimers counter this argument with the opinion that "it's not what you're called but what you answer to" (MC Lyte 1993). Some women of rap take a middle road, concurring that *bitch* can be problematic depending on who uses the term, how it is employed, and to whom one refers. As Queen Latifah explains.

> I don't really mind the term.... I play around with it I use it with my home girls like, "Bitch are you crazy?" Bitch is a fierce girl. [Or.] "That bitch is so crazy, girl." You know, that's not harmful [But.] "This stupid bitch just came down here talking ... ," now that's meant in a harmful way. So it's the meaning behind the word that to me decides whether I should turn it off or listen to it. (1993)

Female MCs revise the standard definition of *bitch*, from an "aggressive woman who challenges male authority" (Penrice 1995) to an aggressive or assertive female who subverts patriarchal rule. Lyndah of the duo BWP explained, "We use 'Bytches' [to mean] a strong, positive, aggressive woman who goes after what she wants. We take that on today ... and use it in a positive sense" (quoted in Donahue 1991).[8]

By the mid- to late 1990s, the "Sista with Attitude" category was augmented with rappers Lil' Kim and Foxy Brown, who conflate fly and hardcore attitudes in erotic lyrics and video performances, bordering both "Fly Girl" and "Sista with Attitude" categories. In doing so, they are designated by some as the "mack divas," "Thelma and Louise of rap" (Gonzales 1997:62), or "bad girls of hip-hop" (Morgan 1997). Foxy Brown, whose name is derived from Pam Grier's 1974 screen character, emulates the powerful, desirable, yet dangerous woman: "I think it's every girl's dream to be fly" (Gonzales 1997:63). Although Lil' Kim's debut album *Hard Core* (1996) and Foxy Brown's *Ill Na Na* (1997) have garnered platinum status, some members of the interpretive community criticize them for being "highly materialistic, violent, lewd" (Morgan 1997:77), an impression exacerbated by their affiliation with male gangsta rap–style crews: Lil' Kim is associated with Junior M.A.F.I.A., and Foxy Brown is connected with The Firm.

The bad girl image also parallels the "badman" character (such as John Hardy, Dolemite, and Stackolee) peculiar to the African American oral narrative. African American oral narratives commonly exploit the "badman" or "bad nigguh" types in the toast, a long poetic narrative form that predates rap.[9] In these narratives, Black badmen boast about their sexual exploits with women, wild drinking binges, and narrow brushes with the law, symbolic of "white power" (Roberts 1989:196). The feminist rendering of "the badman" includes those sistas who brag about partying and smoking "blunts" (marijuana) with their men; seducing, repressing, and sexually emasculating male characters;[10] or "dissin'" (verbally downplaying) their would-be female or male competitors—all through figurative speech.[11]

Some female observers I queried felt that sistas with attitude merely exist on the periphery of rap and are seen as just "shootin' off at the mouth." These artists are not highly respected for their creative skills; rather, they are viewed as misusing sex and feminism and devaluing Black men. In an *Essence* magazine article, hip-hop feminist Joan Morgan states that the new "bad girls of hip-hop" may not have career longevity because "feminism is not simply about being able to do what the boys do—get high, talk endlessly about their wee-wees and what have you. At the end of the day, it's the power women attain by making choices that increase their range of possibilities" (1997:132). Morgan further argues that Black women's power—on- and offstage—is sustained by "those sisters who selectively ration their erotic power" (1997:133).

Despite the controversies, sistas with attitude have acquired respect from their peers for their mastery of figurative language and rhyme. They simply refuse to be second best.

Lesbian

While representatives of the "Queen Mother," "Fly Girl," and "Sista with Attitude" categories came into prominence during the mid- to late 1980s, the "Lesbian" category emerged from the closet during the late 1990s. Not only does the female audience term this category "Lesbian," but the artist who has given recognition to this division is among the first to rap about and address the lesbian lifestyle from a Black woman's perspective. Though other Black rap artists rumored to be gay/lesbian have chosen to remain closeted in a scene described as "notoriously homophobic" (Dyson, quoted in Jamison 1998:AR34), Queen Pen's "Girlfriend," from her debut LP *My Melody* (1997), represents a "breakthrough for queer culture" (Walters 1998:60).[12] "Girlfriend" signifies on or indirectly plays on Black lesbian love interest with a parody of the refrain section of Me'Shell Ndgeocello's "If That's Your Boyfriend (He Wasn't Last Night)." Ndegeocello, who is openly lesbian, appears on "Girlfriend," performing vocals and bass guitar. In "Girlfriend," Queen Pen positions herself as the suitor in a lesbian relationship. While this song may be a "breakthrough for queer culture," other issues still complicate Black female artists' willingness to openly address gay and lesbian culture in their performances.

Black lesbian culture and identity have been concerned with issues of race and role-play, note Lisa M. Walker (1993) and Ekua Omosupe (1991). Drawing on the critical works of Audre Lorde (1982, 1984), Omosupe notes that lesbian identity, similar to feminism, represents white lesbian culture or white women to the exclusion of women of color. In this regard, Black lesbians are at times forced to live and struggle against white male patriarchal culture on the one side and white lesbian culture, racism, and general homophobia on the other (Omosupe 1991:105). Corroborating issues of race privilege raised by the Black lesbian community, Queen Pen contends that certain licenses are afforded to white openly lesbian performers like

Ellen DeGeneres and k.d. lang, who do not have to pay as high a price for their candidness as lesbians of color: "But you know, Ellen [DeGeneres] can talk about any ol' thing and it's all right. With everybody, it's all right. With 'Girlfriend,' I'm getting all kinds of questions" (quoted in Duvernay 1998:88).[13] She continues, "This song is buggin' everyone out right now. [If] you got Ellen, you got k.d., why shouldn't urban lesbians go to a girl club and hear their own thing?" (quoted in Jamison 1998:AR34).

Queen Pen further stresses in performance her play on image, which suggests "role-play," another crucial issue to Black lesbian culture. Walker asserts, "Role-play among black lesbians involves a resistance to the homophobic stereotype ... lesbian as "bulldagger," a pejorative term within (and outside) the black community used to signal the lesbian as a woman who wants to be a man" (1993:886). On her album cover, Queen Pen exudes a "femme" image through wearing lipstick, a chic hairstyle, and stylish dress. However, in performance, as observed in Blackstreet's "No Dignity" (1996), one notices how Queen Pen "drowns out" her femme album cover image by appropriating "B-Boy" gestures (cool pose and bopped gait) commonly associated with male hip-hop culture. Regardless of issues concerning race privilege and role-play, Queen Pen concludes that in "two or three years from now, people will say I was the first female to bring the lesbian life to light [in an open way] on wax. It's reality. What's the problem?" (quoted in Jamison 1998:AR34).

Conclusion

Women are achieving major strides in rap music by continuing to chisel away at stereotypes about females as artists in a male-dominated tradition and by (re)defining women's culture and identity from a Black feminist perspective. Although rap continues to be predominantly male, female MCs move beyond the shadows of male rappers in diverse ways. Some have become exclusively known for their lyrical "skillz," while others have used a unique blend of musical styles or a combination of singer-rapper acts, as is apparent with Grammy awardees Left Eye of TLC and Lauryn Hill.

Women of rap still face, nevertheless, overt sexism regarding their creative capabilities. Female rapper Princesa recalls, "Only when I led them [male producers] to believe that a man had written or produced my stuff did they show interest" (quoted in Cooper 1989:80). Mass-mediation scholar Lisa Lewis notes that, in the popular music arena, "the ideological division between composition and performance serves to devalue women's role in music making and cast doubt on female creativity in general" (1990:57). However, female MCs of the 1990s have defied the sexist repression by writing their own songs, producing records, and even starting their own record companies, as with Salt-N-Pepa's *Very Necessary* (1993), Lauryn Hill's 1999 Grammy Award–winning LP *The Miseducation of Lauryn Hill* (1998), and Queen Latifah's record company, Flavor Unit. Additionally, Queen Latifah's Grammy Award–winning single "U.N.I.T.Y." (1993) challenges those males who use *bitch/ho* appellations in their lyrics.

While the majority of scholarly studies on female rappers locate Black women's voices in rap, they present only a partial rendering of female representation.[14] These works tend to focus on females' attitudes and responses to sexual objectification, ignoring the many roles and issues of women and female rappers. Rap music scholar Tricia Rose says female MCs should be evaluated not only with regard to male rappers and misogynist lyrics "but also in response to a variety of related issues, including dominant notions of femininity, feminism, and black female sexuality. At the very least, black women rappers are in dialogue with one another, black men, black women, and dominant American culture as they struggle to define themselves" (1994:147–148). In rap music performance, a "black female-self emerges as a variation [on] several unique themes" (Etter-Lewis 1991:43).

More importantly, female rappers, most of whom are Black, convey their views on a variety of issues concerning identity, sociohistory, and esoteric beliefs shared by young African American women. Female rappers have attained a sense of distinction through revising and reclaiming Black women's history and perceived destiny. They use their performances as platforms to refute, deconstruct, and reconstruct alternative visions of their identity. With this platform, rap music becomes a vehicle by which Black female rappers seek empowerment, make choices, and create spaces for themselves and other sistas.

Notes

Earlier drafts of this article were presented on the panel "Women Performers as Traditionalists and Innovators" at Resounding Women in World Music: A Symposium sponsored by the World Music Institute and Hunter College/City University of New York Graduate Program in Ethnomusicology, New York, 10–12 November 1995; and as a paper. "'Ain't Nuthin' but a She-Thing' Women. Race and Representation in Rap," at the 42nd Annual Meetings of the Society for Ethnomusicology with the International Association for the Study of Popular Music (USA Chapter), Pittsburgh, 22–26 October 1997. I wish to thank Lou-Ann Crouther, Phyllis May-Machunda, the late Gerald L. Davis, and the anonymous reviewers of the *Journal of American Folklore* for their suggestions on earlier drafts, as well as Corinne Lightweaver, whose invaluable comments contributed to the article's refinement.

1. The following is a list of other artists who make up a roster of female MCs: Antoinette (Next Plateau), Bahamadia (EMI), Conscious Daughters (Priority), Eve (Ruff Ryders), Finesse and Synquis (MCA), Gangsta Boo (Relativity), Heather B (MCA), Lady of Rage (Death Row), Ladybug (Pendulum), MC Smooth (Crush Music), MC Trouble (Motown), Mercedes (No Limit), Nikki D (Def Jam), Nonchalant (MCA), Oaktown's 3–5–7 (Capital), Rah Digga (Flipmode), Solé (Dream Works), and 350 (Rap-a-Lot).
2. Accordingly, sculpting the queen mother's head was established in Benin by King Oba Esigies during the 16th century. Sieber and Walker (1987:93) note that, during Esigies's reign, he commissioned a sculpted head made of bronze of his mother, Idia, and placed it in his palace to commemorate her role in the Benn-Idah war, thereby including, for the first time, queen mothers in the cult of royal ancestors. In addition to Sieber and Walker's work, refer to Ben-Amos 1995 and Ben-Amos and Rubin 1983 for photographs and a brief discussion of queen mother heads of Benin.
3. The Zulu Nation is an organization that was founded in the Bronx during the mid-1970s by DJ Afrika Bambaataa. He contends that the Zulu Nation is a youth organization that incorporates a philosophy of nonviolence and in which inner-city youths compete artistically as break-dancers, rhyming emcees (rappers), disc jockeys, and graffiti artists rather than physically with knives and guns. Bambaataa's Zulu Nation laid the foundation for hip-hop, a youth arts movement comprising the above arts, and an "attitude" rendered in the form of a distinct dress, language, and gesture—all of which is articulated via performance by rap music artists (see Keyes 1996).
4. For a more detailed analysis of this video, see Roberts 1994.
5. Isis once performed with the Black nationalist group X-Clan. After leaving this group, she also adopted a new stage name, Lin Que.
6. "Whatta Man" is adapted from Linda Lyndell's 1968 hit "What a Man."
7. For a more in-depth discussion of this category, refer to the section on female rappers in my book, *Rap Music and Street Consciousness* (Champaign: University of Illinois Press, 2002).
8. Another aspect of speech play is the manner in which sistas with attitude refer to men in their rap songs affectionately or insultingly as "motherfuckas" or "my niggas."
9. For further information about the toast, see Roger Abrahams (1970) and Darryl Dance (1978).
10. This emasculation can occur when sistas with attitude refer to their male competitors or suitors as "motherfuckas" or "niggas." Because the element of signifying is aesthetically appealing in this style of rap, these terms may have both negative and positive meanings depending on context.
11. Examples of selected rap songs that portray the distinct characteristics of sistas with attitude include the following: Boss, "I Don't Give a Fuck" and "Mai Sista Izza Bitch," *Bom Gangstaz* (1993), Bytches with Problems, "Two Minute Brother" and "Shit Popper," *The Bytches* (1991); Da Brat, "Da Shit Ya Can't Fuc Wit" and "Fire It Up," *Funkdafied* (1994); Foxy Brown. "Ill Na Na" and "Letter to the Firm," *Ill Na Na* (1997); Lil' Kim, "Big Momma Thang" and "Spend a Little Doe," *Hard Core* (1996); MC Lyte, "Paper Thin," *Lyte as a Rock* (1988), and "Steady F … king," *Ain't No Other* (1993); Roxanne Shanté, "Big Mama," *The Bitch Is Back* (1992).
12. While "Queen Pen" is a play on "King Pin," Queen Pen uses this moniker to indicate that she "pens" (or writes) her own lyrics. A skill that some believe female MCs lack in comparison with male rappers.

Although "Girlfriend" and other selections on Queen Pen's LP were cowritten and produced by Teddy Riley, inventor of new jack swing style (a rap rhythm and blues hybrid). Queen Pen's real name (Lynise Walters) appears on all songs. In the music industry, it is not unusual for producers to take cowriting credit on their mentees' debut works. The discussion of Riley's input on "Girlfriend" is discussed by Laura Jamison (1998).

13. When asked about "Girlfriend" in her interview in *Rap Pages* with Duvernay (1998), Queen Pen asserts that there are other nonlesbian songs on her debut album *My Melody*, including "Get Away," which discusses domestic violence.

14. For more on this topic, see Berry 1994, Forman 1994, Goodall 1994, Guevara 1987, and Rose 1994.

References Cited

Abrahams, Roger. 1970. *Deep Down in the Jungle. Negro Narrative Folklore from the Streets of Philadelphia.* Chicago: Aldine Publishing.

Ben-Amos, Paula Girshick. 1995. *The Art of Benin.* Rev. edition. Washington, D.C.: Smithsonian Institution Press.

Ben-Amos, Paula Girshick, and Arnold Rubin, eds. 1983. *The Art of Power, the Power of Art: Studies in Benin Iconography.* Los Angeles: Museum of Cultural History.

Berry, Venise T. 1994. Feminine or Masculine: The Conflicting Nature of Female Images in Rap Music. In *Cecilia Reclaimed: Feminist Perspectives on Gender and Music,* ed. Susan C. Cook and Judy S. Tsou, pp. 183–201. Urbana: University of Illinois Press.

Bobo, Jacqueline. 1995. *Black Women as Cultural Readers.* New York: Columbia University Press.

Chyll, Chuck. 1994. Musical Reactions: Sexy Rap or Credibility Gap? *Rap Masters* 7(7):19–20.

Collins, Patricia Hill. 1990. *Black Feminist Thought: Knowledge, Consciousness, and the Politics of Empowerment.* London: Harper Collins Academic.

Cooper, Carol. 1989. Girls Ain't Nothin' but Trouble. *Essence* (April):80, 119.

Dance, Daryl. 1978. *Shuckin' and Jivin': Folklore from Contemporary Black Americans.* Bloomington: Indiana University Press.

Davis, Angela Y. 1998. *Blues Legacies and Black Feminism: Gertrude "Ma" Rainey, Bessie Smith, and Billie Holiday.* New York: Pantheon Books.

Donahue, Phil. 1991. Female Rappers Invade the Male Rap Industry. The Phil Donahue Show Transcript #3216, 29 May.

Duvernay, Ava. 1998. Queen Pen: Keep "EM Guessin." *Rap Pages* (May):86–88.

Etter-Lewis, Gwendolyn. 1991. Black Women's Life Stories: Reclaiming Self in Narrative Texts. In *Women's Words: The Feminist Practice of Oral History,* ed. Sherna Berger Gluck and Daphne Patai, pp. 43–59. New York: Routledge.

Forman, Murray. 1994. Movin' Closer to an Independent Funk: Black Feminist Theory, Standpoint, and Women in Rap. *Women's Studies* 23:35–55.

Gonzales, A. Michael. 1997. Mack Divas. *The Source* (February):62–64.

Goodall, Nataki. 1994. Depend on Myself: T.L.C. and the Evolution of Black Female Rap. *Journal of Negro History* 79(1):85–93.

Green, Kim. 1991. The Naked Truth. *The Source* (November):32–34, 36.

Guevara, Nancy. 1987. Women Writin' Rappin' Breakin'. In *The Year Left,* 2nd ed. Mike Davis, Manning Marable, Fred Pfeil, and Michael Sprinker, pp. 160–175. New York: Verso Press.

Hill, Lauryn. 1994. Panelist. Hip-Hop Summit for New Music, Seminar 15, New York, 20 July.

hooks, bell. 1993. *Sisters of the Yam: Black Women and Self-Recovery.* Boston: South End Press.

Horner, Cynthia. 1993. TLC: The Homegirls with Style! *Right On!* (February):16–17.

Jamison, Laura. 1998. A Feisty Female Rapper Breaks a Hip-Hop Taboo. *Sunday New York Times,* 18 January: AR34.

Keyes, Cheryl L. 1996. At the Crossroads: Rap Music and Its African Nexus. Ethnomusicology 40(2): 223–248. In *Rap Music and Street Consciousness.* 2002. Champaign: University of Illinois Press.

Lawless, Elaine J. 1998. Claiming Inversion: Lesbian Constructions of Female Identity as Claims for Authority. *Journal of American Folklore* 11 (439):3–22.

Leland, John. 1992. Souljah on Ice. *Newsweek,* 29 June: 46–52.

Lewis, Lisa. 1990. *Gender Politics and MTV: Voicing the Difference.* Philadelphia: Temple University Press.

Lorde, Audre. 1982. *Zimi: A New Spelling of My Name.* Trumansburg. N.Y.: Crossing Press.

———. 1984. *Sister Outsider.* Freedom, Calif.: Crossing Press.

MC Lyte. 1993. Musical guest. Arsenio Hall Show, 8 October.

———. 1996. Interview by the author. Irvine, Calif., 11 August.

Morgan, Joan. 1997. The Bad Girls of Hip-Hop. *Essence* (March): 76–77, 132–134.

Nelson, Havelock. 1993. New Female Rappers Play for Keeps. *Billboard*, 10 July 1, 77.

Omosupe, Ekua. 1991. Black/Lesbian/Bulldagger. *differences* 3(2):101–111.

Pearlman, Jill. 1988. Girls Rappin' Round Table. *The Paper* (summer):25–27.

Penrice, Ronda. 1995. Interview by the author. *Manhattan*, 11 November.

Queen Latifah. 1993. Interview by the author. Jersey City. 8 July.

Radner, Joan Newlon, and Susan S. Lanser. 1993. Strategies of Coding in Women's Culture. In *Feminist Messages: Coding in Women's Folk Culture*, ed. Joan Newlon Radner, pp. 1–29. Urbana: University of Illinois Press.

Roberts, Deborah. 1998. Beautiful Women. 20/20, ABC Transcript #1796, 30 March.

Roberts, John W. 1989. *From Trickster to Badman: The Black Folk Hero in Slavery and Freedom*. Philadelphia: University of Pennsylvania.

Roberts, Robin. 1994. "Ladies First": Queen Latifah's Afrocentric Feminist Music Video. *African American Review* 28(2):245–257.

Rogers, E. Charles. 1994. The Salt-N-Pepa Interview. *Rap Masters* 7(7) July:30–31.

Rose, Tricia. 1994. *Black Noise: Rap Music and Black Culture in Contemporary America*. Hanover, N.H.: Wesleyan University Press.

Sieber, Roy, and Roslyn Adele Walker. 1987. *African Art in the Cycle of Life*. Washington, D.C.: Smithsonian Institution Press.

Sister Souljah. 1994. *No Disrespect*. New York: Random House.

Smitherman, Geneva. 1994. *Black Talk: Words and Phrases from the Hood to the Amen Corner*. New York: Houghton Mifflin Co.

Walker, Lisa M. 1993. How to Recognize a Lesbian: The Cultural Politics of Looking Like What You Are. *Signs: Journal of Women in Culture and Society* 18(4):866–889.

Walters, Barry. 1998. My Melody (sound recording review). *Advocate* 755 (17 March):59–60.

Discography

Boogie Boys. 1987[1985]. A Fly Girl. *Rap vs. Rap: The Answer Album*. Priority 4XL-9506.

Boss. 1993. *Born Gangstaz*. Def Jam/Columbia OT 52903.

Bytches with Problems. 1991. *The Bytches*. No Face/RAL CT 47068.

Da Brat. 1994. *Funkdafied*. Chaos/Columbia OT 66164.

Foxy Brown. 1997. *Ill Na Na*. Def Jam 547028.

Funky Four Plus One. Rapping and Rocking the House. *Great Rap Hits*. Sugar Hill SH 246.

Lauryn Hill. 1998. *The Miseducation of Lauryn Hill*. Ruffhouse/Columbia CT69035.

Lil' Kim. 1996. *Hard Core*. Big Beat Records/Atlantic 92733–2.

MC Lyte. 1988. *Lyte as a Rock*. First Priority Music/Atlantic 7 90905–1.

———. 1993. *Ain't No Other*. First Priority Music/Atlantic 7 92230–4.

Missy "Misdemeanor" Elliott. 1997. *Supa Dupa Fly*. The Gold Mind, Inc./EastWest 62062–2.

———. 1999. *Da Real World*. The Gold Mine, Inc./East West 62244–4.

Queen Latifah. 1989. *All Hail the Queen*. Tommy Boy TBC 1022.

———. 1991. *Nature of a Sista'*. Tommy Boy TBC 9007.

———. 1993. U.N.I.T.Y. *Black Reign*. Motown 37463–6370–4.

Queen Pen. 1997. *My Melody*. Lil' Man/Interscope INTC-90151.

Roxanne Shanté. 1992. *The Bitch Is Back*. Livin' Large 3001.

———. 1995. Roxanne's Revenge. *Roxanne Shanté's Greatest Hits*. Cold Chillin'/Warner Brothers 5007.

Salt-N-Pepa. 1986. *Hot, Cool and Vicious*. Next Plateau/London 422–828362–2.

———. 1990. *Black's Magic*. Next Plateau/London 422–828362–2.

———. 1993. *Very Necessary* Next Plateau/London P2–28392.

Sister Souljah. 1992. *360 Degrees of Power*. Epic EK-48713.

TLC. 1992. *Oooooooohhh … On the TLC Tip*. LaFace/Arista 26003–2.

———. 1994. *CrazySexyCool*. LaFace/Arista AC 26009–2.

———. 1999. Unpretty. *FanMail*. LaFace/Arista 26055–4.

Yo-Yo. 1991. *Make Way for the Motherlode*. EastWest/Atlantic 791605–2.

———. 1996. *Total Control*. EastWest/Atlantic 61898.

22

Hip-Hop Feminist

Joan Morgan

Much had changed in my life by the time a million black men marched in Washington. I no longer live in Harlem. The decision had less to do with gunshot lullabies, dead bodies 'round the corner, or the pre-adolescents safe-sexing it in my stairwells—running consensual trains on a twelve-year-old girl whose titties and ass grew faster than her self-esteem—and more to do with my growing desensitization to it all. As evidenced by the zombie-like stare in my neighbors' eyes, the ghetto's dues for emotional immunity are high. And I knew better than to test its capacity for contagion.

So I broke out. Did a Bronx girl's unthinkable and moved to Brooklyn—where people had kids and dogs and gardens and shit. And a park called Prospect contained ol' West Indian men who reminded me of yet another home and everything good about my father.

It is the Bronx that haunts me, though. There a self, long deaded, roams the Concourse, dressed in big bamboo earrings and flare-legged Lees, guarding whatever is left of her memories. I murdered her. Slowly. By sipping miasmic cocktails of non-ghetto dreams laced with raw ambition. I had to. She would have clung so tightly to recollections of monkey bars, sour pickles, and BBQ Bontons, slow dances to "Always and Forever," and tongue kisses *coquito* sweet—love that existed despite the insanities and rising body counts—that escape would have been impossible.

It is the Bronx, not Harlem that calls me back. Sometimes she is the singsong cadences of my family's West Indian voices. Or the childhood memories of girls I once called friends. Sistas who refused the cocktail and had too many babies way too young. Sistas who saw welfare, bloodshed, dust, then crack steal away any traces of youth from their smiles.

Theirs are the spirits I see darting between the traffic and the La Marqueta vibes of Fordham Road. Their visitations dog my equanimity, demanding I explain why this "feminism thing" is relevant to any of their lives. There are days I cannot. I'm too busy wondering what relevance it has in my own.

. . . And then came October 16, the day Louis Farrakhan declared that black men would finally stand up and seize their rightful place as leaders of their communities. . . . It wasn't banishment from the march that was so offensive—after all, black women have certainly convened at our share of closed-door assemblies. It was being told to stay home and prepare food for our warrior kings. What infuriated progressive black women was that the rhetoric of protection and atonement was just a seductive mask for good old-fashioned sexism. . . .

Kristal Brent-Zook, "A Manifesto of Sorts for a New Black Feminist Movement," *The New York Times Magazine.*[1]

The "feminist" reaction to the Million Man March floored me. Like a lot of folks, I stayed home to watch the event. My phone rang off the hook—sista friends as close as round the corner and as far away as Jamaica moved by the awesome sight of so many black men of different hues, classes, and sexual orientations gathered together *peacefully* for the sole purpose of bettering themselves. The significance of the one group in this country most likely to murder each other—literally take each other out over things as trifling as colors or stepping on somebody's sneakers—was not lost on us. In fact, it left us all in tears.

Still, as a feminist, I could hardly ignore that my reaction differed drastically from many of my feminist counterparts. I was not mad. Not mad at all. Perhaps it was because growing up sandwiched between two brothers blessed me with an intrinsic understanding of the sanctity of male and female space. (Maintaining any semblance of harmony in our too-small apartment meant figuring out the times my brothers and I could share space—and the times we could not—with a quickness.)

Perhaps it was because I've learned that loving brothers is a little like parenting—sometimes you gotta get all up in that ass. Sometimes you gotta let them figure it out *on their own terms*—even if it means they screw up a little. So while the utter idiocy inherent in a nineties black leader suggesting women stay home and make sandwiches for their men didn't escape me, it did not nullify the march's positivity either. It's called being able to see the forest *and* the trees.

Besides, I was desperately trying to picture us trying to gather a million or so sistas to march for the development of a new black feminist movement. Highly, highly unlikely. Not that there aren't black women out there actively seeking agendas of empowerment—be it personal or otherwise—but let's face it, sistas ain't exactly checkin' for the f-word.

When I told older heads that I was writing a book that explored, among other things, my generation of black women's precarious relationship with feminism, they looked at me like I was trying to re-invent the wheel. I got lectured ad nauseam about "the racism of the White Feminist Movement," "the sixties and the seventies," and "feminism's historic irrelevance to black folks." I was reminded of how feminism's ivory tower elitism excludes the masses. And I was told that black women simply "didn't have time for all that shit."

While there is undeniable truth in all of the above except the latter—*the shit* black women don't have time for is dying and suffering from exorbitant rates of solo parenting, domestic violence, drug abuse, incarceration, AIDS, and cancer—none of them really explain why we have no black feminist *movement*. Lack of college education explains why 'round-the-way girls aren't reading bell hooks. It does not explain why even the gainfully degreed (self included) would rather trick away our last twenty-five dollars on that new nineties black girl fiction (trife as some of it may be) than some of those good, but let's face it, laboriously academic black feminist texts.

White women's racism and the Feminist Movement may explain the justifiable bad taste the f-word leaves in the mouths of women who are over thirty-five, but for my generation they are abstractions drawn from someone else's history. And without the power of memories, these phrases mean little to nothing.

Despite our differences about the March, Brent-Zook's article offered some interesting insights.

> ... Still, for all our double jeopardy about being black and female, progressive black women have yet to galvanize a mass following or to spark a concrete movement for social change.... Instead of picking up where Ida B. Wells left off, black women too often allow our efforts to be reduced to the anti-lynching campaigns of the Tupac Shakurs, the Mike Tysons, the O.J.

Simpsons and the Clarence Thomases of the world. Instead of struggling with, and against, those who sanction injustice, too often we stoop beneath them, our backs becoming their bridges. . . .

Why do we remain stuck in the past? The answer has something to do with not just white racism but also our own fear of the possible, our own inability to imagine the divinity within ourselves. . . . [2]

I agree. At the heart of our generation's ambivalence about the f-word is black women's historic tendency to blindly defend any black man who seems to be under attack from white folks (men, women, media, criminal justice system, etc.). The fact that the brothers may very well be in the wrong and, in some cases, deserve to be buried *under* the jail is irrelevant even if the victim is one of us. Centuries of being rendered helpless while racism, crime, drugs, poverty, depression, and violence robbed us of our men has left us misguidedly over-protective, hopelessly male-identified, and all too often self-sacrificing.

And yes, fear is part of the equation too, but I don't think it's a fear of the possible. Rather, it is the justifiable fear of what lies ahead for any black woman boldly proclaiming her commitment to empowerment—her sistas' or her own. Acknowledging the rampant sexism in our community, for example, means relinquishing the comforting illusion that black men and women are a unified front. Accepting that black men do not always reciprocate our need to love and protect is a terrifying thing, because it means that we are truly out there, *assed out* in a world rife with sexism and racism. And who the hell wants to deal with that?

Marc Christian was right. *Cojónes* became a necessary part of my feminist armature—but not for the reasons I would have suspected back then. I used to fear the constant accusations—career opportunism, race treason, collusion with "The Man," lesbianism—a lifetime of explaining what I am not. I dreaded the long, tedious conversations spent exorcising others of the stereotypes that tend to haunt the collective consciousness when we think of black women and the f-word male basher, radical literary/academic black women in their forties and fifties who are pathetically separated from real life, burly dreadlocked/crew cut dykes, sexually adventurous lipstick-wearing bisexuals, victims. Even more frightening were the frequent solo conversations I spent exorcising them from my own head.

In time, however, all of that would roll off my back like water.

Cojónes became necessary once I discovered that mine was not a feminism that existed comfortably in the black and white of things. The precarious nature of my career's origins was the first indication. I got my start as a writer because I captured the sexual attention of a man who could make me one. It was not the first time my externals would bestow me with such favors. It certainly would not be the last.

My growing fatigue with talking about "the men" was the second. Just once, I didn't want to have to talk about "the brothers," "male domination," or "the patriarchy." I wanted a feminism that would allow me to explore who we are as women—not victims. One that claimed the powerful richness and delicious complexities inherent in being black girls now—sistas of the post–Civil Rights, post-feminist, post-soul, hip-hop generation.

I was also looking for permission to ask some decidedly un-P.C. but very real questions:

Can you be a good feminist and admit out loud that there are things you kinda dig about patriarchy?

Would I be forced to turn in my "feminist membership card" if I confessed that suddenly waking up in a world free of gender inequities or expectations just might bug me out a little?

Suppose you don't want to pay for your own dinner, hold the door open, fix things, move furniture, or get intimate with whatever's under the hood of a car?

Is it foul to say that imagining a world where you could paint your big brown lips in the most decadent of shades, pile your phat ass into your fave micromini, slip your freshly manicured toes into four-inch fuck-me sandals and have not one single solitary man objectify—I mean roam his eyes longingly over all the intended places—is, like, a total drag for you?

Am I no longer down for the cause if I admit that while total gender equality is an interesting intellectual lectual concept, it doesn't do a damn thing for me erotically? That, truth be told, men with too many "feminist" sensibilities have never made my panties wet, at least not like that reformed thug nigga who can make even the most chauvinistic of "wassup, baby" feel like a sweet, wet tongue darting in and out of your ear.

And how come no one ever admits that part of the reason women love hip-hop—as sexist as it is—is 'cuz all that in-yo-face testosterone makes our nipples hard?

Are we no longer good feminists, not to mention nineties supersistas, if the A.M.'s wee hours sometimes leave us tearful and frightened that achieving all our mothers wanted us to—great educations, careers, financial and emotional independence—has made us wholly undesirable to the men who are supposed to be our counterparts? Men whose fascination with chickenheads leave us convinced they have no interest in dating, let alone marrying, their equals?

And when one accuses you of being completely indecipherable there's really nothing to say 'cuz even you're not sure how you can be a feminist and insist he "respect you as a woman, treat you like a lady, and make you feel safe—like a li'l girl."

In short, I needed a feminism brave enough to fuck with the grays. And this was not my foremothers' feminism.

Ironically, reaping the benefits of our foremothers' struggle is precisely what makes their brand of feminism so hard to embrace. The "victim" (read women) "oppressor" (read men) model that seems to dominate so much of contemporary discourse (both black and white), denies the very essence of who we are.

We are the daughters of feminist privilege. The gains of the Feminist Movement (the efforts of black, white, Latin, Asian, and Native American women) had a tremendous impact on our lives—so much we often take it for granted. We walk through the world with a sense of entitlement that women of our mothers' generation could not begin to fathom. Most of us can't imagine our lives without access to birth control, legalized abortions, the right to vote, or many of the same educational and job opportunities available to men. Sexism may be a very real part of my life but so is the unwavering belief that there is no dream I can't pursue *and achieve* simply because "I'm a woman."

Rejecting the wildly popular notion that embracing the f-word entails nothing more than articulating victimization, for me, is a matter of personal and spiritual survival. Surviving the combined impact of racism and sexism on the daily means never allowing my writing to suggest that black women aren't more than a bunch of bad memories. We *are* more than the rapes survived by the slave masters, the illicit familial touches accompanied by whiskey-soured breath, or the acts of violence endured by the fists, knives, and guns of strangers. We are more than the black eyes and heart bruises from those we believed were friends.

Black women can no more be defined by the cumulative sum of our pain than blackness can be defined solely by the transgenerational atrocities delivered at the hands of American racism. Because black folks are more than the stench of the slave ship, the bite of the dogs, or the smoldering of freshly lynched flesh. In both cases, defining ourselves solely by our oppression denies us the very magic of who we are. My feminism simply refuses to give sexism or racism that much power.

Holding on to that protective mantle of victimization requires a hypocrisy and self-censorship I'm no longer willing to give. Calling rappers out for their sexism without mentioning the complicity of the 100 or so video-hos that turned up—G-string in hand—for the shoot; or defending women's reproductive rights without examining the very complicated issue of *male choice*—specifically the inherent unfairness in denying men the right to choose whether or not *they want* to parent; or discussing the physical and emotional damage of sexism without examining the utterly foul and unloving ways black women treat each other ultimately means fronting like the shit brothers have with them is any less complex, difficult, or painful than the shit we have with ourselves. I am down, however, for a feminism that demands we assume responsibility for our lives.

In my quest to find a functional feminism for myself and my sistas—one that seeks empowerment on spiritual, material, physical, and emotional levels—I draw heavily on the cultural movement that defines my generation. As post–Civil Rights, post-feminist, post-soul children of hip-hop we have a dire need for the truth.

We have little faith in inherited illusions and idealism. We are the first generation to grow up with all the benefits of Civil Rights (i.e., Affirmative Action, government-subsidized educational and social programs) and the first to lose them. The first to have the devastation of AIDS, crack, and black-on-black violence makes it feel like a blessing to reach twenty-five. Love no longer presents itself wrapped in the romance of basement blue lights, lifetime commitments, or the sweet harmonies of The Stylistics and The Chi-Lites. Love for us is raw like sushi, served up on sex platters from R. Kelly and Jodeci. Even our existences can't be defined in the past's simple terms: house nigga vs. field nigga, ghetto vs. bourgie, BAP vs. boho because our lives are usually some complicated combination of all of the above.

More than any other generation before us, we need a feminism committed to "keeping it real." We need a voice like our music—one that samples and layers many voices, injects its sensibilities into the old and flips it into something new, provocative, and powerful. And one whose occasional hypocrisy, contradictions, and trifeness guarantee us at least a few trips to the terrordome, forcing us to finally confront what we'd all rather hide from.

We need a feminism that possesses the same fundamental understanding held by any true student of hip-hop. Truth can't be found in the voice of any one rapper but in the juxtaposition of many. The keys that unlock the riches of contemporary black female identity lie not in choosing Latifah over Lil' Kim, or even Foxy Brown over Salt-N-Pepa. They lie at the magical intersection where those contrary voices meet—the juncture where "truth" is no longer black and white but subtle, intriguing shades of gray.

Notes

1. Kristal Brent-Zook, "A Manifesto of Sorts for a New Black Feminist Movement," *New York Times Magazine* (Nov. 12, 1995). 86.
2. Ibid. 88–89.

23

Seeds and Legacies:

Tapping the Potential in Hip-Hop

Gwendolyn D. Pough

The only thing I'm saying is that the problem is bigger than rap music. If cards need to be plucked, it's not only the rappers who say things some people deem offensive, but also the white financial structure that manufactures and distributes their records. This same structure weaned an entire American generation on sex and violence, so it's little wonder that rappers find such a huge audience hungry for themes involving sex and violence. Rap as a direct reflection of society, will change no sooner than the populace that influences it changes its attitudes.

Cheo Coker, "Who's Gonna Take the Weight?"[1]

It's bigger than Hip-Hop, Hip-Hop, Hip-Hop
It's bigger than Hip-Hop, Hip-Hop, Hip-Hop
One thing 'bout music, when it hit you feel no pain
White folk say it controls your brain
I know better than that, that's game

Dead Prez, "Hip-Hop"[2]

Many would question the subtitle of this article—"Tapping the Potential in Hip-Hop"—specifically the notion that there is indeed any potential to tap in Hip-Hop. Those people would list *ad nauseam* the numerous instances of violence, sexism, and misogyny as well as the glorification of drug use and drug sales described in contemporary rap music. They would list certain rappers who have been arrested for these acts and the recent deaths of young Black male rappers as reason enough to surmise that there is indeed no potential to tap in Hip-Hop. Those same people would probably tell us that this entire generation of young people is a lost cause because of reasons ranging from apathy to selfishness. The Generation X—and more recently Generation O—has been cast aside as the do-nothing generation, a generation of wasted potential. These people probably do not have a clue that Hip-Hop is not rap, while rap is definitely a part of Hip-Hop. They probably do not know that rap is the music and Hip-Hop is the culture.

They probably could not even begin to imagine that some of the Generation Xer's that they have so casually cast aside are far from complacent—they are Hip-Hop activists, Raptivists and about change. In the words of that rap entrepreneur Master P they are "'bout it, 'bout it." And that "'bout it, 'bout it" extends further than clocking dollars, mackin' hos and what have you. That "'bout it, 'bout it" is deeply tied to community building and change. To summarize and condense the epigraphs quoted at the beginning of this article, the negative press and outrage against the music and the culture should be seen as much bigger than anyone could imagine. If we are indeed witnessing a scapegoating or a profiling of minority youth culture, to paraphrase the Reverend Al Sharpton, then it is indeed bigger than Hip-Hop.

As I noted earlier, this movement called Hip-Hop cannot, and should not be reduced to the music that comes out of it. Rap is a part of Hip-Hop, yes, but only a part. Hip-Hop is a state of mind; a way of living and being that expands further then what kind of music one listens to. And there is power there, so much power that some people are scared of it. For example, the largest consuming audience of rap music right now is young White men. Imagine if that same consuming audience became immersed in not just rap music but also a Hip-Hop movement toward change? Can you imagine that? I mean really imagine the future presidents and CEO's of this country's White patriarchal power structure really getting down with a Hip-Hop movement towards change? If you can then you can surely see why the White patriarchal power structure and some White girls too (just ask Mrs. Lynn Cheney and Mrs. Tipper Gore)[3] are scared and starting to condemn and scapegoat the music.

If rap music and Hip-Hop culture could do for little Dick and Jane of the 21st Century what freedom movements and antiwar demonstrations did for little Dick and Jane of the 20th century—meaning give them a political awareness and a cause to fight for—then, it's no wonder white folk are scared of rap music. As a youth movement that crosses race, gender, class, and sexuality, rap music and Hip-Hop culture have the potential to bring people together. We know that rap music can get them on the dance floor. The key is to get them moving in the same direction towards social change. Therefore, this article focuses on Hip-Hop as a state of mind, as a way of life that is tied to a youth movement of change—a youth movement that builds on a legacy of movements against oppression in this country. Hip-Hop culture did not just spring up full-grown. It builds on a past. It has a legacy.

In order to get a fuller account of Hip-Hop's political potential, I want to start by making a link between Hip-Hop and the Black Power Movement. The Black Power Movement of the 1970s was a thriving and vibrant part of many Black communities during the time that many of the founders of the Hip-Hop movement were either being born or coming of age. In fact, just as the Black Power Movement was dying out in the mid-1970s, some of the first Hip-Hop jams were being thrown in parks in the South Bronx.

Author Marvin J. Gladney offers some connections between Hip-Hop culture and the Black Arts Movement—which was the artistic arm of the Black Power Movement—in his article "The Black Arts Movement and Hip-Hop."[4] He recognizes Hip-Hop culture/rap music as the "most recent 'seed' in the continuum of Afrikan-American culture" and notes that it directly follows the Black Arts Movement. He develops three areas of "ideological progression from the Black Arts Movement to Hip-Hop."[5] And he lists them as "1) the elements of anger and rage in the cultural production of Afrikan-American art in the two movements, 2) the ideological need for the establishment of independent Black institutions and business outlets such as schools and publishing and recording companies, and 3) the development of a 'Black Aesthetic' as a yardstick to measure the value of Black art."[6] Gladney draws heavily on the theories of Black Aesthetics scholars and critics such as Addison Gayle, Amiri Baraka, Maulana Karenga, Larry Neal, and Haki R. Madhubuti. In each of these critics' work Gladney finds a need to define Black cultural expression that he feels still exists in Hip-Hop.

However, Gladney's clearest connection between Hip-Hop and the Black Arts Movement occurs in his discussion of "Black rage, anger, and cultural expression." He finds that just as the Black poets of the sixties used their anger to scream out against the injustice of the status quo, rappers offer, "artistic expression designed to cope with urban frustrations and conditions."[7] Others, such as Black Power Movement scholar William Van DeBurg, note rap music as an example of the way "contemporary Black culture continues to reveal its sixties roots."[8] Thus, Hip-Hop culture and rap music did not just spring up full-grown; they are seeds rooted in a legacy of struggle against oppression.

Perhaps the most interesting way in which Hip-Hop culture begins to show its sixties roots and indebtedness to the Black Power Movement is in the Black rhetorical qualities they share; which include the Black rage that Gladney discusses in his work and messages and sayings from the Black Power Movement sampled in rap songs. The rage and anger are consistent in the messages and presences of the Black nationalists and rappers. For example, when the Black Panther Party started "policing the police" and shouting "Off the Pigs" thirty years ago, they set the tone for rappers NWA (Niggas with Attitude) who would later shout, "Fuck the Police" over microphones that would be heard by millions. While the rap group did not have a political program such as the one set up by the Panthers—and they were far from being even remotely considered nationalist rappers—their message of police harassment went just as far. In fact, when the Rodney King beating occurred people pointed to them as prophets of the corrupt conditions in Los Angeles police departments. Also rapper Mos Def's song "Mr. Nigga"[9] is a 21st century remix of Malcolm X's reference that in the eyes of Whites, all Blacks from Ph.D.s to pimps are niggers; Mos Def affirms that not much has changed. He raps:

> ... Checks with O's o-o-o-o-ohs
> Straight all across the globe
> Watch got three time zones
> Keep a digital phone up to his dome
> Two assistants, two bank accounts, two homes
> One problem
> Even with the o's in his check
> The po-po stop him and show no respect
> "Is there a problem officer?"
> Damn straight, it's called race
> That motivate the jake (woo-woo) to give chase
> Say they want you successful, but that ain't the case
> You livin' large, your skin is dark
> They flash a light in your face ...

Mos Def most definitely realizes, just as Malcolm X before him—and as the brutal deaths of Black men from Amadou Diallo and James Byrd have shown—in this land we call America being Black negates respect and even the most basic level of human rights.

Another example of the ways in which there are rhetorical links between the Black Power Movement and Hip-Hop culture can be seen clearly in the message rap of the 1980s. There were numerous attempts to bring a political consciousness to the masses via rap lyrics. Artists such as Public Enemy, X-Clan, Paris, KRS-ONE and Conscious Daughters, to name only a few, produced rap songs with political themes of unity, racial uplift, self-definition, self-determination, and Black diasporas connections. There were also large efforts to end "Black on Black" crime and violence with projects such as "Stop the Violence: Self-Destruction"[10] and KRS-ONE's "Heal: Human Edutainment Against Lies"[11] on the East Coast and the compilation album "We're All in the Same Gang"[12] on the West Coast. Each of these efforts used rap music as a vehicle to stop Black youth from killing one another and brought together a variety of rappers to get that point across.

Although rap music lacks an actual political program in the same way that the Black Arts Movement was connected to the political Black Power Movement, the messages in some rap songs carry the political themes, such as the ones I mentioned earlier, that the Black Power Movement voiced. In the case of rap music/Hip-Hop culture then, we have the rhetorical messages without the political work. However, the current re-birth of message rap is promising a rise in political consciousness and the possibility of a political project. Rapper Common has traveled to Cuba, interviewed Assata Shakur, and participated in Havana's fifth annual National Hip-Hop Conference and Colloquium, which Castro funds acknowledging "rap music as the existing revolutionary voice of Cuba's future."[13] In the U.S. several grassroots organizations aimed at helping youth and inspiring consciousness are using rap music and Hip-Hop culture to do so. For example, we have yet to see the result of the Reverend Al Sharpton's Hip-Hop summit that occurred in late October of last year in New York City and the consciousness and change that it may inspire.

Along similar lines of consciousness and change, new rap duo Dead Prez, in a song fashioned after the Black Panther Party's Ten-Point Platform titled "We Want Freedom,"[14] spouts lyrics like, "Tell me, what you gon' do to get Free / We need more than MCs / We need Hueys and revolutionaries" and "see we all want peace, but the problem is crackers want a bigger piece, got it where niggas can't get a piece." They want to use rap as "propaganda" to jumpstart the movement and spread their revolutionary message. Much like the Black Panthers used their revolutionary rhetoric, guns, and customs to initially attract the masses and get them to listen to their politics, Dead Prez sees rap as a vehicle for reaching the people. Noting their connection to the Panthers, the group states, "We're not trying to be what [late Black Panther] Fred Hampton was, although he was a great man. We can't go back to 1969; we're trying to reach into the future. Chanting on the front line is a valuable way to build a movement, but there is a whole other way that has a lot to do with propaganda."[15] And while propaganda may be the most base level of rhetoric, it is a form of rhetoric that the Black Panthers and certain members of the Hip-Hop community share. These new rappers are simply redefining it to fit contemporary times and the Hip-Hop generation.

A metaphor of the connection between Hip-Hop and the Black Power Movement/Black Panther Party becomes apparent when observing the life of former New York Panther Afeni Shakur. Shakur was a member of the Panther 21—the group arrested and indicted in New York for alleged bomb threats.[16] When Huey P. Newton publicly denounced the Panther 21, a split occurred between the entire New York chapter of the Black Panthers and those Panthers with headquarters in Oakland. This split started a war between East Coast Panthers and West Coast Panthers, and it has been alleged that the FBI fueled this war. Many Black Panthers were killed—reportedly by other Black Panthers. Writers such as Hugh Pearson attribute this intra-Panther war with the ultimate demise of the Party.[17] As Afeni Shakur sat in jail awaiting the trial that would ultimately free her, she grew more and more visibly with-child. Upon her release she gave birth to a child who would become one of Hip-Hop's most brilliant rappers—Tupac Shakur. Tupac claimed an allegiance with California gangsta rappers and became integral to the East Coast/West Coast war that would claim his life, the life of New York rapper Biggie Smalls aka The Notorious B.I.G., and possible others.

I think that it is particularly interesting to note that it has been contended that the FBI also had a hand in starting the East Coast/West Coast war in Hip-Hop that eventually claimed the lives of Biggie Smalls and Tupac Shakur. It was a letter from the FBI denouncing rap group NWA that spirited them to success and thus brought about the rise of West Coast style "gangsta rap" and the death of the political rap that was popular on the East Coast at that time.[18] Gangsta rap's tremendous popularity and East Coast rappers' failure to acknowledge the West Coast as a vital part of the Hip-Hop community caused a great deal of friction on both coasts. However, when we look at the fact that one letter from the FBI stifled the rise of "political/message rap" and ensured an era of gangsta rap, it's difficult not to also recall Hoover's declaration that there will not be another Black messiah unless they (himself and the FBI) made one.[19]

As Afeni gave us Tupac, the Black Power Movement gave us Hip-Hop. Afeni and Tupac then become the physical embodiment for the link between the Black Power Movement and Hip-Hop culture. Both the Black Power Movement and Hip-Hop culture are grassroots movements started by young Black people—in the case of Hip-Hop culture, young black and Latino people. Both movements are known for Black male posturing and are largely masculine discursive spaces. Both worked to disrupt the status quo on varying levels. And the Black Panthers, as the most productive political unit of Black Power Movement, worked to change the existing order in America. They carried guns to disrupt not only police violence, but also the hypocrisy of the United States Constitution. Members of the Hip-Hop movement started their disruption by making music and creating spaces for themselves when everything around them suggested exclusion. Without access to the technology that had come to define music during the disco era, they created a music that disrupted the exclusionary trend. They created parties in the parks because they were not allowed entrance to the posh New York disco clubs. Disco died, but rap is still here. The Black Power Movement left us with a youth movement called Hip-Hop.

While Tupac and his mother Afeni can be viewed a physical embodiment of the connection between Hip-Hop and the Black Power Movement, they can also be viewed as an example of the untapped potential and unfulfilled legacy in rap music. A lot of people thought that Tupac was going to be the next great Black leader. Although his music was conflicted and he walked a thin line between "positive" and "negative," Tupac gave some insightful interviews and made startling observations that left a lot of us waiting for the day that he would come into his true greatness and fulfill the destiny of his legacy to the Black Panther Party; we waited with baited breath, but Tupac never did fulfill his destiny. He never did live up to his legacy. Many scholars, writers, activists, and artists have chronicled the unfulfilled potential of Tupac Shakur. Nikki Giovanni a famed poet from the Black Arts Movement wrote the poem "All Eyez on U." His death spurned many critical articles published by scholarly journals and as well as collection of essays titled, *Tough Love: The Life and Death of Tupac Shakur, Cultural Criticism and Familial Observations.*[20] Public intellectual Dr. Michael Eric Dyson also touches on the untapped potential of Shakur in his controversial book *I May Not Get There With You: The True Martin Luther King Jr.* The book is controversial because among other things, Dyson compares the late Dr. Martin Luther King Jr. to rappers such as Shakur. Dyson writes:

> If we acknowledge that King was an extraordinary man despite his faults, perhaps we might acknowledge that some of our youth have the same potential for goodness that King possessed. (We must remember that if King had died at age twenty-five like Shakur, or twenty-four like the Notorious BIG—or after his first fame as a boycott leader at twenty-six—he might now be remembered as a promising leader who was shown to have borrowed other peoples' words and wives, infractions that in the absence of his later and greater fame we might be less willing to forgive.) In the process, some of these youth, by identifying with King, might rise above their limitations they might also see that they can remake their lives and place their skills in the service of social transformation.

The major point of Dyson's text is that we should begin to take a more critical look at history—a look that does not glorify the past and demonize the present—a look that is not nostalgic but critically conscious. Only then can we begin to establish real change. The truth is that Tupac and to some extent the Notorious BIG had potential that they did not use wisely.

Their music touched the lives of many on a daily basis. Imagine if their messages toward change had been more constant and steadfast. I'm by no means saying that either of these rappers would have been the next Dr. Martin Luther King Jr. and, I don't think that is what Dyson is saying either. I think that Dyson is calling for a mass project of critical reflective consciousness that doesn't look backwards nostalgically for a glorious past, but that looks back in hopes of learning things that would help the youth of today reach their full potential.

In the words of political rap group Dead Prez quoted at the beginning of this talk—"it's bigger than Hip-Hop." Hip-Hop did not spring up full-grown—and it was not created in a vacuum. The legacy of this country is the legacy of the Hip-Hop generation just as much as the legacies of the leaders who worked to change this corrupt society. To paraphrase or shall I say signify on the great poet Langston Hughes' "I Too Sing America," "Hip-Hop Too Raps America." The negative things we see in rap music and Hip-Hop culture are the negative things we see in this country—in this society—if we are honest. Hip-Hop can give us the mirror to the ills of society and to tap that potential we need to look in that mirror and work to change the things we see. The negative legacy of America is what we have to work against. Malcolm X warned us about chickens coming home to roost and we watch them come home time after time, in Columbine on urban streets with drive-bys, all over this country. Think about it and do something.

Notes

1. Coker, Cleo, *Essence Magazine*, August 1994: 62–64.
2. Dead Prez, *Let's Get Free*. Loud Records 2000.
3. Tipper Gore came to national attention in 1985 for helping to launch the Parents Music Resource Center, a group that crusaded to put warning labels on explicit albums. This group comprised primarily of the wives of prominent politicians and business executives testified in front of the Senate Commerce Committee; then-Senator Al Gore was a member of that committee. Lynne Cheney in September 2000 testified before the Senate Committee of Commerce, chaired by John McCain, decrying rapper Eminem as "misogynistie."
4. Gladney, Marvin J. "The Black Arts Movement and Hip-Hop." *Callaloo* 29 (1995): 291–301.
5. Ibid. at 291.
6. Ibid. at 291.
7. Ibid. at 292.
8. Van DeBurg, William L. *New Day in Babylon: The Black Power Movement and American Culture, 1965–1975* Chicago: The University of Chicago Press, 1992 at 307
9. Mos Def, *Black on Both Sides*. Rawkus Records, 1999.
10. Various artists, *Stop The Violence: Self-Destruction*. Jive Records, 1998. $600,000 in proceeds from the record was donated to the National Urban League. See also: various artists, *Hip Hop for Respect*. Rawkus Entertainment, 2000. Rappers, Mos Def and Talib Kweli instituted this project to address the deaths of Amadou Diallo and Tyesha Miller.
11. The purpose of H.E.A.L. was to counter organized lies perpetrated through the educational system, politics and religion that contribute to social problems. The 1992 H.E.A.L. statement, "Before you are a race, a religion or an occupation, you are a human. HEAL YOURSELF."
12. West Coast Rap All-Stars. *We're All in the Same Gang* (12" single). Warner Brothers Records, 1990.
13. Cepeda, Raquel, "Breath Free: In Search of a Definition of Freedom." *Source Magazine* April 2000: 134–138
14. Dead Prez. *Let's Get Free*. Loud Records, 2000.
15. Solomon, Akiba. "Dead Serious." *Source Magazine* April 2000: 150–152.
16. Accused of planning to bomb public spaces, Afeni Shakur, mother of rap artist Tupac Shakur, was a member of the Panther 21 and was imprisoned on more than 200 charges before she was eventually acquitted.
17. Pearson, Hugh. *The Shadow of the Panther, Huey Newton and the Price of Black Power in America*. New York: Addison-Wesley, 1994.

SEEDS AND LEGACIES • 289

18. Dated August 1, 1989, regarding the album, *Straight Outta Compton*. From Milt Ablerich, Assistant Director, Office of Public Affairs—U.S. Justice Department, Federal Bureau of Investigation to Mr. Oui Manganialie, National Promotions Director—Priority Records.

19. J. Edgar Hoover called Martin Luther King, Jr. "the most notorious liar in the country." Accusing King of being a communist, Hoover authorized the wiretapping of King and in attempts to discredit King, spread stories about his sex life.

20. See also Jones, Jacquie, "Time on the Cross," and Keeling, Kara, "A Homegrown Revolutionary?: Tupac Shakur and the Legacy of the Black Panther Party."

24
Never Trust a Big Butt and a Smile

Tricia Rose

If you were to construct an image of rap music via accounts of rap in the established press, you would (besides betraying limited critical instincts about popular culture) probably perceive rap to reflect the violent, brutally sexist reality of a pack of wilding "little Willie Hortons."[1] Consequently, you would wonder what a group of young black women rappers were doing fraternizing with these male rappers and why they seemed to be having such a good time. If I were to suggest that their participation in rap music produced some of the most important contemporary black feminist cultural criticism, you would surely bemoan the death of sexual equality. As Public Enemy's Chuck D has warned regarding the mainstream press, "Don't believe the hype." Sexism in rap has been gravely exaggerated by the mainstream press. Rap is a rich, complex multifaceted African-American popular form whose male practitioners' style and subject matter includes the obsessive sexism of a 2 Live Crew, the wacky parody of Biz Markie, the "edutainment" of Boogie Down Productions, the gangster-style storytelling of Ice Cube, the gritty and intelligent speed rapping of Kool Moe Dee, and the explicit black nationalism of X-Clan. Women rappers are vocal and respected members of the Hip Hop community, and they have quite a handle on what they are doing.

Fortunately or unfortunately (I'm not sure which), most academics concerned with contemporary popular culture and music have avoided sustained critical analysis of rap. A few literary scholars and theorists have explained the historical and cultural heritage of rap as an African-American form, while others have made passing reference to it as an important site of postmodernist impulses or as the prophetic voice of an angry disenfranchised group of young African-Americans.[2] The work on women rappers (while making claims that women rappers are pro-women artists) has been published in popular monthly periodicals and consequently has been limited to short but provocative inquiries.[3]

While any positive, critical attention to rap comes as a welcome relief, almost all of these accounts observe rap music outside of its socio-historical framework, as texts suspended in time. Such distanced readings, especially of a musical form to which it is difficult to gain direct and sustained access, leave open the possibility of grave misreadings regarding meanings and context. Women rappers are especially vulnerable to such misreadings precisely because their presence in rap has been consistently ignored or marginalized, even by those social critics who have published some of the most insightful analyses of rap. This essay, which is part of an extended project on rap music, will try to correct some of these misunderstandings, or as Chuck D states, "give you something that I knew you lacked. So consider me a new jack."[4] Better yet, here's Queen Latifah:

Some think that we can't flow (can't flow)
Stereotypes they got to go (got to go)
I'm gonna mess around and flip the scene into reverse
With what?
With a little touch of ladies first.[5]

The summer of 1989 marked the tenth anniversary of rap music's explosive debut in the recording industry. In honor of its unexpected longevity, Nelson George, a pro-Hip Hop music critic and *Village Voice* columnist, published a sentimental rap retrospective in which he mourned rap's movement from a street subculture into the cold, sterile world of commercial record production. George points out that, until recently, music industry powers have maintained a studied indifference to rap music, but now that rap's "commercial viability has been proven" many major recording companies are signing any half way decent act they can find. What worries George, and rightly so, is that corporate influence on black music has led, in the past, to the dissolution of vibrant black cultural forms and that rap may become the latest victim. The problem is complex, real and requires analysis. However, Nelson George, like media critics generally, imbeds his descriptions of "authentic rap" and fears of recent corporate influence on it in gender-coded language that mischaracterizes rap and silences women rappers and consumers. In his tenth anniversary piece, George traces major shifts in rap, naming titles, artists and producers. He weaves over twenty rap groups into his piece and names not a single female rapper. His retrospective is chock-full of prideful, urban black youth (read men), whose contributions to rap reflect "the thoughts of city kids more deeply than the likes of Michael Jackson, Oprah Winfrey et al." His concluding remarks make apparent his underlying perception of rap:

> To proclaim the death of rap, is to be sure, premature. But the farther the control of rap gets from its street corner constituency and the more corporations grasp it—record conglomerates, Burger King, Minute Maid, Yo! MTV Raps, etc.—the more vulnerable it becomes to cultural emasculation.

For George, corporate meddling not only dilutes cultural forms, it also reduces strapping testosterone-packed men into women! Could we imagine anything worse? Nelson George's analysis is not unusual; his is merely the latest example of media critics' consistent coding of rap music as male in the face of a significant and sustained female presence.

Many social critics who have neglected to make separate mention of women rappers would probably claim that these women are in many ways just "one of the boys." Since they are as tough as male rappers, women rappers fit into George's mind-boggling yet emblematic definition of rap as an "ultra-urban, unromantic, hyperrealistic, neo-nationalist, antiassimilationist, aggressive Afrocentric impulse." For George, and for media critics generally, it is far easier to re-gender women rappers than to revise their own gender-coded analysis of rap music.[6]

Since the summer of 1989, there has been a marked increase in media attention to women rappers. Most of the articles have been written by women and have tried to shed some light on female rappers and offer a feminist analysis of their contributions. I would like to extend some of the themes presented in these pieces by showing how women rappers participate in a dialogue with male rappers and by revising some of the commonly held assumptions about what constitutes "feminist" expression.

As Nancy Guevara notes, the "exclusion and/or trivialization of women's role in Hip Hop" is no mere oversight.[7] The marginalization, deletion, and mischaracterization of women's role in black cultural production is routine practice. Angela Davis extends this criticism by stating that this is "an omission that must be attributed to the influence of sexism." In her article, "Black Women and Music: An Historical Legacy of Struggle," Davis makes three related arguments that are of particular importance here. First, she contests the marginal representation of black women in the documentation of African-American cultural developments and suggests that these representations do not adequately reflect women's participation. Second, she suggests that music (song and dance) are especially productive sites for examining the collective consciousness of black Americans. And third, she calls for a close reexamination of black women's musical legacy as a way to understand black women's consciousness. She writes:

> Music has long permeated the daily life of most African-Americans; it has played a central role in the normal socialization process; and during moments characterized by intense movements for social change, it has helped to shape the necessary political consciousness. Any attempt, therefore, to understand in depth the evolution of women's consciousness within the Black community requires a serious examination of the music which has influenced them—particularly that which they themselves have created.[8]

She continues by offering a close reading of Gertrude "Ma" Rainey's music as a step toward redressing such absences. Dealing with similar issues, Hazel Carby charges that white dominated feminist discourse has marginalized (and I would add often ignored) non-white women and questions of black sexuality. She further argues that representations of black women's sexuality in African-American literature differs significantly from representations of sexuality in black women's blues.[9]

Carby and Davis, while concerning themselves specifically with women's blues, are calling for a multi-faceted analysis of black women's identity and sexuality as represented by their musical production. Stating that "different cultural forms negotiate and resolve different sets of social contradictions," Carby suggests that black women writers have been encouraged to speak on behalf of a large group of black women whose daily lives and material conditions may not be adequately reflected in black women's fiction. For example, the consumption patterns and social context of popular music differ significantly from those of fiction. The dialogic capacity of popular music, especially that of rap music, engages many of the social contradictions and ambiguities that pertain specifically to contemporary urban, working-class black life.

George Lipsitz, applying Mikhail Bakhtin's concept of "dialogic" criticism to popular music, argues that:

> Popular music is nothing if not dialogic, the product of an ongoing historical conversation in which no one has the first or last word. The traces of the past that pervade the popular music of the present amount to more than mere chance: they are not simply juxtapositions of incompatible realities. They reflect a dialogic process, one embedded in collective history and nurtured by the ingenuity of artists interested in fashioning icons of opposition.

Lipsitz's interpretation of popular music as a social and historical dialogue is an extremely important break from traditional, formalist interpretations of music. By grounding cultural production historically and avoiding the application of a fixed inventory of core structures, dialogic criticism as employed by Lipsitz is concerned with how popular music "arbitrates tensions between opposition and co-optation at any given historical moment."[10]

This notion of dialogism is especially productive in the context of African-American music. The history of African-American music and culture has been defined in large measure by a history of the art of signifying, recontextualization, collective memory and resistance. "Fashioning icons of opposition" that speak to diverse communities is part of a rich black American musical tradition to which rappers make a significant contribution. Negotiating multiple boundaries, black women rappers are in dialogue with each other, male rappers, other popular musicians (through sampling and other revisionary practices), and with Hip Hop fans.

Black women rappers are integral and resistant voices in Hip Hop and in popular music generally. They sustain an ongoing dialogue with their audiences and male rappers about sexual promiscuity, emotional commitment, infidelity, the drug trade, racial politics and black cultural history. Rappers interpret and articulate the fears, pleasures and promises of young black women and men whose voices have been relegated to the silent margins of public discourse. By paying close attention to rap music, we can gain some insight into how young African-Americans provide for themselves a relatively safe free-play zone where they creatively address questions of sexual power, the reality of truncated economic opportunity, the pain of racism and sexism and, through physical expressions of freedom, relieve the anxieties of day-to-day oppression.

If you have been following the commercial success of rap music, it is difficult to ignore the massive increase in record deals for women rappers following Salt-N-Pepa's double platinum (two million) 1986 debut album *Hot, Cool and Vicious*. Such album sales, even for a rap album by a male artist, were virtually unprecedented in 1986. Since then, several female rappers, many of whom have been rapping for years (some since the mid-1970s), have finally been recorded and promoted.[11] Says female rapper Ms. Melodie:

> It wasn't that the male started rap, the male was just the first to be put on wax. Females were always into rap, and females always had their little crews and were always known for rockin' house parties and streets or whatever, school yards, the corner, the park, whatever it was.[12]

In the early stages, women's participation in rap was hindered by gender considerations. M.C. Lady "D" notes that because she didn't put a female crew together for regular performances, she "didn't have to worry about getting [her] equipment ripped off, coming up with the cash to get it in the first place, or hauling it around on the subways to gigs—problems that kept a lot of other women out of rap in the early days."[13] For a number of reasons (including increased institutional support and more demand for both male and female rappers), such stumbling blocks have been reduced.

MC Lyte's 1988 release, "Paper Thin," sold over 125,000 copies in the first six months with virtually no radio play. Lady B, who became the first recorded female rapper in 1978, was Philadelphia's top rated D.J. on WUSL and is founder and Editor-in-Chief of *Word Up!*, a tabloid devoted to Hip Hop.[14] Salt-N-Pepa's first single, "Expressions," from their latest album release *Black's Magic*, went gold in the first week and stayed in the number one position on *Billboard*'s Rap Chart for over two months.

But these industry success-markers are not the primary focus here. I intend to show that the subject matter and perspectives presented in many women's rap lyrics challenge dominant notions of sexuality, heterosexual courtship, and aesthetic constructions of the body. In addition, music videos and live performances display exuberant communities of women occupying public space while exhibiting sexual freedom, independence and, occasionally, explicit domination over men. Women's raps grow more and more complex each year and, with audience support, many rappers have taken risks (regarding imagery and subject matter) that a few years ago would have been unthinkable. Through their lyrics and video images, black women rappers—especially Queen Latifah, MC Lyte and Salt-N-Pepa—form a dialogue with working-class black women and men, offering young black women a small but potent culturally-reflexive public space.

In order to understand the oppositional nature of these women rappers, it is important to have at least a sketch of some of the politics behind rap's battle of the sexes. Popular raps by both men and women have covered many issues and social situations that pertain to the lives of young, black working-class teens in urban America. Racism, drugs, police brutality, sex, crime, poverty, education and prison have been popular themes in rap for a number of years. But raps about celebration, dance, styling, boasting and just "gittin' funky" (in Kid-N-Play's words) have been equally popular. Raps about style and prestige sometimes involve the possession of women as evidence of male power. Predictably, these raps define women as commodities, objects and ornaments. Others are defensive and aggressive raps that describe women solely as objects of male pleasure. In rap music, as in other popular genres, women are divided into at least two categories—the "kind to take home to mother" and the "kind you meet at three o'clock in the morning." In Hip Hop discourse, the former is honest and loyal—but extremely rare (decidedly not the girl next door). The latter is not simply an unpaid prostitute, but a woman who only wants you for your money, cars and cash, will trap you (via pregnancy or other forms of manipulation), and move on to another man (probably your best friend). It would be an understatement to suggest that there is little in the way of traditional notions of romance in rap. Sexist raps articulate the profound fear of female sexuality felt by these young rappers and by many young men.

In a recent *Village Voice* interview with ex-NWA member Ice Cube, notorious not only for harsh sexist raps but for brilliant chilling stories of ghetto life, Greg Tate (one of the best Hip Hop social critics) tries to get "some understanding" about the hostility toward women expressed in Ice Cube's raps:

Tate: Do you think rap is hostile toward women?
Ice Cube: The whole damn world is hostile toward women.
Tate: What do you mean by that?
Ice Cube: I mean the power of sex is more powerful than the motherfuckers in Saudi Arabia. A girl that you want to get with can make you do damn near anything. If she knows how to do her shit right, she can make you buy cigarettes you never wanted to buy in life.... Look at all my boys out here on this video shoot, all these motherfuckers sitting out here trying to look fly, hot as a motherfucker, ready to go home. But there's too many women here for them to just get up and leave. They out here since eight o'clock in the morning and ain't getting paid. They came for the girls.[15]

Ice Cube's answer may appear to be a non sequitur, but his remarks address what I believe is the subtext in rap's symbolic male domination over women. Ice Cube suggests that many men are hostile toward women because the fulfillment of male heterosexual desire is significantly checked by women's capacity for sexual rejection and/or manipulation of men. Ice Cube acknowledges the reckless boundaries of his desire as well as the power women can exercise in this sexual struggle. In "The Bomb," Ice Cube warns men to "especially watch the ones with the big derriers" because the greater your desire, the more likely you are to be blinded by it, and consequently the more vulnerable you are likely to be to female domination. From the perspective of a young man, such female power is probably more palpable than any woman realizes. Obviously, Ice Cube is not addressing the institutional manifestations of patriarchy and its effects on the social construction of desire. However, he and many black male rappers speak to men's fears and the realities of the struggle for power in teenage heterosexual courtship in a sexist society.

During the summer of 1990, Bell Biv Devoe, a popular R&B/Rap crossover group, raced up the charts with "Poison," a song about women whose chorus warns men not to "trust a big butt and a smile." The song cautions men about giving in to their sexual weaknesses and then being taken advantage of by a sexy woman whose motives might be equally insincere. The degree of anxiety expressed is striking. "Poison" explains both their intense desire for and profound distrust of women. The capacity of a woman to use her sexuality to manipulate *his* desire for *her* purposes is an important facet of the sexual politics of male raps about women. Bell Biv Devoe are telling men: "You may not know what a big butt and a smile really means. It might not mean pleasure; it might mean danger—poison."

All of this probably seems gravely sexist—so much so that any good feminist would reject it out of hand. However, I would like to suggest that women rappers effectively engage with male rappers on this level. By expressing their sexuality openly and in their own language, yet distinguishing themselves from poisonous and insincere women, black women rappers challenge men to take women more seriously. Black women rappers might respond by saying: "That's right, don't automatically trust a big butt and a smile. We've got plenty of sexual power and integrity, but don't mess with us." I am not suggesting that women have untapped power that once accessed will lead the way to the dismantling of patriarchy. Ice Cube and Bell Biv Devoe's expressions of fear must be understood in the context of their status as men and the inherent social power such a gender assignment affords. But, understanding the fear of female sexuality helps explain the consistent sexual domination men attempt to sustain over women. Without such fears, their efforts would be unnecessary.

Women's raps and my interviews with female rappers display similar fears of manipulation, loss of control, and betrayal at the hands of men. What is especially interesting about women rappers is the way in which they shift the focus of the debate. Male rappers focus on sexually promiscuous women who "want their money" (in rap lingo they are called skeezers) and almost never offer a depiction of a sincere woman. Female rappers focus on dishonest men who seek sex from women (much like the women who seek money from men), and they represent themselves as seasoned women with sexual confidence and financial independence.

During my interview with Salt (one half of the female rap duo Salt-N-Pepa), I pressed her about how she could envision a committed relationship without some degree of emotional dependence. She replied:

> I just want to depend on myself. I feel like a relationship shouldn't be emotional dependence. I, myself, am more comfortable when I do not depend on hugs and kisses from somebody that I possibly won't get. If I don't get them then I'll be disappointed. So if I get them, I'll appreciate them.[16]

Salt's lyrics reflect much of how she feels personally: "You know I don't want to for your money"; "I'm independent, I make my own money, so don't tell me how to spend it"; "You can't disguise the lies in your eyes, you're not a heartbreaker"; "You need me and I don't need you."[17]

Women rappers employ many of the aesthetic and culturally specific elements present in male rap lyrics while offering an alternative vision of similar social conditions. Raps written by women which specifically concern male/female relationships almost always confront the tension between trust and savvy, between vulnerability and control. Women rappers celebrate their sisters for "getting over" on men. Some raps by women such as Icey Jaye's "It's a Girl Thang" mock the men who fall for their tricks. But for the most part, women rappers promote self-reliance and challenge the depictions of women in male raps, addressing the fears about male dishonesty and infidelity that most women share.

Raps written and performed by women regarding male/female relationships can be divided into at least three categories: (1) raps that challenge male dominance over women within the sexual arena, (2) raps, that by virtue of their authoritative stance, challenge men as representatives of Hip Hop, and (3) raps that explicitly discuss women's identity and celebrate women's physical and sexual power. Across these three categories, several popular female rappers and their music videos can serve as illuminating examples.[18]

MC Lyte and Salt-N-Pepa have reputations for biting raps that criticize men who manipulate and abuse women. Their lyrics tell the story of men taking advantage of women, cheating on them, abusing them, taking their money and then leaving them for other unsuspecting female victims. These raps are not mournful ballads about the trials and tribulations of being a woman. Similar to women's blues, they are caustic, witty and aggressive warnings directed at men and at other women who might be seduced by men in the future. By offering a woman's interpretation of the terms of heterosexual courtship, these raps cast a new light on male/female sexual power relations and depict women as resistant, aggressive participants.

Salt-N-Pepa's 1986 single, "Tramp," speaks specifically to black women, warning us that "Tramp" is not a "simple rhyme," but a parable about relationships between men and women:

> Homegirls attention you must pay to what I say
> Don't take this as a simple rhyme
> 'Cause this type of thing happens all the time
> Now what would you do if a stranger said "Hi"
> Would you dis him or would you reply?
> If you'd answer, there is a chance
> That you'd become a victim of circumstance
> Am I right fellas? Tell the truth
> Or else I'll have to show and prove
> You are what you are I am what I am
> It just so happens that most men are TRAMPS.

In the absence of any response to "Am I right fellas?" Salt-N-Pepa "show and prove" the trampings of several men who "undress you with their eyeballs," "think you're a dummy" and "on the first date, had the nerve to tell me he loves me." Salt-N-Pepa's parable, by defining promiscuous *men* as tramps, inverts the social construction of male sexual promiscuity as a status symbol. This reversal undermines the degrading "woman as tramp" image by stigmatizing male promiscuity. Salt-N-Pepa suggest that women who respond to sexual advances are victims of circumstance. It is the predatory, disingenuous men who are the tramps.

The music video for "Tramp" is a comic rendering of a series of social club scenes that highlight tramps on the make, mouth freshener in hand, testing their lines on the nearest woman. Dressed in Hip Hop street gear, Salt-N-Pepa perform the song on television, on a monitor perched above the bar. Since they appear on the television screen, they seem to be surveying and critiquing the club action, but the club members cannot see them. There are people dancing and talking together (including likeable men who are coded as "non-tramps"), who seem unaware of the television monitor. Salt-N-Pepa are also shown in the club, dressed in very stylish, sexy outfits. They act as decoys, talking and flirting with the tramps to flesh out the dramatization of tramps on the prowl, and they make several knowing gestures at the camera to reassure the viewer that they are unswayed by the tramps' efforts.

The club scenes have no dialogue. The tramps and their victims interact only with body language. Along with the music for "Tramp," we hear Salt-N-Pepa's lyrics, which serve respectively as the club's dance music and the video's voice-over narration. Viewing much of the club action from Salt-N-Pepa's authoritative position through the television monitor, we can safely observe the playful but cautionary dramatization of heterosexual courtship. Rapping to a woman, one tramp postures and struts, appearing to ask the stock pick-up line, "What is your zodiac sign, baby?" When she shows disgust and leaves her seat, he repeats the same body motions on the next woman who happens to sit down. Near the end of the video a frustrated "wife" enters the club and drags one of the tramps home, smacking him in the head with her pocketbook. Salt-N-Pepa stand next to the wife's tramp in the club, shaking their heads as if to say "what a shame." Simultaneously, they point and laugh at him from the television monitor. At the end of the video, a still frame of each man is stamped "tramp," while Salt-N-Pepa revel in having identified and exposed them. They leave the club together without men, seemingly enjoying their skill at exposing the real intentions of these tramps.

Salt-N-Pepa are clearly "schooling" women about the sexual politics of the club scene. They are engaged in and critiquing the drama of heterosexual courtship. The privileged viewer is a woman who is directly addressed in the lyrics and can fully empathize with the visual depiction and interpretation of the scenes. The video's resolution is a warning to both men and women. Women: Don't fall for these men either by talking to them in the clubs or believing the lies they'll tell you when they come home. Men: You will get caught eventually and you'll be embarrassed. The "Tramp" video also tells women that they can go to these clubs and successfully play along with the game as long as the power of female sexuality and the terms of male desire are understood.

In her video, MC Lyte has a far less playful response to her boyfriend Sam, whom she catches in the act of flirting with another woman. MC Lyte's underground hit, "Paper Thin," is one of the most scathing raps about male dishonesty/infidelity and the tensions between trust and vulnerability. Lyte has been burned by Sam, but she has turned her experience into a black woman's anthem that sustains an uncomfortable balance between brutal cynicism and honest vulnerability:

> When you say you love me it doesn't matter
> It goes into my head as just chit chatter
> You may think it's egotistical or just very free
> But what you say, I take none of it seriously.
>
> I'm not the kind of girl to try to play a man out
> They take the money and then they break the hell out
> No that's not my strategy, not the game I play
> I admit I play a game, but it's not done that way
> Truly when I get involved I give it my heart
> I mean my mind, my soul, my body I mean every part
> But if it doesn't work out—yo, it just doesn't
> It wasn't meant to be, you know it just wasn't
> So, I treat all of you like I treat all of them
> What you say to me is just paper thin.

Lyte's public acknowledgment that Sam's expressions of love were paper thin is not a source of embarrassment for her, but a means of empowerment. She plays a brutal game of the dozens on Sam while wearing her past commitment to him as a badge of honor and sign of character. Lyte presents commitment, vulnerability and sensitivity as assets, not indicators of female weakness. In "Paper Thin," emotional and sexual commitment are not romantic Victorian concepts tied to honorable but dependent women; they are a part of her strategy, part of the game she plays in heterosexual courtship.

The high energy video for "Paper Thin" contains many elements present in Hip Hop. The video opens with Lyte (dressed in a sweatsuit and sneakers) abandoning her new Jetta because she wants to take the subway. A few members of her male posse follow along behind her, down the steps to the subway tracks. Once in the subway car, her D.J. K-Rock, doubling as the conductor, announces that the train will be held in the station due to crossed signals. While they wait, Milk Boy (her body guard) spots Sam at the other end of the car, rapping heavily to two stylish women. Lyte, momentarily surprised, begins her rhyme as she stalks toward

Sam. Sam's attempts to escape fail; he is left to face MC Lyte's wrath. Eventually, she throws him off the train to the tune of Ray Charles's R&B classic, "Hit the Road Jack," and locks Sam out of the subway station, symbolically jailing him. The subway car is filled with young black teenagers, typical working New Yorkers and street people, many of whom join Lyte in signifying on Sam while they groove on K-Rock's music. MC Lyte's powerful voice and no-nonsense image dominate Sam. The tense, driving music—which is punctuated by sampled guitar and drum sections as well as an Earth Wind and Fire horn section—complement Lyte's hard, expressive rapping style.

It is important that "Paper Thin" is set in public and on the subway, the quintessential mode of urban transportation. Lyte is drawn to the subway and obviously feels comfortable there. She is also comfortable with the subway riders in her video; they are her community. By setting her confrontation with Sam in the subway, in front of their peers, Lyte moves a private problem between lovers into the public arena and effectively dominates both spaces.

When her D.J., the musical and mechanical conductor, announces that crossed signals are holding the train in the station, he frames the video in a moment of communication crisis. The notion of crossed signals represents the inability of Sam and Lyte to communicate with one another, an inability that is primarily the function of the fact that they communicate on different frequencies. Sam thinks he can read Lyte's mind to see what she is thinking and then feed her all the right lines. But what he says carries no weight, no meaning. His words are light, they're paper thin. Lyte, who understands courtship as a game, confesses to being a player, yet expresses how she feels honestly and in simple language. What she says has integrity, weight, and substance.

After throwing Sam from the train, she nods her head toward a young man standing against the subway door, and he follows her off the train. She will not allow her experiences with Sam to paralyze her, but she does have a new perspective on dating. As she and her new male friend walk down the street, she raps the final stanza for "Paper Thin," which sets down the ground rules:

> So, now I take precautions when choosing my mate
> I do not touch until the third or fourth date
> Then maybe we'll kiss on the fifth or sixth time that we meet
> 'Cause a date without a kiss is so incomplete
> And then maybe, I'll let you play with my feet
> You can suck the big toe and play with the middle
> It's so simple unlike a riddle. ...

MC Lyte and Salt-N-Pepa are not alone in their critique of men's treatment of women. Neneh Cherry's "Buffalo Stance" tells men: "You better watch, don't mess with me / No money man can buy my love / It's sweetness that I'm thinkin' of"; Oaktown 3–5–7's "Say That Then" lashes out at "Finger poppin', hip hoppin', wanna be bed rockin'" men; Ice Cream Tee's "All Wrong" chastises women who allow men to abuse them; and MC Lyte's "I Cram to Understand U," "Please Understand" and "I'm Not Havin' It" are companion pieces to "Paper Thin."

Women rappers also challenge the popular conception that male rappers are the only M.C.s who can "move the crowd," a skill that ultimately determines your status as a successful rapper. Black women rappers compete head-to-head with male rappers for status as the preeminent M.C. Consequently, rhymes that boast, signify and toast are an important part of women's repertoire. Antoinette's "Who's the Boss," Ice Cream Tee's "Let's Work," MC Lyte's "Lyte as a Rock," Salt-N-Pepa's "Everybody Get Up," and Queen Latifah's "Dance for Me" and "Come Into My House" establish black women rappers as Hip Hop M.C.s who can move the crowd, a talent that is as important as writing "dope" rhymes. Latifah's "Come into My House" features Latifah as the dance master, the hostess of physical release and pleasure:

Welcome into my Queendom
Come one, come all
'Cause when it comes to lyrics I bring them
In Spring I sing, in Fall I call
Out to those who had a hard day
I've prepared a place on my dance floor
The time is now for you to party. ...
I'm on fire the flames too high to douse
The pool is open
Come Into My House.[19]

As rap's territory expands, so does the material of female rappers. Subjects ranging from racism, black politics, Afrocentrism and nationalism to homelessness, physical abuse of women and children, drug addiction, AIDS and teen pregnancy can all be found in female rappers' repertoire. "Ladies First," Queen Latifah's second release from her debut album, *All Hail the Queen*, is a landmark example of such expansions. Taken together, the video and lyrics for "Ladies First" is a statement for black female unity, independence and power, as well as an anti-colonial statement concerning Africa's southern region. The rap recognizes the importance of black female political activists, offering hope for the development of a pro-female, pro-black, diasporatic political consciousness. A rapid-fire and powerful rap duet between Queen Latifah and her "European sister" Monie Love, "Ladies First" is thus a recital on the significance and diversity of black women. Latifah's assertive, measured voice in the opening rhyme sets the tone:

The ladies will kick it, the rhyme it is wicked
Those who don't know how to be pros get evicted
A woman can bear you, break you, take you
Now it's time to rhyme, can you relate to
A sister dope enough to make you holler and scream?

In her almost double-time verse, Monie Love responds:

Eh, Yo! Let me take it from here Queen
Excuse me but I think I am about due
To get into precisely what I am about to do
I'm conversatin' to the folks who have no whatsoever clue
So, listen very carefully as I break it down to you
Merrily merrily, hyper happy overjoyed
Pleased with all the beats and rhymes my sisters have employed
Slick and smooth—throwing down the sound totally, a yes
Let me state the position: Ladies First, Yes?

Latifah responds, "YES!"

Without attacking black men, "Ladies First" is a wonderful rewriting of the contributions of black women into the history of black struggles. Opening with slides of black female political activists Sojourner Truth, Angela Davis and Winnie Mandela, the video's predominant theme features Latifah as Third World military strategist. She stalks an illuminated, conference table-size map of Southern Africa and, with a long pointer, shoves large chess-like pieces of briefcase carrying white men off white dominated countries, replacing them with large black power style fists. In between these scenes, Latifah and Monie Love rap in front of and between more photos of politically prominent black women and footage of black struggles that shows protests and acts of military violence against protestors. Latifah positions herself as part of a rich legacy of black women's activism, racial commitment and cultural pride.

Given the fact that protest footage rap videos (which have become quite popular over the last few years) have all but excluded scenes of black women leaders or foot soldiers, the centrality of black women's political protest in "Ladies First" is refreshing. Scenes of dozens of rural African women running with sticks raised above their heads toward armed oppressors, holding their ground alongside men in equal numbers and dying in struggle, are rare media images. As Latifah explains:

> I wanted to show the strength of black women in history. Strong black women. Those were good examples. I wanted to show what we've done. We've done a lot; it's just that people don't know it. Sisters have been in the midst of these things for a long time, but we just don't get to see it that much.[20]

After placing a black power fist on each country in Southern Africa, Latifah surveys the map, nodding contentedly. The video ends with a still frame of the region's new political order.

Latifah's self-possession and independence is an important facet of the new cultural nationalism in rap. The powerful, level-headed and black feminist character of her lyrics calls into question the historically cozy relationship between nationalism and patriarchy. The legendary Malcolm X phrase, "There are going to be some changes made here," is strategically sampled throughout "Ladies First." When Malcolm's voice is introduced, the camera pans the faces of some of the more prominent female rappers and D.J.s including Ms. Melodie, Ice Cream Tee and Shelley Thunder. The next sample of Malcolm's memorable line is dubbed over South African protest footage. Latifah evokes Malcolm as part of a collective African-American historical memory and recontextualizes him not only as a leader who supports contemporary struggles in South Africa, but also as someone who encourages the imminent changes regarding the degraded status of black women and specifically black women rappers. Latifah's use of the dialogic processes of naming, claiming and recontextualizing is not random; nor is it simply a "juxtaposition of incompatible realities." "Ladies First" is a cumulative product that, as Lipsitz would say, "enters a dialogue already in progress." It affirms and revises African-American traditions at the same time that it stakes out new territory.

Black women rappers' public displays of physical and sexual freedom challenge male notions of female sexuality and pleasure. Salt-N-Pepa's rap duet, "Shake Your Thang," which they perform with the prominent go-go band E.U., is a wonderful verbal and visual display of black women's sexual resistance. The rap lyrics and video are about Salt-N-Pepa's sexual dancing and others' responses to them. The first stanza sets them in a club "shakin' [their] thang to a funky beat with a go-go swing" and captures the shock on the faces of other patrons. With attitude to spare, Salt-N-Pepa chant: "It's my thang and I'll swing it the way that I feel, with a little seduction and some sex appeal." The chorus, sung by the male lead in E.U., chants: "Shake your thang, do what you want to do, I can't tell you how to catch a groove. It's your thang, do what you wanna do, I won't tell you how to catch a groove."[21]

The video is framed by Salt-N-Pepa's interrogation after they have been arrested for lewd dancing. New York police cars pull up in front of the studio where their music video is being shot, and mock policemen (played by Kid-N-Play and their producer Herbie Luv Bug) cart the women away in handcuffs. When their mug shots are being taken, Salt-N-Pepa blow kisses to the cameraman as each holds up her arrest placard. Once in the interrogation room, Kid-N-Play and Herbie ask authoritatively, "What we gonna do about this dirty dancing?" Pepa reaches across the table, grabs Herbie by the tie and growls, "We gonna do what we wanna do." Outdone by her confidence, Herbie looks into the camera with an expression of shock.

The mildly slapstick interrogation scenes bind a number of other subplots. Scenes in which Salt-N-Pepa are part of groups of women dancing and playing are interspersed with separate scenes of male dancers, co-ed dance segments with Kid-N-Play, E.U.'s lead singer acting as a spokesman for a "free Salt-N-Pepa" movement, and picketers in front of the police station calling for Salt-N-Pepa's release. When he is not gathering signatures for his petition, E.U. chants the chorus from a press conference podium. The camera angles for the dance segments give the effect of a series of park or block parties. Salt-N-Pepa shake their butts for the cameras and for each other while rapping, "My jeans fit nice, they show off my butt" and "I Like Hip Hop mixed with a go-go baby, it's my thang and I'll shake it crazy. Don't tell me how to party, it's my dance, yep, and it's my body."

A primary source of the video's power is Salt-N-Pepa's irreverence toward the morally-based sexual constrictions placed on them as women. They mock moral claims about the proper modes of women's expression and enjoy every minute of it. Their defiance of the moral, sexual restrictions on women is to be distinguished from challenges to the seemingly gender neutral laws against public nudity. Salt-N-Pepa are eventually released because their dancing isn't against the law (as they say, "We could get loose, but we can't get naked"). But their "dirty dancing" also teases the male viewer who would misinterpret their sexual freedom as an open sexual invitation. The rappers make it clear that their expression is no such thing: "A guy touch my body? I just put him in check." Salt-N-Pepa thus force a wedge between overt female sexual expression and the presumption that such expressions are intended to attract men. "Shaking your thang" can create a stir, but that should not prevent women from doing it when and how they choose.

At the video's close, we return to the interrogation scene a final time. Herbie receives a call, after which he announces that they have to release the women. The charges will not stick. Prancing out of the police station, Salt-N-Pepa laughingly say, "I told you so." The police raid and arrests make explicit the real, informal yet institutionally-based policing of female sexual expression. The video speaks to black women, calls for open, public displays of female expression, assumes a community-based support for their freedom, and focuses directly on the sexual desirability and beauty of black women's bodies. Salt-N-Pepa's recent video for "Expression" covers similar ground but focuses more on fostering individuality in young women.

Salt-N-Pepa's physical freedom, exemplified by focusing on their butts, is no coincidence. The distinctly black, physical and sexual pride that these women (and other black female rappers) exude serves as a rejection of the aesthetic hierarchy in American culture that marginalizes black women. There is a long black folk history of dances and songs that celebrate big behinds for men and women (e.g., the Bump, the Dookey Butt, and most recently E.U. and Spike Lee's black chart topper, "Da Butt"). Such explicit focus on the behind counters mainstream definitions of what constitutes a sexually attractive female body. American culture, in defining its female sex symbols, places a high premium on long thin legs, narrow hips and relatively small behinds. The vast majority of white female television and film actresses, musicians and even the occasional black model fits this description. The aesthetic hierarchy of the female body in mainstream American culture, with particular reference to the behind and hips, positions many black women somewhere near the bottom. When viewed in this context, Salt-N-Pepa's rap and video become an inversion of the aesthetic hierarchy that renders black women's bodies sexually unattractive.

Obviously, the common practice of objectifying all women's bodies complicates the way some might interpret Salt-N-Pepa shaking their collective thangs. For some, Salt-N-Pepa's sexual free-dom could be considered dangerously close to self-inflicted exploitation. Such misunderstanding of the racial and sexual significance of black women's sexual expression may explain the surprisingly cautious responses I have received from some white feminists regarding the importance of female rappers. However, as Hortense Spillers and other prominent black feminists have argued, a history of silence has surrounded African-American women's sexuality.[22] Spillers argues that this silence has at least two faces; either black women are creatures of male sexual possession, or else they are reified into the status of non-being. Room for self-defined sexual identity exists in neither alternative. The resistant nature of black women's participation in rap is better understood when we take the historical silence, sexual and otherwise, of black women into consideration. Salt-N-Pepa are carving out a female-dominated space in which black women's sexuality is openly expressed. Black women rappers sport Hip Hop clothing and jewelry as well as distinctively black hairstyles. They affirm a black, female, working-class cultural aesthetic that is rarely depicted in American popular culture. Black women rappers resist patterns of sexual objectification and cultural invisibility, and they also resist academic reification and mainstream, hegemonic, white feminist discourse.

Given the identities these women rappers have fashioned for themselves, it is not surprising that they want to avoid being labeled feminists. During my conversations with Salt, MC Lyte and Queen Latifah, it became clear that these women saw feminism as a signifier for a movement that related specifically to white women. They also thought feminism involved adopting an anti-male position, and they did not want to be considered or want their work to be interpreted as anti-black male.

In MC Lyte's case, she remarked that she was often labeled a feminist even though she did not think of herself as one. Yet, after she asked for my working definition of feminist, she wholeheartedly agreed with my description, which was as follows:

> I would say that a feminist believed that there was sexism in society, wanted to change and worked toward change. [She] either wrote, spoke or behaved in a way that was pro-woman, in that she supported situations [organizations] that were trying to better the lives of women. A feminist feels that women are more disadvantaged than men in many situations and would want to stop that kind of inequality.

MC Lyte responded, "Under your definition, I would say I am." We talked further about what she imagined a feminist to be, and it became clear that once feminism was understood as a mode of analysis rather than as a label for a group of women associated with a particular social movement, MC Lyte was much more comfortable discussing the importance of black women's independence: "Yes, I am very independent and I feel that women should be independent, but so should men. Both of us need each other and we're just coming to a realization that we do."[23] For MC Lyte, feminists were equivalent to devoutly anti-male, white middle-class members of the National Organization of Women.

Queen Latifah was sympathetic to the issues associated with feminism, but preferred to be considered pro-woman. She was unable to articulate why she was uncomfortable with the term "feminist" and preferred instead to talk about her admiration for Faye Wattleton, the black president of Planned Parenthood, and the need to support the pro-choice movement. As she told me:

> Faye Wattleton, I like her. I look up to her. I'm pro-choice, but I love God. But I think [abortion] is a woman's decision. In a world like we live in today you can't use [God] as an excuse all the time. They want to make abortion illegal, but they don't want to educate you in school.[24]

Salt was the least resistant to the term feminism yet made explicit her limits:

> I guess you could say that [I'm a feminist] in a way. Not in a strong sense where I'd want to go to war or anything like that [laughter]. ... But I preach a lot about women depending

on men for everything, for their mental stability, for their financial status, for their happiness. Women have brains, and I hate to see them walking in the shadow of a man.[25]

For these women rappers, and many other black women, feminism is the label for members of a white woman's social movement, which has no concrete link to black women or the black community. Feminism signifies allegiance to historically specific movements whose histories have long been the source of frustration for women of color. Similar criticisms of women's social movements have been made vociferously by many black feminists who have argued that race and gender are inextricably linked for black women—and I would add, this is the case for both black and white women.[26] However, in the case of black women, the realities of racism link black women to black men in a way that challenges cross-racial sisterhood. If a cross-racial sisterhood is to be forged, serious attention must be paid to issues of racial difference, racism within the movement, and the racial blind spots that inform coalition building. In the meantime, the desire for sisterhood among and between black and white women cannot be achieved at the expense of black women's racial identity.

If feminist scholars want to contribute to the development of a women's movement that has relevance to the lives of women of color (which also means working-class and poor women), then we must be concerned with young women's reluctance to be associated with feminism. We should be less concerned with producing theoretically referential feminist theories and more concerned with linking these theories to practices, thereby creating new concrete ways to interpret feminist activity. This will involve broadening the scope of investigations in our search for black women's voices. This will involve attending to the day-to-day conflicts and pressures that young, black working-class women face and focusing more of our attention on the cultural practices that are most important to their lives. Academic work that links feminist theory to feminist practice should be wholeheartedly encouraged, and an emphasis on making such findings widely available should be made. For feminist theorists, this will not simply entail "letting the other speak," but will also involve a systematic reevaluation of how feminism is conceptualized and how ethnicity, class and race seriously fracture gender as a conceptual category. Until this kind of analysis takes place a great deal more often than it does, what any of us say to MC Lyte will remain paper thin.

One of the remarkable talents black women rappers have is their capacity to attract a large male following and consistently perform their explicitly pro-woman material. They are able to sustain dialogue with and consequently encourage dialogue between young men and women that supports black women and challenges some sexist male behavior. For these women rappers, feminism is a movement that does not speak to men; while on the other hand, they are engaged in constant communication with black male audiences and rappers, and they simultaneously support and offer advice to their young, black female audiences. As MC Lyte explains, "When I do a show, the women are like, 'Go ahead Lyte, tell 'em!' And the guys are like, 'Oh, shit. She's right.' "[27] Obviously, such instances may not lead directly to a widespread black feminist male/female alliance. However, the dialogues facilitated by these female rappers may well contribute to its groundwork.

In a world of worst possibilities, where no such movements can be imagined, these black female rappers provide young black women with a small, culturally-reflexive public space. Rap can no longer be imagined without women rappers' contributions. They have expanded rap's territory and have effectively changed the interpretive framework regarding the work of male rappers. As women who challenge the sexist discourse expressed by male rappers yet sustain dialogue with them, who reject the racially-coded aesthetic hierarchies in American popular culture, who support black women and black culture, black female rappers constitute an important voice in Hip Hop and contemporary black women's cultural production generally. As Salt says:

The women look up to us. They take us dead seriously. It's not a fan type of thing; it's more like a movement. When we shout, "The year 1989 is for the ladies," they go crazy. It's the highlight of the show. It makes you realize that you have a voice as far as women go.[28]

Notes

I would especially like to thank MC Lyte, Queen Latifah, and Salt for their generosity and for their incredible talents. I would also like to thank Stuart Clarke for his thoughtful comments and criticism on earlier versions of this article and its title.

1. For a particularly malicious misreading of rap music see David Gates, "The Rap Attitude," *Newsweek Magazine* 19 March 1990: 56–63. While "The Rap Attitude" is an outrageous example, the assumptions made about the use and intent of rap are quite common. Exceptions to misreadings of this nature include Michael Dyson, "The Culture of Hip Hop," *Zeta Magazine* (June 1989): 45–50 and the works of Greg Tate, a *Village Voice* staff writer, who has been covering rap music for almost a decade.

2. See Henry Louis Gates, Jr., "Two Live Crew De-Coded," *The New York Times* 19 June 1990: 31; Bruce Tucker, "Tell Tchaikovsky the News: Postmodernism, Popular Culture and the Emergence of Rock n Roll," *Black Music Research Journal* (Fall, 1989): 271–295; Anders Stephanson, "Interview with Cornell West," *Universal Abandon?: The Politics of Postmodernism*, ed. Andrew Ross (Minneapolis: U of Minnesota P, 1989): 269–286.

3. See the special issue entitled "The Women of Rap!" *Rappin Magazine* (July 1990); Dominique Di Prima and Lisa Kennedy, "Beat the Rap," *Mother Jones* (Sep./Oct. 1990): 32–35; Jill Pearlman, "Rap's Gender Gap," *Option* (Fall 1988): 32–36; Marisa Fox, "From the Belly of the Blues to the Cradle of Rap," *Details* (July 1989): 118–124.

4. Public Enemy, "Don't Believe The Hype," *It Takes a Nation of Millions to Hold Us Back*, Def Jam Records, 1988.

5. Queen Latifah, "Ladies First," *All Hail the Queen*, Tommy Boy Records, 1989.

6. Nelson George, "Rap's Tenth Birthday," *Village Voice* 24 Oct. 1989: 40.

7. Nancy Guevara, "Women, Writin', Rappin', Breakin'," *The Year Left 2*, ed. Mike Davis, et al. (New York: Verso, 1987): 160–175.

8. Angela Davis, "Black Women and Music: A Historical Legacy of Struggle," *Wild Women in the Whirlwind: Afro-American Culture and the Contemporary Literary Renaissance*, ed. Joanne M. Braxton and Andree Nicola McLaughin (New Jersey: Rutgers UP, 1990): 3.

9. Hazel V. Carby, "It Jus Be's Dat Way Sometime: The Sexual Politics of Women's Blues," *Radical America* 20.4 (1986): 9–22.

10. George Lipsitz, *Time Passages: Collective Memory and American Popular Culture* (Minneapolis: U of Minnesota P, 1990): 99.

11. Roxanne Shante was the first commercial breakthrough female artist. Her basement-produced single was "Roxanne's Revenge" (1985).

12. Pearlman 34.

13. Di Prima and Kennedy 34.

14. Pearlman 34.

15. Greg Tate, "Manchild at Large: One on One with Ice Cube, Hip Hop's Most Wanted," *Village Voice* 11 Sept. 1990: 78.

16. Salt (Cheryl James from Salt-N-Pepa), personal interview, 17 Aug. 1990.

17. Salt-N-Pepa, *Black's Magic*, Next Plateau Records, 1990.

18. Salt-N-Pepa, "Tramp," *Cool, Hot and Vicious*, Next Plateau Records, 1986; Salt-N-Pepa, "Shake Your Thang," *A Salt With a Deadly Pepa*, Next Plateau Records, 1988; Queen Latifah, "Ladies First," *All Hail the Queen*, Tommy Boy Records, 1989. As you will see, none of my analysis will involve the music itself. The music is a very important aspect of rap's power and aesthetics, but given my space limitations here and the focus of my argument, I have decided to leave it out rather than throw in "samples" of my own. For an extended cultural analysis of rap's music see Tricia Rose, "Orality and Technology: Rap Music and Afro-American Cultural Theory and Practice," *Popular Music and Society* 13.4 (1989): 35–44.

19. Queen Latifah, "Come Into My House," *All Hail the Queen*, Tommy Boy Records, 1989.

20. Queen Latifah (Dana Owens), personal interview, 6 Feb. 1990.

21. The melody and rhythm section for "Shake Your Thang" is taken from the Iseley Brothers single "It's Your Thang," which was on *Billboard*'s Top Forty charts in the Winter of 1969.

22. Hortense Spillers, "Interstices: A Small Drama of Words," *Pleasure and Danger: Exploring Female Sexuality*, ed. Carol Vance (Boston: Routledge and Kegan Paul, 1984): 73–100.

23. MC Lyte, personal interview, 7 Sep. 1990.

24. Queen Latifah, personal interview.

25. Salt, personal interview.

26. See Carby, Davis and Spillers cited above. Also see bell hooks, *Ain't I a Woman: Black Women and Feminism* (Boston: South End Press, 1982) and *Feminist Theory: From Margins to Center* (Boston: South End Press, 1984); Barbara Smith, ed., *Home Girls: A Black Feminist Anthology* (New York: Kitchen Table, 1983); Cheryl A. Wall, ed., *Changing Our Own Words: Essays on Criticism, Theory and Writing by Black Women* (New Jersey: Rutgers UP, 1989).

27. MC Lyte, personal interview.

28. Salt, personal interview.

Part V
The Message:

Rap, Politics, and Resistance

Mark Anthony Neal

> Never before have you heard so many black male voices yelling at the world.
>
> Chuck D (*Washington Post*, July 31, 1988)

The epigraph quoting Chuck D, lead vocalist of the seminal political hip-hop group Public Enemy, captured the feelings of many as the 1980s came to an end. Driven by almost a decade of down right neglect in the face of Reagan-era domestic policy and the inability of black elected officials to respond adequately to the worst aspects of those policies, a generation of black youth came of age full of rage. Unlike hip-hop's core audience at the time, Chuck D—a half-generation older than this audience—had been exposed to the late stages of the civil rights and black power era. In Public Enemy, Chuck D and cohorts DJ Terminator X, sidekick Flava-Flav, "Minister of Information" Professor Griff, and the S1Ws (Security of the First World), aimed to refashion the "revolution" to the sounds of hip-hop.

In his chapter Mark Anthony Neal remarks that "Chuck D's call for truth, justice and a black nationalist way of life was perhaps the most potent of any political narratives that had appeared on a black popular recording. Public Enemy very consciously attempted to have hip-hop serve the revolutionary vanguard, the way soul did in 1960s." In reality, Public Enemy's 1988 release of *It Takes a Nation of Millions to Hold Us Back* (Def Jam, 1988) may have comprised the apex of political hip-hop. Despite the initial popularity of recordings like *It Takes a Nation of Millions ...* and Boogie Down Productions' (featuring KRS-One) *By All Means Necessary* (Jive, 1988), the subsequent inability of these artists and recordings to inspire a sustained political or social movement lies at the heart of debates about the significance of hip-hop culture as a vehicle for political change.

In her detailed examination of the efforts to organize the hip-hop masses, Angela Ards notes in her chapter, "for many activists, the creation of hip-hop amid social devastation is in itself a political act." Though few critics and scholars would dispute that there is something inherently political about hip-hop music, particularly with regard to how it changed the sonic landscape of urban communities and the recording industry, these theoretical politics are very dissimilar from the concrete politics of resistance and transformation. Can political lyrics within hip-hop—which are not necessarily confined to so-called "conscious" rappers—affect sustained political empowerment among audiences in the absence of grassroots and mainstream political organizing? The chapters in this section consider distinct aspects of a hip-hop–based political movement, examining the shortcomings of political recordings and the attempts by both hip-hop constituencies and those outside of those constituencies to organize on a grassroots level.

As the civil rights and black power movements progressed during the late 1960s and early 1970s, black popular music began to reflect the political tensions that gripped much of the nation at the time. The music of Sly and the Family Stone ("Thankyoufalletinme Be Myself"), The Temptations ("Ball of Confusion"), Freda Payne ("Bring the Boys Home"), and Marvin Gaye ("Inner City Blues") openly confronted police brutality, the Vietnam War, the disenfranchisement of black and poor whites, and the general confusion of the era. Although much of this music had an appeal within the mainstream, there were other artists just beyond the mainstream's radar who found a popular following among young black, white, and Hispanic audiences. Using spoken-word poetry and, at times, West African drum rhythms, two of those acts—Gil Scott-Heron and The Last Poets—spoke directly to the most disaffected of black youth with songs like "The Revolution Won't Be Televised" and "Niggers Are Scared of Revolution," respectively.

Scott-Heron and The Last Poets, as well as other musicians such as The Watts Prophets and Nikki Giovanni, are generally seen as direct precursors to the hip-hop movement and comparisons were drawn when groups like Public Enemy and Boogie Down Productions subsequently emerged. The latter groups were also poster-children for what Ronald A.T. Judy calls "leftist agitprop," meaning they benefited from a commercial culture that found material value in their presence, something that would have been unimaginable with the political groups of the 1960s. In his chapter Clarence Lusane observes that "rap is the voice of alienated, frustrated and rebellious black youth," adding that it is also a factor in the "packaging and marketing of social discontent by some of the most skilled ad agencies and largest record producers in the world."

Todd Boyd argues that the very phenomenon observed by Lusane remains critical to an understanding of the uniqueness of contemporary cultural politics. According to Boyd, the "space between the points where radical political discourse can critique dominant culture and dominant culture becomes financially viable through the selling of this oppositional discourse is the only viable space for a reasoned understanding of contemporary political culture." Boyd specifically examines the popularity of the group Arrested Development and their Afrocentric style among mainstream audiences, like those that comprise the core audience of MTV. Boyd critically notes, "signifiers of leftist political culture are easily corrupted as they are co-opted by the fashion industry of dominant society."

The limits and constraints inherent to the effort to politicize hip-hop audiences within the vortex of the contemporary culture industry frame much of the commentary that is related to the political organization of these audiences. In her chapter Ards identifies three tenets necessary for successfully organizing the hip-hop generation, namely, that such an endeavor must be "youth led and defined"; it must involve "more than a race based political analysis of the issues affecting urban youth"; and it must address the "irony of using hip-hop." Implicit in this analysis is the complication and the reality of deploying a commodity—what hip-hop is for many involved in its production—to forge a social movement. Ards cites activist rapper Boots Riley, of the Oakland-based duo The Coup, who acknowledges that "political rap groups offered solutions only through listening. They weren't part of a movement, so they died out when people saw that their lives were not changing," adding that, "in order for political rap to be around, there has to be a movement that will be around that will make people's lives better in a material sense."

As Ards suggests in her chapter, the "pitfall organizers have to avoid is becoming like advertisers, manipulating youth culture for their own ends." Her referencing of the advertising industry is significant because, as Lusane confirms, "Alcohol companies, already complicit in the disproportionate targeting of the black community for liquor sales were quick to front rap stars to sell their product." Ards's and Lusane's observations are particularly important as several members of the black political and entertainment industry elite have taken an interest in organizing the hip-hop generation. Among the best examples of such efforts are the series of Hip-Hop Summits organized by hip-hop impresario Russell Simmons.

Bakari Kitwana writes in his chapter that the first summit facilitated by Simmons was "impressive in terms of sheer numbers and diverse backgrounds. But where it most seriously came up short was in its failure to incorporate the grassroots segment of hip-hop's cultural movement, especially hip-hop generation activists." Kitwana is careful, however, not to view politicized hip-hop artists as being constitutive of a revolutionary vanguard, warning, "as activist-minded as their lyrics may be, as tuned in as they are to activist concerns, and as much as hip-hop generationers admire their politicized messages and activities, few are in the trenches day to day working to bring about change like those at the forefront of activism in our generation." Instead, Kitwana finds the vanguard in a cadre of young activists, including Ras Baraka (son of the well-known poet and activist Amiri Baraka), AIDs activist Tamara Jones, and Van Johnson, executive director of the Ella Baker Center (named after the legendary civil rights leader) in San Francisco. According to Kitwana, this generation of hip-hop activists "have demonstrated that they are in this for the long haul, not just engaged in a passing fling," yet he laments that "too often voices like these are missing from efforts to create the institutional structure needed to move the hip-hop generation into political power." Ultimately, Kitwana admits, "until hip-hop is recognized as a broad cultural movement, rather than simply an influential moneymaker, those who seek to tap into hip-hop's potential to impact social change should not expect substantive progress."

25

Organizing the Hip-Hop Generation

Angela Ards

Each generation must out of relative obscurity discover its mission, fulfill it, or betray it.

Frantz Fanon, "The Wretched of the Earth"

I have stood in a meeting with hundreds of youngsters and joined in while they sang. "Ain't Gonna Let Nobody Turn Me Around." It's not just a song: it is resolve. A few minutes later I have seen those same youngsters refuse to turn around before a pugnacious Bull Connor in command of men armed with power hoses. These songs bind us together, give us courage together, help us march together.

Martin Luther King Jr., "Why We Can't Wait"

"You'll turn around if they put you in jail," a young black man quips to a peer as counselor LaTosha Brown belts out the classic freedom song.

It's the kickoff of the 21st Century Youth Leadership Movement's annual winter summit, held last December at Tuskegee University in Alabama. In 1985 former SNCC activists and their children founded 21st Century on the anniversary of the Selma marches, which ushered in the 1965 Voting Rights Act. Three times a year the group convenes camps to teach movement history to a generation with little appreciation of its accomplishments. They've heard of sit-ins but little of SNCC. Media sound bites provide piecemeal knowledge of Malcolm X and Martin Luther King, but who was Ella Baker? 21st Century seeks to fill in the gaps before this generation slips through. Yet the paradoxical pull of preparing for the future by building a bridge to the past reveals just how wide the chasm has grown.

"When spirits got low, the people would sing," Brown explains. "The one thing we did right / Was the day we started to fight / Keep your eyes on the prize / Oh, Lord." Her rich contralto, all by itself, sounds like the blended harmonies of Sweet Honey in the Rock, but it's not stirring this crowd of 150 Southern youth. Two fresh-faced assistants bound on stage to join in like cheerleaders at a pep rally. Most of the others, however, take their cues from the older teens, slouched in their seats in an exaggerated posture of cool repose. Brown hits closer to their sensibilities when she resorts to funk. "Say it loud," she calls. "I'm black and I'm proud," they respond. But a brash cry from the back of the room speaks more to their hearts. "Can we sing some Tupac?" Another cracks. "Y'all wanna hear some Busta Rhymes?"

By the weekend's close, 21st Century co-founder Rose Sanders is voicing a sentiment activists who work with young people increasingly share. "Without hip-hop," says Sanders, 53, "I don't see how we can connect with today's youth."

In *Hiphop America*, cultural critic Nelson George writes that this post–civil rights generation may be the first black Americans to experience nostalgia. Although it's proverbial that you can't miss what you never had, or what never truly was, romantic notions of past black unity and struggle—despite the state violence that created the sense of community—magnify the despair of present realities. Public schools are almost as segregated today as at the time of the 1954 *Brown v. Board of Education* ruling. "Jail, no bail"—the civil-disobedience tactic used by sixties activists to dismantle Southern apartheid could just as easily refer to the contemporary incarceration epidemic, ushered in by mandatory minimum sentencing, three-strikes-you're-out laws and the "war on drugs." The voter registration campaigns for which many Southern blacks lost jobs, land and lives are now mocked by the fact that 13 percent of African-American men—1.4 million citizens—cannot vote because of criminal records meted out by a justice system proven to be neither blind nor just.

Hip-hop was created in the mid-seventies as black social movements quieted down, replaced by electoral politics. It has deep sixties cultural and political roots; Gil Scott-Heron and The Last Poets are considered the forebears of rap. But once the institutions that supported radical movements collapsed or turned their attention elsewhere, the seeds of hip-hop were left to germinate in American society at large—fed by its materialism, misogyny and a new, more insidious kind of state violence.

Under the watch of a new establishment of black and Latino elected officials, funding for youth services, arts programs and community centers was cut while juvenile detention centers and prisons grew. Public schools became way stations warehousing youth until they were of prison age. Drugs and the violence they attract seeped into the vacuum that joblessness left. Nowhere was this decay more evident than in the South Bronx, which came to symbolize urban blight the way Bull Connor's Birmingham epitomized American racism—and black and Latino youth in the Boogie Down made it difficult for society to pretend that it didn't see them.

In the tradition of defiance, of creating "somethin' outta nothin'," they developed artistic expressions that came to be known as hip-hop. Rapping, or MC'ing, is now the most well known, but there are three other defining elements: DJing, break dancing and graffiti writing. For most of the seventies hip-hop was an underground phenomenon of basement parties, high school gyms and clubs, where DJs and MCs "took two turntables and a microphone," as the story has come to be told, creating music from the borrowed beats of soul, funk, disco, reggae and salsa, overlaid with lyrics reflecting their alienated reality. On city streets and in parks, hip-hop crews—the peaceful alternative to gangs—sought to settle disputes through lyrical battles and break-dancing competitions rather than violence. On crumbling city walls and subways, graffiti writers left their tags as proof that they'd passed.

Underground tapes showcasing a DJ's skills or an MC's rhymes were all the outside world knew of rap music until 1979, when the Sugar Hill Gang released "Rapper's Delight" on a small independent black label. It wasn't the first rap album: many of the lyrics were recycled from artists with more street credibility. But it was a novelty to the mainstream. The record reached No. 36 on U.S. charts and was a huge international hit, purchased largely by young white males, whose tastes have dictated the way rap music has been marketed and promoted ever since. From those classic "a hip hippin to the hip hip hop" lyrics and risque "hotel-motel" rhymes, rap music has gone through various phases—early eighties message raps, late-eighties

Afrocentricity, early nineties gangsta rap, today's rank materialism—and shows no signs of stopping.

This past February, *Time* trumpeted hip-hop on its cover. "After 20 years—how it's changed America." In the past year it has been the subject of at least five academic conferences—from Howard to Harvard to Princeton to UCLA to NYU. In January 2000, the Postal Service plans to issue a hip-hop stamp. *Nation* colleague Mark Schapiro reports that in Macedonian refugee camps, Kosovar Albanian youth shared tapes of home-grown hip-hop, raging against life in prewar Kosovo. His creation of black and Latino youth whom America discounted is now the richest—both culturally and economically—pop cultural form on the planet.

Given hip-hop's social origins and infectious appeal, there's long been a hope that it could help effect social change. The point of the music was always to "move the crowd," for DJs to find the funkiest part of the record—the "break beat"—and keep it spinning until people flooded the dance floor and the energy raised the roof. In the late eighties, Chuck D of Public Enemy declared rap "the black CNN" and argued that the visceral, sonic force that got people grooving on the dance floor could, along with rap's social commentary, get them storming the streets.

If nothing else, rapping about revolution did raise consciousness. Public Enemy inspired a generation to exchange huge gold rope chains, which the group likened to slave shackles, for Malcolm X medallions. From PE and others like KRS-ONE, X-Clan and the Poor Righteous Teachers, urban youth were introduced to sixties' figures like Assata Shakur and the Black Panther Party, then began to contemplate issues like the death penalty, police brutality, nationalism and the meaning of American citizenship.

These "old school hip-hop headz," in the parlance of the culture, have come of age along with the music. Many of them are activists, artists, educators, academics, administrators, entrepreneurs, hoping to use hip-hop to awaken a younger generation in the way it began to politicize them. Much of this "hip-hop activism" is in New York emanating from the culture's Bronx birthplace, but flashes of organizing are being seen in San Francisco, Los Angeles, Washington, Atlanta and cyberspace.

Last September former Nation of Islam minister Conrad Muhammad launched A Movement for CHHANGE (Conscious Hip Hop Activism Necessary for Global Empowerment) and its Million Youth Voter Registration Drive. El Puente Academy for Peace and Justice in Williamsburg, Brooklyn, has a Hip Hop 101 course that borrows from Paulo Freire's teaching model: educate to liberate. In 1993 the Central Brooklyn Partnership, which has trained people since 1989 to organize for economic justice, opened the first "hip-hop credit union" in Bedford-Stuyvesant to offer low-interest loans. The Prison Moratorium Project, a coalition of student and community activists dedicated to ending prison growth and rebuilding schools, is producing *No More Prisons*, a hip-hop CD featuring Hurricane G, The Coup and Cornel West. In Atlanta, the Youth Task Force works with rap artists Goodie Mobb to teach youth about environmental justice and political prisoners. In the Bay Area, the Third Eye Movement, a youth-led political and arts organization, has initiated a grassroots campaign against police brutality that combines direct action, policy reform and hip-hop concerts that serve as fundraisers, voter education forums and mass demonstrations. The New York chapter of the Uhuru Movement, a black nationalist organization that promotes communal living and self-determination, has as its president Mutulu Olugbala, M1 of the rap group Dead Prez. In cyberspace, Davey D's Hip-Hop Corner, produced by an Oakland radio personality, keeps aficionados up to date on the latest industry trends and issues affecting urban youth. On his own Web site, Chuck D is waging a campaign to get rap artists to plunge into the new MP3 technology, which offers musicians creative control and immediate access to a global audience, bypassing corporate overhead and earning more profits for themselves and, potentially, their communities.

For many activists, the creation of hip-hop amid social devastation is in itself a political act. "To—in front of the world—get up on a turntable, a microphone, a wall, out on a dance floor, to proclaim your self-worth when the world says you are nobody, that's a huge, courageous, powerful, exhilarating step," says Jakada Imani, a civil servant in Oakland by day and a co-founder of the Oakland-based production company Underground Railroad. Concerted political action will not necessarily follow from such a restoration of confidence and self-expression, but it is impossible without it. Radical movements never develop out of despair.

It's too early to say whether the culture can truly be a path into politics and not just a posture, and, if it can, what those politics might be. But what is emerging throughout the country—when the influence of the black church has diminished, national organizations seem remote from everyday life and, in some sense minority youth have to start from scratch—is an effort to create a space where youth of color can go beyond pain to resistance, where alternative institutions, and alternative politics, can develop.

As Tricia Rose, professor of Africana studies and history at New York University and author of *Black Noise: Rap Music and Black Culture in Contemporary America*, puts it, "The creation and then tenacious holding on, of cultural forms that go against certain kinds of grains in society is an important process of subversion." It is "about a carving out of more social space, more identity space. This is critical to political organizing. It's critical to political conscious-ness." Because of its osmotic infusion into the mainstream, Rose argues hip-hop culture could be used to create a conversation about social justice among young people, much as black religious culture influenced the civil rights discourse of the sixties.

> Come on, baby, light my fire / Everything you drop is so tired / Music is supposed to inspire / How come we ain't getting no higher? (Lauryn Hill, "Superstar")

The parallel may stop with broad social appeal. There are critical distinctions between black religious culture and hip-hop that make using hip-hop for social change a complicated gesture suggests Richard Yarborough, English professor and director of the Center for African-American Studies at UCLA. "Black religious culture didn't threaten mainstream white liberals the way hip-hop does," notes Yarborough. "It grew directly out of black social institutions, while hip-hop has few sustained institutional bases. Black religious culture never became fodder for the mainstream commodity economy the way hip-hop has. It provided a central role for black women while the role of women in hip-hop is still problematic. Black religious culture was associated with the moral high ground, while hip-hop is too often linked to criminality."

Indeed, Davey D dubbed 1998 "The Year of the Hip-Hop Criminal." Scores of artists, from Busta Rhymes and DMX to Ol' Dirty Bastard and Sean "Puffy" Combs were arrested that year on charges ranging from assault to drug and weapons possession to domestic and sexual violence. Given the hip-hop mandate to "keep it real," to walk the talk of rap music, the inescapable question becomes: What kind of perspectives are youth tapping into and drawing on in hip-hop music?

At the 21st Century youth camp, students are attending the workshop "Hip-Hop 2 Educate." Discussion facilitator Alatunga asks the students to list the music's major themes, prompting a lugubrious litany, in this order: death, pain, drugs, sex, alcohol, gangbanging, guns, struggling in life, reality, murder and childbirth (an odd inclusion perhaps provoked by Lauryn Hill's joyful ode to her firstborn). The young woman who offers "childbirth" then suggests "love." A fan of Kirk Franklin's hip-hop–inflected gospel says "God." It is Alatunga who suggests "politics." The students duly note it on their list.

For the next exercise, he has each person name a "positive" rapper. The first to respond cite the obvious: Lauryn Hill, Goodie Mobb, Outkast. The rest struggle, coming up with current, though not necessarily politically conscious, chart toppers: Jay-Z, DMX, the whole No Limit family. Gospel singer Fred Hammond is allowed because Kirk Franklin was before. Tupac gets in because everyone feels bad he died before fulfilling his potential. Master P, chief exec of the No Limit label, raises some eyebrows because of his hustler image but slides in because it's argued that the distribution contract he negotiated with Priority Records, which secures him 80 percent of the sales revenue, upsets the classic master-slave relationship between the industry and artists. Alatunga finally draws the line at master marketer Puff Daddy, reminding the group that by "positive" he means political, not just "getting paid."

It's a tricky business fitting culture into politics. Adrienne Shropshire, 31, is a community organizer in Los Angeles with AGENDA (Action for Grassroots Empowerment and Neighborhood Development Alternatives), which came together after the 1992 "Rodney King riots." "Oftentimes the music reinforces the very things that we are struggling against," she says. "How do we work around issues of economic justice if the music is about 'getting mine'? How do we promote collective struggle when the music is about individualism?"

In 1995, AGENDA tried using hip-hop culture in its organizing efforts against Prop 209, the anti-affirmative action ballot measure that eventually passed. Organizers hoped to get youth involved in canvassing around voter education and peer education workshops in schools through open-mike poetry nights. The organizers succeeded in creating a space to talk about social justice issues. They also were able to introduce themselves to artists whom they often failed to reach doing campus-based work. And the events were fun, balancing the unglamorous work of organizing.

Overall, though, Shropshire said, "people didn't make the leap" between raising issues and taking action. They would attend the Friday night poetry reading but pass on the Saturday morning rally. "The attitude was 'If I'm rapping about social justice, isn't that enough?' They wanted to make speeches on the mike, but there was not a critical mass who could take the next step in the process."

This failed experiment forced AGENDA organizers to return to more tried and true techniques: door-to-door canvassing; editorials for local, college and high school newspapers; educational workshops on campuses; collaboration with on-campus student organizations. At their meetings they passed out "action cards" for people to note the areas in which they had expertise: media, outreach, fundraising, event security, etc. And they came to understand that the solid core of people who remained were not the dregs of the hip-hop open-mikes but the die-hard troops who could be counted on over the long haul of a campaign.

As AGENDA learned firsthand the pitfall organizers have to avoid is becoming like advertisers, manipulating youth culture for their own ends. About a decade ago, Tricia Rose recalls, Reynolds Wrap had a campaign with a cartoon figure reciting rhymes over corny beats about using the plastic wrap. Since teenagers rarely purchase Reynolds Wrap, the commercial was rather odd and largely unsuccessful. "But once the advertisers moved into the realm of youth products," says Rose, "then the fusion was complete. There was no leap. You could do sneakers, soda, shoes, sunglasses, whatever, because that's what they're already consuming."

We don't pull no rabbits from a hat / we pull rainbows / from a trash can / we pull hope from the dictionary / n teach it how to ride the subway / we don't guess the card in yo hand / we know it / aim to change it / yeah / we know magic / and don't be so sure that card in yo hand / is the Ace (Ruth Forman, "We Are the Young Magicians")

"I believe in magic," poet/actor Saul Williams chants into the mike at CBGB in New York's East Village, backed up by a live band with violin, viola, drum, bass and electric guitars, and accompanied by a "live performance painting" by Marcia Jones, his partner. In 1996 Williams won the Grand Slam Championship, a competition among spoken-word artists who bring a hip-hop aesthetic to poetry. "Magic," Williams riffs, "not bloodshed," will bring on "the revolution." The transformative power of art is the theme of his hit movie *Slam*, in which Williams plays a street poet cum drug dealer incarcerated for selling marijuana. Through his poetry, and beautiful writing teacher, the protagonist transforms himself and fellow inmates. At the movie's end he raps, "Where my niggas at?" both demanding to know where all the troops are who should be fighting against injustice, and lamenting that they are increasingly in jail. At CBGB, when Williams asks, "Where my wizards at?" the challenge to the hip-hop community to transform society through art is clear.

Later, Williams predicted a "changing of the guard" in hip-hop, from a commodity culture to an arts renaissance that reconnects with hip-hop's sixties Black Arts Movement roots. There are plenty of skeptics. Last September, at a festival of readings, panels and performances in Baltimore and College Park, Maryland, sixties poet Mari Evans argued that while the Black Arts Movement was the cultural arm of a political movement, the work of contemporary artists is "an expression of self rather than the community."

Considering that these are not the sixties and there is not yet a movement to be the arm of, a better analogy would be to the Beat poets of the fifties, whose subversive art prefigured the political tumult that would arise only a few years later, even if they didn't anticipate it. Today, what look like mere social events may represent a prepolitical phase of consciousness building that's integral to organizing. Often, these open-mike nights and poetry slams have politically conscious themes that the poets address in their rhymes. They are also increasingly used for education and fundraising. For instance, Ras Baraka, son of Black Arts father Amiri Baraka, used the proceeds from his weekly Verse to Verse poetry nights in Newark to raise money for his political campaigns for mayor in 1994 and city council in 1998. (He lost both races narrowly, in runoffs.)

Others are developing companies, curriculums and performance spaces to institutionalize hip-hop and reclaim it as a tool for liberation. Mannafest, a performance company, seeks to develop the voice of black London by creating a space where people can express their ideas on political and social issues. This fall the Brecht Forum in New York will sponsor a nine-week "course of study for hip-hop revolutionaries." Akila Worksongs, an artist-representation company, evolved out of president April Silver's work in organizing the first national hip-hop conference at Howard University in 1991. One of its missions is to "deglamorize" hip-hop for school-age kids. About the responsibility of artists, Silver says, "You can't just wake up and be an artist. We come from a greater legacy of excellency than that. Artists don't have the luxury to not be political."

At the Freestyle Union (FSU) in Washington, D.C., artist development isn't complete without community involvement. That philosophy grew out of weekly "cipher workshops," in which circles of artists improvise raps under a set of rules: no hogging the floor, no misogyny, no battling. The last of those, which defies a key tenet of hip-hop, has outraged traditionalists, who see it feminizing the culture. What this transformation has created is a cadre of trained poet-activists, the Performance Corps, who run workshops and panels with DC-based universities, national educational conferences, the Smithsonian Institution and the AIDS Project, on issues ranging from domestic violence to substance abuse and AIDS prevention. This summer FSU and the Empower Program are holding a twelve-week Girls Hip-Hop Project, which tackles violence against women.

Obviously, as Tricia Rose points out, this stretching of the culture, even if it does raise political consciousness, "is not the equivalent of protesting police brutality, voting, grassroots activism against toxic waste dumping, fighting for more educational resources, protecting young women from sexual violence." Toni Blackman, the founder of FSU, admits as much. "As artists," she says, "we're not necessarily interested in being politicians. We are interested in making political statements on issues that we care about. But how do you give young people the tools to decide how to spend their energy to make their lives and the world better?"

It's a good question, but activist/artist Boots of the Oakland-based rap group The Coup laid the challenge far more pointedly in an interview with Davey D in 1996:

> Rappers have to be in touch with their communities no matter what type of raps you do, otherwise people won't relate. Political rap groups offered solutions only through listening. They weren't part of a movement, so they died out when people saw that their lives were not changing. On the other hand, gangsta groups and rappers who talk about selling drugs are a part of a movement. The drug game has been around for years and has directly impacted lives, and for many it's been positive in the sense that it earned people some money. Hence gangsta rap has a home. In order for political rap to be around, there has to be a movement that will be around that will make people's lives better in a material sense. That's what any movement is about, making people's lives better.
>
> In order to have a political movement, you have to have education and consciousness. It's very difficult to mix education and consciousness with capitalism. And most people, when confronted with an option, will pick money over everything else. (Lisa Williamson, aka Sister Souljah)

> It's all about the Benjamins, baby. (Sean "Puffy" Combs, aka Puff Daddy, "No Way Out")

Organizing the hip-hop generation is "an idea whose time has come," says Lisa Sullivan, president of LISTEN (Local Initiative Support Training Education Network), a youth development social change organization in Washington. "But there's no reason to believe that it will happen naturally."

No organizing ever does. The grassroots work that is going on around the country is mostly small, diffuse and underfunded. For it ever to reach a mass scale, Sullivan argues, there will have to be an independent infrastructure to support close-to-the-ground organizing. That means training, coordination and leadership building. It also means money. There is plenty of that among the most successful rappers—for the uninitiated, "the Benjamins" refers to $100 bills—but for the most part they, and the projects they get behind, are in thrall to the corporate ideology that made them stars.

Consider Rock the Vote's Hip-Hop Coalition, designed to register black and Latino youth for the 1996 presidential election using the same model by which rock artists have tried to convince white youth that voting is relevant to their lives. The brainchild of rapper LL Cool J, the Hip-Hop Coalition was led by former Rock the Vote executive director Donna Frisby and involved artists Chuck D, Queen Latifah and Common Sense, among others, registering almost 70,000 youth of color, versus hundreds of thousands of white youth.

This media strategy didn't succeed as Frisby had hoped, so the coalition took its show on the road, staging political forums where rap artists and local politicians talked to teenagers about the political process. What was clear from these open forums was that, besides the political apathy characteristic of most young people, there is a deeper sense of alienation. "African-American and low-income youth feel that the Constitution and the Declaration of Independence were not created with us in mind," says Frisby. "So people felt, the system isn't doing anything to help me, why should I participate in it?"

From these experiences Frisby learned that not only will programs for minority youth always be given short shrift by mainstream underwriters—the Hip-Hop Coalition never got the media support of its white counterpart—but they won't even reach their audience unless they are specifically designed for youth of color. Now she and Chuck D have a new venture, Rappers Educating All Curricula through Hip-Hop (REACH). Building on the Hip-Hop Coalition, REACH is recruiting a cadre of artists as "conduits of learning," making public appearances at schools, juvenile detention centers, community centers. In nurturing more conscious artists, Chuck D and Frisby hope more conscious art will result. The group also plans to develop educational tools incorporating hip-hop songs. "Hip-hop is first and foremost a communication tool," says Chuck D. "For the last twenty years, hip-hop has communicated to young people all across the world, people in different time zones, who speak different languages, teaching them more about English, or black hip-hop lingo, quicker than any textbook can." REACH aims to narrow the cultural and generational gap between teachers and students in the public schools, and to promote the idea that "being smart is being cool."

As described by Chuck D, however, REACH seems in many ways to be an if-you-can't-beat-'em-join-'em approach. To compete for the short attention spans of youth, he says, social change organizations have to be like corporations. "A lot of organizations that have been out there for a long time are not really on young people's minds. In the information age, there are so many distractions. Organizations have to market themselves in a way so that they are first and foremost on young people's minds and supply the answers and options that they might need."

But political organizing isn't about supplying "answers." As Sister Souljah puts it, "Just because you have the microphone doesn't mean you know what you're talking about. Just because you can construct a rhyme doesn't mean that you know how to organize a movement or run an organization." Souljah came to broad public attention during the 1992 presidential campaign when Bill Clinton, gunning for Jesse Jackson to woo the conservative vote, distorted a statement she had made about the LA riots. But before there was Sister Souljah, rap icon, there was Lisa Williamson, activist. At Rutgers University, she was involved in campaigns against apartheid and police brutality. With the United Church of Christ's Commission for Racial Justice, she mobilized young people for various events in the black community and organized a star-studded concert at Harlem's Apollo Theater to fund a summer camp she'd developed. Impressed with her organizing skills, Chuck D christened her "Sister Souljah" and designated her minister of information for Public Enemy.

Today, Souljah is executive director of Daddy's House—the nonprofit arm of Puffy's rap empire, Bad Boy Entertainment—which runs a summer camp for urban youth and provides meals for the homeless during the holidays. "The stars we choose to celebrate are reflections of who we are as a people," she says. "Right now we celebrate those with money, but that has nothing to do with understanding history, culture or understanding your future. And I think that's missing in hip-hop right now."

Last November in an *Essence* profile, Combs said that he wanted to use his popularity and influence to galvanize his generation to exercise their political power in the 2000 presidential election. Last September Master P's nonprofit foundation helped finance the Million Youth March. Rap artists are clearly not political leaders—they might be better described as representatives of their record labels than of their communities—but they do have one obvious role to play if they want to foster activism. While Sullivan embodies the idea of organizing as a fundamentally grassroots undertaking, she knows that it can't survive on sweat alone. "Hip-hop is a billion-dollar industry," she says, "and there are people who can play a venture philanthropist role. But that would require educating them about different ways to be philanthropists." No doubt, Master P and Puffy get capitalism. In 1998, the two were the top-selling rap artists, with Master P earning $57 million and Combs $54 million. But "the $64,000 Question," says Sullivan, "is could [they] become what Sidney Poitier and Harry Belafonte were for the civil rights movement? Those two guys actively financed how people got from Mississippi to Atlantic City," she recalls, referring to the historic all-black Mississippi State delegation, led by Fannie Lou Hamer, that demanded to be seated at the 1964 Democratic convention in place of the state's white segregationists.

Sullivan was the field coordinator of the Children's Defense Fund and, until 1996, manager of its Black Student Leadership Network, a service and child advocacy program. Her subsequent stint as a consultant at the Rockefeller Foundation convinced her that a movement of the hip-hop generation will have to fund itself.

> Traditional foundations are not going to support this work. You have a couple of program officers in the arts and humanities who get how important youth culture is to reaching alienated young people. While they tend to be radical and politicized, the institutions that they money-out from are not anywhere comfortable supporting what a mature hip-hop political agenda could be.

For Sullivan, such an agenda would address three issue areas. Top on the list is the criminal justice system, including police brutality and the incarceration epidemic. "It's the whole criminalization of poor, urban youth," she says. "That's a policy area that folks have got to get a handle on quickly. And it's also a place where our constituency numbers—our power—if organized well, could move the policy agenda away from its current punitive, negative stance." Public education is agenda item number two: "People are being set up. This is the system that is the most dysfunctional in the country, and something drastic has to occur so that people acquire the skills and have a fighting chance in terms of the economic future. A bad public education system feeds a whole generation of young people into the criminal justice system." Finally, activists need to address people losing the vote because of incarceration: "This is about the health of American democracy. What is happening to the hip-hop community around the loss of citizenship is permanently preventing many of us from ever being able to participate in the democratic process."

> If you ain't talkin' about endin' exploitation / then you just another sambo in syndication / always sayin' words that's gon' bring about elation / never doin shit that's gon' bring us vindication / and while we getting strangled by the slavewage grippers / you wanna do the same / and say we should put you in business? / so you'll be next to the ruling class, lyin' in a ditch / 'cuz when we start this revolution all you prolly do is snitch. (The Coup, "Busterismology")

Once all this activism matures, it's hard to say whether it will resemble hip-hop, or the left, as we know it. But a few operations on the ground suggest some necessary features. First off, it has to be youth led and defined.

At the weekly rally for A Movement for CHHANGE, everyone is frisked as they enter the National Black Theater in Harlem, women on the left, men on the right. "Hip-hop minister" Conrad Muhammad the motive force behind the group, is waging a mass voter registration drive in preparation for 2001, when he hopes to sponsor a convention to announce a bloc of young urban voters with the political clout to influence the mayoral agenda. The minister's roots lie in the Nation of Islam, but at the rally he sounds more like a Southern Baptist preacher.

"Would you, please, brother, register today?" Muhammad pleads with a dreadlocked black man sitting with his wife. Their new baby just had a harrowing hospital stay. They're relieved that the baby is healthy and that insurance will pay for the visit, but initially neither was a certainty. After the minister's hour-long pitch, the man is still unconvinced that casting a ballot and then hounding politicians, of any color, will assure strong black communities of healthcare, good schools and intact families.

Voter registration is an odd, and hard, sell coming from a man who, until three years ago, never cast a ballot and, while minister of the Nation of Islam's Mosque #7 in Harlem, preached against it. But Muhammad, 34, tries. It's mid-November 1998, the same week Kwame Ture, aka Stokeley Carmichael, died and the Madd Rapper, aka Deric "D-Dot" Angeletti, ambushed and battered the then–editor in chief of the hip-hop magazine *Blaze*. Someone, Muhammad figures, ought to be the bridge between the civil rights tradition and the hip-hop generation, and it might as well be him.

He appeals to that sense of competition supposedly at the core of hip-hop: "If Kwame at 21 could go down to Lowndes County and register his people to vote, so can we." He appeals to a sense of shame: "This is the talented tenth that Du Bois said was supposed to come up with solutions to the problems of our people, and here they are fighting and killing each other up in corporate offices. Brothers and sisters, you know we got to make a change from that kind of craziness." He goads: "Talkin' 'bout you a nationalist, you don't believe in the system. You're a part of the system!" He suggests outright poverty: "Somebody had to say, 'I'll forgo the riches of this world to make sure that my people are in power.' If Stokeley died with $10 in his pocket I'd be surprised." He pushes the willingness-to-suffer motif that characterized the early civil rights movement: "James Meredith decided to have a march against fear. We need one of those today in the 'hood, where dope is being sold, people are destroying themselves, frivolity and ignorance are robbing this generation of its substance. Meredith marched by himself—of course, he was shot down. You make that kind of stand, you're going to be shot down." At long last, he gets to his point: "If A Movement for CHHANGE can organize the youth, get them off these street corners, get them registered, make them conscious, active players in the political landscape, maybe we can vote Sharpton into office as mayor or Jesse as President."

The grandmothers of the amen gallery in the audience punctuate each exhortation with cheers, and a few raised fists. The young folks quietly mull over the prospects: poverty, suffering, Sharpton, Jesse. At one point, a 17-year-old decked in the "ghetto fabulous" hip-hop style—baggy jeans, boots, black satin do-rag, huge rhinestone studs weighing down each lobe—challenges the voter registration model of political empowerment. "They [politicians] always say things, do things, but soon as they get in office, they don't say and do what they're supposed to. The community that I live in is mostly, like, a drug environment. And they're always talking about, we're going to get the drug dealers, we're going to bust them, we're going to stop all the gangs, we're going to stop all the black-on-black crime, we're going to have our own businessmen. And they never follow their word, so what's the sense in voting?"

"Let's put you in office," says Muhammad. "In 2001, when forty-two City Council seats come up [in New York City], let's run you."

"Run me?" the young brother asks incredulously, biting a delighted grin. He is clearly interested in the idea of being involved, even a leader, in his community. But if these are the terms, he and his peers don't seem so sure.

Second, a mature hip-hop political movement will have more than a race-based political analysis of the issues affecting urban youth. Increasingly, the face of injustice is the color of the rainbow, so a black-white racial analysis that pins blame on some lily-white power structure is outdated. At the 21st Century meeting in Tuskegee the theme of the weekend was miseducation and tracking. In the Selma public schools, however, more than 90 percent of the students are black, so whatever the remedial tracking, it is happening along class lines, instituted by black teachers, principals and superintendents. "All teachers except for the whites told me that I wasn't going to be anybody," says a heavyset, dark, studious young man, who transferred from the public school system to a Catholic school. When he asked many of the black teachers for help, the response was often flip and cutting: "Your mama's smart, figure it out."

Ras Baraka tells of how Black NIA F.O.R.C.E., the protest group he founded while at Howard University in the late eighties, descended on a Newark City Council meeting to oppose an ordinance banning citizens from speaking at its sessions. They were arrested for disrupting city business on the orders of Donald Tucker, a black councilman. "Stuff like 'the white man is a devil' is anachronistic," Baraka says. "The white man didn't make Donald Tucker call the police on us. He did that on his own."

In explaining his actions. Tucker invoked his own history in civil rights sit-ins. "That's their disclaimer to justify doing anything," Baraka says. "If it were white people [jailing peaceful demonstrators], the people would be outraged. The irony is that we went down there singing civil rights songs. We thought we would call the ghosts of Martin Luther King and Medgar Evers and Kwame Ture on their asses, but it didn't even faze them. They have more in common now with the people who oppress us than with us. In that sense the times are changing, so our level of organizing has to change."

Like many activists working on a range of issues across the left in this country, these organizers are beginning to shift focus from civil rights to human rights. As Malaika Sanders, the current executive director of 21st Century, puts it, "Civil rights is based on the state and what the state has defined as the rights of the people." Human rights, on the other hand, is based on the rationale that "no matter who or where I am, I have some basic rights, so it's not about voting rights or what the law is." She argues that human rights presents a more motivating rationale for activism. Whereas a civil rights philosophy—focused on a finite set of principles that define citizenship—can lead to despair as those rights are never fully attained or are subject to the mood of the times, "a human rights approach allows a vision that's bigger than your world or what you think on a day-to-day basis."

On the West Coast, the Third Eye Movement has developed a theory of organizing that goes from civil rights to human rights, from nationalism to internationalism. It couples grassroots organizing with programs and policy analysis, using hip-hop culture not just to educate and politicize but to help young people express their concerns in their own language, on their own terms. Third Eye activists used rap and song to testify before the San Francisco Police Commission in 1997 after Officer Marc Andaya stomped and pepper-sprayed to death Aaron Williams, an unarmed black man. By the sixth week of these appearances, three of the five commissioners had resigned. Their replacements fired Andaya for his brutal police record shortly after being seated. Third Eye also worked recently on the case of Sheila DeToy, a 17-year-old white girl shot in the back of the head by police.

"They've taken hip-hop where it's never been before. They've taken hip-hop ciphers to the evening news," boasts Van Jones, executive director of the Ella Baker Center for Human Rights in San Francisco, one of the principals of Third Eye. Mixed with hip-hop's aggressive attitude, the political message can get "scary," he says. "You won't find it in a traditional civics-class curriculum: We're willing to take issues into our hands if the system won't work. As scary as people thought gangsta rap was, it's nothing compared to young people using hip-hop to express what they're going through and targeting the people who are really responsible."

Jones says he founded the Ella Baker Center—named to honor the soul mother of SNCC—in response to the failures of the civil rights establishment, which had become "too tame and too tired." "I don't believe the true power of the people can be confined to a ballot box," he says, but must express itself in strikes, boycotts, pickets, civil disobedience. "We need to be about the whup-ass. Somebody's fucking up somewhere. They have names and job descriptions. You have to be creative about how you engage the enemy, because if you do it on his terms, the outcome is already known."

Most important, a mature hip-hop movement will have to deal with the irony of using hip-hop. Organizing for social change requires that people tap into their mutual human vulnerability and acknowledge their common oppression before they can bond and band together in solidarity. Though born in and of alienation and extreme social vulnerability, hip-hop culture is not eager to boast of it. Whereas the blues embraced pain to transcend it, hip-hop builds walls to shield against further injury. So getting to that place where the music might once again speak of individual frailty and collective strength is a difficult task.

At a December 12 rally for Mumia Abu-Jamal—co-sponsored by Third Eye and STORM (Standing Together to Organize a Revolutionary Movement), among others—students from the Bay Area crowd the steps of Oakland's City Hall. It's the kind of rally a traditional leftist would recognize. White radicals pass out socialist papers, petitions to end the death penalty and "Free Mumia" decals. Placards and banners quote Malcolm X, Assata Shakur, Che Guevara. The difference is that hip-hop headz take center stage, leaving older white lefties on the periphery with their pamphlets.

It is not exactly a changing of the guard. The rally begins on a shaky note. The Ella Baker Center's youth coordinator, Jasmin Barker, steps to the mike and calls for a moment of silence. Minutes before, the sound system was blaring what "might be called less than conscious rap. It's difficult for some to make the switch from the gangsta lyrics to a spirit of solidarity with Mumia. Barker persists like a schoolmarm and finally gets the reverence she demands. She then calls for a "moment of noise" to put the city government on notice. But it's Saturday. City Hall is closed. Downtown Oakland is empty. If mass demonstrations are for the onlookers, at first glance it seems as if these young activists have made the most basic of organizing errors: staging an action for a targeted constituency that's not even around. But soon enough it's evident that the objective here, this day is to assert a generational identity, a collective sense of political possibility.

"Chill with the sellin' papers while the rally's goin' on," a young brother named Ryan scolds a man passing out *Workers Vanguard* during a step routine by seven Castlemont High School students. They are wearing blue jeans, sneakers, white T-shirts and fluorescent orange decals that say "Free Mumia," distributed by Refuse and Resist. They stand at attention, in single file, each girl holding two empty aluminum cans end to end. The lead girl sets the beat with a syncopated chant: "Mu-miiiiii-aa! Free Mumia, yeah! Mu-miiiiii-aa!" The other six chime in, and the line begins to move like a locomotive, with hands and legs clapping and stomping to recreate the diasporan rhythms that are at the heart of hip-hop.

Speakers pass the mike. Castlemont junior Muhammad, 15, explains the uses of the criminal justice system, from police brutality to the death penalty, to uphold the interests of the ruling class in his own hip-hop lingo. Latifah Simon, founder of the Center for Young Women's Development in San Francisco, relates Mumia's predicament to their lives: "If they should kill Mumia what will they do to you? If they should kill a revolutionary, people got to be in the streets screaming. It was young people like the ones here," she reminds the 300 on the steps of City Hall, "who made the civil rights movement happen." A white kid named Michael Lamb, with UC Berkeley's Poetry for the People collective, pays tribute to Saul Williams and *Slam* in reciting a rap with the refrain "Where my crackers at?" suggesting that the struggle for true democracy in America needs to be an equal opportunity affair.

It is Dontario Givens, 15, who best illustrates the impact a burgeoning hip-hop movement could have on a generation so long alienated. His favorite record at the moment is Outkast's tribute to Rosa Parks, the mother of the civil rights movement. But when his social studies teacher asked him to speak at the rally on behalf of Mumia, his first response was pure hip-hop: "Why should I care?" It took him three weeks to sort through his initial resistance before hitting on that space of empathy and recognition that is the cornerstone of organizing. "What would I want the world to do if I was Mumia?" he asked himself. "Come together and make the revolution."

26

Check Yo Self Before You Wreck Yo Self:

The Death of Politics
in Rap Music and Popular Culture

Todd Boyd

Rap music is the most visible form of African American cultural expression in contemporary society. With its emergence we have also seen a change in African American popular culture specific to the late 1980s and early 1990s. The recent proliferation of African American film and televisual representation, with rap music serving as a primary means of influence, has led to new definitions of contemporary African American popular culture in both the academic and the public domain.[1]

One of the most interesting discussions has involved the thematic resurgence of a politically charged voice that these forms provide a perfect venue for expressing. The rise and eventual fall of this political discourse in popular culture is closely tied to the public presentation of popular forms. In its political dimensions, popular culture, having reached an apex with the release of Public Enemy's second album, *It Takes a Nation of Millions to Hold Us Back* (1988), seems to have functioned as a genre whose popularity had passed, instead of a sustained movement which connected both cultural artifacts and "real" political events, as did similar movements in the late 1960s and early 1970s.[2]

The emergence of gangsta rap has seen an open rejection of politics by those involved. Publicly echoed in Dr. Dre's ever-popular "Dre Day" we hear a complete disregard for "medallions, dreadlocks, and black fists," obvious markers for the more political aspirations of those interested in Black nationalism or what is now commonly called "Afrocentricity." This rejection of a political agenda is consistent with Spike Lee's mainstreaming of the most important figure of Black nationalism, Malcolm X, in the 1992 film by that title. These events mark the end of a political flirtation in rap music and, by extension, African American popular culture.

An interesting case study that examines the highs and lows of political discourse in rap music—similar to what Cornel West calls the "new cultural politics"—and the gradual displacement of this agenda by gangsta rap can be found in the meteoric rise of 1993's Grammy Award–winning best new act, Arrested Development. Using images of a critical spirituality, southern existence, stylized forms of dress, and an overall ideology of Afrocentrism, Arrested Development engaged an empowered critique of both external racism and the internal neglect that set them apart from other rap acts in the early 1990s. This political stance endeared them to many as the embodiment of a progressive discourse surrounding culture, society, and politics.

Rap and the "New Cultural Politics of Difference"

Rap can be used to analyze the mutually illuminating yet divergent categories of race, class, and gender in African American society. More often than not, questions of race dominate both popular and critical discussions about rap music. Though this discussion is undoubtedly important, contemporary society, especially in the post-Reagan/Bush era, forces us to deal with the influence of the class struggle on African American society.

At the same time, an empowered female voice that fuses the issues of race, class, and gender would also open up possibilities for understanding the nuances of contemporary African American culture. As Tricia Rose points out, "through their lyrics and video images, ... black women rappers form a dialogue with working class black women and men, offering young black women a small but potent culturally-reflexive public space" (Rose, 1990, 114). Though this female voice in rap has gained significant momentum over the last few years, there remains much to be desired, both artistically and in terms of intellectual response.[3]

The cultural and economic base of this music emphasizes the African presence in American society, which makes the foregrounding of race and class struggle paramount in understanding this cultural practice. Certain elements of rap music seem to have the potential to exemplify what Cornel West has labeled the "new cultural politics of difference."

> The new cultural politics of difference are neither simply oppositional in contesting the mainstream for inclusion, nor transgressive in the avant-gardist sense of shocking conventional bourgeois audiences. Rather, they are distinct articulations of talented contributors to culture who desire to align themselves with demoralized, demobilized, depoliticized and disorganized people in order to empower and enable social action and, if possible, to enlist collective insurgency for the expansion of freedom, democracy, and individuality. (West, 1990, 19–20)

African American culture is replete with examples of this new cultural politics of difference, particularly in regard to the influence of lower-class politics in understanding race. In many respects, by the late 1980s and the early 1990s, the presentation of anything as an "authentic" reflection of African American culture had to revolve in some way around the exploits and endeavors of the lumpen proletariat. It was necessary in this construction for race and class to consistently inform one another.

The most overt demonstration of this desire for cultural "authenticity" was white rapper Vanilla Ice's claim that he grew up in the midst of African American poverty and was once a victim of gang violence. He was identifying with Blackness based not on his race but on the extent of his association with lower-class African American existence. In other words, his class status made him "Black."

Along the same lines, the all-white rap group Young Black Teenagers claim that Blackness is a "state of mind"—undoubtedly a ghetto mindset. The impetus for forming the rock band in the film *The Commitments* (1991) serves as another example. According to the film's main character, the group members can identify with African American music because of their multiple oppression as Northern Irish working-class Catholics. "The Irish are the Blacks of Europe, and the Dubliners are the Blacks of Ireland, and the Northsiders are the Blacks of Dublin. So say it loud, I'm Black and I'm proud." In this case, race, as expressed through a specific cultural artifact, the music of James Brown, is used to justify an argument rooted in the political economy of class articulation in European society.

Using the "ghetto" or the "'hood" as the dominant metaphor, rap music has vividly presented this emphasis on the lower class. Whereas the earlier days of the genre were dominated by macho posturing, "dick" grabbing, and braggadocio, recently the thematic core of rap music has tended toward a narrative of life in the "'hood." With the advent of West Coast (primarily Los Angeles) rap, the life of a young African American male and his struggle to survive have become a recurrent theme, demonstrating firm entrenchment in the jungle-like setting known as the ghetto.[4] Rappers who resisted this emphasis were regarded as impostors of the tradition. Thus, a concentration on class struggle has been central to defining the cutting edge of rap music during this phase.

The reliance on this now-clichéd narrative and the media's eager embrace of the ghetto lifestyle encouraged the eventual transformation of the "'hood" scenario from initially sublime to utterly ridiculous. Through an intense combination of media manipulation and artistic culpability, the issue of class struggle has been reduced to mere spectacle, as opposed to a sustained critical interrogation of domination and oppression. This genre of rap is becoming the modern-day equivalent of the 1970s "Blaxploitation" film, the earliest examples of which, works of African American grassroots financial struggle turned into valuable products of the culture, were duplicated, depoliticized, and ultimately rendered devoid of all cultural significance.

Rap represents the emotional range of urban, mostly male, existence. At the same time, the commodifying impulses of the music industry have opened a space for selling cultural products that in their very construction undermine the structure that distributes them. It is well known that rap's massive popular audience consists of dominant and marginal audiences. Nor is it a revelation that the capitalistic courting of this massive audience at some level solidifies the music's political message. However, there is a point at which radical political discourse meets the demands of the marketplace and the two merge. The space between the points where radical political discourse can critique dominant culture and dominant culture becomes financially viable through the selling of this contrary discourse is the only available space for a reasoned understanding of contemporary political culture.

West's notion of a "politics of difference" sees the current cultural situation as indicative of an "inescapable double bind." This bind involves the reality of financial dependence that defines the structural dimension of rap music as a metaphorical "escape" from oppressive conditions, much like society's regard for African American professional athletes. The rapper, in this sense, is "simultaneously progressive and co-opted" (West, 1990, 20).

Although a thin theoretical line separates radical political discourse in rap and the commodifying impulses of the dominant culture, our understanding of popular culture requires that we critique both sides. Thus, the contemporary spectacle of the "ghetto" operates primarily to reinforce the dominant society's view of African American culture as a deprived wasteland. "Gangsta" rap offers original commentary on the horrific nuances of ghetto life. In many cases, what was once thought of as a radical critique of repressive state apparatuses, as in NWA's *Fuck tha Police*, has been transformed into a series of unapologetic narratives that celebrate violence, humiliate women, and indulge marijuana use to excess. Race and class struggle have become a series of rhetorical catch phrases and visual signposts absent of any political or social relevance. This overt rejection of politics has now become a theme unto itself—one that is reflective of several larger issues.

Yet what many consider the redundant "nigga in the 'hood" scenario is actually much more complex. Instead of relying solely on this gangsta trend, a small core of rappers have continued to advance what was at one time thought of as a progressive political agenda which analyzes race, class, and in some cases gender through rigorous cultural critique. Foremost in this group of political rappers concerned with cultural politics are Public Enemy, Sister Souljah, KRS-One, and Arrested Development. A certain Afrocentric theme runs through each of the above, yet their individual positions cover a spectrum of topics related to living in late-twentieth-century American society. Nevertheless, none of these acts has had a record of any significance, financially or culturally, in quite some time.

As with the declining significance of Spike Lee as a political voice, though, and of the new Black aesthetic, these political rappers have not been able to link their progressive politics with the ever-changing demands of the music industry or the rap audience; thus their critiques have lately fallen on deaf ears, and their cultural significance has almost completely disappeared. Witness the breakup of the one-time leaders of this political trend, Public Enemy, in the summer of 1995. In contemporary culture it is not only important to bring the political noise, but one must remain significant from an audience perspective as well.

Progressive politics minus the ability to flow lyrically and pump out phat beats has no place in rap culture. This is not to diminish political rap, but to point out that we are analyzing music, as opposed to a rhetoric of pure politics. In addition, the definition of politics, or at least what is political, has changed as the various generational shifts and their class dispositions have occurred.

Arrested Development

The Atlanta-based rap group Arrested Development was the most interesting new act of 1992. The group's male and female members sing as well as rap, while their image is built around the wearing of dreadlocks and African-style clothing. This is in contrast to the image of both the "b-boy" of the East Coast and the West Coast gangsta. Arrested Development suggests a strong stylistic exception to conventions determined by the prevalence of the more popular East and West Coast images; they also can be easily linked with the politics of the new Black aesthetic.

Arrested Development shares its context with a segment of the contemporary African American collegiate audience who use African fashion and hairstyles to demonstrate their political connection to that continent. In this sense, fashion and style function as both icon and commodity. This emphasis on an Afrocentric style not only is a response to the monotonous fashions of other rappers, but also is a rejection of the conservative "preppie" image favored by a certain group of white collegiates, which took on added cultural currency during the Reagan/Bush era. On the other hand, this emphasis on Afrocentricity in fashion becomes easily devalued as it is transformed into a mass commodity. This is the strong contention of Kobena Mercer, who suggests that hairstyles such as the afro and dreadlocks

> counter-politicized the signifier of ethnic devalorization, redefining blackness as a positive attribute, but on the other hand, perhaps not, because within a relatively short period both styles became rapidly depoliticized and, with varying degrees of resistance, both were incorporated into mainstream fashions in the dominant culture. (Mercer, 1990, 251)

This situation demonstrates, once again, the seemingly contradictory nature of political culture in the age of commodity fetishism. Signifiers of leftist political culture are easily corrupted as they are co-opted by the fashion industry of dominant society.

Musically, Arrested Development challenges the traditions of rap, the most visible difference being the use of singing in conjunction with the traditional rapping over beats (this singing style has since become quite popular). The group's songs address topics ranging from homelessness to the search for spirituality and African Americans' connection with Africa. Their popular appeal is demonstrated by their appearance as opening act on the 1992–1993 En Vogue tour, the use of the song "Tennessee" as the theme for the short-lived NBC situation comedy *Here and Now*, their appearance as the only contemporary voice on the soundtrack for Lee's *Malcolm X* (1992), and their selection as both "Best New Artist" and "Best Rap Artist" at the 1993 Grammy Awards.

Arrested Development benefits from a series of other African American acts that have foregrounded a certain leftist bohemian political agenda. Arrested Development belongs to the musical tradition that includes the 1970s band Sly and the Family Stone—this group is sampled on "People Everyday"—the multicultural rhythm and blues group War, and most recently African American female folk singer Tracy Chapman. Yet, the combination of a derivative folk song content, politics associated with the peace movement, and rap is probably best exemplified by the rap organization Native Tongues, of which groups such as De La Soul and A Tribe Called Quest most easily demonstrate this pattern.[5]

A close analysis of Arrested Development's "People Everyday" song and video helps to reveal their political agenda. Using the sample from Sly Stone's track "Everyday People," Arrested Development argues for a kind of cultural innocence or purity. This notion of purity is exemplified through a juxtaposition of the harsh urban realities of the street prominent in contemporary rap and their embrace of the premodern "country" simplicity of a rural landscape. At one level the group attempts to be all-inclusive in its outlook, forwarding an Afrocentric version of political correctness that critiques race, class, and gender, as opposed to privileging the male-dominated discourse that rap has often been guilty of presenting. Yet in doing so the group offers a position that unintentionally erects a class hierarchy while simultaneously trying to destroy existing hierarchies.

The video's time frame spans one day, as marked by the rising of the sun at the beginning of the video and its setting at the conclusion. Thus we are alerted to the concern with time and the extent to which time and space function in defining African American politics. This concern with time is also evident in the title of the album, *3 Years, 5 Months, and 2 Days in the Life of Arrested Development.*

The video begins by calling on multiple aspects of the African oral tradition. Group member Headliner offers a verbal and visual address. After he announces who he is, we get an extreme close-up of his lips. In American society, lips have gone from a regressive stereotype that emphasized the excessive fullness of African American lips through numerous visual objects in American culture (Sambo pictures, lawn jockeys, etc.) to the current trend toward using this fullness as a visual demonstration of one's Africanness. White models and actresses appropriate these features through chemical or surgical treatment as a fashionable sign of what is considered beauty.[6] This modern-day example of exploitiveness is what bell hooks describes as "eating the other."

From this tight close-up, we move to a series of rapidly edited shots that alternate between Headliner's reggae-style call and visual images of the group's response. This visual dimension is edited to visually replicate the verbal call-and-response pattern that the group establishes. It also alternates between black and white and color images and privileges the oral as it motivates the visual direction of the iconography. Thus, oral culture is used in conjunction with the character's motivation of visuals to create a stimulating African American music video.

Through another series of rapidly edited shots, we witness the group's reliance on a strongly rural agrarian aesthetic. Riding on the back of a pickup truck, the equally mixed group of male and female participants are shown in their loosely fitting cast-off-style African clothing, either with their hair in knotty dreadlocks or bald. This emphasis on the rural is supplemented by various shots of the wide-open landscape, dirt roads, wooden porches, and an idyllic series of visual icons that foreground the technologically untainted and morally empowered version of African American life that Arrested Development argues for throughout this album, and especially in the song "People Everyday."

As we witness little children running, playing, and riding their bicycles, and older people enjoying life in a variety of rural settings, we are also clued in to the political agenda that informs Arrested Development. The rejection of modernity that this visual setting evokes harks back to the "pre-New Negro" ideas of Booker T. Washington. These ideas embraced the virtues of southern pastoral living in opposition to the supposed utopic images of the industrialized North. Washington's argument suggested that the independence that was made possible through this rural lifestyle and economy was superior to the technologically mecha-nized economy that was taking hold in northern society. Washington's now-redundant phrase "Lay your buckets down where you are" clearly emphasizes his desire to see the South, in all its simplicity, as the preferred landscape of his contemporaries, and of future generations of African Americans as well.

The angst associated with the dilemma of migration as opposed to settling in the South has numerous other cultural manifestations, including blues singer Juke Boy Bonner's comi-cally titled cut "I'm Going Back to the Country Where They Don't Burn the Buildings Down," soul singer Gladys Knight's hit "Midnight Train to Georgia," August Wilson's play *The Piano Lesson*, Julie Dash's film *Daughters of the Dust*, and Charles Burnett's *To Sleep with Anger*.

Arrested Development modernizes this argument in their first single, "Tennessee." In a video similar to "People Everyday," the group rhetorically engages in a quizzical and at times cynical exploration of African American existence in contemporary society. In a prayer-like address, they wonder aloud about their tenuous place in contemporary though problem-filled America: "Lord I've been really stressed / Down and out, losing ground / Although I am Black and proud / Problems got me pessimistic / Brothers and sisters keep messin' up / Why does it have to be so damn tough?"

The refrain of the song (and incidentally the portion used in the introduction to the short-lived sitcom *Here and Now*) suggests the possibility of freedom and understanding that lies ahead. Speech asks the Lord to "Take me to another place / Take me to another land / Make me forget all the hurt / Let me understand your plan." This spiritually informed intellectual journey, using "Tennessee" as the metaphor of freedom, is not unlike the musical excursions undertaken by John Coltrane during the latter part of his life and career. On the popular *A Love Supreme* and all of his later albums, Coltrane uses spirituality to express his intellectual and creative explorations.

In the same sense, Arrested Development sees "Tennessee" as a site of struggle that informs both past and present: "Walk the streets my forefathers walked / Climb the trees my forefa-thers hung from / Ask those trees for all their wisdom." According to Arrested Development, a return to these humble roots is necessary for an understanding of contemporary society and the place of the African American therein. This is evident in the lines "Now I see the impor-tance of history / Why my people be in the mess that they be / Many journeys to freedom made in vain / By brothers on the corner playing ghetto games." At one level, Arrested Devel-opment offers a political impossibility. Their nostalgia for a romanticized version of early African American culture emphasizes the southern roots of existence, the absence of the modern, and a better quality of life. This seems not only simplistic but untenable considering the difficulties of this style of life within contemporary society. On another level, though, they are able to critique members of their own culture for assisting in the slow destruction of the culture.

Their intellectual posture foregrounds a globally leftist notion of Afrocentric discourse, and some would suggest that this takes rap music in a new direction. Arrested Development criticizes the way that contemporary society has destroyed positive aspects of a supposed earlier communal nature of African American culture, as well as exposed the self-inflicted problems associated with "brothers on the corner," a reference to the urge to romanticize urban Black male ghetto culture in other rap circles. A religiously self-critical orientation is strengthened by the presence of the group's spiritual advisor, Baba Oje, who allows for the emergence of an intellectually empowered voice that points to the future by invoking the past, as opposed to becoming ensconced in the trappings of the present.

Arrested Development's song and video for "People Everyday" extend the practice of self-critique within the African American community, in particular the function of women. The group advocates progressive gender politics, especially given the traditional male rap agenda.

The female rappers/singers in the group have equal voice in defining its political project. This collaborative effort, like the critical academic endeavor undertaken by bell hooks and Cornel West in *Breaking Bread* (1991), demonstrates the possibilities of empowered political discourse that avoids the retreading of misogyny in favor of collective articulation.

During the extended call-and-response segment of "People Everyday," female rapper Aerle Taree responds to Speech's call. She often repeats the last part of his dialogue in order to strengthen her point. At the point where Speech refers to his passivity, "but I ain't Ice Cube," Aerle Taree asserts an unequivocal "Who?" This demonstrates the group members' dialectical self-consciousness regarding Ice Cube's political struggles as well as their reluctance to identify themselves with the militant posture of African American masculinity associated with Ice Cube. The female voice again becomes significant during the video's conclusion, when Montesho Eshe states the "moral" of the story. She summarizes the events and has the "last word," further exemplifying the group's progressive gender politics.

The focal point of "People Everyday" is the issue of gender. The members of Arrested Development, particularly Speech, are contrasted to what they define as a "group of brothers." Throughout the video we see black-and-white shots of African American males who personify media stereotypes of macho working-class behavior. We see this "group of brothers" holding forty-ounce bottles of malt liquor, grabbing their crotches, and laughing among themselves. When an African-attired Black woman approaches, they encircle her. After one of the men grabs her buttock, the others give him "dap" for displaying his masculinity.

The lyrics emphasize this obvious act of sexual harassment. "My day was going great and my soul was at ease / Until a group of brothers started buggin' out / Drinkin' the 40 oz. / Going the nigga route / Disrespecting my Black Queen / Holding their crotches and being obscene." Speech's reference to his "Black Queen" affirms the group's valorization of women.

This segment also demarcates the intellectual politics of Arrested Development from those of their lower-class counterparts, who display their masculine hostility toward African American women and other African Americans who do not fit into their lower-class stereotypes. This is evident in the proclamation that they came to "test speech cuz of my hairdo / And the loud bright colors that I wear, boo / I was a target 'cause I'm a fashion misfit / And the outfit that I'm wearing brothers dissin' it." Speech's African-themed appearance, and by extension his politics, are rejected by the "brothers" as unwelcome in their small ghettoized world. Much like the overpublicized Los Angeles gang culture of identification by "colors," the "brothers" in the video identify not only on the basis of race but on the basis of distinctive class stereotypes, the most prominent of which is clothing and appearance. Thus, like the gangbangers, the "brothers" are presented as destroying their own African American community through debauchery and violence.

This distinction between the politically correct behavior of Arrested Development and the "group of brothers" is based on the difference, according to Speech, between a "nigga" and an "African." In numerous media interviews, Speech defines a "nigga" as someone who realizes that he/she is oppressed and wallows in it; an "African" realizes his/her oppression and through knowledge attempts to overcome it. "Nigga" is often used by rappers who consider themselves products and practitioners of the ghetto life. The "hardest" and often the most confrontational rappers have defined themselves as "niggas" in opposition to the dominant society. For instance, NWA, having called their 1991 album *EFIL4SAGGIN* ("Niggas 4 Life" spelled backward), proclaim that "Real Niggas Don't Die"; Ice T boldly alerts his listeners that "I'm a nigga in America and I don't care what you are" and rejects "African American and Black" as inconsistent with his ghetto identity. Ice Cube has described himself as both "the nigga you love to hate" and "the wrong nigga to fuck wit." In each instance, "nigga" is politicized to indicate class as well as racial politics. This usage often involves a strong identification with the ghetto, but a regressive posture against women. "African" has recently been used to signify a spiritual connection with the continent and an Afrocentric political connection. Flavor Flav of Public Enemy has declared, "I don't wanna be called yo nigga" on the 1991 cut "Yo Nigga," which leads into Sister Souljah's assertion about "African people, too scared to call themselves African" on her 1992 cut "African Scaredy Cat in a One Exit Maze." Calling oneself African is supposed to demonstrate an advanced consciousness that eliminates any connection to America, and affirms one's links with an Afrocentric cultural, political, and spiritual base. Souljah suggests that those who reject this idea are "scared" to reject the ideological opposition that forces them to see America as home.

Arrested Development continually identify themselves as African in "People Everyday." Speech states, "I told the niggas please / Let us past friend / I said please 'cause I don't like killing Africans / But they wouldn't stop / & I ain't Ice Cube / Who? / But I had to take the brothers out for being rude!" Speech shows sympathy in his opposition to "niggas" by implying that they are ultimately "Africans." He also sees their masculine lower-class behavior as part of their definition as "niggas." Speech suggests that if they reject this class-based behavior, they can then be seen as "Africans." Yet in the end, they can aspire no higher than their lower-class status permits, as Speech declares, "That's the story yaw'll / Of a Black man / Acting like a nigga / And get stomped by an African!" This final statement emphasizes the contrast between "nigga" as defined by offensive behavior and African as defined by intellectual and political sophistication.

Much as in the confrontation scene in Lee's *School Daze* (1988) between the "fellas" and the men from the neighborhood at Kentucky Fried Chicken, Arrested Development enunciates class difference within the African American community, but they offer no critical analysis. Representations of class positions are reproduced through the reliance on this stereotyped behavior. Foregrounding this incident increases the possibility for it to replicate the dominant view of lower-class African American males as menacing.

Arrested Development brings an important intellectual and critical dimension to rap music and culture. It breaks away from the redundant "boy 'n the 'hood" scenario, which has become almost counterproductive through the media's overwhelming emphasis of it and the rap community's willingness to participate in such exploitation.

Arrested Development's female members are central to determining and articulating the group's political position. Their collaborative effort helps to provide an empowered position for female speakers without necessarily privileging the male voice. Unfortunately, in comparison to the rest of the rap community, the group's gender politics is uncommon.

Arrested Development's critical Afrocentricity involves an unconscious co-optation of regressive class politics. Through their sophisticated and at times self-righteous political position, they can critique modernity, capitalism, and gender. However, this position does not articulate an empowered position on class. Much like W.E.B. Du Bois's notion of the "talented tenth," (Du Bois, 1993) Arrested Development attempts to close the societal gap on race, but widen it on class, and fails to engage in a political dialogue that could strengthen both areas. While Arrested Development does not blame the victim, they intensify class divisions with their intellectually elitist argument on the ghetto and African American male culture. While they claim to be concerned with "everyday people," it is obvious that they locate the "group of brothers" that they critique somewhere else. Yet as I asserted earlier, my interest in Arrested Development relates to how they open up the dialogue on politics and rap culture through the invocation of their gendered Afrocentric position. Thus, multiple levels of political discourse can now be both demonstrated and juxtaposed within contemporary African American culture.

Arrested Development is clearly linked to a revisionist southern history, and they locate the problems of contemporary African American existence in the limits imposed by urbanization. This critical posture, in light of most other rap music, seems progressive and somewhat liberating. Yet when extrapolated to the larger themes just articulated, this position can be regarded as uncomplicated and ultimately mainstream. With conservative media manipulation of the popular term "political correctness" having all but cut this term off from its originally noble aspirations, Arrested Development can be easily viewed as aligned with this weakened position, as indicated by their public acceptability across race and gender lines. The group indicates in many ways the mainstreaming of Afrocentricity and the death of an earlier revolutionary agenda.

"But I Ain't Ice Cube!"

This limited political agenda, which is furthered by their inability to address the many class inequities in contemporary society, is best understood when comparing Arrested Development to their logical antithesis, Ice Cube, whose political agenda entails the iconic packaging of gangsta culture and the racialized urban American landscape—namely South Central L.A. In a sense, it is Ice Cube and what he represents that motivates much of Arrested Development's critical posture, as alluded to in the refrain "But I ain't Ice Cube" from "People Everyday." Ice Cube functions not only as an extension of the political argument in rap music, but also to expose the limitations of Arrested Development.

Ice Cube's strength lies in his ability to move easily between the general and the specific, simultaneously analyzing individual actions as well as societal oppression. Whereas Arrested Development can be seen in the same tradition as advocating an empowered version of religion, much like James Cone's idea of "Black Liberation Theology" or Albert Cleage's theory of the "Pan-African Orthodox," Ice Cube embraces the controversial tenets of Louis Farrakhan and the Nation of Islam. Unlike Arrested Development, who advocate a return to southern tradition as the solution to the problems of contemporary African American existence, Ice Cube's focus is the inner city in all its blighted glory.

Ice Cube's politics of location is clearly conversant with Burnett's *To Sleep with Anger*. Instead of focusing on the Deep South and the northward migration pattern of the early part of this century so often discussed in popular versions of African American history, Ice Cube, like Burnett, finds critical solace in a neglected segment of African American migration, the westward migration of southwestern (Arkansas, Louisiana, Texas) Blacks to Los Angeles primarily after World War II. Thus, Ice Cube's concerns with history are more contemporary, and in a sense better able to engage certain aspects of present-day culture. Whereas Arrested Development is interested in issues of modernity, Ice Cube is clearly associated with postmodernity.

This postmodern urban agenda is visually underscored through scenes in the "True to the Game" video of the burned-out remains of post-uprising Crenshaw Boulevard—a direct contrast to the rural landscapes that dominate Arrested Development's videos. Ice Cube sees African Americans' self-destruction and the propensity toward assimilating into mainstream society, thus losing one's identity, as the social hindrances to self-empowerment. Though these agenda items are not radically different from those advocated by Arrested Development, it is the urban setting, the embrace of the Nation of Islam, a postmodern criticism of societal institutions, and a rigorous critique of class politics that allow for a clear distinction between the two rap acts.

Ice Cube fuses these ideas into a coherent critical position on the album *Death Certificate*, which brings together the Nation of Islam's notion of race and a concern for the problems within African American society resulting from late commodity culture and the neoconservatism of the Reagan/Bush era. The album is equally divided between what Ice Cube describes as the "Death" and the "Life" sides. On the "Death" side, Ice Cube documents the violently destructive mentality of much of lower-class African American culture. Gangbanging, sexism, wanton violence, and other abusive behaviors are presented without the usual saccharine justification or uninformed rejection, but as harsh realities. This is what he wants to "kill." The "Life" side concerns revitalization and getting at the roots of these societal problems, dealing with them efficiently, and moving on to more concrete solutions.

The "Death" side begins with the funeral of another of Ice Cube's long line of "dead homiez." When Minister Khallid Muhammad of the Nation of Islam eulogizes the victim, he establishes the album's critical posture. Muhammad concludes by stating that the person being eulogized, who we know by this time is Ice Cube, was "the wrong nigga to fuck wit." It is at this point that Ice Cube begins his verbal assault on the racism, conformity, and overall lack of self-expression in contemporary society. Still seeing himself as the ultimate rebel who exists outside of both Black and white society, Ice Cube goes on a verbal rampage, attacking everything from contemporary African American popular music to police brutality. Much as in his opening declaration on *Amerikkka's Most Wanted*, "The Nigga You Love to Hate," Ice Cube revels in his utter disgust with American culture. African American complacency is as detrimental to progress as the most vile forms of white supremacy. Ice Cube's unrelenting attack on these cultural manifestations becomes the core of his identity: the angry Black man, the enraged lyricist.

At the conclusion of the "Death" side we are slowly transformed from sympathetic yet passive listeners into unconscious perpetrators of the very acts and attitudes that reinforce oppressive behavior. Once again, Ice Cube treats African Americans and the dominant society as equal culprits in the continual destruction of African American culture. Yet as the "Life" side begins with the cries of a newborn baby, we are given a glimpse of hope as to the future undoing of the shackles of oppression. Ice Cube implies through the metaphor of "life" that a strong critical, and at times self-critical, posture is necessary to fully understand the dynamics that restrict African American progress and ultimate empowerment in the larger society. The "Life" side proceeds with a critical analysis of sexual harassment, forced patriotism, assimilation, the self-destructive nature of gang violence, and the unwitting rejection of one's culture and soul for financial gain. The "Life" side takes Ice Cube's project to the next level, as he has successfully found a way to neither romanticize nor unequivocally reject the societal problems facing African Americans. Instead, he seems to have found a much-needed ground of critical scrutiny with useful extrapolation for the future. As underscored below by Khallid Muhammad's sermon, the implications of "life" for future directions become the source of potential empowerment.

> No longer dead, deaf, dumb, and blind
> Out of our mind
> Brainwashed with the white man's mind
> No more homicide!
> No more fratricide, genocide, or suicide!
> Look the goddamn white man in his cold blue eyes
> Devil don't even try
> We like Bebe's kids
> We don't die
> We multiply
> You've heard the death side
> So open your black eyes to the resurrection, rebirth, and rise.

In Ice Cube's use of Muhammad's oratorical qualities, Nation of Islam icons ("blue-eyed devil") are fused with icons of the gang subculture ("we don't die, we multiply") and popular African American media culture (Robin Harris's "Bebe's kids") to create an empowered rhetorical articulation that points toward the possibility of a future free of these restraints. Muhammad also relies on a liberatory notion of freedom as expressed through popular religious icons (resurrection, rebirth, and rise), giving new meaning to the at times constraining position that organized religion has always occupied for African Americans. Thus, the "Life" side places contemporary African American culture under a critical microscope, while refusing to relinquish the nature of dominant culture as it separates and ultimately destroys the fabric of African American society.

Central to Ice Cube's political agenda is a critique of the nihilism that exists throughout lower-class African American society. In conjunction with Cornel West's argument in *Race Matters*, where this nihilism is seen in the form of "psychological depression, personal worthlessness, and social despair" (West, 1993, 13), Ice Cube, in the provocative tune, "Us," vividly extents this argument by discussing the contradictory nature of African American culture as it often assumes a posture of victimized helplessness. "Sometimes I believe the hype, man / We mess it up ourselves and blame the white man."

In a society where conservative political criticism of African Americans is abundant and encourages a defensive posture that romanticizes societal problems, Ice Cube has rejected the idea of the "airing of one's dirty laundry in public"—or to use the more succinctly Black phrase, "putting one's business in the street"—in favor of exposing the problems of the community for public debate. This rejection of victimization for an empowered critical agenda goes against the grain of African American public etiquette. But unlike conservative African American critics such as Clarence Thomas, Stanley Crouch, and Shelby Steele, Ice Cube takes a position that cannot be easily co-opted. He uses this self-critical posture as an instance of cultural empowerment. His analysis of race and emphasis on class opens up the dialogue on the problems of contemporary culture, as opposed to closing off this debate through a needed, but often uninformed, cultural deconstruction.

This self-critical duality is exemplified through Ice Cube's commentary on drugs and the subculture within which drugs circulate.

> And all y'all dope dealers
> You as bad as the police
> 'Cause you kill us
> You got rich when you started slingin' dope
> But you ain't built us a supermarket
> So we can spend our money with the blacks
> Too busy buying gold and Cadillacs.

The nightly news is full of stories about the entrenchment of drugs in the African American community and the ghettoized culture that breeds this behavior. Conservatives argue that local dealers should be treated as felons and be given the death penalty. It is no surprise that many African Americans who live in the midst of what amounts to an open-air drug market corroborate elements of this conservative argument out of sheer necessity, as their lives are in constant danger.

On the other hand, in the gangsta rap community from which Ice Cube emerged, many glamorize the lifestyle and economic independence of the drug dealer. Rapper Scarface has even rejected the usual female sexual subservience by stating, "Fuck the bitches / I want money and the power" to demonstrate his complicity with the excesses of late commodity capitalism within the drug culture.

Ice Cube is careful not to fall into either ideological trap as he turns his critique of the drug culture into a positive vision for the community. The drug dealer's embrace of the fetishized commodity—gold and Cadillacs—is seen as hindering an economically informed Black nationalism that allows African Americans to spend their capital within their own self-sufficient communities. Drug dealing is not condemned in terms of "family values" but, as in the case of Gordon Parks Jr.'s *Superfly* (1972), is seen as an imposed necessity that can potentially be turned into an economic means of cultural empowerment.

Ice Cube goes on in "Us" to enunciate the contradictory nature of much within the African American community:

> Us gonna always sing the blues
> 'Cause all we care about is hair styles and tennis shoes
> If you mess with mine
> I ain't frontin'
> 'Cause I'll beat you down like it ain't nothin'
> Just like a beast
> But I'm the first nigga to holler out, peace
> I beat my wife and children to a pulp
> When I get drunk and smoke dope
> Got a bad heart condition
> Still eat hog mauls and chitlins
> Bet my money on the dice or the horses
> Jobless
> So I'm a hoe for the armed forces
> Go to church but they tease us
> With a picture of a blue-eyed Jesus
> Used to call me Negro
> After all this time I'm still bustin' up the chiferow.

His claim that African Americans engage with oppressive economic and cultural forces by an overemphasis on style and commodity culture reflects how corporations target African Americans as the prime market for their products. The Nike/Michael Jordan advertisements are probably the most popular, with the Gatorade slogan "I want to be like Mike" furthering the link between stylish commodity and African American culture. With other shoe companies having entered the fray, ads for athletic shoes are located in an urban environment dominated by African Americans. The proliferation of such products in music videos makes increasingly apparent how mediated slices of African American life have become oversaturated with stylish commodities.

Ice Cube argues that the suturing effects of commodity culture cause those who are oppressed to lose sight of their oppression as a result of this willing yet uncritical relationship with the dominant society. The "singing of the blues" is a direct result of this uneasy identity with popular elements of the dominant culture. African American identity is depoliticized as possessing commodities becomes superior to knowing the political dynamics that fuel consumption.

Witness the recent fashion for the letter *X* on baseball caps and clothing. Originally created as an endorsement for Spike Lee's film about Malcolm X, the letter has become a vulgar postmodern reification of what Jean Baudrillard described as simulation, where signs are detached from all referents and exist simply as signs. A knowledge of Malcolm X, his life, and his philosophies is no longer required. The *X* stands for all of the above and simultaneously allows those wearing it to demonstrate their culture hipness and their stylish political agenda. Ultimately, the *X* loses all association with Malcolm and simply becomes the sign of popular commodity culture. Regardless of a wearer's politics, it becomes the moment's most fashionable statement.

In addition to pointing out the many contradictions of African American life, Ice Cube offers several examples of gaps in relation to the dominant society. His political agenda stresses public self-criticism to force African Americans to deal with internal problems and not use racism as an answer to all questions of oppression. While he acknowledges that racism exists and should not be ignored, he suggests that it often is exacerbated through an uncritical relationship with commodity culture and other self-destructive activities. Ice Cube moves between conservative and liberal positions in making this assertion. The fact that an African American popular figure, albeit a self-proclaimed nationalist, has taken this stance through a strong cultural product opens up a dialogue that allows for solutions to the difficulties imposed by late white supremacist capitalist culture.

Ice Cube also sees another problem facing African American empowerment: attempts to assimilate into mainstream society, especially when it involves compromising one's cultural identity. In a sophisticated class critique, assimilation into middle-class existence is portrayed as consistent with oppression. This argument is clearly articulated through the song and video "True to the Game."

The most informative of Ice Cube's arguments about compromising one's identity appears in the metaphor of musical assimilation—the tendency of many rappers to reject the genre's hard political edge for success in mainstream culture. In Ice Cube's video we see a rapper dressed in what is coded as hard-core clothing—a skullcap, sweatshirt, and work khakis—slowly dissolve into an entertainer attired in red sequins who smiles repeatedly and performs elaborate dance moves. While the immediate reference is pop star Hammer—who in his recent comeback has contradicted his earlier self by embracing gangsta culture—the video implicates all who use the ghettoized trappings of hardcore rap to facilitate their transition into the more lucrative musical mainstream.

The transition from hard-core rapper to pop star is at the expense of one's cultural and class identity. The rapper attempts to change his style for the sake of mainstream culture, only to be exploited and ultimately rejected.

> On MTV
> But they don't care
> They'll have a new nigga next year
> Out in the cold
> No more white fans and no more soul
> And you might have a heart attack
> When you find out black folks don't want you back
> And you know what's worst?
> You was just like the nigga in the first verse
> Stop sellin' out your race
> And wipe that stupid ass smile off your face
> Niggas always gotta show they teeth
> Now I'm gonna be brief
> Be true to the game.

While Black Entertainment Television (BET) and the Miami-based video jukebox THE BOX have long featured African American music videos, receiving play on cable network MTV is now seen as the ultimate mark of crossover success. Ironically, it was only recently, after much initial reservation, that MTV began playing African American music on a regular basis. Though programs such as *Yo MTV Raps* and *MTV Jams* are popular, it is the cable station's association with rock and roll and heavy metal that has made it a symbol of mainstream white culture in the music industry.

Ice Cube's assertion that "they don't care" directly comments on the long-standing exploitive nature of the music industry, as recently exemplified by MTV, and how it has historically used African American culture as trendy and disposable material: "they'll have a new nigga next year." Ice Cube also suggested that once the assimilative rapper, characterized by an excessive smile, has been rejected by mainstream culture, the African American cultural community will have no further need for him. In this sense these rappers, and by extension the desire to assimilate in any form, function as complicit in their own oppression.

Ice Cube has demonstrated through both "Us" and "True to the Game" an empowered class critique of nihilistic individuals as well as societal institutions. This critique is furthered by his continual use of Nation of Islam ideology. Historically the Nation of Islam has been a solid avenue of empowerment for individuals who exist outside mainstream society, in African American society as well as in society as a whole. Their focus on convicts, ex-convicts, and reformed drug abusers, especially African American males, is without equal. Nation of Islam patriarch Elijah Muhammed clearly foregrounds this in the title of his popular book, *Message to the Black Man.* It is no coincidence that Ice Cube's manipulation of this ideology, with the trappings of L.A. gang culture, can forward an empowered critique of those things that entrap the lower-class Black male. The gaps in Arrested Development's elitist critical agenda are here fully exposed.

Yet the limitations to Ice Cube's project lie in the same arena as does his strength. Though the Nation of Islam can critique bourgeois Black society, it cannot empower those who exist outside of the underclass that it so effectively targets. The xenophobic anti-intellectualism and the passive approach to critically engaging mainstream society while existing in it are the point at which this form of critique loses its usefulness. These are the limitations that forced Malcolm X, a true intellectual, to leave the Nation of Islam in search of wisdom elsewhere. And while Ice Cube's clever fusion of Nation of Islam ideology with gangsta iconography is an important form of class critique, it cannot take the questions of race and class to the next level of understanding.

The strength of the Nation of Islam has always been its ability to erect a solid image of defiance. While this is a useful tool in a people's rise to consciousness, defiance should not be the embodiment of all political understanding. If in contemporary society an embrace of the Nation of Islam, which has always been misunderstood as an empowered expression of Black nationalism, is the extent of our historical knowledge, then we are truly at an intellectual impasse. Ice Cube's, and the Nation's, refusal to properly engage a gender critique notwithstanding, it is the limitation of their class critique that ultimately leaves much to be desired.

Much of the political dimension that for a brief period defined rap music, and by extension African American popular culture, has been effectively killed off. Discussions of the resurgence of Black nationalism or attempts to define the elusive term "Afrocentricity" have subsided; in their place we began to hear discussions about the rights to linguistic property: "niggas," "bitches," "hoes," etc. We also began to hear denouncements of the hyperviolent atmosphere surrounding gangsta culture, which eventually led to congressional hearings on the impact that this nihilism is having at a societal level.

The fact that these issues would move outside the rap world into the United States Congress attests to the magnitude of this culture in the larger society. Yet it also wrongly reasserts the "moral imperative" of African American criticism, which has often been the rallying cry for a problematic censorship under the guise of "what's good for our children," as in the critical rejection of a film such as Melvin Van Peebles's *Sweetsweetback's Badass Song* (1971) on these grounds. While these moralistic cries shed no light on the real issues that underlie a systematic suturing of self-hatred with which African Americans have been forced to identify, rap music, in this sense of a new cultural politics, has been a vehicle for the expression of multiple voices—such as Arrested Development and Ice Cube—that have always had difficulty being heard. The real question becomes, when will there be a sustained movement that examines this historical self-hatred, while linking both politics and culture in a way that truly empowers all who subscribe to a liberated notion of existence in an otherwise oppressive society? These concerns clearly prompt Ice Cube's self-critical imperative to "check yo self, before you wreck yo self."

Notes

1. Texts devoted to analyzing rap music and contemporary culture have been appearing with increasing regularity, especially in light of past omissions. For instance, academic texts such as Houston Baker Jr.'s *Rap Music, Black Studies, and the Academy*, Tricia Rose's book *Black Noise: Rap Music and Black Culture in Contemporary America*, and a large segment of Gina Dent's edited volume *Black Popular Culture* are devoted to the subject. In addition, Nelson George, whose work on rap is largely chronicled in *Buppies, B-Boys, BAPS, and Bohos*, and Greg Tate, author of *Flyboy in the Buttermilk*, both former *Village Voice* writers, have gained increased attention as authorities in this regard. The popularity of magazines such as *The Source* and *Vibe* adds to this recent phenomenon.

2. For an extended explanation of the "death of politics" relative to popular culture, see my analysis of Spike Lee's *Malcolm X*, "Popular Culture and Political Empowerment," in the *Cineaste* critical symposium on the same subject.

3. In addition to female rappers such as Salt n Pepa, Queen Latifah, and MC Lyte, whom Rose discusses extensively in her book *Black Noise*, the emergence of West Coast gangsta rap, which is absent from Rose's analysis, does not directly address women rappers such as Yo Yo and Boss, who offer interesting possibilities for the continued exploration of gender issues in rap music.

4. The following West Coast rappers exemplify thematically my argument for Black male angst: Snoop Doggy Dog, Ice-T, the late Easy E, Niggas Wit Attitude (NWA), Compton's Most Wanted (CMW), Tha Dogg Pound, Dr. Dre, King Tee, 2 Pac, Paris, Too Short, Warren G, Coolio, Mack 10, and most notably Ice Cube.

5. As an example, De La's first single, "Me, Myself, and I," critiqued how many rappers assume a monolithic posture instead of being themselves. Thus, they rejected the b-boy style of wearing gold chains, Kangol caps, and lambskin coats for their own stylized attire of uncombed hair and nondescript baggy clothes. As the title, "Me, Myself, and I," states, they were concerned with asserting their own identity, while simultaneously offering a plural definition of "self" and affirming that "Blackness" contained multiple subject positions. This reaffirms the fact that Blackness can be defined from multiple perspectives. De La Soul assumed this posture for their first album, *3 Feet High and Rising*. On their second album they boldly declared that "De La Is Dead," short-circuiting the continuation of this style of rap.

6. The definition of function regarding African American lips in the larger culture can be seen in two recent cinematic examples. Use of the close-up and emphasis on the lips as derogatory stereotype occur in the repeated shots of the African American female radio announcer in the Walter Hill film *The Warriors* (1979). Though the character offers exterior commentary on the plight of the main characters, the street gang the Warriors, as they proceed along the narrative's mysterious path, this character has no identity; she is reduced to her function without recourse to any sustained narrative or visual involvement other than these repeated tight shots that emphasize her "nigger lips."

   More recently, and in contrast to the earlier example, this tight shot of the lips was utilized in Spike Lee's *Do the Right Thing* (1989) with the character of Mr. Señor Love Daddy. In this case, the emphasis on lips becomes an example of the bodily vehicle for the oral tradition. While also functioning as the voice of exterior commentary, Love Daddy is able to articulate the film's rational direction from his empowered position and is also used as a voice of reason in relation to the societal conflicts presented in this film. In addition, Love Daddy connects the film to its oral roots when he engages in a roll call of prominent African American musical figures, both past and present. This use of the lips as vehicle for the oral tradition is also referenced repeatedly throughout *Mo Better Blues* (1990). The film's main character, Bleek Gillam, is shown as being obsessed with his lips as they determine his professional and emotional stability, especially when connected with the jazz that emerges from his trumpet.

   Arrested Development's use of this racial trope can be seen as an extension of Mr. Señor Love Daddy and Bleek's function as oral facilitators within the Spike Lee films. This racial trope is also an embrace of the Africanness of their bodily features, and in turn a rejection of the traditionally Eurocentric standards of beauty in American society. Much like the often-mentioned griot of African society, the lips as visual metaphor, emphasized through extreme close-up in this case, become very useful in exemplifying the oral nature of African American culture. Also, the critique of dominant standards of beauty, at both white and African American levels, can be seen in the group's most prominent female character, who sports a bald head. While Irish female singer Sinead O'Connor is the most visible example of this style in popular white culture, the female participant in Arrested Development uses this stylistic device to affirm the group's Afrocentric cultural project.

References

Baker, Houston, Jr. *Rap Music, Black Studies, and the Academy.* Chicago: University of Chicago Press, 1993.
Baudrillard, Jean. *Simulations.* New York: Columbia University Press, 1983.
Boyd, Todd. Popular Culture and Political Empowerment. *Cineaste* XIX, no. 4 (1993): 12–13.
Cleage, Albert. *The Black Messiah.* New York: Sheed and Ward, 1968.
Cone, James. *Black Theology: A Documentary History.* New York: Orbis Books, 1993.
Dent, Gina, ed. *Black Popular Culture.* Seattle: Bay Press, 1993.
Du Bois, W.E.B. *The Souls of Black Folk.* New York: Knopf, 1993.
George, Nelson. *Buppies, B-Boys, BAPS, and Bohos.* New York: Harper Collins Publishers, 1992.
hooks, bell. *Black Looks: Race and Representation.* Boston: South End Press, 1992.
hooks, bell, and Cornel West. *Breaking Bread: Insurgent Black Intellectual Life.* Boston: South End Press, 1991.
Mercer, Kobena. Black Hair/Style Politics. In *Out There: Marginalization and Contemporary Cultures*, ed. Russell Ferguson, Martha Gever, Trinh T. Minhha, and Cornel West. New York and Cambridge: The New Museum of Contemporary Art and MIT Press, 1990.
Muhammed, Elijah. *Message to the Black Man.*
Rose, Tricia. *Black Noise: Rap Music and Black Culture in Contemporary America.* Boston: University Press of New England, 1994.
Rose, Tricia. Never Trust a Big Butt and a Smile. *Camera Obscura* 23 (1990).
Tate, Greg. *Flyboy in the Buttermilk,* New York: Fireside Press, 1992.
Washington, Booker T. *Up From Slavery.* New York: Dell Publishing, 1965.
West, Cornel. The New Politics of Difference. In *Out There: Marginalization and Contemporary Cultures*, ed. Russell Ferguson, Martha Gever, Trinh T. Minh-ha, and Cornel West. New York and Cambridge: The New Museum of Contemporary Art and MIT Press, 1990.
———. *Race Matters.* Boston: Beacon Press, 1993.

27

The Challenge of Rap Music from Cultural Movement to Political Power

Bakari Kitwana

> Mr. Mayor, imagine this was your backyard
> Mr. Governor, imagine it's your kids that starve imagine your kids gotta sling
> crack to survive, swing a Mac to be live ...
>
> Nas, "I Want to Talk to You"

In June 2001, Rush Communications CEO Russell Simmons convened a hip-hop summit in New York City. With the theme "Taking Back Responsibility," the summit focused its agenda on ways to strengthen rap music's growing influence. The 300 participants included major rap artists and industry executives as well as politicians, religious and community leaders, activists, and scholars. Few forces other than rap music, now one of the most powerful forces in American popular culture, could bring together such a diverse gathering of today's African American leaders. In many ways, the summit signaled hip-hop as the definitive cultural movement of our generation.

As the major cultural movement of our time, hip-hop (its music, fashion, attitude, style, and language) is undoubtedly one of the core influences for young African Americans born between 1965 and 1984. To fully appreciate the extent to which this is true, think back for a moment about the period between the mid-1970s and the early 1980s, before rap became a mainstream phenomenon. Before MTV. Before BET's Rap City. Before the Fresh Prince of Bel Air. Before *House Party* I or II. It is difficult now to imagine Black youth as a nearly invisible entity in American popular culture. But in those days, that was the case. When young Blacks were visible, it was mostly during the six o'clock evening news reports of crime in urban America.

In contrast, today it is impossible not to see young Blacks in the twenty-first century's public square—the public space of television, film, and the Internet. Our images now extend far beyond crime reports. For most of our contemporaries, it's difficult to recall when this was not the case. Because of rap, the voices, images, style, attitude, and language of young Blacks have become central in American culture, transcending geographic, social, and economic boundaries.

To be sure, professional athletes, especially basketball players, have for decades been young, Black, highly visible, and extremely popular. Yet, their success just didn't translate into visibility for young Blacks overall. For one thing, the conservative culture of professional sports, central to their identity, was often at odds with the rebellious vein inherent in the new Black youth culture. While household-name ball players towed the generic "don't do drugs and stay in school" party line, rappers, the emissaries of the new Black youth culture, advocated more anti-establishment slogans like "fuck the police." Such slogans were vastly more in synch with the hard realities facing young Blacks—so much so that as time marched on and hip-hop culture further solidified its place in American popular culture, basketball culture would also come to feel its influence.

Largely because of rap music, one can tune in to the voices and find the faces of America's Black youth at any point in the day. Having proven themselves as marketable entertainers with successful music careers, rappers star in television sit-coms and film and regularly endorse corporate products (such as Lil' Kim—Candies, Missy Elliot—the Gap, and Common, Fat Joe, and the Goodie Mob—Sprite). In the mid-1980s, a handful of corporations began incorporating hip-hop into their advertisement spots. Most were limited to run-of-the-mill product endorsements. By the late 1990s, however, ads incorporating hip-hop—even those promoting traditionally conservative companies—became increasingly steeped in the subtleties of hip-hop culture. Setting the standard with their extremely hip-hop savvy 1994 Voltron campaign, Sprite broke away from the straight-up celebrity endorsement format. Says Coca-Cola global marketing manager Darryl Cobbin, who was on the cutting edge of this advertising strategy: "I wanted to usher in a real authenticity in terms of hip-hop in advertising. We wanted to pay respect to the music *and* the culture. What's important is the value of hip-hop culture, not only as an image, but as a method of communication."

By the late 1990s, advertisers like the Gap, Nike, AT&T, and Sony soon followed suit and incorporated hip-hop's nuances into their advertising campaigns. As a result, the new Black youth culture resonates throughout today's media, regardless of what companies are selling (from soft drinks and footwear to electronics and telecommunications).

Of course, none of this happened overnight. In fact, more important than the commercialization of rap was the less visible cultural movement on the ground in anyhood USA. In rap's early days, before it became a thriving commercial entity, DJ party culture provided the backdrop for this off-the-radar cultural movement. What in the New York City metropolitan area took the form of DJ battles and MC chants emerged in Chicago as the house party scene, and in D.C. it was go-go. In other regions of the country, the local movement owed its genesis to rap acts like Run DMC, who broke through to a national audience in the early 1980s. In any case, by the mid-1980s, this local or underground movement began to emerge in the form of cliques, crews, collectives, or simply kids getting together primarily to party, but in the process rhyming, DJ-ing, dancing, and tagging. Some, by the early 1990s, even moved into activism. In large cities like Chicago, San Francisco, Houston, Memphis, New Orleans, Indianapolis, and Cleveland and even in smaller cities and suburban areas like Battle Creek, Michigan, and Champaign, Illinois, as the '80s turned to the '90s, more and more young Blacks were coming together in the name of hip-hop.

In the early 1980s, the "in" hip-hop fashion for New York City Black youth included Gazelles (glasses), sheepskins and leather bombers (coats), Clarks (shoes), nameplates, and name belts. In terms of language, Five Percenter expressions like "word is bond" were commonplace. These hip-hop cultural expressions in those days were considered bizarre by Black kids from other regions of the country. A student at the University of Pennsylvania at the time, Conrad Muhammad, the hip-hop minister, speaks to this in reminiscing on the National Black Students Unity Conference he organized in 1987:

> Jokers were getting off buses with shower caps on, perms and curls. MTV and BET had not yet played a role in standardizing Black youth culture the way they do today. Young people from different cities weren't all dressing the same way. Brothers and sisters were stepping off buses saying "we're from the University of Nebraska, Omaha." "We're from University of Minnesota." "We're from Cal Long Beach."

But by the early to mid-1990s, hip-hop's commercialized element had Black kids on the same page, regardless of geographic region. In this hip-hop friendly national environment, hip-hop designers like Enyce, Mecca, and FUBU were thriving, multi-platinum sales for rap artists were routine (and dwarfed the 1980s mark of success: gold sales), and hip-hop expressions like "blowin' up," "representin'," and "keepin' it real" worked their way into the conversational language of Black youth around the country. Contrast this to the mid-1980s when even those deep into hip-hop didn't see the extent to which a national cultural movement was unfolding.

"Before the Fresh Fest Tour of 1984, few folks were defining hip-hop culture as hip-hop culture," says Hashim Shomari, author of *From the Underground: Hip-Hop as an Agent of Social Change*. "That was a relatively 1990s phenomenon." Practitioners like Africa Bambaataa, Grandmaster Flash, Fab-Five Freddy, Chuck D, and KRS-One were on the frontlines of those who saw the need to flesh out the definitions. Also, it wasn't until the early 1990s that breakthrough books like Joseph Eure and James Spady's *Nation-Conscious Rap* (1991), Michael Gonzales and Havelock Nelson's *Bring the Noise: A Guide to Rap Music and Hip-Hop Culture* (1991), and Tricia Rose's *Black Noise: Rap Music and Black Culture in Contemporary America* (1994) began to discuss hip-hop as an influential culture that went beyond the commercial.

Without question, rap's national exposure played a key role in the uniform way in which the local cultural manifestations evolved. More recently, given rap's commercial success, alongside limited employment options beyond minimum-wage jobs for young Blacks, hip-hop's cultural movement at the local level is increasingly marked by an entrepreneurial element. On the West Coast, East Coast, in southern and northern cities, and in rural and suburban areas in between, young Blacks are pressing their own CDs and selling them "out the trunk" regionally.[1] Many of them are hoping to eventually put their city on the hip-hop map. What all this around the way activity has in common is that kids are tuned in to the same wavelength via hip-hop, some aspiring to be the next Air Jordan of hip-hop, others engaging in what is to them a way of life without commercial popular culture aspirations, and still others tuning in as a basic engagement with the youth culture of our time.

The commercialized element of this cultural movement and the off-the-radar one fuel each other. The underground element provides a steady stream of emerging talent that in turn gets absorbed into commercialization. That new voice and talent again inspires more discussion (about the art form, new styles, trends, language, and larger issues and themes) and more talent at the local level, which later infuses the commercial manifestation of the cultural movement. Case in point: the more recent wave of talent (say, Master P out of New Orleans, Eve from Philly, and Nelly from St. Louis) is similar to the much earlier waves like the Geto Boys out of Houston and Compton's NWA. Those earlier waves of talent (the Geto Boys, NWA, Too Short, E-40, and others) most certainly provided inspiration for the No Limit Soldiers and Ruff Ryders, who came later. Like the earliest waves of artists, each group represents its distinct region, while tapping into the national movement. In turn, Master P, Eve, and Nelly will influence the next wave of talent breaking from the margins into the mainstream.

It's not exactly a chicken-or-egg question, however. Hip-hop as a culture indisputably emerged in the South Bronx in the late 1970s, and in other parts of the northeast shortly thereafter, before branching out around the country in the early 1980s. What's arguable is the extent to which hip-hop would have become the national cultural movement that it is today without commercialization.

In 1988, rapper Chuck D of the rap group Public Enemy described rap music as "the Black CNN." This was certainly true at the grassroots level at the time. However, the decade of the 1990s proved even more profound as rap music became thoroughly accepted and promoted in mainstream American popular culture. As such, rap provided the foundation for a resounding young Black mainstream presence that went far beyond rap music itself.

Understanding the degree to which the local and commercial are deeply entrenched and interdependent, one can began to grasp the far-reaching effects of hip-hop on young Blacks. As the primary vehicle through which young Blacks have achieved a national voice and presence, rap music transmits the new Black youth culture to a national audience. And in the same way as the mainstream media establishes the parameters for national discussion for the nation at large, rap music sets the tone for Black youth. As the national forum for Black youth concerns and often as the impetus for discussion around those issues, rap music has done more than any one entity to help our generation forge a distinct identity.

Another important aspect of what makes rap so substantive in the lives of young Blacks is its multilingual nature. In addition to beaming out hip-hop culture, rap also conveys elements of street culture, prison culture, and the new Black youth culture. Often all of these elements overlap within rap's lyrics and visual images. In the process, images and ideas that define youth culture for this generation—such as designer clothes, like Sean Jean, Phat Farm, and Tommy Hilfiger, ever-changing styles of dress, and local colloquialisms—are beamed out to a captive national audience. Also transmitted are cues of personal style, from cornrows and baby dreads to body piercing and tattoos.

And finally, even more important than fashion, style, and language, the new Black culture is encoded within the images and lyrics of rap and thus help define what it means to be young and Black at the dawn of the millennium. In the process, rap music has become the primary vehicle for transmitting culture and values to this generation, relegating Black families, community centers, churches, and schools to the back burner.

To be sure, rap marked a turning point, a shift from practically no public voice for young Blacks—or at best an extremely marginalized one—to Black youth culture as the rage in mainstream popular culture. And more than just increasing Black youth visibility, rap articulated publicly and on a mass scale many of this generation's beliefs, relatively unfiltered by the corporate structures that carried it. Even when censored with bleeps or radio-friendly "clean" versions, the messages were consistent with the new Black youth culture and more often than not struck a chord with young Blacks, given our generation's unique collective experiences. At the same time, the burgeoning grassroots arts movement was under way. All was essential to rap's movement into the mainstream and its emergence as the paramount cultural movement of our time.

Although hip-hop has secured its place as a cultural movement, its biggest challenge lies ahead. In the late 1980s when gangsta rap first emerged, community activists and mainstream politicians of the civil rights generation began to challenge rap's content. This criticism forced a dialogue that revealed one of the Black community's best kept secrets, the bitter generational divide between hip-hop generationers and our civil rights/Black power parents.

The key concern was Black cultural integrity: how have the very public images of young Blacks in hip-hop music and culture affected the larger Black community? Central to this discussion was the pervasive use of offensive epithets in rap lyrics, such as "nigga," "bitch," and "ho," all of which reinforce negative stereotypes about Blacks. What was the price of this remarkable breakthrough in the visibility of young Blacks in the mainstream culture? Had young rappers simply transferred images of young Black men as criminals from news reports to entertainment? And finally, had the growing visibility of young Black entertainers further marginalized young Black intellectuals and writers, who have remained nearly invisible?

A handful of responses emerged. The response from the rap industry was unanimous: free speech is a constitutional right. The predominant response from rap artists themselves was a proverbial head in the sand. Most reasoned that the older generation was out of touch with the concerns of hip-hop generationers. Just as our parents' generation was unfamiliar with the music, the thinking went, when it came to other matters of our generation, particularly issues involving hip-hop, they, likewise, didn't know what they were talking about. By and large, the question of rap's attack on Black cultural integrity went unaddressed. In fact, the use of incendiary words like "nigga" and "bitch" has become so commonplace in rap's lyrics that today even those in rap's growing white audience routinely use them when referring to each other and often their Black peers (a matter Spike Lee vaguely touched on in the film *Bamboozled*).

Lately, as the theme of the Simmons summit "Taking Back Responsibility" suggests, hip-hop is again undertaking the critical task of questioning its relationship to the community. David Mays, publisher of the hip-hop magazine *The Source*, and Reverend Al Sharpton held a series of summits eight months prior to the Simmons summit, which called for a code of conduct in light of arrests of numerous rappers and the growing association of rappers with criminality. Minister Conrad Muhammad, dubbed the hip-hop minister for the moral voice he's long brought to the hip-hop community, felt the Mays–Sharpton gathering didn't go far enough. Muhammad called for a summit of Black rap artists, rap industry executives, and activists to discuss ways of holding the hip-hop industry accountable to the Black community. Appalled by Muhammad's moral challenge to the rap industry, Simmons countered Muhammad with a call for his own summit to be held within a few weeks of the Muhammad one.

Simmons, a major player in the rap industry who earlier began flexing his political muscle by reaching out to Democratic Party insiders like Hillary Clinton in her bid for the U.S. Senate, brought together the largest and most media-celebrated summit to date. Joining rap industry insiders were African American notables like minister Louis Farrakhan, NAACP head Kweisi Mfume, U.S. Representative Cynthia McKinney, and scholars Cornel West and Michael Eric Dyson.

The Simmons event was impressive in terms of sheer numbers and diverse backgrounds. But where it most seriously came up short was in its failure to incorporate the grassroots segment of hip-hop's cultural movement, especially hip-hop generation activists. When hip-hop's true influence as a cultural movement is finally understood, events like these will recognize that the very same synergy at the heart of hip-hop's commercial success has also informed our generation's activists and political theorists. Just as some record executives can give us a blue-print for blowin' up rap acts, the ideas that our generation's activists hold about maximizing rap's potential for social change have been seasoned in their day-to-day work and experience. If our generation's cultural movement is to evolve to have a meaningful political impact, the local segments of hip-hop's cultural movement—from hip-hop generation activists to local entrepreneurs to the everyday hip-hop kids on the block—must not only be brought to the table, but must have a major voice.

Furthermore, rather than centering the discussion within our own generation—*and*, yes, including the expertise and insight of our parents' generation—the invitation-only Simmons summit turned to the mostly liberal–integrationist civil rights leadership and music industry executives. The result was predictable: a combination of the traditional music industry call for free speech, which allows for continued blockbuster sales without disrupting the minstrel-esque proven formula for success, and the traditional civil rights activist call for young voters to support Democratic candidates for public office. Neither of these same-game-with-another-name reforms challenge civil righters or industry insiders to do anything different than what they are already doing. Moreover, pushing activists of the civil rights generation to the forefront of this effort is tantamount to casting older-generation R&B singers like Dionne Warwick and Lionel Richie as leads in a 'hood film or featuring them at a concert alongside ODB or Lil' Kim.

Until hip-hop is recognized as a broad cultural movement, rather than simply an influential moneymaker, those who seek to tap into hip-hop's potential to impact social change should not expect substantive progress. A unified front between hip-hop's commercial and grassroots sectors on the issue of sociopolitical action would change the nature of the dialogue. For example, in the same way that the hip-hop community as a cultural movement inherently answered the question, "what is hip-hop culture?" a new inclusive framework inevitably would answer the question, "what do we mean by politicizing the hip-hop generation?" Is our goal to run hip-hop generationers for office, to turn out votes for Democrats and Republicans, to form a third party, or to provide our generation with a more concrete political education?

Indications of the endless possibilities of this unified front approach are evident in the following examples of rap's demonstrated success in extending its influence beyond popular culture.

The Haitian Refugee Crisis

In April 1997, the Fugees held a concert in Port-au-Prince, Haiti, to raise money for local charities and to bring international media attention to the economic and political plight of Haiti's people. Financed mostly by Wyclef Jean, the event was also supported by local companies. Unfortunately, the effort got caught between U.S. foreign policy and the type of corruption that has come to plague new governments on the heels of dictators. As a result, the funds raised never reached the intended charities. Shortly before the event, the Haitian government took control of the fundraiser, including handling all receipts. Afterward they issued a report declaring that the event only broke even. The event did succeed in gaining media attention, however. Beyond that, it demonstrated one way that successful American entertainers can support larger international causes.

Rappers and Mumia Abu-Jamal

One of the major issues of our time has been the disproportionate representation of African Americans in both the penal system and on death row. This issue is critical to a generation that during its lifetime has seen the Black prison population increase from fewer than 250,000 to nearly 1 million. Mumia Abu-Jamal's fight for justice brought the issue to the fore. Abu-Jamal was convicted in 1982 for the murder of Daniel Faulkner, a white Philadelphia cop. He and Faulkner were shot while Abu-Jamal was attempting to break up a confrontation between his brother and the officer. Abu-Jamal was later sentenced to death. Supporters say the former Black Panther was railroaded by a racist police department and received an unfair trial. Abu-Jamal insists that he did not commit the crime and says that he is being punished for his politics. The rap community's participation in Abu-Jamal's fight for justice persists in rap lyrics, in support at rallies, and at anti-death penalty benefits. KRS-One, Channel Live, and other rappers have been among Abu-Jamal's supporters. As a result of these efforts, few hip-hop generation kids are unfamiliar with Abu-Jamal's fight for justice. Most have an opinion on the death penalty and are aware of the inconsistencies in American justice for Blacks and whites.

The Million Man March

The Million Man March was the largest mass gathering in the history of the country. Young Blacks turned out in huge numbers partly because rappers have made it fashionable for Blacks of this generation to support Black causes. Furthermore, rappers like Ice Cube, Ice T, Puff Daddy, Das EFX, Common Sense, and others strongly supported the event. This certainly helped to heighten the importance of the march in the minds of young Blacks.

The Million Youth March

At the eleventh hour, the Million Youth March languished under various obstacles that seemed destined to sabotage the event. Responding to some of the needs to pull the event off, Master

P made a major donation to the event that helped the show to go on. As contributions from hip-hop generation athletes and entertainers to larger causes remain few and far between, the gesture was a much-needed breath of fresh air. In 1998, Danny Glover made a $1 million contribution to TransAfrica, the Washington, D.C.-based organization that lobbies on behalf of U.S. foreign policy toward Africa and the Caribbean Basin. Financial support from the hip-hop community for serious political efforts remains rare. Master P's support for the Million Youth March is an example of how rap artists can make the difference to such efforts.

East Coast/West Coast Conflict

Probably no other event in rap's history has received as much coverage in the mainstream media as the so-called East Coast/West Coast beef—imagined and real antagonism between rappers and fans on the East Coast (mostly New York City) and the West Coast (mostly rappers and fans in Los Angeles). The conflict, which in print often centered on rap labels Death Row and Bad Boy, climaxed with the gangland-style murders of Tupac Shakur in 1996 and Biggie Smalls in 1997. In the wake of their deaths, many rappers participated in efforts to end the seemingly out-of-control antagonisms. From a rapper summit called by Louis Farrakhan's Nation of Islam to rap lyrics denouncing the East-West feud, rappers like Nas, Jay-Z, Common, Snoop, and others succeeded in reducing East-West antagonism.

Social Programs and Foundations

Several rappers have founded social programs and foundations to give back to the communities that produced them; among them are the Wu Charitable Foundation, Camp Cool J, the Refugee Project, Christopher Wallace Foundation, and the Tupac Amaru Shakur Memorial Foundation. All of these organizations focus their efforts on urban youth who lack opportunities and access. Few venture far beyond the typical feel-good effort that boosts the celebrity's publicity. However, some of these programs have features that encourage community responsibility and participation. For example, Daddy's House Social Programs, Sean "P-Diddy" Combs' seven-year-old program for children aged 6–16, sponsors a Saturday school that teaches regular academic courses as well as manhood/womanhood training for teens. Daddy's House also sends a group of children to Ghana and South Africa as part of an Urban Youth Tour. In return, each student makes a presentation to their respective communities when they return home. Lauryn Hill's Refugee Project conducts a mentorship program where each child is assigned two mentors (a college student and a professional). In addition, Camp Hill, the Refugee Project's summer camp, has a required family day component built into the two-week camp, which parents of campers must attend. The Tupac Amaru Shakur Memorial Foundation helps former inmates who are single-parent mothers make the transition back to society. These are examples of community efforts that rappers have supported with their recently acquired wealth. These efforts can serve as a cornerstone for even greater, more cooperative efforts.

Most of the activities concerned with social change have taken place outside of the limelight of rap's growing popularity. In some cases, the activity may seem superficial, but careful examination reveals that some rappers individually and collectively have consistently responded to issues important to this generation. The response may not have always been effective, or even politically correct, but these are the types of activities that have galvanized community-building efforts. The extent of the impact seems to be directly proportionate to the degree that such efforts work themselves deeper into the fabric of hip-hop's cultural movement.

Rap music's ability to influence social change should not be taken lightly. The U.S. Department of Health and Human Services reported that rates of teen pregnancy fell by 4 percent in

1997 and that rates decreased by 17 percent in the 1990s overall. Social policy has had very little impact on this and related issues in the lives of America's poor. In many cases, social policy has only exacerbated the problems. Experts have offered numerous explanations for the decline, but none have considered rap music a factor. Perhaps rap music's influence as a transmitter of ideas should be more carefully considered.

At least one team of researchers at Emory University's Rollins School of Public Health agrees. In a recent study, they found that after Black boys and girls 11–14 years old listened to rappers like Big Pun, the Goodie Mob, and Lil' Kim, they were more knowledgeable about AIDS and were better prepared to discuss safe sex, condom use, and abstinence. "The knowledge they gain about themselves and the disease helps kids make informed decisions about sexual behavior and makes them less likely to engage in risky sexual practices," said Torrence Stephens, lead author of the study. This study adds to the growing body of evidence that hip-hop is much more than entertainment.

In each of these efforts, there is an *informal* exchange between hip-hop's commercial and grassroots sectors. A *formal* unified front could effect even greater change. Here are a few other ways that a unified front could begin to expand rap's influence into social and political arenas.

First, a unified front of rap artists, industry insiders, hip-hop generation activists, and everyday kids on the block could begin to challenge rap's ever-growing listening audience of white youth. How can that relationship build on America's unkept promise of inclusion? If this engagement with Black youth culture is more than simply a fleeting fascination, what will it take to motivate white youth to make the transition from simply enjoying and interacting with hip-hop to using their own power and influence to enhance the quality of American race relations?

In an April 5, 2001, *New York Times* article titled "Pressed Against a 'Race Ceiling,' " Black elected officials lamented the difficulty they have getting elected to statewide office where majority-white populations won't vote for them, a sentiment expressed by New Orleans Mayor Marc Morial in his comments to the *Times*: "People have asked, 'Wouldn't you like to run for the Senate, for governor or attorney general?' And I say, 'Certainly, I'd be interested in that at some point. But in Louisiana they haven't elected a statewide African-American official since the 1880s.' "

Since the passage of the Voting Rights Act of 1965, only one African American has been elected governor and only two have been elected to the U.S. Senate. If rap's white listening audience translated its familiarity and interest in Black youth culture to their voting habits and challenged their parents to deal with the continuing racial contradictions as well, this glass ceiling would be obliterated, and race relations as we know them would never be the same.

Second, young white movers and shakers within the rap industry could be challenged by a unified front to use their knowledge and insight to further narrow the racial divide not only inside the industry but outside of it. Insisting on multi-ethnic hires and diversified staffing in the industry, rather than hiding behind the old excuse "we can't find any qualified ones," and insisting on equal and fair pay across the board would be a good start. Likewise, challenging stereotypical and degrading practices, images, and lyrics in the rap industry is a must.

Third, a unified front could challenge successful rap artists to explore ways of pooling their resources and influence to lead and assist community rebuilding and economic revitalization efforts in poor communities. Activists from the civil rights generation challenged large corporations that do a significant amount of business with African Americans to support development within those communities; a unified front between commercial and around the way hip-hop could do the same. The seemingly endless list of companies marketing products to young Blacks through hip-hop's influence (from those whose ads lace rap music magazines and those who sponsor awards shows to rap labels themselves) should be challenged to reciprocate by supporting community development projects. Such efforts would contribute to and strengthen Black community development and further endear artists to fans. Local community activists will support these efforts to the degree that they improve the day-to-day lives of community residents.

Recently, the Church of God in Christ in West Los Angeles finished building a new $60 million sanctuary with the help of members, who include several major Black entertainers; with their support, a vision became a reality. In another effort, the 2000 Watts Foundation created by MTV VJ and R&B singer Tyrese is bringing together corporate sponsors to build a community center in Watts, Tyrese's hometown. Efforts like these provide models for future projects.

Fourth, a united front could challenge the rap industry to finally resolve the issue of hip-hop's responsibility to Black cultural integrity. Rappers like Chuck D, Queen Latifah, Lauryn Hill, Will Smith, and Common have long tried to raise the bar on lyrical content. Community activists like C. Delores Tucker and Calvin Butts and more recently Conrad Muhammad have challenged rap artists and the industry to do more to make socially responsible lyrics as pervasive in hip-hop as those that advance stereotypes. Along with the mainstreaming of rap throughout the 1990s, elements of street culture and prison culture have become more and more dominant in rap lyrics, compounding the now decade-old problem of stereotypical images in hip-hop.

Just as problematic is hip-hop's growing tendency to cross over into the adult entertainment industry—from the soft porn images of rap music videos and the XXX hip-hop video *Doggystyle* (a Snoop Dogg/Larry Flynt joint venture) to emerging magazines that blur the lines between pornography and hip-hop. Not only is hip-hop a major force in the lives of hip-hop generationers at the older end of the age group, but it also heavily impacts those at the younger end of the spectrum, some of whom are just approaching their teenage years. The commercial rap industry must begin to more seriously weigh the impact of exposing children to age-inappropriate (adult) situations. A unified front could develop workable approaches for addressing these issues. As Muhammad and Simmons squared off, Bill Stepheney, political activist and CEO of Stepson Media, put it succinctly in his comments to the *New York Post* (May 8, 2001): "What is the line that we [artists and industry executives] are unwilling to cross for profits? Is there a line? Or is it completely laissez-faire?"

Finally, the "Taking Back Responsibility" summit should be applauded for advocating artist development. Much more can and should be done in this area. An ongoing alliance between those in the commercial industry and those at the grassroots level would inevitably build on the Black community's traditional call for self-determination through greater Black ownership, control, and influence within the industry beyond being "the show." The current generation of rap industry insiders needs to develop a new generation of songwriters, performers, and music industry executives with real power and ownership within the industry. Kalamu Ya Salaam, activist-poet and former executive director of the New Orleans Jazz and Heritage Foundation, identified this need as part of the solution to America's long-standing race problem. In his *What Is Life: Reclaiming the Black Blues Self* (Third World Press, 1994), he proposes the music industry as an important sector for Black economic development:

> A current possible solution is what I call horizontal economic development at a mass level in a specific economic sector. The traditional vertical mode of economic development is simply individual wealth generated by climbing the earnings ladder in a given field. The miscellaneous array of athletes and entertainers celebrated in *Ebony* and *Black Enterprise* are a prime example of this in our community. . . . African Americans must make a concerted effort to carve out a significant niche in the . . . music business. . . . It offers the broadest

array of opportunities for a diversity of skill areas while remaining focused in a particular economic sector.... The music business is one of the few segments of the modern American economy in which [African Americans] have any significant leverage....

The real challenge of integration is to capture control of economic development. We are the creative labor of a significant portion of the music industry. Now is the time to become the controllers of the fruit of our labor. African Americans desperately need economic development and a move on the music industry is a feasible route. We make the music. Now, let's make the money.

A working unified front would greatly enhance rap's potential to contribute to needed sociopolitical transformations. The real question is this: why should hip-hop generationers continue to participate in and support a multibillion dollar industry if it fails to in any way address the critical problems facing our generation? What good is rap music if it does nothing more than give young Blacks the opportunity to "dance to our own degradation" (as Black studies scholar Maulana Karenga has noted) and if it enriches only a few at the expense of the many? If rap is to stand as not only the most significant cultural movement of our time but one of history's most salient, and I believe it will, hip-hop generationers both inside and outside of the rap music industry must rise to the challenge. All the components for a mass political movement in our lifetime are in place and functioning—but separate. Do we dare join them together?

Note

1. My emphasis here is on Black youth—no disrespect to the countless folks of other racial and ethnic groups down with hip-hop. This is not to say that Latino and to a lesser extent Asian and Native American youth have not been influential in and touched by hip-hop culture. Neither is it meant to ignore the distinctiveness of Caribbean Americans. More recently white kids, a large segment of hip-hop's listening audience, are jumping into the fray. Nevertheless, rap music indisputably remains dominated by Black youth in both its commercial and local manifestations.

28
Rap, Race, and Politics

Clarence Lusane

> Whatever may be the conditions of a people's political and social factors … it is generally within the culture that we find the seed of opposition, which leads to the structuring and development of the liberation movement.
>
> Amilcar Cabral[1]

For many black youths in the United States, in the words of the classic song by War, the world is a ghetto. Trapped in and witness to cycles of violence, destitution and lives of desperation, their aspirations and views find expression in political behavior, social practice, economic activities, and cultural outlets. These streams came together and informed a culture of resistance that has been termed Hip Hop whose most dynamic expression is in the form of rap music. On the one hand, rap is the voice of alienated, frustrated and rebellious black youth who recognize their vulnerability and marginality in post-industrial America. On the other hand, rap is the packaging and marketing of social discontent by some of the most skilled ad agencies and largest record producers in the world. It's this duality that has made rap and rappers an explosive issue in the politics of power that shaped the 1992 U.S. elections and beyond. It's also this duality that has given rap its many dimensions and flavors; its spiraling matrix of empowerment and reaction.

Influenced by a tradition of oral leaders and artists, from Malcolm X, Martin Luther King and Nikki Giovanni to Gil Scott Heron and the Last Poets, young black cultural activists evolved from the urban cosmos of the early 1980s ready for rap. Denied opportunity for more formal music training and access to instruments due to Reagan-era budget cuts in education and school music programs, turntables became instruments and lyrical acrobatics became a cultural outlet. Initially underground, by the late 1980s, rap and the broad spectrum of Hip Hop had become the dominant cultural environment of young African-Americans, particularly males.

Following the historic example of the cultural modes of the civil rights and Black Power movements, rap has had an international impact. Just as the Vietnamese sang civil rights freedom songs, so have the political imperatives of rap traversed the globe and found expression in venues from Mexico to India. In Czechoslovakia, local rappers rap about the struggle of being young and penniless. Wearing baseball caps and half-laced sneakers, youth in the Ivory Coast have found a bond in the music. Australian rappers kick it about the mistreatment of the

Aborigine people. Tributes to the victims of U.S. atomic bombs form the substance of local rappers in Japan.[2]

The cultural power of rap as global protest music is undeniable. To understand the genesis of this power, however, requires a return to the source. It is rap's impact on the economics, politics and gender issues in the African-American community that must be examined, if only briefly, to sense its significance, possibilities and contradictions. The enemies of rap, as one observer noted, have gone after "the message, the messenger and the medium."[3] And it is not just whites who have dismissed and criticized rap. As Salim Muwakkil wrote in *In These Times*, "for many middle-class black Americans, rap is ... a soundtrack for sociopaths."[4]

Hip Hop Capitalism

From slave town to Motown, from Bebop to Hip Hop, black music has been shaped by the material conditions of black life. Contextually, today's black youth culture flows out of the changes that affected the political economy of U.S. capitalism over the last two decades. Incremental economic and social gains made in the late 1960s and the 1970s were destroyed with a vengeance in the Reagan and Bush years. Many observers of black politics saw the handwriting on the wall when Reagan came into power. In 1982, political writer Manning Marable prophesied:

> The acceleration of black unemployment and underemployment, the capitulation of many civil rights and Black Power leaders to the Right, the demise of militant black working-class institutions and caucuses, and the growing dependency of broad segments of the black community upon public assistance programs and transfer payments of various kinds; these interdependent realities within the contemporary black political economy are the beginning of a new and profound crisis for black labor in America.[5]

Thus, in the late 1980s and early 1990s, the material basis for the production and reproduction of black youth alienation is the growing immiseration of millions of African-American working-class families. Between 1986 and 1992, according to the Census Bureau, an additional 1.2 million African-Americans fell below the poverty line.[6] As stunning as that may be, the Bush administration achieved the same result in half the time. A report issued by the Children's Defense Fund documents that 841,000 youth fell into poverty in the first two years of the Bush administration, affecting, in some cities, as many as two-thirds of minority children.[7] The official poverty rate for blacks is 32.7 per cent, 10.2 million people, which is higher than for Hispanics (28.7 per cent), Asians (13.8 per cent), or whites (11.3 per cent).[8]

Most critical, however, has been the unemployment situation of African-American youth and what has happened to black youth economically over the last three decades. Since 1960, black youth suffered the largest decline in employment of all component groups of all races. In 1986, in the middle of the Republican years, black teenage unemployment was officially as high as 43.7 per cent. In October 1992, six years later, the numbers remained virtually unchanged, with black youth unemployment officially at 42.5 per cent.[9] One does not have to agree with the rantings and rage of Ice T, Sister Souljah or other rappers to unite with their sense of isolation, anger and refusal to go down quietly. Ignored and "dissed" by both major political parties and much of what passes for national black leadership, is it any wonder that Ice Cube reflects the views of so many youth when he sings:

> Do I have to sell me a whole lot of crack
> For decent shelter and clothes on my back?
> Or should I just wait for President Bush
> Or Jesse Jackson and Operation PUSH?[10]

It was, then, perfectly logical that Hip Hop culture should initially emerge most strongly in those cities hardest hit by Reaganomics with large minority youth populations—New York, Los Angeles, Houston and Oakland. For many of these youth, rap became not only an outlet for social and political discourse, but also an economic opportunity that required little investment other than boldness and a competitive edge. In a period when black labour was in low demand, if one could not shoot a basketball like Michael Jordan, then the entertainment industry was one of the few legal avenues available for the get-rich consciousness that dominated the social ethos of the 1980s.

Rap music is big business. According to the *Los Angeles Times*, in 1990 rap brought in $600 million (in that year, two rap albums alone—admittedly from the "soft" end of the spectrum—Hammer's *Please Hammer Don't Hurt 'Em* and the white group, Vanilla Ice's, *To the Extreme* sold 14 million copies just in the United States, while the hard-hitting Public Enemy's *Fear of a Black Planet* and Digital Underground's *Sex Packets* also sold over a million each); in 1991, sales rose to about $700 million.[11] 2 Live Crew's *As Nasty as They Wanna Be*, the subject of law suits and arrests, sold more than two million copies. In their debut album, *Straight Outta Compton*, NWA sold over a million copies and followed that up in 1992 by breaking all sales records with their *Efil4zaggin* (Niggaz 4 life spelled backwards) album. The album sold an unprecedented 900,000 copies in its first week of release and later went on to sell millions.[12]

Rap is attractive because it requires generally low-investment costs for the corporations. According to one producer, a rap album can be produced for less than $50,000, while an equivalent album for an established rock group or popular R&B group can cost $100,000–300,000. And while rap artists are signed with a bewildering frenzy, they are also dropped more rapidly than musicians from other music forms. If an artist or group doesn't do well within the first six to eight weeks of their release, they are often sent packing.

Annually, young black consumers age 15–24 spend about $23 billion a year in the United States, of which about $100 million is spent on records and tapes.[13] African-Americans, however, are not the main purchasers of rap as, increasingly, rap is being bought by non-blacks. A survey taken in mid-1992 found that 74 per cent of rap sold in the first six months of that year was bought by whites.[14] This is one reason why every major record company and communications conglomerate, from Sony to Atlantic, has made significant investments in rap music.

For many rappers, Hip Hop capitalism promises both riches and racial integrity. Rappers found that they could yell at the system and be paid (highly) by it at the same time. A legitimate desire and need for economic empowerment could be turned into profit with only minor ideological adjustments and rationalizations about "free speech" by capital. Some of those who have been the target of censorship, such as rapper Ice T, would argue that free enterprise will only let free speech go so far. As he says in his song "Freedom of Speech":

> Freedom of Speech
> That's some mutherfuckin' bullshit
> You say the wrong thing
> They'll lock your ass up quick

In the laissez-faire capitalist atmosphere that dominated the early years of modern rap, a number of black entrepreneurs were able to enter the business and become highly successful. Queen Latifah's Flavor Unit Management and Records is home to popular groups such as Nikki D, Black Sheep, D Nice, Pete Rock & CL Smooth, and Naughty by Nature.

No one better symbolizes the contradictory aspirations of the rappers than Russell Simmons and his phenomenal achievements with Rush Communications and its rap label, Def Jam. By any estimation, Rush Communications is huge. Home to top rap groups such as Public Enemy, Run DMC and Big Daddy Kane and producer of the highly rated, hip hop-ish cable comedy series Def Comedy Jam, Simmons has transformed what was essentially a small basement operation into a $34 million conglomerate. Rap artists at Rush have earned ten gold records, six platinum records, and two multiplatinum records. Plans are afoot to expand the conglomerate into film production and even sell public stock. Rush Communications is the thirty-second largest black-owned business in the United States and the second largest black-owned entertainment company.[15]

As CEO, Simmons earns an estimated $5 million annually. Usually attired in sneakers, sweatsuits and baseball caps, Simmons is a major driving force behind the music and in attacking the racist structures of the popular music business that have historically reduced the role of African-American to that of powerless entertainer.

Simmons' success and efforts are as laudable as they are remarkable. They do not represent, however, a break from the economic system that is responsible for the misery that forms the substance of the music that Rush produces. The commodification of black resistance is not the same as resistance to a society built upon commodification. Rap artists, even those who obtained some level of economic power and independence, are still slaves to a market system that requires an economic elite and mass deprivation.

It's critical to note that it has been more than just the multinational recording industry that has benefited from the reduction of black culture to the circumscribed limits of Hip Hop. The alcohol, tennis shoe, clothing, hat and film industries have boomed as a result of the new markets that have opened up or expanded, based on the spread of Hip Hop and the often exploitative use of rap artists in advertising.

Alcohol companies, already complicit in the disproportionate targeting of the black community for liquor sales, were quick to front rap stars to sell their product. (One group that did not buy into the hype was Public Enemy. After McKenzie River Corp illegally used PE's Chuck D's voice in one of their commercials, PE went on the offensive and denounced malt liquor sales, used the company for $5 million and recorded a song, "One Million Bottlebags," criticizing the practice of selling the brew mainly in the black community.)[16] Ice Cube, Eric B. & Rakim, EPMD, the Geto Boys, Compton's Most Wanted, Yo! MTV Rap's Fab Freddie and Yo-Yo—who was not even drinking age at the time—were all used to sell highly potent malt liquor. Sexually-suggestive scripts also attempted to convince consumers that malt liquors are aphrodisiacs. Yo-Yo would moan that St Ides Malt Liquor "puts you in the mood [and] makes you wanna go oooh." Ice Cube claimed that with St Ides you could "get your girl in the mood quicker" and that the beverage would make your "jimmy thicker." The alcohol content of St Ides, Elephant, Magnum, Crazy Horse, Olde English 800, Red Bull Malt Liquor, PowerMaster and other malt beers is greater than regular beer—nearly twice as great in some cases. Malt beer accounts for only about 3 per cent of all beer sold, yet more than 30 per cent of its sales are in the black community.

This exploitation of these rappers' popularity was denounced by community activists and black health advocates around the country. Makani Themba of the Marin Institute in California pointed out astutely that the beer companies were "appropriating a very important part of our culture to sell what is a dangerous product for many of these kids."[17]

Rap's impact on the Hollywood film industry has also been significant. Across the spectrum, rap has found its way into the soundtrack and themes of movies both big and small. Black films, in particular, have been built around the symbols of Hip Hop and black resistance, even as the substance of most of the films has retained a profound commitment and defense of middle-class, bourgeois culture and values.

Official Hollywood has produced an avalanche of films targeted at the black community in the last few years that have run the gamut from gratuitously violent action dramas, such as "New Jack City" and "Trespass," to absurdly embarrassing comedies, such as "True Identity" and "Sister Act." Spike Lee, who embodies much of Hip Hop's contradictory strengths and weaknesses, along with other black directors, actors and producers, has challenged the standard fare and attempted to create a new generation of black films that honestly reflect black youth culture.

Hollywood has been willing to produce both these types of films for a very simple reason: with a relatively small investment there is the potential for large returns. While African-Americans constitute only about 12 per cent of the U.S. population, they make up about 25 per cent of the movie-going audience.[18] John Singleton's *Boyz N the Hood*, for example, which starred rapper Ice Cube, cost about $6 million to produce and raised at least $57 million. This translates into a profit of roughly $51 million. *House Party (I)*, by the Hudlin Brothers, starring rappers Kid 'N Play, cost a paltry, by Hollywood standards, $2.5 million and brought in $26 million in revenue for a cool $23.5 million in profits. Spike Lee's *Jungle Fever* cost about $13 million and raised $31 million in sales. The dirt cheap *Straight Outta Brooklyn* cost $327,000 and brought back $2,173,000.[19]

In all of these films and many more, the background music is rap and Hip Hop is the atmosphere in which mainly moral tales are told and the politics of liberalism are preached. From Public Enemy to Digital Underground to Arrested Development, every genre of rap is represented. Many rappers are finding it a smooth move from rapping to acting. The Ices, T and Cube, are the most active of the rapper-actor set, but are being followed closely by Queen Latifah, the Fresh Prince, Kid 'N Play, 2Pac, and LL Cool J, all of whom have made movies and television appearances.

The political economy of Hip Hop, i.e., its capacity to open markets, maximize profits, and commodify legitimate grief and unrest, is the material basis that drives it forward. However, the nature of Hip Hop, its political soul, is to provoke and agitate.

Fear of a Black Planet: The Politics of Provocation

> Nightmare. That's what I am
> America's nightmare
> I am what you made me
> The hate and evil that you gave me …
> America, reap what you sow.
>
> 2 Pac

The dominant ideological trend of the rappers is black nationalism. Universally wedded to the notion that black leadership, for the most part, has sold out, the black nationalist rhetoric of Hip Hop becomes a challenging and liberating political paradigm in the face of surrender on the part of many political forces in the black community. While there are leftist rappers, such as the Disposal Heroes of Hiphoprisy and KRS-One, who to some extent embody Jesse Jackson's Rainbow Coalition notion of politics, most range from the soft-core nationalism of Arrested Development to the hard-core nationalist influenced raps of the political and gangsta rappers.

In particular, minister Louis Farrakhan and his Nation of Islam have had tremendous influence on the political views of black youth, in general, and of rappers, more specifically. Ice Cube, for example, joined the organizeation, stating that, "To me, the best organization around for black people is the Nation of Islam."[20] And a whole set of Muslim rappers has come on the scene. This includes groups such as Brand Nubian, Poor Righteous Teachers, King Sun, Movement Ex and Paris, who created his own mini-controversy when he wrote the song "Bush Killer"—the title of which should be explanation enough.

Other nationalist groups and movements have also emerged, such as the hard-core cultural nationalist Blackwatch movement, centered in New York, which sees itself as building a national black youth movement. It is spearheaded by the group X-Clan and includes other rappers such as Isis, Professor X and Queen Mother Rage.

In modern rap, Public Enemy (PE) is the leading, though by no means only, force espousing a black nationalist ideology. Public Enemy's Chuck D, recognized by many as the leader of radical rap, calls Hip Hop music "black folks' CNN."[21] Although many newer and more provocative rappers have come on the scene, PE can still be controversial with the best of them and maintains its reputation as the "Black Panthers" of rap[22]—for example, with the release in 1992 of its "By the Time I Get to Arizona" rap and video. In Arizona, the reactionary former Republican governor, Evan Mecham, had rescinded the state holiday celebrating the birthday of the Reverend Martin Luther King, Jr. This made it virtually the only state in the nation that did not officially honor King. Indeed, Mecham went as far as to state that "King didn't deserve a holiday and that blacks needed jobs more than another day off." Boycotts and protests over the issue cost the state an estimated $360 million.

In Public Enemy's video, a white governor is blown to bits by a car bomb, a white state senator is poisoned and members of the state legislature are gunned down. Chuck D's song leaves no mistaking his intent: "I'm on the one mission to get a politician," he says, and "until we get some land, call me the trigger man." Coretta Scott King denounced both PE and the video: "We do not subscribe to violence as a way to achieve any social or economic ends." PE was also soundly condemned by other civil rights leaders both inside and outside of Arizona.

In interviews, Chuck D stated that he viewed King as far more militant by the time of his death than he is generally portrayed as being, both by the media and by civil rights leaders. Chuck D claimed that if King were alive today, he would probably be referred to as "Martin Luther King Farrakhan."[23]

Rap's rage interjected itself into the world of black politics in 1992 in other ways. Its most celebrated entrance into black political life occurred when the then presidential candidate, Bill Clinton, shot a stinging criticism at rapper Sister Souljah for provocative remarks attributed to her following the Los Angeles uprising. In an interview with the *Washington Post*, Souljah is reported to have said, "I mean if black people kill black people every day, why not have a week and kill white people."[24] Although she said that the statement had been taken out of context, and subsequent examination of the full text of her interview seems to support her contention, her remarks set off a firestorm of white protest and a wave of black defensiveness. Both Clinton and Souljah had been invited to speak (a day apart) at a meeting of Jesse Jackson's National Rainbow Coalition. Jackson was taken to task by Clinton for inviting Souljah to speak—he went as far as to equate her with the racist demagogue, David Duke.

Most black observers asserted that Clinton bludgeoned Jackson with Souljah in order to win back to the Democrats white support that had fled to the Republicans over the last several elections. Although Reagan and Bush had played the race card effectively in their previous campaigns, Clinton's move appeared to be a preemptive strike. As one reporter noted, "Move over Willie Horton. Sister Souljah has arrived."[25] While it may be some exaggeration to say that Clinton owed his triumph to Souljah, he received more media attention for his willingness to make a calculated attack on her and Jackson than he did for his pleas for racial harmony. His rise in the polls, particularly and almost exclusively among whites, in June and July of 1992, was due in no small part to this tactical hit. While blacks responded negatively to the attack by three to one, whites, by three to one, showed a favorable response.[26]

But while many in the Hip Hop and black communities denounced Clinton, at least one rapper found some common ground with the new president. Clinton (and his vice president Al Gore) could be seen during the inaugural festivities rocking to the rhymes of long-time popular rapper LL Cool J. Illustrating the way in which form can be divorced from content, Cool J delivered the following conciliatory rap:

'93 unity, you and me
time to party with Big Bill and Hillary ...
We're making history, a landslide victory
Raise the flag, blast the mag, let the plane fly
Pack the bags and tell George and Barbara Bush bye.[27]

Gangsta Rap

Much of rap's political pedagogy comes from the so-called gangsta rappers. Dismissed by many as vulgar, profane, misogynist, racist, anti-Semitic and juvenile—accusations that carry a great deal of validity—gangsta rap, at the same time, reflects and projects what scholar Robin D. G. Kelley calls "the lessons of lived experiences."[28] In a sense, Cube, NWA, Too Short, the Geto Boys and others are the "organic intellectuals" of the inner-city black poor, documenting as they do their generally hidden conditions and lifestyle choices. Naughty by Nature's "Ghetto Bastard" is a captivating and engrossing piece of verbal literature and sociology. This autobiographical tale of a black male teenager's urban experience is a brilliant exposition of what Foucault has termed the "insurrection of subjugated knowledges." The song is rich in a wide array of themes—absent ghetto fathers, the attractiveness of lumpen activities, the racist assumptions of the education system, the vicissitudes of consumer culture, dilapidated housing and the ever-present threat of violence—that reflect an experience that is collectively endured, daily, by millions of African-Americans. It's social anthropology with rhythm. Naughty by Nature's Treach projects the anger and frustration of many when he raps,

Say somethin' positive, well positive ain't where I live
I live right around the corner from West Hell
Two blocks from South Shit and once in a jail cell[29]

An examination of today's rap songs quickly demonstrates that the principal topic of the music is the social crisis engulfing working-class black America. Unlike the moralistic preaching, escapism or sentimentality that defines most popular music, including the moderated rap of Hammer, hard-core rappers detail the unemployment, miseducation, discrimination, homicides, gang life, class oppression, police brutality and regressive gender politics that dominate the lives of many black youth. The macho boasting, misogyny, violent fantasies and false consciousness exist side by side with an immature, but clear, critique of authority, a loathing of the oppressive character of wage labor, a hatred of racism and an exposé of Reaganism.

Many rappers, for example, address the racist character of the nation's war on drugs. Although blacks make up only about 15 per cent of the nation's drug users, they are close to 50 per cent of those arrested on drug charges, mainly for possession. The drug war's collateral damage continues to grow in what one senate committee calls a "$32 billion failure."[30] Raps like NWA's "Dope Man," Ice T's "New Jack Hustler," Ice Cube's "The Product" and CPO's "The Wall" all expose the bankruptcy of the war on drugs and its deadly impact on the black community. And Houston's Geto Boys, notorious for their brutal depictions of women, address the contradictions of drug dealing in their hit "Mind Playing Tricks on Me." Pinpointing the anxiety and frustration of a young drug dealer, the song struggles to find a human character in what has become a media stereotype. They state in one passage:

Can't keep a steady hand
Because I'm nervous
Every Sunday morning, I'm in service

> Praying for forgiveness
> And trying to find an exit out the business[31]

Debates over police brutality were also forced into the public arena as a result of rap songs. While the video of the Rodney King beating introduced many in the United States to the reality of police brutality in the black, the rap community noted that it had been discoursing about the issue for years. In his 1987 "Squeeze the Trigger," Ice T links the police attitude with police murders:

> Cops hate kids, kids hate cops.
> Cops kill kids with warnin' shots.[32]

In a similar vein, NWA also addresses the issue of police brutality as well as the issues of racial oppression, violence, black-on-black crime, self-hatred, unemployment and human rights— often all in the same song. Their signature song, "F*** Tha Police," embodies a street-felt rage that resonates through the entire national black community:

> Fuck the police coming straight from the underground
> A young nigger got it bad 'cause I'm brown
> I'm not the other color
> Some people think
> They have the authority to kill a minority
> Fuck that shit, 'cause I ain't the one
> For a punk motherfucker with a badge and a gun
> to be beaten on, and thrown in jail[33]

Other rappers also address what has become a virtually black-only experience: police shootings. In their "Behind Closed Doors," W.C. and the MAAD Circle rhyme:

> I'm being charged for resisting arrest
> But it was either catch a bullet or be beaten to death[34]

Or, in Ice Cube's "Endangered Species":

> Every cop killer goes ignored
> They just send another nigger to the morgue[35]

Los Angeles, in particular, has been notorious for its police killings and for the way the police view the black community as a war zone. Under the leadership of the (now departed) police chief Daryl Gates, the LAPD viewed young blacks as unredeemable urban terrorists who were best kept locked up, contained or eliminated. (Under the cover of fighting the drug war, for example, LAPD initiated Operation Hammer which, time and time again, invaded the black community and, on 9 April 1988, arrested 1,453 young blacks.)[36]

In 1992, Ice T returned to this theme with his song "Cop Killer," which generated a massive counter-reaction from conservative luminaries, such as George Bush, Dan Quayle, Oliver North, and the National Rifle Association. His flight of fantasy this time, however, advocated a pro-active preventative measure:

> I got my 12-gauge sawed off
> I got my headlights turned off
> I'm 'bout to bust some shot off

> I'm 'bout to dust some cops off.
> Cop killer, better you than me.
> Cop killer, fuck police brutality.[37]

Not surprisingly, there have been moves to censor rap. One organization active in this is the Parents Music Resource Center (PMRC) founded by Tipper Gore (wife of former vice president Al Gore) and Susan Baker (wife of Bush's campaign manager, James Baker). In 1985, PMRC led the movement that forced congressional hearings on record labeling. Record companies succumbed to the pressure and began to put warning labels on rap and rock music felt to be obscene and too explicit. The first album to have a warning label placed on it was Ice T's *Rhyme Pays*. Evidence indicates that most of the groups targeted for labeling are black. In a 1989 newsletter put out by PMRC, every song listed as having warning labels was done by a black artist. Other groups calling for censorship of rap records have been more explicitly racist. Missouri Project Rock passed out information packets that criticized "race-mixing" and called Martin Luther King "Martin Lucifer King."[38]

Tipper Gore battled Ice T on the Oprah Winfrey show and wrote about it in the *Washington Post*. In an article titled "Hate, rape and rap," she justifiably criticized some of the vile sexist statements made by rappers, particularly Ice T. In words that specifically seem to be addressed to Ice T, she said, "We must raise our voices in protest and put pressure on those who not only reflect this hatred but also package, polish, promote and market it; those who would make words like 'nigger' acceptable."[39] In highly moral tones, she then unconvincingly attempted to make a link between rap music and rape.

One of Ice T's responses was to write a song, "Freedom of Speech." In the song, he attacks Gore personally. He says:

> Think I give a fuck about a silly bitch named Gore?
> Yo, PMRC, here we go, war![40]

The Evil that Men Do: Rap's Phallo-Centric Musings

Gender issues in rap remain controversial. From its earliest days to the present, women and more than a few men have rightfully condemned much of rap music as misogynist and degrading to women. National Council of Negro Women president Dorothy Height states: "This music is damaging because it is degrading to women to have it suggested in our popular music that [women] are to be abused."[41] Former head of the NAACP, Benjamin Hooks, echoes that sentiment. He says, in reference to the music, "our [black] cultural experience does not include debasing women."[42]

Scholar Marilyn Lashley is uncompromising in her denunciation of the portrayal of women in rap music. It is "explicitly and gratuitously sexual, occasionally bestial and frequently violent. These images, in the guise of 'art and music,' exploit, degrade and denigrate African-American women as well as the race. They encourage sexual harassment, exploitation and misogyny at their best and sexual abuse at their worst," she states.[43]

Others, mainly men, have defended these projections as part of a continuity in black culture that is not as harmful as it appears. No less than Harvard scholar and cultural critic Henry Louis Gates walks softly on this turf, he pooh-poohs the uproar by stating that the male rappers are playing out the old black tradition of "signifying,"[44] a practice that is relatively harmless and culturally important. Some have attempted to justify the degradation of women by arguing for the singular uplifting of black males. Ice Cube, for example, argued in an interview with Angela Davis that black women have to wait for black men to be uplifted first.[45]

Rap has become a forum for debating the nature of gender relations among black youth. The name-calling, descriptions of graphic rapes and other negative encounters between young black women and men dominate the music's gender politics. For many of the rap groups, their songs are one long extended sex party. This aspect of the music has also drawn fire, though many of the male rappers have argued that they are engaging in meaningless fantasies. However, as one feminist correctly pointed out, it's "not so much the issue of sex as an obsession, but that of sex as a violent weapon against women." She goes on to say that songs like "Treat Her Like a Prostitute," "One Less Bitch," "Pop that Coochie," "Baby Got Back," "Me So Horny," "That Bitch Betta Have My Money" and "She Swallowed It" "not only desensitize their audiences to violence against women, they also help rationalize and reinforce a nihilistic mentality among those who already suffer from the effects of ghetto reality."[46] The escalating incidence of rape and sexual harassment against women in general, and black women in particular, underscores her concerns.

A number of positive female rappers have emerged to challenge the musical and ideological dominance of the male rappers. Strong women, such as Queen Latifah, Monie Love, Queen Mother Rage, Isis and MC Lyte, have produced popular songs that have advocated positive relations among men and women, called for sisterhood and projected what scholar Patricia Hill Collins calls an "Afrocentric feminist epistemology."[47]

In one of her first songs, "Latifah's Law," Queen Latifah, who has also managed rap groups, makes it clear that she sees herself, and demands to be seen, as an equal to the male rappers:

> The ladies will kick it, the rhyme is wicked
> Those who don't know how to be pros get evicted
> A woman can bear you, break you, take you
> Now its time to rhyme. Can you relate to
> A sister dope enough to make you holler and scream?[48]

In addition, some rap male and gender-mixed groups, such as the Disposal Heroes of Hiphoprisy and Arrested Development, have shown that a positive perspective on black female and male relations is possible.

But, for every (social) action, there is an opposite and equal (social) reaction. Hard-core female rappers, such as Bytches With Problems, Nikki D, Hoes With an Attitude and LA Starr, have come on the scene and demonstrated that they can be as vulgar, blasphemous and homicidal as the men. BWP's Lyndah and Tanisha, whose records are distributed by mega-corp Columbia Records, have been called the "Thelma and Louise" of rap.[49] In song after song, they gun down men, cops and anyone else who crosses or is perceived to have crossed their path. When they are not committing homicide, they are busy either screwing men to death or ripping them off. All the while, they hold high the banner of women's liberation.

In their song "Shit Popper," they denounce woman beating by advising sisters to:

> Wait until he goes to bed,
> then give him three to the head,
> leave his motherfucking ass for dead.[50]

While addressing important themes, such as date rape and adultery, their solutions, more often than not, are to just blow the suckers away.

It is ironic that BWP, like many of the hardcore women's groups, are produced by men who also write many of the lyrics. That women producers and managers are far and few between is one of the main reasons why the music remains so misogynist. Progressive women rappers complain incessantly about how difficult it is for their music to be produced. Even some of the songs produced by the political, usually black nationalist, rappers run counter to women's liberation. While eschewing the violence and sexual exploitation of the hard-core gangsta rappers, groups such as Public Enemy and X-Clan will often project a romanticized notion of black womanhood that does not fundamentally challenge male domination. More critically, they will also use language that fundamentally reinforces the power relations of gender oppression.

As one scholar noted, for many, the rappers are "urban griots dispensing social and cultural critiques."[51] While this may be true, the nature of those critiques is simultaneously painfully naive and incredibly insightful; abjectly dehumanising and rich in human spirit. Rap's pedagogy, like the initial stages of all pedagogies of oppressed people, emerges incomplete, contradictory and struggling for coherence. If we look closely, the birth and evolution of rap tell us as much about the current state of black America as rap's content and form.

At the same time, we must be careful not to reduce African-American culture to the commodities and political ambiguities of Hip Hop. Music forms, including jazz and blues and other non-Hip Hop cultural expression deserve criticism, reaffirmation and validation. In the end, Hip Hop is neither the cultural beast that will destroy black America nor the political panacea that will save it, but is a part of the ongoing African-American struggle constantly reaching for higher and higher modes of liberation.

Notes

1. Amilcar Cabral, "National liberation and culture," in *Return to the source* (New York, Africa Information Service, 1973), p. 43.
2. See articles on rap worldwide by B. Bollag, K. Noble, J. Bernard and S. Weisman in *New York Times* (23 August 1992).
3. Robin Givhan, "Of rap, racism and fear: why does this message music seem so menacing?," *San Francisco Chronicle* (6 August 1992).
4. Quoted in Kathleen M. Sullivan, "2 Live Crew and the cultural contradictions of Miller," *Reconstruction* (Vol. I, no. 2, 1990), p. 23.
5. Manning Marable, "The crisis of the black working-class: an economic and historical analysis," *Science & Society* (Summer 1982), p. 156.
6. National Urban League, *The state of black America 1993* (New York, National Urban League, 1993), p. 168.
7. Barbara Vobejda, "Children's poverty rose in '80s; suburbs, rural areas also show increase," *Washington Post* (12 August 1992).
8. Press release, U.S. Department of Commerce, Bureau of Census, 3 September 1992.
9. See *The state of black America*, op. cit. and K. Jennings, "Understanding the persisting crisis of black youth unemployment" in J. Jennings (ed.), *Race, politics and economic development* (New York, 1992).
10. Ice Cube, "A bird in the hand," *Death Certificate* (Priority Records, 1991).
11. Paul Grein, "It was feast or famine in '90 certs; platinum ranks thin, but smashes soar," *Billboard* (12 January 1991), p. 9.
12. See John Leland, "Rap and race," *Newsweek* (29 June 1992), p. 49, and James T. Jones IV, "NWA's career gets a jolt from lyric's shock value," *USA Today* (21 June 1991).
13. Bruce Horovitz, "Quincy Jones, Time Warner launch rap lovers magazine," *Los Angeles Times* (15 September 1992).
14. Chuck Philips, "The uncivil war: the battle between the establishment and the supporters of rap opens old wounds of race and class," *Los Angeles Times* (19 July 1992).
15. Christopher Vaughn, "Simmons' rush for profits," *Black Enterprise* (December 1992), p. 67.
16. D. Hickley, "Rapper in brew-haha over rights to his voice," *New York Daily News* (26 August 1991).
17. Media Action Alert issued by the Marin Institute, 23 July 1991.
18. See Karen Grigsby Bates, 'They've gotta have us," *New York Times Magazine* (14 July 1991), p. 18, and Lewis Beale, "'Boyz' in your hood?," *Washington Post* (3 March 1992).
19. "Black video distribution," *Washington Post* (8 March 1992), and Carla Hall, "Breaking down the color barrier," *Washington Post* (24 September 1991).
20. Ice Cube and Angela Davis, "Nappy happy," *Transition* (no. 58, 1992), p. 191.
21. Leland, op. cit.
22. K. Carroll, "One black nation under a groove," *Black Arts Bulletin* (October 1992).
23. See R. Harrington, "Public Enemy's twisted tribute," *Washington Post* (19 January 1992).
24. David Mills, "Sister Souljah's call to arms," *Washington Post* (13 May 1992).
25. Juan Gonzalez, "Bill hits low note in rap of Souljah," *New York Daily News* (17 June 1992).

26. Thomas B. Edsall, "Black leaders view Clinton strategy with mix of pragmatism, optimism," *Washington Post* (28 October 1992).
27. Richard Harrington, "At the memorial, songs in the key of hope," *Washington Post* (18 January 1993).
28. Robin D. G. Kelley, "Straight from underground," *The Nation*, p. 796.
29. Naughty by Nature, "Ghetto Bastard," *Naughty by Nature* (Tommy Boy Records).
30. *The president's drug strategy: has it worked*, Majority Staff of the Senate Judiciary Committee and the International Narcotics Control Caucus, September 1992.
31. D. Mills, "The Geto Boys, beating the murder rap," *Washington Post* (15 December 1991).
32. Ice T, "Squeeze the trigger," *Rhyme Pays* (Sire Records, 1987).
33. NWA, "F*** tha Police," *Straight Outta Compton* (Ruthless Records, 1988).
34. W. C. and the MAAD Circle, "Behind Closed Doors," *Ain't a Damn Thing Changed* (Priority Records, 1991).
35. Ice Cube, "Endangered Species (Tales from the Darkside)," *AmeriKKKa's Most Wanted* (Priority Records, 1990).
36. Mike Davis, *City of Quartz* (New York, 1990), p. 268.
37. Ice T, "Cop Killer," *Body Count* (Time-Warner, 1991).
38. Sullivan, op. cit.
39. Tipper Gore, "Hate, rape and rap," *Washington Post* (8 January 1990).
40. Ice T, "Freedom of Speech" (Rhyme Syndicate, 1990).
41. "Other rappers accused of 'nasty' influence," *Washington Times* (16 June 1992).
42. Ibid.
43. Marilyn Lashley, "Bad rap," *Washington Post* (25 September 1992).
44. "Other rappers accused of 'nasty' influence," op. cit.
45. Cube and Davis, op. cit., p. 186.
46. Sonja Peterson-Lewis, "A feminist analysis of the defenses of obscence rap lyrics," *Black Sacred Music* (Summer 1991), p. 78.
47. P. H. Collins, *Black feminist thought: knowledge, consciousness, and the politics of empowerment* (Boston, 1990).
48. J. D. Eure and J. G. Spady, *Nation Conscious Rap* (New York, 1991), p. 148.
49. K. Carroll, "Word on Bytches with problems," *Black Arts Bulletin* (Vol. 1, no. 8), p. 1.
50. Ibid.; Bytches With Problems, "Shit Popper," *The Bytches* (RAL Records, 1991).
51. M. E. Dyson, "Performance, protest and prophecy in the culture of Hip Hop," *Black Sacred Music* (Summer 1991), p. 22.

29

Postindustrial Soul:
Black Popular Music at the Crossroads

Mark Anthony Neal

> Life on the margins of postindustrial urban America is inscribed in hip hop style, sound, lyric and thematics. Situated at the "crossroads of lack and desire," hip hope emerges from the deindustrialized meltdown where social alienation, prophetic imagination, and yearning intersect. Hip hope is a cultural form that attempts to negotiate the experiences of marginalization, brutally truncated opportunity, and oppression within the cultural imperatives of African-American and Caribbean history, identity, and community. It is the tension between the cultural fractures produced by postindustrial oppression and the binding ties of black cultural expressivity that sets the critical frame for the development of hip hop.
>
> Tricia Rose, *Black Noise*, 1994

The emergence of the postindustrial city radically altered black communal sensibilities in the late 1970s and 1980s. Intense poverty, economic, collapse, and the erosion of viable public space were part and parcel of the new urban terrain that African-Americans confronted. Culled from the discourse of the postindustrial city, hip-hop reflected the growing visibility of a young, urban, and often angry so-called "underclass." Aesthetically the genre drew on diverse musical sensibilities like James Brown and the Parliament/Funkadelic collection and on black oral traditions like the prison toasts, "The Dozens," and the Black Arts poets of the 1960s. As the genre represented a counternarrative to black middle-class mobility, it also represented a counternarrative to the emergence of a corporate-driven music industry and the mass commodification of black expression. Relying largely on word of mouth and live performance as a means of promotion, hip-hop may represent the last black popular form to be wholly derived from the experiences and texts of the black urban landscape.

The emergence of hip-hop in the postindustrial city was far removed from the daily realities of an expanding black middle class. Inspired in part by Smokey Robinson's *A Quiet Storm* and the lusher recordings of Gamble and Huff, black popular recordings began to reflect the sensibilities of the black middle class. The subsequent Quiet Storm format, popularized on many radio stations with large black audiences, allowed the black middle class the cultural grounding that suburban life could not afford them, while maintaining a distinct musical subculture that affirmed their middle-class status and distanced them from the sonic rumblings of an urban underclass.

By the mid-1980s, both an urban-based working class/underclass and suburban middle class exhibited symptoms of "postindustrial nostalgia." Loosely defined as a nostalgia that has its basis in the postindustrial transformations of black urban life during the 1970s, many contemporary cultural workers began to appropriate the narratives and styles of black life in black urban spaces prior to the structural and economic changes of postindustrial transformations. While most visible in the burgeoning new black cinema of the late 1980s and 1990s, postindustrial nostalgia is also reflected in the popular music industry. The prevalence of nostalgia-based narratives in black popular culture would have particular effects on the maintenance of intradiasporic relations, at once providing the aural and visual bridge to reaffirm diverse communal relations, particularly those across the generational divide, while underscoring the black middle class' general refusal to adequately engage the realities of the Black Public Sphere in the postindustrial era.

Quiet Storms: Soul and Survival in the Suburbs

Excepting the trio of Holland, Dozier, and Holland, William "Smokey" Robinson has been the most influential black singer/songwriter/producer of his generation. After a long and productive collaboration with the Miracles, Robinson embarked upon a solo career in the early 1970s. Possessing one of the most gifted and distinct falsettos in the history of popular music, Robinson's songwriting skills, best exemplified by songs like "My Girl," "Ooh Baby, Baby," and "Shop Around," were no longer on the critical edge in the early 1970s. Momentarily regaining his creative energies, Robinson release his first "concept" recording with the 1975 classic *A Quiet Storm*. *A Quiet Storm* reflected the changing dynamics of popular music in the 1970s.

Some twenty years plus after the emergence of the 33-rpm long-playing format, artists began experimenting with longer recordings that often features self-contained themes examined over the course of the entire album. This was a concept that Album Oriented Rock (AOR) exploited to its fullest commercial potential with groups like Led Zeppelin and The Eagles. Marvin Gaye was the first black artist to embrace this concept with large commercial success with his 1971 recording *What's Going On,* though Isaac Hayes's groundbreaking *Hot Buttered Soul* charted this territory with some success among black audiences before Gaye's crossover success. These changes in popular music represented the first opportunities for black artists to experiment with improvisation and arrangement outside of the gene of jazz and partially ended the reign of the 45-rpm recording as the only viable commercial format for popular music. Hayes's eighteen-minute reworking of Jimmy Webb's "By the Time I Get to Phoenix," and Donny Hathaway's gospel-tinged recording of Bobby Scott's "He Ain't Heavy, He's My Brother," from *Donny Hathaway* (1970) are two of the best examples of this new creative terrain for black artists. Though neither attracted mainstream appeal—Hayes commercial breakthrough occurred with the soundtrack to *Shaft* and Hathaway's only mainstream success occurs with pop-soul duets with Roberta Flack—these recordings laid the foundation for the later artistic achievements of Flack, Earth, Wind and Fire, and Barry White. It was in this context that Robinson made his own self-contained suite of romance recordings in 1975.

Robinson's seven-minute title track to *A Quiet Storm* surprised him by becoming the aesthetic cornerstone of a more upscale and sophisticated soul sound that would captivate an older, mature, and largely black middle-class audience that relished its distance from a deteriorating urban landscape. The cover art to *A Quiet Storm* finds a pensive Robinson examining woodland terrain with a black Shetland pony, an image that was unthinkable as cover art for a black recording artist a generation earlier, though Robinson's cover photo appealed to the sensibilities and desires of a newly emerging black middle class. Covering traditional soul themes like love lost, love found, and love betrayed, the entire first side of the album, recorded as a suite, is held together by the sounds of whispering winds, hence the recording's title.

As important as the recording was to Robinson's then-fading career, it proved more important to black radio programmers searching for programming that would appeal to a growing black middle class with disposable income, as a Howard University communications student appropriated Robinson's title and introduced the Quiet Storm format to black radio programmers. The generally late-night format basically consisted of soul ballads interspersed with some jazz and possibly a little contemporary blues. By the early 1980s, the format was a fixture in virtually every major radio market that programmed black or, as it came to be known by the late 1980s, urban contemporary music.[1] For Quiet Storm audiences, this format offered a welcome reprieve from disco and funk, both of which were arguably driven by working-class youth audiences. While the Quiet Storm format was in part shaped by middle-class sensibilities, particularly given its Howard University roots, it cut across class lines because it appealed to adult sensibilities. Most notably, these recordings were in most cases devoid of any significant political commentary and maintained a strict aesthetic and narrative distance from issues relating to black urban life.

Artists like PIR stalwarts Harold Melvin and the Blue Notes and the O'Jays were all at home in this format. The solo careers of Patti Labelle and Teddy Pendergrass were in part shaped by their appeal to Quiet Storm audiences. Tracks like Labelle's "If Only You Knew" and Pendergrass's "Turn Out the Lights" are still Quiet Storm staples. Vocal groups like Atlantic Starr, The Whispers, Frankie Beverly and Maze, as well as solo acts like Denice Williams, Peabo Bryson, Stephanie Mills, Roberta Flack, and Jeffrey Osborne offered Quiet Storm audiences an aesthetic connection to the traditions of black popular music, particularly as postindustrial transformations further eroded public spaces in black communities and disco dance clubs migrated from black locales into more mainstream provinces. Furthermore, as time passed, some elements of the black middle class were decreasingly responsible for familial relations in black urban centers and began to successfully develop institutions within their own provinces, like churches and other social groups predicated on a common middle-class experience.

Gamble and Huff perhaps exploited this phenomenon best by always carefully packaging their recordings with potential pop Top-40 singles and Quiet Storm type album cuts. The O'Jays 1978 release *So Much Love,* is a case in point. Though the infectious pop-soul ditty "Use Ta Be My Girl" is still their highest charting single, the album's "Cry Together" has gone on to become a Quiet Storm classic. More importantly, much of this was occurring with little or no corporate interference, in that this market, dominated by black middle-class consumers who often equated consumption with acceptance in "integrated" America, was virtually ignored by the major corporate labels. Veteran soul singer Tyrone Davis's 1979 release "In the Mood" is such an example. Signed to the Columbia/CBS label, promotion of Davis's album *In the Mood* was lost in the shuffle of releases by younger black artists like Earth, Wind and Fire and Michael Jackson. Despite this the title track found a market niche among black audiences who were attracted to Davis's old-styled soul balladry.

By the mid-1980s, Luther Vandross and Anita Becker were perhaps the two artists who most benefited from the development of Quiet Storm radio. A veteran of stage musicals and commercials, Vandross achieved some success with his guest appearance with the disco group Change on its 1980 release *The Glow of Love,* in which Vandross sang lead vocals on the title track and the exquisite "Searching." While "Never Too Much," the lead single of his first Epic/CBS recording, garnered considerable support from black and white audiences alike, it was Vandross's own seven-minute arrangement of the Hal David and Burt Bacharach song "A House Is Not a Home," that gave him his reputation as a definitive soul balladeer. On subsequent releases like *Forever, For Always, For Love* (1982), *Busy Body* (1984) which included a startling remake of the Carpenter's "Superstar," and *The Night I Fell in Love* (1985), Vandross established himself as an innovative singer/arranger and producer, particularly within the context of Quiet Storm radio.

With stellar sales among black listeners, Vandross's crossover success began with the release of his fifth recording, *Give Me the Reason,* in 1986. This success occurs at precisely the same moment crossover audiences were embracing Anita Baker's 1986 release *Rapture.* Possessing limited vocal range but a highly distinctive vocal quality, Baker attracted attention among black audiences as lead singer of the group Chapter 8 during the late 1970s and with her debut solo release, *The Songstress,* on the independent Beverly Glen label in 1983. Baker's jazz-flavored major label debut on the Elektra/Warner label found support among black radio and contemporary jazz stations that were embracing the pop-jazz of artists like David Sanborn, Grover Washington, Jr., and a still relatively unknown Kenny G. What is notable here is that the commercial successes of Vandross and Baker were overshadowed by the commercial appeal of another form of black music that developed largely in the shadows of black middle-class mobility and in the ruins of an eroding urban landscape. While mature black audiences supported the music and performances of what Nelson George has called "retro-nuevo" soul, corporate labels focused their attention on the crossover appeal of three young black men from Hollis, Queens, Run-DMC, who along with their white protégés, The Beastie Boys, sold more than six million records of a "new" genre of music known as hip-hop or rap.[2]

Postindustrial Context(s): Hip-Hop, Postindustrialism, and the Commodification of the Black Underclass

Despite national rhetoric that suggested the contrary, the Black Public Sphere of the postindustrial city represented a de facto state of racial segregation that was, arguably, much more insidious than segregated black spaces prior to the Civil Rights movement. Lacking an indigenous economic base, these new social constructs developed largely as bureaucratic props of the federal government, as the postindustrial economy institutionalized a veritable nation of displaced workers, as integral cogs in the federal government's economy and industry of misery.[3] Meanwhile public institutions, already taxed by black middle-class flight and the inability of the black working class to negotiate the economic burdens of community maintenance, were literally destroyed as part of the spatial logic of the postindustrial city. As Tricia Rose relates in her seminal text on hip-hop music:

> The city's poorest residents paid the highest price for deindustrialization and economic restructuring.... In the case of the South Bronx, which has frequently been dubbed the "home of hip-hop culture," these larger postindustrial conditions were exacerbated by disruptions considered an "unexpected side effect" of the larger politically motivated policies of "urban renewal." In the early 1970s, the renewal [*sic*] project involved massive relocations of economically fragile people of color from different areas of New York City into parts of the South Bronx. Subsequent ethnic and racial transition in the South Bronx was not a gradual process that might have allowed already taxed social and cultural institutions to respond self-protectively; instead, it was a brutal process of community destruction and relocation executed by municipal officials.[4]

Thus black urban populations were affected by economic and social transformations both internal and external to the traditional Black Public Sphere. In the quest to create a functional postindustrial environment, the masses of multiracial working-class and working-poor people were some of the most expendable urban resources human resources that, a half-century earlier were enticed to migrate to urban spaces in support of industrial development. As urban development changed in response to technological "advancement" and economic restructuring, so did social and economic investment in working-class communities. As John Mollenkopf suggests in his texts on the emergence of postindustrial cities like New York, "The magnificence of the Manhattan central business and shopping district and the resurgence of luxury residential areas may be juxtaposed to the massive decay of the city's public facilities and poor neighborhoods."[5] Many working-class communities and their inhabitants were deemed as peripheral to the mechanisms of the postindustrial city as high finance and the consumerist desires of a growing managerial class influenced municipal development, including well-publicized tax breaks to corporate entities that remained within certain munic-ipalities without any specific commitment to their lower-tier workers. This phenomenon further challenged working-class communities as a diminishing tax base led to cuts in munic-ipal and later federal aid, thus instigating a further spiral into poverty and community erosion for many working-class communities. Under the banner of "urban renewal," the black working class and working poor were marginalized and isolated from the engines of the postindustrial city—the privatization of public space in downtown areas being emblematic—and instead exposed to intense poverty and rampant unemployment, which subsequently challenged traditional desires to maintain community.

Poverty within the postindustrial city featured spatial dimensions that also altered African-American efforts to build and maintain urban communities. As David Theo Goldberg states, "The segregated space of formalized racism is over-determined. Not only is private space restricted by the constraints of poverty, so too is public institutional space."[6] By the mid-1970s, Goldberg's thesis found its logical icon in the sprawling federal housing projects that largely replaced the kitchenette tenements of black urban spaces in the North and Midwest.[7] Goldberg's "living space of poverty" acknowledges an urban landscape that privileges the private and the local—the manifestation of fractured communal relations and the pervasive aura of social isolation. Though many federal housing projects represented a marked improve-ment over the quality of urban housing prior to the Civil Rights movement, the very logic of federally subsidized "low-income" housing meant that the poorest blacks would be socially and economically isolated from the mechanisms of the postindustrial city in neighborhoods that were acutely overcrowded and lacked the necessary public and institutional space to build and maintain communal sensibilities. This social isolation has been defined by sociologist William Julius Wilson as "lack of contact or of sustained interaction with individuals and institutions that represent mainstream society."[8] Though isolation from mainstream culture remains a substantial barrier to survival in the postindustrial city, the fracturing of communal relations within the African-American diaspora has had a more profound effect on the black poor as communal exchange, critique, and other communal relations that were integral to black survival in the industrial era were severed by regional and spatial dislocations within the Black Public Sphere and economic and political transformations beyond it.

Given the paucity of private and public space, it was no surprise that the private and the public began to conflate, as the familial, communal, and social "dysfunction" of the African-American experience entered into mainstream public discourse. While dysfunction exists in many communal settings, regardless of race, class, and social location, African-American dysfunc-tion was mass mediated and commodified for mass consumption via network news programs, Hollywood films like *Fort Apache,* and television programs like *Starsky and Hutch* and *Baretta.* By the late 1970s, the commodification of the black poor or underclass as human spectacle became a standard trope of mass culture, parlaying a clear sense of social difference from "blackness" for many mainstream consumers, including an emerging black middle class. My point is not to suggest that "dysfunction" among white communities was not present in mass culture, but that the mass-mediated images of the black underclass often served as the only images available to mainstream consumers, whereas a diversity of images for the white ethnic experience was often presented for consumption, albeit rife with its own internal markers of class and social difference. Many of the experiences of the "ghettocentric" poor were essentialized as a representative sample of the broader black community, to the obvious detriment of many segments of the African-American diaspora including the black poor. For instance, mass-mediated misrepresentations of the black poor often validated the rhetoric of conservative politicians like Ronald Reagan who opposed increased federal spending for social programs, by deemphasizing the roles of racism, poor education, inadequate health care, and the collapse of industrial-based economies and by instead projecting drug addiction, laziness, and the inferiority of African-American culture as the primary culprits of black misery.

The rather vivid imagery of black urban spaces within mass culture was further enhanced by the layout of communal spaces in many urban communities. For example, many of the federally subsidized housing projects of the Northeast and Midwest—Chicago's Cabrini-Greene comes to mind—represented the inverted logic of Jeremy Bentham's Panopticon, by providing surveillance from the bottom. Though I am not suggesting that the federal housing projects were part of some conspiracy to manage the black masses, the high visibility of such housing, with its distinct architecture that privileged more efficient use of urban space over livability and the concentration of the black poor within such spaces, increased notions that such communities were socially isolated from mainstream life and thus to be feared and neglected. Of course, in many locales like the Compton and Watts districts in Los Angeles, technological advancements in policing have allowed many police departments the ability to "patrol" black urban spaces via helicopters or "ghetto-birds."[9] Such developments countered historical examples where black isolation was often accompanied and defined by invisibility. To the contrary, in the postindustrial era, the black masses continued to be marginalized but remained highly visible within varying social constructs.

In response to poverty and unemployment, an illicit economy emerged as a primary conduit for economic survival among some segments of the postindustrial city. Illicit activities like petty thievery, numbers running, prostitution, and even drug dealing had been a small part of the informal economy of segregated black spaces throughout the twentieth century. For example, one of the few black patrons of the "Harlem Renaissance" was West Indian numbers runner Casper Holstein, who helped finance the Urban League's literary awards in 1926 from his profits.[10] What radically changed the nature of the informal economy of the Black Public Sphere in the post–Civil Rights era is the intensity of the economic collapse, accompanied by massive unemployment within those spaces and the emergence of an illegal drug that is perhaps the most destructive element to emerge within the contemporary Black Public Sphere.

Crack cocaine was a unique drug; its emergence exemplified the paradox of consumptionist desire in the midst of intense poverty. In his exhaustive examination of postindustrial Los Angeles, Mike Davis writes of the cocaine trade:

> Like any "ordinary business" in an initial sales boom, the cocaine trade had to contend with changing relations of supply and demand.... Despite the monopsonistic position of the cartels vis-à-vis the producers, the wholesale price of cocaine fell by half. This, in turn, dictated a transformation in sales strategy and market structure. The result was a switch from *haute cuisine* to fast food, as the Medellin Cartel, starting in 1981 or 83 (accounts differ), designated Los Angeles as a proving ground for the mass sales of rock cocaine or crack.[11]

To counter the flattening of demand for cocaine, a less expensive form of cocaine was introduced into poor communities within postindustrial cities like Los Angeles, New York, and Detroit in an effort to expand markets. Not only did crack cocaine increase demand for cocaine nationally, crack cocaine created its own thriving market. It featured a short, intense high that was highly addictive and thus offered "more bang for the buck." As Cornel West has suggested, the intensity of crack cocaine addiction mirrored the intensity of consumptionist desire in America.[12] The craving for the type of stimulant that crack cocaine provided made it popular among those who desired transcendence from the everyday misery of postindustrial life. In this regard, crack cocaine addiction resembled the historical examples of religion, recreational sex, and dancing as temporal releases from the realities of African-American life in the twentieth century. Crack cocaine differed from these aforementioned examples in that it also helped destroy communal relations within the Black Public Sphere as crack cocaine addiction led to increased black-on-black crime and the emergence of illicit sex acts "performed" within distinctly public forums where sex acts were exchanged often for drug money or drugs themselves.

More compellingly, the crack cocaine trade was attractive as a counter to poverty within the postindustrial city. As Davis maintains in *City of Quartz*, the crack cocaine industry was introduced to postindustrial Los Angeles after large numbers of blue collar workers were displaced from the industrial plant economy that was largely responsible for black migration from the South into Los Angeles immediately after World War II. The postindustrial transformation of Los Angeles, including the emergence of Japanese imports, effectively mitigated many of the economic and social gains made by the black working class in the post–World War II era. Furthermore, many African-Americans, particularly young black men, were excluded from both the service and the high-tech industries that were developing in the region, leading to unemployment rates well over 40 percent among black youth.[13] The significant demand for crack cocaine and the relative ease with which in could be produced on-site made the crack cocaine trade an attractive alternative to the abject poverty that defined the postindustrial experience for many blacks.

What was unique about the crack cocaine industry for many African-Americans is that it attempted to counter a poverty that was itself constructed against commodified images of wealth and consumption. Unlike previous periods of widespread poverty that existed somewhat in isolation of mainstream wealth, the impoverished masses within America generally faced a barrage of commodified images of wealth and consumption via television, film, and other organs of mass culture, as self-worth increasingly came to be defined by the ability to consume. African-American youth were particularly subject to this barrage of wealth and consumption as part of the first real generation of American youth socialized by television.[14] As mentioned previously, African-American youth investment in television was intensified as a corollary to corporate annexation of black popular expression, marking the post–Civil Rights generation(s) of African-American youth as the first who could readily consume the iconography of "blackness." As street-level sellers and producers of crack cocaine, African-American youth found a way to escape poverty and to consume as a measurement of self-worth. Thus unlike other ethnic groups who used the drug trade as a foundation to build upon "legitimate wealth"—Mario Puzo's examples in the *Godfather* chronicles immediately come to mind—African-American youth involved in the crack cocaine industry simply invested in material icons of wealth like cars, cellular phones, jewelry, and au couture fashions instead of transforming such wealth into familial or communal efforts to rebuild community. Furthermore, African-American youth interest in the crack cocaine industry was particularly profound because of the "juvenization of poverty" among many urban groups. In Los Angeles County, for instance, more than 40 percent of children lived below or just above the official poverty line. This mirrored a doubling of children in poverty across the state of California in just a generation.[15] These trends were further realized in many postindustrial urban environments across the nation.

What emerged in the shadows of many of these developments was a distinct African-American youth culture whose basic sentiments were often incompatible with mainstream African-American leadership and mainstream culture in general. In its worst case, it was a culture personified by gang turf wars over the control of the crack cocaine industry, a culture described by Michael Eric Dyson as a "ghettocentric juvenocracy" where economic rule and illegal tyranny is exercised by a cadre of young African-American males over a significant portion of the black urban landscape.[16] It is at this end of the spectrum that the postindustrial realities of black life continue to challenge the very idea of community as drive-by shootings and subsequent police occupation continue to rip communities apart by militarizing public spaces. At the more positive end of the spectrum a distinct discourse of African-American youth, with obvious regional variations, emerged to narrate, critique, challenge, and deconstruct the realities of postindustrial life. Hip-hop music and culture represented such a discourse.

The Discourse(s) of Hip-Hop: Resistance, Consumption, and African-American Youth Culture

While many African-American youth were not privy to the everyday realities of the black urban experience, a distinct urban-based African-American youth culture emerged in the mid- to late 1970s. Prior to World War II African-American youth culture was largely hidden from mainstream culture, subsumed within the parameters of segregated black spaces. The zoot suit riots and explosion of bebop music represented the first real glimpse into African-American youth culture for those beyond the confines of segregated urban spaces. Though bebop was essentially an aesthetic movement driven by the sensibilities of black male musicians, some well into their thirties who were reacting to racism in the North, the movement was given its energy and stylistic acumen by African-American youth who embraced the movement as a form of transcendence/resistance from the everyday drudgery of their existence. Zoot suits, the lindy-hop, and jive were all the nuances that African-American youth brought to the subculture of bebop music.

Historically African-American youth culture has rarely been driven by ideological concerns, but instead has embraced, appropriated, and reanimated existing structures, organizations, and institutions that African-American youth perceived as empowering them within various social, cultural, and economic constructs. Many of the stylistic excesses associated with African-American youth culture were conscious efforts to deconstruct and critique mass-mediated images of African-American youth. The impact of African-American youth culture on existing political and social movements was perhaps most profound when black youth embraced the Civil Rights movement of the early 1960s. The lunch-counter sit-ins, marches, and Freedom Summer bus rides were all emblematic of the impact of black youth culture on the movement. The development of the Student Nonviolent Coordinating Committee (SNCC), often referred to as the youth wing of the traditional Civil Rights movement, was a recognition on the part of the traditional leadership of the importance of black youth to mass social movement.

That importance was further realized when African-American youth began to reject the strategies of the traditional Civil Rights leadership and embraced the nationalist leanings of the Nation of Islam and later the Black Panther Party. The Black Panther Party, whose members were often culled from youth street gangs like the Slausons in south-central Los Angeles and the Blackstone Rangers in Chicago, personified African-American youth culture's ability to impact upon mainstream culture both within and beyond the Black Public Sphere.[17] Not surprisingly, such overtly political organizations gave way to less-inspiring constructs as a direct response to the collapse of the Civil Rights/Black Power movements and the increased commodification of wealth and consumption within mass culture. Thus the return to street-level gangs like the Crips and Bloods in Los Angeles or the Black Spades in New York City where emblematic of the belief within African-American youth culture that mass consumption and the accumulation of wealth for mass consumption were the most viable means of social transcendence afforded them in the post–Civil Rights era. The introduction of the crack cocaine industry into black urban spaces further enhanced such notions well into the 1990s.

Hip-hop music and culture emerged as a narrative and stylistic distillation of African-

American youth sensibilities in the late 1970s. Hip-hop differed from previous structures influenced by African-American youth in that it was largely predicated and driven by black youth culture itself. The fact that hip-hop emerged as a culture organic to African-American youth in urban spaces reflects the aforementioned social isolation afforded black youth and the conscious effort by many corporate capitalists to develop a popular music industry largely anchored by the sensibilities of American youth. Given this context, it was perfectly natural that the most profound aesthetic movement in black popular music in the post–Civil Rights era would be profoundly influenced by black youth culture. In reality, African-American youth appropriated many diverse examples of black expressive culture, including the Jamaican Toast tradition, and created an aesthetic movement that was uniquely tailored to their historic moment and their own existential desires.

I maintain that the emergence of hip-hop, which appeared in a rudimentary state in the mid-1970s, was representative of a concerted effort by youth urban blacks to use mass-culture to facilitate communal discourse across a fractured and dislocated national community. As Rose states, "Rappers' emphasis on posses and neighborhoods has brought the ghetto back into the public consciousness. It satisfies poor youth black people's profound need to have their territories acknowledged, recognized and celebrated."[18] While much of this activity was driven by the need to give voice to issues that privilege the local and the private within the postindustrial city—thus the overdetermined constructions of masculinity, sexuality, criminality, and even an urban patriarchy—hip-hop's best attempts at social commentary and critique represented traditions normalized and privileged historically in the Black Public Sphere of the urban North. Arguably the most significant form of counterhegemonic art in the black community over the last twenty years, the genre's project questions power and influence politically in the contexts of American culture and capitalism, the dominance of black middle-class discourse, but most notably the "death of community" witnessed by African-American youth in the postindustrial era.

Despite its intense commodification, hip-hop has managed to continuously subvert mass-market limitations by investing in its own philosophical groundings. Like bebop before it, hip-hop's politics was initially a politics of style that created an aural and stylistic community in response to the erosion of community with the postindustrial city. Perhaps more that any other previous popular form, hip-hop thrived on its own creative and aesthetic volatility by embracing such volatility as part of its stylistic traditions. This has allowed the form to maintain an aesthetic and narrative distance from mass-market limitations, though I must acknowledge that it is often a transient moment. As Tricia Rose suggests, "Developing a style nobody can deal with—a style that cannot be easily understood or erased, a style that has the reflexivity to create counter-dominant narratives against a mobile and shifting enemy—may be one of the most effective ways to fortify communities of resistance and *simultaneously* reserve the right to communal pleasure."[19]

Commercial disinterest in the form during its developing years allowed for its relatively autonomous development. Relying largely on word of mouth and live performance as a means of promotion, hip-hop represents the last black popular form to be wholly derived from the experiences and texts of the black urban landscape. In the aftermath of disco and corporate America's considerable retreat from its commitment to producing and distributing black popular music, hip-hop was allowed to flourish in public spaces and on several independent recording labels. Hip-hop's live performances were largely predicated on the recovery of commodified black musical texts, for the purpose of reintegrating these texts into the organic terrain of black urban communities. According to critic Paul Gilroy:

> Music recorded on disk loses its preordained authority as it is transformed and adapted....
> A range of de/reconstructive procedures—scratch mixing, dubbing, toasting, rapping, and

beatboxing—contribute to new layers of local meaning. The original performance trapped in plastic is supplemented by new contributions at every stage. Performer and audience alike strive to create pleasures that can evade capture and sale as cultural commodities.[20]

Like bebop, hip-hop appropriated popular texts, often refiguring them to serve hip-hop sensibilities. This phenomenon contextually questions and ultimately undermines the notion of corporate ownership of popular music and would have legal ramifications well into the decade of the 1990s.[21] Gilroy's comments are instructive in that even as hip-hop became a thoroughly commodified form in the late 1980s, its ability to mine the rich musical traditions of the African-American diaspora through the process of sampling allowed the form to privilege local and specific meanings historically aligned with organic sites of resistance and recovery.

For African-American youth, hip-hop music also allowed them to counter the iconography of fear, menace, and spectacle that dominated mass-mediated perceptions of contemporary black life by giving voice to the everyday human realities of black life in ways that could not be easily reduced to commodifiable stereotypes. The release of Grandmaster Flash and the Furious Five's "The Message" was a prime example of these sensibilities in the early stages of hip-hop. Recorded and released in 1982 to mainstream critical acclaim, it is the first hip-hop recording to be accorded such praise. Part of the recording's obvious appeal to mainstream critics was its unmitigated and "authentic" portrayal of contemporary black urban life. "The Message" was the first significant political recording produced in the postsoul era, representing an astute critique of the rise and impact of the Reagan right on working-class and urban locales.

Melle Mel's narrative portrays the transformation of the individual spirit within a context that offers little or no choice or freedom for those contained within it. Within Melle Mel's text, the fate of the individual spirit living within the parameters of the postindustrial urban landscape has been consigned at birth to live a short and miserable life. Representative of the genre, hip-hop was perhaps the first popular form of black music that offered little or no hope to its audience. The fatalistic experience has become a standard trope of urban-based hip-hop—"The Message" is but one clarion example of this. Juxtaposing diminishing hope and the rampant materialism of the underground economy of the urban landscape, Melle Mel identifies a ghetto hierarchy that ghetto youth have little choice but to invest in. Here, Melle Mel is cognizant of the "role model" void produced by middle-class flight and the lack of quality institutions to offset the influence of the illicit underground economy. In this context, Melle Mel identifies the failure of inner-city schools to provide a necessary buffer against urban malaise.

Seven years after the release of "The Message," more than 600,000 black men ages twenty to twenty-nine were either incarcerated, paroled, or on probation. The American prison population doubled over the twelve-year period from 1977 to 1989.[22] What Stevie Wonder had emphatically prophesied in "Living for the City" had become a stark and inescapable reality for the urban constituency that Melle Mel represented in "The Message." Using dated tropes of black masculinity and political resistance, Melle Mel considers a penal system that is incapable of producing rehabilitated individuals and has become a site of sexual violence between men. If the ideological imagination of the Black Power movement was partially related to the reintroduction of a hypermasculine patriarchy within the black community, Melle Mel's imagery of black male rape is an assertion that the Civil Rights/Black Power eras were far removed historically and intellectually from the landscape of the postindustrial city. In the end, Melle Mel transforms his ghetto narrative into a contemporary slave narrative, in which the protagonist chooses death at his own hands as opposed to incarceration and enslavement.[23]

The closing moments of "The Message" find members of Grandmaster Flash and the Furious Five engaged in casual banter on a street corner in New York. The group is shortly confronted by members of the NYPD who immediately accuse them of and arrest them for some unnamed crime. In a comic moment, one of the group members asserts, "But we're Grandmaster Flash and the Furious Five," to which a cop responds, "What is that, a gang?" and proceeds with his arrest. While the scene on one level acknowledges the lack of status afforded hip-hop artists within mainstream culture, a recurring theme in hip-hop, it also is a thinly veiled appropriation of a similar moment during Stevie Wonder's "Living for the City." I suggest that a comparison of the two recordings adequately details the changes within the postindustrial urban landscape over a period of nine years.

The most significant difference in the two texts is the fact that Wonder's protagonist migrates from the American South, during what is the very last stages of the black migration from the South in the twentieth century. Melle Mel's protagonist was born in the urban North, and thus could never invest in the type of promise that was articulated in the oppositional meanings of the mass migration. It is this lack of hope that remains a constant marker of the differences detailed in both narratives. While Wonder's protagonist is unwittingly introduced to the economic subculture of the urban North, Melle Mel's protagonist makes a conscious choice to invest in the economic subculture of the postindustrial city, precisely because of the lack of educational and economic opportunities that Wonder's protagonist envisioned in the urban North in the first place. Both artists are critical of the lack of rehabilitation that takes place in the American penal system, though the world that Wonder's protagonist returns to after prison is more closely aligned to the world that Melle Mel's character is born into.

The death of Melle Mel's protagonist suggests that the continuing transformation of the urban landscape will produce an environment that is as unlivable as it is unbearable and perhaps unnameable, within Melle Mel's narrative imagination. For example, neither Wonder nor Grandmaster Flash could foretell the coming threat of crack addiction within the black community, though Melle Mel would document its presence on his solo recording "King of the Streets" in 1984, almost two years before mainstream culture would acknowledge the presence of what is defined as a "smokable, efficient, and inexpensive" drug, that produces "hyperactive, paranoid, psychotic, and extremely violent" addicts.[24] The introduction of crack cocaine into the black urban landscape would arguably have as much effect on the quality of life within the postindustrial city as black middle-class flights and the postindustrial economy. Hip-hop music and the burgeoning "ghetto" cinema that emerges from within its traditions were both uniquely poised to represent the realities of contemporary black urban life within mainstream culture. In their best moments, these cultural narratives create critical exchange within the vast constituencies of the African-American diaspora. In their worse moments, these narratives were too often interpreted by a dislocated black middle-class as the products of individuals who lack the civility and determination that befit their middle class sensibilities. Almost a full century after the first articulation of the "New Negro," the old Negro had been transformed from southern migrant to urban ghetto dweller, and the black middle class was equally disdainful of both.

Despite recordings like "The Message," early hip-hop recordings rarely ventured beyond themes associated with the everyday experiences of urban-based African-American youth. Because of hip-hop's intimate connection to African-American youth culture, its narratives usually mirrored whatever concerns were deemed crucial to black youth. Like the music that echoed throughout black dance halls in the 1930s and 1940s, the "party and bullshit" themes of most early hip-hop represented efforts to transcend the dull realities of urban life, including body-numbing experiences within low-wage service industries and inferior and condescending urban school systems. Though hip-hop represented an art form that countered mainstream sensibilities and clearly could be construed as a mode of social resistance, in and of itself, it was not invested with political dimensions, at least not any more so than African-American youth culture contained within itself. At best hip-hop represented a distinct mode of youthful expression primed to serve as a conduit for political discourse as it coincided with the sensibilities of black youth. Jesse Jackson's first presidential campaign in 1984 and the reemergence of Louis Farrakhan and the Nation of Islam represented two distinct though related phenomena that would politicize black youth and thus politicize some aspects of hip-hop music in the early to mid-1980s.

On the surface Jesse Jackson's presidential campaign in 1984 was largely rooted in the discourse of the traditional Civil Rights movement and thus was not initially attractive to hip-hop's primary constituency. The Civil Rights movement and electoral politics, for that matter, were often interpreted as being marginal to the primary concerns of the black urban poor. The failure of the increased numbers of black elected officials in various municipalities to adequately empower the black poor in those municipalities is one of many issues responsible for such interpretations. But Jackson's campaign, which was publicly parlayed as the first serious attempt at the presidency by an African-American—Shirley Chisholm's efforts in 1972 largely removed the black political landscape—attracted tacit support throughout the African-American diaspora because of its historic meaning.

Louis Farrakhan's public support of Jackson's efforts offered the Nation of Islam leader the mainstream visibility, if not credibility, that the Nation of Islam had not been afforded since the death of Malcolm X. Though Farrakhan's black nationalist politics and critiques of white supremacy were often oppositional to the broad mainstream appeal that Jackson craved and needed to be seriously considered for the presidency, his momentary alliance with Jackson gave him access to the black masses, particularly the urban masses who had long rejected the style of political activism that Jackson personified. Particularly appealing to black urban youth was Farrakhan's willingness, like his late mentor Malcolm X, to speak forcefully about the nature of American race relations and the evils of white supremacy. Farrakhan's penchant for rhetoric, which often bordered on anti-Semitism, effectively demonized him among main-stream pundits, and his subsequent outlaw status further attracted black youths who felt themselves demonized in mainstream culture. Farrakhan's inability to project lasting solutions to the problems that face the urban poor did not deter support from black youth, in that his channeling of black rage in a national context validated the black rage that black youth often expressed within their own personal and local contexts. Farrakhan's rage, within the context of the increasing misery of urban life, provided the impetus for segments of the hip-hop community channel their own critiques of white supremacy and expressions of black rage into their music.

The group Public Enemy was perhaps the most accomplished at projecting black rage as a political discourse that would prove attractive to the youth audiences that hip-hop garnered. Born and raised on the fringes of the Black Panther Party, Public Enemy leader Chuck D intu-itively understood the attractiveness of black nationalism to urban youth in the 1960s and attempted to reintroduce many of those themes to black youth within a contemporary social and aesthetic context. Chuck D's political rhetoric for the Reagan era was initially and cautiously presented on Public Enemy's first recording, *Yo! Bum Rush the Show,* in 1987. It failed to attract black youth audiences, mostly because much of the music was undanceable, heresy for those who are serious about making music popular among black youth. Moreover, given black radio's initial rejection of hip-hop and the subtle transformation of the music from a live/public form of expression to one increasingly produced in a studio for mass consumption, it was imperative for its survival that hip-hop be conducive to the types of public spaces where black youth were most likely to convene. Dance halls or clubs continued to be the most accessible spaces for black youth to congregate, so the challenge for those who were interested in presenting hip-hop as political discourse was to make sure the music was danceable. Public Enemy later recorded a succession of twelve-inch releases that were not necessarily any more danceable than those found on *Yo! Bum Rush the Show,* but instead challenged and dared black youth to dance to them, much the way bebop artists dared black youth to lindy-hop to their self-styled musical tomes.

The sonic cacophony of "Rebel Without a Pause" and "Bring the Noise" represented the vanguard of hip-hop production styles. Chuck D's driving baritone was the perfect foil for the "organized confusion" that was a staple of Public Enemy's producers, The Bomb Squad. These innovations proved enticing to both a mainstream public and black youth, who were perhaps tired of the unimaginative drum machine programming that had come to dominate the genre. *It Takes a Nation to Hold Us Back,* released in the late spring of 1988, represented Public Enemy's vision for hip-hop's role in galvanizing a political vanguard in the post–Civil Rights era. As Greg Tate wrote at the time of the recording's release:

> Nation of Millions is a declaration of war on the federal government, and that unholy trinity—black radio programmers, crack dealers, and rock critics. . . . For sheer audacity and specificity Chuck D's enemies list rivals anything produced by the Black Liberation Army or punk—rallying for retribution against the Feds for the Panthers' fall ("Party for your Right to Fight"), slapping murder charges on the FBI and CIA for the assassinations of MLK and Malcolm X ("Black Steel in the Hour of Chaos"), assailing copyright law and the court system ("Caught, Can I Get a Witness").[25]

Chuck D's call for truth, justice, and a black nationalist way of life was perhaps the most potent of any political narratives that had appeared on a black popular recording. Public Enemy very consciously attempted to have hip-hop serve the revolutionary vanguard, the way soul did during the 1960s. Despite Public Enemy's vast popularity among black and white youth audiences, their 1960s-style rhetoric raised old antagonisms from those further on the political right as well as mainstream African-American leaders concerned about both the group's militancy and its obvious connections to Farrakhan and the Nation of Islam.

Chuck D clearly saw hip-hop as an alternative medium for black youth and their fellow travelers to access political and social reality as constructed by Public Enemy. Nowhere was this more evident than on the song "Don't Believe the Hype," where Chuck D offers a compelling argument for media education. Chuck D characterizes mainstream media as misinformed and malicious in their distribution of misinformation. Chuck D's narrative constitutes a counternarrative to mainstream attacks on the social and political commentary reflected in the work of the group. In an effort to democratize the mainstream critical establishment, the Public Enemy front man links his experiences to John Coltrane. Coltrane's jazz explorations in the 1960s were also criticized by a biased and misinformed critical establishment. Chuck D embraces a nationalist argument that suggests that critiques of black popular culture are best performed by those immersed in the organic culture that produces it. Within Chuck D's worldview, hip-hop represents the most natural environment in which to critique the social and political experiences of an urban-based African-American constituency. Black radio's early rejection of hip-hop, excepting the few late-night programming slots given to well-known hip-hop DJs in the major markets, reflected the sentiments of the black middle class regarding hip-hop and in part reflected a historical trend among the black middle class regarding popular art forms that emerge from the black working-class experience.

But Public Enemy's resuscitation of 1960s-style black political rhetoric was often problematic, particularly when considering that the group's primary constituents were not likely to provide the type of critique that was necessary to realize Chuck D's lofty goals. Chuck D's politics were particularly problematic in the area of gender, where tracks like "She Watch Channel Zero" could have been used as a chorus for Reagan's attacks on "welfare queens," as the track suggested that black women who watch soap operas are partially to blame for the precarious predicament of black children. Public Enemy's failure to adequately critique the ideals they espoused was of course logical in the type of vacuum that their rhetoric was reproduced in. The erosion of communal exchange that marked the post–Civil Rights period, also denied the movement the ability to critique itself in ways that would allow it to be self-sustaining and progressive. Thus a younger generation of activists emerged, many of whom were not privy to the type of communal processes that were crucial to black political discourse prior to the Civil Rights movement, and they appropriated the ideological themes of the era without the benefit of critiquing these themes to make them more applicable to a contemporary context. The fact that groups like Public Enemy were unable to critique the sexism inherent to much of black political thought in the 1960s is particularly disheartening in that black women have been the most outspoken critics of the movement's shortcomings, particularly in regard to gender issues.[26] Unfortunately, Public Enemy's political shortcomings were easy to ignore, as Greg Tate relates: "Were it not for the fact that Nation is the most hellacious and hilarious dance record of the decade, nobody but the converted would give two hoots about PE's millenary desires."[27]

The release of *It Takes a Nation of Millions to Hold Us Back* coincided with several industry initiatives that offered hip-hop much more accessibility and visibility. Two years after the release of Run-DMC's landmark *Raisin' Hell* recording, many independent recording labels that featured hip-hop entered into distribution deals with corporate conglomerates. The Def Jam label's sale to conglomerate CBS/Columbia was strikingly reminiscent of the conglomerate's relationship with Gamble and Huff more than a decade earlier. With distribution outlets increased and cooperate labels having more money to spend on artist development, hip-hop began its growth as one of the more popular music genres, this despite all of the negative connotations associated with it within mainstream society. Never radio-friendly, hip-hop got a necessary promotional boost with the debut of *Yo MTV Raps* on MTV in the fall of 1988. Music video opened hip-hop to an audience of mid-Americans youths, who relished in the subversive "otherness" that the music and its purveyors represented. By the time Gangsta rap (an often cartoonish portrayal of black masculinity, ghetto realism, and gangster sensibilities) became one of the most popular genres of hip-hop, a significant portion of the music was largely supported by young white Americans.

Despite such successful recordings as *Fear of a Black Planet* (1990) and *Apocalypse '91 ... The Enemy Strikes Black* (1991), *It Takes a Nation ...* , would be the apex of politically infused hip-hop and Public Enemy's popularity among black youth. The failure of explicit political discourse to remain an integral part of hip-hop was influenced by various dynamics. Placing a premium on lyrical content, artists like Public Enemy, Boogie Down Productions featuring KRS-One, Paris, X-Clan, former Public Enemy member Professor Griff, and Michael Franti and the Disposable Heroes of Hiphoprisy all failed to grasp the significance of producing music that would be considered danceable by the black masses they aimed to attract. As Tate surmised about Public Enemy's first recording, many of these artists produced music that consistently "moved the crowd off the floor."[28] The simultaneous emergence of NWA (Niggas with Attitude), whose production by Dr. Dre effectively altered the hop-hop landscape by removing the industry focus away from the East Coast and New York specifically, should have been instructive to artists with explicit political designs. Lacking a cohesive ideology but possessing an accessible critique of poverty, economic exploitation, and police brutality in postindustrial Los Angeles, NWA recordings like "Fuck the Police," from *Straight Out of Compton* (1988), ingratiated them to those who shared their experience and craved a funky beat. Ironically it was NWA's antipolice anthem that drew the most attention from federal agencies like the FBI and not the more ideologically sound rhetoric of groups like Public Enemy or Boogie Down Productions.

Ultimately, political hip-hop was undermined by hip-hop's own internal logic that often privileged constant stylistic innovation, both in narrative and musical content, as a response to intense commodification. Thus as Todd Boyd suggests, political hip-hop "seems to have functioned as a genre whose popularity had passed, instead of a sustained movement which connected both cultural artifacts and 'real' political events."[29] But political hip-hop was also challenged by efforts of segments of mainstream culture to control or "police" hip-hop, efforts that would ultimately transfer control of the genre away from its organic purveyors and limit access to the form in communal settings where alternative interpretations could be derived which countered mass-mediated presentations of the genre. These threats to hip-hop's ability to function as conduit for communal exchange came from those already entrusted to police black youth, the insurance industry and corporate America, the latter of which slowly began to continue their aborted effort to fully annex the black popular recording industry.

Fear of a Black Commodity: The Policing, Criminalization, and Commodification of Hip-Hop Culture

In November 1992, Spike Lee produced and directed the cinematic epic *Malcolm X*. The fact that the most visible icon of black political resistance over the past thirty years was the focus of a Hollywood film would suggest that the efforts of groups like Public Enemy and X-Clan had successfully altered the landscape of mainstream American culture. Only three years earlier another Spike Lee film, *Do the Right Thing*, which featured Public Enemy's now-classic recording "Fight the Power," was criticized for potentially stirring the black masses to violence in response to the film's vivid portrayal of race relations in a fictional Brooklyn neighborhood.[30] Several months before the release of Lee's *Malcolm X*, the city of Los Angeles exploded in violence in response to the acquittal of the police officers involved in the videotaped beating of black motorist Rodney King. On the surface the communal response to the highly controversial court decision further suggested that hip-hop had succeeded in producing a visible and influential political vanguard. But *Malcolm X* was instead released to much mainstream acclaim for the film, its director, and its star, Denzel Washington, who earned an Academy Award nomination for his portrayal of the black nationalist icon. The revolutionary vanguard that Lee, Public Enemy, Louis Farrakhan, and Malcolm X's memory supposedly inspired were instead to found "Rolling wit Dre." While such a reality clearly suggests that the political expediency that some hip-hop artists tried to instill in black expressive culture had been subsumed by the economic interests of a cadre of middle-class black artists driven by the demands of corporate capitalism, it also reflected the limits placed on political expression in an era where public expressions of identity and self-determination are so readily commodified and mediated for mass consumption, particularly when such consumption could in fact distribute values contrary to those valued in mainstream culture.

Following the highly influential solo efforts of former NWA comrade Ice Cube, whose recordings *AmeriKKKa's Most Wanted* (1990), *Death Certificate* (1991), and *The Predator* (1992) captured hip-hop's creative imagination, Dr. Dre released his first solo recording, *The Chronic,* in the autumn of 1992. Dr. Dre's musical ode to "good weed" and the self-styled lifestyles of postindustrial gangsters had all but solidified the Los Angeles area as the dominant creative and commercial force in hip-hop and the "G-Funk" of Dr. Dre and his protégés Snoop Doggy Dog and Warren G as the dominant production style. The underlying influences of G-Funk, or as it came to be known among mainstreams pundits, "gangsta rap," included narratives as diverse as the fiction of Iceberg Slim, the music of Parliament-Funkadelic, and Brian De Palma's 1983 remake of the film *Scarface*. Within contemporary black male culture, particularly that located within poverty-stricken urban spaces, the film had long been embraced as a contemporary example of a postimmigration attempt at pursuing the American Dream. Like the cocaine industry that framed the film's core themes, crack cocaine served a similar purpose in the real-life narratives of the young black men that the film appeals to. The culture and industry of crack's intimate relationship to the culture and industry of hip-hop would be realized with *The Chronic* and Dr. Dre's stirring production style.

The introduction of the G-Funk was largely framed by efforts of various social forces to curtail and control the popularity of hip-hop and its potential use as a conduit for oppositional discourse(s). Though Public Enemy's efforts to create a political insurgency for the 1980s were destined to fail because they existed beyond an actual political movement rooted in legitimate political concerns, and the efforts of NWA, while more closely aligned to sensibilities of black urban youth, ultimately lacked the political sophistication to be a legitimate threat to mainstream society, both efforts held the potential to galvanize popular resistance to some of mainstream culture's core sensibilities. Nowhere was this more evident than the response from law enforcement agencies in the aftermath of NWA's "Fuck tha Police." The circulation of the recording, which critiques police violence against black youth, instigated an unprecedented response from the assistant director of the FBI, who charged the group with advocating violence against law enforcement officers. The notoriety of the song was used against the group as law enforcement officers in several cities openly challenged the group to perform the song in concert with threats of detaining them or shutting down their shows.[31]

The policing of NWA reflected an increasingly common trend to criminalize hip-hop artists, their audiences, and the music itself. Thus seemingly random, incidental acts of violence and criminal activity occurring at hip-hop concerts were characterized as social intolerable communal acts capable of destroying the civility of mainstream society. Very often these random exchanges were instigated by the treatment that young concertgoers received from arena security, as many venues forced ticket holders to be searched for drugs, weapons, or any other paraphernalia that could be defined as counter to mainstream sensibilities. As Tricia Rose relates:

> The public school system, the police, and the popular media perceive and construct young African Americans as a dangerous internal element in urban America; an element that, if allowed to roam freely, will threaten the social order; an element that must be policed. Since rap music is understood as the predominate symbolic voice of black urban males, it heightens this sense of threat and reinforces dominant white middle class objections to urban black youths who do not aspire to (but are haunted by) white middle class standards.[32]

Mainstream reaction to hip-hop concerts, particularly the reactions of law enforcement agencies, was rooted in deeply held historical concerns about the congregation of African-Americans in public spaces. These concerns were heightened and legitimized within mainstream society in the post–World War II period as African-American youth began to assert themselves socially, culturally, and politically and in the process publicly question various forms of social authority that countered their own desires. Thus the criminalization of African-American youth in mass media contributed to the type of social paranoia already existent in American society, particularly since most major concert venues were in locations most suitable for access by white middle-class suburbanites. Thus in the eyes of many suburban whites, hip-hop concerts in places like Long Island's Nassau Coliseum represented a temporary threat to the day-to-day stability of white suburban life. The historic policing of public spaces where blacks often congregated often had a profound impact on the ability of African-Americans to build and maintain community, and such was the case when young African-Americans congregated at the local clubs and concert venues where the core values of the "hip-hop" generation were distributed and critiqued.

Despite such efforts to curtail community building within the hip-hop "community," hip-hop concerts remained a thriving industry for various promoters, performers, and venue operators, though increased collusion on the part of venue operators, the insurance industry, and law enforcement agencies began to erode acceptable public spaces for an art form, itself predicated on the lack of viable public space in black communities. The insurance industry had a particularly compelling impact by raising venue insurance rates for hip-hop concerts in relations to the public paranoia associated with hip-hop performances, in effect making the promotion of such events a distinct financial risk. Common strategies included the denial of insurance for any promoter who promoted a show where "significant" violence erupted or even a tenfold increase in the minimum insurance allowed to cover a hip-hop event. What was insidious about this practice is that the criminalization of hip-hop in mainstream society effectively helped mask racist efforts to deny black expression, as venue operators and insurance companies regularly facilitated concerts by white acts whose concerts also featured random and incidental acts of criminality, without the constraints placed on hip-hop artists. As Tricia Rose suggests, such efforts mirrored previous efforts to control the influence of jazz music via cabaret laws.[33]

As the number of venues willing to present hip-hop concerts evaporated, mass media increasingly dominated the presentation of not only mainstream critiques of hip-hop, but hip-hop itself. The social and public policing of hip-hop and its audiences coincided with the corporate annexation of the hip-hop industry and a subsequent period of intense commodification. Increasingly as programs like MTV's *Yo! MTV Raps* and major recording labels like SONY and Warner Brothers became the primary outlets to access hip-hop discourse, the discourse itself was subject to social controls rooted in corporate attempts to mainstream hip-hop for mass consumption. So successful were these efforts initially that Oakland-based rapper MC Hammer could legitimately claim Michael Jackson's "King of Pop" title, as he attempted to do upon the release of his 1991 recording *Too Legit to Quit*.[34] Part and parcel of Hammer's success was the mainstreaming of the iconography of black youth culture—Hammer's clothes and hairstyles were as appealing to young white as his music—and the distribution of narratives that were palatable to mainstream sensibilities even if they were often nonsensical.

But hip-hop's notoriety was also a stimulus for its own commercialization as recording labels carefully distributed recordings and videos to be accessed via alternative video outlets like the Black Entertainment Channel's (BET) *Rap City* or viewer request channels like *The Box*, who were more willing to present videos from artists who rejected mainstream impositions. This was particularly effective in the marketing of "gangsta rap" as the subgenre's notoriety and the notoriety of its artists correlated directly to recording sales. Like the jazz performers that Norman Mailer so eloquently describes in his essay "The White Negro," the apolitical "G," who stood at the center of the G-funk universe, proved attractive to young whites who viewed hip-hop as a conduit for oppositional expression and the "G" as a model for oppositional behavior. Via hip-hop music and videos, the antisocial behavior of "fictional" black drug dealers was embraced by many young whites as a mode of social resistance, though this influence was manifested in stylistic acumen and not political mobilization.

Hip-hop artists became the spokespersons for stylistic developments within black youth culture and hip-hop the vehicle for which these styles would be commodified for mass consumption both within and beyond mainstream culture. Clothing designers and companies as diverse as Timberland, Starter, Tommy Hilfiger, and even haute couture designers like Versace benefited from the visibility of hip-hop artists who willingly used their bodies, music, and videos—often without remuneration—to market these products. Of course the attraction of black youth to these products is the manifestation of complex identity issues where black youth equate social status with mass consumerism. Much of what is today a multibillion-dollar industry was stabilized when the black middle-class entrepreneurial spirit collided with corporate capitalist desire as hip-hop artists and fellow travelers begin to exploit hip-hop's mainstream influence for financial gain beyond recording contracts. Thus black entrepreneurs like Karl Kani and hip-hop artists like the WU-Tang Clan, who started a line of clothing called WU Wear, became petit bourgeois exploiters of hip-hop's popularity. These developments mirrored changes from within the recording industry itself that would have tremendous impact on hip-hop culture.

Reflecting the furious consolidation that has taken place in the entertainment industry, more than 80 percent of all music recorded in the United States was controlled by six major corporate entities. Black popular forms accounted for approximately 25 percent of the total sales of recorded music. Exploiting the black nationalist/capitalist rhetoric among the black working class and middle-class elite, still marginalized even after two decades of Civil Rights legislation, many corporate entities would turn "ghetto pop" producers into contemporary ghetto merchants. Arista/BMG for example, run by Clive Davis, was once home to three distinct boutique labels run by Antonio Reid and Kenneth Edmonds (LaFace), Sean "Puffy" Combs (Bad Boy) and until recently, Dallas Austin (Rowdy). While Quincy Jones and Gamble and Huff were seasoned songwriters, producers, and businesspersons, many of the ghetto pop vanguard were only a few years removed from high school and lacked any definitive critical perspectives beyond the marketing of their respective boutique labels. Many of these artist/producers remain distanced from the real seats of power within their respective corporate homes—power that could be defined along the lines of point or sole ownership of recording masters, control over production and promotional costs, and the authority to hire and replace internal staff members.[35] In many regards, many of these ghetto merchants are little more than glorified managers or overseers, involved in what was little more than a twenty-first century plantation operation.

Stephen Haymes's work on urban pedagogy and resistance constructs a broader paradigm to interpret the connection between contemporary hip-hop and mass consumer culture. In his work Haymes suggests that the intense commodification of African-American culture and the changes in the consumption habits of the black masses is rooted in structural changes linked to the process of American Fordism.[36] Historically linked to efforts to raise workers' wages as a vehicle to increase consumption, Fordism is the concept around which much of the industrial labor force has been structured throughout the twentieth century, as higher wages and concepts of leisure helped promote the burgeoning advertising industry, which emerged to help stimulate and institutionalize consumptionist desire in industrial workers. The consumptionist ethic became as valuable as the work ethnic in the construction of Americanness. But as Haymes further suggests, the failure of the Fordist model to counter market saturation in the post–Civil Rights era led to the emergence of a subsequent model, which he refers to as neo-Fordism, designed to both integrate the black populace into mainstream markets and increase consumption. As he states, "Unlike the strategy of Fordism, which sought to fuel demand by integrating the industrial working class via higher wages, neo-Fordism aimed, through an expanded welfare state, to fuel demand and economic growth by also integrating poor and working-class blacks into the American Dream."[37]

Of course much of this state-sanctioned expansion collapsed with the emergence of the Reagan right in the early 1980s, though the logic of neo-Fordism continued as the advertising industry increasingly became the vehicle by which not only goods and services were promoted but lifestyles and identities were constructed and consumed. This was partially achieved through the process of niche marketing, where specific products were aimed at various populations based on income, social status, race, gender, and ethnicity. What is important here is that individuals no longer consumed products, but also the social status and lifestyle that particular products represented. Accordingly, the high visibility of au couture fashions and other emblems of conspicuous wealth within hip-hop served to stimulate desire and consumption that transcended the structural realities of many black urban youth; processes that were often construed as forms of resistance against the invisibility and misery associated with black urban life. Not surprisingly, such marketing trends occur during an era when much of black popular expression has in fact been annexed by the engines of corporate capitalism and thus black popular expression is placed in the service of stimulating consumption among the very masses for whom the American Dream was inaccessible throughout much of the twentieth century.

In less than a decade, hip-hop culture had been transformed from a subculture primarily influenced by the responses of black urban youth to postindustrialization into a billion-dollar industry in which such responses were exploited by corporate capitalist and the petit bourgeois desires of the black middle class. The latter developments offered little relief to the realities of black urban youth who remained hip-hop's core constituents, though the economic successes of hip-hop artists and the black entrepreneurs associated with contemporary black popular music were often used to counter public discussions about the negative realities of black urban life. Economic issues aside, corporate control of black popular expression, often heightened the contradictions inherent in music produced across an economically deprived and racially delimited urban landscape. As Rose relates:

> In the case of rap music, which takes place under intense public surveillance ... contradictions regarding class, gender, and race are highlighted, decontextualized, and manipulated so as to destabilize rap's resistive elements. Rap's resistive, yet contradictory, positions were waged in the face of a powerful, media-supported construction of black urban America as a source of urban social ills that threaten social order. Rappers' speech acts are heavily shaped by music industry demands, sanctions, and prerogatives. These discursive wars are waged in the face of sexist and patriarchal assumptions that support and promote verbal abuse of black women.[38]

Within this context, discourse(s) of resistance were undermined by narratives with privileged patriarchal, sexist, and even misogynistic ideals, that were themselves taken out of their organic contexts. In the past, socially problematic narratives were critiqued and distributed according to communal sensibilities in a process that maintained the contextual integrity in which the narratives were produced. Ironically the most visible critiques of hip-hop and ghetto pop emit from black middle-class groups who are in part responsible for the fractured quality of social and political narratives produced by black urban youths in the postindustrial city.

Postindustrial Nostalgia: Mass Media, Memory, and Community

In the spring of 1994, talk show host Arsenio Hall ended his successful run as host of *The Arsenio Hall Show*, a nighttime talk and variety show. Only a year earlier, Hall had celebrated the fifth anniversary of his show with a rousing rendition of Sly Stone's "Thank You (Falettinme Be Mice Elf Agin)" led by soul singer Bobby Womack and soul recluse Sly Stone himself. The song's performance was a metaphor for the show itself, as the show served as a vehicle for the presentation of black popular culture on black popular culture's own terms. Though Hall's own hyperblack antics often broached the worst stereotypes associated with black men, including his insatiable desire to fawn over white women guests, Hall and his audiences reveled in the insiderisms that mainstream America was not privy, but was so willing to consume. For a six-year period, *The Arsenio Hall Show* remained a fixture in African-American households, precisely because it represented a link to community and black expressive culture, as Hall used his own memories of black Cleveland as a springboard to personify contemporary black anxieties and concerns through humor. *The Arsenio Hall Show* was crucial to the hip-hop community because Hall allowed his show to be a forum for their concerns, not just as performers, but as public spokespersons and critics for their communities. Thus it was not unusual for Hall to interview the likes of KRS-One or female hip-hop artist YO-YO about the complexities of hip-hop and black urban life. Like *Soul Train* a generation earlier, Hall's show was an audiovisual remnant to seminal black public spaces that promoted communal exchange and critique. Though Hall's interviews often lacked depth, he covered an astounding diversity of issues and personalities.

Hall's late-night television show ended as Spike Lee premiered his seventh film, his first since *Malcolm X* appeared in late 1992. Personified by cultural workers like filmmaker Lee, the black middle class responded to the proliferation of ghetto imagery and "ghetto pop" that appeared in commodified form on television, film, and black radio stations with a nostalgic return to the 1970s. Lee's 1994 film *Crooklyn* is an example of what I call postindustrial nostalgia, loosely described as a nostalgia that has its basis in the postindustrial transformations of black urban life during the 1970s. While the pop-cultural texts of the 1970s have proved to be huge commodities for this generation of black cultural producers, I maintain that these nostalgic turns yearn more for the historic period they consume as opposed to the profit motives that inspire their appropriation and reanimation, as the decade of the 1970s marked the increasing tensions of a burgeoning postindustrial economy and the continued erosion of the Black Public Sphere. It is the realization of these tensions that frame the major concerns of the largely autobiographical *Crooklyn*.

Perhaps the opening sequence of *Crooklyn* best suggests Lee's foci for the film. Minus Lee's usual bravado and self-indulged wit, the film opens with the sounds of Russell Thompkins Jr.'s stirring falsetto from the recording, "People Make the World Go 'Round." Very clearly a film more about people than ideas, community than ideology, *Crooklyn* places the black family and community at the center of the film. Notions of people and community resonate throughout the film from the imagery of the opening sequence to continuous musical reminders like the Stylistics's "People Make the World Go 'Round" and Sly Stone's "Everyday People." Indeed as the closing credits begin to roll and we are treated to a "Soul Train line" circa 1975, one is reminded of the centrality of music and dance to black life and of the communal purposes such cultural activities have historically played for people within the African-American diaspora. Films like Lee's *Crooklyn* or Robert Townsend's nostalgic *The Five Heartbeats*, were clearly intended to counter the influence of ghettocentric filmmaking as represented by *New Jack City, Boyz N the Hood*, and *Menace II Society*.

Crooklyn introduces us to the Carmichael family as they attempt to negotiate the schisms of the postindustrial urban North and an eroding public sphere, as such schisms begin to threaten their multiethnic Brooklyn community. The Carmichael family members represent animate metaphors for the realities of postindustrial Black America. Both mother and father figures represent complex issues regarding the location of black women and men in the workforce, the potential effects of integration, and the challenges faced by organic cultural producers, who can no longer be sustained by the community they live in and have little or no value in the marketplace. Meanwhile, the unbridled fascination of the Carmichael children when confronting black images on the television in the form of *Soul Train* and Afro-sheen commercials portends the uncritical consumption of black images and sounds that stifle contemporary black youth sensibilities. The family patriarch, Woody Carmichael, is in many ways a living embodiment of the marginalization of high African-American art in the black community as well as a useful example of the lack of public spaces provided specifically for jazz music and jazz musicians. Woody confronts a world where the valued practice of African-American musicianship has given way to the demands of a recording industry that values less experimental and more formulaic approaches to popular music as well as an eroding public sphere that can no longer economically sustain jazz musicians.

The changes in the recording industry during that era are reflected in the two-volume soundtrack of classic soul from the late 1960s and 1970s, a period marked by corporate efforts to annex the black popular music industry. The two-decades-old catalogs of artists like Marvin Gaye, Teddy Pendergrass, and the O'Jays sold more than one hundred thousand units apiece in early 1995 to a largely black middle class consumer base weary of contemporary black popular music. Black radio would in turn respond to this commercial shift by radically changing programming formats to acquiesce to the taste and buying power of their middle-class audiences. Under the banner of "Classic Soul and Progressive R&B," many urban contemporary stations would begin programming classic soul recordings with upscale and less offensive (read: more adult) contemporary R&B. RKO Broadcasting, in a fairly interesting and innovative move, would purchase a rival station that exclusively featured "ghetto pop," transfer many of their younger DJs to the newly acquired station, and change the initial station's format to the "Classic Soul and Progressive R&B" format. This of course gave the parent company the opportunity to nurture two distinctly different audiences bases.[39]

Within the context of the black popular music tradition, this trend toward "nostalgia programming" provided invaluable access to a digitized aural Chitlin' Circuit for younger generations of artists and audiences. Part of this curiosity was peaked initially by the use of classic soul and soul jazz samples by innovative hip-hop producers who may have been introduced to the musical texts as kids. Within the context of a middle-class critique of contemporary black popular culture, the emergence of "postindustrial" narratives offers few lasting solutions to the continued erosion of African-American diasporic relations. By embracing the soul narratives of twenty years ago, the black middle class yearns for a social and cultural landscape that they were, in part, responsible for transforming. In addition, while there should be some balance in the marketing and production of black popular music forms, ghetto pop, and hip-hop, particularly that which is derived from the real-life tension of young urban life, deserve to be supported. The production of many of these ghettocentric narratives partially reflects the black middle class' refusal to address these issues within the context of African-American diasporic relations.

Postindustrial nostalgia was not limited to the social imagination of the black middle class, however. It was also a construct of contemporary black youth, who attempted to reconstruct community, history, and memory by embracing communal models from previous historical eras. The erosion of the Black Public Sphere provided the chasm in which the hip-hop generation was denied access to the bevy of communally derived social, aesthetic, cultural, and political sensibilities that undergirded much of black communal struggle throughout the twentieth century, fracturing the hip-hop generation and the generations that will follow from the real communal history of the African-American diaspora. It is within this context that mass culture fills the void of both community and history for contemporary black youth, as it becomes the terrain in which contemporary hip-hop artists conflate history and memory in an effort to reconstruct community. The recording "Things Done Changed" from the debut release of the late Notorious B.I.G. (aka Biggie Smalls) is such an example.[40] Within his narrative, the Notorious B.I.G. reconstructs a community where young children engaged in games in various public spaces and where a communal ethic existed to support activities like cookouts and block parties. Though the artist was raised in the postindustrial era in a black urban community that was not immune to poverty, crime, or random violence, he chose to highlight the type of communal exchanges that dominated his childhood experiences. Even in his memories of hanging on street corners and drinking beer, he chose to forget the high unemployment and school dropout rates that black urban youth have faced for the past twenty-five years, effectively affording many black youths of Notorious B.I.G.'s generation the time to hang out on the street corners.

The point here is not to question the accuracy of the narrative but to note that it contains a sense of community that the author clearly finds missing within black urban life in the

1990s. Even more telling is his reading of how these changing dynamics have altered familial relations as a segment of black youth prey on their parents and other adults within the community. This aspect of communal erosion is so significant that many black adults have chosen to ignore decades of police brutality and have subjected their communities to an intensified police presence in order to control black youth. While Notorious B.I.G.'s narrative fails to convey some of the complexities of this reality, he clearly articulates a sense of community collapse and suggests that this collapse is partially connected to a generational divide within the African-American diaspora. While "Things Done Changed" adequately documents the impact of community erosion, other hip-hop artists used other modes of nostalgia to advance solutions to the plight of contemporary blacks.

The release of Arrested Development's *3 Years 5 Months and 2 Days in the Life of* ... in 1992 represented a challenge to the status quo in hip-hop as its Afrocentric "grunge" style distanced them from both gangsta rap and the political narratives of Public Enemy and KRS-One. As Todd Boyd suggests, Arrested Development shared its context with the emergence of a generation of black collegiates who used African garb and hairstyles to articulate their connection to the African continent.[41] As the group's name suggests, many of the recording's tracks were critical of the impact of migration and urbanization on the black community. Throughout the recording, but especially on tracks like "People Everyday" and "Tennessee," the group's lead vocalist articulated a notion of difference within the African-American diaspora that has its basis in class difference but is articulated as a difference between black rural and urban culture. The recording represented a clear revision of historic class sensibilities that posited southern migrants as the primary threat to black middle-class development in the urban North and Midwest. Within Arrested Development's framework, urbanization had clearly destroyed traditional black communal and familial sensibilities.

The track "Tennessee" perhaps best exemplified Arrested Development's use of nostalgia to counter the impact of urbanization on the black community. The track, which shares its postmigration theme with songs like the Gladys Knight and the Pips classic "Midnight Train to Georgia," represents an open rejection of black urban life. As many black creative artists and intellectuals ponder a vision of communal empowerment on par with the role "Promised Land" migration narratives played in the early to mid-twentieth century and emancipation narratives played in the antebellum period, Arrested Development lead vocalist Speech asserts that the American South will be the focus of the next stage of communal movement.[42] Using Tennessee as a symbol for this movement, Speech articulates his concern for his peers and his desire to reconnect with an African-American spiritual past. Speech's use of the American South as a metaphor for black homespaces is of course nothing new. As Farah Jasmine Griffin and Ralph Ellison both suggested, many migrants attempted to re-create southern homespaces within industrialized urban spaces, but the migrants were also clear about their memories of the Deep South's racial oppression, violence, and segregation.

As a postmigration narrative, "Tennessee" differs from traditional migration narratives in its suggestion that traditional black communal and familial values had been lost precisely because the most malicious aspects of the American South are no longer present to galvanize the black community as witnessed in the charcoal drawing of a lynching that serves as a subtext for the song's music video. But to read "Tennessee" as a rejection of the hard-fought political and social gains won as a corollary to mass migration and urbanization is to misread the song's text.[43] Given the proliferation of Afrocentric iconography that was present in the group's music videos and publicity photos, "Tennessee" clearly represents a contemporary metaphor for the African continent, as is suggested in the song's chorus, which states, "Take me to another place / Take me to another land.... "[44] While a mass-migration movement to the African continent is perhaps more politically credible in the late twentieth century than it was in Marcus Garvey's era, Speech is not suggesting a return to Africa but instead posits the

American South and its physical terrain as the connection to forms of African spiritually that have been lost to migration and urbanization. The point here is not whether a return to the South would stimulate economic development in the black community, decrease homelessness, or affect public policy in any way, but rather how African spirituality could be one of the vehicles by which community could be reconstructed.

Several artists would embrace various modes of nostalgia to reconstruct a seminal relationship within the African-American diaspora. For instance, bisexual artist Me'Shell Ndegeocello uses the iconography of black plantation life to affirm same-sex love in a period of heightened homophobia. On the track "Mary Magdalene" from her recording *Peace Beyond Passion,* she states, "I imagine us jumpin' the broom."[45] The phrase "jumpin' the broom" was initially used by enslaved blacks in the antebellum period to signify marriage between slaves, when the legality of such was severely challenged. Here the phrase is appropriated to signify lesbian marriage in an era when the idea of homosexual and lesbian marriages is being sharply criticized and attacked in mainstream culture. Ndegeocello's use of the symbolic imagery of black marriage at once reaffirms her status in the African-American diaspora, even as black homosexuals and lesbians are being marginalized within that community, while linking the struggles of contemporary homosexuals and lesbians to the African-American tradition of social protest and resistance.

In another example, hip-hop artist Method Man appropriated the melody of the Marvin Gaye and Tammi Terrell's classic "You're All I Need to Get By" for his recording "I'll Be There for You/You're All I Need to Get By." The recording, which featured contemporary soul vocalist Mary J. Blige, used the Ashford and Simpson composition to reaffirm heterosexual relationships in the postindustrial era. The recording, which represented one of the more popular affirmations of the continuity of African-American expressive culture, highlights the role of popular music as a primary conduit to express various continuities within the African-American diaspora. Such continuities were perhaps undermined when the Coca-Cola Co. used both the original Gaye/Terrell recording and Method Man/Blige update in a commercial to signify a generation gap within the black community, a generation gap that was bridged according to the company, because of the continuity of Coca-Cola in the lives of black families. The commercial again highlights the increasingly intimate relationship between memory, history, and the marketplace.

Driven by his own realization of the commercial value of ghetto narratives and his own middle-class and nationalistic sensibilities, Spike Lee has been one of the few contemporary black cultural workers to successfully integrate the often oppositional taste within both urban working-class/underclass locales and segments of the black middle class. The first volume of the *Crooklyn* soundtrack contains a hip-hop recording from a trio of solo artists, Buckshot, Special Ed, and Masta Ace, who combine their efforts under the banner of the Crooklyn Dodgers. The recording entitled "Crooklyn" is a stunning acknowledgment of postindustrial transformation within black urban spaces as mediated through the increased presence of mass culture. Within the context of the "Crooklyn Dodger" narrative, the erosion of black public life is represented by television sitcoms, in an interesting conflation of contemporary communal crises, 1970s television icons, and designer fashions.[46] The memories of the traditional Black Public Sphere of the early 1970s are contained, specifically in the narrative of a black sitcom like *What's Happening.* In one regard, this narrative serves to deconstruct romantic recollections of black public life, while also identifying the pervasive impact of mass culture on the lives of African-Americans. Consistent with hip-hop's own project, the artists use mass-market-produced imagery and meanings to parlay their narrative concerns.

The recording, which is sandwiched between broadcast accounts of the 1955 World Series, including Jackie Robinson at bat, highlights a phenomenon perhaps organic to post–Civil Rights generations of African-American youth. While memories of national and international events have been mass-mediated in the twentieth century through print organs, radio, and later television—how many people remember World War II via *Life* magazine's coverage?—*Crooklyn* highlights how some of the seminal memories of community life are mass-mediated via television for the generation of black youth that emerged immediately after the Civil Rights era. My point here is not to delegitimize these memories, particularly given the role television has played in socializing African-American youth since the early 1970s, but to suggest that contemporary efforts to reconstruct community would most likely also be mediated through mass culture, though not necessarily via television.

Notes

1. George discusses the birth of Quiet Storm radio in *The Death of Rhythm and Blues*, 131–35, 172–73.
2. George defines "retronuevo" as black music that embraces the past to "create passionate, fresh expressions, and institutions." *The Death of Rhythm and Blues*, 186–88.
3. My commentary here is not of an effort to engage in debates about welfare reform, but to acknowledge the bureaucratic realities associated with many federal programs, particularly in their ineffectiveness in countering the general misery associated with black urban life.
4. Rose, *Black Noise: Rap Music and Black Culture in Contemporary America*, 30.
5. Mollenkopf, *Dual City*, 8.
6. Goldberg, "Polluting the Body Politic," *Racism, the City and the State*, 52.
7. Ibid., 51–52.
8. Wilson, *The Truly Disadvantaged*, 60.
9. Davis, *City of Quartz*, 250–53.
10. Lewis, *When Harlem was in Vogue*, 129–30.
11. Davis, *City of Quartz*, 311.
12. West, *Prophetic Thought in Postmodern Times*, 122.
13. Davis, *City of Quartz*, 304–305.
14. Jerry Mander addresses the relationship between American youth and television in his text *Four Arguments for the Elimination of Television*.
15. Davis, *City of Quartz*, 306.
16. Dyson, *Race Rules*, 140–45.
17. Davis, *City of Quartz*, 293–300
18. Rose, *Black Noise*, 11.
19. Ibid., 61.
20. Gilroy, "One Nation Under a Groove," *Small Acts*, 39–40.
21. The litigation between Chic and Sugar Hill records over the use of "Good Times" was just the first of many celebrated sampling cases, of which the 1991 legal battle between artists Biz Markie and singer/songwriter Gilbert O'Sullivan is the most notorious. Many artists have dealt with this problem by simply giving sampled artists songwriting credit, though given the history of pop music, these credits simply enhanced the financial coffers of corporate entities who controlled the publishing rights.
22. Marable, *Race, Reform and Rebellion*, 194–96.
23. Manning Marable offers a credible argument in his text *How Capitalism Underdeveloped Black America*, that the increased rates of black male incarceration is related to the use of prison inmates in the maintenance of municipal works and services. Marable believes that the use of prison inmates in such a way is representative of a modern form of enslavement.
24. Marable, *Race, Reform and Rebellion*, 1972.
25. Tate, *Flyboy in the Buttermilk*, 125.
26. The works of black women like Angela Davis, Kathleen Cleaver, and Elaine Brown exemplify the type of necessary critique and reflection that needs to take place to more adequately consider the success and failures of the Civil Rights/Black Power era.
27. Tate, *Flyboy in the Buttermilk*, 126.
28. Ibid.
29. Boyd, *Am I Black Enough for You*, 39.
30. I am referring here to Joe Kleine's review of the film for *New Yorker* magazine in June 1989.
31. Rose, *Black Noise*, 128–30.
32. Ibid., 126.
33. Ibid., 130–35.

34. Despite a recording career that has been inconsistent at best and well-publicized financial problems, MC Hammer remains the best-selling hip-hop artist of all time.
35. During the summer of 1996 Combs renegotiated his deal with Arista/BMG, giving him ownership of his label's recording masters over a period of time. At the time of Comb's deal Reid and Edmonds were rumored to renegotiate along the same terms, issues of autonomy and product ownership were at the core of Andre Harrell's severed relationship with Uptown/MCA, the label he founded in the autumn of 1995. Harrell was subsequently chosen to lead Motown into the twenty-first century with considerably more autonomy and prestige than was offered at the boutique he founded in 1986, though his failure to produce new acts led to his forced resignation in August 1997.
36. Haymes, *Race Culture and the City*, 36–39.
37. Ibid., 37.
38. Rose, *Black Noise*, 104.
39. RKO owns both Hot 97 and KISS-FM in New York City. Hot 97, which is dedicated to a twenty-four-hour ghetto pop and hip-hop format, has also brought in popular artists, including former *Yo MTV Raps* hosts Dr. Dre and Ed Lover, to host segments of their programming. Ed and Dre, as they are affectionately known, are the station's morning drive-time hosts. WBLS-FM, the only-black owned station in the market, responded to these shifts only after RKO's experiment proved successful.
40. Notorious B.I.G., "Things Done Changed," *Ready to Die* (Arista/Bad Boy, 78612–73000–2).
41. Boyd, *Am I Black Enough for You?*, 43–50.
42. I am thinking here of works like Samm Art-William's *Home,* Cornel West's *Prophetic Fragments,* Farah Jasmine Griffin's *Who Set You Flowin'?,* and Spike Lee's film *Crooklyn* and *Clockers,* which all consider the lack of communal vision in the aftermath of the migratory movement.
43. Arrested Development, "Tennessee," *3 Years, 5 Months and 2 Days in the Life of ...* (Chrysalis 1992).
44. Ibid.
45. Michelle Ndegeocello, "Mary Magdelene," *Peace Beyond Passion* (Maverick/Reprise 1996).
46. The Crooklyn Dodgers, "Crooklyn," *Music From the Motion Picture Crooklyn* (MCA 1994).

References

Boyd, Todd. *Am I Black Enough for You?* South Bend: Indiana University Press, 1997.
Davis, Mike. *City of Quartz: Excavating the Future in Los Angeles.* New York: Verso, 1990.
Dyson, Michael Eric. *Race Rules: Navigating the Color Line.* New York: Addison Wesley, 1996.
George, Nelson. *The Death of Rhythm and Blues.* New York: Pantheon, 1988.
Gilroy, Paul. *Small Acts.* New York: Serpent's Tail, 1993.
Goldberg, David Theo. "Polluting the Body Politic:" Racist Discourse and Urban Location. *Racism, the City and the State,* Malcolm Cross and Michael Keith, eds. New York: Routledge, 1993.
Griffin, Farah Jasmine. *"Who Set You Flowin?": The African-American Migration Narrative.* New York: Oxford University Press, 1995.
Haymes, Stephen. *Race, Culture and the City: A Pedagogy for Black Urban Struggle.* Albany: State University of New York Press, 1995.
Lewis, David Levering. *When Harlem was in Vogue.* New York: Oxford University Press, 1989.
Mander, Jerry. *Four Arguments for the Elimination of Television.* New York: William Morrow, 1978.
Marable, Manning. *How Capitalism Underdeveloped Black America.* Boston: South End Press, 1983.
———. *Race Reform and Rebellion: The Second Reconstruction in Black America, 1945–1992.* Jackson: University Press of Mississippi, 1993.
Mollenkopf, John, and Manuel Castells, eds. *Dual City: Restructuring New York.* New York: Russell Sage Foundation, 1991.
Rose, Tricia. *Black Noise: Rap Music and Black Culture in Contemporary America.* Hanover: Wesleyan University Press, 1994.
Tate, Greg. *Flyboy in the Buttermilk: Essays on Contemporary America.* New York: Simon & Schuster, 1992.
West, Cornel. *Prophetic Fragments.* Trenton. Africa World Press, 1988.
———. *Prophetic Thought in Postmodern Times.* Monroe, Maine: Common Courage Press, 1993.
Wilson, William Julius. *The Truly Disadvantaged: The Inner City, the Underclass, and Public Policy.* Chicago: University of Chicago Press, 1987.

Part VI
Looking for the Perfect Beat:
Hip-Hop Aesthetics
and Technologies of Production

Murray Forman

As several of the chapters in Part I explain, technology figures prominently in hip-hop's creative process. This is especially true of rap music, although once the media production and diffusion of hip-hop are factored into the equation, technology's deep influence in virtually all of hip-hop's constituent forms is evident. Despite a central impact, it is essential not to adopt a technological determinist position identifying technology as the motivating force in the change and evolution of cultural practices; technology has never been the sole drive of hip-hop's development. Rather, the technologies of hip-hop are culturally inflected at diverse scales of effect, woven into prevailing social contexts, and enfolded within the systems of production and exchange that are prone to transition in the face of historically specific stimuli. As Langdon Winner notes, "what matters is not technology itself, but the social and economic systems in which it is embedded" (1986: 20).

This is not to suggest, however, that technology is benign since virtually every form of technology has the potential to extend power in ways both scripted and unscripted. An example, in the late 1970s Bronx, was the illegal hijacking of electricity from city sources to rechannel the "juice" to drive mighty sound systems at impromptu block parties. Through the amplification of disco, funk, and the first break beats, a new means of imposing a radical presence in the public spaces of the city parks and streets was discovered, producing cultural events that were accessible, meaningful, and fun for those close enough to palpably experience the powerful bass reverberations as the DJ worked "the wheels of steel." As numerous interviews and casual anecdotes affirm, more than a few of these original hip-hop jams were broken up with the arrival of the New York constabulary who, reasserting hegemonic power and authority, saw that the sound systems were summarily unplugged and dismantled.

Rap music traditionally relies on the appropriation and reassignment of music technologies, especially the turntable, mixer, and vinyl record, which, in the hands of DJ trailblazers such as Afrika Bambaataa, Kool DJ Herc, Grandmaster Flash, or Grand Wizard Theodore, were employed in ways unforeseen by corporate manufacturers. The turntable was transformed from a playback unit mainly associated with domestic forms of musical reception to an instrument of production that facilitated new musical styles to be performed in alternative public contexts. Describing the merging of electronic technologies with emergent aesthetic sensibilities, Iain Chambers writes:

> Rap is New York's "sound system"; the black youth culture of Harlem and the Bronx successfully twisting technology into new cultural shape. Rap is sonorial graffiti, a musical spray

that marries black rhythms and the verbal gymnastics of hip street talk to a hot DJ patter over an ingenious manipulation of the turntable. (1985: 190)

The practice of rocking a beat between two turntables, aided by electronic mixers rebuilt with efficient cross fade switches and, at times, small rudimentary rhythm boxes, gradually developed into a full-fledged DJ art form through the late 1970s and into the 1980s. Hip-hop historians such as David Toop (1984), Steve Hager (1984), Dick Hebdige (1987), and many others have recounted the historical roots of the DJ from Jamaican dance halls to the streets and parks in the Bronx and Harlem, charting the gradual ascendance of a new hybrid urban aesthetic as the Caribbean DJ practices, including the musical influences of Jamaican reggae and Puerto Rican or Cuban salsa, were blended with U.S. soul, R&B, and funk music.

With the advent of studio recording in 1979 when the Sugarhill Gang released "Rapper's Delight" on Sugar Hill Records, rap DJs and producers increasingly combined their turntable skills with the technical possibilities of the studio, further enhancing the sonic range of hip-hop's urban soundtrack. Many of the prominent DJs from this period are on record lamenting the shift to studio production (Fricke & Ahearn, 2002), suggesting that the industrial structures of the recording business displaced the primacy of live performances and eroded the caliber of rap talent that was up to this point measured by the ability to "rock a party." By the mid-1980s, digital sound sampling had become a standard technological component of music production, again modifying the standards and skills involved in rap music production. Sampling was rapidly integrated into rap's studio arsenal, introducing radical capabilities that transformed the way music was conceived and constructed while simultaneously challenging the music industry's legal authority inscribed in copyright law. Most early applications of sound sampling technology involved the digital excision of brief rhythm "breaks" or song passages from previously recorded material including familiar choruses, catchy lyrical phrases, or distinct vocal exhortations such as James Brown's inimitable screams.

Apart from constructing a bridge between musical antecedents and the present, digital sampling can imbue an element of authenticity on newer tracks as the patina of the past seeps into the new mix. The hiss or pop of old vinyl records provides a sonic link to the original recording by referencing its age and wear through what are, in most conventional recording contexts, deemed as imperfections. DJ's or producer's tastes and cultural capital are also on display with their selection of classic recordings from the past, especially as they seek more compelling or obscure material to distinguish their musical creations. While James Brown, George Clinton, or the Gap Band are today regarded as classic, if obvious, sources for rap's sonic appropriation, it requires considerable knowledge to seek out exotic, unfamiliar, or forgotten tracks for an interesting horn progression, bass rhythm, or melodic signature. After twenty-five years of rap recording, rap and hip-hop tracks are themselves constant sources in a repository of sound available to producers who are just as inclined to employ a snippet of a recent rap hit as they are to include a beat from a time-proven funk masterpiece.

Technological innovation and the history of creative production and interpretive strategies lie at the core of Andrew Bartlett's chapter. Citing often irreverent or contestatory practices of black cultural production, Bartlett establishes a viable link between antebellum spirituals or postemancipation work songs and contemporary hip-hop and rap music. With an emphasis on strategic production practices involving "selective adaptation" and radical cultural performance techniques, Bartlett contributes a valuable perspective on the cultural politics within which black youths forge their art. As in past contexts of African American cultural production, youth of the hip-hop generation turn existing musical forms toward sonic communication, envisioning today's electronic and digital mechanisms as objects that facilitate the dissemination of African American cultural values, ideals, and aesthetics.

Early rap artists were often derided as mere copyists—or worse—and rap often initially struggled for artistic legitimacy among its critics even as it proved its commercial might. Clearly, rap does not need legitimization in the sense that it might be "rescued" from the slag heap of popular culture, and Richard Shusterman argues for the creative and artistic virtue of rap by aligning its forms and practices with classic literary and visual arts as well as with aspects of philosophical inquiry and the representation of deeper human values and ideals. Employing a close reading of Stetsasonic's "Talkin' All that Jazz," Shusterman's research is less concerned with justifying rap's existence than with providing a broader cultural understanding of its value status and aesthetic contributions to long-standing artistic traditions, in the process more firmly connecting hip-hop studies with traditional academic approaches in the humanities.

Greg Dimitriadis in his chapter emphasizes the point that hip-hop is experienced bodily as well as cognitively, elaborating the affective range within which hip-hop is made meaningful within broad cultural contexts. As he explains, the aesthetic properties of rap changed in the mid-1980s as new forms of production and reception that diminished the primacy of live hip-hop emerged, placing primary significance on recorded rap and its musical and lyrical forms of expression. Dimitriadis assesses the impact of the emergent emphasis on "verbal discourse" in rap and the concurrent positioning of hip-hop within the mass media flows of national and global dissemination. As he explains, these shifts have often constrained live production and limited audience congregation in public performance contexts while attenuating the centralized authority of the corporate entertainment industry.

Opening his chapter with an anecdote, Nelson George identifies a generational dissonance that has crystallized due to the reliance—some might say overreliance—among hip-hop producers on the prior creative labor of soul, R&B, and funk artists of the 1960s, 1970s, and 1980s. George appropriately locates the digital sampler within a lineage of electric instruments that black artists have mastered, altering the aesthetic and musical soundscape of their respective eras. As much as the twin turntables of the DJ, the digital sampler emerged as a studio staple, becoming an essential piece of equipment for hip-hop producers before mass-produced compact discs, production software, or MP3 technologies were available for studio and home recording. Sampling is not a rigid, unchanging practice, and George explains the transitions in sampling itself as different producers throughout the 1980s and 1990s employed it in various contexts.

Mark Dery's close analysis of Public Enemy's production practices and the group's sophisticated approach to sound and recording illuminates the creative process that gave rise to one of the most challenging and innovative musical acts to emerge in the late 1980s. In his chapter, Dery equates Public Enemy's radical political agenda and its incendiary lyrical discourses with an uncompromising revolutionary aesthetic agenda, explaining how the production is integrated into an overall sonic performance of resistance. The emphasis in this chapter is on how technology is tied into the politics of sound, and extensive interviews with Public Enemy producer Hank Shocklee and front-men Flavor Flav and Chuck D illuminate how the group's artistic and political orientation is inseparable from an overarching aesthetic sensibility.

In his chapter, Rickey Vincent locates hip-hop in relation to "funk" that is constituted as both a musical form and a powerful essence of the black cultural aesthetic. As Vincent explains, in its musical formation funk is a complex and sophisticated genre that permeates hip-hop. He illustrates how regional variations and idiosyncratic styles among artists and producers further extend the range of musical genres and subgenres that funk has fundamentally influenced. By delineating a panoply of cultural forces and the concurrent intermixing of formal musical elements, Vincent stresses the fact that hip-hop's musical outpouring is entirely heterogeneous and the evolution of rap is established through diverse aesthetic manifestations of "the funk."

Even as it evolved as a foundation of the sonic construction of rap recordings, digital sound sampling challenged the existing copyright law, provoking debates about ownership and creative appropriation, in the process raising the specter of musical thievery within the recording industry. Thomas Shumacher's chapter isolates copyright law as yet another site in which rap's creative approaches have disrupted the prevailing order, necessitating a reconsideration of the ways that law and culture are linked and the implications of their relations. Shumacher analyzes several of the landmark copyright infringement cases (especially those involving Biz Markie and 2 Live Crew) that focused on rap from a legalistic perspective, reminding us of the particular arguments that were leveled against rap sampling at the time and of the arguments for the defense. This chapter also presents a theoretically informed examination of the technological aspects of sampling, the role of the author, and the status of the original recording, framing these issues in the context of African American musical traditions and a black cultural aesthetic.

References

Chamber, Iain. 1985. *Urban Rhythms: Pop Music and Popular Culture.* London: Macmillan.

Fricke, Jim, and Charlie Ahearn. 2002. *Yes Yes Y' All: The Experience Music Project Oral History of Hip-Hop's First Decade.* Cambridge, MA: Da Capo Press.

Hager, Steven. 1984. *Hip Hop: The Illustrated History of Break Dancing, Rap Music, and Graffiti.* New York: St. Martin's Press.

Hebdige, Dick. 1987. *Cut 'n' Mix: Culture, Identity and Caribbean Music.* London: Comedia.

Toop, David. 1984. *The Rap Attack: African Jive to New York Hip-Hop.* Boston: South End Press.

Winner, Langdon. 1986. *The Whale and the Reactor: A Search for Limits in an Age of High Technology.* Chicago: University of Chicago Press.

30

Airshafts, Loudspeakers, and the Hip Hop Sample:

Contexts and African American Musical Aesthetics

Andrew Bartlett

The art of digital sampling in (primarily) African American hip hop is intricately connected to an African American/African diasporic aesthetic which carefully selects available media, texts, and contexts for performative use. Thomas Porcello explains that digital sampling allows one

> to encode a fragment of sound, from one to several seconds in duration, in a digitised binary form which can then be stored in computer memory. This stored sound may be played back through a keyboard, with its pitch and tonal qualities accurately reproduced or, as is often the case, manipulated through electronic editing. (69)

Porcello concludes, perhaps rightly, but in any case reductively, that "rap musicians have come to use the sampler in an oppositional manner which contests capitalist notions of public and private property by employing previously tabooed modes of citation" (82).

When *popular* discussions of rap or hip hop come around to digital sampling, they often do so by way of telling metaphors. Public Enemy's Hank Shocklee asserts that "rap culture" is "becoming more of a scavenger culture" when "mixing all the colors together" (Kemp 20); Mark Costello and David Foster Wallace liken sampling to "holding music at gunpoint" (57); and a March 1991 *Keyboard* magazine article refers to sampling as "audio junkyard collisions" (Dery, "Tommy" 64).

The oral pedagogical techniques hip hop artists utilize have maintained what Porcello calls "three capabilities of the sampler—the mimetic/reproductive, the manipulative[,] and the extractive" (69), and these capabilities reveal, among other things, what W.E.B. Du Bois in 1903 called "second sight" (5)—that process by which the "minority" knows the majority not only better than the obverse, but often better than the "majority" knows itself. Du Boisian second sight is not reserved for quietly ideological activity, but has historically been exercised in a thoroughly public and thoroughly popular forum—and thus a forum in need of contextualization—the African American musical performance.

In his study of African American musical aesthetics *Black Talk: How the Music of Black America Created a Radical Alternative to the Values of Western Literary Tradition*, Ben Sidran relies heavily on a distinction between literate and oral "*approaches* to perception and the organization of information" (3). This distinction, Sidran notes, is not concrete: Whereas "literacy freezes concept, as it were, through the use of print" (xxiv), the so-called oral mode relies on "basic actionality" (5), a functional elaboration, often through performance, that allows communication and perception a massive spectrum of referents. Whether Sidran's distinctions are accepted in full or not, there is a clear continuum in which African American artists have put things learned by listening into action by way of *performance*. Greg Tate argues that one of the most extraordinary transformations in African American aesthetic history—Miles Davis's late 1960s and 1970s electric band—was the result of an act of listening: "What Miles heard in the music of P-Funk progenitors James Brown, Jimi Hendrix, and Sly Stone was the blues impulse transferred, masked, and retooled for the space age through the lowdown act of *possession*" (73). The closeness of listening and performative possession becomes all the more clear as hip hop artists appropriate bits and pieces of numerous musics and nonmusical sounds into their performative matrices. And this appropriative process is hardly novel, despite digital technology, in the 1980s or 1990s.

References to Harlem in early Duke Ellington compositions—"Harlem Speaks" (1935), "Echoes of Harlem" (1936), and "Harlem Air Shaft" (1940)—often concern what Ellington heard in the community. Indeed, Ellington explained "Harlem Air Shaft" as a composition explicitly heard before it was written and arranged:

> You get the full essence of Harlem in an air shaft. You hear fights, you smell dinner, you hear people making love. You hear intimate gossip floating down. You hear the radio. An air shaft is one great big loudspeaker. You see your neighbor's laundry. You hear the janitor's dogs. The man upstairs' aerial falls down and breaks your window. You smell coffee.... An air shaft has got every contrast.... You hear people praying, fighting, snoring.... I tried to put all that in my *Harlem Air Shaft*. (Shapiro & Hentoff 224–25)

While "literate" Western culture is a stereotype at a certain point, it is so because Western culture(s) have largely fetishized reading as a function solely of print and the sole mode of learning and subsequent "actionality," whether musical or not. Ellington's exegesis for "Harlem Air Shaft" points to a musical actionality that *reads* context for potential material. The resultant composition is an evocative interchange. The *text* Ellington reads in order to offer the listener his performed reading is an evocative prompt which conjures up the possibility of composition and performance, and the narrative Ellington offers as discussion of his compositional technique shows that the evocative prompt goes to the listener as well. We are supposed to experience the "great big loudspeaker" where "every contrast" is possible at once.

This expansive idea of musical composition and performance is the center around which contemporary hip hop constellates. Possibilities for simultaneous contrast are enhanced—if not revolutionized—by the art of digital sampling so prevalent in hip hop and yet so seldom elaborated within the hip hop texts themselves. Within the musical performance is the kernel of the theoretical conviction that "the great big loudspeaker," a multi-sensory extravaganza, can be actualized performatively.

In her essay "The Race for Theory," African American feminist critic Barbara Christian points out that

> people of color have always theorized—but in forms quite different from the Western form of abstract logic. And I am inclined to say that our theorizing (and I intentionally use the verb rather than the noun) is often in narrative forms, in the stories we create, in riddles and proverbs, in the play with language, since *dynamic rather than fixed ideas seem more to our liking*. (336; italics added)

The textual "theorizing" Christian discusses has virtually always been present in African American musical aesthetics, as John Miller Chernoff's exploration of African and African diasporic traditions through his experiences as a drumming student in Ghana make clear.

Chernoff says early in his *African Rhythms and African Sensibility* that "the variations from formal and familiar structures in an actual performance are what count most in distinguishing and appreciating artistic quality in a certain type of music" (30). While Chernoff apparently sees them as separable—*variation* as a process and *structure* as a quasi-static model—"formal and familiar structures" are, in the African American tradition, intimately related, de facto, to controlled and cultivated variation.

Using Ghanian drumming and other "folk traditions" (an admittedly dubious designation which suggests an age-old dichotomy between folklore and art) in the context of hip hop sampling has to take into account the question of musical technology and the contexts for exercising that technology historically in the U.S. Obviously, sound recordings are not and have not always been widely available. Perhaps the best history of the *technology* (my term) of early African American music is John Lovell, Jr.'s *Black Song: The Forge and the Flame—The Story of How the Afro-American Spiritual Was Hammered Out*, a book rarely mentioned in bibliographies of African American historical material.[1] Using *technology* as a rubric for discussing the spirituals may seem out of place, but the components of musical performance—whether instruments or not—are technological by virtue of their presence in the performance. In *Black Song*, Lovell notes the slave's "special attitude toward the Bible, his selectivity with respect toward its contents, and his special way of turning Biblical materials to imaginative purpose" (255). Although this "turning" is complex and never altogether clear, the power of the oral pedagogical tradition has its origins here. While Eugene D. Genovese points out that "the estimate by W.E.B. Du Bois that, despite prohibition and negative public opinion, about five percent of the slaves had learned to read by 1860 is entirely plausible *and may even be too low*" (563; italics added), widespread selective adaptation of Biblical material had to have occurred by way of listening, rather than reading. Lovell writes,

> The Biblical item is selected most often for … symbolization of the deliverer or overcoming the oppressors; inspiration from notable accomplishments under impossible circumstances (the slave considered himself a potential accomplisher in a universe where he had little or no hope but great expectation); and exemplification of the workings of faith and power. (257)

Rather than the *literal* learning of the Biblical text, there was, Lovell observes, a "thin Bible" (262) spread throughout Southern plantations as the highest textual technology that afforded singing opportunity (masters were placated by religious texts being sung) and momentary empowerment. "Nearly all of the Biblical personages the slave poet dealt with," writes Lovell, "were involved in upheaval and revolution (Moses, Daniel, David, the Hebrew children, Samson, Elijah, Gideon, Jesus, Paul)" (228).

The dissemination of Biblical knowledge does not perplex historians of slavery or the spirituals, but the *functionality* (Sidran's "actionality") of Biblical material relied on another disseminative presence:

> How a group without newspapers or any mass media, and mostly without the ability to read or write, kept informed on … the news of the day, inventions and discoveries, the approach of underground agents, the details about David Walker and Nat Turner, the ebb and flow of wars … can hardly be explained. The incontrovertible fact is that all this happened by a regular system…. From this kind of communication, and the resultant close interrelationships, the songs acquired impetus, ideas for poetic development, and power for dissemination. (Lovell 121)

A "regular system" of dissemination made performative space available for the carefully cultivated Biblical references, paired up with potent ideological commentary. The spiritual text is as much a chronicle of slave culture, a "massive archiving," as it is a religious document. Here I intend the term *culture* as John Miller Chernoff has defined it: "A culture may perhaps best be considered … a dynamic style with which people organize and orient themselves to act through various mediators" (36). The dynamic style of organization through "various mediators" is, for Chernoff, and here, overtly musical.

David Coplan makes the important observation that "ultimately it is not any systemic logic of music as organised sound but rather *the nature of metaphoric enactment* that prevents the analytic reduction of music performance to other levels of action" (123; italics added). While Coplan is concerned with the metaphoric bridges musical performance builds between performers and the society around them in South Africa, metaphoric enactment is important in the African American context as well. Coplan says,

> In musical performances, metaphors fuse several realms of experience into single, encapsulating images linked to the formation of personal identity.… The images of performance embody values and characteristics that people identify, at some level, with themselves. (123)

Lovell, for example, discusses the centrality of *motion* to the spirituals: "In his mind, the slave was constantly on the move, partly because of his desire for a new life and partly because of his fascination with moving vehicles" (247). From the use of "arks and chariots," obvious Biblical references, Lovell charts the metaphorical usage of the railroad train in the spirituals (which is replete in jazz traditions as well):

> Songs about trains are a minor miracle. The railroad train did not come into America until the late 1820s; it did not reach the slave country to any great extent until the 1830s and 1840s. Even then, the opportunities of the slave to examine trains closely were limited. Yet, before 1860, many spiritual poems exploited the train: its seductive sounds, speed and power, its recurring schedules, its ability to carry a large number of passengers at cheap rates, its implicit democracy. (249)

Performatively, the train's potency was tonal, ideational, and not altogether explainable as a literally *technological* presence; this is further indication of a "regular system" of dissemination. The technology ran from the machine implications into the implications of the notion of *mass* transit itself. Inevitably, the "seductive sounds, speed and power" found their way into a rhythmic matrix that virtually every chronicler of African American and African diasporic performative aesthetics discusses.

Besides being frequent in hip hop discourse, associations of the African American rhythmic matrix with labor are common when dealing with early music like the spirituals. This is not to say that singing was confined to the fields or the "yard," but Harold Courlander's comment about prison gang songs in the early twentieth century is germane here: "A song starting out as a description of the prisoners' work shifts into a narration of the Noah story. The thread that binds the two parts together is *the pounding of the hammers*" (99; italics added). The rhythm of labor is expropriated carefully. Lawrence Levine observes that "the work song … allow[s] the workers to blend their physical movements and psychic needs with other workers" (215) and quotes Bruce Jackson to underscore an earlier, harsher evocative prompt: "'By incorporating the work with theirs, by, in effect, co-opting something they are forced to do anyway, they make it *theirs* in a way it otherwise is not'" (215). Prompting an actional method of taking possession, the work became *frame*work for song.

The expropriation of work rhythms as a method for taking possession of one's physical labor is situated at an aesthetic/economic crossroads that long antedates the recording of work songs. In *Singing the Master: The Evolution of African American Culture in the Plantation South*, Roger D. Abrahams explores how "constantly ... within each other's gaze" (37) slaves (unwillingly) and the white-planter class participated in the evolution of not only *African* American culture but American popular culture in general. Abrahams focuses attention on an end-of-harvest celebration at which slaves were called upon to shuck enormous amounts of corn:

> Corn ... was not a demanding crop, since it might be cut away at any time and left in the field. The corn needing shucking would accumulate until all the other crops had been harvested.... Thus, the communal shucking of the corn was not crisis work, but rather the final act in the harvesting of the grain which provided the basic food resource for slaves and domestic animals. (74–75)

That the institution of corn shucking, from the "white" side of the gaze, was a "display event" (23) can be explained by the fact that corn shucking was not "crisis work" and that, as Abrahams further notes, Southern planters tended to cling "to many of the more aristocratic features which had characterized the Cavalier perspective in England" (65), particularly "ever more theatrical opportunities by which their public postures of power might better be appreciated" (40).

Briefly, an overseer or master elected two "captains" who picked "teams" which raced against each other to finish shucking their assigned pile of the corn harvest first. With the recognition of "the most powerful voice" came the selection of a leader from the slave community "to stand on top of the corn pile and lead the singing" (325). Abrahams points out more generally about "slave life" and singing that

> few observers ... failed to notice the importance of call-and-response singing. All [accounts] focus on the sense of power produced by the *overlapping* of the leader's voice with the voices of the chorus as they engaged with each other antiphonally. (91; italics added)

It is the centrality of "overlapping" that echoes throughout the African American musical tradition. From the vocalized overlap to the individualized instrumental meandering of much jazz, a constant is Thompsonian (as in Robert Farris Thompson) "apart playing," in which "a central performer interacts in counterpoint or some other contrasting mode with the rest of the performing group."[2] Of equal importance in the work/play matrix Abrahams discusses is the *overlap* of English quasi-aristocratic display and the actional engagement of the display opportunity, which slave singers found well (enough)-suited for their own performances.

The corn-shucking event—complete with the festivities that followed the shucking labor—is an oft-ignored aesthetic event which, Abrahams notes,

> has received scant attention from historians. Doubtless this is because it represents such an apparent capitulation to the image of the happy slave purveyed by the planter-apologists for slavery. (21)

But Abrahams locates the corn-shucking event as a pivotal occasion for white onlookers to learn "slave style." The "slave" qualification here is vital, as recognition of an *African* style would counteract the white dominant practice of inculcating the slave into the person at every turn. From this onlooker learning comes the institutionalization of the white "vernacular artist," who appears variously throughout the nineteenth century, "on the minstrel stage, the lecturer's platform, or the written page" (145). Vernacular artistry, for white performers, was a function of "an ardent effort to bring to the stage *studied imitations* of slave styles of singing and dancing and celebrating" (133).

What we find here is the central presence of *imitation* in an emergent Anglo-American popular culture. While the corn-shucking event sits at the economic and aesthetic crossroads, every opportunity afforded slaves at that crossroads is transformatively worked into a multi-level aesthetic performance which whites tried to duplicate *exactly*, even to the point of using specific "tales of random encounters" to give their nineteenth-century stage acts authenticity. Regarding blackface entertainment and white minstrelsy, Abrahams notes that

> the authenticity of the material itself became an important feature of presentation for these singers and dancers wearing blackface.... By the end of the nineteenth century such authenticating stories had become almost conventional, so often had the theme been embellished upon by the most successful writers of the time: Joel Chandler Harris, Lafcadio Hearn, Mark Twain, and George Washington Cable. (142)[3]

While Anglo-American popular culture became saturated with the problematics of authenticity and the establishment of a standard for "vernacular artistry," singularity again was fetishized. That is, a one-to-one, unmediated knowledge of slave life offered "an abundance of stylized ways of acting, singing, and dancing" (142) in American popular culture. White minstrelsy in blackface did not rest once the performance was authenticated; instead, it reinforced a singular expression of what Joel Williamson describes as an organic society in which African Americans were considered and treated as innately incapable of operating beyond a social sphere of servitude and, ironically, the aping of the master class.

In opposition to this is the multiplicity of performatively engaged, metaphorically enacted *texts* worked into the slaves' performances during corn-shucking events (and elsewhere). When we read William Cullen Bryant's reminiscence of a post-corn-shucking celebration in which the "commander," called on to speak after dinner, confesses "his incapacity for public speaking," and in turn asks "a huge black man named Toby to address the company in his stead," we see a non-musical but nonetheless performative actionality that draws on numerous discourses. Toby, Bryant writes,

> came forward, demanded a piece of paper to hold in his hand, and harangued the soldiery. It was evident that Toby had listened to stump-speeches in his day. He spoke of "de majority of Sous Carolina," "de interests of de state," "de honor of ole Ba'nwell district," and these phrases he connected by various expletives and sounds of which we could make nothing. (qtd. in Abrahams 225)

From the "piece of paper" Toby "demanded," to his "political" discourse, Bryant can see nothing *coherent*, perhaps because of the "various expletives," etc. In any case, Toby appears not to have tried exact replication of any *specific* stump speech; rather, he used the tone and the pose and the props. In other words, this metaphoric enactment makes Thomas Porcello's map of the digital sampler's functions, "the mimetic/reproductive, the manipulative[,] and the extractive" (69), begin to look like an ahistorical overview of African American aesthetics rather than a comment on postmodern technology. I would add to Porcello's analysis the constant element of simultaneity. Distinguishing between mimesis and the actional uses of that process—that is, manipulation and extraction of one's stylized signature—is difficult, if not impossible.

Following the corn-shucking competition, slaves and guests—those who *worked* and those who *watched*, respectively—were treated by the plantation master to a large feast at which the captain of the winning team would make a speech, and following the feast the slaves, again, would become the spectacle. With the setting up of a platform dance floor, the entertainment began. Wood below the slaves' feet kept up the "multimetrical effects" (93) that were, Abrahams suggests, a pervasive presence throughout the dancing and music making, from "patting" to the ring shout. While patting (clapping) "created a field of rhythm in which each performer respond[ed] to a basic beat," it did so in an asymmetrically harmonious fashion: "By doubling or tripling the time, breaking each beat into doublets or triplets, a performer produced a rolling effect that played against the master pulse without necessitating an actual change in the basic meter" (95).

Abrahams further locates the "apart playing" of the dances which white planters watched from the distance of the owner's gaze. With the dancer's hips as the "center of gravity," there was division and cohesion, paradoxically engaged at once: "Thus the flexibility and fluidity of black dancing arises from the division of the body at the pelvis, with the upper body playing against the lower much as individual dancers or singers playfully oppose themselves to the rest of the performing community" (98–99). This bodily intertextuality, under the gaze of the planter class, presented a much more communally fluid aesthetic, contrary to "European social dancing," in which "the body is maintained as a single unit of behavior" (98).[4] The overlapping is multi-directional, with the body functioning similarly to the grouped voices.

The body in hip hop is again foregrounded, with the solid thumping of the backbeat speaking directly to the flexibility necessary to negotiate what Tricia Rose calls "the complex web of institutional policing to which all rappers are subject" (276). The contestation over "public space" Rose discusses was initiated in the early eighties with break dancing and the renegotiation of urban space to include the bodily appropriation of prerecorded music. Subsequent escalation of musics tailored specifically for breaking widened hip hop's appeal, as did the appropriative use of recognizable pop fragments which "hooked" listeners. Rose argues that the very musical signifiers, both samples and raps, that evoke comparisons to animalism in white mainstream journalism carry "the power of Black collective memory," which initiates the automaticity of the body's appropriation of the digital sounds. These " … cultural markers, and responses to them are," Rose asserts, "in a sense 'automatic' because they immediately conjure Black collective experience" (286). From the outlandish space costumes Sun Ra and his various Arkestras sported over the decades from the 1950s to the 1990s, to the space age rhetoric and massive stage shows of George Clinton's Parliament in the 1970s, to the current streamlined (and newly mass-marketed) hip hop style, the body has been vital as a locus within and around which theorizing performance occurs.

Commonly working in tandem with the "cultural markers" of sampling in hip hop is the thump of the sampled bass/rhythm line, that beat which signals the automaticity of the body's appropriation of digital sound. Repetition supplies a groove within which the rap can be executed and to which the audience can dance. Balanced against deep bass repetitions are the variations which other sampled material (and the rap) supplies. This complex sonic arrangement has an important analog in Chernoff's drumming experiences: "In essence, if rhythmic complexity is the African alternative to harmonic complexity, then the repetition of *responsive* rhythms is the African alternative to the development of a melodic line" (55).

It may be a tired story at this point,[5] but it is important to explicate briefly the re-emergence of a cross-roads aesthetics—where performance merges, balances, and elaborates rhythmic complexity and "the repetition of responsive rhythms" with renewed fluidity in what would become hip hop. Houston Baker quotes Jazzy Jay from a June 19, 1988, *Village Voice* article:

> "We'd find these beats, these heavy percussive beats, that would drive the hip hop people on the dance floor to breakdance. A lot of times it would be a two-second spot, a drum beat, a drum break, and we'd mix that back and forth, extend it, make it twenty minutes long." ("Hybridity" 199)

Baker's genealogy of hip hop ("the Rap Race," as he calls it) reaches back to DeeJay Kool Herc, a Jamaican national who came to New York in 1967 and brought with him the Jamaican dance hall/recording techniques of "dub" and "talk over," formative aesthetic techniques that have explosively invigorated popular culture in the United States.

In a 1991 essay on hip hop, Elizabeth Wheeler argues that "fragmentation and reassembly describe both black music and black history" (199). In light of this "fragmentation" Dick Hebdige's vague, early 1960s, "One day" reassembly-genealogy-scenario of dub and talk-over offers this portrait of then-producer King Tubby "working in his studio mixing a few 'specials' (i.e. exclusive recordings)":

> He began fading out the instrumental track, to make sure that the vocals sounded right. And he was excited by the effect produced when he brought the music back in. So ... he cut back and forth between the vocal and instrumental tracks and played with the bass and treble ... until he changed the original tapes into something else entirely. (83)

From the studio, with the knobs and controls close by, it is but a transference of technology to the live dance hall and eventually the New York "disco," where performative reassembly happens live. In a 1973 article "The Impact of Technology on Rhythm and Blues," April Reilly points out with some trepidation that

> authorities of the music industry have observed that modern music has become more and more "the creature of the control room and less the documentation of a musical event." As a result, we have for the first time in history the phenomenon of "a musical entity being created that has its first existence on tape." *The tape is, indeed, the performance.* (140)

Indeed Reilly's comment that, in the late '50s and early '60s, " ... the live-performance concert was the occasion that offered the audience the opportunity to appreciate the music, skills, and talents of the R&B artist" (140) specifies an historical era at the tail end of two decades which Ronald L. Morris points out had seen a 40 percent decline in "night club and dance hall dates" (192).[6] While Reilly says that the "live concert of yesteryear was a total theatrical experience, as distinguished from the primarily listening experience that it is today" (141), the work of King Tubby, et al. turned a static product into fluid process.

Rather than succumb to an industry specification for a product that would relegate live performances to promotional support for a recent release, DJs and performers picked up the variation-prompt. Houston Baker says,

> Why listen—the early hip hop DJs asked—to an entire commercial disc if the disc contained only twenty (or two) seconds of worthwhile sound? Why not work that sound by having two copies of the same disc on separate turntables, moving the sound on the two tables in DJ-orchestrated patterns, creating thereby a worthwhile sound? The result was an indefinitely extendable, varied, reflexively signifying hip hop sonics. ("Hybridity" 200)[7]

Greg Tate illustrates the transformation thus: "The advent of hip hop can be said to have contributed ... radical acts of counterinsurgency, turning a community of passive pop consumers into one of creative ... producers" (154).

Production, in the sense Tate uses the term, also refers literally to an economic process which has allowed numerous African American performing artists and aesthetic improvisationalists to earn a living, to work profitably, successfully, and critically, often by utilizing Porcello's "previously tabooed modes of citation" (82).

Working the turntables, Public Enemy's Chuck D insists, is not far removed from the lofty plateau of *musicianship*, from which sampling is often looked down upon as unoriginal:

... when Terminator X rocks the beat back and forth, it gives the music a real feel, almost like playing real drums.... You gotta understand that when the deejay cuts the record in and out, it's almost like a live drummer's kick.... Deejays like Jeff or X are able to play the turntables like somebody else might play the guitar.... If you strum a guitar or play the keys, the real creativity lies in your ability to make those strings or those keys do something original. (Dery, "Public Enemy" 85–86)

The turntable places the record at the center of the hip hop performance, turning the notion of musical virtuosity on its head by using prerecorded material not only as rhythm but also as melody and harmony. The questions of authorship, musicianship, "creativity," and "originality" are, thus, problematized. Like the purveyors of African American improvisational jazz, whether bebop or the so-called "new thing" of the 1960s and onward, hip hop artists have to negotiate the charge of being labeled musically unfit. They do so with the aid of the growing complexities of sampling.

It is this re-cognition of the multiform possibilities for records that makes hip hop, ultimately, what Houston Baker calls a "massive archiving" ("Hybridity" 200). The hip hop archive serves as a miniaturized repository for vast interactive historical material—interactive because all archival material is handled by the archivist, who listens carefully (with Du Boisian "second sight") for the beats and snippets which will accompany and be accompanied by vocalized narrative. The pro-active artistic process which utilizes and makes *functional* what is heard backdrops hip hop from start to finish.[8] Indeed, the fascination with sounds of myriad shapes, pitches, and durations that characterizes the Chicago avant-garde continuum (including Henry Threadgill, the Art Ensemble of Chicago, Anthony Braxton, et al.) ups the aesthetic ante considerably for African American musical aesthetics overall, serving to "archive" an immeasurable range of sonics.[9]

The "massive archiving" Baker alludes to is also the backdrop to the various military/robber metaphors rampant throughout hip hop criticism and commentary. Like Tricia Rose, who excellently explores "the exercise of institutional and ideological control over Hip Hop and the manner in which the Hip Hop community (e.g., fans and artists) relate and respond to this context" (277), my focus here is on popular depictions of sampling, mostly in music periodicals. Ethnomusicologist Louise Meintjes argues in a 1990 essay that Paul Simon's album *Graceland* "operates as a sign which is principally interpreted by means of the notion of collaboration" (37). Listeners, Meintjes continues, go through a series of "interpretive moves" which link "formal stylistic components" to the listener's "unique set of accumulated musical and social experiences," and the preponderance of "social experiences" (49) lead to judgments based on the *social* collaboration at hand as much as, if not more than, the musical collaboration.

Sampling in hip hop is not collaboration in any familiar sense of that term. It is a high-tech and highly selective archiving, bringing into dialogue by virtue of even the most slight representation—"a short horn blast, a James Brown scream, a kick or snare drum" (Kemp 20)—any range of "voices." The transformation enacted in hip hop's "radical acts of counterinsurgency" hinge on the recording, which turns, as Tate notes, the "community of passive pop consumers into one of creative ... producers" (154). This transformation addresses Rose's tripartite summary of her concerns with the politics of hip hop: "It is not just what one says, it is where one can say it, how others react to what one says, and whether one has the means with which to command public space" (276–77). De La Soul's Posdnuos says,

We don't exclude anything from playing a part in our music. I think it's crazy how a lot of rappers are just doing the same thing over and over—Parliament/Funkadelic/James

Brown—and all that. I bought Steely Dan's *Aja* when it first came out, and "Peg" was a song I always loved, so when it came down to making my own music, that was definitely a song I wanted to use.... It doesn't make any difference whether a sample is from James Brown, Cheech and Chong, Lee Dorsey, or a TV theme; if there's something that catches my ear, I'll use it. (Dery, "Tommy" 70)

High-tech selection allows this form of archiving/orchestration to act similarly, albeit in a different context of virtuosity, to the various jazz "archivings" often read and re-read by critics and historians. So we have the ever-pivotal bebop evoked by Q-Tip, on A Tribe Called Quest's *The Low End Theory*:

> Back in the days when I was a teenager
> before I had status and before I had a pager
> you could find the abstract by listenin' to hip hop.
> My pops used to say it reminded him of bebop.
> I said well Daddy don't you know that things go in cycles.

The mention of bebop is fitting, because the conscious and often referred to selectivity of pop tunes and chord structures which took flight in the 1940s and '50s does, indeed, look like hip hop—of course in proportion to the technology available. Indeed jazz lexicographer Robert S. Gold locates one of the earliest uses of the term *lick* in popular music criticism in a 1932 *Melody Maker* article: "They manage to steal a 'lick' from an American record" (188–89). References to African American musical aesthetics and their relationships to "American" products have consistently relied on theft to dismiss or explain these aesthetics.

Musicologist James Patrick's 1975 essay "Charlie Parker and Harmonic Sources of Bebop Composition: Thoughts on the Repertory of New Jazz in the 1940s" brought briefly to jazz discourse, "by analogy to text substitution in medieval music," the term *melodic contrafact* (3). The contrafact is an expropriated piece of another tune, brought in as the basis for the composition/performance at hand. It is not always localizable as its own entity, however:

> ... many contrafact compositions derive at least in part from solo improvisations on well-known tunes and the blues. In general there are two possibilities. The original solo line (or a close variant) may appear as part of a composition either in its original (or similar) harmonic context or in a completely different harmonic context. The original material may often be nothing more than a pet phrase which becomes formalized as an incipit of a contrafact composition. (7)[10]

The bebop use of contrafact harmonies cannot really be isolated except insofar as players of the era perfected their playing in small ensembles outside regular gigs but always within earshot of the emerging ubiquity of recognizable popular music.

Dizzy Gillespie points out that "when we borrowed from a standard we added and substituted so many chords that most people didn't know what song we really were playing" (Gillespie and Fraser, 209). Many players, though, put a more ideological spin on their doings. With the move "downtown" in the New York jazz crucible of the 1940s, players had to accommodate requests and the (white) desire to be entertained in a familiar fashion. Max Roach says,

> When we got downtown, people wanted to hear something they were familiar with, like "How High the Moon," "What Is This Thing Called Love?" Can you play that? So in playing these things, the black musicians recognized that the royalties were going back to these people, like ASCAP, the Jerome Kerns, the Gershwins. So one revolutionary thing that

happened, they began to write parodies on the harmonic structures.... If I have to play it, I will put my own particular melody on that progression.... If you made a record, you could say, "This is an original." (Gillespie and Fraser 209)

The statement *This is an original* points handily and dually to the issue of technological dissemination and the treatment generally afforded what became, by virtue of dissemination, communal knowledge.

Roach's enthusiasm for his appropriation of previously copyrighted music is, of course, shortsighted on the level of legal ownership. However, communal knowledge has perhaps always been the basis for selectivity and appropriative utility in African American aesthetics. Lawrence Levine quotes Newman White from his 1928 *American Negro Folksongs*:

> The notes of the songs in my whole collection, show nothing so clearly as the tendency of Negro folk-song to pick up material from any source and, by changing it or using it in all sorts of combinations, to make it definitely its own. (196)

I quote this passage not to equate bop or hip hop with White's version of "Negro folk-song," but rather to illustrate further and historicize the question of originality and ownership vis-à-vis communal knowledge.[11]

Communal knowledge in the 1990s initiates a discussion of issues like intellectual property rights. Currently, hip hop artists like EPMD credit those works they have digitally sampled in this fashion: "This recording *embodies* portions of the recording and composition 'The Message' by Grand Master Flash and the Furious Five; appears courtesy of Sugar Hill Records."[12] Embodiment and its physical implications intensify Newman White's confounded observations of performative appropriations of communal knowledge. While exactitude is mandatory contemporaneously, James Patrick, when faced with a specific Dizzy Gillespie solo figure reminiscent of Louis Armstrong, could assert that "it is ... likely that these phrases and thousands of others were simply 'in the air' and had become associated with familiar harmonic contexts" (10).

This "in the air" ubiquity of phrases and progressions is not simply an historical product of the phonograph or other technology, just as sampling is not simply an historical product of the digital technology now widely available. The propensity for selective expropriation, for the dually directed evocative prompt, gains more and more exposure as time goes on. This propensity in the African American musical text is akin to the blues singer whose power is in the "anonymous (nameless) voice issuing from the black (w)hole" which "comprises the 'already said' of Afro-America" (Baker, *Blues* 5, 206). Traces of the "original" are lost in translation, whether digitally sampled or instrumentally improvised. Technology serves and has served well the dissemination of important aesthetic elements. Levine points out that "Negroes living far apart could now share not only styles, but experiences, attitudes, folk wisdom, expressions, in a way ... simply not possible before the advent of the phonograph" (231). Contrary to April Reilly's fear of the rise of industrial technology in music production, Levine contends that " ... records can be seen as bearers and preservers of folk traditions" (231).[13]

The evolution of American popular culture happens with African American culture at its hub. The popularity of *authentic* entertainment in African American idioms would become highly prevalent in the early twentieth century.[14] What needs to be looked at and looked for in the future is the *theorizing* Barbara Christian discusses. From slavery days to emancipation to the early-to-mid twentieth century, the musico-social collaborations between African American aesthetics and available texts become variously more obvious and more oblique. With digital sampling, expropriated material is (often minutely and momentarily) recognizable, yet placed so that it often sounds radically anomalous, especially when the sampled material is overlapped or layered.

Porcello quotes a 1988 *Billboard* magazine article from which he draws on record producers who "have often claimed that rap records using [sampling] techniques are simply pioneering a new phase in popular music's already extensive history of recycling source material" (72). This recycling stands historically situated at an aesthetic/economic crossroads still of great importance today. Hip hop sampling has a disseminative function which tends to be ignored, especially if we refer to the sample as *recycling* and be done with it. Public Enemy's Chuck D. says,

> "Our music is filled with bites, bits of information from the real world, a world that's rarely exposed. Our songs are almost like headline news. We bring things to the table of discussion that are not usually discussed, or at least not from that perspective." (Dery, "Public Enemy" 93)

In no way do I want to *equate* any two aesthetic expressions, but historically such cultivations of discursive space have been constant and constantly a function of available resources. The contingencies of historical situations resist, I think, any dismissals which often attend associations with general pop culture.

Nearly 175 years ago these cultivations of discursive space were the central focus of a growing (white) authenticating impulse that spawned an *imitative* popular culture. African American musical aesthetics are historically little concerned with the exactitude of *imitation*. The "massive archiving" Houston Baker insists on is centrally present as a highly selective aesthetic/economic/historical catalog. Regarding his drumming in Ghana John Miller Chernoff says,

> In more than one sense, music carries the mark of tradition to an occasion, and at a rudimentary level it thus signifies the traditional solidarity of a community; but aesthetically, the music involves people with their community in a more dynamic way, thus recreating the tradition, and … the nature of this involvement is the key to understanding the integrative power of the music. (125)

So the massive archiving stands to signify and theorize communality. With sampling technology, this solidarity may be the aim, but issues of authenticity, ownership, and property seem part and parcel of high-tech aesthetic exercises. And as the disjuncture seen by some in hip hop sampling indicates to them the fragmentation of post-modernity, there is a simultaneous inability to see the *act's* vibrant connectedness in historical relation to African American aesthetics.

Notes

1. Ishmael Reed makes this observation in a review of Harold Courlander's *Treasury of Afro-American Folklore* (152). In my own work, I rarely see any mention of Lovell's *Black Song*.
2. Abrahams (91–92) alludes to Robert Farris Thompson's term *apart playing*, first coined in 1966.
3. Note especially that Abrahams uses *success* here rather than a valuative term like *best*, or even *noted*, to describe these writers. *Success* obviously means monetary support, and this points further to the institution of the black body/encounter as an authenticating force in whose presence either redemption or profit occurs.
4. Zora Neale Hurston points out that adornment, asymmetry, and angularity are key polyphonic features of African American art and that African American dance not only incorporates these elements but acts as a "realistic suggestion" in light of the fact that "no art can ever express all the variations conceivable" (56).

5. Several good histories of hip hop and rap exist, the best of which, *Rap Attack*, is authored by David Toop and comes in two volumes. The examples that follow are more useful for their hemeneutics than is Toop's study—thus its absence.

6. Morris quotes a *Time* magazine story on the American Federation of Musicians from May 7, 1956, that used 1930 as a "base year" with "99,000 live dates open to musicians.... by 1954 only 59,000 night club and dance hall dates were available, a decline of 40% in two decades" (192).

7. The importance here of a "reflexively signifying" aesthetic is at the heart of hip hop and its aesthetic continuum. Baker's juxtaposition of this concept with the phrase indefinitely extendable needs clarification, perhaps, precisely because the "commercial disc" relies so much on indefinito extendability as a marketing device.

8. As an indication of the "massiveness" of the hip hop archive, Mark Dery says Public Enemy DJ/producer Hank Shocklee estimates his record collection at "nearly 19,000 records" ("Hank" 83).

9. For more on this, see Lock, Radano, and Wilmer.

10. The presence of "pet phrases" is central to the modes of collaboration, both social and musical, present throughout jazz history. Leonard and, later, Ogren discuss these interactions and collaborations in jazz's formative years, with soloists who would themselves become icons for later generations of players.

11. Royalties and credits have always ridden alongside the controversies over the explicitness of rap, but in a more muted "high legal" discourse which seeks to curtail hip hop artists' use of the sampler.

12. Liner notes to EPMD's "Nobody's Safe Chump," *Business Never Personal*.

13. For more on expropriation in jazz, see Gabbard.

14. See Ogren for further discussion here, especially of the growing nostalgia evident in club settings (The Plantation Club, Club Alabam, etc.).

Works Cited

Abrahams, Roger D. *Singing the Master: The Evolution of African American Culture in the Plantation South*. New York: Pantheon, 1992.

Baker, Houston A. Jr. *Blues, Ideology, and Afro-American Literature: A Vernacular Theory*. Chicago: U of Chicago P, 1987.

———. "Hybridity, the Rap Race, and Pedagogy for the 1990s." *Technoculture*. Ed. Constance Penley and Andrew Ross. Minneapolis: U of Minnesota P, 1991. 197–209.

Chernoff, John Miller. *African Rhythm and African Sensibility: Aesthetics and Social Action in African Musical Idioms*. Chicago: U of Chicago P, 1979.

Christian, Barbara. "The Race for Theory." *Making Face, Making Soul (Haciendo Caras): Creative and Critical Writings by Feminists of Color*. Ed. Gloria Anzaldua. San Francisco: Aunt Lute, 1990. 335–45.

Coplan, David. "The Urbanization of African Music." *Popular Music 2: Theory and Method*. Cambridge: Cambridge UP, 1982. 113–29.

Costello, Mark, and David Foster Wallace. *Signifying Rappers: Rap and Race in the Urban Present*. New York: Ecco, 1990.

Courlander, Harold. *Negro Folk Music U.S.A.* New York: Columbia UP, 1963.

Dery, Mark. "Hank Shocklee: Bomb Squad Declares War on Music." *Keyboard* Sept. 1990. 82–96.

———. "Public Enemy: Confrontation." *Keyboard* Sept. 1990. 81–96.

———. "Tommy Boy X 3: Digital Underground, Coldcut, and De La Soul Jam the Beat with Audio Junkyard Collisions." *Keyboard* Mar. 1991. 64–78.

Du Bois, W. E. B. *The Souls of Black Folk*. 1903. New York: Penguin, 1989.

Ellington, Duke. *Music Is My Mistress*. New York: Doubleday, 1973.

Gabbard, Krin. "The Quoter and His Culture." *Jazz in Mind: Essays on the History and Meanings of Jazz*. Ed. R. T. Buckner and Steven Weiland. Detroit: Wayne State UP, 1991, 92–111.

Genovese, Eugene D. *Roll, Jordan, Roll: The World the Slaves Made*. New York: Pantheon, 1974.

Gillespie, Dizzy, and Al Fraser. *To BE, or not to ... BOP*. New York: Doubleday, 1979.

Gold, Robert S. *A Jazz Lexicon*. New York: Knopf, 1964.

Hebdige, Dick. *Cut 'N' Mix: Culture, Identity, and Caribbean Music*. London: Comedia, 1987.

Hurston, Zora Neale. "Characteristics of Negro Expression." 1935. *The Sanctified Church*. Berkeley: Turtle Island, 1983. 49–68.

Kemp, Mark. "Issue by Issue: The Death of Sampling." *Option Magazine* Mar.–Apr. 1992. 20.

Leonard, Neil. *Jazz and the White Americans*. Chicago: U of Chicago P, 1962.

Levine, Lawrence. *Black Culture and Black Consciousness: Afro-American Folk Thought from Slavery to Freedom*. Oxford: Oxford UP, 1977.

Lock, Graham. *Forces in Motion: Anthony Braxton and the Meta-Reality of Creative Music, Interviews and Tour Notes, England 1985*. London: Quartet, 1988.

Lovell, John, Jr. *Black Song: The Forge and the Flame—The Story of How the Afro-American Spiritual Was Hammered Out*. 1972. New York: Paragon House, 1986.

Meintjes, Louise. "Paul Simon's Graceland and the Mediation of Musical Meaning." *Ethnomusicology* 34.1 (1990): 37–73.

Morris, Ronald L. *Wait Until Dark: Jazz and the Underworld, 1880–1940*. Bowling Green: Bowling Green U Popular P, 1980.

Ogren, Kathy J. *The Jazz Revolution: Twenties America and the Meaning of Jazz*. New York: Oxford UP, 1989.

Patrick, James. "Charlie Parker and Harmonic Sources of Bebop Composition: Thoughts on the Repertory of New Jazz in the 1940s." *Journal of Jazz Studies* 2.2 (1975): 3–23.

Porcello, Thomas. "The Ethics of Digital Audio Sampling: Engineers' Discourse." *Popular Music* 10.1 (1991): 69–84.

Radano, Ronald. *New Musical Figurations: Anthony Braxton's Cultural Critique*. Chicago: U of Chicago P, 1993.

Reed, Ishmael. *Shrovetide in Old New Orleans*. 1978. New York: Avon, 1979.

Reilly, April. "The Impact of Technology on Rhythm and Blues." *Black Perspective in Music* 1.2 (Fall 1973): 136–46.

Rose, Tricia. "'Fear of a Black Planet': Rap Music and Black Cultural Politics in the 1990s." *Journal of Negro Education* 60.3 (1991): 276–90.

Shapiro, Nat, and Nat Hentoff. *Hear Me Talkin' to Ya: The Story of Jazz as Told by the Men Who Made It*. 1955. New York: Dover, 1966.

Sidran, Ben. *Black Talk: How the Music of Black America Created a Radical Alternative to the Values of Western Literary Tradition*. 1971. New York: Da Capo, 1981.

Tate, Greg. *Flyboy in the Buttermilk: Essays on Contemporary Music*. New York: Simon, 1992.

Thompson, Robert Farris. "An Aesthetic of the Cool: West African Dance." *African Forum* 2.2 (1966): 85–102.

Toop, David. *Rap Attack: African Jive to New York Hip Hop*. Boston: South End P, 1984.

———. *Rap Attack, Number 2: African Rap to Global Hip Hop*. London: Serpent's Tail, 1992.

Wheeler, Elizabeth. "'Most of My Heroes Don't Appear on No Stamps': The Dialogics of Rap." *Black Music Research Journal* 11.2 (1991): 193–216.

Williamson, Joel. "The Genesis of the Organic Society." *The Crucible of Race: Black-White Relations in the American South since Emancipation*. New York: Oxford UP, 1984. 11–43.

Wilmer, Valerie. *As Serious As Your Life: The Story of the New Jazz*. London: Allison & Busby, 1977.

Discography

EPMD. *Business Never Personal*. Chaos/Sony, 1992.

A Tribe Called Quest. "Excursions." *The Low End Theory*. Zomba, 1418-2-J, 1991.

31
Public Enemy:
Confrontation

Mark Dery

Elvis was a hero to most
But he never meant shit to me you see
Straight up racist that sucker was
Simple and plain
Mother fuck him and John Wayne
'Cause I'm black and proud
I'm ready and hyped plus I'm amped
Most of my heroes don't appear on no stamps
Sample a look back you look and find
Nothing but rednecks for 400 years if you check
Don't worry be happy
Was a number one jam
Damn if I say it you can slap me right here
(Get it) let's get this party started right
Right on, c'mon
What we got to say
Power to the people no delay
To make everybody see
In order to fight the powers that be

"Fight the Power" from *Fear of a Black Planet*

Bart Simpson is black. Or at least he is in New York, where black teenagers sport T-shirts depicting a dark-skinned version of the popular cartoon character, his nappy hair shaved in the razorcut "fade" favored by Arsenio Hall and homeboys everywhere. Gold tooth glinting, black Bart bellows, "I've got the power!" A legend beneath the drawing identifies him, simply, as "Radical Dude."

Bart Simpson is a radical dude for radical times. On political and economic fronts, the time-honored hegemony of the wealthy, white, gray-haired, heterosexual male is being openly challenged by an ever-expanding non-white population. In higher education, the unabashed Eurocentrism of college curricula has been called into question, while all across America suburban youth are blurring the boundaries between WASP and Afro-American subcultures.

West Coast surf punks, their blond mops teased into dreadlocks, bang their heads to Bad Brains, 24–7 Spyz, and other black thrash bands; East Coast B-boys, baseball caps cocked at just the right angle, pump black fists to 3rd Bass, Everlast, and other white rappers.

In the midst of this charged atmosphere, a militant, '60s-style Afrocentrism is on the rise. African amulets and T-shirts bearing the slogan "you wouldn't understand—It's a black thing" are popping up everywhere, the names of Marcus Garvey and Malcolm X are invoked with religious fervor, and an "I'm mad-as-Hell-and-I'm-not-going-to-take-it-anymore" attitude prevails.

Nowhere is this groundswell more evident than in hip-hop, where Niggas With Attitude (NWA), Ice-T, Schooly-D, X Clan, and other rap groups with radical agendas abound. By far the best known and best-selling of these bands is Public Enemy, the Black Panthers of rap, whose stage show includes a khaki-clad security force performing precision drills with plastic Uzis, and whose logo is a rifle's-eye view of a black man, the crosshairs of the gun trained on his chest.

Public Enemy—a loose confederation of producers, publicists, bodyguards, and demagogues centered around a core trio of rapper/rhetorical bomb thrower Chuck D (Carlton Ridenhour), rapper/prankster Flavor Flav (William Drayton), and deejay Terminator X (Norman Rogers)—call themselves "prophets of rage," and for good reason. If the fear, frustration, and fury—mostly fury—of American blacks could be distilled into something dark and deadly, corked in a bottle, and left to sit on an unwatched shelf, waiting to explode in a shower of foam and flying glass, you'd have Public Enemy. The grooves of *Yo! Bum Rush the Show*, *It Takes a Nation of Millions to Hold Us Back*, and this year's *Fear of a Black Planet* (all on Def Jam, dist. by Columbia) are haunted by the ghosts of slaves flogged to death, Southern blacks lynched on trumped-up charges of raping white women, civil rights activists killed by Klansmen, Michael Stewart beaten to death by New York City Transit Police, Michael Griffith chased into the headlights of an oncoming car in Howard Beach, and Yusef Hawkins shot in Bensonhurst.

At a time when the 15-second sound bite can bust the balls of the biggest power brokers, in a country where few radio and television stations are minority-owned, rap, as Chuck D has observed, is black America's TV station. By extension, Public Enemy is that station's most incendiary channel; setting the airwaves crackling with hortatory broadcasts such as "Countdown to Armageddon," "Don't Believe the Hype," "Rebel without a Pause," "Welcome to the Terrordome," "Anti-Nigger Machine," and "Leave This Off Your Fu*kin' Charts." In 1990, the media is all-powerful, and those who do not control it are controlled by it. Hollywood, which has traditionally portrayed blacks as Aunt Jemimas and Stepin Fetchits, still prefers the white-washed—pun intended—*Driving Miss Daisy* vision of race relations to the grittier black perspective offered by Spike Lee's *Do the Right Thing*. D's lyrics, conversely, address oppression from a black perspective.

Public Enemy's backing tracks are every bit as political as its lyrics. Part morality play, part *musique concrète*, part blueprint for the building of a mind-blowing bomb, the band's music is a noisy collage of sputtering Uzis, wailing sirens, fragments of radio and TV commentary about the band itself, and key phrases lifted from rousing speeches by famous black leaders, all riding on rhythms articulated by constantly changing drum voices. Off-kilter loops, aliased or scratchy samples, and high-pitched spiralling sounds add to the overall feeling that the listener has been airlifted into the heart of a riot.

Rap, by definition, is political music. Fabricated from stolen snatches of prerecorded music by smash-and-grab producers who frequently thumb their noses at copyright laws, it is the musical equivalent of shoplifting. Created by musical illiterates whose instruments are samplers, turntables, and wide-ranging record collections, it bum-rushes the academy, challenging the Eurocentric definition of the word "musician" and leaving graffiti all over the ivy-clad halls. To ithyphallic metalheads, fusion speedfreaks, prog rockers, and others who still worship at the altar of technical virtuosity in pursuit of itself, rap is the musical equivalent of a—forgive the pun—Black Mass. Satanists invert Christian iconography by hanging the crucifix upside down and reciting the Lord's Prayer backwards; rappers invert the natural—read "European"—order of things by stripping music of its harmonic content and supplanting it with rhythm, timbre, and boasting, bullying, wisecracking lyrics delivered in a voice that hovers between speech and song. Rap's plaster-cracking volume functions simultaneously as a metaphor for empowerment ("Today the button on my boombox, tomorrow the world") and as the artistic parallel to fingernails on a blackboard, setting establishment teeth on edge in much the same way that Bob Dylan's snotty whine or Johnny Rotten's adenoidal yawp did in earlier times. As visionary rock critic Lester Bangs noted in his essay "A Reasonable Guide to Horrible Noise," "I am firmly convinced that one reason for the popularity of rap music, like disco and punk before it, is that it's utterly annoying to those of us whose cup of blare it isn't."

All of which has insured that rap, like speed metal, hardcore, and atonal avant-gardism, has received little shelf space in mainstream retail stores and little airplay on mainstream radio. Until now, that is. Suddenly, after a decade of struggling in the shadows, rap is big business, and Public Enemy is a prime example of that success. *It Takes a Nation* sold over 800,000 copies and nailed the Number One spot on *Billboard*'s Top Black Albums chart, while *Fear* hit the platinum mark within a week of its release. Ruben Rodriguez, senior vice president of Black Music at Columbia Records, was quoted in one of that label's press releases: "What's happening with Public Enemy is unbelievable. The album is selling across the board to all demographics and nationalities."

Public Enemy was formed at Long Island's Adelphi University, where hip-hop fans and media maven Bill Stephney hosted *The Mr. Bill Show*, a rap program broadcast on WBAU, the school's student-run radio station. Graphic artist Chuck D and local party promoters Hank and Keith Shocklee signed on as deejays for the *Super Spectrum Mix Show*. Now and again, a colorful lunatic named William Drayton would stage an in-studio performance called "the claustrophobia attack." In 1986, Rick Rubin offered Stephney a position in his newly-formed all-rap label, Def Jam. Stephney threw his hat in the ring, and it wasn't long before Chuck D, Drayton, and the rest of the on-the-air deconstruction crew were signed. Released under the name Public Enemy, *Yo! Bum Rush the Show* hit the racks in 1987, and included "Public Enemy No. 1," a more-or-less authentic version of the rude, rough-edged audio collage that had first knocked WBAU listeners on their ears.

Since then, a firestorm of controversy has raged around Public Enemy, much of it sparked by the band's now-departed "Minister of Information," Professor Griff (Richard Griffin). In a May 1989 interview with the *Washington Times*, Griff opined that "the Jews are wicked. And we can prove this." He further observed that Jews are responsible for "the majority of wickedness that goes on across the globe." Liberal rock critics and Jewish leaders peppered the band with rhetorical volleys from every angle, and Griff lit out for the territories. He is now the leader of his own band, the Last Asiatic Disciples, signed to Skyywalker Records.

Like many rap bands, Public Enemy continues to be haunted by charges of anti-Semitism, misogyny, homophobia, and race hate. D espouses the teachings of Nation of Islam leader Louis Farrakhan, whose bigoted remarks about Jews scuttled Jesse Jackson's presidential campaign. The band's "Media Assassin" Harry Allen recently mailed journalists copies of *The Cress Theory of Color Confrontation and Racism (White Supremacy)*, a pamphlet full of Social Darwinist foamings about Caucasians being genetically inferior due to a lack of pigmentation. To add fuel to the fire, *Fear* features "Welcome to the Terrordome," whose machine-gunned lines "Crucifixion ain't no fiction / So-called chosen frozen / Apology made to whoever pleases / Still they got me like Jesus" seem to revive the nasty, age-old tactic of charging Jews with deicide. Then again, Chuck D has compared himself to Marcus Garvey, Nat Turner, and other historical figures; there may be nothing more sinister than a Narcissus complex in evidence here. *Fear* also contains "Meet the G That Killed Me," whose opening stanza ("Man to man / I don't know if they can / From what I know / The parts don't fit") could be construed either as gleeful gay-bashing or a forthright statement of Black Muslim teachings regarding homosexuality. In a recent *Pulse!* interview, D seemed to suggest the latter, stating flatly, "I think [homosexuality] is a violation of God's law. The original purpose of sex is reproduction, and it's a fact that a man cannot reproduce with another man—the parts don't fit."

In the final analysis, it is important to remember that while rap is political, rappers are not politicians. Like callow young men of all races, they often fall prey to macho posturing, misogyny, and xenophobia. The jury is still out on Public Enemy's politics, but one thing is certain: Their music, in its finest moments, throws the pitiless light of truth on all that is mean and venal in a country whose president rode to the Oval Office on Willie Horton's back, a country where the sanctity of the flag is the subject of impassioned debate while oil spills foul the seas and radioactive waste sullies the earth, a country where women's wombs are public property, a country where the mouth of the artist is gagged with a sticker that reads "Warning: Parental Advisory." It is the right music for wrongheaded times.

Chuck D

Rap, with its use of samplers and turntables as musical instruments, has created a new definition for the word "musician." But there are still a lot of musicians, many of them readers of this magazine, who think to themselves, "Give me a break! These guys can't even play a real instrument!" What do you say to people who condemn you for the fact that your creativity lies in areas that much of the academic musical community refuses to recognize as musical?

Well, it's almost like somebody trying to tell you about intelligence. How can you measure intelligence when people are gifted in so many areas? This is one particular area that, sonically, creates an impression, demands a response, and for that reason requires a certain skill. I mean, if a conventional musician saw a guy like Jazzy Jeff on the turntables—man, he's a musician if there ever was one! And when Terminator X rocks the beat back and forth, it gives the music a real feel, almost like playing real drums, you know what I'm saying? You gotta understand that when the deejay cuts that record in and out, it's almost like a live drummer's kick. In fact, the first thing you hear usually is a kick, and the backcue is usually a snare sound. Deejays like Jeff or X are able to play the turntables just like somebody else might play the guitar. These guys make an art out of what they're doing, taking that basic sound and making it do strange new things. If you strum a guitar or play the keys, the real creativity lies in your ability to make those strings or those keys do something original. And I think the ability of myself and Hank [Shocklee] and the rest of our production team is to arrange individual sounds into a pattern, each one complementing the other to create something that's a driving force.

There's always been an element of syncopation in black music, from African village music with its ever-present shekeres to Jimi Hendrix with his wah-wah pedal. Aren't rap deejays just replacing those thousand-year-old shakers?

Exactly! But it can be anybody in the production team who adds that extra bit of percussion, that extra bit of drive. People who listen to black music listen to different songs in different ways, like some people might be moving to the bass line, some might be moving to that kick drum, some people might be moving to something inside the music—a pulse that's just driving them. So people listen to music in different ways, and that should be acknowledged and respected. When we put together our music, we try to put together layers that complement each other, and then the voice tries to complement that, and the theme tries to complement that, and then the song itself tries to complement the album as a whole, fitting into the overall context. There's all kinds of little intricate parts. It's not just what people perceive to be a standard type of groove. Sometimes a vocal sample can move the groove along. Soul and funk are a lot of things; they can just be the way somebody's speaking, you know what I'm saying?

We work with a lot of computers and drum machines and digital instruments, so it's important that we play as much of the music in manually as we can. Also, fuck-ups are not bad. Like, our first record, "Public Enemy No. 1" [from *Yo! Bum Rush the Show*] was something that you just could not program, because when I made that tape, I made it off of two cassette decks, splicing part of this record. A couple of the splices were off, but the rap over it was on. The loop wasn't perfect: You might hear the beat jump and shit like that. But when I did the rhyme over it, the rhyme was perfect, the rhyme being controlled by the rhymer, who can kind of ride the bumps. It gives it more of a natural feel, like an imperfect drummer was behind him. That's what made the soul and funk come out of it. Now, when we reworked for the album, we programmed a new loop, and it just didn't feel the same, so we started doing it manually, and that's what kept that same ethic, you know? And in "Rebel without a Pause" [from *It Takes a Nation of Millions to Hold Us Back*], we programmed that weird screechy sound. It was sampled to have a clean sound, and it just didn't feel right, so we cut the amount of time in that siren sample, redid it with, like, a two-bit sampling rate, which made it really gritty-sounding, almost unpresentable, and then we looped that at a point where it was kind of imperfect. That's what made the record have more soul, have more funk.

That's an interesting point, that dirt equals funkiness.
Well, I think the arrangement of a song is what makes a sound, clean or dirty, funky. Sometimes you've got a funky groove, but if the vocals don't ride it right, it takes the funk away. But funk is something that I don't think you can really put a finger on, you gotta feel it.

How conscious was the injection humor, through Flavor Flav, into your music? Public Enemy's message is very heavy, the music is very hard, and he seems to save it at times from crumpling under its own weight.
Exactly. He's like lubrication to the whole machine. He adds that looseness—or, at least, that *perception* of looseness, know what I'm saying? He keeps it from being so serious, keeps it from being like straight vodka with no chaser. It's the chaser that makes it lighter, easier for people to handle. That's necessary when you're trying to get something across. I mean, the types of teachers I liked when I was in school were those who were teaching you but, at the time, they weren't *tight*, you know what I'm saying? The classes where I learned the most were the ones that were just boom, boom, boom, where the teacher would get funny a couple of times and the class would get to the point where you'd start losing yourself. So I think that looseness helps the music.

Also, the key is that when you speak about oppression from a black point of view, you're able to come up with all kinds of things that are not presented in today's media—things that are just as new to black America as they are to white America. Logically laying out of a situation so that you can throw out a solution is good, but also just throwing the problems up there on the board inspires people to come up with their own solutions. One of the things that makes Public Enemy different from the Clash or anybody else before is that this stuff is so straight up and real, to the point where we're just saying, "Yo, man, what the fuck is up?" and any black man on the block, 18 to 25, will know what we're talking about. It's only been spoken about, up 'til now, by people behind pulpits and lecterns—people like Marc Garvey, Malcolm X, Martin Luther King, Huey Newton of the Black Panther party. But none of those energetic, exciting personalities expanded into the area of music, so we decided to do that.

You've often said that Public Enemy is one of the first artists to fuse radical politics with black music. But what about the Last Poets, or Gil-Scott Heron?

The thing about the Last Poets and Gil-Scott Heron is that they were into a jazz-type approach, doing poetry over a beat. When rap music came along, it was poetry over a beat too, but *in time*. More important than the Last Poets or Gil-Scott Heron, to us, was James Brown. His record, "Say It Loud, I'm Black and I'm Proud" [available on *Billboard's Top R&B Hits*, Rhino] had the most impact because it was danceable and yet you still thought about it. What really influenced me and other rappers was guys like Kool Herc, Afrika Bambaataa, Grandmaster Flash, Eddie Cheeba, and D.J. Hollywood, because they kept the rhythm happening, you know what I'm saying? They rocked the groove, and the groove was funk and soul, which was different from jazz.

See, rap comes from the idea of a deejay working a party. A lot of our decisions are still based on that structure. We figure the thing that makes people really respond is changes in beats-per-minute. At one time, most of the rap music coming out was around 99 to 102 beats per minute, and that's what made us do "Bring the Noise" [from *It Takes a Nation* ...], where we jetted it up to 109. On *It Takes a Nation* ... a lot of things were even higher, and we changed the whole approach to rap by putting a different rhyme style over it. We tried to make that album like Marvin Gaye's "Let's Get It On" in a fast, hectic rhythm. Then once we'd established that pattern, everybody followed Young MC and all those guys started getting up there. So with *Fear of Black Planet*, we decided, "Well, if everything's going to be *this* way now, we'll go *that* way!" And things slowed down.

When Public Enemy hit the scene, hip hop was dominated by rappers—L.L. Cool J, Run-D.M.C.—who used these 4/4 hard rock beats with Billy Squier and AC/DC crunch chords dropped in the pocket. You guys introduced this shuffling, eight-note feel. Where did that come from?

Well, you know, if it hadn't been for Run-D.M.C. setting a precedent, there wouldn't be no Public Enemy. Run-D.M.C. is the phenomenon of the '80s. They were *it*. This was way before the Steve Tyler thing [*i.e.*, Run D.M.C.'s collaboration with Aerosmith on "Walk This Way"], which was really kind of an aftermath. I'm talking about how they came into rap music with a different approach, one that magnified the power of the beat, the rhythm behind their rapping, where as before the whole thing was just about rhymes. Run-D.M.C. had the power and the yelling and the rage on top of it, riding it which made you just say, "Damn, this shit is controlling me!" That just crossed over out of the black community. "Sucker MCs" and "Rock Box" [from *Run-D.M.C.*], even without the guitar, transcended, because the beat was strong and the rhythm was strong and the image they projected was hard and black: "This is what we're about, we're only into this, and we don't give a fuck if you into this or not because we're having a damn good time and we believe in what we're doing!" Their records made people look at rap and say, "Well, that's some legit shit!"

It's almost as if rap became rock at that point, because before that, it was really a subcategory of disco. Early rappers, like Kurtis Blow and Grandmaster Flash, used backing tracks that sounded very much like disco.

Well, in 1977 and '78, the New York clubs were playing disco, which was the type of records the record companies were making, and the B-boys who were trying to find different grooves would rock what they had. Some of the other stuff they had was music from the early- and mid-'70s; they would rock those, and those would become the classics—Kool & the Gang, tunes from the Stax era, Thin Lizzy, Aerosmith, the incredible Bongo Band, all that stuff. The guys in the Bronx were looking for *beats*, you know? But when the record companies came around in 1979, their whole thing was coming up with a band that would emulate some of that New York era where guys were rhyming on top of disco beats, so you never really heard the actual beat up front. I remember when Run-D.M.C. first came out—we were some of the first people to play it, on our radio show—and

I remember saying, "This is the shit we was looking for." The beats was *large*. Before that, rap music had the beat and the bass line way in the back.

You mentioned your WBAU show. What was that like?
We did so many innovative things. For example, we used to mix our program under the emcees. Not rhyming emcees, but personality jocks who read off dedications and live commentary with hectic scratching underneath it. We developed it into an art so that we would find a hole in the music where we was able to talk, and then when we stopped talking it would just increase and get more hectic. It's the only time I've ever heard of anybody doing this, and it was an exciting period because each one of those radio shows could have been a record.

Isn't that what you're doing now—making radio shows on your records, with samples flying out of the wings and people screaming over the songs?
Right. We try to make records with something happening every second, from beginning to end. We try not to leave any space between songs on our albums. It's taboo. If you're listening to something for an hour, it's almost like listening to the radio, and on the radio, dead air cancels you out. You've got to do something with the dead air. When I buy a tape and I play it and there's dead air between the songs, that dead air is telling me to take that tape off, so my finger automatically goes to the eject button and I put another tape in. I don't want to give people that subliminal command to eject, because an eject is a reject, you know what I'm saying? You gotta make them listen to the whole side. So since our first album, that's always been our format.

Is your whole approach defined by any sort of production philosophy?
Well, our whole thing in making rap music that's innovative involves all three steps: recording it, mastering it, pressing it, always making sure that it's *loud*. *Fear of a Black Planet* didn't play loud enough in the first shipments; somebody in the plant turned it down, unauthorized, because he thought the type of tape it was on would break up. You know, that's a problem with our music: Some of the people in the plants are old and they're thinking technically, but technical is not really the case in point when it comes to this type of music.

What is the case in point?
That it's *loud*! It doesn't have to be clear; it just gots to be boomin'! A good 80% of the people who listen to rap music listen to it with their car systems all the way up. You gotta understand when you talk about rap music that this whole thing revolves around a car mentality. A lot of these guys got them fat speakers in the back, and they want to turn that shit up and hear those back speakers go *booooommm*. Sometimes guys turn the bass *all* the way up, like they do in Miami or Atlanta or New Orleans, and they won't even hear no words—just *booooommm*.

One thing that's helped us is that we study different regions in rap. Rap has different feels and different vibes in different parts of the country. For example, people in New York City don't drive very often, so New York used to be about walking around with your radio. But that doesn't really exist anymore. It became unfashionable because some people were losing their *lives* over them, and also people didn't want to carry them, so now it's more like, "Hey, I've got my Walkman." For that reason, there's a treble type of thing going on; they're not getting too much of the bass. So rap music in New York City is a headphone type of thing, whereas in Long Island or Philadelphia, where in order to get anywhere you gotta drive so people have cars by the time they're 16 or 17 years old, rap is more like, "Well, I got my speakers in my car and I'm turning my sound all the way up." It's more of a bass type of thing. In some cities, they're into Jeeps now. In the West, in L.A., they're into low riders—big cars you can put a four-way system in, with speakers in the front doors and in back, so that it becomes more of a wraparound sound. I know it sounds crazy, but this is some shit that's probably being explained for the first time.

How did your knowledge of all these different regional preferences affect your mix of Fear of a Black Planet?

I try to write a lot of different songs for different regions, using those regional sounds. "Power to the People" represents the sound of the Southeastern part of the United States, with that fast-paced [Roland TR-] 808-based feel—a Miami type of electro-boogie groove, a "Planet Rock" type of thing, which they're still into down there. The BPM is somewhere around 125. It uses a different rhyme style than most hip-hop. "Brothers Gonna Work It Out" has a more funky movement; it's more New Yorky. "Anti-Nigger Machine" is basically New York because it has a bass twang in it and it's more laid back; it's a sinister soul type of groove. "Burn Hollywood Burn" is a typical, upbeat, *It Takes a Nation* type of thing, which would appeal to all areas because it's so fast.

What is the BPM threshold for rap? Will we ever hear somebody rapping over hardcore or speed-metal rhythms?

Well, "War at 33–1/3" [from *Fear of a Black Planet*] is at 128 beats per minute which is the fastest thing I've ever rapped to, rapping right on top of the beat. I wanted to do something around 155, but it would have gotten to a point where it was just crazy. The lyrics are flying by so fast, you can't even figure out what I'm saying, even though I work at saying every single word clearly. It's important that people understand the words because what we're saying means something.

How was "Contract on the World Love Jam," that bizarre little sound collage on Fear of a Black Planet, *constructed?*

A lot of the samples on "Contract" came from me taping radio stations, taking bites of interviews and commercials. Sometimes I might go through the dial, just sampling at random, keeping it on a cassette, listen to the cassette, and say, "Well, being that I'm the lyric writer, how should I arrange these fragments so they'll add up to a kind of a song?" That's how "Contract" came along.

A lot of the time, Eric "Vietnam" Sadler, Hank [Shocklee], Keith [Shocklee], and I will be hanging, and I might be playing records, and we'll take some bites and put them together and construct a groove. We've used the [E-mu] SP-12 and the Akai S900 a lot, of course. We just started using a Macintosh for certain things—tailoring samples and sequencing. I can't tell you much about it because that's Eric's and Keith's department.

The interesting thing about "Contract" is that it's not really propelled by the usual hammering groove: It sloshes and slops all over the place, like waterlogged musique concrète. When you put it on the record as the opener, weren't you worried that some B-boys out in the 'burbs would say, "Man, what is this noise?"

Naww, we never get worried, 'cause there's nothing to get worried about except bad health. We just said, "This is a new approach." At the same time, I know that things like that can't be over a minute and a half, two minutes; they have to be short, and they have to lead violently into something that's moving and funky in the mode that rap fans would except. That's why you hear the voice say, "There is something changing on the face of this planet today: Public Enemy," *bam, bam, bam,* samples coming up, and then bam!, right into the jam, almost like four passes and a slam dunk. If it doesn't do that, you'd lose 'em on the album.

We approach every record like it was a painting. Sometimes, on the sound sheet, we have to have a separate sheet just to list the samples for each track. We used about 150, maybe 200 samples on *Fear of a Black Planet*. "Fight the Power" has, like, 17 samples in the first ten seconds. For example, there's three different drum loops that make one big drum loop: One is a standard Funkadelic thing, another is a Sly thing, and I think the third one is the Jacksons. Then we took some sounds from a beat box. The opening lick is the end of a Trouble Funk record, processed with doubling and reverb. And the chorus is music going backwards.

Our music is all about samples in the right area, layers that pile on each other. We put loops on top of loops on top of loops, but then in the mix we cut things away. To get them in time, we hear the basic groove on the SMPTE or the sync pattern and just line them up. It's just like mixing records. Eric and Keith or Hank will have a basic track where they'll already have hunted out the snare sounds, the bass sounds, the hi-hat sounds, and then we construct it from that point, arranging it, overdubbing 30-second samples and bits of tracks.

Being that I'm the lyric writer, I have to come up with something that will correspond with these particular tracks. Sometimes, of course, the words come first. I'll come up with a point of view or a title, then I search for a track or a beat that will fit that title, and then I'll write the lyrics because I have that point of view already laid out. But the title always comes first. That way, you know where you're going: It helps me to key on a theme, even though it might not be used in the song. You're going to Pittsburgh, you gotta get a map, right?

On a more philosophical plane, do you think that rap is the rebel music of '90s youth, white or black?
Rap is a new way of communicating, and I think the message rappers are communicating is opening up a lot of eyes and ears. Is it rebel music? Well, the thing that makes rap alarming to some people is that it's coming from a different perspective. There's a lot of young white guys around the country who are saying, "Hey, the type of individual I'd most like to be like is Ice Cube [of Niggas With Attitude] or Run [of Run-D.M.C.]." That's what makes it rabble-rousing rebel music. Guys like Axl Rose [of Guns and Roses] are radicals within a genre of music that's considered old by today's white teenagers. They're just saying, "We're daring to be openly racist because we want you to notice us," but basically the music isn't that different from the next guy's music. Now, people might want to say the same thing about Public Enemy and rap music in general, but you can't say that there's no difference between rap and metal! The other thing that makes rap so radically different is what we're talking about and who's responding to it. It's not about black guy to black guy anymore, and that's what makes it so eyebrow-raising. Our music is filled with bites, bits of information from the real world, a real world that's rarely exposed. Our songs are almost like headline news. We bring things to the table of discussion that are not usually discussed, or at least not from that perspective.

What's your take on white rap? Does that old cliché about white people not being able to play the blues apply to hip-hop? Is 3rd Bass deemed good only because they've managed to sound black?
I think rap deals with being real, and you just do what you do and be who you are. You gotta understand, 3rd Bass are who they are because they grew up in a black community in Brooklyn, so they're not faking or fronting. The Beastie Boys grew up in your basic white community and related to a different lifestyle than 3rd Bass. But people will accept that in the black community, and the black community is still the core audience for hip-hop—the barometer of acceptance. Where the Beasties lost their acceptance was when they left Def Jam, the Rick Rubin/Russell Simmons connection, the foundation that kind of legitimized them. That hurt them, the perception that they left their roots, their black base. The black audience said, "Well, we only liked you because you were down with Run D.M.C.," and the white audience said, "Hmmm, it seems like the Beastie Boys aren't so hip anymore because the black audience isn't into them."

Will there ever be a white rapper who sounds white and is still accepted by the black audience— a rapper with a degree in philosophy who sounds like he's rapping with a pipe clenched in his teeth?
It's hard to say if that'll happen or not. The black audience in rap is basically a male audience, and usually black guys accept white males as able to play ball on their own terms, you know what I'm saying? A lot of black guys respect Larry Bird, although it took a lot of black guys a while to warm up to him, but then they saw him sinking those baskets and

beating brothers on a face-to-face confrontation, so they had to say, "Yo, Larry Bird's a *bad* motherfucker!" But that acceptance didn't come over night, you know what I'm saying? So it's sort of the same thing in rap. It's a male thing, so for white guys to appeal to a black audience, it's basically going to have to be a 3rd Bass type of situation. Or on a sex symbol level, possibly, like a George Michael thing, where you have a few black women saying, "Ooo, he's bad," where black guys are like, "Yo, dissolve that motherfucker." But rap music has a black male base, and the fellahs wanna hear some bad muthafuckah spankin' them lyrics with funk, soul, rage, and truth!

Is that your job description?
My job is to write shocking lyrics that will wake people up. Take "Welcome to the Terror-dome." How could I talk about 1989 and not talk about the band's confrontation with the Jewish community? It would've been false! But no matter what, if I mention the word "Jew" on a record, if I'm not explicitly praising the Jewish community, that record will be deemed anti-Semitic because people would just hear that word in a rap song by a group that allegedly said something about the Jewish community and interpret it accordingly. But I had to tell people what happened and how it happened, and a line like "Tell the rab to get off the rag" is about what happened. I told Rabbi Cooper, "Listen, I'll take care of the situation, don't worry about it, calm down," and his attitude was, like, "Everything's cool, I just want to know what's going on. These things can't happen, and if this is your group member, it doesn't make things look good for the rest of the group."

You went to New York's Holocaust Museum shortly after all of this happened. What sort of an impression did that make on you?
If affected me, sure, but most of it was stuff I already knew. You gotta understand, we as black people know all about the Holocaust because you can't get away from it. You hear about it, see it on TV where *Time/Life* is selling you books on Hitler and the SS. You're getting it every day, practically for years and years. But the whole point that when it comes time for the Black Holocaust to be talked about, a holocaust which took place over a longer period of time and initiated the destruction of a whole chunk of the African continent, people say, "Well you know, that was then, this is now." That brings anger from the black community which says, "Hell, our whole holocaust is consistently being covered over. Not that, but our holocaust is still going on!" The ball rolls by its damn self, you know what I'm saying? Now, black people want to kill themselves. That pattern of self-hate has been established, and all Public Enemy is saying is, "We need something to stop the self-hate." When you see something like the Holocaust Museum, you get inspired because you say "Well, shit, we as black people need about 30 of these, one in each city!"

If you're so intent on breaking the cycle of hatred and violence, why the paramilitary trappings, the plastic Uzis, and the martial exercises and H. Rap Brown type of rhetoric?
First of all, something like "Miuzi Weighs a Ton" [from *Yo! Bum Rush the Show*] is a metaphor about how my tongue and mind rattle off rhymes and I dissolve emcees, all that.

Now, as far as us using plastic Uzis in our stage show, you gotta understand that there's a certain way of how America approaches the black situation, and that's with force. The system of white world supremacy is dominated by a white male mindset and structure. The only way to defeat this most of the time is to convince people [by] using the same methods. What the Uzis represent, as explained many times in interviews, is that the gun was used by Europeans to abduct black people out of their peaceful setting in Africa, dragging them around the world for capitalist exploitative purposes. Black people today are still controlled by weapons. In black communities, the police are looked upon as terrorists; that uniform is a part of a bigger structure. Historically, black people have looked at police as no different from the first people who put the slaves on ships and took them to America.

A lot of times, to be self-defensive in this society, you have to say, "No, uh-uh, you not takin' my spear, you not takin' my soul, you not takin' my beliefs, you not takin' my culture, no fuckin' more!" So we symbolize this attitude with guys onstage in uniforms, doing tight moves, just like the police, but these are police people of culture.

All rap music is a reflection of what is, and things are the way they are because they were made to be that way from a plan that was set up before by white male slaveowners, and that's why the most we can do is make a change. Yeah, somebody's gonna come along and say the wrong thing, but maybe he's learning. You don't blame the untaught, you blame the teachers, and how can you blame a student if there's no teachers? If you're just coming through life, learning by experience, you're at the level of an animal, and your animal instincts teach you to survive, so you'll do anything you can to survive as an individual. Rap music is just an avenue of communication, a way of speaking about what's on your mind and how you feel, and if things don't get better, you're gonna have rappers out there saying, "Yo! Fuck that, I'm gonna kill everybody I see!" You've yet to see a record that says, "Kill the white man tomorrow," because a record company's not gonna pick that up, but that's a feeling shared by a lot of brothers out there that can't get theirs. It's all of our jobs to make sure that that attitude gets pushed away to the side, but it can only get pushed away if everybody gets his, which brings us to the economic thing. As long as a lot of brothers are have-nots, that attitude is gonna persist, and it's gonna come out through the music they make.

Another thing that makes rap even more threatening is that the sons and daughters of a lot of these people who are hopping and screaming and crying about it are so into it! If Public Enemy was just a black community thing, maybe it would just be a minor concern, but here you got guys like this guy I keep running into on talk shows, I forgot his name, and his son is, like, "Pop, I don't give a fuck about none of that shit. I'm just a Public Enemy fan!" Which presents a problem for this guy 'cause he's a Jewish father and his kid don't care nothin' about any of that political shit.

One last question: Is Public Enemy a rock band?
You gotta understand, rock is black music. That's why Little Richard has such an attitude, because rock and roll is the shit they set up on a black foundation. It wouldn't exist without that rhythm, that groove. Rock and roll isn't just the Rolling Stones, you know? So, yes, Public Enemy is a rock and roll band.

Hank Shocklee

"BOMB SQUAD" LEADER DECLARES WAR ON MUSIC
Condemnations roll from the mouth of Hank Shocklee like cadenced commandments from a storefront preacher. "We don't *like* musicians. We don't *respect* musicians. The reason why is because they look at people who do rap as people who don't have any knowledge. As a matter of fact, it's quite the opposite. We have a *better* sense of music, a *better* concept of music, of where it's going, of what it can do."

Speaking from the office of his new label, Sounds Of Urban Listening (SOUL), Public Enemy's longtime producer can back up his words—with noise. Squalling sirens, banshee police whistles, snares that kick like shotguns, all melt into a cacophonous symphony orchestrated by Shocklee behind the band's urgent sermonizing. Conservatory grads may blanch at these roiling textures, but rap initiates will recognize them as evidence of a striking artistic sensibility.

Classrooms, theory textbooks, are even the pristine sensibilities of R&B balladry mean nothing to Public Enemy. Though work on SOUL cut into Shocklee's involvement on *Fear of a Black Planet*, his imprimatur is stamped all over the album, in its riotous intensity and refusal to follow rap or pop formulas. Where most hip-hoppers are content to rhyme over skeletal rhythm loops and stark textures, Public Enemy and its four-man "bomb squad" production team—Chuck D, Eric Sadler, and brothers Keith and Hank Shocklee—strive to integrate all elements into a single, fist-in-your-face sonic blow.

Shocklee is a study in contradiction. His family is musical, yet his method is specifically *anti*-musical. His goal is to create a feeling of live performance, warts and all, through manipulating samples, with as little live playing as possible—preferably none at all. While the sound behind Public Enemy may strike traditionalists as chaotic, he insists that his work is essentially similar to that of his precursors in R&B: "To fill the gap where the bass, drums, keyboards, and horns left off, a lot of companies in the '70s put an orchestra behind the singers. Public Enemy does the same thing, but instead of hiring an orchestra, we fill the space with samples."

Shocklee's approach traces to what he feels his music stands for. "In dealing with rap, you have to be innocent and ignorant of music," he insists. "Trained musicians are not ignorant to music, and they cannot be innocent to it. They understand it, and that's what keeps them from dealing with things out of the ordinary. For example, certain keys have to go together because you have this training and it makes musical sense to you. Also, because musicians create music from nothing, that means they want to utilize a lot more than what's necessary. They can create any sound, any texture, any chord, any key in the universe. They're saying, 'Look, I can do more. Let me display my talent.' But as rappers, we don't have that musical sense. We say that your talent might be just playing one note. We go by what feels good. Since we're using [sampling] machinery, we have to calculate for a lot of stuff that musicians hear— and a lot of things they do *not* hear. We might use a black key and a white key playing together because it works for a particular part. A musician will go, 'No, those are the wrong keys. The tones are clashing.' We don't look at it that way."

From the beginning, Shocklee and Chuck D conceived of Public Enemy as "a musician's *nightmare*." "We took whatever was annoying, threw it into a pot, and that's how we came out with this group," Shocklee recalls. "We believed that music is nothing but organized noise. You can take anything—street sounds, us talking, whatever you want—and make it music by organizing it. That's still our philosophy, to show people that this thing you call music is a lot broader than you think it is."

Inspired initially by such projects as Brian Eno's and David Byrne's *My Life in the Bush of Ghosts*, he took to sampling in the mid-'80s as a means of taking the sounds of everyday life and, through organizing them, creating his kind of music. Armed with an Akai S900 and S1000, an Ensoniq EPS, and his collection of nearly 19,000 records, Shocklee and his colleagues splashed tactile landscapes behind Chuck D, Flavor Flav, and Professor Griff on "Rebel without a Pause," "Edge of Panic," "Night of the Living Baseheads," "Black Steel in the Hour of Chaos"—message after vivid message, each one a careful match of voice and accompaniment.

"When I look at a track, I say, 'Okay, we know what it sounds like. Now, what does this track *look* like? Does it look like a Chuck D track?' See, if I took a typical Salt-n-Pepa track, or an Eric B. & Rakim track, that wouldn't work, because Chuck is an intense person, so you can't come up with something that's not intense. Therefore, I put this wall of noise around Chuck, because his voice is very commanding. It's like Pat Summerall, who was the announcer on the NFL *Game of the Week*. We always called him the Voice of God—and he was doing football! So Chuck's intensity is, instead of music being behind it, he's like Pat Summerall announcing this *war* that's about to take place.

"With Flavor, the stuff is a little more in key. The *music* is in key, but the agitation is that *Flavor* is not! On '911 Is a Joke,' Flav is out of key purposely! When you put him in key, it gets syrupy—too close to music. See, when you add noise on top of noise, you gonna tune everybody out. But with Flavor, he becomes the noise, because he is annoying!"

After talking through each song with the band, Shocklee begins his work by putting a rhythm track together. His drum machine of choice is the E-mu SP-1200, "because it allows you to do everything with a sample. You can cut it off, you can truncate it really tight, you can run a loop in it, you can cut off certain drum pads. The limitation is that it sounds white, because it's rigid. The Akai Linn [MPC-60] allows you to create more of a feel; that's what Teddy Riley uses to get his swing beats. For an R&B producer, the Linn is the best, because it's a slicker machine. For house records, you want to use a [Roland] TR-808, because it has that charging feel, like a locomotive coming you. But every rap producer will tell you that the 1200 is still the ultimate drum machine.

Shocklee's approach to drum machine parallels his meticulous pursuit of disc or dance. "Drum machines are nothing but computers," he points out. "Each one measures time differently, but each one still puts time in a numerical value. Now, human beings don't have a numerical value. We can vary from a hundredth of a second to a tenth of a second within a fraction of that second, so you can't really calculate that fluid situation. So we might push the drum sample to make it a little bit out of time, to make you feel uneasy. We're used to a perfect world in music, to seeing everything revolve in a circle. When that circle is off by a little bit, that's weird. It's like bouncing a ball with some kind of bubble in it, so it goes off to the side somewhere. It's not predictable. That's the situation we develop in our music.

Since samples are his medium, Shocklee bristles at suggestions—even from the musical heroes whose guitar squeals, drum hits, and demands to "*Hit me!*" fill his library—that his is a parasitic art. "If they're bothered that I use their riff, then those guys are no longer musicians," he declares. "They're now lawyers and accountants trying to keep track of every little sound they've created. That's not what music is about. Music is about creating new things.

"That's why I'm pissed off about a lot of jazz musicians. The new guys who are coming up only mimic what they've heard in past. And jazz was never like that. It was always an exploration music. It explored new levels, new sounds, new things. There was never a formula for jazz. I mean, Thelonius Monk didn't care about keys, notes, tones, anything. He wanted his music to be spontaneous and as alive as possible.

"That's why I'm waiting for the day when there comes a new set of musicians who don't give a fuck about none of that stuff. Once the live musicians get to that point, then you're gonna see a real resurgence."

Robert L. Doersa

Cold Lampin' with Flavor Flav

Flavor Flav (born William Drayton) is hip-hop's answer to jive jocks, Screamin' Jay Hawkins, Cab Calloway, and Salvador Dali, all rolled into one. Rarely seen without his trademark mirrored shades, he often wears an outsized clock around his neck—the b-boy equivalent of the White Rabbit's pocket watch, perhaps; he has even, in the video for "Fight the Power," sported a Mad Hatter-type topper. Goggle-eyed and rubber-faced, he plays Dr. Seuss to Chuck D's scowling demagogue, mugging, striking vaudeville poses, and razzing the crowd with his patented Muttley snigger and rafter-rattling "Yeahhhh Boyeeee!!" Currently at work on his solo debut, *Lifestyles of the Rich and Flav*, due out early next year, he offers this crash course in hip-hop semiotics.

"I write about what I see every day in life, but I put it in such a form to where you gotta really dig your nails in deep to find out what I'm talking about, you know what I'm saying? I come up with a lot of new words and slang phrases, put it all in a tricky form, in street language. I take it through a whole science project.

"I'm definitely inspired by those old jazz scatters and jive talkers. I used to listen to Redd Foxx albums way back in the days when he used to have some explicit lyrics on his albums, and Gil-Scott Heron—man, he's one of my idols. But my biggest poetic influence is the Last Poets. I used to recite everything from their records, and that poetry stuck with me.

"I can understand the politics of everything, but I'm not really into digging up old books and blowing the dust off the covers. Chuck puts book knowledge on the records, but if you can't understand what Chuck is saying 'cause his words are too high science for you, then I'll come and break it down on the street level. Flavor Flav portrays a street character."

32
Hip-Hop:
From Live Performance to Mediated Narrative

Greg Dimitriadis

Hip hop culture originated during the mid-1970s as an integrated series of live community-based practices.[1] It remained a function of live practice and congregation for a number of years, exclusive to those who gathered together along NYC blocks, in parks, and in select clubs such as the now famous Harlem World or T-Connection. Early MCs (or "rappers") and DJs, graffiti artists and breakdancers, forged a "scene" entirely dependent upon face-to-face social contact and interaction. Indeed, the event itself, as an amalgam of dance, dress, art and music, was intrinsic to hip hop culture during these years. As one might expect, the art's earliest years went largely unrecorded and undocumented. However, in 1979, Sugarhill Records, a small label in New Jersey, released a single entitled "Rapper's Delight." It was an unexpected event for many of hip hop's original proponents, those pioneers immersed in the art's early live scene. Grandmaster Flash comments:

> I was approached in '77. A gentleman walked up to me and said, "We can put what you're doing on record." I would have to admit that I was blind. I didn't think that somebody else would want to hear a record re-recorded onto another record with talking on it. I didn't think it would reach the masses like that. I didn't see it. I knew of all the crews that had any sort of juice and power, or that was drawing crowds. So here it is two years later, and I hear "To the hip-hop, to the bang to the boogie," and it's not Bam, Herc, Breakout, AJ. Who is this? (quoted in George 1993, p. 49)

Many of those who were a part of early hip hop were also puzzled and asked similar questions. This all-but-unknown group, The Sugarhill Gang, was not a part of the early hip hop scene in any real sense, as Grandmaster Flash makes clear. "Rapper's Delight" clearly ruptured the art form's sense of continuity as a live practice known to all its "in group" members. This rupture was a defining one for hip hop as it marked the art's entrance into the public sphere of worldwide cultural discourse, where it has remained ever since. The decentralized face-to-face social dynamic which marked early hip hop has thus given way to a different dynamic, one mediated by way of commodity forms such as vinyl, video and CD. These configurations have separated hip hop's vocal discourse (i.e., "rap") from its early contexts of communal production, encouraging closed narrative forms over flexible word-play and promoting individualized listening over community dance. This shift towards in-studio production has affected the art in a number of crucial ways, most especially by redefining hip hop culture by and through the relatively more narrow and more easily appropriated idiom of "rap music."

Hip hop emerged from the experiences and practices of economically disadvantaged Afro-American, Latin, and Afro-Caribbean youths. These youths—early hip hop practitioners and participants—formed a culture distinct from that of the dominant order. This culture was marked by a whole series of integrated practices, including dance, music and visual art. It is important to note that this aesthetic integration was nurtured by the availability of spaces for face-to-face interaction and communication. The availability of such autonomous space is crucial for "marginalized" groups, a point Katrina Hazzard-Gordon makes well throughout her book *Jookin': The Rise of Social Dance Formations in African-American Culture* (1990).

In her study, Gordon explores how community dance and social interaction have been linked to the availability of different kinds of "dance arenas," including "jooks, honky-tonks, and after-hours joints" (Hazzard-Gordon 1990, p. 76). Gordon defines "dance arena" as "any institution of social interaction in African-American life in which secular social dancing plays an integral part" (1990, p. ix). Such spaces, she notes, have allowed "esthetic and technical commonalities" to be retained throughout the histories of African and African-American dance (1990, p. 18). These commonalities are, of course, not biologically determined, but rather are the product of body-to-body socialization processes made possible through the availability of dance spaces.

The particular form of dancing most associated with hip hop's formative years is "break-dancing." This art's seminal role in hip hop's history is noted by early dancer Crazy Legs: "See, the whole thing when hip-hop first started was the music was played in the parks and in the jams for the dancers, and those dancers were B-Boys" (quoted in Fernando, Jr. 1994, p. 17). Pioneering DJ Afrika Bambaataa elaborates upon the role of dance in hip hop's origins, pointing out that his influential Zulu Nation began as a breakdance crew:

When I seen that hip-hop started rising with myself and Kool Herc, I decided to switch the Organization [a Zulu Nation prototype], after a two-year run, into the Zulu Nation. Then, once the Zulu Nation came out, it was basically just a break-dance crew—the Zulu Kings and Queens and later the Shaka Kings and Shaka Queens. And then as it progressed, years after, it became more than that. (quoted in Fernando, 1994, p. 7)

The connection between dance and music is intrinsic to understanding African and African-inspired musics. Music is not a reified discourse in these cultures, an attitude brought by Africans to the Americas, where maintaining flexible contexts for social interaction became a method for survival. Chris Small writes, "Music itself ... hardly exists as a separate art from dance, and in many African languages there is no separate word for it, although there are rich vocabularies for forms, styles and techniques" (1987, p. 24).

The role of dance in hip hop history, however, is often understated or ignored, especially by critics with logocentric biases. The constant search for meaning through rap's vocal content alone has led to much cross-cultural misunderstanding, especially concerning the role of social dance. The link between protest lyrics and social resistance, for example, is often assumed, while the body itself is often ignored or dismissed. However, as Susan McClary notes:

The musical power of the disenfranchised—whether youth, the underclass, ethnic minorities, women or gay people—more often resides in their ability to articulate different ways of construing the body, ways that bring along in their wake the potential for different experiential worlds. (1994, p. 34)

New ways of being in the world, "new forms of subjectivity" (Foucault 1982, p. 216) if you will, can thus be located and nurtured in and through the body itself, a point Stuart Hall echoes in his article "What Is This 'Black' in Black Popular Culture?" (Hall 1992, p. 27).

By engaging in a myriad of experiential and representational practices, the body can connect with "experiential worlds" different from those articulated by dominant orders. Community dance is pivotal here as it allows the self to experience these "new forms of subjectivity," while placing the self within a group context. Individuals exploring different ways of being in collective contexts is the prelude and precursor to all important social or political action. Hip hop club activity in the late 1970s thus offered sites of resistance as potent as the social realism or protest discourses of the late 1980s and early 1990s. However, most critics still fetishize these discourses alone and ignore the ways in which community space has been contested and bodies have been constrained, controlled, and liberated.

The integration of dance with music is, again, crucial to understanding African and African-inspired musics, such as blues or jazz. Unlike composed "classical" European forms (arts which are represented by some sort of written score), such musics are brought to life through live production and concurrent improvisation. Such arts often reflect a more flexible lyrical or musical aesthetic than do Western arts such as classical European music. Peter Manuel notes this distinction in his *Popular Musics of the Non-Western World*:

> Since the Renaissance on, there has been a strong tendency for Western musical pieces to be sectionally structured, goal-oriented, discrete units with a clear sense of dramatic climax and closure; genres as diverse as sonatas, pop ballads, Tin Pan Alley tunes, and Beatles songs all exhibit this "song" format. Such an organized format contrasts with open-ended, expandable or compressible approaches used in narrative epics, *juju* music, *ch'in* variations, and, indeed, most musical genres outside of Western bourgeois traditions, which often operate more through repetition and variation of short motifs. (1988, p. 23)

Many Western musics rely, in short, on closed narrative, while "most musical genres outside of Western bourgeois traditions" do not. For example, Afro-American blues, when performed live, is a flexible art form, one which relies on a fluid interchange between floating verses, rhymed couplets, and other vocal tools. The performers need to maintain a kind of flexibility as they engage different kinds of crowds in different kinds of social settings. Christopher Small notes:

> The verses sung by the blues performer consist of a succession of rhyming couplets, with the first line repeated, making three lines to a stanza. Each of these stanzas stands independently, not as part of a narrative sequence as in a ballad; indeed, it is rare for a blues performance to tell a story.... The form in which the blues performance is cast relates to the orality and the improvised nature of the art; the repeated first line can give the singer time to think of a punch-line, while the absence of narrative thread gives a freedom to the improvising artist, allowing him or her not only to insert lines and even whole stanzas from any number of sources but also to shape the performance, in the time-honoured African and Afro-American way, as the social situation develops between singer and listeners. (1987, pp. 199–200)

The absence of a strict narrative thus allows for a kind of spontaneity appropriate to live production and performance. Neither performers nor audiences are aware of any particular story's outcome, allowing for an open-ended and engaging social experience. Small notes further:

> The musician regards himself as responsible, not just for the sounds that he makes, but for the whole social progress of the event, for its success as a human encounter. The musician

as he improvises responds not only to the inner necessities of the sound world he is creating but also to the dynamics of the human situation as it develops around him. It is his task to create not just a single set of sound perspectives which are to be contemplated and enjoyed by listeners, but a multiplicity of opportunities for participation along a number of different perspectives. (1987, p. 295)

By creating a text open to different interpretations or perspectives, performers allow for various points of intersection between themselves and the audience.

By contrast, post-Renaissance classical musics have come to claim a kind of autonomy from social contexts, allowing more room for single-perspective narrative or narrative progression *per se*. Composer Aaron Copeland betrays how intrinsic narrative is to the ideals of Western music-making in his bestselling book, *What to Listen for in Music*:

It is insufficient merely to hear music in terms of the separate moments at which it exists. You must be able to relate what you hear at any given moment to what has just happened before and what is about to come afterward. In other words, music is an art that exists in point of time. In that sense it is like a novel, except that the events of a novel are easier to keep in mind, partly because real happenings are narrated and partly because one can turn back and refresh one's memory of them. (1988, p. 6)

Copeland's metaphor for the extended composition as a novel is both apt and telling. The novel, like the composed classical European piece, demands attention to a larger continually unfolding structure. This larger structure often demands "delayed gratification" as an ideal of music appreciation.[2] One listens with an ear towards what has happened and what will happen. Physical engagement is, accordingly, downplayed in favor of polite listening.

Composed pieces, in broad contrast to dance musics, have a kind of autonomy across time and space. They can be worked with and thought about in a context entirely separate from their point of production. The written or sound recording introduces and eventually facilitates this autonomy from socially specific contexts, reducing musical experiences or performances to "music-object[s]," thus placing the entirety of the piece at the fingertips of the listener and potential composer (Small 1987, p. 43). Such composers are less apt to privilege "repetition and variation of short motifs" and more apt to take a linear approach to their art, constructing pieces which place phrases in narrative order, implying beginnings, middles, and ends, suggesting progression. The recording thus allows for a manipulation (often a splitting up and ordering) of sound bytes, in a manner similar to the way movable type allows for a manipulation of language. Both technologies encourage the construction of longer narrative paradigms separate from their immediate contexts of production (e.g., dance spaces).

These contexts of production often embrace much more than music itself. Early hip hop, again, was comprised of a number of interlocking and integrated practices, including graffiti writing and (as noted) breakdancing, arts which reflected hip hop's rough and abrupt "cut and mix" aesthetic in visual art and physical movement, respectively (Hebdige 1987, pp. 136–48). Tricia Rose notes hip hop's "cross-fertilization" of practices in her book *Black Noise*:

Stylistic continuities were sustained by internal cross-fertilization between rapping, break-dancing, and graffiti writing. Some graffiti writers, such as black American Phase 2, Haitian Jean-Michel Basquiat, Futura, and black American Fab Five Freddy produced rap records. Other writers drew murals that celebrated favorite rap songs (e.g., Futura's mural "The Breaks" was a whole car mural that paid homage to Kurtis Blow's rap of the same name). Breakdancers, DJs, and rappers wore graffiti-painted jackets and tee-shirts. DJ Kool Herc was a graffiti writer and dancer first before he began playing records. Hip hop events featured breakdancers, rappers, and DJs as triple-bill entertainment. Graffiti writers drew murals for DJ's stage platforms and designed posters and flyers to advertise hip hop events. (Rose 1994, p. 35)

This hip hop aesthetic, broadly speaking, allows for sharp and abrupt discontinuities or "cuts" as it encourages continuity by way of the all-important "mix." Breakdancing, one case in point, relies on a sharp "segmentation and delineation of various body parts" as arms and legs are manipulated to juxtapose the smooth and the circular with the abrupt and the linear. Part of the art's visual appeal lies in its ability to engage—and resolve—such apparent dichotomies. The sharp fragmentation of individual body parts gives the art a feeling of indeterminacy, evoking a postmodern aesthetic. However, fluid execution gives the dance an overriding sense of cohesion, a feeling of "asymmetry as balance" (Hazzard-Gordon 1990, p. 18). Hip hop's instrumentals resolve many of these same dichotomies as the DJ juxtaposes a steady and continuous beat with rough and abrupt "breaks" between turntables. This "cut and mix" duality is crucial for understanding why hip hop has had such a lasting appeal for so many for so long. Hip hop engages the postmodern present in its stress on the discontinuous and the contingent while it nurtures a community building musical tradition rooted in the oral.

The earliest books on the subject of hip hop did not see fit to separate hip hop's musical discourse from dance and aerosol art. Steven Hager's *Hip Hop: The Illustrated History of Break Dancing, Rap Music, and Graffiti* (1984) illustrates this cohesion of practice in its very title. Yet, Tricia Rose notes "Unlike breakdancing and graffiti, rap music had and continues to have a much more expansive institutional context within which to operate. Music is more easily commodified than graffiti, and music can be consumed away from the performance context" (Rose 1994, p. 58). Because music is most easily "consumed away from the performance context," it has emerged as hip hop's most visible signifier. The majority of peoples now exposed to rap (including most artists) are receiving this exposure by way of an "institutional context" which has only commodified hip hop's musical discourse. Note that the full title of Tricia Rose's 1994 book on hip hop is *Black Noise: Rap Music and Black Culture in Contemporary America*. Her title places "rap music" at the forefront, while Hagar's work (written a decade before Rose's) highlights "hip hop" and "breakdancing."

Hip hop's musical discourse was at one point integrated in the context of live social interaction and dance. This integration accounts for early hip hop's unorchestrated sound (relative to later endeavours). Early rappers, for example, often had a number of floating chants such as "shock the house" or "throw your hands in the air"—chants which framed freestyle rhymed couplets, calls to members of the audience, or short non-semantic vocable routines. Rhymed tales or stories were a part of the music, but such stories were usually not related to some longer thematic song-structure. "Rapper's Delight," for example, was just that— 14-plus minutes of sprawling enjoyment rather than a coherent narrative with a beginning, a middle and an end. The following is a brief excerpt from the 1979 release:

> I got a little face and a pair of brown eyes
> All I'm here to do, ladies, is hypnotize
> Singin' on 'n on on 'n on
> The beat don't stop until the break of dawn
> And singin' on 'n on on 'n on
> Like a hot butter pop the pop the pop
> Di bi di bi, pop the pop pop you don't dare stop
> Come alive y'all, and give me what you got

Note the use of rhymed couplets ("I got a little face and a pair of brown eyes / All I'm here to do, ladies, is hypnotize"), artist-audience chants ("Come alive y' all, and give me what you got"), and vocable routines ("Di bi di bi, pop the pop pop you don't dare stop"). Clearly, like much early rap, "Rapper's Delight" is in the rich and varied Afro-American rhetorical tradition, a tradition explored and explicated by critics such as Roger Abrahams and Henry Louis Gates, Jr.

Many early "crews" or groups, like The Sugarhill Gang, had three or more members. Most often these groups were loosely structured, members delivering and trading verses, rhymes and chants in a flexible and non-thematic manner. The Treacherous Three, The Cold Crush Brothers, The Fantastic Five, and The Furious Five (Grandmaster Flash's crew) are all key examples of such early collectives. These artists, again, did not have a strictly orchestrated or linearly composed approach to the art. Engaging crowds—both individually and as a group— was more important than delivering clearly composed narrative "messages."

A 1979 performance (captured on tape) featuring Grandmaster Flash and the Furious Five at T-Connection clearly evinces this flexible approach to live performance. The Furious Five trade boasts, brags and chants throughout the night, as members enter and exit the verbal flow often and seemingly at will. There is absolutely no evidence of a clearly organized and delineated song structure here. Rather, loose boasts and brags (about themselves, each other, and Grandmaster Flash) and loose chants (such as "wanna hit the top" and "to the beat y' all") are most important. These boasts and chants are often repeated with slight variations, further evincing the absence of a narrative song-structure. Indeed, "repetition and variation of short motifs" is of primary import, both in The Furious Five's vocals and in Flash's instrumental track (Manuel 1988, p. 23). As Peter Manuel notes, such patterns mark musics outside of the dominant Western tradition, musics that often depend on small-scale interaction between artists and audiences.

Grandmaster Flash's opening quote gives voice to the more context-specific nature of the early live performance. Flash speaks of knowing all the "crews" at the time, all those drawing crowds. Hip hop, once again, was dependent upon face-to-face interaction and small-scale mediation during the late 1970s. The event itself was more important than any particular separable discourse to its earliest devotees. Flash's question—who would want to hear a record of a record with someone talking over it?—attests to this sense of aesthetic integration. Hip hop, as a concrete experience all about the particulars of a complex multi-tiered social event, is privileged here (however implicitly) for Flash. Early hip hop reflected this sense of live practice in its sound, in its spacious dance grooves, in its stress on the particularities of time and place, in its flexible word play. It took time for more accessible choruses, themes, and longer narratives to be introduced as a vital part of the art.

Run-DMC was the first group to work successfully with the recorded medium and its temporal and sonic constraints. The group made the most out of the three- to four-minute song structure, composing pieces such as the popular 1983 single "It's Like That." This single, like many that would follow, employs the traditional popular song structure, including the use of a chorus ("It's like that and that's the way it is") and theme (the trials of poverty). In addition, collective delivery—often used as a loose, non-thematic framing devise by early collectives such as the Cold Crush Brothers—is employed here in an organized and thematic manner. Run-DMC exposed rap to much wider audiences, ultimately bringing it into the mainstream of American popular culture. Yet, it should be noted that the media form which Run-DMC consolidated and commodified was the easily duplicatable aural form. And along with opening up this medium they effectively diminished the importance of two other dimensions of hip hop culture born along with rap music—graffiti and breakdancing.

The emergence of rap music in commodity form resulted, thus, in a very basic redefinition of hip hop culture. A key example of how language-use shifted to prioritize rap music over and above integrated communal participation will prove helpful here. Run-DMC gave wide currency to the term "b-boy" during the mid-1980s, employing it freely in songs such as "Sucker M.C.'s." Lines such as "cold chill at a party in a b-boy stance," for example, imply the laid back street-corner aesthetic which would become the group's trademark. However, the term meant more than stance and attitude early on. In a rather symbolic and telling moment, Mr. Wiggles, a member of the early breakdance crew the Rock Steady Crew, comments on seeing Run-DMC live in concert:

> The first rappers to get on a mike and call themselves B-boys, who did know how to B-boy, was Run-DMC. And that group did impress 'em. Everybody thought *this* was a B-boy: anybody who posed like that like with an attitude. So when I went to see my first Run-DMC jam, I was saying these brothers are gonna get on the mike and they gonna break, because they call themselves B-boys. I got there; they didn't B-boy. I was upset, so I said what the phukk is this? That was the first time I ever seen a rapper call himself a B-boy just 'cause he could jam. (quoted in Allah 1993, p. 55)

Thus, what it means to be a part of the culture shifted at this time, as attention focused on hip hop's vocal discourse alone. In group face-to-face interaction in a live setting took a back seat to a more codified notion of the art. Performers had only to "jam" now, giving consummate priority to the recorded or aural medium of transmission. Many Old School pioneers, those immersed in the art's early live scene, those *not* as accustomed to the confines of vinyl, were, as a result, made obsolete. Bill Adler notes:

> Few debuts in the history of rock have been as momentous as the assassination attempt called "It's Like That"/"Sucker M.C.'s." With this one record, Run-D.M.C. not only laid the foundation for the next five years of rap, they incidentally created what is now referred to as the Old School. Rappers who'd recorded before Run—as had such notable acts as Grandmaster Flash & The Furious Five, The Fearless Four, The Treacherous Three, The Cold Crush Brothers, and The Sugarhill Gang—were suddenly Old School. (1991, p. 5)

Attention thus shifted to rap's verbal discourse during these years, decreasing the importance of dance, live congregation, and those who could create a live scene. This shift allowed, however, a number of very creative and talented vocalists to emerge for a brief and thrilling period. An amazing group of singles and albums by artists such as Eric B. & Rakim, Big Daddy Kane, Boogie Down Productions (KRS-One), and Kool G Rap & D.J. Polo were released during the mid-to-late 1980s, making these years a "golden era" in rap for many. Rap music, as a self-conscious art form, flowered with these performers turned poets.

Rakim, for example, takes rap lyric to a new level on tracks such as "Follow the Leader," released in 1988. No longer are boasts and brags dependent upon face-to-face interaction and communication. Rakim claims a more consummate control over his listeners, employing "rhyme displays that engrave deep as X-rays." Rakim blurs the line between his words and their invisible and all-penetrating means of transmission here as throughout the single. The power to communicate, always intrinsic to orality, is thus intensified by an acknowledgement of the mass-disseminated media forms now so much a part of rap. "Follow the Leader," like other singles by Eric B. & Rakim, including "In the Ghetto" (1990) and "Let the Rhythm Hit 'Em" (1990), are among the most fondly remembered by many hip hop aficionados today.

However, the widening reach of rap music offered more than aesthetic possibilities. A kind of black nationalist identity politics became apparent in rap during the late 1980s as its community stretched irretrievably beyond local boundaries. A brief example of how the recorded medium engendered black nation building within the idiom will prove illuminating.

Public Enemy released a song in 1987 entitled "Raise the Roof" off of the album *Yo! Bum Rush the Show*. An aggressive boasting and bragging track, it contains the line, "It takes a nation of millions to hold me back." There are very definite political overtones here and throughout the track, as chaotic abandonment bordering on the riotous is evoked (reminiscent, perhaps, of Martha and the Vandella's "Dancing in the Street"). Yet, at best, the language here is coded, not explicit. The first-person "I" abounds throughout, reflecting the loose kinds of self-aggrandisement which were so much a part of early party rap. A radical social consciousness was emerging in rap, though it was tied to the local, to a party tradition.

Public Enemy's next album, *It Takes a Nation of Millions to Hold Us Back*, however, was quite different from *Yo! Bum Rush the Show*. Note that the more personal "me" from "Raise the Roof" has been replaced here by the more inclusive "us," reflecting the album's encompassing black nationalistic theme. Their political agenda became more pronounced on this second release as evinced by track titles such as "Rebel Without a Pause," "Prophets of Rage," and "Party for Your Right to Fight."

Indeed, Chuck D and Flavor Flav wed a pro-black stance with Nation of Islam ideology on "Party for Your Right to Fight" as well as on others, such as "Bring the Noise." Terms such as "devil" and "Asiatic" abound throughout, referencing the intricate genesis beliefs preached by Nation founders W.D. Fard and Elijah Muhammad. The Nation of Islam became a pronounced force in rap at this point in time, its blend of militancy and pro-black ideology finding enthusiastic support among many young Afro-Americans.

Public Enemy's radical new conception of the idiom as a nation building force was intrinsically a part of their new and innovative uses of mass-disseminated technology. Unlike most early rap albums, *It Takes a Nation of Millions to Hold Us Back* is not a collection of singles. Rather, *It Takes a Nation* is structured as a 58-minute self-contained radio broadcast, its individual songs linked together along conceptual lines. Tracks are interspersed with portions of a UK concert, static, the sound of a radio dial turning, and bits and pieces of radio shows. Communication itself became most important as Public Enemy envisioned an Afro-American community that could be linked together through postmodern media technology. Thus, their second release marked a shift in the rap aesthetic. Community performance and entertainment on a decentralized scale gave way to worldwide mediation by and through centralized recording media. Rap became, in short, an idiom that could create solidarities beyond the boundaries of face-to-face communication.

The relationship between technology and nation building is explored by Benedict Anderson in his book *Imagined Communities: Reflections on the Origin and Spread of Nationalism* (1991). He notes, early on, that nations are "imagined communities" which foster feelings of deep solidarity between peoples who do not know each other and might never meet each other:

> [A nation] is *imagined* because the members of even the smallest nation will never know most of their fellow-members, meet them, or even hear of them, yet in the minds of each lives the image of their communion.... It is imagined as a *community*, because, regardless of the actual inequality and exploitation that may prevail in each, the nation is always conceived as a deep, horizontal comradeship. (Anderson 1991, pp. 6–7)

As Anderson observes, mass-disseminated technology—most notably print-technology or "print-capitalism"—was essential to envisioning these large scale "imagined communities." This revolutionary technology "made it possible for rapidly growing numbers of people to think about themselves, and to relate to others, in profoundly new ways" throughout disparate areas in Western Europe beginning in the eighteenth century (Anderson 1991, pp. 11, 36). Similarly, recorded technology allowed artists such as Public Enemy to envision their audience as a wide and encompassing nation within a nation, one which transcended any and all local contexts of production. Indeed, unity was the cry of the moment late in the decade, as groups such as X-Clan and Boogie Down Productions stressed similar (though not identical) black nationalist aesthetics on albums such as *To the East, Blackwards* and *By All Means Necessary* (respectively).

It is an ironic and uncomfortable reality that so-called "gangsta rap" emerged at almost exactly the same point in time on the West Coast that Public Enemy and other nationalist rappers did on the East. While many have attempted to draw sharp distinctions between the lyric content of "positive pro-black" artists such as Public Enemy and "negative gangsta rap" artists such as NWA (Niggas With Attitude), these groups share at least one formal characteristic. Both groups encountered and engaged hip hop as a mass-mediated, primarily verbal, art form—one no longer continually negotiated and processed in live practice and performance. Public Enemy's shows, for example, seem less like small-scale community performances and more like major-label rock extravaganzas. Elaborate props and rigid codification all give their performances a kind of large scale grandiosity foreign to most early—clearly less formal—hip hop music. The group, for example, is often flanked on stage by the Security of the First World (or the S1Ws), a paramilitary "outfit" which carries fake Uzi submachine guns, dresses in camouflage, and does an elaborate stage show behind band leaders Chuck D and Flavor Flav. NWA, now disbanded, shared a similar aesthetic. The group made a similar use of elaborate stage-props, including "Do Not Cross—Police Line" tape, which was spread across the group's performance space on occasion. The message, again, was "Do Not Cross" the line between those on stage and those off stage. Like many popular rock stars, both artists replicated their album tracks on stage ("in concert") with maximum amounts of spectacle and pageantry, formalizing the line between artist and audience.

This stress on mass-mediation and large-scale dissemination, as opposed to small-scale community performance, helped to forge in rap a more "informational" narrative-based music. The now familiar "rap as ghetto reporter" equation entered West Coast parlance during this period as Chuck D's oft quoted "rap as black America's CNN" entered that of the East. Former NWA member Ice Cube notes:

I give information to the people in Atlanta, that the people in Atlanta never even thought about. It's a form of unity, it does form a unity that we're startin' to put together.... [Rap is] a formal source to get our ideas out to a wider group of peers. (quoted in Cross 1993, p. 206)

Characters, plots and "messages" became most important for West Coast "gangsta rap" as the art's verbal discourse alone was severed from its context of live congregation and production. "Repetition and variation of short motifs" was replaced by narrative story telling within a closed song-structure.

An example from Ice Cube's work will prove helpful. "Dead Homiez" is from Ice Cube's *Kill at Will* EP, released a short time after his first album, *AmeriKKKa's Most Wanted*. Cube tells a vivid story on this track, narrating, in the first-person, his experiences at the funerals of friends who died early and violent deaths. The track, it is important to note, does not stress word play or metaphor and no sense of artist-audience interaction is acknowledged in this text. This is not a music created for the purpose of engaging live crowds. Rather, "Dead Homiez" communicates straightforward information, albeit with passion and emotional clarity. The video for this track is similarly poignant, and follows the action of the song faithfully. For example, the line "I still hear the screams from his mother," is accompanied by—appropriately enough—a grieving woman.

Indeed, the video became a much more prevalent part of rap during the late 1980s and early 1990s, primarily through the influence of MTV's *Yo! MTV Raps*. The video medium reinforced prevailing currents in hip hop music during this period, moving it towards a kind of literality that was exceedingly appropriate for all kinds of mass-mediation. The gun-carrying gangster was and is capable of signifying parallel messages in both sight and sound. For example, there was a clear link early in rap between the power to communicate orally and the power of a weapon. The microphone was often metaphorically referred to both as a gun and as a phallus. However, after about 1989, with the increasing importance of the video, there was a move to a kind of literality rooted in the visual. The gun came to signify (referentially) a gun and a gun alone. The power of this symbol stood on its own. Realism in the realm of the mass-mediated became more important than engaging live crowds or working with the language itself.

The "gangsta rap" narrative struck a chord in American popular culture, most especially with solvent, young, white teens. Artists such as Ice-T, NWA, Eazy-E, Dr. Dre, Ice Cube, MC Ren, and Snoop Doggy Dogg reached platinum-plus status, prompting artists and record companies alike to attempt to replicate their formula for success. Part of the wide cultural currency of the "gangsta" comes from the universally extractable nature of his narrative. The violent outlaw, living his life outside of dominant cultural constraints, solving his problems through brute power and domination, is a character-type with roots deep in American popular lore. Indeed, the gangster holds a very special place in the American popular imagination. He embodies such capitalist values as rugged individualism, rampant materialism, strength through physical force, and male domination, while he rejects the very legal structures which define that culture. He is both deeply inside and outside of mainstream American culture, his position not unlike that which Afro-Americans have occupied in the Americas for over 400 years. It is not surprising that the black gun-toting gangster has had such limitless appeal for so many young males, both black and white. The "gangsta" is a "romantic" figure, a ready-made tool for male teen rebellion. The following is from Ice-T's single "New Jack Hustler":

> Hustler, word, I pull the trigger long
> Grit my teeth
> Spray till every brother's gone
> Got my block sewn, armored dope spots
> Last thing I sweats, a sucka punk cop
> Move like a king when I roll, hops
> You try to flex, bang
> Another brother drops
> You gotta deal with this
> Cause there's no way out
> Why? Cash money ain't never gonna play out
> I got nothin to lose, much to gain
> In my brain, I gotta capitalist migraine
> Gotta get paid tonight
> To keep my hustle right
> Quick when I speak, check my freak
> Keep my game tight
> So many girls on my jock
> Think I'm a movie star
> Nineteen, I got a fifty thousand dollar car
> Go to school, I ain't goin' for it
> Kiss my butt, bust the cork on the Moet
> Cause I don't wanna hear that crap
> Why? I rather be a New Jack Hustler
> H-U-S-T-L-E-R Hustler[3]

Ice-T's "New Jack Hustler" embodies the super-gangster character-type. Sexist ("check my freak"), violent ("spray till every brother's gone"), utterly materialistic ("I gotta capitalist migraine"), and all but impenetrable ("keep my game tight"), Ice-T creates a larger than life bad guy along the big screen lines of Don Corleone or Al Pacino's *Scarface*. Indeed, many "gangsta rap" singles and albums have a strong visual feel to them and a number of popular artists working within the genre, including Ice Cube, Ice-T, and MC Eiht, have made a successful transition to film. "New Jack Hustler" was, in fact, originally contained on the *New Jack City* soundtrack, an action film which features Ice-T as an undercover cop. Ice-T blurs the line between "ghetto reporting" and cinematic fantasy in this film, as have many rap artists entering the realm of American popular culture.

The gangster narrative has become an intrinsic part of the art, engendering an entire musical genre. Its wild financial success has helped to shape the contours of rap's present landscape, the "language" through which rappers articulate their raps. Most artists today acknowledge the genre either implicitly or explicitly, as values such as "hardness" and "realness" now dominate across the board. "Hard-core" artists of the early-to-mid 1990s such as Nas, Redman, Lords of the Underground, Naughty by Nature, Casual, and Das EFX have all embraced the violently impenetrable outlaw stance on some level, though they have all proclaimed a love for rap as an art form as well. They have all also employed performance tools such as word play and freestyle-sounding delivery though they are all operating on a popularly determined landscape both in medium and message.

The following is "Time 4 Sum Aksion," from Redman's debut album, *Whut? Thee Album.* It offers a particularly apt example of rap's current state:

> Let's get ready to rumble!
> In this corner we have the funk bodysnatcher
> P Funkadelic and I gotcha
> Hard enough that I can chew a whole bag of rocks
> Chew an avenue, chew an off street, an off block
> Then turn around and do the same damn thing to a soloist
> 'Cause Reggie Noble's pissed
> I'll crush the whole brain frame
> 'Cause you couldn't maintain the funk
> That have your rap style for lunch, chump
> 'Cause '92, I take a whole crew
> Give 'em a punch of the funk
> Knock all of their gold tooth loose (pow!)
> To show you what type of stuff I'm on, you can't puff or sniff it
> Because I was born with it, the Funkadelic devil
> Hit you with a rap level of 10, then 1, 2, 3, you're pinned
> I get action
> So everybody jump with your rump
> If you like the way it sounds, punk pump it in your back trunk
> And let loose with the juice when I do rock
> I'm too hot
> Some say I got more juice than 2Pac[4]
> Straight outta Jersey, you heard me, my brother
> I'm laughing (he he he he)
> *Time, Time 4, Time 4 Sum Aksion*

Redman is clearly displaying a flexible control over language in this frenetic non-narrative piece. His delivery resonates with freestyle vocal improvisation, a practice intrinsic to rap's continuum as a live practice. Lines such as "And let loose with the juice when I do rock / I'm too hot / Some say I got more juice than 2Pac," seem to tumble out of his mouth freely and without effort. This control over language is crucial, for Redman frames "Time 4 Sum Aksion" as a vocal "battle" or competition. Such "battles" have been an intrinsic part of hip hop almost from its inception. Artists such as The Cold Crush Brothers and The Fantastic Five routinely engaged in verbal "cutting" contests during the late 1970s and early 1980s, as did jazz musicians and blues singers before them. "Time 4 Sum Aksion" has much of the sprawling energy of such battles, though it is very much contained within a kind of pop formalism.

The chorus "*Time, Time 4, Time 4 Sum Aksion,*" for example, frames the song's three verses, one of which is printed above. Such devices became important as hip hop left the context of live dance-hall production and entered the realm of the recorded. Early face-to-face battles were, as one might imagine, more dialogic than were later popular recordings such as "Time 4 Sum Aksion." Early competitors both knew each other and had to react to each other's challenges. Boasts and brags and insults were often personalized during these early battles, an aesthetic clearly evinced during a famous match between Kool Moe Dee and Busy Bee Starski at Harlem World in 1981.

During the competition, Kool Moe Dee insults Busy Bee's trademark "bom ditti bom" routine ("Busy Bee I don't mean to be bold but put that 'Bom ditti bom' bullshit on hold") as well as his general lack of originality. Busy Bee, according to Kool Moe Dee, "bit" his name from Lovebug Starski and "hugs" other MC's "jocks." Note that these insults are both individualized and center upon the act of MCing itself. Redman's single is, in contrast, inscribed within a one-sided gangster narrative, a narrative that often blurs the line between rhetorical competition and violent threat. Lines such as "Give 'em a punch of the funk / Knock all of their gold tooth loose" are neither personalized nor contained clearly within the realm of the performance. Redman places himself explicitly within the "gangsta rap" genre when he raps, "straight outta Jersey," an allusion to NWA's seminal album, *Straight Outta Compton*. Tricia Rose notes that much of today's hardcore rap is directly indebted to "gangsta rap":

> During the later 1980s Los Angeles rappers from Compton and Watts, two areas severely paralyzed by the postindustrial economic redistribution, developed a West Coast style of rap that narrates experiences and fantasies specific to life as a poor young, black, male subject in Los Angeles. Ice Cube, Dr. Dre, Ice-T, Ezy-E, Compton's Most Wanted, W.C. and the MAAD Circle, Snoop Doggy Dog, South Central Cartel, and others have defined the gangsta rap style. The Los Angeles school of gangsta rap has spawned other regionally specific hardcore rappers, such as New Jersey's Naughty By Nature, Bronx-based Tim Dog, Onyx and Redman, and a new group of female gangsta rappers, such as Boss (two black women from Detroit), New York–based Puerto Rican rapper Hurricane Gloria, and Nikki D. (Rose 1994, p. 59)

Redman, thus, recoups much of rap's freestyle energy on "Time 4 Sum Aksion," though he is operating within a context made popular and prevalent by West Coast gangster narratives.

Rap is today driven by the closed song-structure. The closure of rap's narrative structure has come as a parallel phenomenon to the increasing lack of space for live production and congregation. The majority of rap is now produced in-studio and is received in solitary settings, such as in jeeps, home stereos and Walkmans. While many people are exposed to rap in such decentralized settings, the art itself is increasingly constituted through a centralized recording industry. This industry has reified hip hop's vocal content alone and has downplayed the significance of dance, graffiti, and other face-to-face community building practices. Brian Cross sums up much in his *It's Not About a Salary: Rap, Race and Resistance in Los Angeles*:

> Hiphop in LA today is a community of bedrooms, occasional open mikes and airwaves. In homes all over the city people gather around turntables, record collections, SP1200s and MPC60s and conjure worlds that intersect with and absorb reality. Connected by a network of tapes, hard to find samples, a nomadic and often underground club scene, and places like the open mike at the Good Life, different perspectives are shared, microphone techniques are invented and beatbrokers collage new soundtracks for urban survival. (Cross 1993, p. 64)

Cross notes that spaces for community production are limited in LA. "Occasional open mikes" seem the closest thing the city has to offer to a live scene. Rather, people gather together around turntables, record collections, SP1200s and MPC60 samplers in more private contexts, such as in bedrooms. The community is constituted vicariously, linked together by an available number of recordings. Cross notes that such mass-mediation of rap engenders flexible "soundtracks for urban survival," allowing great numbers of people to cope with a violent and hostile reality.

Yet, how strong are these support systems? The spaces which have traditionally nurtured Afro-American community interaction and congregation are now all-but gone. Such spaces, as noted throughout, are vital for people of colour dealing with life in often hostile and alienating territory. Indeed, while a sense of rebellion and resistance is certainly fostered by many of rap's contemporary mass-mediated narratives, one wonders how strong—or better, how resilient—are the bonds formed by their mass-dissemination. One wonders whether a vibrant and varied "hip hop culture" can exist by way of a popularly constituted "rap music" idiom.

Notes

1. Special thanks to Charles Keil, William Youngren, William Fischer, Rob Bowman, Bruce Jackson, Larry Chisolm, Michael Frisch and John Wright all of whom commented upon and critiqued this project in its various stages.
2. See Leonard Meyer's *Emotion and Meaning in Music* (1956) as well as Charles Keil's rebuttal piece, "Motion and feeling through music" (1966), republished in *Music Grooves* (1994).
3. The above was copied directly from the liner notes to Ice-T's *O.G. Original Gangster*. Certain differences exist between this text and the text as performed.
4. Rapper 2Pac starred in a film entitled *Juice*, hence Redman's reference.

References

Adler, B. 1991b. Album notes to *Run-DMC: Greatest Hits 1983–1991*. Profile Records.

Allah, B. 1993. "Can't Stop the Body Rock," *Rappages*, June, pp. 54–7.

Anderson, B. 1991. *Imagined Communities: Reflections on the Origin and Spread of Nationalism* (London).

Copeland, A. 1988. *What to Listen for in Music* (New York).

Cross, B. 1993. *It's Not About a Salary: Rap, Race and Resistance in Los Angeles* (London).

Fernando, Jr., S. H. 1994. *The New Beats: Exploring the Music, Culture, and Attitudes of Hip-Hop* (New York).

Foucault, M. 1982. "The Subject and Power," in *Michel Foucault: Beyond Structuralism and Hermeneutics.* H. Dreyfus and P. Rabinow (Chicago), pp. 208–26.

George, N. 1993. "Hip-Hop's Founding Fathers Speak the Truth," *The Source*, November, pp. 44–50.

Hager, S. 1984. *Hip Hop: The Illustrated History of Break Dancing, Rap Music, and Graffiti* (New York).

Hall, S. 1992. "What Is This 'Black' in Black Popular Culture?," in *Black Popular Culture*, ed. G. Dent (Seattle), pp. 21–33.

Hazzard-Gordon, K. 1990. *Jookin': The Rise of Social Dance Formations in African-American Culture* (Philadelphia).

Hebdige, D. 1987. *Cut 'n Mix: Culture, Identity and Caribbean Music* (London).

Keil, C., and Feld, S. 1994. *Music Grooves* (Chicago).

Manuel, P. 1988. *Popular Musics of the Non-Western World* (New York).

McClary, S. 1994. "Same as It Ever Was: Youth Culture and Music," in *Microphone Fiends: Youth Music & Youth Culture*, eds. A Ross and T. Rose (New York), pp. 29–40.

Meyer, L. 1956. *Emotion and Meaning in Music* (Chicago).

Rose, T. 1994. *Black Noise: Rap Music and Black Culture in Contemporary America* (New England).

Small, C. 1987. *Music of the Common Tongue* (London).

Additional Reading

Abrahams, R. 1970. *Deep Down in the Jungle: Negro Narrative Folklore From the Streets of Philadelphia* (Chicago).

Adler, B. 1991. *Rap: Portraits and Lyrics of a Generation of Black Rockers* (New York).

Baker, Jr., H. 1993. *Black Studies, Rap, and the Academy* (Chicago).

Bourdieu, P. 1977. *Outline of a Theory of Practice* (Cambridge).

Dent, G. (ed.) 1992. *Black Popular Culture* (Seattle).

During, S. (ed.) 1993. *The Cultural Studies Reader* (New York).

Evans, D. 1982. *Big Road Blues* (Berkeley).

Foucault, M. 1977. *Discipline and Punish: The Birth of the Prison* (New York).

Gates, Jr., H. L. 1988. *The Signifying Monkey: A Theory of African-American Literary Criticism* (New York).

Grossberg, L., Nelson, C., and Treichler, P. (eds) 1992. *Cultural Studies* (New York).

Hebdige, D. 1991. *Subculture: The Meaning of Style* (London).

Jackson, B. 1974. *Get Your Ass in the Water and Swim Like Me: Narrative Poetry from the Black Oral Tradition* (Cambridge).

Jones, L. 1963. *Blues People: Negro Music in White America* (New York).

Keil, C. 1991. *Urban Blues* (Chicago).

Murray, A. 1976. *Stomping the Blues* (New York).

Ogren, K. 1989. *The Jazz Revolution: Twenties America and the Meaning of Jazz* (New York).

Sidran, B. 1981. *Black Talk* (New York).

Southern, E. 1983. *The Music of Black Americans: A History* (New York).

Toop, D. 1991. *Rap Attack 2: African Rap to Global Hip Hop* (New York).

West, C. 1993. *Keeping Faith: Philosophy and Race in America* (New York).

Discography

Boogie Down Productions, *By All Means Necessary*, Jive. 1097–4-J. 1988.

Boogie Down Productions, *Criminal Minded.* Sugarhill. SHCD 5255. 1991.

EPMD, *Strictly Business.* Fresh. CDRE-82006. 1988.

Eric B. & Rakim, *Paid in Full.* 4th & Broadway. CCD 4005. 1987.

Eric B. & Rakim, *Follow the Leader.* Uni. UNIC-3. 1988.

Eric B. & Rakim, *Let the Rhythm Hit'Em.* MCA. MCAC-6416. 1990.

Ice Cube, *AmeriKKKa's Most Wanted.* Priority. 4XL57120. 1990.

Ice Cube, *Kill at Will.* Priority. E4V7230. 1990.

Ice-T, *O.G. Original Gangster.* Sire/Warner Brothers. 9 26492–2. 1991.

Keith Murray, *The Most Beautifullest Thing in This World.* Jive. 01241–41555–4. 1994.

Kool G Rap & D.J. Polo, *Road to the Riches.* Cold Chillin'/Warner Brothers. 9 25820–2. 1988

Kool G Rap & D.J. Polo, *Wanted: Dead or Alive.* Cold Chillin'/Warner Brothers. 9 26165–2. 1990.

L.L. Cool J, *Radio.* Def Jam. FCT 40239. 1985.

Nas, *Illmatic.* Columbia. CK 57684. 1994.

N.W.A., *Straight Outta Compton.* Priority. 4XL57102. 1988.
Public Enemy, *Yo! Bum Rush the Show.* Def Jam. BCT 40658. 1987.
Public Enemy, *It Takes a Nation of Millions to Hold Us Back.* BWT 44303. Def Jam. 1988.
Redman, *Whut? Thee Album.* RAL/Chaos/Columbia. OK 52967. 1992.
Run-D.M.C., *Together Forever: Greatest Hits 1983–1991.* Profile. PCD-1419. 1991.
Sugarhill Gang, "Rapper's Delight." Sugarhill. VID-153RE-BW. 1979.
Various Artists, *Hip Hop Heritage Volume One.* Jive. 1291–4-J. 1989.
Yo Yo, *Make Way for the Motherlode.* East West. 7 91605–2. 1991.

33
Sample This

Nelson George

Mase got the ladies, Puff drives Mercedez
take hits from the '80s, don't it sound so crazy

Mase, "Bad Boy," 1997

On a Sunday morning in 1988 I was a guest, along with producer-songwriter Mtume and a couple of other music industry types, on Bob Slade's *Week in Review*, a radio show on New York's KISS-FM. We were kicking it about African-American culture and Mtume was wailing hip hop upside its head. The man who wrote '80s standards like Roberta Flack's "The Closer I Get to You" and Stephanie Mills's "I Never Knew Love Like This Before," Mtume is one of the most articulate, thoughtful musicians I've ever encountered. He was a political activist with Ron Karenga's nationalist U.S. organization in the '60s (with whom he survived a shoot-out with the Panthers). He played with Miles Davis during his controversial funk period and went on to write and produce for Flack, Mills, Levert, and Phyllis Hyman as well as with his own band. Mtume's wide musical experience, balanced by his grounding in street politics, has given him a provocative perspective on the evolution of black culture and music.

Mtume spent much of this particular Sunday morning blasting hip hop record production for its slavish reliance on record sampling. He charged that "this is the first generation of African-Americans not to be extending the range of the music" and that the resulting record-ings "were nothing but Memorex music." To further illustrate his creative disdain, Mtume made a bold analogy: sampling James Brown's drum beats in a hip hop album was like me sticking chapters from James Baldwin in my books and claiming the words as mine.

Now let me be clear here. Mtume wasn't totally against sampling as a musical tool. What he was objecting to was the use of sampling as a substitute for musical composition. It upset him that so many hip hop producers had no understanding of theory, could play no instru-ments, and viewed a large record collection as the only essential tool of record making. He charged that this made for lazy musicians and listeners. If obscenity is what the general public chiefly criticizes in hip hop as a social statement, the musically astute have long expressed contempt for its rampant sampling.

Listening to KISS-FM that morning was Daddy-O (Glenn Bolton) of Brooklyn's Stet-sasonic, a six-member crew composed of rappers, a DJ, and a live drummer, who boldly proclaimed themselves a hip hop band. Just as Mtume's cold-blooded critique of sampling reflected the widespread disdain of soul-generation musicians for the use of sampling (especially when done without crediting the source recordings), Stetsasonic's response to his comments spoke to hip hop's warrior aesthetic: when challenged, dis back.

Stetsasonic's answer was "Talkin' All That Jazz," a most articulate defense of sampling that became the band's signature hit. Released in 1988, "Jazz," which itself was based on a loop made from sampling '70s keyboardist Lonnie Liston Smith's instrumental "Expansions," argued: "Tell the truth, James Brown was old / 'til Eric and Rak came out with "I Got Soul" / Rap brings back old R&B and if we would not / people could have forgot." This was a reference to Eric B. & Rakim's use of several James Brown samples and singer Bobby Byrd's vocal in "You Know You Got Soul." Mtume didn't appreciate the line "You said it wasn't art / So now we're gonna rip you apart," and he certainly wasn't impressed with Stetsasonic's reply.

Sampling represents the kind of generational schism that tore through the rock world when folk purists chastised Bob Dylan for plugging in electric instruments in 1965 and jazz purists attacked Miles Davis for rejecting acoustic instruments in the early '70s. (Coincidentally, Mtume was Miles's percussionist for much of that period.) What continues to be debated is whether sampling is a tragic break with African-America's creative musical traditions or a radical, even transcendental, continuation of them.

New Toys

Since the end of World War II, technology has been a driving force in moving black music ahead—it has given musicians tools and opened possibilities their old instruments never suggested. While Charlie Christian, an extraordinary jazz musician, was the first to explore the possibilities of the electric guitar, it was country boys from the South and Midwest, men like Muddy Waters and Chuck Berry, who electrified the blues, giving rural music a hard, loud, citified sheen that set the stage for rock 'n' roll. Monk Montgomery, a bass player in Lionel Hampton's dance-crazy postwar big band, was the first to tour with the Fender bass guitar, an instrument that, along with the electric guitar and larger trap drum kits, recalibrated the sound of American dance music.

Quincy Jones once told me that the bass guitar's sound was "so imposing in comparison to the upright bass … it couldn't have the same function. You couldn't have it playing 4/4 lines because it had too much personality. Before the electric bass and the electric guitar, the rhythm section was the support section, backing up the horns and piano. But when they were introduced everything upstairs had to take a backseat…. The old style didn't work anymore and it created a new language."

Similarly, Stevie Wonder's embrace of the Moog synthesizer in the '70s again revamped pop. As Wonder announced with *Music of My Mind* and then elaborated on in a series of masterpieces (*Innervisions, Fulfillingness' First Finale, Songs in the Key of Life*), sounds filtered through then-novel computer technology could give an adventurous composer access to traditional sounds (strings, horns) and a wide range of new sonic textures. Just as the big bands were overwhelmed by enhanced rhythm sections of the '50s, Wonder's synthesizer-driven albums had a ripple effect throughout popular music. One by-product of the synthesizer's versatility was that it eventually drove most of the great African-American bands of the '70s to either shrink or disband in its wake.

At the tail end of the '70s the Fairlight Computer Musical Instrument appeared out of Australia. Sampling was not the main feature of this machine, though many musicians utilized it for that. With a Fairlight you could digitize a real sound, manipulate its pitch or tone, and then replay it. English artists such as the estimable Peter Gabriel and lesser acts like Heaven 17 and the Human League utilized the Fairlight in the early '80s. So did R&B producer Kashif and Earth, Wind & Fire, on its abysmal *Powerlight* album.

Around 1981 the E-mu Emulator, the first pure sampler, was developed and put on the market in the United States. This digital device, and the many others that followed, possessed the ability to store, manipulate, and play back any sound that had been stored in it. No musical expertise was needed to use it, though there is an inherent musicality required to understand how elements from various recordings can be arranged to create something new. But to make it work, you just had to know how to push the buttons.

Legend has it that the Emulator was first used in hip hop to capture the drum sound from an old record, which became the centerpiece of rap record production, by accident. Marley Marl was doing a remix in either 1981 or 1982 and was trying to sample using his Emulator when "accidentally a snare went through," as he told Harry Allen. He loved the sound of this old snare on his remix and realized "I could take any drum sound from any old record, put it in here and get that old drummer sound on some shit."

Kurtis Blow claimed that in 1983 he used a Fairlight to snatch the "one, two" countdown from "A.J. Scratch," making the first sample loop, using go-go band Trouble Funk's "Pump It Up," on his hip hop standard "If I Ruled the World."

Before hip hop, producers would use sampling to disguise the absence of a live instrument. If a horn was needed or a particular keyboard line was missing, a pop producer might sample it from another record, trying to camouflage its artificiality in the process. However, a hip hop producer, whose sonic aesthetic was molded by the use of break beats from old records pulled from dirty crates, wasn't embarrassed to be using somebody else's sounds. Recontextualizing someone else's sounds was, after all, how hip hop started. For example, producer Marley Marl became known for the "dusty" quality of his productions. In his records for Big Daddy Kane, Biz Markie, and L.L. Cool J, you could damn near hear the pops, scratches, and ambient noise of old vinyl.

To the post-soul generation that makes and consumes rap—people who grew up using remote controls, microwaves, and video games—employing an E-mu SP-1200 (favored by Public Enemy's producers) or an Akai MPC-60 (utilized by Teddy Riley) to sample, then loop and surround with other percussive elements is making music and no amount of bitching can change that.

Sample That

In 1979, the Sugar Hill house band replayed Chic's "Good Times" to provide musical backing for "Rapper's Delight." Eighteen years later, Sean "Puff Daddy" Combs sampled Diana Ross's "I'm Coming Out" to provide musical backing for the Notorious B.I.G.'s "Mo Money Mo Problems"—both sampled songs were written by the team of the late Bernard Edwards and Nile Rodgers. The Sugar Hill Gang, and many of the early studio band–generated rap records, used live musicians to replicate the feel of a DJ spinning. They may have been trying to create a sound that black radio DJs felt more comfortable airing, but it had nothing to do with the way authentic rap was made or sounded. Rather, this strategy reflected the sensibility of the soul-era producers who controlled the recording process at Sugar Hill, Enjoy, and elsewhere.

Sampling's flexibility gave hip hop–bred music makers the tools to create tracks that not only were in the hip hop tradition but allowed them to extend that tradition. For them the depth and complexity of sounds achievable on a creatively sampled record have made live instrumentation seem, at best, an adjunct to record making. Records were no longer recordings of instruments being played—they had become a collection of previously performed and found sounds.

Hip hop's sampling landmarks were both recorded in the late '80s by two acts from Long Island. The power of the first, Public Enemy's *It Takes a Nation of Millions to Hold Us Back* from 1988, is not simply its evocation of the Black Panthers, the Nation of Islam, and fearless brothers confronting anti-Nigga Machines. All that rhetoric is intensified with heavy-metal vigor by a tapestry of samples that set standards few have come close to since.

Greg Tate described it as "a songcraft from chipped flecks of near forgotten soul gold. On *Nation* a guitar vamp from Funkadelic, a moan from Sly, a growl abducted from Bobby Byrd aren't rhythmically spliced in but melodically sequenced into colorful narratives. Think of Romare Bearden." The revered African-American painter used color, texture, and collage (photos, ads, fabric) in a visual approach that is comparable in many ways to what the Bomb Squad production team achieved with *Nation*. Pulling from the Nation of Islam's Sister Ava Muhammad, a John Coltrane solo, an Anthrax rock riff, and scores of other sound sources, *Nation* fulfilled the visionary promise of sampling as an agitprop tool.

Equally visionary was De La Soul's whimsical debut, *3 Feet High and Rising*, a 24-track collection of raps, songs, puns, skits, and amused good feeling that was released a year after *Nation*. While P.E. looked for sounds that articulated anger and contempt, De La Soul sought bemused, off-handed noises and deceptively childlike melodies: De La Soul's "Eye Know" features Steely Dan's "Peg" rubbing up against Otis Redding's "Dock of the Bay," and on "Say No Go" Sly Stone fragments meet the Hall and Oates hook from "I Can't Go for That." Over these crafty Prince Paul–produced tracks, rappers Trugoy and Posdnuos intone their lyrics with a witty, conversational ease.

It Takes a Nation and *3 Feet High and Rising* were both products of a more carefree environment regarding sampling. Producers in the '80s tended to make liberal use of musical samples and were not as concerned about copyright issues. That philosophy has been replaced by greater sophistication on the part of everyone involved—the record labels, the producers, and especially those with catalogs that have been heavily sampled, who are now eternally vigilant. After "Rapper's Delight" hit the charts in 1979, Edwards and Rodgers eventually sued and got full songwriting credit (and royalties) on the Sugar Hill Gang hit. The case was widely covered, but sampling still went on for years before attorneys really caught on to how lucrative sampling could be for the original sound creators.

There is an evident racial aspect to this wake up-call. It was only when progressive groups such as P.E. and De La Soul began expanding beyond black music for samples that the form truly attracted negative attention. When rock or pop musicians found that—horror of horrors!—a rap group was using their music, they tended to go after the offense with an outrage that spoke to their contempt for the form. Old R&B performers on the whole were not aggressive enough, or maybe they were just more used to being ripped off. Prince Paul, a member of Stetsasonic when they made "Talkin' All That Jazz," was, along with De La Soul's other members, sued for using a bit of a song by the '60s band the Turtles on De La Soul's "Transmitting Live from Mars," resulting in a costly out-of-court settlement.

The most damaging example of anti–hip hop vindictiveness in a sample case came from a most unlikely source. In 1992, the gentle-voiced '70s balladeer Gilbert O'Sullivan sued Cold Chillin'–Warner Bros. signee Biz Markie for unauthorized use of his 1972 hit "Alone Again (Naturally)." But instead of sticking up Biz and his record companies for a substantial royalty on all records sold—which he was certainly entitled to—O'Sullivan successfully forced Warner Bros. to recall all pressings and stop selling the album until the song was removed. The resulting loss of visibility severely damaged Biz Markie's career as a rapper and sent a chill through the industry that is still felt.

Obviously, sampling hasn't disappeared from hip hop, but the level of ambition in using these samples has fallen. The high-intensity sound tapestries of P.E. have given way to often simple-minded loops of beats and vocal hooks from familiar songs—a formula that has grossed Hammer, Coolio, and Puff Daddy millions in sales and made old R&B song catalogs potential gold mines.

The most audacious uses of sampling in the '90s has not come from hip hop proper but from acts directly influenced by hip hop aesthetics (the Beastie Boys, Beck, Tricky, Forest for the Trees) and from those for whom hip hop is but one key point of reference (Prodigy, the Chemical Brothers). The gulf between instruments and sampling, bridged by hip hop, is now a given in progressive dance music around the world. Hip hop moved sampling technology to a central place in record making, the same way R&B did the electric guitar and bass in the '50s and Stevie Wonder did the synthesizer in the '70s.

That undisputable fact doesn't always cheer me. Sometimes when I hear a record I grew up with—say, Diana Ross's Bernard Edwards and Nile Rodgers produced "I'm Coming Out"—reused in a contemporary record, I get pissed. I rail against the lack of creativity in the hip hop generation. I long for old familiar sounds to remain in their original context and for younger musicians, with new approaches, to dominate the musical mainstream.

But those are the cries of an old-school purist and this decade's culture has little use for such arguments. My answer to the question—is or isn't sampling an extension of African-American tradition?—is a straight-forward no *and* yes. If creating new notes, new chords, and harmonies is what the African-American musical tradition is about, then sampling is not doing that. However, if that tradition means embracing new sounds, bending found technology to a creator's will in search of new forms of rhythm made to inspire and please listeners, well then sampling is as black as the blues. Sampling has changed the way a generation hears, and hip hop was central to that change. To quote Run-D.M.C., "It's like that and that's the way it is!"

A side note: Up to this day Mtume, who spent much of the '90s creating the hip hop–flavored score for Fox's *New York Undercover*, continues to be a vocal critic of rap's overuse of sampling, doing it now from his regular spot giving commentary Sunday mornings on WRKS in New York. Even the fact that "Juicy Fruit," the biggest hit his band enjoyed, has become an extremely popular sample—used quite prominently (and one imagines lucratively) in the Notorious B.I.G.'s "Juicy"—hasn't softened his opinion, though he no longer calls it "Memorex music." No, on that he's moved on. These days he calls it "artistic necrophilia" and has a good laugh.

34

"This Is a Sampling Sport":[1]

Digital Sampling, Rap Music, and the Law in Cultural Production

Thomas G. Schumacher

Everyday life invents itself by poaching in countless ways on the property of others.

de Certeau, 1984: xii

Introduction

Digital audio sampling poses several interesting challenges to existing intellectual property right laws, and by looking at the specific case of rap music, a form that is in many ways based on the opportunities presented by sampling technology, these confrontations are highlighted.[2] This article questions both the philosophical bases and common law decisions surrounding intellectual property through a critique of their understanding of individual authorship and creativity. Ultimately, copyright law is *property* law, and its foundation in notions of creativity and originality therefore have to be seen within the complex of capitalist social relations. Even so, because much of the discourse surrounding the question of copyright concerns itself with the creative process and the circulation of cultural products, it becomes necessary to address the ways in which sampling technology is able to highlight some of the contradictions in the foundational principles of jurisprudence. Sampling, in general and here in the particular case of rap music, forces us to reconceptualize these bases of copyright doctrine for both technological and cultural reasons—the former because digital reproduction accentuates existing understandings of "copying" and poses its own challenge to the ways in which we have to think about the process of production, the latter because rap highlights how different cultural forms and traditions are founded on different understandings of creativity and originality. Finally, because under capitalism the cultural form is necessarily the commodity form, because "the real creative subject within copyright law ... is capital" (Bettig, 1992: 150), current intellectual property rights articulate the limits of the cultural raw materials available for musical production as well as defining the formal boundaries of acceptable end-products. Gaines (1991: 9) points out that this limitation is "self-correcting" through the "double movement of circulation and restriction." Copyright is enabling of certain forms of discourse while prohibiting others in the ideological balance of "free expression" and profitability. Therefore, copyright becomes an issue for discussions of so-called free expression. In order to enter the fray, it is necessary to look at existing definitions of copyright within legal discourse.

Copyright and the Structuring of Noise in Legal Discourse

> The authority of the sovereign's law depends on the establishing of unambiguous proper meanings for words.... Such absolute meaning requires the possibility of absolute knowledge, of a logos in which meaning and word coalesce as law. The absolute political state is necessarily logocentric because it depends on law, which in turn depends on the univocal meaning of words, ... a point at which knowledge and language attain an identity that can serve as an absolute authority.
>
> Ryan, 1982: 3

> Music, the quintessential mass activity, like the crowd, is simultaneously a threat and a necessary source of legitimacy; trying to channel it is a risk that every system of power must run.
>
> Attali, 1985: 14

The copyright problems caused by digital audio sampling concern basically those inhering in the sound recording (McGraw, 1989). Copyright protection for music is divided between the underlying composition and the sounds "fixed in a tangible medium." The latter received protection only in 1971 as an amendment to the 1909 Copyright Act in an effort to control widespread record piracy, and are defined as:

> works that result from the fixation of a series of musical, spoken, or other sounds, but not including the sounds accompanying a motion picture or other audio visual work, regardless of the nature of the material objects, such as disks, tapes, or other phonorecords, in which they are embodied. (17 USC, s.101)

Under the 1976 Copyright Act, only those sounds which were "fixed" on or before 15 February 1972 are protected (17 USC, s.102(a)) and protection subsists only in "original works of authorship." Authorship is the capturing of sound in a tangible medium, not the production of those sounds. Importantly, most musicians or performers as well as engineers and producers contractually deliver the right of authorship to the record company (this is the "circle-p" copyright).[3] The originality required for copyright protection is *de minimis* and does not have to be novel, ingenuous or aesthetically meritorious (HR Rep. No. 94–1476, 94th Cong., 2d Sess. 1, 51 (1976); Fishman, 1989: 205). Originality means nothing more than a designation of origin with a particular author (*Burrow-Giles Lithographic Co.* v. *Sarony*, 111 US 53, 57–58 (1884)). As Gaines (1991: 63) has stated it, "all works originating from an individual are individual works of authorship." Hence, in order for a sample to be copyrightable, it must be original. While simple sounds of a snare drum may not be protected,

> the "signature sample," an identifiable sound of an artist taken live or from a recording, which is then dropped into a musical composition, may possess the required degree of personality to warrant copyrightability. (McGraw, 1989: 159)

Prevost (1987: 8) has stated that "it is difficult to imagine a musical performance that does not have originality sufficient to qualify for copyright."[4]

After proving copyrightability and the ownership of copyright, the plaintiff must show that there was an actual "recapture of original sounds" (Prevost, 1987: 9) and that the taking was more than *de minimis*, i.e., that it was substantially similar. In the case of sampling, however, the taking is exactly similar (an exact reproduction), so the question becomes one of determining if the taking was significant. This leads back to the protectability of sounds—if a sound is copyrightable, it will probably be substantial enough to be infringed. Thom has rather crassly suggested that the extent of the taking be judged by looking at "the artistic and *financial* importance of the portion(s) copied or appropriated" (Thom, 1988: 324; emphasis added). In any event, "the question turns on whether the similarity relates to a substantial portion of the plaintiff's work, not whether the material constitutes a substantial portion of the defendant's work" (McGraw, 1989: 164).

With these foundational points of law in mind, the three extant U.S. court decisions on sampling and copyright provide another segue into legal doctrine. The first case to be decided on the subject of sampling and copyright was *Acuff-Rose Music Inc.* v. *Campbell* (754 F.Supp. 1150 (MD Tenn. 1991)) in which the holders of the copyright of Roy Orbison's "Oh, Pretty Woman" enjoined Luther Campbell of the rap group 2 Live Crew for their use of a sample in the song "Pretty Woman" from the album *As Clean As They Wanna Be.* Acuff-Rose Music denied 2 Live Crew's management the license request to parody the Orbison song and sued Luther Campbell and 2 Live Crew's record company, Luke Skyywalker Records, after the release of "Pretty Woman" for copyright infringement and two tort claims of interference with business relations and prospective business advantage (under Tennessee state law), in spite of the fact that the album acknowledged Orbison and Dees (the co-writer) and Acuff-Rose as holding rights to the song. The defendants argued that their use of "Oh, Pretty Woman" was a parody and was therefore protected as fair use under 17 USC, s.107 of the Copyright Act (754 F.Supp. at 1152). While the tort claims are less important for this article's purposes, the claim of fair use as a defense in sampling cases is an important one. The statutory law of copyright in s.107 suggests that the courts consider four factors in determining a fair use defense:

> The purpose and character of the use, including whether such a use is of a commercial nature or is for non-profit educational purposes;
>
> The nature of the copyrighted work;
>
> The amount and substantiality of the portion used in relation to the copyrighted work as a whole; and
>
> The effect of the use upon the potential market for or value of the copyrighted work.

The courts have indicated that these factors are minimally required but are not exclusive in determining fair use (see *Harper & Row Publishers, Inc.* v. *Nation Enterprises*, 471 US 539, 560).

In deciding the *Acuff-Rose* case, the court considered each of these points in turn. First, Congress listed parody as one of the purposes of fair use which might be granted and common law has traditionally allowed this. Because 2 Live Crew's record was sold for profit, this is an important point. However, a finding of parody is not a presumptive finding of fair use; therefore, the other factors have to be weighed as well (745 F.Supp. at 1115, quoting *Fisher* v. *Dees*, 794, F.2d 432, 435 (9th Cir. 1986)). The second factor in fair use determines whether the copyrighted work (not the subsequent work) is "creative, imaginative, and original, ... and whether it represented a substantial investment of time and labor made in anticipation of financial return" (quoting *MCA, Inc.* v. *Wilson*, 677 F.2d 180, 182). The original can be (must be?) for profit, the derivative work cannot. The court in *Acuff-Rose* decided that "since 'Oh, Pretty Woman' is a published work, with creative roots, this factor weighs in favor of the plaintiff" (754 F. Supp. at 1156). In other words, it is impossible to infringe on a work which is not original itself. Third, the courts addressed the question of the substantiality and amount of quotation. While the 2 Live Crew song was a substantial use, the court maintained that "the question about substantial similarity cannot be divorced from the purpose for which the defendant's work will be used" (754 F.Supp. at 1156). Because the defendant's work was a parody, the court maintained that a greater use was allowed. In *Elsmere Music* v. *National Broadcasting Co.* (623 F.2d 252 (1980)) the court held that "a parody frequently needs to be more than a fleeting evocation of the original in order to make its humorous point" (at 253). The courts maintained in *Acuff-Rose* that 2 Live Crew's parody did not invoke too much of the original. Lastly, the court held that the defendant's work would not have a detrimental effect on the market of the original, perceptively noting that "the intended audience for the two songs is entirely different" (754 F. Supp at 1158).

The decision in *Acuff-Rose* was appealed to the Sixth Circuit Court of Appeals and was reversed and remanded because it held that "Pretty Woman" was not a fair use (972 F.2d 1429 (6th Cir. 1992)). Even if "Pretty Woman" is a parody (which the Circuit Court had difficulty granting), its purpose as a for-profit song (i.e. its commodity status) outweighed its character as parodic (972 F.2d at 1437). The Appellate Court also held that "Oh, Pretty Woman" was a copyrightable work, but reversed the District Court's decision that the amount of the taking was not an infringement. Here, the Circuit Court's opinion becomes convoluted as they argue that "near verbatim taking of the music and meter of a copyrighted work without the creation of a parody is excessive taking" (at 1438) even though they admit that "we will assume ... that 2 Live Crew's song is a parody" (at 1435). The court then held, following *Sony Corp. of America* v. *Universal City Studios, Inc* (464 US 417, 451), that it is not necessary to show any certain future harm and that a commercial use is presumptively unfair (972 F.2d at 1438). However, as Judge Nelson states in his dissenting opinion, the "Betamax" case cited above involved a copying which did not involve any "alteration of the copied material" (972 F.2d at 1443). A commercial use which transforms the original is different from one which does not. Overall, the result of this appeal has been that sampling has not been afforded a fair use defense on the grounds of parody (keeping in mind that each instance would still have to be decided on a case-by-case basis). Luther Campbell has had a writ of certiorari granted by the Supreme Court to finally decide whether or not 2 Live Crew's parody was a fair use under s.107 (123 L.Ed.2d 264), and the outcome of this case will be significant for future sampling parody claims.

Before the *Acuff-Rose* Circuit Court decision, a second case was handed down by the U.S. District Court in New York. In *Grand Upright Music* v. *Warner Bros Records* (780 F.Supp. 182 (SDNY 1991)), the court held that Biz Markie's sample of three words and portions of music from Gilbert O'Sullivan's "Alone Again (Naturally)" was an infringement of copyright. The case does not present the legal problems that arose in *Acuff-Rose* because quite simply the clearance was not obtained for the use of the samples and there was no formal fair use defense, and Warner Brothers was ordered to discontinue the sale of the Biz Markie recording. However, the defense's claim that "because others in the 'rap music' business are also engaged in illegal activity" they should be excused, although dismissed as "totally specious" by the judge, is an interesting comment on widespread musical practice. Perhaps buoyed by the preliminary success of 2 Live Crew at the District Court level, this line of argument suggests that the counsel may have been hoping for an even wider interpretation of originality for sampling. The ruling in favour of the plaintiffs, however, had wide effect and was reported extensively in the popular press (*New York Times*, 8 January 1992: C13, 21 April 1992: C13, for example).[5]

The most recent sampling case to be decided is *Boyd Jarvis* v. *A&M Records et al.* (1993 US Dist. LEXIS 10062, filed 27 April 1993; 827 F.Supp. 282). In this case, Robert Clivilles and David Cole used samples of Boyd Jarvis's song "The Music's Got Me" in their "Get Dumb! (Free Your Body)." Interestingly in this case, the court considered the specific issue of the digital audio sampling of uncopyrightable portions of an original. The court points out that "the simple fact of copying is not enough to prove an improper appropriation" (note 2 in text). Because in the case of sampling there is not a question that copying took place, the courts have to determine whether the sample is an unlawful one. Infringement is decided if "the value of a[n original] work may be substantially diminished even when only a part of it is copied, if the part that is copied is of great qualitative importance to the work as a whole"

(*Werlin* v. *Reader's Digest Association*, 528 F.Supp. 451, 463 (SDNY 1981)) and, as in *Grand Upright*, if the defendants appropriated elements that are "original." While the court held that non-copyrightable elements of a song should be factored out in determining the extent of appropriation, it ruled that the series of "oohs" and "moves" and the phrase "free your body" were in fact copyrightable expressions. The court concluded that the fact this was a sampling case in which direct appropriation took place "says more than what can be captured in abstract legal analysis." The court ultimately agreed with the judge in *Grand Upright* when it found here that "there can be no more brazen stealing of music than digital sampling."

This sentiment is the same as that expressed in the vast majority of legal literature on the subject of audio sampling. The subject first emerged for legal scholars with the "problems" of mastermix recordings in which DJs would spin different records together over borrowed beat tracks (Prevost, 1987). Since then, more than a dozen law review articles have appeared addressing the challenges of sampling to copyright doctrine—even before the courts supplied a case on which to comment. While McGraw's (1989) study presents a fairly even-handed investigation of the relevant portion of the Copyright Act, most others have been less sympathetic to samplers.[6] A number of the articles worry about the future place of "live" musicians and the general impact of sampling on presumably more "authentic" musical creators. Wells (1989: 705) is characteristic in his quip that "ultimately, digital samplers are thieves" (see also McGiverin, 1987; Thom, 1988; Newton, 1989; Moglovkin, 1990; Small, 1991). The other primary concerns of legal theorists has been the economics of sampling. Authors have drawn attention to the ways in which sampling is seen as a threat to the livelihood of record companies, and this is seen as a motivation to prosecute samplers (Giannini, 1990; Houle, 1992). Characteristic of this view is Fishman who argues that while the courts have successfully balanced free speech interests against those of profitability in the past, sampling upsets that balance and is therefore "a substantial economic threat" to musicians and the industry (Fishman, 1989: 223). The other concern is that sampling upsets the balance of copyright doctrine itself: "the law can ill afford to linger during the exponential growth of the legal complexities that encompass this technology" (Moglovkin, 1990: 174). Finally, Houle (1992: 902) has expressed the underlying belief of these authors when he states that only through prosecuting samplers "will the true creativity be spawned and true genius discovered."

What this article maintains is that legal doctrine, through its assigning of copyrights to corporate subjects and its definition of originality as origin in the individual author, is a contradictory discourse—one that allows for its own contradiction even as it seeks to secure unambiguous meanings. Even though, after *Bleistein* v. *Donaldson Lithographing Co.*, authorship can now be assigned to corporate entities instead of artists, and even though originality has come to mean origination (here, the "fixing" of sound), copyright is still influenced by the ideological construct of the "author" as a singular "origin" of artistic works (Jaszi, 1991).[7] As the three extant cases show, these contradictions have been consistently resolved in the interests of copyright holders. The significance of copyrights to further accumulation by record companies is being supported at the expense of more dialogic forms of cultural production. The technological practice of sampling and the specific case of rap music highlight these issues.

Looking for Benjamin's Orchid: Technology, Authenticity and Authorship in Popular Music

> That is to say, in the studio the mechanical equipment has penetrated so deeply into reality that its pure aspect freed from the foreign substance of equipment is the result of a special procedure.... The equipment-free aspect of reality here has become the height of artifice; the sight of immediate reality has become an orchid in the land of technology.
>
> Benjamin, 1968: 233

Walter Benjamin early on argued that the technological reproduction of artistic works has an impact on them. His argument is that through the process of mechanical reproduction, the artifact loses its "aura" and "detaches the reproduced object from the domain of tradition." Instead of a single art object, there now exists "a plurality of copies" (Benjamin, 1968: 221). One effect of this is that the copy can then be used in different ways than the original could have been, "and in permitting the reproduction to meet the beholder or listener in his own particular situation, it reactivates the object reproduced" (Benjamin, 1968: 221). This "shattering of tradition" takes the object of art and moves it from both the realm of cult-inspired awe and artistic authenticity to a new social function:

> for the first time in world history, mechanical reproduction emancipates the work of art from its parasitical dependence on ritual. To an ever greater degree the work of art reproduced becomes the work of art designed for reproducibility.... But the instant the criterion of authenticity ceases to be applicable to artistic production, the total function of art is reversed. Instead of being based on ritual, it begins to be based on another practice— politics. (Benjamin, 1968: 224)

The work of art is now seen as having lost an aura of authenticity and as having gained a foundation in relations of power. However, the structures of intellectual property rights are founded on notions of the work of art that has its aura intact. Statute and common law definitions of originality and authenticity still presume that the aura of the author remains intact after the processes of technological mediation. In order to understand Benjamin's point about artifice and reality in technologized art, it becomes necessary to look at the practices of musical production.

As Steve Jones has pointed out, the different technical apparatuses like sampling that are available and are used in the making of popular music are an important part of that process and need to be part of an understanding of musical production:

> The effects those [sonic and compositional] limitations [of equipment used for the fixation of sound] have on the composition and realization ... of music play a critical role in the production of popular music. Therefore, it is at the level of composition and realization that one should begin to analyze the relationship of technology and popular music, for it is at that level that popular music is formed. (Jones, 1993: 7)

However, the relationship between technology and music is not altogether obvious: for one thing, the precise moment of realization becomes less clear (Frith, 1987a: 65). Clearly, no recorded music is simply the recording of a live event—even "live" recordings are the product of mixing and post-production work. The very uncertainty of the precise musical moment is a product of the ideological mystification of the production process that conceals the constructedness of musical sound. As Doane explains in the context of recorded sound in film,

> the rhetoric of sound is the result of a technique whose ideological aim is to conceal the tremendous amount of work necessary to convey an effect of spontaneity and naturalness. What is repressed in this operation is the sound which would signal the existence of the apparatus. (Doane, 1980: 55)

The arrival of the apparatus in the form of sampling is a reminder that there is more to a recording than simply the virtuosity of the performers.[8]

There is a need to reconceptualize the musical process to include an understanding that technological knowledge, not just knowledge of particular instruments, is now an integral part of the process of popular music production (Jones, 1993). The sounds that we think of as original or authentic are themselves the product of the production process. As Tankel (1990) has shown, the process of remixing is a recoding of the musical text and engineers are as much a part of the recorded sound as musicians. One engineer put it this way:

> I don't know if you've ever tried to make a sample, but making one is a real pain in the ass. Everybody thinks, oh, sample, oh, I just play a note and that's it. It's a lot harder than that, because of the vagaries of the machine once you get it in and once you get it out. (Jones, 1993: 108)

This engineer goes on to explain the different procedures for refining the sample in order to put it into a usable form and points out "it's just not as easy as it *sounds*" (Jones, 1993: 109; emphasis added). Durant (1990) points out that sampling has created a new technological literacy that is necessary for modern musical production. Indeed, Porcello (1991) notes that engineers are unemployable if they do not know how to sample effectively.[9]

The production of music is not something that is tainted by the effects of technology; rather, music is constituted by technology through and through. As Frith explains,

> The "industrialization of music" can't be understood as something that happens *to* music but describes a process in which music itself is made—a process, that is, which fuses (and confuses) capital, technical, and musical arguments. (Frith, 1987b: 54)

All of popular music is the product of technology, and it becomes important to look at those "relations [which] exist between different technical and practical elements at play in any changing context of musical production" (Durant, 1990: 180). By looking at the process of production, we see that technologized music is the product of not just auteur-musicians but of the work of musicians and engineers alike. We cannot go back to some pre-industrial form of music. The "demand for authenticity in popular music is a false request, because such a demand is made with the assumption that music exists in some pure form" (Jones, 1993: 208). The practices of making music cannot be usefully detached from the conditions of their existence; therefore, in the age of digital reproduction, the search for a singular musical moment is a search in vain. Gaines points out that,

> while sound recording is certainly mechanical or electronic "copying," it produces neither a "copy" of the acoustic event nor a "copy" of the notational system in which the underlying composition has been encoded. It is more likely a "sample" of an acoustic event stored in another form such as paper roll, magnetic tape, pressed vinyl, or compact disc. (Gaines, 1991: 131)

As with Benjamin's orchid, popular music is now so imbricated with technology that its "reality" can no longer be assigned to a pre-industrial authenticity but is instead constituted by its technical processes.[10]

Frith and Durant's understanding above of the connection between popular music and technology (i.e. that music is part of a productive process that necessarily involves the engagement of the productive apparatus) forces us to interrogate the role of the author or musician in the productive process itself. Traditional aesthetics and copyright philosophy depend on a strong notion of authorship and are situated within humanist ideologies of the creative *artiste*. However, after the industrialization of art, as described by Benjamin for cinema, the role of the producer has changed. As Lyotard has argued,

> that the mechanical and the industrial should appear as substitutes for hand and craft was not in itself a disaster—except if one believes that art is in its essence the expression of an individuality of genius assisted by an elite craftsmanship. (Lyotard, 1984: 74)

That is, the end of the dominance of the aura of a work of art is only a problem insofar as this end further discredits the myth of the individual creator. In the case of sampling technology in musical production, the abolition of the aura signals the insertion of different subjects into the creative process, namely those of DJs, engineers and producers.

Foucault (1977) provides some interesting comments on the social function of the author. He points out that the role of the name of an author is not simply that of the proper name, which distinguishes between different subjects; rather the name of an author serves to distinguish between different texts, separating them and marking them distinct from others. Moreover, not all texts (e.g., bureaucratic forms, receipts, now the post-it note) necessarily require (or are granted) authorship. For Foucault, the question becomes one of understanding not only which texts are designated as authored, but also analyzing the conditions for authorial discourse. Thus Foucault says that "the function of an author is to characterize the existence, circulation, and operation of certain discourses within society" (Foucault, 1977: 124). The designation of authorship for a text signifies for that text a certain social significance that the anonymous text does not possess. The author then becomes a function of social discourses.

According to Foucault, there are four characteristics of the "author-function" in discourse. One is that it is not universal or constant, that is, certain forms of discourse do not always require authorship for validity (e.g., the use of authorship in scientific discourse over time has generally changed to one of anonymity). Second, the attribution of authorship is not automatic or "spontaneous" simply by connecting individuals and discourses. Instead, it is a result of a "complex operation whose purpose is to construct the rational entity we call an author" (Foucault, 1977: 127). The characteristics that we localize as belonging to an author of a particular type are for Foucault projections onto that individual of our interaction with the text. Thus the qualities that we would characterize as constituting the author of a musical piece are those that we choose to locate in the individual to whom authorship is attributed. Combined with the first characteristic, it is important to remember that these characteristics are not transhistorical or culturally universal but rather are transformed over time. The next characteristic of the author-function concerns the presence of the author in the text. In discourses that do not have authorship, the use of personal pronouns points directly towards the writer; however, in authored texts, the reference to "I" is never exact and therefore signals a generality of the text which the reader encounters. Thus the author-function in an authored text does not refer to an actual individual but to a subject position that remains open to the reader.

Most importantly for purposes of understanding authorship and copyright, however, is the characteristic of authored discourse that Foucault (1977: 130) says "is tied to the legal and institutional systems that circumscribe, determine, and articulate the realm of discourses." Authored texts are always a form of property—they are "objects of appropriation" (Foucault, 1977: 124). Foucault notes that this author-function has been linked to transgression, first by assigning authorship to discourses that were to be punished—misappropriation. He goes on to say that

> it was a gesture charged with risks long before it became a possession caught in a circuit of property values. But it was at the moment when a system of ownership and strict copyright rules were established ... that the transgressive properties always intrinsic to the act of writing became the forceful imperative of writing. (Foucault, 1977: 125)

Now writing, in general, again becomes a dangerous activity through conferring "the benefits of property" (Foucault, 1977: 125). What this analysis of authorship provides for a current understanding of copyright law is in its approach to the category of author as historically situated and constructed. Moreover, it is the granting of copyright to authors that situates them in the dynamics of power. From Benjamin we see that the work in the age of reproduction is no longer authentic, but it is firmly situated in politics. This politics is the politics of authorship, and from Foucault we see that not every discourse stands equal before the law.

Sampled recordings are not granted an author-function the way that supposedly individually created recordings are. Given that the myth of the pre-technological musician is abolished in the age of electronic reproduction, the specific practices of sampling become transgressive.[11] Porcello notes also the problems of authorship and copyright when he states that

> after Foucault, it is hard to imagine how any particular instance of interaction with a text does not itself create a new text (thus satisfying the conditions of the older aesthetic anyway), which is why the author is a spurious category for Foucault, and why the sampler's physical and functioning fusing of documentary and reproductive capabilities—which serves to throw the authorial producer of sound into a binary electronic limbo—has so thoroughly frustrated a legal model of copyright which is based on assumptions that one can clearly separate producers from consumers and texts from their readings. (Porcello, 1991: 77)

The DJ's interaction with the prerecorded sound of another unsettles the idea of the audio text as sealed and final to be consumed in preordained ways. The text is now part of the aural collage (Korn, 1992) as it becomes temporarily fixed to other samples in the record.

Transgression on the Turntable: Rap and Intertextuality

> I found this mineral that I call a beat
> I paid zero
> I packed my load 'cause it's better than gold
> People don't ask the price, but its sold
> They say that I sample, but they should
> Sample this, my pit bull
> We ain't goin' for this
> They said that I stole this
> Can I get a witness?
>
> Public Enemy, "Caught, Can We Get A Witness?"

The Foucauldian analysis of authorship reveals the intertextuality of the text, i.e., the connections between texts that are (arbitrarily) separated from one another by the name of the author. As Gaines (1991: 77) has stated, "the very concept of authorship overrides the generic and conventional indebtedness that would mark words as the product not so much of individuals as of societies." The text is historically suited within aesthetic traditions which contextualize cultural production. Rap music can be seen as part of a tradition of Black culture that Gates (1988) has drawn attention to as being double-voiced and which he calls "Signifyin(g)." Signifyin(g) is the practice of formal revision and intertextual relation between texts and refers to "the manner in which texts seem concerned to address their antecedents. Repetition, with a signal difference, is fundamental to the nature of Signifyin(g)" (Gates, 1988: 51). Meaning is created in the tradition of Signifyin(g) through the formal revision of patterns of representation, i.e., through the inflection of previous texts in new texts. Further, Gates states that

> Signifyin(g), in other words, is the figurative difference between the literal and the metaphorical, between surface and latent meaning.... Signifyin(g) presupposes an "encoded" intention to say one thing but to mean quite another. (Gates, 1988: 82)

That is to say, meaning operates at several levels and does not lend itself to surface-level decodings. Signifyin(g) is a form of Black discourse, one that significantly relies on the intertextual referencing of previous texts in its making of meaning.[12] Rap's "double-voiced discourse" (Stephens, 1991) is premised on the practices of intertextuality such that the rap song (through both aural and verbal cues) contains within it the inflected "voice" of its antecedent "other" (Bakhtin, 1981; Volo_inov, 1973).[13]

The case of rap also highlights the ways in which notions of authorship and originality do not necessarily apply across forms and cultural traditions—not because of any inherent worth or quality of different musics, but because different musical practices defy the universals of legal discourse. Frith (1987a: 63) points out that "copyright law defines music in terms of nineteenth-century Western conventions and is not well suited to the protection of Afro-american musicians' improvisational art." The formal practices of Signifyin(g) in rap music defy traditional definitions of authorship because they are ultimately premised on referencing the other and by explicitly relying on previous utterances.

The specific case of rap music challenges both the accepted understandings of musical practice and the dominant definitions of pop form, both of which are situated within capitalist social relations. Gaines's analysis presents the development of technological means for capturing sound—for giving sound its materiality—as one way in which sound has been able to become copyrightable, hence its status as a "protected property-appendage" (Gaines, 1991: 119). Sampling is a way of appropriating this property, of subverting the proprietary status of sound and allows for a new kind of poaching on the aural commons. Toop notes that scratching and sampling have "led to creative pillage on a grand scale and [have] caused a crisis for pre-computer-age concepts of artistic property" (Frith, 1986: 276). By selecting recorded sounds and reusing them in new recordings, rap music offers its critique of the ownership of sound. Porcello (1991: 82) argues that "rap musicians have come to use the sampler in an oppositional manner which contests capitalist notions of public and private property by employing previously tabooed modes of citation." It is rap's very flaunting of its intertextuality that poses the challenge to copyright law. Porcello continues:

> Rap musicians may be engaging in opposition at the level of praxis, but there is an ideological war occurring over the sign as well. The connotative meanings behind each term may be read as attempts to define appropriate sampling practice, at a discursive level, within both industry structures and pop aesthetics. (Porcello, 1991: 84, n.5)

As the DJ samples, there is a simultaneous critique of the ownership of sound and "Rockist"[14] aesthetics that remain tied to the romantic ideals of the individual performer. Rap forces an expansion of these definitions of musicality. Its meaning-making practices that rely on intertextual referencing via the sample demonstrate the different ways in which the struggle over originality is waged in divergent musical traditions. Because rap music and the practice of sampling change the notion of origin (the basis of copyright) to one of origins, it becomes transgressive in the Foucauldian sense and an infringement of copyright law in the eyes of the courts.

Intellectual Property Is Theft: Copyright and "Free Speech"

> In society, however, the producer's relation to the project, once the latter is finished, is an external one, and its return to the subject depends on his [sic]

relations to other individuals. He does not come into possession of it directly. Nor is its immediate appropriation his purpose when he produces in society. *Distribution* steps between the producers and the products, hence between production and consumption, to determine in accordance with social laws what the producer's share will be in the world of products.

Marx, 1973: 94

Copyright is a political and economic not a moral matter.

Frith, 1987a: 73

As Marx states here, the relationship between a musician and her or his musical product is not a natural one but is determined by social relations. The first step towards a critical understanding of copyright is to acknowledge that "copyright law is not a statement of ethical principle but a device to sustain a *market* in ideas" (Frith, 1988: 123). As Bettig (1992) has shown, the development of copyright philosophy has been more to secure the rights of capital in the sphere of cultural production. In the decisions that have come down on digital audio sampling, the courts have ruled consistently in favor of the owners of intellectual property, thereby reinscribing the relation of exteriority between producers and capital and securing the rights of the corporate legal subject over the concerns of cultural expression. Bettig (1992: 152) comments that "intellectual property rights continue to be utilized to gain or maintain market advantages by an increasingly oligopolistic and multinational culture industry." It is this development that has concerned many observers.

Rosemary Coombe has shown how the organization of intellectual property law (and its interpretation in the courts) is a limiting force on the free expression of ideas.[15] She echoes Frith when she points out that copyright and intellectual property in general functions solely to secure the market values of cultural artefacts.[16] Ultimately, however, this function limits the possible forms of expression. While certain signs retain cultural meanings even after (or in spite of the fact that) they are owned as intellectual property, the law prevents the free circulation of those signs. Coombe charges that

> by objectifying and reifying cultural forms—freezing the connotations of signs and symbols and fencing off fields of cultural meaning with "no trespassing" signs—intellectual property laws may enable certain forms of political practice and constrain others. (Coombe, 1991: 1866)

This brings us back to Gaines's point about the double movement of circulation and restriction in the law. While allowing certain forms of cultural expression to exist, others are restricted. As Coombe's study of trademark shows, the determination of this process is not innocent:

> the more powerful the corporate actor in our commercial culture, the more successfully it may immunize itself against oppositional (or ironic or simply mocking) cultural strategies to "recode" those signifiers that most evocatively embody its presence in postmodernity. (Coombe, 1991: 1874)

In other words, capital is able to control the patterns of signification that are most suited to its needs. While it is easy at this point to lapse into an instrumentalist or reductive argument about base and superstructure, even a careful analysis reveals that the political and economic structures are in place which facilitate the interests of capital. Durant gloomily suggests that if the issues of copyright are not resolved favorably, then the production knowledges involved in sampling will be "largely *cut off from* the possibility of responding to developments in musical culture expressed in the form of quotation or imitation" (Durant, 1990: 195). This appears to be true.

However, an analysis of sampling also draws our attention to other issues of critical importance. Digital technology is:

> disrupting the implicit equation of artists' "ownership" of their creative work and companies' ownership of the resulting commodities—the latter is being defended by reference to the former. (Frith, 1986: 276)

As I have shown in this article, sampling technology challenges the concept of the singular artist as the only embodied voice in the text. The ways in which copyright law understands the creative process and its assigning of property on that basis is confronted by the intertextual artifact. Jaszi points to this as a central contradiction in copyright doctrine when he states that

> the overall incoherence of the law's account of "authorship" may be best understood as reflecting a continuing struggle between the economic forces that (at least in the abstract) would be best served by the further depersonalization of creative endeavor and the ideological persistence of an increasingly inefficient version of individualism. (Jaszi, 1991: 501–2)

It is not altogether clear that the interests of the record companies would not be served by the widespread use of samplers, given their status as commodities whose profits are generated for these corporations (McGiverin, 1987: 1730); the struggle over appropriate sampling practices in rap and other dance-based forms is currently seeking to resolve this contradiction in the dance halls over the court rooms.

Gaines points out that sometimes the very ways in which capital seeks to realize its accumulation may actually speed up the "production of a common culture, a culture which can be inflected oppositionally" (Gaines, 1991: 228). As the culture industries seek the widest possible circulation of their products, the meanings of those products then gain such a purchase that they become part of the public domain: "what the proprietors of popular signs will always come up against is the predictable and desired result of their own popularity—imitation, appropriation, re-articulation" (Gaines, 1991: 232). The litigation surrounding sampling has been an effort to prevent just this. Record companies, as owners of the copyrights to the recorded sounds, have tried to take back what have become widely popular tracks from the DJs and engineers who are using them in new mixes.

Collins and Skover (1993) present a "cultural" analysis of free expression that they call "pissing in the snow." They suggest that actual speech practices (not idealized ones from legal theory) assume a Carnivalesque quality in that they tend not to abide by existing rules or laws. In the Carnival of popular culture, speech is directed more by the demands of listeners than by a fear of infringement:

> The "anarchistic" quality of the Carnival is fundamentally at war with the notion of a government of laws. The very character of the Carnival is to push all boundaries, including the fixed lines of law. (Collins and Skover, 1993: 802)

The other thing that this article has tried to show, however, is that the Carnival is also often at odds with the very medium of its circulation—the market. This article has advocated (at least implicitly) the freedom of unauthorized sampling, much in the spirit of the Carnival that respects no boundaries. What it has also shown is that "what cannot be tolerated by the gatekeepers of the Carnival, however, is dissent which poses a clear and present danger to the amusement culture and its economy" (Collins and Skover, 1993: 802).

Notes

1. Public Enemy, "Caught, Can We Get a Witness" (*It Takes a Nation of Millions to Hold Us Back*, Def Jam Records, 1988).
2. I would like to thank Priyadarshini Jaikumar-Mahey and Joseph Foley for their comments on an earlier version of this paper.
3. The ownership of the copyright of a sound recording grants three rights:

   > to reproduce the copyrighted work in copies or phonorecords (the right to duplicate the sound recording in a fixed form that directly or indirectly recaptures the actual sounds fixed in the recording);

   > to prepare derivative works based on the copyrighted work (the right to create a derivative work in which the actual sounds fixed in the sound recording are rearranged, remixed, or otherwise altered in sequence or quality); and

   > to distribute copies or phonorecords of the work to the public by sale or other transfer of ownership, or by rental, lease, or lending. (17 USC ss. 106 and 114)

   This excludes the right to control public performance that is attached to the copyright of the underlying composition (and hence why it is ASCAP and BMI which are involved in litigation in public performance cases, not the record companies; see Morgan, 1980).
4. As Frith (1987a: 64) points out, "originality, in short, can be difficult to define in a business in which similarity (the hit formula) is at a premium." That is, record companies do not have an interest in a record being so "original" that it does not attract a wide audience! The avant-garde, while "original" by romantic definitions, has not always proved commercially viable.
5. Indeed, the success of Grand Upright Music spurred on other suits to recover from unauthorized samples. In a significant case, Aaron Fuchs of Tuff City Records tried to sue Sony and Def Jam Records for the unauthorized use of drum beats from a song by the Honeydrippers. This case, although it was settled out of court, is significant because most drum beat samples are not cleared. Should this decision have come down in favour of Fuchs, rap music would have become prohibitively expensive because it would have required the clearance of all samples used, no matter how small (see *Billboard*, 11 January 1992: 71, 23 May 1992: 4, 30 May 1992: 8, 6 June 1992: 6).
6. For a sympathetic reading of sampling and copyright, see Marcus (1991) who suggests a licensing scheme to alleviate the problem; Hempel (1992) who argues that being sampled does not necessarily deprive the original author the rights of copyright; Korn (1992) who advocates a fair use defense for samples as parodies of pre-existing texts; and Brown (1992) who suggests amending the Copyright Act to allow for short samples.
7. Jaszi (1991: 459) argues that:

   > Legal scholars' failure to theorize copyright relates to their tendency to mythologize "authorship," leading them to fail (or refuse) to recognize the foundational concept for what it is—a culturally, politically, economically, and socially constructed category rather than a real or natural one.

8. Some critics of sampling maintain that the sampler is still invisible. Small (1991: 108) claims that "the practice of digital sampling is not common knowledge to the untutored public at this time" and therefore is guilty of unfair competition by confusion of origin. On the other hand, Goodwin (1990: 263) maintains that pop fans "have grown used to connecting *machines* and *funkiness*" suggesting that their presence is recognized by audience members. Ultimately, listeners' perceptions remain an empirical question, but the theoretical point that sampling practice challenges traditional understandings of the productive process still obtains.
9. It is important to remember the distinction between the "threat" of "piracy" of recordings and the practice of sampling. As Jones (1993: 117) points out, "even though it appears that sampling allows artists to reclaim or recontextualize sound, it must be remembered that sampling is a *production* method and not a means of distribution" and is therefore distinct from the challenge of "piracy" to corporate profits. Sampling's recording is quite distinct from the practices of illegal record pressing (the problem which brought the 1971 amendment to the 1909 Copyright Act) and home-taping—the industry's menace in the 1980s. This point is missed sorely by Thom (1988) who confuses the two in making points of law.
10. Andrew Goodwin's (1990: 259) assertion that digital reproduction allows a "mass production of the aura" in which "*everyone* may purchase an 'original'" seems to me to miss the point. Benjamin's argument is that the performer's presence is lost in technological mediation; even under conditions where the studio performance is reproduced "exactly" using digital technology (disregarding contentions about the "warmth" of analogue recordings), the performer is still absent. It may be that the affect of popular music no longer relies exclusively on the presence of the author, as in the ways in which DJ-based musical cultures upset the meaning of "live" performances.

11. It is important to remember that copyright needs an "author-function" but not necessarily an "author." Gaines points this out when she states that:

> we should not be surprised that Anglo-American intellectual property law is formally unaccommodating to the human subject bearing natural rights, because copyright doctrine is nothing more or less than a right to prohibit copying by others. Actual authors, in other words, are irrelevant to the operation of a copyright system. (Gaines, 1991: 64)

It is the record companies as rights-holders who are enjoining samplers, not necessarily individual author-subjects. This is one of the fundamental contradictions in legal theory: its reliance on the myth of the original, individual author coupled with the abandonment of the author-subject for the corporate rights-holding-subject.

12. Importantly, Gates does not maintain that the tradition of Signifyin(g) is metaphysically connected to conditions of race, nor is it part of an essential nature outside of history. Instead, "blackness" for Gates (1988: 121) means "the specific uses of literary language that are shared, repeated, critiqued, and revised."

13. For a descriptive presentation of the ways in which reggae DJs are also part of a multi-voiced Black discourse, see Hebdige (1987). A more analytical presentation of the position of reggae within Black diasporic culture is provided by Gilroy (1987).

14. Most criticism of popular music remains firmly tied to the aesthetics and affects of rock music—a form which is facilitated by copyright doctrine through its reliance on virtuosity and artistry, especially in the excesses of 1970s progressive rock and its aftermath. The implications of this are that different forms are judged by rock's presumed universal standards to be "less creative" as a new high culture/low culture divide is instituted between the more "serious" rock and pop (or other dance-based forms).

Bradby (1993: 156) has recently pointed out how rock's ideology of virtuosity has not applied equally to men and women performers and has not allowed "women's performances to be 'authentic' in the ways that men's are." Moreover, she argues that modernist ideologies of the creative process "are kept alive especially by the 'expert' writing of the male rock press and among male groups and producers" (Bradby, 1993: 164). In this way, the discourse of authorship and originality can be seen as gendered.

15. Coombe points out that legal theory does not address the problem of how meanings are fixed and dialogue is prevented. Legal theorists she says,

> fail to examine the differential power that social agents have to make their meanings mean something and the material factors that constrain signification and its circulation in the late twentieth-century. Legal theory perhaps defines itself *as* theory by its loathing to address specific processes of hegemonic struggle or the political economies of communication in a late capitalist era. (Coombe, 1991: 1860)

16. See also Helfand (1992) who points to the convergence in court interpretations of the logics of copyright, trademark, and Lanham Act s. 43 (a) which, "led by a small handful of major character owners" (Helfand, 1992: 627), has had the effect of preventing fictional characters from falling into the public domain and therefore "unavailable for new expressive uses" (Helfand, 1992: 654).

References

Attali, J. (1985) *Noise: The Political Economy of Music* (trans. by B. Massumi). Manchester: University of Manchester Press.

Bakhtin, M.M. (1981) in M. Holquist (ed.), *The Dialogic Imagination* (trans. by C. Emerson and M. Holquist). Austin: University of Texas Press.

Benjamin, W. (1968) "The Work of Art in the Age of Mechanical Reproduction," pp. 217–51 in H. Arendt (ed.), *Illuminations.* New York: Schocken.

Bettig, R.V. (1992) "Critical Perspectives on the History and Philosophy of Copyright," *Critical Studies in Mass Communication*, 9(2): 13–55.

Bradby, B. (1993) "Sampling Sexuality: Gender, Technology and the Body in Dance Music," *Popular Music*, 12(2): 155–76.

Brown, J.H. (1992) "'They Don't Make Music the Way They Used To': The Legal Implications of 'Sampling' in Contemporary Music," *Wisconsin Law Review*, No. 6: 1941–91.

Collins, R.K.L. and D.M. Skover (1993) "Pissing in the Snow: A Cultural Approach to the First Amendment," *Stanford Law Review*, 45(3): 783:80.

Coombe, R.J. (1991) "Objects of Property and Subjects of Politics: Intellectual Property Laws and Democratic Dialogue," *Texas Law Review*, 69(7): 1853–80.

de Certeau, M. (1984) *The Practice of Everyday Life* (trans. by S. Rendall). Berkeley, CA: University of California Press.

Doane, M.A. (1980) "Ideology and the Practice of Sound Editing and Mixing," pp. 47–56 in T. DeLaurentis and S. Heath (eds.), *The Cinematic Apparatus*. New York: St. Martin's.

Durant, A. (1990) "A New Day for Music? Digital Technologies in Contemporary Music-Making," pp. 175–96 in P. Hayward (ed.), *Culture, Technology, and Creativity in the Late Twentieth Century*. London: John Libbey.

Fishman, L.D. (1989) "Your Sound or Mine?: The Digital Sampling Dilemma," *St John's Journal of Legal Commentary*, 4(2): 205–23.

Foucault, M. (1977) "What Is an Author?," pp. 113–38 in D.F. Bouchard (ed. and trans.), *Language, Counter-memory, Practice*. Ithaca, NY: Cornell University Press.

Frith, S. (1986) "Art versus Technology: The Strange Case of Popular Music," *Media, Culture, and Society*, 8(3): 263–79.

Frith, S. (1987a) "Copyright and the Music Business," *Popular Music*, 7(1): 57–75.

Frith, S. (1987b) "The Industrialization of Popular Music," pp. 53–77 in J. Lull (ed.), *Popular Music and Communication*. Newbury Park, CA: Sage.

Frith, S. (1988) "Video Pop: Picking up the Pieces," pp. 88–130 in S. Frith (ed.), *Facing the Music*. New York: Pantheon.

Gaines, J.M. (1991) *Contested Culture: The Image, the Voice, and the Law*. Chapel Hill, NC: University of North Carolina Press.

Gates, H.L., Jr. (1988) *The Signifying Monkey: A Theory of African-American Literary Criticism*. New York: Oxford University Press.

Giannini, M. (1990) "The Substantiality Similarity Test and its Use in Determining Copyright Infringement Through Digital Sampling," *Rutgers Computer and Technology Law Journal*, 16(2): 509:30.

Gilroy, P. (1987) *There Ain't No Black in the Union Jack': The Cultural Politics of Race and Nation*. Chicago, IL: University of Chicago Press.

Goodwin, A. (1990) "Sample and Hold: Pop Music in the Digital Age of Reproduction," pp. 258–73 in S. Frith and A. Goodwin (eds.), *On Record: Rock, Pop, and the Written Word*. New York: Pantheon.

Hebdige, D. (1987) *Cut 'n' Mix*. New York: Routledge.

Helfand, M.T. (1992) "When Mickey Mouse Is as Strong as Superman: The Convergence of Intellectual Property Laws to Protect Fictional Literary and Pictorial Characters," *Stanford Law Review*, 44(3): 623–74.

Hempel, S.C. (1992) "Are Samplers Getting a Bum Rap?: Copyright Infringement or Technological Creativity," *University of Illinois Law Review*, No. 2: 559–91.

Houle, J.R. (1992) "Digital Audio Sampling, Copyright Law and the American Music Industry: Piracy or Just a Bad 'Rap'?," *Loyola Law Review*, 37(4): 879–902.

Jaszi, P. (1991) "Toward a Theory of Copyright: The Metamorphoses of 'Authorship,'" *Duke Law Journal*, No. 2: 455–502.

Jones, S. (1993) *Rock Formation: Music, Technology, and Mass Communication*. Newbury Park, CA: Sage.

Korn, A. (1992) "Renaming that Tune: Aural Collage, Parody and Fair Use," *Golden Gate University Law Review*, 22(3): 321–70.

Lyotard, J.-F. (1984) *The Postmodern Condition: A Report on Knowledge* (trans. by G. Bennington and B. Massumi). Minneapolis, MN: University of Minnesota Press.

McGiverin, B.J. (1987) "Digital Sound Sampling, Copyright and Publicity: Protecting Against the Electronic Appropriation of Sounds," *Columbia Law Review*, 87(8): 1723–45.

McGraw, M. (1989) "Sound Sampling Protection and Infringement in Today's Music Industry," *High Technology Law Review*, 4(1): 147–69.

Marcus, J. (1991) "Don't Stop that Funky Beat: The Essentiality of Digital Sampling to Rap Music," *Hastings Communications and Entertainment Law Journal*, 13(4): 767–90.

Marx, K. (1973) *Grundrisse* (trans. by M. Nicolaus). New York: Penguin.

Moglovkin, T.C. (1990) "Original Digital: No More Free Samples," *Southern California Law Review*, 64(1): 135–74.

Morgan, B. (1980) "Sound Recording Copyright Law—Its Application to the Performance of Records and Tapes," *Cumberland Law Review*, 11(1): 447–63.

Newton, J.S. (1989) "Digital Sampling: The Copyright Considerations of a New Technological Use of Musical Performance," *Hastings Communications and Entertainment Law Journal*, 11(4), 671–713.

Porcello, T. (1991) "The Ethics of Digital Audio-Sampling: Engineers Discourse," *Popular Music*, 10(1): 69–84.

Prevost, J.V.A. (1987) "Copyright Problems in Mastermixes," *Communication and Law*, 9(4): 3–30.

Ryan, M. (1982) *Marxism and Deconstruction: A Critical Articulation*. Baltimore, MD: Johns Hopkins University Press.

Small, D. (1991) "To Catch a Thief: Unauthorized Digital Sampling of Copyrighted Musical Works," *Thurgood Marshall Law Review*, 17(1): 83–112.

Stephens, G. (1991) "Rap Music's Double-voiced Discourse: A Crossroads for Interracial Communication," *Journal of Communication Inquiry*, 15(2): 70–91.

Tankel, J.D. (1990) "The Practice of Recording Music: Remixing as Recording," *Journal of Communication*, 40(3): 34–46.

Thom, J.C. (1988) "Digital Sampling: Old-fashioned Piracy Dressed Up in Sleek New Technology," *Loyola Entertainment Law Journal*, 8(2): 297–336.

Volo_inov, V.N. (1973) *Marxism and the Philosophy of Language* (trans. by L. Matejka and I.R. Titunik). Cambridge, MA: Harvard University Press.

Wells, R.M. (1989) "You Can't Always Get What You Want But Digital Sampling Can Get You What You Need!," *Akron Law Review*, 22(4): 691–706.

35

Challenging Conventions
in the Fine Art of Rap

Richard Shusterman

> ... rapt Poesy,
> And arts, though unimagined, yet to be.
>
> > Shelley, *Prometheus Unbound*

Rap is today's fastest-growing genre of popular music, but also the most maligned and perse-cuted. Its claim to artistic status is drowned under a flood of abusive critique, acts of censor-ship, and commercial cooptation.[1] This should not be surprising. For rap's cultural roots and main following belong to the black underclass of American society, and its militant black pride and thematizing of the ghetto experience represent a threatening siren to that society's complacent status quo. Given this political incentive for undermining rap, one can readily find aesthetic reasons that seem to discredit it as a legitimate art form. Rap songs are not even sung, only spoken or chanted. They typically employ neither live musicians nor original music; the sound track is instead composed from various cuts (or "samples") of records already made and often well known. Finally, the lyrics seem to be crude and simple-minded, the diction substandard, the rhymes raucous, repetitive, and frequently raunchy. Yet, as my title suggests, these same lyrics insistently lay claim to and extol rap's status as poetry and fine art.[2]

I wish to examine more closely the aesthetics of rap, or "hip hop" (as the cognoscenti often call it).[3] Since I enjoy this music, I have a personal stake in defending its aesthetic legitimacy. But the cultural issues and aesthetic stakes are much larger. For rap, I believe, is a postmodern popular art that challenges some of our most deeply entrenched aesthetic conventions, conventions that are common not only to modernism as an artistic style and ideology but to the philosophical doctrine of modernity and its sharp differentiation of cultural spheres. Yet while challenging such conventions, rap still satisfies the most crucial conventional criteria for aesthetic legitimacy that are generally denied to popular art. It thus undermines any rigid distinction between high and popular art made on purely aesthetic grounds, just as it calls into question the very notion of such grounds. To substantiate these claims, I first consider rap in terms of postmodern aesthetics. But since aesthetic legitimacy is best demonstrated by actual critical perception, I devote most of my effort to a close reading of a representative rap, which shows how the genre can answer the major aesthetic indictments against popular art.

Postmodernism is a vexingly complex and contested phenomenon, and its aesthetic thus resists clear and unchallengeable definition. Nonetheless, certain themes and stylistic features are widely recognized as characteristically postmodern, which is not to say that they cannot also be found in some modernist art.[4] These include recycling and appropriation rather than unique and original creation, the eclectic mixing of styles, the enthusiastic embracing of mass-media technology and culture, the challenging of modernist notions of aesthetic autonomy and artistic purity, and an emphasis on the localized and temporal rather than the putatively universal and eternal. Whether or not we call these features postmodern, rap exemplifies and often consciously highlights them, and they are essential to an adequate understanding of rap.

Appropriative Sampling

Artistic appropriation is the historical source of hip-hop music and still remains the core of its technique and a central feature of its aesthetic form and message. The music derives from selecting and combining parts of prerecorded songs to produce a "new" sound track. This sound track, produced by the DJ on a multiple turntable, constitutes the musical background for the rap lyrics. These in turn are frequently devoted both to praising the DJ's inimitable virtuosity in sampling and synthesizing the appropriated music and to boasting of the lyrical and rhyming power of the rapper (called the MC). While the rapper's vaunting self-praise often highlights his sexual desirability, commercial success, and property assets, these signs of status are all presented as secondary to and derived from his verbal power.

Some whites may find it difficult to imagine that verbal virtuosity is greatly appreciated in the black urban ghetto. But sociological study reveals that it is very highly valued there; and anthropological research shows that asserting superior social status through verbal prowess is a deeply entrenched black tradition that goes back to the griots in West Africa and has long been sustained in the New World through such conventionalized verbal contests or games as "signifying" or "the dozens."[5] Failure to recognize the traditional tropes, stylistic conventions, and constraint-produced complexities of African-American English (such as semantic inversion and indirection, feigned simplicity, and covert parody—all originally designed to conceal the real meaning from hostile white listeners)[6] has induced the false belief that all rap lyrics are superficial and monotonous, if not altogether moronic. But an informed and sympathetic close reading will reveal in many rap songs not only the cleverly potent vernacular expression of keen insights but also forms of linguistic subtlety and multiple levels of meaning, whose polysemic complexity, ambiguity, and intertextuality can sometimes rival that of high art's so-called open work.[7]

Like its stylized, aggressively boasting language, rap's other most salient feature—its dominant funky beat—can be traced back to African roots, to jungle rhythms that were taken up by rock and disco and then reappropriated by the rap DJs, musical cannibals of the urban jungle. But for all its African heritage, hip hop was born in the disco era of the mid-seventies in the grim ghettos of New York—first the Bronx, then Harlem and Brooklyn. As it appropriated disco sounds and techniques, it undermined and transformed them, much as jazz (an earlier black art of appropriation) had done with the melodies of popular songs. But in contrast to jazz, hip hop did not take mere melodies or musical phrases, that is, abstract musical patterns exemplifiable in different performances and thus bearing the onto-logical status of "type entities." Instead, it lifted concrete sound-events, prerecorded token performances of such musical patterns. Thus, unlike jazz, its borrowing and transfiguration did not require creative skill in composition or in playing musical instruments but only in manipulating recording equipment. DJs in ordinary disco clubs had developed the technique of cutting and blending one record into the next, matching tempos to make a smooth transition without violently disrupting the flow of dancing. Dissatisfied with the tame sound of disco and commercial pop, self-styled DJs in the Bronx adopted this technique of cutting in order to concentrate and augment those parts of the records that could provide for better dancing (Toop 1984, 151).

In short, hip hop clearly began as dance music to be appreciated through movement, not mere listening. It was originally designed only for live performance (at dances held in homes, schools, community centers, and parks), where one could admire the dexterity of the DJ and the personality and improvisational skills of the rapper. And even when the groups moved from the street to the studio where they could use live music, the DJ's role of appropriation was not generally abandoned and continued to be thematized in rap lyrics as central to the art.[8]

From the basic technique of cutting between sampled records, hip hop developed three other formal devices that contribute significantly to its sound and aesthetic: "scratch mixing," "punch phasing," and simple "scratching." The first is simply overlaying or mixing certain sounds from one record with those of another already playing.[9] Punch phrasing is a refinement of such mixing, in which the DJ moves the needle back and forth over a specific phrase of chords or drum slaps of a record so as to add a powerful percussive effect to the sound of the other record playing all the while on the other turntable. The third device is a more wild and rapid back-and-forth scratching of the record, too fast for the recorded music to be recognized but productive of a dramatic scratching sound that has its own intense musical quality and crazed beat.

These devices of cutting, mixing, and scratching provide rap with a variety of forms of appropriation that seem as versatile and imaginative as those of high art—as those, say, exemplified by Marcel Duchamp's mustache on the Mona Lisa, Robert Rauschenberg's erasure of a De Kooning canvas, and Andy Warhol's multiple re-representations of prepackaged commercial images. Rap also displays a variety of appropriated content. Not only does it sample from a wide range of popular songs, it feeds eclectically on classical music, TV theme songs, advertising jingles, and the electronic music of arcade games. It even appropriates nonmusical content, such as media news reports and fragments of speeches by Malcolm X and Martin Luther King.

Though some DJs took pride in appropriating from very unlikely and arcane sources and sometimes tried to conceal (for fear of competition) the exact records they were sampling, there was never any attempt to conceal the fact that they were working from prerecorded sounds rather than composing their own original music. On the contrary, they openly celebrated their method of sampling. What is the aesthetic significance of this proud art of appropriation?

First, it challenges the traditional ideal of originality and uniqueness that has long enslaved our conception of art. Romanticism and its cult of genius likened the artist to a divine creator; it advocated that his works be altogether new and express his singular personality. Modernism, with its commitment to artistic progress and the avant-garde, reinforced the dogma that radical novelty was the essence of art. Though artists have always borrowed from one another's works, the fact was generally ignored or implicitly denied through the ideology of originality, which posed a sharp distinction between original creation and derivative borrowing. Postmodern art such as rap undermines this dichotomy by creatively deploying and thematizing its appropriation to show that borrowing and creation are not at all incompatible. It further suggests that the apparently original work of art is itself always a product of unacknowledged borrowings, the unique and novel text always a tissue of echoes and fragments of earlier texts.

Originality thus loses its absolute originary status and is reconceived so as to include the transfiguring reappropriation and recycling of the old. In this postmodern picture there are no ultimate, untouchable originals, only appropriations of appropriations and simulacra of simulacra; so creative energy can be liberated to play with familiar creations without fear that it thereby denies itself the opportunity to be truly creative by not producing a totally original work. Rap songs simultaneously celebrate their originality and their borrowing.[10] And as the dichotomy of creation/appropriation is challenged, so is the deep division between creative artist and appropriative audience; transfigurative appreciation can take the form of art.

Cutting and Temporality

Rap's sampling style also challenges the work of art's traditional ideal of unity and integrity. Since Aristotle, aestheticians have often viewed the work as an organic whole so perfectly unified that any tampering with its parts would destroy the whole. Moreover, the ideologies of romanticism and *art for art's sake* have reinforced our habit of treating art works as transcendent and virtually sacred ends in themselves, the integrity of which should be respected and never violated. In contrast to this aesthetic of austere organic unity, rap's cutting and sampling reflects the "schizophrenic fragmentation" and "collage effect" characteristic of the postmodern aesthetic.[11] In contrast to an aesthetic based on devotional worship of a fixed, untouchable work, hip hop offers the pleasures of deconstructive art—the thrilling beauty of dismembering (and rapping over) old works to create new ones, dismantling the prepackaged and wearily familiar into something stimulatingly different.

The DJ's sampling and the MC's rap also highlight the fact that the apparent unity of the original artwork is often an artificially constructed one, at least in contemporary popular music, where the production process is frequently quite fragmented: an instrumental track recorded in Memphis, combined with a back-up vocal from New York and a lead voice from LA. Rap simply continues this process of layered artistic composition by deconstructing and differently reassembling prepackaged musical products and then superimposing the MC's added layer of lyrics so as to produce a new work. But rap does this without the pretense that its own work is inviolable, that the artistic process is ever final, that there is ever a product that should be so fetishized that it could never be submitted to appropriative transfiguration. Instead, rap's sampling implies that an artwork's integrity as object should never outweigh the possibilities for continuing creation through use of that object. Its aesthetic thus suggests the Deweyan message that art is essentially more process than finished product—a welcome message in our culture, where the tendency to reify and commodify all artistic expression is so strong that rap itself is victimized by this tendency while defiantly protesting it.

In defying the fetishized integrity of artworks, rap also challenges traditional notions of their monumentality, universality, and permanence. No longer are admired works conceived in Eliotic fashion as "an ideal order" of "monuments" existing timelessly and yet preserved through time by tradition.[12] In contrast to the standard view that "a poem is forever," rap highlights the artwork's temporality and likely impermanence, not only by appropriative deconstructions, but by explicitly thematizing its own temporality in its lyrics. For example, several songs by BDP include lines like "Fresh for 88, you suckers" or "Fresh for 89, you suckers."[13] Such declarations of date imply a consequent admission of datedness; what is fresh for 88 is apparently stale by 89, and so superseded by a new freshness of 89 vintage. But, by rap's postmodern aesthetic, the ephemeral freshness of artistic creations does not render them aesthetically unworthy, no more than the ephemeral freshness of cream renders its sweet taste unreal. For the view that aesthetic value can only be real if it passes the test of time is simply an entrenched but unjustified presumption, ultimately deriving from the pervasive philosophical bias that equates reality with the permanent and unchanging.

By refusing to treat artworks as eternal monuments for permanent hands-off devotion, by reworking works to make them work better, rap also questions their assumed universality. Although it typically avoids violently excluding white society, hip hop is proudly localized as "ghetto music," thematizing its roots in and commitment to the black urban ghetto and its culture. The lyrics focus on features of ghetto life that whites and middle-class blacks would rather ignore: pimping, prostitution, and drug addiction, as well as rampant venereal disease, street killings, and oppressive harassment by white policemen. Most rappers define their local allegiances in very specific terms, often not simply by city but by neighborhood, such as Compton, Harlem, Brooklyn, or the Bronx.

Eclecticism, History, and Autonomy

If rap's freewheeling eclectic cannibalism violates high modernist conventions of aesthetic purity and integrity, its belligerent insistence on the deeply political dimension of culture challenges one of the most fundamental artistic conventions of modernity: aesthetic autonomy. Modernity, according to Max Weber and others, was bound up with the project of occidental rationalization, secularization, and differentiation, which disenchanted the traditional religious world view and carved up its organic domain into three separate and autonomous spheres of secular culture: science, art, and morality, each governed by its own inner logic of theoretical, aesthetic, or moral-practical judgment.[14] This tripartite division was of course powerfully reflected and reinforced by Immanuel Kant's critical analysis of human thinking in terms of pure reason, practical reason, and aesthetic judgment.

In this division of cultural spheres, art was distinguished from science as not being concerned with the formulation or dissemination of knowledge, since its aesthetic judgment was essentially nonconceptual and subjective. It was also sharply differentiated from the practical activity of the realm of ethics and politics, which involved real interests and appetitive will (as well as conceptual thinking). Instead, art was consigned to a disinterested, imaginative realm, which Friedrich Schiller (1795) later described as the realm of play and semblance. As the aesthetic was distinguished from the more rational realms of knowledge and action, it was also firmly differentiated from the more sensate and appetitive gratifications of embodied human nature—aesthetic pleasure residing rather in a distanced, disinterested contemplation of formal properties.

Hip hop's genre of "knowledge rap" (or "message rap") is dedicated to the defiant violation of this compartmentalized, trivializing, and eviscerating view of art and the aesthetic. Such rappers repeatedly insist that their role as artists and poets is inseparable from their role as insightful inquirers into reality and as teachers of truth, particularly those aspects of reality and truth that get neglected or distorted by establishment history books and contemporary media coverage. KRS-One of BDP claims to be not only "a teacher and artist, startin' new concepts at their hardest," but a philosopher and a scientist.[15] In contrast to the media's political whitewash, stereotypes, and empty escapist entertainment, he proudly claims: "I'm tryin' not to escape, but hit the problem head on / By bringing out the truth in a song.... It's simple; BDP will teach reality / No beatin' around the bush, straight up; just like the beat is free / So now you know a poet's job is never done. / But I'm never overworked, cause I'm still number one."[16]

Of course, the realities and truths that hip hop reveals are not the transcendental eternal verities of traditional philosophy, but rather the mutable yet coercive facts and patterns of the material, sociohistorical world. Yet this emphasis on the temporally changing and malleable nature of the real (reflected in rap's frequent time tags and its popular idiom of "knowing what time it is")[17] constitutes a respectable and tenable metaphysical position associated with American pragmatism. Though few may know it, rap philosophers are really "down with" Dewey, not merely in metaphysics but in a noncompartmentalized aesthetics that highlights social function, process, and embodied experience.[18]

"Knowledge rap" not only insists on uniting the aesthetic and the cognitive but equally stresses the idea that practical functionality can be part of artistic meaning and value. Many rap songs are explicitly devoted to raising black political consciousness, pride, and revolutionary impulses; some make the powerful point that aesthetic judgments, and particularly the question of what counts as art, involve political issues of legitimation and social struggle in which rap is engaged as progressive praxis and which it advances by its very self-assertion as art. Other raps function as street-smart moral fables, offering cautionary narratives and practical advice on problems of crime, drugs, and sexual hygiene (e.g., Ice-T's "Drama" and "High Rollers," Kool Moe Dee's "Monster Crack" and "Go See the Doctor," BDP's "Stop the Violence" and "Jimmy"). Finally, rap has been used effectively to teach writing and reading skills and black history in the ghetto classroom.[19]

Rap also challenges another well-entrenched modernist convention of artistic purity: the idea that a proper aesthetic response requires distanced contemplation by a transcendental and temperately disinterested subject. Against this aesthetic of distanced, disengaged, formalist judgment, rap advocates one of deeply embodied participatory involvement, with content as well as form. Rappers want to be appreciated primarily through energetic and impassioned dance, not through immobile contemplation and dispassionate study.[20] Queen Latifah, for example, insistently commands her listeners, "I order you to dance for me." For, as Ice-T explains, the rapper "won't be happy till the dancers are wet" with sweat, "out of control" and wildly "possessed" by the beat, as indeed the captivating rapper should himself be possessed so as to rock his audience with his God-given gift to rhyme.[21]

This aesthetic of divine yet bodily possession is strikingly similar to Plato's account of poetry and its appreciation as a chain of divine madness extending down from the divine Muse through the artists and performers to the audience, a seizure which for all its divinity was criticized as regrettably irrational and inferior to true knowledge.[22] More importantly, the spiritual ecstasy of divine bodily possession should remind us of Vodun and the metaphysics of African religion to which the aesthetics of Afro-American music has indeed been traced.[23]

What could be farther from modernity's project of rationalization and secularization, what more inimical to modernism's rationalized, disembodied, and formalized aesthetic? No wonder the established modernist aesthetic is so hostile to rap and to rock music in general. If there is a viable space between the modernist rationalized aesthetic and an altogether irrational one whose rabid Dionysian excess must vitiate its cognitive, didactic, and political claims, this is the space for a post-modern aesthetic.[24] I think the "fine art" of rap inhabits that space, and I hope it will continue to thrive there.

Thus far I have presented rap as a challenging violator of traditional artistic conventions. Why, then, still call it art? True, its lyrics proudly claim it is art—performative self-assertion being a crucial means of achieving such status. But mere self-assertion is not enough to establish the arthood or aesthetic character of an expressive form; the claim must be convincing. Primarily, of course, conviction must come from experience; we must feel a work's artistry and aesthetic power impress itself on our senses and intelligence. But theoretical justification can also help extend art's limits by assimilating previously unaccepted forms into art's honorific category. One proven strategy for such assimilation is showing that despite obvious deviance from established conventions, an expressive form still meets enough of the more crucial criteria to warrant recognition of its artistic or aesthetic legitimacy. Popular art is often refused such legitimacy because of an alleged failure to meet such criteria, particularly those of complexity and depth, creativity and form, artistic self-respect and self-consciousness.

While rap may be the most denigrated of popular arts, its better works can, I think, satisfy these central artistic criteria. The best way to demonstrate this is not by general polemics and pleading but by looking closely at a concrete specimen of the genre. I therefore turn to a close reading of "Talkin' All That Jazz," by the Brooklyn crew Stetsasonic. It is neither my favorite rap nor the one I think most artistically sophisticated. I choose it for its popularity and representative character, as proven by its selection in a number of rap LP anthologies,[25] and because it highlights some of the central aesthetic issues that rap raises.

Though the aim of my close reading is to show this rap's aesthetic richness, the very method of reading—that is, presenting and analyzing this rap as inscribed text—will involve ignoring some of its most important aesthetic dimensions and its intended mode of aesthetic appropriation. For I shall be abstracting from its crucial dimensions of sound, since the printed page captures neither the music nor the oral phrasing and intonation of the lyrics (a point of pride and style among rappers). Nor can it convey the complex aesthetic effects of the multiple rhythms and tensions between the driving musical beat and the word stress of the rap delivery, which in contrast to popular songs maintains its own speech rhythms.[26] A full appreciation of a rap song's aesthetic dimensions would require not merely hearing it but dancing to it, feeling its rhythms in movement as the genre emphatically means us to. The printed medium of our written culture precludes this, thereby suggesting more generally the inherent difficulties in appreciating and legitimating oral culture by academic means so deeply entrenched and trapped in the written.

Nonetheless, if rap can satisfy aesthetic standards in its impoverished form as written poetry, *a fortiori* it can meet them in its rich and robust actuality as music and rhythmic speech. Recognizing, then, that a rap is aesthetically much more than its text, let us see how the text itself can sustain a claim to aesthetic status in terms of the central criteria I have mentioned.

> *Talkin' All That Jazz*
> Well, here's how it started,
> Heard you on the radio
> Talk about rap,
> Sayin' all that crap
> About how we sample,
> Give an example.
> Think we'll let you get away with that.
> You criticize our method
> Of how we make records
> You said it wasn't art,
> So now we're gonna rip you apart.
> Stop, check it out my man.
> This is the music of a hip-hop band.
> Jazz, well you can call it that.
> But this Jazz retains a new format.
> Point, when you misjudged us
> Speculated, created a fuss,
> You've made the same mistake politicians have,
> Talkin' all that Jazz.
>   . . . [musical break]
> Talk, well I heard talk is cheap.
> Well, like beauty, talk is just skin deep.
> And when you lie and you talk a lot,
> People tell you to step off a lot.
> You see you misunderstood,
> A sample's just a fact,
> Like a portion of my method,
> A tool. In fact,

It's only of importance when I make it a priority,
And what we sample of is a majority.
But you are a minority, in terms of thought,
Narrow minded and poorly taught
About hip-hop's aims and the silly games
To embrace my music so no one use it.
You step on us and we'll step on you.
You can't have your cake and eat it too.
Talkin' all that Jazz.
   ... [musical break]
Lies, that's when you hide the truth,
It's when you talk more jazz than proof.
And when you lie and address something you don't know,
It's so whacked that it's bound to show.
When you lie about me and the band, we get angry.
We'll bite our pens and start writin' again.
And the things we write are always true,
Sucker, so get a grip now we're talkin' about you.
Seems to me that you have a problem,
So we can see what we can do to solve them.
Think rap is a fad; you must be mad
'Cause we're so bad, we get respect you never had.
Tell the truth, James Brown was old,
Till Eric and Rak' came out with "I got soul."
Rap brings back old R & B
And if we would not
People could have forgot.
We want to make this perfectly clear:
We're talented and strong and have no fear
Of those who choose to judge but lack pizazz,
Talkin' all that jazz.
   ... [musical break]
Now we're not tryin' to be a boss to you.
We just wanna get across to you
That if you're talkin' jazz
The situation is a no win.
You might even get hurt my friend.
Stetsasonic, the hip-hop band,
And like Sly and the Family Stone
We will stand
Up for the music we live and play
And for the song we sing today.
For now, let us set the record straight,
And later on we'll have a forum and
A formal debate.
But it's important you remember though,
What you reap is what you sow.
Talkin' all that jazz.
Talkin' all that jazz.
Talkin' all that jazz.

Complexity

At first glance this song seems simple enough, perhaps too simple to warrant aesthetic consideration. It lacks the trappings of erudite allusion, opaque elision, and syntactico-semantic obscurity, which constitute the characteristic complexity of modernist poetry. Its straight-forward statement, paucity of metaphor, and repeated clichés suggest that it is simplistically shallow and devoid of any complexity or depth of meaning. But semantic complexity is richly enfolded within its seemingly artless and simple language. The song's multiple levels of meanings are detectable from the very title, and indeed encapsulated in its key word, "jazz." Jazz has, of course, at least two relevant but radically different and differently valorized meanings in the poem's context. The first concerns jazz as a musical art form originating in Afro-American culture, long opposed and discredited by the cultural establishment, but by now culturally legitimated throughout the world. The second sense concerns the most common slang use of jazz as "lying and exaggerated talk; also idle and foolish talk"; or "stuffy foolish-ness: humbug."[27]

This ambiguity and privileging opposition within the very meaning of jazz—its positively valorized standard usage as a musical art over its slang (hence less "legitimate") usage as lies and pretentious talk—is developed into a central theme of this rap and seems central to rap in general. "Talkin' All That Jazz" simultaneously exploits and questions this privileging oppo-sition, presenting rap as a force involved with legitimating the illegitimate, exposing the sociopolitical factors involved in such legitimation and challenging the legitimacy of the powers denying legitimacy to rap. In confronting these issues, the song in turn raises deeply philosophical questions about the nature of truth and art and about their sources of authority. For art, we should remember, though now culturally sacralized, was itself sometimes delig-itimated as pretentious lies and idle foolishness.

In order to dismiss this kind of reading from the outset, one might be tempted to argue that the term *jazz* is adequately disambiguated by the context of the title, and certainly by the complete song. For the phrase "talkin' all that jazz" seems to suggest that we are concerned not at all with jazz as positive music but only with negative *talk* and lies, specifically the pretentious, foolish lies that constitute the uninformed criticism of hip hop, the personified source of which is the confrontational target or "you" of the poem. "Heard you on the radio / Talk about rap, / Sayin' all that crap." The identification of talkin' jazz with lies and foolish talk is confirmed by linking it with the discourse of politicians ("You've made the same mistake politicians have / Talkin' all that Jazz"), and it certainly seems clinched by the lines "Lies, that's when you hide the truth, / It's when you talk more jazz than proof. / And when you lie and address something you don't know, / It's so whacked that it's bound to show."

But just as it is identified with negative lies, talkin' jazz is also positively identified as musical art by the very topic of the song—rap as an art. For, we must ask, what is rap but talkin' jazz? It is not merely jazz-related instrumental music nor even lyrics sung to jazz rhythms or tunes. The most distinctive feature of rap music is that it is defiantly talk rather than song, the word *rap* being a slang synonym for talk. And the linking of rap music with jazz is confirmed in the first stanza: "This is the music of a hip-hop band. / Jazz, well you can call it that. / But this jazz retains a new format."

These lines embody even more semantic complexities of valorization. The band accepts its identification with jazz as the most respected black cultural form and tradition to which hip hop is genealogically attached; but the acceptance is somewhat hesitant. For rap does not want to be seen as a mere variety of established jazz, not even of progressive jazz; rather, it insists on its originality. Rap's jazz, unlike standard jazz already appropriated by the establishment, "retains a new format," sustains novelty and freshness by maintaining a closer link to changing popular experience and vernacular expression (to the "majority" of the street). There is the hint that hip hop is thus truer to the original spirit of jazz; and there is also the hint that jazz has somehow been tainted through its past treatment by the cultural establishment and through its accommodating compliance with that treatment.[28] For surely the establishment's initial rejection of jazz as wildly exaggerated and foolish music helped give the term its negative slang meaning of foolish pretension and untruth; and this abiding negative meaning maintains a sense of the original rejection, which seems to introduce a troublingly negative trace in even its standard meaning as music and raises the lingering question of whether this music is truly art in the standard sacralized sense in which classical music obviously is.

These deep ambiguities of jazz are most cleverly manipulated by Stetsasonic to make the case for rap as an art. The meaning of jazz as pretentious lies, based both on its identification with art rather than truth and on its further rejection as serious art, is in turn used to dismiss as pretentious lying the renewed rejection of new jazz in the form of rap. The rappers reject as "talkin' jazz" the allegedly legitimate discourse of those who ignorantly reject rap as degenerate, appropriative talkin' jazz. The band at once employs and reverses the jazz versus serious truth distinction by asserting that their talking jazz is true (and true art), while the supposedly serious discourse of the antirap, antijazz critics is really talkin' jazz in the negative sense; for the latter are altogether misinformed, "narrow minded and poorly taught." Their allegedly true talk about true art is neither truth nor art but ignorant palaver devoid of critical understanding or creative pizzazz. In contrast to the weak "whacked" lies of its bigoted critics, rap's lines "are always true." Moreover, they are not mindlessly and carelessly uttered like the "cheap" condemnatory "crap" of radio talk, but instead thoughtfully composed in writing[29] and then performed by artists who are "talented and strong" and committed to original expression in this "new format." Thus, in contrast to its denunciatory criticism, rap is claimed to display both truth and artistry; a claim that this rap artfully demonstrates by its ingeniously double-edged and inversive method of asserting it.

Though complexity of meaning and witty twists of argument are undeniably found here, it may be denied that they are actually intended or that they exist for the real rap audience. Perhaps they are merely the product of our academic habit of reading (indeed, even torturing) texts to find ambiguities. Reading rap in this complex way, one might argue, is unfaithful to the spontaneity and simplicity of the genre and its audience. Moreover, by suggesting that simpler responses are inferior understandings, it serves to expropriate the art from its popular use and from the people who use it. Such a process, where intellectualized modes of appropriation are used to transform popular into elite art, is a virtual commonplace of cultural history.[30]

This line of objection to my interpretive reading is serious enough to demand immediate response. First, there is no compelling reason to limit the rap's meaning to explicit authorial intentions; its meaning is also a function of its language, a social product beyond the determining control of the individual author. The ambiguities of "jazz" and the cultural conflicts and history they embody are already there in the language through which the author must speak, whether he intends them or not. Similarly, since art can be appreciated in many ways and on many levels, new modes of appreciation by new audiences cannot be outlawed as necessarily disenfranchising those of the original audience. This only happens when the new intellectualized forms insist on imposing a privileged or exclusionary status as legitimate. But whatever our view on the intentional fallacy and the primacy of intended audience, I think the ambiguities and inversions are too prominent and pointed here to be unintended. Moreover, the average rap audience is very well equipped to understand them. For precisely this sort of ambiguity and inversion is basic to the black linguistic community.

Afro-American English is saliently ambiguous. For example, while "nigger" in white English is univocally a term of abuse, in black speech it is just as often "a term of affection, admiration, approval" (Holt 1972, 155). The reasons for its greater ambiguity should be obvious.

"Negro slaves were compelled to create a semi-clandestine vernacular" to express their desires while disguising them from the hostile scrutiny of their overseers, and they did so by giving ordinary English words specific black meanings along with their standard ones (Brown 1972, 135). One crucial method of multiplying meanings was by inverting them. Since language both embodies and sustains societal power relations, this method of inversion is particularly significant, both as a source of protest and as a source of extremely subtle linguistic skill.[31] It also, of course, helped make the black community especially adept at and familiar with the encoding and decoding of ambiguous and inverted messages. Rap fans, then, through their ordinary linguistic training, have typically mastered a wittily indirect communicative skill, which one researcher regards as "a form of verbal art,"[32] and which enables them readily to process texts of great semantic complexity if the content is relevant to their experience. Thus, Stetsasonic's ambiguous, inversive play on the notion of "talkin' jazz" is hardly beyond the reach of the rap audience, even if it is far less obvious than the text's most transparent and by now commonplace inversion of "bad" to mean good. ("Think rap is a fad; you must be mad / 'Cause we're so bad, we get respect you never had.")

Philosophical Content

Rap can be intellectually rewarding, not merely because of the stimulation linked to its polysemic complexity, but also because of its philosophical insights. For just as popular art has been condemned as inevitably superficial because of its simplistic, undemanding semantic structures, it is similarly condemned for being devoid of any deep content.

Since popular art's use of clichés is often held to be a prime cause of its bland shallowness, something should be said to vindicate the obvious clichés in "Talkin' All That Jazz." For the song is studded with some of the most trite and most commonplace proverbs: "Talk is cheap"; "Beauty is ... just skin deep"; "You can't have your cake and eat it too"; "What you reap is what you sow." However, within the particular context of this rap, these proverbs acquire new meanings that not only depart from but challenge the clichés of cultural thought that they normally embody. First and most simply, by their very use in arguments against the cultural cliché that rap is not art, these proverbs lose their bland, commonplace character. Second, their use is aesthetically justified as a reinforcing verbal counterpart to the method of appropriative sampling that forms the major theme of this rap. For just as rap DJs cannibalize familiar prepackaged musical phrases to create an original sound by placing them in new contexts, so the MC can appropriate old proverbs and give them new significance by his recontextualizing application of them in his rap.

Consider the first two clichés about truth and beauty, which together form a couplet: "Talk, well I heard talk is cheap. / Well, like beauty, talk is just skin deep." So conjoined in this rap's specific context, these clichés are anything but simplistic and commonplace in meaning. Instead, they undermine with ambiguity the simple, common truths they standardly express while also suggesting philosophical theses on the nature of language, beauty, and aesthetic judgment which radically diverge from and challenge commonplace dogma on these issues.

Of course, "talk is cheap" can surely be understood here in its standard sense; it costs nothing, requires no effort, knowledge, or talent to blast rap with ignorant criticisms. Such uninformed "talkin' jazz" is worthless, cheap talk. The proverb's standard sense also suggests the commonplace opposition between mere talk (which is easy but effects nothing) and real action or performance, which not only costs effort but actually does something. And Stetsasonic employ this opposition in the contrast they draw between the "narrow-minded" critics who, lacking the pizazz to create art, simply talk about and "judge" it, and, on the other hand, the rap artists who are "talented and strong" and fearless enough to act and create rather than merely "speculate" with "cheap talk."

However, over and against these standard senses, the contextual content of the rap is urging, more strikingly, that so-called cheap talk is not really so cheap at all. It is instead very costly. First, its ignorant maligning of rap deceives the public, insults and persecutes rap artists and their audience, and thereby creates a confusing "fuss" over the nature of hip hop. The clichéd distinction between talk and action is thus challenged by showing that mere talk can constitute an action having costly consequences. This argument is painfully confirmed by the actual facts of rap's condemnation and persecution by people totally unfamiliar with the music who rely on the hearsay of others who are themselves as disinclined to listen to rap as to let it be heard.[33] Moreover, as "Talkin' All That Jazz" also argues, the seemingly cheap condemnatory talk of the critics will end up costing them dearly as well; for "when you lie and you talk a lot, / People tell you to step off a lot." Injured by their "talk about rap / Sayin' all that crap," Stetsasonic violently warn rap's denouncers of the high price of such cheap talk: "You said it wasn't art, / So now we're gonna rip you apart."

If uninformed "cheap" talk can have such powerful effects, what is the source of discourse's power and authority? If "talkin' jazz" can be false criticism or true art, if discourse in general can be taken as lies or truth, what determines discursive truth or aesthetic legitimacy? These heady philosophical issues are ingeniously linked in the same clichéd couplet, where talk (or discourse) is identified with beauty as being "just skin deep." Here again we see how the specific rap context provides a bland old cliché with radically new meaning. Given rap's ghetto roots and its aesthetic rejection and persecution as black music, the complaint that beauty is just skin deep is transformed from the hackneyed critique of beauty's superficiality (its concern with surface appearance) and comes to embody the powerfully provocative charge that beauty is connected with racial bias, with reactions linked to the surface color of skin. In more general terms, aesthetic judgment is not the pure, lofty, and disinterested contemplation of form it is standardly taken to be; instead, it is profoundly conditioned and governed by sociopolitical (including racial) prejudices and interests.

Thus, in contrast to the clichéd view that sees truth and beauty as altogether independent of power relations, this rap emphasizes the different power relations involved in determining truth and aesthetic legitimacy. Two sources of discursive authority are located. The first is sociopolitical power as manifested and exercised, for example, by the control of media and political institutions. Though uninformed and inimically biased, the antirap critics deliver their verdicts through the pervasive, legitimating medium of radio. Their condemnation of rap as devoid of aesthetic merit and unworthy of artistic status can therefore pass for truth, since it is broadcast without challenge by the dominant media and thus receives the aura of expertise and authority typically associated with views propagated through privileged channels of mass communication. Rappers, on the other hand, particularly those with an underground political message, have been denied similar radio access, let alone equal time, to present and defend their art. Truth and artistic status are thus in large part issues of sociopolitical control. The song reinforces this message when it links rap's artistic denunciation and denial by the media with the mistakes of politicians who disvalue and disenfranchise the black community. With an implied pragmatist epistemology that puts no store in social truths no one believes or in artistic status no one recognizes, the song suggests that the truth of rap's artistic status is not something independently there to be discovered but rather something that must be made; and it can be made only by challenging and overcoming the established, establishment truth of rap's artistic illegitimacy. The song urges and itself represents such a challenge. Given the serious sociopolitical interests and stakes involved in the struggle for artistic legitimation, the rappers realize that this struggle is an essentially violent one; and to defend hip hop against its media critics, they are prepared to use violence: "You said it wasn't art, / So now we're gonna rip you apart." The threat of violence is seriously intended, for it is repeated later in the song, warning anyone who sounds off against rap: "You might even get hurt my friend."[34]

Aware of the connection between artistic status and sociopolitical power, the rappers also realize that the establishment's rejection of hip hop can be opposed by attacking the contradictions and weaknesses of its sociopolitical base. While American society claims to be a liberal democracy with free speech and majority rule, this is contradicted by its censorship of rap and, more generally, by its cultural leader's tendency to identify true art with only high art, even though the majority of Americans find more aesthetic satisfaction in the arts of popular culture. In defending their music against its media critics, Stetsasonic argue that these elitist cultural czars are overstepping the democratic power base that empowers their judgments. In terms of taste they "are a minority"; just as "in terms of thought" they are "narrow-minded and poorly taught / About hip hop's aims" for a more democratic and emancipatory black popular art.[35] In contrast, the rappers defend their art by aligning it with the majority. Their insistence that "what we sample of is a majority" aims to justify not only their method of sampling but their resultant musical creation by suggesting that they reflect popular taste and majority interests.

"Talkin' All That Jazz" not only appeals to rap's majoritarian democratic power base, but, through its own polemic, seeks to mobilize and expand rap's popular support. One of its polemical strategies involves the politics of personal pronouns. The whole song is structured on the opposition between "you" and "us." On the narrowest literal level, the "us" is simply Stetsasonic, the hip hop band that is singing this song. Ordinarily this could suggest that the listening audience would be part of the "you" to whom the song is addressed; and it is of course addressed to its audience. Since the song is, however, an angry protest, it takes care to address its audience not as a "you" but instead distinguishes them, at the very outset, from the confrontational "you" of its hostile message—the radio's antirap critic. For the vast majority of the song's audience are not radio speakers but only listeners.

The audience is further encouraged to assimilate themselves to the celebrated "we" of the song by their opposition to the confrontational "you" who is aggressively attacked as an ignorant and untalented but powerfully oppressive and hypercritical minority. The "we" thus comes to mean not only Stetsasonic but the whole hip-hop community whose cause they are advocating. And it reaches still farther by appealing to those who are not yet fans of hip hop but can identify with it because of their common opposition to the media and political authorities against which this song and hip hop generally are defiantly struggling. Anyone resentful of the weak, "whacked" babblings of media figures and politicians, anyone angry with our society's authoritative spokesmen and their iniquitous exercise of power, any artist (or athlete or laborer) incensed at being negatively judged by critics lacking the talent, strength, or pizazz to perform what they haughtily criticize; to all such people, and their number is legion, this song should appeal through its impassioned spirit of protest and thus should enlist increasing support for rap, outside its original and core ghetto audience.

This strategy of gaining acceptance for rap by widening the sociocultural base of its support is shrewdly pursued through at least three other rhetorical devices. First, in the third stanza, rap is linked to (and "brings back") the music of rhythm and blues (R & B), arguably the source of all rock music and a genre that achieved great popularity among white audiences not only in America but throughout the world. This implicit appeal to a wider and also white audience is subtly developed in the last stanza's invocation of Sly and the Family Stone, a group that, though led by a black (Sly Stone) and committed to black pride, also expressed a pluralistic spirit of brotherhood (manifest in its composition by blacks and whites, men and women) and was extremely popular with white audiences.[36]

Sandwiched between the invocations of Sly and of R & B, we find a third strategy for making rap more acceptable to the general audience: a reassurance that rap's claim to artistic legitimacy is not a demand for hegemony. In promising "we're not tryin' to be a boss to you," the "Stets" reassure the unconverted audience of hip hop that their aim is simply to be heard, not to silence others, even if they are prepared to "hurt" those whose "talkin' jazz" seeks to censure and censor rap. In proposing the goal and hope of peaceful pluralistic coexistence (as opposed to the "no-win" situation of violent cultural strife), the rappers are cleverly appealing to one of American society's most widely held and deeply cherished tenets, the freedom of pluralist tolerance. If we are tempted to dismiss this ideal as mere bourgeois liberal ideology, it remains effective as an argument to those pervaded by that ideology, and its scope is actually far wider. For it also reemerges in the utopian visions of Marxists like Theodor Adorno, whose sociopolitical (and aesthetic) ideal is "difference without domination." The advocacy of such ideals, of course, adds yet another aspect to the rich philosophical content of this song.

I conclude my discussion of this content by briefly noting the second source of discursive and aesthetic authority that the song recognizes. This is the charismatic authority of artistic and rhetorical power. If truth and artistic status depend on a sociocultural power structure, this structure is not permanently fixed but is instead a changing field of struggle. And one way a population's beliefs and tastes can be transformed is by the expressive power of the discourse or art presented to them, though of course their appreciation of this power will always rest on some of their antecedent beliefs and tastes that remain in place.[37] Thus, the song suggests, we listeners can come to reject the critics' talkin' jazz as lies and instead recognize rap's talkin' jazz as art, truth, and proof by sensing their relative expressive power. While the critic's discourse is palpably weak ("so whacked that it's bound to show") and lacks "pizzazz," rap's discourse proves its truth and artistic status by its punch and power, by being "talented and strong."

Such proof through perceptual persuasion is not a confused aberration but an important form of argument in aesthetics and elsewhere;[38] and this song, a rap manifesto in rap, is clearly meant to represent such a perceptually persuasive proof of rap's artistic status by its own specific artistic power. Stetsasonic do not pretend to provide an exhaustive survey or extended "formal debate"; they claim "to set the record straight" about rap and its record-sampling distortions within the mere space of a record by the convincing and exemplary appeal of "the song [they] sing today": a self-consciously self-asserting and arguably self-validating declaration of the truth that rap is art.

Artistic Self-Consciousness, Creativity, and Form

This self-conscious self-assertion of artistic status is more important than it might seem, for artistic self-consciousness is regarded by many aestheticians as an essential feature of art.[39] Thus, one reason why popular arts have been denied artistic status is that they fail to claim it. They do not, Adorno and Horkheimer argue (1944, 121), even "pretend to be art" but rather accept their status as entertainment industries. They do not, Bourdieu argues, insist on their own aesthetic legitimacy but instead meekly accept the dominant high-art aesthetic that essentially negates them.[40] Lacking the requisite artistic self-consciousness and self-respect to claim artistic status, popular art does not merit or achieve it. However true this may be for other popular arts, it cannot be said for rap. Stetsasonic, like countless other rappers, "stand / Up for the music [they] live and play," aggressively claiming and proudly celebrating rap as an art.

"Talkin' All That Jazz" evinces at least five aspects of this proud artistic self-consciousness, apart from its firm assertion of artistic status. First, since art is something that stands out from ordinary conduct and humdrum experience by its superior skill and quality, this song insists on rap's superior talent, strength, and pizazz vis-à-vis ordinary cheap talk. Second, if art's essentially historical character means that to be a work of art is to belong to an artistic tradition, the song underlines rap's connection to such a tradition. It does this most pointedly by first describing itself as a new kind of jazz, thus aligning itself with the black musical form most widely recognized as legitimate art; and then further connecting itself with "old R & B," the established popularity of which is said to be enhanced or insured through rap's "bring[ing] back" of its rhythms. There are also the more specific and intricate intertextual links to Sly Stone, James Brown, and the rap crew Eric and Rakim, which give a fuller sense of rap's place in and shaping of a continuing artistic tradition—one that involves both the recognition and contestation that any healthy and fruitful tradition must display.[41]

A very important aspect of recent artistic tradition (and one often regarded as essential to the very nature of art) is art's oppositional stance. Many maintain like Adorno that art—to qualify as such, to display its defining originality and distinction from the ordinary—must somehow take a stand against a generally accepted but unacceptable reality or status quo (artistic or societal), even if this opposition be expressed only implicitly by art's fictionality or by the difficulties it poses for ordinary comprehension. Popular arts, they argue, cannot display such opposition because their popularity requires an appeal to the most commonly accepted views and standards and to the most elementary modes of understanding. Thus, these so-called arts must not be granted true artistic status.[42]

Whether or not such an oppositional character is indeed essential to art, it is certainly present in rap, not only explicitly but often self-consciously. Violent protest of the status quo—the establishment culture and media, the politicians and police, and the representations and realities they all seek to impose—is, as we have seen, a central and often thematized feature of many rap lyrics. But "Talkin' All That Jazz" most clearly exemplifies rap's self-consciousness as *artistic* opposition, attacking and defying the cultural czars who deny rap aesthetic legitimacy or artistic status. Moreover, apart from this explicit content, its very form, its dramatic monologue of confrontational discourse, is structured by the oppositional stance.

Two other central features of modern artistic consciousness are frequently taken to be essential for any art worthy of the name and are just as frequently denied to the products of popular culture: concern for creativity and attention to form. Both can be connected to art's allegedly requisite oppositional character. For art's creative injunction to be new implies at least some opposition to the old and familiar, while preoccupation with form rather than content seems to reverse our ordinary cognitive and practical concerns (and thus has come to define for some the specifically aesthetic attitude).[43] Both these creative and formalist concerns are powerfully present in "Talkin' All That Jazz," and their demonstration will conclude my aesthetic account of this rap and of rap in general.

Though its method of appropriative sampling challenges romantic notions of unique novelty and pure originality, rap claims to be creative. It moreover insists that originality can be manifested in the revisionary appropriation of the old, whether this be old records or the old proverbs that "Talkin' All That Jazz" samples but creatively endows with new meanings. Indeed, "Talkin' All That Jazz" is all about rap's acute consciousness of its novelty as an artistic form, a consciousness painfully sharpened by rap's having been persecuted as such. With its talking rather than singing, sampling rather than composing or playing, rap's departure from traditional music provoked the denial of its legitimacy, even as a popular art. But in the economy of two lines, Stetsasonic cleverly establish rap's link to artistic tradition through its connection with jazz, while at the same time reaffirming the genre's creative divergence and importance as a new artistic form. "Jazz, well you can call it that / But this jazz retains a new format." Moreover, the single phrase that rap "*retains* a new format" (rather than, say, *inventing* one) ingeniously captures the complex paradox of artistic tradition and innovation that Eliot labored to express: the idea that art can and must be novel to be traditional (and traditional to be novel), that one cannot conform to our artistic tradition by simply conforming to it, since artistic tradition is one of novelty and deviation from conformity.

Rap thus refutes the dogma that concern for form and formal experimentation cannot be found in popular art.[44] It moreover displays the thematized attention to artistic medium and method often regarded as the hallmark of contemporary high art. Sampling is not only rap's most radical formal innovation (since some earlier pop songs experimented with speech rather than song); it is also the most concerned with rap's artistic medium—recorded music. And, not surprisingly, it is extremely contested, in the courts of law as well as the court of culture. The aesthetic defense of sampling constitutes the motivating theme of "Talkin' All That Jazz," which from the outset links the issue of rap's artistic legitimacy with that of its sampling method.

> Well, here's how it started
> Heard you on the radio
> Talk about rap,
> Sayin all that crap
> About how we sample,
> Give an example.
> Think we'll let you get away with that.
> You criticize our method
> Of how we make records
> You said it wasn't art,
> So now we're gonna rip you apart.

In order to defend rap's claim to be creative art, sampling must be defended from the obvious and plausible charge that it is just the stealing or copying of already existing songs. The defense is that rap's sampling is not an end in itself, an attempt to reproduce or imitate already popular records, but rather a formal technique or "method" to make from old fragments new songs with "a new format," by innovative manipulation of the technical media of the recording industry: records, turntables, tapes, etc. As with any artistic method or "tool," sampling's aesthetic significance or value depends on how it is used ("It's only of importance when I make it *a priority*") and thus ultimately needs to be judged within particular concrete contexts; thus, the maligning critics are enjoined to "give an example" of how sampling vitiates rap's artistry. Stetsasonic moreover assert that sampling is only "a portion" of rap's method and not always its highest priority. This message and their challenge to "give an example" are formalistically reinforced by the fact that the actual use of sampling and scratch mixing in "Talkin' All That Jazz" is relatively negligible.

Aware that rap's innovative technique of sampling might be dismissed as an ephemeral gimmick, Stetsasonic explicitly answer the "mad" critics who "think rap is a fad" devoid of creative potential and staying power, by pointing to the "strong" talent of its artists and the enduring "respect" it has won among its growing audience. And the Stets are not just "talkin' jazz." For while the pop culture pundits thought rap would barely survive a season when it appeared in 1979, it is finally achieving some critical recognition. "Now as the 90's begin," writes *New York Times* critic Jon Pareles, rap "is both the most startlingly original and fasted growing genre in popular music."[45]

But while granting its creative originality, Pareles questions rap's achievement of coherent form. Its techniques of sampling and mixing and its fragmented, mass-media mentality prevent the creation of ordered form and logical structure, resulting in songs fractured by "dislocations and discontinuities" where "rhythm is paramount and non sequiturs are perpetual." The songs "don't develop from a beginning to an end," thus giving the sense that "a song could be cut off at any moment." This is certainly true for some rap, and perhaps for that which most immediately attracts attention and hostility by its deviation from accepted form. But it is at best a very partial and exaggerated account of the genre as a whole. For rap is full of songs firmly structured either on clear narrative development or on coherent logical argument. The narrative form includes the many celebratory ballads of the rapper's exploits and the equally numerous cautionary moral exempla about drugs, venereal disease, and the life of crime. The logical format is exemplified by many of rap's songs of protest and black pride, including its frequent manifestoes of rap's self-pride. "Talkin' All That Jazz" falls into this last category, and its formal and logical coherence is undeniable.

It is composed of four clearly structured stanzas, which, though of slightly unequal length, are equally framed by the same instrumental interlude that at once distinguishes and connects them. These stanzas are further formalistically united by their closing with the same oneline refrain, which is also the song's title. Finally, while this closing line appears once in each of the first three stanzas, in the fourth and final stanza it is given three times, as if to recall, reinforce, and sum up the three preceding stanzas and their arguments.

The song's argument in defense of rap is also very coherently structured. The first stanza begins with the condemnation of rap and sampling followed by the threatening, protesting counterclaim of rap's creative artistic status. The second proceeds to refute rap's condemnation by explaining the role of sampling, stressing rap's popular appeal, and pointing to the elitist narrowness and ignorance of its condemnatory critics while continuing the threat of retaliatory violence ("You step on us and we'll step on you"). Stanza three continues the theme of "angry" retaliation against the maligning lies of rap critics while further justifying rap's legitimacy both in terms of the truth, talent, and strength it displays and because of its connection with and renovating preservation of the artistic tradition of Afro-American music. The final stanza, while reinforcing this traditional link and maintaining the song's proud "stand" of resistance and threat of violence, also extends an invitation of peaceful coexistence to rap's as yet unconverted audience, showing that they need not be afraid of granting rap artistic legitimacy. This closing advocacy of pluralistic tolerance (of "not tryin' to be a boss") does not come from the fear of rap's weakness in the face of critical scrutiny. Rap is ready for "a formal debate," but only when it can have an adequate "forum" (i.e., a public space) within which to express itself, a forum that the media and cultural establishment have so far denied it.

Here again we have the insightful and ingeniously telescoped linking of the aesthetic and the political. The struggle for aesthetic legitimacy (a symptom of more general social struggles) can only achieve the form of refined and carefully reasoned debates about form when one can enjoy the security of being heard. The rappers are still struggling for that hearing, and to get it Stetsasonic must "for now" speak more urgently and violently, so less formally. If the denigration and suppression of rap's voice incites violent protest rather than sweet aesthetic reasonings, the enemies of rap are themselves responsible ("What you reap is what you sow").

This prioritization of getting a hearing before going into a formal debate, of securing expressive legitimacy before concentrating on intricacies of form, can be taken as a critical but defensive self-commentary on this song's own formal status, and it raises a crucial formalist issue that rap must face. For while "Talkin' All That Jazz" achieves formal unity and logical coherence, it remains formalistically more simple and traditional than many other raps, which talk much less about sampling but instead apply it much more extensively, complexly, and emphatically. But while such songs produce a far more radically "new format," it is one far more susceptible to Pareles' charge of formal incoherence.

This suggests a tension between rap's aims of formal innovation and its satisfaction of the formal coherence required of art. For rap's artistic innovation, particularly its technique of sampling, is closely connected with elements of fragmentation and the breaking of forms. This tension between formal innovation and already appreciable formal coherence is the formal debate in which rap is now actively engaged. It is still in the process of testing the limits of its innovative techniques and the formal sensibilities of its audience in order to find the right balance—a form that is both new and yet somehow assimilable to our changing aesthetic tradition and sensibility. Less than fifteen years old, rap is still far from a solution and from artistic maturity. It will attain neither if it is not first accorded the artistic legitimacy necessary to pursue its own development and that of its audience without the oppression and dismissive abuse of the cultural establishment and without the compulsion to sell out to the most immediate and crassest of commercial pressures.

"Talkin' All That Jazz," a song advocating rap's new format while remaining comfortably close to traditional form, is an appeal for such legitimacy, and an appealing one because of the way it meets traditional aesthetic criteria. It thus provides us intellectuals with a more tempting invitation to enter the formal debate about rap, a debate that it defers to the future and that only the future will resolve.

Notes

1. Rap's censorship became national news when 2 Live Crew were banned and arrested in Florida in the summer of 1990, but it was prevalent long before then. Of course, more recently, rap has proven too popular not to be coopted and absorbed (in its milder forms) by the established media. Its rhythms and style have been adopted by mainstream mass-media advertising, and one mild-mannered rapper (Fresh Prince) was given his own prime-time major network show. For more details on rap's censorship and rap's complex relation to mass-media culture and technology, see the chapter on rap in *Pragmatist Aesthetics: Living Beauty, Rethinking Art*, in which I develop many of this chapter's points.

2. See, for example, Ice-T's "Hit the Deck," which aims to "demonstrate rappin' as a fine art." There are countless other raps that emphatically declare rap's poetic and artistic status; among the more forceful are Stetsasonic's "Talkin' All That Jazz"; BDP's "I'm Still #1," "Ya Slippin'," "Ghetto Music," and "Hip Hop Rules"; and Kool Moe Dee's "The Best."

3. Hip hop actually designates an organic cultural complex wider than rap. It includes breakdancing and graffiti, and also a stylized but casual style of dress, where hightop sneakers became high fashion. Rap music supplied the beat for the breakdancers; some rappers testify to having practiced graffiti; and hip-hop fashion is celebrated in many raps, one example being Run-DMC's "My Adidas."

4. For a more detailed account of the aesthetic dimension of postmodernism, see Shusterman 1989.

5. See, for example, Abrahams 1964; this study of a Philadelphia ghetto revealed that speaking skills "confer high social status," and that even among young males, "ability with words is as highly valued as physical strength" (31, 59). Studies of Washington and Chicago ghettos have confirmed this. See Hannerz 1969, which shows that verbal skill is "widely appreciated among ghetto men" not only for competitive practical purposes but for "entertainment value" (84–85); see also Kochman 1972. Along with its narrower use to designate the traditional and stylized practice of verbal insult, black signifying has a more general sense of encoded or indirect communication, which relies heavily on the special background knowledge and particular context of the communicants. For an impressively complex and theoretically sophisticated analysis of signifying as such a generic trope and its use "in black texts as explicit theme, implicit rhetorical strategy, and as a principle of literary history," see Gates 1988, 89.

6. Such linguistic strategies of evasion and indirection (which include inversion, shucking, tomming, marking, and loud-talking, as well as the more generic notion of signifying, are discussed at length in Kochman 1972, Holt 1972, and Mitchell-Kernan 1972.

7. I later try to demonstrate some of this rich complexity by a close reading of Stetsasonic's "Talkin' All That Jazz."

8. See, for example, Ice-T's "Rhyme Pays," Public Enemy's "Bring the Noise," Run-DMC's "Jam-master Jammin'," and BDP's "Ya Slippin'."

9. It is called scratch mixing not only because the manual placement of the needle on particular tracks scratches the records but because the DJ hears the scratch in his ear when he cues the needle on the track to be sampled before actually adding it to the sound of the other record already being sent out on the sound system.

10. See, for example, Public Enemy's "Caught, Can We Get a Witness," Stetsasonic's "Talkin' All That Jazz," and BDP's "I'm Still #1," "Ya Slippin'," and "The Blueprint." The motivating image of this last rap highlights the simulacral notion of hip-hop originality. In privileging their underground style as original and superior to "the soft commercial sound" of other rap, they connect its greater originality with its greater closeness to rap's ghetto origins: "You got a copy, I read from the blueprint." But a blueprint is itself a copy, not an original; indeed, it is a simulacrum or representation of a designed object that typically does not yet (if it will ever) exist as a concrete original object.

11. See Jameson 1984, 73–75. This is not to deny that rap ever achieves any unity or formal coherence of its own; I argue below that it does in "Talkin' All That Jazz."

12. For a critique of this early view of Eliot's and for an explanation of the reasons why Eliot himself abandoned it in formulating his later theory of tradition, see Shusterman 1988, 156–67.

13. See, respectively, "My Philosophy" and "Ghetto Music." The lyrics of "Ya Slippin' " and "Hip Hop Rules" respectively date themselves as 1987 and 1989. Public Enemy's "Don't Believe the Hype" has a 1988 time tag, and similar time tags can be found in raps by Ice-T, Kool Moe Dee, and many others.

14. See, for example, Habermas 1985, 1–22.

15. See BDP's "My Philosophy" and "Gimme Dat, (Woy)." The lyrics of their knowledge rap "Who Protects Us from You?" describe it as "a public service announcement brought to you by the scientists of Boogie Down Productions." In the jacket notes to their albums *Ghetto Music* and *Edutainment*, KRS-One describes himself as "Metaphysician."

16. See "I'm Still #1." For BDP's attack on establishment history and media and its stereotypes, see especially "My Philosophy," "You Must Learn," and "Why Is That."

17. This phrase and notion, for example, provide the central theme of Kool Moe Dee's "Do You Know What Time It Is?"

18. For an account of Dewey's aesthetics and its contemporary relevance, see Shusterman 1992, chap. 1.

19. The best example of this is Gary Byrd, a New York radio DJ who developed a literacy program based on rap. For more details, see Toop 1984, 45–46.

20. Grandmaster Flash complained that, because of the novelty and virtuosity of his cutting, "the crowd would stop dancing and just gather round like a seminar. This is what I didn't want. This wasn't school, it was time to shake your ass." Quoted from Toop 1984, 72.

21. See Queen Latifah's "Dance for Me" and Ice-T's "Hit the Deck." For a similar emphasis on the mesmerizing possession and physically and spiritually moving power of rap in both performer and audience, see Kool Moe Dee's "Rock Steady" and "The Best."

22. The point is made most explicitly in Plato's *Ion*. The direction and valorization of this chain of divine madness is wittily reversed in a song by Kool Moe Dee ("Get the Picture"), where his hypnotic rapping is identified with "knowledge" and "telling you the truth," which brings the rapper's possessed audience up to the level of the gods, challenging their supremacy and captivating them as well: "I start to float / On the rhymes I wrote / Ascending to a level with the gods and I tote / Loads and mounds of people / As they reach new heights / A half a mile from heaven is the party site / And I'm the attraction. / The gods will be packed in / Coming out of their pockets for me to rock it / And Acting / Like they've never ever been entertained / They try to act godly but they can't maintain / ... And Venus would peak on every word I speak / Zeus would get loose / Fully induced. / I'll make Apollo's rhymes sound like / Mother Goose. / By night's end Mercury is so hyped / He'd spread the word / That there's a god of the mic / Captivating all the other gods / By the masses / Described as a dark-skinned brother in glasses."

23. See, for example, Ventura 1986 and Thompson 1984.

24. For more discussion of these two notions of aesthetics, see Shusterman 1989.

25. It is, for example, the only song to appear on both the popular *Yo, MTV Raps* and *Monster TV Rap Hits* albums.

26. Nor does my printed transcription of the lyrics convey that they are delivered in an antiphonic style by three voices that alternate irregularly between lines and sometimes within the very same line, adding to the rap's jumpy syncopated style and formal complexity.

27. I take these definitions from *Funk and Wagnall's Standard Desk Dictionary* and *Webster's Collegiate Dictionary*. The *Random House Dictionary* conveys essentially the same meaning of "insincere, exaggerated, or pretentious talk."

28. Rap is far more outspoken in its black pride and challenge of white cultural and political domination than jazz, which is not surprising, since the latter evolved in a black experience much closer to slavery.

29. This emphasis on rap as deliberately composed writing rather than mere talk highlights rap's claim to literacy as well as artistry. The poem does not, however, draw a firm dichotomy between talking as lies and writing as truth; for in presenting the truth to their hostile critics, the rappers are not only writing but "talkin' about you."

30. See, for example, Levin's (1988) excellent study of America's transfiguration of Shakespeare and opera from popular to elite art.

31. As Holt (1972) explains: "Blacks clearly recognized that to master the language of whites was in effect to consent to be mastered by it through the white definitions of caste built into the semantic/social system. Inversion therefore becomes the defensive mechanism which enables blacks to fight linguistic, and thereby psychological entrapment.... Words and phrases were given reverse meanings and functions changed. Whites, denied access to the semantic extensions of duality, connotations, and denotations that developed within black usage, could only interpret the same material according to its original singular meaning ... enabling blacks to deceive and manipulate whites without penalty. This protective process, understood and shared by blacks became a contest of matching wits ... [and a] form of linguistic guerilla

warfare [that] protected the subordinated, permitted the masking and disguising of true feelings, allowed the subtle assertion of self, and promoted group solidarity" (155).

32. See Mitchell-Kernan 1972, 326–27. This form of verbal art is one that in fine Deweyan fashion is extremely continuous with and enhancive of ordinary life. We should not forget that rapping was a linguistic style before it went musical, and this sense of rapping, of course, remains.

33. An FBI director, for example, issued an official warning regarding a rap by N.W.A. (Niggers With Attitude), without ever hearing the song; a survey of the protest mail received by the group revealed that none of these antirap critics had in fact heard the song in question or were at all familiar with other rap music. Such hearsay-based animosity has resulted in cancellations of rap concerts and the censoring and confiscation of rap records. For more details on these matters, see Marsh and Pollack 1989.

34. The violence of this struggle often exceeds the domain of mere symbolic violence. Beyond critique and counter-critique, the establishment exercises the actual violence of censorship and police coercion, while the rap forces employ the retaliatory violence of rap's blasting noise (which is thematized in many rap songs) and the threat of physical violence born of extended frustration and oppression. These two forms of retaliatory violence are emphasized and cleverly linked in Spike Lee's *Do the Right Thing*, in which the violent silencing of loud rap leads to a neighborhood riot.

35. The contradictions of the democratic establishment's censoring repudiation of rap is pointedly expressed in the title song of Ice-T's album *Freedom of Speech … Just Watch What You Say*, and in the very name of the crew Public Enemy, which mischievously plays on the two different meanings of "public" here in sharp contradiction: the institutionally official versus truly representative of the people.

36. See Marcus 1975, 82. The book contains an excellent chapter devoted to Sly Stone's career (55–111).

37. Hence, the song's appeal to the antecedent beliefs of democratic majoritarianism and pluralistic tolerance, and to the antecedent tastes for R & B and Sly and the Family Stone.

38. I discuss this form of argument in considerable detail in Shusterman 1978, 1981, 1986, and 1988.

39. Wollheim (1968), for example, speaks of "the perennial and ineradicable self-consciousness of art" (16). Indeed, twentieth-century art has been so preoccupied with the concept of art that Danto (1986) can speak of art as having turned into its own philosophy.

40. See Bourdieu (1979, 41, 48, 395), where he is led to suggest that popular culture's implicit acceptance of its denied artistic status means that in a sense "there is no popular art."

41. For an elaboration of this point, see Shusterman 1988, 157–64, 170–90.

42. See Adorno and Horkheimer 1944; Adorno 1970, 320–23, 340–41; van den Haag 1957, 504–36, esp. 514–18; and Broudy 1972, 110–12.

43. See Bourdieu 1979, 3, 30–35.

44. See, for example, Bourdieu 1979, 32–33, and Kaplan 1967, 53.

45. Pareles 1990, 1, 28. Many rap songs, particularly those that trace and celebrate the history of hip hop, explicitly flaunt rap's stunning success at outlasting the critics' constant predictions of its early demise and thereby argue for its value and rich creative potential in terms of its staying power. See, for example, BDP's "Hip Hop Rules."

References

Abrahams, Roger. [1964] 1970. *Deep Down in the Jungle: Negro Narrative Folklore from the Streets of Philadelphia.* Chicago: Aldine Press.

Adorno, Theodor Wiesengrund. [1970] 1984. *Aesthetic Theory.* Translated by C. Lenhardt. London: Routledge & Kegan Paul.

Adorno, Theodor Wiesengrund, and Max Horkheimer. [1944] 1986. *Dialectic of Enlightenment.* Translated by John Cumming. New York: Continuum.

Bourdiue, Pierre. [1979] 1984. *Distinction: A Social Critique of the Judgment of Taste.* Translated by Richard Nice. Cambridge, Mass.: Harvard University Press.

Broudy, Harry. 1972. *Enlightened Cherishing: An Essay on Aesthetic Education.* Urbana: University of Illinois Press.

Danto, Arthur. 1964. The Artworld. *Journal of Philosophy* 61: 571–584.

———. 1986. *The Philosophical Disenfranchisement of Art.* New York: Columbia University Press.

Gates, Henry Louis, Jr. 1988. *The Signifying Monkey: A Theory of Afro-American Literary Criticism.* New York: Oxford University Press.

Habermas, Jürgen. [1970] 1988. *On the Logic of the Social Sciences.* Translated by Shierry Weber Nicholsen and Jerry A. Stark. Cambridge, Mass.: MIT Press.

Hannerz, Ulf. 1969. *Soulside: Inquiries into Ghetto Culture and Community.* New York: Columbia University Press.

Holt, Grace Sims. "Inversion" in Black Communication. In Kochman 1972, 152–159.

Jameson, Frederic. 1984. Postmodernism, or the Cultural Logic of Late Capitalism. *New Left Review* 146: 53–92.

Kochman, Thomas. Toward an Ethnography of Black American Speech Behavior. In Kochman 1972, 241–264.

———, ed. 1972. *Rappin' and Stylin' Out: Communication in Urban Black America.* Urbana: University of Illinois Press.

Levin, Lawrence. 1988. *Highbrow/Lowbrow: The Emergence of Cultural Hierarchy in America.* Cambridge, Mass.: Harvard University Press.

Marcus, Greil. [1975] 1982. *Mystery Train: Images of America in Rock 'n Roll Music.* New York: Dalton.

Marsh, Dave, and Phyllis Pollack. 1989. Wanted for Attitude. *Village Voice,* October 10, 33–37.

Mitchell-Kernan, Claudia. Signifying, Loud-Talking, and Marking. In Kochman 1972, 315–335.

Pareles, Jon. 1990. How Rap Moves to Television's Beat. *New York Times,* January 14, sec. 2.

Schiller, Friedrich. [1795] 1982. *On the Aesthetic Education of Man.* Translated by Elizabeth M. Wilkinson and L.A. Willoughby. Oxford: Clarendon Press.

Shusterman, Richard. 1986. Convention: Variations on a Theme. *Philosophical Investigations* 9: 36–55.

———, 1981. Evaluative Reasoning in Criticism. *Ratio* 23: 141–157.

———, 1978. The Logic of Interpretation. *Philosophical Quarterly* 28: 310–324.

———, 1989. Postmodernism and the Aesthetic Turn. *Poetics Today* 10: 605–622.

———, 1992. *Pragmatist Aesthetics: Living Beauty, Rethinking Art.* Oxford: Basic Blackwell.

———, 1988. *T.S. Eliot and the Philosophy of Criticism.* New York: Columbia University Press.

Thompson, Robert Farris. 1984. *Flash of the Spirit: African and Afro-American Art and Philosophy.* New York: Random House, Vintage Books.

Toop, David. 1984. *The Rap Attack: African Jive to New York Hip Hop.* Boston: South End Press.

van den Haag, Ernest. 1957. Of Happiness and of Despair We Have No Measure. In *Mass Culture: The Popular Arts in America,* edited by Bernard Rosenberg and David Manning White, 504–536. Glencoe, Ill.: Free Press.

Ventura, Michael. 1986. *Shadow Dancing in the USA.* Los Angeles: J.P. Tarcher.

Wollheim, Richard. [1968] 1975. *Art and Its Objects: An Introduction to Aesthetics.* Harmondsworth: Penguin Books.

36
Hip-Hop and Black Noise:
Raising Hell
Rickey Vincent

> Don't push me 'cause I'm close to the edge.
>> Grandmaster Flash and the Furious Five

With the aesthetic demise of black popular music, the *soul* of the people as it was expressed in the music went underground. The underground music of the eighties was generated by a new youth movement of deejays and emcees from every urban uptown, high-tech synthesizer wizards from around the world, and crafty old-school musicians all interpreting the impulse of The Funk. Eighties funk was a noisy, rugged, and tense interpretation of an African music and value system, fueled in part by the desperation of the inner cities. The monstrous, apocalyptic Hip Hop tracks of Grandmaster Flash and the Furious Five featuring Melle Mel, the bone-crushing bass drum throbs and hysterical yelps of Run-D.M.C., and the relentlessly thick, funk grind of Trouble Funk's live performances all reflected the intensity of eighties music—a music too desperate, too articulate, and too meaningful for so-called black radio.

The irrelevance of black radio was underscored in three major markets, the now-legendary New York Hip Hop scene, Washington, D.C.'s nonstop Go Go funk clubs, and the San Francisco Bay Area's international and interracial "World Beat" fiasco. All three locales generated an authentic, people-oriented music culture from the bottom-up, yet only one claimed national prominence—and even this was accomplished despite a profound lack of radio airplay.

New York Hip Hop

The New York Hip Hop scene is now a well-oiled legend, a mythic tale that has made its way into the pantheon of rock and roll folklore. The booming sounds and break mixes of DJ Kool Herc at midsummer Bronx block parties in the mid-seventies, the turntable wizardry of Jazzy Jay, Afrika Bambaataa, and DJ Hollywood at South Bronx disco clubs, and proto-rapping styles of Grandmaster Flash, DJ Hollywood, and Eddie Cheeba took mixing disco singles from a fad, to an art form, to a cultural symbol of resilience by the late 1970s. Youngsters in this environment abandoned their illusions of making music with bands, and instead lined up turntables and developed hyped mixing techniques such as the percussive record rotation known as *scratching*, the sound-strobe effect of *transforming*, and an ability to mix an endless supply of music onto synchronous, danceable beats. Adroit Hip Hop deejays could take the wickedest breakdowns of certain records—mixing them with identical copies—and repeat the breaks, sustaining a level of total *hype*. Craftier mixers rendered the entire history of recorded music into a scrap heap of the beat fragments at their disposal. Once just the stage-setters, the presenters of music, Hip Hop deejays became the *artists* as they took snippets of sounds, jingles, commercials, nursery rhymes, and pop standards and mixed them into a new, post-modern collage with a funky dance beat.

The culture of Hip Hop had developed to the point in 1979 where New Jersey–based producer Sylvia Robinson (of "Pillow Talk" fame) took the chance and recorded fifteen minutes of the Sugarhill Gang and took Hip Hop to national prominence with "Rapper's Delight." With catchy all-purpose rhymes that *everyone* seemed to have memorized, "Rapper's Delight" was the hippest novelty single in years. Yet members of the scene knew it was more than a fad.

Shortly thereafter, Robinson signed a seven-member set from the Bronx known as Grandmaster Flash and the Furious Five, creators of the most politically charged rap record of the early 1980s: "The Message." Lead rapper Melle Mel's scathing realism and charged animosity ("Don't—push—me—cause I'm close—to—the—*edge!*") caught the music scene off guard, for there was nothing to compare "The Message" to. It's not as if Teddy Pendergrass or Al Green had some social message of their own circulating on black radio at the time. The summer of 1982 was the heyday of the Gap Band and the much-awaited second album of slick-funk band The Time; Rick James was "Standing on the Top"; and the electric blues of Zapp, whose music was a celebration of high-tech grooves and relatively lightweight working-class lyrics, was bugging people out.

"The Message" was a window into the urban underworld that was never heard before on the radio—and unlike most rap records, it *was* heard on the radio. The despair, anger, and claustrophobia of life in the inner city was brought to the public *uncut*: "I can't take the smell / I can't take the noise / I got no money to move out / I guess I got no choice." As the voice of a forgotten social strata—poor black males from the inner city—Flash and his mates served a *political* function, by giving a voice to the voiceless. Not since Marvin Gaye's "What's Goin' On" in 1971 had social commentary been taken as seriously.

While Grandmaster Flash, lead rapper Melle Mel, and the rest of the Furious Five delivered a series of compelling, graphic, and grooving singles for Sugarhill, namely the gurgling anti-cocaine chant "White Lines," the grim "New York, New York" and "Survival (The Message II)," and the apocalyptic "Beat Street Breakdown," the group's popularity was lost in the wave of early eighties Hip Hop/break-dancing movies (such as *Crush Groove, Wild Style*, and *Breakdance*) and decidedly less political rappers Whodini, LL Cool J, and the upstart Run-D.M.C.

With the advent of powerful new machines capable of delivering concussions with electric drumbeats, a new form of funk emerged to support the rap sensation. Towering, metallic-sounding clanks became the percussion sound of choice, a crushing effect that reflected the urban soundscape of crashing cars, trash cans, and gunfire, all set against the backdrop of towering steel skyscrapers. With industrial-strength beats and yelling rap styles in vogue by 1984, a newfangled sound took hold: an industrial funk beat that thrived on minimalism. A booming electric bass "drum" (known as an 808) provided an unreal eardrum-splitting bump sound, followed by crashing symbols on the two and four counts, and a funk track was born. New York rap duo Whodini's 1984 anthem "Five Minutes of Funk" is an example of minimalist, crashing funk beats—with a simple two-note keyboard melody on top, the beat sold on its own as an instrumental.

The outrageously loud rappers Joseph (Run) Simmons and Darryl (D.M.C.) McDaniels scorched listeners with loud raps engineered over even louder beats. The pair created a stoopid-fresh sound that fit the noise of rock guitars as easily as ghetto raps. With songs like

"Rock Box," "It's Like That," and "King of Rock," Run-D.M.C. began an assault on rock radio, blowing out pop notions of goofy, loud rock music that had rock buyers and music critics in a quandary. On the band's crossover 1986 album *Raising Hell*, they performed a duet with the almost-forgotten rock act Aerosmith, covering the band's earlier hit "Walk This Way," and reviving Aerosmith's stalled career. With the viciously loud riffs on Run-D.M.C. records hitting the streets, the radio, and even MTV, hard-rock fans by the millions flocked to the rap record bins in search of that elusive monster chord, the lifeblood of hard rock. (Accelerating the hype of funky rap tracks with a rock and roll sensibility was the "discovery" of three trash-talking punks that called themselves the Beastie Boys.) Even without overtly political lyrics, loud, hard-rocking rap music was threatening to overturn the music industry status quo by bringing new life to rock and roll from an urban black source. But the real instigator of the global Hip Hop movement—a true threat to the system—was a funkateer from the Bronx known as Afrika Bambaataa.

Afrika Bambaataa

If any single player in eighties music established himself as the instigator of electro-funk, it was the New York–bred Afrika Bambaataa. Taking his (legal) name from the sixties film *Zulu*, of the South African Zulu Nation tribe, Bambaataa began his musical exploits as a deejay in the Bronx, later becoming leader of his own Zulu Nation, a street organization of break dancers, graffiti writers, deejays, and emcees. His first large-selling musical effort was a high-tech beat known as "Planet Rock," released on Tommy Boy Records in 1982. With the requisite booming bass, slick, spacey synthesizer riffs, and Bambaataa's distorted vocals, "Planet Rock" was an anthem of futuristic-minded club dancers everywhere. The record jump-started the Tommy Boy Records sound, from which flowed a stream of synthesizer beat–laden dance singles. Artists such as the Jonzun Crew, Planet Patrol, and Bambaataa became the second nationally known rap perpetrators after the successes of Sugarhill. Their works also influenced the emerging electro-disco sounds coming from Chicago known as "house" music, as well as the Miami bass grooves of bands such as Maggotron, and the digitized lechery of the Egyptian Lover in Los Angeles.

But Bambaataa had a greater scheme of things on his mind. With his 1983 single "Renegades of Funk," he began mixing African chants onto his kicking electro-funk tracks, and he presented his band, the Soul Sonic Force, as a posse of crazy black superheroes in the tradition of George Clinton's Dr. Funkenstein and Parliament-Funkadelic. Bambaataa also began a tradition of acknowledging large numbers of people as influences on his record sleeves, giving credit to Sly and the Family Stone, Clinton, Bootsy Collins, and James Brown, among others. Bambaataa would take the cycle full circle when he hooked up with the Godfather of Soul himself in 1984 to record "Unity," a rather noisy tribute to the old and new traditions of funk as they converged.

Bambaataa's cosmic concepts, historical understandings, and humility in the midst of stardom flew in the face of the ego-tripping of most airplay-friendly Hip Hop, and he remained underground, influencing such later so-called Afro-centric rap artists as the Jungle Brothers, Public Enemy, X-Clan, and De La Soul. Many of Bambaataa's efforts were simply ahead of their time, such as his duet with James Brown, recorded three years before sampling of Brown's work became the centerpiece of so many rap tracks. His incorporation of Clinton's P-Funk imagery was ridiculed by many in the eighties, yet in the mid-1990s, anything with references to Clinton's works is given instant credibility. The contemporary black music style of remaking seventies records and the showcasing of older artists on state-of-the-art beats were all pioneered by Bambaataa.

Bambaataa's crowning artistic achievement was the 1988 Capital Records LP *The Light*, in which he delivered a grand scenario of global liberation. He designed logos and symbols that represented his vision of "Peace, Unity, Love, and Fun," he wrote at length about the ills of the world on his liner notes, and he brought together a collection of artists that reflected the clout of a superstar. Guest artists on *The Light* included the reggae superstar Yellowman, George Clinton and Bootsy Collins, the pop rhythm band UB40, vocalists Boy George, Tim Hutton from the new wave act Cabaret Voltaire, ex-LaBelle singer Nona Hendryx, P-Funk vocalist Gary "Mudbone" Cooper, Bernard Fowler, and many other industry heavyweights in the production studio.

Brilliant, insightful monster jams such as "World Racial War," "Clean Up Your Act," a scorching remake of Aretha Franklin's "Something He Can Feel," and a fifteen-minute Hip Hop/Go-Go fusion set "Sho Nuff Funky" delivered the necessary humps to justify Bambaataa's bold themes—but it wasn't enough. "They were really scared of that album," Bambaataa recalled in 1994. The double-length album was stuffed into a single record for American distribution by Capitol Records (a British import of *The Light* on double album is a grand spectacle of album audiovisuals), a fight over the single release led to the record abandoning all promotion, and the record was a flop.

Afrika Bambaataa did his best to maintain the funk-oriented aspect of urban music in New York, and to this day he is revered and respected as the Godfather of Hip Hop. As the years go by, and his innovations have become standard aspects of modern music, Afrika Bambaataa's role in music history will be confirmed.

Industrial Funk

With Bambaataa's influence, instrumental funk tracks were just as popular as New York rappers by 1984. With the demise of the P-Funk Empire in 1980, many of the innovations in funk beats were produced overseas. The German duo known as Kraftwerk was well known to club deejays with their hits "Trans Europe Express," and the 1981 radio hit "Numbers," neither of which had any "human" instruments associated with them. The British techno-trio known as Art of Noise hit the country in February 1984 with a loud, stumbling brand of danceable beat tracks, debuting with "Beat Box" and following with one of the all-time industrial funk tracks, "Close (to the Edit)," in the summer.

A swarming, international funk sound came from the Talking Heads, led by Scottish-born David Byrne, whose 1984 album and film *Stop Making Sense* served to link the catchy new wave sound with The Funk, providing some of the strongest and loudest funk from a white band since the Average White Band back in 1974. A unique spinoff group from the Talking Heads, the Tom Tom Club, led by bassist Tina Weymouth, generated a club classic, "Genius of Love," in 1982, one of the most sampled records of the eighties. Lyrics in the record praised funksters such as James Brown, Bohannon, and Bootsy Collins. One reason for the oozing funk flow of the Talking Heads and the Tom Tom Club was P-Funk keyboardist Bernie Worrell, who recorded with the group, performed with them on *Soul Train*, toured with the Talking Heads, and can be seen in the *Stop Making Sense* performance film.

While many early eighties pop artists dabbled in funk hooks and funky grooves (such as the B-52s' "Planet Claire," Peter Gabriel's "Shock the Monkey," Gary Numan's "Cars," and Queen's 1980 classic "Another One Bites the Dust"), one master musician surfaced on a collision course through funk and Hip Hop. Keyboardist Herbie Hancock, himself a veteran of Miles Davis's groundbreaking sixties quintet and his own Headhunters jazz-funk innovations, continued to dabble in electronic music. In 1982 Hancock asked his new manager, a young Bay Area promoter and New York Hip Hop freak named Tony Meilandt, to put together some Hip Hop tracks, and Meilandt recruited the talents of bassist and producer Bill Laswell (who would go on to become the most important industrial funk producer of the era) and a brilliant local New York deejay known as Grandmixer D.S.T. The resulting collaboration was a masterpiece of Hip Hop beats and multilayered keyboard tracks that hit the streets in 1983 as "Rockit." With the supporting album delivering a wicked fusion of traditional instruments, masterfully threaded chords, and melodies locked into industrial strength Hip Hop tracks and rhythms, Hancock's *Future Shock* album was much more than a Grammy-winning hit, it was a *phenomenon.* In many ways Herbie's spectacular combinations of future and past delivered a high-tech catharsis that brought the industrial funk era to its zenith, just as it was beginning. By the time of Herbie's brilliant "Hardrock" follow-up in 1984, Hip Hop was undergoing another one of its predictions of demise. Yet the beats kept coming.

While Herbie's funk legend grew, Bill Laswell's influence as a pioneer in industrial funk also expanded as a result of "Rockit." As an accomplished bass player as well as a technician, Laswell was able to extract a vast range of sounds and moods for a variety of artists—while maintaining a thick, bass-heavy musical foundation. His monster funk productions—beginning with his classic 1983 *Basslines* album, and moving on to stomping grooves for Afrika Bambaataa and punk superstar John (Johnny Rotten) Lydon's duet of "World Destruction" (under the name Time Zone), Manu Dibango's "Electric Africa," the Last Poets' gripping "Get Movin'," and albums by Massacre and his band Material—put an indelible stamp on the eighties funk sound.

A series of independent labels began to thrive in the new noisy marketplace. Celluloid Records, On U Sound Records, Def Jam, Tommy Boy, Island, Rough Trade, World Records, and Manhattan Records delivered the sounds for artists such as African Head Charge, Afrika Bambaataa, Time Zone, Tackhead, Fats Comet, Mark Stewart and the Mafia, and others. What these acts had in common was a loud, almost scraping, rugged edge to their beats, with sound effects such as suctions, metallic scratches, or rapid-fire bass drum stutters that gurgled along under distorted voices or chants, barely recognizable melodic riffs, phased guitar solos, and a distinctly fonky bass. These ingredients all mixed into a chaotic stew that reflected the sparse feel of urban isolation and eighties Cold War tension.

The most prolific purveyors of this new fonk, the On-U-Sound collective, based in London and led by arranger Adrian Sherwood, captured the bleak, tense feel of life in the eighties by hiring the rhythm section of legendary rap label Sugarhill Records: Doug Wimbish on bass, Skip Macdonald on guitar and synthesizers, and Keith LeBlanc on an assortment of drums. The three players called themselves Tackhead and became *the* rhythm section of the underground—as central to industrial fonk as Sly Dunbar and Robbie Shakespeare were to the eighties reggae sound. With uncredited yet legendary tracks such as "Rapper's Delight," "White Lines," and "The Message" for Sugarhill; the 1984 dub track of Malcolm X, "No Sell Out," which featured the first samplings of Brother Malcolm's voice over a (killer) funky beat track; and the phenomenal Artists United Against Apartheid compilation in 1985 all featured the signature grooves of the Tackhead trio. While hits were rare from this unit, their sound was unmistakable, as bassist Wimbish had the voluminous tones to drive rooster-poot fonkiness into the most deliberately technified tracks his buddies could come up with. P-Funk album artist and music critic Pedro Bell summed up the Tackhead sound by saying that "they are the P-Funk of the eighties, they are what P-Funk should have been doing now."

The similarities between Tackhead and George Clinton's P-Funk were actually quite strong. The daring and irrepressible Clinton experimented with hypnotic hooks played in sequence backwards on his classic 1982 smash "Atomic Dog"; a backward bass line on his 1986 hit "Do Fries Go with That Shake," and bone-crushing thumps on tracks like "Double Oh Oh" and "Bullet Proof." (One of Clinton's best spin-off projects of the decade was his baby brother Jimmy Giles's Jimmy G and the Tackheads album *Federation of Tackheads*—not to be confused with the industrial band Tackhead.) But the digital direction of Clinton's work only served to remind people of the distance his music had gone from the *real fonk.* To find it in the eighties, one would have to go to *Chocolate City,* and hit the Go Go clubs.

Go Go

At first glance looking like nothing more than large and loud R&B acts onstage, Go Go bands such as Trouble Funk, E.U., Rare Essence, Redds and the Boys, and their mentor Chuck Brown & the Soul Searchers, delivered the strongest, hottest, truest monster funk experience of the decade. Storming the Washington, D.C., club scene with long, percussion-filled jam sessions often consisting of only two- or three-hour-long "songs," propelled by a steady, punishing funk beat, the music at the Go Go clubs (such as the Black Hole or the Coliseum) in D.C. in the early eighties became known exclusively as Go Go music.

The Go Go beat is *hard-core* funk—a thick and slow bass groove, overlayed with a relentless counterpunching timbale or conga beat, jazzy horn breaks, chants of audience participation, and catchy lyrics or riffs from well-known dance hits, all delivered with a raw edge that rejected the digitized notions of eighties R&B heard on the radio. While the Go Go beat is an urban funk explosion, the approach to the music had more to do with the endless rhythms of Afro-Caribbean dance styles such as reggae, calypso, and salsa—all of which thrive on rhythmic energy, rather than hit records.

On his *Good to Go* compilation liner notes, writer Nelson George has described the Go Go beat as "local music with an international heart," a "ritual of black celebration" that fulfills its role "with an African beauty that connects the links between Rio de Janeiro, Kingston, Havana and Lagos." Yet the primary impulse of the Go Go beat is the outrageous irony of the proximity of the grim urban circumstances of the District of Columbia black community (the Go Go clientele) with the seat of the federal government: Congress and the *White* House. The contrast between the whitewashed political doublespeak of the capital and the heart wrenching realism of the funk tracks played on D.C.'s south side underscored the fonkiest of truths—as Nelson George put it, "that the distance between lofty American dreams and 1980s black reality is frighteningly huge."

The Godfather of the Go Go beat is Chuck Brown, bandleader of the Soul Searchers since 1968. A tireless performer, Brown made his mark playing club dates year after year, developing his particular brand of R&B, one with a simple, steady, nonstop funky groove on the bottom, with lots of room to operate and improvise on top. "I'd been trying to get drummers to play that particular groove for the longest time," Brown told journalist Adam White. "The beat is so simple most drummers don't like to play it."

With the success of his 1978 smash hit "Bustin' Loose," a groove Chuck Brown had been performing for three years before recording, the Go Go scene was finally given its spark. Inspired by Brown and the far-reaching funk of Clinton's apocalyptic P-Funk vibe (a uniquely appropriate fan base of P-Funk resides in D.C., the original "Chocolate City" referred to by Clinton in a 1975 hit, and the seat of most of black America's problems, the U.S. government), other bands began to take up their own brand of heavy, horny dance music. Locked into the endless funk groove, mimicking the dialogue on pop tunes and P-Funk hits, bands such as Trouble Funk, Rare Essence, Redds and the Boys, and E.U. were going strong by 1984. (It is important to note that anything can be played over a Go Go beat, and for three hours a night, everything was going in the mix.)

Trouble Funk

Independently producing themselves on TF Records, and later with the help (and hype) of Maxx Kidd and D.E.T.T. Records, Trouble Funk blasted ahead of the pack onto the D.C. Go Go scene. Featuring the loud and aggressive lead vocals of 250-plus-pound bass player and singer "Big Tony" Fisher, guitarist Robert "Dyke" Reed, and keyboardist James Avery, and always supporting at least *three* drummers, led by Timothy "T-Bone" David, Alonzo Robinson, and Mack Carey, Trouble Funk was a nonstop funk machine. The Trouble Funk groove was ferocious—and it never let up. Nine men strong, kicking a drum splattering, stupefying fat funk chunk from all directions, a Trouble Funk Jam session burned the roof off the house. A Trouble Funk performance was a required initiation for those who wanted to be ultimate funkateers.

They were also the most adept Go Go group at capturing their sound on record. Scoring their first album deal on Sylvia Robinson's Sugarhill label in 1982, the record featured the club classic "Pump Me Up" and their anthem "Drop the Bomb." From there a series of twelve-inch singles hit the streets on D.E.T.T. Records, another one becoming a deejay's classic, the hypnotically hype "Trouble Funk Express" (a networking of the Kraftwerk electro-hit "Trans Europe Express"). Their 1984 double album *In Times of Trouble* is a collector's item—a densely packed set of churning funk chops on one disc, while one live song covers both sides of the second disc.

The band was then picked up by Island Records and promoted in a variety of ways, beginning with a central role in the Island Visual Artist film *Good to Go*. Filmed in and around the D.C. Go Go scene in 1984, and starring pop singer and actor Art Garfunkel as a wayward journalist, *Good to Go* was billed as the breakthrough film for Go Go, one that would do for Trouble Funk and Go Go what *The Harder They Come* had done for Jimmy Cliff and reggae music in 1972. Power struggles and poor filmmaking delayed release and left the film—and the many bands on the soundtrack, such as Chuck Brown, E.U., and Trouble Funk's most vicious hit "Still Smokin'"—out of the spotlight. (It's still worth checking out on video under the name *Short Fuse*.) Island then reissued an earlier "live" recording for Trouble Funk recorded for D.E.T.T. (the second disc of *Times of Trouble*) and set about repackaging the group yet again.

Island's final effort with the band was the ill-fated *Trouble Over Here*. For this record, the band was given a slick, bright-colored, candy-coated angular look, with slices in their Afros—in the style of Cameo—betraying the homeboy image of the band. Many of the beats are tinny and thin, as if Big Tony left his bass at home when the set was recorded. Even guest producer Bootsy Collins couldn't salvage the band's sound on "Times of Trouble," an otherwise strong opening cut that set the slick tone for a record with monumental potential that manages to jam hard yet, like most eighties funk, still falls short.

Few Go Go hits ever scored on the charts, and even fewer were known nationally, but the driving Go Go beat persisted throughout the 1980s, infesting many classic Hip Hop dance tracks such as Curtis Blow's percussion-rich 1985 hit "If I Ruled the World," Doug E Fresh's 1985 "The Show," and Salt 'N Pepa's monster 1987 groove "Shake Your Thing," which was performed as a duet with E.U. (Experience Unlimited).

The most serious effort to "cross over" Go Go music was accomplished through Spike Lee's film *School Daze*, a fictionalized romp through a black college fraternity pledge week, in which the final party song, "Da Butt," is performed by E.U. Written by jazz performer and bassist Marcus Miller (veteran of Miles Davis's eighties efforts), the groove was slow and simple enough, yet it took the genius of E.U. lead singer Greg "Sugarbear" Elliot to bring it on home. With lyrics like "Tina's got a big ole butt / Darlene's got a big ole butt," the idea of the song caught on all too easily, but the *beat* was another thing. Slow and heavy, bass-driven and bouncy, "Da Butt" sounded like *nothing* on the radio in 1987, and filmmaker Lee struggled against enormous pressure from his label to release a different single from the soundtrack. But he stuck to his guns and scored a No. 1 R&B hit. Meanwhile, in a mysterious break from industry formula, every effort to follow up with Go Go songs fell off the charts like a brick in the water.

Despite the efforts of industry heavies such as Afrika Bambaataa, Curtis Blow, and Run-D.M.C., all of whom incorporated Go Go tracks in their music of the late eighties, the Go Go sound was all but forgotten by the time of the political upheaval of rap music in 1988. Despite the politics, missed opportunities, and industry indifference, there is a gold mine of classic monster funk from Washington, D.C., festering around record bins nationwide.

World Beat

Another unique eighties musical phenomenon occurred across the country with the same energy and local enthusiasm of the Go Go scene. The international dance music scene of the San Francisco Bay Area in the mid-1980s was a thriving, compelling movement of music and politics that dared to expose the questions relating music to social movements. "World Beat," as it came to be known, was tied in part to the simmering Anti-Apartheid and Central American support movements in the Bay Area, as well as the many multicultural undercurrents in the region. Driven mostly by African and Caribbean rhythm players setting out a catchy Afro-pop rhythm, with pop stylists, activists, and rappers taking on the vocals, bands like Zulu Spear, Big City, Mapenzi, and the Looters rode the wave of Afro-pop that was spread by acts like King Sunny Ade, the Nigerian political leader and bandleader Fela Anikulapo Kuti, and the efforts of rock superstars such as Paul Simon (*Graceland*) to perform with African players. The international eighties pop trend of African music was enjoying an organic synthesis in the Bay Area with the many other cultures—Asian-Americans, Mexican-American salsa, black funk, jazz and blues, rock singers, and the struggling Hip Hop scene.

Destined for pop saturation, the World Beat scene died before it could be "crossed over," in part because of the schizoid nature of the bands (typically overqualified lifelong players on rhythm instruments and late-coming art school graduates taking lead singing roles). Ironically, some of the most potent funk in the Bay Area came from the World Beat scene. The Looters, fueled by the monstrously loud bass playing of Jim Johnson and his guitarist brother Joe and led by the almost maniacal Matt Callahan's rough voice and radical politics, sounded like a cross between the Clash and Earth, Wind & Fire, stirring up songs with catchy, accessible rhythms that were driven with strident, compelling lyrics such as this riff from "See the World": "Lady what you got in the basket / what you bringin' here to trade / is it grapefruit / is it banana / maybe it's a hand grenade." The militant group managed to score one stirring album on Island Records, *Flashpoint*, which was destined to make political rockers like U2 and Little Steven sound like lightweights, but the disc never took off and is now out of print.

One act that never even made it to print was arguably the area's favorite, the Freaky Executives, perhaps the only truly organic funk band from the scene. The Freakys won the Bay Area's Best Ethnic Band award in 1986, the "Bammies," as they are called, smoking the stage while the other rock monoliths Journey, Huey Lewis, Santana, and the Grateful Dead looked on. "They had San Francisco locked up. They had the whole Bay Area locked up for a minute," recalled Dewayne Wiggins, bassist for Tony! Toni! Tone!. Even without a record, the Freaky Executives stirred up a storm across the bay. They were incessantly hip and funky, with the polish and theatrics of Morris Day and The Time, but kicked multilayered jazzy bridges and pace changes in their set that spoke more of a modern-day Tower of Power. The group could *jam* like Graham Central Station, smoke Latin percussion workouts like Santana, Stomp Monster Funk and break down into desperate ballads like Hubert Tubbs (who sang lead on the live version of "You're Still a Young Man" by Tower of Power). One local writer reviewing the Freakys claimed that lead singer Piero El Malo "generated enough sexuality to croon the panties off a nun." Even renowned and discriminating P-Funk scribe Pedro Bell, upon hearing demos of the band in 1987, called me to ask, "Who *are* the Freaky Executives?" Their highly percussive rhythm mix was a funk-centered total music experience, in the vein of the best Go Go, but just like the Go Go groups, they were lost in the storm in the production studio. Determined to sign on with a major label (Warner Bros.), the group's handlers pared down their sound to fit the R&B "format" until the horns were gone, the highly percussive mix was replaced by a drum machine, and the band's style was reduced to a weak imitation of the Minneapolis sound. Their furious live energy and antiestablishment irreverence that inspired acts across Northern California was wasted in an effort to "fit the format" of so-called "black radio."

While some of the players continue to perform, it is nevertheless a tragic commentary on a music industry that is so far from the realities of local communities that the best act in the area is dismantled. What's worse, it's likely that every city in the nation has its own Freaky Executives, an all-star band with the most potential for success that is only known by its imitations.

Bay Area Funk

While the Freakys would go down in flames, Bay Area funk would thrive in a variety of separate forms in the eighties. Out of the blue, the Berkeley-based Timex Social Club scored an international hit with "Rumors" in 1986, with a unique fusion of soul and rap. The Oakland-based trio of Tony! Toni! Tone! produced a deceptively familiar funky soul sound in their sparse, catchy hits like "Little Walter," "Blues," and "Feels Good." With the help of producers Denzil Foster and Thomas McElroy, the homegrown trio balanced their earthy, Oakland roots feel with the dubious state of the art, and made it to the top. "We used to sit around the garage and jam fat shit like 'Hair' by Larry Graham," bassist Dewayne Wiggins recalled. Foster and McElroy's efforts also produced the crossover group Club Noveau, the ill-fated Nation Funktasia, and the "Funky Divas" themselves, En Vogue. The hard-core rock scene also produced such funk-based dinosaurs as Primus, Psychofunkapus, and the Limbomaniacs, all of whom managed eccentric records of their own in the eighties.

Funk Rock

Rock bands had little trouble incorporating The Funk into their hot and heavy eighties chops. It was much easier for a funky white act to play whatever they liked and get recorded. The first album of the offbeat and whimsical funky rock band Jane's Addiction, for example, was a *live recording* of the act at a small club. (Can you name *any* black artist in the past twenty years whose first album was a live recording?) The absurd, bass-heavy stomps of Primus, led by the almost indecipherable lead singer and bassist Les Claypool, defy all the formulas of rock, pop, and funk, yet they *jam*, and their sound is their own.

Claypool's irreverent splatterings on bass are one of a kind, yet he frequently showcases the riffs of his idol, bassist Larry Graham, in concert. The San Jose-based Limbomaniacs fused hard rock riffs and Go Go beats on their uniquely odorous *Stinky Grooves* LP in 1989 that featured cameos from Bootsy Collins and Maceo Parker. (Limbo's drummer "Brain" went on to record with the P-funk metal band Praxis in 1993.)

The versatile Red Hot Chili Peppers have enjoyed a vast range of styles—mixing folk, rock and blues, speed-metal, ska, and The Funk into their sound, and performing covers of such funk classics as Sly Stone's "If You Want Me to Stay," the Meters' "(Hollywood) Africa," and Stevie Wonder's "Higher Ground." Led by the cantankerous Anthony Kiedis's vocals and the preposterous chops of Flea Balzary on bass, the Chili Peppers are devout and cloned funkateers who have steadily given props to The Funk since George Clinton produced their second album, *Freaky Stylee*, in 1985. (When the Chili Peppers won a Grammy Award for their 1992 hit "Give It Away," they invited the entire P-Funk Mob to play with them onstage, and the chaotic performance is now a classic.) Their style and attitude is exquisitely funky, as their LP producer in 1985, George Clinton, put it: "rock out with your cock out, and play like you got a big dick." As white ambassadors of the contagious funk groove, the Chili Peppers have taken The Funk to new heights (and given props to the original funk along the way). Yet the original funk bands, most notably the P-Funk All Stars—bands that patented the versatile formula of funk rock—have been denied access to the exposure and freedom enjoyed by white bands.

The Black Rock Coalition

The problems involved in the music industry's treatment of black bands that did not play stereotypical R&B came to a head in New York in 1985. The area's hottest rock band was the all-black hard rock quartet Living Colour, led by the phenomenal guitarist Vernon Reid. Despite numerous awards and a rabid fan base (which included rock and roll superstar Mick Jagger), the band could not get a recording contract. Their sound and image was defined as black rock, once again a hybrid category designed in reaction to the artificially whitened music known at the time as rock.

In the 1980s, the concept of black rock took on severe political overtones: Many artists realized the inherent racism in the industry, as MTV began its operation in 1981 with an apparent policy of airing no black videos, and the "urban contemporary" radio format was purview to disco-dance black music. It was clear that marketing a black artist in the rock format was not acceptable to the decision makers in the business. The segregation was so intense that Vernon Reid, *Village Voice* writer Greg Tate, and others founded a New York–based organization called the Black Rock Coalition, a "united front of musically and politically progressive Black artists and supporters" who produced the following manifesto that reads in part:

> The BRC also opposes those racist and reactionary forces within the American music industry which deny Black artists the expressive freedom and economic rewards that caucasian counterparts enjoy as a matter of course. For white artists, working under the rubric "rock" has long meant the freedom to expropriate any style of Black music—funk, reggae, blues, soul, jazz, gospel, salsa, ad infinitum—then sell it to the widest possible audience. We too claim the right of creative freedom and total access to American and international airwaves, audiences and markets. . . .

> Rock and roll is Black music and we are its heirs. Like our forebears—Chuck Berry, Jimi Hendrix, Sly Stone, Funkadelic, and LaBelle, to name but a few—the members of the BRC are neither novelty acts, nor carbon copies of the white bands who work America's Apartheid Oriented Rock circuit.

By performing concerts with experimental acts and lobbying for their exposure, the BRC opened the door for a number of artists to gain a foothold in their own particular flavors of funky black jazz-rock. With the many cross-blendings of styles that occur on local stages across New York, strong self-defined acts continue to pop up on the scene. Performers such as Steve Coleman, Me'Shell NdegeOcello, John Paul Burelly, James "Blood" Ulmer, and Kelvyn Bell's Kelvynator are tireless innovators in the hard-driving music of New York's underground jazz-rock-funk scene. As the 1990s roll on, however, the apartheid-oriented rock circuit continues to operate, as the majority of successful New York bands remain on independent labels and out of the spotlight.

In the 1980s The Funk became more harsh and intense, as a direct reflection of the growing intensity of oppression that fell upon America's funky people. It would only increase in the 1990s as urban Hip Hop became the primary medium for the rebel/funk expression.

Essential Eighties Underground Funk

Afrika Bambaataa/Planet Rock: absurd and irreverent Nigs in space vibe
Afrika Bambaataa & James Brown/Unity (12"): noisy and chaotic tribute to the God-father
Afrika Bambaataa/Beware, The Funk Is Everywhere: vicious, throbbing industrial fonk
Afrika Bambaataa/The Light: exquisitely enlightened, ruthless grooves

Grandmaster Flash & the Furious Five/The Message: original album packed with jams
Grandmaster Flash & the Furious Five/Beat Street: boldest political rap of the decade
Run-D.M.C./Run-D.M.C.: here come the heavyweights
Run-D.M.C./Raising Hell: awesome package of catchy hooks, funny raps, and thick funk
Beastie Boys/License to Ill: trashy white boys mix the funk like pros
Herbie Hancock/Future Shock: groundbreaking industrial funk sessions. Killer
Herbie Hancock/Hardrock: a second helping of rough-edged industrial funk
Herbie Hancock/Perfect Machine: slick, overproduced collaboration with Bootsy and Sugar-
    foot
Malcolm X/No Sellout (12"): groundbreaking Tackhead beat track featuring Malcolm X voice
Tackhead/The Game (12"): insanely hard industrial funk beat
Fats Comet/Eat the Beat (12"): bizarre, thumping throb track
Artists United Against Apartheid/Sun City: magnificent political message; monstrous funk
Sly & Robbie/Language Barrier: wicked extended riffs, yet somewhat confined
Sly & Robbie/Rhythm Killers: ridiculous, rock hard riffs, expanded by P-Funk guest players
Bill Laswell/Basslines: oozing funk jazz from industrial funk pioneer and producer
Various/Celluloid Trilogy: awesome cross-section of best underground grooves of the decade
Gettovetts/Missionaries Moving: thoroughly noisy and conceptual industrial New York rap
Praxis/Transmutation: modern funk fusion masterpiece, features Bootsy, Bernie, and others
Art of Noise/Who's Afraid Of . . . : best and most thumping industrial funk from Britain
Kraftwerk/Numbers: quirky and ethereal digitized funk beats from German trio
Talking Heads/Remain in Light: scandalous, offbeat, nastay new-wave funk
Talking Heads/Speaking in Tongues: deeply thumping funk disguised as modern rock
Talking Heads/Stop Making Sense: live session features keyboard work of guest Bernie Worrell
Tom Tom Club/Tom Tom Club: complex, silly, and cute mix of grooves. Features "Genius of
    Love"
Trouble Funk/Drop the Bomb: relentless and totally hype percussion overload
Trouble Funk/In Times of Trouble: awkward mix of studio efforts and vicious live tracks
Trouble Funk/Saturday Night Live: incredible live session. Absolutely essential
Trouble Funk/Trouble Over Here: overproduced disappointment
Various Go Go bands/Paint the White House Black: strong and stirring set of nasty funk
Various Go Go bands/Good to Go soundtrack: scattered samplings of Go Go from movie
    Short Fuse
Looters/Flashpoint: unheralded political funk rock of the future
Red Hot Chili Peppers/Freaky Stylee: wicked and ridiculous. Produced by George Clinton
Red Hot Chili Peppers/Mother's Milk: tight and yet still preposterous
Red Hot Chili Peppers/Blood Sugar Sex Magik: deep, strong, and stanky
Primus/Suck On This: grungy and thick, like all their stuff
Fishbone/Truth & Soul: tight and spastic, like all their stuff
Living Colour/Vivid: tight and noisy black-rock breakthrough
Brand New Heavies/Brand New Heavies: noble effort to bring back real funk and soul
Me'Chell NdegeOchello/Plantation Lullabies: ruthless bass-driven rap and funk
"The Message" Grandmaster Flash & the Furious Five. Written by E. Fletcher, M. Glover, S.
    Robinson, J. Chase. Sugarhill Music. Used by permission.
"They were really scared of that album." Telephone interview with Afrika Bambaataa in
    February, 1995.
"They are the P-Funk of the eighties". Telephone interview with Pedro Bell in 1987.
"Ritual of black celebration." Nelson George quoted from liner notes to Good to Go sound-
    track, Island Records, 1986.
"The distance between lofty American dreams and 1980s black reality." Ibid.

"The beat is so simple most drummers don't like to play it." Chuck Brown quoted from Billboard Book of #1 R&B Hits, Adam White, p. 252.

"Maybe it's a hand grenade." "See the World" by the Looters. Written by the Looters, 1985. Used by permission.

"Jam fat shit like 'Hair' by Larry Graham." Telephone interview with Dewayne Wiggins in June, 1995; "they had the whole Bay Area locked up for a while," telephone interview with Dewayne Wiggins in August, 1995.

"Rock out with your cock out, and play like you got a big dick." George Clinton quoted in Tower Pulse, June, 1985, p. 30. Thanks to Linda Tosetti for her research.

"America's Apartheid Oriented Rock circuit." BRC manifesto, courtesy of Greg Tate.

Part VII
I Used to Love H.E.R.:
Hip-Hop in/and the Culture Industries
Mark Anthony Neal

On his 1994 disc *Resurrection*, Chicago-based rapper Common (Sense) recorded a song titled "I Used to Love H.E.R." On the surface, the song was about a failed relationship but, in fact, Common used "H.E.R." as a metaphor to talk about his relationship with hip-hop and hip-hop's relationship to the Culture Industries. In the recording, Common questions hip-hop's fixation with the "gangsta" culture (taking a clear shot at "Left Coast" artists like Ice Cube and N.W.A., who responded in kind) and hypersexual imagery. The track becomes the basis of a nearly decade-long narrative where artists such as The Roots ("Act Too [The Love of My Life]") and Erykah Badu (the Grammy Award-winning "Love of My Life") also question hip-hop's transition from an organic, grassroots art form to a transnational commodity. All are clear in their opinions that hip-hop's entry into the mainstream has fundamentally changed its production, distribution, reception, and function as an art form. The chapters in Part VII explore from myriad vantages the kind of crisis that Common alludes to in "I Used to Love H.E.R."

While early purveyors of hip-hop clearly had commercial interests in the music, there was little expectation that hip-hop would transcend its distinctly localized existence and become a primary cog in the mainstream music industry. In her chapter, M. Elizabeth Blair suggests that the anxieties among hip-hop artists and critics over the genre's intense engagement with the mainstream marketplace is rooted in the belief, of some, that the "industrialization of music means a shift from active musical production to passive pop consumption, the decline of cultural traditions and community." Throughout her chapter, Blair examines the evolving relationship between commercial products and ideological meaning, citing the ways that commercial products undergo a transformation, from being advertised as a basic social utility to their alignment with "certain cultural symbols, or in connection with specific group practices, or for use in subcultural activities," finally acquiring value among mass culture industries that change subcultural meanings "into more marketable, less radical meanings." One of the best examples of this cultural dynamic has been the subordination of dance (break dancing and other forms of social dance associated with hip-hop) as one of the four original elements of what became hip-hop.

In her seminal chapter on the role of dance in hip-hop culture, scholar Katrina Hazzard-Donald observes, "although the wide acceptance of hip-hop music and exploitation of hip-hop in the advertising and popular music industries has on one level robbed the dance of its original significance, hip-hop still functions in the places of its origin." But Hazzard-Donald is quick to add that "most mainstream Americans will never see the subtle codes, gestures, and meanings of hip-hop as they are displayed in African American communities."

Blair's analysis and Hazzard-Donald's remarks seem to suggest that the anxieties of Common and others are well founded, yet as S. Craig Watkins observes in his chapter, "popular media culture is perhaps best understood as a perpetual theater of struggle in which the forces of containment and resistance remain in a constant state of negotiation, never completely negating each other's presence or vigor." For some rappers, hip-hop's engagement with the mainstream has forced them to renegotiate between long-standing narratives within the black community that have equated mainstream acceptance with "selling out" and basic desires to craft a lifestyle out of their skills and visibility as rap artists.

In his chapter Keith Negus notes, "in the struggle against racism and economic and cultural marginalization, and in an attempt to 'live the American dream,' rap has also been created as a self-conscious business activity as well as a cultural form and aesthetic practice."

Ted Swedenburg explains in his chapter that it is also "rappers' fundamental connection to a young black community ... that allows them to get paid without selling out." In his view, "getting paid ... means achieving their due as artists and as representatives of a creative and oppressed community." Citing the examples of so-called "conscious rappers" who would seem less invested in mainstream acceptance, Swedenburg suggests that "conscious rappers also aren't selling out because their strategy is to deploy the market to disseminate crucial political messages to the widest possible audience."

Moreover, as Watkins writes, "at the same moment that black youth have become especially vulnerable to shifts in the postindustrial economy and political landscape, they, too, have gained unprecedented access to the technologies of communications media," adding that "what has emerged in the process is the structuring of a historically distinct terrain upon which the varying repertoires of black youth cultural production dramatically reorganize the scope and possibilities of social and political struggle from the margins."

Both Eric K. Watts and Keith Negus, in their chapters, suggest there is a deeper relationship to be found between the "street" and the tenets of mass cultural production. Citing the case of archetypal gangsta rap group N.W.A. and their song "One Less Bitch," Watts observes in his chapter that "Eazy E's (Eric Wright) misogynistic protestation can be profitably exploited by more than just a mass-marketed culture industry. If we listen carefully, we can discern how N.W.A. gleefully acknowledge participation in their self-promotion as 'niggas' who condemn women by limiting their self-realization to the status of 'bitches' and 'hoes' in a perverse dramatization of street oriented relations." In Watts's view, the N.W.A. track represents a "commercialized spectacle designed to thrust the street code through the doors of corporate boardrooms." Perhaps obvious in this analysis is the shared investment that a group like N.W.A. and mass cultural producers have in exporting sexism and misogyny to those who have desires to consume such practices; less obvious are ways that, as Watts explains, "there exist a spectacularly symbiotic relationship between the dictates of the street code and an energetic American consumerism."

Part of the explanation for this relationship, according to Watts, "resides in the fact that consumerism is in the midst of symbolically reproducing the street code, commodifying it in the form of an easy-to-open package of hip." Watts adds, "this awesome replication and consumption of street-coded imagery is significant precisely because the processes of spectacular consumption are implicated ... in the validation of what becomes reasonable street protocol." Negus concurs, noting that "street intelligence is about 'knowing markets' and 'knowing consumers' and, like street marketing, it involves employing conventional business activities that are elided through the discourse of the street, denying that this is similar to the other activities that are daily being conducted and initiated from the corporate suite."

Unfortunately for many rappers, the theoretical implications of the conflation of the street ethos and corporate America have little to do with the everyday struggles they face as artists—employees—working within multinational corporations.

In two separate interviews, former Def Jam president Carmen Ashhurst-Watson and Rap Coalition founder Wendy Day discuss some of the pitfalls faced by rappers within corporate music environments. Day, who has been at the forefront of efforts to acquire health insurance and pension plans for rap artists, admits to Norman Kelley in his chapter that the "average rapper really doesn't want to know how the business works; they just want fame and the women; they don't even want the money, because if they wanted money they would learn how it works and learn how to manipulate that to get the money." Such inattentiveness creates a perilous situation for artists working within an industry that Ashhurst-Watson suggests is "really, in its institutional design, a very plantation like system."

In Ashhurst-Watson interview in Tricia Rose's chapter, she gives deeper meaning to her analogy. Commenting on the practice of record companies to sign new acts to six to eight album contracts, Ashhurst-Watson states, "most acts—not just rappers—do not make it through the first contract. So the record company locks you up for a significant portion of your career, because the average pop group barely makes it through half of an average contract." The dire economic realities of the recording industry, as they relate to the average individual artist, have led some artists to establish their own labels within the mainstream recording industry. Ashhurst-Watson cautions, however, that such set-ups have little impact on the basic exploitative practices within the popular music industry: "Are you just going to be a slave that gets beat up? Or are you going to be an overseer, be someone who is higher up in the hierarchy? Those distinctions are real for you as a person. And these artist-owned companies gives them the institutional structure to produce and develop new talent."

Wendy Day describes the contract-signing process and the "point-system" that it is based on in her interview with Norman Kelley. According to Day, "every contract, even though they are different, includes a point-system." Points loosely relate to the percentage that artists earn in royalties from the total sales of a recording after the artists pay off advances —referred to as "recoupables"—given to them for studio time, production costs, and the like. Day observes that "when you're an artist and you pay back everything that's recoupable, you don't get to keep the masters (the master recordings). In fact you don't have anything to show but fame. You don't get to keep shit." Ashhurst-Watson explains that the situation is even more tenuous for female performers who "rarely come to negotiation sessions with high powered legal representation," adding that they "generally hire lawyers for whom they are the first or second or third client. It's very rare to see a woman rapper walk in with seasoned counsel."

37

Commercialization of the Rap Music Youth Subculture

M. Elizabeth Blair

Rap music, with its boastful rhymes and synthesizer-created claps and pops, has moved out of the inner cities and into the mainstream of popular culture. Mass media advertisers have recognized the value of using rap to sell their products, even though they do not always have a thorough understanding of the subculture from which it came. Pepsi-Cola, Coca-Cola, and British Knights footwear company have all signed popular rap artists to promote their products. While there are a few rappers who have greatly benefited from this level of commercial success, others are concerned that as rap moves into the mainstream, they will not be given the appropriate credit and compensation. In his introduction to *The Rap Attack*, Tony Van Der Meer states the problem with the commercialization of rap music:

> There is nothing wrong with one community learning the cultural forms produced by another, if it respects their specific shapes and meanings. There is something horribly wrong with a dominant community repeatedly co-opting the cultural forms of oppressed communities, stripping them of their vitality and form, the heritage of their creators and then popularizing them. The result is bleached Pepsi culture masquerading as the real thing. This is what threatens to dilute the real feeling and attitude of hip hop preventing its genuine forms the freedom to fully develop. The expression of Black people is transformed when it is repackaged without any evidence remaining of the Black historical experience. (1984, 4–5)

Black artists may have good reason for concern. Historically, blacks have not been able to reap the financial rewards from the musical forms that were uniquely theirs. The blues, jazz, gospel, soul, funk and rap are all musical styles that originated within the black community. In the 1950s and early 1960s, most major record producers were interested in promoting only white artists, such as Elvis Presley, to perform rock and roll music that had previously been recorded by black artists. The white performer was instrumental in promoting the acceptance of the musical style among mainstream audiences. According to Peterson and Berger, black rhythm and blues performers were most often the victims of the "cover tactic," where major "white" companies would quickly record and market a version of a fast-selling song recorded by a smaller independent "black" company (162). The development and acceptance of rock and roll was in many ways similar to the development of rap in the late 1980s and the development of jazz in the 1920s. Some of the first rap concerts, like some of the first rock and roll concerts, were plagued by riots, leading people to believe that this new music was corrupting today's youth. These public reactions parallel the moralistic reaction against jazz in the 1920s.

According to Peterson and Berger, this controversy indicates that the music was viewed as important and radically different from the music that preceded it (166).

How does a subcultural phenomenon such as rap become integrated into the mainstream of mass culture? In the past, a number of other youth subcultures have gained some level of notoriety (e.g., punk rock subculture), but few have achieved the same level of commercial success that has been achieved by the rap subculture. What is it about rap that has captured the interest and dollars of so many people? What meaning does it have for them?

Youth subcultures have been often organized around music. For example, there was the punk rock subculture, which originated in England in the 1970s. The quintessential punk event involved gathering together to hear a live band, while slamming into other dancers, jumping up and down or jumping off the stage into the audience. Rude and antisocial behavior was highly encouraged, so that this music would remain more meaningful as an expression of rebellion than overly-commercialized pop music. The heavy metal subculture also provided an identity and haven for young people who were disenchanted with home, school, jobs and churches, the acceptable institutions of their parents. Lull called these types of movements (including rap) "oppositional" subcultures, because they represent loosely organized resistance to social institutions, values and practices (29). There develops a common bond between performer and listener through shared meanings, not only in the lyrics but also in the style and sound of the music itself. In the 1950s, sociologist David Riesman observed that young people were using popular music to create socially shared meanings and common states of awareness. The popular music was a primary source of conversation and predicting the next hit became a way of maintaining status within one's peer group (Lewis 138). These subcultures develop their own distinct values and fashions that serve as the price of entry into the particular group.

Historically, much subcultural music has come from oppressed groups defined by socio-economic class (Lull 6). For example, folk singers like Woody Guthrie and Pete Seeger were banned from the mainstream media because they reflected interests of the poor. For many minority youngsters, rap has become a voice reflecting not only rebellion against adults but alienation from the majority culture. Some rap reflects a youth rebellion against all attempts to control black masculinity in the street and home. Since most children in the inner city grow up with a single female parent, some male rappers may oppress women to make themselves feel more powerful (Hanna 190).

Behind each style of music there is a local scene where involvement with the music and its accompanying fashions becomes an important part of the lives of the fans. Rap music originated in the Southeast Bronx of New York City, where some street gangs decided to put their energies into creative pursuits. Rap started as a verbal competition and is related to the African-American tradition of word battles such as "playing the dozens." Rap developed in the Bronx as part of the hip hop subculture, along with breakdancing and graffiti art. Hip hop parties (known as "house parties") usually included a show provided by a disc jockey, rappers, dancers and graffiti artists, who provided the decor. The first rap music was happy party music and often involved nonsensical bragging between males.

Since about 1945, technological advances have played an important part in determining what type of popular music is recorded and promoted by the mass media. For example, the initial popularity of rock and roll was largely due to the rapid diffusion of radio and television. Shows like *American Bandstand* promoted the music, and radios became commonplace in the teenagers' cars and bedrooms (Wicke 35). Rap music also developed and became popular largely because of recent advances in recording and computing technology, which allows the relatively easy manipulation of musical sounds. In some ways, rap music is the ultimate commercial product, because its main features have often been borrowed from other, successfully tried-and-true products (Goodwin 85). Initially, rap music involved competition among DJs to develop the most creative sampling of records. Old Monkees tunes, TV themes (such as *Gilligan's Island*) as well as funk and rhthym-and-blues classsics were all borrowed and sampled in unusual ways. Often the original tune was unidentifiable because DJs would alternate between two different turntables, repeating the drum sequence from each record a number of times.

Because of its emphasis on borrowing previous hits and altering them to fit the rap style, it is not surprising that the first widely-successful national rap hit was a remake of a popular rock tune. This introduction of rap into the mainstream was accomplished by a three-man group known as Run-DMC. Their interpretation of the song "Walk This Way," originally a hit for the white rock group Aerosmith, sold 3.3 million copies, and demonstrated to both artists and producers that rap was not just a passing phase (McKinney 66). Since that time, rap has diversified considerably and much of the recent rap music could be described as a crossover between rap and some other style, such as pop, funk or rhythm-and-blues.

Rap has moved off the East coast and prominent rappers are popping up all over the country. Though originally a male phenomenon, many prominent female rappers are now expressing their unique points of view (DiPrima 32). The most important development in recent rap music is that it has become more political, and serious intelligent messages about life in urban black neighborhoods have replaced the emphasis on nonsensical party-type lyrics (Adler 56–59).

The criticism that rap has become too commercialized stems from a similar criticism that has often been expressed about all types of popular music. To some, the industrialization of music means a shift from active musical production to passive pop consumption, the decline of cultural traditions and community. Pop music is a classic case of what Marx called alienation, when something human is taken from us and is returned in the form of a commodity. Pop stars are made magical, such that we can only possess them via cash transactions in the marketplace (Frith 50).

Since the 1970s, several sociologists have proposed that Marxian hegemony theory provides a good explanation of how a subcultural trend, such as rap, becomes popular and is then commercialized by the mass media. The concept of hegemony means the way in which an entire ideological complex of beliefs, values and attitudes that function for the sustenance of the ruling class comes to dominate every aspect of society. Though originally proposed by Karl Marx in *The German Ideology*, the idea was further elaborated by the Italian theoretician Antonio Gramsci. He viewed hegemony as a process where the dominant class uses its privileged access to ideological institutions of that society, such as religion, education, and the media to propagate its values and reinforce its position (Sallach 41). Gramsci believed that the most effective aspect of hegemony is found in the suppression of alternative views through the establishment of parameters that define what is legitimate, reasonable, sane, practical, good, true and beautiful. A consequence of the hegemonic process is that groups who do not benefit from the dominant view, that are farthest outside the mainstream, tend to have value systems that are fragmented, inconsistent and confused. This tendency for views to become increasingly fragmented as one descends the class structure is due to the fact that their "alternative" viewpoints are suppressed by forces in the dominant ideology.

Domhoff suggests that the upper class exerts a predominant, yet indirect, influence on the mass media through corporate advertising (44). The power of corporate advertisers is both ideological and economic. For example, advertisers are often hesitant to support a program which contains controversial viewpoints or when viewers are considered to be less wealthy. The TV show *Gunsmoke* was canceled when it was in the top ten of the Nielson ratings because the audience was older, rural and down-scale (Gitlin 254).

Gottdiener proposed a model of mass culture that is inspired by Marxian hegemony theory, but is at the same time critical of that theory. He suggests a semiotic approach for explaining the influence of various subcultures, particularly youth subcultures associated with certain musical styles, on the mass culture. Hegemonists believe that consciousness of the masses is either "false" (they perceive illusion and not reality) or "contradictory" (they are confused and their judgment is fragmented). According to hegemony theory, the abilities of the lower classes to realize their own oppression are short-circuited because of the industrial control of consciousness by the ruling class. However, this assertion commits the fallacy of idealism by implying that the mental activity of individuals can be separated so easily from the material conditions of their existence that consciousness can be false (Gottdiener 983). Gottdiener perceives his view to be opposed to the false consciousness theory. The semiotic approach assumes that the production of meaning takes place by virtue of a social relation, such as reciprocal linkages between producers and users as mediated through mass cultural objects. By focusing explicitly on symbols and their exchange, the model can specify where meaning is created, communicated and received. This model assumes that social groups of all kinds including powerful as well as less powerful groups are understood to be bearers of meaning. "Mass" culture is made up of various individual subcultures, which vary in the extent to which they interact with the dominant ideology in society. Before there is a "mass" culture there must be "culture," meaning the conceptual forms and accumulated knowledge by which social groups organize everyday experience. The "mass" culture develops as a result of dynamic meaning creation from groups that may or may not be closely allied with the dominant ideology.

Gottdiener visualized the production and control of ideological meanings as operating in three separate stages. In the first stage, producers produce objects for their exchange value, whereas purchasers of these objects desire them for their use value. The link between the producers and consumers occurs when the producers communicate an image for the product, usually through advertising. Products are surrounded with a web of social significance from the outset through advertising as a further inducement to purchase, creating value above and beyond the basic utility of the product. For example, a pair of trousers is no longer just an article of clothing, but also a social symbol, promising the wearer youthfulness, sportiness, or an exotic aura, making him look like a "man of the world" or whatever else the imaginative variations of the advertising experts on the theme of trousers might be (Wicke 78–79). Successful transfunctionalization of goods from exchange value to desirable use-value status has been achieved by several large sporting goods companies. The manufacturers of Reebok, Puma, Nike and Adidas sneakers are making huge profits because their shoes have become accepted not only as the most technologically advanced, but also as stylish and prestigious. These manufacturers did not intentionally market these products to appeal to the rap subculture, but their products were subsequently adopted by this group, becoming part of its identifiable look.

In the second stage, users modify objects of mass consumption in order to express certain cultural symbols, or in connection with specific group practices, or for use in subcultural activities. This is when culture is actually created by the users of the object. The primary use value of the object is transformed, so that the object becomes a sign of belonging to a subculture. In some cases, the commodity may have become so personalized that it is no longer effective in its primary function. Throughout the history of popular music, youth subcultures have used insignificant everyday objects to develop a material context of cultural behavior that is stable enough to allow those meanings and values which the music embodies for them to be projected onto these material possessions (Wicke 80). The meanings are often class specific and are based upon the particular experiences of the interpreter. It is for this reason that commercial entities cannot completely exploit and manipulate consumers. Even though advertisers have been accused of controlling the consciousness of the purchaser, most advertisers would testify that their efforts to "control" consumers are often unsuccessful. The youth subcultures transform everyday objects to show that they are different from the mainstream, using clothing and hairstyles as weapons or visible insults in a cultural war (80).

Wicke describes the Mod subculture during the 1960s in Great Britain to show how youth subcultural trends are often tied to social class frustrations. The Mods were primarily working-class youth who grew up during a time when there was increased prosperity for their parents but little hope of them being able to achieve the same level of affluence. The Mods reacted to their frustration in achieving this level of affluence by consuming in excess. Their outward appearance matched that of mannequins in the department store windows. They hung out in nightclubs that were usually reserved only for the high society in-crowd. Their cultural form parodied the ideology of the consumer society and at the same time expressed the hopelessness of achieving that level of prosperity and social class. Their cult bands were the Who, the Kinks, and the Rolling Stones, as well as some lesser known groups. When the Who sang "My Generation," the line "Hope I die before I get old" was seen by the Mods as one way to escape the clutches of the bourgeois ideology (Wicke 85).

Rap music also expresses the economic and social frustration of many young people from the inner city. Originally, rappers borrowed the dance beat from the disco music of the 1970s to create their own style of party music. It has been observed that dancing is one arena in which blacks confront whites and win. Many blacks see dance as their province and are threatened when whites try to challenge their territory by "dancing black" (Hanna 85).

Rap is possibly the commercial equivalent of what the Marxist writer Adorno called part-interchangability or pseudo-individualization, two methods of capitalist production (Goodwin 76). Part-interchangability is when mass-produced parts from one product line are used in another "different" product. In rap music, this process occurred when the disc jockey took old recordings from a number of artists ranging from James Brown to the Rolling Stones, pieced them together and extended the drum break to form a new instrumental composition. Pseudo-individualization is when the "same" products are made to seem different by the use of individual gimmicks, such as promoting a particular "star" image or adding some guitar licks or drum riffs that are characteristic of a particular performer.

During the third stage of Gottdiener's model, the producers of mass culture decide to capitalize on these subcultural trends. The transfunctionalized objects produced by the subculture become the raw material for cultural production by the mass culture industries. During this process, subcultural meanings are changed by mass producers (such as advertisers) into more marketable, less radical meanings. A rather pessimistic Marxist would probably view this third stage as being extremely important to the process of ideological control, the ideology that benefits capitalist production. It is evident that big business is making big money from the impact and influence of the rap culture. Major record companies have signed popular rap artists and advertisers are using these stars and their music to promote products. Two Saturday-morning cartoons, "Hammerman" and "Kid N Play," feature animated characterizations of rap stars Hammer and Kid N Play. There is an M.C. Hammer doll and a Vanilla Ice doll. Middle-class rapper Will Smith (aka the Fresh Prince) has his own prime-time comedy series, *The Fresh Prince of Belair*, and rapper Ice T has starred in several major motion pictures.

The history of popular music tells us that once a subcultural form is totally removed from its original context, that subculture ceases to exist. Wicke relates how the enormously popular British television series *Ready, Steady, GO!* led to the end of the Mod subculture. The show was part of a vast publicity machine that ensured a profit for mod-style goods (Wicke 88–89). The Mod style no longer said "I'm different from the mainstream" and soon a new teenage subculture, known as the Rockers, emerged from the underprivileged strata of working-class Britain.

Gottdiener concludes that Marxist theorists who advocate ideological domination fail to appreciate the importance of the relative autonomy of subcultural life. It is true that the consumption habits of individuals are so manipulated by the mass culture industries as to transform the production of meaning by subcultures into a managed market purchase. But this does not always happen because consciousness itself cannot be controlled. There are no two people in the world who will perceive any given stimulus musical or otherwise in exactly the same way. Fortunately, there will always be groups who desire to distinguish themselves from the mainstream and produce meanings for cultural objects that are independent of the logic of exchange value and dominant cultural sensibilities. Interestingly, these two sources of cultural production (mass-producers and subcultures) are dependent on each other.

Television advertising provides an excellent medium for examining the influence of rap on the mainstream audience. Because children and teens are the major consumers of rap music, as well as products associated with its identifiable look, it is only logical that rap would be used to promote products to these age groups. Nine hours of children's Saturday morning television were collected in both October of 1990 and October of 1991. The programming and ads were videotaped on three consecutive Saturdays from the three major networks. All the ads were examined carefully to determine whether or not rap was used. In the first year (October 1990), there were 11 commercials judged by the author to contain rap. To be considered as rap music, words had to be spoken in rhythm and not sung to a melody. Rap music was usually accompanied by typical rap fashion and behaviors, such as wearing sneakers, baseball caps and workout suits, speaking into microphones and breakdancing.

Two of the rap ads promoted products within the "Barbie doll" line and are considered by the author to be the least true to the typical rap style, in comparison to the other rap ads in the sample. For instance, rap is predominantly a black male expression, while each of the characters in these two commercials is a white female. The products advertised, Barbie Trading Cards and the "Cool Tops" Skipper doll, seem totally incompatible with the rap meanings of rebellion and socio-economic deprivation. Barbie has traditionally been very materialistic, upscale and white in her image. The little girls who appeared in the ad were shown dancing together and mouthing the words to the rap song. Their style of dance and clothing is more disco-like than hip hop.

Interestingly, all of the white male rappers to appear in the sample were cartoon characters. "Barney Rubble" was a rappin' detective who plays a joke on his old pal Fred Flintstone, who is led to believe that someone is stealing his Pebbles cereal. Once again, the characters of Barney Rubble and Fred Flintstone are incompatible with the values and meanings inherent in rap. They are both lovable family men and can be considered as the cartoon versions of Ralph Cramden and Ed Norton from the old *Honeymooners* TV show. They were originally portrayed as working class men with traditional 1950s values.

The second white male rapper in the sample shared the spotlight with a rapping teddy bear. In this cartoon ad, a "Campbell Kid" and a rapping Teddy Bear take turns doing the rap for Teddy Bear soup. Although the ad is clever, kids may feel that they are being insulted or manipulated by advertisers who are trying just a bit too hard to be "cool" and do not quite make it. Both characters in the ad have the reputation of being cuddly, child-like and All-American, like Mom, hot dogs and apple pie. Kids would not naturally associate these two cultural symbols with rap music.

The third white male rapper was "Punchy" from Hawaiian Punch, who looks like a little Hawaiian tourist. Hawaiian Punch does not have a very strong symbolic meaning for most people, so a rap approach in this case may be as good as any. Rap definitely is not Hawaiian, but maybe it is not incompatible with the punch part, since "Punchy" usually hits his pal in the nose when he asks him for a drink.

The most unusual rapper in the sample was the "Chicken McNuggets" from McDonald's, which looked like little brown puppets with baseball caps. In this hilariously ridiculous ad, Ronald McDonald is shown doing a few breakdancing moves. I'm afraid that even small children would consider this to be either stupid or insulting. Ronald McDonald is usually portrayed as being extremely kind, light-hearted and child-like. The macho image of the rapper and breakdancer is highly incompatible with these McDonaldland characters.

The next four ads were from a related line of Lego's products for boys. These four commercials were very similar, except that they advertised different toys (pirate ship, spaceship, etc.). These ads were the most true to the original rap style. Three boys were shown playing with the toy and then dancing and rapping at the end of the ad. The boy leading the group and mouthing the words to the rap is black and he has two white boys on each side of him who appear to be backup singers. These ads are fairly compatible with the use of rap for several reasons. First, it is a product for boys and so the macho image of rap is probably appealing to the target audience. Second, since characters like pirates are supposed to be nasty and rebellious, this type of image probably does not hurt the product either. Third, a black male is used as the rapper, which is typical in the original rap style.

The last commercial, which advertises the Hot Wheels Racer, is very similar to the format of the previously discussed Lego ads. A black boy is shown rapping about the toy car, while two white boys in the background are playing with the cars and watching the rapper. The use of rap is probably fairly effective here, because the product is for boys, a black male is used, and the rap is intelligently presented.

The sample of ads from one year later showed that rap was used much less frequently and seemingly more discriminantly than the year before. There were three ads that clearly used rap and one that used a style of music that might be considered a combination of pop and rap. Apparently, the Lego ads were successful because the Pirate collection was still being advertised, using exactly the same commercial. A second, but new, Lego ad was also being aired, using the same approach (the "Blacktron" collection). The third rap ad appeared only once in the entire nine hours of programming, and was promoting Hershey's chocolate bars. This ad is beautifully executed and is quite a tribute to the rap style. The main slogan in the ad is "Pure milk chocolate … Can you handle it?" There is a black boy wearing a headset mike, who is leading the rap in an imaginary chocolate factory. The camera on occasion switches to a disc jockey surrounded by a space-age turntable console, who scratches the record to the beat. Near the rapper are several children breakdancing on an assembly line and providing some "backup" rapping. These dancers include boys and girls, both black and white. It seems that this commercial would be quite effective. It is so catchy and attractive that it makes chocolate seem hip, cool and fun. It is hard to believe that this ad was only shown once, perhaps to keep the concept from wearing thin. The fourth ad utilized a combination of rock and rap, and was used to advertise Campbell's Dinosaur soup. All of the characters are cartoons, either Campbell kids or dinosaurs. The dinosaurs are playing musical instruments in rock music style as the Campbell kids dance to the beat. There is a break in the song and one of the dinosaurs raps to the beat, holding a microphone. The final shot of the dancers features the entrance of a black Campbell kid who does a few breakdancing moves as several white Campbell kids dance in the background. This ad is entertaining and clever. It features a danceable beat that would facilitate memory of the ad and encourage children to join in the fun. Because this ad does not strictly emphasize rap, it avoids taking on the harshness of the true rap style, and does so in an effective way.

Conclusion

Evidence indicates that rap music has moved into the third stage of Gottdiener's model, in which a subcultural trend is sanitized by the producers of the mass culture. In October of 1990, advertisers seemed to believe that because rap was popular, kids would like any message in which rap was used. However, in 1991, it appears that advertisers have learned that rap may not be appropriate for all children's products and that rap must be presented in a "cool" or "hip" way. It is less compatible with characters that are nice, child-like, family-oriented or All-American.

These findings are consistent with the evidence that indicates that producers of mass culture have only limited control in their attempted "manipulation" of consumers. This has been the general conclusion of several researchers who have examined the usefulness of hegemony theory in a contemporary, free-market society. In his analysis of the hegemonic process in television entertainment, Gitlin says " … capitalism implies a certain sensitivity to audience taste, taste which is never wholly manufactured. Shows are made by guessing at audience desires and tolerances. ... " Alternative material is routinely incorporated into the dominant body of cultural production (Gitlin 263). Vallas examined occupational worker classes in order to come to the following conclusion: " ... members of subordinate classes have not uncritically embraced the tenets of the dominant ideology; rather they regard its premises with great skepticism ... members of privileged classes commonly believe that both the normative and empirical statements in the dominant ideology are true, most of the lower classes do not" (64). Even the popular music industry has resisted total domination by corporate interests, such that many successful products have been the ones that give more control to the consumer. Home taping and cassette recorders have given fans a new means of control over their sounds and have been the thorn in the side of the recording industry ever since. Sampling of records in hip hop music has undermined the status of the record as a finished product and has created a legal nightmare in terms of challenges to previously existing copyright laws (Frith 69–70).

Nevertheless, there is also evidence that the mass-culture industries are presenting rap in ways that they expect to be more acceptable to mainstream audiences. It is somewhat unfortunate that the mass culture industries have the power to dominate the development and diffusion of rap music, because most of the producers have little understanding about the subculture from which it originates. For most Americans, exposure to the life and cultural of others takes place through the agency of mass culture. This is the most unfortunate outcome for a subculture in which many young people hoped that rap would be a "way out" for disadvantaged youth and a chance that others might listen to what they have to say.

Works Cited

Adler, Jerry, Jennifer Foote, and Ray Sawhill. "The Rap Attitude." *Newsweek* 19 Mar. 1990: 56–59.

DiPrima, Dominique. "Beat The Rap." *Mother Jones* Sept.-Oct. 1990: 32–36, 80–82.

Domhoff, G. Williams. *Who Rules America?* Englewood Cliffs, NJ: Prentice, 1967.

Frith, Simon. "Industrialization of Popular Music." *Popular Music and Communication.* 2nd ed. Ed. James Lull. Newbury Park, CA: Sage, 1992: 49–74.

Gitlin, Todd. "Prime Time Ideology: The Hegemonic Process in Television Entertainment." *Social Problems* Feb. 1979: 251–66.

Goodwin, Andrew. "Rationalization and Democratization." *Popular Music and Communication.* 2nd ed. Ed. James Lull. Newbury Park, CA: Sage, 1992: 75–100.

Gottdiener, Mark. "Hegemony and Mass Culture: A Semiotic Approach." *American Journal of Sociology* 90.5 (1985): 979–1001.

Gramsci, Antonio. *Selections from the Prison Notebooks.* Eds. Quentin Hoare and Geoffrey Smith. London: Lawrence and Wishart, 1971.

Hanna, Judith Lynne. "Popular Music and Social Dance." *Popular Music and Communication.* 2nd ed. Ed. James Lull. Newbury Park, CA: Sage, 1992: 176–95.

Lull, James. "Popular Music and Communication: An Introduction." *Popular Music and Communication.* 2nd ed. Ed. James Lull. Newbury Park, CA: Sage, 1992: 1–32.

Marx, Karl, and Friedrich Engels. *The German Ideology.* New York: International P, 1969.

McKinney, Rhoda E. "What's Behind the Rise of Rap." *Ebony* June 1989: 66–70.

Peterson, Richard A., and David G Berger. "Cylces in Symbol Production: The Case of Popular Music." *American Sociological Review* Apr. 1975: 158–73.

Riesman, David. "Listening to Popular Music." *American Quarterly* 1 (1950): 359–71.

Sallach, David L. "Class Domination and Ideological Hegemony." *The Sociological Quarterly* Winter 1974: 38–50.

Toop, David. *The Rap Attack.* Boston: South End, 1984, 4–5

Vallas, Steven Peter. "Workers, Firms and the Dominant Ideology: Hegemony and Consciousness in the Monopoly Core." *The Sociological Quarterly* 32.1 (1991): 61–83.

Wicke, Peter. *Rock Music: Culture, Aesthetics and Sociology.* Cambridge: Cambridge UP, 1990.

38
Dance in Hip-Hop Culture
Katrina Hazzard-Donald

A cyclical quality distinguishes African American dance from dance elsewhere in the African diaspora. That is, an African American dance appears, then goes underground or seems to die out, only to emerge twenty or so years later as a "new" dance.[1] Consider Cuban rumba, Brazilian samba, Jamaican skank, or any number of dances that have originated in black Atlantic cultures; these dances, which have become familiar nationally and internationally, seem to have continuous rather than cyclical histories.

Rumba, the national dance and rhythm of Cuba, more than any other dance genre reflects the aesthetic sentiments and historical self-characterizations of the Cuban people. As in many New World African dances, including those appearing the United States, rumba uses derision, polymeter, mimetic characterization and, often, biting commentary. Cuba is rumba; its daily rhythms at work and play contribute to the rumba consciousness. In rumba various aspects of life are expressed and overlaid with a strong mimetic mating dialogue between male and female.[2]

In Brazil the throbbing syncopations of samba have inspired samba schools and competitions in which large numbers of Brazilians actively participate. Like Cuban rumba, Brazilian samba is a genre that expresses the national character and is familiar to old and young alike.

Like many popular dances in the United States, both samba and rumba originated among working-class and lower-class members of black communities only to be adopted and often modified by the "white" and upper-strata segments of society. The dances survive, largely intact, despite the contestation and class conflict that accompany their dissemination.

In contrast the cyclical nature of African American secular dance may reflect unique social forces; the rapidity with which the dance vocabulary is recycled and renamed in African American dance appears to be a by-product of the ever changing U.S. commodity market, which continually demands new dance material. The popular-culture market and industry are also international in scope, so that African American vernacular/popular dance eventually shows up in places such as Cuba or Sri Lanka.[3]

As influential as the external demands are, however, African American popular cultural creation is also driven by a desire for uniqueness and a tendency toward embellishment referred to as "the will to adorn" by anthropologist Zora Neale Hurston, which provide African American youth with wide parameters for unique expressiveness. Popular creation appears to change, even if only slightly, from one generation to the next.[4]

Shifting circumstances of class stratification and work, particularly as they impact on the changing African American national identity and character, also shaped the general movement of African American popular dance as a primarily agricultural labor force changed to one engaged in proletarian and other forms of urban labor. Immediately after Emancipation and the mass migration of rural freedmen into the cities and industries of both the South and North, African American secular social dance began to lose its rural character and take on more urban characteristics. The rural dances were marked by flat-footedness, bent or crouched postures, and group dancing rather than partnered couples. In the approximately sixty years of peak migration north, dances such as shuckin' corn, pitchin' hay, and milkin' the cow gave way to dances with more upright postures, less flat-footedness, and names that reflected a new urban reality.[5] But even today, after more than three-quarters of a century of proletarianization, African Americans still include agrarian references in their dance and in their music, particularly the blues.

Urbanization and proletarianization also transformed partnering relationships; the group and community-oriented dancing typical of rural dancing gave way to the single couple, with emphasis on sexual coupling. Subjected to less community scrutiny and participation, partners on the urban dance floor were alone with each other and required no contact with others. This isolation of the couple was a significant departure from the traditional circle and line dances familiar in both West African culture and in the dances of the rural bondsman and freedman. Traditional West African dances and even the Euro-American forms could not proceed without the participation of a sizeable community. Even so, the rural, community-oriented character of African American social dance was not completely obliterated. Evidence of this rural and community orientation surfaces in any group dance that does not emphasize sexual coupling. Think of dances such as the Madison, the continental, the birdland, the surplus, the bus stop and the most recent, the electric slide—group dances with little or no partnering relationships—these are all single-line dances. Double-line dances such as stroll and the soul train line require two lines, formed according to gender, and facing each other in a potential partnering arrangement. In both the stroll and the soul train line, dancers commonly featured a movement in which the partners move down the center between the lines; this limited partnering offered an opportunity for cooperation, but it was by no means required. Other evidence of rural influence can be observed in the mimetic character of African American dances. Dances such as the chicken (and its variation, the funky chicken), the horse, the snakehips, the pony, and milking the cow refer directly to the rural environment.

At any given moment in African American cultural history the working classes have had (and today have) a working repertoire of about half a dozen up-to-date dances from which to choose, and a general repertoire of around thirty.[6] There is no shortage of creative recycling. Each generation of African American youth, it seems, recalls demonstrating what they think is a new dance step, only to be told that their elders did that same dance twenty, thirty, forty, or more years ago. I had that experience many times as a young street dancer in Cleveland, Ohio. Like a language, the basic vocabulary of African American dance is passed along.[7] As did many of my peers, I learned it both in my home and "in the street" with my peer group. Former Cotton Club performer Howard "Stretch" Johnson and I once compared historical and regional variations on a number of dances. I asked him if he had ever heard of a dance called the twine. Yes, he had, and as we each demonstrated the versions we had learned, we agreed that his 1920s New York version, imported from "down South," was far more flat-footed and rooted into the earth than mine. My 1960s urban, midwestern version was more upright, lighter, with less weight in the arm strokes and freer movement in the legs and feet. After comparing a number of dances and making similar observations on all of them, we jointly concluded that his bent, flat-footed version of the dances might reflect a time when upright postures in African American dance were not well tolerated by white audiences. Many whites who attended the minstrel theater in particular are not ready to see Africans in postures that suggested anything but the bent, flat-footed, crouched, lowered head of the old "buck-dancing" styles. Since there a widespread and influential exchange of dance material between the vernacular popular-folk dances and the black professional performance tradition, many early versions of recycled popular dances bore that stamp of theatrical and plantation subservice, particularly when performed before a white audience. This was probably true as well on the southern plantation, since slaves were often called upon to entertain their master and his guests. The cakewalk, a dance that utilized exaggerated upright postures, was the notable exception.

The cakewalk is believed to have originally ridiculed the arrogant, upright, erect postures of the slaveholding class; it was a dance of derision.[8] The widespread change from the old Uncle Tom postures, bent and cowardly, to the more upright dancing styles appears simultaneously with the return of African American GIs from World War I and the heaviest recruitment of black male workers by northern industry.[9] African Americans had a new national pride and self-consciousness, reflected in the phrase "the new Negro," in the theater dance style of the "class acts," and in the slogan "All tap, no Tom." Performers like Eddie Rector purged the old postures from their routines.[10] Later in the popular-dance arena the lindy hop struck a new cord of defiance, public self-redefinition, and cultural pride.

Supporting these new dance trends in both the popular theater and in the rent parties, dance halls, honky-tonks, after-hours joints, and jooks were the significant numbers of black men who were increasingly being employed in industry or jobs related to or dependent upon industrial production: in factories, steel mills, auto plants, and the post office, and on the construction crews laying the nation's roads and later the new interstate highways. Both the economy and the community offered support for forming and maintaining African American families. Black men's lives were considerably less stressful and economically insecure than they would later become. This trend toward a positive environment for marriage and family was clearly expressed in the urban song and dance styles emerging and dominating African American popular culture between 1920 and the mid-1970s.

The themes of security, marriage, mating, sexual coupling, heartbreak, and cheating became more popular and well developed in the music and dance era of rhythm and blues. Blacks, like many other Americans, enjoyed the postwar prosperity and security of the forties, fifties, and sixties. For those who remained marginally employed, the thriving alternative economy—particularly "the numbers"—provided supplemental and, for some, occasional full-time employment.[11] But even the alternative economy had at its foundation African American male breadwinners, for without the wealth generated by African American male labor and the income of working black men, and to a lesser extent women, "the numbers" would not have thrived. The labor of many African American women was an important supplement to that of the men. All this would change.

In the 1960s a number of economic and social changes began to transform the culture-creating environment of African American life. First, the state-sponsored educational, social, and economic programs in black communities, many of them born of the sixties, suffered large funding cuts and were phased out. The remaining jobs were privately funded for relatively short periods, affording workers little job security. Nevertheless, some of these programs served as centers of community activism as well as providing employment and economic services such as job training. The Job Corps, street academies, Model Cities, drug education and abuse treatment, Opportunities Industrialization Center, and black-culture community centers and programs became focal points for those on the bottom of society who wanted to make it, thus providing an additional buffer to economic deprivation and instilling hope and societal concern. Many of these programs had youth orientations; most focused at least some of their energies on young people. At these focal points culture was generated, reworked, challenged, and disseminated.

Second, while racial integration brought about many positive changes, it also resulted in the demise or weakening of some traditional black economic networks and institutions. For example, the old "numbers" or "policy" games were converted into state-controlled lotteries, and specialized "race" products and services, such as those related to hair and beauty, were drawn into the mainstream. The third, and by no means least, important change was the uprooting of U.S. industry, marked by corporate flight and the move to a service-based economy. The loss of manufacturing jobs disproportionately affected black men who headed households; as the percentage of black male unemployment began a steady rise, the percentage of female-headed households began to increase dramatically.

By the late 1960s and early 1970s popular music and dance had become increasingly political as the industrial base that supported much black cultural creation eroded; the politicized forms of popular music and dance were successfully challenged by the apolitical, slick dance and music called disco. Disco gave voice to a newly empowered economic strata, the yuppie, and the midlevel service worker.[12] Despite the social, political, and economic accomplishments that their grandparents and parents had struggled for, African American youth inherited economically unstable and eroded ground for their hopes and dreams. Vicious attacks on all phases of the black movement deprived this generation of a viable social movement through which to work against their frustrations and for their economic needs. Where would this generation of African American youth find employment? Where would they find the working, productive male role models so necessary to the health of any community? With what material would they create their dreams? In the midst of rapidly worsening social conditions, how could this generation find meaning in their community's traditional music and dance forms as their predecessors had? Would they create utterly new dance and music forms that spoke more directly to their unique experiences in a world without its former industrial base? In this era of African American male economic insecurity, of popular conspicuous consumption (e.g., the brazen display of designer labels and brand names), of widening gaps between rich and poor, and of a moribund social movement for black and minority inclusion, hip hop emerged.

Why Hip Hop?

Hip hop is an expressive cultural genre originating among lower- and often marginalized working-class African American youth; it has West Indian influences, particularly dance hall, dub, and DJ style.[13] The genre includes rapping and rap music, graffiti writing, particular dance styles (including breakdancing), specific attire, and a specialized language and vocabulary. Hip hop appears at the crucial juncture of postindustrial stagnation, increased family dissolution, and a weakened struggle for black economic and political rights. Might one expect the pressures of mutually antagonistic social forces such as high unemployment, heightened job competition, and expectations of conspicuous consumption to influence both the popular expressive culture and the culture-creating apparatus of a community? I say yes. It is no coincidence that many youth of the hip hop generation have never known the relative security that some of their parents and even grandparents knew.

Hip hop dance is clearly masculine in style, with postures assertive in their own right as well as in relation to a female partner. In its early stages, hip hop rejected the partnering ritual between men and women; at a party or dance, hip hop dance was performed between men or by a lone man. About 1973 or 1974 I attended a dance given by African American students at Cornell University. I took the initiative and asked a young man to dance; on refusing my invitation, he explained that he couldn't dance with women, that the way he danced unsuitable for dancing with women. He proceeded to give me a demonstration how that was so, running through several dance steps that I had seen performed by Fred "Rerun" Berry and the Lockers. Correctly performed, the dance did not allow for female partnering;

it was a purely male expression and rarely performed by females. Particularly in early hip hop the male does not assume the easygoing, cool, confident polish characteristic of earlier popular-dance expression. Even in its early stages hip hop dancing aggressively asserted male dominance.

Waack and Breakin'

Hip hop dance can be characterized in three stages; waack, breakdancing, and rap dance. Waack dancing appears about 1972. Dance moves such as locking (later known on the East Coast as pop-locking), the robot, and the spank, along splits and rapidly revolving spins combined with unexpected freezes, were part of waack's outrageous style.[14] Here the fusion of theatrical expectation and outrageous showmanship occurs that would mark later hip hop styles known as break-dancing.

A staple in the vocabularies of waack, breaking, and, to a lesser degree, rap dance was the pop and lock, a movement technique that was part of the jerk in the late 1950s before that dance left black communities and crossed over to mainstream America in the mid to late 1960s. (The mainstream version is almost unrecognizable to the dancers who performed the original.) The pop and lock is both a way of handling the body and a movement quality in which a jerking and freezing of movement takes place. In this particular style a segmented body part such as the foot or hand initiates a free-flowing, undulating movement that flows up the leg or arm and ends with a jerking and freezing in place. It can be done with almost any combination of body parts but is most often performed with the torso, arms, and legs. The pop-and-lock technique could also be observed in the snakehips, as that dance was performed by the Cotton Club's Earl "Snakehips" Tucker in the 1920s.[15] Going farther back, a dance called the snakehips was popular in the Georgia Sea Islands and throughout the antebellum plantation South, and I have no reason to doubt that it resembled the version I learned in a 1950s midwestern African American community.[16]

As with later stages of development, clothing was an essential part of hip hop style. Big apple hats (an oversized style cap popularized by the late Donny Hathaway and soon to be replaced by Kangol caps, then by baseball caps); knickers, or suspenders with baggy pants, or pants tucked into striped knee socks; open-laced combat boots (soon to be replaced by open-laced sneakers); sun visors—all were part of waack's style of dress. Through mass-media exposure, particularly on the TV dance show *Soul Train*, the dance group the Lockers and the Outrageous Waack Dancers popularized the early hip hop dancing styles, helped along by TV sitcoms such as *What's Happening*, featuring Fred "Rerun" Berry. Rerun was often allowed short solos to demonstrate the early hip hop dance and clothing style. Both the Waacks' and Lockers' dancing was full of jerks and staccato movement, with up-and-down motion providing the center from which flashy embellishments such as high kicks and sudden unexpected turns emanated.

Breakdancing, the second stage of hip hop dancing, draws on a traditional and familiar concept in African American music, dance, and verbal arts: competitive one-upmanship. In music, breaking appears in the cutting contests of Harlem rent-party musicians, or in the competitive dialogue between musician and dancer. Look for it in the verbal arts of toasting, signifying, burnin', or "cutting his mouth out," usually performed with rhyming dexterity, articulation, and style; this verbal skill is highly valued in certain contexts. The principle of competitive dialogue shows up in African American street rhyme (e.g., the Signifying Monkey, Stackolee, and Shine rhymes), in the ritual of insult known as "the dozens," in contemporary rap music, and in a sacred context in the African American sermon.[17] It is not surprising that the competitive acrobatics involved in breakdancing were labeled *breaking* or that this traditional principle provides the form through which rappers and DJs would express themselves.

It is generally agreed that breaking as a dance style emerged around 1973 or 1974, concurrent with disco but confined to the African American youth subculture of male street associations known as crews. Breakdancing involved acrobatics that used headspins, backspins, moonwalking (a recycled version of the late 1950s, early 1960s dance the creep), waving, and the robot; it was mediated by a preparatory step known as top rockin' and pressed into competitive virtuosity. By 1976 the Zulus, a group of African American teenagers from the Bronx (the Zulu Nation formed as an alternative to the gangs in that community), had perfected the top rockin' footwork, backspins, and headspins. By 1978 many black youth had given up breaking and moved on to DJing, but the dance form would be rejuvenated among Puerto Rican youth, who took it up later than blacks and extended its longevity.[18]

Breaking's introduction to the general public by the mass media in April 1981 surely marked the beginning of its decline as a functional apparatus for competitive challenge among rival groups or individuals. Breakdancers began rehearsing in order to be discovered and appear in movies or for competitive street exhibition rather than practicing to compete with a rival. Far more acrobatic than either preceding or subsequent hip hop dance forms, without competition breaking loses its thrust, its raison d'être. Movement into the mainstream negated its status as countercultural by redefining it from a subcultural form to one widely accepted and imitated, a move that inadvertently linked breakers with the society that had previously excluded them. Breaking became so popular that it was featured as entertainment in the opening extravaganza of the 1984 Olympics.

Rap Dancing

The third stage of hip-hop dance, which I will label rap dance, developed a response to the popularity and athletic requirements of breaking. Combining aspects of both breaking and waack, it is influenced and cross-fertilized by a less athletic form of popular dance, house dancing, which uses much of the traditional African American vocabulary. Further influenced by the older rhythm-and-blues dances of the 1950s and 1960s, rap dance is male oriented, even male dominated, but unlike breakdancing not exclusively male. Its movements suit male–female partnering better than those of either waack or breaking, but less well than older popular dance forms such as the lindy hop or the rhythm-and-blues dances.

Like the lindy hop, hip hop dance is often athletic, youth oriented, and competitive, but rap dancing, and hip hop dance generally, require considerably less cooperation between partners. In the era of both rhythm and blues and the lindy hop, the contingencies of African American life required and fostered a firmer cooperation and interdependence from the racial group and the extended family to an extent virtually unknown to most of today's young hip hoppers. The lindy demonstrates a celebratory exuberance foreign to the break-dancing phase of hip hop dance and largely absent from the other two phases as well. This exuberance was fed by the celebration of the individual bound by in-group solidarity, community accountability, and cooperation.

Though I would not categorize rap dance as a dance of celebration, it does appear to celebrate male solidarity, strength, and competitiveness, themes that might be expected to emerge via the social dance in an era of high black male unemployment and of scarce jobs for which men are increasingly forced to compete with women. At the same time, the lack of commitment to the traditional partnering ritual also breaks with at least one function found in earlier African social dancing: selecting a romantic partner. Dancers who want to couple off romantically must return to the dance styles of a previous era. Hip hop shows no trace of the male-leadership themes expressed in the lindy and its 1950s and 1960s variants (the strand, offtime, jitterbug, and hand dancing), although they are still observable in the slow drag variations of what is now called slow dancing.

I was ambivalent about the hip hop phenomenon until I noticed the dancing that accompanied the rapping; it was energetic, athletic, and noticeably male dominated, using a very African movement vocabulary. It revived movements that had been out of popular use for thirty years, like splits and rapidly revolving turns (movements still employed by performers). "Splits have made a comeback," I thought. Over time I observed more of this "new" dancing and spoke with African American youth about where they got their dance steps. Many had learned them from friends, but most of the young people I spoke with in West Philadelphia also identified several dance steps with a popular hip hop artist or said that they learned the step from watching a particular performer. This indicated to me that the interplay between the popular/vernacular dance and the black commercial performer is still very strong. In observing rap dance I have seen the following traditional African American dances or dance fragments recycled and recontextualized: the black bottom, roach, Watusi, splits, boogaloo, mashed potatoes, funky butt (funky bottom, boodie green, 'da butt), chicken, four corners, worm, snakehips, and horse (old and new versions). I have also observed the use of traditional opposition or counterpoint as well as traditional characteristics such as percussive phrasing, polyrhythm, derision, mimetic play, and competition.

The rappers whose dance movements best encompass and personify the extremes in the genre of hip hop movement are Flavor Flav, of the group Public Enemy, and M.C. Hammer. Flavor Flav resembles the contemporary urban Esu-Elegba, or deity (principle) of uncertainty and unpredictability, also known as the trickster deity.[19] M.C. Hammer's well-choreographed movements draw directly from a strong rhythm-and-blues tradition. Hammer credits James Brown, a rhythm-and-blues artist, as the most powerful influence on his dance-performance style.

Contemporary rap dances such as the pump, running man, and Roger Rabbit, as well as the dance styles from a concurrent genre, house dancing, all exhibit structural and functional continuity with previous dances. House dancing and rap dance are cross-fertilizing each other. Like most African dance styles, these exhibit angularity, asymmetry, polyrhythmic sensitivity, derision themes, segmentation and delineation of body parts, earth-centeredness, and percussive performance.[20] To this list we can add apart dancing.

Apart dancing describes dancing in which the partners do not touch each other during the dance, yet the commitment to the partnering ritual is clear; this quality helps characterize both the traditional West African dance styles and many dance styles in African communities in the Americas. In the old rhythm-and-blues forms, apart dancing was a dominant theme, and little competition between partners emerged. Individual virtuosity often took the form of display rather than challenge as a dominant governing principle. Themes of challenge pervade both breakdancing and rap dance to a greater degree than occurs in either waack dancing or the older rhythm-and-blues dances such as the twist, the slop, or the horse. Challenge could and did emerge in these older dances, however, particularly when there was a dispute to be settled.

What Hip Hop Dance Says

The richness of gesture and motion in hip hop dance, as in numerous other forms of popular American dance styles that develop among marginalized African American, West Indian, and Puerto Rican youth, reflects the effect of social and economic marginalization on their lives.

Competitiveness in hip hop dance occurs not only against these backdrops but also with strained gender relations thrown into the mix. Since U.S. society regards young African American males as threatening, attitudes of fear and suspicion restrict their entry into the mainstream service economy as well as other areas of mainstream life. That economy thus more easily absorbs African American female workers than males; add the effects of the feminist movement on black women's attitudes toward traditional female roles, and you have raised the potential for cultural expression of rivalry and self-assertion between black and women.

Hip hop dance permits and encourages a public (and private) male bonding that simultaneously protects the participants from and presents a challenge to the racist society that marginalized them. This dance is not necessarily observer friendly; its movements establish immediate external boundaries while enacting an aggressive self-definition. Hip hop's outwardly aggressive postures and gestures seem to contain and channel the dancer's rage.

The whole of African American dance reflects the postures and gestures that African Americans esteem. Observe today's popular dancing and note how important unpredictability is; reflected in the term "fresh" and emphasized in the new movement styles, this unpredictability has a certain logic that calls forth praise and admiration.

Hip hop dance reflects an alienation not only of young African American males from mainstream society and of African American males from females but also of one African American generation from another. Despite the many continuities and similarities to earlier dances, hip hop represents a clear demarcation between generations in ways previously unknown in African American dance culture. Because of its athletic nature, its performance in popular arenas is largely confined to those under about twenty-five years of age. This might reflect the commodity market's emphasis on youth; it certainly coincides with current marketing strategies that appeal to the "cult of youth," strategies that do not exclude African American cultural commodities. Or it might simply reflect the cultural leadership of young black men in creating African American dances.

Although hip hop dance possesses an air of defiance of authority and mainstream society that reflects a critical vision observable in earlier dances of derision, it lacks the dominant or strongly stated derision that one finds in such as the PeeWee Herman or the Patty Duke of the 1970s, or even the cake-walk. True, hip hop's critical vision comes out of a marginalized youth culture with its own language, its own values and symbols, its own dance and style, yet unlike a true counterculture, hip hop does not reject the mainstream materialism of designer leisure wear, brand-name kicks, expensive cars, and (until recently) dookie gold.[21] Perhaps this embracing of materialism by the later hip hop stylists modifies or otherwise influences the emergence of derision themes, but this connection is by no means clear-cut.

Still, as dance has done for youth in other times, hip hop dance does more than express the view of the social and economic outsider, or even of the wanna-be insider. It encompasses a highly functional system of symbols that affect individual identity development, peer-group status, and intergroup dynamics and conflict.[22] For example, youth in New York City used the breaking form of hip hop to settle lower-level gang disputes and assert territorial dominance. A similar function for dancing was observed among gang members in Chicago in the late 1950s and early 1960s: "Dancing is even more important in Vice Lord life. Almost all Vice Lords take intense pride in their dancing ability and lose few opportunities to demonstrate it."[23]

Malcolm X describes the importance of dancing ability in facilitating peer-group inclusion for him: "Like hundreds of thousands of country-bred Negroes who had come to the Northern black ghetto before me, and have come since, I'd also acquired all the other fashionable ghetto adornments—the zoot suits and conk that I have described, liquor, cigarettes, then reefers—all to erase my embarrassing background. But I harbored one secret humiliation: I couldn't dance."[24]

I have understood the significance of dance in negotiating peer-group inclusion since childhood. As in many African American communities, dancing was important among the young people I knew for peer-group status and acceptance. In the mid-1950s a dance known as the slop was extremely popular.[25] I heard my peers joyfully discussing this dance that I knew nothing about, and I felt excluded. One day I asked an older girl (about twelve or thirteen years old), Thelmari

Workman, who lived downstairs from me, to demonstrate the dance for me. She teased me, taunted me, told me that I was "too little to learn the slop." She had me crying. I begged her, "Thelmari, please, please teach me how to do the slop." I knew that dance could help me to belong with my peers and garner admiration from within my community, and it could open an entire new realm of being, self-definition, and socialization.[26]

Just as the jookers and jitterbugs of another era were given their monikers, African American working- and lower-class youth who participate in the hip hop genre, who adopt its persona as their personal presentation style, are sometimes called b-boys, b-girls, or hip hop people.[27] Like their forerunners, they are the product of a specific sociohistoric backdrop and time-bound cultural experience. And like the *rumbista* with Cuban rumba and the *sambista* with Brazilian samba, hip hop people identify with, embrace, and live the genre completely, however short-lived it may be.

The hip hop persona emphasizes converting postures that in another context would indicate alienation and defeat into postures of self-assurance in the face of unbeatable odds. For instance, holding one's arms crossed high on the chest might be interpreted as an insecure and withdrawing posture; in hip hop dance I interpret this posture as affirming African American maleness, strength, and readiness for physical and sexual competition. It also indicates the vision of an inside observer who is simultaneously on the outside. "Laying in the cut," this observer sees something invisible to most people; his bobbing head and crossed arms reaffirm this secretly observed universal truth.

Though hip hop music and dance are today enjoyed by virtually every socioeconomic segment of American society, hip hop postures and presentation are born of the African-derived core culture of the street, and they are still used to negotiate a place there. Fear was among the general white public's initial reaction to the latter-day hip hop genre. I have observed young men with hip hop carriage and in hip hop attire—sneaker laces open, baseball cap, sweatsuit—listening to and carrying their beat boxes blasting rap music in the public space of the street, and I have observed whites threatened and intimidated by their presence.

Talkin' the Talk and Walkin' the Walk in the Mainstream

But the image of hip hop dance and music is changing, influenced by women's entry into the genre, by the media, and by the adoption of hip hop by the popular-music and advertising industries. The recent entry of females into the rap recording and video industry has challenged the hard, male-dominated, often misogynist hip hop identity reflected in the themes of some rap songs. Women are talkin' the talk of hip hop; they are dancing and creating new dance materials as well as recycling older dances and crosscultural black dances such as the butterfly in ways that voice the moral, romantic, and political concerns, the aesthetic preferences, the needs and desires of this generation.[28]

Since the popular market has recently embraced hip hop as a marketing strategy, movement and music once identified with African American, West Indian, and Latino male street associations are being used to sell everything from pastry to autos, and they are being incorporated into aerobics classes and exercise videos.

At the same time, widespread acceptance of hip hop music has led to modifications in the masculine, confrontive nature of the dance, resulting in less athletic new dances that can be performed to hip hop music. Hip hop songs are increasingly danceable, even using the movement of a previous era. For television and movies, in dance competitions, and in commercials, professional choreographers have adopted hip hop energy and style.

Although the wide acceptance and exploitation of hip hop in the advertising and popular-music industries has on one level robbed the dance of its original significance, hip hop still functions in the places of its origin. Most mainstream Americans will never see the subtle codes, gestures, and meanings of hip hop as they are displayed in African American communities, and that is true of much dance originating in African American culture.

Meanwhile, the aspects of hip hop that can be commercialized will affect daily rhythms of mainstream American life, but even watered down, hip hop's influence will have profound and enduring effects on American culture.

Notes

1. Chadwick Hansen, "Jenny's Toe: Negro Shaking Dances in America," *American Quarterly* 19 (1967): 554–563.
2. For accounts and analyses of rumba, see Yvonne Daniel, *Rumba: Dance and Social Change in Contemporary Cuba* (Bloomington: Indiana University Press, 1995). See also Janheinz Jahn, *Muntu: The New African Culture* (New York: Grove, 1961).
3. In July 1990 I observed breakdancing in a cabaret in Havana. The crew, attired in open-laced sneakers, baseball caps, and baggy trousers or jeans, performed popping and locking, headspins, backspins, and moonwalking that rivaled any I have observed in the United States. Television, videotape, and returning relatives were sources for cultural transference from the United States to Cuba. As far back as 1983 I was informed by Sri Lankan students at Cornell University in Ithaca, New York, that breakdancing was being attempted in Sri Lanka. One male student in particular was avidly learning the new moves in order to carry them back to his homeland. For accounts of the international impact of hip hop, see "A Newcomer Abroad, Rap Speaks Up," *New York Times*, Arts and Leisure section, August 23, 1992, which discusses the emergence of hip hop in Russia, China, India, West Africa, Eastern Europe, Britain, France, and Mexico.
4. Zora Neale Hurston, "Characteristics of Negro Expression," in *Negro Anthology*, ed. Nancy Cunard (New York: Negro Universities Press, 1969), 44.
5. Renamed the toilet stool, the dance milkin' the cow appears in the urban Midwest, Cleveland, Detroit, and Gary, Indiana, in the late 1940s and early 1950s; the footwork and lateral pelvic isolation goes on to become part of a popular 1960s dance, the Watusi, and later reappears once more in the late 1970s as the rock.
6. Regional variation in this repertoire becomes less pronounced when dances have popular media exposure, and it is even less apparent generally than it was in the past. Today regional variation is short lived.
7. For a discussion of dance's language-like properties, see Judith Lynn Hanna, *To Dance Is Human: A Theory of Non-Verbal Communication* (Chicago: University of Chicago Press, 1988).
8. For accounts of the cakewalk, see Tom Fletcher, *The Tom Fletcher Story—100 Years of the Negro in Show Business* (New York: Burdge, 1954); see also "Cakewalk King: 81-Year-Old Charles E. Johnson Still Dreams of New Comeback with Dance Step of Gay 90s," *Ebony*, February 1953, 99–102, and Lynne Fauley Emery, *Black Dance from 1619 to Today*, 2d ed. (Princeton, N.J.: Princeton Book Co., 1988). It is interesting to note that waack, a 1970s hip hop style of dance, used high kicks similar to those used in the cakewalk. My current research leads me to question the interpretation of the cakewalk as purely imitative of exaggerated Euro-American postures. There are numerous dances in West Africa that use the leg in high kicks or extensions. Dances such as sabar, in Senegal, use high leg raises and arched erect spines.
9. Florette Henri, *Black Migration: Movement North, 1900–1920* (Garden City, N.Y.: Anchor, 1976).
10. Marshall Stearns and Jean Stearns, *Jazz Dance* (New York: Macmillan, 1966), 285–297. African American performers who worked the TOBA (Theater Owners Booking Association) circuit responded to the demand for subservient postures with the phrase "All tap, no Tom," indicating that they were not willing to perform Uncle Tom postures in their dance routines. Interview with Howard "Stretch" Johnson, former Cotton Club and TOBA performer and brother-in-law of Lincoln Perry: whose stage name was Step 'n Fetchit, New Paltz, New York, December 1979.
11. "The numbers" was an illegal lottery played in black communities. See St. Clair Drake and Horace Cayton, *Black Metropolis* (New York: Harper & Row, 1962). See also Harold Gosnell, *Negro Politicians* (Chicago: University of Chicago Press, 1935); J. Saunders Redding, "Playing the Numbers," *North American Review* 238, December 1934); and George J. McCall, "Symbiosis: The Case of Hoodoo and the Numbers Racket," *Social Problems* 10 (Spring 1963): 361–371.
12. That the famous Motown sound came out of Detroit, Michigan, is no coincidence. The Motor City was a midwestern industrial center that employed thousands of African American men and women in auto production. This economic base provided a sociocultural and economic backdrop for a particular type of popular-culture creation. The Motown sound found a ready market in the black communities of Detroit, Cleveland, Gary, Pittsburgh, and other centers of heavy industry with large Southern first- and second-generation migrant populations.

13. The vainglorious boasting, sexual innuendo (recently labeled sexist), and mocking commentary on a wide range of topics including social issues, racism, economics and politics have existed in Trinidadian calypso for at least sixty years. Trinidian calypso, with its high level of improvisation and verbal dexterity requirements, was the most influential musical form in the English-speaking Caribbean until the early 1970s commercial emergence of Jamaican reggae. In the mid-1970s Jamaican bands began experimenting with and integrating calypso's verbal improvisation into their music. Jamaican DJs scatted over reggae records, intersecting with traditional American scatting heard over transistor radios in the Caribbean. Known as "toasting" (not to be confused with the African American toast rhyme, though culturally similar), this technique was mastered, recorded, and popularized by artists like U Roy and Big Youth and can be heard today in the running rap style of Shabba Ranks. Jamaican and other West Indian immigrants to the United States brought their musical styles with them, and in the 1970s toasters could be heard on the streets of South Bronx, an economically marginalized community with significant West Indian, African American, and Puerto Rican populations. Many of the early rappers and DJs like Afrika Bambaataa had West Indian parents at home and absorbed the strong West Indian influences. See "The Forgotten Caribbean Connection," *New York Times*, August 23, 1992, Pop Music section.

14. "The 'Outrageous' Waack Dancers," *Ebony*, August 1978, 64. I observed similar popping and locking in a sacred ceremony to the deity Shango in Cuba in July 1990, and the movement can be observed in dances to Shango in Nigeria. Interviews with Abiodune Adekunle, Nigerian Yoruba devotee of Shango, Philadelphia, March 1991 and with Unoboje Aisiku, Nigerian Yoruba, May 1992.

15. Interview with Charles "Honi" Coles, Ithaca, New York, March 1980. During an after-dinner chat at a mutual friend's home, Honi performed the old snakehips dance the way he had seen Earl Tucker perform it. Watching Coles perform it made me realize that the 1950s dance move known as poppin' the hips, which I learned around 1957, was an updated version of the 1920s snakehips.

16. Georgia Writers Project, *Drums and Shadows* (Athens: University of Georgia Press: 1940), 115; Stearns, *Jazz Dance*, 235–238.

17. For an excellent commentary on the importance of verbal dexterity among African Americans, both on the mainland and in the Caribbean, see Roger D. Abrahams, *The Man of Words in the West Indies* (Baltimore: Johns Hopkins University Press, 1983); see also Abrahams, "Playing the Dozens," *Journal of American Folklore* 75: 209–220, and *Deep Down in the Jungle: Negro Narrative Folklore from the Streets of Philadelphia* (Hatboro, Pa.: Folklore Associates, 1964); Lawrence W. Levine, *Black Culture and Black Consciousness* (New York: Oxford University Press, 1977), 298–366.

18. Steven Hager, *Hip Hop* (New York: St. Martin's, 1984), 81–90. I learned the moonwalk in the late 1950s or early 1960s in Cleveland, Ohio, as a dance named the creep. Michael Jackson, who popularized it as the moonwalk, was born in 1958 just as the creep was emerging and gaining popularity; he could have seen it performed or learned it in the midwestern community of Gary, Indiana, where he grew up the child of a steel-mill employee.

19. During performance, Flavor Flav bears a striking resemblance to other New World African performers— King Warrin of the John Canoe celebrations, Haiti's Baron Samedi, and even the Uruguayan "el Gramillero." All exhibit aspects of Esu-Elegba. See Ira De A. Reid, "The John Canoe Festival," *Phylon* 3 (4): 350, 356; Dougald MacMillan, "John Kuners," *Journal of American Folklore* 39 (January–March 1926): 53–57; Margaret Shedd, "Carib Dance Patterns," *Theater Arts Monthly* 17 (January 1933): 65–77; Paulo deCarvalho Neto, "The Candombe, a Dramatic Dance from Afro-Uruguayan Folklore," *Journal of the Society for Ethnomusicology* 5 (1962): 164–174; and Katrina Hazzard-Gordon, "Dancing to Rebalance the Universe: African-American Secular Dance," *Journal of Physical Education, Recreation & Dance* 62 (February 1991): 36. Flavor Flav and other rappers pronounce the word "boy" as "bwoy," drawing out the "wo" and giving it an "oi" sound. Melville J. Herskovits comments on Africanized speech patterns in Jamaica and Suriname: "In addition we found correspondences in such pronunciations as 'bwoy' for 'boy.'" See *The Myth of the Negro Past* (Boston: Beacon, 1990), 282.

20. John Szwed, "Musical Adaptation among Afro-Americans," *Journal of American Folklore* 82 (April–June 1969); Hurston, "Characteristics of Negro Expression."

21. *Kicks*, the name given to the designer sneakers worn by the youth, is a term at least forty years old in many African American communities. *Dookie gold* refers to the large gold chains admired and desired by some youth.

22. Katrina Hazzard-Gordon, "Afro-American Core Culture Social Dance: An Examination of Four Aspects of Meaning," in *Perspectives of Black Popular Culture*, ed. Harry Shaw (Bowling Green, Ohio: Bowling Green State University Popular Press), 46; see also Roy Milton Clark, "Dance Party as a Socialization Mechanism," *Sociology and Sociological Research* 58 (1974).

23. R. Lincoln Keiser, *The Vice Lords* (New York: Holt, Rinehart & Winston, 1969), 52. The dance–martial arts form known as *capoeira* also serves this purpose. See Bira Almeida, *Capoeira, a Brazilian Art Form* (Richmond, Calif.: North Atlantic, 1981).

24. Alex Haley with Malcolm X, *The Autobiography of Malcolm X* (New York: Grove, 1966), 56.

25. The slop today is known as the George Jefferson, named for the main character in a TV sitcom, who performed it on a number of occasions.

26. For further discussion of the function of dance in African American culture, see Hazzard-Gordon, "Afro-American Core Culture Social Dance," 46.

27. Interview with North Philadelphia youth who participate in the hip hop genre, Philadelphia, December 1990. I found the label "hip hop people" used when no other term fit. It is used in North Philadelphia among lower- and working-class black youth only to describe those who wear the appropriate clothes, listen to rap, and immerse themselves in the genre through the verbal and nonverbal language. The appropriate terms to describe hip hop participants, formerly "b-boy" or "b-girl," seem to have changed as hip hop becomes widely accepted.

28. For a discussion of female rappers, see "Female Rappers Invade the Male Rap Industry," *Donahue Transcripts*, show #0529–91, transcript #3216, May 29, 1991; Tricia Rose, "Never Trust a Big Butt and a Smile," *Camera Obscura*, no. 23 (May 1990) 108–130; "The Women of Rap," *Rappin Magazine*, July 1990; Jill Pearlman, "Rap's Gender Gap," *Option*, Fall 1988, 32–36; and Nancy Guevara, "Women, Writin', Rappin', Breakin'," in *The Year Left* 2, ed. Mike Davis et al. (New York: Verso, 1987), 160–175. The butterfly is a dance imported to East Coast cities from Jamaican dancehall style.

39

Wendy Day, Advocate for Rappers

Norman Kelley

Wendy Day is the founder of Rap Coalition, a not-for-profit organization set up to help rap artists.

NORMAN KELLEY: How long have you been doing this?

WENDY DAY: Five years. I started in March 1992. I was in corporate America prior to running Rap Coalition. My background was advertising and sales, and I was very fortunate in that I made quite a bit of money. I was in Montreal at the time and I decided to come back to America, come home. I had quite a bit of money and I knew I wanted to do something to help people. I wanted to combine the money that I had with my entire business background. I have a masters degree in African-American studies and I knew I wanted to do something within the black community but wasn't quite sure as to what. I've always loved rap music since the early 1980s and I decided to take the money and start Rap Coalition. It's been five and a half years and no looking back.

NORMAN KELLEY: Was there anything like an event or series of events that precipitated you starting the coalition?

WENDY DAY: Not necessarily. It was the system that bothered me. As I mentioned, I have a degree in African-American studies and white folk have been robbing black folk since time began. So I knew I wanted to do something as a white person to sort of balance out that injustice that's been done for five hundred years. I wanted to do something that would balance that scale and I chose rap music, because it's the music I'd been listening to since the Cold Crush Brothers, since Grandmaster Flash. It's the music that has always been there for me. When I was happy, I listened to rap. When I was sad, I listened to rap. When I was tired, I listened to rap. When I was energetic, I listened to rap. So the music was my escape in my life; it was there.

When I came back to the United States I knew I wanted to do something. I started studying the music business because I'm not one to jump in without learning what the climate is. I studied the music business for about eight months, and in that time period, Eric B and Rakim got jerked and X Clan got jerked, and those were two of my favorite groups—they and Public Enemy were what I was listening to. They were my favorite artists and I couldn't understand why no one stepped in to help these guys, and that's really what did it. It wasn't like one thing made me do it. It was a series of events up until that time, you know, for the past five hundred years, that led me to want to do something. But that was the straw that broke the camel's back.

NORMAN KELLEY: How did your training in corporate America help you?

WENDY DAY: The funny thing about corporate America is that you kind of learn to dance for a dollar. You learn to do what you have to do to get the job done. My background was sales and marketing and I was always very good with people. So the first thing I did with Rap Coalition was introduce very high-powered attorneys to rappers, because that seemed the one piece of the equation that was missing and the average rapper does not have access to— Madonna's attorney. So I started meeting people. I would just show up on their door steps—attorneys'—and set up meetings with them and tell them what my plans were, what I was trying to accomplish. My thinking was that Madonna's attorney makes more money than God, so chances are good that this person could probably afford to do some pro-bono work. And I also come from the belief that human nature is basically good. So somebody who had the opportunity to help somebody else probably would if that opportunity was brought to them.

I sort of acted as matchmaker between up-and-coming rap artists and very powerful attorneys. That's really what the company's first mission was. We still do that, and it's been very successful in that a lot of attorneys have taken a lot of pro-bono cases. And they are more than qualified to handle them. They are not people right out of school who don't have the time to handle it. They are very busy professionals who take one or two extra cases, in some cases five. My attorneys are handling five different pro-bono cases right now.

NORMAN KELLEY: How many attorneys does Rap Coalition have?

WENDY DAY: About seventy.

NORMAN KELLEY: What's the structure of Rap Coalition? Is there a structure?

WENDY DAY: Yes and no. It's a loose structure. The most important aspect of the company is being able to change in order to fill needs. As the music industry changes—and it changes almost every day—so does the company, to meet those needs. We have some basic underlying principles that we go by.

NORMAN KELLEY: Which are … ?

WENDY DAY: Pulling people out of bad deals. Introducing people to attorneys. We have a series of educational programs, and probably as important is changing the attitude of the general public in terms of what rap music really is. That's an important one. But because the industry changes so quickly, all of the other projects are based on what the need of the day is, the need of the week, the need of the month. We have an office here in New York, an office in Chicago. By the end of the year I hope to have an office in L.A. as well.

NORMAN KELLEY: It is interesting that you as a white person are doing this. Have you ever given any thought as to why a black person isn't or blacks themselves aren't doing this?

WENDY DAY: Funny, that's usually the first question I'm asked. I think there is a problem with a white person running a black organization. I personally have a problem with that. I know my motives and I know my agenda, so if somebody has to do it and it's not a black person, I'm glad it's me. But I understand why it is a problem that a black person is not running the organization. On the flip side, there are a lot of places that my skin color gets me into and a lot of situations that my skin color gets me into. Someone from Atlantic Records is much more comfortable negotiating a deal with me than with someone who doesn't look like him or her. That's just a human nature kind of attribute. It's wrong, but it is a reality. You're dealt a certain hand in life and you play that hand.

NORMAN KELLEY: You understand that black artists have been ripped off since the 1920s. I understand this, but why aren't today's black intellectuals or black leaders looking into this? Is it that they don't care?

WENDY DAY: I don't know if they care. I know that Nelson George [a black writer who covered hip hop when it was breaking; author of *The Death of Rhythm & Blues, Buppies, B-Boys, Baps, and Bohos,* and *Hip Hop America*] cares. I know he seems to endeavor more into the film side of it. I think because this is not as glamorous, and because he has the contacts.... He's real good friends with Russell Simmons. Why hasn't he written some sort of exposé? I'm sure he's seen it firsthand. Why hasn't he done in music what he's done in film? Maybe he has and I'm just not all up in his business. I don't know why that is, but people do know that exploitation exists.

There's no investigative journalism in music whatsoever, you know. I read *Source* magazine, I read all the magazines, even the ones you have never heard of. Craig Mack was on the cover of *Rap Pages* last month and Allen Gordon wrote an article called "Prince Among Thieves," talking about the different aspects of how he has been taken advantage of and how naïve he is. It was a great article, don't get me wrong, and I'm excited because it's a start, but it wasn't from the angle of the big bad music industry fucking over Craig Mack. It came from a stance that Craig Mack is naïve and that's the problem. It sort of blamed the victim. That seems to be the direction that criticism in music goes. People write books about the actual history of rap or the more glamorous side of things, but there is no tell-all.

NORMAN KELLEY: Rap really became big during the mid-eighties when Run-D.M.C. proved its crossover appeal. From what I've been reading, sixty percent of those who buy rap are white kids.

WENDY DAY: I bet it is a higher percentage than that.

NORMAN KELLEY: Now, is this a matter of the tail leading the dog? Do you have black kids following someone like Puffy because he's getting paid? The question is, are these artists doing it, their particular style and content, because they want to do it, or are they responding to market demands?

WENDY DAY: It's a trend. That's where the shift came. That's exactly where the shift came. It used to be that the artist would lead the market. Now, it's the market leading the artist. That's exactly the shift that occurred that inspired me to do the Rap Olympics. If we can bring the feeling of success to those who have skills rather than just those making money ... And I'm not saying just get rid of the money-making aspect. I love that young black people are getting paid, you just don't know. I love that and I would never take that away from anybody. I just want to see the concept of success in rap music expanded a little more—not changed, but expanded to included some of the real successes.

Let's use Puffy as an example—and I'm not trying to single him out; it's just that he's in my brain right now. If Puffy were sitting here right now, today, and I said, "You know what? There's a kid in Augusta, Georgia, who's making rhymes that are creating social change," Puffy would think that's as cool as fuck. He would love that, even though he has a lot of money and he's not about that. He would love that somebody was doing that. That kid's a success—even though you don't know who he is, Puffy doesn't know who he is, and maybe even I don't know who he is. But the point is, that kid is a success. The problem is that the rest of the world doesn't see it as a success because they see Puffy as success. That's the yardstick that they are judging people by. But because of the credibility that he has, that Puffy has, because of the money he has, if he got up on a podium, like that Lotto commercial, where his voice could be heard everywhere, and said, "This kid from Rhythm and Poetry in Augusta, Georgia, is a success because he's actually keeping kids in school and keeping kids off the street or whatever social change issue he's dealing with," kids would say, "Oh, Puffy says he's a success, therefore he's a success."

NORMAN KELLEY: Let's talk about your relationship with the Nation of Islam.

WENDY DAY: I worked a lot with the Nation of Islam and when I first went to Farrakhan's house, I was ecstatic. To me, it was a symbol of success that I had achieved a level of recognition for what I do. It's pretty cool to be at a meeting at the minister's house and you're the only white person there—and he pointed that out.

NORMAN KELLEY: Why were you there?

WENDY DAY: For the Rap Summit.

NORMAN KELLEY: What happened at that summit?

WENDY DAY: Basically, we discussed that lyrical content needed to change; that the black-on-black crime that exists in the lyrics is dead, it has to go away now.

NORMAN KELLEY: Is there a movement toward that?

WENDY DAY: There has been. There has been for about two years. There has been a huge backlash against gangsta rap.

NORMAN KELLEY: Did you think it was going to last?

WENDY DAY: I thought it'd be gone two years ago.

NORMAN KELLEY: It's still there.

WENDY DAY: Sure it is. Sure it is. Especially when you leave New York. I traveled through the Midwest a lot. There's a group called the Wild West Society, and they have less than socially redeeming lyrics. The lyrical content is not positive. So when you get into the Midwest and you have people buying hundreds of thousands of politically incorrect messages, it's kind of hard to tell them to stop. How do you tell Tupac, "Don't write a song like 'Toss It Up.' Make only songs like 'Brenda Has a Baby'?" You can't. Because the buying public buys it. That's the bottom line.

NORMAN KELLEY: How do you, as the president of Rap Coalition, deal with people like C. Delores Tucker and William Bennett, critics of rap? Have you ever met them?

WENDY DAY: I have two opinions. One is my personal opinion and one is my professional opinion. As the founder of Rap Coalition, it is my job to support rap artists. Rap artists can do no wrong. When I'm out in public and somebody says, "Twisted's lyrics are wrong because he degrades black women and he talks about black-on-black crime," I will defend him to the umpteenth degree.

NORMAN KELLEY: What would you defend?

WENDY DAY: It's his right to express whatever his wants: First Amendment rights, blah, blah, blah. He's chronicling what he sees in his area of Chicago, which is called Kaytown. So he has the right to chronicle what he sees. If you don't like his lyrical content, change his lifestyle. Change the problems of the ghetto in Chicago and his lyrics will change. Then I have—Wendy-as-a-person's opinion—a problem with his lyrical content, and he knows that. I've sat down with him and said, "You know what? This shit is dead, this whole black-on-black crime thing. You have got a slave mentality. You're a lost soul and it's really pathetic." That's the personal opinion, but I would never voice that publicly. At Rap Coalition, it is my job to protect and support him. C. Delores Tucker and William Bennett are the enemies. They have never been in the situations that rap artists have been in. So I can understand why they find it odd. I understand what their goals are. I know they are trying to protect children, they're trying to protect women from misogyny. I understand that exactly. I don't have a problem with what they are trying to accomplish; I have a problem with the way they are going about it.

NORMAN KELLEY: Which is?

WENDY DAY: By attacking—attacking the messenger but not the message. If they had sat down, one on one, with a Snoop Dogg or a Tupac and tried to accomplish it that way and tried to educate Snoop on their position, I wouldn't have a problem with that. But the fact is they didn't even meet with them; they went immediately to the media and started rabble-rousing. To me, it seems that this is their agenda, but they are going about it in such a wrong way. Are they just an Al Sharpton? Are they just trying to get press? Are they media whores? That's kind of my take on it: They are media whores. Because when the cameras aren't running, what are they doing that is really making a difference? Are they really making a difference? C. Delores has been around for three years and she has accomplished less than I have in three weeks. So how dedicated is she to her cause?

NORMAN KELLEY: How would you define the relationship between the music industry and rappers?

WENDY DAY: The relationship? Rappers don't really want to be part of the industry.

NORMAN KELLEY: Why is that?

WENDY DAY: I'm not exactly sure why they don't want to be part of the industry, but they are sort of removed from the whole thing. I'm generalizing. The average rapper really doesn't want to know how the business works; they just want fame and the women; they don't even want the money, because if they wanted money they would learn how it works and learn how to manipulate that to get the money. And they don't. They don't even read the contract, for the most part.

NORMAN KELLEY: But don't they understand that by not reading the contract …

WENDY DAY: By the time they get here they do. By the time they get here they have been jerked. And if they are coming to my panel discussions to learn how the industry works, they are already on a superior mental plane, because they know: Study the industry, and then make your move. You wouldn't get on a basketball court with Michael Jordan if you didn't know how to play basketball, right?

NORMAN KELLEY: Is that what you tell some of them?

WENDY DAY: Yeah.

NORMAN KELLEY: What's their response?

WENDY DAY: When they think about it, they go, "Yeah … you're right." If you don't study the game and, more important, how he moves, you'll never win. So why are you going to get on the court and look like an asshole? Why are you going to go to Atlantic Records and look like an asshole?

NORMAN KELLEY: What is it that they see initially?

WENDY DAY: Fame. They see a video with Jay-Z driving down the street in a Lexus. They hear Puffy on the radio every three minutes. They have a perception of this great lifestyle where you're famous and everybody loves you. Nobody hates you; everybody loves you. And you can fuck any woman you want. The president's wife? No problem. You can have her if you want her. So it's this whole misconception of more money then God and never having to worry about paying a bill. Waaaay too many women, and love from tons of adoring fans. And that's what they see and that's what they want. But it really isn't like that at all. To get to a level of Puffy is so much work. So much work. It's work and it's money. You have to have somebody behind you dumping tons of money into your project. Because you can be the greatest rapper with the best record, but if you don't have the right people working it, not getting the right publicity, not getting the right radio play, it's not going to go anywhere.

NORMAN KELLEY: How does the music industry view rap?

WENDY DAY: Let me preface this by saying this is not my opinion at all. It depends on the label. Obviously, Puffy is going to have a different view than a Craig Talbot who runs Atlantic Records, but for the most part it's "a bunch of dumb niggers," and I can see it in the deals that they offer. They front-load deals, they meaning record companies.

NORMAN KELLEY: What do you mean by front-load?

WENDY DAY: Front-load means they dangle money in your face. "Here's a hundred and fifty thousand dollars." They don't even talk about what you're going to get down the road. I'm generalizing again, not all labels are the same, but they say, "Okay, these guys are disposable. We'll get them to sign for a BMW or a bunch of sneakers, and a little bit of cash. We'll make a gazillion dollars and when they are not making money any more—fuck 'em. Who cares what happens to them?" And that's the perception, not just for rappers but for artists in general. Black artists in general have it even rougher because of the whole stereotype that's going on. There are stereotypes in everything. There are stereotypes about Jewish people. There are stereotypes about Middle Eastern people. But we live in a country where it is acceptable to degrade black people, and it is acceptable among both my race and black folk.

NORMAN KELLEY: What are the typical aspects of a bad contract?

WENDY DAY: First of all, there is not a typical contract. A contract is really an agreement between you and me. We sit down and you say, "Wendy, you have talent in painting toenails. So I'm going to dump five thousand dollars into you and you're going to go out and paint toenails. You've been doing it for free, but you're going to charge five dollars from now on and you're going to pay me half of everything you make until you pay me back the initial investment." That's a contract. It's not like there's a set contract for people who paint toes. Or people who lend money to people who paint toes. There is no such thing as a set contract. It's impossible to take a book like *This Business of Music* and go to the record label contract that is printed in it, then Xerox and use it, because every situation is different.

NORMAN KELLEY: But don't record companies have standard contracts?

WENDY DAY: No, they don't. They really don't. If you work for a record label, you're thinking about signing me, the rapper. There's a legal department that is going to ask me what I want or they are going to go to my lawyer, which is the preferable situation, and say, "What does this kid want?" Or they are just going to print out a contract that is as much to their benefit as possible. But each rapper comes in at a different position. Some of them have a vibe on the street and everyone knows who they are. Some of them have gotten unsigned hype in *Source*. They come at different levels. Some are straight out of school, they've never rapped a lick in their life, and they get signed. Some are Puffy's best friends. They all come in at different levels, so there are different incentives that a label has to sign them, and the contract is going to reflect that.

NORMAN KELLEY: Is Rap Coalition trying to get a bare minimum of standardization? And if so, what?

WENDY DAY: Every contract, even though they are different, includes a point system. What "points" means is this: you give me five thousand dollars to make a record and once I pay that back to you out of my royalties, I get to keep a percentage of my royalties. A good deal would be somewhere between twelve and fifteen points. That means I get twelve to fifteen percent of the net retail selling price, which, when you think about it, really sucks—but I want to be a star so I'm willing to sign to that, and that's the status quo. So a label can get away with that.

Okay, you may decide that instead of giving me twelve, to give me nine points. I've seen them as low as six. Ice Cube gave Cam six points and he signed it. Naughty by Nature gets eighteen points. They didn't start off at eighteen. I don't remember what they began with. Scarface is at thirteen. Why is Scarface at thirteen points and Naughty by Nature at eighteen points? I bet if I pull the statistics on them they sell about the same amount of units. Why is that? It's because Scarface and Naughty by Nature don't talk, but I talk to both of them and then I bring information back to both of them. I tell Scarface that they are getting eighteen. I tell them that he's getting thirteen. That's my job. My job is to educate them. What they do with that information is on them. I can't make them renegotiate their contracts. I can refer them to attorneys and accountants who can. But Scarface never will because he feels that Little Jay, his label, is working in his best interest. He doesn't have a clue. He doesn't realize it's about Jay getting rich, not Scarface getting rich. And Scarface doesn't care because whenever he needs money, he goes to Jay, and Jay just gives it to him.

NORMAN KELLEY: And any money that Jay gives him ...

WENDY DAY: Is recoupable. When you're an artist and you pay back everything that's recoupable, you don't get to keep the masters. In fact, you don't have anything to show for it except fame. You don't get to keep shit. It is stated in almost every contract that if you leave the record label, you can't perform the songs you did for them for five years. It's usually not enforced, but what happens when the first group pisses off the labels? George Michaels pissed off the record company so badly that they may be the first ones to enforce that rule.

I have a huge problem with that whole *recoupable* element and not getting to own one's masters. I'd like to see the artists get to own their masters. I don't think the record labels should profit that much. I would like to change the laws so that you could nullify the contract if you could prove that a company was operating unfairly. I'd like the percentage to change and I don't know how far the law can go to do that. It may just have to be that we all get together and say that no one is going to sign a contract for under twelve percent. Actually, it should be higher.

I got Twisted fifty percent. He owns half his masters, he owns half of everything. And he has complete creative control. He can say, "No, I'm not doing that" on anything—on marketing, music, on how much money they spend. In fact, he did it on his first video. They wanted to spend a hundred thousand dollars, and he said, "No, I'm not spending more." He wanted to spend only fifty thousand because he knew he would have to pay it back. But he agreed on seventy-five because he didn't want to rock the boat. The point is, he felt that he saved twenty-five thousand dollars that he could put into another area—street promotions. He has a phenomenal contract. My point is, it is possible … it's possible. They wanted him that badly and it was the price they were willing to pay.

40

The Business of Rap:

Between the Street and the Executive Suite

Keith Negus

Rap has usually been approached as an aesthetic form of African-American expression: a resistant, oppositional, countercultural style created via the appropriation of technology and existing musical signs and symbols (scratching, sampling, mixing), drawing on a long tradition of diasporic creativity (with varying inflections of both an essentialist and anti-essentialist argument that point both back to and away from the slave routes of the Atlantic). Although the music industry has been referred to and acknowledged by a few writers,[1] most of the writing has tended to concentrate on cultural criticism[2] and locate the "politics" of rap within the domain of a cultural struggle conducted across the broad terrain of "consumption" that is lived outside the world of the corporate entertainment industry.

This perspective has clearly demonstrated that rap has been made as a cultural practice that involves the quite explicit creative appropriation of existing sounds, images and technologies and their reconstitution as a new art form. The creation of rap has also highlighted the tangible connecting points that link the often inadequate concepts of "production" and "consumption," and has illustrated how consumption can *become* production. In the process, creative practice and aesthetic discourse have produced a particular type of cultural-political identity which can be understood in terms of a long tradition of black creative activity, not only within the United States (Fernando Jr, 1995; Vincent, 1996) but within the context of a diaspora of the black Atlantic (Gilroy, 1993).

This chapter is not a direct challenge to such an account but an attempt to add a further dimension to the arguments and knowledge through which rap is understood as both a musical genre and cultural practice. My argument is that to understand rap, both in the past and its potential in the future, then cultural explanations alone are not enough. Rap is also a very particular U.S. business. As Kevin Powell wrote in a magazine profile of the highly successful Death Row Records, prior to the death of Tupac Shakur and the imprisonment of Suge Knight:

> There is no way to truly comprehend the incredible success of Death Row Records—its estimated worth now tops $100 million—without first understanding the conditions that created the rap game in the first place: few legal economic paths in America's inner cities, stunted educational opportunities, a pervasive sense of alienation among young black males, black folk's age-old need to create music, and a typically American hunger for money and power. The Hip Hop Nation is no different than any other segment of this society in its desire to live the American dream. (Powell, 1996, p. 46)

In the struggle against racism and economic and cultural marginalization, and in an attempt to "live the American dream," rap has also been created as a self-conscious business activity as well as a cultural form and aesthetic practice. A skim through consumer magazines such as *The Source* or *Vibe*, publications that address both artists and fans (often at the point where the two merge), reveals frequent references to issues of "career planning" and business management, often presented as a form of educational intelligence. A typical article in *The Source* began in the following way:

> We all have dreams, aspirations and goals ... things that we dream of but for whatever reason don't follow through on. For many of us, that dream is getting into the recording industry. So before you just dive with reckless abandon into the murky waters of the biz, here are some steps that might make the going a bit easier.
>
> Knowledge: Go to the library and do your homework. This will give you a basic knowledge of the day-to-day operations of an independent label. It's also very important that you do an internship at an independent label (a minimum of 6 months). Make contacts, ask questions and take notes. It is important that you are able to experience, first-hand, the struggles you will inevitably face.
>
> Business plan: As in starting any business, you must have a plan. You need a 5-year business plan that includes a projected budget. Your business plan should reflect you. You're the one who has to live by it. (Payton, 1997, p. 96)

The article then goes on to cover other issues under the subheadings of cash, legal counsel, operating a business, communication, artist, production, manufacturing and distribution and promotion—throwing quite a different light on to the idea of rap spontaneously emerging from "the streets" (an issue I shall come back to shortly).

In a similar way, a reading of trade magazines such as *Billboard* will turn up a number of articles in which rap artists and entrepreneurs, whether Suge Knight or Chuck D, explicitly discuss their commercial strategies and business plans or where executives such as Angelo Ellerbee, President of Double XXposure, discusses his "charm school for rap artists" (Snyder, 1996). As Bahamadia commented during the promotion for her first album:

> You have to understand that this is a business. When you sign your name on the dotted line on your contract you are literally a walking human business as well as a human being. So you have to study this business, ask questions, educate yourself and have a plan B and a plan C. (Fitzgerald, 1996, pp. 22–23)

I hope that in some small way this chapter might educate and inform. I also wish to argue that, to understand what rap might mean and its potential as a form of cultural expression and communication, it's also necessary to understand it as a business that links—and perhaps more significantly separates—artist and audience in quite distinct ways. In very broad terms, this chapter follows the central theme set out earlier in this book by considering how the industry sets up structures of organization and working practices to produce culture and also by highlighting the way that broader culture processes and practices connect with the industry—the uneasy relationship between the genre culture of rap and the corporate cultures of the music industry.

In developing the theoretical focus I outlined earlier, I shall illustrate these dynamics by analyzing how the industry organizes the production of rap in a very specific way and bases working practices on a particular construction of knowledge about the social world. The approach to the relationship between rap music and the recorded entertainment industry that I am proposing here is more complex than the often narrated tales of co-optation, exploitation and forced compromise to a commercial agenda, although these pressures are certainly not absent. At the same time, it is an attempt to avoid the celebration of black entrepreneurialism or the endorsement of rap as a type of material success-oriented "fun capitalism."[3]

The title of this chapter, "Between the street and the executive suite," signals a further broad argument and general theme that weaves throughout. First, it signals the way in which rappers who have often been identified solely with "the street" are also executives. I consider this important, for while the portrayal of rap artists as creative iconoclasts from the margins certainly reclaims a value for activities that have been devalued, it fails to adequately acknowledge that rap is, potentially, not "outside" or bursting out from the periphery but central to the development of the practices and aesthetics of the contemporary music industry. However, this is not simply to replace rap artists and entrepreneurs at the center of a fun type of capitalism. Instead, my aim is to raise questions about *why* and *how* rap has remained "on the street"—materially and discursively. Here "the street" operates as a metonym for a particular type of knowledge which is deployed by executives throughout the music industry, a type of knowledge which legitimates the belief that rap *is* and *should be* outside the corporate suite. Hence, I use the theme of the street and executive suite to signal the way in which the discourse of the street (and the mythical "being in touch" with it) is integral to how the music industry deals with rap practices. One consequence is that this maintains a separation of experiences and contributes to the ongoing reproduction of the broader economic, cultural, and racialized divisions across which r 'n' b and rap have been and continue to be made.

In approaching rap in these terms, this chapter ... is a deliberate attempt to try and steer a course away from the dichotomy between modernist despair at the power and influence of corporate commodity production and postmodernist celebration of the possibilities provided by cultural consumption and appropriation. It is also an attempt to suggest that the politics of culture need not simply be waged on one side or the other, but during a significant series of connections and relational practices which connect production and consumption and the articulations through which the corporate organization and music industry occupations are linked to broader cultural formations.

Corporate Decisions and Cultural Divisions: The Major Companies and the Black Music Department

To understand how the recording industry has come to deal with black music in general and rap in particular, it's necessary to recall ... how the industry, and specifically the U.S. music business, deals with different genres. As I discussed, the major record companies use a technique known as portfolio management in order to divide labels, genres and artists into strategic business units, making visible the performance, profile and financial contribution of each division. Well-established genres are often referred to as "cash cows." A genre such as rap, however, despite the revenues it has continued to generate, may be classified as a "wild cat" by industry analysts who are uncertain about its future aesthetic changes and nervous when trying to predict "potential market growth," and by business personnel who are uncomfortable with the politics of black representation foregrounded by the genre and anxious about confronting political pressure from the moral opponents of rap (these issues I shall elaborate over the following pages).

It is within the context of corporate strategies of portfolio management that the major companies and their labels have come to deal with black music in separate divisions. Historically, the contemporary management of rhythm and blues within separate formally defined corporate entities can be traced back to a reorganization of the music business that occurred during the late 1960s and early 1970s. The creation of "black divisions" during this period was a response to commercial opportunity, social and political pressure and cultural changes.

A number of factors contributed to this. One involved pressure from activists associated with the civil rights movement and the National Association for the Advancement of Colored People, who urged the major labels to give a more equitable remuneration to black artists and sought greater representation for industry personnel. Additional pressure came from the so-called Fairplay Committee. This was a group, associated with DJs and radio personnel, that managed to combine what many supported as "commendable aims" (a fair deal for African-American artists and music industry staff) with alleged acts of intimidation and violence and a desire to extort money through being "the prime collector of payola for all black disc jockeys" (Wade and Picardie, 1990, p. 175).[4]

A further influence came from within the major companies themselves, where senior executives were beginning to reassess how they dealt with different types of music. After commissioning research, the major companies selectively followed the key recommendations of a 1971 report for CBS by the Harvard Business School, that had advocated the formation of black music divisions.[5] This was for many executives a logical restructuring and response to promotional practices and radio broadcasting which had dealt separately with African-American recordings through a series of euphemisms which began with the term "race music" during the 1920s (Garofalo, 1994, 1997). Reebee Garofalo (1993) has also pointed out that when the "race music" labels of the 1920s (such as Black Swan, Merit and Black Patti) were hit by the Great Depression, they were bought up by major labels (such as OKeh and Paramount) and maintained as a distinct "race music" series, kept separate from other parts of the catalogue. Hence, although the major labels began setting up black music divisions and departments from the early 1970s, the practices upon which this built can be traced back throughout the twentieth century.

One benefit of such a practice is that these divisions have provided a space for black staff within a company, people who may not otherwise have gained employment in the music business. These separate divisions have also ensured that musicians are managed by personnel with knowledge, skills, and understanding of their music (not all of whom are black, obviously). However, staff within the black divisions have experienced an unstable and uncertain existence. One of the most significant disadvantages is that the department can easily be cut back, closed down or restructured by the corporation (whether this is due to an assessment that the genre has changed or simply because cuts have to be made). A similar fate can befall many departments when exposed as business units, from the cutting of the smallest Latin division in the 1980s to the reorganization of the largest hard rock division in the wake of the rise of post-Nirvana "alternative rock" in the early 1990s.

However, it is often the black music division that is subject to greater cutting than others. A notorious example of this occurred in February 1996 when Capitol Records closed its urban division, canceling the contracts of most artists and sacking eighteen members of staff (most of them black). This was yet another example of EMI's drastic restructurings. On this occasion the company publicly explained that they had closed this division so as to concentrate resources on their "stars" (such as Bonnie Raitt and Richard Marx) and their modern rock artists (Everclear and Radiohead). In the week that this occurred, I happened to have an interview arranged with Havelock Nelson, a *Billboard* writer who, over the years, has been involved in organizing various hip hop workshops and educational events. As he remarked: "This happens so much whenever there is a budget cut to be made; it's always the black department that suffers."[6]

For J.R. Reynolds (1996), another columnist working for *Billboard*, this event represented "the systematic extermination of black music at Capitol Records" and "cut the company's ties to the r 'n' b community." As such, this was far from simply an "economic" decision. Reynolds pointed out that it could not be justified in market terms: in 1995 r 'n' b and rap had sold 132 million albums and accounted for over 21 per cent of the music market in the U.S.[7]

Despite the corporate reasoning presented to the press, the "commercial" strategies of music corporations are not simply business decisions alone, but are informed by a number of value judgments and cultural beliefs. In this instance, whatever the dynamic within the company, to many outsiders this looked suspiciously like racism and a distinct lack of commitment (in terms of staff and investment) to sustain an involvement in black music and what Nelson George (1989) has called the "rhythm and blues world." George has used this phrase to refer to the "extramusical" significance of rhythm and blues as an "integral part" and "powerful symbol" for "a black community forged by common political, economic and geographic conditions" (1989, p. xii).

Hence, one issue here is that of occupational insecurity. The music industry is a notoriously insecure place to work, but black music divisions can be particularly unstable. For as long as they have been in existence the variously named r 'n' b/black/urban divisions have been chopped and changed. They have been closed down and reopened as a way of dealing with financial booms and slumps, and staffed and restaffed as senior management has continually changed its thinking about how to deal with r 'n' b. Recent shifts include the transition from appointing senior staff with backgrounds in promotion during the middle of the 1980s to heading the black divisions with attorneys, artists' managers and producers in the early 1990s, and then bringing in artists and producers in the middle of the 1990s.[8] This instability was rather ironically signaled by a panel organized for a music business convention by the coalition Sista Friends, entitled "You're Not Really in the Record Business Until You've Been Fired."[9]

This instability intersects with a broader issue of historical continuity. Although numerous African-American executives have contributed to the formation of the modern music industry and the history of recorded popular music, all have continued to occupy a "precarious position" (Sanjek, 1997). The black music divisions have not been allowed the space to establish their own agenda. One conspicuous point here is that there are very few senior black executives within the corporate hierarchy who are above the black division and hence involved in the decision about closing down business units or restaffing existing departments. This is frequently acknowledged within the industry and has been emphasized by Garofalo, who has noted that "black personnel have been systematically excluded from positions of power within the industry" (1994, p. 275). There is a strong sense, and a justifiable belief held by many in the industry, that the black divisions have not been allowed to develop a continuity and a sense of history that is consonant with the African-American contribution to U.S. musical culture.

This issue was publicly raised by Andre Harrell, whose music industry career has seen him move from performer (in the act *Dr Jekyll and Mr Hyde*), to head of Uptown Records (a joint venture with MCA which broke acts such as Mary J. Blige and Heavy D and The Boyz) to President and CEO of Motown for a few years in the middle of the 1990s. While at Motown he observed:

> Black music is becoming *the* music of the popular culture. Because of that, companies are repositioning their priorities and trying to get in the game. But as black music becomes more important, there should be more black presidents and black chairmen. As soon as the black executive's artist reaches platinum, suddenly the artist and manager have to deal with the president of the corporation, because *he* controls the priorities at pop radio. The black executive becomes obsolete. As his music gets bigger, his power diminishes. He's more or less told, "Go find the next act and establish it." ... That's why young black executives don't get to become the old chairmen—the wise men who've seen it and done it. They get to stay hot black executives so long as their instincts are hot ... the black executive is not given the opportunity to become the business *and* the music. Why not? Why shouldn't he be the one that everybody reports to? When you get an act that sells 5 million—at a major company— the black executive's out of the room. But when there's some sort of problem, the major

label looks at the black executive: "Why can't you handle this act?" When the artist hires a violent manager and the violent manager is coming up to the record company the label's like: "How did it get to this?" How? Because *they* [the white executives] couldn't see it coming. Because *they're* not sensitive to his issues. By then the relationship between the record company and the artist is dysfunctional. And the black executive gets blamed and fired. But *they* created the monster.

When I had the artist, I talked to his mother, his girlfriend, his babies' mother with the two children, dealt with his drug counsellor, and whatever other dysfunctional Generation X problems he has. He'd call me late at night.

But he feels like they're just business people. And they *don't* understand. And they *might* be racist. He's comin' with all that energy. Even if they like him as a person, he still has 400 years of issues he has to get over to accept them. And they have a lot of work to do to gain his trust and respect. (DeCurtis, 1995, p. 94, emphasis in original)

Harrell spoke these words with considerable experience, highlighting how racial identity, racism and the history of racial antagonism inform relationships that are often blandly referred to as "business decisions" within the corporate suite. Ironically, Harrell did not last long in his post at Motown, but his comments were publicly vindicated just under two years after the publication of this interview. It was then that PolyGram (the current owners of Motown and the corporation which had appointed Harrell) removed Eric Kronfeld, their domestic music president, from the board after he made "several racially insulting remarks" in relation to the company's R&B act Dru Hill. Alain Levy, PolyGram President, immediately appointed Clarence Avant who became the company's first African-American director (Johnson, 1997).

It is within the context of this history that the music industry began dealing with rap (or not dealing with rap) during the 1980s. At one point it seemed that the major companies had neither the inclination, the understanding, nor the skills to deal with rap. It was partly anxiety, partly lack of expertise and incomprehension on the part of the majors that allowed many small companies to carve out a considerable niche during the 1980s. It's often claimed that the small companies were in touch with "the streets." But it is not as straightforward as this— the large companies have also allowed small labels to carve out such a niche.

Independents on the Street: Keeping It outside the Corporation

If one way in which the major companies have attempted to manage African-American music has involved the continual cutting and restructuring of their R&B division, the other has been based on a series of changing relationships with minor companies. There is a familiar explanation offered for why so many successful rap recordings have come from independent labels: they are "closer to the street." It's a view held by many observers of the music industry. As Tricia Rose has written:

It became apparent that the independent labels had a much greater understanding of the cultural logic of hip hop and rap music, a logic that permeated decisions ranging from signing acts to promotional methods. Instead of competing with smaller, more street-savvy labels for new rap acts, the major labels developed a new strategy: buy the independent labels, allow them to function relatively autonomously, and provide them with production resources and access to major retail distribution. (1994a, p. 7)

This perspective draws on the long-running argument that changes in popular music are driven by the activities of independent companies. There is an element of truth in this claim;

it is often easier to identify a new sound and participate in its circulation from outside the gatekeeper-riddled systems of the major companies. It should also be acknowledged that many black independent companies are also attempting to assert their autonomy and self-sufficiency (George, 1989). However, this is a partial and rather too neat and tidy explanation of why rap has ended up *produced* on so many small labels, even if the artists do tend to be *marketed* and *distributed* by the major companies.

There are a number of ways in which this argument has been challenged. One counter-claim has proposed that rap has been somewhat closer to the middle-class suburb than the street. According to David Samuels:

> Since the early 1980s a tightly knit group of mostly young, middle-class, black New Yorkers, in close concert with white record producers, executives and publicists, has been making rap music for an audience that industry executives concede is composed primarily of white suburban males. (1995, p. 242)

There would seem much evidence to support such a claim. Many of those involved with the influential "street savvy" labels—such as Tom Silverman at Tommy Boy, and Russell Simmons and David Harleston at Def Jam, were from educated and middle-class backgrounds. The backgrounds and actions of various artists, such as De La Soul or Chuck D, for example, could also be cited to support this argument.[10]

Yet, this claim is equally partial. In terms of production, rap has, since it first began to appear on recordings, been produced from multiple points of origin with distinct inflections of geographical place (Houston, Atlanta, Los Angeles, Washington, Philadelphia, Georgia), class identity (De La Soul or NWA), ethnic representation (Fugees, Tres Delinquents, Cypress Hill), urban, rural differences (Arrested Development, Smoothe Da Hustler). Not only has rap been stylistically diverse, this diversity has been created across complex identity amalgams. Hence, it is misleading and partial to collapse these variances into any straightforward model of inspiration from the streets or collusion of the black middle class with white executives.

Equally, the idea that the integrity of rap is undermined because a large part of consumption can be located within the white suburb is also simplistic. A strong case against this claim has been argued by Rose (1994a), who has pointed out that purchasing statistics do not in any straightforward way equal "consumption." Sales figures—such as "75 per cent of rap records are owned by white teenagers" (Whalen, 1994, p. 12)—cannot account for the complex ways in which rap is *circulated* and how recordings are appreciated, used and re-used. Young males in the white suburbs may have the disposable income to purchase a recording that will sit on a shelf looking cool, while, in contrast, black urban youth may circulate recordings and listen to them repeatedly, record them, mix them—there may be a much higher "pass-along-rate" (Rose, 1994a).

What does seem clear is that, as rap has been and continues to be made, appreciated and circulated, it has intersected with and crossed numerous borders of class, neighborhood, gender, ethnic label and "national" belonging. Yet it has not been crossing many divisions *within* the music industry. There are two distinct, but interrelated, regimes of containment I want to identify here: first, organizational practices through which rap is confined to a specific "position" within the industry and not accorded as much investment (economic, staff, time) as other types of music; and second, those through which a particular type of knowledge finds expression in a discourse of "the street." These simultaneously deny the complexities I have just referred to, and in doing so construct a simplistic commercial cultural "reality" for rap production that is easily accommodated to the management practices adopted by the music industry.

Major Anxieties: Affiliations, Representations and Expectations

One of the characteristics of rap that initially confused the major companies was the way that rap proposed a series of working relationships across different musical entities: cliques, collectives, affiliations and group and label identities that connected together different "bands" and individual performers. This is signified in the continual appearance of performers on each other's recordings and the way that this establishes very specific networks of affiliation and alliances, e.g., the performers who have grouped around such entities as The Dogg Pound, Dr Dre's Aftermath and Puff Daddy and The Family.

The genre culture of rap posits a different notion of musical practice, not only in the well-documented use of existing musical elements and technologies but in terms of the idea of a "career" and sense of belonging to a musical entity. This is quite a contrast from that of the stable, bounded and predictable rock unit or pop band, the solo performer and self-sufficient singer-songwriter which the industry has become competent at producing and comfortable in dealing with. Rap posits a fluid series of affiliations and associations, alliances and rivalries—occasionally serious, and usually related to neighborhood and representation.[11] These affiliations are lived across various group and individual identities.

This is connected to another issue which the industry has also found uncomfortable, the representation of "the real" or what is often referred to as "being real" and the politics of identity which has accompanied this. This aspect has often received more superficial mass media coverage than serious debate about the issue that it raises and has frequently been reduced to simple arguments about profanity and the generic imagery of violence and misogyny that has characterized so-called gangsta rap. The "discussion" is often informed by a simple stimulus–response model of media effects and an aesthetic reductionism through which rap becomes merely lyrics. One consequence is that there have been overt political pressures put on record companies—from "community" organizations, government and state forces—and this has further encouraged the major companies to distance themselves from the genre culture of rap.[12]

Further judgments made by staff within business affairs and international departments have also had a decisive influence on the acquisition and drawing up of contracts for rap artists. There are two "business decisions" here which are far more than straightforward commercial judgments. First is an assessment of the ongoing revenue that can be generated from rap: what is referred to as "catalogue value." Rap tracks are routinely compared to conventional songs and it is asserted that they cannot be "covered"—re-recorded, re-sung, re-performed by other artists. Hence, rap tracks are judged to have a short catalogue shelf life, in terms of their ability to bring in ongoing copyright revenue from their re-use.[13] In addition, the revenue that rap can generate during any assumed "shelf life" is considered to be less than other types of music. In the words of one corporate attorney:

> Music publishing and rap is a nightmare because so much of it is parts of songs. You know, they have, like, one-eighth of this song and two-thirds of another song … because everything is owned by someone else that can make those deals less expensive, but also less lucrative for the publishers than otherwise.… The publisher looks at how much they can collect on a particular album, and sometimes because of the number of samples on the album the amount they can collect can be pretty low.[14]

As Thomas Schumacher has observed in his discussion of sampling and copyright law, rap "highlights the ways in which notions of authorship and originality do not necessarily apply across forms and cultural traditions" (1995, p. 265). Not only do they not apply, they pose problems for the "universals of legal discourse" (Schumacher, 1995, p. 265). Hence, the music industry copyright system, itself established upon culturally coded assumptions about the character of a composition and performance which can be traced back to the nineteenth century (Frith, Ed., 1993), is inscribed into these business relationships and informs these apparently straightforward "commercial" decisions. One consequence is that rap is perceived to be less attractive in terms of the criteria through which long-term catalogue value is accorded. Hence, less will be paid to artists as advances and royalties, because less can be earned.[15]

A further pragmatic business judgment that affects the amount invested in rap is the assumption that it does not "travel well." Here a strand of racist anxiety that permeates the international music industry manages to combine with a narrow aesthetic evaluation. One senior executive in an international department remarked that he had sat in meetings and heard rap recordings being referred to as "too black" for international promotion,[16] a broad sweeping claim that is justified specifically with the assertion that lyrically rap is "parochial"— although the history of popular music is littered with parochial lyrics appearing in numerous places around the world. While rap does foreground poetic vocal performance, it is misleading to imply that this works simply as lyrics and not as an emotional performative sound event. This argument from within the industry, like Tony Mitchell's claim that U.S. rap has remained "resolutely local" (1996, p. 26), seems to reduce the genre's aesthetic complexity and rhythmic, harmonic and melodic cosmopolitanism to rap lyrics.

Hence, there are a number of ways in which the music industry seeks to contain rap within a narrow structure of expectations: through confinement within a black division; through arm's-length deals in an attempt to avoid dealing with various alliances and affiliations; through judgments about rap's long-term historical and geographical potential to endure. One consequence is a straightforward lack of investment, and the adoption of practices to keep investment down (it is easier to deal with production units than to invest in staff and office space within company). At the same time, rather than bringing the culture—the people, the practices—into the industry, the major companies have tended to maintain a sharp border. This can be contrasted with the treatment of rock in the late 1960s and early 1970s. During this period there was a noticeable and often commented upon movement from the rock subculture and so-called counter-culture into the music industry—a period when the "revolutionaries" were on CBS (as one marketing slogan proclaimed at time).[17] This has continued, with a new wave of young white males recruited into the U.S. music industry in the early 1990s following the success of Nirvana and the stabilization of grunge into modern or alternative rock. As Joe Levy, a music writer for a number of years, observed in 1996:

> I have not seen R&B and hip hop have the same impact that the big boom in alternative rock had on the industry. Certainly two years ago there was this influx of young people in their twenties going to labels as A and R people and vice presidents of this or that, and these were almost uniformly young white kids who were coming into work alternative rock in the wake of Nirvana.... There's a career path in the industry that has to do with alternative rock and I don't necessarily know that it's there for rap and R&B.[18]

Rap personnel have not been embraced or recruited in the same way. For example, when Capitol closed its black music division the company dropped most of its artists and moved only a few acts over to the EMI label. The company publicly announced that this was because EMI had the expertise to deal with them. Yet a few weeks later, when I interviewed Davitt Sigerson, President of EMI Records, and asked him to explain how he deals with rap, he said:

> I don't have anyone doing R&B A&R. What I've adopted as a model is to have a bunch of different production deals or first-look arrangements with entrepreneurs who bring me stuff ... it's a very affiliative sort of creative community and process and I don't need to be in a camp.[19]

Earlier I referred to George's use of the term "rhythm and blues world" to suggest that R&B is more than a genre of music. Likewise, George has characterized rap culture as a "post-civil rights, ultra-urban, unromantic, hyperrealistic, neonationalistic, anti-assimilationist, aggressive Afro-centric impulse" (George, 1992, p. 93). In the above discussion I have highlighted how these genre cultures relate to the organization of the major companies and inform major independent relationships within the music industry, suggesting that rap culture is kept at a distance from the main offices of the corporations. Despite the influence of rap and hip hop on the aesthetics of music, video, television, film, sport, fashion, dancing and advertising, the potential of this broader cultural formation to make a contribution to music industry business practices is not encouraged. Indeed, as I now want to argue, this distance is maintained by the discursive practices articulated through the myth of the street.

Rebels, Indies, and the Street

I have already suggested that the major companies tend to *allow* rap to be produced at independent companies and production units, using these producers as an often optional and usually elastic repertoire source. This is not to deny the struggles of artists and entrepreneurs for both autonomy from the recognition by the major music companies. However, I am stressing the above point because I think we need to be wary of the increasingly routine rhetoric and romanticization of rap musicians as oppositional rebels "outside" the corporate system, or as iconoclasts in revolt against "the mainstream"—a discourse that has often been imposed upon rap and not necessarily come from participants within hip hop culture itself. In addition, it is important to remember that small companies are not spontaneously or straightforwardly inclined to be more in tune with new musical developments. That certain independent labels (such as Atlantic, Stax, or Def Jam) have been so at specific historical moments is beyond dispute. But most rap labels have very soon entered into formalized and fairly standard commercial relationships characteristic of those between major and minor companies, a division of labor based on a production/distribution split. Despite such close ties, the making of rap is usually explained with numerous references to "the street."

In very general terms, rap is often associated with the street by senior executives when talking about different types of music. For example, Kevin Conroy, Senior VP of Marketing at BMG, remarked that, compared to other styles, rap and hip hop "is a business that really grows from the streets."[20] In a similar way, the corporate *Advertising Age* once informed its readers, "The streets where a rap album begins, of course, are very far from the suburban record stores where it ends up" (Whalen, 1994, p. 12). As Michael Rosenblatt, Senior VP of Artist and Repertoire at MCA, remarked, aware that he was using a somewhat clichéd idea: "A lot of the rap does happen on the small labels because rap is much more of a street thing, it happens on the street. I know it sounds trite, but it really does."[21]

Apart from these very general associations of rap with the street, there are two further and more formal ways in which "the street" is articulated. First, in terms of "taking it to the streets"—what is often referred to as street marketing. Second, in terms of "bringing it from the streets"—frequently referred to as "street intelligence." Both practices involve formalized management practices and systematic commercial procedures that are by no means peculiar to rap or R&B.

Taking It to the Streets

The promotion and marketing of rap, like other genres of music, involve the use of techniques that, elsewhere, I have characterized as "promotional war games" due to the way that they are referred to by staff within record companies through a number of "war-like metaphors"

(Negus, 1992). So, for example, when Capitol still had a presence in black music, the label's rap promotion unit was called "Capitol Punishment," and the head of the section was referred to as the "chief commander and warden" (Nelson, 1994, p. 26). The term "sniping" is routinely used to refer to fly-posting bills that make no reference to the record label involved, merely signaling the name of the act and tracks or album. The so-named "street teams" (largely made up of college or radio DJs) have been described as "right there in the trenches"[22] and as engaging in "reconnaissance missions into urban enterprise zones" (Rubin, 1997, p. 99). When I spoke to David Harleston, then Senior VP of the Black Music Collective at MCA, he referred to "the use of guerrilla marketing tactics and street promotion." When I rather naively asked what this might involve, he explained:

> Well, it's going to places where consumers are and hitting them where they live. So we no longer just rely on radio or rely on video, which are both very important. We also promote at barber shops and swap meets and things like that and … playgrounds where folks are shooting basketball … we have street teams who hit people with singles and flyers and stickers and stuff like that…. When you take a rap project to radio, radio wants to know that the street is behind it before they'll commit to it. You can't go to radio cold.[23]

The term "street marketing" is shorthand for building an interest in a track or artists through a long process that can involve circulating recordings to influential party-givers, using word-of-mouth networks, approaching local radio mix shows and college radio and promoting through stickers and flyers placed in public places where the targeted "demographic" will take notice. This was institutionalized by Loud Records, a label half-owned by BMG, in their promotion of a number of acts, particularly the Wu-Tang Clan. As Steve Rifkind, Chairman of Loud Records, has claimed:

> I can tell a record company in two days if they have a record or not…. We know that kid from the time he steps out of his house, every step he's making, where he's going to hang out, what's the scoop on where to eat lunch at, where he's getting his hair cut, what's the cool way to get it cut, what's the cool record store to go to. We know all these things, and before we attack we get all the information from the street first. (quoted in Rubin, 1997, p. 99)

Prior to forming Loud Records, Rifkind had established his reputation by promoting recordings by acts such as Boogie Down Productions and Brand Nubian. He followed this by promoting Nike sports gear, spending some time with Nike founder Phil Knight. This gave him the experience that he drew upon when formulating a strategy for selling the Wu-Tang Clan. In his own words: "a kid who's going to buy a pair of Nikes is the same kid who's going to buy a Wu-Tang record" (quoted in Rubin, 1997, p. 100).

The ultimate aim of street marketing is to build up such a "buzz" that the radio stations will feel that they have to programme a recording as they themselves will want to be heard to be "in touch with the streets." As Marcus Morton, VP of Rap Promotion for EMI, commented:

> You have to have the DJs and the people that are the trend-setters. They kind of herd the sheep around. They have to like it. And everybody else—y' know, if you look at the people that program the crossover stations, nine out of ten of them think that they are the hippest thing on the planet, but in reality they're not. They listen to somebody else. Which is either their DJ—that's why you have a mix show DJ because he's supposed to be really in tune with the streets and really in tune with what's going on. And he's supposed to play it on his show and then translate it back to the people who run the stations so that they can put it into regular rotation.[24]

In practice, the activity of "street marketing" relies upon a number of well-developed acts of persuasion that have been deployed within various industries for a number of years. This includes utilizing the "personal influence" of key opinion-formers, "selecting target markets," using concepts of "followers" and "niches," and "branding" and "positioning" products.[25] These practices are not peculiar to rap, but are used when selling a range of products throughout the entertainment and fashion industries. As Terri Rosi, VP of Black Music Marketing for BMG Distribution, commented when I remarked that "there's a lot of talk about 'the street' ": "I know and that's very annoying because the end result is that you talk about 'the street' but you really want it on radio and you want it on MTV."[26]

Bringing It from the Street

As implied in Rifkind's comments about following the movements of "the kids," street teams are also responsible for information gathering and feeding that data back to headquarters. This is sometimes described as an informal process of intuitively hanging out in colleges, neighborhood record stores, clubs, playgrounds and parties, an experiential process of "developing an instinct" by keeping an ear and eye on what is going on. However, the process is also far from spontaneous and is organized in comparable ways to other types of information gathering. To quote from Terri Rosi once more, this time at length:

> It is systematized. You have a guy out there called a street promotion person who is hanging out in stores and clubs and talking to people, and he may even actually go into a college campus. He may be wherever people gather that are those people. He has to learn his marketplace and know where he's supposed to go. They put up stickers in advance so when it comes two months, three months later, "well, yes, I know the ABC band," or whatever. So in that sense, it is a form of street intelligence and you get feedback and you learn after a while who can pick the hit, you figure that out, but it's very people-intense. You're out there, you're moving, talking and working and doing all that kinda stuff.... We've got twenty of them all across the country, and there will be one person in the record company who works with the street team. So they give their reports, where it's going to work, where it's not going to work and their reputation is on the line. I can't tell you that I'm the street person in Oakland and tell you, "Man, this is gonna jam," and then I ship these records in there and nobody likes it at all. Because, well, "Who did you talk to?" ... You don't want to lose your job because you didn't do the right thing. So, yes, in that way it is very systematized.[27]

Street intelligence is about "knowing markets" and "knowing consumers" and, like street marketing, it involves employing conventional business management techniques based on monitoring, data gathering and accumulation. Yet these conventional marketing practices and business activities are elided through the discourse of the street, denying that this is similar to the other activities that are daily being conducted and initiated from the corporate suite.

More Than Music: Rap, Fashion and Product Endorsement

I referred to Steve Rifkind's association with the Nike company and highlighted how this influenced the way Loud Records presented and promoted the Wu-Tang Clan. From the days when Run DMC made reference to Adidas in their songs to the appearance of Coolio and Method Man on the catwalk to present Tommy Hilfiger's new 1996 fashions, clothing has been central to the marketing and making of rap. This has been increasingly recognized by magazines such as *The Source* (which accrue a large part of their revenue from the clothing and sports shoe manufacturers who place advertisements in their pages), performers (who have been increasingly endorsing different products and creating their own lines of clothing), and record labels. As Jim Parham, Director of Sales at Tommy Boy, remarked when explaining how the music and merchandizing were being brought closer together:

> We are gradually tying the music into the clothing. Right now the clothing is sort of an entity unto itself, but the way it originally started was that we made clothing items as promotional items for the music or the label and they were really popular, so we developed it into an actual selling line and we will hopefully be expanding that in the next couple of years.[28]

Many rap musicians have recognized such connections and formed their own successful companies. Notable here is Wu-Wear, the clothing and accessory company established by the Wu-Tang Clan. This company has stores throughout the United States where you can purchase T-shirts, socks, baggy jeans, coffee mugs, and keychains, all featuring the distinctive Wu-Bat brand logo. Like other companies, Wu-Wear has recognized the importance of music video for promoting clothing as much as for selling music. As Mike Clark, CEO of Wu-Wear, observed: "Videos are hands down the best advertising you can have" (quoted in Edwards and Stein, 1998, p. 71). Not surprisingly, the Wu-Tang Clan themselves wear their own clothing in their videos. But, like other major clothing companies, they have sought other celebrity endorsements, and artists including Bjork and Rage Against The Machine have publicly worn Wu-Wear, as have various athletes. In 1997 the company made $10 million (Edwards and Stein, 1998) and also signed a deal with the Federated Department Store retail corporation, the owners of Macy's and Bloomingdale's (Parker, 1997). As Public Enemy's Chuck D proclaimed in an advertisement which appeared in *The Source* of September 1996 and in which he was launching his own Rap Style International: "So You Wanna Be in the Music Business … Whatcha' Gonna Wear?"

The business of rap is about more than music and clothes and can embrace all manner of consumer products, visible and audible in the way that Queen Latifah has appeared in a box of cereal during an advertisement for Frosted Cheerios, as LL Cool J has been rapping in advertising for major league baseball, and as Method Man has appeared on billboards dressed in Reebok clothing while KRS-One was promoting Nike. "Business awareness" and the range of revenue sources that can be linked to the genre have been recognized by numerous rap performers. As Allen S. Gorden "Tha Ebony Cat" explained, discussing the range of endorsement opportunities being pursued by different artists and companies: "In an increasingly complex, often hostile, marketplace, many rappers are refining their portfolio by pursuing endorsement opportunities" (1997, p. 98). Whether or not rap culture might enter the corporate suites and boardrooms of the major record labels, the discourse of portfolio management has certainly entered the business of rap.

Culture, Industry, and Rap

This chapter has focused on how the making of rap is managed by the music industry, and it has been highlighted how various corporate strategies, which utilize the technique of portfolio management as a way of allocating staff, artists, and investment, directly intersect with the deployment of a particular type of knowledge used to understand the world and to produce a "reality" that informs the perceptions and activities of staff. It is not that there are organizational structures (such as the black music division and deals with small production companies): it is that these are operated according to a particular type of knowledge through which the world is imagined in a particular way, a knowledge that depends upon many systematic data-collecting techniques. At the same time, uncritically received cultural assumptions and common-sense ideas about the social location of rap are continually articulated to notions of the street. In many ways this situation is symptomatic of broader social relation-ships and beliefs about rap culture and the way in which these intersect with and become "part" of the industry—a process that requires much more empirical and theoretical work before it can be fully understood, but which I have tried to evoke through the idea of "culture producing an industry." Such broader cultural political tensions are structured into what are often taken to be straightforward economic, organizational and business practices, activities that are lived by those working within the industry as if they are merely responding to "the world out there." One significant consequence is that the rhythm and blues world and the genre culture of rap in particular are kept at a distance from the dominant interests and agendas within the main offices of the music corporations.

Yet rap produced in the United States has managed to move out from such regimes of containment—both at home and abroad. There is a final twist. The physical and discursive borders erected by the organizational arrangements and knowledge practices of the contem-porary music industry have meant that rap music and musicians have not been "co-opted" or invited into the boardroom in quite the same way as have other types of music and their makers, most notably the way in which rock moved from the street to the executive suite.[29] Often denied direct access, offered licensing deals, lower budgets, poorer contracts, or simply cut from the roster when there is a financial crisis, rap has (partly out of necessity) been able to generate alternative resources, and through these the genre has continually reinvented and redefined itself in those spaces and places designated (for want of terminology rather than as a transparent description of a "reality") as "underground." That rap musicians have managed continually to redefine the style itself while crossing social and cultural barriers, both within the U.S. and beyond is a process which has occurred despite, rather than because of, the ways in which the recording industry has sought to organize the production of contemporary popular music.

Notes

1. Notable here is Tricia Rose (1994a) who notes the importance of independent labels and the significance of video in the distribution of rap. She is also careful to acknowledge that the commercial marketing of rap has produced a contradictory situation whereby the music is affirmative of black identity, yet can also be used by corporations such as McDonald's, Coke, and Nike in ways that are directly connected to anx-ieties about U.S. cultural imperialism. Rose (1994b) has also discussed rap in relation to the general con-tractual arrangements operating within the music industry, particularly in an interview with Carmen Ashurst-Watson. Also notable here is Reebee Garofalo's (1997) discussion of the music industry and rap in his history of popular music, and Nelson George's coverage of rap within the context of his critique of the music industry and its role in the "death of rhythm and blues" and formation of post-soul culture (1989, 1992).
2. A useful collection of essays is Adam Sexton (ed.) (1995).
3. An argument proposed by Ann Marlowe who has stated that: "For some time now the problem with cap-italism hasn't been that it doesn't work but that it's no longer fun. Opposition culture has failed to make good on this.... The business of rap is just business, yet it looks like fun" (1995, p. 223).
4. Discussed at length in relation to Atlantic and Stax Records in Wade and Picardie (1990).
5. For a more detailed discussion of this report see George (1989).
6. Personal interview, New York City, 27 February 1996.
7. See Reynolds (1996) and Rosen (1996). See also Clark-Meads (1996) for a discussion of Capitol redefin-ing their "core business."
8. These types of changes are discussed in Sandler (1995).
9. Referred to by J.R. Reynolds in "Confab Covers Urban Industry Issues" *Billboard*, 18 May 1996, p. 20.
10. Backgrounds of various producers, artists and entrepreneurs are discussed in Fernando Jr (1995).
11. Most notable here is the well-publicized East–West NYC–LA dispute which, in the early to mid-1990s, became focused in a series of highly public confrontations between those associated with Death Row Records and Bad Boy Records.
12. Most notably C. Delores Tucker, Chairwoman of the National Political Congress of Black Women, and William Bennett (previously Ronald Reagan's Secretary of Education) put pressure on Time-Warner

shareholders. Likewise (then) Senator Bob Dole continually accused Warner Music and other labels of "putting profits ahead of common decency" and "glamorizing violence." For a perspective on this and its impact from within the industry see Nunziata (1995). One immediate consequence was that Michael Fuchs, Chairman CEO of Warner Music Group, announced that the company would form label groups made up of an A and R person, label head, someone from business affairs and legal personnel to judge the suitability of future releases, with particular attention paid to lyrics. On this point see Jeffrey (1995). In addition, when MCA purchased Interscope, the label that had been distributing recordings by Death Row Records, Doug Morris, CEO of MCA Music Entertainment, publicly announced that the company had an option "not to release any music it deems objectionable" (Morris, 1996).

13. This was most explicitly raised by a senior executive at a major corporate group when explaining how the company would strategically assess the value of different musical genres. It was an off-the-record interview.
14. Personal interview, Paul Robinson, Associate General Counsel, Warner Music Group, New York City, 13 February 1996.
15. This is acknowledged within the industry, but I was unable to obtain any verifiable figures.
16. This was again an off-the-record interview.
17. For discussion of recruitment from rock subculture into the industry, see Chapple and Garofalo (1977) and Frith (1983).
18. Personal interview, Joe Levy, *Details Magazine*, New York City, 22 March 1996.
19. Personal interview, New York City, 19 March 1996.
20. Personal interview, New York City, 5 April 1996.
21. Personal interview, New York City, 6 February 1996.
22. Greg Peck, a former VP of Black Music at Warner Music, quoted in Reynolds (1995, p. 26).
23. Personal interview, Universal City, Los Angeles, 6 May 1996.
24. Personal interview, EMI, Los Angeles, 24 April 1996.
25. All similar to many referred to in textbook guides to marketing; see, for example, Kotler (1994).
26. Personal interview, Terri Rosi, VP Black Music Marketing, BMG Distribution, New York City, 11 April 1996.
27. Personal interview, Terri Rosi, VP Black Music Marketing, BMG Distribution, New York City, 11 April 1996.
28. Telephone interview, 15 April 1996.
29. For an argument about the co-optation of rock, see Chapple and Garofalo (1977). For a discussion of the way in which rock has been central rather than peripheral, or oppositional, to the development of the modern recording industry, see Frith (1983).

References

Chapple, S. and Garofalo, R. (1977) *Rock 'n' Roll is Here to Pay*, Chicago: Nelson Hall.

DeCurtis, A. (1995) Dre Day, *Vibe*, December, pp. 92–94.

Edwards, T. and Stein, J. (1998) Getting Giggy With a Hoodie: Young Black Designers are Giving Urban Fashions Street Appeal, *Time*, Vol. 151, No. 1, pp. 71–72.

Fernando, Jr., S.H. (1995) *The New Beats: Exploring the Music Culture and Attitudes of Hip-Hop*, Edinburgh: Payback Press.

Fitzgerald, T. (1996) Uknowhowsheduit, *Beat Down*, Vol. 4, No. 2, pp. 22–23.

Frith, S. (1983) *Sound Effects, Youth, Leisure and the Politics of Rock 'n' Roll*, London: Constable.

———— (ed.) (1993) *Music and Copyright*, Edinburgh: Edinburgh University Press.

Garofalo, R. (1994) Culture Versus Commerce: The Marketing of Black Popular Music, *Public Culture*, Vol. 7, No. 1, pp. 275–288.

———— (1997) *Rockin' Out, Popular Music in the USA*, Needham Heights, Mass.: Allyn and Bacon.

George, N. (1989) *The Death of Rhythm and Blues*, London: Omnibus.

———— (1992) *Buppies, B-Boys, Baps and Bohos*, London: HarperCollins.

Gilroy, P. (1993) *The Black Atlantic, Modernity and Double Consciousness*, London: Verso.

Gorden, A. (1997) It All Adds Up, *The Source*, January, p. 98.

Jeffrey, D. (1995) Warner's Fuchs Pledges Scrutiny, *Billboard*, 14 October 1995, p. 1/91.

Johnson, R. (1997) PolyGram: The Hits Just Keep on Coming. Racial Tensions at Record Label, *Fortune*, Vol. 36, No. 12, p. 40.

Kotler, P. (1994) *Marketing Management; Analysis, Planning, Implementation and Control*, New Jersey: Prentice Hall.

Mitchell, T. (1996) *Popular Music and Local Identity: Rock, Pop and Rap in Europe and Oceania*, Leicester: Leicester University Press.

Morris, C. (1996) MCA Purchases 50% of Interscope: Gangsta Rap Issue Minimized by Execs, *Billboard*, 2 March 1996, p. 13/84.

Negus, K. (1992) *Producing Pop: Culture and Conflict in the Popular Music Industry*, London: Edward Arnold.

Nelson, H. (1994) Rap: In an Ever-Shifting Climate, Rap Holds Steady and Grows Strong, *Billboard*, 26 November 1994, p. 25/46.

Nunziata, S. (1995) The Year in Business, *Billboard*, 23 December 1995, p. YE–10.

Parker, A. (1997) Wu-Wear Urban Clothing Chain Opens Store in Norfolk Va, *Virginia Pilot*, 2 May 1997, p. 5.

Payton, T. (1997) Set It Off, *The Source*, January, p. 96.

Powell, K. (1996) Live From Death Row, *Vibe*, Vol. 4, No. 1, February, pp. 44–50.

Reynolds, J. (1995) Rap Confab Assembles Nation, *Billboard*, 11 November 1995, p. 26.

———— (1996) Capitol Records Setting a Bad Example, *Billboard*, 9 March 1996, p. 18.

Rose, T. (1994a) *Black Noise: Rap Music and Black Culture in Contemporary America*, Hanover, NH: Wesleyan University.

———— (1994b) Contracting Rap; An Interview with Carmen Ashurst-Watson in A. Ross and T. Rose (eds) *Microphone Fiends*, London: Routledge.

Rosen, C. (1996) Capitol Moves Urban Division to EMI: 18 Staffers Laid Off, *Billboard*, 9 March 1996, p. 3.

Rubin, M. (1997) Secrets of the Ch-Ching, *Spin*, October, pp. 95–102.

Samuels, D. (1995) The rap on rap: The "Black music" that isn't either, in A. Sexton (ed.) *Rap on Rap: Straight-Up Talk on Hip-Hop Culture*, New York: Delta, pp. 241–52.

Sandler, A. (1995) Big Labels Ride Black Music Bandwagon, *Variety*, 28 August 1995, Vol. 360, p. 13.

Sanjek, D. (1997) One Size Does Not Fit All: The Precarious Position of the African-American Entrepreneur in Post WW2 American Popular Music, *American Music*, Vol. 15, No. 4, pp. 535–62.

Schumacher, T. (1995) This is a Sampling Sport: Digital Sampling, Rap Music and the Law in Cultural Production, *Media, Cutlure and Society*, Vol. 17, pp. 253–73.

Sexton, A. (ed.) (1995) *Rap on Rap: Straight-Up Talk on Hip-Hop Culture*, New York: Delta.

Snyder, M. (1996) Artist Support Groups, *Billboard*, 8 June 1996, p. 30/44.

Vincent, R. (1996) *Funk, the Music, the People and the Rhythm of the One*, New York: St Martin's Press.

Wade, D. and Picardie, J. (1990) *Music Man, Ahmet Ertegun, Atlantic Records and the Triumph of Rock 'n' Roll*, New York: W.W. Norton.

Whalen, J. (1994) Rap Defies Traditional Marketing, *Advertising Age*, No. 65, 12 March 1994, p. 12.

41

Contracting Rap:

An Interview
with Carmen Ashhurst-Watson

Tricia Rose

Carmen Ashhurst-Watson has been involved in media, film and television organization-building and production for twenty years. She began working with hip hop impressario Russell Simmons in the mid-1980s, and as of 1990 became president of Def Jam Recordings. Since 1991, Ashhurst-Watson has been president of Rush Communications, the parent company of Simmons' media empire and the second largest black-owned entertainment company in the United States, which has—in addition to music—three major subdivisions for film, television and fashion. In my animated conversation with Ashhurst-Watson, she dropped science on rap artists' contracts, black radio, capitalism, sexism in the music business and more. Here it is ... hardcore.

TRICIA ROSE: Before I turned the recorder on, I asked what I thought would be a throwaway question—your answer will probably shock folks as it shocked me. So let's begin there: how many rap demo tapes do you receive and how many of those would you be interested in?

CARMEN ASHURST-WATSON: Out of about a thousand tapes, we might be interested in one or two.

TR: Given that, describe the process of discovering a band.

CAW: First of all, it is extremely rare for a group to come to the attention of a record company just off the street, and it's very rare that any such group that would come to the attention of a record company wouldn't have a large body of work. By the time a record company is interested in a group, they've already been tried and tested somewhere. They have a local following, or a friend who's an artist who brought them to the label, or they used to DJ for an established artist. It is very, very rare that somebody came up with one song idea, did a tape in their basement, and then brought it to somebody. Usually, a rapper has done several hundred songs and picked three of the several hundred that somebody likes before he's even in the league of being commercially viable. The most recent discovery story that people mention is Kris Kross. It's this great story of two kids who were found in a shopping mall by an agent or manager. By the time they were in this mall, they had already been performing there and in other local places for two years, and had a body of songs from which this guy could choose. So, yes, he did see them in this environment, but he didn't actually discover them performing for the first time.

Most of Def Jam's new groups are actually brought to our attention by our artists. Onyx, the most recent find, was brought in by Jam Master Jay who knew them and had seen them perform. They had been struggling together for some time—Onyx had a different kind of music, but when Jay got his own label, he remembered them. We found L.L. Cool J because he lived in the same neighborhood with Run-DMC.

TR: Nowadays, the markets for performing are not that great. You're saying that Kris Kross performed in the mall. Where would Onyx perform without a label, without a record contract? Why would a small club owner allow them to perform given their rough and rugged image and explicit lyrics?

CAW: Well, for the most part they're allowed to perform because they perform for free or real cheap. They do local club dates, they might be the DJ at a party in their neighborhood or something like that. There are local amateur shows or talent shows which feature competition amongst rappers. They get their experience by freestyling and battling other rappers in jam sessions. Freestyling is the primary mode of competition for rappers before they come to a label. Freestyling is not really a commercially viable style of rap—it is more of a training ground. There might be some tapes of freestyling that would make it on to underground radio, but that's a precommercial market. It is very important in terms of their development as artists: it certainly would be important to be able to have that skill for live concerts once they start touring, but nobody's going to put out a record of freestylers at the moment.

TR: Not yet! [Laughs] So by the time you get a viable demo from a band, the group is fairly seasoned, and because of their experience they already understand themselves in terms of marketing categories?

CAW: They may think so. What most groups think of themselves, and what the record business requires or expects of them, are often very far apart. Helping the group to understand that their idea of what's marketable might not be really marketable in the year that they get the record deal is the job of the A & R department (artist and repertoire) and/or the management. But they at least have a sense of themselves as a group, they have a sense of who has the best lyrics, who has the best style, who is going to be the lead, whatever. Sometimes, though, the record company might say, "That guy really isn't the lead. This other one has more personality." But, generally speaking, and certainly with Def Jam and Russell Simmons, he pretty much tries to work with the personalities as the group established them. His contribution might be, "This is the kind of music that's selling. Can you add two songs to your repertoire that fit this?" For example, right now gangsta rappers are the big thing. If they look like the kind of group that has the capacity to do that, then he might suggest they do some gangsta-style songs. With Nikki D as an example, she was not really as hardcore when she came to Def Jam. Then hardcore women rappers became popular. He knew that she had the capacity to do that, and he told her that she could and should work some of it into her repertoire, so she went back and worked on some hardcore raps.

TR: Let's diverge there for a moment. That's actually something I find disturbing and problematic about the way the market works in relationship to rap. I bought Yo-Yo's and MC Lyte's new records, and they're basically both coming off as hardcore female rappers. I'm not suggesting that their initial image wasn't also a performance, but it certainly wasn't as market-driven. But now, it seems as if all these women have to come out superhard to even remain in the game, whereas there still seems to be a much wider range of personae for male rappers. How much do you think this trend is about shaping the market or following a lead set by fans? When someone makes two or three gangsta cuts, is that following the gangsta style or is that perpetuating the gangsta style?

CAW: It's a little bit of both. The trick with marketing is that you have to do something that the market is already comfortable with, but you have to do something that's a little ahead at the same time. It's finding that balance which is the mark of a good marketer [realizes pun & laughs]. Sometimes a group cannot carry what the market is used to. When De La Soul first came out, there wasn't anything even remotely related to daisy rap; that just wasn't even happening. There was no way to think of what De La Soul are doing as gangsta rap, or hard or street rap, or militant rap—they just didn't fit. If they don't fit but they have good music, they have a good stage presence, and we can do something with it, then we'll just market them as new, or different, and work that. You have to find what makes the group unique. The underlying decision about Nikki D was that, whatever her original image, it wasn't so distinct or unique that it could be pushed as a separate entity. In those cases we look at her strong suits. She really is good at delivering fast lyrics, and she's very clever with her wording. There were a lot of people who did that, but she can, in fact, deliver stronger lyrics than most.

TR: It'll be interesting to see how Salt-N-Pepa respond to this trend. I heard their new album is coming out pretty soon, so it'll be really interesting to see what direction they take, since they're not as easily fit into the hardcore image.

CAW: They have an additional problem, in terms of marketing, and that is longevity, which is very difficult to achieve. The audience for all youth music, not just rap, has a very short attention span. A record is hot for three or four months maximum, and then it becomes an oldie, right? So then the key becomes how you can make the old record have the sustenance of an oldie.... There are a lot of old records that just die, and there are old records that you want to hear next year. There's some mental connection you have to them. Kids today remember all the words, just like we remember all the words to Motown songs. They even have that same relationship to the music, but not to every song. To become an act whose records have that kind of relationship to the fans, so that you end up having a body of material that has a long sales life, is the difference between a professional music group and a flash-in-the-pan music group.

TR: Most rap-derived independent labels haven't been around long enough to have these "professional," top-shelf bands. Most rappers haven't been around long enough to really have multiple records until recently.

CAW: In terms of the conversation we're having, that's important, because a record company can't survive without groups that have *catalogue* and *future*. That's how record companies survive. Most rap labels, or independent labels, were presumed to be short-term business deals, because rap was not perceived as something with a history, and its future was highly questionable, according to music business executives. It's only now that rap labels—and there are really only four—who are in a position to do this survive this transition, who have acts with catalogue and future, and these are: Def Jam, Tommy Boy, Uptown and Profile. Ruffhouse is getting there, but their big-name promising acts like Kris Kross and Cypress Hill are new. Priority is profitable because they have N.W.A.

TR: They have Young MC and Yo-Yo, too.

CAW: Right. The difference between a flash-in-the-pan label and a label that has longstanding groups is that the latter have more money to give to other groups, are able to take a risk on younger groups. It's like having the rap equivalent of Bruce Springsteen or Paul Simon. Those guys on those big labels—they provide the support base for the record company because they make sure that you have basic sales, which helps you cut deals with retailers, helps you get records on the radio, and provides money that you can use to support other groups. So, for a record label to survive, it has to have groups with both past and future.

TR: Let's talk about this notion that rap has changed the rules about black music and the historical legacy of black musicians softening or diluting the blackness of the music in order to cross over to a white (and much larger) audience. There is a commonly held belief that rap has been "accepted by the mainstream on its own terms," that is, without compromise. It seems to me that what is really interesting about rap is that the notion of crossover doesn't emerge until long after rap has a prominent commercial presence. Run-DMC was accused of trying to cross over with rock samples, but frankly that was a misinterpretation of what they were doing. You had your first commercial successes like "Rapper's Delight," ...

CAW: Kurtis Blow with "The Breaks."

TR: Yeah, Kurtis Blow, but I'm not sure he was a crossover attempt, because in effect, he was still very much in line with what rap was up to—he just happened to cross over with what he was already doing. He wasn't quite like the groups who were polished up and made to look like what a mainstream American audience would want/expect them to look like. So why is it, and how is it, that Def Jam or Russell had the confidence, or vision to promote rap as a hardcore black music? What was the logic behind that, and why did he think it would work?

CAW: Russell Simmons thought it would work because he saw it working on a smaller scale. He would go to clubs, and while the white kids didn't necessarily understand the music, they liked the style. The idea of wearing sneakers all the time was something that white rebellious kids could do. They might have a different kind of sneaker [laughs], but they liked the idea of being able to go to a party and wear sneakers and jeans as opposed to getting dressed up. In fact, this "slumming" was actually more comfortable for white kids than it was for many middle-class black kids. Middle-class black kids thought that when you went out on a Friday night you were supposed to get dressed up. White kids liked to dress down. So the rapper's image looked a lot more like ...

TR: ... like Saturday night for white kids ...

CAW: ... right, and Russell observed that from hanging out with Rick Rubin and other guys. So he figured that he could sell it, that it was something that he could get them to appreciate just on the rebellious tip, as opposed to understanding rap or music aesthetically. He sold rap music as a style. He felt that, if he could sell it as a stylistic package, then the music and stuff would come later. The core audience would be street kids who knew the music, who would actually imitate rappers, which is something white kids would not feel they could do. White kids would feel that they could imitate the look—the sneakers, the hats, whatever, and look cool. So Russell reasoned that, if he could combine those two, then he had a hit.

TR: Doesn't that sound a lot like early rock and roll?

CAW: It's exactly like early rock and roll.

TR: But what makes rap different, then? It seems to me that the marketing history is somewhat different; the music seems to have retained a black edge to it for a much longer period of time. Fifteen years into recorded rock 'n' roll history and we had to remind folks that black musicians were the core inventors. Now, fifteen years into rap's recording history we've got Snoop Doggy Dogg and Onyx.

CAW: Because white people really can't do it very well, or it has taken them a very, very long time. Singing was different; you could go to school and learn to sing. [Laughs] Or you were already crooning. For Pat Boone to move from Andy Williams-type songs to black songs was not such a leap; the lyrical line was somewhat familiar. Rapping is a much harder skill to develop from the ground up. Certainly scratching is a different thing; people didn't even believe it was a skill. For a long time, they thought it was something that you threw together. Like breakdancing, rapping and scratching is something that you really have to master. It isn't like anybody could just flop down and spin around on their back.

TR: Also rock 'n' roll was in many ways more of a mixture of white country music genres with black blues and R&B. These sounds were more closely related to one another. What about consumption, though? Even though there are not many white rappers, there are plenty of white B-boys and B-girls. They wear the clothes, and they're buying the black versions of the music. In other words, what white kids would do in rock 'n' roll is buy Pat Boone, rather than buy Chuck Berry, but now they're buying Chuck D.

CAW: But for a long time, there was no equivalent Pat Boone in rap. It wasn't until the Beastie Boys that you had a white group who was trying to rap. In fact, they were the biggest-selling rap act ever! Until Vanilla Ice came along—now he's the closest thing to Pat Boone in rap.

TR: Why is that?

CAW: Same thing. White kids bought Pat Boone, so they bought Beastie Boys! And then Vanilla Ice. The way I see it, the Beastie Boys, to their credit, did not attempt to pretend to be black. Their rap was pretty much the idiotic, rebellious, middle-class, "I don't like my parents" kind of rap. They didn't try to be urban. They were just rap kids who rapped rather than sang. For example, *License to Ill*, their 1986 record, they had a real ill image, and they sold it to white kids. At that point, white kids in general thought that the only real difference between rap and R&B was that for one you spoke and for the other you sang. It was a while before they caught on that there was a skill involved in rapping.

TR: But I think that a lot of white kids thought of the Beastie Boys as real rappers—as in—they rapped like black kids—even though most black rap fans could hear major stylistic differences. But, let's go back to the question of crossover. Even though the marketing wasn't intended that way, basically what you're saying is that white people buy white people's music more regularly. Beastie Boys were a little bit different because they in fact weren't trying to imitate black artists completely—they brought a kind of rock/punk style to their rapping. Whereas Vanilla Ice, who was obviously trying to be a white Negro, clearly couldn't really rap that well, but he still outsold everybody. How do you explain that?

CAW: By the time Vanilla Ice appeared, rap was a very familiar sound. When the Beastie Boys came out, black kids knew about rap, and black kids on the East Coast knew a lot about rap. Even though it was popular, it was still fairly limited. The Beastie Boys were essentially introducing a lot of the rest of the country to this music. By the time Vanilla Ice came out, rap was already fairly well known. There had been some rap movies, there were some rap lyrics on commercials, and L.L. Cool was big, so there were other "safe" black rappers around. There was a body of work that white kids could feel comfortable with, and then Vanilla Ice came along and attempted to be the Elvis Presley of rap. He sold more records— eight million, I think—than anybody else.

TR: He outsold Hammer and Tone-Loc.

CAW: Hammer is first; then there's Vanilla Ice, and then there's Beastie Boys. So the three rap artists with the greatest sales are the black guy who's rap was like a white imitation of a black rapper and the two white groups who imitated black rappers. [Laughter] Those are the three lead sales, to this day.

TR: You've said before that early rap frightened mainstream record companies. Exactly what was it that frightened them?

CAW: Record companies say that the early rappers—with the exception of a Kurtis Blow or a Dougle Fresh—most of them like Afrikka Bambaataa or Grand Master Flash or the Sugar Hill Gang—had pretty rough management. The people who were involved on the business end of early rap music were people who were, in fact, frightening, whether they were just sort-of frightening, or pretty rough-looking guys, or very tough. They also found the images of the artists frightening. Rappers were not tuxedo-wearing black guys, they dressed like working-class kids—which translated into looking like the black guys you feared would mug you on the street. The management and the rappers frightened black industry people, much less white people. But record companies also have their own thugs, too—and Dannen's book *Hit Men* is testimony to all of that. The difference is more of a matter of criminal style. Record company criminals are more accustomed to doing you out of your money, and telling you that they're going to buy you a whole bunch of Rolls-Royces, and then use up all of your money and own you. But, in rap, the criminal process is different. People literally have shot people, and have been shot—it was a new phenomenon for these people! [Laughs] Gun fights were not a part of regular business practices—they were more accustomed to drugs, laundering money, that kind of criminal element, not 'round-the-way, straight-up street hoods.

TR: So they were afraid both of the music and of the people that they felt they had to work with in order to sell it.

CAW: They were afraid of the people they had to work with, and that's why they were afraid of the music. The music was a little difficult to embrace because they couldn't be sure how long people would listen to songs that were not sung. That would be something they would think of as more of a novelty, but that's a different kind of fear. They might be afraid to put a whole bunch of money into that act. . . . But that's similar to any other kind of novelty in the mind of a record company executive. A couple of the independent labels started one or two acts that they believed in, and they started a label as part of the process of getting a distribution deal for the group or for the record. But they did not expect the label to remain viable. They were just trying to develop a way to sell their particular rapper. So it was a while before the bigger record companies, the Sonys and Warner Brothers, began taking rap seriously as a genre with longevity. So the big guys really left to the independent labels the job of finding the new rap acts and putting all the energy into working with them. That meant that rap acts had smaller budgets and much fewer resources, generally. This eventually contributed to sampling problems. If a rap producer had a choice between paying legal fees to clear samples or cleaning up your last demo in the studio to make the music better, they will put the money into the record. It was a while before people even started chasing rappers for sample clearance. Since they had so little money to work with, they couldn't see investing it in sample clearances, especially five or seven years ago when it seemed a small and distant problem. But having less money also limited rappers' ability to produce music with a lot of a complexity or depth to the cuts, because they just did not have that much time to spend in the studio. It's not until Public Enemy's *Nation of Millions* (1988) that the music begins to have elaborate musical layering.

TR: That's true, but you are referring to a certain kind of musical complexity, because there was a different kind of complexity, rhythmically and sonically, going on even when there were limited production funds. Say, Eric B. and Rakim's first album, *Paid In Full* (1986), which precedes Public Enemy's *Nation of Millions*, is pretty extraordinary in its sonic and rhythmic arrangements.

CAW: Right, but I'm pretty sure that Hank Shocklee was the first rap producer to make a conscious decision to put a lot of money into production. It is a difficult decision to make—it is also a gamble. The money used to produce the record comes from the record company's advance to the artist against royalties. So, it is really your money that you're using to make the record, (something that a lot of artists don't realize). Artists get a check for one hundred fifty thousand dollars and that's the first time they've ever seen a check with that many zeros and their name on it. From that money they have to produce the record and they have to live off that money for months, sometimes a year or longer, until they get royalty payments.

TR: And they have to sell enough records so that the first one hundred fifty thousand dollars worth of royalties which they have already spent can be recouperated by the record company. After that, they see payment number one. It could be years before they see any money, right?

CAW: That's correct. Because of that, a lot of groups get crazy because they have all of this money, and then really in order to survive they have to tour. They have to be able to have a performance career in order to live once they've cut the first record. Actually, you could cut the first record and then not have it released for quite a while, so there's potentially a large time gap. So you have to know to take your cut off the hundred and fifty grand, take your thirty thousand dollars, which is all you're going to get to live on, and God help you if you've got a group of five! If you've got a group of two, that's fine; if you've got a big group, then you're cutting it up five ways and still have to make the record.

TR: You've got to get a day job.

CAW: Right, or tour. Once your record comes out, you have to do a lot of touring, which is basically free promotion stuff. You've got to go around and talk to radio stations, talk to the retailers, and so on. You don't really get paid for that; your expenses might get covered, but you don't really get paid. And then touring becomes a problem for rappers after 1985— after the Long Beach, California Arena gang melee. The mainstream press, which had already begun to presume that rap concerts are dangerous, really went to town. This is a serious problem because their capacity to make money diminishes dramatically when they are frozen out of the largest arenas. The cost of putting on a rap show increased phenomenally after that because the insurance rates went up.... So the ticket prices went up. Before, you could have a show that only had two groups; now you have to have a show that's going to have five groups lined up to cover expenses. Each group gets less money, the ticket price is higher, and moving the groups around costs more. So now, the touring options for rappers are fewer and their need to tour for income is as great as ever.

Who's Zoomin' Who? Rights, Contracts and Ownership

TR: Let's talk about the question of publishing rights. Why is it important for artists to have the publishing rights to their lyrics and songs, and why have so many artists relinquished these rights? Do rappers, as compared with other artists, tend to have more of their publishing rights, or less?

CAW: There are three profitable areas for artists. The first is when you record the music and you sell records. You get some money off the direct sale of the record—this is called royalties. The second is if somebody else records your record, or if your record gets used in something other than the original song that you recorded, like a commercial, or on a sound track—this is called publishing. The third is if it gets played on radio—this is performance. So you get money from your royalties on records sold from your record company, you get licensing fees from the publisher, and you get money from performance from ASCAP or BMI, or now SESAC, which is a smaller version of ASCAP or BMI. Most of the time, when new groups are starting out and come to the record company, the publishing rights don't seem like a big deal to them. They're really focused on royalties and getting a record made. The other thing they might be interested in is touring opportunities—going out and performing live—getting some money for that. So record companies have a tendency to say. "Well, give me those publishing rights," and that becomes something that the record companies get from the group, and the group gets fifty percent and the record company keeps fifty percent of the publishing rights. The group can say, "No, I'm not going to give up my publishing, I want to keep my publishing" and then become a publisher of themselves. Keeping one's publishing rights is a major undertaking and it's also a major contract negotiation item. But the average new group doesn't even think about publishing.

TR: Even today? Even today they still don't know that publishing is a major source of income?

CAW: No. And it isn't necessarily so, unless you produce a catalogue of material. If you're only going to be a flash-in-the-pan group, fighting over publishing doesn't really make that much sense anyway. It only makes sense if you're going to have a body of work, because you're not going to make a killing on each and every song. It's when you have a body of well-known work that publishing rights matter. People might want that Public Enemy sound, and they might go through your catalogue to use it. But generally speaking, rap catalogues have not had a whole lot of revenue strength, because they were so lyric-driven rather than tune-driven. The music is important to rap, but not as valuable in terms of publishing rights. Often the rap tune wasn't original with the rap song. They relied heavily on samples from somebody else, so it was James Brown who would make the money rather than Eric B. and Rakim, because rappers' tunes are not completely original—most of the songs are comprised of samples. So, they have to pay the other publishers for the right to use that material.

TR: So the publishing rights, then, become important with the larger acts that have what you're calling a history or catalogue. Since most bands sign those standard multiyear contracts before they expect to have a history, the ones that become successful don't necessarily have any publishing rights.

CAW: Publishing is often an area for renegotiation. They often start out with a fifty-fifty split, then they might move to seventy-five–twenty-five. Sometimes they move to eighty-five–fifteen. A super-large group might get all the publishing rights back. As they get more successful you review your contract for things to give the group.

TR: How long are these contracts, generally speaking?

CAW: They're not set by years, they are set by album, so usually bands are signed for six to eight albums.

TR: Most rappers haven't even gotten through half of their first contract—they can't even think about renegotiating!

CAW: That's right. Most acts—not just rappers—do not make it through the first contract. So the record company locks you up for a significant portion of your career, because the average pop group barely makes it through half of an average contract. If a pop group makes three records, that's a successful act!

TR: So the record companies lock the artist up for six to eight albums so that they can be sure to cash in on the acts that might get big after the first few album attempts. I suppose that, from their vantage point, it's the second three records that have the potential to make the big money—if they get made at all.

CAW: That's correct. So when you come to them, you come as a new act with not much negotiating power, because the record company is going to have to lay out all this money, and
it's a lot of money. I don't want to understate how much it costs. To get the record distributed nationally—to get twenty copies of every record into every record store in the
country—is a big financial undertaking. To get radio stations to play this record—every radio
station has a forty-song cap on its three-week play list—to get your record to be one of
those forty costs money.

TR: Forty out of how many songs?

CAW: About five thousand. [Notes shocked look on my face] It's a lot of songs. And some of
those spaces get snapped up automatically by established groups. If a Janet Jackson record
comes out, they'll make space for it, so that's one less space that you can compete for. And
then there are different formats—black radio has one format, adult contemporary has
another, so you've got to pick which stations will carry this record. For rap, you have to put
a lot of energy into underground stuff—making sure that DJs get it and play it in clubs so
that people will start demanding it. You might have to put a lot of money into getting the
video done so that it will be on TV and people will start demanding it. There are lots of
other monies that you have to expend in order to put pressure on radio to play this record.
Radio has to get a sense that people want to hear the record.

TR: What kind of investment is this? Let's just talk numbers. Let's say I'm a new rapper—
Sweet Tricia, and I get my one hundred fifty thousand dollars advance from my royalties to
make the record and so on. Where are all the rest of these expenses coming from?

CAW: Some of it also comes out of your royalties. Some of the marketing money wouldn't, that
would be another point of negotiation. Certainly a portion of the music video and
publicity costs comes out the artist's percentage. Promotion, for example, sending the
group around on a tour to convince radio to love them, that might not come out. Selling
the record to radio—that wouldn't come out of royalties. Neither might the artwork for your
posters. Some of it might, some of it might not. If you wanted any special packaging, that
would certainly come out of the royalties, but if you just had standard packaging, the label
pays for that. Distribution costs are covered by the label.

TR: Those distribution costs are factored into the price of the CD and the number of records
and CDs that you choose to press. The vast majority of the expenses are coming out of the
musician's pocket in the long haul, and yet record companies still consider it expensive to
front the money. Since they've got the next ten years of the artist's productivity to draw on
for profit, they can recoup one way or another. So, what's the big expense? Why do record
companies cry the "it cost so much" blues?

CAW: From a record company's position, I'd have to say, "Gee, this is pretty much a win-win
situation."

TR: Even you have to admit that!

CAW: Oh, without question! But the only spot where that doesn't work is if the record bombs,
and a significant portion of the records bomb. So that every Public Enemy album is
covering for No Face [laughs], BWP and so on. So you've got to cover for failures. And you
also have to decide when you're going to cut your losses. You have the option to release
them from the contract if you don't think they're going to be productive.

TR: So what's the minimum sales figure that would save a group from being released from
their contract?

CAW: Mmm, about two hundred thousand.

TR: But that seems like a pretty solid initial fan base.

CAW: Yeah. If they sold two hundred thousand on the first record, you would keep them; if they sold two hundred thousand over the course of three records, no.

TR: So, Def Jam's ability to market certain artists may have an effect on sales?

CAW: That's right. In that kind of case, you can get stuck because the artist can really get a lot of advances. ...

TR: But that's a negotiation problem. The record company is going to basically fight as hard as it can to lower its advance to the artist, unless they feel a band is a total smash and they just know it.

CAW: That's right. But that's a rarity.

TR: As I understand it, smaller record companies have distribution deals with larger record companies, and some have production and distribution deals. What are the differences between the two?

CAW: A distribution deal is where you, the independent label, are paying in advance for the cost of making the record, and you show up at the major label with a demo master tape ready to be pressed. A production/distribution deal is one in which the major label advances to you, the smaller label, the money to pay for the production of the record. So you give most of that, or a significant portion of that, to the artist to make a record. Then the record company becomes more involved with helping you pick the studio, figuring out who the engineer is and managing the costs. A joint venture deal is when the major label and the independent is splitting costs fifty-fifty including overhead. The larger company takes distribution costs and marketing costs off the top. So a distribution deal has the most uneven power relationship and a joint venture is much closer to partnership.

TR: How common are joint venture deals?

CAW: Distribution deals are more common than joint venture deals.

TR: In the same way that the artist is at a disadvantage negotiating with the record company, an independent record company is at a disadvantage negotiating with a major, right?

CAW: Even though an independent company can have great records and great artists, they have very limited distribution outlets; they have no way to get that record to everybody across the country. You cannot sit in New York and make sure that your record is being sold in Boise, Idaho, unless you have some nationwide distribution system.

TR: Nationwide distribution is dominated and completely controlled by the six major labels, right?

CAW: Right. Warner Brothers, Sony, EMI, Polygram, MCA and BMG; only one of which—Time-Warner—is American-owned, by the way. (At this point, Japan owns Sony and MCA, EMI is British-owned, Polygram is owned by a Dutch company and BMG is German-owned.) So, if you want your record distributed widely, if you want it on two hundred radio stations simultaneously, if you want it on all the video outlets at the same time, you've got to hook up with these six corporations. The small record companies are concerned about getting the record into every retail outlet, and making sure that the retailer puts the name tag on the record so that the artist is not just under the "F"s but under her name, right? They want to make sure that the record is selling at the front of the store when it first comes out, and that there's a picture of the group in the store. All of those things make a difference in sales. A small label doesn't have the money to do that, so the first deal you make with a major record company would be, "For every record that we sell, we'll give you twenty-five points." (Points are percentages out of one hundred percent of how the royalties/profits get divided.) You, the small record label, then, have to go to an artist and say, "I'm going to give you fifteen points, and I keep ten." In reality, you don't tell the group you're going to keep ten, because you don't reveal how many points you have to distribute.

TR: That's really how it works? The independent label keeps less than what they give the artist?

CAW: Yes, but I'm taking ten percent of artist A and ten percent of artist B, so my ten percents add up. You're only getting this one fifteen percent. Michael Jackson's got a very lucrative deal. He's reputed to have the most lucrative deal in the industry, at thirty percent. But most artists do not expect to get anywhere near that. Some artists with big deals might get eighteen, twenty, twenty-two, twenty-four, percent. After the artist's cut, the independent label works with the remaining percentage. So, of course, the independent label tries to negotiate with the major label to pay some of these expenses. An independent label might say, "I don't want anything taken off my profits for distribution costs." Then the major label tells you how much they spent, and you basically have their word as proof. Who's to say that a company didn't keep your profits and called it distribution costs? So it can become sort of like a company town thing.

TR: As Chuck D has said, show business is five percent show and ninety-five percent business.

CAW: It's really, in its institutional design, a very plantation-like system. Not just for rappers, but across the board for all artists. The record industry is very plantation-like. Every rung down gets less and less of the pie, and the artists are at the bottom.

TR: What does this mean about the possibility for creative control? What are your thoughts about this profoundly confining and unequal relationship?

CAW: The primary issue in the music business is profit. So, even black record executives with a conscience are trapped by the rules of the institution. Artists on all labels get exploited, some get exploited less than others. Really big-name stars get exploited less, but what they get paid is not commensurate with the profits that they generate, and their creative control expands only as much as the company feels they can sell this new product. This is one of the reasons so many artists behave in temperamental ways that seem juvenile and irrational, and it explains why label executives accept artists' quirkiness and artists' negative behavior and so on. When record companies give them the limo, or the girls, or whatever else they give them, it's not out of some largess or because they think it is fair compensation. It's like ...

TR: ... the European settlers giving tobacco and beads to Native Americans in exchange for land ...

CAW: Yeah, right.... It really is like that. It's very difficult for an artist to break out of these lengthy contracts. It's very rare for an artist to be able to be both an artist and a businessperson, and to get some control over their career at that level. That's very, very hard and frustrating.

TR: Given that, then what is the significance of rapper-owned record companies like N.W.A's Ruthless Records, Luther Campbell's Skywalker Records, or Flavor Unit Records. Is this artist-owned label phenomena really something that could redistribute the power in the industry?

CAW: I think it will be a very, very long time before power is actually redistributed in the industry, especially now that the industry is owned by these multinational conglomerates who are utilizing the entertainment industry to fuel much bigger enterprises. Sony bought

Columbia records to help them sell hardware. It's not as if they had this burning desire to sell Public Enemy records. [Mutual laughter] They're trying to sell electronic equipment. Artists' work sells interactive television, it sells video games—each artist is a pindrop, a pinhead on this much bigger mosaic. The record industry is worried about its strategic positioning in relationship to the film industry or records versus television versus telecommunications versus phone companies; that's the kind of jockeying they're doing. They're not talking about Public Enemy versus Bruce Springsteen.

These artist-controlled labels are not really going to change the balance of power in the industry. What they can do is facilitate an artist getting more control of his or her own individual career. Mind you, for the individual artist, this is a profound difference. Are you just going to be a slave that gets beat up? Or are you going to be an overseer, be someone who is higher up in the hierarchy? Those distinctions are real for you as a person. And these artist-owned companies gives them the institutional structure to produce and develop new talent. So, when a rapper brings in new talent, having a company can mean the difference between getting a flat fifty thousand dollars discovery fee and a thank-you from the larger record label, and being able to negotiate a long-term investment in that artist's career. Suppose that artist becomes a big seller …

TR: Like Jam Master Jay and his "discovery" of the rap group Onyx.

CAW: That's right. But for most acts who've brought a new hot group to the attention of a label, up until now, somebody would thank them, maybe give them some money, and they would have no relationship with that act whatsoever, nor would they see any profits for their efforts. Somebody as famous as Gladys Knight, who discovered the Jackson Five, didn't get money. She just got a thank-you from Berry Gordy.

TR: I'd go bald over that one.

CAW: This is an industry-wide phenomena, it's not just rap-related. But because rappers are such a small and insulated group, and because the labels that rap music profits helped found are few and highly visible, you can see this dynamic more clearly in this genre.

I Can Live Without My Radio

TR: One of the things that you alluded to at the Princeton conference was the significance of the major record labels and the entertainment industry at large realizing that rappers could sell products to white middle America. They seemed to have overcome their fear of B-boys. An image of some rapper selling Coke, they decided, was not going to traumatize the middle-American family gathered wholesomely around their living room television screen. In fact, rappers seemed to stimulate sales among the wanna-be hip. This meant the rappers would soon become viable outlets for sales revenues in Hollywood and for general advertising. How was this fear overcome? What changed?

CAW: Well, the key is that the B-boy will never really come to your home, right? [Laughs] He can only appear on the screen. He can only come through that hamburger. He can only come through that sneaker style, whatever.

TR: He's fully mediated by a commodity …

CAW: … and so he's fully safe. The first big rapper who made this transition was Fresh Prince. When television producers selected a rapper for a white middle-class television audience, it was a light-skinned guy from Philadelphia from a middle-class background. Even when he was rapping full-time, Fresh Prince's raps were "Parents Just Don't Understand," and "Nightmare on My Street." He was as much a comedic poet as a rapper. Because of his image and talent, they were able to market him as a fresh-faced kid with a little ghetto flavor. He had a little edge to him because he used black slang. But that was as much as Hollywood or the mainstream television audience really saw. They found a rapper who would be safe but at the same time appear cutting-edge. The only other place you could see rap was on the *Cosby Show*. Theo, the Huxtable's son, grew up listening to rap in a very safe context. This was significant because these were black people whom middle-class White Americans know and understand, who are accepting this music in their lives and homes. Of course, in reality it wasn't true. Black middle-class adults have not been supportive of rap and black radio was refusing to play rap.

TR: Why did black radio reject rap music?

CAW: Advertising. All radio is local—even when they advertise nationally, the vast majority of things that they sell, even when they sell McDonald's ads, are being sold for the local outlet. McDonald's, the Cadillac dealership, the Seaman's furniture store and so on—they want to be assured that when they advertise to a radio station's listenership that this audience is not going to come to the store and steal from it or break it up. Radio station advertising salespeople censored themselves. They were sure—even before they were rejected—that local stores would not want to appear as if they were advertising to rap's core listening audience: young black teenagers.

TR: The promotion and the advertising departments at black radio feel as if they have to convince the advertisers that their listeners are not hoodlums, but that they're upstanding black people?

CAW: ... who have money.... But rappers, or the rapper image, was an image that was frightening to your local store owners. They did not want to up the number of black kids who are coming into their store with baggy pants and their hats on backwards.

TR: Do you think the radio stations are right about rap fans and correct in deciding to affirm advertiser's fears?

CAW: I think black radio and the advertisers overreacted. I think that a lot of the products that they sell weren't going to be attractive to that audience anyway. A fourteen-year-old kid isn't really that interested in going to Seaman's furniture store and certainly isn't by definition a thief. And black radio really could have utilized rap music to expand its advertising base, because there are a lot of stores and companies who do want to sell to a young black audience as well as the other audiences who listen to black radio. But black radio has spent most of its time trying to "upgrade" its advertisers, that is, trying to get the more prestigious sponsors. They were trying to upgrade the image of their audience by courting advertisers who are associated with higher-class demographics. To be fair, black radio's attempts to upgrade its local advertising base is also related to its inability to reserve the big national advertising spots, since advertisers presume that black radio has a smaller audience which spends less money. Some of it is sheer numbers: there are a lot more white folks in this country than black folks. So a bigger part of black radio's advertising dollar comes from these local stores. Rock or pop stations can more easily get a national ad for McDonald's, a Colgate, Tide, and all of that. But black radio doesn't get that as easily, so their dependence on these smaller, local outlets is much more significant.

The main problem with black radio's response to rap music is that they didn't wait for Seaman's and so on, to reject the audience. The radio executives decided in advance, "Since we're afraid of these kids and think they are going to mug us, we know that Seaman's won't want them." And that was the beef that Russell Simmons has had with black radio. So black radio's rejection of rap, combined with the touring problems, really limits rap's media access. It has also led to rap's disproportionate dependence on video outlets for visibility. There was no other way—except for smaller club dates (which is a specialized market) for kids to hear or see rap performed. If you're trying to sell records to the kid who's not allowed to stay out on Friday night past midnight, [laughs] or who can only go to one party, you've got to get on radio, you've got to get on TV.

TR: But I do hear some rappers on New York black radio stations. How did they get through?

CAW: Since there are a number of rap groups that are considered "respectable," black radio has relaxed their silent rap ban. And at the same time, rap defines "cool" for this generation, and black radio doesn't want to be corny! On black radio, you can get rappers who have made the Top 10 or Top 20 rotation. The occasional big group gets played, like an L.L. Cool J, on white radio. But the bulk of rap's artists still depend on college radio, on listener-sponsored radio and on other alternative outlets.

TR: Who listens to black radio?

CAW: Black radio's audiences are actually considerably older than rap's audience. Rap music's audiences are twelve to thirty years old, while black radio's audiences are twenty-four to forty years old. There's really a hole in the radio demographic for young black people.

TR: Since there is no real radio market for teenagers they rely on video culture, which explains why MTV's mining of rap video was so lucrative. But there were still advertiser's concerns for MTV and for BET (Black Entertainment Television). They also seem to contain rap programming to keep advertisers happy. What if someone started a twenty-four-hour rap show? Could you find advertisers and make tons of money?

CAW: The question is, can you? And that's what we're trying to figure out.

Women in the Music Business

TR: Let's talk about the gender issues in rap and in the music business, in general. How and where do women function in the music business?

CAW: Well, it's good news and bad news. Women are a bigger presence than you would think at the executive level in the entertainment business in general, and in the music business specifically. At the *absolute top*, very few women run record labels, not one is running a major label. There are women who run particular departments, and Sylvia Rhone runs a label. But the bad news is that women do not make anywhere near the same salary for the same positions. These are not small salary differences, we're talking about at least a twenty thousand-dollar-a-year gap and more. And there are very few women who are at the level at which stock options or equity in the company are offered, those kind of things which are normal in the old boy network are not passed on to women, no matter how high up the corporate ladder they may be. This is true for women of any color. So the record business is not particularly different from other industries. What makes it especially noticeable in the music business is the fact that women are heavily relied upon for the nurturing of artists. Keeping your artists happy, keeping them in line, and keeping them working along with you is a key part of the record business. We talked about this whole plantation thing—well, if the slaves uprise, you're in a lot of trouble, so women are used to negotiate artist's emotional needs. You will notice that women will dominate publicity, artist development, product management—all those "keep the artist happy" departments. We do not dominate sales, we do not dominate business affairs, we do not dominate marketing.

TR: What about everyday work conditions for women? I've heard a number of horror stories.

CAW: It's a very macho industry across the board, not just with rappers. There's a lot of foul and sexist language that is routine. The things that Anita Hill said she heard from Clarence Thomas over a four-year period, I might hear in a morning. My boss, if he wants to tell me I did a good job, he'll call me up and say, "Carmen, I'm on your dick!" Should I say, "Look, this is sexual harassment, I shouldn't have to hear that," or do I take the props (praise)? That's the kind of decision that women have to make literally by the hour—not by the day, not by the week, but by the hour. It's at that level of conversation all the time. Rappers also use verbal disrespect, verbal abuse and constant sexual innuendo in their interaction with women employees. By contrast, rockers have groups of girls or groupies around them a lot more than rappers. So you, as a woman executive or woman in artist development in a rock division, might be asked to cover for the rocker who leaves some girl drunk and battered in the back of his car. Part of your job can require you to cover for really blatant sexism, sexual harassment and abuse. It's hard to fight because it is so routine for the rockers to abuse women on that level. In my experience, rappers are not often that physically abusive.

TR: Clearly, the culture of the music industry is profoundly sexist, and yet fully depends on women to manage their primary investments. Is it that they're more threatened by women's presence because the male executives are more dependent on women to keep things running smoothly? What do you think motivates their behavior?

CAW: There is a mutual love-hate relationship between the record company and the artist. For the record company, there's the basic: "We need these artists," but there's also the belief that "Artists come a dime a dozen." So the people who take care of the dime-a-dozens are treated as dime-a-dozens people, too. The sexism travels more like that.

TR: So the abusive logic of the industry has reverbatory effects going all the way up the ladder.

CAW: Right, and up in the upper echelons of executive management, they consider women and girls one of the perks of their job.

TR: Let's bring it down to the rap context. You're saying that rappers are much more likely to be verbally abusive but not physically abusive. What about the day-to-day contact between rappers and women employees? I spoke to a black female video producer who said that she sometimes has to speak to rappers through her male coworkers because she can't get these rappers to respect her role as a producer and do what she's asking them to do. They'll call her "sweetheart" throughout the video shoot, lick their lips at her, constantly undermine her authority.

CAW: There's no question that the reason rappers work with me is their sense that Russell thinks I protect his money, period. And I'm older. The fact that I have a body of professional skills is irrelevant, absolutely irrelevant to them. It's as if I am Russell's business wife, not his romantic woman. Their fear is that if they don't treat me with respect then Russell will be mad at them, not "Carmen deserves respect." There is no woman who's respected at Def Jam who does not have Russell to watch her back. This is true for most of the upper-level female executives in the music business.

TR: So what happens to the women who don't have that sort of patriarchal protection, women who are independent producers or work for very small labels?

CAW: The same thing that happens to the black female producer you mentioned earlier. You literally end up having to find the man who is going to front for you. Or you have the physical size and diva status to establish authority against the odds. Even then, all powerful women are at some point labeled a "bitch" for exercising their power—often they are called bitches to their faces. I had to put one artist out of the office because he told a woman staff person that he wanted her to suck his dick, straight up. I said, "You can't come back in here until you apologize to her." And we had to get Russell and Lyor Cohen to back us up, to agree to tell this artist that he couldn't come back in the building. But it was not an automatic decision.

TR: You had to persuade them that this was a legitimate reason to demand an apology?
CAW: No, in this case they backed me up immediately, but if the rapper had been somebody who had been selling a lot of records, I'm not sure that I would have won.

TR: What about women rappers and women music producers? You've described an environment in which women employees are treated in a consistant and extremely sexist manner. Are women rappers treated like their male counterparts, since they are potentially equal money-makers?
CAW: Women rappers have a special set of concerns: one, record companies have not yet found a sure-fire sales strategy for female rappers' work and two, female rappers have less business savvy and are less aggressive negotiators. They rarely come to negotiation sessions with high-powered legal representation. I'm not quite sure why that is, but they generally hire lawyers for whom they are the first or second or third client. It's very rare to see a woman rapper walk in with seasoned counsel. The power of your counsel to represent and protect you has a serious effect on your image with the record label. Too often, women rappers' records are categorized as "We're waiting to see what's going to happen with this artist." They are not considered. "This is the breakout one." So oftentimes they don't get promoted as well, and the initial assessment becomes a self-fulfilling prophecy.

At the same time, women rappers as a group have some clout because everybody's waiting to see who's going to be the break-out woman rapper. People are trying to see who's going to be the Diana Ross of this music. And that person has not yet arrived.

42

Black Youth and the Ironies of Capitalism

S. Craig Watkins

[I]n the struggles of urban youths for survival and pleasure inside of capitalism, capitalism has become their greatest friend and greatest foe. It has the capacity to create spaces for their entrepreneurial imaginations and their "symbolic work," to turn something of a profit for some, for them to hone their skills and imagine getting paid. At the same time, it is also responsible for a shrinking labor market, the militarization of urban space, and the circulation of the very representations of race that generate terror in all of us at the sight of young black men and yet compels most of America to want to wear their shoes.

Robin D.G. Kelley[1]

Although African American filmmaking is the primary locus of inquiry, the scope of my analysis is considerably broader. It is difficult to understand the significance of filmmakers like Spike Lee and the Hughes brothers in American cinema without situating their arrival on the cultural stage in relation to the social transformations that reorganize the material and symbolic worlds inhabited by black youth. The creative labor of African American filmmakers takes place upon a complicated sphere from which the production of blackness, a historically situated racial signifier, proliferates across many sites.[2] But before discussing African American filmmaking practices specifically, it is important to consider the historical formations and decisive shifts that transform the social landscapes, everyday experiences, and cultural productions of black youth more generally.

According to sociologist David Brain, cultural production is the "collective production of skills and practices which enable social actors to make sense of their lives, articulate an identity, and resist with creative energy the apparent dictates of structural conditions they nonetheless reproduce."[3] The cultivation of skills that allow them to participate in a rapidly expanding and global communications media culture enables black youth to produce a broad range of cultural products. The most arresting features of black youth popular cultural productions represent distinct forms of agency, struggle, and social critique. But the vigorous commodification of African American cultural productions also develops complicated features.

The study of popular media culture generally oscillates between two opposing poles: containment or resistance. Whereas the former maintains that the ideas, values, and representations that shape popular media discourses are determined by the dominant classes, the latter argues, alternatively, that popular cultures have the capacity to subvert dominant ideologies and regimes of representation.[4] Yet popular media culture is remarkably more complex than the containment/resistance binary opposition implies. Similar to the social world from which it is produced, popular media cultures are marked by instability and change. It is, in fact, one of the main locations where the struggle for ideological hegemony is waged. But as Stuart Hall explains, this "struggle for [ideological dominance] is never about pure victory or pure domination[;] it is always about shifting the balance of power in relations of culture."[5] From this view, then, popular media culture is perhaps best understood as a perpetual theater of struggle in which the forces of containment and resistance remain in a constant state of negotiation, never completely negating each other's presence or vigor.

While the different spheres of commercial media culture—television, film, music, video, and the Internet—function as sources of pleasure and entertainment, they also perform a pivotal role in patterning the cultural and ideological landscape. The popular media productions created by black youth represent a distinct sphere of cultural production. Any serious consideration of black cultural productions must examine the relationship between several interlocking factors: the specific culture industries within which these productions are organized; the changing landscape of communications media technologies; emergent mood shifts and sensibilities that lead to the creation of new collective identities; and finally, the unsettled social world within which black youth cultural practices take shape. Sociologist Herman Gray argues that commercial media culture is an essential location to think and theorize about African American culture, representation, and politics. Gray reminds us that "commercial culture serves as both a *resource* and a *site* in which blackness as a cultural sign is produced, circulated, and enacted."[6]

Commercial forms of popular culture are a rapidly growing field of study. Scholars and social historians are beginning to understand it as a plentiful and remarkably revealing reservoir of practices and formations that are inextricably linked to the changing contours of American life: urbanization/suburbanization, technological innovation, and shifting conceptions of racial, gender, class, and sexual identities. Commercial forms of popular media culture, for example, are central to how we (re)produce and experience socially constructed formations like race.

More precisely, my aim is to more fully explain the increasingly complex ways in which young African Americans have mobilized around a changing racial and popular media landscape. Moreover, it is a story about how the pulsing gestures, performances, and representations practiced by black youth are structured, in large part, by the profound ways in which they experience the changing contours of American life. The focus on the production of black youth cultural styles and popular movements also recognizes that a notable feature of the late twentieth century, as Stuart Hall and Martin Jacques write, "is the proliferation of sites of antagonism and resistance, and the appearance of new [actors], new social movements, new collective identities—an enlarged sphere for the operation of politics, and new constituencies for change."[7]

My research pivots around a particular site of antagonism and resistance—the sphere of popular media culture—and more precisely, the ferment and creative energy that drive the cultural innovations of African American youth and their strategic participation on this terrain. The buoyant surge in black youth popular cultural production raises important questions about the evolving disposition of cultural and representational politics in a media-saturated universe. Early critics of "mass culture" demonstrated concern that popular media culture was controlled by and for the dominant classes. But this view fails to consider how popular media culture functions as a site of intense ideological struggle. Quite simply, can the commercial media, long regarded by many critical theorists as the modern-day "opium of the masses," function as a location of counterideological struggle? Similar to other institutional milieus, commercial media also develop specific antagonisms. So as new subjects gain access to the most prominent sites of media and representation, the possibilities for new collective identities, social movements, and distinct modes of struggle are also established.

To contend that cultural innovation and production among black youth have flourished and achieved a discernible niche in the arena of popular media culture is certainly a tenable position. This is not to imply that African American youth have only recently begun to cultivate spaces for producing cultural objects and expressing themselves but rather that the symbolic practices created by the post–civil rights generation have achieved greater visibility and resonance in the global popular culture economy. But before discussing some of the specific attributes of black youth agency, I would like to consider an initial question first: Why have cultural innovation and production among black youth exploded or, as they might boast, "blown up"? Even more to the point, how has the social, political, and historical terrain on which black youth cultural productions do their work enabled them to intervene in the remaking of society in ways that are more visible, invigorating, and problematic?

The New World Order: Black Youth and the Racialization of Crisis

> Oh you know what else they trying to do, make a curfew especially for me and you. The traces of the new world order, time is gettin' shorter if we don't get prepared people its gone be a slaughter. My mind won't allow me to not be curious. My folks don't understand, so they don't take it serious. But every now and then, I wonder if that gate was put up to keep crime out, or our ass in?
>
> Goodie Mob[8]

A cursory glance at the cultural landscape—music, video, film, television, advertising, and sports—reveals that the expressive cultures created by African Americans play a lively role in patterning the racial and gender identities of youth as well as the general popular culture scene. The precarious relationship between youth subcultures, media technology, and commercial culture has been the subject of numerous inquiries.[9] Still, despite the fact that we can speak broadly of youth cultural practices, it is essential to appreciate the historical specificities that enable distinct formations of youth culture to take shape. Historian Robin D. G. Kelley reminds us that, "unlike more mature adults, young people are in the process of discovering the world as they negotiate it. They are creating new cultures, strategies of resistance, identities, sexualities, and in the process generating a wider range of problems for authorities whose job it is to keep them in check."[10]

Admittedly, it is difficult to pinpoint with precision when and why a distinctive mood shift or transition in youth cultural production originates. However, it is possible to identify those factors that work, more or less, to establish the circumstances from which youth popular culture formations emerge. Certainly, any discussion of late twentieth-century black youth cultural practices that does not consider the social context that situates their agency would be severely impaired.

So why have cultural innovation and production among black youth exploded? One approach might look solely at the innovators of the new symbolic practices that lead to the creation of new popular culture products. This can be called the genius view of cultural innovation because it presupposes that certain periods of cultural production are the result of talented individuals.[11] However, a more discerning approach would seek to understand the historical particularities that produce the resources and opportunities that unleash and enable the creative energies of cultural producers. Moreover, this view understands that the creative labor of cultural producers does not take place in a vacuum. Innovators of new symbolic practices and cultural products do their work in relation to other cultural producers and within specific social historical contexts. Like all historical actors, then, black youth operate within the context of structural and historical constraints not of their own making.

Consequently, any serious interrogation of the symbolic efficacy of black youth cultural practices must understand their social, economic, and political milieu. Sociologist Ann Swidler states that "unsettled times"—that is, periods of great disorder and transition: population shifts; wars; social, economic, or moral crisis—tend to create moments of fierce struggle, instability, and social action.[12] New ideas, social movements, and ideological strategies are mobilized to make sense of societal flux and instability. In the process, the ideas, belief systems, and symbolic terrain of a given period become more fragile and increasingly vulnerable to competing ideological worldviews. Similarly, dominant cultures produce "emergent" social formations that cultivate alternative/oppositional practices and ideologies that modify hegemonic practices and cultural discourses.[13]

To be sure, the presumed "dominant ideologies" of any given period do not always penetrate and shape the consciousness, ideas, and practices of aggrieved populations.[14] In fact, dominant economic and political classes do not consistently fashion consensus in ways that legitimate their authority. This view of culture and society seems especially plausible when thinking about the United States in the late twentieth century, a period of tremendous political agitation and social discord.

The ideological and political formations of the postindustrial United States are marked by profound social, economic, and cultural transition. Moreover, this period of transition has established the conditions for the construction of different crisis scenarios, both real and imagined. In the process, crisis-tinted discourses are mobilized to make sense of and effectively manage the flux and uncertainty that abound. Even in cases where crises may in fact be real, they are typically *made* intelligible and, as a result, are defined, shaped, interpreted, and explained. For instance, a complex assemblage of crisis discourses revolves around the postindustrial ghetto. The ghetto has become an intensely charged symbol, particularly as it patterns discourses about crime and personal safety, welfare, familial organization, and the disintegration of American society.

African American (and Latino) youths are prominently figured in the crisis scenarios that stage some of the more contentious social and political episodes of the late twentieth century. Some researchers contend that increases in violent crimes, teen pregnancy, female-headed households, and welfare dependency can be *partially* explained by the sheer growth in the number of young people, particularly black and Latino, residing in many cities across the United States.[15] Moreover, the concentration of black and Latino youth in postindustrial cities corresponds with structural changes in the postindustrial economy, especially the movement of industry and meaningful employment opportunities away from the communities in which they are most likely to live.[16]

One of the peculiar developments of postwar economic transformations is what economist Juliet Schor describes as an increase in work hours for some segments of the population and the overproduction of idleness for others.[17] Schor argues that, as the U.S. economy and the labor market continue to undergo substantive reorganization, they are increasingly unable to provide work for some segments of the population. One of the persistent tensions in the postindustrial economy is the widespread erosion of meaningful employment opportunities for poor, inner-city youth. As the labor-force participation of black youth hovers around chronically low levels, both their real and perceived prospects for upward mobility become more grim. Indeed a tenacious set of factors restricts the social and economic mobility of poor youth: inadequate schools, lower levels of educational attainment, low self-esteem and personal confidence, discriminatory hiring practices, and racially inflected tensions on the job site.[18]

As the face of urban poverty in the United States continues to evolve, one of the distinguishing features is the growing number of youth who now live in poverty-stricken households, a trend not replicated across other industrialized nations.[19] Cultural critic Mike Davis writes: "[C]orrelated to the economic peripheralization of working-class blacks has been the dramatic *juvenation of poverty* amongst all innercity ethnic groups."[20] By the end of the 1980s, roughly 20 percent of America's youth were poor. And while youth and single-parent mothers represent a disproportionate share of the poor, the probability of being a poor child is not equal across racial/ethnic groups. In fact, research consistently indicates that African American children are significantly more likely to grow up in impoverished households and neighborhoods than their white counterparts.[21] By the end of the eighties, an astonishing 44 percent of African American youth were living in poverty. In contrast, 38 percent of Latino and 11 percent of white youth lived in similar conditions.

The incorporation of African American youth into a broad complex of crisis scenarios develops specific social and political dimensions. Black youth tend to be concentrated in poor communities that have been the primary targets of the post-1960s conservative social and political backlash packaged in numerous movements: antigovernment, antitaxes, antiwelfare, and anticrime. The drive to correct the perceived excesses of "big government" has ignited a broad-based movement of disinvestment in inner-city job training, social, education, and crime-prevention programs. Ghetto youth are prominent icons in the seemingly indefatigable efforts of an emboldened conservatism committed to the enforcement of "traditional values," law and order, and personal responsibility. But the association of black youth with social instability is indelibly marked by the production and popular dissemination of the "underclass" label.

The making of the "underclass" label is congruous with the general rise of social-issue conservatism in post-1960s American political culture. Social-issue conservatism is the explicitly focused debate about values, morality, behavior, two-parent households, and respect for authority. While cultural issues have historically shaped American politics, they have been elevated from a peripheral to a central role.[22] One journalist goes so far as to argue that whereas politicians and political consultants operate from the assumption that economic issues drive electoral politics, "values matter most."[23] However, the author's focus on issues like crime, welfare, and affirmative action suggests that perhaps "race matters most." The "values matter most" contention is at best disingenuous, but it nevertheless illustrates how conservatives have attempted to elevate what are increasingly racialized themes above concerns about the inherent nature and instabilities of capitalism as the central dilemma in American social and political life.

Contemporary discourses about African Americans are increasingly patterned by sensational representations of the black "underclass." Sociologist Herbert Gans maps the evolution of the "underclass" label and its absorption into mainstream social and political discourse. Despite the newness of the label, it plays a definitive role in shaping popular discourses about race, poverty, and social change in general. According to Gans, the term has passed through three descriptive stages: economic, racial, and finally behavioral.[24] By the 1970s, he argues, descriptions of the term turned decisively behavioral as news journalists began to devote substantial time and coverage to the proliferation of social dislocations in poor ghetto communities.[25] The emphasis on the alleged deviance of the poor refashions "culture-of-poverty" explanations of poverty and strengthens the notion that misbehavior is the primary culprit in the reproduction of poor ghetto communities.[26]

The "underclass" is customarily portrayed as one of the most distressing social problems facing the United States. Stephen Hilgartner and Charles Bosk have proposed what they call the public arenas model for understanding the rise of social problems.[27] According to the model, social problems are collectively defined, selected, framed, and disseminated within a dynamic arena of public discourse. In this arena, a broad population of potential problems competes against each other for attention and notoriety. Given the vast number of potential social problems, only a few are able to capture the attention of the public and major institutions. As a result, social problems are necessarily stratified: problems considered the most urgent occupy the top of the "social problems ladder," while those achieving little or no public cognizance are typically positioned near the bottom.

Furthermore, Hilgartner and Bosk contend that the career of a social problem variegates over time and hinges on its ability to capture the attention of the institutions that have the power and resources to effectively define the problem for broad public consumption. These institutions, in effect, *make* the social problem and render it intelligible to the broader public. The carrying institutions include, for example, the cinema, made-for-television movies, news media organizations, book publishing, and political parties. These are the major institutions that select, define, and disseminate social problems to the public. Because of the vast population of potential problems, creators of social problems must package them in dramatic terms. Once a social problem achieves prominence in one arena, it may then begin to saturate other arenas. When multiple carrying institutions devote substantial attention to a particular problem, it develops a "celebrity" status. Moreover, the problem begins to dominate public, and especially media, discourse.

Visualizing the Underclass, Representing Danger

> Today's dangerous classes included segments of the diverse communities of racial and ethnic minorities; young people who exhibit some degree of independence from their elders' direction and values. . . . The likelihood that the identified group creates danger—crime, urban decay, challenge to authority—is an article of faith, as both the public and the policymakers point to high levels of urban disorder, family dissolution, and unwed motherhood. . . . What is needed to construct them as enemies is a bridge between group identity and an experience of social threat—a neighborhood mugging . . . or the dramatic depiction of a murder on the nightly news—that is familiar to many people.
>
> Diana Gordon[28]

It only takes a quick glance at legislative and electoral politics, the news media, public opinion polls, or popular entertainment culture to recognize that the "underclass," and poor youth especially, has attained the dubious distinction of being a celebrity social problem. The absorption of the "underclass" label into mainstream vocabulary corresponds with the social and economic transformations that configure postindustrial life. And even though the label circulates as if it were ideologically neutral, representations of the "underclass" are sharply coded in both racial and gender terms. Moreover, historian Michael Katz maintains that the label implies that the problem of late twentieth-century urban poverty is profoundly novel in character and kind, and unprecedented in scope.[29]

Take, for example, the proliferation of news media discourses that play a leading role in framing public perceptions of postindustrial ghetto life. Perhaps even more than social scientists or politicians, the news media industry has played a crucial role in coloring the public discourses that render the "underclass" seemingly more intelligible. The television news industry is a distinct sphere of commercial media and discourse production. Unlike most of television entertainment, it is nonfictional—in other words, real. But the news media is a peculiar blend of fact and artifice. Thus, while news media journalists deal with real-world phenomena, they do so in a way that is always selective and interpretive.[30]

News discourse is one of the primary means by which a society comes to know itself. In their analysis of television news, Richard Campbell and Jimmie Reeves contend that it is "a spectacle of surveillance that displays a range of cultural performances—all of which articulate visions of order by representing legitimate authority, reproducing commonsense, and visualizing deviance."[31] The news media are also an important site of racial discourse. In fact, part of the evolving role of the news media industry has been to determine what is most newsworthy about race, construct images and definitions of race, and pattern the range of potential connotations the idea of race produces. For example, television news discourse typically constructs African Americans as conflict-generating and problematic.[32] And though it would be faulty to conclude that the news media are the primary agent in the racial fissures that percolate throughout the late twentieth century, the way in which television news frames race certainly occupies a crucial position on the embattled terrain of racial conflict.

The news media serve several functions at once.[33] A primary purpose is to provide their mass audience with information and descriptions of events that take place in the world. However, another less obvious function is the news media's role as a mechanism of social control. The news media, to be sure, can be viewed as a central component of the social control processes that define and produce meaning about what constitutes difference and deviance. In this particular role, as explained by Ericson, Baranek, and Chan, the news media are a kind of "deviance-defining elite" that play a key role in constituting visions of order, stability, and change and in influencing the control practices that accord with these visions.[34] News media organizations specialize in visualizing—and accordingly, defining—deviant behavior for their audience. In the process, the news media also reproduce commonsense notions of civility, social order, and community consensus. Moreover, the focus on deviance develops an entertainment angle that appeases the commercial interests of news media organizations. Cognizant of its role in commercial television entertainment and the competition for ratings, the television news industry relies heavily on dramatic, sensational, and titillating images in order to attract and hold a wide viewing audience.[35]

The preponderance of television news stories highlighting black youth, violence, and the arrival of crack cocaine in the middle 1980s stands out as a dramatic orchestration of a "moral panic" and demonstrates how news media organizations aid in shaping the way social problems are selected, defined, packaged, and disseminated to the public.[36] Campbell and Reeves maintain that the news media's construction of the cocaine crisis in the 1980s embodied the racial, gender, and class tensions that shaped the most celebrated crisis scenarios of the period.[37] The authors argue that, with the emergence of crack cocaine, the news media developed a "siege" narrative that replaced earlier news stories regarding cocaine use. This rewriting of the cocaine narrative shifted from *class*-coded themes focusing on recreational drug use and therapy to *race*-coded themes focusing on violence, criminality, and punishment. Using production techniques like clandestine footage, the news media began to serve as a surveillance device, built largely on visual clichés that portrayed the burgeoning crack cocaine economy in hyper-villainous terms.[38] The authors persuasively claim that this particular rewriting of the cocaine narrative fit the demonology of racial conservatism, stigmatized poor inner-city youth, and played a central role in legitimating, for example, the "hard" disciplinary ethos of social control initiatives like the war on drugs.[39]

A main set of organizing themes in the "underclass" discourse is the alleged social pathologies of ghetto youth. To be sure, the connection of black youth with illegal drugs, gangs, and violence performs a distinct role in shaping how many of the crisis scenarios of the period were understood. More crucially, inner-city youth arouse public anxiety and precipitate what Diana Gordon describes as "the return of the dangerous classes."[40] Members of the dangerous classes, she argues, are believed to pose a threat to the personal safety of law-abiding citizens and, if unchecked, to the social, economic, and moral order of the larger society. Accordingly, black and Latino youth are prominently figured in the widely shared notion that inner cities—and by association, their racially coded populations—constitute a fiscal and moral strain on national resources. Subsequently, some of the salient crisis scenarios coloring the postindustrial United States have been redefined. In the process, meanings about race, class, gender, and youth undergo substantial revisions.

In many ways, the "underclass" is as much a cultural construction as it is a sociological reality. At stake, of course, is how the widespread impoverishment of black youth is comprehended. To be sure, before any society can create new laws and mobilize punitive measures for the express purpose of controlling those portrayed as dangerous, it must conduct a sufficient amount of ideological work in order to legitimate the use of coercion. In essence, the general public must be made to feel vulnerable, to feel that the stability of the moral and social order is threatened, thus necessitating dramatic acts to preserve social order. Representing ghetto youth as dangerous is not simply a symbolic exercise; it has serious implications for social policy and also influences the social control mechanisms put in place to restore a sense of order. Indeed, initiatives like the war on drugs, school dress codes, and evening curfews achieve their popular status precisely because of the work that crisis discourses perform in the criminalization of black youth.[41] The perceived dangerousness of the urban poor legitimates the deployment of the coercive technologies of the state and the adoption of elaborate crime management operations.

It is within this social context that the cultural productions of black youth amass energy and ever-increasing ingenuity. The transformations of urban ghetto life situate different formations of racial discourse and enable them to take shape. One aim of black youth popular culture is to redefine the crisis scenarios that prominently figure young African Americans. The symbolic practices of black youth develop distinct styles, moods, and imaginative contours that engage a broad spectrum of cultural producers—journalists, politicians, scholars—about African American life. The explosive surge in popular cultural productions by black youth prompts a reconsideration of how unsettled times reinvigorate not only social control discourses but resistive discourses, too. This is not to suggest that social and economic dislocations are the determinate causes of black youth cultural productions. Instead, I am suggesting that the ways in which black youth experience a rapidly changing society and how they practice cultural politics to express these experiences correspond.

Paradoxically, the intensification of racial and economic polarization in the United States produces space for the emergence of cultural practices that derive much of their symbolic efficacy from locations of marginality. The popularization of black youth expressive cultures is an excellent case in point. Despite high rates of poverty, joblessness, and criminal arrests, black youth occupy a dynamic role in the shaping of the popular cultural landscape. Many of the major culture industries—sports, television, advertising, music, cinema—incorporate the innovative styles and expressive cultures of black youth in order to appeal to their respective markets and revitalize their own commercial viability. Ironically, social isolation and economic marginalization contribute to the energy and imaginative capacities that enable black youth to participate effectively in the ever-expanding universe of popular media culture. In the process, black youth have accumulated significant amounts of symbolic capital.[42]

So despite the currency of conservative discourses, black youth have mobilized their own discourses, critiques, and representations of the crisis-colored scenarios in which they are prominently figured. More important, young African Americans are acutely aware of the social world in which they live and the vast structural inequalities that impose severe restrictions on their economic mobility. All members of society exercise some measure of agency—that is, capacity to exert some degree of power over the social arrangements and institutions that situate their lives. Faced with the increasing trend toward structurally enforced idleness and state-sanctioned coercion, black youth have fought diligently to create spaces of leisure, pleasure, and opposition from the social structures and institutional arrangements that influence their life chances.

How do black youth maneuver to contest and destabilize the growing tide of racial conservatism? Ironically, at the same moment that black youth have become especially vulnerable to shifts in the postindustrial economy and the political landscape, they, too, have gained unprecedented access to the technologies of communications media. What has emerged in the process is the structuring of a historically distinct terrain upon which the varying repertoires of black youth cultural production dramatically reorganize the scope and possibilities of social and political struggle from the margins. Indeed, the popular cultures of black youth reveal that they experience, interpret, and make sense of the world in ways that are both historically specific and highly performative.

The Making of the Hip Hop Nation: The Social Transformation of Black Youth Culture

It was not long before similarly marginalized black and Hispanic communities in other cities picked up on the tenor and energy in New York hip hop. Within a decade, Los Angeles County (especially Compton), Oakland, Detroit, Chicago, Houston, Atlanta, Miami, Newark, and Trenton, Roxbury, and Philadelphia, have developed local hip hop scenes that link various regional postindustrial urban experiences of alienation, unemployment, police harassment, social, and economic isolation to their local and specific experience via hip hop's language, style, and attitude.... In every region, hip hop articulates a sense of entitlement and takes pleasure in aggressive insubordination.

Tricia Rose[43]

Despite the widespread popularity of black youth expressive culture and the vast amount of critical attention it currently receives, our understanding of the historical processes that situate its varied articulations remains underdeveloped. The relationship between African American youth and communications media technology is also underexamined. The histories of black youth and their relationship to commercial media culture, to be sure, remain largely unwritten. Black youth continue to create new cultural practices and products that penetrate and reconfigure the production and distribution strategies that govern the culture industry. Moreover, the collective mobilization around popular media technologies by black youth raises intriguing questions about their participation in a vast and rapidly expanding communications media and information economy.

Sociologist Claude Fischer explains that the study of technology and society is commonly informed by technological determinism.[44] According to Fischer, the determinism model views a technology as an autonomous or external "force" that "impacts" social life. The main assumption from this view is that technology dictates changes that are far-reaching and fundamental in scope. Further, it is assumed that a technology produces homogeneous consequences for the larger society. In other words, the impact of a technology on members of society is believed to be uniform.

Critics of technological determinism maintain that while technology can and often does lead to change, the process is socially rather than technologically determined. Moreover, Fischer argues, the determinism view fails to appreciate how specific technologies are adopted by particular members of society and used in ways that accommodate specific intentions and priorities. Fischer writes: "[O]nce we have understood the genesis of a technology, its development and promotion, we can begin looking at consequences. Here we should ask: Who adopted the device? With what intention? How did they use it? What role did it play in their lives? How did using it alter their lives?"[45] According to Fischer, the value of this position is that it emphasizes the agency and intentionality of those who use technology. Fischer adds, "[P]eople are neither 'impacted' by an external force, nor are they the unconscious pawns of a cultural Geist. Instead of being manipulated, they manipulate."[46]

Technological determinism typically informs how the relationship between black youth and popular media culture is comprehended. For example, it is commonly argued that communications media exercise unrelenting power in shaping the worldviews, behavior, and lived experiences of black youth.[47] There are at least two immediate problems with this position. First, it does not adequately specify how media technology has entered and altered the social lives of black youth. Second, and perhaps more important, it does not address how black youth manipulate media technology and, in the process, reshape the sphere of popular media culture.

Take as an example the study of black youth by historian Carl Nightingale.[48] Nightingale contends that analysts of the black urban poor fail to understand the way in which black youth are connected to the larger mainstream culture. Whereas theories about economic, spatial, and cultural alienation emphasize the exclusion of black youth from the mainstream, Nightingale seeks to understand the problematic ways in which mainstream culture penetrates the lived experiences of black youth.[49] Furthermore, he directs his critical gaze toward popular media culture and its "impact" on the racial, gender, and economic identities of black youth. The exploration of the relationship between black youth and the commercial media is certainly an important site of study. But the framing of his inquiry presumes technological determinance. It is taken for granted that the practices of black youth are rigidly conditioned by the media and corporate strategies of consumer socialization. However, it is equally important to consider how black youth influence the culture industry, the cultural marketplace, and consumer trends. In other words, it is important to understand that youth are not simply passive victims of commercial media culture but are actively involved in its making.

The emergence of hip hop culture illustrates black youth agency. In many ways, hip hop represents a particular species of social movement. The movement is made possible by new social and economic arrangements, technological innovations, and the global dissemination of U.S. popular media cultures. Sociologists broadly define social movements as collective efforts to produce social change.[50] Any attempt to discuss hip hop as a movement demands careful delineation because it is variously preoccupied with style, performance, opposition, leisure, consumption, representation, and entrepreneurship. First, this particular movement takes place on the field of popular culture, a site not immediately discerned as political, or capable of producing social change. Second, hip hop is invigorated by the creative labor of a constituency not ordinarily regarded as interested in effecting social change: youth. Third, like social movements in general, hip hop enables its participants to imagine themselves as part of a larger community; thus, it produces a sense of collective identity and agency. To be sure, this particular movement constitutes a distinct mode of intervention in the social world.

Communications media have become an especially important location for both individual and collective agency. Many black youth believe that the sphere of popular media culture is an especially important space in which to articulate many of their frustrations and grievances with their disproportionate membership in the growing ranks of the underemployed/unemployed, impoverished, and incarcerated. Ironically, and as Kelley points out, capitalism has been both a foe and a friend of black youth. Within the interstices of late twentieth-century capitalism, black youth have fought to create productive spaces to counter the dominant discourses deployed to both demonize and discipline them. The hip hop movement has developed into a fertile reservoir of youth cultural production. In fact, numerous expressive cultures have been created in the process: graffiti art, break dancing, and most notably, rap music. The origins of hip hop are difficult to record precisely.[51] And while my focus is on African American youth, hip hop has never been an exclusively "black thing." Many of the creative elements of hip hop developed in correspondence with the postwar migrations and subsequent shifting racial geography of New York City. The interaction between Latino, Afro-Caribbean, and African American expressive cultures established the conditions for the development of alternative modes of youth expression.[52]

The evolution and transformation of hip hop are patterned by class, generational, and gender cleavages. These three markers of differentiation within the African American community make crucial imprints on black popular culture. According to cultural critic Todd Boyd, the most recent generational shifts in black popular culture came into view with the passing of what he refers to as the ideology of the race man, animated best by Bill Cosby.[53] This particular period of black cultural production, Boyd contends, reflected the views and aspirations of a generation concerned with civil rights, assimilation, and the production of what are often alluded to as respectable or "positive" images of black Americans. Further, Boyd maintains that a new black popular culture sensibility—the new black aesthetic (NBA)—supplanted the race man ideology sometime during the middle to late 1980s. This particular generation of black cultural producers—he uses Spike Lee and Wynton Marsalis as illustrations—came of age after the protests of the 1960s and represented the first creative community of African Americans to benefit from the resources and networks made available because of greater access to higher education. This generation practiced a black American version of bourgeois nationalism that emphasized the infiltration of mainstream institutions. These two periods or regimes of cultural politics were informed by a middle-class sensibility that distinguishes them from the most recent generational shift in black popular culture—a shift that is related to the ascendancy of hip hop as a leading signifier of black culture.

Whereas the first two periods are shaped by middle-class priorities and notions of assimilation and respectability (the Cosby era) and new conceptions of black-style politics and upward mobility (the new black aesthetic), the succeeding shift identified by Boyd is governed by a hardcore ghetto sensibility that represents a radical break. This particular generation eschews both the comportment of social acceptability and the racial chic of neo-black nationalist politics. More specifically, Boyd argues that the emergence of hardcore ghetto iconography altered the orbit of black popular culture and is representative of working-class definitions of blackness that contest bourgeois-inflected definitions. While the transitions and breaks that distinguish one period from the other are never total, Boyd's analysis does help to further elucidate class differentiation within the African American community and its implications for a varied terrain of cultural politics and production.

The issue of gender is equally important. While it is true that hip hop is shaped by narratives that emphasize male hegemony, pleasure, and desire, it is important to emphasize that female cultural practices also inflect this particular movement. In her analysis of black youth culture, Tricia Rose maintains that most academic and popular discourses tend to marginalize the presence and contributions of women to hip hop. The presence of females has been integral if not always adequately recognized. Although the commercial media landscape is overwhelmingly dominated by men, women continue to forge new territories for their active involvement and pleasure. The hip hop scene is no different. Indeed, as many female authors point out, women have long struggled to gain access to and control over the resources and sites that animate the production of hip hop culture.[54]

If hip hop is preeminently a generational discourse, it is also a historically specific formation that articulates with the shifting contours of the late twentieth century. The dominant themes expressed in hip hop develop their creative shape in relation to a social world in which new forms and sites of political antagonism proliferate. Romanticized descriptions of hip hop portray its emergence as an explicit reaction against the racially conservative policies of the Reagan presidency. However, the seeds of this movement were planted much earlier. The elaboration of hip hop preceded the Reagan years; in fact, the movement began to blossom in the mid- to late 1970s.[55] The creators of hip hop devoted immense energy to carving out spaces of pleasure and recreation in the face of an eroding urban infrastructure devastated by a diminishing tax base, decaying public schools and parks, drugs, and political retreat from the redistributive policies born from the civil rights era.[56] Hip hop began in public parks, on street corners, in subway terminals, and in apartment basements. It soon moved to community centers, dance clubs, radio airwaves, and later the visual media—music video, television, and cinema—thus accentuating what analysts claim is one of the central themes in the movement: the struggle over public space, who occupies it, and how its resources are put to use.

Yet it is the subsequent role of technology and the commodification of hip hop, more than anything else, that continues to drive and animate provocative debates about the relationship between youth, cultural production, and commercial media culture. Does the intrusion of technology and commodification—most notably, the mass production, distribution, and merchandising of rap music—conspire to dull the oppositional edges of hip hop? Moreover, is the participation of black youth in the popular cultural economy a legitimate expression of opposition? These questions, of course, rekindle debates about the capacity of commercial culture to contain oppositional cultural practices. But rather than view technology and commercial culture as resources that prohibit creative action, I would like to invert this idea and consider an alternative proposition instead: How do technology and commercial culture enable new repertoires of black youth agency and cultural production?

The use of technology to produce media cultural products was viewed by the early critics of commercial culture as an indication that mass production would enforce standardization and stifle creativity.[57] But technological innovations in the production of popular music, for example, facilitate the opposite effect: creativity has flourished, and new musical styles and genres continue to thrive.[58] Yet technology only provides the possibility for new practices to take shape; individuals adopt a technology and use it in creative ways that lead to new cultural formations. In the case of rap music production, digital technology, sampling machines, multitrack recording devices, and video forge new creative frontiers for "fresh" innovations and formations of youth culture.[59] The innovation of rap music production suggests that technology does not manipulate individuals but rather that individuals adopt and manipulate technology to accommodate their intentions.

Furthermore, the intersection of hip hop and technology vividly illustrates what Michael Schudson calls the integrative effects of mass-mediated culture on modern societies.[60] The electronic dissemination of hip hop has proved to be powerfully integrative. By that, I mean it has established the conditions for mobilizing a youth culture that is rapidly becoming global in scope as it connects youth from disparate conditions and places. For example, it would be impossible to make reference to the "hip hop nation" without the broadcasting capabilities of media technology. One of the most impressive attributes of the electronic media is their capacity to connect people and organize collective identities despite physical distance.[61] The communications media enable new forms of access to and association among communities that transcend geographical boundaries. The growth and spread of hip hop culture are an illustrative example.

While its origins in the United States are typically traced back to the urban polyglot of postindustrial New York City, the hip hop movement has expanded far beyond the local youth cultures of its social and geographical base. The electronic dissemination of hip hop multiplies its constituency, complicates its articulations, and serves as the primary circuit through which youth have been able to produce an expanding sphere of influence within the rapidly evolving global media village. To be sure, the hip hop nation is an "imagined community."[62] But as Schudson points out, all communities are fictive in the sense that "personal identification with any grouping of people beyond those one encounters face to face in daily life depends on an imagined leap."[63] So while black youth in New York City, Mexican American youth in East Los Angeles, and black youth in Brixton, London, do not literally know each other, the various media technologies—music, video, film, print, and cyberspace—allow them to communicate, interact, and create new collective identities. In addition, it is the increasing prowess of media technology through which youth have been able to mobilize competing discourses about the varied social, economic, and political currents that continue to alter their lives. Hip hop, then, develops both local and global particularities that build a broad terrain for youth production and discourse.[64]

Whereas early critics of "mass" media culture viewed technology as stifling creativity and encouraging passivity, they were even less optimistic about the effects of commodification on culture. The diffusion of hip hop throughout the different spheres of commercial culture is commonly viewed as undermining the authenticity of this youth practice. For example, it is common to see the sartorial styles made popular in hip hop merchandised and packaged in suburban shopping malls. The contention, however, that commercial culture subverts the intentions and resistive qualities of hip hop is, at best, misguided. Tricia Rose insists that this critique obscures the fact that many of the original participants in hip hop (i.e., break dancers, rappers, disc jockeys) were in fact concerned with monetary compensation for their creative labor. Further, she makes the crucial point that "the contexts for creation in hip hop were never fully outside or in opposition to commodities, they involved struggles over public spaces and access to commodified materials, equipments, and products of economic viability."[65] Still, it must be acknowledged that, as the popularity and profits of hip hop soared, the rap industry has changed substantially. The major shift, according to Rose, is not that hip hop suddenly became commercial but rather that "control over the scope and direction of the profit making process"[66] has shifted from local black and Latino entrepreneurs to the major media and entertainment industries.

The corporatization of hip hop is undeniable. Since its popularization in the early 1980s, the profits of hip hop–related products have increased exponentially. As a result, the linkage of corporate strategies and marketing techniques with the expressive cultures of black youth undeniably alters the trajectory of hip hop. But the corporatization of hip hop reflects a more general trend toward the global spread of consumer culture made possible by new media technologies, marketing techniques, distribution patterns, and a wider conception of consumer markets as well as potential profits. It is indeed difficult to imagine any aspect of cultural life that has not been influenced by corporate culture.[67] In the case of hip hop, then, what has taken place is the joining of an urban street and youth aesthetic with the technological resources and distribution muscle of corporate organizations.

But the corporatization of hip hop seems only to enliven rather than to stifle the struggle to control its commercial vigor. Similar to other subcultural practices, hip hop creates its own symbolic universe and commodities. Furthermore, hip hop has made more explicit the political nature of popular culture. When emergent cultural practices disrupt the social equilibrium, they usually provoke the dominant culture to take some kind of action as a means of maintaining order.[68] Dick Hebdige argues that the process of recuperation typically comes in the form of co-optation and commodification or labeling. I would like to discuss the former.

The commodification of rap produces paradoxical results. For instance, recognition by the music industry—the Grammy and American Music Awards—validates its place as an "official" genre of popular music and therefore stimulates production. But commodification also domesticates and defuses rap of some of its subversive energy. Once distributed on a mass scale, rap is packaged and made more palatable, rendered at once a consumable good and profitable merchandise. But is commodification simply a form of containment? In other words, does the packaging of hip hop erode its oppositional possibilities? While it is true that the transformation of hip hop into a vast assortment of commodities alters its course, it is presumptuous to view commodification as the utter erasure of black youth agency and cultural politics. For as Hebdige points out:

[T]he relationship between the spectacular subculture and the various industries which service and exploit it is notoriously ambiguous. After all, such a subculture is concerned first and foremost with consumption. ... It communicates through commodities even if the meanings attached to those commodities are purposefully distorted or overthrown. It is therefore difficult in this case to maintain any absolute distinction between commercial exploitation on the one hand and creativity/originality on the other, even though these categories are emphatically opposed in the value systems of most subcultures.[69]

It would be a mistake to assume that black youth have been idle in, or even resistant to, efforts to merchandise hip hop. For as historian Robin D.G. Kelley reminds us, black youth meticulously hone their expressive cultures and forms of play and leisure into income-generating practices.[70] Few today understand the exuberant and sometimes subtle ways in which black youth maneuver to exploit a cultural marketplace that generates a seemingly endless flow of commodities produced to satisfy changing consumer desires and tastes. One of the most striking ironies of late twentieth-century capitalism is the simultaneous structural and economic displacement of black youth along with the emergence of a voracious appetite for the cultural performances and products created by them. In the process, some black youth have been able to translate their creative labor into social and economic mobility as they carve out small entrepreneurial enclaves while still practicing, in their unique way, "small acts" of opposition.

Dipannita Basu sharply illuminates this point in her observation of Los Angeles's hip hop community.[71] Basu asserts that participation in commercial culture by black youth is *not* a sign of surrender to the recuperative powers of capitalism but is instead a crucial element in their attempt to counter some of its most crippling effects. In fact, many youth do not view association with the popular culture industry as a form of "selling out." In her discussion of the burgeoning rap industry in Los Angeles, Basu writes: "[R]ap music has given a substantial number of black youth a world view, a political philosophy, a language, and lifestyles that have in turn become the articulating principles for economic activity, from creativity to business, from music to films, magazines, clothing, and a whole host of auxiliary position."[72]

Admittedly, it is difficult to imagine that striving for and achieving economic success in a capitalist society are oppositional. Such practices are typically viewed as complying with rather than subverting the dominant priorities of capital accumulation. But as Basu claims, black youth do not see a contradiction in their efforts to "get paid" and simultaneously contest the institutional practices that severely limit their prospects for social and economic mobility. No action or gesture is inherently oppositional. Social context determines the extent to which practices develop oppositional characteristics. The potential economic benefits and prestige associated with rap music production are viewed as a direct challenge to a social and economic structure that is becoming increasingly impenetrable for a number of black youth. From the perspectives of black youth, then, the production of popular commodities and economic success belie the widespread belief that they are criminal-minded and lack industriousness, intelligence, and a commitment to work.[73] So even though black youth turn their symbolic practices and creative skills into work that reproduces the master ideal of capital accumulation (a principle that historically works to their disadvantage), it is work that enables some to escape the serial employment and menial labor widely regarded as humiliating, stigmatizing, and oppressive.[74]

Angela McRobbie has described youth subcultures as practices that are both productive and empowering. According to McRobbie, the styles and commodities created by youth do more than just publicize subcultures. These practices also provide opportunity for cultivating skills that can be utilized to provide access to substantive employment or even self-employment. She writes: "[T]his involvement can be an empowering experience, particularly for young people with no access to the skills and qualifications acquired as a matter of course by those other young people destined for university and for the professions. Subcultures are often ways of creating job opportunities as more traditional careers disappear. In this undocumented, unrecorded and largely 'hidden economy' sector, subcultures stand at one end of the culture industry spectrum and the glamorous world of the star system and the entertainment business at the other."[75] To the degree that hip hop has produced an alternative economy that provides the resources and opportunities for black youth to exert their own creative energies and also realize their entrepreneurial ambitions, it can be viewed as a formation that enlivens rather than subverts the ability of youth to more effectively negotiate social and economic deprivation.

Consequently, rather than challenge the legitimacy of capitalism, black youth confront a more immediate problem—how to turn the contradictory contours of capitalism to their advantage. The strategic movement of black youth into commercial culture does not intend to destroy a flourishing information and entertainment economy. On the contrary, their skillful interventions drive the production and commodification of cultural products. Still, while it is true that they do not seek to subvert the notion of capital accumulation, black youth do seek to play a more substantial role in the rapidly expanding frontier of communications media and information technology. Describing this distinctive generational ethos, journalist Kevin Powell writes: "[T]he hip hop nation is no different than any other segment of this society in its desire to live the American dream. Hip hop, for better or for worse, has been this generation's most prominent means for making good on the long promises of the civil rights movement."[76] Black youth maneuver to exploit those emergent spaces that are opening up in the new information economy. And in the process of struggling for that space, black youth continue to shape the popular cultural world in which we all live.

It should also be noted that while some hip hop purists claim that commodification erodes the subversive demeanor and style of hip hop, the youth culture did not develop explicitly political expressions until after the road to commercial success had been paved. In truth, the earliest rap recordings were mostly first-person narratives that boasted about the acquisition of status-conferring objects: jewelry, designer clothing, and women. And though narratives that portrayed women as sources of heterosexual male pleasure were certainly political, they did not embody the counterideological themes that would later be labeled "message rap."[77] The production of message rap developed as the rap genre was becoming commercial. Indeed, the arrival of rap groups like Public Enemy in the late 1980s signaled a decisive turn in the politicization of rap lyrics. Thus, it is quite possible to argue that by enlarging the creative terrain of rap production, commodification, ironically, forged open spaces that now include styles and performances that nourish rather than impoverish resistive discourses.

Yet we must also bear in mind that black youth are operating on historical terrain clearly not of their own making. Moreover, the sphere of popular media culture is only one of numerous sites where the struggle for hegemony is waged. Additionally, the transformative powers of each site differ. For example, the symbolic efficacy of holding a political office (Newt Gingrich) versus occupying a niche in the arena of popular music production (Ice Cube) differs in kind and extent. Therefore, it must be acknowledged that the potency of black youth intervention on the field of popular culture has serious limitations for effecting social change. Still, it must also be noted that oppositional practices come in different guises and are governed by different intentions. Black youth are acutely aware of the social world they inhabit and that current structural arrangements produce limited opportunities for their generation. This particular formation of black youth culture is, then, a strategic attempt to make use of the fissures produced by social, economic, and technological change.

So while it is true that hip hop did not originate as an explicit critique of the rising tide of racial conservatism, its growth, evolution, and multiple deployments illustrate how the cultural politics, moods, energies, and lived experiences of everyday life provide black youth with the resources and imaginative capacities to respond creatively to material and symbolic domination. The evolution of hip hop teaches us, as cultural critic Michael Dyson writes, "that history is made in unexpected ways, by unexpected people with unexpected results."[78] As youth continue to re-create hip hop, they also continue to penetrate and shape the popular media cultures, which are becoming global in scope. In fact, hip hop has generated a broad range of cultural products that enlarge its creative community and sphere of influence. The diffusion of hip hop throughout mainstream culture has led to the creation of new independent record labels, magazines, television programs, and advertising campaigns.[79] More important, the success and spread of hip hop culture have forged open productive spaces for young cultural producers beyond the field of popular music.

Like their contemporaries in the production of rap music, black filmmakers attempt to exercise similar modes of agency and intervention in the intensely mobile world of information technology. Whereas the producers of rap attempt to manipulate the new technologies and distribution systems that govern popular music production, filmmakers, in like fashion, attempt to manipulate the new technologies and distribution systems that govern popular film production. But because commercial film is a more expensive arena of production, breaking through industry barriers is a far more formidable task. Besides, the commercial film industry is extremely insular, and practices of nepotism and cronyism are customary. The producers of commercial film tend to constitute a closed inner circle whose members are constantly recycled within the industry. Commercial film is a profession that requires specialized training, large sums of capital, and expensive equipment. Discussing the costs involved in film production, Robert Withers writes:

> Perhaps only architecture can begin to rival it in the amount of capital required for production, and in the potential demand for laborers. The high cost of filmmaking has always placed limitations on the kind of work filmmakers could do, and the financial risk involved has consistently affected the relationship between producers and audiences.... Because of its high cost, film production is generally controlled or influenced by those powers in a society that command financial resources and determine how products are distributed.[80]

It is perhaps the high cost of film production that, historically, has limited the effective participation of African American filmmakers. However, for a select group of African American filmmakers, the transformation of the popular cultural landscape and the popularization of black youth expressive cultures changed the prospects for their own filmmaking careers.

Also, the production of black cinema is driven by the constant search for new consumer markets and expressive cultures to exploit. Historically conditioned opportunities in the production of popular film create productive spaces for the post–civil rights generation of African Americans that did not exist for previous generations. This is not to suggest that African Americans have never participated in the production of film but rather that the combination of a new film industry landscape, a changing cultural marketplace, and a more vibrant black culture industry establishes a creative environment in which the film narratives created by African American filmmakers attain greater commercial value. These particular arrangements work to give a small group of African American filmmakers a precarious niche along the production hierarchy of commercial film.[81]

The creation of popular cultural movements like hip hop suggests that black youth struggle to mobilize their own meanings about and representations of societal change. George Lipsitz argues that the emergence of new cultural producers and popular movements is made possible by the very economic shifts that also produce historically distinct forms of social and economic inequality: flexible accumulation.[82] It is crucial to point out, however, that the new formations in capitalism and the global spread of communications media do not intentionally produce new popular movements or expressive cultures. Rather, the new economic regimes, media technologies, and popular culture economy provide the resources and opportunities that make it possible for new symbolic practices to be created by historically situated cultural producers. The immediate challenge, then, is to further examine how the new mediascape enables black youth to creatively intervene in the making of the larger popular cultural universe.

Notes

1. Kelley (1997, 224).
2. Herman Gray (1995) contends that commercial media culture is a primary site for producing discourses about and representations of blackness.
3. See Brain's (1994) theoretical discussion of the relationship between the production of symbolic artifacts and the reproduction of social relations and social-political hierarchies.
4. Hall (1981b) discusses the theoretical tension between these two positions.
5. Hall (1992, 24).
6. Gray (1995, 2).
7. Hall and Jacques (1990, 17).
8. This is a quote from a popular rap song by the Goodie Mob (1995).
9. For some good examples of this genre of scholarship, see Hebdige (1979). Willis (1977), Frith (1981), Lipsitz (1990), Gilroy (1993), Gray (1995), Rose (1994b), McRobbie (1991), and Boyd (1997).
10. Kelley (1994b, 11).
11. See Griswold (1994).
12. Swidler (1986).
13. For a more elaborate discussion of what Raymond Williams refers to as dominant, emergent, and residual forms of culture, see Williams (1977).
14. For a more elaborate critique of the dominant ideology thesis, see Abercrombie et al. (1980).
15. For an example of this view, see Wilson (1987).
16. For a succinct, yet informative, discussion of the transformation of urban life and the construction of postindustrial cities, see Katz (1989, 124–84).
17. Schor (1991, 39–41).
18. For engaging explorations on the schooling of black and poor Americans, see Kozol (1991). Kirschenman and Neckerman (1991) discuss the discriminatory hiring practices of employers against black youth. Anderson (1980) also addresses the racially inflected tensions black youth face on the job site. For a discussion of the self-esteem and confidence of poor black youth, see Nightingale (1993).
19. The Center for the Study of Social Policy (1992) reports that the United States has a greater percentage of its youth living in poverty than other advanced capitalist nations.
20. M. Davis (1992, 306).
21. Center for the Study of Social Policy (1992) and Lerner (1995).
22. Edsall and Edsall (1992).
23. Wattenberg (1995).
24. For a full discussion of the three phases, see Gans (1995).
25. A variety of symbol handlers and cultural producers have played a role in the making of the "underclass" label. While the work of social scientists and politicians has been important, the news-reporting conventions and visual strategies employed by the national news media played a crucial role in the broad circulation and use of the label. In 1977, *Time* magazine ran a cover-story feature on the "underclass." The photos accompanying the story focused primarily on black and Latino poor inner-city residents. Also, in 1978, ABC News produced a prime-time news-story feature that focused on dislocated youth and the escalation of juvenile delinquency. The feature was titled "Youth Terror: The View Behind the Gun." Moreover, what is interesting about this news piece is that it is unnarrated. The producers of the program elected to create a documentary-style news report that certainly appealed to viewers as an authentic representation of black and Latino youth dislocation. In the late 1980s, CBS News produced the feature "The Vanishing Black Family," which also visualized the "underclass" for television viewers. To be sure, black and Latino youth have been central in the creation and visualization of the label. For analysis of the formation and politics of the label, see Katz (1991 and 1989), Gans (1995), and Lemann (1991).
26. The culture-of-poverty position essentially argues that the poor suffer not from structural and economic problems but rather from cultural deficiencies. The emphasis from this perspective is on family history, lifestyles, and the behavior of the poor. The term itself was born from the work of anthropologist Oscar Lewis (1968), who coined it to describe the rural poor in Mexico. The concepts behind the term, however, have been fashioned to discuss and explain the poor in the United States. Whereas Lewis developed the term to discuss how the poor adapt to impoverished conditions in ways that tend to facilitate the reproduction of poverty, the manner in which conservatives have claimed and defined the culture-of-poverty discourse seems to blame impoverished conditions on the culture and behavior of the poor. For a critique of the term, see, for example, Katz (1989 and 1991), Wilson (1987), and Steinberg (1981).
27. For a full discussion of the public arenas model, see Hilgartner and Bosk (1988).
28. Gordon (1994, 125–26).
29. Katz writes, "[T]he term underclass offers a convenient metaphor for use in commentaries on inner-city crises because it evokes three widely shared perceptions: novelty, complexity, and danger. Conditions

within inner cities are unprecedented; they cannot be reduced to a single factor; and they menace the rest of us. The idea of the underclass is a metaphor for the social transformation embedded in these perceptions" (1991, 3).

30. To be sure, the specific manner in which the news media work to suppress their ideological dimensions in the selection, organization, packaging, and presentation of news is also crucial. For example, Campbell (1991) stresses that TV news stories operate as "narratives" that follow familiar boundaries of plot, character, setting, problem, resolution, and synthesis. Tuchman (1979) and the Glasgow University Media Group (1980) focus on how filmic conventions tend to legitimate news's claims of representational facticity. Hall (1981a) argues that television news conceals its ideological operations by offering itself as authentic visual transcriptions of the "real world."

31. Campbell and Reeves (1994, 38).

32. For studies of how the news media construct images and definitions of race, see, for example, Hartman and Husband (1981), Dijk (1987), Entman (1990 and 1994), and Jacobs (1996). The growing body of literature suggests that the news media typically address issues of racial conflict and protest rather than racism.

33. For a discussion of the function of the news media, see Gans (1979, 290–99).

34. Ericson, Baranek, and Chan (1987) examine how the news media produce images and definitions of deviance.

35. TV news can be viewed as a form of popular culture due, primarily, to its role in TV entertainment and the formulaic conventions that news workers employ. During the last few decades, many of the local news media affiliates have adopted a strategy referred to by some critics as "If it bleeds, it leads." This is a reference to the fact that producers of television news often shape the content and form of broadcast news in ways that can compete for higher ratings and higher revenue. In particular, television news stories are increasingly accompanied by graphic images and horrific descriptions of murders, acts of terrorism, and plane crashes.

36. In his discussion of the media's discovery of the mods and rockers, Cohen (1972) defines a moral panic as follows:

> Societies appear to be subject, every now and then, to periods of moral panic. A condition, episode, person, or group of persons emerges to become defined as a threat to societal values and interests; its nature is presented in a stylized and stereotypical fashion by the mass media ... and other right-thinking people.... Socially accredited experts pronounce their diagnoses and solutions; ways of coping are evolved or (more often) resorted to; the condition ... deteriorates and becomes more visible. Sometimes the object of the panic is quite novel and at other times it is something which has been in existence long enough, but suddenly appears in the limelight. Sometimes the panic is passed over and forgotten, except in folklore and collective memory; at other times it has more serious and long-lasting repercussions and might produce such changes as those in legal and social policy or even in the way society conceives itself. (p. 28)

37. For a more detailed analysis, see Campbell and Reeves (1994).

38. Clandestine footage usually involves a TV camera crew's following a drug bust, or drug raid, into someone's place of residence.

39. Reeves and Campbell (1994) argue that the (re)writing of the cocaine narrative follows a journalistic rite of inclusion/exclusion. The authors write: "[R]ites of inclusion are not centrally about Us versus a marginal Them, but, instead, are devoted generally to the edification and internal discipline of those who are within the fold. Rites of inclusion are, in other words, stories about Us: about what it means to be Us; about what it means to stray away from Us ... about what it means to be welcomed back to Us" (p. 39). Alternatively, rites of exclusion "are preoccupied with sustaining the central tenets of the existing moral order against threats from the margins. News reports that operate in this domain emphasize the reporter's role of maintaining the horizons of common sense by distinguishing between the threatened realm of Us and the threatening realm of Them" (pp. 41–42).

40. See Gordon (1994).

41. Various local ordinances in cities like Los Angeles; Dallas and Austin, Texas; Minneapolis; and New Orleans have been established to exercise greater control over youth. The enforcement of dress codes is a direct attempt to discipline the body. For example, in Irving, Texas, a suburb of Dallas, a large mall recently prohibited the wearing of baseball caps backward, baggy pants, or other "gang" paraphernalia. Many cities have also turned to nightly curfews that generally target black and Latino youth. See M. Davis (1992) for a discussion of how curfews are arbitrarily enforced in Los Angeles.

42. I use the term *symbolic capital* in this instance similarly to Bourdieu (1990), who refers to the capacity of cultural creators to enforce meaning, label, and define our world. I should also note that the symbolic capital gained by a rapper like Ice Cube in the commercial culture arena works differently, for instance, than the symbolic capital gained by a political figure like Newt Gingrich in the arena of legislative poli-

tics. Both are cultural producers. Both also attempt to pattern discourses about urban ghetto life. However, their efforts to shape the symbolic landscape take place on different terrain. More important, there is a differential in the kind and extent of power each terrain provides.

43. Rose (1994, 60).

44. Fischer contends that the study of technology and society can be broadly divided into two areas: technological determinism and symptomatic approaches. For a complete discussion of these two approaches, see Fischer (1992, 8–21).

45. Ibid., 17.

46. Ibid.

47. Indeed, the persistent call for regulating control over media content is driven by the belief that youth are especially impressionable and therefore vulnerable to media messages. Thus, the introduction of the V-chip is a more recent illustration of how prevalent technological determinism is in the larger public imagination.

48. Nightingale's (1993) study examines the experiences of black youth in Philadelphia.

49. For a more detailed discussion of the various alienation theories on black urban poverty, see Nightingale (1993).

50. Social movements come in different forms. Immediate examples of social movements include the civil rights movement, New Right conservatism, and feminism. Some representative work on social movements and social theory can be found in Morris's (1984) analysis of the civil rights movement and its relationship to the black church and political networks or the classic theoretical statement on the contexts and content of movements by Piven and Cloward (1979).

51. While hip hop is commonly associated with black American youth, the imprint, for example, of Caribbean musical forms on hip hop is clearly evident. Elsewhere, U.S. cultural critic Tricia Rose (1994b) and British cultural critics Isaac Julien and Paul Gilroy map out the African diasporic elements embedded in rap. See, for example, Gilroy (1993) and Julien's independent film feature *The Darker Side of Black* (1994). Julien discusses, for example, the similarities between gangsta rap in the United States and dance hall reggae in Jamaica (Grundmann 1995).

52. See Toop (1984), Guevara (1987), and Rose (1994b) for discussions of the formation of hip hop culture.

53. See Boyd (1997) for a more elaborate analysis of the class and generational dimensions of black popular culture forms.

54. See Guevara (1987) and Rose (1994b) for examples of this genre of scholarship. Also, Carby (1986) discusses the sexual politics of black women and the production of blues music.

55. For an interesting journalistic history of hip hop culture, see Owen (1994–95).

56. For discussions of the relationship between the transformation of urban life and the formation of hip hop culture, see, for example, Rose (1994b), Kelley (1994b), Cross (1994), and Boyd (1997). For an excellent discussion of the social and political retreat from racial equality, see Steinberg (1995).

57. The pessimistic viewpoints regarding the influence of electronically produced popular media cultures over capitalist societies were vehemently expressed by members of the Frankfurt school. For an example of this view, see Adorno and Horkheimer (1989). Also, for a history of the theories, ideas, and significance of the Frankfurt school approach, see Wiggershaus (1994). For an example of how the Frankfurt school influenced media studies, see Rosenberg and White (1957).

58. See, for example, Gendron (1987) and Kealy (1982).

59. See Rose (1992) for an informative discussion of the relationship between new music-recording technologies and rap music production.

60. Schudson (1994) considers how communications media technology establishes a context for societal integration and nation building.

61. See Meyrowitz (1985) for an intriguing analysis of how electronic forms of media transform social behavior and relations.

62. Anderson (1983) examines some of the factors crucial to how members imagine themselves to be part of a national culture.

63. Schudson (1994, 24).

64. I do not want to suggest that hip hop is expressed in a uniform fashion. For instance, rap varies sharply across regions, styles, subgenres, and gender. Nor do I want to suggest that there is a monolithic constituency operating within the hip hop community. Indeed, different subjective positions, ideas, and experiences are communicated through hip hop, thus creating a vastly diverse body of discourses and cultural practices. See Cross (1994) for a discussion of how hip develops locally specific features.

65. Rose (1994b, 40).

66. Ibid.

67. For example, the Internet, the Olympic Games, collegiate athletics, and national political party conventions have all been uniquely transformed as a result of their relationship to the corporate sphere. For a more complete discussion of the corporatization of culture, see Schiller (1989).

68. Williams (1977) discusses the relationship between what he calls hegemonic, residual, and emergent cultures. Williams argues that dominant, or hegemonic, cultures must always contend with emergent cultures that are constantly struggling to destabilize the hegemonic center.
69. Hebdige (1979, 94–95).
70. Kelley (1994a).
71. Basu's analysis (1997) is based on observational studies of how the rap music recording industry has created niches of entrepreneurship for black youth in Los Angeles.
72. Basu (1997). Greg Tate, a longtime observer and analyst of hip hop, contends that rap music is arguably the first black American expressive culture that African Americans have commercially exploited as much as, if not more than, whites.
73. For a candid discussion of white (and black) employer perceptions of black youth, see, for example, Kirschenman and Neckerman (1991).
74. See Anderson (1980) for an analysis of the disdain black youth developed toward menial labor.
75. McRobbie (1994, 161–62).
76. Powell (1996, 46) discusses hip hop culture as an avenue of social mobility for some black youth in the context of Death Row Record label, a successful producer of gangsta rap in particular.
77. For a discussion of the rise, vitality, and contradictions of message rap, see Allen (1996).
78. Dyson (1996, 77).
79. Take, for example, the rap entrepreneur Russell Simmons. Simmons started out as a rap performer but soon realized that his talents were best put to use on the business side of the hip hop industry. Using rap music as his core product, Simmons has created a multimillion-dollar entertainment company that features television sitcoms, cable television specials, and clothing merchandise (Hicks 1992). Simmons talks openly about the commercial viability of rap and the drive by many African Americans to exploit its commercial success (Marriott 1992).
80. Withers (1983, 8).
81. African American filmmakers who have achieved a notable degree of commercial success tend to be male graduates from prestigious film programs and business schools. For example, Spike Lee attended New York University film school, and John Singleton received several awards for writing while attending the University of Southern California filmic writing program. Reginald and Warrington Hudlin received their training from Harvard and Yale Universities, respectively. George Jackson, a successful producer of black films, graduated from Harvard Business School.
82. Lipsitz (1994) considers how changes in technology and the globalization of popular media cultures generate the possibility for aggrieved populations to engage in new forms of cultural production and resistance.

References

Abercrombie, Nicholas, et al. 1980. *The Dominant Ideology Thesis.* London: G. Allen & Unwin.

Adorno, Theodor W., and Max Horkheimer. 1989. *Dialectic of Enlightenment.* New York: Continuum.

Allen, Ernest. 1996. Making the Strong Survive: The Contours and Contradictions of Message Rap. In *Droppin' Science: Critical Essays on Rap Music and Hip Hop Culture*, edited by Eric Perkins. Philadelphia: Temple University Press.

Anderson, Benedict. 1983. *Imagined Communities: The Origins and Spread of Nationalism.* London: Verso.

Anderson, Elijah. 1980. Some Observations of Black Youth Employment. In *Youth Employment and Public Policy*, edited by Bernard E. Anderson and Isabel V. Sawhill, 64–87. Englewood Cliffs, N.J.: Prentice Hall.

Basu, Dipannita. 1997. The Economics of Rap Music: An Examination of the Opportunities and Resources of African Americans in the Business of Rap Music. Paper presented at the American Sociological Association Annual Meeting, Toronto, Ontario.

Boyd, Todd. 1997. *Am I Black Enough for You?: Popular Culture from the 'Hood and Beyond.* Bloomington: Indiana University Press.

Brain, D. 1994. Cultural Production as 'Society in the Making': Architecture as an Exemplar of the Social Construction of Cultural Artifacts. In *The Sociology of Culture: Emerging Theoretical Perspectives*, edited by Diana Crane. Cambridge, Mass.: Blackwell.

Campbell, Richard. 1991. *60 Minutes and the News: A Mythology for Middle America.* Urbana: University of Illinois Press.

Carby, Hazel. 1986. It Jus Be's Dat Way Sometime: The Sexual Politics of Women's Blues. *Radical America* 20, no 4: 9–22.

Center for the Study of Social Policy. 1992. *Kids Count: Data Book: State Profiles of Child Well-Being.* Washington, D.C.: Center for the Study of Social Policy.

Cohen, Stanley. 1972. *Folk Devils and Moral Panics: The Creation of the Mods and Rockers.* London: MacGibbon & Kee.

Cross, Brian. 1994. *It's Not about a Salary: Rap, Race, and Resistance in Los Angeles*. London: Verso.

Davis, Mike. 1992. *City of Quartz: Excavating the Future in Los Angeles*. New York: Vintage.

Dijk, Teun A. Van. 1987. *Communicating Racism*. Newbury Park, Calif.: Sage.

Dyson, Michael Eric. 1996. *Between God and Gangsta Rap: Bearing Witness to Black Culture*. New York: Oxford University Press.

Edsall, Thomas, with Mary Edsall. 1992. *Chain Reaction: The Impact of Race, Rights, and Taxes on American Politics*. New York: Norton.

Entman, Robert. 1990. Modern Racism and the Image of Blacks in Local Television News. *Critical Studies in Mass Communication* 7, no. 4 (December): 332–45.

———. 1994. Representation and Reality in the Portrayal of Blacks on Network Television News. *Journalism Quarterly* 71, no. 3 (autumn): 509–520.

Ericson, Richard V., Patricia M. Baranek, and Janet B.L. Chan. 1987. *Visualizing Deviance: A Study of News Organization*. Toronto: Toronto University Press.

Fischer, Claude. 1992. *America Calling: A Social History of the Telephone to 1940*. Berkley: University of California Press.

Frith, Simon. 1981. *Sound Effects: Youth, Leisure, and the Politics of Rock 'n' Roll*. New York: Pantheon Books.

Gans, Herbert J. 1979. *Deciding What's News: A Study of CBS Evening News, NBC Nightly News, Newsweek, and Time*. New York: Pantheon Books.

———. 1995. *The War against the Poor: The Underclass and Antipoverty Policy*. New York: Basic Books.

Gendron, B. 1987. Theodor Adorno Meets the Cadillacs. In *Studies in Entertainment*, edited by T. Modleski. Bloomington: University of Indiana Press.

Gilroy, Paul. 1993. *The Black Atlantic: Modernity and Double Consciousness*. Cambridge, Mass.: Harvard University Press.

Glasgow University Media Group. 1980. *More Bad News*. London: Routledge.

Gordon, Diana R. 1994. *The Return of the Dangerous Classes: Drug Prohibition and Policy Politics*. New York: Norton.

Gray, Herman. 1995. *Watching Race: Television and the Struggle for "Blackness."* Minneapolis: University of Minnesota Press.

Griswold, Wendy. 1994. *Cultures and Societies in a Changing World*. Thousand Oaks, Calif.: Pine Forge Press.

Grundmann, Roy. 1995. Black Nationhood and the Rest of the West: An Interview with Isaac Julien. *Cineaste* 21, no. 1–2 (winter-spring): 28–30.

Guevara, Nancy. 1987. Women Writin' Rappin' Breakin'. In *The Year Left 2: Essays on Race, Ethnicity, Class, and Gender*, edited by Mike Davis et al. New York: Verso.

Hall, Stuart. 1981a. The Determinations of News Photographs. In *The Manufacture of News: Social Problems, Deviance, and the Mass Media*, edited by Stanley Cohen and Jack Young. London: Constable.

———. 1981b. Notes on Deconstructing the Popular. In *People's History and Socialist Theory*, edited by Raphael Samuel. London: Routledge.

———. 1992. What Is This 'Black' in Black Popular Culture? In *Black Popular Culture*, edited by Gina Dent. Seattle: Bay Press.

Hall, Stuart, and Martin Jacques, eds. 1990. *New Times: The Changing Face of Politics in the 1990s*. London: Verso.

Hartman, Paul, and Charles Husband. 1981. The Mass Media and Racial Conflict. In *The Manufacture of News*, edited by Stanley Cohen and Jack Young. London: Constable.

Hebdige, Dick. 1979. *Subculture: The Meaning of Style*. London: Methuen.

Hicks, Jonathan. 1992. A Big Bet on the Godfather of Rap. *New York Times*, June 14, sec. 3, pp. 1, 6.

Hilgartner, Stephen, and Charles L. Bosk. 1988. The Rise and Fall of Social Problems: A Public Arenas Model. *American Journal of Sociology* 94, no. 1:53–78.

Jacobs, Ronald N. 1996. Civil Society and Crisis: Culture, Discourse, and the Rodney King Beating. *American Journal of Sociology* 101, no. 5:1238–1272.

Katz, Michael B. 1989. *The Undeserving Poor: From the War on Poverty to the War on Welfare*. New York: Pantheon Books.

———. 1991. *The "Underclass" Debate: Views from History*. Princeton, N.J.: Princeton University Press.

Kealy, Edward R. 1982. Conventions and the Production of the Popular Music Aesthetic. *Journal of Popular Culture* 16, no. 2 (fall): 100–115.

Kelley, Robin D.G. 1994. *Race Rebels: Culture, Politics, and the Black Working Class*. New York: Free Press.

———. 1997. Playing for Keeps: Pleasure and Profit on the Postindustrial Playground. In *The House That Race Built: Black Americans, U.S. Terrain*, edited by Wahneema Lubiano. New York: Pantheon.

Kirschenman, Joleen, and Kathryn M. Neckerman. 1991. "We'd Love to Hire Them, but …": The Meaning of Race for Employers. In *The Urban Underclass*, edited by Christopher Jencks and Paul E. Peterson. Washington, D.C.: Brookings Institution.

Kozol, Jonathan. 1991. *Savage Inequalities: Children in America's Schools*. New York: Crown.

Lemann, Nicholas. 1991. *The Promised Land: The Great Black Migration and How It Changed America.* New York: Knopf.

Lewis, Oscar. 1968. The Culture of Poverty. In *On Understanding Poverty: Perspectives from the Social Sciences,* edited by D.P. Moynihan. New York: Basic Books.

Lipsitz, George. 1990. *Time Passages: Collective Memory and American Popular Culture.* Minneapolis: University of Minnesota Press.

———. 1994. *Dangerous Crossroads: Popular Music, Postmodernism, and the Poetics of Place.* London: Verso.

Marriott, Michael. 1992. Hip-Hop's Hostile Takeover: Rap Joins the Mainstream. *New York Times,* September 22, sec. 9, p. vi.

McRobbie, Angela. 1991. *Feminism and Youth Culture: From "Jackie" to "Just Seventeen."* Boston: Unwin Hyman.

———. 1994. *Postmodernism and Popular Culture.* New York: Routledge.

Meyrowitz, Joshua. 1985. *No Sense of Place: The Impact of Electronic Media on Social Behavior.* New York: Oxford University Press.

Morris, Aldon. 1984. *The Origins of the Civil Rights Movement: Black Communities Organizing for Change.* New York: Free Press.

Nightingale, Carl Husemoller. 1993. *On the Edge: A History of Poor Black Children and Their American Dreams.* New York: Basic Books.

Owen, Frank. 1994–95. Back in the Days. *Vibe* (December–January): 66–68.

Piven, Frances Fox, and Richard A. Cloward. 1979. *Poor People's Movements: Why They Succeed, How They Fall.* New York: Pantheon Books.

Powell, Kevin. 1996. Live from Death Row. *Vibe* (February): 44–50.

Reeves, Jimmie, and Richard Campbell. 1994. *Cracked Coverage: Television News, Reaganism, and the Journalistic Crusade against Cocaine Use.* Durham, N.C.: Duke University Press.

Rose, Tricia. 1992. Black Texts/Black Contexts. In *Black Popular Culture,* edited by Gina Dent. Seattle: Bay Press.

———. 1994a. Black Males and the Demonization of Rap Music. In *Black Male: Representations of Masculinity in Contemporary American Art,* edited by Thelma Golden. New York: Whitney Museum of American Art. Distributed by N.H. Abrams.

———. 1994b. *Black Noise: Rap Music and Black Culture in Contemporary America.* Hanover, N.H.: Wesleyan University Press.

Rosenberg, Bernard, and David Manning White, eds. 1957. *Mass Culture: The Popular Arts in America.* Glencoe, Ill.: Free Press.

Schiller, Herbert I. 1989. *Culture Inc.: The Corporate Takeover of Public Expression.* New York: Oxford University Press.

Schot, Juliet B. 1991. *The Overworked American: The Unexpected Decline of Leisure.* New York: Basic Books.

Schudson, Michael. 1994. Culture and the Integration of National Societies. In *The Sociology of Culture: Emergent Theoretical Perspectives,* edited by Diana Crane. Cambridge, Mass.: Blackwell.

Steinberg, Stephen. 1982. *The Ethnic Myth: Race, Ethnicity, and Class in America.* Boston: Beacon Press.

———. 1995. *Turning Back: The Retreat from Racial Justice in American Thought and Policy.* Boston: Beacon Press.

Swidler, Ann. 1986. Culture in Action: Symbols and Strategies. *American Sociological Review* 51: 273–286.

Toop, David. 1984. *The Rap Attack: African Hand Jive to New York Hip Hop.* Boston: South End Press.

Tuchman, Gaye. 1978. *Making News: A Study in the Construction of Reality.* New York: Free Press.

Wattenberg, Ben. 1995. *Values Matter Most: How Republicans or Democrats or a Third Party Can Win and Renew the American Way of Life.* New York: Free Press.

Wiggershaus, Rolf. 1994. *The Frankfurt School: Its History, Theories, and Political Significance,* translated by Michael Robertson. Cambridge, England: Polity Press.

Williams, Raymond. 1977. *Marxism and Literature.* New York: Oxford University Press.

Willis, Paul. 1977. *Learning to Labor: How Working Class Youth Get Working Class Jobs.* New York: Columbia University Press.

Wilson, William Julius. 1987. *The Truly Disadvantaged: The Inner City, the Underclass, and Social Policy.* Chicago: University of Chicago Press.

Withers, Robert S. 1983. *Introduction to Film.* New York: Barnes and Noble Books.

43

Homies in The 'Hood:

Rap's Commodification of Insubordination

Ted Swedenburg

Despite the much-heralded advances of multiculturalism in the U.S. academy, our discussions of radical, oppositional and/or postmodernist practices within the field of popular culture still tend to focus on white artists, whose practices are taken as paradigmatic of cultural resistance. The major studies of postmodern culture, while acknowledging the significance of the proliferation of "other" voices within popular culture (or the arts in general), too rarely *define* cultural insubordination on the basis of their practices. When "other" cultural forms of expression are considered, they all too often serve simply to confirm already established models of resistance and thereby function as further instances of the same.

A similar situation prevails in academic analyses and histories of pop music in the U.S. and the UK. According to the most influential studies, written chiefly by leftist white males, the great moments in the history of modern Anglo-American pop music are variously said to be: (1) the emergence of rock 'n' roll in the mid-1950s; (2) the Beatles-led "English invasion" of 1963–1964 and the subsequent growth of youth protest rock in the 1960s; (3) punk and post-punk in the late 1970s and early 1980s; (4) the "new authenticity" of the 1980s; (5) techno-dance music. The various figures who epitomize oppositional pop culture are: the Sex Pistols for Greil Marcus; the Talking Heads or the punks for Dick Hebdige; Bruce Springsteen for Lawrence Grossberg; the "deconstructivists" Public Image Ltd and the Gang of Four for Iain Chambers; high-tech dance-pop artists New Order and S'Express for Terry Bloomfield—all white, U.S. or UK, artists.[1] While the major academic rock critics usually acknowledge black musicians' essential contributions to pop and occasionally write sympathetic and informative accounts of black artists,[2] their tendency is still to treat black music as an *influence*, a source for white musicians to mine. Thus Elvis' greatness is said to stem from his creative and combustive fusion of black rhythm 'n' blues with hillbilly music; the Rolling Stones were fueled by the driving beats of Chuck Berry and Chicago blues; the genius of the English punk aesthetic is that it constituted a white "translation" of the black "ethnicity" manifested in reggae;[3] the Talking Heads' signal contribution is their imaginative amalgamation of funk and Afropop with the quirky sensibilities of new wave; and so on. What defines the great and progressive *breaks* in these narratives of postwar pop music are the moments when white artists tapped into the energy and innovation of black musical forms, harnessed them for commercial success, and "integrated" them into the white pop music arena.[4] In such accounts, it is almost as if white pop artists make "culture" out of black musicians' "nature."[5] The "home" turf from which these critics theorize oppositional culture, therefore, is a white cultural milieu. As Simon Frith observes, "what we're dealing with in cultural studies of popular music ... are academic not working-class fantasies ... [and] what's at stake in such writings are what it means to be male, to be white, to be middle-class."[6]

Although black musicians (usually "crossovers" like Jimi Hendrix or Michael Jackson) receive a measure of credit and critical attention in these accounts, it is the great white artists who ultimately epitomize the moments of breaks and innovation, who merit serious study, and whose practices provide the foundation for the dominant theoretical models of cultural resistance and creativity. Within the field of Cultural Studies, black musical forms and their relation to social insubordination remain seriously understudied. Despite the important recent work of black cultural critics like Nelson George, Paul Gilroy, Cornel West and Greg Tate (not to mention earlier studies of black music such as those of LeRoi Jones, Charles Keil and Ben Sidran)[7] the hegemonic narrative of rock's progressive moments has yet to be displaced. (Note that my focus here is on *academic* accounts of rap's place within pop music. There are some exceptional critics writing for the popular music press, particularly the *Village Voice* and *Spin*, who do highlight African-Americans' role in pop music; by contrast, writers for *Rolling Stone* tend to be more conservative, classicist, and whiteboy-rock-centric.)

Rap's recent domination of U.S. pop charts (from M.C. Hammer to NWA to P.M. Dawn to Kriss Kross), testimony of its growing "crossover" appeal, should be an occasion for progressive white academics to rethink our conceptions of our music-cultural "home." We need to begin asking the questions: what would pop music historical narratives and theories look like if one took figures like Little Richard, James Brown, Otis Redding, Aretha Franklin, Parliament-Funkadelic or Afrika Bambaataa as paradigmatic practitioners of cultural oppositionality, as artists whose aesthetic innovations and complex relations to social movements qualify them as central figures in the history of pop music? If Cultural Studies based its models of cultural resistance and creativity on the practices of such African-American artists rather than primarily on white ones, our narratives of contemporary pop music and conceptions of postmodernism might look considerably different. The long moment of rap, which shows no signs of dissipation (unlike punk, which peaked after two to three years), merits our close critical attention because its practices enact precisely such a reinscription of pop cultural history. Rap, moreover, is arguably *more* significant—politically and aesthetically—than punk, which is privileged by so many critics as the last significant radical movement in rock.[8] This is not to suggest simply replacing the old pop narrative with one based exclusively on African-American models of cultural resistance, but rather that we engage with rap's challenge in order to rethink and redefine our conception of our pop-culture "home."

I proceed by comparing the practices of rap to canonical treatments of rock or postmodernist oppositionality. Most of my examples are drawn from four strands of this ever-evolving and proliferating musical form: (1) the "hard" or "serious" nationalist rap of Public Enemy and Boogie Down Productions; (2) the playful cultural-nationalist rap of the Native Tongues Posse (Jungle Brothers, A Tribe Called Quest, De La Soul); (3) the "gangster rap" of Ice-T, NWA, and Ice Cube; and (4) women's rap (Queen Latifah, M.C. Lyte, Yo-Yo), which is complexly linked to the other trends.[9]

Funky Detournement

In *Lipstick Traces*, Greil Marcus tracks one of the sources of punk radicalism to the situationist practice of *détournement*, which involves "the theft of aesthetic artifacts from their contexts"—thereby negating their original value—and the diversion of those artifacts "into contexts of one's own devise." *Détournement*, Marcus writes, is "a politics of subversive quotation."[10] Rap, too, practices a kind of *détournement*—but with a vengeful difference. Ever since rap's early days—when DJs manipulated records on two turntables, shifting between them to cut up, scratch and extend the sounds embedded in their grooves—until today—when rap artists deploy *the* most advanced techniques of digital computer recording[11]—rap DJs have constructed the musical collages or "mixes," over which the MCs declaim their rhymes, out of prerecorded, or "détourned" sound.

Yet rappers do not "détourn" in exactly the same way as punks or situationists, for rap is not simply about the devaluation or negation of earlier artistic elements in order to reinvest them in a different context.[12] This is certainly *part* of rappers' strategy when they sample snippets of sound by established white rock stars—such as Lou Reed's "Walk on the Wild Side" (A Tribe Called Quest's "Can I Kick It"), Steve Miller's "Gangster of Love" (Geto Boys' horrifyingly misogynist rap of the same name), Led Zeppelin's "Kashmir" (Schooly D's "Signifying Rapper"). By placing such instantly recognizable rock riffs in the context of black music, rap artists "reinvest" them as black. They thereby assert African-Americans' familiarity with, and claim to, the segregated rock heritage, while proclaiming the largely unacknowledged debt of that heritage to the work of black musicians. (They also demonstrate a startling talent for uncovering and recycling riffs and hooks of rock music, simply because they sound so good.)[13] The practice of sampling white rock 'n' rollers, forcing "classic rock" into a "ghetto" environment, buttresses the claim of Public Enemy's leader Chuck D that rap *is* rock 'n' roll.[14] Challenging the prevailing rock 'n' roll narrative, rappers assert that James Brown's band or Parliament-Funkadelic may be the greatest ever rock bands in the world.

Something similar occurs when, in a lighter vein, everyday sounds from the mass media, such as themes from television shows, are sampled over rap's unmistakably hard and funky African-American beats. When the campy themes of "I Dream of Jeannie" or "The Munsters" are yanked out of their "natural" (white) environment and thrust into a seemingly foreign (black) context, what is performed is an act of theft and tribute that exposes the apartheid character of "our" mass media culture through mock integration.[15] Picture Rap Brown or Eldridge Cleaver showing up on reruns of "Leave it to Beaver," "Ozzie and Harriet," or "Father Knows Best" to disrupt those shows' rosy, "happy days" vision of U.S. culture, and you begin to understand the effect. When rap DJs raid hegemonic white culture they contest its seeming universal character; at the same time, by showing how "at home" they are in U.S. pop culture, rappers demonstrate how different that culture might look from a two-toned perspective. (Listen, for instance, to De La Soul's masterpiece, *Three Feet High and Rising*, replete with a game-show theme and samples from Liberace and Johnny Cash.) Rap exemplifies how African-Americans' historically subordinate position in North America, dating from the days of slavery, has afforded them a sensibility that Paul Gilroy calls "double vision"[16] and W.E.B. Du Bois has termed "double-consciousness"—a feeling of "twoness," of "always looking at one's self through the eyes of others."[17] This doubled way of seeing/knowing enables an incisive style of collage.

Master practitioners of "serious" rap like Public Enemy as well as "hard" gangster rappers like Ice-T, NWA (Niggers with Attitude), the Geto Boys, and Schooly D, frequently produce mixes so hard and slammin' that the listener cannot mentally pick apart their elements.[18] One simply *feels* the razor's edge of sound, produced by a tumultuous amalgam of dentist drills, Uzi blasts, squealing tires, boomin' bass, and video game bleeps. And what one apprehends through hardcore mixes, as tactile and auditory sensation, is the din of urban hell or (to cite Public Enemy) "the hour of chaos," "the edge of panic." Hard rap is "aural paranoia," in Costello and Wallace's felicitous formulation.[19] "Armageddon," Public Enemy shouts over the screech of air-raid sirens, "is in effect" ("Countdown to Armageddon"). These are "homeboys" conveying the dread atmosphere of a home community in dire crisis. Eardrum-shattering sounds straight from the deindustrialized home front, aural depictions of the underclass that, in Cornel West's words, "embodies a kind of walking nihilism of pervasive drug addiction, pervasive alcoholism, pervasive homicide, and an exponential rise in suicide."[20] It's a kind of soundscape version of the dystopian images purveyed in William Gibson's cyberpunk novels and sci-fi films like *The Terminator* or *Robocop*. But this bad future is *now*, as if the atom bomb or toxic catastrophe had hit the South Bronx or Compton. Hence the cataclysmic title of Public Enemy's latest release, *Apocalypse 91 ... The Enemy Strikes Black*. And if you're a white listener, you sense that the rage and anger emanating from this soundscape is aimed directly at *you*, something like the sensation produced by reading the crime novels of Chester Himes.[21]

Yet even as you are pummelled by the sonic booms of a state of emergency, you are also hit with the funkiest of dance music, due to rap's most fundamental element—the rhythm, the groove, the beat, supplied by Black R 'n' B, funk and soul. These prerecorded sounds, citations from virtually all eras and genres of postwar black popular music, are "détourned" not to *negate* their value but to pay *homage* to them. The energy, the creativity, the sheer *funkiness* of yesterday's and today's black artists is reemphasized, recast, learned and appreciated anew by a younger generation of listeners, whenever a few recognizable (or previously unknown) bars of these inimitable grooves appear in another context.[22]

A complex system of montage or pastiche which makes visible hidden or forgotten connections between apparently unrelated—because forcibly segregated—musical forms;[23] which cheerfully plunders the (white) icons and debris of the mass media, which creates an aura of calamity even as it compels the body to dance; which reanimates and celebrates an occulted cultural history, this is surely different *détournement*, more sophisticated, more urgent, than anything ever imagined by punk.

Deconstructive Authenticity

Rap also partakes of, while distinguishing itself from, another contemporary pop practice that we can loosely term deconstructivism. Deconstructivism, according to the critics, names the moment when punk and post-punk turned away from 1960s concerns for rock "authenticity," away from the desire for an organic relation between rockers and the youth community or "the street," and embraced a practice of exposing music as artifice, as a construction of sound and image. These artists hoped that by revealing pop music's elements, they would disrupt music's taken-for-grantedness and defamiliarize pop consumption patterns.[24] This formalist pop tendency, which stressed the constructed nature and exposed the seams of the musical product, as well as the subcultural identities associated with it, should sound familiar, since "deconstructivist" musicians and their music-magazine theorists were heavily influenced by poststructuralist and post-modernist theory. (In one celebrated instance, the successful "deconstructivist" group, Scritti Politti, even issued a single entitled "I'm in Love with Jacques Derrida.")

Rappers' "musical massacre" of prerecorded sounds (the term is Rakim's, of the group Eric B and Rakim)—the technique through which DJs compose the mix—qualifies them for membership in the pop "deconstructivist" camp. For rappers certainly blast open "the illusion of the stability and integrity of the popular song form," as Forest Pyle puts it.[25] But their project is not merely about formal innovation or exposing musical artifice. Rap actually *undoes* the favored oppositions of postmodernist thought which contrasts formal and moral radicalism, which opposes the artificial and the authentic. While engaging in cutting-edge formal innovation, rap artists equally articulate an ethico-political agenda that, according to Paul Gilroy, is both utopian and pragmatic.[26]

This ability to combine the aesthetic and the political is enabled by rap's connection to a community. While for post-1960s, post-punk musicians and their theorists, all "notions of community ... are outmoded"[27] (and presumably naïve and essentialist), rappers still adhere strongly to a notion of the community and relate to it as "organic intellectuals."[28] But theirs is not necessarily a simplistic vision, for they do not assume that this community is pre-given and exists "naturally" but realize that it must be constructed and created, against all odds, in the face of the threat of decimation. Rappers sustain their dialectical relation to their target audience, composed centrally (although not exclusively) of young urban blacks, through an inventive yet authentic use of street language, through the hard realism of their lyrical depiction of black urban experience, and through the razor-sharp mix that Public Enemy call the "loud sound pound to make the brothers proud" ("Terminator X to the Edge of Panic"). Thus rap harnesses avant-garde musical inventiveness to African-American oral forms of expression with a long and continuous tradition.[29]

It is particularly in collective rites of performance, such as live concerts, that the community is recreated and affirmed. In these rituals of pride and protest, where the music is heard in alternative, social modes of consumption, a "moral, even a political community" is defined, according to Paul Gilroy.[30] At a Public Enemy (PE) concert in Seattle in August 1990, nearly the entire audience rapped along with the group, an amazing spectacle of collective orality given the lengthy and complicated character of PE lyrics. Public Enemy broke after every four or five songs to give "speech seminars" on current social and political issues. Nearly half of the audience was white—typical of PE concerts and its audience. Among other things, white kids learned from PE leader Chuck D that the group's "pro-black" posture "doesn't mean anti-white," and they joined enthusiastically in collective fist-pumping as PE opened the song, "Don't Believe the Hype," with a Malcolm X sample: "Too black, too strong." Young whites, too, are addressed by PE—not as central to the collectivity, but decentered—set apart from, yet still part of, the ritual of protest.

Sellin' Out or Gettin' Paid?

But it is rappers' fundamental connection to a young black community—a community "imagined" yet real—that allows them to get paid without selling out. "Selling out," of course, was a major issue for 1960s protest rockers, and it remained an ethico-political concern for punks; post-punkers finessed the issue by abandoning any notion of loyalty to a community, since community, after all, was a fiction. But for rappers, getting paid—"so let's just pump the music up and count the money," Rakim intones on "Paid in Full"—means achieving their due, as artists and as representatives of a creative and oppressed community. The operative slogan for hard rappers in the 1990s appears to be "Black Is Beautiful, Money Is Powerful" (Jungle Brothers, on "Beads on a String"). These rappers are party to a long collective memory of forefathers (yes, the bias is male) who *did not* get paid, who received neither the financial success nor the critical acclaim they deserved. And according to Public Enemy, even when the likes of Wilson Pickett, Red Foxx and James Brown *did* make some money, the IRS ("International Rape System" according to PE) went after them: "The bigger the black get / the bigger the Feds want / A piece of that … booty" ("Who Stole the Soul"). So if rappers do earn a few "dead presidents" (Rakim's mocking term for dollar bills) for their labors, they're only getting their just rewards, and their success begins to rectify previous injustices. The efforts of rappers (particularly Chuck D) to network and to create black businesses (and jobs) in the 'hood (neighborhood) are also regarded as nationalist warrants for 'gettin' paid." For such reasons, hard rappers are rarely accused of selling out, since the successful rapper is seen as representing the community and its desires for recognition. "I get paid," chants Kool Moe Dee, "to rock the nation" ("I Go to Work").

"Conscious" rappers also aren't selling out because their strategy is to deploy the market to disseminate crucial political messages to the widest possible audience. "The revolution *will* be marketed," asserts Public Enemy producer Bill Stephney.[31] Like punks, rappers view crisis as "the best salesman";[32] like Malcolm McLaren, pop situationist and Svengali of the Sex Pistols, they're trying to make "cash from chaos."[33] They critique mass culture from within, in the belief that, as Chuck D puts it, "white American business will sell the sword to cut its own throat."[34] Rappers play on capital's insatiable demand for new, sensational, and different products, a need that is partially responsible for turning "otherness" and "ethnicity" into the latest hip commodities.[35] Yet many rappers (the hardcore, not Young MC or MC Hammer) manage to make commodities out of otherness without appearing to be co-opted. They avoid mainstreaming, in part because the novelty and thrill of hard rap stems from its up-yours, fuck y' all attitude.[36] Rappers' posture of menacing danger appears mysteriously cool and soulful to the white listener, while sending a chilly frisson down his/her spine; whereas for the young black, the cold scariness of rap (cf. the Geto Boys' "Mind Playing Tricks on Me") is merely realism. Therefore rap sells in both markets. And because a hostile attitude is marketable and commercially successful, rappers can retain control of the message and keep it undiluted.

And the message *is* dangerous, if continuing governmental and media attacks on rap are any measure. Million-selling rap artists still experience difficulty in gaining access to concert halls due to obstacles in obtaining insurance and media hysteria about violence ostensibly inherent in rap audiences; dance clubs are phasing out rap from coast to coast due to official harassment.[37] In August 1989, the FBI sent a "warning letter" to NWA's record company after its release of "Fuck tha Police." In the fall of 1990, it was reported that the Justice Department had issued an internal memorandum concerning seven rap artists (including NWA, Ice-T, Public Enemy, 2 Live Crew and Sir Mix-A-Lot) "whose music advocates violence against law enforcement officers."[38] And campaigns to censor rap, by criminalizing the performance of "obscene" lyrics, banning rap from public libraries, and making it illegal to sell to minors, are occurring in communities from coast to coast. Rap is not about dangerous attitude and posing simply for the sake of making a threat, the posture punk often seemed to adopt. The lyrics and the "loud sound pound" convey a real air of crisis, a vivid depiction of the mood of life in hellish circumstances. The brutal verisimilitude of rap's lyrics and sound, Costello and Wallace argue,[39] makes it more powerful, more incendiary than punk.

The marketing revolution is that no other popular musical genre is so overtly oppositional. What is remarkable is how well political rap *sells* (Public Enemy's *Fear of a Black Planet* sold one million copies in its first week of release, with virtually zero airplay). While rappers espouse no single, unitary political message, 1960s-style black nationalism, complete with samples from the speeches of Malcolm X and Louis Farrakhan, is hegemonic. Rappers deal critically with issues ranging from homelessness, police harassment, drug dealing, crack addiction, to gang-bangin'; more recently they have taken up child abuse (Ice-T, "The House") and date rape (A Tribe Called Quest, "The Infamous Date Rape"). There are raps variously promoting world peace, safe sex (using a "jimmy hat" or condom), female pride (Queen Latifah's "Ladies First"), and low-cholesterol vegetarian diets (A Tribe Called Quest, "Ham and Eggs"). And at their August 1990 Seattle concert, Public Enemy's Chuck D seized the time to attack U.S. military intervention in the Gulf—one of the first, isolated public expressions of opposition to be heard during that long fall and winter of super-patriotism. Ice-T, known chiefly as a "gangsta" rapper and emerging movie star (*New Jack City*), closed his *O.G. Original Gangster*, which was completed on 15 January 1991, with this remarkable spoken message:

> By now the war has probably started and a whole bunch of people have probably died out there in the desert over some bullshit.... I feel bad about all the brothers and sisters gettin' pulled right out of their neighborhoods, all the cities and small towns in America, to go over there and fight for the bullshit that most of them don't really have anything to do with.... I'd like to send this special shout out: fuck the police, fuck the FBI, fuck the DEA, fuck the CIA.... ("Ya Shoulda Killed Me Last Year")

Rap was one of the rare popular cultural arenas where anti-Gulf war sentiment was voiced.[40] Few U.S. popular artists, I would argue, have ever so successfully commodified such messages of insubordination.

Rappers are also intervening in the debate over multiculturalism and Eurocentric college curricula. Afrocentricity is a key platform for many 1990s rap artists and marks the increasing visibility of what has been dubbed "Nation-Conscious Rap."[41] Perhaps the foremost Afrocentric rap "text" is Public Enemy's *Fear of a Black Planet*, which attacks white European cultural hegemony and argues that if whites would only abandon Caucasian arrogance they could easily live in harmony with the world's majority non-white populations. Chuck D calls this the "Jackass Theory"—"Just Acting Caucasian Kills a Simple Solution."[42] Whites, Public Enemy argues, need to acknowledge that there is no such thing as pure white (or pure black, for that matter), that "white comes from black / No need to be confused" ("Fear of a Black Planet"). Due to the impact of such messages, "conscious" rappers like Chuck D, KRS-One of Boogie Down Productions, and Queen Latifah have emerged as important popularizers of Afrocentricity and are much in demand as speakers on college campuses where racism, multiculturalism and ethnic studies requirements are burning issues.

Crossing Over

As suggested above, hardcore and Afrocentric rappers enjoy a significant and enthusiastic white audience. In many areas, in fact, "hardcore" rap is heard more readily on community and college radio stations than on black commercial ones. There are a number of reasons why young whites are attracted to rap, among them a countercultural or political identification with "rebel music," as well as a desire to be on the cultural cutting edge by consuming rap's avant-garde hipness. For their part, many hardcore rappers see no contradiction between advocating a black nationalist agenda and forging cultural/political alliances with sympathetic whites, and so they actively work to build crossover audiences. Their citations of white rockers might be regarded as part of this strategy of alliance-building. Some rappers have even collaborated and/or toured with white rock musicians. A recent noteworthy joint effort is the amazing Public Enemy-Anthrax remake of Public Enemy's "Bring the Noise," on which whiteboy metal band Anthrax backs PE's Chuck D and Flavor Flav with grunge-adelic drums and guitars, and even raps a few verses. Public Enemy recently toured with Anthrax, while Ice-T is working and touring with *black* metal band Body Count.

Although some whites like the notorious "rap perpetrator" Vanilla Ice have profited by mainstreaming rap, the genre by-and-large remains remarkably impervious to such rip-offs. It was precisely because rap's image is so bound up with street credibility that Vanilla Ice was compelled to invent a phony autobiography in which he claimed to have spent a great deal of time with "brothers" in the 'hood, who taught him to rap. Perhaps audience knowledge of his inauthenticity explains the miserable commercial failures of the Ice-man's recent releases. But, on the other hand, white rappers like 3rd Bass, who learned their rhyming styles through an apprenticeship in the black streets, are judged to have mastered the genre and are respected as honest and creative practitioners.[43]

Other U.S. "minority" groups are also employing rap as message vehicle and expression of cultural pride. Hispanic participation in the hip-hop scene dates back to the late 1970s, when Puerto Ricans were active in creating the breakdance, graffiti and rap scene of the South Bronx.[44] But despite their long involvement in rap, barrio homeboys (but not homegirls) have only recently achieved wide visibility. Among today's high-profile Latino rappers are LA's Kid Frost, who drops rhymes in English and *Calo* (East LA southwestern Spanish) on his hit "La Raza" (from *Hispanic Raising Panic*), the supergroup Latin Alliance (featuring Puerto Ricans, Chicanos, Cubans, Spaniards and Nicaraguans), and Cypress Hill. If rap, as Paul Gilroy suggests, is part of a diasporic-transnational Atlantic (Africa, America, the Caribbean, Britain) culture,[45] barrio hip-hoppers are "hispanicizing" this malleable art form. They infuse it with Latin percussion, *cholo* (Chicano gangster) slang, mariachi horns, celebrations of lowriding, Santana guitar riffs, blasts against INS and police harassment ("Pigs," Cypress Hill), in the "high-tech Aztec" style of performance artist

Guillermo Gómez-Peña. Latino rappers assert and construct a distant pan-Latino diasporic cultural identity while acknowledging African connections (rapper Mellow Man Ace, who performs solo and with Latin Alliance, is Afro-Cuban) and creating possibilities for Afro-Latino linkages. Kid Frost even argues, based on early Puerto Rican involvement in hip-hop, that "Rap is not a black art form, rap is an urban art form."[46]

Rap is also being embraced by minority communities of Europe, where the term "black" has a rather different and expanded referent than in the U.S., often including South Asians and Middle Easterners. In Britain, female rappers (like Monie Love, the Cookie Crew, and the Wee Papa Girls) seem to occupy a more prominent position than do women in the U.S. hip-hop scene. And the rap messages of British blacks are usually less nationalist or hardcore than those of their U.S. counterparts. Rebel MC, for instance, who advocates a "black white unite" line, celebrates his biracial background—something virtually unthinkable for a U.S. rapper.

By 1989, rap had also taken hold among the young *franco-maghrébins* and *franco-africains* of the *banlieues*, the suburban French ghettos. These youths, marginalized by the educational and economic systems and still regarded as *immigrés* rather than settlers, are adapting African-American rap to their own purposes: to assert their cultural creativity; to protest against the socio-economic system (*"Ce monde est caca, pipi, cacapipi-taliste"*—C Solaar); to organize against drugs and black-on-black violence; and to promote self-education. *Rappeurs* and *rappeuses* affirm their connections to Africa (North as well as sub-Saharan) while inflecting colloquial French with inventive *franglais* and *verlan* (slang based on the reversal of syllables).[47] Elsewhere in Europe, one finds rappers like Leila K, the teenage daughter of Moroccan immigrants living in Sweden who delivers rhymes in proficient black street English and whose single, "Got to Get," recorded in Sweden, was a 1990 U.S. dance hit.

The Limits of Streetwise, Afrocentric Rap

Despite rappers' creativity and crossover appeal, there are a number of inherent limitations to its "hardcore" orientation. Sometimes, as in the "gangsta" releases of NWA or the Geto Boys, the high premium on hard "street reality" gives rise to ghetto visions that resemble blaxploitation films—rap as *Super Fly II*.[48] NWA's sensationalized street violence has sold so well that it has inspired a slew of Compton-style imitators, who seem to feed what Stuart Alan Clarke calls the U.S. political culture's "enormous appetite for images of black men misbehaving."[49] Gangsta rappers' concern to sound "real" leads, in some instances, to increasingly excessive and outrageous depictions of the street: in the case of the Geto Boys, something like *Shaft* meets *Nightmare on Elm Street*. Occasionally the "prophets of rage" (the title of a PE song) seem to be turning into the profits of rage, as some gangsta rhymers appear less concerned with fighting stereotypes than in selling them.

There are also qualifications one would want to make about rap's political positions. Hardcore, "conscious" rap generally espouses a 1960s-style nationalist vision of community, often inspired by black Islamic leaders like Louis Farrakhan and Elijah Muhammad, that can be inimical to cross-racial dialogue. Public Enemy and, more recently, Ice Cube champion the Farrakhan-led Nation of Islam, although they are not full-fledged members and tend to sample the Nation's ideology rather than preach it.[50] A number of prominent rappers, like Poor Righteous Teachers, Rakim, and Brand Nubian, belong to the Five Percent Nation, an Islamic sect which believes that the black man is God and that whites are genetically inferior white devils.[51] The Afrocentric group X-Clan (led by Professor X, son of New York City militant Sonny Carson) see whites as sun-deprived and culturally deficient "cave-boys." Political rappers spray Malcolm X soundbites throughout their mixes, but even those seeking out white audiences only sample the pre-Mecca Malcolm. Rap audiences never hear the Malcolm who, towards the end of his life, said of the white man, "If you attack him because he is white, you give him no out. He can't stop being white. We've got to give the man a chance."[52]

There is also the question of what it means when artists rise to prominence in the absence of an effective black political leadership able to reach urban black youth. Rappers' awareness of the fact that many young black homies will only listen to them has led many to stress a message of "positivity." According to PE's Chuck D, since the only blacks who achieve national prominence are athletes and musicians, "we've got a little bit more responsibility than the average white musician that comes along and just wants to talk about his dick."[53] But rappers' political importance can sometimes be grossly overestimated, as when they are compared in significance and theoretical sophistication to Malcolm X or the Black Panthers—and especially if the message stresses the development of black capitalism rather than "self-determination."

Another critical issue is hip-hop machismo. Nationalist rap tends to relegate women to second place, to supporting roles, and at best "respects" them as "mothers" and "queens" ("Black Woman," Jungle Brothers; "Revolutionary Generation," Public Enemy). While conscious rap encourages black youth to read African-American historians and theorists, the book lists it promotes are notable for the virtual invisibility of prominent black women writers like Angela Davis, Toni Morrison, or bell hooks.[54] Gangsta rap (NWA, Ice Cube, Geto Boys) lyrics meanwhile are pervaded by derogatory references to women as bitches, hoes (whores) and skeezers (gold-diggers). Well-publicized incidents such as the beating of rap TV show host Dee Barnes by Dr Dre of NWA and the arrests of PE's Flavor Flav for assaulting his girlfriend and failing to pay child support, as well as the artists' justifications ("Goddamn right I hit her, and I'd hit her again," said Flav[55]) have focused more attention on rap's "woman problem."

But in the last three years a powerful crew of female rappers like Queen Latifah, Monie Love, MC Lyte, Shazzy, Yo-Yo, and BWP (Bytches With Problems) have joined ranks with an earlier generation of women rappers (Salt 'n' Pepa, Roxanne Shanté) to confront such sexist attitudes and depictions. As Tricia Rose has shown, women rappers are challenging male dominance in the sexual arena, contesting men's hegemony as rap performers, and putting forward strong images of women. While many women rappers are uncomfortable with the label feminist—especially because they see feminism as an anti-male position which might cut them off from African-American men—their lyrical practices are explicitly pro-women.[56] Yet the nationalist ethos nonetheless imposes limits on how far some women rappers are willing to challenge male behavior, as exemplified by the position of Sister Souljah (part of the Public Enemy crew, and now a solo artist): "The white male power structure has made our men insane: how can we hold them responsible?"[57]

The Hip-Hop Nation's relation to the Queer Nation is less encouraging, for most rap espouses a brand of maleness that seems to root its authenticity on putdowns of gays. Public Enemy's negative assessment of homosexuality ("Man to man / I don't know if they can / From what I know / The parts don't fit," on "Meet the G that Killed Me") seems like a positively polite "dis" compared to rappers' usual rampant gay-bashing, in which the term faggot is employed as an everyday term of abuse. Hardcore, street-authentic rappers relentlessly push a form of masculinity that Marlon Riggs dubs black macho—a monolithic construction of a strong, unflinching man who is counterposed to the sissy/faggot.[58] While there are, as far as I know, *no* openly gay rappers, at least the playful image of groups like De La Soul (on their first release), PM Dawn, Dream Warriors, and Arrested Development offers audiences some alternative models to an otherwise unrelentingly tough and anti-gay vision of rap masculinity. But there are some cracks in the hardcore-homophobe edifice—witness Ice-T's recent positive rhymes: "She wanna be lez / He wanna be gay / Well I'm straight so nigga / Have it your way" ("Straight Up Nigga").[59]

Fightin' the Power

Despite such shortcomings, rap is a crucial political-cultural phenomenon that confounds many hegemonic notions about the nature of oppositional expressive culture. For hard rap manages to be on the musical cutting edge with its sophisticated "mangl[ing] of technology"[60] and simultaneously rooted in "authentic" traditional practices of orality. Rappers refuse to abandon their loyalty to a community, all the while maintaining a complicated conception of how communities are constructed and re-created. Rap practitioners assert an identity politics that often seems essentialist, separatist, and even supremacist, while simultaneously working effectively to forge new transracial identities and solidarities.[61] Hardcore homeboys and homegirls manipulate the market mechanisms to promulgate social change and communicate the dire atmosphere of urban emergency. Conscious rap advocates a strong sense of African-American history, yet understands how histories are created and are sites of struggle.

Rap, therefore, is a kind of a field in which mobile oppositional practices are possible. No single position is occupied for long, rather rappers shuttle between what are usually regarded as mutually exclusive positions. Thus they engage in complicated movements between essentialist and constructionist poles; they work within ideology while trying to transform it; they engage simultaneously in separatism and coalition-building; their sounds are avant-garde and mass cultural; they advocate Afrocentricity and hybridity.[62] And all the while they intervene in efforts to, as Public Enemy puts it, "Fight the powers that be."

In addition to enjoining us to recast our theories of oppositional culture, the rap attack also demands new narratives of pop culture history. Such histories must be reconceptualized, not as a linear, white-focused narrative, but as movements along multiple lines of influence, counter-influence, attraction and repulsion. At the minimum, this narrative must start from an assumption of the dominant and crucial contribution of African-Americans to contemporary popular music. Its heroes and central figures can no longer simply be white boys. Yet in keeping with the mobility and fluidity of the phenomena we are tracking, these narratives would key in on zones of syncretism, crossover, creative fusion, and inter-culturation.[63] We also need to concentrate our research on non-white subcultures and countercultures. Beats, hippies and punks cannot be our only models of opposition—we must investigate, for instance, b-boys and b-girls, hip-hoppers, gangsters, and their antecedents. Our new narratives must be two-toned, a manifestation of double consciousness.

Postscript: Rap and the LA Insurrection

In the rush to find anyone who could make sense of the events in South-Central Los Angeles of April and May 1992, the mainstream media, which usually maligns rap music, began to seek out rappers. Thus readers of mainstream newspapers were treated to an unprecedented spate of articles on rap, which pointedly refrained from criticizing rappers for advocating violence (and also eschewed censuring their sexism and homophobia—rap is virtually the only entertainment form excoriated for such sins) and instead respectfully analyzed rap lyrics—particularly LA rappers like NWA, Ice-T, and Ice Cube—which for years have been explaining and expressing the festering conditions and rage that prompted the insurrection.[64] Even President Bush got a crash course on the 'hood when he invited minority members of the White House staff to lunch. On being told about Ice Cube, George Herbert Walker Bush responded, with the usual Presidential perspicacity and syntax, "I know that rap is the music where it rhymes."

But soon it was back to race relations as usual in the USA, as both political parties hunted for 1992 Willie Hortons (in order to fend off the threat of H. Ross Perot) and found likely candidates in rap. Democratic Presidential candidate Bill Clinton (now President elect) tried to revive his flagging campaign with a well-publicized attack on "raptivist" Sister Souljah. Addressing the Jesse Jackson–led Rainbow Coalition, Clinton compared Sister Souljah's explanation of why LA black youths decided to kill whites—rather than each other—for a change, to the racism of neo-Nazi David Duke. His remarks were a blatant attempt to win conservative white votes by proving that he does not pander to "black racism." Meanwhile, Vice President Dan Quayle, also working to consolidate white support,[65] attacked Time-Warner because its subsidiary released an album by Ice-T's Body Count that includes the song "Cop Killer." "They are making money off a record," the family-values veep intoned, "that is suggesting it's OK to kill cops, and that is wrong." Ice-T explained that the song is the complaint of a homie "fed up with police brutality."[66] Meanwhile the Bloods and Crips' detailed program for rebuilding and redeveloping LA, which calls for replacing the welfare system with jobs, a massive rehabilitation of schools, and the incorporation of former gang members into a community-based police force, is being scandalously ignored.[67]

Notes

This article is based on a paper presented at the annual meetings of the American Anthropological Association, New Orleans, December 1990. A shout-out to Ewan Allinson, Angelika Bammer, Lata Mani, Fred Pfeil, Lousia Schein, Gregory Stephens, and Mike Woost for suggestions and criticisms.

1. G. Marcus, *Lipstick Traces: A Secret History of the Twentieth Century*, Harvard University Press, Cambridge 1989; D. Hebdige, *Hiding in the Light*, Routledge, London 1988, pp. 233–44, and *Subcultures*, Methuen, London 1979; L. Grossberg, "Putting the Pop Back into Postmodernism" in A. Ross (ed.), *Universal Abandon? The Politics of Postmodernism*, University of Minnesota Press, Minneapolis 1988, pp. 167–90; I. Chambers, *Urban Rhythms*, Macmillan, Basingstoke 1985; T. Bloomfield, "It's Sooner Than You Think, or Where Are We in the History of Rock Music?" *New Left Review*, no. 190, 1991, pp. 59–81.
2. For instance D. Hebdige's *Cut 'n' Mix: Culture, Identity and Caribbean Music*, Methuen, London 1987 and G. Marcus' chapter on Sly Stone in *Mystery Train*, E. P. Dutton, New York 1976, pp. 75–111. Hebdige's *Subcultures* and *Hiding in the Light, op. cit.*, are better known, easier to obtain, and more frequently cited than *Cut 'n' Mix*.
3. Hebdige, *Subcultures, op. cit.*, p. 64.
4. P. B. Harper, "Synesthesia, "Crossover," and Blacks in Popular Music," *Social Text*, no. 23, 1989, p. 118.
5. I owe this insight to Lata Mani. See her "Cultural Theory, Colonial Texts: Reading Eyewitness Accounts of Widow Burning," in L. Grossberg *et al.* (eds.), *Cultural Studies*, Routledge, New York 1992, p. 393.
6. S. Frith, "The Cultural Study of Popular Music" in L. Grossberg *et al.* (eds.), *Cultural Studies, op. cit.*, p. 180.
7. See N. George, *The Death of Rhythm & Blues*, E. P. Dutton, New York 1989; P. Gilroy, *There Ain't No Black in the Union Jack*, Hutchinson, London 1987; "One Nation under a Groove: The Cultural Politics of 'Race' and Racism in Britain" in D.T. Goldberg (ed.), *Anatomy of Racism*, University of Minnesota Press, Minneapolis 1990, pp. 263–82; "It Ain't Where You're From, It's Where You're At … The Dialectics of Diasporic Identification," *Third Text*, no. 13, 1991, pp. 3–16; C. West, "On Afro-American Popular Music: From Bebop to Rap," in *Prophetic Fragments*, William B. Eerdmans/Trenton: Africa World Press, Grand Rapids 1988, pp. 177–87; "Postmodernism and Black America," *Zeta Magazine* vol. 1, no. 6, 1988, pp. 27–29; "Black Culture and Postmodernism," in B. Kruger and P. Mariani (eds.), *Remaking History*, Bay Press, Seattle 1989, pp. 87–96; G. Tate's regular columns in the *Village Voice* some of which have now been collected in his *Flyboy in the Buttermilk*, Simon and Schuster, New York 1992; L. Jones, *Blues People*, Quill, New York 1963; C. Keil, *Urban Blues*, University of Chicago Press, Chicago 1966; B. Sidran, *Black Talk*, Da Capo Press, New York 1981 (1971).
8. For instance, Marcus, *Lipstick Traces, op. cit.* See also J. Savage's 600-page *England's Dreaming*, Faber and Faber, London 1991.
9. Gilroy ("It Ain't Where You're From," *op. cit.*, p. 7) discusses the first three strands of rap but does not deal with women rappers.
10. Marcus, *Lipstick Traces, op. cit.*, pp. 168, 170; see also K. Knab (ed. and trans.), *Situationist International Anthology*, Bureau of Public Secrets, Berkeley 1981, pp. 8–14, 55–56.
11. See D. Sanjek, "'Don't Have to DJ No More.' Sampling and the 'Autonomous' Creator," MS, 1991.
12. Knab, *op. cit.*, p. 55.
13. Personal communication from Ewan Allinson.

14. Quoted in M. Dery, "Public Enemy Confrontation," *Keyboard*, vol. 16, no. 9, 1990, p. 96.
15. M. Costello and D.F. Wallace, *Signifying Rappers*, The Ecco Press, New York, 1990, p. 67.
16. Gilroy, "One Nation Under a Groove," *op. cit.*, p. 280.
17. W.E.B. Du Bois, *The Souls of Black Folk*, New American Library, New York 1969 (1903), p. 45.
18. Costello and Wallace, *op. cit.*, p. 25.
19. *Ibid.*, p. 25.
20. A. Stephenson, "Interview with Cornel West," in A. Ross (ed.), *Universal Abandon? The Politics of Post-modernism*, University of Minnesota Press, Minneapolis 1989, p. 276.
21. This observation is courtesy of James Knippling. On rap's relation to urbanism, see E. Allinson, "'War on 33$^1/_3$': Hearing Hip-Hop Through Pragmatism," paper presented at the Mid-Atlantic American Culture/Popular Culture Association conference, Buffalo, November 1991.
22. Other black musical genres, not (immediately) associated with dance grooves, are also being incorporated by some rappers; for instance, Arrested Development's reinscription of gospel and blues, and Gang Starr's incorporation of jazz.
23. See M. Taussig, *Shamanism, Colonialism, and the Wild Man*, University of Chicago Press, Chicago 1987, p. 369.
24. S. Frith, "Frankie Said" in Alan Tomlinson (ed.), *Consumption, Identity, and Style*, Routledge, London 1990, p. 175.
25. F. Pyle, "Poetical Terror: The Word, the Beat and the Noise (Theses on Interference)," paper presented at the Popular Culture Association conference, Toronto 5 March 1990, p. 10.
26. Gilroy, "One Nation Under a Groove," *op. cit.*, p. 278.
27. D. Hebdige, from *Hiding in the Light*, cited by T. Brennan, "Writing from Black Britain," *The Literary Review*, vol. 34, no. 1, 1990, p. 6.
28. C. West, "The Dilemma of the Black Intellectual," *Cultural Critique*, no. 1, 1985, p. 114.
29. Cf. H.L. Gates, *The Signifying Monkey: A Theory of African-American Literary Criticism*, Oxford University Press, New York 1988, pp. 44–124; T. Kochman, *Black and White Styles in Conflict*, University of Chicago Press, Chicago 1981; T. Kochman (ed.), *Rappin' and Stylin' Out*, University of Illinois Press, Urbana 1972; D. Toop, *The Rap Attack: African Jive to New York Hip Hop*, South End Press, Boston 1984; D. Wepman et al. *The Life: The Lore and Folk Poetry of the Black Hustler*, Holloway House, Los Angeles 1976.
30. Gilroy, "One Nation Under a Groove," *op. cit.*, pp. 275, 277.
31. Quoted in J. Leland, "Do The Right Thing," *Spin*, vol. 5, no. 6, 1989, p. 70.
32. Costello and Wallace, *op. cit.*, p. 104.
33. Marcus, *Lipstick Traces, op. cit.*, pp. 17–18.
34. Quoted in G. Boyd, "Prophet of Rage: Public Enemy," *The Rocket*, April 1989, p. 23.
35. C. Fusco, "Managing the Other," *Lusitania*, vol. 1, no. 3, 1990, pp. 77–83.
36. Costello and Wallace, *op. cit.*, pp. 33–34.
37. P. Lang, "Tough Times for Rap Music Clubs," *San Francisco Chronicle*, 10 January 1992, p. 1.
38. R.T. White, "Seattle," *Pulse!*, December 1990, p. 32.
39. Costello and Wallace, *op. cit.*, p. 33.
40. G. Tate, "Can We Drop the Bomb on the White Boy Too?," *Village Voice*, 12 March 1991, pp. 29–32.
41. See J.D. Eure and J.G. Spady (eds.), *Nation Conscious Rap*, P.C. International Press, New York 1991.
42. F. Owen, "Public Service," *Spin*, vol. 6, no. 3, 1990, p. 57.
43. P. Benjamin, "Two Funky White Boys," *Village Voice*, 9 January 1990, pp. 33–37.
44. N. Guevara, "Women Writin' Rappin' Breakin'" in M. Davis et al. (eds.), *The Year Left*, Verso, London 1987, pp. 161–62; M. del Barco (producer and narrator), "Que Pasa?: Latino Rappers and Hip-hop," National Public Radio broadcast.
45. P. Gilroy, "Ethnic Absolutism" in L. Grossberg *et al.* (eds.), *Cultural Studies*, Routledge, New York 1992, pp. 187–98.
46. Quoted by G. Stephens, "Droppin' Science: Rap Music's Postmodern Critique," Masters Thesis, California State University–Hayward 1990, p. 75. See also Stephens in *New Formations*, Spring 1992, no. 16.
47. R. Mèzouane, "Le rap, complainte des maudits," *Le Monde Diplomatique*, December 1990, pp. 4–5; B. Zakri and P. Azoulay, "Cru, Vrai, Hard," *Actuel*, February 1991, pp. 84, 87–90.
48. N. George, "Video Blaculinity," *Village Voice*, 25 December 1991, p. 28.
49. S.A. Clarke, "Fear of a Black Planet," *Socialist Review*, vol. 21, nos. 3&4, 1991, p. 40.
50. N. George, "Everyday People," *Village Voice*, 17 September 1991, p. 30.
51. C. Ahearn, "The Five Percent Solution," *Spin*, vol. 6, no. 11, 1991, pp. 55–57, 76; H. Allen, "Righteous Indignation," *The Source*, March/April 1991, pp. 49–53.
52. M. Riggs, "Black Macho Revisited: Reflections of a Snap! Queen," *Black American Literature Forum*, vol.

25, no. 2, 1991, p. 394; G. Breitman (ed.), *Malcolm X Speaks*, Pathfinder Press, New York 1989 (1965), p. 213.

53. R. Christgau and G. Tate, "Chuck D All Over the Map," *Village Voice Rock & Roll Quarterly*, Fall 1991, p. 14.

54. Eure and Spady, *op.cit.*, pp. 417–21; N. George (ed.), *Stop the Violence*, Pantheon, New York 1990, pp. 75–76.

55. *Option*, May/June 1992, pp. 28–29.

56. Tricia Rose, "Never Trust a Big Butt and a Smile," *Camera Obscura*, no. 23, 1990, pp. 117, 126–27. See also M. Wallace, "Women Rap Back," *Ms*, November 1990; Dominique Di Prima and Lisa Kennedy, "Beat the Rap," *Mother Jones*, September/October 1990, pp. 32–36.

57. Quoted by J. Morgan, "Ghosts," *Village Voice*, 17 September 1991, p. 36.

58. Riggs, *op. cit.*

59. The vigorously anti-homophobic Disposable Heroes of Hiphoprisy ("Language of Violence") appeared on the scene after this article was completed. Disposable Heroes advocate a complicated politics that is pro-black but critical of nationalism, green-socialist, anti-imperialist, personal-political, and hybridity-positive. Their cultural politics merit a separate article, but it is still too early to know if they will win "street credibility."

60. Costello and Wallace, *op. cit.*, p. 116.

61. Stephens, *op. cit.*, p. 89.

62. My thinking about these issues has been enabled by Chela Sandoval's "U.S. Third World Feminism: The Theory and Method of Oppositional Consciousness in the Postmodern World," *Genders*, no. 10, Spring 1991, pp. 1–24.

63. See, for example, K. Mercer, "Black Hair/Style Politics," *New Formations*, no. 3, 1987, pp. 33–54; S. Perry, "Ain't No Mountain High Enough: The Politics of Crossover," in S. Frith (ed.), *Facing the Music*, Pantheon, New York 1988, pp. 51–87.

64. For instance, A. Light, "Rappers Sounded Warning," *Rolling Stone*, 9–23 July 1992, pp. 15–17.

65. Perot, for his part, was aggressively wooing black voters with an anti-racist entrepreneurialism, until his gaffe of addressing a predominantly black audience as "you people" damaged the credibility of these overtures.

66. *New York Times*, 10 June 1992, p. 9.

67. A. Cockburn, "Beat the Devil," *The Nation*, 1 June 1992, pp. 738–39.

44

An Exploration
of Spectacular Consumption:
Gangsta Rap as Cultural Commodity

Eric K. Watts

Gangsta rap narratives are treated as testimonials that provoke conflicted strategies for constituting urban African American male identity and social intercourse. I argue that hard-core
rap artistry participates in a complex and fluid set of economic exchange relations among the
lived experiences of artists, the operations of a consumer culture, and the dictates of rap music
industry. The concept of "spectacular consumption" is posited as a discursive template for
understanding how rhetorical strategies of self-promotion in gangsta rap artistry alter and
are altered by the sophisticated interdependence among private, public, and economic spheres.

> I'm a product of your sins / though you say I never heard of ya / a killer, a dope dealer,
> gangsta / murderer, merciless maniac / monarch of manipulation / primary focus of your
> local police station … (C.P.O., 1992, p. 51)

> It's really sick / young brothers and sisters today have a lack of understanding about what it
> really means to be Black … (Ice Cube, 1991)

> The Spectacle is the moment when the commodity has attained the total occupation of social
> life … (Debord, 1983)

In 1991, *Rolling Stone* magazine, usually considered to be a liberally hip source of music
criticism, seemed to be at a loss to explain the success of the latest album by Niggaz With Attitude (N.W.A.). "Hell has apparently frozen over," proclaimed the lead to the *Rolling Stone*
story detailing the meteoric rise of N.W.A.'s last album as well as the phenomenal popularity
of the so-called "gangsta rap" genre (Wilson, 1994, p. B25). The editors of the magazine
seemed stupefied when they lamented that the "album was released without a single, a video,
or even a track suitable for radio play. So how did it get to the top?" ("Beating up," 1991, p. 65).
The answer to such an inquiry is both deceptively simple and surprisingly complex. It appears
simple when we assume that market strategists can sell the average American consumer any
kind of cultural expression, especially the racially provocative and perverse impulses of hard-
core hip hop (Cocks, 1991; see also McAdams, 1991). Since it is both traditional and trendy
for mainstream America to exploit and relish black cultural artifacts (hooks, 1990), the glim-
mering presence of gangsta rap merely stands as another example of a smart, expert market
procedure. On the other hand, the answer becomes more complex if we shift from a perspective promoted by an overbearing consumer calculus and move toward a perspective that

explores the ways in which consumerism is altered in correspondence with rap artistry's "political soul" of agitation and mobilization (Lusane, 1994b, p. 58). By shifting perspectives, we are encouraged to assess its "popularity" with a more meaningful discursive frame.

In an effort to explore the controversial and contradictory musical genre known as "gangsta rap," I develop a frame that recognizes the complex interactions among the material conditions of urban living, artistic production, and the culture industry, thus rectifying the problem of analytical isolation often experienced when taking a particular approach to cultural criticism. That is, many scholars have concerned themselves with the structure of hip hop discourse as a means of understanding its symbolic force (Dyson, 1996; see also Rose, 1994). Some critics have deconstructed the machinery of mass reproduction, treating the artifact as mere product of power (Crane, 1992; see also Jameson, 1991; Ewen, 1988). Still other analysts have viewed sociological data gathered in urban communities as the key to unlocking the secrets of hip hop discourse (Lusane, 1994a; see also Bell, 1992; Anderson, 1990). I offer an alternative frame based on the concept of "spectacular consumption" as an interpretive schema for defining and clarifying the relations among hip hop culture, gangsta rap narratives, and the interposition of an expanding rap industrial complex into the American culture industry.

In *Society of the Spectacle*, Guy Debord (1983) describes the spectacle as a general condition in a society oriented toward mass consumerism as a way of life. Moreover, the spectacle is constitutive of a separation of sign and signified wherein the market value of the detached image gets magnified—made spectacular—through the processes of mass production and distribution. Importantly, the spectacle is fully realized when the enhanced appearance of the image becomes more significant than the social world it previously represented. Jean Baudrillard (1993) argues that post-industrial societies have perfected modes of artistic replication so as to nearly eradicate the relationship between the sign and the signified, modifying the essence of both. Thus, spectacular consumption describes a process through which the lifeworld of the artist, the meaning of representation, and the operations of the culture industry get transformed based upon terms generated by public consumption of the art.

Elijah Anderson's (1994) conception of "street" and "decent" orientations can be used as a means of ordering and assessing the conflicted and brutal representations of urban living reproduced in the artistic performances of gangsta rap. I will demonstrate the way in which the social configurations of these orientations serve as rhetorical resources for the discursively captured and occupied sites of urban survival and conquest. Gangsta rap narratives are inscribed with compelling rationales concerning making a living in urban America. Artists attempt to offer good reasons supporting the strategies their narrative protagonists use to "make ends." And so, I hope not only to describe and evaluate rap strategies and the lifeworlds that promote them, but by understanding their service to spectacular consumption, critique the character of their relationship with the production of their mass appeal. I argue that the dialectical energies produced by the confrontation between the "street" and "decent" orientations to effecting better urban living provoke conflicting rhetorical strategies for civic life. These narrative strategies enter into a pact with American cultural outlets and are selectively enhanced so that urban (and suburban) youth can share in an artist's attempt to "live large" by replicating and consuming the imagery. I also contend that spectacular consumption can, in part, be seen as the cause and effect of a reproduction of the "street" orientation as the means for successful performance in both public and private sectors. Thus, spectacular consumption's tendency to commodify, over-value, and sell the "street" orientation must be recognized and critiqued. Lastly, I intend to show how this seller's market advertising gangsta rap artistry, in more than just a figurative way, also provides the "juice" for the invention of creative possibilities for reconstituting the terms of "making ends." But, in order to see more clearly the "public" and "private" self-performances of many urban youth and to hear the words of dissent and "dissing," let us begin our exploration on the streets.

The Street Orientation of the "Young and the Ruthless"

Playing on the name of a popular daytime soap opera, ABC's *World News Tonight's* Peter Jennings labeled the teenage perpetrators of crime "the young and the ruthless" as he reported the grim statistics on the escalation in violent teenage crime. The criminal activity of today's youth, as well as the likelihood of their meeting with violent death had risen several hundred percentage points since 1988 (*World News Tonight*, 1994). But, as so often happens in these days of hit-and-run reporting, the story veered away from any substantive account of poverty, unemployment, drug abuse, broken dreams and shattered hearts to discuss President Clinton's crime bill. What frequently escapes public scrutiny is the fact that people living in these communities are pulled by contentious orientations toward self-empowerment and survival. However, for the University of Pennsylvania's Elijah Anderson, what the popular media overlooks in its search for tidy conclusions to its grim headlines becomes the special site of sociological inquiry.

Anderson (1994) identifies two conflicting worldviews ordering social interaction in urban America—"street" and "decent." According to Anderson, the "street" orientation is represented as a culture "whose norms are often consciously opposed to those of mainstream society" (Anderson, 1994, p. 82). On the streets, a different set of rules and guidelines structure interpersonal interaction, and one's ignorance of them can lead to unfortunate consequences. Thus, even though the majority of families in urban environments promote "decent" values, their children must be schooled in the ways of the street for self-defense. Conversely, a "decent" family is a loving, nurturing unit that has internalized traditional, mainstream American values—especially those associated with education and a strong work ethic. Children from these families tend to have a vital respect for themselves and others, constructing social and psychical living quarters out of the lessons passed on through meaningful interaction with community "old heads" (Anderson, 1990, p. 65). This issue is important for the present study for two reasons. First, many of the vital directions about the performance of "blackness" and "black manhood," as themes in a larger historical drama, get reproduced and passed on within these relationships.[1] Second, Anderson ascribes values associated with American morality to the "decent" orientation.

By contrast, since thoroughly street-oriented youth have little in the way of parental guidance and support in the home, they come of age in accordance with the outlaw code. And, "at the heart of the code is the issue of respect—loosely defined as being treated 'right,' or granted the deference one deserves" (Anderson, 1994, p. 83). Urban youth, whether oriented predominantly toward "street" or "decent," learn at an early age that aggression and toughness earn respect among peers. Being able to handle affronts, verbally and physically, is a valuable skill on the streets. As such, one's capacity to "dis" others while not being "dissed" enhances one's reputation and self-image. Given the fact that many of our youth come of age in urban centers blighted with poverty and an educational system overwhelmed and underfunded, it sometimes follows that our kids see themselves as damaged or deficient. Therefore the street environment poses a dangerously exciting game; a kind of "ghetto-rama" where players are eager to "campaign for respect" (Anderson, 1994, p. 86). The dictum is clear: the greater one's ability to decipher and execute the street code, the greater one's self-worth.

For inner-city young males in particular, the street code not only structures their daily interactions with others who are also "campaigning for respect," but provides them with precarious rites of passage into "manhood" (Anderson, 1990, p. 165). There is a complex relationship among the acquisition of material possessions, the maintenance of "juice" or respect, and the concept of manhood. A street-oriented young man has a particularly heightened sense of the importance of self-presentation because the respect others give him is disproportionately based on whether others see him as a potential threat. That is, his bearing and comportment in public are based on sending the undeniable message that he is not someone to be messed with.

To make matters more volatile, the assembly of expensive items for show enhances his juice. Jackets, sneakers, jewelry, cars, and women are treated as "trophies" (Anderson, 1994, p. 88) that demonstrate and create self-worth. As Ray Dog, of the Mighty RSO, says "[t]hat shit built up your self esteem" ("Reality check," 1994, p. 67). However, since to own it is to risk its loss, the flow of juice demands the defense of its wells. And therein lies the potentially deadly rub. For the more expensive the item, the more valuable the prize seems to another, the more likely he will be "stepped to" (confronted or challenged), the more frequent will be acts of physical violence and interpersonal crime. Since this brutal form of social intercourse is promoted and legitimized by the street code, his earnest participation in it already produces a certain amount of regard. In fact, his willingness to play the game signals his "readiness" for the street-coded manhood rituals. Meanwhile, those attempting to circumvent the code are judged as weak and are thus subject to attack precisely because they are viewed as easy prey.

Explicit in the dynamics of the street code is an award system for the unabashed use of aggression in lieu of diplomacy in social relations. Accordingly, a black male's "manhood" seems to rest on negotiating the combative terrain of the streets so as not to get "punked out," "beat down," or generally abused. Throw into this confrontational formula crack cocaine, gangs, and guns, and it is no wonder the black community is reeling from multiple blows delivered by its youthful citizenry and increasingly uncoupling from what some black and white leaders refer to as a "lost generation" (Vogel, 1994, p. 56). Paradoxically, Anderson and others adamantly argue that it is exactly the community "old heads" who must take a stand and initiate the young men into a more meaningful manhood, one steeped in the diverse and rich cultural history of family and black community ritual, rather than ruthless and rugged adventurism.

Given the unforgiving street orientation and its self-promoting norms, a generation of black youth left to find its own means of attaining selfhood has been accused of producing packs of "predators" who consume weaker or more "decent" youth to feed their voracious but delicate personae. Concomitantly, inner-city youth argue that running in gangs is an inevitable and necessary form of self-preservation. At a recent "gangsta rap summit," MC Eiht, formerly of Compton's Most Wanted, had this to say about the function and formation of gangs:

> I couldn't see school. I couldn't see a job, I couldn't see moms, nobody. All I seen was the 'hood, the colors and I'm out there. I didn't give a fuck. Nigga put a strap [gun] in my hand. I had back [support] from about fifty niggas. So I didn't have to worry 'bout a nigga. All I had to do was throw on my khakis and my sweatshirt, put my rag in my back pocket and mothafuckas was intimidated by that shit. . . . ("Reality check," 1994, p. 67)

In any case, Anderson contends that the street-oriented black male is dissociated from the values corresponding to the traditional black family; he makes "the [street-coded] concept of manhood a part of his very identity, [but] he has difficulty manipulating it—it often controls him" (Anderson, 1994, p. 92). And it is precisely this sense of careening, intimidating public display that has alarmed civil authorities. "Ironically, this perceived dangerousness has become important to the public self-identity of many local black men." It is of special import that "[t]he public awareness is color-coded: white skin denotes civility, law-abidingness, and trust-worthiness, while black skin is strongly associated with poverty, crime, incivility, and distrust" (Anderson, 1990, p. 168, p. 208).

With the mass production of gangsta rap and its massive array of detractors and supporters, with the public tribulation over violent street crime, the mounting concern over abuse against women and children, and racial tensions strangling important public debate, you may wonder aloud while reading the next section of this essay whether or not the '70s funk group, War, was on to something when it announced "The World Is a Ghetto."

Consumerism Meets Gangsta-ism: The Selling of a Street Code and Shock Appeal

Undeniably one of the most meaningful accomplishments of gangsta artistry has been to open a window on the daily, gritty grind of inner-city living. The social dynamics of the 'hood were largely obscure to mainstream America until the protestations of hard-core hip hop in the mid to late 1980s. Artists like Ice-T, Schooly-D, and N.W.A. emerged from the hip hop underground with shocking and touching portrayals of life and death. Other performers such as The Geto Boys, Tupac Shakur, Too Short, Warren G., D.J. Quik, and Snoop Doggy Dogg began to take us on tours of their blighted neighborhoods, forcing us to witness a devastating procession of human roadkill. Gangsta artists relate to us stories about pimps, pushers, "niggas," "hoes," and "bitches," both real and imagined, who, like deer, are terrified and mesmerized by the dazzling headlights of oncoming perversion and mayhem.

In the 1980s, the West Coast quickly established itself as the center of foul-mouthed agitation, mainly through the music of N.W.A. On their first full-length album, *Straight Outta Compton*, the members of N.W.A., Easy-E, Dr. Dre, Ice Cube, MC Ren, and Yella, proudly announced that America was "now about to witness the power of street knowledge" (N.W.A., 1988). N.W.A. set the pace and the standard for gruesome and controversial passion on tracks like "Gangsta, Gangsta," where Ice Cube introduced himself as "a crazy mothafucka from around the way," and on "If It Ain't Ruff," where we came to know the troublesome and turbulent persona of MC Ren. Part of the significance of N.W.A. was that they realized that rebellious street norms could be exploited for economic gain and made to serve rhetorical ends. On "Parental Discretion Is Advized," N.W.A. warns us that there are necessarily some black issues and street-coded performances that will fall outside of mainstream America's comfortable understanding. Moreover, the promotion of the street code by America's political economy constitutes a conspiracy because it justifies the imposition of a form of marshal law in the ghetto. To punctuate this point, N.W.A. waves a defiant middle finger in the face of racist and oppressive social institutions on their infamous track, "Fuck Tha Police." In the song, a cop is dragged into "N.W.A. court," tried and "found guilty of bein' a red-neck, white-bred, chicken-shit mothafucker ... "[2] As Ice Cube explained in a later interview, "[i]t's like fuck Uncle Sam. We just narrowed it down to the police. Because the black kid out there don't give a fuck about who's mayor or who's governor or who's the president ... the police is the government in the ghetto" (Baraka, 1991, p. 33).

Having confirmed the financial viability of a hard-core street aesthetic (*Straight Outta Compton* sold 2 million copies), N.W.A., along with the self-proclaimed "Original Gangster," Ice-T, helped set in motion an impulse to describe and manipulate the horrors of the "United States Ghetto" ("Reality check," 1994, p. 70). Thus, artists began articulating a chaotic world where young urban males, locked in the grip of an unrelenting and unrepentant street code, are pressured to become what Compton's Most Wanted referred to as "trigger happy niggas" who are "ready for the apocalypse. ... " (Ice Cube, 1992). Ice Cube (1990, 1992) seems thoroughly prepared for self-destruction when he speaks of "genocide" on "Endangered Species," and on "Now I Gotta Wet 'Cha" relishes the murders of those he views as doing him wrong: "Now wet mothafuckas all bloody 'cause a bullet will mold yo ass like silly putty ... comin' out yo back, Mr. Mack / now they got your guts in a sack. ... " Similarly, Ice-T (1991a) gives this account of where he's from: "I'm from South Central, fool, where anything goes / snatch you out of your car so fast you get whiplash ... gang-bangers don't carry no switch blades / every kid's got a tech-nine or hand grenade / 37 killed last week in a crack war / hostages tied up and shot in a liquor store / nobody gives a fuck … " Note the Geto Boys' classic trip into the deranged psychosis of a paranoid psychopath:

> Thinkin' I got to fuck somebody before the weekend / the sight of blood excites me / shoot you in the head, sit down and watch you bleed to death / I hear the sound of your last breath / shouldn't have been around, I went all the way left / you was in the right place with me at the wrong time I'm a psychopath in a minute, lose my fuckin' mind…. (Geto Boys, 1989)

Musical artists dramatizing the street code depict violent confrontation as a black ghetto norm, present misogyny as an organizing principle of sexual relations, and equate this mentality with mental illness. Underlying this characterization of the street code is the assumption that hip hop's so-called social pathologies are derived from America's ills. Despite the belief by legislators, politicians, and black community leaders that the civil rights movement secured human dignity for African Americans, gangsta rap artists maintain that those social institutions designed to promote human dignity and preserve civil order actually contributed to the reinforcement of the street code. Ice Cube (1990) strongly concurs with this assessment and offers a tremendous description of this process on the track, "The Product." In this song, Ice Cube highlights the role that prison plays in hardening an already rigid street code. Similarly, Snoop Doggy Dogg, premiering on Dr. Dre's (1992) first solo effort, laments in the song "Li'l Ghetto Boy," that "I spent four years in the county [jail] with nothin' but convicts around me / but now I'm back at the pound and we expose ways for the youth to survive / some think it's wrong, but we tend to think it's right. … " Also, Tupac Shakur (1993) alludes to the manufacture of an oppressive selfhood on "Keep Ya Head Up," when he remarks that "I was give [sic] this world, I didn't make it. … "

Interestingly, in this song ostensibly dedicated to bolstering the spirits of black urban women, Tupac Shakur also identifies what is arguably the production line for much of the misogynistic tendencies in hard-core hip hop. Recall that Anderson contends that the street etiquette validates the objectification of women in terms of their potential sexual and "juice" values, and in the process discredits the historical and cultural significance of black womanhood (Anderson, 1990). In song after song, black women are assumed to be "skeezers" or "hoodratz" (*Compton's Most Wanted*, 1992). And so, a street-oriented young man may view a woman as a pawn to be played in the larger chess game for respect. The "ownership" of an attractive young woman builds a young man's self-esteem in a way similar to the donning of a fresh, new pair of Air Jordans. But, since the development of genuine affection is discouraged by the street credo of acquisition, this social-exchange dynamic encourages female abuse. Therefore, it is ironic that as Tupac raps for the elevation of women, in tracks like "I Get Around" he relies on the very code that compels him to put them down. In gangsta artistry, women are routinely referred to as "hoes" and "bitches" who justify their degradation by scheming against men, using sex as a lure for financial gain. The population of artists who frequently represent women in this manner is too large to characterize fully here, but N.W.A.'s (1991) "One Less Bitch" serves as a prime example:

> In reality, a fool is one who believes that all women are ladies / A nigga is one who believes that all ladies are bitches / And all bitches are created equal / to me, all bitches are the same / money-hungry, scandalous groupie hoes! / that's always ridin' on a nigga's dick / always in a nigga's pocket / and when a nigga runs outta money, the bitch is gone in the wind / to me, all bitches ain't shit. …

Easy E's (Eric Wright) misogynistic protestations can be profitably exploited by more than just a mass-marketed culture industry. If we listen carefully, we can discern how N.W.A. gleefully acknowledge participation in their self-promotion as "niggas" who condemn women by limiting their self-realization to the status of "bitches" and "hoes" in a perverse dramatization of street-oriented relations. Not only is manhood mutated into "nigger-hood," and the black female mystique twisted into prostitution, but N.W.A. suggest that their caricatures should be taken as such. That is, they consistently hint that their "raging erections" (Reynolds, 1991, p. 27) display what Nelson George (1992, p. 156) calls "cartoon machismo," a commercialized spectacle designed to thrust the street code through the doors of corporate boardrooms.

As "maniacs" and "lunatics" stalk our city streets, as car-jackers murder tourists for the keys to rental cars, and as this mayhem is sampled and shipped to record stores so that the marketers of the shameless are "once again beatin' on your mothafuckin' eardrums" (N.W.A., 1991), we find ourselves doing an absurd kind of public dance, both retreating and advancing to the frenzied cadence of spectacular consumption. Long gone are the days of wine and roses and whimsical waltzes in New York City's Central Park. Now we participate in a media-orchestrated bump-and-grind—a wild "wilding" where our social sensibilities are gang raped (Baker, 1993). This spectacle makes for great TV because consumers love to talk about hating to eat it (Hughes, 1993), and since the intensity of the pleasure of perverse consumption is directly related to our gross diet, we want nastier stuff to digest. Indeed, Americans can't seem to get enough of this commercial indigestion because somehow we all sense that there is an essential void we need to fill.

As we peer down the dark and frequently dangerous streets of our urban communities, the sense of a psychical abyss can overwhelm us. Listen to Elijah Anderson's voice as it echoes softly into that openness:

> Simply living in such an environment places young people at special risk of falling victim to aggressive behavior. Although there are often forces in the community which can counteract the negative influences ... the despair is pervasive enough to have spawned an oppositional culture ... [t]his hard reality can be traced to the profound sense of alienation from mainstream society and its institutions felt by many poor inner-city black people, particularly the young. The code of the streets is actually a cultural adaptation to a profound lack of faith.... (Anderson, 1994, pp. 81–82)

And so perhaps the "young and the ruthless" show symptoms of social heresy because they suffer from a kind of dis-ease transmitted by "[l]iving in a post-industrial, Reagan-molded, increasingly-racist, anti-immigrant, less tolerant, more sexist, Jesse-dissing, King-beating, Quayle-spelling, Clarence Thomas-serving America. ... " (Lusane, 1992, p. 37). It is hardly surprising that, given the apparent loss of hope in urban America, hard-core rap would be center stage in the searing debate about how to save our children (Saunders, 1994).

As generational wisdom and black-folk beliefs fall into the gulf separating the "old heads" and the "young bloods," historical, cultural discontinuity is displayed through acts of mutual cynicism. Reporting on an interview with the President of the National Political Congress of Black Women, Kierna Dawsey makes this disturbing observation: "Although some of us will, it's a little scary that Dr. [Dolores] Tucker would assume that Snoop Doggy Dogg, or me for that matter, cares that she marched with King ... [a]t this very moment, the gap between the generations in Black America is as wide as the Sahara. 'Kids have it better today,' she tells me. Really?" (Dawsey, 1994, pp. 58–59). As lessons learned through a "street" orientation seemingly take the place of black-folk lifestyles inscribed within a "decent" orientation, and as "music in the combat zone" (Pareles, 1990) irritates the antagonism between the two worldviews, cultural critics of diverse ideological hues are looking toward the heavens for spiritual guidance regarding the "hole in our soul."

Using the "down-home" idiom that rebukes a philistine-like, anti-blues, dead aesthetic,

Martha Bayles (1994, pp. 3–4), in *Hole in Our Soul*, documents the tailspin that popular culture has endured since the rebellious, yet devoted '60s generation. Bayles traces the evolution of the black folk spiritual through the blues and jazz factions to what she perceives as the decadence of today's pop music scene. Of particular importance is the manner in which Bayles demonstrates the joint influences of a peculiarly American aesthetic and an overblown consumer economy on pop music and on black artistry.

This Harvard graduate provides a comprehensive account of African New World music and details its trials and tribulations as it participates in a conscious effort at cultural reclamation. She takes Theodor Adorno to task for not really understanding the psychical motivations of jazz and, after negotiating the diverse ideological terrain of modernity, she arrives at the threshold of "postmodernity," which is when she claims nearly all things go wrong for art. Instead of the triumph of postmodernity over modernity, the victory of popular culture over "high" culture, Bayles contends that at least some strains of postmodernism are fetid achievements of "perverse modernism" over modernism. Moreover, Bayles (1994, p. 387) believes that perverse modernism exhibits the ability of a Western "civilization" to champion an aesthetic that seeks, as its guiding principle, to destroy the idea of morality as such. By this she means that despite postmodernity's claims of a liberating aesthetic, one that blurs distinctions so as to undermine oppressive forms of elitism, Bayles argues that perverse modernism thrives by promoting the myth that there is no "good" (read "moral") art. Ensconced in this myth is the conception that the vulgar subverts elitism and that the masses can celebrate their common experiences through the cultural reproduction of the mundane. Since this move also eliminates the restrictions that morality used to place on art through the dictates of "fine taste," it follows that the baser, more "obscene" the artifact, the more palatable its form for mass consumption.

At this point, perverse modernism is prepared to pounce and capitalize on the seediest forms of cultural expression, with the skillful support of some culture industry brokers. For Bayles (1994, p. 345), gangsta rap answers the call for self-perversion because it caters to its own lowest common denominator. By obscuring the fact that some "popular" music can also be "good" in terms of decency and morality, perverse modernism provokes a jubilee wherein patrons feast on the vile and vicious, at the same time provoking the awkward question, what is *really* what?

I want to be careful here because this question cannot be answered simply by saying that art imitates life, or that the music is just entertainment (Jones, 1993), or that rappers talk "the real shit" (Shecter, 1991, p. 24). What we need to do at least is to delve into the interstices of popular cultural production. The battle lines in the debate over whether or not hard-core rap possesses insightful commentary or seeks to merely shock and incite are nearly as blurry as the lines between art and life itself in post-industrial American entertainment (Hughes, 1993). But we need to understand that this is only part of the scenario. By linking rap theatrics with punk and heavy metal imagery, Bayles paints a larger picture that includes the accusation that a European Anglocized aesthetic strategy fosters the perverted turn for youthful desire. The fact that black art has historically performed at the core of a white pleasure principle leads this critic to the poignant, yet overly determined conception that the insatiable hunger of predominantly white youth dictates the flow of "aggressive noise dominated [*sic*] sound; obscene violent lyrics; and emotions ranging from sadistic lust to nihilistic rage" (Bayles, 1994, p. 342). In sum, Bayles (1994) puts her point this way: "As we've seen, obscenity is the preferred weapon of those willing to do anything to get a rise out of the public. The faces are black, but the strategy is *European*: seek out a submerged anti-social custom that is considered marginal even by its participants, drag it kicking and screaming to the surface, and celebrate it as 'art' " (p. 352, my emphasis).

The fact that so-called gangsta rap narratives are complex collages of social proclamations booming out of previously muffled throats-angry, confused, frustrated voices speaking from what Robin D.G. Kelley (1992) calls the "social and spatial fringes" of our society—is a precious one. Lest we forget: the Geto Boys' Robert Shaw, a.k.a. Bushwick Bill, was actually shot in the head during a suicidal tirade (DeCurtis, 1991); 22-year-old Calvin Broadus did roll with the Long Beach Insane Crips before his album *Doggystyle* went multi-platinum and before he was charged with and tried for murder (Wilson, 1994; "Witnessess," 1995); the handsome and charismatic Tupac Shakur couldn't learn important lessons about becoming a man at home (Powell, 1994), and so he gleaned them from the street code pervasive in Marin City, California, and was charged with assaulting a limousine driver and shooting two off-duty Atlanta police officers, was convicted of sodomizing a fan in his hotel room and was recently murdered during a drive-by shooting ("Three rap sheets," 1995). Similarly, Chris Wallace, a.k.a. The Notorious B.I.G., was gunned down outside a Los Angeles night club (Kinnon, 1997); the 2-year-old son of the Wu-Tang Clan's, U-God, was critically injured in a Staten Island drive-by (Alexander, 1994); and the very real brilliance of Dr. Dre cannot excuse the fact that he man-handled the female host of a rap video show because he reportedly felt he was dissed on the air ("Microphone check," 1991).

My point is not simply that these artists exemplify a "street" orientation in their artistry and in their lives, but that there exists a spectacularly symbiotic relationship between the dictates of the street code and an energetic American consumerism. It looks somewhat like this: Taking Elijah Anderson at his word, we appreciate the manner in which the street code legitimates aggression in the pursuit of juice and manifests it in material possession. As rap artists graphically explore this reality, the processes of spectacular consumption become vivid. Gangsta rap artistry vivifies harsh imagery and its consumption establishes a set of exchange relations among public culture, rap music, and the rap industrial complex.[3] Moreover, these exchange relations legitimate themselves by pointing to increased market consumption and by increasing the status of some of its more talented spokespersons. For example, *Time* magazine asserted that N.W.A. climbed to No. 1 by "bearing down as hard as it always had," and by not selling out (Cocks, 1991, p. 78). Similarly, *The New York Times* suggested that "market research had shown demand for harsher lyrics," and so Rap-A-Lot records urged the Geto Boys to go insane (Pareles, 1990, p. 29). Therefore, as the street code gets explosively commodified and artists get juiced beyond their maddest dreams, they are compelled to maintain their celebrity status by "authenticating" their self-presentations in increasingly grittier street terms. And as rappers scramble to position themselves beyond the range of the kind of humiliating parody that 3rd Bass leveled at Vanilla Ice in their video, "Pop Goes the Weasel," their magnified rage and profiteering gets portrayed as the way it really is—everywhere. What this also means is that artists, encouraged to display the ferocity of street knowledge on and offstage, perform outrageous and seamless characters. The Harvard-trained former editor of *The Source* gives us this illuminating piece of reporting: "When N.W.A. hit No. 1, mainstream America was dumbfounded." "*People* magazine wanted to catch the group casually at home, sitting on their couch and smiling," a spokesperson from Priority told us. "I tried to explain to some 40-year-old white woman that they don't sit on their couch and smile. They're gangsters for God's sake' " (Shecter, 1991, p. 24). And so it would seem that Guy Debord (1983) was incisive when he argued that the "spectacle is not a collection of images, but a social relation mediated by images" (p. 4).

Undeniably there are those young men who have so thoroughly internalized the street code that, if they were not clever or talented artists, they would have a hard time putting the "street" orientation aside long enough to get through a standard job interview, but this issue only grazes the point. The hyper-reality and hyperbole of gangsta rap is constitutive of dynamic exchange relationships that make moot nearly all discussions of what is "real." If Snoop Doggy Dogg can appear on the Fox network with a harem of "trophies," boast about how he doesn't "love 'dem hoes" on the now-expired *Arsenio Hall Show*, roll through Long Beach and choose among many adoring fans while keeping a watchful eye out for Bloods or others who are just itching to "step to" the star (Hampton, 1993), what's the point of bickering about a distinction between fact and fiction?

Todd Shaw's argument that "Too Short" is a character and that he is a "businessman" who isn't "brainwashed by the shit I sing" (Dennis, 1992) has merit, but it doesn't resolve this dilemma. American popular culture is today constitutive of the vigorous exchange relations of spectacular consumption—an intensely overblown interactive consumer network where some black (and white) folk gladly sell their "souls" for a thrill ride toward ultimate juice and "manhood." Meanwhile, on the streets of the "United States Ghetto" rap artistry is celebrated as the profit-making industry that it most assuredly is and hailed for allowing brothers and sisters in the 'hood to share in the dissing of society's repressive institutions and leadership. In short, many hip hop enthusiasts are so because they get a chance to make something out of nothing, to participate in the transposition of poverty into profit by "punking out" America. And so, perhaps it's more meaningful to say that gangsta rap is neither fact, fiction nor some exotic combination, but part of an *overdose of commercialized reality*; that it constitutes some of the ugly and obscene excesses of pop culture and is constitutive of the mess we've gotten ourselves into; that it poses as death-on-a-stick, a low-fat, low-calorie poison that is sure to satisfy anyone's "appetite for destruction."

Part of the explanation resides in the fact that consumerism is in the midst of symbolically reproducing the street code, commodifying it in the form of an easy-to-open package of hip (Lacayo, 1994). This awesome replication and consumption of street-coded imagery is significant precisely because the processes of spectacular consumption are implicated not only in the validation of what becomes reasonable street protocol, but also in the promotion of strategies that can get anyone "jocked" by an entire MTV generation. And although I share Jonathan Alter's (1993) pained query, "How did we get to a point where 'art' became a code word for money?" (p. 67), there is a bit more at stake here than a requiem for a Platonic idealism in music.

For all the strengths of *Hole in Our Soul*, Bayles, in my opinion, not only overstates her case for perversion, but badly misreads the righteously imaginative funk of George Clinton and the political protestations of Chuck D. Part of the problem is that she treats rap discourse in precisely the same terms as holistic cultural movements. In truth, she doesn't engage rap as discourse at all, but understands it as the static feedback from the electrified colloquy of mass consumerism. And as piercing and insightful as she is when discussing our perverted "hole," she overlooks the fragments, traces, or momentary utterances of "soul" found in the ruptured speech of rappers like Ice-T and KRS-One. For example, Bayles (1994) derides KRS-One, of Boogie Down Productions, for his gangsta-style message on their debut album, *Criminal Minded*, and, therefore, backhandedly dismisses subsequent releases with the clipped retort, "[b]ut it was too late" (p. 353). Too late for what? In a single stroke, Bayles reveals a cultivated prejudice not only against hard-core rap, but against the recuperative energies of rhetoric. As a social production, the marketed articulations of the street code provoke idioms that speak synecdochically in our behalf. As such, they are vast and vital representations of our lost-and-found cultures and histories. Bayles exerts great energy describing gangsta rap's menacing "noise," but has very little sense of its evocative and provocative features; that is, the myriad ways in which rap performance invents life-affirming possibilities for "making ends." Perhaps, therefore, it is not surprising that this critic does not actively engage in the act of criticism.

With this said, the final section of this essay critiques the discursive competition between distinct rhetorical norms of black communal tradition, illuminating what counts as a reasonable lifestyle. Through a textual analysis of a selected rap text, I will demonstrate how the rhetorical resources of both the "decent" and "street" orientations constitute an important dialectical relationship in gangsta rap narrative. I will argue that this dialectic provides resistance against consuming impulses through inquiries into and assertions of strategic means for transfiguring urban livelihood.

The Street Hustler's Spectacular Paradox

Before both the "Cop Killer" controversy and the Warner Brothers split with Ice-T over "creative differences" (*USA Today*, 1993, p. D2), the motion picture *New Jack City* propelled the former gang member-turned-rapper into movie stardom. The successful soundtrack of the same name contained a virulent trek into the mind of gangsta. In "New Jack Hustler," Ice-T participates in a perverse spectacle in which the Hustler is consumed by a street-provoked obsession with materialism and consumes others with a voracious street-coded persona. By this I mean that the Hustler's identity is constituted through a near-seamless rapport with a street code composed of a consumer-dominated rationality. In the text, a commodified street code encourages the kind of behavior that translates into ghettoized profit and power.

> Hustler! / word, I pull the trigger long / grit my teeth, spray 'till every nigga's gone / got my block / sewn up my dope spot / last thing I sweat, some sucka punk cop / move like a king when I road hop / you try to flex, bang! / another nigga drop / you gotta deal with this 'cause ain't no way out / why? / cash money ain't never gonna play out / I got nothin' to lose, much to gain / in my brain I gotta capitalist migraine / I gotta get paid tonight, you mothafuckin' right / pickin' my grip, check my bitch, keep my game tight…. (Ice-T, 1991a)

From the outset the Hustler surveys his kingdom and metes out brutal forms of territorial control. When a dispute arises the challenger is violently dismissed. If we inspect the warrant supporting the Hustler's authority, we understand that it is defined in correspondence with a kind of virtual reality where aggressive norms are legitimized by a profit-oriented street code (ain't no way out … cash money ain't never gonna play out). The fact that the Hustler feels as if he has "nothin' to lose" suggests the important point that he is apparently detached from a worldview that instills a sense of immanent self-worth based on communal forms of support and guidance. In this brief excerpt, we begin to understand how a Hustler views the conditions in which his selfhood is constituted.

> So many hoes on my jock, think I'm a movie star / nineteen, I gotta $50,000 car / go ta school? / I ain't goin' for it / kiss my ass / bust the cap on the Moet / 'cause I don't wanna hear that crap / Why? I'd rather be a new jack hustler. …

The beginning of an enormous tension is revealed to us here. A traditionally stable form of initiation into social values and "manhood," the educational system, gets summarily dismissed in favor of a street-coded market consumption. Listen to this same rationale in an interview with MC Eiht: "If you gave a child an option, you can hang on the streets, sell dope, have the cars, the bitches or you can go to school eight hours a day, come home, can't go outside, go to church. You tell me which one you gonna pick? I'm going for the streets goddammit" ("Reality check," 1994, p. 74). Eiht's comment illustrates the notion that the "decency" orientation garners none of the precious commodity of juice for urban youth. Moreover, women are treated as "hoes" and "bitches" precisely because the Hustler views all community relations through a prism of street-jaded consumerism. These degrading labels signal women's status and value in a seemingly exigent materialistic hierarchy. But also notice that women are *jocking him* because of his enhanced status as trophy. The terms for this distorted social structure are, as Anderson points out, provided by a reckless "street" orientation that undermines traditional black folk sources of authority. In effect, then, the Hustler, in describing his justification for his way of life, clarifies the conditions for the development of his self-image.

This conception of nihilistic bravado, absurdly framed by an illusion of invincibility, begins to crack open, however, to reveal the inner chambers of the Hustler's psyche.

> What's up, you say you wanna be down? / ease back, a mothafucka get beat down / out my face, fool / I'm the illest / bullet proof / I die harder than Bruce Willis / got my crew in effect, I bought a new Jag / so much cash gotta keep it in Hefty bags / all I think about is t's and g's / imagine that, me workin' in Mickey D's / that's a joke 'cause I'm never gonna be broke / when I die it'll be bullets and gunsmoke / you don't like my lifestyle? / fuck you! / I'm rollin' with the new jack crew / and I'm a hustler. ...

With this latest turn we can see how the Hustler's social identity seems manufactured by Guy Debord's splendid machinery. The Hustler defines himself in terms brokered by an orientation that replicates humanity as commodity. Thus, it is easy to understand why to be broke is a fate worse than death ("never gonna be broke ... bullets and gunsmoke"). Since the Hustler's being is constituted through the pressures of a street code, and since it seems to be a foregone conclusion that one will meet with some kind of untimely death in the ghetto (Foster, 1994), poverty represents a kind of living nothingness. In a moving way, then, gangsta rap articulates an important perspective on the sad stasis of discharged personhood—the cultivated refusal by a cannibalistic consumer society to own up to its inability to meet its fabulous promises for livelihood. And so, the Hustler is a spectacular facade whose public performances both refute and sustain his status as a glamorous image. Debord (1983, p. 12) reminds us that this paradox is integral to the spectacle because one's brilliant *appearance* conceals the contradiction.

> Here I come, so you better break north / as I stride my gold chains glide back and forth / I care nothin' 'bout you, and that's evident / all I love is my dope and dead presidents / sound crazy? well it isn't / the ends justifies the means, that's the system / learned that in school, then I dropped out / hit the streets, checked the grip, and now I got clout / I had nothin' and I wanted it / you had everything and you flaunted it / turned the needy into the greedy / with cocaine my success came speedy. ...

The Hustler seems systematically trained for brutality. The ends-means rationale he references is not only influential in his production as a trophy, it binds him to the street orientation. The Hustler demonstrates an utter lack of consideration for the welfare of anyone. Not only does he allude to the prominence of degenerate consumption ("you had everything"), he internalizes the distorted lesson ("learned that in school") and executes its systems logic with cold efficiency ("with cocaine my success came speedy"). Importantly, notice how the glare of the spectacle ("you *flaunted* it") illuminates one potential set of strategies, while overshadowing alternative schemes constitutive of "decent" black communal processes. Materialism is presented here as everything that determines the Hustler's identity.

> Got me twisted, jammed into a paradox / every dollar I get another brother drop / Maybe that's the plan and I don't understand / Goddamn! / you got me sinkin' in quicksand / but since I don't know ain't never learned / I gotta get paid / I got money to earn / with my posse out on the ave, buck my sounds, crack a forty and laugh / cool out and watch my new Benz gleam / is this a nightmare or the American dream?

What we witness here is a kind of textual revelation (revolution?). Formerly, the Hustler only understood his social world in terms of a rigidly enforced mentality of street consumption. But here the Hustler briefly reconsiders his behavior from a different standpoint. The idea that his rampaging impulses may have been constituted through a devastating alliance between perverse materialism and a ruthless street ethic virtually flickers before his eyes. But, his overdetermined selfhood rationalizes the potential insight away.

By examining both the pragmatic and symbolic modes of production for the street code we find a social structure that emerges out of harsh economic despair. Also, by understanding that the code valorizes the campaign for respect and manhood in terms of the brutal acquisition of material goods, we can appreciate that in the absence of black folk values and cultural ritual, black personhood under these conditions can be constituted as "thug life" (Powell, 1994, p. 37). The Hustler's tale dramatizes the (near) triumph of street nihilism and individualism over the social responsibility traditionally embraced and celebrated by a vital black community. In other words, the Hustler is blinded by the glare of materialism, constitutes his social identity in accordance with the street code, and actualizes his self-worth as an objectified street agent by objectifying others; that is, by blinding others with the oppressive glare of his materialistic presence.[4] And, "maybe that's the plan. ... "

The rupture that the dialectic of the street/decent orientations creates in the text is fantastic. For an instant the Hustler re-orients his perception in terms of previously unrecognized values constitutive of black community (another *brother*—not nigga—drop) and vaguely apprehends the outlines of potential "genocidal catastrophe. ... " This dramatic shift in perspective is important in understanding that the competing rhetorical resources of the "street" and "decent" orientations destabilize the normativity of *both* orientations in the text. Jeffrey Louis Decker (1990) provides a valuable discussion of the symbolic process of dominance and subversion in *The Interpretation of American Dreams: The Political Unconscious in American Literature and Culture*. In brief, Decker argues that the meta-narrative of the American Dream denies harsh realities, while making poetic arguments on behalf of materialism. Put another way, the American Dream, as an endearing and enduring literary trope or ideograph, provides mythic justification for spectacular consumption. This is accomplished, says Decker (1990), because the American Dream demonstrates a mode of self-promotion fueled by a fictionalized "ideal of possibility" (p. 3) if you do the right thing. Gangsta rap disputes and sustains this warrant by drawing upon competing lifestyle codes as its chief rhetorical resources. And so, as Decker points out that there are other ways of dreaming, gangsta rap provides conflicted and contradictory testimony for the American Dream.

While "cooling out," the Hustler's insight into the absurd and unreasonable constitution of the American Dream is nearly blotted out by the gleam of a trophy of the Dream—the "new Benz." But the Hustler tacitly knows that the answer to his question, "Is this a nightmare or the American Dream?" must be *yes to both*. The Hustler's nightmare is exposed in a horrific collage of some of the sights and sounds of ghetto life:

> So think twice if you comin' down my block / you wanna journey through hell? / well shit gets hot / pregnant teens, children scream / life is weighed on the scales of a triple beam / you don't come here much and you better not / wrong move—bang—ambulance, cops / I gotta get more money than you got / so what if some mothafucka gets shot. ...
>
> That's how the game is played, another brother slain / the wound is deep but they givin' us a bandaid / my education's low, but I got long dough / I'm raised like a pitbull, my heart pumps nitro / sleep on silk, lie like a politician / my uzi's my best friend, cold as a mortician / lock me up, it's genocidal catastrophe / there'll be another one after me. ...

The psychical struggle the Hustler experiences here is remarkable. The dialectical perspective allows him to see the nightmare *despite* the brilliance of the Dream. This paradoxical image is produced by the conflicting rhetorical demands placed on the discourse by the "street" and "decent" orientations. Viewed in this way, the Hustler's tale is about how social economic processes bolstered by the American Dream and encoded in the materialistic aspect of street relations conceal nightmarish effects. Indeed, the "decent" orientation provokes the reference to a history of oppression as well as the speculation about forms of abuse ("with cocaine … education's low … raised like a pitbull"). However, this resistant space is always susceptible to the dictates of a street code that, through market impulses, becomes virtually consubstantial with realizing the American Dream. And so, in these final sections of this track, the Hustler partially recognizes the terms of his subjection, but continues to participate in it.

This precarious positioning is also evident if we emerge from the textual world of the "Hustler" and confront Tracy Marrow's (Ice-T) rap artistry. "New Jack Hustler" is a conflicted narrative because Ice-T uses a dialectical lens as a kind of refractory tool; he bends visions of reality so as to both blend and distinguish arguments justifying aggressive acquisition and the communal life it threatens. Ice-T (1991b) performs a similar maneuver in "Original Gangster," where he raps "for the brothers just like myself / dazed by the game and the quest for extreme wealth. …" In this way, Ice-T constitutes an important confrontation of worldviews. Ice-T's comments on being imprisoned in the "jungle" reveal a source of destabilization for meaning: "The greatest tragedy in the ghetto is watching people become accustomed to the prospect of a bleak future.… I see the frustrations of this mind-set so clearly; I'm basically a product of it" (Marrow & Siegmund, 1994, p. 13). However, if this is so, then, gangsta rap's use of the "street" orientation allows for economic *possibility* while the "decent" orientation is constitutive of *impossibility*. Or, is it the other way around?

Conclusions

Yes, the Hustler is ultimately consumed by his own spectacle. However, the final line of the song, "there'll be another one after me," compels a fundamental question: What kind of social knowledge will emerge next? A hustler's? This question, in turn, maintains the destabilizing energy of the text. This is so because a critical audience is invited to further question and intervene in the commercial reproduction of social identity and knowledge (Rasmussen & Downey, 1991). We are shown a particular perspective on making a living in post-industrial America and on the flaws of strategies distinguished by individuation and profit.

Having made his name (not to mention his money) in hip hop, Ice-T represents some of the best and worst of perverse consumerism. His successes demonstrate the effectiveness of a rap discursive strategy that disrupts the strict polarity of the "street" and "decent" orientations. While his compelling brand of public discourse supports the mass appeal of the "street" orientation, his interrogation of *what it means to be successful* provides for moments of critical reflection. Indeed, these moments are crucial for it seems as though in order for gangsta rap to maintain its popularity, it increasingly has to submit to a form of tragic humiliation: The influence of market consumption on rap artistry is patently denied by the oft-repeated assertion of street authenticity. This refutation not only obscures corporate power, but it reifies a dangerous social equation. As rappers depict themselves as prowling "niggas," their popularity, as I mentioned before, relies on their "authenticating" these performances. And so black manhood is degraded within the dynamic intersticiality of "ghettonomics." This symbiosis among street dictates and market strategy is both revealed and strengthened by the gangsta artist's spectacular presence. However, for this dialectic to fulfill itself, it must do more than provoke talk about poverty and crime and how brothers are stuck in a market-induced dilemma. It must do more than mediate argumentative tensions through the imagery of despair and material deliverance. It must broker the articulation of the conditions under which an orientation can be rebuked, revised, or rejected.

To achieve this understanding, I contend that critics need to pay more attention to the terms of exchange and interaction among cultural performances, regulatory institutions, and the contours of our public culture. We must carefully assess the modes of transference and redefinition invented by and invested in speech performances. The areas, or "venues," occupied by these performances are, as Thomas Farrell (1993, pp. 284–285) elucidates, powerfully conflicted to the extent that the normative constraints exerted upon discourse can be called into question by interested others. It is this participatory stake that gives rise to the forms of rhetorical recuperation and transformation that Bayles dismisses. Surveying the ground of this stake allows critics to recognize, for example, how so-called gangsta rap narratives are colonized by strategic interests of culture industry, are constitutive of the unique and crucial interests of urban youth, and are re-inscribing the rules of a spectacular game (Roberts, 1995). In order to reflect upon, to question, the features and forms of spectacular consumption (the exhibition and exchange of bodies, assaults, sex, drugs, and treasures) critics need to become acquainted with the "performance conditions" of various realms (McKerrow, 1990, p. 24). To do so our epistemologies will need to resemble organic relations among diverse social practices. They could extend from within a kind of nexus where rhetoric benefits from anthropology, argument from aesthetics, and economics from semiotics. Framing the matter differently, my analysis clarifies the fact that it has become increasingly difficult to assess the character of conflicted, mediated cultural performances precisely because they cohabit in multiple social spheres at once. It is also increasingly pressing that we do so.

Notes

1. Anderson (1990, 1994) is not suggesting that institutions like the African American church and school systems have no important role in this process, only that they are, or ideally should be, secondary to traditional and non-traditional family structures.
2. This inflammatory track provoked an equally incendiary letter of protest by the FBI.
3. These exchange relations can be powerfully binding. Following the death of Tupac Shakur, the now jailed CEO of Death Row Records, Marion "Suge" Knight, told a reporter that he doesn't want "to give up gangsta rap, not at all. It is the real shit. It's not about us [record executives]. It's about the community; it's about our people, and we can't turn our backs on them." Not to mention the $100 million the record label earned in 1996 (Farley, 1996, p. 70).
4. This model was dramatized by Grand Master Flash and the Furious Five more than 15 years ago. As one of the first rap groups to explicitly discuss the root causes of living conditions in the ghetto, their song, "The Message," lamented that "a child is born with no state of mind / blind to the ways of mankind the places you'll stay and where you'll play looks like one big alleyway / you'll admire all the number book takers, thugs, pimps, and pushers, and big money makers / drivin' big cars, spendin' 20s and 10s / and you'll wanna grow up to be just like them!" (Grand Master Flash and the Furious Five, 1992, p. 152).

References

Alexander, D. (1994). Life is hectic. *The Source*, 56, 22.

Alter, J. (1993, November 29). Let's Stop Crying Wolf on Censorship. *Newsweek*, 81, 67.

Anderson, E. (1990). *Streetwise: Race, class, and change in an urban community*. Chicago: University of Chicago Press.

Anderson, E. (1994, June). The code of the streets. *Atlantic Monthly*, 24, 81–94.

Baker, H., Jr. (1993). *Rap and the academy*. Chicago: University of Chicago Press.

Baraka, R. (1991). Endangered species. *The Source*, 24, 33.

Baudrillard, J. (1993). *Symbolic exchange and death*. London: Sage Publications.

Bayles, M. (1994). *Hole in our soul: The loss of beauty and meaning in American popular music*. New York: The Free Press.

Beating up the pop charts. (1991, August 8). *Rolling Stone*, 66, p. 65.

Bell, D. A. (1992). *Faces at the bottom of the well: The permanence of racism*. New York: Basic Books.

Cocks, J. (1991, July 1). A nasty jolt for the pop charts. *Time*, 74, p. 78.

Compton's Most Wanted. (1992). *Music to driveby*. New York: Epic Records.

C.P.O. (1992). Ballad of a menace. In L. A. Stanley & J. Morley (Eds.), *Rap: The lyrics* (p. 51). New York: Penguin Books.

Crane, D. (1992). *The production of culture: Media and the urban arts*. London: Sage Publications.

Dawsey, K. M. (1994). Caught up in the (gangsta) rapture. *The Source*, 56, 58–59.

Debord, G. (1983). *Society of the spectacle*. Detroit: Black and Red Press.

Decker, J. L. (1990). *The interpretation of American dreams: The political unconscious in American literature and culture*. Unpublished doctoral dissertation, Brown University, Providence, RI.

DeCurtis, A. (1991, June 27). Geto Boy Bushwick Bill shot in head. *Rolling Stone*, 66, p. 17.

Dennis, R. (1992). Pimpin' ain't easy. *The Source*, 35, 35.

Dr. Dre. (1992). Li'l ghetto boy. On *The chronic*. |Compact disk|. Los Angeles: Interscope Records.

Dyson, M. E. (1996). *Between God and gangsta rap: Bearing witness to black culture*. New York: Oxford University Press.

Ewen, S. (1988). *All consuming images: Politics of style in contemporary culture*. New York: Basic Books.

Farley, C. J. (1996, September 30). From the driver's side: gangsta rap mogul "Suge" Knight finally breaks his silence on Tupac Shakur's murder. *Time*, 79, p. 70.

Farrell, T. B. (1993). *Norms of rhetorical culture*. New Haven, CT: Yale University Press.

Foster, D. (1994). The disease is adolescence. *Utne Reader*, 36, 50–56.

George, N. (1992). *Buppies, b-boys, baps, & bohos: Notes on post-soul black culture*. New York: Harper-Collins Publishers.

Geto Boys. (1989). Mind of a lunatic. In *Grip it! On that other level*. |Compact Disk|. Houston: Rap-A-Lot Records.

Grand Master Flash and the Furious Five. (1991). The message. In L.A. Stanley & J. Morley (Eds.), *Rap: The lyrics* (p. 152). New York: Penguin Books.

Hampton, D. (1993). G-down. *The Source*, 48, 64.

hooks, b. (1990). *Yearning: Race, gender, and cultural politics*. Boston: South End Press.

Hughes, R. (1993). *Culture of complaint: The fraying of America*. New York: Oxford University Press.

Ice Cube. (1990). Endangered species. In *Kill at will*. |Compact disk|. Hollywood: Priority Records.

Ice Cube. (1991). Us. In *Death certificate*. |Compact disk|. Los Angeles: Priority Records.

Ice Cube. (1992). Now I gotta wet'cha. In *The predator*. |Compact disk|. Los Angeles: Priority Records.

Ice-T. (1991a). New Jack hustler. In *New Jack city*. |Compact disk|. New York: Giant Records.

Ice-T. (1991b). Original gangster. In *Original gangster*. |Compact disk|. Los Angeles: Warner Bros. Records.

Jameson, F. (1991). *Postmodernism, or, the cultural logic of late capitalism*. Durham, NC: Duke University Press.

Jones, J. T., IV. (1993, November 3). Art or anarchy? Gunplay spurs rap debate. *USA Today*, p. D1.

Kelley, R. D. G. (1992, June 8). Straight from underground. *The Nation*, p. 794.

Kinnon, J. B. (1997, June). Does rap have a future? *Ebony*, p. 76.

Lacayo, R. (1994, August 8). If everyone is hip … is anyone hip? *Time*, 77, 48–55.

Lusane, C. (1992, September). Rap, race, and rebellion. *Z Magazine*, 28, p. 37.

Lusane, C. (1991a). *African Americans at the crossroads: The restructuring of black leadership and the 1992 elections*. Boston: South End Press.

Lusane, C. (1994b). Rap, race, and politics. *Alternative Press Review*, 1, 58.

Marrow, T., & Siegmund, H. (1994). *The ice opinion*. New York: St. Martin's Press.

McAdams, J. (1991, November 23). Credibility and commerciality. *Billboard*, p. R-4.

McKerrow, R. (1990). The centrality of justification: Principles of warranted assertability. In D. Williams & M. Hazen (Eds.). *Argumentation theory and the rhetoric of assent* (pp. 17–32). Tuscaloosa, AL: University of Alabama Press.

Microphone check. (1991). *The Source*, 28, 18.

N.W.A. (1988). Straight outta Compton. In *Straight outta Compton*. |Compact disk|. Hollywood: Priority Records.

N.W.A. (1991). One less bitch. In *Niggaz4life*. |Compact disk|. Hollywood: Priority Records.

Pareles, J. (1990, October 7). Gangster rap: Life and music in the combat zone. *The New York Times*, p. 29.

Powell, K. (1994, February). This thug's life. *Vibe*, 2, p. 37.

Rasmussen, K., & Downey, S. D. (1991). Dialectical disorientation in Vietnam war films: Subversion of the mythology of war. *Quarterly Journal of Speech*, 77, 176–195.

Reality check. (1994). *The Source*, 56, 67–74.

Reynolds, S. (1991, November 2). Rap's reformation. *New Statesman Society*, p. 27.

Roberts, J. (1995, December 18). A piece of the action. *Newsweek*, 83, 48.

Rose, T. (1994). *Black noise: Rap music and black culture in contemporary America*. Hanover, MA: Wesleyan University Press.

Saunders, M. (1994, May 25). The oversimplification of "gangsta rap." *Boston Globe*, p. 30.

Shakur, T. (1993). Keep ya head up. In *Strictly 4 my N.I.G.G.A.Z* … ⌐Compact disk⌐. New York: Atlantic Records.

Shecter, J. (1991). Real niggaz don't die. *The Source*, 24, 24.

Three rap sheets, one R. I. P. (1995, April 10). *Newsweek*, 83, p. 74.

USA Today. (1993, January 20). p. D2.

Vogel, J. (1994). Throw away the key: Juvenile offenders are the Willie Hortons of the '90s. *Utne Reader*, 39, 56–60.

Wilson, Y. (1994, May 31). Back beat of pain and anger in music. *The San Francisco Chronicle*, p. B25.

Witnesses in rapper trial alter stories. (1995, December 5), *The Los Angeles Times*, p. B1.

World News Tonight with Peter Jennings. (1994, July). *ABC News*. New York.

Permissions

Part I   Hip-Hop Ya Don't Stop: Hip-Hop History and Historiography

Banes, Sally. 1985. "Breaking," in *Fresh: Hip Hop Don't Stop*, Nelson George, Sally Banes, Susan Flinker, and Patty Romanowski. New York: Sarah Lazin. Reprinted by permission of the publisher.

Castleman, Craig. 1982. "The Politics of Graffiti," in *Getting Up: Subway Graffiti in New York*. Cambridge, MA: M.I.T. Press. pp. 135–157. Reprinted by permission of the publisher.

Holman, Michael. 1984. "Breaking: The History," in *Breaking and the New York City Breakers*. New York: Freundlich Books. pp. 45–59. Reprinted by permission of the author.

Ford, Robert Jr. 1978. "Jive Talking N.Y. DJs Rapping Away in Black Discos," *Billboard*. May 5, p. 3(c) 1978 VNU Business Media, Inc. Used with permission from *Billboard* magazine.

Ford, Robert Jr. 1979. "B-Beats Bombarding Bronx," *Billboard*. July 1, p. 65 (c) 1979 VNU Business Media, Inc. Used with permission from *Billboard* magazine.

George, Nelson. 1993. "Hip-Hop's Founding Fathers Speak the Truth." *The Source*, no. 50. November 1993, pp. 44–50. Reprinted by permission of the author.

Part II   No Time for Fake Niggas: Hip-Hop Culture and the Authenticity Debates

Dyson, Michael Eric. 1993. "The Culture of Hip-Hop," in *Reflecting Black: African-American Cultural Criticism*. Minneapolis: University of Minnesota Press. pp. 3–15. Reprinted by permission of the author.

Flores, Juan. 2000. "Puerto Rocks: Rap, Roots, Amnesia," in *From Bomba to Hip-Hop: Puerto Rican Culture and Latino Identity*. New York: Columbia University Press. pp. 115–139. Reprinted by permission.

Gilroy, Paul. 1992. "It's a Family Affair," in *Black Popular Culture*, edited by Gina Dent. Seattle: Bay Press. pp. 303–316. Reprinted by permission.

Kelly, Raegan. 1993. "Hip Hop Chicano: A Separate but Parallel Story," in *It's Not About a Salary: Rap, Race + Resistance in Los Angeles*, by Brian Cross. New York: Verso. pp. 65–76. Reprinted by permission of the publisher.

Judy, R.A.T. 1994. "On the Question of Nigga Authenticity," in *boundary 2*, 21:3. pp. 211–230. Copyright, 1994, Duke University Press. All rights reserved. Used by permission of the publisher.

Kelley, Robin D.G. 1997. "Looking for 'the Real Nigga': Social Scientists Construct the Ghetto," in *Yo' Mama's Disfunktional: Fighting the Culture Wars in Urban America*. Copyright © 1997 by Robin D.G. Kelley. Reprinted by permission of Beacon Press, Boston.

Part III   Ain't No Love in the Heart of the City: Hip-Hop, Space, and Place

Part IV   I'll Be Nina Simone Defecating on Your Microphone: Hip-Hop and Gender

Part V   The Message: Rap, Politics, and Resistance

Part VI   Looking for the Perfect Beat: Hip-Hop Aesthetics and Technologies of Production

Part VII   I Used to Love H.E.R.: Hip-Hop in/and the Culture Industries

Watkins, S. Craig, 1998. "Black Youth and the Ironies of Capitalism," in *Representing: Hip-Hop Culture and the Production of Black Cinema.* Chicago: University of Chicago Press. Reprinted by permission of the publisher.

Swedenburg, Ted. 1992. "Homies in the 'Hood: Rap's Commodification of Insubordination," in *New Formations.* vol. 18, November. pp. 53–66. Reprinted by permission of the publisher.

Watts, Eric K. 1997. "An Exploration of Spectacular Consumption: Gangsta Rap as Cultural Commodity," in *Communication Studies,* vol. 48, Spring. pp. 42–58. Reprinted by permission.

Index